CRIMINAL LAW

CASES, MATERIALS AND TEXT

Seventh Edition

By

Phillip E. Johnson
Jefferson E. Peyser Professor Emeritus
University of California, Berkeley

Morgan Cloud
Charles Howard Candler Professor of Law
Emory University

AMERICAN CASEBOOK SERIES®

WEST
GROUP

A THOMSON COMPANY

Mat #18196549

610 Opperman Drive
P.O. Box 64526
St. Paul, MN 55164–0526
1–800–328–9352

Printed in the United States of America

ISBN 0–314–25649–0

To Shelby, Kate, and Jessica

MC

*

Preface

The seventh edition thoroughly updates this casebook, but retains both the essential materials and basic order of the chapters as they appeared in previous editions. The new materials were carefully selected to enrich the book without altering either its basic structure or contents. Instructors who have used previous editions will be at home in this new edition, but will find the new materials helpful in linking traditional concepts with recent developments in many areas of substantive criminal law.

Criminal Law is a fascinating subject, and one which law students ought to enjoy. It is, of course, an important area of law practice, and even lawyers who practice in other areas will find that they will be asked to advise their clients on questions of criminal liability. Lawyers also tend to become judges, or legislators, or members of bar committees. In these positions, they frequently deal with issues pertaining to criminal justice and criminal law reform.

An introductory course in criminal law does not purport to teach everything that lawyers ought to know about this subject. The enormous problems of correctional policy, for example, must be addressed elsewhere. Legal doctrine is an important part, but only a part, of what lawyers ought to know about criminal justice. This casebook is designed with the goal of presenting materials that the instructors and students will find to be both interesting and important.

The casebook's style reflects that goal. Judicial opinions tend to be lengthy and repetitious. Judges and their law clerks are primarily concerned with demonstrating that their premises and conclusions are soundly reasoned and supported by authority, so they often make copious use of citations and quotations from those authorities. For teaching purposes, a much leaner presentation of judicial reasoning in these opinions is preferable. The cases have been edited rigorously to provide students with the materials they need, but no more. Most citations and footnotes have been eliminated, and the footnotes that remain are not necessarily numbered as in the original opinion. These condensed opinions are designed for effective teaching, not as sources to be cited in legal documents.

On the other hand, the complete factual background is presented in cases where that background seemed particularly significant. In some cases, additional information from independent sources is supplied in footnotes or within brackets, and in some instances concise fact summaries placed within brackets replace the opinions' unnecessarily lengthy fact statements.

Christopher Bly, Ellen Chung, Tracy Slavens, Sara Covington, and Jim Chen provided outstanding research assistance during the preparation of the Seventh Edition.

The sections of the Model Penal Code are copyrighted by the American Law Institute, and are reprinted with the permission of that distinguished Institute. The selections in Chapter Six by Mirjan Damaska are from his article *Evidentiary Barriers to Conviction and Two Models of Criminal Procedure*, 121 U.Pa.L.Rev. 536 (1973), and are used by permission of the University of Pennsylvania Law Review.

PHILLIP E. JOHNSON
University of California,
Berkeley

MORGAN CLOUD
Emory University

Summary of Contents

Page

Table of Contents

*

The Bill of Rights

Amendment I

Congress shall make no law respecting an establishment of religion, or prohibiting the free exercise thereof; or abridging the freedom of speech, or of the press; or the right of the people peaceably to assemble, and to petition the Government for a redress of grievances.

Amendment II

A well regulated Militia, being necessary to the security of a free State, the right of the people to keep and bear Arms, shall not be infringed.

Amendment III

No Soldier shall, in time of peace be quartered in any house, without the consent of the Owner, nor in time of war, but in a manner to be prescribed by law.

Amendment IV

The right of the people to be secure in their persons, houses, papers, and effects, against unreasonable searches and seizures, shall not be violated, and no Warrants shall issue, but upon probable cause, supported by Oath or affirmation, and particularly describing the place to be searched, and the persons or things to be seized.

Amendment V

No person shall be held to answer for a capital, or otherwise infamous crime, unless on a presentment or indictment of a Grand Jury, except in cases arising in the land or naval forces, or in the Militia, when in actual service in time of War or public danger; nor shall any person be subject for the same offence to be twice put in jeopardy of life or limb; nor shall be compelled in any criminal case to be a witness against himself, nor be deprived of life, liberty, or property, without due process of law; nor shall private property be taken for public use, without just compensation.

Amendment VI

In all criminal prosecutions, the accused shall enjoy the right to a speedy and public trial, by an impartial jury of the State and district wherein the crime shall have been committed, which district shall have been previously ascertained by law, and to be informed of the nature and cause of the accusation; to be confronted with the witnesses against him; to have compulsory process for obtaining witnesses in his favor, and to have the Assistance of Counsel for his defence.

Amendment VII

In Suits at common law, where the value in controversy shall exceed twenty dollars, the right of trial by jury shall be preserved, and no fact tried by jury, shall be otherwise re-examined in any Court of the United States, than according to the rules of the common law.

Amendment VIII

Excessive bail shall not be required, nor excessive fines imposed, nor cruel and unusual punishments inflicted.

Amendment IX

The enumeration in the Constitution, of certain rights, shall not be construed to deny or disparage others retained by the people.

* * *

Amendment XIV

Section 1. All persons born or naturalized in the United States, and subject to the jurisdiction thereof, are citizens of the United States and of the State wherein they reside. No State shall make or enforce any law which shall abridge the privileges or immunities of citizens of the United States; nor shall any State deprive any person of life, liberty, or property, without due process of law; nor deny to any person within its jurisdiction the equal protection of the laws.

* * *

Section 5. The Congress shall have power to enforce, by appropriate legislation, the provisions of this article.

Table of Cases

The principal cases are in bold type. Cases cited or discussed in the text are roman type. References are to pages. Cases cited in principal cases and within other quoted materials are not included.

C

D

E

F

G

S

T

U

V

W

X

Y

Table of Model Penal Code Sections

*

CRIMINAL LAW

CASES, MATERIALS AND TEXT

Seventh Edition

*

Chapter 1

BASIC CULPABILITY DOCTRINES

INTRODUCTION

The Latin maxim *Actus non facit reum, nisi mens sit rea*, was translated by Blackstone as "an unwarrantable act without a vicious will is no crime at all." Other terms besides "vicious will" that are frequently used to translate *mens rea* are "criminal intent," and "culpability." Criminal offenses therefore require an "actus reus" and "mens rea," a guilty act accompanied by a guilty mind. To use more modern language, a defendant is not guilty unless he or she performed the wrongful act with the required culpability. The purpose of this chapter is to introduce the student to the problems of culpability in general, developing understanding of concepts and techniques of analysis that will be important in subsequent chapters as we consider specific crimes and defenses.

Chapter One consists of four sections. Sections A through C deal with major doctrinal areas and problems of the traditional criminal law, which developed gradually through a process of case decision and statutory codification. These traditional concepts and terms are still the basis of criminal law in many of the states and in the federal system. Section D provides an introduction to the concepts employed in the Model Penal Code, which has been the basis for penal code reform in about half of the states.

A. THE TRADITIONAL CONCEPTS

REGINA v. FAULKNER

Ireland, Court of Crown Cases Reserved, 1877.
13 Cox Crim.Cases 550.

[The prisoner, a seaman, was convicted of "feloniously, unlawfully, and maliciously" setting fire to a ship. Testimony indicated that he entered the hold for the purpose of stealing rum from the cargo. He bored a hole in the cask and then, after removing some rum, attempted to plug it. During this operation he was holding a lighted match, with the result that somehow the rum caught fire and the ship was completely destroyed. The trial judge instructed the jury that "although the prisoner had no actual intention of burning the vessel, still if they found he was engaged in stealing the rum, and that the fire took place in the manner above stated, they ought to find him guilty." The Court of Crown Cases Reserved twice heard argument on the appeal, and before the second argument the trial judge amended the record to add the following sentence: "It was conceded that the prisoner had no actual intention of burning the vessel and I was not asked to leave any question to the jury as to the prisoner's knowing the probable consequences of his act, or as to his reckless conduct."]

BARRY, J. A very broad proposition has been contended for by the Crown, namely, that if, while a person is engaged in committing a felony, or, having committed it, is endeavouring to conceal his act, or prevent or spoil waste consequent on that act, he accidently does some collateral act, which if done wilfully would be another felony either at common law or by statute, he is guilty of the latter felony. I am by no means anxious to throw any doubt upon, or limit in any way, the legal responsibility of those who engage in the commission of felony, or acts *mala in se;* but I am not prepared without more consideration to give my assent to so wide a proposition. No express authority either by way of decision or *dictum* from judge or text writer has been cited in support of it. The authorities mainly relied upon are those which lay down that if homicide or the burning of a house be the direct, though unintended result of an act felonious or *malum in se,* the perpetrator will be guilty of murder or manslaughter or arson, as the case may be. As regards the case of homicide they may be referred to principles applicable to that class of offence, the authorities as to arsons are more in point, but they all put the case of an act felonious or *malum in se,* wilfully done and directly causing the ultimate injury. As to whether there may be any substantial distinction between the act of lighting the match in the present case, and the shooting at the deer with the felonious intent in the authorities cited, or whether this doctrine of construction, wilfulness or malice extends to any but felonies at common law, I shall not pronounce any opinion, as I shall consider myself bound for the purpose of this case by the authority of Reg. v. Pembliton (12 Cox C.C. 607).[a]

That case must be taken as deciding that to constitute an offence under the Malicious Injuries to Property Act, sect. 51, the act done must be in fact intentional and wilful, although the intention and will may (perhaps) be held to exist in, or be proved by, the fact that the accused knew that the injury would be the probable result of his unlawful act, and yet did the act reckless of such consequences. The present indictment charges the offence to be under the 42nd section of the same Act, and it is not disputed that the same construction must be applied to both sections. I confess that, as at present minded, I am not altogether

a. Pembliton threw a stone at some persons with whom he had been fighting, and the stone went over their heads and broke a window. The jury specifically found that he intended to injure the persons but not to break the window. The Court of Criminal Appeal quashed his conviction for maliciously damaging property because the jury did not find that he knew that there was a window nearby which the stone was likely to hit.—ed.

satisfied with that decision so far as it seems to be rested upon the construction to be given to the words "unlawfully and maliciously" in that particular statute. To constitute the crime of arson at common law, the setting fire to the house must be unlawful and malicious, yet it is not disputed that a person firing a shot with a felonious intent, and thereby unintentionally burning a house, is guilty of feloniously burning it; and certainly it seems difficult to see why the words "unlawful and malicious," when used to describe the essential attributes of the burning of a house as an offence at common law are to receive a different interpretation for the same words when used in the statute, the object of which is simply to place the burning of a house and the burning of a ship in the same legal category. Perhaps the true solution of the difficulty is that the doctrine of constructive malice or intention only applies to cases where the mischief with which the accused stands charged would be, if maliciously committed, an offence at common law. * * * I shall, under the circumstances of the case before us, act on the authority of Reg. v. Pembliton, without pledging myself to adopt its reasoning or conclusion under a different state of facts. * * *

FITZGERALD, J. I concur in opinion with my brother Barry, and for the reasons he has given, that the direction of the learned judge cannot be sustained in law, and that therefore the conviction should be quashed. I am further of opinion that in order to establish the charge of felony under sect. 42, the intention of the accused forms an element in the crime to the extent that it should appear that the defendant intended to do the very act with which he is charged, or that it was the necessary consequence of some other felonious or criminal act in which he was engaged, or that having a probable result which the defendant foresaw, or ought to have foreseen, he, nevertheless, persevered in such other felonious or criminal act. The prisoner did not intend to set fire to the ship—the fire was not the necessary result of the felony he was attempting; and if it was a probable result, which he ought to have foreseen, of the felonious transaction on which he was engaged, and from which a malicious design to commit the injurious act with which he is charged might have been fairly imputed to him, that view of the case was not submitted to the jury. On the contrary, it was excluded from their consideration on the requisition of the counsel for the prosecution. Counsel for the prosecution in effect insisted that the defendant, being engaged in the commission of, or in an attempt to commit a felony, was criminally responsible for every result that was occasioned thereby, even though it was not a probable consequence of his act or such as he could have reasonably foreseen or intended. No authority has been cited for a proposition so extensive, and I am of opinion that it is not warranted by law. * * *

KEOGH, J. I have the misfortune to differ from the other members of the Court. * * * I am * * * of opinion, that the conviction should stand, as I consider all questions of intention and malice are closed by the finding of the jury, that the prisoner committed the act with which he was charged whilst engaged in the commission of a substantive felony.

On this broad ground, irrespective of all refinements as to "recklessness" and "wilfulness," I think the conviction is sustained; and although, if necessary, prepared to decide this case irrespective of Reg. v. Pembliton, I think I could distinguish this case from Pembliton, in which the Judges appear to have been carried away by the very specific and negative findings of the jury as to the intention of the defendant.

PALLES, C.B. I concur in the opinion of the majority of the Court, and I do so for the reasons already stated by my brother Fitzgerald. I agree with my brother Keogh that from the facts proved the inference might have been legitimately drawn that the setting fire to the ship was malicious within the meaning of the [statute]. I am of opinion that that inference was one of fact for the jury, and not a conclusion of law at which we can arrive upon the case before us. There is one fact from which, if found, that inference would, in my opinion, have arisen as matter of law, as that the setting fire to the ship was the probable result of the prisoner's act in having a lighted match in the place in question; and if that had been found I should have concurred in the conclusion at which Mr. Justice Keogh has arrived. In my judgment the law imputes to a person who wilfully commits a criminal act an intention to do everything which is the probable consequence of the act constituting the *corpus delicti* which actually ensues. In my opinion this inference arises irrespective of the particular consequence which ensued being or not being foreseen by the criminal, and whether his conduct is reckless or the reverse. * * *

Conviction quashed.

Note

The terms traditionally used in criminal statutes to describe the *mens rea* or culpability required for conviction—"maliciously", "willfully", "feloniously"—are far from self-defining. Statutory definitions frequently are of little help. For example, Section 7 of West's Ann. California Penal Code states only that "the words 'malice' and 'maliciously' import a wish to vex, annoy, or injure another person, or an intent to do a wrongful act, established either by proof or presumption of law." This lack of precision requires the courts to decide such basic questions as whether a defendant is guilty of the "malicious" or "willful" destruction of property if he inadvertently but negligently destroys it, or whether some greater degree of culpability such as wanton disregard of a known substantial risk or actual intent to destroy the property is required. In making those decisions the courts often invoke the "legislative intent," but it is likely that legislatures often use these standard terms reflexively, without giving much thought to what they are supposed to mean.

In United States v. Bishop, 412 U.S. 346 (1973) the Supreme Court construed "willfully" as used in two sections of the Internal Revenue Code. 26 U.S.C.A. § 7206 provides felony punishment for any person who "*willfully* makes and subscribes any return, * * * which contains or is verified by a written declaration that it is made under the penalties of perjury, and which he does not believe to be true and correct as to every material matter * * *"

§ 7207 is a misdemeanor statute punishing "any person who *willfully* delivers or discloses" to the Internal Revenue Service any return "known by him to be fraudulent or false as to any material matter * * *" Because all tax returns are signed under penalties of perjury, it is practically impossible for a taxpayer filing a fraudulent return to commit the misdemeanor without at the same time committing the felony. Feeling that there ought to be a distinction between the two offenses, the Court of Appeals held that the term "willfully" as used in the felony statute required proof of "an evil motive and bad faith," but that the same term as used in the misdemeanor statute required proof only of "unreasonable, capricious, or careless disregard for the truth or falsity" of the return. The Court of Appeals was trying to draw a very sensible distinction between purposeful or knowing fraud for the more serious crime, and mere recklessness disregard of the truth for conviction of a misdemeanor.

The Supreme Court reversed, holding that "willfully" has the same meaning in both statutes, and that it connotes "a voluntary, intentional violation of a known legal duty." This holding gave a consistent definition of the term, but failed to make sense of the legislative scheme for grading punishments. Section 7 of West's Ann. California Penal Code states that "the word 'willfully,' when applied to the intent with which an act is done or omitted, implies simply a purpose or willingness to commit the act, or to make the omission referred to. It does not require any intent to violate law, or to injure another, or to acquire any advantage."

A further source of difficulty arises when a particular offense has more than one factual element. Suppose, for example, that a statute punishes only the intentional destruction of *government* property. Does a defendant violate this statute if he does not know or have reason to know that the property he intentionally destroys belongs to the government? Even if the definition of the culpability term used is clear, it may be difficult to determine which elements of the *actus reus* it was meant to modify. Many crimes have more than one factual element, and the level of culpability required for each may be quite different. For example, 18 U.S.C.A. § 111 (West 2000) punishes anyone who "forcibly assaults" any federal officer "while engaged in or on account of the performance of official duties." The assault must be intentional, but the accused need not have any knowledge or reason to know that the victim is a federal officer, or that he is engaged in the performance of his official duties. United States v. Feola, 420 U.S. 671 (1975). That brings us to the next case.

UNITED STATES v. YERMIAN

Supreme Court of the United States, 1984.
468 U.S. 63, 104 S.Ct. 2936, 82 L.Ed.2d 53.

JUSTICE POWELL delivered the opinion of the Court. * * *

Respondent Yermian was convicted in the District Court of Central California on three counts of making false statements in a matter within the jurisdiction of a federal agency, in violation of [18 U.S.C.] § 1001.[1]

1. That section provides in full: "Whoever, in any matter within the jurisdiction of any department or agency of the United States knowingly and willfully falsifies,

The convictions were based on false statements respondent supplied his employer in connection with a Department of Defense security questionnaire. Respondent was hired in 1979 by Gulton Industries, a defense contractor. Because respondent was to have access to classified material in the course of his employment, he was required to obtain a Department of Defense Security Clearance. To this end, Gulton's security officer asked respondent to fill out a "Worksheet For Preparation of Personnel Security Questionnaire."

In response to a question on the worksheet asking whether he had ever been charged with any violation of law, respondent failed to disclose that in 1978 he had been convicted of mail fraud. In describing his employment history, respondent falsely stated that he had been employed by two companies that had in fact never employed him. The Gulton security officer typed these false representations onto a form entitled "Department of Defense Personnel Security Questionnaire." Respondent reviewed the typed document for errors and signed a certification stating that his answers were "true, complete, and correct to the best of [his] knowledge" and that he understood "that any misrepresentation or false statement * * * may subject [him] to prosecution under section 1001 of the United States Criminal Code."

After witnessing respondent's signature, Gulton's security officer mailed the typed form to the Defense Industrial Security Clearance Office for processing. Government investigators subsequently discovered that respondent had submitted false statements on the security questionnaire. Confronted with this discovery, respondent acknowledged that he had responded falsely to questions regarding his criminal record and employment history. On the basis of these false statements, respondent was charged with three counts in violation of § 1001.

At trial, respondent admitted to having actual knowledge of the falsity of the statements he had submitted in response to the Department of Defense Security Questionnaire. He explained that he had made the false statements so that information on the security questionnaire would be consistent with similar fabrications he had submitted to Gulton in his employment application. Respondent's sole defense at trial was that he had no actual knowledge that his false statements would be transmitted to a federal agency.[2]

conceals or covers up by any trick, scheme, or device a material fact, or makes any false, fictitious or fraudulent statements or representations, or makes or uses any false writing or document knowing the same to contain any false, fictitious or fraudulent statement or entry, shall be fined not more than $10,000 or imprisoned not more than five years, or both."

2. Respondent maintained this defense despite the fact that both the worksheet and the questionnaire made reference to the Department of Defense, and the security questionnaire signed by respondent was captioned "Defense Department." The latter document also contained a reference to the "Defense Industrial Security Clearance Office," stated that respondent's work would require access to "secret" material, and informed respondent that his signature would grant "permission to the Department of Defense to obtain and review copies of [his] medical and institutional records." Nevertheless, respondent testified that he had not read the form carefully before signing it and thus had not noticed either the

Consistent with this defense, respondent requested a jury instruction requiring the Government to prove not only that he had actual knowledge that his statements were false at the time they were made, but also that he had actual knowledge that those statements were made in a matter within the jurisdiction of a federal agency. The District Court rejected that request and instead instructed the jury that the Government must prove that respondent "knew or should have known that the information was to be submitted to a government agency." Respondent's objection to this instruction was overruled, and the jury returned convictions on all three counts charged in the indictment.

The Court of Appeals for the Ninth Circuit reversed, holding that the District Court had erred in failing to give respondent's requested instruction. 708 F.2d 365 (C.A.9 1983) * * *.

The only issue presented in this case is whether Congress intended the terms "knowingly and willfully" in § 1001 to modify the statute's jurisdictional language, thereby requiring the Government to prove that false statements were made with actual knowledge of federal agency jurisdiction. The issue thus presented is one of statutory interpretation. Accordingly, we turn first to the language of the statute. * * * The statutory language requiring that knowingly false statements be made "in any matter within the jurisdiction of any department or agency of the United States" is a jurisdictional requirement. Its primary purpose is to identify the factor that makes the false statement an appropriate subject for federal concern. Jurisdictional language need not contain the same culpability requirement as other elements of the offense. Indeed, we have held that "the existence of the fact that confers federal jurisdiction need not be one in the mind of the actor at the time he perpetrates the act made criminal by the federal statute." United States v. Feola, 420 U.S. 671, 676–677, n. 9 (1975). Certainly in this case, the statutory language makes clear that Congress did not intend the terms "knowingly and willfully" to establish the standard of culpability for the jurisdictional element of § 1001. The jurisdictional language appears in a phrase separate from the prohibited conduct modified by the terms "knowingly and willfully." Any natural reading of § 1001, therefore, establishes that the terms "knowingly and willfully" modify only the making of "false, fictitious or fraudulent statements," and not the predicate circumstance that those statements be made in a matter within the jurisdiction of a federal agency. Once this is clear, there is no basis for requiring proof that the defendant had actual knowledge of federal agency jurisdiction. The statute contains no language suggesting any additional element of intent, such as a requirement that false statements be "knowingly made in a matter within federal agency jurisdiction," or "with the intent to deceive the federal government." On its face, therefore, § 1001 requires that the Government prove that false statements were made knowingly and willfully, and it unambiguously dispenses with any requirement that

words "Department of Defense" on the first page or the certification printed above the signature block.

the Government also prove that those statements were made with actual knowledge of federal agency jurisdiction.[7] * * *

Respondent argues that absent proof of actual knowledge of federal agency jurisdiction, § 1001 becomes a "trap for the unwary," imposing criminal sanctions on "wholly innocent conduct." Whether or not respondent fairly may characterize the intentional and deliberate lies prohibited by the statute (and manifest in this case) as "wholly innocent conduct," this argument is not sufficient to overcome the express statutory language of § 1001. Respondent does not argue that Congress lacks the power to impose criminal sanctions for deliberately false statements submitted to a federal agency, regardless whether the person who made such statements actually knew that they were being submitted to the Federal Government. That is precisely what Congress has done here. In the unlikely event that § 1001 could be the basis for imposing an unduly harsh result on those who intentionally make false statements to the Federal Government, it is for Congress and not this Court to amend the criminal statute.[14]

Both the plain language and the legislative history establish that proof of actual knowledge of federal agency jurisdiction is not required under § 1001. Accordingly, we reverse the decision of the Court of Appeals to the contrary.

It is so ordered.

JUSTICE REHNQUIST, with whom JUSTICE BRENNAN, JUSTICE STEVENS and JUSTICE O'CONNOR join, dissenting. * * *

Notwithstanding the majority's repeated, but sparsely supported, assertions that the evidence of Congress' intent not to require actual knowledge is "convincing," and "unambiguous," I believe that the language and legislative history of § 1001 can provide no more than a guess as to what Congress intended. I therefore think that the canon of statutory construction which requires that ambiguity concerning the ambit of criminal statutes be resolved in favor of lenity is applicable here. * * *

Seemingly aware of the broad range of conduct that § 1001 could sweep within its scope under today's interpretation, the Court apparently does not hold that the words "in any matter within the jurisdiction of

7. Because the statutory language unambiguously dispenses with an actual knowledge requirement, we have no occasion to apply the principle of lenity urged by the dissent.

14. In the context of this case, respondent's argument that § 1001 is a "trap for the unwary" is particularly misplaced. It is worth noting that the jury was instructed, without objection from the prosecution, that the Government must prove that respondent "knew or should have known" that his false statements were made within the jurisdiction of a federal agency.

As the Government did not object to the reasonable foreseeability instruction, it is unnecessary for us to decide whether that instruction erroneously read a culpability requirement into the jurisdictional phrase. Moreover, the only question presented in this case is whether the Government must prove that the false statement was made with *actual* knowledge of federal agency jurisdiction. The jury's finding that federal agency jurisdiction was reasonably foreseeable by the defendant, combined with the requirement that the defendant had actual knowledge of the falsity of those statements, precludes the possibility that criminal penalties were imposed on the basis of innocent conduct.

any department or agency of the United States" are jurisdictional words *only* and that *no* state of mind is required with respect to federal agency involvement. Instead, the Court suggests that some lesser state of mind may well be required in § 1001 prosecutions in order to prevent the statute from becoming a "trap for the unwary." Accordingly, it expressly declines to decide whether the trial judge erred in its jury instructions in this case.

In my view, the Court has simply disregarded the clearest, albeit not conclusive, evidence of legislative intent and then has invited lower courts to improvise a new state of mind requirement, almost out of thin air, in order to avoid the unfairness of the Court's decision today. I think that the Court's opinion will engender more confusion than it will resolve with respect to the culpability requirement in § 1001 cases not before the Court. And, unfortunately, it tells us absolutely nothing about whether respondent Yermian received a proper jury instruction in the case that is before the Court.

If the proper standard is something other than "actual knowledge" or "reasonable foreseeability," then respondent is entitled to a new trial and a proper instruction under that standard. * * * Here, respondent's alternative argument for a "recklessness" standard, if accepted, mandates affirmance of the Court of Appeals' judgment below that he is entitled to a new trial. If the Court is unwilling to decide the issue itself, I believe that at a minimum it must remand for a decision on the issue, rather than simply leaving the propriety of respondent's conviction in a state of limbo.[a]

PEOPLE v. HOOD

Supreme Court of California, 1969.
1 Cal.3d 444, 82 Cal.Rptr. 618, 462 P.2d 370.

TRAYNOR, C.J. * * *

[After an evening of drinking, defendant Hood and his companions forced their way into the home of Hood's former girlfriend. When the police arrived and attempted to arrest Hood, there was a struggle in the course of which Hood grabbed the arresting officer's gun and shot him once in each leg. The jury convicted Hood of assault with a deadly weapon upon a peace officer (Count I) and assault with intent to murder (Count III). The court reversed the conviction on Count I because of an error in the jury instructions not here relevant.]

The judgment must also be reversed as to count III, for the court gave hopelessly conflicting instructions on the effect of intoxication.[3]

a. Following the decision in *Yermian*, the Court of Appeals held that no culpable mental state of any kind is required with respect to the element of federal jurisdiction in § 1001. United States v. Green, 745 F.2d 1205 (9th Cir.1984).—ed.

3. The court instructed:

Although the court correctly instructed the jury to consider the evidence that defendant was intoxicated in determining whether he had the specific intent to commit murder, it followed that instruction with the complete text of CALJIC No. 78 (revised)[a] which applies to crimes that require proof only of a general criminal intent. The court in no way made clear to the jury that the latter instruction did not apply to the

"To constitute the crime of assault with intent to commit murder there must exist an assault and, in the mind of the perpetrator, a specific, preconceived intent to kill a human being.

"In a crime such as that of which defendant David Keith Hood, is charged in Count Three of the indictment, there must exist a union or joint operation of act or conduct and a certain specific intent.

"In the crime of Assault With Intent to Commit Murder (Penal Code Section 217), there must exist in the mind of the perpetrator the specific intent to murder a human being, and unless such intent so exists that crime is not committed.

"In the crime of assault with intent to commit murder of which the defendant, David Hood, is accused in count III of the indictment, a necessary element is the existence in the mind of the defendant of the specific intent to commit murder.

"If the evidence shows that the defendant was intoxicated at the time of the alleged offense, the jury should consider his state of intoxication in determining if defendant had such specific intent.

"Intoxication of a person is voluntary if it results from his willing partaking of any intoxicating liquor, drug or other substance when he knows that it is capable of an intoxicating effect or when he willingly assumes the risk of that effect as a possibility.

"Our law provides that 'no act committed by a person while in a state of voluntary intoxication is less criminal by reason of his having been in such condition.'

"This means that drunkenness, if the evidence shows that the defendant was in such a condition when allegedly he committed the crime charged, is not of itself a defense in this case. It may throw light on the occurrence and aid you in determining what took place, but when a person in a state of intoxication, voluntarily produced by himself, commits a crime such as that (any of those) charged against the defendant in this case, the law does not permit him to use his own vice as a shelter against the normal legal consequences of his conduct."

a. The Court is referring to the final three paragraphs of the instruction quoted in the previous footnote. CALJIC is a book of pattern jury instructions for use in criminal cases. California trial judges rarely draft their own jury instructions, because they are afraid of committing reversible error. Instead, they normally try to select the appropriate CALJIC instructions, modifying them slightly in some cases to fit the particular case. Use of such pattern instructions in California and other states has been attacked on two grounds: (1) They are drafted primarily with a view to satisfying the appellate courts, and only secondarily with a view to educating the jury; and (2) they are necessarily couched in generalities, which may not be very helpful to a juror in deciding a specific case.

Written copies of the instructions are not ordinarily given to jurors. In Commonwealth v. Oleynik, 568 A.2d 1238 (Pa.1990), the Pennsylvania Supreme Court reversed a conviction because the trial judge had sent with the jury written instructions pertaining to the specific issues most in dispute in the trial. The court explained that "Where a jury is permitted to take with them written instructions during their deliberations, a question may arise as to the appropriate application of the written instruction when resolving an issue in the cause. In such a case, it is highly probable the jury would resort to its interpretation of the written instructions in reaching its verdict. Where the jury is required to rely upon the oral instructions given by the judge in his charge, if disagreement arises concerning the oral instructions, it is more likely that the jury would seek further instructions from the judge to resolve the question. When an issue is resolved by further instructions from the court, that procedure insures that misconceptions are not permitted to infect the deliberative process. On the other hand, when a jury is left to its own devices to interpret a written instruction, the possibility of a misconception is significantly enhanced. Moreover, the submission of written instructions would tend to encourage the jury to ignore the court's general instruction and focus upon the written instructions supplied to them. This undue emphasis on portions of the charge has the potential of undermining the integrity of the deliberative process."—ed.

charge of assault with intent to commit murder. The giving of such conflicting instructions with respect to a crime requiring proof of a specific intent is error. That error was clearly prejudicial in this case. There was substantial evidence that defendant was drunk. He testified that he was not aware that he ever had the gun in his possession or fired it. Its discharge during the scuffle could be reconciled with an intent to kill, an intent to inflict only bodily injury, or with no intent to fire it at all. Had the jury not been given conflicting instructions on the significance of defendant's intoxication, it is reasonably probable that it would have reached a result more favorable to defendant on Count III.

To guide the trial court on retrial, we consider the question of the effect of intoxication on the crime of assault with a deadly weapon. * * *

[Earlier California cases had held, consistent with the law in many other jurisdictions, that assault is a general intent crime which may be committed recklessly. Thus, one who deliberately fired a gun in the direction of another could be convicted of assault with a deadly weapon even if he intended to miss. Later California cases disapproved these earlier decisions insofar as they held that an assault could be predicated on reckless conduct. Noting that the California Penal Code defines an assault as "an unlawful attempt, coupled with a present ability, to commit a violent injury on the person of another," the later cases concluded that "one could not very well 'attempt' or try to 'commit' an injury on the person of another if he had no intent to cause any injury to such other person." The cases left unclear whether assault was to be considered a general intent or specific intent crime.]

The distinction between specific and general intent crimes evolved as a judicial response to the problem of the intoxicated offender. That problem is to reconcile two competing theories of what is just in the treatment of those who commit crimes while intoxicated. On the one hand, the moral culpability of a drunken criminal is frequently less than that of a sober person effecting a like injury. On the other hand, it is commonly felt that a person who voluntarily gets drunk and while in that state commits a crime should not escape the consequences.

Before the nineteenth century, the common law refused to give any effect to the fact that an accused committed a crime while intoxicated. The judges were apparently troubled by this rigid traditional rule, however, for there were a number of attempts during the early part of the nineteenth century to arrive at a more humane, yet workable, doctrine. The theory that these judges explored was that evidence of intoxication could be considered to negate intent, whenever intent was an element of the crime charged. [S]uch an exculpatory doctrine could eventually have undermined the traditional rule entirely, since some form of *mens rea* is a requisite of all but strict liability offenses. To limit the operation of the doctrine and achieve a compromise between the conflicting feelings of sympathy and reprobation for the intoxicated offender, later courts both in England and this country drew a distinction between so-called specific intent and general intent crimes.

Specific and general intent have been notoriously difficult terms to define and apply, and a number of text writers recommend that they be abandoned altogether. Too often the characterization of a particular crime as one of specific or general intent is determined solely by the presence or absence of words describing psychological phenomena—"intent" or "malice," for example—in the statutory language defining the crime. When the definition of a crime consists of only the description of a particular act, without reference to intent to do a further act or achieve a future consequence, we ask whether the defendant intended to do the proscribed act. This intention is deemed to be a general criminal intent. When the definition refers to defendant's intent to do some further act or achieve some additional consequence, the crime is deemed to be one of specific intent. There is no real difference, however, only a linguistic one, between an intent to do an act already performed and an intent to do that same act in the future. * * *

We need not reconsider our position * * * that an assault cannot be predicated merely on reckless conduct. Even if assault requires an intent to commit a battery on the victim, it does not follow that the crime is one in which evidence of intoxication ought to be considered in determining whether the defendant had that intent. It is true that in most cases specific intent has come to mean an intention to do a future act or achieve a particular result, and that assault is appropriately characterized as a specific intent crime under this definition. An assault, however, is equally well characterized as a general intent crime under the definition of general intent as an intent merely to do a violent act.[b]

Therefore, whatever reality the distinction between specific and general intent may have in other contexts, the difference is chimerical in the case of assault with a deadly weapon or simple assault. Since the definitions of both specific intent and general intent cover the requisite intent to commit a battery, the decision whether or not to give effect to evidence of intoxication must rest on other considerations.

A compelling consideration is the effect of alcohol on human behavior. A significant effect of alcohol is to distort judgment and relax the controls on aggressive and anti-social impulses. Alcohol apparently has less effect on the ability to engage in simple goal-directed behavior, although it may impair the efficiency of that behavior. In other words, a drunk man is capable of forming an intent to do something simple, such as strike another, unless he is so drunk that he has reached the stage of unconsciousness. What he is not as capable as a sober man of doing is exercising judgment about the social consequences of his acts or controlling his impulses toward anti-social acts. He is more likely to act rashly and impulsively and to be susceptible to passion and anger. It would therefore be anomalous to allow evidence of intoxication to relieve a man of responsibility for the crimes of assault with a deadly weapon or simple assault, which are so frequently committed in just such a manner * * *.

b. Subsequently, in People v. Rocha, 3 Cal.3d 893, 92 Cal.Rptr. 172, 479 P.2d 372 (1971), the California Supreme Court held that assault is a "general intent" crime, requiring only the general intent to commit a battery.—ed.

Those crimes that have traditionally been characterized a[illegible] specific intent are not affected by our holding here. The [illegible] mental activity between formulating an intent to commit a ba[illegible] formulating an intent to commit a battery for the purpose of rapi[illegible] killing may be slight, but it is sufficient to justify drawing a line between them and considering evidence of intoxication in the one case and disregarding it in the other. Accordingly, on retrial the court should not instruct the jury to consider evidence of defendant's intoxication in determining whether he committed assault with a deadly weapon on a peace officer or any of the lesser assaults included therein. * * *

Note

The traditional approach to the use of intoxication as a defense can most accurately be described as thoroughly confused. The "hornbook" rule is that intoxication may be used to show lack of a "specific intent" where specific intent is an element of the crime, but not to show lack of "general intent" where the crime requires only general intent. That sounds simple enough, but no one has been able to explain satisfactorily why this distinction makes sense, or even how we are to tell the difference between specific and general intent when we have to do so.

Some authorities say that a crime is one of specific intent when its definition includes a special mental element which is required above and beyond any mental state required with respect to the actus reus of the crime. Examples would include such crimes as "assault with intent to commit rape," "breaking and entering a dwelling with the intent to commit a felony therein" (i.e. burglary), "kidnapping for the purpose of ransom," and "making false statements with the intent to defraud." In all these and similar cases, the definition of the crime explicitly includes an action and a further specified intent or purpose. It seems to follow that *any* evidence that tends to disprove the presence of this intent should be admissible to be evaluated by the jury. For example, an extremely drunken person might enter another person's dwelling out of confusion, and lack the intent to steal even though appearing to be a burglar. Intoxication is not *per se* a defense to burglary, but a defendant's intoxicated condition may bear on whether he had the required specific intent.

Somewhat less obviously, attempt is usually considered to be a specific intent crime because one cannot attempt something unless one has an intent to bring about certain consequences. The term "battery"—an unlawful use of force or violence upon the person of another—does not similarly connote a subjective intention to bring about forbidden consequences. For this reason, it is usually held that battery is a crime of general intent, which may be committed recklessly or even negligently. If the California statute punished "assault *or battery* on a police officer" the defendant's intoxication could easily be excluded as irrelevant in cases of battery. Because "assault" is defined as an *attempt* to commit a battery, and because the statute does not separately punish the completed battery, the crime appears to be one of specific intent. Nonetheless, the California courts eventually held simple assault to be a general intent crime on the ground that it is "simpler" to form an intent to commit battery than an intent to rape or kill. See People v.

Rocha, supra Ch. 1, § A. In People v. Mendoza, 18 Cal.4th 1114, 77 Cal.Rptr.2d 428, 959 P.2d 735 (1998), the California Supreme Court noted that, despite various amendments to the applicable statutes, "the basic framework that *Hood* established for designating a criminal intent as either specific or general for these purposes [admission of evidence of voluntary intoxication to negate intent] has survived." 18 Cal.4th at 1128.

Chief Justice Traynor's opinion correctly explains that the usual effect of alcohol is to "distort judgment and relax the controls on aggressive and anti-social impulses" rather than to make one incapable of forming an intent. To put it simply, a person can be very drunk and yet intend to kill, or inflict an injury, or steal. To the extent that this is true, and to the extent that judges and juries are capable of distinguishing between the kind of intoxication that relaxes inhibitions and that which negates intent, use of intoxication as a defense will rarely be successful, whether the crime is one of general or specific intent. Presumably, the argument for excluding evidence of intoxication must rest either on the premise that the jury is likely to become confused and think that it should acquit the defendant if intoxication caused him to do something he would not have done if sober, or on the premise that the testimony about intoxication is likely to waste a great deal of the court's time in the majority of cases where it is not relevant to intent.

GARNETT v. STATE

Court of Appeals of Maryland, 1993.
332 Md. 571, 632 A.2d 797.

MURPHY, CHIEF JUSTICE.

Maryland's "statutory rape" law, prohibiting sexual intercourse with an underage person is codified in Maryland Code § 463, which reads in full:

"Second degree rape.

(a) What constitutes.—A person is guilty of rape in the second degree if the person engages in vaginal intercourse with another person:

(1) By force or threat of force against the will and without the consent of the other person; or

(2) Who is mentally defective, mentally incapacitated, or physically helpless, and the person performing the act knows or should reasonably know the other person is mentally defective, mentally incapacitated, or physically helpless; or

(3) Who is under 14 years of age and the person performing the act is at least four years older than the victim.

(b) Penalty.—Any person violating the provisions of this section is guilty of a felony and upon conviction is subject to imprisonment for a period of not more than 20 years."

Subsection (a)(3) represents the current version of a statutory provision dating back to the first comprehensive codification of the criminal law by the Legislature in 1809. Now we consider whether under the present statute, the State must prove that a defendant knew the complaining witness was younger than 14 and, in a related question, whether it was error at trial to exclude evidence that he had been told, and believed, that she was 16 years old.

Raymond Lennard Garnett is a young retarded man. At the time of the incident in question he was 20 years old. He has an I.Q. of 52. His guidance counselor from the Montgomery County public school system, Cynthia Parker, described him as a mildly retarded person who read on the third-grade level, did arithmetic on the 5th-grade level, and interacted with others socially at school at the level of someone 11 or 12 years of age. Ms. Parker added that Raymond attended special education classes and for at least one period of time was educated at home when he was afraid to return to school due to his classmates' taunting. Because he could not understand the duties of the jobs given him, he failed to complete vocational assignments; he sometimes lost his way to work. As Raymond was unable to pass any of the State's functional tests required for graduation, he received only a certificate of attendance rather than a high-school diploma.

In November or December 1990, a friend introduced Raymond to Erica Frazier, then aged 13; the two subsequently talked occasionally by telephone. On February 28, 1991, Raymond, apparently wishing to call for a ride home, approached the girl's house at about nine o'clock in the evening. Erica opened her bedroom window, through which Raymond entered; he testified that "she just told me to get a ladder and climb up her window." The two talked, and later engaged in sexual intercourse. Raymond left at about 4:30 a.m. the following morning. On November 19, 1991, Erica gave birth to a baby, of which Raymond is the biological father.

Raymond was tried on one count of second degree rape under § 463(a)(3). At trial, the defense twice proffered evidence to the effect that Erica herself and her friends had previously told Raymond that she was 16 years old, and that he had acted with that belief. The trial court excluded such evidence as immaterial, explaining that even a good faith mistake as to age was no defense. The court found Raymond guilty. It sentenced him to a term of five years in prison, suspended the sentence and imposed five years of probation, and ordered that he pay restitution to Erica and the Frazier family. * * *

II

* * * Section 463(a)(3) does not expressly set forth a requirement that the accused have acted with a criminal state of mind, or mens rea. The State insists that the statute, by design, defines a strict liability offense, and that its essential elements were met in the instant case when Raymond, age 20, engaged in vaginal intercourse with Erica, a girl under 14 and more than 4 years his junior. Raymond replies that the criminal law exists to assess and punish morally culpable behavior. He

says such culpability was absent here. He asks us either to engraft onto subsection (a)(3) an implicit mens rea requirement, or to recognize an affirmative defense of reasonable mistake as to the complainant's age. Raymond argues that it is unjust, under the circumstances of this case which led him to think his conduct lawful, to brand him a felon and rapist.

III

* * * It is well understood that generally there are two components of every crime, the actus reus or guilty act and the mens rea or the guilty mind or mental state accompanying a forbidden act. The requirement that an accused have acted with a culpable mental state is an axiom of criminal jurisprudence. Writing for the United States Supreme Court, Justice Robert Jackson observed: "The contention that an injury can amount to a crime only when inflicted by intention is no provincial or transient notion. It is as universal and persistent in mature systems of law as belief in freedom of the human will and a consequent ability and duty of the normal individual to choose between good and evil." Morissette v. United States, 342 U.S. 246, 250–252 (1952).

To be sure, legislative bodies since the mid–19th century have created strict liability criminal offenses requiring no mens rea. Almost all such statutes responded to the demands of public health and welfare arising from the complexities of society after the Industrial Revolution. Typically misdemeanors involving only fines or other light penalties, these strict liability laws regulated food, milk, liquor, medicines and drugs, securities, motor vehicles and traffic, the labeling of goods for sale, and the like. [Citations] Statutory rape, carrying the stigma of felony as well as a potential sentence of 20 years in prison, contrasts markedly with the other strict liability regulatory offenses and their light penalties.

Modern scholars generally oppose the concept of strict criminal liability. Professors LaFave and Scott summarize the consensus that punishing conduct without reference to the actor's state of mind fails to reach the desired end and is unjust:

> "It is inefficacious because conduct unaccompanied by an awareness of the factors making it criminal does not mark the actor as one who needs to be subjected to punishment in order to deter him or others from behaving similarly in the future, nor does it single him out as a socially dangerous individual who needs to be incapacitated or reformed. It is unjust because the actor is subjected to the stigma of a criminal conviction without being morally blameworthy. Consequently, on either a preventive or retributive theory of criminal punishment, the criminal sanction is inappropriate in the absence of mens rea."

LaFave & Scott, *Criminal Law* (2d ed. 1986), at 248, quoting Herbert L. Packer, "Mens Rea and the Supreme Court," 1962 Sup.Ct.Rev. 107, 109.

* * *

Conscious of the disfavor in which strict criminal liability resides, the Model Penal Code states generally as a minimum requirement of culpability that a person is not guilty of a criminal offense unless he acts purposely, knowingly, recklessly, or negligently, i.e., with some degree of mens rea. Model Penal Code § 2.02 (Official Draft and Revised Comments 1980). The Code allows generally for a defense of ignorance or mistake of fact negating mens rea. The Model Penal Code generally recognizes strict liability for offenses deemed "violations," defined as wrongs subject only to a fine, forfeiture, or other civil penalty upon conviction, and not giving rise to any legal disability.[2]

The commentators similarly disapprove of statutory rape as a strict liability crime. In addition to the arguments discussed above, they observe that statutory rape prosecutions often proceed even when the defendant's judgment as to the age of the complainant is warranted by her appearance, her sexual sophistication, her verbal misrepresentations, and the defendant's careful attempts to ascertain her true age. * * *

Two sub-parts of the rationale underlying strict criminal liability require further analysis at this point. Statutory rape laws are often justified on the "lesser legal wrong" theory or the "moral wrong" theory; by such reasoning, the defendant acting without mens rea nonetheless deserves punishment for having committed a lesser crime, fornication, or for having violated moral teachings that prohibit sex outside of marriage. Maryland has no law against fornication. It is not a crime in this state. Moreover, the criminalization of an act, performed without a guilty mind, deemed immoral by some members of the community rests uneasily on subjective and shifting norms. "[D]etermining precisely what the 'community ethic' actually is [is] not an easy task in a heterogeneous society in which our public pronouncements about morality often are not synonymous with our private conduct." LaFave & Scott, supra, at 411. * * *

IV

The legislatures of 17 states have enacted laws permitting a mistake of age defense in some form in cases of sexual offenses with underage persons. * * *

In addition, the highest appellate courts of four states have determined that statutory rape laws by implication required an element of mens rea as to the complainant's age. In the landmark case of People v. Hernandez, 61 Cal.2d 529 (1964), the California Supreme Court held that, absent a legislative directive to the contrary, a charge of statutory

2. With respect to the law of statutory rape, the Model Penal Code strikes a compromise with its general policy against strict liability crimes. The Code prohibits the defense of ignorance or a reasonable mistake of age when the victim is below the age of ten, but allows it when the critical age stipulated in the offense is higher than ten. Model Penal Code, * * * §§ 213.1, 213.6(1). The drafters of the Code implicitly concede that sexual conduct with a child of such extreme youth would, at the very least, spring from a criminally negligent state of mind. The available defense of reasonable mistake of age for complainants older than ten requires that the defendant not have acted out of criminal negligence.

rape was defensible wherein a criminal intent was lacking; it reversed the trial court's refusal to permit the defendant to present evidence of his good faith, reasonable belief that the complaining witness had reached the age of consent. [But see, People v. Olsen, 36 Cal.3d 638 (1984), holding that a good faith, reasonable mistake of age is *not* a defense to a charge of lewd or lascivious conduct with child under the age of 14 years.—ed.] * * *

V

We think it sufficiently clear, however, that Maryland's second degree rape statute defines a strict liability offense that does not require the State to prove mens rea; it makes no allowance for a mistake-of-age defense. The plain language of § 463, viewed in its entirety, and the legislative history of its creation lead to this conclusion. * * *

Section 463(a)(3) prohibiting sexual intercourse with underage persons makes no reference to the actor's knowledge, belief, or other state of mind. As we see it, this silence as to mens rea results from legislative design. First, subsection (a)(3) stands in stark contrast to the provision immediately before it, subsection (a)(2) prohibiting vaginal intercourse with incapacitated or helpless persons. In subsection (a)(2), the Legislature expressly provided as an element of the offense that "the person performing the act *knows or should reasonably know* the other person is mentally defective, mentally incapacitated, or physically helpless." Code, § 463(a)(2) (emphasis added). In drafting this subsection, the Legislature showed itself perfectly capable of recognizing and allowing for a defense that obviates criminal intent; if the defendant objectively did not understand that the sex partner was impaired, there is no crime. That it chose not to include similar language in subsection (a)(3) indicates that the Legislature aimed to make statutory rape with underage persons a more severe prohibition based on strict criminal liability. * * *

Second, an examination of the drafting history of § 463 during the 1976 revision of Maryland's sexual offense laws reveals that the statute was viewed as one of strict liability from its inception and throughout the amendment process. * * *

This interpretation is consistent with the traditional view of statutory rape as a strict liability crime designed to protect young persons from the dangers of sexual exploitation by adults, loss of chastity, physical injury, and, in the case of girls, pregnancy. See Michael M. v. Sonoma County Superior Court, 450 U.S. 464, 470 (1981). The majority of states retain statutes which impose strict liability for sexual acts with underage complainants. We observe again, as earlier, that even among those states providing for a mistake-of-age defense in some instances, the defense often is not available where the sex partner is 14 years old or less; the complaining witness in the instant case was only 13. * * *

Maryland's second degree rape statute is by nature a creature of legislation. Any new provision introducing an element of mens rea, or permitting a defense of reasonable mistake of age, with respect to the offense of sexual intercourse with a person less than 14, should properly result from an act of the Legislature itself, rather than judicial fiat. Until then, defendants in extraordinary cases, like Raymond, will rely upon the tempering discretion of the trial court at sentencing.

JUDGMENT AFFIRMED, WITH COSTS.

BELL, JUDGE, dissenting.

* * * I do not dispute that the legislative history of § 463 may be read to support the majority's interpretation that subsection (a)(3) was intended to be a strict liability statute. Nor do I disagree that it is in the public interest to protect the sexually naive child from the adverse physical, emotional, or psychological effects of sexual relations. I do not believe, however, that the General Assembly, in every case, whatever the nature of the crime and no matter how harsh the potential penalty, can subject a defendant to strict criminal liability. To hold, as a matter of law, that § 463(a)(3) does not require the State to prove that a defendant possessed the necessary mental state to commit the crime, i.e. knowingly engaged in sexual relations with a female under 14, or that the defendant may not litigate that issue in defense, offends a principle of justice so rooted in the traditions of conscience of our people as to be ranked as fundamental and is, therefore, inconsistent with due process. * * *

I would hold that the State is not relieved of its burden to prove the defendant's intent or knowledge in a statutory rape case and, therefore, that the defendant may defend on the basis that he was mistaken as to the age of the prosecutrix. The analysis I would employ is that developed for use in self defense cases, perfect and imperfect. Before the State's burden affirmatively to prove the defendant's mental state kicks in, the defendant must have generated the issue by producing "some evidence" supporting his or her claim of mistake of fact. If the defendant generates the issue, the State must prove beyond a reasonable doubt that the act was committed without any mistake of fact—that the defendant acted intentionally and knowingly. * * *

Obviously, and the majority concurs, "statutory rape" is not merely a public welfare offense; it simply does not "fit" the characteristics of such an offense: it is a felony, not a misdemeanor. In striking contrast to "other strict liability regulatory offenses and their light penalties," the potential penalty of 20 years imprisonment is not a light penalty; unlike the "garden variety" strict liability penalty, the penalty under section 463(a)(3), is neither so insignificant that it can be ignored as a criminal sanction, nor so slight that the fate of the defendant can be ignored. * * * I respectfully dissent.

Note

By definition, a person cannot commit a specific intent crime unless he had the required specific intent. Although the case law is not without contradiction and confusion on the point, it follows that any mistake of fact or law, whether reasonable or unreasonable, is a defense to a specific intent crime if because of it the defendant lacked the required intent. Thus, one is not guilty of theft if he takes the property of another believing it to be his own property, however unreasonable he may be in that belief. (The crime of theft requires a "specific intent" to deprive another person of his property.) Of course, the belief must be an honest one, and the jury will not necessarily credit a defendant's testimony that he formed an honest belief upon totally unreasonable grounds.

The traditional rule with respect to general intent crimes is that a mistake of law does not excuse at all, and a mistake of fact excuses only (1) if it was reasonable and (2) if the defendant's conduct would have been lawful had the facts been as he believed them to be. The mistake does not excuse if it was not based on reasonable grounds, or if the defendant would have been committing some other crime had the facts been as he thought.

As the majority opinion in *Garnett* indicates, many American jurisdictions follow the rule than even a reasonable mistake of age does not excuse a defendant who engaged in forbidden sexual conduct with a person under the "age of consent." This harsh doctrine is sometimes justified on vague considerations of public policy, and sometimes on the theory that the defendant's conduct would have been at least immoral, and in some cases illegal, even if the facts had been as he reasonably supposed. Several states have abandoned the majority rule with respect to statutory rape prosecutions, and recognized reasonable mistake of age as an affirmative defense. See State v. Guest, 583 P.2d 836 (Alaska 1978); State v. Elton, 680 P.2d 727 (Utah 1984).

Consent is a defense to a charge of forcible rape, but not to a charge of "statutory rape" or to a charge of rape of a person who was incapable of consent due to mental illness or retardation. A mistaken belief that the victim was consenting is also a defense, provided that the mistake was reasonable in the circumstances. The English House of Lords held in a very controversial decision that a mistake of fact as to consent is a defense to the "general intent" crime of rape even if the mistake was unreasonable. In Director of Public Prosecutions v. Morgan, (1975) 2 All E.R. 347, 61 C.A. 136, three men were convicted of raping Morgan's wife and Morgan was convicted of aiding and abetting them. The three men testified that Morgan invited them to come to his house and have intercourse with his wife, and that he assured them that his wife would be willing but would pretend to resist. The trial judge instructed the jury that a mistaken belief that the victim of a rape was consenting was a defense only if it was reasonable. A majority of the House of Lords held that the defendants could not be said to "intend" to commit rape if they honestly believed that the victim was consenting, even if they were unreasonable in forming that belief. The House of Lords nonetheless affirmed the convictions, holding that no reasonable jury could have believed the defendants' testimony. (An American appellate court probably would not be as willing to evaluate the credibility of defense testimony.) Even though the convictions were affirmed, the decision sparked severe criticism because in the view of many commentators it seemed to encourage bogus defenses in rape cases. The holding in *Morgan* on unreasonable mistake of fact is contrary to the established American rule.

BRYAN v. UNITED STATES

Supreme Court of the United States, 1998.
524 U.S. 184, 118 S.Ct. 1939, 141 L.Ed.2d 197.

JUSTICE STEVENS delivered the opinion of the Court.

I

In 1968 Congress * * * amended the Criminal Code to include detailed provisions regulating the use and sale of firearms. As amended, 18 U.S.C. § 922 defined a number of "unlawful acts;" subsection (a)(1) made it unlawful for any person except a licensed dealer to engage in the business of dealing in firearms. Section 923 established the federal licensing program and repeated the prohibition against dealing in firearms without a license, and § 924 specified the penalties for violating "any provision of this chapter." Read literally, § 924 authorized the imposition of a fine of up to $5,000 or a prison sentence of not more than five years, "or both," on any person who dealt in firearms without a license even if that person believed that he or she was acting lawfully. As enacted in 1968, § 922(a)(1) and § 924 omitted an express scienter requirement and therefore arguably imposed strict criminal liability on every unlicensed dealer in firearms. The 1968 Act also omitted any definition of the term "engaged in the business" even though that conduct was an element of the unlawful act prohibited by § 922(a)(1).

In 1986 Congress enacted the Firearms Owners' Protection Act (FOPA), in part, to cure these omissions. The findings in that statute explained that additional legislation was necessary to protect law-abiding citizens with respect to the acquisition, possession, or use of firearms for lawful purposes. FOPA therefore amended § 921 to include a definition of the term "engaged in the business,"[5] and amended § 924 to add a scienter requirement as a condition to the imposition of penalties for most of the unlawful acts defined in § 922. For three categories of offenses the intent required is that the defendant acted "knowingly;" for the fourth category, which includes "any other provision of this chapter," the required intent is that the defendant acted "willfully."[6] The

5. "(21) The term 'engaged in the business' means—* * *

"(C) as applied to a dealer in firearms, as defined in section 921(a)(11)(A), a person who devotes time, attention, and labor to dealing in firearms as a regular course of trade or business with the principal objective of livelihood and profit through the repetitive purchase and resale of firearms, but such term shall not include a person who makes occasional sales, exchanges, or purchases of firearms for the enhancement of a personal collection or for a hobby, or who sells all or part of his personal collection of firearms...."

6. Title 18 U.S.C. § 924(a)(1) currently provides:

"Except as otherwise provided in this subsection, subsection (b), (c), or (f) of this section, or in section 929, whoever—

"(A) knowingly makes any false statement or representation with respect to the information required by this chapter to be kept in the records of a person licensed under this chapter or in applying for any license or exemption or relief from disability under the provisions of this chapter;

"(B) knowingly violates subsection (a)(4), (f), (k), (r), (v), or (w) of section 922;

"(C) knowingly imports or brings into the United States or any possession thereof any

§ 922(a)(1)(A) offense at issue in this case is an "other provision" in the "willfully" category.

II

The jury having found petitioner guilty, we accept the Government's version of the evidence. That evidence proved that petitioner did not have a federal license to deal in firearms; that he used so-called "straw purchasers" in Ohio to acquire pistols that he could not have purchased himself; that the straw purchasers made false statements when purchasing the guns; that petitioner assured the straw purchasers that he would file the serial numbers off the guns; and that he resold the guns on Brooklyn street corners known for drug dealing. The evidence was unquestionably adequate to prove that petitioner was dealing in firearms, and that he knew that his conduct was unlawful. There was, however, no evidence that he was aware of the federal law that prohibits dealing in firearms without a federal license.

Petitioner was charged with a conspiracy to violate 18 U.S.C. § 922(a)(1)(A), by willfully engaging in the business of dealing in firearms, and with a substantive violation of that provision. After the close of evidence, petitioner requested that the trial judge instruct the jury that petitioner could be convicted only if he knew of the federal licensing requirement, but the judge rejected this request. Instead, the trial judge gave this explanation of the term "willfully:"

> "A person acts willfully if he acts intentionally and purposely and with the intent to do something the law forbids, that is, with the bad purpose to disobey or to disregard the law. Now, the person need not be aware of the specific law or rule that his conduct may be violating. But he must act with the intent to do something that the law forbids."

Petitioner was found guilty on both counts. On appeal he argued that the evidence was insufficient because there was no proof that he had knowledge of the federal licensing requirement, and that the trial judge had erred by failing to instruct the jury that such knowledge was an essential element of the offense. The Court of Appeals affirmed. It concluded that the instructions were proper and that the Government had elicited "ample proof" that petitioner had acted willfully. Because the Eleventh Circuit has held that it is necessary for the Government to prove that the defendant acted with knowledge of the licensing requirement, United States v. Sanchez–Corcino, 85 F.3d 549, 553–554 (C.A.11 1996), we granted certiorari to resolve the conflict.

III

The word "willfully" is sometimes said to be "a word of many meanings" whose construction is often dependent on the context in

firearm or ammunition in violation of section 922(*l*); or

"(D) willfully violates any other provision of this chapter,

"shall be fined under this title, imprisoned not more than five years, or both."

which it appears. Most obviously it differentiates between deliberate and unwitting conduct, but in the criminal law it also typically refers to a culpable state of mind. As a general matter, when used in the criminal context, a "willful" act is one undertaken with a "bad purpose." In other words, in order to establish a "willful" violation of a statute, "the Government must prove that the defendant acted with knowledge that his conduct was unlawful." Ratzlaf v. United States, 510 U.S. 135, 137 (1994).

Petitioner argues that a more particularized showing is required in this case for two principal reasons. First, he argues that the fact that Congress used the adverb "knowingly" to authorize punishment of three categories of acts made unlawful by § 922 and the word "willfully" when it referred to unlicensed dealing in firearms demonstrates that the Government must shoulder a special burden in cases like this. This argument is not persuasive because the term "knowingly" does not necessarily have any reference to a culpable state of mind or to knowledge of the law. As Justice Jackson correctly observed, "the knowledge requisite to knowing violation of a statute is factual knowledge as distinguished from knowledge of the law." Thus, in United States v. Bailey, 444 U.S. 394 (1980), we held that the prosecution fulfills its burden of proving a knowing violation of the escape statute "if it demonstrates that an escapee knew his actions would result in his leaving physical confinement without permission." And in Staples v. United States, 511 U.S. 600 (1994), we held that a charge that the defendant's possession of an unregistered machine gun was unlawful required proof "that he knew the weapon he possessed had the characteristics that brought it within the statutory definition of a machine gun." It was not, however, necessary to prove that the defendant knew that his possession was unlawful. Thus, unless the text of the statute dictates a different result, the term "knowingly" merely requires proof of knowledge of the facts that constitute the offense.

With respect to the three categories of conduct that are made punishable by § 924 if performed "knowingly," the background presumption that every citizen knows the law makes it unnecessary to adduce specific evidence to prove that "an evil-meaning mind" directed the "evil-doing hand." More is required, however, with respect to the conduct in the fourth category that is only criminal when done "willfully." The jury must find that the defendant acted with an evil-meaning mind, that is to say, that he acted with knowledge that his conduct was unlawful.

Petitioner next argues that we must read § 924(a)(1)(D) to require knowledge of the law because of our interpretation of "willfully" in two other contexts. In certain cases involving willful violations of the tax laws, we have concluded that the jury must find that the defendant was aware of the specific provision of the tax code that he was charged with violating. See, e.g., Cheek v. United States, 498 U.S. 192, 201 (1991). Similarly, in order to satisfy a willful violation in *Ratzlaf*, we concluded that the jury had to find that the defendant knew that his structuring of cash transactions to avoid a reporting requirement was unlawful. See 510 U.S., at 138, 149. Those cases, however, are readily distinguishable. Both the tax cases and *Ratzlaf* involved highly technical statutes that presented the danger of ensnaring individuals engaged in apparently innocent conduct. As a result, we held that these statutes "carve out an exception to the traditional rule" that ignorance of the law is no excuse and require that the defendant have knowledge of the law. The danger of convicting individuals engaged in apparently innocent activity that motivated our decisions in the tax cases and *Ratzlaf* is not present here because the jury found that this petitioner knew that his conduct was unlawful.

Thus, the willfulness requirement of § 924(a)(1)(D) does not carve out an exception to the traditional rule that ignorance of the law is no excuse; knowledge that the conduct is unlawful is all that is required. * * *

One sentence in the trial court's instructions to the jury, read by itself, contained a misstatement of the law. In a portion of the instructions that were given after the correct statement that we have already quoted, the judge stated: "In this case, the government is not required to prove that the defendant knew that a license was required, nor is the government required to prove that he had knowledge that he was breaking the law." If the judge had added the words "that required a license," the sentence would have been accurate, but as given it was not.

Nevertheless, that error does not provide a basis for reversal for four reasons. First, petitioner did not object to that sentence, except insofar as he had argued that the jury should have been instructed that the Government had the burden of proving that he had knowledge of the federal licensing requirement. Second, in the context of the entire instructions, it seems unlikely that the jury was misled. Third, petitioner failed to raise this argument in the Court of Appeals. Finally, our grant of certiorari was limited to the narrow legal question whether knowledge of the licensing requirement is an essential element of the offense.

Accordingly, the judgment of the Court of Appeals is affirmed.

[JUSTICE SOUTER's concurring opinion is omitted.]

JUSTICE SCALIA, with whom THE CHIEF JUSTICE and JUSTICE GINSBURG join, dissenting.

Petitioner Sillasse Bryan was convicted of "willfully" violating the federal licensing requirement for firearms dealers. The jury apparently found, and the evidence clearly shows, that Bryan was aware in a general way that some aspect of his conduct was unlawful. The issue is whether that general knowledge of illegality is enough to sustain the conviction, or whether a "willful" violation of the licensing provision requires proof that the defendant knew that his conduct was unlawful specifically because he lacked the necessary license. On that point the statute is, in my view, genuinely ambiguous. Most of the Court's opinion is devoted to confirming half of that ambiguity by refuting Bryan's various arguments that the statute clearly requires specific knowledge of the licensing requirement. The Court offers no real justification for its implicit conclusion that either (1) the statute unambiguously requires only general knowledge of illegality, or (2) ambiguously requiring only general knowledge is enough. Instead, the Court curiously falls back on "the traditional rule that ignorance of the law is no excuse" to conclude that "knowledge that the conduct is unlawful is all that is required." In my view, this case calls for the application of a different canon—"the familiar rule that, where there is ambiguity in a criminal statute, doubts are resolved in favor of the defendant." [Citations]

Section 922(a)(1)(A) of Title 18 makes it unlawful for any person to engage in the business of dealing in firearms without a federal license. That provision is enforced criminally through § 924(a)(1)(D), which imposes criminal penalties on whoever "willfully violates any other provision of this chapter." The word "willfully" has a wide range of meanings, and "its construction [is] often * * * influenced by its context." [Citations] In some contexts it connotes nothing more than "an act which is intentional, or knowing, or voluntary, as distinguished from accidental." United States v. Murdock, 290 U.S. 389, 394 (1933). In the present context, however * * * the United States concedes (and the Court apparently agrees) that the violation is not "willful" unless the defendant knows in a general way that his conduct is unlawful.

That concession takes this case beyond any useful application of the maxim that ignorance of the law is no excuse. Everyone agrees that § 924(a)(1)(D) requires some knowledge of the law; the only real question is which law? The Court's answer is that knowledge of any law is enough—or, put another way, that the defendant must be ignorant of every law violated by his course of conduct to be innocent of willfully violating the licensing requirement. The Court points to no textual basis for that conclusion other than the notoriously malleable word "willfully" itself. Instead, it seems to fall back on a presumption (apparently derived from the rule that ignorance of the law is no excuse) that even where ignorance of the law is an excuse, that excuse should be construed as narrowly as the statutory language permits.

I do not believe that the Court's approach makes sense of the statute that Congress enacted. I have no quarrel with the Court's assertion that "willfully" in § 924(a)(1)(D) requires only "general" knowledge of illegality—in the sense that the defendant need not be able to recite chapter and verse from Title 18 of the United States Code. It is enough, in my view, if the defendant is generally aware that the actus reus punished by the statute—dealing in firearms without a license—is illegal. But the Court is willing to accept a mens rea so "general" that it is entirely divorced from the actus reus this statute was enacted to punish. That approach turns § 924(a)(1)(D) into a strange and unlikely creature. Bryan would be guilty of "willfully" dealing in firearms without a federal license even if, for example, he had never heard of the licensing requirement but was aware that he had violated the law by using straw purchasers or filing the serial numbers off the pistols. The

Court does not even limit (for there is no rational basis to limit) the universe of relevant laws to federal firearms statutes. Bryan would also be "act[ing] with an evil-meaning mind," and hence presumably be guilty of "willfully" dealing in firearms without a license, if he knew that his street-corner transactions violated New York City's business licensing or sales tax ordinances. (For that matter, it ought to suffice if Bryan knew that the car out of which he sold the guns was illegally double-parked, or if, in order to meet the appointed time for the sale, he intentionally violated Pennsylvania's speed limit on the drive back from the gun purchase in Ohio.) Once we stop focusing on the conduct the defendant is actually charged with (i.e., selling guns without a license), I see no principled way to determine what law the defendant must be conscious of violating.

Congress is free, of course, to make criminal liability under one statute turn on knowledge of another, to use its firearms dealer statutes to encourage compliance with New York City's tax collection efforts, and to put judges and juries through the kind of mental gymnastics described above. But these are strange results, and I would not lightly assume that Congress intended to make liability under a federal criminal statute depend so heavily upon the vagaries of local law—particularly local law dealing with completely unrelated subjects. If we must have a presumption in cases like this one, I think it would be more reasonable to presume that, when Congress makes ignorance of the law a defense to a criminal prohibition, it ordinarily means ignorance of the unlawfulness of the specific conduct punished by that criminal prohibition.

That is the meaning we have given the word "willfully" in other contexts where we have concluded it requires knowledge of the law. See, e.g., *Ratzlaf*, 510 U.S., at 149 ("To convict Ratzlaf of the crime with which he was charged, . . . the jury had to find he knew the structuring in which he engaged was unlawful"); Cheek v. United States, 498 U.S. 192, 201 (1991) ("The standard for the statutory willfulness requirement is the 'voluntary, intentional violation of a known legal duty.' . . . [T]he issue is whether the defendant knew of the duty purportedly imposed by the provision of the statute or regulation he is accused of violating"). The Court explains these cases on the ground that they involved "highly technical statutes that presented the danger of ensnaring individuals engaged in apparently innocent conduct." That is no explanation at all. The complexity of the tax and currency laws may explain why the Court interpreted "willful" to require some awareness of illegality, as opposed to merely "an act which is intentional, or knowing, or voluntary, as distinguished from accidental." *Murdock*, 290 U.S., at 394. But it in no way justifies the distinction the Court seeks to draw today between knowledge of the law the defendant is actually charged with violating and knowledge of any law the defendant could conceivably be charged with violating. To protect the pure of heart, it is not necessary to forgive someone whose surreptitious laundering of drug money violates, unbeknownst to him, a technical currency statute. There, as here, regardless of how "complex" the violated statute may be, the defendant would have acted "with an evil-meaning mind."

It seems to me likely that Congress had a presumption of offense-specific knowledge of illegality in mind when it enacted the provision here at issue. Another section of the Firearms Owners' Protection Act, Pub.L. No. 99–308, 100 Stat. 449, prohibits licensed dealers from selling firearms to out-of-state residents unless they fully comply with the laws of both States. 18 U.S.C. § 922(b)(3). The provision goes on to state that all licensed dealers "shall be presumed, for purposes of this subparagraph, in the absence of evidence to the contrary, to have had actual knowledge of the State laws and published ordinances of both States." Like the dealer-licensing provision at issue here, a violation of § 922(b)(3) is a criminal offense only if committed "willfully" within the meaning of § 924(a)(1)(D). The Court is quite correct that this provision does not establish beyond doubt that "willfully" requires knowledge of the particular prohibitions violated: the fact that knowledge (attributed knowledge) of those prohibitions will be sufficient does not demonstrate conclusively that knowledge of other prohibitions will not be sufficient. But though it does not demonstrate, it certainly suggests. To say that only willful violation of a certain law is criminal, but that knowledge of the existence of that law is presumed, fairly reflects, I think, a presumption that willful violation requires knowledge of the law violated.

If one had to choose, therefore, I think a presumption of statutory intent that is the opposite of the one the Court applies would be more reasonable. I would not, however, decide this case on the basis of any presumption at all. It is common ground that the statutory context here requires some awareness of the law for a § 924(a)(1)(D) conviction, but the statute is simply ambiguous, or silent, as to the precise contours of that mens rea requirement. In the face of that ambiguity, I would invoke the rule that "ambiguity concerning the ambit of criminal statutes should be resolved in favor of lenity," United States v. Bass, 404 U.S., at 347 (1971).

* * *

I respectfully dissent.

LAMBERT v. CALIFORNIA

Supreme Court of the United States, 1957.
355 U.S. 225, 78 S.Ct. 240, 2 L.Ed.2d 228.

Mr. Justice Douglas delivered the opinion of the Court.

Section 52.38(a) of the Los Angeles Municipal Code defines "convicted person" as follows:

> "Any person who, subsequent to January 1, 1921, has been or hereafter is convicted of an offense punishable as a felony in the State of California, or who has been or who is hereafter convicted of any offense in any place other than the State of California, which

offense, if committed in the State of California, would have been punishable as a felony."

Section 52.39 provides that it shall be unlawful for "any convicted person" to be or remain in Los Angeles for a period of more than five days without registering; it requires any person having a place of abode outside the city to register if he comes into the city on five occasions or more during a 30-day period; and it prescribes the information to be furnished the Chief of Police on registering.

Section 52.43(b) makes the failure to register a continuing offense, each day's failure constituting a separate offense.

Appellant, arrested on suspicion of another offense, was charged with a violation of this registration law. The evidence showed that she had been at the time of her arrest a resident of Los Angeles for over seven years. Within that period she had been convicted in Los Angeles of the crime of forgery, an offense which California punishes as a felony. Though convicted of a crime punishable as a felony, she had not at the time of her arrest registered under the Municipal Code. At the trial, appellant asserted that § 52.39 of the Code denies her due process of law and other rights under the Federal Constitution, unnecessary to enumerate. The trial court denied this objection. The case was tried to a jury which found appellant guilty. The court fined her $250 and placed her on probation for three years. * * *

We must assume that appellant had no actual knowledge of the requirement that she register under this ordinance, as she offered proof of this defense which was refused. The question is whether a registration act of this character violates due process where it is applied to a person who has no actual knowledge of his duty to register, and where no showing is made of the probability of such knowledge.

We do not go with Blackstone in saying that "a vicious will" is necessary to constitute a crime, for conduct alone without regard to the intent of the doer is often sufficient. There is wide latitude in the lawmakers to declare an offense and to exclude elements of knowledge and diligence from its definition. * * * But we deal here with conduct that is wholly passive—mere failure to register. It is unlike the commission of acts, or the failure to act under circumstances that should alert the doer to the consequences of his deed. The rule that "ignorance of the law will not excuse" is deep in our law, as is the principle that of all the powers of local government, the police power is "one of the least limitable." On the other hand, due process places some limits on its exercise. Engrained in our concept of due process is the requirement of notice. Notice is sometimes essential so that the citizen has the chance to defend charges. Notice is required before property interests are disturbed, before assessments are made, before penalties are assessed. Notice is required in a myriad of situations where a penalty or forfeiture might be suffered for mere failure to act. * * *

Registration laws are common and their range is wide. Many such laws are akin to licensing statutes in that they pertain to the regulation of business activities. But the present ordinance is entirely different. Violation of its provisions is unaccompanied by any activity whatever, mere presence in the city being the test. Moreover, circumstances which might move one to inquire as to the necessity of registration are completely lacking. At most the ordinance is but a law enforcement technique designed for the convenience of law enforcement agencies through which a list of the names and addresses of felons then residing in a given community is compiled. The disclosure is merely a compilation of former convictions already publicly recorded in the jurisdiction where obtained. Nevertheless, this appellant on first becoming aware of her duty to register was given no opportunity to comply with the law and avoid its penalty, even though her default was entirely innocent. She could but suffer the consequences of the ordinance, namely, conviction with the imposition of heavy criminal penalties thereunder. We believe that actual knowledge of the duty to register or proof of the probability of such knowledge and subsequent failure to comply are necessary before a conviction under the ordinance can stand. As Holmes wrote in The Common Law, "A law which punished conduct which would not be blameworthy in the average member of the community would be too severe for that community to bear." Its severity lies in the absence of an opportunity either to avoid the consequences of the law or to defend any prosecution brought under it. Where a person did not know of the duty to register and where there was no proof of the probability of such knowledge, he may not be convicted consistently with due process. Were it otherwise, the evil would be as great as it is when the law is written in print too fine to read or in a language foreign to the community.

Reversed.

MR. JUSTICE BURTON, dissents because he believes that, as applied to this appellant, the ordinance does not violate her constitutional rights.

MR. JUSTICE FRANKFURTER, whom MR. JUSTICE HARLAN and MR. JUSTICE WHITTAKER join, dissenting.

The present laws of the United States and of the forty-eight States are thick with provisions that command that some things not be done and others be done, although persons convicted under such provisions may have had no awareness of what the law required or that what they did was wrongdoing. The body of decisions sustaining such legislation, including innumerable registration laws, is almost as voluminous as the legislation itself. * * *

Surely there can hardly be a difference as a matter of fairness, of hardship, or of justice, if one may invoke it, between the case of a person wholly innocent of wrongdoing, in the sense that he was not remotely conscious of violating any law, who is imprisoned for five years for conduct relating to narcotics, and the case of another person who is placed on probation for three years on condition that she pay $250, for failure, as a local resident, convicted under local law of a felony, to register under a law passed as an exercise of the State's "police power."[1] Considerations of hardship often lead courts, naturally enough, to attribute to a statute the requirement of a certain mental element—some consciousness of wrongdoing and knowledge of the law's command—as a matter of statutory construction. Then, too, a cruelly disproportionate relation between what the law requires and the sanction for its disobedience may constitute a violation of the Eighth Amendment as a cruel and unusual punishment, and, in respect to the States, even offend the Due Process Clause of the Fourteenth Amendment.

But what the Court here does is to draw a constitutional line between a State's requirement of doing and not doing. What is this but a return to Year Book distinctions between feasance and nonfeasance—a distinction that may have significance in the evolution of common-law notions of liability, but is inadmissible as a line between constitutionality and unconstitutionality. * * *

If the generalization that underlies, and alone can justify, this decision were to be given its relevant scope, a whole volume of the United States Reports would be required to document in detail the legislation in this country that would fall or be impaired. I abstain from entering upon a consideration of such legislation, and adjudications upon it, because I feel confident that the present decision will turn out to be an isolated deviation from the strong current of precedents—a derelict on the waters of the law. Accordingly, I content myself with dissenting.

Note

The maxim that "ignorance of the law is no defense" is overbroad. It is important to distinguish between two quite different types of ignorance: (1) ignorance of the existence of a particular criminal prohibition; and (2) ignorance or mistake about an element of the crime. A defendant who marries two women not knowing that bigamy is a crime is an example of the first situation; a defendant who remarries after obtaining an apparently valid (but actually invalid) divorce is an example of the second situation.

The law is clear that it is no defense to a bigamy charge that the defendant did not know that it was unlawful to have more than one spouse at the same time. But suppose that the defendant believed that he was free to remarry because (1) he thought his former spouse was dead; (2) his former spouse had told him falsely that she had obtained a divorce; or (3) he had obtained a divorce in a foreign court which he mistakenly thought was valid due to his ignorance of the law governing foreign divorces. If the defendant has a defense in either of the first two cases, then it would seem that the third case should be treated similarly, although it is based upon "ignorance of the law." The Supreme Court of Delaware reversed a bigamy

1. This case does not involve a person who, convicted of a crime in another jurisdiction, must decide whether he has been convicted of a crime that "would have been punishable as a felony" had it been committed in California. Appellant committed forgery in California, and was convicted under California law. Furthermore, she was convicted in Los Angeles itself, and there she resided for over seven years before the arrest leading to the present proceedings.

conviction of a man who had remarried after receiving an erroneous assurance from a reputable attorney that his out-of state divorce from his first wife was valid. Long v. State, 44 Del. 262, 65 A.2d 489 (1949). See also People v. Vogel, 46 Cal.2d 798, 299 P.2d 850 (1956).

Courts frequently do not understand or observe the distinction between the two types of mistake of law. In a 1982 California decision a woman named Snyder was convicted of "possession of a concealable firearm by a convicted felon." She had been convicted previously of the felony of sale of marijuana, on the basis of a bargained plea that involved no jail sentence. She offered to prove that her attorney had advised her that she was pleading guilty to a misdemeanor, and that (believing that she was not a felon) she had subsequently registered to vote and voted.

The trial court refused to admit any evidence of her mistaken belief that her prior conviction was a misdemeanor, and refused to instruct the jury that her knowledge of the felony conviction was an element of the firearm charge. The California Supreme Court held by a narrow majority that the trial court was correct because ignorance of the law is no defense. The dissenters conceded that lack of knowledge that it was a crime for a felon to possess a concealable firearm would not be a defense, but argued that "a mistaken impression as to the legal effect of a collateral matter may mean that a defendant does not understand the significance of his conduct and may negate criminal intent." People v. Snyder, 32 Cal.3d 590, 186 Cal.Rptr. 485, 652 P.2d 42 (1982).

Of course, the legislature can always make knowledge of a legal matter relevant by specifically incorporating it as an element of the offense. Whether it has done so is a question of statutory interpretation. A court that is favorably disposed may infer such a requirement from general language such as "without lawful authority." In People v. Weiss, 276 N.Y. 384, 12 N.E.2d 514 (1938), the defendants were convicted of seizing or kidnapping another "with intent to cause him, without authority of law, to be confined or imprisoned * * *." They testified that they seized and confined the victim in the mistaken belief that he was involved in the Lindbergh baby kidnapping. The New York Court of Appeals in a 4–3 decision reversed the convictions because the trial judge had refused to instruct the jury that the defendants should be acquitted if they believed in good faith belief that they had legal authority to seize and confine the victim. The dissent argued that "the intent applies to the seizing and to the confining," and not to the absence of legal authority.

Mistake of law was raised as a defense in a notorious case growing out of the "Watergate" scandals. Barker and Martinez were prosecuted for conspiracy to violate the civil rights of a certain psychiatrist. The defendants had participated in a burglary of the psychiatrist's office to obtain records of a former patient, Daniel Ellsberg, who was suspected of leaking classified documents. The burglars had been recruited by one Howard Hunt, a sometime White House aide with a background in covert CIA operations. The defendants claimed that Hunt had led them to believe that the operation was officially authorized in the interests of national security, and that they had reasonably believed in the apparent authority of Hunt to convey such an authorization. The trial court ruled as a matter of law that such a mistake as to the scope of Hunt's legal authority was no defense.

A closely divided panel of the Court of Appeals reversed the convictions, holding that the trial judge should have instructed the jury to return a verdict of not guilty if the defendants honestly and reasonably relied on the apparent authority of Hunt to authorize the operation. United States v. Barker, 546 F.2d 940 (D.C.Cir.1976). Compare United States v. Ehrlichman, 546 F.2d 910 (D.C.Cir.1976), where the same court held that former presidential assistant John Ehrlichman, who had actually approved the operation on behalf of the President, was not entitled to claim a similar defense. The majority decision in the *Barker* case has been subjected to powerful criticism. See the dissenting opinion of Judge Leventhal, 546 F.2d at 957.

Ignorance of the scope or existence of the criminal prohibition itself probably ought to be a defense when the offense is an unusual one and the defendant had no reasonable opportunity to learn about it. This consideration probably best explains the holding in Lambert v. California, supra. The Supreme Court distinguished *Lambert* in United States v. Freed, 401 U.S. 601 (1971). In that case the district court dismissed an indictment charging possession of hand grenades not registered under the National Firearms Act because it did not allege that the defendant knew that the hand grenades were not registered. The Court reversed, holding that the Act was a "regulatory measure" which did not require knowledge or "scienter" as to the element of non-registration. Distinguishing *Lambert,* the opinion of Mr. Justice Douglas asserted that "Being in Los Angeles is not *per se* blameworthy," whereas "one would hardly be surprised to learn that possession of hand grenades is not an innocent act." In other words, the nature of the conduct was such as to give notice of the likelihood of some regulation.

UNITED STATES v. GARRETT

United States Court of Appeals, Fifth Circuit, 1993.
984 F.2d 1402.

GARWOOD, CIRCUIT JUDGE:

On December 18, 1990, Regina Kay Garrett was a ticketed passenger for and attempted to board flight 457 of L'Express Airlines, a regularly scheduled commercial commuter airline, from New Orleans to Alexandria, Louisiana. Passing through the New Orleans airport security, Garrett was stopped when the security guard monitoring the X-ray scanner noticed a dark mass in the hand bag that Garrett had placed on the conveyor belt. A consensual search of the bag was conducted and a small hand gun was discovered therein. The gun, a Browning .25 caliber semi-automatic, was loaded with six rounds in the magazine and one in the chamber. Garrett told security personnel that she had forgotten that the gun was in her purse.[a]

a. News reports indicate that airport security officials confiscate 2,000 to 3,000 weapons annually. When the Garrett case arose in the early 1990s, approximately 2,500 firearms were seized each year. See McDowell, Guns at Airports: A Common Problem, N.Y. Times, Dec. 29, 1992, at A12. Nearly a decade later, similar numbers of weapons were being seized. See John Sullivan & Randy Kennedy, Armed Intruder Exposes Limits of Air Security, N.Y. Times, July 29, 2000, at A1 (estimating 2,000 weapons seized each year); and Michael Moss, A Nation Challenged: Airport Security, U.S. Airport Task Begins with Hiring, N.Y. Times, Nov. 23, 2001, at A1 (estimat-

Garrett was charged with attempting to board an aircraft with a concealed weapon in violation of the Federal Aviation Act (the Act or the statute).[b] Garrett waived her right to a jury trial and the cause was tried by consent before a United States Magistrate Judge. Garrett was found guilty and sentenced to five years' probation and a $25 special assessment. As a special condition of probation, the magistrate ordered Garrett to reside for six months in a halfway house. * * *

On appeal, Garrett * * * argues that her conviction is invalid because the magistrate did not find that she had actual knowledge that the gun was in her purse. The government's position is that § 1472(*l*)(1) is a strict liability offense and contains no intent requirement whatsoever. The magistrate, eschewing both extremes, declared that "this Court is of the opinion that it would be consistent with Fifth Circuit jurisprudence and the United States Constitution to apply a 'should have known' standard to this misdemeanor offense." We agree.

In determining whether section 1472(*l*)(1) contains a mens rea requirement, our overarching task is to give effect to the intent of the Congress. The Congress is fully capable of creating strict liability crimes when it is their intent to do so. Of course, the Congress cannot do so in a way that transgresses constitutional boundaries. Accordingly, to give due respect both to the will of the Congress and the mandate of the Constitution, we construe the acts of Congress, whenever possible, so as to avoid raising serious constitutional questions.

Our effort to discern Congress' intent must begin, of course, with the statute's language. By its explicit terms, the statute makes no mention of mens rea. But before going any further, we reject a textual argument made by the government. That § 1472(*l*)(1) contains no mens rea requirement, the government maintains, must be inferred from the fact that the very next subsection does so explicitly.[16] To be sure, the fact that § 1472(*l*)(2) speaks of willful or reckless violations of § 1472(*l*)(1)

ing 3,000 weapons seized annually). Even celebrities are not immune from weapons seizures. Among the celebrities reported to have been caught with weapons at airports are singer and pianist Harry Connick, Jr., who was arrested in New York's John F. Kennedy International Airport for this offense. The Times reports that, "Most of those arrested ... are like Mr. Connick: they say they simply forgot they were carrying guns to the airport." McDowell, *supra*.—ed.

b. On July 5, 1994, the aircraft piracy and other aircraft offenses which previously appeared in the Appendix to Title 49, United States Code, were recodified in Title 49 by Public Law No. 103–272, § 1(e), 108 Stat. 1244. The statute referred to in *Garrett*, 49 U.S.C. App. § 1472(*l*), now is codified in 49 U.S.C. § 46505. At the time Garrett was apprehended, 49 U.S.C. App. § 1472(*l*) provided in pertinent part:

"(1) With respect to any aircraft in, or intended for operation in air transportation or intrastate air transportation, whoever—(A) while aboard, or while attempting to board such aircraft has on or about his person or his property a concealed deadly or dangerous weapon which is, or could be, accessible to such person in flight; ... shall be fined not more than $10,000 or imprisoned not more than one year, or both."—ed.

16. 49 U.S.C. App. § 1472(*l*)(2) provided:

"Whoever willfully and without regard for the safety of human life, or with reckless disregard for the safety of human life, shall commit an act prohibited by paragraph (1) of this subsection, shall be fined not more than $25,000 or imprisoned not more than five years, or both."

is convincing evidence that one need not act willfully or recklessly to violate § 1472(*l*)(1). One cannot infer from § 1472(*l*)(2), however, that § 1472(*l*)(1) contains no mens rea requirement whatsoever. There is a range of culpability between recklessness or willfulness, on the one hand, and total blamelessness, on the other, the most familiar of which is ordinary negligence. Therefore, the absence of knowledge is not the necessary converse of willfulness. So too, in some contexts, it takes more than knowledge for a violation to be willful. See, e.g., Cheek v. United States, 498 U.S. 192 (1991) (conviction for willful failure to file a federal income tax return and willful evasion of income taxes requires the voluntary, intentional violation of a known legal duty). * * *

The requirement of mens rea as predicate to criminal liability is a fundamental precept of the Anglo–American common law. * * * So deeply rooted is this tradition that it is presumed that the Congress intended to incorporate some requirement of mens rea in its definition of federal crimes, although that presumption is rebuttable. [Citations] In short, we will presume that Congress intended to require some degree of mens rea as part of a federal criminal offense absent evidence of a contrary congressional intent. * * *

This presumption is well established in the case law of this Circuit. A seminal case in this regard is United States v. Delahoussaye, 573 F.2d 910 (5th Cir.1978), in which defendants were convicted of duck hunting in violation of federal regulations promulgated pursuant to the Migratory Bird Treaty Act, 16 U.S.C. § 703 et seq. These regulations prohibit the shooting of migratory game birds over a baited field. Reasoning that hunters might innocently violate these regulations by hunting over a field without knowledge that it was baited, we held that "a minimum form of scienter—the 'should have known' form—is a necessary element of the offense." "Any other interpretation," we said, "would simply render criminal conviction an unavoidable occasional consequence of duck hunting."

In United States v. Anderson, 885 F.2d 1248 (5th Cir.1989)(en banc), defendant was convicted of violating the National Firearms Act, 26 U.S.C. § 5681 et seq. Concluding that this Court's "precedent permitting conviction of certain felonies without proof of mens rea ... is aberrational in our jurisprudence," id. at 1249, we reversed his conviction on the ground that the government had failed to prove that he knew that the guns were automatic weapons (and hence prohibited by the Act). * * *

In United States v. Wallington, 889 F.2d 573 (5th Cir.1989), defendant was convicted of divulging information that he had obtained within the scope of his official duties as a United States Customs agent in violation of 18 U.S.C. § 1905. We rejected his arguments that the statute was overbroad and vague by construing it narrowly to apply only to information that the employee knows to be confidential. "We do not believe that Congress intended to create strict criminal liability and impose prison sentences of up to one year for innocent disclosures of information."

In United States v. Nguyen, 916 F.2d 1016 (5th Cir.1990), defendant was convicted of possessing and importing a threatened species of sea turtle (caretta caretta) in violation of the Endangered Species Act, 16 U.S.C. § 1531 et seq. We affirmed and held that the Act contained no specific intent requirement: "it is sufficient that Nguyen knew that he was in possession of a turtle. The government was not required to prove that Nguyen knew that this turtle is a threatened species or that it is illegal to transport or import it." We distinguished *Anderson*, and refrained from reading into the Act a more demanding mens rea requirement, because Congress had made its intent clear: "The [House] committee explicitly stated that it did 'not intend to make knowledge of the law an element of either civil penalty or criminal violations of the Act.' "

Here, the text of § 1472(*l*)(1) provides no indication that the Congress intended to depart from the default rule of requiring some mens rea. Nor is there anything in the legislative history of the Federal Aviation Act that would lead us to believe that the Congress intended § 1472(*l*)(1) to be a wholly strict liability offense. At the same time, we think that a serious due process problem would be raised by application of this statute, which carries fairly substantial penalties, to someone who did not know and had no reason to know that he was carrying a weapon. Avoiding such a construction of § 1472(*l*)(1), moreover, would comport with the so-called "rule of lenity"—the principle that ambiguous criminal statutes should be construed in favor of the defendant. Therefore, in light of the principles laid down by the Supreme Court and our case law, we cannot conclude that the Congress intended § 1472(*l*)(1) to reach persons acting without any mens rea whatsoever. * * *

Having declined to construe section 1472(*l*)(1) as a strict liability crime, it remains to be determined what level of mental culpability will support a conviction under it. We believe that the minimum level of scienter—the "should have known" standard—is appropriate and consistent with our case law.

The touchstone in our analysis is the severity of the punishment authorized by the statute. A violation of section 1472(*l*)(1) is punishable by a fine of up to $10,000 and a prison sentence of up to one year. Therefore, a violation of section 1472(*l*)(1), although a non-petty offense,[21] is still a misdemeanor.

21. Petty offenses are statutorily defined as those punishable by not more than six months in prison or a $5,000 fine. The petty/non-petty distinction is an important one in our law because a defendant charged with a non-petty offense has a right to a jury trial, whereas virtually no petty offenses require jury trials. [Citations] There is some support for the notion that those crimes for which a jury trial is required are also the ones for which some degree of mens rea should be required. See Hopkins, Mens Rea and the Right to Trial by Jury, 76 Cal. L. Rev. 391, 397, 415–16 (1988)(arguing that the right to a jury trial includes the right to have a jury pass upon one's "moral blameworthiness" or mens rea). An offense that carries a punishment of one year or less, but more than six months, is statutorily defined as a Class A misdemeanor. Any offense for which a sentence of

We believe that a "should have known" standard is consistent with our prior cases in this area. This case is most akin to *Delahoussaye*, in which we also applied a "should have known" standard. In *Delahoussaye*, as here, the crime at issue was a misdemeanor, although one punishable by a maximum of only six months in prison rather than one year. We decline today to go as far as *Anderson*, in which we required actual knowledge, because the crime at issue in that case was a felony that carried a possible sentence of ten years imprisonment.

We conclude that one violates section 1472(*l*)(1) if, but only if, she either knew or should have known that the concealed weapon in question was on or about her person or property while aboard or attempting to board the aircraft.

There is ample evidence in the record to support the magistrate's conclusion that Garrett should have known that she was carrying the gun when she attempted to board by going through security. Garrett testified that she had traveled by air many times and that she was aware that it was illegal to try to bring a gun through airport security. And if she needed any reminder, there were two large signs in the area of the security checkpoint. The first sign, printed with large white letters upon a bright red background, stated: "CARRY NO WEAPONS OR EXPLOSIVES BEYOND THIS POINT: VIOLATORS ARE SUBJECT TO PROSECUTION UNDER FEDERAL CRIMINAL STATUTES REQUIRING PENALTIES AND/OR IMPRISONMENT." ¶ The sign also had an image of a pistol and a knife over which was superimposed a circle and a diagonal line. The other sign displayed a list of "Federal Safety and Security Inspection Rules" and informed passengers, among other things, that, "Federal regulations prohibit persons from having a FIREARM, explosive or incendiary device on or about their person or accessible property when entering or in an airport sterile area or while aboard an aircraft."

It is also relevant that the gun was in Garrett's hand bag. Garrett testified that she owns and uses seven or eight purses and that she did not remember when she put the gun in this particular bag, which was described at trial as a large leather satchel. She stated that she did not put the gun in the bag on the day of the flight, nor did she think that day to check the bag for it. On the other hand, she testified that she knew that she previously had carried the gun in that particular bag. Garrett also testified that she had put her wallet, checkbook, and makeup in the bag on the day in question. It is inferable that she would have used the bag during the day. We think it patently reasonable to require individuals in such circumstances to be aware of the presence of a firearm in their purse or equivalent bag, or, indeed, to infer that they actually have such knowledge.

In short, there is sufficient evidence in the record to support the magistrate's finding that Garrett should have known that she was carrying a firearm. * * * AFFIRMED.

more than one year may be imposed is a felony.

Note

In response to the September 11, 2001, terrorist attacks on the World Trade Center and the Pentagon, Congress enacted the Uniting and Strengthening America by Providing Appropriate Tools Required to Intercept and Obstruct Terrorism Act of 2001, Pub. L. No. 107–56, which President Bush signed into law on October 26, 2001. More commonly referred to as the "USA Patriot Act," this legislation included provisions both amending several existing federal criminal statutes and enacting a number of new offenses. Because the terrorists hijacked commercial airliners to commit their crimes, and because of the public outrage at these crimes, this legislation could have served as an opportunity to convert the crime of attempting to board an aircraft with a concealed weapon into a strict liability offense. Congress instead retained the mens rea requirement of "should have known" applied in *Garrett.*

Various provisions of the "USA Patriot Act" utilized mens rea concepts common in federal legislation. For example, Congress enacted 18 U.S.C. § 1993, which makes it a felony to *willfully* engage in a variety of acts, including damaging or destroying mass transportation vehicles or facilities or personnel, or using biological agents or toxins as weapons in connection with mass transportation vehicles or facilities. The Act also created 18 U.S.C. § 2339, which makes it a felony for a person to harbor or conceal "any person who he *knows, or has reasonable grounds to believe*, has committed or is about to commit," terrorist acts violating the terms of listed federal statutes. The Act also added a new 18 U.S.C. § 175b, which prohibits an extensive list of "restricted person[s]," from shipping certain biological agents or toxins in interstate or foreign commerce. The crime is defined without reference to any mens rea element in § 175b(a), but § 175b(c) imposes penalties, including prison sentences of up to ten years, for anyone who "*knowingly* violates this section."

B. REGULATORY OFFENSES AND STRICT LIABILITY

MORISSETTE v. UNITED STATES

Supreme Court of the United States, 1952.
342 U.S. 246, 72 S.Ct. 240, 96 L.Ed. 288.

MR. JUSTICE JACKSON delivered the opinion of the Court.

This would have remained a profoundly insignificant case to all except its immediate parties had it not been so tried and submitted to the jury as to raise questions both fundamental and far-reaching in federal criminal law, for which reason we granted certiorari.

On a large tract of uninhabited and untilled land in a wooded and sparsely populated area of Michigan, the Government established a practice bombing range over which the Air Force dropped simulated bombs at ground targets. These bombs consisted of a metal cylinder about forty inches long and eight inches across, filled with sand and enough black powder to cause a smoke puff by which the strike could be located. At various places about the range signs read "Danger—Keep

Out—Bombing Range." Nevertheless, the range was known as good deer country and was extensively hunted.

Spent bomb casings were cleared from the targets and thrown into piles "so that they will be out of the way." They were not stacked or piled in any order but were dumped in heaps, some of which had been accumulating for four years or upwards, were exposed to the weather and rusting away.

Morissette, in December of 1948, went hunting in this area but did not get a deer. He thought to meet expenses of the trip by salvaging some of these casings. He loaded three tons of them on his truck and took them to a nearby farm, where they were flattened by driving a tractor over them. After expending this labor and trucking them to market in Flint, he realized $84.

Morissette, by occupation, is a fruit stand operator in summer and a trucker and scrap iron collector in winter. An honorably discharged veteran of World War II, he enjoys a good name among his neighbors and has had no blemish on his record more disreputable than a conviction for reckless driving.

The loading, crushing and transporting of these casings were all in broad daylight, in full view of passers-by, without the slightest effort at concealment. When an investigation was started, Morissette voluntarily, promptly and candidly told the whole story to the authorities, saying that he had no intention of stealing but thought the property was abandoned, unwanted and considered of no value to the Government. He was indicted, however, on the charge that he "did unlawfully, wilfully and knowingly steal and convert" property of the United States of the value of $84, in violation of 18 U.S.C. § 641, which provides that "whoever embezzles, steals, purloins, or knowingly converts" government property is punishable by fine and imprisonment. Morissette was convicted and sentenced to imprisonment for two months or to pay a fine of $200. The Court of Appeals affirmed, one judge dissenting.

On his trial, Morissette, as he had at all times told investigating officers, testified that from appearances he believed the casings were cast-off and abandoned, that he did not intend to steal the property, and took it with no wrongful or criminal intent. The trial court, however, was unimpressed, and ruled: "He took it because he thought it was abandoned and he knew he was on government property. * * * That is no defense. * * * I don't think anybody can have the defense they thought the property was abandoned on another man's piece of property." The court stated: "I will not permit you to show this man thought it was abandoned. * * * I hold in this case that there is no question of abandoned property." The court refused to submit or to allow counsel to argue to the jury whether Morissette acted with innocent intention. It charged: "And I instruct you that if you believe the testimony of the government in this case, he intended to take it. * * * He had no right to take this property. * * * And it is no defense to claim that it was abandoned, because it was on private property. * * * And I instruct you to this effect: That if this young man took this property (and he says he did), without any permission (he says he did), that was on the property of the United States Government (he says it was), that it was of the value of one cent or more (and evidently it was), that he is guilty of the offense charged here. If you believe the government, he is guilty. * * * The question on intent is whether or not he intended to take the property. He says he did. Therefore, if you believe either side, he is guilty." Petitioner's counsel contended, "But the taking must have been with a felonious intent." The court ruled, however: "That is presumed by his own act."

The Court of Appeals suggested that "greater restraint in expression should have been exercised", but affirmed the conviction because, "As we have interpreted the statute, appellant was guilty of its violation beyond a shadow of doubt, as evidenced even by his own admissions." Its construction of the statute is that it creates several separate and distinct offenses, one being knowing conversion of government property. The court ruled that this particular offense requires no element of criminal intent. This conclusion was thought to be required by the failure of Congress to express such a requisite and this Court's decisions in United States v. Behrman, 258 U.S. 280, and United States v. Balint, 258 U.S. 250.

I

In those cases this Court did construe mere omission from a criminal enactment of any mention of criminal intent as dispensing with it. If they be deemed precedents for principles of construction generally applicable to federal penal statutes, they authorize this conviction. Indeed, such adoption of the literal reasoning announced in those cases would do this and more—it would sweep out of all federal crimes, except when expressly preserved, the ancient requirement of a culpable state of mind. We think a résumé of their historical background is convincing that an effect has been ascribed to them more comprehensive than was contemplated and one inconsistent with our philosophy of criminal law.

The contention that an injury can amount to a crime only when inflicted by intention is no provincial or transient notion. It is as universal and persistent in mature systems of law as belief in freedom of the human will and a consequent ability and duty of the normal individual to choose between good and evil. A relation between some mental element and punishment for a harmful act is almost as instinctive as the child's familiar exculpatory "But I didn't mean to," and has afforded the rational basis for a tardy and unfinished substitution of deterrence and reformation in place of retaliation and vengeance as the motivation for public prosecution. Unqualified acceptance of this doctrine by English common law in the Eighteenth Century was indicated by Blackstone's sweeping statement that to constitute any crime there must first be a "vicious will." Common-law commentators of the Nineteenth Century early pronounced the same principle, although a few exceptions not relevant to our present problem came to be recognized.

Crime, as a compound concept, generally constituted only from concurrence of an evil-meaning mind with an evil-doing hand, was congenial to an intense individualism and took deep and early root in American soil. As the states codified the common law of crimes, even if their enactments were silent on the subject, their courts assumed that the omission did not signify disapproval of the principle but merely recognized that intent was so inherent in the idea of the offense that it required no statutory affirmation. Courts, with little hesitation or division, found an implication of the requirement as to offenses that were taken over from the common law. The unanimity with which they have adhered to the central thought that wrongdoing must be conscious to be criminal is emphasized by the variety, disparity and confusion of their definitions of the requisite but elusive mental element. However, courts of various jurisdictions, and for the purposes of different offenses, have devised working formulae, if not scientific ones, for the instruction of juries around such terms as "felonious intent," "criminal intent," "malice aforethought," "guilty knowledge," "fraudulent intent," "wilfulness," "*scienter*," to denote guilty knowledge, or "*mens rea*," to signify an evil purpose or mental culpability. By use or combination of these various tokens, they have sought to protect those who were not blameworthy in mind from conviction of infamous common-law crimes.

However, the *Balint* and *Behrman* offenses belong to a category of another character, with very different antecedents and origins. The crimes there involved depend on no mental element but consist only of forbidden acts or omissions. This, while not expressed by the Court, is made clear from examination of a century-old but accelerating tendency, discernible both here and in England, to call into existence new duties and crimes which disregard any ingredient of intent. The industrial revolution multiplied the number of workmen exposed to injury from increasingly powerful and complex mechanisms, driven by freshly discovered sources of energy, requiring higher precautions by employers. Traffic of velocities, volumes and varieties unheard of came to subject the wayfarer to intolerable casualty risks if owners and drivers were not to observe new cares and uniformities of conduct. Congestion of cities and crowding of quarters called for health and welfare regulations undreamed of in simpler times. Wide distribution of goods became an instrument of wide distribution of harm when those who dispersed food, drink, drugs, and even securities, did not comply with reasonable standards of quality, integrity, disclosure and care. Such dangers have engendered increasingly numerous and detailed regulations which heighten the duties of those in control of particular industries, trades, properties or activities that affect public health, safety or welfare.

While many of these duties are sanctioned by a more strict civil liability, lawmakers, whether wisely or not, have sought to make such regulations more effective by invoking criminal sanctions to be applied by the familiar technique of criminal prosecutions and convictions. This has confronted the courts with a multitude of prosecutions, based on statutes or administrative regulations, for what have been aptly called "public welfare offenses." These cases do not fit neatly into any of such accepted classifications of common-law offenses, such as those against the state, the person, property, or public morals. Many of these offenses are not in the nature of positive aggressions or invasions, with which the common law so often dealt, but are in the nature of neglect where the law requires care, or inaction where it imposes a duty. Many violations of such regulations result in no direct or immediate injury to person or property but merely create the danger or probability of it which the law seeks to minimize. While such offenses do not threaten the security of the state in the manner of treason, they may be regarded as offenses against its authority, for their occurrence impairs the efficiency of controls deemed essential to the social order as presently constituted. In this respect, whatever the intent of the violator, the injury is the same, and the consequences are injurious or not according to fortuity. Hence, legislation applicable to such offenses, as a matter of policy, does not specify intent as a necessary element. The accused, if he does not will the violation, usually is in a position to prevent it with no more care than society might reasonably expect and no more exertion than it might reasonably exact from one who assumed his responsibilities. Also, penalties commonly are relatively small, and conviction does no grave damage to an offender's reputation. Under such considerations, courts have turned to construing statutes and regulations which make no mention of intent as dispensing with it and holding that the guilty act alone makes out the crime. This has not, however, been without expressions of misgiving.

The pilot of the movement in this country appears to be a holding that a tavernkeeper could be convicted for selling liquor to an habitual drunkard even if he did not know the buyer to be such. Barnes v. State, 1849, 19 Conn. 398. Later came Massachusetts holdings that convictions for selling adulterated milk in violation of statutes forbidding such sales require no allegation or proof that defendant knew of the adulteration. Departures from the common-law tradition mainly of these general classes, were reviewed and their rationale appraised by Chief Justice Cooley, as follows: "I agree that as a rule there can be no crime without a criminal intent, but this is not by any means a universal rule. * * * Many statutes which are in the nature of police regulations, as this is, impose criminal penalties irrespective of any intent to violate them, the purpose being to require a degree of diligence for the protection of the public which shall render violation impossible." People v. Roby, 1884, 52 Mich. 577, 579, 18 N.W. 365, 366.

After the turn of the Century, a new use for crimes without intent appeared when New York enacted numerous and novel regulations of tenement houses, sanctioned by money penalties. Landlords contended that a guilty intent was essential to establish a violation. Judge Cardozo wrote the answer: "The defendant asks us to test the meaning of this statute by standards applicable to statutes that govern infamous crimes. The analogy, however, is deceptive. The element of conscious wrongdoing, the guilty mind accompanying the guilty act, is associated with the concept of crimes that are punished as infamous. * * * Even there it is not an invariable element. * * * But in the prosecution of minor offenses there is a wider range of practice and of power. Prosecutions for petty penalties have always constituted in our law a class by themselves. * * * That is true, though the prosecution is criminal in form." Tenement House Department of City of New York v. McDevitt, 1915, 215 N.Y. 160, 168, 109 N.E. 88, 90.

* * * Before long, similar questions growing out of federal legislation reached this Court. Its judgments were in harmony with this consensus of state judicial opinion, the existence of which may have led the Court to overlook the need for full exposition of their rationale in the context of federal law. In overruling a contention that there can be no conviction on an indictment which makes no charge of criminal intent but alleges only making of a sale of a narcotic forbidden by law, Chief Justice Taft, wrote: "While the general rule at common law was that the *scienter* was a necessary element in the indictment and proof of every crime, and this was followed in regard to statutory crimes even where the statutory definition did not in terms include it * * * there has been a modification of this view in respect to prosecutions under statutes the purpose of which would be obstructed by such a requirement. It is a question of legislative intent to be construed by the court. * * *" United States v. Balint, supra.

He referred, however, to "regulatory measures in the exercise of what is called the police power where the emphasis of the statute is evidently upon achievement of some social betterment rather than the punishment of the crimes as in cases of *mala in se*," and drew his citation of supporting authority chiefly from state court cases dealing with regulatory offenses.

On the same day, the Court determined that an offense under the Narcotic Drug Act does not require intent, saying, "If the offense be a statutory one, and intent or knowledge is not made an element of it, the indictment need not charge such knowledge or intent." United States v. Behrman, supra.

Of course, the purpose of every statute would be "obstructed" by requiring a finding of intent, if we assume that it had a purpose to convict without it. Therefore, the obstruction rationale does not help us to learn the purpose of the omission by Congress. And since no federal crime can exist except by force of statute, the reasoning of the Behrman opinion, if read literally, would work far-reaching changes in the composition of all federal crimes. * * *

It was not until recently that the Court took occasion more explicitly to relate abandonment of the ingredient of intent, not merely with considerations of expediency in obtaining convictions, nor with the *malum prohibitum* classification of the crime, but with the peculiar nature and quality of the offense. We referred to "* * * a now familiar type of legislation whereby penalties serve as effective means of regulation", and continued, "such legislation dispenses with the conventional requirement for criminal conduct—awareness of some wrongdoing. In the interest of the larger good it puts the burden of acting at hazard upon a person otherwise innocent but standing in responsible relation to a public danger." But we warned: "Hardship there doubtless may be under a statute which thus penalizes the transaction though consciousness of wrongdoing be totally wanting." United States v. Dotterweich, 320 U.S. 277, 280–281.

Neither this Court nor, so far as we are aware, any other has undertaken to delineate a precise line or set forth comprehensive criteria for distinguishing between crimes that require a mental element and crimes that do not. We attempt no closed definition, for the law on the subject is neither settled nor static. The conclusion reached in the *Balint* and *Behrman* cases has our approval and adherence for the circumstances to which it was there applied. A quite different question here is whether we will expand the doctrine of crimes without intent to include those charged here.

Stealing, larceny, and its variants and equivalents, were among the earliest offenses known to the law that existed before legislation; they are invasions of rights of property which stir a sense of insecurity in the whole community and arouse public demand for retribution, the penalty is high and, when a sufficient amount is involved, the infamy is that of a felony, which, says Maitland, is " * * * as bad a word as you can give to man or thing." State courts of last resort, on whom fall the heaviest burden of interpreting criminal law in this country, have consistently retained the requirement of intent in larceny type offenses. If any state has deviated, the exception has neither been called to our attention nor disclosed by our research.

Congress, therefore, omitted any express prescription of criminal intent from the enactment before us in the light of an unbroken course of judicial decision in all constituent states of the Union holding intent inherent in this class of offense, even when not expressed in a statute. Congressional silence as to mental elements in an Act merely adopting into federal statutory law a concept of crime already so well defined in common law and statutory interpretation by the states may warrant quite contrary inferences than the same silence in creating an offense new to general law, for whose definition the courts have no guidance except the Act. Because the offenses before this Court in the Balint and Behrman cases were of this latter class, we cannot accept them as authority for eliminating intent from offenses incorporated from the common law. Nor do exhaustive studies of state court cases disclose any well considered decisions applying the doctrine of crime without intent to such enacted common-law offenses, although a few deviations are notable as illustrative of the danger inherent in the Government's contentions here. * * *

Of course, the jury, considering Morissette's awareness that these casings were on government property, his failure to seek any permission for their removal and his self-interest as a witness, might have disbelieved his profession of innocent intent and concluded that his assertion of a belief that the casings were abandoned was an afterthought. Had the jury convicted on proper instructions it would be the end of the matter. But juries are not bound by what seems inescapable logic to judges. They might have concluded that the heaps of spent casings left in the hinterland to rust away presented an appearance of unwanted and abandoned junk, and that lack of any conscious deprivation of property or intentional injury was indicated by Morissette's good character, the openness of the taking, crushing and transporting of the casings, and the candor with which it was all admitted. They might have refused to brand Morissette as a thief. Had they done so, that too would have been the end of the matter.

Reversed.

UNITED STATES v. WEITZENHOFF

United States Court of Appeals, Ninth Circuit, 1993.
1 F.3d 1523.

FLETCHER, CIRCUIT JUDGE:

Michael H. Weitzenhoff and Thomas W. Mariani, who managed the East Honolulu Community Services Sewage Treatment Plant, appeal their convictions for violations of the Clean Water Act ("CWA"), 33 U.S.C. §§ 1251 et seq., contending that (1) the district court misconstrued the word "knowingly" under section 1319(c)(2) of the CWA; * * * [other issues omitted]. We affirm the convictions and sentence.

Facts and Procedural History

In 1988 and 1989 Weitzenhoff was the manager and Mariani the assistant manager of the East Honolulu Community Services Sewage Treatment Plant ("the plant"), located not far from Sandy Beach, a popular swimming and surfing beach on Oahu. The plant is designed to treat some 4 million gallons of residential wastewater each day by removing the solids and other harmful pollutants from the sewage so that the resulting effluent can be safely discharged into the ocean. The plant operates under a permit issued pursuant to the National Pollution Discharge Elimination System ("NPDES"), which established the limits on the Total Suspended Solids ("TSS") and Biochemical Oxygen Demand ("BOD")—indicators of the solid and organic matter, respectively, in the effluent discharged at Sandy Beach. During the period in question, the permit limited the discharge of both the TSS and BOD to an average of 976 pounds per day over a 30–day period. It also imposed monitoring and sampling requirements on the plant's management.

The sewage treatment process that was overseen by Weitzenhoff and Mariani began with the removal of large inorganic items such as rags and coffee grounds from the incoming wastewater as it flowed through metal screens and a grit chamber at the head of the plant. The wastewater then entered large tanks known as primary clarifiers, where a portion of the organic solids settled to the bottom of the tanks. The solid material which settled in the primary clarifiers, known as primary sludge, was pumped to separate tanks, known as anaerobic digesters, to be further processed. Those solids that did not settle continued on to aeration basins, which contained microorganisms to feed on and remove the solids and other organic pollutants in the waste stream.

From the aeration basins the mixture flowed into final clarifiers, where the microorganisms settled out, producing a mixture that sank to the bottom of the clarifiers called activated sludge. The clarified stream then passed through a chlorine contact chamber, where the plant's sampling apparatus was, and emptied into the plant's outfall, a long underground pipe which discharged the plant's effluent into the ocean through diffusers 1,100 to 1,400 feet from shore (the "Sandy Beach outfall").

Meanwhile, the activated sludge that had settled in the final clarifiers was pumped from the bottom of the clarifiers. A certain portion was returned to the aeration basins, while the remainder, known as waste activated sludge ("WAS"), was pumped to WAS holding tanks. From the holding tanks, the WAS could either be returned to other phases of the treatment process or hauled away to a different sewage treatment facility.

From March 1987 through March 1988, the excess WAS generated by the plant was hauled away to another treatment plant, the Sand Island Facility. In March 1988, certain improvements were made to the East Honolulu plant and the hauling was discontinued. Within a few weeks, however, the plant began experiencing a buildup of excess WAS. Rather than have the excess WAS hauled away as before, however, Weitzenhoff and Mariani instructed two employees at the plant to dispose of it on a regular basis by pumping it from the storage tanks directly into the outfall, that is, directly into the ocean. The WAS thereby bypassed the plant's effluent sampler so that the samples taken and reported to Hawaii's Department of Health ("DOH") and the EPA did not reflect its discharge.

The evidence produced by the government at trial showed that WAS was discharged directly into the ocean from the plant on about 40 separate occasions from April 1988 to June 1989, resulting in some 436,000 pounds of pollutant solids being discharged into the ocean, and that the discharges violated the plant's 30–day average effluent limit under the permit for most of the months during which they occurred. Most of the WAS discharges occurred during the night, and none was reported to the DOH or EPA. DOH inspectors contacted the plant on several occasions in 1988 in response to complaints by lifeguards at Sandy Beach that sewage was being emitted from the outfall, but Weitzenhoff and Mariani repeatedly denied that there was any problem at the plant. In one letter responding to a DOH inquiry in October 1988, Mariani stated that "the debris that was reported could not have been from the East Honolulu Wastewater Treatment facility, as our records of effluent quality up to this time will substantiate." One of the plant employees who participated in the dumping operation testified that Weitzenhoff instructed him not to say anything about the discharges, because if they all stuck together and did not reveal anything, "they [couldn't] do anything to us."

Following an FBI investigation, Weitzenhoff and Mariani were charged in a thirty-one-count indictment with conspiracy and substantive violations of the Clean Water Act ("CWA"), 33 U.S.C. §§ 1251 et seq. At trial, Weitzenhoff and Mariani admitted having authorized the discharges, but claimed that their actions were justified under their interpretation of the NPDES permit. The jury found them guilty of six of the thirty-one counts. [Weitzenhoff was sentenced to twenty-one months and Mariani thirty-three months imprisonment. Each filed a timely notice of appeal.]

Discussion

A. Intent Requirement

Section 1311(a) of the CWA prohibits the discharge of pollutants into navigable waters without an NPDES permit. Section 1319(c)(2) makes it a felony offense to "knowingly violate section 1311, 1312, 1316, 1317, 1318, 1321(b)(3), 1328, or 1345 . . ., or any permit condition or limitation implementing any of such sections in a permit issued under section 1342."

Prior to trial, the district court construed "knowingly" in section 1319(c)(2) as requiring only that Weitzenhoff and Mariani were aware that they were discharging the pollutants in question, not that they knew they were violating the terms of the statute or permit. According to appellants, the district court erred in its interpretation of the CWA and in instructing the jury that "the government is not required to prove that the defendant knew that his act or omissions were unlawful," as well as in rejecting their proposed instruction based on the defense that they mistakenly believed their conduct was authorized by the permit. Apparently, no court of appeals has confronted the issue raised by appellants. * * *

As with certain other criminal statutes that employ the term "knowingly," it is not apparent from the face of the statute whether "knowingly" means a knowing violation of the law or simply knowing conduct that is violative of the law. We turn, then, to the legislative history of the provision at issue to ascertain what Congress intended.

In 1987, Congress substantially amended the CWA, elevating the penalties for violations of the Act. Increased penalties were considered necessary to deter would-be polluters. With the 1987 amendments, Congress substituted "knowingly" for the earlier intent requirement of "willfully" that appeared in the predecessor to section 1319(c)(2). The Senate report accompanying the legislation explains that the changes in the penalty provisions were to ensure that "criminal liability shall . . . attach to any person who is not in compliance with all applicable Federal, State and local requirements and permits and causes a POTW [publicly owned treatment works] to violate any effluent limitation or condition in any permit issued to the treatment works." Similarly, the report accompanying the House version of the bill, which contained parallel provisions for enhancement of penalties, states that the proposed amendments were to "provide penalties for dischargers or individuals who knowingly or negligently violate or cause the violation of certain of the Act's requirements." Because they speak in terms of "causing" a violation, the congressional explanations of the new penalty provisions strongly suggest that criminal sanctions are to be imposed on an individual who knowingly engages in conduct that results in a permit violation, regardless of whether the polluter is cognizant of the requirements or even the existence of the permit.

Our conclusion that "knowingly" does not refer to the legal violation is fortified by decisions interpreting analogous public welfare statutes. The leading case in this area is United States v. International Minerals & Chem. Corp., 402 U.S. 558 (1971). In *International Minerals*, the Supreme Court construed a statute which made it a crime to "knowingly violate [] any ... regulation" promulgated by the ICC pursuant to 18 U.S.C. § 834(a), a provision authorizing the agency to formulate regulations for the safe transport of corrosive liquids. The Court held that the term "knowingly" referred to the acts made criminal rather than a violation of the regulation, and that "regulation" was a shorthand designation for the specific acts or omissions contemplated by the act. "Where ... dangerous or deleterious devices or products or obnoxious waste materials are involved, the probability of regulation is so great that anyone who is aware that he is in possession of them or dealing with them must be presumed to be aware of the regulation." * * *

Appellants seek to rely on the Supreme Court's decision in Liparota v. United States, 471 U.S. 419 (1985) to support their alternative reading of the intent requirement. *Liparota* concerned 7 U.S.C. § 2024(b)(1), which provides that anyone who "knowingly uses, transfers, acquires, alters, or possesses [food stamp] coupons or authorization cards in any manner not authorized by [the statute] or regulations" is subject to a fine or imprisonment. The Court, noting that the conduct at issue did not constitute a public welfare offense, distinguished the *International Minerals* line of cases and held that the government must prove the defendant knew that his acquisition or possession of food stamps was in a manner unauthorized by statute or regulations.

Subsequent to the filing of the original opinion in this case, the Supreme Court decided two cases which Weitzenhoff contends call our analysis into question. See Ratzlaf v. United States, 114 S.Ct. 655 (1994); Staples v. United States, 114 S.Ct. 1793 (1994). We disagree.

The statute in *Ratzlaf* does not deal with a public welfare offense, but rather with violations of the banking statutes. The Court construed the term "willfully" in the anti-structuring provisions of the Bank Secrecy Act to require both that the defendant knew he was structuring transactions to avoid reporting requirements and that he knew his acts were unlawful. The Court recognized that the money structuring provisions are not directed at conduct which a reasonable person necessarily should know is subject to strict public regulation and that the structuring offense applied to all persons with more than $10,000, many of whom could be engaged in structuring for innocent reasons. In contrast, parties such as Weitzenhoff are closely regulated and are discharging waste materials that affect public health. The *International Minerals* rationale requires that we impute to these parties knowledge of their operating permit. This was recognized by the Court in *Staples*.

The specific holding in *Staples* was that the government is required to prove that a defendant charged with possession of a machine gun knew that the weapon he possessed had the characteristics that brought it within the statutory definition of a machine gun. But the Court took pains to contrast the gun laws to other regulatory regimes, specifically those regulations that govern the handling of "obnoxious waste materials." It noted that the mere innocent ownership of guns is not a public welfare offense. The Court focussed on the long tradition of widespread gun ownership in this country and, recognizing that approximately 50% of American homes contain a firearm, acknowledged that mere ownership of a gun is not sufficient to place people on notice that the act of owning an unregistered firearm is not innocent under the law.

Staples thus explicitly contrasted the mere possession of guns to public welfare offenses, which include statutes that regulate " 'dangerous or deleterious devices or products or obnoxious waste materials,' " and confirmed the continued vitality of statutes covering public welfare offenses, which "regulate potentially harmful or injurious items" and place a defendant on notice that he is dealing with a device or a substance "that places him in 'responsible relation to a public danger.' " "In such cases Congress intended to place the burden on the defendant to ascertain at his peril whether [his conduct] comes within the inhibition of the statute." Id. at 1798 (citations and internal quotations omitted).

Unlike "guns [which] in general are not 'deleterious devices or products or obnoxious waste materials,' *International Minerals*, supra, at 565, that put their owners on notice that they stand 'in responsible relation to a public danger,' " *Staples*, 114 S.Ct. at 1800, the dumping of sewage and other pollutants into our nation's waters is precisely the type of activity that puts the discharger on notice that his acts may pose a public danger. Like other public welfare offenses that regulate the discharge of pollutants into the air, the disposal of hazardous wastes, the undocumented shipping of acids, and the use of pesticides on our food, the improper and excessive discharge of sewage causes cholera, hepatitis, and other serious illnesses, and can have serious repercussions for public health and welfare.

The criminal provisions of the CWA are clearly designed to protect the public at large from the potentially dire consequences of water pollution, and as such fall within the category of public welfare legislation. *International Minerals* rather than *Liparota* controls the case at hand. The government did not need to prove that Weitzenhoff and Mariani knew that their acts violated the permit or the CWA. * * *

We AFFIRM both the convictions and Mariani's sentence.

The petition for rehearing en banc was circulated to the full court. An active judge of this court requested a vote as to whether the case should be reheard en banc. Less than the required majority of the non-recused active judges voted to take the case en banc.

No further petitions for rehearing or rehearing en banc will be entertained. The mandate shall issue forthwith.

KLEINFELD, CIRCUIT JUDGE, with whom CIRCUIT JUDGES REINHARDT, KOZINSKI, TROTT, and THOMAS G. NELSON join, dissenting from the order rejecting the suggestion for rehearing en banc.

* * * We have now made felons of a large number of innocent people doing socially valuable work. They are innocent, because the one thing which makes their conduct felonious is something they do not know. It is we, and not Congress, who have made them felons. The statute, read in an ordinary way, does not. If we are fortunate, sewer plant workers around the circuit will continue to perform their vitally important work despite our decision. If they knew they risk three years in prison, some might decide that their pay, though sufficient inducement for processing the public's wastes, is not enough to risk prison for doing their jobs. We have decided that they should go to prison if, unbeknownst to them, their plant discharges exceed permit limits. Likewise for power plant operators who discharge warm water into rivers near their plants, and for all sorts of other dischargers in public and private life. If they know they are discharging into water, have a permit for the discharges, think they are conforming to their permits, but unknowingly violate their permit conditions, into prison they go with the violent criminals.

The statute does not say that. The statute at issue makes it a felony, subject to three years of imprisonment, to "knowingly violate[ ] . . . any permit condition or limitation." * * * In this case, the defendants, sewage plant operators, had a permit to discharge sewage into the ocean, but exceeded the permit limitations. The legal issue for the panel was what knowledge would turn innocently or negligently violating a permit into "knowingly" violating a permit. Were the plant operators felons if they knew they were discharging sewage, but did not know that they were violating their permit? Or did they also have to know they were violating their permit? Ordinary English grammar, common sense, and precedent, all compel the latter construction.

As the panel opinion states the facts, these two defendants were literally "midnight dumpers." They managed a sewer plant and told their employees to dump 436,000 pounds of sewage into the ocean, mostly at night, fouling a nearby beach. Their conduct, suggests that they must have known they were violating their National Pollution Discharge Elimination System (NPDES) permit. But we cannot decide the case on that basis, because the jury did not. The court instructed the jury that the government did not have to prove the defendants knew their conduct was unlawful, and refused to instruct the jury that a mistaken belief that the discharge was authorized by the permit would be a defense. Because of the way the jury was instructed, its verdict is consistent with the proposition that the defendants honestly and reasonably believed that their NPDES permit authorized the discharges. * * *

If we were to accept as a general rule the Government's suggestion that dangerous and regulated items place their owners under an obligation to inquire at their peril into compliance with regulations, we would undoubtedly reach some untoward results. Automobiles, for example, might also be termed "dangerous" devices and are highly regulated at both the state and federal levels. Congress might see fit to criminalize the violation of certain regulations concerning automobiles, and thus might make it a crime to operate a vehicle without a properly functioning emission control system. But we probably would hesitate to conclude on the basis of silence that Congress intended a prison term to apply to a car owner whose vehicle's emissions levels, wholly unbeknownst to him, began to exceed legal limits between regular inspection dates.

Congress made it a serious felony "knowingly" to violate permit limitations on discharge of pollutants. The harsh penalty for this serious crime must be reserved for those who know they are, in fact, violating permit limitations.

Note

Strict liability is not entirely limited to the so-called "regulatory" or "public welfare" offenses, or to violations that carry only a relatively small penalty and do not involve moral stigma. As we saw in the preceding section, the crime of statutory rape is usually held to be one of strict liability with respect to the "victim's" age. There is ancient authority for the proposition that a man may be convicted of bigamy even though he believed his first wife to be dead, or of adultery although he did not know that his paramour was married. Such cases do not clearly distinguish between negligence and intent, however, and probably would not be followed in this more permissive age.

Aggravating factors that operate to make a relatively less serious crime into a more serious one are frequently matters of strict liability. For example, the distinction between "grand" and "petty" theft depends upon the objective value of the goods stolen, not their value in the mind of the thief. The felony-murder rule imposes both *strict* and *vicarious* liability for all persons involved in certain dangerous felonies. The felon who commits the killing is *strictly* liable for murder even if it was accidental, and all others participating in the felony are *vicariously* guilty of murder, even though they did not participate in the killing. Scholarly commentators have been critical of this harsh doctrine, but American state legislators have been convinced that it is fair to make a person who intentionally participates in a dangerous felony strictly liable for the consequences.

Finally, the doctrine that ignorance of the law, or at least the criminal law, is no defense could be said to impose a form of strict liability. Perhaps what is involved here is more accurately described as a doctrine of negligence, however: we think that people ought to know the criminal law (except in the rare cases where ignorance is an excuse) whether they do know it or not.

When courts and scholars refer to strict liability in the criminal law, they ordinarily have in mind not the examples just discussed, but a category of so-called regulatory offenses where strict liability is the rule rather than the exception. This category refers to a body of offenses that have emerged since the Industrial Revolution, offenses that typically involve commercial activities such as the selling of unsafe or unhealthy products or environmental pollution. The classic justification for this area of strict liability is that given by Supreme Court Justice Robert Jackson in the *Morissette* opinion.

Most scholarly commentators have found this justification for strict liability offenses unconvincing. Ordinarily, the criminal law is supposed to punish only the blameworthy. To be sure, it is easier to enforce the law if the prosecution does not have to carry a burden of proof on such difficult questions as intent or negligence, but it is equally true that the traditional criminal law could be enforced more efficiently if it were not necessary to prove criminal intent, the absence of excuse, and other difficult matters. The fact that so many defenses are permitted in the traditional criminal law reflects the importance of punishing only the blameworthy.

No one has demonstrated that criminal penalties are uniquely necessary or effective in protecting the public from unsafe products or environmental pollution, and in the absence of such a showing there is no apparent justification for violating a fundamental principle of criminal liability. Moreover, the courts have sometimes applied the "regulatory offense" theory even to statutes that carry a penalty of years in prison and considerable moral stigma. In United States v. Balint, 258 U.S. 250 (1922), for example, the Supreme Court held that an indictment for selling narcotics did not have to charge that the defendants knew, or ought to have known, what they were selling. In United States v. Freed, 401 U.S. 601 (1971), the court invoked the regulatory offense theory in holding that an indictment for possession of unregistered hand grenades need not allege that the defendant knew the grenades to be unregistered. The crime was punishable by up to ten years in prison and a fine of $10,000.

Some strict liability statutes also impose *vicarious* liability: i.e., the owner or supervisor of an enterprise may be held liable for a violation committed by his agent or employee even though he was personally not involved in the conduct in question. For example, the owner of a tavern may be convicted of unlawfully selling liquor to a minor even if the sale was made by a bartender without the owner's knowledge or approval. A few courts have held, however, that it is unconstitutional to impose a jail sentence in this situation. See State v. Guminga, 395 N.W.2d 344 (Minn.1986); Commonwealth v. Koczwara, 397 Pa. 575, 155 A.2d 825 (1959).

Strict liability may also be unconstitutional when it affects specific constitutional rights, such as the First Amendment protection of freedom of expression. In United States v. X–Citement Video, Inc., 513 U.S. 64 (1994), the defendant was charged with violating a federal statute for distributing pornographic films featuring an underage actress. The federal statute made it a crime to "knowingly transport, receive, or distribute * * * any visual depiction," *if* "(A) the producing of such visual depiction involves the use of a minor engaging in sexually explicit conduct"; and "(B) such visual depiction is of such conduct." The Court of Appeals for the Ninth Circuit held that "knowingly" modified only the verbs immediately following, that the statute did not require knowledge either of the sexually explicit character of the conduct depicted or that the actress was a minor, and that as so construed the statute was unconstitutional on its face. The Supreme Court reversed. The majority opinion by Chief Justice Rehnquist conceded that the Ninth Circuit's holding was the most natural way of reading the statute, but nonetheless held that Congress probably did not mean the statute to impose strict liability in view of the injustice this could cause and the constitutional problems strict liability would raise in this context. The Supreme Court therefore interpreted (or rewrote) the statute to require knowledge both of the sexual explicit nature of the conduct and of the underage status of the actress.

C. THE CONDUCT REQUIREMENT

PEOPLE v. NEWTON

California Court of Appeal, First District, 1970.
8 Cal.App.3d 359, 87 Cal.Rptr. 394.

RATTIGAN, ASSOCIATE JUSTICE. Huey P. Newton appeals from a judgment convicting him of voluntary manslaughter. * * *

[The facts of this famous case are set out in great detail in the court's opinion. Briefly, Newton was charged with murdering Oakland Police Officer Frey, with wounding Frey's partner, Officer Heanes, and with kidnapping a bystander. The trial court dismissed the kidnapping charge, and the jury found Newton not guilty on the charge of assaulting Heanes but guilty of the voluntary manslaughter of Frey. The key prosecution witness was a bus driver who testified that he saw Newton fire several shots into Frey's body, the last while Frey was lying on the ground. Newton testified that he did not kill Frey or wound Heanes. According to his account, Frey arrested him arbitrarily, and then after bullying him drew a revolver and shot him in the stomach. After being shot, Newton remembered nothing until he regained consciousness in a hospital. An eminent psychiatrist named Dr. Bernard Diamond testified that Newton's recollections were compatible with the gunshot wound he had received, and that such a wound very frequently produces a profound reflex shock reaction which may cause a loss of consciousness.

The trial judge correctly instructed the jury on the elements of murder, and on the California doctrine of "diminished capacity." This doctrine allows a California defendant to argue that his mental condition at the time of the killing was such that he could not form the "malice aforethought" required for a conviction of murder. If accepted by the jury, such a defense reduces the crime from murder to manslaughter. He did not instruct the jury on self-defense or the defense of unconsciousness, because the defense withdrew the request it had originally made for instructions on these doctrines.]—ed.

Where not self-induced, as by voluntary intoxication or the equivalent * * * unconsciousness is a complete defense to a charge of criminal homicide. "Unconsciousness," as the term is used in the rule just cited, need not reach the physical dimensions commonly associated with the term (coma, inertia, incapability of locomotion or manual action, and so on); it can exist—and the above-stated rule can apply—where the subject physically acts in fact but is not, at the time, conscious of acting. The statute underlying the rule makes this clear,[11] as does one of the unconsciousness instructions originally requested by defendant. Thus the rule has been invoked in many cases where the actor fired multiple gunshots while inferably in a state of such "unconsciousness" including some in which the only evidence of "unconsciousness" was the actor's own testimony that he did not recall the shooting.

Where evidence of involuntary unconsciousness has been produced in a homicide prosecution, the refusal of a requested instruction on the subject, and its effect as a complete defense if found to have existed, is prejudicial error. The fact, if it appears, that such evidence does not inspire belief does not authorize the failure to instruct: "However incredible the testimony of a defendant may be he is entitled to an instruction based upon the hypothesis that it is entirely true."

Defendant did not request instructions upon unconsciousness; as we have seen, his original request therefor was "withdrawn." But a trial court is under a duty to instruct upon diminished capacity, in the absence of a request and upon its own motion, where the evidence so indicates. The difference between the two states—of diminished capacity and unconsciousness—is one of degree only: where the former provides a "partial defense" by negating a specific mental state essential to a particular crime, the latter is a "complete defense" because it negates capacity to commit any crime at all. Moreover, evidence of both states is not antithetical; jury instructions on the effect of both will be required where the evidence supports a finding of either. We hold, therefore, that the trial court should have given appropriate unconsciousness instructions upon its own motion in the present case, and that its omission to do so was prejudicial error.

The error was prejudicial *per se* because the omission operated to deprive defendant of his constitutional right to have the jury determine every material issue presented by the evidence. Actual prejudice, moreover, is perceptible in the present case. The voluntary manslaughter

11. Penal Code section 26 provides in pertinent part that "All persons are capable of committing crimes except those belonging to the following classes: * * * Five—Persons who *committed the act charged without being conscious thereof.*" (Italics added.)

verdict indicates the jury's decision that defendant shot Officer Frey, but that the jurors found (1) provocation by the officer or (2) diminished capacity on defendant's part, or both. As defendant alone testified to both events, it appears that the jury believed him as to either or both. But, if they fully believed his testimony with respect to his asserted unconsciousness, they had been given no basis upon which to acquit him if they found it to be true. Defense counsel, in fact, argued to the jury defendant's, and Dr. Diamond's, testimony on this subject. Absent instructions upon the legal effect of unconsciousness as a complete defense, the argument was necessarily limited and essentially ineffective. It further appears that the jury gave some thought, at least, to acquitting defendant upon a finding of justifiable homicide.[13]

Under these circumstances, it is "reasonably probable" that a result more favorable to him—i.e., a verdict acquitting him of the homicide, based upon unconsciousness as a complete defense—would have been reached if the omitted instruction had been given.

The Question of Invited Error

As defendant's point on the omission of unconsciousness instructions is thus valid on its merits, the question is whether he is precluded from asserting it on appeal because his original request for such instructions was "withdrawn." He contends in effect that he withdrew his request for [the unconsciousness instructions] only because the trial court forced him to choose between them and * * * [an] instruction on diminished capacity. The trial court denied this claim when defense counsel asserted it on motion for new trial; nevertheless, the judge's remarks at trial suggest that he (the judge) thought the jury should be given instructions on diminished capacity *or* unconsciousness, but not upon both.

If the trial court entertained this view at the time of its remarks, it was in error: the defenses of diminished capacity and unconsciousness were "entirely separate," and neither incompatible nor mutually exclusive, under the evidence. In any event, while the deficient record does not clearly substantiate counsel's claim that the trial court forced him to a choice, it does not wholly refute him, either; and it tends to explain the court's failure to instruct upon both defenses, upon its own motion, whether counsel correctly understood the situation or not. * * *

The self-defense instructions originally requested by defendant were wholly inconsistent with his testimony that he did not kill Officer Frey or shoot Officer Heanes. Accordingly, we can discern a "deliberate tactical purpose" in his counsel's withdrawing the request for them.

13. The jurors deliberated for four full days, during which they were twice reinstructed, by request, on murder in both degrees, voluntary manslaughter, provocation, heat of passion, diminished capacity, and assault. On one of these occasions, they apparently asked for instructions on "justifiable homicide," which had not been given in the first instance (and were not given when requested). * * *

It also bears mentioning that, during their lengthy deliberations, the jurors asked to see, and were shown, the bullet wounds in defendant's body.

Defendant's denial of the shootings, however, went no further than his own conscious recollections as recited in his testimony; the denial was not inconsistent with the hypothesis that he fired a gun while—and not before—he was in a state of "unconsciousness" as such state has been previously defined herein. Against the substantial evidence that it was he who shot Officer Frey, the instructions he requested on diminished capacity afforded him partial defenses at best. As only instructions upon unconsciousness offered a complete defense, his counsel's "withdrawal" of them, or the failure to press for them, is irreconcilable with "deliberate tactical purpose" on counsel's part.

The "withdrawal" of the critical instructions * * * can perhaps be ascribed to "neglect or mistake" or "ignorance or inadvertence" on the part of defense counsel. Whatever the reason for it, though, no "deliberate tactical purpose" appears and we can conceive of none. Under these circumstances, the "invited error" doctrine does not foreclose defendant from asserting his point on the appeal. Since we have sustained the point on its merits, the judgment must be reversed. * * *

PEOPLE v. DECINA

Court of Appeals of New York, 1956.
2 N.Y.2d 133, 157 N.Y.S.2d 558, 138 N.E.2d 799.

FROESSEL, JUDGE. * * *

[Decina was convicted of negligent homicide after his automobile struck and killed four children because he had suffered an epileptic seizure at the wheel. Both he and the prosecution appealed from the trial court's order granting a new trial because of an error in the admission of evidence.]

We turn first to the subject of defendant's cross appeal, namely, that his demurrer should have been sustained, since the *indictment* here does not charge a crime. The indictment states essentially that defendant, *knowing* "that he was subject to epileptic attacks or other disorder rendering him likely to lose consciousness for a considerable period of time", was culpably negligent "in that he *consciously* undertook to and *did operate* his Buick sedan on a public highway" (emphasis supplied) and "while so doing" suffered such an attack which caused said automobile "to travel at a fast and reckless rate of speed, jumping the curb and driving over the sidewalk" causing the death of 4 persons. In our opinion, this clearly states a violation of section 1053–a of the Penal Law * * *.

Assuming the truth of the indictment, as we must on a demurrer, this defendant knew he was subject to epileptic attacks and seizures that might strike *at any time*. He also knew that a moving motor vehicle uncontrolled on a public highway is a highly dangerous instrumentality capable of unrestrained destruction. With this *knowledge*, and without anyone accompanying him, he deliberately took a chance by making a conscious choice of a course of action, in disregard of the consequences which he knew might follow from his conscious act, and which in this case did ensue. How can we say as a matter of law that this did not amount to culpable negligence within the meaning of section 1053–a?

To hold otherwise would be to say that a man may freely indulge himself in liquor in the same hope that it will not affect his driving, and if it later develops that ensuing intoxication causes dangerous and reckless driving resulting in death, his unconsciousness or involuntariness at that time would relieve him from prosecution under the statute. His awareness of a condition which he knows may produce such consequences as here, and his disregard of the consequences, renders him liable for culpable negligence, as the courts below have properly held. To have a sudden sleeping spell, an unexpected heart or other disabling attack, without any prior knowledge or warning thereof, is an altogether different situation, and there is simply no basis for comparing such cases with the flagrant disregard manifested here. It is suggested in the dissenting opinion that a new approach to licensing would prevent such disastrous consequences upon our public highways. But would it—and how and when? The mere possession of a driver's license is no defense to a prosecution under section 1053–a; nor does it assure continued ability to drive during the period of the license. It may be noted in passing, and not without some significance, that defendant strenuously and successfully objected to the district attorney's offer of his applications for such license in evidence, upon the ground that whether or not he was licensed has nothing to do with the case. Under the view taken by the dissenters, this defendant would be immune from prosecution under this statute even if he were unlicensed. Section 1053–a places a personal responsibility on each driver of a vehicle—whether licensed or not—and not upon a licensing agency.

* * *

[The court then upheld the trial court's order granting a new trial.]

DESMOND, JUDGE (concurring in part and dissenting in part). * * * No *operation* of an automobile in a reckless manner is charged against defendant. The excessive speed of the car and its jumping the curb were "caused", says the indictment itself, by defendant's prior "attack and loss of consciousness". Therefore, what defendant is accused of is *not* reckless or culpably negligent driving, which necessarily connotes and involves consciousness and volition. The fatal assault by this car was after and because of defendant's failure of consciousness. To say that one drove a car in a reckless manner in that his unconscious condition caused the car to travel recklessly is to make two mutually contradictory assertions. One cannot be "reckless" while unconscious. One cannot while unconscious "operate" a car in a culpably negligent manner or in any other "manner". The statute makes criminal a particular kind of knowing, voluntary, immediate operation. It does not touch at all the involuntary presence of an unconscious person at the wheel of an uncontrolled vehicle. To negative the possibility of applying section 1053–a to these alleged facts we do not even have to resort to the rule that all criminal statutes are closely and strictly construed in favor of the citizen and that no act or omission is criminal unless specifically and in terms so labeled by a clearly worded statute. * * *

Just what is the court holding here? No less than this: that a driver whose brief blackout lets his car run amuck and kill another has killed that other by reckless driving. But any such "recklessness" consists necessarily not of the erratic behavior of the automobile while its driver is unconscious, but of his driving at all when he knew he was subject to such attacks. Thus, it must be that such a blackout-prone driver is guilty of reckless driving, whenever and as soon as he steps into the driver's seat of a vehicle. Every time he drives, accident or no accident, he is subject to criminal prosecution for reckless driving or to revocation of his operator's license. And how many of this State's 5,000,000 licensed operators are subject to such penalties for merely driving the cars they are licensed to drive? * * *

A whole new approach may be necessary to the problem of issuing or refusing drivers' licenses to epileptics and persons similarly afflicted. But the absence of adequate licensing controls cannot in law or in justice be supplied by criminal prosecutions of drivers who have violated neither the language nor the intendment of any criminal law. * * *

COMMONWEALTH v. PESTINIKAS

Superior Court of Pennsylvania, 1992.
421 Pa.Super. 371, 617 A.2d 1339.

WIEAND, J.:

The principal issue in this appeal is whether a person can be prosecuted criminally for murder when his or her failure to perform a contract to provide food and medical care for another has caused the death of such other person. The trial court answered this question in the affirmative and instructed the jury accordingly. The jury thereafter found Walter and Helen Pestinikas guilty of murder of the third degree in connection with the starvation and dehydration death of ninety-two (92) year old Joseph Kly. [Each defendant was sentenced to serve a term of imprisonment for not less than five (5) years nor more than ten (10) years.] On direct appeal from the judgment of sentence, the defendants contend that the trial court misapplied the law and gave the jury incorrect instructions. * * *

Joseph Kly met Walter and Helen Pestinikas in the latter part of 1981 when Kly consulted them about prearranging his funeral. In March, 1982, Kly, who had been living with a stepson, was hospitalized and diagnosed as suffering from Zenker's diverticulum, a weakness in the walls of the esophagus, which caused him to have trouble swallowing food. In the hospital, Kly was given food which he was able to swallow and, as a result, regained some of the weight which he had lost. When he was about to be discharged, he expressed a desire not to return to his stepson's home and sent word to appellants that he wanted to speak with them. As a consequence, arrangements were made for appellants to care for Kly in their home on Main Street in Scranton, Lackawanna County.

Kly was discharged from the hospital on April 12, 1982. When appellants came for him on that day they were instructed by medical personnel regarding the care which was required for Kly and were given a prescription to have filled for him. Arrangements were also made for a visiting nurse to come to appellants' home to administer vitamin B–12 supplements to Kly. Appellants agreed orally to follow the medical instructions and to supply Kly with food, shelter, care and the medicine which he required.

According to the evidence, the prescription was never filled, and the visiting nurse was told by appellants that Kly did not want the vitamin supplement shots and that her services, therefore, were not required. Instead of giving Kly a room in their home, appellants removed him to a rural part of Lackawanna County, where they placed him in the enclosed porch of a building, which they owned, known as the Stage Coach Inn. This porch was approximately nine feet by thirty feet, with no insulation, no refrigeration, no bathroom, no sink and no telephone. The walls contained cracks which exposed the room to outside weather conditions. Kly's predicament was compounded by appellants' affirmative efforts to conceal his whereabouts. Thus, they gave misleading information in response to inquiries, telling members of Kly's family that they did not know where he had gone and others that he was living in their home.

After Kly was discharged from the hospital, appellants took Kly to the bank and had their names added to his savings account. Later, Kly's money was transferred into an account in the names of Kly or Helen Pestinikas, pursuant to which moneys could be withdrawn without Kly's signature. Bank records reveal that from May, 1982, to July, 1983, appellants withdrew amounts roughly consistent with the three hundred ($300) dollars per month which Kly had agreed to pay for his care. Beginning in August, 1983 and continuing until Kly's death in November, 1984, however, appellants withdrew much larger sums so that when Kly died, a balance of only $55 remained. In the interim, appellants had withdrawn in excess of $30,000.

On the afternoon of November 15, 1984, when police and an ambulance crew arrived in response to a call by appellants, Kly's dead body appeared emaciated, with his ribs and sternum greatly pronounced. Mrs. Pestinikas told police that she and her husband had taken care of Kly for 300 dollars per month and that she had given him cookies and orange juice at 11:30 a.m. on the morning of his death. A subsequent autopsy, however, revealed that Kly had been dead at that time and may have been dead for as many as 39 hours before his body was found. The cause of death was determined to be starvation and dehydration. Expert testimony opined that Kly would have experienced pain and suffering over a long period of time before he died.

At trial, the Commonwealth contended that after contracting orally to provide food, shelter, care and necessary medicine for Kly, appellants engaged in a course of conduct calculated to deprive Kly of those things necessary to maintain life and thereby cause his death. The trial court instructed the jury that appellants could not be found guilty of a malicious killing for failing to provide food, shelter and necessary medicines to Kly unless a duty to do so had been imposed upon them by contract. The court instructed the jury, inter alia, as follows:

> In order for you to convict the defendants on any of the homicide charges * * * you must first find beyond a reasonable doubt that the defendants had a legal duty of care to Joseph Kly.
>
> There are but two situations in which Pennsylvania law imposes criminal liability for the failure to perform an act. One of these is where the express language of the law defining the offense provides for criminal [liability] based upon such a failure. The other is where the law otherwise imposes a duty to act.
>
> Unless you find beyond a reasonable doubt that an oral contract imposed a duty to act upon Walter and Helen Pestinikas, you must acquit the defendants.

Appellants contend that this was error. * * *

The applicable law appears at 18 Pa.C.S. § 301(a) and (b) as follows:

> (a) General rule.—A person is not guilty of an offense unless his liability is based on conduct which includes a voluntary act or the omission to perform an act of which he is physically capable.
>
> (b) Omission as basis of liability.—Liability for the commission of an offense may not be based on an omission unaccompanied by action unless:
>
> (1) the omission is expressly made sufficient by the law defining the offense; or
>
> (2) a duty to perform the omitted act is otherwise imposed by law.

With respect to subsection (b), Toll, in his invaluable work on the Pennsylvania Crimes Code, has commented

> . . . [Subsection (b)] states the conventional position with respect to omissions unaccompanied by action as a basis of liability. Unless the omission is expressly made sufficient by the law defining the offense, a duty to perform the omitted act must have been otherwise imposed by law for the omission to have the same standing as a voluntary act for purposes of liability. It should, of course, suffice, as the courts now hold, that the duty arises under some branch of the civil law. If it does, this minimal requirement is satisfied, though whether the omission constitutes an offense depends as well on many other factors. Toll, Pennsylvania Crimes Code Annotated, § 301, at p. 60, quoting Comment, Model Penal Code § 2.01 (emphasis added). * * *

Consistently with [the weight of authority] we hold that when the statute provides that an omission to do an act can be the basis for criminal liability if a duty to perform the omitted act has been imposed by law, the legislature intended to distinguish between a legal duty to act and merely a moral duty to act. A duty to act imposed by contract is legally enforceable and, therefore, creates a legal duty. It follows that a failure to perform a duty imposed by contract may be the basis for a charge of criminal homicide if such failure causes the death of another person and all other elements of the offense are present. Because there was evidence in the instant case that Kly's death had been caused by appellants' failure to provide the food and medical care which they had agreed by oral contract to provide for him, their omission to act was sufficient to support a conviction for criminal homicide, and the trial court was correct when it instructed the jury accordingly.

Our holding is not that every breach of contract can become the basis for a finding of homicide resulting from an omission to act. A criminal act involves both a physical and mental aspect. An omission to act can satisfy the physical aspect of criminal conduct only if there is a duty to act imposed by law. A failure to provide food and medicine, in this case, could not have been made the basis for prosecuting a stranger who learned of Kly's condition and failed to act. Even where there is a duty imposed by contract, moreover, the omission to act will not support a prosecution for homicide in the absence of the necessary mens rea. For murder, there must be malice. Without a malicious intent, an omission to perform duties having their foundation in contract cannot support a conviction for murder. In the instant case, therefore, the jury was required to find that appellants, by virtue of contract, had undertaken responsibility for providing necessary care for Kly to the exclusion of the members of Kly's family. This would impose upon them a legal duty to act to preserve Kly's life. If they maliciously set upon a course of withholding food and medicine and thereby caused Kly's death, appellants could be found guilty of murder. * * *

Having found no valid reason for disturbing the jury's verdicts, we conclude that the judgments of sentence must be, as they are, AFFIRMED. [Concurring opinions omitted.]

Dissenting opinion of McEwen, J.

The author of the majority opinion has, in his customary fashion, provided so persuasive an expression of view upon this trying issue that one can hardly be resolute in dissent, particularly since I wholeheartedly concur with the conclusion of the majority that there is ample evidence upon which to sustain the homicide convictions of appellants. Nonetheless, I must respectfully depart the company of my eminent colleagues who find that the trial court properly instructed the jury that the failure to perform a civil contract, though simple omission alone, is sufficient to meet the voluntary act requirements of Section 301 of the Crimes Code.

The majority quite correctly observes that "appellants' culpable conduct, according to the evidence, was not limited merely to an omission to act. It consisted, rather, of an affirmative course of conduct calculated to deprive Kly of the food and medical care which was otherwise available to him and which was essential to continued life. It included efforts to place Kly beyond the ability of others to provide such needs." Thus, while I would grant appellants a new trial, it is to be emphasized as certain and sure that appellants are not entitled to an arrest of judgment since a reading of even the limited portions of the record available to this Court discloses sufficient evidence to support a finding by the jury that appellants' omission (failure to perform the contract) would not have resulted in the death of Joseph Kly except for the voluntary acts of the appellants, including the removal of their victim, Joseph Kly, to a remote area of Scott Township where he did not have access to a phone, store, or friends, and the active concealment of his whereabouts from those who might otherwise have assisted him. * * *

The attorney for the Commonwealth, however, while relating in his brief to this Court that appellants "not only . . . failed to provide Mr. Kly with proper care, food and shelter they had agreed to, but, additionally, they took deliberate steps to prevent others from doing so", presumably deemed it strategically prudent to refrain in the trial court from arguing that those deliberate acts were sufficient to establish liability for criminal homicide and thereby render the provisions of Section 301(b)(2) irrelevant in this prosecution. As a result, one of the issues which this Court must now decide is whether appellants are correct when they argue that the charge to the jury contained error since Pennsylvania law does not permit a finding that a breach, by omission, of a civil contract will suffice as an "act" for purposes of criminal liability where the duty to act arises only by virtue of the contract and not under a statute or other ordinance or regulation. After intense and concerned reflection, I find myself obliged to agree that the trial court erred when it instructed the jury that appellants could be found guilty of criminal homicide based solely upon a finding of a breach by omission of an oral contract. * * *

While a minority of other jurisdictions have sustained convictions for involuntary manslaughter under similar circumstances, see: State v. Brown, 129 Ariz. 347, 631 P.2d 129 (1981); Davis v. Commonwealth, 230 Va. 201, 335 S.E.2d 375 (1985), *Anno*, Homicide by withholding food, clothing or shelter, 61 ALR3d 1207 (1975), the function of this Court is to interpret and apply the provisions of the criminal law in accordance with the intent of the legislature of Pennsylvania. My review of case law from this and other jurisdictions as well as our legislature's use of the phrase in other sections of the Crimes Code and in a number of other statutes has persuaded me that the legislature, in employing the phrase "imposed by law", intended that the phrase denote duties specifically imposed by a statute, ordinance or administrative regulation, and not duties voluntarily assumed by private individuals.

Thus, it is that I dissent. DEL SOLE, J. joins this dissent.

COMMONWEALTH v. CALI

Supreme Judicial Court of Massachusetts, 1923.
247 Mass. 20, 141 N.E. 510.

BRALEY, J. The defendant having been indicted, tried and convicted under G.L. c. 266, § 10, of burning a building in Leominster belonging to Maria Cali, which at the time was insured against loss or damage by fire, with intent to injure the insurer, the case is here on his exceptions to the denial of his motion for a directed verdict, and to rulings at the trial.

* * *

The only evidence as to the origin, extent and progress of the fire were the statements of the defendant to the police inspector, and as a witness. The jury who were to determine his credibility and the weight to be given his testimony could find notwithstanding his explanations of its origin as being purely accidental, that when all the circumstances were reviewed he either set it, or after the fire was under way purposely refrained from any attempt to extinguish it in order to obtain the benefit of the proceeds of the policy, which when recovered, would be applied by the mortgagee on his indebtedness. If they so found, a specific intent to injure the insurer had been proved. The motion and the defendant's requests in so far as not given were denied rightly.

The instructions to the jury that:

> "If a man does start an accidental fire what is his conduct in regard to it? A question—as if after the fire has started accidentally, and he then has it within his power and ability to extinguish the fire and he realizes and knows that he can, and then he forms and entertains an intent to injure an insurance company, he can be guilty of this offense. It is not necessary that the intent be formed before the fire is started,"

—also show no error of law. It is true as the defendant contends, that if he merely neglected in the emergency of the moment to act, his negligence was not proof of a purpose to commit the crime charged.

The intention, however, to injure could be formed after as well as before the fire started. On his own admissions the jury were to say whether when considered in connection with all the circumstances, his immediate departure from the premises for his home in Fitchburg, without giving any alarm, warranted the inference of a criminal intent or state of mind, that the building should be consumed.

Exceptions overruled.

Note

The criminal law punishes only conduct, not mere thoughts or dispositions, but an omission to do something that one has a duty to do is treated as a form of "conduct." The American rule that there is no duty to assist a stranger in need of rescue, which applies to both civil and criminal liability, has been the subject of frequent criticism.[a]

The American rule drew heated attention in a 1998 incident which did not involve a criminal prosecution. David Cash, then aged 18, went with his friend Strohmeyer to a Nevada casino, where Strohmeyer raped and murdered a 7–year-old girl. Cash knew what Strohmeyer was doing and may have watched it, but he did nothing either to aid the victim or to prevent the crime. He also made statements to investigators indicating that he felt no remorse for the victim but only for his friend. Prosecutors concluded that Cash had violated no law, but there were bitter protests against his presence on the University of California's Berkeley campus when he appeared there to attend classes as a nuclear engineering student. Strohmeyer was sentenced to life imprisonment without eligibility for parole. See New York Times, October 4, 1998, Page A29, Column 1, "Campus Peers Shun Student Who Did Not Report Child's Killing."

The Penal Codes of some European countries punish failure to rescue or assist persons in serious danger in many circumstances in which Anglo–American law would impose no duty to act. See Feldbrugge, "Good and Bad Samaritans," 14 Am.J.Comp.L. 630 (1966). As a rule, however, the European statutes do not treat failure to rescue as homicide when death results, but as a separate crime with a lesser penalty.

A bodily movement is not "conduct" unless it is voluntary, i.e. directed by the will. For example, the Alabama Court of Appeals reversed a conviction for public drunkenness of a man who was arrested by police in his own home while drunk, and then taken out onto a public highway. The defendant's appearance in public was involuntary, and so he committed no crime. Martin v. State, 31 Ala.App. 334, 17 So.2d 427 (1944). Similarly, the defendant in *Decina* was not "driving" the automobile, negligently or otherwise, during the period when he was having an epileptic fit.

The same principle applies even to strict liability crimes. The issue arose in a New Zealand case where the defendant was charged with permitting a motor vehicle to be on a road without displaying a "warrant of fitness" in the manner prescribed by law. The parties stipulated that the warrant was properly displayed when the defendant parked his car, but it was subsequently somehow detached from the windshield before his return. The New Zealand Supreme Court reversed the conviction because "there was no opportunity at all to take a different course, and any inactivity on the part of the appellant after the warrant was removed was involuntary and unrelated to the offense." Kilbride v. Lake, [1962] N.Z.L.R. 590.

Many statutes prohibit "possession" of some substance. Ordinarily these statutes specify that it is only "knowing" possession of (say) narcotics which is prohibited and so the prosecution must prove that the defendant was aware of the contraband nature of the substance possessed. Even when the word "knowing" is omitted from the statute, however, an important mental element remains because it is inherent in the term "possession." For

a. Hawaii and Wisconsin enacted legislation in 1984 imposing misdemeanor penalties upon persons who fail to summon assistance for victims of assaultive crimes, if they could do so without peril to themselves or others. Vermont has long imposed a statutory duty upon bystanders to give reasonable assistance in any emergency where serious harm is threatened. See Hawaii Rev.Stat. § 663–1.6; Wis.Stat.Ann. 940.34; Vt.Stat.Ann. tit. 12, § 519.

example, in People v. Gory, 28 Cal.2d 450, 170 P.2d 433 (1946), the defendant, a jail prisoner, was charged with possession of marijuana found in his personal locker. He testified that he had no idea how the marijuana came to be placed in the locker. The court interpreted the California narcotic statute as it then read to impose strict liability, so that the defendant could be properly convicted without regard to whether he knew that the substance he possessed was marijuana. It further held, however, that he could not be said to "possess" any object unless he had knowledge of the presence of the object within his dominion and control. In other words, the mere fact that he possessed the locker did not mean that he possessed the marijuana found within it. If he knew that the substance was in his locker, however, he could be said to possess marijuana even if he thought it was tobacco.

The requirement of a voluntary act presents difficult problems of philosophy and policy when a defendant claims that he engaged in seemingly goal-directed activity following a "blackout." The defendant in People v. Newton, supra, may have been unconscious in some sense, but it was plainly not the same sense in which a sleeping person is unconscious. It is difficult to say how many American states recognize unconsciousness or "automatism" as a defense distinct from insanity in such circumstances. See Fulcher v. State, 633 P.2d 142 (Wyo.1981); State v. Caddell, 287 N.C. 266, 215 S.E.2d 348 (1975); People v. Grant, 71 Ill.2d 551, 17 Ill.Dec. 814, 377 N.E.2d 4 (1978); N. Morris, Madness and the Criminal Law 211–18 (1982).

Recognition of such an unconsciousness defense may have important procedural consequences. In a number of states, the defendant is required to plea a defense of insanity before trial (thus eliminating the advantage of surprise), and to prove it by a preponderance of the evidence. If he succeeds, the verdict is "not guilty by reason of insanity," and special mental commitment procedures usually follow. The claim that the defendant's act was not voluntary because he was unconscious need not be specially pleaded, and the defendant need not prove he was unconscious but only that there is a reasonable doubt on the matter. (But see, State v. Caddell, supra which places the burden of proof on the defense.) If he is successful, the verdict is a plain "not guilty", and he is subject only to such mental commitment procedures as apply generally to persons not accused of criminal activity.

Conceivably, an unconsciousness defense might result in the outright release of a very dangerous individual. In Regina v. Charlson, (1955) 1 W.L.R. 317, 39 Cr.App.R. 37, the defendant was charged with aggravated assault for hitting his ten-year-old son on the head with a hammer and throwing him into a river. Medical experts testified that he was not suffering from any "mental disease", but that the attack was caused by the pressure of a cerebral tumor on the brain which made him subject to fits of uncontrollable purposeless violence. The judge instructed the jury that he was not guilty "if his actions were purely automatic and his mind had no control over the movement of his limbs." A verdict of acquittal followed. The House of Lords subsequently held that the defense of automatism (as distinguished from insanity) is not available "where the only cause alleged for the unconsciousness is a defect of reason from disease of the mind." Bratty v. Attorney–General for Northern Ireland, (1961) 3 W.L.R. 965, 3 All E.R. 523. The relationship between automatism and insanity is considered further in Chapter 4.

The criminal conduct and the required culpability must occur at the same time. Note, however, that where a particular result (e.g. death) is an element of a crime, the result may occur after the conduct is completed. Thus, in the *Decina* case, the negligent driving occurred before the epileptic seizure, and the impact and death subsequently. The requirement that the conduct and culpability occur at the same time can lead to some interesting intellectual puzzles. For example, in Thabo Meli v. Regina, [1954] 1 All E.R. 373 (P.C.), the defendants attacked the victim intending to kill him. Believing he was dead when in fact he was alive, they rolled him over a cliff where he subsequently died from exposure rather than from the original act. The conduct that caused the death was not accompanied by an intent to kill, and the murderous assault did not cause the death. If one considers the two acts separately, the defendants might be guilty of attempted murder *and* negligent homicide. Instead, the court considered the series of events to be a single transaction and upheld a verdict of guilty of murder.

D. THE MODEL PENAL CODE REFORM

The Model Penal Code

Section 1.13. General Definitions

In this Code, unless a different meaning plainly is required:

(1) "statute" includes the Constitution and a local law or ordinance of a political subdivision of the State;

(2) "act" or "action" means a bodily movement whether voluntary or involuntary;

(3) "voluntary" has the meaning specified in Section 2.01;

(4) "omission" means a failure to act;

(5) "conduct" means an action or omission and its accompanying state of mind, or, where relevant, a series of acts and omissions;

(6) "actor" includes, where relevant, a person guilty of an omission;

(7) "acted" includes, where relevant, "omitted to act";

(8) "person," "he" and "actor" include any natural person and, where relevant, a corporation or an unincorporated association;

(9) "element of an offense" means (i) such conduct or (ii) such attendant circumstances or (iii) such a result of conduct as

(a) is included in the description of the forbidden conduct in the definition of the offense; or

(b) establishes the required kind of culpability; or

(c) negatives an excuse or justification for such conduct; or

(d) negatives a defense under the statute of limitations; or

(e) establishes jurisdiction or venue;

(10) "material element of an offense" means an element that does not relate exclusively to the statute of limitations, jurisdiction, venue or to any other matter similarly unconnected with (i) the harm or evil,

incident to conduct, sought to be prevented by the law defining the offense, or (ii) the existence of a justification or excuse for such conduct;

* * *

Section 2.01. Requirement of Voluntary Act; Omission as Basis of Liability; Possession as an Act

(1) A person is not guilty of an offense unless his liability is based on conduct which includes a voluntary act or the omission to perform an act of which he is physically capable.

(2) The following are not voluntary acts within the meaning of this Section:

(a) a reflex or convulsion;

(b) a bodily movement during unconsciousness or sleep;

(c) conduct during hypnosis or resulting from hypnotic suggestion;

(d) a bodily movement that otherwise is not a product of the effort or determination of the actor, either conscious or habitual.

(3) Liability for the commission of an offense may not be based on an omission unaccompanied by action unless:

(a) the omission is expressly made sufficient by the law defining the offense; or

(b) a duty to perform the omitted act is otherwise imposed by law.

(4) Possession is an act, within the meaning of this Section, if the possessor knowingly procured or received the thing possessed or was aware of his control thereof for a sufficient period to have been able to terminate his possession.

Section 2.02. General Requirements of Culpability

(1) Minimum Requirements of Culpability. Except as provided in Section 2.05,[a] a person is not guilty of an offense unless he acted purposely, knowingly, recklessly or negligently, as the law may require, with respect to each material element of the offense.

(2) Kinds of Culpability Defined.

(a) *Purposely.* A person acts purposely with respect to a material element of an offense when:

(i) if the element involves the nature of his conduct or a result thereof, it is his conscious object to engage in conduct of that nature or to cause such a result; and

a. 2.05 deals with "violations," which are non-criminal regulatory offenses punishable only by a fine or forfeiture.—ed.

(ii) if the element involves the attendant circumstances, he is aware of the existence of such circumstances or he believes or hopes that they exist.

(b) *Knowingly.* A person acts knowingly with respect to a material element of an offense when:

(i) if the element involves the nature of his conduct or the attendant circumstances, he is aware that his conduct is of that nature or that such circumstances exist; and

(ii) if the element involves a result of his conduct, he is aware that it is practically certain that his conduct will cause such a result.

(c) *Recklessly.* A person acts recklessly with respect to a material element of an offense when he consciously disregards a substantial and unjustifiable risk that the material element exists or will result from his conduct. The risk must be of such a nature and degree that, considering the nature and purpose of the actor's conduct and the circumstances known to him, its disregard involves a gross deviation from the standard of conduct that a law-abiding person would observe in the actor's situation.

(d) *Negligently.* A person acts negligently with respect to a material element of an offense when he should be aware of a substantial and unjustifiable risk that the material element exists or will result from his conduct. The risk must be of such a nature and degree that the actor's failure to perceive it, considering the nature and purpose of his conduct and the circumstances known to him, involves a gross deviation from the standard of care that a reasonable person would observe in the actor's situation.

(3) Culpability Required Unless Otherwise Provided. When the culpability sufficient to establish a material element of an offense is not prescribed by law, such element is established if a person acts purposely, knowingly or recklessly with respect thereto.

(4) Prescribed Culpability Requirement Applies to All Material Elements. When the law defining an offense prescribes the kind of culpability that is sufficient for the commission of an offense, without distinguishing among the material elements thereof, such provision shall apply to all the material elements of the offense, unless a contrary purpose plainly appears.

(5) Substitutes for Negligence, Recklessness and Knowledge. When the law provides that negligence suffices to establish an element of an offense, such element also is established if a person acts purposely, knowingly or recklessly. When recklessness suffices to establish an element, such element also is established if a person acts purposely or knowingly. When acting knowingly suffices to establish an element, such element also is established if a person acts purposely.

(6) Requirement of Purpose Satisfied if Purpose Is Conditional. When a particular purpose is an element of an offense, the element is established although such purpose is conditional, unless the condition negatives the harm or evil sought to be prevented by the law defining the offense.

(7) Requirement of Knowledge Satisfied by Knowledge of High Probability. When knowledge of the existence of a particular fact is an element of an offense, such knowledge is established if a person is aware of a high probability of its existence, unless he actually believes that it does not exist.

(8) Requirement of Wilfulness Satisfied by Acting Knowingly. A requirement that an offense be committed wilfully is satisfied if a person acts knowingly with respect to the material elements of the offense, unless a purpose to impose further requirements appears.

(9) Culpability as to Illegality of Conduct. Neither knowledge nor recklessness or negligence as to whether conduct constitutes an offense or as to the existence, meaning or application of the law determining the elements of an offense is an element of such offense, unless the definition of the offense or the Code so provides.

(10) Culpability as Determinant of Grade of Offense. When the grade or degree of an offense depends on whether the offense is committed purposely, knowingly, recklessly or negligently, its grade or degree shall be the lowest for which the determinative kind of culpability is established with respect to any material element of the offense.

Section 2.04. Ignorance or Mistake

(1) Ignorance or mistake as to a matter of fact or law is a defense if:

(a) the ignorance or mistake negatives the purpose, knowledge, belief, recklessness or negligence required to establish a material element of the offense; or

(b) the law provides that the state of mind established by such ignorance or mistake constitutes a defense.

(2) Although ignorance or mistake would otherwise afford a defense to the offense charged, the defense is not available if the defendant would be guilty of another offense had the situation been as he supposed. In such case, however, the ignorance or mistake of the defendant shall reduce the grade and degree of the offense of which he may be convicted to those of the offense of which he would be guilty had the situation been as he supposed.

(3) A belief that conduct does not legally constitute an offense is a defense to a prosecution for that offense based upon such conduct when:

(a) the statute or other enactment defining the offense is not known to the actor and has not been published or otherwise reasonably made available prior to the conduct alleged; or

(b) he acts in reasonable reliance upon an official statement of the law, afterward determined to be invalid or erroneous, contained in (i) a statute or other enactment; (ii) a judicial decision, opinion or judgment; (iii) an administrative order or grant of permission; or (iv) an official interpretation of the public officer or body charged by law with responsibility for the interpretation, administration or enforcement of the law defining the offense.

(4) The defendant must prove a defense arising under Subsection (3) of this Section by a preponderance of evidence.

Section 2.08. Intoxication

(1) Except as provided in Subsection (4) of this Section, intoxication of the actor is not a defense unless it negatives an element of the offense.

(2) When recklessness establishes an element of the offense, if the actor, due to self-induced intoxication, is unaware of a risk of which he would have been aware had he been sober, such unawareness is immaterial.

(3) Intoxication does not, in itself, constitute mental disease within the meaning of Section 4.01.[12]

(4) Intoxication which (a) is not self-induced or (b) is pathological is an affirmative defense if by reason of such intoxication the actor at the time of his conduct lacks substantial capacity either to appreciate its criminality [wrongfulness] or to conform his conduct to the requirements of law.

(5) Definitions. In this Section unless a different meaning plainly is required:

(a) "intoxication" means a disturbance of mental or physical capacities resulting from the introduction of substances into the body;

(b) "self-induced intoxication" means intoxication caused by substances which the actor knowingly introduces into his body, the tendency of which to cause intoxication he knows or ought to know, unless he introduces them pursuant to medical advice or under such circumstances as would afford a defense to a charge of crime;

(c) "pathological intoxication" means intoxication grossly excessive in degree, given the amount of the intoxicant, to which the actor does not know he is susceptible.

Note

The American Law Institute's Model Penal Code has had a large and continuing influence on the development of the criminal law since its promulgation in 1962. Approximately half the states have revised their Penal Codes since 1962 (many other states and the federal government have considered revisions), and the Model Code has heavily influenced the drafting of most of these revisions. In addition, state and federal courts frequently cite the Model Code as authority on points not covered in their own codes.

12. Section 4.01 defines the "insanity" defense.—ed.

The federal courts of appeal, for example, chose to adopt the Model Code's insanity test into federal law in the absence of Congressional legislation. (But see the Federal Insanity Defense Reform Act of 1984, infra, Chapter 4.)

The basic culpability provisions reprinted above have been widely copied in the state Penal Code revisions, and are generally considered by scholarly commentators to be a substantial improvement upon the traditional law doctrines described in the preceding sections of this chapter. These culpability provisions are relatively non-ideological and technical in character: the purpose is to provide a legislature with adequate concepts and terminology to achieve whatever substantive policy goals in criminal law it happens to have. At this point, students should consider how the Code has attempted to resolve the conceptual difficulties previously identified in the traditional criminal law. The following commentary is designed to help law students to absorb the very special logic of the Model Penal Code approach to culpability analysis. For a very thorough critique of the Model Penal Code's culpability provisions, see Robinson and Grall, "Element Analysis in Defining Criminal Liability: The Model Penal Code and Beyond," 35 Stan.L.Rev. 681 (1983).

Section 1.13 contains the general definitions. Of critical importance here is to understand what is meant by an "element of an offense" and a "*material* element of an offense." Practically everything that the prosecution has to prove is included within the definition of "element." This includes such "procedural" matters as that the crime occurred within the jurisdiction of the court, and within the time period provided by an applicable statute of limitations. The more important category, however, consists of the "material" elements: those that go to the criminality or wrongfulness of the activity as opposed to the merely procedural elements. What is a little difficult to grasp, until one gets used to the idea, is that what we would ordinarily call defenses to the charge are classified as negative "material elements." The material elements of homicide thus include not only the killing of the human being, but also the lack of self-defense or any other justification or excuse for the crime. If the homicide is being prosecuted in, say, Texas, the fact that the victim was killed within that state is a non-material element.

Section 2.01 provides, consistent with traditional law doctrine, that all criminal liability must be based on voluntary activity. The California statute involved in People v. Newton, supra page 52, stated that a defendant was not guilty if he "committed the act charged without being conscious thereof." The Model Penal Code would put it slightly differently: a defendant who is not conscious is not acting at all.

Section 2.02 is the most important section in the entire Code and contains a number of rules for resolving conceptual difficulties with regard to "culpability," the Model Penal Code term for what was previously called mens rea. Subsection (1) states some important starting points. First, strict liability is provided only for non-criminal "violations," which are punished merely by financial penalties. There is no criminal strict liability, strictly speaking. Second, this subsection provides that one must have the required degree of culpability with respect to *each material element of the offense.* The significance of this way of putting it will become clearer as we go on.

The four types of culpability—purposely, knowingly, recklessly and negligently—replace traditional terms like "willfully" and "maliciously." The meaning of these terms can perhaps best be grasped by considering the following example. An anarchist throws a bomb into the royal carriage, killing the king, the king's valet, the royal coachman, and a bystander on the street. The assassin's purpose was to kill the king. He knew that the bomb would also kill the valet (who was riding in the coach) but sincerely regretted this inevitable consequence of the assassination. He told a friend beforehand that he was aware that the bomb might possibly kill the coachman, but he hoped that the coachman would survive. He never thought about the possibility that any bystanders might be injured or killed, but this possibility was sufficiently likely that he ought to have foreseen it. The anarchist purposely killed the king, knowingly killed the valet, recklessly killed the coachman, and negligently killed the bystander.

This analysis may give the reader the misleading impression that each of these crimes is of a different degree and carries a different penalty. That is not necessarily the case: in fact, the Model Penal Code homicide provision punishes all the killings as murder except that of the bystander. The distinction between purpose and knowledge is significant only in a small number of doctrinal areas, principally conspiracy and accessorial liability. The culpability terms and definitions are for the assistance of the legislature, which decides on policy grounds how to make use of them.

The distinction between reckless and negligent activity is particularly significant. Recklessness involves conscious risk creation; negligence involves the failure to perceive a risk of which one ought to have been aware. At times, a person is justified in going ahead despite the awareness or presence of risk. A surgeon may perform a brain operation even though it is risky, and a contractor may build a suspension bridge even though there is a known risk that some workers may be injured or killed. Criminal liability results only when the risk was "unjustifiable," and the second sentence in the definition of each term explains what the drafters meant by "unjustifiable."

Section 2.02(3) gives a rule of construction in case the legislature fails to specify the appropriate level of culpability. For example, if the statute punishes "causing injury to a police officer," the defendant is liable if he caused the injury purposely, knowingly, or recklessly—but not if he caused the injury merely negligently. Unlike the other degrees of culpability, negligence involves no conscious wrongdoing. Some authorities have argued that there should be no criminal liability for negligence, on the theory that there is no true blameworthiness where one is merely inattentive or stupid. The Code does not go that far, but it does presume that liability for negligence is the exception rather than the norm, and so such liability is imposed only where the legislature expressly so provides.

Section 2.02(4) is aimed at the problem illustrated by United States v. Yermian, supra p. 5. To continue with the example stated in the preceding paragraph, a defendant is not guilty of "causing injury to a police officer" unless he disregarded not only a risk of injury, but also a risk that the person injured might turn out to be a police officer. Of course, the lower culpability term incorporates the higher terms. A person is guilty of causing injury to a police officer if he recklessly injured a person whom he knew to be an officer. *Section 2.02(5)* makes this explicit.

Section 2.02(6) deals with the problem of conditional purpose. A burglar who enters a home with the purpose of committing rape if the occupant rejects his advances is guilty of burglary even though he may have hoped that the use of force would not be necessary. Compare, State v. Irwin, 55 N.C.App. 305, 285 S.E.2d 345 (1982). Irwin, a jail prisoner, held a knife to the throat of a matron and threatened to kill her if anyone resisted his attempt to escape. He said, "I don't want to hurt this woman but I don't have any choice." The North Carolina Court of Appeals held that as a matter of law he was not guilty of "assault with intent to kill" because the intent was conditional and the defendant never had occasion to carry out his threat.

Section 2.02(7) deals with the problem of "willful blindness." The meaning of this provision is illustrated by the opinions in United States v. Jewell, the case which follows this Note. That case also illustrates the tendency of courts in "traditional" jurisdictions to cite the Model Penal Code as authority even though it has not been enacted.

Section 2.02(8) provides a rule of construction that should be necessary only if the legislature fails to revise all applicable statutes to replace obsolete terms such as "willfully." *Section 2.02(9)* states the correct doctrine with respect to ignorance of the law: knowledge of the existence or meaning of the criminal prohibition itself is not an element of the offense.

Section 2.02(10) is an important provision which may run counter to common sense intuitions. Suppose that a defendant kills a person by intentionally shooting him in the heart under the honest but thoroughly mistaken belief that the victim is about to kill him. The killing is done purposely, but the defendant is merely negligent with respect to a material negative element of the crime: lack of a self-defense justification. (If this is unclear, review the definition of "material element" in Section 1.13.) The defendant is guilty of negligent homicide, not murder.

Section 2.04(1) is entirely superfluous; it states nothing that is not already implicit in Section 2.02. The drafters of the Code felt it necessary to commit this redundancy because of the danger that courts would read pre existing limits on mistake (particularly mistake of law) into the Code.

Section 2.04(2) is another provision that can best be illustrated with a simple example. Suppose that a jurisdiction makes it a felony to possess heroin and a misdemeanor to possess cocaine. A defendant is charged with possessing heroin; he says that he thought the substance was cocaine. The appropriate verdict is guilty on the heroin charge (assuming the substance really is heroin), but the sentence should be for a misdemeanor.

Section 2.04(3) deals with the circumstances under which a mistake as to the existence or meaning of the criminal prohibition itself may be a defense. There has been some opposition to enacting this type of provision, because of the danger that public officials may claim official authorization for acts which violate the civil liberties of citizens. The decision in United States v. Barker, supra Ch. 1, § A, may indicate that there is some substance to these fears.

Section 2.08 provides a special rule for intoxication, a rule which runs counter to the general logic of the Code. If a defendant is charged with reckless conduct, he can be convicted even if he did not consciously disregard the risk. This provision has been controversial. Some state codes omit it and permit intoxication to be considered, like any other evidence, insofar as it tends to negate the culpability required for the crime. That was initially the position of the drafters of the Model Penal Code itself, but they were eventually persuaded that drunkenness so severe as to destroy temporarily the actor's powers of perception and judgment is the moral equivalent of recklessness. Note that recklessness is in a sense the Model Penal Code equivalent for the discredited term "general intent," and it is ironical that the Code was not able to avoid the need to have a special and somewhat illogical rule governing voluntary intoxication.

When the intoxication is not voluntary (as when a practical joker spikes the punch bowl with LSD, or when the actor has an unusual reaction to a mild intoxicant due to factors beyond his control or knowledge) the rule is different. In this circumstance intoxication excuses if it was so severe that the defendant lacked "substantial capacity" to control his conduct, the Model Penal Code test for legal insanity.

The following cases illustrate the use of the Model Penal Code's culpability provisions by the courts and by state legislatures:

UNITED STATES v. JEWELL

United States Court of Appeals, Ninth Circuit, 1976.
532 F.2d 697 (en banc).

Browning, Circuit Judge:

* * *

It is undisputed that appellant entered the United States driving an automobile in which 110 pounds of marihuana worth $6,250 had been concealed in a secret compartment between the trunk and rear seat. Appellant testified that he did not know the marijuana was present. There was circumstantial evidence from which the jury could infer that appellant had positive knowledge of the presence of the marihuana, and that his contrary testimony was false. On the other hand there was evidence from which the jury could conclude that appellant spoke the truth—that although appellant knew of the presence of the secret compartment and had knowledge of facts indicating that it contained marijuana, he deliberately avoided positive knowledge of the presence of the contraband to avoid responsibility in the event of discovery. If the jury concluded the latter was indeed the situation, and if positive knowledge is required to convict, the jury would have no choice consistent with its oath but to find appellant not guilty even though he deliberately contrived his lack of positive knowledge. Appellant urges this view. The trial court rejected the premise that only positive knowledge would suffice, and properly so.

Appellant tendered an instruction that to return a guilty verdict the jury must find that the defendant knew he was in possession of marihuana. The trial judge rejected the instruction because it suggested that "absolutely, positively, he has to know that it's there." The court said,

"I think, in this case, it's not too sound an instruction because we have evidence that if the jury believes it, they'd be justified in finding he actually didn't know what it was—he didn't because he didn't want to find it."

The court instructed the jury that "knowingly" meant voluntarily and intentionally and not by accident or mistake. The court told the jury that the government must prove beyond a reasonable doubt that the defendant "knowingly" brought the marihuana into the United States (count 1: 21 U.S.C. § 952(a)), and that he "knowingly" possessed the marihuana (count 2: 21 U.S.C. § 841(a)(1)). The court continued:

> The Government can complete their burden of proof by proving, beyond a reasonable doubt, that if the defendant was not actually aware that there was marijuana in the vehicle he was driving when he entered the United States his ignorance in that regard was solely and entirely a result of his having made a conscious purpose to disregard the nature of that which was in the vehicle, with a conscious purpose to avoid learning the truth.

The legal premise of these instructions is firmly supported by leading commentators here and in England. Professor Rollin M. Perkins writes, "One with a deliberate antisocial purpose in mind * * * may deliberately 'shut his eyes' to avoid knowing what would otherwise be obvious to view. In such cases, so far as criminal law is concerned, the person acts at his peril in this regard, and is treated as having 'knowledge' of the facts as they are ultimately discovered to be." J. Ll. J. Edwards, writing in 1954, introduced a survey of English cases with the statement, "For well-nigh a hundred years, it has been clear from the authorities that a person who deliberately shuts his eyes to an obvious means of knowledge has sufficient *mens rea* for an offence based on such words as * * * 'knowingly.'" Professor Glanville Williams states, on the basis both English and American authorities, "To the requirement of actual knowledge there is one strictly limited exception. * * * [T]he rule is that if a party has his suspicion aroused but then deliberately omits to make further enquiries, because he wishes to remain in ignorance, he is deemed to have knowledge." Professor Williams concludes, "The rule that wilful blindness is equivalent to knowledge is essential, and is found throughout the criminal law."

The substantive justification for the rule is that deliberate ignorance and positive knowledge are equally culpable. The textual justification is that in common understanding one "knows" facts of which he is less than absolutely certain. To act "knowingly," therefore, is not necessarily to act only with positive knowledge, but also to act with an awareness of the high probability of the existence of the fact in question. When such awareness is present, "positive" knowledge is not required.

This is the analysis adopted in the Model Penal Code. Section 2.02(7) states: "When knowledge of the existence of a particular fact is an element of an offense, such knowledge is established if a person is aware of a high probability of its existence, unless he actually believes that it does not exist." As the Comment to this provision explains, "Paragraph (7) deals with the situation British commentators have denominated 'wilful blindness' or 'connivance,' the case of the actor who is aware of the probable existence of a material fact but does not satisfy himself that it does not in fact exist." * * *

Appellant's narrow interpretation of "knowingly" is inconsistent with the Drug Control Act's general purpose to deal more effectively "with the growing menace of drug abuse in the United States." Holding that this term introduces a requirement of positive knowledge would make deliberate ignorance a defense. It cannot be doubted that those who traffic in drugs would make the most of it. This is evident from the number of appellate decisions reflecting conscious avoidance of positive knowledge of the presence of contraband—in the car driven by the defendant or in which he is a passenger, in the suitcase or package he carries, in the parcel concealed in his clothing.

It is no answer to say that in such cases the fact finder may infer positive knowledge. It is probable that many who performed the transportation function, essential to the drug traffic, can truthfully testify that they have no *positive* knowledge of the load they carry. Under appellant's interpretation of the statute, such persons will be convicted only if the fact finder errs in evaluating the credibility of the witness or deliberately disregards the law.

It begs the question to assert that a "deliberate ignorance" instruction permits the jury to convict without finding that the accused possessed the knowledge required by the statute. Such an assertion assumes that the statute requires positive knowledge. But the question is the meaning of the term "knowingly" in the statute. If it means positive knowledge, then, of course, nothing less will do. But if "knowingly" includes a mental state in which the defendant is aware that the fact in question is highly probable but consciously avoids enlightenment, the statute is satisfied by such proof. * * * In the language of the instruction in this case, the government must prove, "beyond a reasonable doubt, that if the defendant was not actually aware * * * his ignorance in that regard was *solely* and *entirely* a result of * * * a conscious purpose to avoid learning the truth."[21]

* * *

No legitimate interest of an accused is prejudiced by such a standard, and society's interest in a system of criminal law that is enforceable and that imposes sanctions upon all who are equally culpable requires it.

21. We do not suggest that the instruction given in this case was a model in all respects. The jury should have been instructed more directly (1) that the required knowledge is established if the accused is aware of a high probability of the existence of the fact in question, (2) unless he actually believes it does not exist.

The deficiency in the instruction does not require reversal, however. Appellant did not object to the instruction on this ground either below or in this court. Since both of the elements referred to are implied in the instruction, the deficiency in the instructions is not so substantial as to justify reversal for plain error.

The conviction is affirmed.

ANTHONY M. KENNEDY, CIRCUIT JUDGE, with whom ELY, HUFSTEDLER and WALLACE, CIRCUIT JUDGES, join (dissenting).

* * *

In light of the Model Penal Code's definition, the "conscious purpose" jury instruction is defective in three respects. First, it fails to mention the requirement that Jewell have been aware of a high probability that a controlled substance was in the car. It is not culpable to form "a conscious purpose to avoid learning the truth" unless one is aware of facts indicating a high probability of that truth. To illustrate, a child given a gift-wrapped package by his mother while on vacation in Mexico may form a conscious purpose to take it home without learning what is inside; yet his state of mind is totally innocent unless he is aware of a high probability that the package contains a controlled substance. Thus, a conscious purpose instruction is only proper when coupled with a requirement that one be aware of a high probability of the truth.

The second defect in the instruction as given is that it did not alert the jury that Jewell could not be convicted if he "actually believed" there was no controlled substance in the car. The failure to emphasize, as does the Model Penal Code, that subjective belief is the determinative factor, may allow a jury to convict on an objective theory of knowledge—that a reasonable man should have inspected the car and would have discovered what was hidden inside. One recent decision reversed a jury instruction for this very deficiency—failure to balance a conscious purpose instruction with a warning that the defendant could not be convicted if he actually believed to the contrary. United States v. Bright, 517 F.2d 584, 586–89 (2d Cir.1975).

Third, the jury instruction clearly states that Jewell could have been convicted even if found ignorant or "not actually aware" that the car contained a controlled substance. This is unacceptable because true ignorance, no matter how unreasonable, cannot provide a basis for criminal liability when the statute requires knowledge. A proper jury instruction based on the Model Penal Code would be presented as a way of defining knowledge, and not as an alternative to it.

* * *

Although the defense counsel did not fully anticipate our analysis of the conscious purpose instruction, he came close. (1) He gave a reason for his objection—that the instruction would allow conviction without proof of the scienter element. (2) He further suggested adding "an addendum" to warn the jury against misinterpreting the instruction. We believe these objections were sufficient to require reversal on appeal unless the deficiencies in the instruction were harmless error.

We do not question the sufficiency of the evidence in this case to support conviction by a properly-instructed jury. As with all states of mind, knowledge must normally be proven by circumstantial evidence.

There is evidence which could support a conclusion that Jewell was aware of a high probability that the car contained a controlled substance and that he had no belief to the contrary. However, we cannot say that the evidence was so overwhelming that the erroneous jury instruction was harmless. Accordingly, we would reverse the judgment on this appeal.

STATE v. COATES

Supreme Court of Washington, 1987.
107 Wash.2d 882, 735 P.2d 64.

DORE, JUSTICE.

Steven Kenneth Coates appeals his conviction of assault in the third degree. * * * The conviction is affirmed.

Facts

At approximately 11:30 p.m. on September 15, 1984, as Matt Long drove home from his job as a Hanford patrolman, he observed a blue Thunderbird strike another automobile. This second car pulled to the side of the road, but the Thunderbird continued; the officer followed the Thunderbird. Approximately a half mile farther, the Thunderbird's engine died, and it also pulled off to the side of the road. The officer stopped his vehicle behind the car. The defendant exited the driver's side and walked toward the officer's vehicle. Long identified himself as a police officer and told defendant that he should return to the accident scene. Defendant replied that he was a Navy corpsman and could help if anyone were injured. Defendant returned to his car, spoke briefly with his passenger Dana Soderquist, and then agreed to walk back to the scene of the accident.

As they approached the scene, the officer and defendant observed a police vehicle with emergency lights flashing. Defendant stared at the lights for a few moments, then said that he would not return to the scene. By this time Officer Long had come to question defendant's mental stability, so he agreed that defendant could return to his own car. As they neared the officer's truck, the defendant stabbed Officer Long twice in the back, and then returned to his car. * * *

[A detective named Hodge questioned defendant about the assault at the jail after advising him of his rights.] Defendant, who was obviously intoxicated, said he could not believe anyone could have been stabbed. Replying to the detective's question as to what had happened, the defendant said that he and the officer fell * * *. [A] Breathalyzer test, administered over 4 hours after the accident and assault, showed defendant as having a blood alcohol level of .16 percent. * * *

At trial Long testified to the circumstances of the assault. Defendant denied all wrongdoing, testifying that he could not remember the hit-and-run incident or the assault. Defendant stressed that he had consumed a great deal of alcohol that evening. Upon defense counsel's request, the trial judge instructed the jury on the "intoxication defense" and on the State's burden of proving that defendant's intoxication did not prevent the defendant from forming the particular requisite mental state. Over defense counsel's objection, however, the trial judge instructed the jury that this defense applies only where the mental state is intent, knowledge, or recklessness. The trial judge specifically precluded the jury from considering Coates' intoxication in determining whether he was guilty of the lesser-included offense of third degree (negligent) assault. The jury found defendant not guilty of second degree assault, but guilty of assault in the third degree. * * *

The voluntary intoxication statute provides:

> No act committed by a person while in a state of voluntary intoxication shall be deemed less criminal by reason of his condition, but whenever the actual existence of any particular mental state is a necessary element to constitute a particular species or degree of crime, the fact of his intoxication may be taken into consideration in determining such mental state.

* * * When the Legislature adopted the new criminal code, it replaced the concept of general and specific intent with four levels of culpability: intent, knowledge, recklessness, and negligence. At the same time, the Legislature amended the intoxication statute so as to refer to "particular mental state" rather than "purpose, motive, or intent."

Criminal negligence is defined as a person's "[failure] to be aware of a substantial risk that a wrongful act may occur and his failure to be aware of such substantial risk constitutes a gross deviation from the standard of care that a reasonable man would exercise in the same situation." Criminal negligence is the requisite mental state in the crime of assault in the third degree. Because this mental state is based on a reasonable person standard, evidence of defendant's voluntary intoxication can not work in any way to negate or obviate the mental state. Because of his intoxication, a particular defendant may not act with intent or knowingly inflict grievous bodily harm. Nonetheless, if a reasonable person would have avoided the wrongful act, and the defendant's failure to do so is a gross deviation from this reasonable course of conduct, the defendant has acted with criminal negligence.

In the present case, the "wrongful act" was the stabbing. Defendant's claimed reason for failing to be aware that the victim was being stabbed was evidently defendant's own intoxication. A reasonable person would not have stabbed the victim, and defendant's action was a gross deviation from the reasonable course of conduct. Consequently defendant was criminally negligent despite his intoxication. This is the proper interpretation to be given the definition of criminal negligence. The trial court did not err in precluding the jury from considering voluntary intoxication as a defense to the charge of third degree assault. * * *

DOLLIVER, ANDERSEN, CALLOW and DURHAM, JJ., concur.

PEARSON, CHIEF JUSTICE (dissenting).

* * * The majority holds that voluntary intoxication can never be a defense to criminal negligence. The voluntary intoxication statute provides that "whenever the actual existence of any particular mental state is a necessary element to constitute a particular species or degree of crime, the fact of [the defendant's] intoxication may be taken into consideration in determining such mental state." The defendant contends this defense applies to all four of the particular mental states defined in [the Code]: namely, intent, knowledge, recklessness, and criminal negligence. The State argues that public policy considerations require the courts to limit the intoxication defense to the three most culpable mental states, excluding criminal negligence. * * *

As originally enacted, the intoxication statute referred not to "particular mental state", but rather to "particular purpose, motive or intent". This court interpreted this phrase to apply to "specific intent" crimes, but not to "general intent" crimes. When the Legislature adopted the new criminal code, it replaced the concepts of general and specific intent with four levels of culpability: intent, knowledge, recklessness and criminal negligence. At the same time, the Legislature amended the intoxication statute to refer to "particular mental state" rather than "purpose, motive or intent". These amendments appear to extend the intoxication defense to all crimes in which one of the four mental states set forth in constitutes an element of the crime. Under the rule of lenity, criminal statutes should be construed strictly against the State and in favor of the accused. If the Legislature desires to limit the scope of the defense to crimes involving all mental states other than criminal negligence, it is free to amend the statute to reflect that desire. Until then, a defendant should be entitled to an instruction permitting the jury to determine whether the defendant's intoxication precluded formation of the requisite mental state of criminal negligence.

The Legislature on the one hand states that intoxication does not make an act "less criminal", and on the other states that intoxication "may be taken into consideration" by the jury in determining whether the defendant acted with the requisite mental state. These propositions are contradictory. If a particular mental state must be proved, and the jury may consider the defendant's intoxication in determining whether the defendant acted with that mental state, intoxication must be a defense to a criminal act * * * For the foregoing reasons, I dissent.

Utter and Brachtenbach, JJ., concur.

PEOPLE v. MARRERO

Court of Appeals of New York, 1987.
69 N.Y.2d 382, 515 N.Y.S.2d 212, 507 N.E.2d 1068.

Bellacosa, Judge.

[Defendant, a corrections officer at a federal prison, was convicted of unlawful possession of a pistol under a statute containing an exemption for "peace officers," as defined in another statute. The statutory definition of "peace officer" included "correction officers of any state correction facility or of any penal correctional institution." The trial court dismissed the charge on the ground that defendant was a peace officer, but the Appellate Division ruled by a 3–2 vote that only state and not federal corrections officers were covered by the statutory definition. At the ensuing criminal trial the court refused to instruct the jury that it should acquit defendant if he reasonably believed himself to be a peace officer under the statutory definition.]

* * * Defendant claimed at trial that there were various interpretations of fellow officers and teachers, as well as the peace officer statute itself, upon which he relied for his mistaken belief that he could carry a weapon with legal impunity.

The starting point for our analysis is the New York mistake statute as an outgrowth of the dogmatic common-law maxim that ignorance of the law is no excuse. The central issue is whether defendant's personal misreading or misunderstanding of a statute may excuse criminal conduct in the circumstances of this case. * * *

The common-law rule on mistake of law was clearly articulated in Gardner v. People, 62 N.Y. 299. In Gardner, the defendants misread a statute and mistakenly believed that their conduct was legal. The court insisted, however, that the "mistake of law" did not relieve the defendants of criminal liability. The statute at issue, relating to the removal of election officers, required that prior to removal, written notice must be given to the officer sought to be removed. The statute provided one exception to the notice requirement: "removal * * * shall only be made after notice in writing * * * unless made while the inspector is actually on duty on a day of registration, revision of registration, or election, and for improper conduct." The defendants construed the statute to mean that an election officer could be removed without notice for improper conduct at any time. The court ruled that removal without notice could only occur for improper conduct on a day of registration, revision of registration or election. In ruling that the defendant's misinterpretation of the statute was no defense, the court said: "The defendants made a mistake of law. Such mistakes do not excuse the commission of prohibited acts * * * " This is to be contrasted with People v. Weiss, 276 N.Y. 384, 12 N.E.2d 514 where, in a kidnapping case, the trial court precluded testimony that the defendants acted with the honest belief that seizing and confining the child was done with "authority of law". We held it was error to exclude such testimony since a good-faith belief in the legality of the conduct would negate an express and necessary element of the crime of kidnapping, i.e., intent, without authority of law, to confine or imprison another. Subject to the mistake statute, the instant case, of course, falls within the *Gardner* rationale because the weapons possession statute violated by this defendant imposes liability irrespective of one's intent.

The desirability of the *Gardner*-type outcome, which was to encourage the societal benefit of individuals' knowledge of and respect for the law, is underscored by Justice Holmes' statement: "It is no doubt true that there are many cases in which the criminal could not have known that he was breaking the law, but to admit the excuse at all would be to encourage ignorance where the law-maker has determined to make men know and obey, and justice to the individual is rightly outweighed by the larger interests on the other side of the scales" (Holmes, The Common Law, at 48 [1881]).

The revisors of New York's Penal Law intended no fundamental departure from this common-law rule in Penal Law § 15.20, which provides in pertinent part:

* * *

> "2. A person is not relieved of criminal liability for conduct because he engages in such conduct under a mistaken belief that it does not, as a matter of law, constitute an offense, unless such mistaken belief is founded upon an official statement of the law contained in (a) a statute or other enactment * * * (d) an interpretation of the statute or law relating to the offense, officially made or issued by a public servant, agency, or body legally charged or empowered with the responsibility or privilege of administering, enforcing or interpreting such statute or law."

This section was added to the Penal Law as part of the wholesale revision of the Penal Law in 1965. When this provision was first proposed, commentators viewed the new language as codifying "the established common law maxim on mistake of law, while at the same time recognizing a defense when the erroneous belief is founded upon an 'official statement of the law' " (Note, Proposed Penal Law of New York, 64 Colum.L.Rev. 1469, 1486 [1964]).

The defendant claims as a first prong of his defense that he is entitled to raise the defense of mistake of law under section 15.20(2)(a) because his mistaken belief that his conduct was legal was founded upon an official statement of the law contained in the statute itself. Defendant argues that his mistaken interpretation of the statute was reasonable in view of the alleged ambiguous wording of the peace officer exemption statute, and that his "reasonable" interpretation of an "official statement" is enough to satisfy the requirements of subdivision (2)(a). However, the whole thrust of this exceptional exculpatory concept, in derogation of the traditional and common-law principle, was intended to be a very narrow escape valve. Application in this case would invert that thrust and make mistake of law a generally applied or available defense instead of an unusual exception which the very opening words of the mistake statute make so clear, i.e., "A person is not relieved of criminal liability for conduct * * * unless" (Penal Law § 15.20). * * *

The prosecution [argues] that one cannot claim the protection of mistake of law under section 15.20(2)(a) simply by misconstruing the meaning of a statute but must instead establish that the statute relied on actually permitted the conduct in question and was only later found to be erroneous. To buttress that argument, the People analogize New York's official statement defense to the approach taken by the Model Penal Code (MPC). Section 2.04 of the MPC provides:

> "Section 2.04. Ignorance or Mistake.
>
> * * *
>
> "(3) A belief that conduct does not legally constitute an offense is a defense to a prosecution for that offense based upon such conduct when * * * (b) he acts in reasonable reliance upon an official statement of the law, *afterward determined to be invalid or erroneous,* contained in (i) a statute or other enactment" (emphasis added).

Although the drafters of the New York statute did not adopt the precise language of the Model Penal Code provision with the emphasized clause, it is evident and has long been believed that the Legislature intended the New York statute to be similarly construed. In fact, the legislative history of section 15.20 is replete with references to the influence of the Model Penal Code provision. * * *

It was early recognized that the "official statement" mistake of law defense was a statutory protection against prosecution based on reliance of a statute that did in fact authorize certain conduct. * * * While providing a narrow escape hatch, the idea was simultaneously to encourage the public to read and rely on official statements of the law, not to have individuals conveniently and personally question the validity and interpretation of the law and act on that basis. If later the statute was invalidated, one who mistakenly acted in reliance on the authorizing statute would be relieved of criminal liability. That makes sense and is fair. To go further does not make sense and would create a legal chaos based on individual selectivity.

In the case before us, the underlying statute never in fact authorized the defendant's conduct; the defendant only thought that the statutory exemptions permitted his conduct when, in fact, the primary statute clearly forbade his conduct. Moreover, by adjudication of the final court to speak on the subject in this very case, it turned out that even the exemption statute did not permit this defendant to possess the weapon. It would be ironic at best and an odd perversion at worst for this court now to declare that the same defendant is nevertheless free of criminal responsibility.

The "official statement" component in the mistake of law defense in both paragraphs (a) and (d) adds yet another element of support for our interpretation and holding. Defendant tried to establish a defense under Penal Law § 15.20(2)(d) as a second prong. But the interpretation of the statute relied upon must be "officially made or issued by a public servant, agency or body legally charged or empowered with the responsibility or privilege of administering, enforcing or interpreting such statute or law." We agree with the People that the trial court also properly rejected the defense under Penal Law § 15.20(2)(d) since none of the interpretations which defendant proffered meets the requirements of the statute.

* * * We recognize that some legal scholars urge that the mistake of law defense should be available more broadly where a defendant misinterprets a potentially ambiguous statute not previously clarified by judicial decision and reasonably believes in good faith that the acts were legal * * *.

We conclude that the better and correctly construed view is that the defense should not be recognized, except where specific intent is an element of the offense or where the misrelied upon law has later been properly adjudicated as wrong. Any broader view fosters lawlessness * * *.

If defendant's argument were accepted, the exception would swallow the rule. Mistakes about the law would be encouraged, rather than respect for and adherence to law. There would be an infinite number of mistake of law defenses which could be devised from a good-faith, perhaps reasonable but mistaken, interpretation of criminal statutes, many of which are concededly complex. Even more troublesome are the opportunities for wrong minded individuals to contrive in bad faith solely to get an exculpatory notion before the jury. These are not in terrorem arguments disrespectful of appropriate adjudicative procedures; rather, they are the realistic and practical consequences were the dissenters' views to prevail. Our holding comports with a statutory scheme which was not designed to allow false and diversionary stratagems to be provided for many more cases than the statutes contemplated. This would not serve the ends of justice but rather would serve game playing and evasion from properly imposed criminal responsibility. Accordingly, the [conviction] should be affirmed.

HANCOCK, JUDGE (dissenting).

* * * It is fundamental that in interpreting a statute, a court should look first to the particular words of the statute in question, being guided by the accepted rule that statutory language is generally given its natural and most obvious meaning. Here, there is but one natural and obvious meaning of the statute: that if a defendant can establish that his mistaken belief was "founded upon" his interpretation of "an official statement of the law contained in * * * statute" he should have a defense. No other natural and obvious meaning has been suggested * * *.

Defendant stands convicted after a jury trial of criminal possession of a weapon in the third degree for carrying a loaded firearm without a license. He concedes that he possessed the unlicensed weapon but maintains that he did so under the mistaken assumption that his conduct was permitted by law. On defendant's motion before trial the court dismissed the indictment, holding that he was a peace officer as defined by [the relevant statute]. The People appealed and the Appellate Division reversed and reinstated the indictment by a 3–2 vote. Defendant's appeal to this court was dismissed for failure to prosecute and the case proceeded to trial. The trial court rejected defendant's efforts to establish a defense of mistake of law under Section 15.20(2)(a). He was convicted and the Appellate Division has affirmed * * *.

The precise phrase in the Model Penal Code limiting the defense to reliance on a statute "afterward determined to be invalid or erroneous" which, if present, would support the majority's narrow construction of the New York statute, is omitted from Penal Law § 15.20(2)(a). How the Legislature can be assumed to have enacted the very language which it has specifically rejected is not explained.

As an alternate interpretation of Penal Law § 15.20(2)(a) the majority suggests that the Legislature intended that the statute should afford a defense only in cases involving acts *mala in se* such as People v. Weiss, supra, where specific intent is an element of the offense. Again such construction is at odds with the plain wording of Penal Law § 15.20(2)(a) and finds no support in the statutory history or the literature. There are, moreover, other fundamental objections to such construction which, we believe, rule out any possibility that the Legislature could have intended it. The essential quality of evil or immorality inherent in crimes *mala in se* (murder, robbery, kidnapping, etc.) is incompatible with the notion that the actor could have been operating under a mistaken belief that his conduct did not, as a matter of law, constitute an offense. There are no policy or jurisprudential reasons for the Legislature to recognize a mistake of law defense to such crimes. On the contrary, it is not with such inherently evil crimes but with crimes which are *mala prohibita*—i.e., the vast network of regulatory offenses which make up a large part of today's criminal law—where reasons of policy and fairness call for a relaxation of the strict "ignorantia legis" maxim to permit a limited mistake of law defense.

Nor does it seem possible that the Legislature could have intended to permit a mistake of law defense only in the limited circumstance where it had already been permitted prior to the enactment of the statute, i.e., to negate a specific element of the charge. Such a reading, contrary to the statute's plain meaning, makes Penal Law § 15.20(2)(a) superfluous. * * *

We believe that the concerns expressed by the majority are matters which properly should be and have been addressed by the Legislature * * *.

Chapter 2

DISCRETION AND THE RULE OF LAW

INTRODUCTORY NOTE

Chapter Two examines the exercise of discretion by legislators, police officers, prosecutors, jurors and judges. Each of these groups exercises discretion as they perform their duties in the criminal justice system. Legislators decide what conduct should be outlawed, police officers decide whether to arrest those suspected of criminal acts, prosecutors decide what crimes and which criminals to prosecute, juries can convict or acquit, and judges not only impose sentences, they also judge the constitutionality of the behavior by the other participants in the criminal justice system.

The phrase "equal justice under law" inscribed in the façade above the doors of the Supreme Court's building suggests an image of law as a system of rules applied evenly to individuals so that the consequences of conduct can be predicted with fair accuracy. Yet at a fundamental level, an inherent conflict exists between our commitment to law as a system of rules known in advance and applied equally to all, and our acceptance of discretion as a necessary means of limiting the harshness and arbitrariness of fixed rules.

In our legal system, criminal prohibitions and penalties must be enacted by a legislature and applied only prospectively. We do not allow a legislature to impose criminal punishment on an individual directly through a Bill of Attainder, or to change the definition of a crime or the penalty for it retroactively. Statutes must be capable of reasonably precise interpretation, or the courts may hold them to be "void for vagueness."

On the other hand, outcomes in individual cases inevitably depend on the judgments of a variety of individuals, rather than on the inflexible application of pre-ordained rules. Police officers do not have to arrest, prosecutors do not have to prosecute, juries do not have to convict (even when the evidence is overwhelming), and judges or parole boards frequently have broad discretion over the term of confinement that will actually be served and over the amount of the fine or restitution that will have to be paid. Because of this discretion, anachronistic laws can remain on the books for years without ever being enforced, and offenders who cooperate with the prosecution or attract the sympathy of the judge or jury may be treated very differently from individuals who are less cooperative, or more unpopular.

There is no simple solution to the conflict between rules and discretion. It seems to be impossible to devise in advance rules that can be applied to achieve acceptable results in all cases without the tempering influence of human judgment in individual cases. But opportunities for individualized judgment are also opportunities for favoritism and unfair discrimination. Prosecutors plausibly claim that they must have broadly drafted statutes to use as weapons against organized crime, and yet such statutes can be invoked selectively against persons who are not organized criminals. There is much to be said for giving judges discretion to put dangerous violent offenders in prison for a long time, and also to "give a second chance" to offenders who seem unlikely to repeat their crimes if released, but such discretion can lead to extreme disparity in punishment among similar offenders because different judges will apply different criteria. If we choose to restrict our officials with inflexible rules, we get one set of disadvantages, and if we choose to give them broad discretion we get another.

The materials in this chapter illustrate certain areas of the substantive criminal law in which the conflict between rules and discretion is most acute.

Section A introduces the topic of discretion by examining problems that arise under loitering statutes intended to give police officers discretionary authority to accomplish a number of socially desirable goals, including intervening before serious crimes occur. The materials in Part B introduce fundamental questions about the nature of the conduct that is sufficiently culpable to warrant legislation making this conduct a crime. These questions include the relationship between morality and the criminal law, the authority of legislatures to outlaw "immoral" conduct, and the scope of the authority of the judiciary to invalidate laws enacted by the other branches of government. Section C examines issues related to the exercise of discretion in sentencing, while Section D explores problems raised by the exercise of discretion when the sentence imposed is the death penalty.

A. VAGUENESS, STRICT CONSTRUCTION, AND THE PRINCIPLE OF LEGALITY

PAPACHRISTOU v. CITY OF JACKSONVILLE

Supreme Court of the United States, 1972.
405 U.S. 156, 92 S.Ct. 839, 31 L.Ed.2d 110.

Mr. Justice Douglas delivered the opinion of the Court.

This case involves eight defendants who were convicted in a Florida municipal court of violating a Jacksonville, Florida, vagrancy ordinance.[1] Their convictions, entailing fines and jail sentences (some of which were suspended), were affirmed by the Florida [appellate courts]. * * *

At issue are five consolidated cases. Margaret Papachristou, Betty Calloway, Eugene Eddie Melton, and Leonard Johnson were all arrested early on a Sunday morning, and charged with vagrancy—"prowling by auto."

Jimmy Lee Smith and Milton Henry were charged with vagrancy—"vagabonds."

Henry Edward Heath and a co-defendant were arrested for vagrancy—"loitering" and "common thief."

Thomas Owen Campbell was charged with vagrancy—"common thief."

Hugh Brown was charged with vagrancy—"disorderly loitering on street" and "disorderly conduct—resisting arrest with violence."

The facts are stipulated. Papachristou and Calloway are white females. Melton and Johnson are black males. Papachristou was enrolled in a job-training program sponsored by the State Employment Service at Florida Junior College in Jacksonville. Calloway was a typing and shorthand teacher at a state mental institution located near Jacksonville. She was the owner of the automobile in which the four defendants were arrested. Melton was a Vietnam war veteran who had been released from the Navy after nine months in a veterans' hospital. On the date of his arrest he was a part-time computer helper while attending college as a full-time student in Jacksonville. Johnson was a tow-motor operator in a grocery chain warehouse and was a lifelong resident of Jacksonville.

At the time of their arrest the four were riding in Calloway's car on the main thoroughfare in Jacksonville. They had left a restaurant owned by Johnson's uncle where they had eaten and were on their way to a night club. The arresting officers denied that the racial mixture in the car played any part in the decision to make the arrest. The arrest, they said, was made because the defendants had stopped near a used-car lot which had been broken into several times. * * *

Jimmy Lee Smith and Milton Henry were arrested between 9 and 10 a.m. on a weekday in downtown Jacksonville, while waiting for a friend

1. Jacksonville Ordinance Code § 26–57 provided at the time of these arrests and convictions as follows:

"Rogues and vagabonds, or dissolute persons who go about begging, common gamblers, persons who use juggling or unlawful games or plays, common drunkards, common night walkers, thieves, pilferers or pickpockets, traders in stolen property, lewd, wanton and lascivious persons, keepers of gambling places, common railers and brawlers, persons wandering or strolling around from place to place without any lawful purpose or object, habitual loafers, disorderly persons, persons neglecting all lawful business and habitually spending their time by frequenting houses of ill fame, gaming houses, or places where alcoholic beverages are sold or served, persons able to work but habitually living upon the earnings of their wives or minor children shall be deemed vagrants and, upon conviction in the Municipal Court shall be punished as provided for Class D offenses."

Class D offenses at the time of these arrests and convictions were punishable by 90 days imprisonment, $500 fine, or both. * * *

who was to lend them a car so they could apply for a job at a produce company. Smith was a part-time produce worker and part-time organizer for a Negro political group. He had a common-law wife and three children supported by him and his wife. He had been arrested several times but convicted only once. Smith's companion, Henry, was an 18-year-old high school student with no previous record of arrest.

This morning it was cold, and Smith had no jacket, so they went briefly into a dry cleaning shop to wait, but left when requested to do so. They thereafter walked back and forth two or three times over a two-block stretch looking for their friend. The store owners, who apparently were wary of Smith and his companion, summoned two police officers who searched the men and found neither had a weapon. But they were arrested because the officers said they had no identification and because the officers did not believe their story.

Heath and a codefendant were arrested for "loitering" and for "common thief." Both were residents of Jacksonville, Heath having lived there all his life and being employed at an automobile and body shop. Heath had previously been arrested but his codefendant had no arrest record. Heath and his companion were arrested when they drove up to a residence shared by Heath's girlfriend and some other girls. Some police officers were already there in the process of arresting another man. When Heath and his companion started backing out of the driveway, the officers signaled to them to stop and asked them to get out of the car, which they did. Thereupon they and the automobile were searched. Although no contraband or incriminating evidence was found, they were both arrested, Heath being charged with being a "common thief" because he was reputed to be a thief. The codefendant was charged with "loitering" because he was standing in the driveway, an act which the officers admitted was done only at their command.

Campbell was arrested as he reached his home very early one morning and was charged with "common thief." He was stopped by officers because he was traveling at a high rate of speed, yet no speeding charge was placed against him.

Brown was arrested when he was observed leaving a Jacksonville hotel by a police officer seated in a cruiser. The police testified he was reputed to be a thief, narcotics pusher, and generally opprobrious character. The officer called Brown over to the car, intending at that time to arrest him unless he had a good explanation for being on the street. Brown walked over to the police cruiser, as commanded, and the officer began to search him, apparently preparatory to placing him in the car. In the process of the search he came on two small packets which were later found to contain heroin. When the officer touched the pocket where the packets were, Brown began to resist. He was charged with "disorderly loitering on the street" and "disorderly conduct—resisting arrest with violence." While he was also charged with a narcotics violation, that charge was *nolled*.

* * *

This ordinance is void for vagueness, both in the sense that it fails to give a person of ordinary intelligence fair notice that his contemplated conduct is forbidden by the statute, and because it encourages arbitrary and erratic arrests and convictions.

* * *

The poor among us, the minorities, the average householder are not in business and not alerted to the regulatory schemes of vagrancy laws; and we assume they would have no understanding of their meaning and impact if they read them. Nor are they protected from being caught in the vagrancy net by the necessity of having a specific intent to commit an unlawful act.

The Jacksonville ordinance makes criminal activities which by modern standards are normally innocent. "Nightwalking" is one. Florida construes the ordinance not to make criminal one night's wandering; only the "habitual" wanderer or as the ordinance describes it "common night walkers." We know, however, from experience that sleepless people often walk at night, perhaps hopeful that sleep-inducing relaxation will result.

Luis Munoz–Marin, former Governor of Puerto Rico, commented once that "loafing" was a national virtue in his Commonwealth and that it should be encouraged. It is, however, a crime in Jacksonville.

"[P]ersons able to work but habitually living on the earnings of their wives or minor children"—like habitually living "without visible means of support"—might implicate unemployed pillars of the community who have married rich wives.

"[P]ersons able to work but habitually living on the earnings of their wives or minor children" may also embrace unemployed people out of the labor market, by reason of a recession or disemployed by reason of technological or so-called structural displacements.

Persons "wandering or strolling" from place to place have been extolled by Walt Whitman and Vachel Lindsay. The qualification "without any lawful purpose or object" may be a trap for innocent acts. Persons "neglecting all lawful business and habitually spending their time by frequenting * * * places where alcoholic beverages are sold or served" would literally embrace many members of golf clubs and city clubs.

* * *

Another aspect of the ordinance's vagueness appears when we focus, not on the lack of notice given a potential offender, but on the effect of the unfettered discretion it places in the hands of the Jacksonville police. Caleb Foote, an early student of this subject, has called the vagrancy-type law as offering "punishment by analogy." Such crimes, though long common in Russia, are not compatible with our constitutional system. We allow our police to make arrests only on "probable cause," a Fourth and Fourteenth Amendment standard applicable to the States as well as to the Federal Government. Arresting a person on suspicion, like arresting a person for investigation, is foreign to our system, even when the arrest is for past criminality. Future criminality, however, is the common justification for the presence of vagrancy statutes.

A presumption that people who might walk or loaf or loiter or stroll or frequent houses where liquor is sold, or who are supported by their wives or who look suspicious to the police are to become future criminals is too precarious for a rule of law. The implicit presumption in these generalized vagrancy standards—that crime is being nipped in the bud—is too extravagant to deserve extended treatment. Of course, vagrancy statutes are useful to the police. Of course they are nets making easy the round up of so-called undesirables. But the rule of law implies equality and justice in its application. Vagrancy laws of the Jacksonville type teach that the scales of justice are so tipped that even-handed administration of the law is not possible. The rule of law, evenly applied to minorities as well as majorities, to the poor as well as the rich, is the great mucilage that holds society together.

The Jacksonville ordinance cannot be squared with our constitutional standards and is plainly unconstitutional.

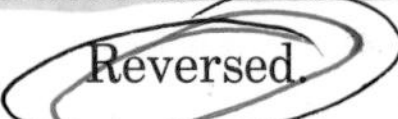

Reversed.

The Model Penal Code

Section 250.6. Loitering or Prowling

A person commits a violation if he loiters or prowls in a place, at a time, or in a manner not usual for law-abiding individuals under circumstances that warrant alarm for the safety of persons or property in the vicinity. Among the circumstances which may be considered in determining whether such alarm is warranted is the fact that the actor takes flight upon appearance of a peace officer, refuses to identify himself, or manifestly endeavors to conceal himself or any object. Unless flight by the actor or other circumstance makes it impracticable, a peace officer shall prior to any arrest for an offense under this section afford the actor an opportunity to dispel any alarm which would otherwise be warranted, by requesting him to identify himself and explain his presence and conduct. No person shall be convicted of an offense under this Section if the peace officer did not comply with the preceding sentence, or if it appears at trial that the explanation given by the actor was true and, if believed by the peace officer at the time, would have dispelled the alarm.

Note

The Supreme Court's holding in *Papachristou* sealed the fate of the old-style vagrancy statutes, which most legal scholars had long assumed to be obviously unconstitutional. The only surprising thing about the case is that police in some communities were still making arrests and even obtaining convictions under such statutes as late as 1972. The enduring question which the *Papachristou* decision did not settle is whether the police should have some authority to deal with "suspicious characters" who seem to them to be up to no good but who have not as yet done anything to justify an arrest for a conventional offense.

The essential point at issue was put succinctly by Professor Louis Schwartz, a distinguished liberal law professor who was one of the two principal drafters of the Model Penal Code. He explained the rationale behind the American Law Institute's resolution of the problem as follows:

"While the law obviously must be changed to eliminate medieval, unconstitutional provisions and practices, the Institute took cognizance of a very real problem of public safety and police administration and refused to drop all vagrancy-loitering legislation as some urged. The fearful householder who observes a dark figure lurking in an alley behind his home, the woman who notices a burly stranger apparently hiding in the park shrubbery, these citizens are entitled to some police action to dispel their alarm. Section 250.6 spells out an appropriate law-enforcement response." Schwartz, The Model Penal Code: An Invitation to Law Reform, 49 A.B.A. J. 447, 454 (1963).

The contrary view is that the police should leave lurking "dark figures" and "burly strangers" alone until they do something that provides some more tangible basis for alarm. It is also fair to note that the situation where an alarmed citizen demands action from the police is the exception rather than the norm; in the litigated cases the police ordinarily make the arrest without prompting from citizens. See e.g, City of Akron v. Rowland, 67 Ohio St.3d 374, 618 N.E.2d 138 (1993), holding unconstitutional a statute punishing "loitering * * * in a manner and under circumstances manifesting the purpose to engage in [unlawful] drug-related activity."

The police interest in such cases is not primarily to prosecute and convict the suspect for violating the loitering ordinance, but to use the ordinance as authority to detain the suspect for investigation of conventional criminal offenses such as theft or possession of contraband. Convictions for violations of loitering ordinances are rare, and the constitutionality of those ordinances usually arises in a prosecution for some more conventional offense that depends upon evidence obtained following an arrest for loitering. If the loitering arrest was unlawful, then the evidence obtained in a search incident to that arrest should be excluded.

As a justification for police investigation of "burly strangers" and lurking "dark figures" the vagrancy and loitering statutes have to some extent been superseded by the "stop and frisk" authority approved by the Supreme Court in Terry v. Ohio, 392 U.S. 1 (1968). An officer who does not have probable cause to arrest a suspect for a particular crime may lawfully detain him on the street for a brief period to investigate further and may "frisk" him for concealed weapons if the officer reasonably suspects that the suspect may be engaged in some type of criminal activity and if he has reason to fear that the suspect may be armed. Police therefore have some authority to detain a suspicious character to ask him what he is doing, and even to frisk him, but what is their authority if he answers that he is doing "nothing," and that his name is "John Doe?"

In states having statutes following the pattern of Model Penal Code § 250.6, the police may presumably arrest such a person on the ground that he has not truly identified himself or explained what he is up to. The Supreme Court dealt with the constitutionality of this approach to the problem in Kolender v. Lawson, 461 U.S. 352 (1983). Lawson made something of a career of walking about streets and highways in southern California in a manner that attracted the attention of police officers. He was arrested about 15 times in a two-year period, and convicted once, on a charge of violating West's Ann. California Penal Code Section 647(e). This statute punished as a misdemeanant anyone who "loiters or wanders upon the streets or from place to place without apparent reason or business and who refuses to identify himself and to account for his presence when requested by any peace officer so to do, if the surrounding circumstances are such as to indicate to a reasonable man that the public safety demands such explanation." State court decisions had held that a person validly stopped under this section must provide a "credible and reliable identification" to avoid conviction.

The Supreme Court opinion by Justice O'Connor held that the requirement that the identification be credible and reliable made the statute "void for vagueness," because it left too much discretion in the hands of the police to determine whether the identification offered by a suspect was credible and reliable. This holding gave support to the view, taken by several state courts, that loitering statutes based on the Model Penal Code formula are unconstitutional. The states are about evenly split on the question, however, and so the next case is included here to indicate that loitering statutes based upon the Model Penal Code still have some support in the state courts.

CITY OF MILWAUKEE v. NELSON

Supreme Court of Wisconsin, 1989.
149 Wis.2d 434, 439 N.W.2d 562.

DAY, JUSTICE.

Nelson was arrested by two Milwaukee police officers for violating Milwaukee City Ordinance 106–31(1)(a), which [is substantially identical to Model Penal Code § 250.6, supra.] At approximately 7:30 p.m., the two officers observed Mr. Nelson on a street corner in front of a tavern called the Cobra Club. The area was allegedly a high crime area with reported drug trafficking, loitering, and public drinking. "No loitering" signs were posted at each of the four corners of the intersection near where the arrest occurred. From about a block and a half away, the officers, using binoculars, observed Nelson and another person shaking hands with pedestrians and automobile passengers. The handshake was described as a clasping of the fingers together, twisting them back and forth and then reclasping them. The handshakes were characterized as "friendly." Nelson would approach the automobiles and lean toward the passenger door, resting his hands just inside the window. At no time did the officers observe an exchange of money or other items. They did not know Nelson and they had no information that he was a suspect or was wanted in connection with any crime. After about fifteen minutes, the officers approached Nelson and his companion in their squad car and Nelson and his companion hurriedly entered the tavern. The officers circled the block and returned to their initial observation point. Shortly thereafter, Nelson and the other person emerged from the tavern and resumed shaking hands with pedestrians and automobile passengers. The officers waited another five to ten minutes and then reapproached Nelson in their squad car. Nelson quickly reentered the tavern. This time, however, the officers followed him inside and asked him what he was doing outside the tavern to which he replied "nothing." Nelson was then arrested for loitering.

Nelson was "patted down" but no weapon was found. He was placed in a police van which took him to the police station. Shortly after Nelson had left the van, it was searched and a twenty-five caliber handgun was discovered. Nelson admitted the gun was his, that he had concealed it in his pants, and that he had placed it in the van. He also stated he had stolen the handgun. Nelson was subsequently charged with [carrying a concealed weapon and theft.]

In a separate action Nelson pled guilty in municipal court to violating the loitering ordinance. On the criminal charges, however, Nelson's counsel filed a motion to suppress evidence obtained from an illegal arrest [on the theory that the loitering ordinance was unconstitutional].

The Milwaukee Loitering Ordinance is patterned after § 250.6 of the Model Penal Code. [The opinion described the great prestige of the American Law Institute and the care that was taken in drafting the Model Penal Code. The Court went on to explain that the ALI thoroughly considered the constitutional implications of the Supreme Court's decision in the *Papachristou* case, and that there is a split of authority among the state supreme courts as to whether loitering ordinances similar to Model Penal Code § 250.6 are unconstitutional under the Supreme Court's holding in Kolender v. Lawson, which is described in the preceding note.]

Vagueness

A statute or ordinance is unconstitutionally vague if it fails to afford proper notice of the conduct it seeks to proscribe or if it encourages arbitrary and erratic arrests and convictions. The test to determine vagueness is whether the statute or ordinance is so obscure that men of ordinary intelligence must necessarily guess as to its meaning and differ as to its applicability.

One is not in violation of the ordinance by just "loitering." Rather, one must be loitering or prowling "in a place, at a time, or in a manner not usual for law-abiding individuals under circumstances that warrant alarm for the safety of persons or property in the vicinity." Certain factors are listed which may be considered in determining whether alarm is warranted: flight at the appearance of a police officer, failure to identify oneself, and attempts to conceal oneself or objects. Although flight and failure to answer an officer's question by itself may be a constitutionally protected activity, surrounding circumstances may lead such action to constitute probable cause that an offense has been committed.

Furthermore, the police must give the suspect the opportunity to "dispel any alarm which would otherwise be warranted" prior to an arrest if such circumstances are possible. If no such opportunity is given, there can be no conviction of the offense. Ultimately, it is the trier of fact who decides if the suspect's explanation "would have dispelled any alarm," not the police officer.

Impossible standards of clarity are not required. * * * We conclude the ordinance is not unconstitutional on grounds of vagueness.

Overbreadth

The ordinance is also challenged on overbreadth grounds. A statute or ordinance is overbroad when its language, given its normal meaning, is so sweeping that its sanctions may be applied to conduct which the state is not permitted to regulate. An ordinance which is overbroad is one which burdens or punishes activities which are constitutionally protected.

We find it highly unlikely that someone taking a stroll, sitting on a park bench, seeking shelter in a doorway from the elements, or shaking hands while politically campaigning, would be doing so in a place, at a time, or in a manner not usual for law-abiding individuals under circumstances that warrant alarm to police officers for the safety of persons or property within the vicinity. * * * On an overbreadth challenge this court found untenable an argument that the Milwaukee "Loitering of Minors" ordinance would impermissibly apply to a minor walking home from work, or standing while waiting for a bus after the curfew hour. This court held that the curfew ordinance "is to prevent the undirected or aimless conduct of minors during the curfew hours." Milwaukee v. K.F., 145 Wis.2d at 48, 426 N.W.2d 329. Here too, the ordinance is not aimed at constitutionally protected conduct but at conduct which causes alarm for the safety of persons or property. * * *

The decision of the court of appeals is affirmed.

SHIRLEY S. ABRAHAMSON, JUSTICE (dissenting).

* * * The word "loitering" connotes the act of hanging around without any apparent purpose. A law that prohibits loitering without further definition is unconstitutionally vague because it fails to distinguish between innocent conduct and conduct calculated to cause harm. Such a law fails to give adequate notice of what conduct is proscribed. * * *

In this case the defendant's response to the officer's question of what he was doing was "nothing." The very essence of loitering is "doing nothing." "Doing nothing" may be very suspicious conduct and "nothing" is hardly an explanation of one's conduct. But clearly the ordinance cannot constitutionally make a person culpable for doing nothing.

Courts have concluded that similar identification and explanation requirements in loitering laws are void for vagueness because they do not provide a standard for law enforcement officers to determine what a suspect has to do in order to satisfy the requirement. * * *

The Milwaukee ordinance gives the suspect, upon being stopped, the opportunity to dispel any alarm, and thus avoid arrest. Like the statute in *Kolender,* the Milwaukee ordinance leaves the definition of this "opportunity" entirely up to the individual judgment of the police officer making the stop. It is the police officer who determines, without significant guidance from the ordinance, what circumstances cause "alarm", and it is the police officer who decides, again without significant guidance from the ordinance, whether the suspect has adequately dispelled that alarm by identifying himself or herself and explaining his or her presence and conduct. The ordinance leaves all of the critical definitions up to the discretion of law enforcement and so, under *Kolender,* it violates the federal Constitution.

The majority observes that "ultimately, it is the trier of fact who decides if the suspect's explanation would have dispelled any alarm, not the police officer." It is important, however, to recognize that availability of a trial after arrest in no sense obviates the constitutional requirement that laws include minimal guidelines to govern law enforcement officials. * * * Accordingly I dissent.

Note On "Gang Loitering"

In 1992, the Chicago City Council enacted a "Gang Congregation Ordinance," which prohibited "criminal street gang members" from loitering with one another or with other persons in any public place. Findings attached to the Ordinance established that a continuing increase in criminal street gang activity was largely responsible for an escalation of violent and drug related crimes, which had the effect of intimidating law-abiding citizens in some neighborhoods and making them feel they were virtual prisoners in their own homes. The City Council found that "aggressive action is necessary to preserve the city's streets and other public places so that the public may use such places without fear," and that the city "has an interest in discouraging all persons from loitering in public places with criminal gang members." The resulting Ordinance provided in pertinent part that:

(a) Whenever a police officer observes a person whom he reasonably believes to be a criminal street gang member loitering in any public place with one or more other persons, he shall order all such persons to disperse and remove themselves from the area. Any person who does not promptly obey such an order is in violation of this section.

(b) It shall be an affirmative defense to an alleged violation of this section that no person who was observed loitering was in fact a member of a criminal street gang.

(c) As used in this section:

(1) "Loiter" means to remain in any one place with no apparent purpose.

(2) "Criminal street gang" means any ongoing organization, association in fact or group of three or more persons, whether formal or informal, having as one of its substantial activities the commission of one or more of the criminal acts enumerated in paragraph (3), and whose members individually or collectively engage in or have engaged in a pattern of criminal gang activity.

. . .

(5) "Public place" means the public way and any other location open to the public, whether publicly or privately owned. . . .

(e) Any person who violates this Section is subject to a fine of not less than $100 and not more than $500 for each offense, or imprisonment for not more than six months, or both. In addition to or instead of the above penalties, any person who violates this section may be required to perform up to 120 hours of community service pursuant to section 1–4–120 of this Code.

During the three years of its enforcement, the Chicago police issued over 89,000 dispersal orders and arrested over 42,000 persons for violating the Ordinance. Gang-related crimes declined in number, but there was a hotly contested debate over whether or to what extent enforcement of the Ordinance contributed to the decline. In 1997 the Illinois Supreme Court held the Ordinance unconstitutional as "void for vagueness." Chicago v. Morales, 177 Ill.2d 440, 227 Ill.Dec. 130, 687 N.E.2d 53 (Ill. 1997), *affd.* in City of Chicago v. Morales, 527 U.S. 41 (1999). The Illinois court observed that the Ordinance drew no distinction between innocent conduct and conduct calculated to cause harm or fear. "People with entirely legitimate and lawful purposes will not always be able to make their purposes apparent to an observing police officer. For example, a person waiting to hail a taxi, resting on a corner during a job, or stepping into a doorway to evade a rain shower has a perfectly legitimate purpose in all these scenarios; however, that purpose will rarely be apparent to an observer. * * * Although the proscriptions of the ordinance are vague, the city council's intent in its enactment is clear and unambiguous. The city has declared gang members a public menace and determined that gang members are too adept at avoiding arrest for all the other crimes they commit. Accordingly, the city council crafted an exceptionally broad ordinance which could be used to sweep these intolerable and objectionable gang members from the city streets." 687 N.E.2d, at 60–64.

The United States Supreme Court suggested that a more direct yet limited attempt to achieve the ordinance's goals would be constitutionally acceptable:

"The basic factual predicate for the city's ordinance is not in dispute. As the city argues in its brief, 'the very presence of a large collection of obviously brazen, insistent, and lawless gang members and hangers-on on the public ways intimidates residents, who become afraid even to leave their homes and go about their business. That, in turn, imperils community residents' sense of safety and security, detracts from property values, and can ultimately destabilize entire neighborhoods.' The findings in the ordinance explain that it was motivated by these concerns. We have no doubt that a law that directly prohibited such intimidating conduct would be constitutional, but this ordinance broadly covers a significant amount of additional activity. Uncertainty about the scope of that additional coverage provides the basis for respondents' claim that the ordinance is too vague." 527 U.S. at 51–52.

STATE v. ANONYMOUS

Superior Court of Connecticut, Appellate Division, 1978.
34 Conn.Sup. 689, 389 A.2d 1270.

DAVID M. SHEA, JUDGE.

The defendant was found guilty by a jury of disorderly conduct in violation of General Statutes § 53a–182(a)(2) and of harassment in violation of General Statutes § 53a–183(a)(3). She has appealed assigning error in the denial of her motion to set aside the verdict. * * * In this appeal she claims that the charge to the jury was deficient in that it failed to circumscribe the language of the two statutes involved within the limits required by the first amendment prohibition against restrictions upon freedom of speech, and she also claims error in a ruling upon evidence.

From the statements of facts in the briefs it appears that the jury could have found that on the day of the alleged offenses the complaining witness and her friend were traveling to work when they passed the defendant in another car. When the car in which the complainant was riding turned into the parking lot of the restaurant where she worked, the defendant's car, which had been following, drove up close to the complainant, who had by then emerged from her car, and the defendant shouted from the car window that the complainant was a "tramp," that her mother was a whore and had gone to bed with the defendant's husband, and that the defendant was "going to get" the complainant this time. While the defendant was making these insulting remarks, the complainant and her companion walked toward the restaurant and entered. This incident was the basis for the disorderly conduct charge.

On the same evening the defendant telephoned the complainant at the restaurant where she was working. After the complainant was called to the phone, she heard the defendant repeat substantially the same insults as those which had been made earlier in the parking lot of the restaurant. The harassment charge was based upon this telephone call.

I

The defendant claims that her conviction under General Statutes § 53a–182(a)(2) was a violation of her constitutional right of free speech because of the overbroad language of the statute, which the trial court failed to confine within constitutional limits. The pertinent portion of the statute provides: "A person is guilty of disorderly conduct when, with intent to cause inconvenience, annoyance or alarm, or recklessly creating a risk thereof, he ... (2) by offensive or disorderly conduct, annoys or interferes with another person...." The charge gave the jury the statutory definitions of "intentionally" and "recklessly." "Offensive conduct" was described as "conduct which under contemporary community standards is so grossly offensive to a person who actually overhears it or sees it as to amount to a nuisance." "Disorderly conduct" was explained as meaning "such conduct as outrages the sense of public decency" and also conduct which "must annoy or interfere with another person." Standard dictionary definitions of "annoy" and "interfere" were also given.

In summation, the court stated that "the test, then, of this statute is what people of common intelligence and common sense would understand would be annoyance or interference with another person, which intentionally causes or has an intention to cause inconvenience, annoyance, or alarm, or which recklessly creates a risk of causing inconvenience, annoyance, or alarm of another person." In accordance with an exception taken by the defendant at the conclusion of the charge, the jurors were again instructed that there had to be a "specific intent of causing inconvenience, annoyance, or alarm and not just a general bad intent to do something wrong to somebody."

Although she filed no such request to charge and took no such exception to the charge before the trial court, defendant now claims error in the failure to instruct the jurors that they could not convict her unless they found that she had uttered "fighting words" to the victim, as that term is used in Chaplinsky v. New Hampshire, 315 U.S. 568. [Connecticut cases have] held that a claim raised for the first time on appeal will be considered where the defendant has clearly been deprived of a fundamental constitutional right and a fair trial. The claim of the defendant in this case that her first amendment freedoms were violated by the instructions given to the jury would fall within that rule.

In *Chaplinsky,* supra, a statute which forbade addressing "any offensive, derisive or annoying word to any other person who is lawfully in any street or other public place" was upheld as not infringing upon freedom of speech because the state court had construed the broad language of the statute as forbidding no words except those having "a direct tendency to cause acts of violence by the persons to whom, individually, the remark was addressed." "Fighting words"—those which by their very utterance inflict injury or tend to incite an immediate breach of the peace—have never been deemed to fall within the protection of the first amendment. Id., 572. There can be no question but that the remarks attributed to the defendant in this case could reasonably have been found to constitute "fighting words." Nevertheless, the defendant may assert her claim of overbreadth if the statute as explained in the charge would have permitted her conviction without a finding by the jury that her utterance had a substantial tendency to provoke violence on the part of the complainant. * * *

Despite the evident care with which the charge was framed, we cannot say that it limited the broad language of the statute to prohibit only those expressions having a substantial tendency to provoke violent retaliation or other wrongful conduct. At least where speech in a public place is involved, an instruction that a conviction may be had for conduct which is "so grossly offensive . . . as to amount to a nuisance" or which "outrages the sense of public decency" or which causes "inconvenience, annoyance, or alarm" exceeds the narrow scope of permissible restrictions on freedom of speech.

The state argues that the infirmity of the statute as construed by the trial court is cured by the requirement in § 53a–182(a)(2) of a specific intention "to cause inconvenience, annoyance or alarm." Several of the disorderly conduct statutes deemed to have been overbroad in the absence of a "fighting words" limitation have contained similar provisions necessitating proof of intention as an element of the crime. That feature has not evoked any judicial comment suggesting that the "fighting words" restriction may be supplanted by such a provision. If the prohibition of conduct which "annoys or interferes with another person" is overbroad because it reaches constitutionally protected speech, that deficiency would not be remedied by requiring a mental element defined in terms of similar latitude as provided by § 53a–182(a)(2) ("intent to cause inconvenience, annoyance or alarm, or recklessly creating a risk thereof"). In no significant way does the addition of that element alleviate the inhibiting effect upon freedom of expression, which is the essential rationale of the overbreadth doctrine.

We conclude that the failure of the charge to limit the application of § 53a–182(a)(2) to "fighting words" in accordance with Chaplinsky v. New Hampshire, supra, deprived the defendant of a fundamental constitutional right.

II

The defendant claims that her conviction for harassment in violation of § 53a–183(a)(3) also infringed upon her constitutional right to freedom of speech. The statute, which she claims is overbroad without some judicial gloss limiting its application to "fighting words," provides in the portion involved that "[a] person is guilty of harassment when: . . . (3) with intent to harass, annoy or alarm another person, he makes a telephone call, whether or not a conversation ensues, in a manner likely to cause annoyance or alarm." The charge provided the jurors with definitions of the words "harass," "annoy" and "alarm" and instructed them that if they found that the defendant had made a telephone call with the intention to harass, annoy, or alarm, and that the telephone call did harass, annoy, or alarm another person, then the defendant would be guilty of the offense. No exception was taken with respect to the deficiency in the charge now claimed, but we must, nevertheless, consider the matter to determine whether the record indicates that the defendant has been deprived of a fundamental constitutional right.

As venerated a place as freedom of speech may hold in the constitutional scheme, reasonable regulation of the place and manner of its exercise has been upheld consistently. Where the means of communication involves an intrusion upon privacy, the right of free expression must be balanced against the right to be let alone. A telephone is not a public forum where, in vindication of our liberties, unreceptive listeners need be exposed to the onslaught of repugnant ideas. The overbreadth principle is not violated by the unrestricted scope of the messages which the statute may ban because it is the manner and means employed to communicate them which is the subject of the prohibition rather than their content. The statute is not flawed because a recital on the telephone of the most sublime prayer with the intention and effect of harassing the listener would fall within its ban as readily as the most scurrilous epithet. The prohibition is against purposeful harassment by means of a device readily susceptible to abuse as a constant trespasser upon our privacy. That words may be the instrument of annoyance does not insulate such wrongful conduct from criminal liability. We conclude that it was not necessary to limit the application of § 53a–183(a)(3) to "fighting words" as claimed by the defendant. * * *

There was no error in the conviction of the defendant for harassment in violation of § 53a–183(a)(3) under the first count of the information; there was error in the conviction of the defendant for disorderly conduct in violation of § 53a–182(a)(2) under the second count of the information, the judgment is set aside, and that count of the information is remanded for a new trial.

Note

The preceding case had a lengthy subsequent history. After her conviction was affirmed by the state appellate courts, defendant Gormley filed a petition for habeas corpus in the federal courts to challenge her telephone harassment conviction. The federal Court of Appeals upheld the statute and the conviction, reasoning that "the possible chilling effect on free speech of the Connecticut statute strikes us as minor compared with the all-too-prevalent and widespread misuse of the telephone to hurt others." Gormley v. Director, Connecticut State Department of Probation, 632 F.2d 938 (2d Cir.1980). The Supreme Court denied a writ of certiorari, with an unusual dissenting opinion by Justice White which pointed out that a number of state courts have invalidated substantially equivalent statutes as being unconstitutionally overbroad. Justice White's opinion, reported at 449 U.S. 1023, provides a useful review of the conflicting decisions.

Section 415 of the California Penal Code punishes anyone who "maliciously and willfully disturbs the peace or quiet of any neighborhood or person, by loud or unusual noise, or by tumultuous or offensive conduct * * *." The California Supreme Court considered the constitutionality of this statute in In re Bushman, 1 Cal.3d 767, 83 Cal.Rptr. 375, 463 P.2d 727 (1970). The defendant, an attorney and a licensed private pilot, was upset because of the poor condition of a runway at the local airport. To dramatize his complaint, he brought a bucket of debris collected from the runway to a meeting of the Airport Board and emptied the bucket over the chairman's desk and papers. The California Supreme Court upheld the statute but reversed the conviction. It construed the statute to punish only "disruption of public order by acts that are themselves violent or that tend to incite others to violence." The opinion did not define "violence," but indicated that the defendant's conduct could have been punished under that limiting construction. The opinion did not make clear whether dumping the bucket was itself a "violent" act, or whether it was punishable as likely to provoke a violent response from the chairman (who in fact hit the defendant in retaliation). In any case, the conviction was reversed because the jury had not been properly instructed. The facts recited by the California Supreme Court also suggested that the court may have been troubled by the terms of Bushman's sentence and probation. It noted that "the court required petitioner to make a prompt and sincere apology to the president and members of the airport district board of directors; * * * *to resign as newly elected president of the airport board*; and to submit himself to the local bar association for possible disciplinary action." (emphasis supplied) 1 Cal. 3d at 776, n. 3.

See also, People v. Dietze, 75 N.Y.2d 47, 550 N.Y.S.2d 595, 549 N.E.2d 1166 (1989) where the New York Court of Appeals held unconstitutional a statute punishing "abusive or obscene language" because the statute could not fairly be construed as limited to "fighting words." The case involved a hateful defendant who approached a mentally retarded mother and her son, called the woman a "bitch" and her son a "dog," and threatened to "beat the crap out of" the mother at some time in the indefinite future. According to the opinion, "complainant fled in tears and reported the incident to authorities. Defendant had been aware of the complainant's mental limitations and had, on a prior occasion, been warned by a police officer about arguing with her again."

The court held that even "abusive speech" is constitutionally protected unless couched in words "which, by their utterance alone, inflict injury or tend naturally to evoke immediate violence or other breach of the peace." But why didn't the verbal humiliation itself "inflict injury," regardless of whether it was likely under the circumstances to provoke a violent reaction from the victim?

SCREWS v. UNITED STATES

Supreme Court of the United States, 1945.
325 U.S. 91, 65 S.Ct. 1031, 89 L.Ed. 1495.

MR. JUSTICE DOUGLAS announced the judgment of the Court and delivered the following opinion, in which the CHIEF JUSTICE, MR. JUSTICE BLACK and MR. JUSTICE REED concur.

This case involves a shocking and revolting episode in law enforcement. Petitioner Screws was sheriff of Baker County, Georgia. He enlisted the assistance of petitioner Jones, a policeman, and petitioner Kelley, a special deputy, in arresting Robert Hall, a citizen of the United States and of Georgia. The arrest was made late at night at Hall's home on a warrant charging Hall with theft of a tire. Hall, a young negro about thirty years of age, was handcuffed and taken by car to the court house. As Hall alighted from the car at the court-house square, the three petitioners began beating him with their fists and with a solid-bar blackjack about eight inches long and weighing two pounds. They claimed Hall had reached for a gun and had used insulting language as he alighted from the car. But after Hall, still handcuffed, had been knocked to the ground they continued to beat him from fifteen to thirty minutes until he was unconscious. Hall was then dragged feet first through the court-house yard into the jail and thrown upon the floor dying. An ambulance was called and Hall was removed to a hospital where he died within the hour and without regaining consciousness. There was evidence that Screws held a grudge against Hall and had threatened to "get" him.

An indictment was returned against petitioners—one count charging a violation of § 20 of the Criminal Code, and another charging a conspiracy to violate § 20. Sec. 20 provides:

"Whoever, under color of any law, statute, ordinance, regulation, or custom, willfully subjects, or causes to be subjected, any inhabitant of any State, Territory, or District to the deprivation of any rights, privileges, or immunities secured or protected by the Constitution and laws of the United States, or to different punishments, pains, or penalties, on account of such inhabitant being an alien, or by reason of his color, or race, than are prescribed for the punishment of citizens, shall be fined not more than $1,000, or imprisoned not more than one year, or both."[a]

The indictment charged that petitioners, acting under color of the laws of Georgia, "willfully" caused Hall to be deprived of "rights, privileges, or immunities secured or protected" to him by the Fourteenth Amendment—the right not to be deprived of life without due process of law; the right to be tried, upon the charge on which he was arrested, by due process of law and if found guilty to be punished in accordance with the laws of Georgia; that is to say that petitioners "unlawfully and wrongfully did assault, strike and beat the said Robert Hall about the head with human fists and a blackjack causing injuries" to Hall "which were the proximate and immediate cause of his death." A like charge was made in the conspiracy count.

The case was tried to a jury. The court charged the jury that due process of law gave one charged with a crime the right to be tried by a jury and sentenced by a court. On the question of intent it charged that ". . . if these defendants, without its being necessary to make the arrest effectual or necessary to their own personal protection, beat this man, assaulted him or killed him while he was under arrest, then they would be acting illegally under color of law, as stated by this statute, and would be depriving the prisoner of certain constitutional rights guaranteed to him by the Constitution of the United States and consented to by the State of Georgia."

The jury returned a verdict of guilty and a fine and imprisonment on each count was imposed. The Circuit Court of Appeals affirmed the judgment of conviction, one judge dissenting. 5 Cir., 140 F.2d 662. The

a. This section is presently codified as 18 U.S.C.A. § 242. It still provides for a fine of no more than $1,000 and imprisonment for not more than one year, except that if death results from the violation the defendant may be imprisoned for any term of years or for life.—ed.

case is here on a petition for a writ of certiorari which we granted because of the importance in the administration of the criminal laws of the questions presented.

I

We are met at the outset with the claim that § 20 is unconstitutional, insofar as it makes criminal acts in violation of the due process clause of the Fourteenth Amendment. The argument runs as follows: It is true that this Act as construed in United States v. Classic, 313 U.S. 299, 328, was upheld in its application to certain ballot box frauds committed by state officials. But in that case the constitutional rights protected were the rights to vote specifically guaranteed by Art. I, § 2 and § 4 of the Constitution. Here there is no ascertainable standard of guilt. There have been conflicting views in the Court as to the proper construction of the due process clause. The majority have quite consistently construed it in broad general terms. Thus it was stated in Twining v. New Jersey, 211 U.S. 78, 101, that due process requires that "no change in ancient procedure can be made which disregards those fundamental principles, to be ascertained from time to time by judicial action, which have relation to process of law and protect the citizen in his private right, and guard him against the arbitrary action of government." In Snyder v. Massachusetts, 291 U.S. 97, 105, it was said that due process prevents state action which "offends some principle of justice so rooted in the traditions and conscience of our people as to be ranked as fundamental." The same standard was expressed in Palko v. Connecticut, 302 U.S. 319, 325, in terms of a "scheme of ordered liberty."

It is said that the Act must be read as if it contained those broad and fluid definitions of due process and that if it is so read it provides no ascertainable standard of guilt. * * *

But the general rule was stated in Ellis v. United States, 206 U.S. 246, 257, as follows: "If a man intentionally adopts certain conduct in certain circumstances known to him, and that conduct is forbidden by the law under those circumstances, he intentionally breaks the law in the only sense in which the law ever considers intent." Under that test a local law enforcement officer violates § 20 and commits a federal offense for which he can be sent to the penitentiary if he does an act which some court later holds deprives a person of due process of law. And he is a criminal though his motive was pure and though his purpose was unrelated to the disregard of any constitutional guarantee.

The treacherous ground on which state officials—police, prosecutors, legislators, and judges—would walk if indicated by the character and closeness of decisions of this Court interpreting the due process clause of the Fourteenth Amendment. A confession obtained by too long questioning; the enforcement of an ordinance requiring a license for the distribution of religious literature; the denial of the assistance of counsel in certain types of cases; the enforcement of certain types of anti-picketing statutes; the enforcement of state price control laws; the requirement that public school children salute the flag—these are illustrative of the kind of state action which might or might not be caught in the broad reaches of § 20 dependent on the prevailing view of the Court as constituted when the case arose. Those who enforced local law today might not know for many months (and meanwhile could not find out) whether what they did deprived someone of due process of law. The enforcement of a criminal statute so construed would indeed cast law enforcement agencies loose at their own risk on a vast uncharted sea.

If such a construction is not necessary, it should be avoided. * * *

II

We recently pointed out that "willful" is a word "of many meanings, its construction often being influenced by its context." Spies v. United States, 317 U.S. 492, 497. At times the word denotes an act which is intentional rather than accidental. But when used in a criminal statute it generally means an act done with a bad purpose. In that event something more is required than the doing of the act proscribed by the statute. An evil motive to accomplish that which the statute condemns becomes a constituent element of the crime. And that issue must be submitted to the jury under appropriate instructions.

An analysis of the cases in which "willfully" has been held to connote more than an act which is voluntary or intentional would not prove helpful as each turns on its own peculiar facts. Those cases, however, make clear that if we construe "willfully" in § 20 as connoting a purpose to deprive a person of a specific constitutional right, we would introduce no innovation. The Court, indeed, has recognized that the requirement of a specific intent to do a prohibited act may avoid those consequences to the accused which may otherwise render a vague or indefinite statute invalid. The constitutional vice in such a statute is the essential injustice to the accused of placing him on trial for an offense, the nature of which the statute does not define and hence of which it gives no warning. But where the punishment imposed is only for an act knowingly done with the purpose of doing that which the statute prohibits, the accused cannot be said to suffer from lack of warning or knowledge that the act which he does is a violation of law. The requirement that the act must be willful or purposeful may not render certain, for all purposes, a statutory definition of the crime which is in some respects uncertain. But it does relieve the statute of the objection that it punishes without warning an offense of which the accused was unaware. * * *

It is said, however, that this construction of the Act will not save it from the infirmity of vagueness since neither a law enforcement official nor a trial judge can know with sufficient definiteness the range of rights that are constitutional. But that criticism is wide of the mark. For the specific intent required by the Act is an intent to deprive a person of a right which has been made specific either by the express terms of the Constitution or laws of the United States or by decisions interpreting them. Take the case of a local officer who persists in enforcing a type of ordinance which the Court has held invalid as violative of the guarantees of free speech or freedom of worship. Or a local official continues to select juries in a manner which flies in the teeth of decisions of the Court. If those acts are done willfully, how can the officer possibly claim that he had no fair warning that his acts were prohibited by the statute? He violates the statute not merely because he has a bad purpose but because he acts in defiance of announced rules of law. He who defies a decision interpreting the Constitution knows precisely what he is doing. If sane, he hardly may be heard to say that he knew not what he did. Of course, willful conduct cannot make definite that which is undefined. But willful violators of constitutional requirements, which have been defined, certainly are in no position to say that they had no adequate advance notice that they would be visited with punishment. When they act willfully in the sense in which we use the word, they act in open defiance or in reckless disregard of a constitutional requirement which has been made specific and definite. When they are convicted for so acting, they are not punished for violating an unknowable something. * * *

The difficulty here is that this question of intent was not submitted to the jury with the proper instructions. The court charged that petitioners acted illegally if they applied more force than was necessary to make the arrest effectual or to protect themselves from the prisoner's alleged assault. But in view of our construction of the word "willfully" the jury should have been further instructed that it was not sufficient that petitioners had a generally bad purpose. To convict it was necessary for them to find that petitioners had the purpose to deprive the prisoner of a constitutional right, e.g. the right to be tried by a court rather than by ordeal. And in determining whether that requisite bad purpose was present the jury would be entitled to consider all the attendant circumstances—the malice of petitioners, the weapons used in the assault, its character and duration, the provocation, if any, and the like.

It is true that no exception was taken to the trial court's charge. Normally we would under those circumstances not take note of the error. But there are exceptions to that rule. And where the error is so fundamental as not to submit to the jury the essential ingredients of the only offense on which the conviction could rest, we think it is necessary to take note of it on our own motion. Even those guilty of the most heinous offenses are entitled to a fair trial. Whatever the degree of guilt, those charged with a federal crime are entitled to be tried by the standards of guilt which Congress has prescribed.

Since there must be a new trial, the judgment below is

Reversed.

MR. JUSTICE RUTLEDGE, concurring in the result. * * * [S]tatutory specificity has two purposes, to give due notice that an act has been made criminal before it is done and to inform one accused of the nature of the offense charged, so that he may adequately prepare and make his defense. More than this certainly the Constitution does not require. All difficulty on the latter score vanishes, under § 20, with the indictment's particularization of the rights infringed and the acts infringing them. * * *

In the other aspect of specificity, two answers, apart from experience, suffice. One is that § 20, and § 19, are no more general and vague, Fourteenth Amendment rights included, than other criminal statutes commonly enforced against this objection. The Sherman Act[b] is the most obvious illustration.

Furthermore, the argument of vagueness, to warn men of their conduct, ignores the nature of the criminal act itself and the notice necessarily given from this. Section 20 strikes only at abuse of official functions by state officers. It does not reach out for crimes done by men in general. Not murder per se, but murder by state officers in the course of official conduct and done with the aid of state power, is outlawed. These facts, inherent in the crime, give all the warning constitutionally required. For one, so situated, who goes so far in misconduct can have no excuse of innocence or ignorance.

Generally state officials know something of the individual's basic legal rights. If they do not, they should, for they assume that duty when they assume their office. Ignorance of the law is no excuse for men in general. It is less an excuse for men whose special duty is to apply it, and therefore to know and observe it. If their knowledge is not comprehensive, state officials know or should know when they pass the limits of their authority, so far at any rate that their action exceeds honest error of judgment and amounts to abuse of their office and its function. When they enter such a domain in dealing with the citizen's rights, they should do so at their peril, whether that be created by state or federal law. For their sworn oath and their first duty are to uphold the Constitution, then only the law of the state which too is bound by the charter. Since the statute, as I think, condemns only something more than error of judgment, made in honest effort at once to apply and to follow the law, officials who violate it must act in intentional or reckless disregard of individual rights and cannot be ignorant that they do great wrong. This being true, they must be taken to act at peril of incurring the penalty placed upon such conduct by the federal law, as they do of that the state imposes. * * *

We have in this case no instance of mere error in judgment, made in good faith. It would be time enough to reverse and remand a conviction, obtained without instructions along these lines, if such a case should arise. Actually the substance of such instruction was given in the wholly adequate charge concerning the officer's right to use force, though not to excess. When, as here, a state official abuses his place consciously or grossly in abnegation of its rightful obligation, and thereby tramples underfoot the established constitutional rights of men or citizens, his

b. This statute, which punishes the making of contracts and conspiracies "in restraint of trade," was held constitutional in Nash v. United States, 229 U.S. 373 (1912).—ed.

conviction should stand when he has had the fair trial and full defense the petitioners have been given in this case. * * *

My convictions are as I have stated them. Were it possible for me to adhere to them in my vote, and for the Court at the same time to dispose of the cause, I would act accordingly. The Court, however, is divided in opinion. If each member accords his vote to his belief, the case cannot have disposition. Stalemate should not prevail for any reason, however compelling, in a criminal cause or, if avoidable, in any other. My views concerning appropriate disposition are more nearly in accord with those stated by Mr. Justice Douglas, in which three other members of the Court concur, than they are with the views of my dissenting brethren who favor outright reversal. Accordingly, in order that disposition may be made of this case, my vote has been cast to reverse the decision of the Court of Appeals and remand the cause to the District Court for further proceedings in accordance with the disposition required by the opinion of Mr. Justice Douglas.

[The opinion of MR. JUSTICE MURPHY, dissenting from the reversal of the judgments of conviction, is omitted. He argued that petitioners, who knew very well that they were violating the victim's constitutional rights, should not be heard to complain that the meaning of the statute might be uncertain in other, quite different situations.]

MR. JUSTICE ROBERTS, MR. JUSTICE FRANKFURTER and MR. JUSTICE JACKSON, dissenting. * * *

All but two members of the Court apparently agree that insofar as § 20 purports to subject men to punishment for crime it fails to define what conduct is made criminal. As misuse of the criminal machinery is one of the most potent and familiar instruments of arbitrary government, proper regard for the rational requirement of definiteness in criminal statutes is basic to civil liberties. As such it is included in the constitutional guaranty of due process of law. But four members of the Court are of the opinion that this plain constitutional principle of definiteness in criminal statutes may be replaced by an elaborate scheme of constitutional exegesis whereby that which Congress has not defined the courts can define from time to time, with varying and conflicting definiteness in the decisions, and that, in any event, an undefined range of conduct may become sufficiently definite if only such undefined conduct is committed "willfully."

It is not conceivable that this Court would find that a statute cast in the following terms would satisfy the constitutional requirement for definiteness:

> "Whoever WILLFULLY commits any act which the Supreme Court of the United States shall find to be a deprivation of any right, privilege, or immunity secured or protected by the Constitution shall be imprisoned not more than, etc."

If such a statute would fall for uncertainty, wherein does § 20 as construed by the Court differ and how can it survive? * * *

It is as novel as it is an inadmissible principle that a criminal statute of indefinite scope can be rendered definite by requiring that a person "willfully" commit what Congress has not defined but which, if Congress had defined, could constitutionally be outlawed. Of course Congress can prohibit the deprivation of enumerated constitutional rights. But if Congress makes it a crime to deprive another of any right protected by the Constitution—and that is what § 20 does—this Court cannot escape facing decisions as to what constitutional rights are covered by § 20 by saying that in any event, whatever they are, they must be taken away "willfully." It has not been explained how all the considerations of unconstitutional vagueness which are laid bare in the early part of the Court's opinion evaporate by suggesting that what is otherwise too vaguely defined must be "willfully" committed. * * *

The Government recognizes that "this is the first case brought before this Court in which § 20 has been applied to deprivations of rights secured by the Fourteenth Amendment." It is not denied that the Government's contention would make a potential offender against this act of any State official who as a judge admitted a confession of crime, or who as judge of a State court of last resort sustained admission of a confession, which we should later hold constitutionally inadmissible, or who as a public service commissioner issued a regulatory order which we should later hold denied due process or who as a municipal officer stopped any conduct we later should hold to be constitutionally protected. The Due Process Clause of the Fourteenth Amendment has a content the scope of which this Court determines only as cases come here from time to time and then not without close division and reversals of position. Such a dubious construction of a criminal statute should not be made unless language compels.

That such a pliable instrument of prosecution is to be feared appears to be recognized by the Government. It urges three safeguards against abuse of the broad powers of prosecution for which it contends. (1) Congress, it says, will supervise the Department's policies and curb excesses by withdrawal of funds. It surely is casting an impossible burden upon Congress to expect it to police the propriety of prosecutions by the Department of Justice. Nor would such detailed oversight by Congress make for the effective administration of the criminal law. (2) The Government further urges that, since prosecutions must be brought in the district where the crime was committed, the judge and jurors of that locality can be depended upon to protect against federal interference with State law enforcement. Such a suggestion would, for practical purposes, transfer the functions of this Court, which adjudicates questions concerning the proper relationship between the federal and State governments, to jurors whose function is to resolve factual questions. Moreover, if federal and State prosecutions are subject to the same influences, it is difficult to see what need there is for taking the prosecution out of the hands of the State. After all, Georgia citizens sitting as a federal grand jury indicted and other Georgia citizens sitting as a federal trial jury convicted Screws and his associates; and it was a

Georgia judge who charged more strongly against them than this Court thinks he should have.

Finally, the Department of Justice gives us this assurance of its moderation:

> "(3) The Department of Justice has established a policy of strict self-limitation with regard to prosecutions under the civil rights acts. When violations of such statutes are reported, the Department requires that efforts be made to encourage state officials to take appropriate action under state law. To assure consistent observance of this policy in the enforcement of the civil rights statutes, all United States Attorneys have been instructed to submit cases to the Department for approval before prosecutions or investigations are instituted. The number of prosecutions which have been brought under the civil rights statutes is small. * * * "

But such a "policy of strict self-limitation" is not accompanied by assurance of permanent tenure and immortality of those who make it the policy. Evil men are rarely given power; they take it over from better men to whom it had been entrusted. There can be no doubt that this shapeless and all-embracing statute can serve as a dangerous instrument of political intimidation and coercion in the hands of those so inclined. * * *

Note

Sheriff Screws was found not guilty at the retrial. The frequency of racially motivated attacks by law enforcement officers and the unlikelihood of convictions (or even prosecutions) in state court systems dominated by segregationists meant that the vaguely drafted Reconstruction era federal Civil Rights Act had to be pressed into service if there was to be any prospect of justice in these cases. According to constitutional theory, however, a statute which is vaguely written, or judicially interpreted so as to be open-ended, is unconstitutional and may not be used even against a defendant as worthy of punishment as Screws. Whatever the decision in *Screws* may be thought to mean, it apparently does not mean that a defendant must actually know that his actions are unconstitutional in order to be convicted under the Civil Rights Act. In United States v. Ehrlichman, 546 F.2d 910 (D.C.Cir.1976), the former presidential assistant was charged with conspiring to violate the Fourth Amendment rights of a Los Angeles psychiatrist by entering his office without a warrant for the purpose of seizing medical records relating to Daniel Ellsberg, a former patient then under indictment for publishing top secret documents. Ehrlichman contended that he believed that the President had authority to authorize such a "break-in" in the interests of national security, and that President Nixon had delegated this authority to him. In other words, he claimed to have believed that his actions were within a "national security" exception to the Fourth Amendment's prohibition of unreasonable searches and seizures, and that he therefore lacked the specific intent to violate the Constitution even if his belief was erroneous. The trial judge instructed the jury that such a belief would be no defense, and the federal court of appeals affirmed the resulting conviction. The opinion stated that: "Specific intent under Section 241 does not require an actual awareness on the part of the conspirators that they are violating constitutional rights. It is enough that they engage in activity which interferes with rights which as a matter of law are clearly and specifically protected by the Constitution." 546 F.2d at 928. In effect the court held that Ehrlichman's belief in the legality of the search, based on the facts known to him, was unreasonable as a matter of law. Compare, United States v. Barker, supra.

B. LAW, MORALITY, AND JUDICIAL AUTHORITY

Many legal rules mirror, and some are derived from, religious precepts or moral codes. For many crimes, the intersection of law and morality is not troubling. No controversy arises from the fact that secular laws criminalizing homicide and theft correspond with the commands of particular religions that "thou shalt not kill" and "thou shall not steal." Serious disputes have arisen in England and the United States, however, over the validity of some legal rules derived from religious traditions and moral codes, particularly laws criminalizing some types of sexual conduct.

During the middle of the twentieth century, English lawmakers and scholars vigorously debated the legitimacy of some of these rules. The debate was triggered in part by the 1957 Report of the Committee on Homosexual Offenses and Prostitution (the Wolfenden Report) to the Secretary of State for the Home Department. The most controversial recommendation made by this Committee was that "homosexual behavior between consenting adults in private should no longer be a criminal offense."

The most influential criticisms of this recommendation were raised by Sir Patrick Devlin. Devlin summarized the main thread of his argument in this way:

> "* * * Society cannot live without morals. Its morals are those standards of conduct which the reasonable man approves. A rational man, who is also a good man, may have other standards. If he has no standards at all he is not a good man and need not be further considered. If he has standards, they may be very different; he may, for example, not disapprove of homosexuality or abortion. In that case he will not share in the common morality; but that should not make him deny that it is a social necessity. A rebel may be rational in thinking that he is right but he is irrational if he thinks that society can leave him free to rebel.
>
> "A man who concedes that morality is necessary to society must support the use of those instruments without which morality cannot be maintained. The two instruments are those of teaching, which is doctrine, and of enforcement, which is the law. If morals could be taught simply on the basis that they are necessary to society, there would be no social need for religion; it could be left as a purely personal affair. But morality cannot be taught in that way. Loyalty is not taught in that way either. No society has yet solved the

problem of how to teach morality without religion. So the law must base itself on Christian morals and to the limit of its ability enforce them, not simply because they are the morals of most of us, nor simply because they are the morals which are taught by the established Church—on these points the law recognizes the right to dissent—but for the compelling reason that without the help of Christian teaching the law will fail." Patrick Devlin, *Morals and the Criminal Law*, in The Enforcement of Morals 24–25 (1965).

Devlin's thesis was contested by the famous English scholar, H.L.A. Hart. The Hart–Devlin debate was conducted on both sides of the Atlantic in lectures, articles, and books, and space constraints prohibit a comprehensive discussion of their complex arguments. On the central issue of the enforcement of sexual morality by legal sanctions, however, the nature of the dispute is clear. Hart embraced, with some qualifications, John Stuart Mill's argument that "The only purpose for which power can rightfully be exercised over any member of a civilised community against his will is to prevent harm to others," at least in the context of the enforcement of sexual morality. H.L.A. Hart, Law, Liberty, and Morality 4 (1963). Hart argued against the unquestioned imposition of the values of democratic majorities:

> "It seems fatally easy to believe that loyalty to democratic principles entails acceptance of what may be termed moral populism: the view that the majority have a moral right to dictate how all should live. This is a misunderstanding of democracy which still menaces individual liberty. * * *
>
> "The central mistake is a failure to distinguish the acceptable principle that political power is best entrusted to the majority from the unacceptable claim that what the majority do with that power is beyond criticism and must never be resisted. No one can be a democrat who does not accept the first of these, but no democrat need accept the second." *Id.*, at 79.

More recently, these issues have been revisited in litigation in the United States. Although questions about the legal enforcement of morality and the proper allocation of political and legal power within our democratic institutions have arisen in a variety of contexts, nowhere have they been raised more starkly than in the following cases which determined the constitutionality of the Georgia statute criminalizing sodomy.

BOWERS v. HARDWICK

Supreme Court of the United States, 1986.
478 U.S. 186, 106 S.Ct. 2841, 92 L.Ed.2d 140.

JUSTICE WHITE delivered the opinion of the Court.

In August 1982, respondent Hardwick (hereafter respondent) was charged with violating the Georgia statute criminalizing sodomy[1] by committing that act with another adult male in the bedroom of respondent's home. After a preliminary hearing, the District Attorney decided not to present the matter to the grand jury unless further evidence developed.

Respondent then brought suit in the Federal District Court, challenging the constitutionality of the statute insofar as it criminalized consensual sodomy.[2] He asserted that he was a practicing homosexual, that the Georgia sodomy statute, as administered by the defendants, placed him in imminent danger of arrest, and that the statute for several reasons violates the Federal Constitution. The District Court granted the defendants' motion to dismiss for failure to state a claim. * * *

A divided panel of the Court of Appeals for the Eleventh Circuit reversed * * * [holding] that the Georgia statute violated respondent's fundamental rights because his homosexual activity is a private and intimate association that is beyond the reach of state regulation by reason of the Ninth Amendment and the Due Process Clause of the Fourteenth Amendment. * * *

[W]e granted the Attorney General's petition for certiorari questioning the holding that the sodomy statute violates the fundamental rights of homosexuals. We agree with petitioner that the Court of Appeals erred, and hence reverse its judgment.

This case does not require a judgment on whether laws against sodomy between consenting adults in general, or between homosexuals in particular, are wise or desirable. It raises no question about the right or propriety of state legislative decisions to repeal their laws that criminalize homosexual sodomy, or of state-court decisions invalidating those laws on state constitutional grounds. The issue presented is whether the Federal Constitution confers a fundamental right upon homosexuals to engage in sodomy and hence invalidates the laws of the many States that still make such conduct illegal and have done so for a

1. Georgia Code Ann. § 16–6–2 (1984) provides, in pertinent part, as follows:

"(a) A person commits the offense of sodomy when he performs or submits to any sexual act involving the sex organs of one person and the mouth or anus of another....

"(b) A person convicted of the offense of sodomy shall be punished by imprisonment for not less than one nor more than 20 years.... "

2. John and Mary Doe were also plaintiffs in the action. They alleged that they wished to engage in sexual activity proscribed by § 16–6–2 in the privacy of their home and that they had been "chilled and deterred" from engaging in such activity by both the existence of the statute and Hardwick's arrest. The District Court held, however, that because they had neither sustained, nor were in immediate danger of sustaining, any direct injury from the enforcement of the statute, they did not have proper standing to maintain the action. The Court of Appeals affirmed the District Court's judgment dismissing the Does' claim for lack of standing, and the Does do not challenge that holding in this Court.

The only claim properly before the Court, therefore, is Hardwick's challenge to the Georgia statute as applied to consensual homosexual sodomy. We express no opinion on the constitutionality of the Georgia statute as applied to other acts of sodomy.

very long time. The case also calls for some judgment about the limits of the Court's role in carrying out its constitutional mandate.

* * *

[R]espondent would have us announce, as the Court of Appeals did, a fundamental right to engage in homosexual sodomy. This we are quite unwilling to do. It is true that despite the language of the Due Process Clauses of the Fifth and Fourteenth Amendments, which appears to focus only on the processes by which life, liberty, or property is taken, the cases are legion in which those Clauses have been interpreted to have substantive content, subsuming rights that to a great extent are immune from federal or state regulation or proscription. Among such cases are those recognizing rights that have little or no textual support in the constitutional language.

Striving to assure itself and the public that announcing rights not readily identifiable in the Constitution's text involves much more than the imposition of the Justices' own choice of values on the States and the Federal Government, the Court has sought to identify the nature of the rights qualifying for heightened judicial protection. In *Palko* v. *Connecticut*, 302 U.S. 319, 325, 326 (1937), it was said that this category includes those fundamental liberties that are "implicit in the concept of ordered liberty," such that "neither liberty nor justice would exist if [they] were sacrificed." A different description of fundamental liberties appeared in *Moore* v. *East Cleveland*, 431 U.S. 494, 503 (1977), where they are characterized as those liberties that are "deeply rooted in this Nation's history and tradition."

It is obvious to us that neither of these formulations would extend a fundamental right to homosexuals to engage in acts of consensual sodomy. Proscriptions against that conduct have ancient roots. Sodomy was a criminal offense at common law and was forbidden by the laws of the original 13 States when they ratified the Bill of Rights. In 1868, when the Fourteenth Amendment was ratified, all but 5 of the 37 States in the Union had criminal sodomy laws. In fact, until 1961, all 50 States outlawed sodomy, and today, 24 States and the District of Columbia continue to provide criminal penalties for sodomy performed in private and between consenting adults. Against this background, to claim that a right to engage in such conduct is "deeply rooted in this Nation's history and tradition" or "implicit in the concept of ordered liberty" is, at best, facetious.

Nor are we inclined to take a more expansive view of our authority to discover new fundamental rights imbedded in the Due Process Clause. The Court is most vulnerable and comes nearest to illegitimacy when it deals with judge-made constitutional law having little or no cognizable roots in the language or design of the Constitution. * * * There should be, therefore, great resistance to expand the substantive reach of those Clauses, particularly if it requires redefining the category of rights deemed to be fundamental. Otherwise, the Judiciary necessarily takes to itself further authority to govern the country without express constitutional authority. The claimed right pressed on us today falls far short of overcoming this resistance.

Respondent, however, asserts that the result should be different where the homosexual conduct occurs in the privacy of the home. He relies on *Stanley* v. *Georgia*, 394 U.S. 557 (1969), where the Court held that the First Amendment prevents conviction for possessing and reading obscene material in the privacy of one's home: "If the First Amendment means anything, it means that a State has no business telling a man, sitting alone in his house, what books he may read or what films he may watch."

Stanley did protect conduct that would not have been protected outside the home, and it partially prevented the enforcement of state obscenity laws; but the decision was firmly grounded in the First Amendment. * * * Plainly enough, otherwise illegal conduct is not always immunized whenever it occurs in the home. Victimless crimes, such as the possession and use of illegal drugs, do not escape the law where they are committed at home. *Stanley* itself recognized that its holding offered no protection for the possession in the home of drugs, firearms, or stolen goods. And if respondent's submission is limited to the voluntary sexual conduct between consenting adults, it would be difficult, except by fiat, to limit the claimed right to homosexual conduct while leaving exposed to prosecution adultery, incest, and other sexual crimes even though they are committed in the home. We are unwilling to start down that road.

Even if the conduct at issue here is not a fundamental right, respondent asserts that there must be a rational basis for the law and that there is none in this case other than the presumed belief of a majority of the electorate in Georgia that homosexual sodomy is immoral and unacceptable. This is said to be an inadequate rationale to support the law. The law, however, is constantly based on notions of morality, and if all laws representing essentially moral choices are to be invalidated under the Due Process Clause, the courts will be very busy indeed. Even respondent makes no such claim, but insists that majority sentiments about the morality of homosexuality should be declared inadequate. We do not agree, and are unpersuaded that the sodomy laws of some 25 States should be invalidated on this basis. * * *

CHIEF JUSTICE BURGER, concurring.

I join the Court's opinion, but I write separately to underscore my view that in constitutional terms there is no such thing as a fundamental right to commit homosexual sodomy.

As the Court notes, the proscriptions against sodomy have very "ancient roots." Decisions of individuals relating to homosexual conduct have been subject to state intervention throughout the history of Western civilization. Condemnation of those practices is firmly rooted in Judeao–Christian moral and ethical standards. Homosexual sodomy was a capital crime under Roman law. During the English Reformation when powers of the ecclesiastical courts were transferred to the King's Courts, the first English statute criminalizing sodomy was passed. Blackstone described "the infamous *crime against nature*" as an offense of "deeper malignity" than rape, a heinous act "the very mention of which is a disgrace to human nature," and "a crime not fit to be named." The common law of England, including its prohibition of sodomy, became the received law of Georgia and the other Colonies. In 1816 the Georgia Legislature passed the statute at issue here, and that statute has been continuously in force in one form or another since that time. To hold that the act of homosexual sodomy is somehow protected as a fundamental right would be to cast aside millennia of moral teaching.

* * *

JUSTICE POWELL, concurring.

I join the opinion of the Court. I agree with the Court that there is no fundamental right—*i.e.*, no substantive right under the Due Process Clause—such as that claimed by respondent Hardwick, and found to exist by the Court of Appeals. This is not to suggest, however, that respondent may not be protected by the Eighth Amendment of the Constitution. The Georgia statute at issue in this case, Ga. Code Ann. § 16–6–2 (1984), authorizes a court to imprison a person for up to 20 years for a single private, consensual act of sodomy. In my view, a prison sentence for such conduct—certainly a sentence of long duration—would create a serious Eighth Amendment issue. Under the Georgia statute a single act of sodomy, even in the private setting of a home, is a felony comparable in terms of the possible sentence imposed to serious felonies such as aggravated battery.[1]

In this case, however, respondent has not been tried, much less convicted and sentenced.[2] * * *

1. Among those States that continue to make sodomy a crime, Georgia authorizes one of the longest possible sentences. See Ala. Code § 13A–6–65(a)(3) (1982) (1-year maximum); Ariz. Rev. Stat. Ann. §§ 13–1411, 13–1412 (West Supp. 1985) (30 days); Ark. Stat. Ann. § 41–1813 (1977) (1-year maximum); D. C. Code § 22–3502 (1981) (10-year maximum); Fla. Stat. § 800.02 (1985) (60-day maximum); Ga. Code Ann. § 16–6–2 (1984) (1 to 20 years); Idaho Code § 18–6605 (1979) (5-year minimum); Kan. Stat. Ann. § 21–3505 (Supp. 1985) (6-month maximum); Ky. Rev. Stat. § 510.100 (1985) (90 days to 12 months); La. Rev. Stat. Ann. § 14:89 (West 1986) (5-year maximum); Md. Ann. Code, Art. 27, § § 553–554 (1982) (10-year maximum); Mich. Comp. Laws § 750.158 (1968) (15-year maximum); Minn. Stat. § 609.293 (1984) (1-year maximum); Miss. Code Ann. § 97–29–59 (1973) (10-year maximum); Mo. Rev. Stat. § 566.090 (Supp. 1984) (1-year maximum); Mont. Code Ann. § 45–5–505 (1985) (10-year maximum); Nev. Rev. Stat. § 201.190 (1985) (6-year maximum); N. C. Gen. Stat. § 14–177 (1981) (10-year maximum); Okla. Stat., Tit. 21, § 886 (1981) (10-year maximum); R. I. Gen. Laws § 11–10–1 (1981) (7 to 20 years); S. C. Code § 16–15–120 (1985) (5-year maximum); Tenn. Code Ann. § 39–2–612 (1982) (5 to 15 years); Tex. Penal Code Ann. § 21.06 (1974) ($200 maximum fine); Utah Code Ann. § 76–5–403 (1978) (6-month maximum); Va. Code § 18.2–361 (1982) (5-year maximum).

2. It was conceded at oral argument that, prior to the complaint against respondent Hardwick, there had been no reported decision involving prosecution for private homosexual sodomy under this statute for several decades. See Thompson v. Aldredge, 187 Ga. 467, 200 S.E. 799 (1939). Moreover, the State has declined to present the criminal charge against Hardwick to a grand jury, and this is a suit for declaratory judgment brought by respondents challenging the validity of the statute. The history of nonenforcement suggests the moribund

JUSTICE BLACKMUN, with whom JUSTICE BRENNAN, JUSTICE MARSHALL, and JUSTICE STEVENS join, dissenting.

This case is no more about "a fundamental right to engage in homosexual sodomy," as the Court purports to declare, than *Stanley* v. *Georgia* was about a fundamental right to watch obscene movies, or *Katz* v. *United States* was about a fundamental right to place interstate bets from a telephone booth. Rather, this case is about "the most comprehensive of rights and the right most valued by civilized men," namely, "the right to be let alone."

The statute at issue denies individuals the right to decide for themselves whether to engage in particular forms of private, consensual sexual activity. The Court concludes that § 16–6–2 is valid essentially because "the laws of . . . many States . . . still make such conduct illegal and have done so for a very long time." But the fact that the moral judgments expressed by statutes like § 16–6–2 may be " 'natural and familiar . . . ought not to conclude our judgment upon the question whether statutes embodying them conflict with the Constitution of the United States.' " Like Justice Holmes, I believe that "[it] is revolting to have no better reason for a rule of law than that so it was laid down in the time of Henry IV. It is still more revolting if the grounds upon which it was laid down have vanished long since, and the rule simply persists from blind imitation of the past." I believe we must analyze respondent Hardwick's claim in the light of the values that underlie the constitutional right to privacy. If that right means anything, it means that, before Georgia can prosecute its citizens for making choices about the most intimate aspects of their lives, it must do more than assert that the choice they have made is an " 'abominable crime not fit to be named among Christians.' "

I

* * *

First, the Court's almost obsessive focus on homosexual activity is particularly hard to justify in light of the broad language Georgia has used. Unlike the Court, the Georgia Legislature has not proceeded on the assumption that homosexuals are so different from other citizens that their lives may be controlled in a way that would not be tolerated if it limited the choices of those other citizens. Rather, Georgia has provided that "[a] person commits the offense of sodomy when he performs or submits to any sexual act involving the sex organs of one person and the mouth or anus of another." Ga. Code Ann. § 16–6–2(a) (1984). The sex or status of the persons who engage in the act is irrelevant as a matter of state law. In fact, to the extent I can discern a legislative purpose for Georgia's 1968 enactment of § 16–6–2, that

character today of laws criminalizing this type of private, consensual conduct. Some 26 States have repealed similar statutes. But the constitutional validity of the Georgia statute was put in issue by respondents, and for the reasons stated by the Court, I cannot say that conduct condemned for hundreds of years has now become a fundamental right.

purpose seems to have been to broaden the coverage of the law to reach heterosexual as well as homosexual activity.[1] * * *

II

A

The Court concludes today that none of our prior cases dealing with various decisions that individuals are entitled to make free of governmental interference "bears any resemblance to the claimed constitutional right of homosexuals to engage in acts of sodomy that is asserted in this case." While it is true that these cases may be characterized by their connection to protection of the family, the Court's conclusion that they extend no further than this boundary ignores the warning * * * against "clos[ing] our eyes to the basic reasons why certain rights associated with the family have been accorded shelter under the Fourteenth Amendment's Due Process Clause." We protect those rights not because they contribute, in some direct and material way, to the general public welfare, but because they form so central a part of an individual's life.

Only the most willful blindness could obscure the fact that sexual intimacy is "a sensitive, key relationship of human existence, central to family life, community welfare, and the development of human personality." The fact that individuals define themselves in a significant way through their intimate sexual relationships with others suggests, in a Nation as diverse as ours, that there may be many "right" ways of conducting those relationships, and that much of the richness of a relationship will come from the freedom an individual has to *choose* the form and nature of these intensely personal bonds.

* * *

III

* * *

The assertion that "traditional Judeo–Christian values proscribe" the conduct involved cannot provide an adequate justification for § 16–6–2. That certain, but by no means all, religious groups condemn the behavior at issue gives the State no license to impose their judgments on the entire citizenry. The legitimacy of secular legislation depends instead on whether the State can advance some justification for its law beyond its conformity to religious doctrine. Thus, far from buttressing his case, petitioner's invocation of Leviticus, Romans, St. Thomas Aquinas, and

1. Until 1968, Georgia defined sodomy as "the carnal knowledge and connection against the order of nature, by man with man, or in the same unnatural manner with woman." Ga. Crim. Code § 26–5901 (1933). In Thompson v. Aldredge, 187 Ga. 467, 200 S. E. 799 (1939), the Georgia Supreme Court held that § 26–5901 did not prohibit lesbian activity. And in Riley v. Garrett, 219 Ga. 345, 133 S.E. 2d 367 (1963), the Georgia Supreme Court held that § 26–5901 did not prohibit heterosexual cunnilingus. Georgia passed the act-specific statute currently in force "perhaps in response to the restrictive court decisions such as *Riley*," Note, The Crimes Against Nature, 16 J. Pub. L. 159, 167, n. 47 (1967). * * *

sodomy's heretical status during the Middle Ages undermines his suggestion that § 16–6–2 represents a legitimate use of secular coercive power.[6] * * *

[Part IV of this dissenting opinion and Justice Stevens' dissenting opinion are omitted.]

POWELL v. STATE

Supreme Court of Georgia, 1998.
270 Ga. 327, 510 S.E.2d 18.

Opinion: BENHAM, CHIEF JUSTICE.

Anthony San Juan Powell was charged in an indictment with rape and aggravated sodomy in connection with sexual conduct involving him and his wife's 17–year-old niece in Powell's apartment. The niece testified that appellant had sexual intercourse with her and engaged in an act of cunnilingus without her consent and against her will. Powell testified and admitted he performed the acts with the consent of the complainant. In light of Powell's testimony, the trial court included in its jury charge instructions on the law of sodomy. The jury acquitted Powell of the rape and aggravated sodomy charges and found him guilty of sodomy, thereby establishing that the State did not prove beyond a reasonable doubt that the act was committed "with force and against the will" of the niece. Powell brings this appeal contending the statute criminalizing acts of sodomy committed by adults without force in private is an unconstitutional intrusion on the right of privacy guaranteed him by the Georgia Constitution. * * *

* * * [W]e address appellant's constitutional challenge to O.C.G.A. § 16–6–2 (a). In so doing, we are mindful that a solemn act of the General Assembly carries with it a presumption of constitutionality that is overturned only when it is established that the legislation "manifestly infringes upon a constitutional provision or violates the rights of the people...." Appellant contends that the statute criminalizing intimate sexual acts performed by adults in private and without force impermissibly infringes upon the right of privacy guaranteed all Georgia citizens by the Georgia Constitution.[1]

6. The theological nature of the origin of Anglo–American antisodomy statutes is patent. It was not until 1533 that sodomy was made a secular offense in England. 25 Hen. VIII, ch. 6. Until that time, the offense was, in Sir James Stephen's words, "merely ecclesiastical." 2 J. Stephen, A History of the Criminal Law of England 429–430 (1883). Pollock and Maitland similarly observed that "[t]he crime against nature ... was so closely connected with heresy that the vulgar had but one name for both." 2 F. Pollock & F. Maitland, The History of English Law 554 (1895). The transfer of jurisdiction over prosecutions for sodomy to the secular courts seems primarily due to the alteration of ecclesiastical jurisdiction attendant on England's break with the Roman Catholic Church, rather than to any new understanding of the sovereign's interest in preventing or punishing the behavior involved. Cf. 6 E. Coke, Institutes, ch. 10 (4th ed. 1797).

1. Privacy rights protected by the U.S. Constitution are not at issue in this case. Thus, not applicable to this discussion [is] Bowers v. Hardwick, 478 U.S. 186, 191–192, 106 S. Ct. 2841, 92 L. Ed. 2d 140 (1986), where the U.S. Supreme Court ruled that

The right of privacy has a long and distinguished history in Georgia. In 1905, this Court expressly recognized that Georgia citizens have a "liberty of privacy" guaranteed by the Georgia constitutional provision which declares that no person shall be deprived of liberty except by due process of law. Pavesich v. New England Life Ins. Co., 122 Ga. 190, 197 (50 S.E. 68) (1905). The *Pavesich* decision constituted the first time any court of last resort in this country recognized the right of privacy, making this Court a pioneer in the realm of the right of privacy. * * * Since that time, the Georgia courts have developed a rich appellate jurisprudence in the right of privacy which recognizes the right of privacy as a fundamental constitutional right, "having a value so essential to individual liberty in our society that [its] infringement merits careful scrutiny by the courts."

In *Pavesich*, the Court found the right of privacy to be "ancient law," with "its foundation in the instincts of nature[,]" derived from "the Roman's conception of justice" and natural law, making it immutable and absolute. The Court described the liberty interest derived from natural law as "embracing the right of man to be free in the enjoyment of the faculties with which he has been endowed by his Creator, subject only to such restraints as are necessary for the common good." "Liberty" includes "the right to live as one will, so long as that will does not interfere with the rights of another or of the public," and the individual is "entitled to a liberty of choice as to his manner of life, and neither an individual nor the public has the right to arbitrarily take away from him his liberty." The *Pavesich* Court further recognized that the "right of personal liberty" also embraces "[t]he right to withdraw from the public gaze at such times as a person may see fit, when his presence in public is not demanded by any rule of law...." Stated succinctly, the Court ringingly endorsed the "right 'to be let alone' so long as [one] was not interfering with the rights of other individuals or of the public."

* * * This Court has determined that a citizen's right of privacy is strong enough to withstand a variety of attempts by the State to intrude in the citizen's life. * * * Georgia's strong public policy in favor of open government was required to bend in favor of the individual's right of privacy when matters about which the public had no legitimate concern were at issue. It is clear from the right of privacy appellate jurisprudence which emanates from *Pavesich* that the "right to be let alone" guaranteed by the Georgia Constitution is far more extensive that the right of privacy protected by the U.S. Constitution, which protects only those matters "deeply rooted in this Nation's history and tradition" or which are "implicit in the concept of ordered liberty...."[3]

the right of privacy protected by the U.S. Constitution did not insulate private sexual conduct between consenting homosexual adults from state proscription because the U.S. Constitution did not "extend a fundamental right to homosexuals to engage in acts of consensual sodomy * * *".

3. It is a well-recognized principle that a state court is free to interpret its state constitution in any way that does not violate principles of federal law, and thereby grant individuals more rights than those provided by the U.S. Constitution. Thus, a state court may interpret a state constitu-

While Georgia citizens' right to privacy is far-reaching, that is not to say that the individual's right to privacy is without limitation. The *Pavesich* court recognized that the right could be waived by the individual; could be subsumed when the individual was required to "perform public duties ...", and had to yield "in some particulars ... to the right of speech and of the press." * * * [W]e have ruled that a defendant may not successfully assert a privacy right when the acts [of sexual assault] are committed: in a public place; in exchange for money; or with those legally incapable of consenting to sexual acts.

Today, we are faced with whether the constitutional right of privacy screens from governmental interference a non-commercial sexual act that occurs without force in a private home between persons legally capable of consenting to the act. While *Pavesich* and its progeny do not set out the full scope of the right of privacy in connection with sexual behavior, it is clear that unforced sexual behavior conducted in private between adults is covered by the principles espoused in *Pavesich* since such behavior between adults in private is recognized as a private matter by "[a]ny person whose intellect is in a normal condition...." Adults who "withdraw from the public gaze" to engage in private, unforced sexual behavior are exercising a right "embraced within the right of personal liberty." We cannot think of any other activity that reasonable persons would rank as more private and more deserving of protection from governmental interference than unforced, private, adult sexual activity. We conclude that such activity is at the heart of the Georgia Constitution's protection of the right of privacy.

Having determined that appellant's behavior falls within the area protected by the right of privacy, we next examine whether the government's infringement upon that right is constitutionally sanctioned. As judicial consideration of the right to privacy has developed, this Court has concluded that the right of privacy is a fundamental right and that a government-imposed limitation on the right to privacy will pass constitutional muster if the limitation is shown to serve a compelling state interest and to be narrowly tailored to effectuate only that compelling interest. * * * The State fulfills its role in preventing sexual assaults and shielding and protecting the public from sexual acts by the enactment of criminal statutes prohibiting [rape; aggravated sodomy; statutory rape; child molestation and aggravated child molestation; enticing a child for indecent purposes; sexual assault of prisoners, the institutionalized, and the patients of psychotherapists; bestiality; sexual assault of a dead human being; public indecency; prostitution, pimping, pandering; solicitation of sodomy; masturbation for hire; incest; sexual battery and aggravated sexual battery], and by the vigorous enforcement of those

tional provision as affording more protection to citizens than have the federal courts in interpreting a parallel provision of the federal constitution. * * * Georgia is not alone in providing its citizens with a broader right of privacy than that provided by the federal constitution. Appellate courts in [Montana, Tennessee, Kentucky, Texas, and New Jersey] have all interpreted the right of privacy guaranteed by their respective state constitutions as being more extensive than that provided by the U.S. Constitution.

laws through the arrest and prosecution of offenders. In light of the existence of these statutes, the sodomy statute's *raison d'être* can only be to regulate the private sexual conduct of consenting adults, something which Georgians' right of privacy puts beyond the bounds of government regulation.

* * *

The State also maintains that the furtherance of "social morality," giving "due regard to the collective will of the citizens of Georgia," is a constitutional basis for legislative control of the non-commercial, unforced, private sexual activity of those legally capable of consenting to such activity. It is well within the power of the legislative branch to establish public policy through legislative enactment. It is also without dispute that oftentimes the public policy so established and the laws so enacted reflect the will of the majority of Georgians as well as the majority's notion of morality. However, "it does not follow ... that simply because the legislature has enacted as law what may be a moral choice of the majority, the courts are, thereafter, bound to simply acquiesce."

In undertaking the judiciary's constitutional duty, it is not the prerogative of members of the judiciary to base decisions on their personal notions of morality. Indeed, if we were called upon to pass upon the propriety of the conduct herein involved, we would not condone it. Rather, the judiciary is charged with the task of examining a legislative enactment * * * to ensure that the law meets constitutional standards. While many believe that acts of sodomy, even those involving consenting adults, are morally reprehensible, this repugnance alone does not create a compelling justification for state regulation of the activity. * * *

We conclude that O.C.G.A. § 16–6–2, insofar as it criminalizes the performance of private, unforced, non-commercial acts of sexual intimacy between persons legally able to consent, "manifestly infringes upon a constitutional provision" which guarantees to the citizens of Georgia the right of privacy. Appellant was convicted for performing an unforced act of sexual intimacy with one legally capable of consenting thereto in the privacy of his home. Accordingly, appellant's conviction for such behavior must be reversed.

Judgment reversed. All the Justices concur, except CARLEY, J., who dissents.

SEARS, JUSTICE, concurring.

* * * In this opinion, this Court in no way usurps the legislative function of promulgating social policy. Rather, in an inspired opinion, a majority of this Court today has fulfilled its constitutional responsibility within the American tripartite system of checks and balances. As well stated in the majority opinion, merely because the legislature has enacted a law which may impact upon the public's moral choices, courts are not "bound to simply acquiesce." It is the duty of this Court, and all courts, to ensure that, absent a compelling state interest, legislative acts

do not impinge upon the inalienable rights guaranteed by our State Constitution. * * *

* * *

The individual's right to freely exercise his or her liberty is not dependent upon whether the majority believes such exercise to be moral, dishonorable, or wrong. Simply because something is beyond the pale of "majoritarian morality" does not place it beyond the scope of constitutional protection. * * *

* * *

CARLEY, JUSTICE, dissenting.

"The responsibility of this Court ... is to construe and enforce the Constitution and laws of the [State] as they are and not to legislate social policy on the basis of our own personal inclinations." The issue in this case is not whether private and consensual acts of sodomy should be legal or illegal in Georgia, because that question has already been resolved by the General Assembly. Under the unambiguous provisions of O.C.G.A. § 16–6–2 (a), commission of an act of sodomy is against the criminal law of this state, and performance of such an act in private between consenting adults is not exempted from that statutory prohibition. Therefore, the only issue presented for decision is whether the General Assembly has the constitutional authority to prohibit such conduct. * * * Today, however, a majority of this Court concludes that our state constitution does confer upon the citizens of Georgia a fundamental right to engage in a consensual act which the majority itself concedes, as it must, that many Georgians find "morally reprehensible." I believe that, in so holding, the majority not only misconstrues the Constitution of Georgia, but that it also violates the fundamental constitutional principle of separation of powers. * * *

The premise of the majority is that the right of privacy guaranteed by the Georgia Constitution grants to the citizens of this state the right to engage in private consensual sodomy. Unlike the constitutions of some other states, the Georgia Constitution contains no express recognition of a right to privacy. That right stems entirely from this Court's holding in *Pavesich* * * * In accordance with *Pavesich*, an individual's liberty and, hence, his privacy is not completely unrestricted, but is subject to " 'such restraints as are necessary for the common welfare.' "

* * *

More importantly, however, the majority cites no authority as support for its adoption of the novel proposition that the constitutionality of a criminal statute is somehow dependent upon whether anyone other than the actual participants themselves are adversely affected by the proscribed act. Presumably, under this new standard, the State can no longer enforce laws against fornication or adultery. Thankfully, the majority includes incest among those sexual acts which it will continue to permit the State to proscribe as criminal. However, the majority offers no analytical or conceptual distinction between the crimes of sodomy and incest when committed by consenting adults. Neither a public performance of the proscribed sexual act, an exchange of money nor the use of force is an element of either offense as defined by the General Assembly. The only conclusion to be drawn is that the majority simply has decided that legislative proscription of the right of adults to engage in consensual sodomy is now politically incorrect and unconstitutional, but that it still is politically correct and constitutional for the General Assembly to prohibit adult relatives from engaging in consensual sexual intercourse. The majority opinion will have anomalous results. For example, it remains criminal for a father and his adult daughter or stepdaughter to engage in consensual sexual intercourse, but they may now lawfully perform consensual acts of anal and oral sodomy.

Moreover, the majority does not purport to limit to sexual offenses the application of its new found authority to declare this state's criminal statutes unconstitutional. By equating the general constitutional guarantee of "liberty" to all Georgia citizens with the right of each individual citizen to engage in self-indulgent but self-contained acts of permissiveness, it appears that the majority has now called into constitutional question any criminal statute which proscribes an act that, at least to the satisfaction of a majority of this Court, does not cause sufficient harm to anyone other than the actual participants. Thus, to give but one example, the constitutionality of criminal laws which forbid the possession and use of certain drugs has suddenly become questionable.

* * * Simply put, commission of what the legislature has determined to be an immoral act, even if consensual and private, is an injury against society itself. "The protection of 'societal order and morality' [is] a 'substantial government interest.' " The law "is constantly based on notions of morality, and if all laws representing essentially moral choices are to be invalidated under the Due Process Clause, the courts will be very busy indeed."

* * *

Retaining the long-standing proscription on sodomy may or may not be good public policy, but it is a public policy determination which, as a matter of constitutional law, only the General Assembly can make. * * * By holding that the constitutional guarantee of "liberty" precludes the General Assembly from enacting an express ban on the commission of consensual private acts of sodomy, the Court has usurped the legislative authority of the General Assembly to establish the public policy of this state.

* * *

C. SENTENCING DISCRETION

PEOPLE v. POINTER

California Court of Appeals, First District, 1984.
151 Cal.App.3d 1128, 199 Cal.Rptr. 357.

KLINE, PRESIDING JUSTICE.

Our principal inquiry in this case is whether a woman convicted of the felony of child endangerment (Pen.Code, § 273a, subd. (1)) and found to be in violation of a custody decree (§ 278.5) may, as a condition of probation, be prohibited from conceiving a child. * * *

I.

Appellant, Ruby Pointer, has at all material times been the devoted adherent of a rigorously disciplined macrobiotic diet. She is also the mother of two children, Jamal and Barron, who at the time of trial were, respectively, two and four years of age. Appellant imposed an elaborate macrobiotic regime on both children despite the objections of Barron's father and despite the repeated advice of her physician, Dr. Gilbert Carter, that such diet was inappropriate and unhealthy for young children. Dr. Carter additionally advised appellant that breastfeeding Jamal while she was herself on a macrobiotic diet was hazardous for the infant.

In October 1980, more than a year prior to the trial, Barron's father sought the assistance of Children's Protective Services, a county agency that investigates complaints of child abuse and neglect. Donald Allegri, a social worker with the agency thereupon met with appellant and, after seeing the children, strongly urged her to immediately consult Dr. Loretta Rao, a pediatrician. Appellant brought Barron to Dr. Rao for examination, but not Jamal. Upon learning that Jamal had not been examined by Dr. Rao, Allegri phoned appellant's regular physician, Dr. Carter, and expressed his deep concern over Jamal's condition.

On November 8, 1980, Dr. Carter spent nearly two hours with appellant and both children. He was shocked when he observed Jamal and stated "God, Ruby, God, how could you do this? How could you not take care of your baby?" Dr. Carter reiterated the dangers of breastfeeding Jamal while she was on a macrobiotic diet, importuned her to modify her own diet and recommended increased calories and protein for the child. Dr. Carter also urged her to consult Dr. Rao, who, because she was herself a vegetarian, he thought might be able to more strongly influence appellant. Appellant disregarded Dr. Carter's advice and at this time did not consult Dr. Rao.

Two days later Dr. Carter again saw appellant and Jamal and observed that the child remained malnourished and significantly underdeveloped. He again pressed appellant to visit Dr. Rao and she again declined to do so. During a telephone conversation nearly two weeks later, Dr. Carter repeated his warning of the severity of Jamal's condition and urged appellant once more to visit Dr. Rao or, in the alternative, bring the child to a hospital emergency room. Appellant vaguely indicated that she would "take care of things."

When on November 25th appellant finally brought Jamal to Dr. Rao she was informed that the child, who was emaciated, semicomatose, and in a state of shock, was dying and in need of immediate hospitalization. Appellant demurred, telling Dr. Rao that she wanted to consult others and would return later. Appellant resisted hospitalization because she felt Jamal might intravenously be fed "preservatives" and suffer a rash. Dr. Rao thereupon called the police, who arrived in five minutes and ordered Jamal hospitalized at once. As a result of emergency procedures the child's life was saved.

During Jamal's hospitalization, appellant surreptitiously brought him macrobiotic food despite warnings not to do so and continued to breastfeed him even after being told that her milk contained high levels of sodium that endangered the child.

Upon his discharge from the hospital, Jamal was placed in a foster home. While ostensibly visiting him there, appellant abducted the child and fled to Puerto Rico with him and her other son. An agent of the FBI located appellant and the children in a housing project in Puerto Rico, and arrested her. The agent testified at trial that appellant's living quarters were rather squalid and that the only foodstuffs he observed were bags of beans, some millet, a few other grains and noodles. After appellant waived her *Miranda* rights, she admitted to the agent that she had abducted Jamal from the foster home. She did so, she stated, because the woman who managed the home fed Jamal eggs and sugar and did not respect his dietary habits. She said Jamal was "getting fat" and that she did not like it.

When the children returned to California it was determined that as a result of diet and maternal neglect Barron was seriously underdeveloped and Jamal had suffered severe growth retardation and permanent neurological damage.

On the facts just briefly described, appellant was found guilty by a jury of violation of Penal Code sections 273[a] and 278.5. She was thereafter sentenced to five years probation on the conditions that she serve one year in county jail; participate in an appropriate counseling program; not be informed of the permanent whereabouts of Jamal (who was placed in foster care) and have no unsupervised visits with him; have no custody of any children, including her own, without prior court approval; and that she not conceive during the probationary period. Appellant chal-

a. Section 273a provides in pertinent part: "(1) Any person who, under circumstances or conditions likely to produce great bodily harm or death, . . . willfully causes or permits any child to suffer, or inflicts thereon unjustifiable physical pain or mental suffering, or having the care or custody of any child, willfully causes or permits the person or health of such child to be injured, or willfully causes or permits such child to be placed in such situation that its person or health is endangered, is punishable by imprisonment in the county jail not exceeding one year, or in the state prison for 2, 3 or 4 years."—ed.

lenges this last condition as an unconstitutional restriction of her fundamental rights to privacy and to procreate. * * *

The condition of probation prohibiting conception, to which we now turn, was imposed only after thoughtful consideration by the trial judge, who fully appreciated the extraordinary nature of his action. As he stated at the sentencing hearing, "I have never considered imposing as a condition of probation the requirement that someone not conceive during the period of probation, and I have never considered requiring as a condition of probation that a defendant not have custody of her children without approval by the sentencing court following a hearing, but that's certainly what I intend to do in this case. This is an extremely serious case."

This assessment is supported by the record. The lengthy probation report repeatedly emphasized appellant's denial of responsibility for her actions and inability or unwillingness to alter her conduct, as well as the high likelihood that, if permitted to do so, she would in the future continue to endanger the health and indeed the lives of her children. Though the report expressed the view that appellant's understanding and acceptance of responsibility would not be enhanced by incarceration in prison and did not recommend a state prison term, it did point out that such confinement would at least prevent appellant from "interfering or attempting to interfere in the treatment and special education of her sons and that she will also not become pregnant and endanger another small child in the future."

In this connection, Dr. Barbara O. Murray, a psychologist who examined appellant at the direction of the court, reported that appellant "is extremely reluctant to take any forms of chemicals or medication [and] * * * would not comply with such a requirement if it were imposed. Thus, if required to take birth control pills, for example, it first of all would be extremely difficult to monitor or supervise such a condition, and the likelihood of noncompliance would be inordinately high. Thus, if such an alternative is ultimately considered desirable by the court, it might be more advisable simply to incarcerate her now rather than wait for her to violate probation." Dr. Murray also concluded that "any new born child to Ms. Pointer would encounter similar risks as those of her previous children." This conclusion is consistent with the views of Dr. Rao, who stated that appellant suffers "an altered state of reality" that can not easily be reformed. * * *

The validity of the condition of probation with which we are here concerned must first be assessed in terms of its reasonableness. The test of the reasonableness of a condition of probation [established by California case law is] as follows: "A condition of probation will not be held invalid unless it (1) has no relationship to the crime of which the offender was convicted, (2) relates to conduct which is not in itself criminal, and (3) requires or forbids conduct which is not reasonably related to future criminality." [Citations] * * *

Applying this test to the facts of the instant case, we conclude that the condition in question is reasonable. Unlike People v. Dominguez, 256 Cal.App.2d 623, 64 Cal.Rptr. 290 (1967), where the court found a similar condition invalid because the defendant's future pregnancy was unrelated to the crime of robbery and had no reasonable relation to future criminality, in this unusual case the condition is related to child endangerment, the crime for which appellant was convicted. Although cases in other jurisdictions have concluded that a condition of probation that a defendant not become pregnant has no relation to the crime of child abuse or to future criminality [Citations], those cases relied heavily upon the fact that the abuse could be entirely avoided by removal of any children from the custody of the defendant. This case is distinguishable, however, because of evidence that the harm sought to be prevented by the trial court may occur before birth. Since the record fully supports the trial court's belief that appellant would continue to adhere to a strict macrobiotic diet despite the dangers it presents to any children she might conceive, we cannot say that the condition of probation prohibiting conception is completely unrelated to the crime for which appellant was convicted or to the possibility of future criminality.

Our determination that the condition of probation is reasonably related to the offense of which appellant was convicted and to possible future criminality, which are the factors measured by the *Dominguez* test, does not, however, end our inquiry. For where a condition of probation impinges upon the exercise of a fundamental right and is challenged on constitutional grounds we must additionally determine whether the condition is impermissibly overbroad.

There is, of course, no question that the condition imposed in this case infringes the exercise of a fundamental right to privacy protected by both the federal and state constitutions. Nor is there any question that for this reason the condition must be subjected to special scrutiny to determine whether the restriction is entirely necessary to serve the dual purposes of rehabilitation and public safety. * * *

The challenged condition was apparently not intended to serve any rehabilitative purpose but rather to protect the public by preventing injury to an unborn child. We believe this salutary purpose can adequately be served by alternative restrictions less subversive of appellant's fundamental right to procreate. Such less onerous conditions might include, for example, the requirement that appellant periodically submit to pregnancy testing; and that upon becoming pregnant she be required to follow an intensive prenatal and neonatal treatment program monitored by both the probation officer and by a supervising physician. If appellant bears a child during the period of probation it can be removed from her custody and placed in foster care, as was done with appellant's existing children, if the court then considers such action necessary to protect the infant.

Though at the sentencing hearing the prosecutor claimed that the probation department and the local children's protective services agency lacked the resources for such intensive probation supervision, there is no evidence on this issue before us. Nor does the record or common sense provide any reason to believe it would be any more difficult to determine whether appellant is pregnant for purposes of enforcing prenatal care requirements than it would be to determine whether she is pregnant for purposes of enforcing the condition here challenged. Indeed, in at least one critical respect we believe it would be *less* difficult; and the reason relates to another troublesome aspect of the challenged condition.

Although the trial judge stated at the sentencing hearing that he would not order appellant to have an abortion if she became pregnant, he also stated that "If she violates probation in this case, I would be sending her to prison; I can assure you of that. I expect her to live up to every single, solitary term and condition of probation." This stern admonition doubtless made it apparent to appellant that in the event she became pregnant during the period of probation the surreptitious procuring of an abortion might be the only practical way to avoid going to prison. A condition of probation that might place a defendant in this position, and, if so, be coercive of abortion, is in our view improper.

In any event, the dilemma that might well confront appellant if she conceived in violation of the condition imposed[12] renders it unlikely she would voluntarily reveal any pregnancy. Less restrictive conditions aimed at protecting the child in utero and after birth would not so clearly induce resistance to the disclosure of pregnancy. To this extent, less restrictive alternative conditions would be easier to monitor and enforce and therefore better protect against the harm sought to be avoided by the trial court.

We conclude that the condition of probation prohibiting conception is overbroad, as less restrictive alternatives are available that would feasibly provide the protections the trial court properly believed necessary. In order to provide the trial court an opportunity to devise a specific alternative condition or conditions we reverse only that portion of the judgment prohibiting conception as a condition of probation and remand for resentencing consistent with the views herein expressed. In all other respects the judgment is affirmed.

UNITED STATES v. ELY

United States Court of Appeals, Seventh Circuit, 1983.
719 F.2d 902.

POSNER, CIRCUIT JUDGE.

David Ely was indicted in 1979 along with two other men, Dawson and Griswold, for distributing and conspiring to distribute cocaine. Ely

12. It deserves to be noted that the condition imposed did not include a prohibition on sexual intercourse. As the trial judge stated at the sentencing hearing: "I would never require somebody to have no sexual activity; I don't think that's even suggested." The conceded fact that even the best birth control measures sometimes fail raises the possibility that appellant could conceive despite reasonable precautions to comply with the condition imposed. This might also occur if, as defense counsel pointed out at the time of sentencing, appellant reasonably relied on a sex partner's false representation that he had undergone a vasectomy.

was an intermediate distributor, Dawson his source, and Griswold a dealer whom Ely supplied with cocaine that he obtained from Dawson. Griswold and Dawson pleaded guilty and were sentenced to 10 and 15 years in prison, respectively. Dawson moved for a reduction of sentence under Rule 35(b) of the Federal Rules of Criminal Procedure, the motion was denied, he appealed, and this court affirmed. Ely failed to appear in court with the others and became a fugitive. The government then filed a superseding indictment against him that included two counts of failing to appear. * * *

Ely entered into a plea agreement with the government under which he pleaded guilty to one count of distributing and one count of conspiring to distribute cocaine and to both counts of failing to appear. The government agreed to drop other cocaine charges and not to prosecute Ely for attempted bank robbery or illegal possession of firearms—charges that might have been lodged against him on the basis of the circumstances of his arrest in 1982. The plea agreement was silent as to the sentence. After receiving the presentence report, the judge sentenced Ely to the maximum term of 15 years on each of the narcotics counts, to be served consecutively and to be followed by ten years of supervision (a special term of parole of five years, plus five years of probation) for the failure-to-appear offenses. * * *

Ely received a 30–year prison sentence and will not be eligible for parole until he has served one-third of it. Since Ely was 30 years old when he was sentenced, he will be at least 40 when he is released from prison, and he will not be free from government supervision till he is 70. His codefendants received much lighter sentences. Ely's dealer-customer, Griswold, received a 10–year prison term and Ely's supplier, Dawson—a presumptively bigger fish than Ely—received 15 years, a sentence this court described as "very harsh" in upholding the district judge's refusal to reduce it, 642 F.2d at 1063. (One judge on the panel dissented, on the ground that the district judge had failed to exercise his sentencing discretion.) In the last fiscal year for which statistics are available, the average prison sentence for distributing Schedule II drugs (such as cocaine) was approximately five years in the nation as a whole (but it was six and one-half years in the Central District of Illinois), and fewer than 25 percent of the convicted defendants received more than five years (exactly 50 percent in the Central District). A number of offenders, however, received much longer sentences.

We do not understand Ely to be arguing that his sentence exceeds the statutory maximum or that, considered apart from the sentences meted out to his codefendants, it is so disproportionate to the gravity of his crime that it violates the due process clause of the Fifth Amendment or the cruel-and-unusual punishment clause of the Eighth Amendment. In Solem v. Helm, 463 U.S. 277 (1983), the Supreme Court held for the first time that a noncapital punishment could be so disproportionate to the defendant's crime as to violate the Eighth Amendment. But Helm had been sentenced to life imprisonment, with no possibility of parole, for committing a $100 fraud. * * * Ely has not made a comparable showing of disproportion. Not only is his sentence lighter than Helm's, but large-scale trafficking in narcotics is not comparable to penny-ante fraud. Many people, whose views must have been influential with Congress given the penalties that it imposed for such trafficking, consider the drug traffic enormously destructive.

The only basis for Ely's challenge to the sentence is that the district judge abused his discretion by giving Ely a much longer sentence than either of his codefendants. The scope of appellate review of a judge's determination of how long, within statutory limits, to make a sentence is extremely limited. "A reviewing court may not change or reduce a sentence imposed within the applicable statutory limits on the ground that the sentence was too severe unless the trial court relied on improper or unreliable information in exercising its discretion or failed to exercise any discretion at all in imposing the sentence." United States v. Fleming, 671 F.2d 1002, 1003 (7th Cir.1982). * * * The only power we have that might be applicable to this case, therefore, is the power to remand for resentencing if the district judge failed to exercise his sentencing discretion—for example, failed to read the presentence report, or listen to what the defendant or his lawyer had to say, or in short attend responsibility to the performance of his awesome duty of fixing the punishment that, within the statutory limits, will fit the crime and the criminal.

Although there is no direct evidence that the judge here failed to exercise his sentencing discretion, we may assume that if a judge sentences similar offenders to greatly disparate terms for the same crime, without any explanation, an inference arises that he failed to exercise his discretion. * * * Ely tries to invoke this principle by pointing out as we have said that his codefendants received lighter sentences than he. But their circumstances were different. Griswold, a retail dealer, sold a much smaller quantity of drugs than Ely (street value: $18,000). Though below Dawson in the chain of distribution, Ely sold to the agents, for $33,000, a substantial amount of cocaine (more than a pound) having an estimated street value of $175,000, which was almost as much as the street value of Dawson's sale ($212,000). And whereas Dawson's criminal record was, limited to one conviction for possession of marijuana, Ely had been convicted of robbery and sentenced to 21/2 to 71/2 years in prison, and had violated his state parole and become a federal fugitive when he failed to appear for his trial in 1979. Moreover, the circumstances of his arrest in 1982, disclosed in the presentence report, suggest that Ely has a propensity to violence. He was traveling in a car that had been wired by the FBI. By his own statement he was en route to rob a bank and was armed; and he was arrested after the FBI heard him say he would steal a car in the vicinity of the bank and shoot any police officer who tried to stop him. So besides having committed serious narcotics offenses, being a convicted robber, and having been a fugitive for three years, Ely made a threat, that in the circumstances cannot be dismissed as idle, to take human life. All these were pertinent considerations in sentencing, all were before the district judge in a presentence report the factual accuracy of which is not contested, and they prevent us from concluding that Ely's sentence is so disproportionate and unexplained that the district judge must not have exercised his sentencing discretion and should be told to try again.

There is an undoubted paradox in the fact that while if Ely had stood trial, been convicted, and been sentenced just to probation he could have gotten plenary appellate review of his conviction, he cannot obtain plenary appellate review of the judge's decision to sentence him to 30 years in prison on his plea of guilty. But we are unwilling to broaden the extremely narrow scope of appellate review of sentences. All other considerations to one side, Judge Friendly's warning, which is even more timely today than when delivered a decade ago, that a general power of appellate review of sentences would end the federal appellate court system as we know it, must give us pause. Friendly, Federal Jurisdiction: A General View 36 (1973).

The judgment of the district court is Affirmed.

STATE v. OXBORROW

Supreme Court of Washington, 1986.
106 Wash.2d 525, 723 P.2d 1123.

DURHAM, JUSTICE.

Kenneth D. Oxborrow challenges the trial court's imposition of consecutive 10–and 5–year prison terms under the Sentencing Reform Act of 1981 (the SRA), for the crimes of first-degree theft and violation of a cease and desist order in connection with the sale of securities. * * *

In 1979, Oxborrow and two other persons started the Wheatland Investment Company. Oxborrow told potential investors that he would place their monies into the commodities and futures markets and promised a return of approximately 2 percent per week on their investments. As Oxborrow attracted more and more investors, he began to pay off prior investors with the money obtained from newer investors, creating an elaborate pyramid scheme. In all, Oxborrow obtained over $58 million, of which only $45 million was returned to the investors. At most, Oxborrow placed only 10 percent of his investors' monies into the commodities and futures markets. He appropriated a large portion of the remainder to satisfy his own extravagant tastes. During this period, he purchased two Rolls–Royce automobiles, a Cadillac limousine, several airplanes and an oceanside resort cabin worth several hundred thousand dollars. He decorated his office and home with fine leather furniture, expensive antiques and imported Chinese rugs. Other portions of his investors' monies were used to cover past debts and to finance his own private business ventures. * * * Over 500 investors lost everything they had invested. Oxborrow's victims included pensioners, the elderly and the blind. He allegedly gained the confidence of some investors by making a show of his own supposedly ethical and honest behavior; large pictures of Jesus and other Christian items were on prominent display throughout his home and office.

On August 2, 1984, Oxborrow was served with a cease and desist order which directed him to stop selling or offering for sale any unregistered securities. This order was aimed at Oxborrow's investment scheme. Oxborrow ignored the order and ultimately accepted an additional $1 million from various investors. However, near the end of August, when he saw that he would be unable to pay back all his investors, he approached an attorney for advice. His attorney contacted the prosecuting attorneys for both the United States and Grant County to discuss Oxborrow's investment scheme and soon commenced plea bargaining. For ease of prosecution, the Grant County Prosecuting Attorney was designated to represent the combined interests of prosecutors from the 15 affected Washington counties.

On October 31, 1984, Oxborrow pled guilty to theft in the first degree, and to willful violation of a cease and desist order. * * * Under the SRA, the presumptive sentence ranges for these crimes are 0–90 days and 0–12 months respectively, since Oxborrow had no previous criminal history. The statutory maximum sentences are 10 years in each case. The Prosecutor recommended that Oxborrow serve concurrent 10–and 5–year sentences for the two crimes, for a total term of 10 years. Instead, the trial court sentenced Oxborrow to consecutive 10–and 5–year sentences for a total term of 15 years. * * *

The Sentencing Reform Act of 1981 created presumptive sentencing ranges for most felonies based on the seriousness of the crime and the offender's criminal history. The sentencing court may impose any sentence within the presumptive range that it deems appropriate. However, the court may also impose a sentence outside the range (an exceptional sentence) if it finds, "considering the purpose of this chapter, that there are substantial and compelling reasons justifying an exceptional sentence." The SRA provides a nonexclusive list of aggravating and mitigating factors which the sentencing court may consider in imposing an exceptional sentence.

Either the defendant or the State may appeal an exceptional sentence. * * *

> To reverse a sentence which is outside the sentence range, the statute provides that the reviewing court must find: "(a) Either that the reasons supplied by the sentencing judge are not supported by the record which was before the judge or that those reasons do not justify a sentence outside the standard range for that offense; or (b) that the sentence imposed was clearly excessive or clearly too lenient."

As Oxborrow readily admits, the trial court's reasons for going outside the standard range are supported by the record and these reasons also unquestionably justify the imposition of an exceptional sentence; thus, subsection (a) is inapplicable. The issue here is if the duration of

Oxborrow's exceptional sentence was justified, or, as Oxborrow argues, was "clearly excessive".

The SRA does not define the term "clearly excessive" nor otherwise explicitly indicate the standard of review to be used in determining if a particular sentence is "clearly excessive". However, three important sources—the language of the SRA itself, the express recommendations of the Sentencing Guidelines Commission, and the Washington courts' previous interpretation of identical language in the Juvenile Justice Act—clearly indicate that the sentencing court's decision regarding length of an exceptional sentence should not be reversed as "clearly excessive" absent an abuse of discretion. We hereby adopt that standard of review. * * *

In passing, we note that Oxborrow has urged this court to adopt the so-called "Minnesota rule", which generally limits exceptional sentences to no more than twice the presumptive sentence range. We decline to do so for several reasons. First, there is no statutory authority for applying such a rule, and no indication that the Legislature intended to impose this arbitrary limit on exceptional sentences. Second, if this rule were strictly applied in the present case, Oxborrow could be sentenced to no more than 180 days for the first-degree theft charge, a grossly inappropriate punishment given the facts of the case. Finally, even the Minnesota courts have had difficulty in applying the "doubling rule". A number of cases have failed to strictly abide by the rule and have allowed greater sentences upon a finding of "severe" aggravating circumstances. [Citations]

Applying the abuse of discretion standard, we conclude that Oxborrow's sentence is not clearly excessive. [The statute] provides a list of aggravating factors that the sentencing court may consider when imposing an exceptional sentence:

"(3) The offense was a major economic offense or series of offenses, so identified by a consideration of any of the following factors: (a) The offense involved multiple victims or multiple incidents per victim; (b) The offense involved attempted or actual monetary loss substantially greater than typical for the offense; (c) The offense involved a high degree of sophistication or planning or occurred over a lengthy period of time; (d) The defendant used his or her position of trust, confidence, or fiduciary responsibility to facilitate the commission of the offense".

Oxborrow's crimes fulfill all of the listed criteria for a "major economic offense". Considering only his activities subsequent to July 1, 1984, he defrauded at least 50 investors of over $1 million by the use of a highly sophisticated pyramid scheme in which he grossly abused his position of trust. * * * Surely this is the quintessential crime for which the Legislature contemplated a maximum sentence. We find no abuse of discretion.

Oxborrow next contends that the trial court exceeded its authority under the SRA by imposing consecutive, rather than concurrent, 10–and 5–year sentences. He further claims that even if the consecutive sentences are not illegal per se, the length of the consecutive sentences may not exceed the presumptive sentence ranges for his crimes. We disagree.

RCW 9.94A.400(1)(a) and (b) allow for consecutive sentences only for persons convicted of "three or more serious violent offenses". * * * In all other instances, the sentences are to be concurrent. Oxborrow's crimes admittedly do not meet the requirements of RCW 9.94A.400 for consecutive sentences.

However, former RCW 9.94A.390(4)(h) lists as an "aggravating circumstance" the possibility that: "The operation of the multiple offense policy of RCW 9.94A.400 results in a presumptive sentence that is clearly too lenient in light of the purpose of this chapter.... "The Legislature thus recognized that the limitations on consecutive sentences in RCW 9.94A.400 might be inappropriate in exceptional cases. * * *

We next turn to RCW 9.94A.120(13), which provides: "A departure from the standards in RCW 9.94A.400(1) and (2) governing whether sentences are to be served consecutively or concurrently is an exceptional sentence subject to the limitations in subsections (2) and (3) of this section, and may be appealed by the defendant or the state."

The sentencing court thus may impose consecutive sentences even if RCW 9.94A.400 does not so provide, but in such a case, the sentencing court must provide "substantial and compelling reasons" for its decision, set forth in written findings of fact and conclusions of law. RCW 9.94A.120(2) and (3). There is no requirement that the length of the consecutive sentences not exceed the presumptive range; rather, when the consecutive sentences result in a total term exceeding the presumptive range, the defendant may appeal this sentence in the same way he would appeal any sentence outside the presumptive range.

Here, Oxborrow's presumptive sentence range was 0–12 months (using the longer of his two presumptive sentence ranges for first-degree theft and violation of the cease and desist order), and his consecutive sentences total 15 years. This brings him within RCW 9.94A.210(4) which mandates reversal of the sentencing court's decision if (a) the reasons given by the sentencing judge do not justify a sentence outside the presumptive range, or (b) the total sentence is clearly excessive. As earlier indicated, Oxborrow does not challenge the adequacy of the trial court's reasons for imposing an exceptional sentence, but claims only that the sentence is "clearly excessive". Thus, we apply the abuse of discretion test to Oxborrow's claim. Although the trial court did not make a separate listing of factors to justify both its decision to sentence Oxborrow to a term beyond the presumptive range on each of the two counts and to make those terms run consecutively, the same factors would apply to each decision. Oxborrow could have been sentenced to consecutive 10–year terms, a total of 20 years, for his crimes; the trial court chose instead to impose a total term of 15 years. We hold that the trial court acted within its authority in imposing consecutive sentences and did not abuse its discretion in so doing. * * *

The sentences of the trial court are affirmed.

DOLLIVER, C.J., and CALLOW, J., concur.

DORE, J., concurs in result only.

ANDERSEN, JUSTICE (concurring).

I fully concur with the majority opinion authored by JUSTICE DURHAM, and the conclusion that there is no statutory or other compelling reason to adopt Minnesota's arbitrary "doubling rule". In fairness to the concurring/dissenting opinion, however, it seems obvious to me that, as a practical matter, an exceptional sentence of no more than twice the length of the presumptive sentence will on appellate review be less likely to be held to constitute an abuse of discretion than one which probes the outermost limits of the statutory maximum. The egregious facts of this case amply justify the sentence imposed herein. There was no abuse of discretion; the sentence was not "clearly excessive."

BRACHTENBACH, J., concurs.

UTTER, JUSTICE (concurring in part; dissenting in part).

I agree with the majority that the crimes committed by Oxborrow justify a sentence of 15 years. I disagree, however, with the majority's adoption of the "abuse of discretion" standard of review for criminal sentences. The reasons given by the majority for its conclusion are unsupported by the language of the act or its legislative history. I also disagree with the majority's rejection of Minnesota's "doubling" rule.

[Justice Utter pointed out that the SRA does not require the "abuse of discretion" standard, that the recommendation of the Sentencing Guidelines Commission advocating that standard was not accepted by the legislature, and that the SRA is significantly different in philosophy and language from the earlier Juvenile Justice Act. Determination of the appropriate standard of review was left to the judiciary, which should employ the standard of review that best carries out the sentence reform objectives of the SRA.] In other areas of law, appellate review traditionally serves as a legal mechanism to reconcile the myriad decisions of individual trial judges. Under indeterminate sentencing schemes of criminal law, however, appellate courts are unable to produce a useful set of guiding principles. * * * The sentencing powers of the judges are so unconfined that, except for frequently monstrous maximum limits, they are effectively subject to no law at all. Everyone with the least training in law would be prompt to denounce a statute that merely said the penalty for crimes "shall be any term the judge sees fit to impose." A regime of such arbitrary fiat would be intolerable in a supposedly free society, to say nothing of being invalid under our due process clause. But the fact is that we have accepted unthinkingly a criminal code creating in effect precisely that degree of unbridled power. Appellate review of sentencing decisions therefore is a key element in sentence reform. * * *

The abuse of discretion standard is extremely deferential. Under this standard an appellate court will overturn a trial court's decision only if the court's action was "manifestly unreasonable, or exercised on untenable grounds, or for untenable reasons." [Citation] Only one Washington court has ever reversed a criminal sentence as an abuse of discretion. Under this standard appellate courts cannot conduct the review necessary to achieve the uniformity and proportionality envisioned by the drafters of the Sentencing Reform Act. * * *

An abuse of discretion standard of review is appropriate when (1) concerns of judicial economy dictate that the trial court be responsible for the decision, or (2) the trial judge is in a better position to make the decision because he can observe the parties. Neither circumstance is present here. First, in the Sentencing Reform Act the Legislature addressed concerns of judicial economy by authorizing appeal of only those sentences that are exceptional. Second, the Sentencing Reform Act has shifted the focus of a sentencing decision from observation of the individual defendant to objective consideration of statutory policies and guidelines. The length of an exceptional sentence thus should now be based on articulated factors instead of intuition, and a reviewing court can now weigh the factors considered by the trial court against the requirements of the act when it reviews a decision. * * *

The majority also rejects the Minnesota "doubling" rule. The Minnesota Supreme Court has ruled that generally a court that imposes a sentence outside of the sentencing guidelines should not impose a sentence more than double the presumptive sentence length. However, in "severe aggravating circumstances" the court will affirm longer sentences. In this case I would hold that "severe aggravating circumstances" support Oxborrow's 15–year sentence. * * *

However, even though I agree with the majority that in this case the trial court properly imposed a sentence more than twice the length of the presumptive sentence, I do not agree that this court should categorically reject Minnesota's rule. * * * When Minnesota's determinate sentencing guidelines first came into effect, many Minnesota judges were unused to the seemingly short sentences. These judges were not accustomed to the fact that determinate sentences represent "real" time, during which no opportunity for parole exists. As a result, Minnesota trial court judges frequently imposed sentences close to the statutory maximum in cases that did not warrant such long incarceration. The doubling rule has helped Minnesota judges impose sentences that are more uniform and proportional, and empirically closer to the standards established by the Minnesota Legislature. * * *

This court should follow the example of the Minnesota court and attempt to establish a body of common law principles for imposing exceptional sentences. The length of a Washington presumptive sentence often is only a fraction of the length of the statutory maximum sentence, and Washington judges are as unused to these short sentences as the Minnesota judges were. Without the doubling rule a trial court has no guidance whatsoever when deciding where to fix the exceptional sentence. The doubling rule is necessary to insure that the principled guidelines envisioned by the drafters of the Sentencing Reform Act become reality.

A major hope of those who have advocated sentencing reform of this type has been that it would produce a "common law" of sentencing, in which the time-honored methods of the common law-reasons for decisions, appellate review of those reasons and the further articulation and rearticulation of reasons in the light of new circumstances—would be applied to sentencing. * * * If this expectation is met, sentencing decisions in Washington will, to a significantly greater extent than ever before, be based on principle and guided by reason, and much of the promise of the reform will be realized.

The Washington Legislature chose to leave some discretionary power in the trial courts when it established the Sentencing Reform Act of 1981. Throughout the act, however, the Legislature balances discretion against guidelines and restrictions. Appellate review is the act's most important check on the discretionary power of trial court judges to impose exceptional sentences. I do not agree with the majority that this court should review exceptional sentences only for abuses of discretion. This court should adopt the Minnesota doubling rule, and this court shall also subject exceptional sentences to the full power of review.

PEOPLE v. STRINGHAM

California Court of Appeal, First District, 1988.
206 Cal.App.3d 184, 253 Cal.Rptr. 484.

POCHE, ACTING PRESIDING JUSTICE.

[Stringham appeals his conviction of second degree murder and kidnapping. The evidence at trial showed that Stringham and others beat and abducted Paul Snipes, whom they suspected of having "ripped them off." Stringham in particular participated in the brutal beating and passed a gun to a confederate who used it to kill Snipes. Stringham was originally charged with murder by torture, a capital offense, but the prosecutor agreed to accept a bargained guilty plea to voluntary manslaughter. The prosecutor explained that he was agreeing to reduce the charge because he might be unable to obtain the testimony of two key witnesses, including a detective (Williams) who had obtained a confession from Stringham but who had subsequently suffered a heart attack. Members of Snipes' family vigorously objected to the plea bargain, and accused the prosecutor and judge of bias because Stringham's mother was employed by the county probation department. The local trial judge disqualified himself, and a judge (Buffington) was brought in from another county to conduct the case. Judge Buffington indicated at a hearing on January 23, 1987, that he wanted further time to study the case before deciding what sentence to impose.]

After determining that Snipes' parents were present, Judge Buffington inquired of them "I take it that you and your family are saying that I should not accept this plea?" Mr. Snipes answered affirmatively, and said that he had been told by a probation officer "I had the right to make a statement here." Replying that "You will have a right," Judge Buffington was asked by Mr. Snipes if "the decision is to be made today whether to accept this plea today or not. Is that correct so far?" Judge Buffington responded "Yes, sir, basically," and then permitted Mr. Snipes to read a statement in which Mr. Snipes passionately excoriated the plea bargain * * * [and concluded by saying]: "Guy Stringham is a murderer and should be charged accordingly." Judge Buffington gave Mr. Snipes permission to "write a letter to the Court" with any additional comments. "I'll consider the letter. I'll consider your comments in making the decision that I have to make." After conferring with counsel for both sides regarding the materials he could examine to familiarize himself with the case, Judge Buffington continued matters until January 30th.

On January 30th the court conducted a hearing at which the parties earnestly requested acceptance of the plea bargain. The prosecutor outlined several perceived obstacles to convicting defendant for murder, one of the difficulties being the likely unavailability of Detective Williams. Judge Buffington, however, was unsatisfied that Williams could not be produced, and his review of the preliminary examination transcript and the other materials designated by the parties for his perusal persuaded him that "there's a case to be tried here." He therefore rejected the bargain and set a March trial date. [Detective Williams did testify at this trial. Defendant was convicted of second degree murder and kidnapping and given consecutive sentences.]

[The court held that Judge Buffington had authority to reject or accept the plea bargain at the sentencing hearing, and to postpone his decision until he had time to study the record and arguments.] * * * It is also at the sentencing hearing that the victim or the victim's next of kin may appear pursuant to § 1191.1.[10] That statute was enacted as part of an initiative measure entitled "The Victim's Bill of Rights," the general goal of which was to promote the rights of victims of crime. The specific goal of § 1191.1 was to mandate a previously optional procedure; to require the judge to listen to and consider the views of the victim. * * * § 1191.1 entitles victims and other designated persons to appear at "all sentencing proceedings." [Defendant argues] that matters had not proceeded to the sentencing stage where Mr. Snipes would be entitled to be heard.

The hearing Judge Buffington convened on January 23 was a "sentencing proceeding" within the meaning of § 1191.1. * * * In assuming that a "sentencing proceeding" involves nothing more than

10. Section 1191.1 provides in pertinent part: "The victim of any crime, or his or her parent or guardian if the victim is a minor, or the next of kin of the victim if the victim has died, has the right to attend all sentencing proceedings * * * and shall be given adequate notice by the probation officer of all sentencing proceedings concerning the person who committed the crime.

"The victim, or his or her parent or guardian if the victim is a minor, or next of kin has the right to appear, personally or by counsel, at the sentencing proceeding and to reasonably express his or her views concerning the crime, the person responsible, and the need for restitution. The court in imposing sentence shall consider the statements of victims, parents, or guardians, and next of kin made pursuant to this section and shall state on the record its conclusion concerning whether the person would pose a threat to public safety if granted probation. * * * "

the arraignment for judgment and the pronouncement of sentence, defendant gives too narrow a reading to the term. A sentencing proceeding is a concept of considerable flexibility. It may encompass motions for a new trial, motions in arrest of judgment and attacks on a plea of guilty. Doubts as to the defendant's sanity may be raised and resolved. Charges, enhancements, and special circumstance findings may be stricken. Supplemental probation reports may be ordered. * * * The manifest purpose of the electorate in enacting § 1191.1 would be frustrated if victims or next of kin were deprived of the opportunity to acquaint the court with their opinion concerning the propriety of a plea bargain. * * *

Defendant's attack on the substance of Mr. Snipes' remarks is also unavailing. In enacting § 1191.1 the people * * * gave Mr. Snipes the right "to reasonably express his * * * views concerning the crime, the person responsible, and the need for restitution." Mr. Snipes was not concerned with restitution, but he did have strong views regarding the crime and defendant's responsibility. The victim was not idealized ("He became addicted to drugs and did resort to thievery to support his addiction"), and in any event a murdered person's parent can hardly be expected to maintain an angelic impartiality. Mr. Snipes' remarks, which did not elicit a single objection from either the defense or the prosecution, were not hasty or ill-considered. * * * His bottomline conclusion ("Guy Stringham is a murderer and should be charged accordingly") dealt directly with defendant's responsibility and culpability for the crimes charged. Following his own independent examination, Judge Buffington agreed with that conclusion. More importantly, so did the jury.

Booth v. Maryland (1987) 482 U.S. 496, does not constitute a basis for invalidating Mr. Snipes' statement. The court in *Booth,* taking pains to limit its holding to capital cases, held that introduction of a "Victim Impact Statement" at the sentencing phase of a capital murder trial violated the Eighth Amendment because it "can serve no other purpose than to inflame the jury and divert it from deciding the case on the relevant evidence concerning the crime and the defendant." Mr. Snipes was not addressing the finder of fact at the sentencing phase of a capital trial.

Affirmed.

Note

The laws pertaining to criminal sentencing are different in every jurisdiction, and undergo frequent change. The cases in this subchapter are included to illustrate a variety of issues relating to the exercise and review of sentencing discretion.

During the 1950s and 1960s, expert opinion tended to favor indeterminate sentences with an emphasis upon rehabilitation of offenders. For example, the Model Penal Code (Official Draft 1962) disfavors mandatory minimum sentences, except possibly for murderers. Murder under the MPC is a felony of the first degree, for which a sentence with a life maximum and a 1 to 10 year minimum may be imposed. A section [§ 6.02(b)] makes murderers ineligible for probation, but the drafters put this section in parentheses to indicate that the American Law Institute "neither approved nor disapproved this formulation." With this tentative exception the Code makes all convicted persons eligible for probation, and even legislates a presumption in favor of a probationary disposition. Section 7.01 states that a sentencing court should not impose a sentence of imprisonment unless "imprisonment is necessary for protection of the public because:

> "(a) there is undue risk that during the period of a suspended sentence or probation the defendant will commit another crime; or
>
> "(b) the defendant is in need of correctional treatment that can be provided most effectively by his commitment to an institution; or
>
> "(c) a lesser sentence will depreciate the seriousness of the defendant's crime."

The Commentary states that "The Institute wholly rejected the idea that when public protection does not require imprisonment, the state is nevertheless justified in imposing the misery of prison on someone solely because the person has done something very bad and therefore 'deserves' a severe penalty." Rather, "The common sense of the matter, borne out in the main by available research, is that it is better to maintain the offender in the environment in which he must eventually learn to live rather than to place him in one that contains all of the artificial, and potentially harmful, factors of imprisonment." The decision to place quotation marks around the word "deserves" reflects the essential philosophy behind the Code: retribution or "just deserts" is obsolete and inhumane as a justification for imprisonment. The objectives of the Code are utilitarian rather than punitive: to deter offenses, to restrain and rehabilitate offenders, and to maintain public respect for the law. The same philosophical objectives lay behind the Institute's decision to expand the insanity defense, a subject explored in Chapter 4 of this book.

No state was as consistent in abandoning retributive or punitive sentencing policies as the Model Penal Code recommended, but many endorsed the basic concept that the duration of confinement should be discretionary and determined mainly by utilitarian considerations. Before 1976, California was the state most thoroughly committed to the idea that criminal sentences should be indeterminate. The judge merely sentenced the offender to "the term prescribed by law," which often was one year to life in prison. The actual period of confinement (and the subsequent period of parole supervision) was set by the Adult Authority, an administrative agency which exercised practically unsupervised discretion. The penological premise of the system was that the prisoner should be held until "cured" of his criminal propensities, but in fact the Adult Authority applied rules of thumb in most cases to make the punishment roughly fit the crime. The system was effective in inducing inmates to obey prison rules and giving them an incentive to participate in rehabilitative programs, although the degree of sincerity with which they did this was sometimes questionable. It was also useful in controlling the size of the prison population, since by shortening all sentences a few months the Authority could substantially reduce the prison population.

All this changed with the passage of the Determinate Sentencing Act of 1976. For most crimes short of murder, this Act provides for definite terms of confinement, with the judge having a narrow range of discretion to select the low, middle, or high term for the particular offense. Enhanced terms may be imposed for such things as weapons use, prior convictions, or multiple crimes. The system is extremely complex and confusing, and appellate courts in California now spend a great deal of their time resolving disputes about the interpretation of the Determinate Sentencing Act and its many subsequent amendments. Because the amendments have tended to raise the level of penalties, and because discretionary parole release is greatly restricted, the system is inflexible and is leading to a crisis of prison overcrowding. In part to relieve this pressure, and in part to restore the incentives to inmates to observe prison rules and participate in rehabilitative programs, the California Legislature has provided that an inmate may earn "good time" credits of up to 50 percent of the sentence.

The California experience illustrates the difficulties involved in having the legislature prescribe precise rules to govern the exercise of sentencing discretion. State legislators tend to have neither the time nor the background for developing a thoroughly rational and coherent sentencing scheme, and they are exposed to political pressures that tend to influence them to raise sentences above the level that the prison system can reasonably accommodate. These considerations have led some state legislatures to delegate the task of promulgating sentencing rules or guidelines to an independent commission, which presumably has more expertise and a degree of insulation from political pressure. The leading examples of states adopting this approach are Minnesota and Washington. The basic idea is that the sentencing commission provides guidelines to ensure consistency and rationality in sentencing, and the judges who actually impose the sentences either follow the guidelines or state reasons for departing from them. Sentences that depart from the guidelines can be appealed by either the prosecution or defense and will be modified if the appellate court determines that the stated reasons are insufficient to justify the departure.

The Federal Sentencing Guidelines, which are based in principle on the Minnesota model, went into effect in 1987. Judge Posner's opinion in United States v. Ely, supra, illustrates the practice in federal criminal cases under the system that previously prevailed. Judges had considerable discretion and could impose either definite or indefinite terms, and in either case the Parole Board had further discretion to determine the actual period of confinement. Appellate review of discretionary sentencing decisions was available only where the judge failed to exercise discretion at all (e.g. by sentencing everybody to the maximum), or where the judge expressly relied upon an unlawful consideration. As Judge Posner's opinion indicates, this system resulted in considerable disparity among similar offenders sentenced by different judges, with little hope for effective appellate review (although the Parole Board could mitigate unusually harsh sentences to some extent by granting early parole).

When Congress set up the United States Sentencing Commission in 1984, its principal goals were to reduce sentencing disparity and to provide "honesty in sentencing" by setting realistic terms of imprisonment which convicts would actually serve, as opposed to apparently lengthy sentences which were in practice largely negated by early parole release. The constitutionality of the mixed legislative-judicial role of the United States Sentencing Commission was strongly challenged as a violation of the separation of powers doctrine, but the Supreme Court upheld the Guidelines in United States v. Mistretta, 488 U.S. 361 (1989). For a good brief introduction to the Guidelines, see Breyer, "The Federal Sentencing Guidelines and the Key Compromises Upon Which They Rest," 17 Hofstra L. Rev. 1 (1988).

The Federal Sentencing Guidelines were greeted with hostility by some federal judges, whose objections often included the complaint that the Guidelines limited judicial discretion in sentencing. Consider, for example, the following description of the Guidelines found in a book co-authored by Judge Cabranes of the United States Court of Appeals for the Second Circuit: "But the new regime sought to strip [federal judges] of authority to determine the purposes of criminal sentencing, the factors relevant to sentencing, and the proper type and range of punishment in most cases." KATE STITH & JOSE A. CABRANES, FEAR OF JUDGING: SENTENCING GUIDELINES IN THE FEDERAL COURTS 1 (1998). See also, *Criticizing Sentencing Rules, U.S. Judge Resigns*, N.Y. TIMES, Sept. 30, 1990, at A22 (former U.S. District Court Judge J. Lawrence Irving, commenting that if he stayed on the bench he would have no choice but to follow the law, and concluding "I just can't, in good conscience, continue to do this."); Torry, Saundra, *Some Judges Decide a Lifetime on the Federal Bench is Too Long*, WASH. POST, Jan. 20, 1992, at F5 (quoting former U.S. District Court Judge Raul Ramirez as complaining that the guidelines turned judges into "nothing more than computers wearing robes").

The change from indeterminate to determinate sentencing reflects a shift away from the utilitarian and rehabilitative emphasis of the Model Penal Code. The California Determinate Sentencing Act, for example, stated explicitly in its Preamble that "the purpose of imprisonment is punishment." Today it is again respectable to say that convicted persons should receive the punishment they deserve, and the emphasis is on equality of treatment in the imposition of punishment rather than providing the minimum incarceration consistent with the protection of the public.

D. CAPITAL PUNISHMENT

INTRODUCTORY NOTE

At common law murder was subject to an automatic death sentence, subject of course to the sovereign prerogative of mercy. This rule prevailed in England until 1957. Mandatory death penalties were also characteristic of American law during the nation's early history. Where murder was divided into degrees, first degree murder was punished by death and second degree murder by lengthy imprisonment. During the nineteenth century, most American jurisdictions abandoned the mandatory death sentence for murder, and left the discretion to choose between death and imprisonment to the court or the jury. The situation as liberal reformers saw it in the late 1960's was described by the President's Commission on Law Enforcement and Administration of Justice in its *Task Force Report: The Courts* (1967):

> The most salient characteristic of capital punishment is that it is infrequently used. During 1966 only 1 person was executed in the United States; the trend over the last 36 years shows a substantial decline in the number of executions, from a high of 200 in 1935 to last year's low of 1. All available data indicate that judges, juries, and Governors are becoming increasingly reluctant to impose or authorize the carrying out of a death sentence. Only 67 persons were sentenced to death by the courts in 1965, half the number of death sentences imposed in 1961; and 62 prisoners were relieved of their death sentences by commutation, reversals of judgment, or other means. In some States in which the penalty exists on the statute books, there has not been an execution in decades.
>
> This decline in the application of the death penalty parallels a substantial decline in public and legislative support for capital punishment. According to the most recent Gallup Poll, conducted in 1966, 47 percent of those interviewed were opposed to the death penalty for murder, while 42 percent were in favor of it; a poll conducted in 1960 on the same question reported a majority in favor of the death penalty. Since 1964 five States effectively abolished capital punishment. There are now eight States in which the death penalty is completely unavailable and five States in which it may be imposed only for exceptional crimes such as murder of a prison guard or an inmate by a prisoner serving a life sentence, murder of a police officer, or treason. In 1965 Great Britain experimentally suspended use of the death penalty for five years. [The suspension of capital punishment in Great Britain continues to this day, although there is substantial public support for reviving it and the issue continues to be debated.]

The trend in public opinion was reversed in the 1980s, with polls measuring as high as 80% approval. As of 1967, however, it seemed to opponents of capital punishment that they would before long win the battle of public opinion and prevail in the legislatures. Meanwhile, they mounted a powerful legal attack in the federal courts against the enforcement of the death penalty. Four major points were at issue:

(1) *Exclusion of "scrupled" jurors.* Prosecutors in many jurisdictions were permitted to challenge for cause any prospective jurors who indicated that they were opposed to capital punishment or had conscientious scruples about imposing it. Because a large proportion of the population of the United States opposed the death penalty, such challenges increasingly resulted in juries unrepresentative of the community as a whole. Moreover, studies indicated that "death qualified" jurors tended to favor the police and prosecution on other issues as well, whereas persons voicing opposition to capital punishment frequently tended to be more sympathetic to the defense. In

other words, a jury inclined to sentence to death may also be inclined to convict. In Witherspoon v. Illinois, 391 U.S. 510 (1968), a majority of the Supreme Court held that "a sentence of death cannot be carried out if the jury that imposed or recommended it was chosen by excluding veniremen for cause simply because they voiced general objections to the death penalty or expressed conscientious or religious scruples against its infliction." Although it reversed the death sentence in the case before it, the Court declined to reverse the guilty verdict, finding the evidence before it insufficient to establish that "death qualified" juries were biased on the issue of guilt. The opinion also suggested that the states could continue to excuse jurors in capital cases who expressed a determination to vote automatically against imposing capital punishment without regard to the evidence, or who indicated that their attitude towards capital punishment would prevent them from making an impartial decision as to guilt or innocence.

(2) *Discriminatory Enforcement.* Studies by prominent sociologists gave academic support to the common perception that the death penalty for rape in southern states was discriminatorily enforced against black men convicted of raping white women. A federal Court of Appeals found the statistical evidence inadequate to support a finding that the death penalty was discriminatorily enforced in a particular Arkansas county, however. See Maxwell v. Bishop, 398 F.2d 138 (8th Cir.1968), reversed on other grounds 398 U.S. 262 (1970). The Supreme Court did not confront the question of discriminatory enforcement directly until its decision in McCleskey v. Kemp, 481 U.S. 279 (1987), by which time the Court had already held that the death penalty may not be imposed for crimes such as rape and robbery, which do not involve the taking of human life. In *McCleskey*, the Court rejected a claim based upon disputed statistical analyses that the death penalty was being imposed disproportionately upon defendants convicted of killing white victims.

(3) *Lack of Standards.* None of the states with discretionary capital punishment provided the court or jury with any legal standards to guide it in exercising its life or death decision. Discretion without standards is common in the area of criminal sentencing, but arguably the existence of unfettered and unguided discretion is particularly objectionable when a decision has to be made between life and death. In McGautha v. California, 402 U.S. 183 (1971), the Supreme Court found it "quite impossible to say that committing to the untrammelled discretion of the jury the power to pronounce life or death in capital cases is offensive to anything in the Constitution." The majority went on to observe that "The States are entitled to assume that jurors confronted with the truly awesome responsibility of decreeing death for a fellow human will act with due regard for the consequences of their decision and will consider a variety of factors, many of which will have been suggested by the evidence or by the arguments of defense counsel. For a court to attempt to

catalog the appropriate factors in this elusive area could inhibit rather than expand the scope of consideration, for no list of circumstances would ever be really complete. The infinite variety of cases and facets to each case would make general standards either meaningless 'boiler plate' or a statement of the obvious that no jury would need." 402 U.S. at 207–208.

(4) *Cruel and Unusual Punishment.* After the *McGautha* decision, most observers were surprised when the Court decided in Furman v. Georgia, 408 U.S. 238 (1972), that all the discretionary death penalty statutes then in effect violated the Eighth Amendment's prohibition of "cruel and unusual punishments," made applicable to the states by the Due Process Clause of the Fourteenth Amendment.

Each of the nine Justices wrote a separate opinion. Only Justices Brennan and Marshall argued that infliction of the death penalty under modern conditions was inherently unconstitutional. The three other Justices in the majority (Douglas, Stewart, and White) each held the death penalty statutes unconstitutional only on the ground that they were being applied arbitrarily and capriciously. Mr. Justice Stewart put it most vividly: "These death sentences are cruel and unusual in the same way that being struck by lightning is cruel and unusual. For, of all the people convicted of rapes and murders in 1967 and 1968, many just as reprehensible as these, the petitioners are among a capriciously selected random handful upon whom the sentence of death has in fact been imposed." 408 U.S. at 309–310. Mr. Justice White concluded that as "the death penalty is exacted with great infrequency even for the most atrocious crimes * * * there is no meaningful basis for distinguishing the few cases in which it is imposed from the many cases in which it is not." 408 U.S. at 313. Mr. Justice Douglas stressed the widely held belief that the supreme penalty is applied only to racial minorities, the poor, and other unprivileged persons. Chief Justice Burger and Justices Blackmun, Powell and Rehnquist dissented, arguing that whether capital punishment should be retained or abolished is a question for the Congress and the various state legislatures.

The *Furman* decision held unconstitutional only those statutes which imposed a standardless discretionary death penalty. Because the Court was so divided, the implications of the decision for other types of statutes were most unclear. Some states reacted to *Furman* by changing their laws to provide a mandatory death penalty in some circumstances. [Of course, such penalties are never truly mandatory, because of the possibility that prosecutors or juries will use their discretion to evade the law, and because of the possibility of executive clemency.] Other states added standards and procedural safeguards to their death penalty laws, but left the judge or jury some discretion. The constitutionality of these post-*Furman* statutes was at issue in the following case.

GREGG v. GEORGIA

Supreme Court of the United States, 1976.
428 U.S. 153, 96 S.Ct. 2909, 49 L.Ed.2d 859.

MR. JUSTICE STEWART, MR. JUSTICE POWELL, and MR. JUSTICE STEVENS announced the judgment of the Court and filed an opinion delivered by MR. JUSTICE STEWART.

I

[The prosecution's evidence at trial showed that Gregg and a companion named Allen were hitchhiking when they were picked up by Simmons and Moore. According to Allen, Gregg wantonly shot and killed Simmons and Moore for the purpose of robbery. Gregg testified and claimed that he shot the two men in self defense. The jury convicted Gregg on two counts of robbery and two counts of murder.]

At the penalty stage, which took place before the same jury, neither the prosecutor nor the petitioner's lawyer offered any additional evidence. Both counsel, however, made lengthy arguments dealing generally with the propriety of capital punishment under the circumstances and with the weight of the evidence of guilt. The trial judge instructed the jury that it could recommend either a death sentence or a life prison sentence on each count. The judge further charged the jury that in determining what sentence was appropriate the jury was free to consider the facts and circumstances presented by the parties, if any, in mitigation or aggravation.

Finally, the judge instructed the jury that it "would not be authorized to consider [imposing] the sentence of death" unless it first found beyond a reasonable doubt one of these aggravating circumstances:

One—That the offense of murder was committed while the offender was engaged in the commission o[f] two other capit[a]l felonies, to-wit the armed ro[b]bery of [Simmons and Moore].

Two—That the offender committed the offense of murder for the purpose of receiving money and the automobile described in the indictment.

Three—The offense of murder was outrageously and wantonly vile, horrible and inhuman, in that they [*sic*] involved the depravity of the mind of the defendant.

Finding the first and second of these circumstances, the jury returned verdicts of death on each count. The Supreme Court of Georgia affirmed the convictions and the imposition of the death sentences for murder. After reviewing the trial transcript and the record, including the evidence, and comparing the evidence and sentence in similar cases in accordance with the requirements of Georgia law, the court concluded that, considering the nature of the crime and the defendant, the sentences of death had not resulted from prejudice or any other arbitrary factor and were not excessive or disproportionate to the penalty applied in similar cases.

The death sentences imposed for armed robbery, however, were vacated on the grounds that the death penalty had rarely been imposed in Georgia for that offense and that the jury improperly considered the murders as aggravating circumstances for the robberies after having considered the armed robberies as aggravating circumstances for the murders.

We granted the petitioner's application for a writ of certiorari challenging the imposition of the death sentences in this case as "cruel and unusual" punishment in violation of the Eighth and the Fourteenth Amendments.

II

The Georgia statute, as amended after our decision in Furman v. Georgia, retains the death penalty for six categories of crime: murder, kidnapping for ransom or where the victim is harmed, armed robbery, rape, treason, and aircraft hijacking. The capital defendant's guilt or innocence is determined in the traditional manner, either by a trial judge or a jury, in the first stage of a bifurcated trial.

If trial is by jury, the trial judge is required to charge lesser included offenses when they are supported by any view of the evidence. After a verdict, finding, or plea of guilty to a capital crime, a presentence hearing is conducted before whomever made the determination of guilt. The sentencing procedures are essentially the same in both bench and jury trials. At the hearing:

> [T]he judge [or jury] shall hear additional evidence in extenuation, mitigation, and aggravation of punishment, including the record of any prior criminal convictions and pleas of guilty or pleas of nolo contendere of the defendant, or the absence of any prior conviction and pleas: Provided, however, that only such evidence in aggravation as the State has made known to the defendant prior to his trial shall be admissible. The judge [or jury] shall also hear argument by defendant or his counsel and the prosecuting attorney ... regarding the punishment to be imposed. § 27–2503. (Supp.1975).

The defendant is accorded substantial latitude as to the types of evidence that he may introduce. Evidence considered during the guilt stage may be considered during the sentencing stage without being resubmitted.

In the assessment of the appropriate sentence to be imposed the judge is also required to consider or to include in his instructions to the jury "any mitigating circumstances or aggravating circumstances otherwise authorized by law and any of [10] statutory aggravating circumstances which may be supported by the evidence...." § 27–2534.1(b) (Supp.1975). The scope of the nonstatutory aggravating or mitigating circumstances is not delineated in the statute. Before a convicted defendant may be sentenced to death, however, except in cases of treason or aircraft hijacking, the jury, or the trial judge in cases tried without a jury, must find beyond a reasonable doubt one of the 10 aggravating circumstances specified in the statute.[9] The sentence of death may be imposed only if the jury (or judge) finds one of the statutory aggravating circumstances and then elects to impose that sentence. If the verdict is death the jury or judge must specify the aggravating circumstance(s) found. In jury cases, the trial judge is bound by the jury's recommended sentence.

In addition to the conventional appellate process available in all criminal cases, provision is made for special expedited direct review by the Supreme Court of Georgia of the appropriateness of imposing the sentence of death in the particular case. The court is directed to consider

9. The statute provides in part:

"(a) The death penalty may be imposed for the offenses of aircraft hijacking or treason, in any case.

"(b) In all cases of other offenses for which the death penalty may be authorized, the judge shall consider, or he shall include in his instructions to the jury for it to consider, any mitigating circumstances or aggravating circumstances otherwise authorized by law and any of the following statutory aggravating circumstances which may be supported by the evidence:

"(1) The offense of murder, rape, armed robbery, or kidnapping was committed by a person with a prior record of conviction for a capital felony, or the offense of murder was committed by a person who has a substantial history of serious assaultive criminal convictions.

"(2) The offense of murder, rape, armed robbery, or kidnapping was committed while the offender was engaged in the commission of another capital felony, or aggravated battery, or the offense of murder was committed while the offender was engaged in the commission of burglary or arson in the first degree.

"(3) The offender by his act of murder, armed robbery, or kidnapping knowingly created a great risk of death to more than one person in a public place by means of a weapon or device which would normally be hazardous to the lives of more than one person.

"(4) The offender committed the offense of murder for himself or another, for the purpose of receiving money or any other thing of monetary value.

"(5) The murder of a judicial officer, former judicial officer, district attorney or solicitor or former district attorney or solicitor during or because of the exercise of his official duty.

"(6) The offender caused or directed another to commit murder or committed murder as an agent or employee of another person.

"(7) The offense of murder, rape, armed robbery, or kidnapping was outrageously or wantonly vile, horrible or inhuman in that it involved torture, depravity of mind, or an aggravated battery to the victim.

"(8) The offense of murder was committed against any peace officer, corrections employee or fireman while engaged in the performance of his official duties.

"(9) The offense of murder was committed by a person in, or who has escaped from, the lawful custody of a peace officer or place of lawful confinement.

"(10) The murder was committed for the purpose of avoiding, interfering with, or preventing a lawful arrest or custody in a place of lawful confinement, of himself or another.

"(c) The statutory instructions as determined by the trial judge to be warranted by the evidence shall be given in charge and in writing to the jury for its deliberation. The jury, if its verdict be a recommendation of death, shall designate in writing, signed by the foreman of the jury, the aggravating circumstance or circumstances which it found beyond a reasonable doubt. In nonjury cases the judge shall make such designation. Except in cases of treason or aircraft hijacking, unless at least one of the statutory aggravating circumstances enumerated in section 27–2534.1(b) is so found, the death penalty shall not be imposed." § 27–2534.1 (Supp.1975).

The Supreme Court of Georgia, in Arnold v. State, 236 Ga. 534, 224 S.E.2d 386 (1976), recently held unconstitutional the portion of the first circumstance encompassing persons who have a "substantial history of serious assaultive criminal convictions" because it did not set "sufficiently clear and objective standards."

"the punishment as well as any errors enumerated by way of appeal," and to determine:

(1) Whether the sentence of death was imposed under the influence of passion, prejudice, or any other arbitrary factor, and

(2) Whether, in cases other than treason or aircraft hijacking, the evidence supports the jury's or judge's finding of a statutory aggravating circumstance as enumerated in section 27.2534.1(b), and

(3) Whether the sentence of death is excessive or disproportionate to the penalty imposed in similar cases, considering both the crime and the defendant. § 27–2537 (Supp.1975).

If the court affirms a death sentence, it is required to include in its decision reference to similar cases that it has taken into consideration.

A transcript and complete record of the trial, as well as a separate report by the trial judge, are transmitted to the court for its use in reviewing the sentence. The report is in the form of a six and one-half page questionnaire, designed to elicit information about the defendant, the crime, and the circumstances of the trial. It requires the trial judge to characterize the trial in several ways designed to test for arbitrariness and disproportionality of sentence. Included in the report are responses to detailed questions concerning the quality of the defendant's representation, whether race played a role in the trial, and, whether, in the trial court's judgment, there was any doubt about the defendant's guilt or the appropriateness of the sentence. A copy of the report is served upon defense counsel. Under its special review authority, the court may either affirm the death sentence or remand the case for resentencing. In cases in which the death sentence is affirmed there remains the possibility of executive clemency.

III

We address initially the basic contention that the punishment of death for the crime of murder is, under all circumstances, "cruel and unusual" in violation of the Eighth and Fourteenth Amendments of the Constitution. * * *

[After reviewing the precedents, the plurality opinion concluded that the Eight Amendment's prohibition of cruel and unusual punishments must draw its meaning from "the evolving standards of decency which mark the progress of a maturing society," so that a particular form of punishment which was regarded as acceptable by the Framers of the Amendment may be nonetheless unconstitutional today. The plurality concluded that, to be acceptable under the Eighth Amendment, a punishment must not violate contemporary standards of decency, and it must accord with the "dignity of man," which means that it must not be "excessive." A punishment is excessive if it involves the unnecessary and wanton infliction of pain, or if it is grossly out of proportion to the seriousness of the crime. The plurality stated further, however, that it would presume the validity of any punishment selected by a democratically elected legislature, because the judgment of the legislature weighs heavily in ascertaining contemporary moral standards. Those who challenge such a legislative judgment bear a heavy burden of proof.]

Four years ago, the petitioners in *Furman* and its companion cases predicated their argument primarily upon the asserted proposition that standards of decency had evolved to the point where capital punishment no longer could be tolerated. * * * The petitioners in the capital cases before the Court today renew the "standards of decency" argument, but developments during the four years since *Furman* have undercut substantially the assumptions upon which their argument rested. Despite the continuing debate, dating back to the 19th century, over the morality and utility of capital punishment, it is now evident that a large proportion of American society continues to regard it as an appropriate and necessary criminal sanction.

The most marked indication of society's endorsement of the death penalty for murder is the legislative response to *Furman.* The legislatures of at least 35 States have enacted new statutes that provide for the death penalty for at least some crimes that result in the death of another person. And the Congress of the United States, in 1974, enacted a statute providing the death penalty for aircraft piracy that results in death. These recently adopted statutes have attempted to address the concerns expressed by the Court in *Furman* primarily (i) by specifying the factors to be weighed and the procedures to be followed in deciding when to impose a capital sentence, or (ii) by making the death penalty mandatory for specified crimes. But all of the post-*Furman* statutes make clear that capital punishment itself has not been rejected by the elected representatives of the people.

In the only statewide referendum occurring since *Furman* and brought to our attention, the people of California adopted a constitutional amendment that authorized capital punishment, in effect negating a prior ruling by the Supreme Court of California that the death penalty violated the California Constitution.

The jury also is a significant and reliable objective index of contemporary values because it is so directly involved. * * * It may be true that evolving standards have influenced juries in recent decades to be more discriminating in imposing the sentence of death. But the relative infrequency of jury verdicts imposing the death sentence does not indicate rejection of capital punishment *per se.* Rather, the reluctance of juries in many cases to impose the sentence may well reflect the humane feeling that this most irrevocable of sanctions should be reserved for a small number of extreme cases. Indeed, the actions of juries in many States since *Furman* is fully compatible with the legislative judgments, reflected in the new statutes, as to the continued utility and necessity of capital punishment in appropriate cases. At the close of 1974 at least 254 persons had been sentenced to death since *Furman,* and by the end of March 1976, more than 460 persons were subject to death sentences. * * *

The death penalty is said to serve two principal social purposes: retribution and deterrence of capital crimes by prospective offenders.

In part, capital punishment is an expression of society's moral outrage at particularly offensive conduct. This function may be unappealing to many, but it is essential in an ordered society that asks its citizens to rely on legal processes rather than self-help to vindicate their wrongs. * * * Retribution is no longer the dominant objective of the criminal law, but neither is it a forbidden objective nor one inconsistent with our respect for the dignity of men. Indeed, the decision that capital punishment may be the appropriate sanction in extreme cases is an expression of the community's belief that certain crimes are themselves so grievous an affront to humanity that the only adequate response may be the penalty of death.

Statistical attempts to evaluate the worth of the death penalty as a deterrent to crimes by potential offenders have occasioned a great deal of debate. The results simply have been inconclusive. * * * The value of capital punishment as a deterrent of crime is a complex factual issue the resolution of which properly rests with the legislatures, which can evaluate the results of statistical studies in terms of their own local conditions and with a flexibility of approach that is not available to the courts. Indeed, many of the post-*Furman* statutes reflect just such a responsible effort to define those crimes and those criminals for which capital punishment is most probably an effective deterrent.

In sum, we cannot say that the judgment of the Georgia legislature that capital punishment may be necessary in some cases is clearly wrong. * * * We hold that the death penalty is not a form of punishment that may never be imposed, regardless of the circumstances of the offense, regardless of the character of the offender, and regardless of the procedure followed in reaching the decision to impose it.

IV

We now consider whether Georgia may impose the death penalty on the petitioner in this case. * * *

[The plurality held that the Georgia statutory scheme previously described adequately protects against arbitrary or capricious death sentences because it (1) provides a bifurcated trial at which the defendant has an opportunity to present evidence relating to mitigation at a time when it can no longer prejudice him on the question of guilt; (2) provides standards (see footnote 9, supra) to guide the jury's decision which require the jury to consider the circumstances of the crime and the criminal before it recommends sentence; and (3) provides automatic appeal of death sentences to the state supreme court, which reviews each sentence to determine whether it was imposed under the influence of passion or prejudice, whether the evidence supports the jury's finding of a statutory aggravating circumstance, and whether the sentence is disproportionate compared to sentences imposed in similar cases. The plurality then rejected the petitioner's arguments that the statutory standards were too vague and broad to guide jury discretion effectively and that the existence of unchecked discretionary power in prosecutors, juries, and the Governor created a likelihood of arbitrary and capricious decisions.]

For the reasons expressed in this opinion, we hold that the statutory system under which Gregg was sentenced to death does not violate the Constitution. Accordingly, the judgment of the Georgia Supreme Court is affirmed.

It is so ordered.

MR. JUSTICE WHITE, with whom THE CHIEF JUSTICE and MR. JUSTICE REHNQUIST join, concurring in the judgment.

* * *

The threshold question in this case in whether the death penalty may be carried out for murder under the Georgia legislative scheme consistent with the decision in Furman v. Georgia, supra. In *Furman,* this Court held that as a result of giving the sentencer unguided discretion to impose or not to impose the death penalty for murder. The penalty was being imposed discriminatorily, wantonly and freakishly and so infrequently that any given death sentence was cruel and unusual. Petitioner argues that, as in *Furman,* the jury is still the sentencer; that the statutory criteria to be considered by the jury on the issue of sentence under Georgia's new statutory scheme are vague and do not purport to be all inclusive; and that, in any event, there are *no* circumstances under which the jury is required to impose the death penalty. Consequently, the petitioner argues that the death penalty will inexorably be imposed in as discriminatory, standardless, and rare a manner as it was imposed under the scheme declared invalid in *Furman.*

* * *

Petitioner also argues that decisions made by the prosecutor—either in negotiating a plea to some offense lesser than capital murder or in simply declining to charge capital murder—are standardless and will inexorably result in the wanton and freakish imposition of the penalty condemned by the judgment in *Furman.* I address this point separately because the cases in which no capital offense is charged escape the view of the Georgia Supreme Court and are not considered by it in determining whether a particular sentence is excessive or disproportionate.

Petitioner's argument that prosecutors behave in a standardless fashion in deciding which cases to try as capital felonies is unsupported by any facts. Petitioner simply asserts that since prosecutors have the power not to charge capital felonies they will exercise that power in a standardless fashion. This is untenable. Absent facts to the contrary it cannot be assumed that prosecutors will be motivated in their charging decision by factors other than the strength of their case and the likelihood that a jury would impose the death penalty if it convicts. Unless prosecutors are incompetent in their judgments the standards by which they decide whether to charge a capital felony will be the same as those by which the jury will decide the questions of guilt and sentence. Thus defendants will escape the death penalty through prosecutorial charging decisions only because the offense is not sufficiently serious; or because the proof is insufficiently strong. This does not cause the system to be standardless anymore than the jury's decision to impose life imprisonment on a defendant whose crime is deemed insufficiently serious or its decision to acquit someone who is probably guilty but whose guilt is not established beyond a reasonable doubt. Thus the prosecutor's charging decisions are unlikely to have removed from the sample of cases considered by the Georgia Supreme Court any which are truly "similar." If the cases really were "similar" in relevant respects it is unlikely that prosecutors would fail to prosecute them as capital cases; and I am unwilling to assume the contrary.

Petitioner's argument that there is an unconstitutional amount of discretion in the system which separates those suspects who receive the death penalty from those who receive life imprisonment a lesser penalty or are acquitted or never charged seems to be in final analysis an indictment of our entire system of justice. Petitioner has argued in effect that no matter how effective the death penalty may be as a punishment, government, created and run as it must be by humans, is inevitably incompetent to administer it. This cannot be accepted as a proposition of constitutional law. Imposition of the death penalty is surely an awesome responsibility for any system of justice and those who participate in it. Mistakes will be made and discriminations will occur which will be difficult to explain. However, one of society's most basic tasks is that of protecting the lives of its citizens and one of the most basic ways in which it achieves the task is through criminal laws against murder. I decline to interfere with the manner in which Georgia has chosen to enforce such laws on what is simply an assertion of lack of faith in the ability of the system of justice to operate in a fundamentally fair manner.

* * *

I therefore concur in the judgment of affirmance.

MR. JUSTICE BRENNAN, dissenting.

This Court inescapably has the duty, as the ultimate arbiter of the meaning of our Constitution, to say whether, when individuals condemned to death stand before our Bar, "moral concepts" require us to hold that the law has progressed to the point where we should declare that the punishment of death, like punishments on the rack, the screw and the wheel, is no longer morally tolerable in our civilized society. My opinion in Furman v. Georgia concluded that our civilization and the law had progressed to this point and that therefore the punishment of death, for whatever crime and under all circumstances, is "cruel and unusual" in violation of the Eighth and Fourteenth Amendments of the Constitution. I shall not again canvass the reasons that led to that conclusion. I emphasize only that foremost among the "moral concepts" recognized in our cases and inherent in the Clause is the primary moral principle that the State, even as it punishes, must treat its citizens in a manner consistent with their intrinsic worth as human beings—a punishment must not be so severe as to be degrading to human dignity. A judicial determination whether the punishment of death comports with human dignity is therefore not only permitted but compelled by the Clause. * * *

The fatal constitutional infirmity in the punishment of death is that it treats members of the human race as nonhumans, as objects to be toyed with and discarded. It is thus inconsistent with the fundamental premise of the Clause that even the vilest criminal remains a human being possessed of common human dignity. As such it is a penalty that subjects the individual to a fate forbidden by the principle of civilized treatment guaranteed by the Clause. * * *

MR. JUSTICE MARSHALL, dissenting.

In *Furman* I concluded that the death penalty is constitutionally invalid for two reasons. First, the death penalty is excessive. And second, the American people, fully informed as to the purposes of the death penalty and its liabilities, would in my view reject it as morally unacceptable.

Since the decision in *Furman,* the legislatures of 35 States have enacted new statutes authorizing the imposition of the death sentence for certain crimes, and Congress has enacted a law providing the death penalty for air piracy resulting in death. I would be less than candid if I did not acknowledge that these developments have a significant bearing on a realistic assessment of the moral acceptability of the death penalty to the American people. But if the constitutionality of the death penalty turns, as I have urged, on the opinion of an *informed* citizenry, then even the enactment of new death statutes cannot be viewed as conclusive. In *Furman,* I observed that the American people are largely unaware of the information critical to a judgment on the morality of the death penalty, and concluded that if they were better informed they would consider it shocking, unjust, and unacceptable. * * *

Even assuming, however, that the post-*Furman* enactment statutes authorizing the death penalty renders the prediction of the views of an informed citizenry an uncertain basis for a constitutional decision, the enactment of those statutes has no bearing whatsoever on the conclusion that the death penalty is unconstitutional because it is excessive. An excessive penalty is invalid under the Cruel and Unusual Punishments Clause "even though popular sentiment may favor" it. The inquiry here, then, is simply whether the death penalty is necessary to accomplish the legitimate legislative purposes in punishment, or whether a less severe penalty—life imprisonment-would do as well.

The two purposes that sustain the death penalty as nonexcessive in the Court's view are general deterrence and retribution. In *Furman,* I canvassed the relevant data on the deterrent effect of capital punishment. The available evidence was convincing that capital punishment is not necessary as a deterrent to crime in our society.

* * *

The other principal purpose said to be served by the death penalty is retribution. * * * The concept of retribution is a multifaceted one, and any discussion of its role in the criminal law must be undertaken with caution. On one level, it can be said that the notion of retribution or reprobation is the basis of our insistence that only those who have broken the law be punished, and in this sense the notion is quite obviously central to a just system of criminal sanctions. But our recognition that retribution plays a crucial role in determining who may be punished by no means requires approval of retribution as a general justification for punishment. It is the question whether retribution can provide a moral justification for punishment—in particular, capital punishment—that we must consider.

My Brothers STEWART, POWELL, and STEVENS offer the following explanation of the retributive justification for capital punishment:

> "The instinct for retribution is part of the nature of man, and channeling that instinct in the administration of criminal justice serves an important purpose in promoting the stability of a society governed by law. When people begin to believe that organized society is unwilling or unable to impose upon criminal offenders the punishment they 'deserve,' then there are sown the seeds of anarchy—of self-help, vigilante justice, and lynch law."
>
> This statement is wholly inadequate to justify the death penalty. As my Brother BRENNAN stated in *Furman,* "there is no evidence whatever that utilization of imprisonment rather than death encourages private blood feuds and other disorders." It simply defies belief to suggest that the death penalty is necessary to prevent the American people from taking the law into their own hands.

In a related vein, it may be suggested that the expression of moral outrage through the imposition of the death penalty serves to reinforce basic moral values—that it marks some crimes as particularly offensive and therefore to be avoided. The argument is akin to a deterrence argument, but differs in that it contemplates the individual's shrinking from anti-social conduct not because he fears punishment, but because he has been told in the strongest possible way that the conduct is wrong. This contention, like the previous one, provides no support for the death penalty. It is inconceivable that any individual concerned about conforming his conduct to what society says is "right" would fail to realize that murder is "wrong" if the penalty were simply life imprisonment.

The foregoing contentions—that society's expression of moral outrage through the imposition of the death penalty preempts the citizenry from taking the law into its own hands and reinforces moral values—are not retributive in the purest sense. They are essentially utilitarian in that they portray the death penalty as valuable because of its beneficial results. These justifications for the death penalty are inadequate because the penalty is, quite clearly I think, not necessary to the accomplishment of those results.

There remains for consideration, however, what might be termed the purely retributive justification for the death penalty—that the death penalty is appropriate, not because of its beneficial effect on society, but because the taking of the murderer's life is itself morally good. Some of the language of the plurality's opinion appears positively to embrace this notion of retribution for its own sake as a justification for capital punishment. * * *

Of course it may be that these statements are intended as no more than observations as to the popular demands that it is thought must be responded to in order to prevent anarchy. But the implication of the statements appears to me to be quite different—namely, that society's judgment that the murderer "deserves" death must be respected not simply because the preservation of order requires it, but because it is appropriate that society make the judgment and carry it out. It is this latter notion, in particular, that I consider to be fundamentally at odds with the Eighth Amendment. The mere fact that the community demands the murderer's life in return for the evil he has done cannot sustain the death penalty, for as the plurality reminds us "the Eighth Amendment demands more than that a challenged punishment be acceptable to contemporary society." To be sustained under the Eighth Amendment, the death penalty must "[comport] with the basic concept of human dignity at the core of the Amendment," and the objective in imposing it must be "[consistent] with our respect for the dignity of other men." Under these standards, the taking of life "because the wrong-doer deserves it" surely must fall, for such a punishment has as its very basis the total denial of the wrongdoer's dignity and worth.

Note

On the same day that it decided Gregg v. Georgia, the Supreme Court struck down the death penalty statutes of North Carolina and Louisiana. The North Carolina statute provided a mandatory death sentence for all persons convicted of first degree murder. The Louisiana statute also provided a mandatory sentence for first degree murder, but defined this crime more restrictively than other states and required that the jury be instructed on second degree murder and manslaughter in every capital case without regard to whether the evidence provided any basis for such instructions. The Justices who formed the plurality in Gregg v. Georgia held that mandatory death sentences for all persons convicted of a particular crime without regard to individual circumstances depart markedly from contemporary standards of decency and invite unchecked jury discretion in the form of nullification of the letter of the law. The plurality observed that states had enacted mandatory death statutes after the *Furman* decision not because the legislators or voters really wished to do so, but because they interpreted Furman v. Georgia to require the elimination of discretion. Justices Marshall and Brennan, who opposed capital punishment in any form, joined with the three Justices in the plurality to hold the North Carolina and Louisiana statutes unconstitutional. Woodson v. North Carolina, 428 U.S. 280 (1976); Roberts v. Louisiana, 428 U.S. 325 (1976).

The Supreme Court narrowed the circumstances under which capital punishment may be imposed in Coker v. Georgia, 433 U.S. 584 (1977). Coker escaped from a Georgia prison, where he had been serving various sentences for murder, rape, kidnapping, and aggravated assault. Shortly after the escape he raped and kidnapped an adult woman at knife point after robbing her husband. The jury found aggravating circumstances and sentenced Coker to death. The Supreme Court reversed. The plurality opinion for four Justices held that a sentence of death for the crime of rape of an adult woman was grossly disproportionate and excessive punishment forbidden by the Cruel and Unusual Punishment clause. The plurality reasoned that rape does not compare in seriousness with murder because it does not involve the taking of human life. Justices Brennan and Marshall concurred, holding to their view that the death penalty is always unconstitutional, and Justice Powell concurred separately on the ground that the death penalty may not be imposed for a rape unless it was committed with excessive brutality or with serious, lasting harm to the victim. Chief Justice Burger dissented in an opinion joined by Mr. Justice Rehnquist.

In Lockett v. Ohio, 438 U.S. 586 (1978), the Supreme Court reviewed a case in which an Ohio judge sentenced to death a woman convicted of driving the getaway car in a pawn shop robbery in the course of which another robber, Parker, had shot and killed the pawnbroker. The Ohio death penalty statute had been revised after *Furman* to eliminate the discretion which that case had seemed to condemn. As revised, it required the judge to impose a death sentence for such a felony murder unless he found by a preponderance of the evidence that (1) the victim had induced or facilitated the offense; or (2) it was unlikely that the defendant would have committed the offense but for the fact that she was "under duress, coercion, or strong provocation;" or (3) the offense was primarily the product of her psychosis or mental deficiency. The judge found that none of these circumstances were present and that he was therefore required to impose a death sentence. The state's primary witness was Parker, who pleaded guilty and testified against Lockett pursuant to a plea bargain by which he escaped the death penalty. The prosecutor offered to permit Lockett herself to plead guilty to voluntary manslaughter and aggravated robbery, with a 25–year maximum, but she rejected the offer. The Supreme Court overturned the death sentence on the ground that the Ohio statute unduly limited the mitigating circumstances which should be considered on behalf of the defendant in a capital case. See also, Eddings v. Oklahoma, 455 U.S. 104 (1982).

Disputes continue to arise about what information a jury can or must consider in capital punishment cases. For example, in Simmons v. South Carolina, 512 U.S. 154 (1994), the Supreme Court held that when the defendant's future dangerousness was an issue for jury consideration, and the only alternative punishments available were either the death penalty or life imprisonment without the possibility of parole, due process required that the jury must be informed of the defendant's ineligibility for parole. Subsequent amendments to the South Carolina death penalty statute provided that if a jury failed to agree unanimously that the prosecution had proven the existence of a statutory aggravating circumstance beyond a reasonable doubt, the jury made no sentencing recommendation and the trial judge could sentence the defendant either to life imprisonment or a mandatory minimum sentence of thirty years. On the other hand, if the jury found that an aggravating circumstance existed, it could either recommend the death penalty or life imprisonment. The South Carolina statute specified that "life imprisonment means until death of the offender." In Shafer v. South Carolina, 532 U.S. 36 (2001), the defendant had been sentenced to death under this statute after the trial judge had refused to instruct the jury on parole ineligibility if an aggravating circumstance was found to exist, even after the deliberating jury sent the trial judge questions asking whether someone convicted of murder could become eligible for parole. The Supreme Court reversed the death sentence, finding that "South Carolina has consistently refused to inform the jury of a capital defendant's parole eligibility status," and reaffirming that a sentencing jury must be informed that a life sentence carries no possibility of parole "whenever future dangerousness is at issue in a capital sentencing proceeding." The Supreme Court reversed yet another South Carolina death sentence on the same grounds during its next term. Kelly v. South Carolina, 534 U.S. 246 (2002).

ARAVE v. CREECH

Supreme Court of the United States, 1993.
507 U.S. 463, 113 S.Ct. 1534, 123 L.Ed.2d 188.

JUSTICE O'CONNOR delivered the opinion of the Court.

I

The facts underlying this case could not be more chilling. Thomas Creech has admitted to killing or participating in the killing of at least 26 people. The bodies of 11 of his victims—who were shot, stabbed, beaten, or strangled to death—have been recovered in seven States. Creech has said repeatedly that, unless he is completely isolated from humanity, he likely will continue killing. And he has identified by name three people outside prison walls he intends to kill if given the opportunity.

Creech's most recent victim was David Dale Jensen, a fellow inmate in the maximum security unit of the Idaho State Penitentiary. When he killed Jensen, Creech was already serving life sentences for other first-degree murders. Jensen, about seven years Creech's junior, was a nonviolent car thief. He was also physically handicapped. Part of Jensen's brain had been removed prior to his incarceration, and he had a plastic plate in his skull.

The circumstances surrounding Jensen's death remain unclear, primarily because Creech has given conflicting accounts of them. In one version, Creech killed Jensen in self defense. In another—the version that Creech gave at his sentencing hearing—other inmates offered to pay Creech or help him escape if he killed Jensen. Creech, through an intermediary, provided Jensen with makeshift weapons and then arranged for Jensen to attack him, in order to create an excuse for the killing. Whichever of these accounts (if either) is true, the Idaho Supreme Court found that the record supported the following facts:

> "Jensen approached Creech and swung a weapon at him which consisted of a sock containing batteries. Creech took the weapon away from Jensen, who returned to his cell but emerged with a toothbrush to which had been taped a razor blade. When the two men again met, Jensen made some movement toward Creech, who then struck Jensen between the eyes with the battery laden sock, knocking Jensen to the floor. The fight continued, according to Creech's version, with Jensen swinging the razor blade at Creech and Creech hitting Jensen with the battery filled sock. The plate imbedded in Jensen's skull shattered, and blood from Jensen's skull was splashed on the floor and walls. Finally, the sock broke and the batteries fell out, and by that time Jensen was helpless. Creech then commenced kicking Jensen about the throat and head. Sometime later a guard noticed blood, and Jensen was taken to the hospital, where he died the same day." State v. Creech, 670 P.2d 463, 465 (Idaho 1983), cert. denied, 465 U.S. 1051 (1984).

Creech pleaded guilty to first-degree murder. The trial judge held a sentencing hearing in accordance with Idaho Code § 19–2515(d) (1987). After the hearing, the judge issued written findings in the format prescribed by Rule 33.1 of the Idaho Criminal Rules. Under the heading "Facts and Argument Found in Mitigation," he listed that Creech "did not instigate the fight with the victim, but the victim, without provocation, attacked him. [Creech] was initially justified in protecting himself." Under the heading "Facts and Argument Found in Aggravation," the judge stated:

> "The victim, once the attack commenced, was under the complete domination and control of the defendant. The murder itself was extremely gruesome evidencing an excessive violent rage. With the victim's attack as an excuse, the ... murder then took on many aspects of an assassination. These violent actions ... went well beyond self-defense. ..."

"... The murder, once commenced, appears to have been an intentional, calculated act."

The judge then found beyond a reasonable doubt five statutory aggravating circumstances, including that Creech, "by the murder, or circumstances surrounding its commission, ... exhibited utter disregard for human life." He observed in this context that "after the victim was helpless [Creech] killed him." Ibid. Next, the judge concluded that the mitigating circumstances did not outweigh the aggravating circumstances. Reiterating that Creech "intentionally destroyed another human being at a time when he was completely helpless," the judge sentenced Creech to death.

After temporarily remanding for the trial judge to impose sentence in open court in Creech's presence, the Idaho Supreme Court affirmed. The court rejected Creech's argument that the "utter disregard" circumstance is unconstitutionally vague, reaffirming the limiting construction it had placed on the statutory language in State v. Osborn, 631 P.2d 187 (Idaho 1981): * * * "We conclude that the phrase is meant to be reflective of acts or circumstances surrounding the crime which exhibit the highest, the utmost, callous disregard for human life, i.e., the cold-blooded, pitiless slayer." *Creech*, supra, at 370, (quoting *Osborn*, supra, at 418–419).

After independently reviewing the record, the Idaho Supreme Court also held that the evidence clearly supported the trial judge's findings of aggravating and mitigating circumstances, including the finding that Creech had exhibited "utter disregard for human life." Then, as required by Idaho law, the court compared Creech's case to similar cases in order to determine whether his sentence was excessive or disproportionate. The court emphatically concluded that it was not: "We have examined cases dating back more than 50 years and our examination fails to disclose that any such remorseless, calculating, cold-blooded multiple murderer has ... ever been before this Court."

[Creech filed a petition for writ of habeas corpus in federal court.] The Court of Appeals for the Ninth Circuit agreed with Creech that the "utter disregard" circumstance is unconstitutionally vague. 947 F.2d 873 (1991). * * *

II

This case is governed by the standards we articulated in Walton v. Arizona, 497 U.S. 639 (1990), and Lewis v. Jeffers, 497 U.S. 764 (1990). In *Jeffers* we reaffirmed the fundamental principle that, to satisfy the Eighth and Fourteenth Amendments, a capital sentencing scheme must "suitably direct and limit" the sentencer's discretion" so as to minimize the risk of wholly arbitrary and capricious action." The State must "channel the sentencer's discretion by clear and objective standards that provide specific and detailed guidance, and that make rationally reviewable the process for imposing a sentence of death."

In *Walton* we set forth the inquiry that a federal court must undertake when asked to decide whether a particular aggravating circumstance meets these standards:

> "The federal court ... must first determine whether the statutory language defining the circumstance is itself too vague to provide any guidance to the sentencer. If so, then the federal court must attempt to determine whether the state courts have further defined the vague terms and if they have done so, whether those definitions are constitutionally sufficient, i.e., whether they provide some guidance to the sentencer."

Where, as in Idaho, the sentencer is a judge rather than a jury, the federal court must presume that the judge knew and applied any existing narrowing construction. Id., at 653.

Unlike the Court of Appeals, we do not believe it is necessary to decide whether the statutory phrase "utter disregard for human life" itself passes constitutional muster. The Idaho Supreme Court has adopted a limiting construction, and we believe that construction meets constitutional requirements.

Contrary to the dissent's assertions, the phrase "cold-blooded, pitiless slayer" is not without content. Webster's Dictionary defines "pitiless" to mean devoid of, or unmoved by, mercy or compassion. The lead entry for "cold-blooded" gives coordinate definitions. One, "marked by absence of warm feelings: without consideration, compunction, or clemency," mirrors the definition of "pitiless." The other defines "cold-blooded" to mean "matter of fact, emotionless." It is true that "cold-blooded" is sometimes also used to describe "premeditation," Black's Law Dictionary 260 (6th ed. 1990)—a mental state that may coincide with, but is distinct from, a lack of feeling or compassion. But premeditation is clearly not the sense in which the Idaho Supreme Court used the word "cold-blooded" in *Osborn*. Other terms in the limiting construction—"callous" and "pitiless"—indicate that the court used the word "cold-blooded" in its first sense. "Premeditation," moreover, is specifically addressed elsewhere in the Idaho homicide statutes; had the *Osborn* court meant premeditation, it likely would have used the statutory language.

In ordinary usage, then, the phrase "cold-blooded, pitiless slayer" refers to a killer who kills without feeling or sympathy. We assume that legislators use words in their ordinary, everyday senses, and there is no reason to suppose that judges do otherwise. The dissent questions our resort to dictionaries for the common meaning of the word "cold-blooded," but offers no persuasive authority to suggest that the word, in its present context, means anything else.

The Court of Appeals thought the *Osborn* limiting construction inadequate not because the phrase "cold-blooded, pitiless slayer" lacks meaning, but because it requires the sentencer to make a "subjective determination." We disagree. We are not faced with pejorative adjectives such as "especially heinous, atrocious, or cruel" or "outrageously or wantonly vile, horrible and in-human"—terms that describe a crime as a whole and that this Court has held to be unconstitutionally vague. See, e. g., Shell v. Mississippi, 498 U.S. 1 (1990) (per curiam). The terms "cold-blooded" and "pitiless" describe the defendant's state of mind: not his mens rea, but his attitude toward his conduct and his victim. The law has long recognized that a defendant's state of mind is not a "subjective" matter, but a fact to be inferred from the surrounding circumstances. * * *

Determining whether a capital defendant killed without feeling or sympathy is undoubtedly more difficult than, for example, determining whether he was previously convicted of another murder. But that does not mean that a State cannot, consistent with the Federal Constitution, authorize sentencing judges to make the inquiry and to take their findings into account when deciding whether capital punishment is warranted. This is the import of *Walton*. In that case we considered

Arizona's "especially heinous, cruel, or depraved" circumstance. The Arizona Supreme Court had held that a crime is committed in a "depraved" manner when the perpetrator "relishes the murder, evidencing debasement or perversion," or "shows an indifference to the suffering of the victim and evidences a sense of pleasure in the killing." We concluded that this construction adequately guided sentencing discretion, even though "the proper degree of definition of an aggravating factor of this nature is not susceptible of mathematical precision." 497 U.S. at 655.

The language at issue here is no less "clear and objective" than the language sustained in *Walton*. Whether a defendant "relishes" or derives "pleasure" from his crime arguably may be easier to determine than whether he acts without feeling or sympathy, since enjoyment is an affirmative mental state, whereas the cold-bloodedness inquiry in a sense requires the sentencer to find a negative. But we do not think so subtle a distinction has constitutional significance. The *Osborn* limiting construction, like the one upheld in *Walton*, defines a state of mind that is ascertainable from surrounding facts. Accordingly, we decline to invalidate the "utter disregard" circumstance on the ground that the Idaho Supreme Court's limiting construction is insufficiently "objective."

Of course, it is not enough for an aggravating circumstance, as construed by the state courts, to be determinate. Our precedents make clear that a State's capital sentencing scheme also must "genuinely narrow the class of defendants eligible for the death penalty." Zant v. Stephens, 462 U.S. 862, 877 (1983). When the purpose of a statutory aggravating circumstance is to enable the sentencer to distinguish those who deserve capital punishment from those who do not, the circumstance must provide a principled basis for doing so. If the sentencer fairly could conclude that an aggravating circumstance applies to every defendant eligible for the death penalty, the circumstance is constitutionally infirm. See Cartwright, 486 U.S. at 364 (invalidating aggravating circumstance that "an ordinary person could honestly believe" described every murder); Godfrey, 446 U.S. 420 at 428–429 ("A person of ordinary sensibility could fairly characterize every murder as 'outrageously or wantonly vile, horrible and inhuman' ").

Although the question is close, we believe the *Osborn* construction satisfies this narrowing requirement. The class of murderers eligible for capital punishment under Idaho law is defined broadly to include all first-degree murderers. And the category of first-degree murderers is also broad. It includes premeditated murders and those carried out by means of poison, lying in wait, or certain kinds of torture. In addition, murders that otherwise would be classified as second degree,—including homicides committed without "considerable provocation" or under circumstances demonstrating "an abandoned and malignant heart" (a term of art that refers to unintentional homicide committed with extreme recklessness),—become first degree if they are accompanied by one of a number of enumerated circumstances. For example, murders are classified as first degree when the victim is a fellow prison inmate, or a law enforcement or judicial officer performing official duties; when the defendant is already serving a sentence for murder; and when the murder occurs during a prison escape, or the commission or attempted commission of arson, rape, robbery, burglary, kidnapping, or mayhem. In other words, a sizable class of even those murderers who kill with some provocation or without specific intent may receive the death penalty under Idaho law.

We acknowledge that, even within these broad categories, the word "pitiless," standing alone, might not narrow the class of defendants eligible for the death penalty. A sentencing judge might conclude that every first-degree murderer is "pitiless," because it is difficult to imagine how a person with any mercy or compassion could kill another human being without justification. Given the statutory scheme, however, we believe that a sentencing judge reasonably could find that not all Idaho capital defendants are "cold-blooded." That is because some within the broad class of first-degree murderers do exhibit feeling. Some, for example, kill with anger, jealousy, revenge, or a variety of other emotions. In *Walton* we held that Arizona could treat capital defendants who take pleasure in killing as more deserving of the death penalty than those who do not. Idaho similarly has identified the subclass of defendants who kill without feeling or sympathy as more deserving of death. By doing so, it has narrowed in a meaningful way the category of defendants upon whom capital punishment may be imposed.

Creech argues that the Idaho courts have not applied the "utter disregard" circumstance consistently. He points out that the courts have found defendants to exhibit "utter disregard" in a wide range of cases. This, he claims, demonstrates that the circumstance is nothing more than a catch-all. The dissent apparently agrees. The State, in turn, offers its own review of the cases and contends that they are consistent. In essence, the parties and the dissent would have us determine the facial constitutionality of the "utter disregard" circumstance, as construed in *Osborn*, by examining applications of the circumstance in cases not before us.

As an initial matter, we do not think the fact that "all kinds of ... factors," may demonstrate the requisite state of mind renders the *Osborn* construction facially invalid. That the Idaho courts may find first-degree murderers to be "cold-blooded" and "pitiless" in a wide range of circumstances is unsurprising. It also is irrelevant to the question before us. * * * The Idaho Supreme Court upheld Creech's death sentence in 1983—before it had applied *Osborn* to any other set of facts. None of the decisions on which the dissent relies, or upon which Creech asks us to invalidate his death sentence, influenced either the trial judge who sentenced Creech or the appellate judges who upheld the sentence. And there is no question that Idaho's formulation of its limiting construction has been consistent. The Idaho Supreme Court has reaffirmed its original interpretation of "utter disregard" repeatedly, often reciting the definition given in *Osborn* verbatim. * * * In light of the consistent narrowing definition given the "utter disregard" circumstance by the Idaho Supreme Court, we are satisfied that the circumstance, on its face, meets constitutional standards.

III

Creech argues alternatively that the "utter disregard" circumstance, even if facially valid, does not apply to him. He suggests—as did the Court of Appeals and as does the dissent,—that the trial judge's findings that he was provoked and that he exhibited an "excessive violent rage" are irreconcilable with a finding of "utter disregard." The Idaho Supreme Court, Creech claims, did not cure the error on appeal. There also appears to be some question whether the other murders that Creech has committed, and the self-defense explanations he has offered for some of them, bear on the "utter disregard" determination.

These are primarily questions of state law. * * * The posture of the case, moreover, makes it unnecessary for us to reach the remaining arguments. The Court of Appeals granted Creech relief on two other claims: that the trial judge improperly refused to allow him to present new mitigating evidence when he was resentenced in open court, and that the judge applied two aggravating circumstances without making a finding required under state law. On the basis of the first claim, Creech is entitled to resentencing in state trial court. Accordingly, we hold today only that the "utter disregard" circumstance, as defined in *Osborn*, on its face meets constitutional requirements. The judgment of the Court of Appeals is therefore reversed in part and the case remanded for proceedings consistent with this opinion.

It is so ordered.

JUSTICE BLACKMUN, with whom JUSTICE STEVENS joins, dissenting.

* * * The Idaho Supreme Court has determined that under our cases Idaho's statutory phrase, "utter disregard for human life," requires a limiting construction, and respondent does not challenge the Court of Appeals' conclusion that the phrase, unadorned, fails to meet constitutional standards. This is understandable. Every first-degree murder will demonstrate a lack of regard for human life, and there is no cause to believe that some murders somehow demonstrate only partial, rather than "utter" disregard. Nor is there any evidence that the phrase is intended to have a specialized meaning—other than that presented by the Idaho Supreme Court in its limiting constructions—that might successfully narrow the eligible class. The question is whether *Osborn's* limiting construction saves the statute.

Under *Osborn*, an offense demonstrates "utter disregard for human life" when the "acts or circumstances surrounding the crime . . . exhibit the highest, the utmost, callous disregard for human life, i.e., the cold-blooded, pitiless slayer." Jettisoning all but the term, "cold-blooded," the majority contends that this cumbersome construction clearly singles out the killing committed "without feeling or sympathy." As an initial matter, I fail to see how "without feeling or sympathy" is meaningfully different from "devoid of ... mercy or compassion"—the definition of "pitiless" that the majority concedes to be constitutionally inadequate.

Even if there is a distinction, however, the "without feeling or sympathy" test, which never has been articulated by any Idaho Court, does not flow ineluctably from the phrase at issue in this case: "cold-blooded." I must stress in this regard the rather obvious point that a "facial" challenge of this nature—one alleging that a limiting construction provides inadequate guidance—cannot be defeated merely by a demonstration that there exists a narrowing way to apply the contested language. The entire point of the challenge is that the language's susceptibility to a variety of interpretations is what makes it (facially) unconstitutional. To save the statute, the State must provide a construction that, on its face, reasonably can be expected to be applied in a consistent and meaningful way so as to provide the sentencer with adequate guidance. The metaphor "cold-blooded" does not do this. * * *

In its eagerness to boil the phrase down to a serviceable core, the majority virtually ignores the very definition it cites. Instead, the majority comes up with a hybrid all its own—"without feeling or sympathy"—and then goes one step further, asserting that because the term "cold-blooded" so obviously means "without feeling," it cannot refer as ordinarily understood to murderers who "kill with anger, jealousy, revenge, or a variety of other emotions." That is incorrect. In everyday parlance, the term "cold-blooded" routinely is used to describe killings that fall outside the majority's definition. In the first nine weeks of this year alone, the label "cold-blooded" has been applied to a murder by an ex-spouse angry over visitation rights, a killing by a jealous lover, a revenge killing, an ex-spouse "full of hatred," the close-range assassination of an enemy official by a foe in a bitter ethnic conflict, a murder prompted by humiliation and hatred, killings by fanatical cult members, a murderer who enjoyed killing, and, perhaps most appropriately, all murders. [Citing newspaper articles] All these killings occurred with "feelings" of one kind or another. All were described as cold-blooded. The majority's assertion that the Idaho construction narrows the class of capital defendants because it rules out those who "kill with anger, jealousy, revenge, or a variety of other emotions" clearly is erroneous, because in ordinary usage the nebulous description "cold-blooded" simply is not limited to defendants who kill without emotion.

In legal usage, the metaphor "cold blood" does have a specific meaning. "Cold blood" is used "to designate a willful, deliberate, and premeditated homicide." Black's Law Dictionary 260 (6th ed. 1990). As such, the term is used to differentiate between first-and second-degree murders. * * * Murder in cold blood is, in this sense, the opposite of murder in "hot blood." Arguably, then, the *Osborn* formulation covers every intentional or first-degree murder. An aggravating circumstance so construed would clearly be unconstitutional. * * *

As noted above, the Idaho courts never have articulated anything remotely approaching the majority's novel "those who kill without feeling or sympathy" interpretation. All kinds of other factors, however, have been invoked by Idaho courts applying the circumstance. For example, in State v. Aragon, 690 P.2d 293 (Idaho 1984), the killer's cold-bloodedness supposedly was demonstrated by his refusal to render aid to his victim and the fact that "his only concern was to cover up his own participation in the incident." In State v. Pizzuto, 810 P.2d 680, 712 (Idaho 1991), a finding of "utter disregard" was held to be supported by evidence that the defendant "approached Mr. Herndon with a gun, then made him drop his pants and crawl into the cabin where he proceeded to bludgeon the skulls of both of his victims with a hammer. He then left them lying on the floor to die and Mr. Herndon was left lying on the floor of the cabin convulsing." And, in the present case, the trial judge's determination that Creech exhibited utter disregard for human life appears to have been based primarily on the fact that Creech had "intentionally destroyed another human being at a time when he was completely helpless." Each of these characteristics is frightfully deplorable, but what they have to do with a lack of emotion—or with each other, for that matter—eludes me. Without some rationalizing principle to connect them, the findings of "cold-bloodedness" stand as nothing more than fact-specific, "gut-reaction" conclusions that are unconstitutional under Maynard v. Cartwright, 486 U.S. 356 (1988).

The futility of the Idaho courts' attempt to bring some rationality to the "utter disregard" circumstance is glaringly evident in the sole post-*Osborn* case that endeavors to explain the construction in any depth. In State v. Fain, 774 P.2d 252 cert. denied, 493 U.S. 917 (Idaho 1989), the court declared that the "utter disregard" factor refers to "the defendant's lack of conscientious scruples against killing another human being." Thus, the latest statement from the Idaho Supreme Court on the issue says nothing about emotionless crimes, but, instead, sweepingly includes every murder committed that is without "conscientious scruples against killing." I can imagine no crime that would not fall within that construction. * * *

I would affirm the judgment of the Court of Appeals.

Chapter 3

CRIMINAL HOMICIDE

A. MURDER: THE MEANING OF MALICE AFORETHOUGHT

HOLMES v. DIRECTOR OF PUBLIC PROSECUTIONS

House of Lords, 1946.
(1946) A.C. 588, 31 Crim.App.R. 123, (1946) 2 All E.R. 124.

VISCOUNT SIMON: * * *

[Appellant was convicted of murdering his wife. The Court of Appeal affirmed the conviction, but appellant obtained leave to appeal to the House of Lords because the case involved a point of law of exceptional public importance.]

The point of law is whether CHARLES, J., was right in telling the jury that, upon the evidence at the trial, and having regard to the law, it was not open to the jury to find a verdict of manslaughter, and that the statement by the accused's wife to him that she had been unfaithful to him was not such provocation as could justify a verdict of manslaughter instead of murder. More generally, the question we have to consider is what are the respective functions of judge and jury in such cases, and how the law draws the line between instances of provocation which would, and those which cannot, make it proper for the jury to be left to decide on the facts on the appropriate verdict.

The appellant killed his wife, according to his own evidence, on the night of Sunday or in the early hours of Monday, Nov. 18 or 19 of last year, in the kitchen of the house where they lived. On the previous Saturday he had telegraphed to a Mrs. X, who lived in a different part of the country and with whom he admitted that he had previously had sexual relations, that she might expect him on the Sunday or Monday; he travelled on the Monday to Mrs. X and told her that his wife had left him. In fact, his wife's dead body was discovered next day in the room where he had killed her. She had received a severe wound on the head caused by the hammer-head for breaking coal which was close to his hand, and she had many bruises on her body, but the final cause of death was manual strangulation. The appellant's story was that there was a quarrel between them on the Saturday night originating from some persons winking in the direction of his wife in a public house that evening; he said that he had entertained suspicions of his wife's conduct with regard to other men in the village, and that there had been some suggestion made to him with regard to her and his own younger brother. The quarrel, he said, culminated in his wife saying, "Well, if it will ease your mind, I have been untrue to you," and she went on, "I know I have done wrong, but I have no proof that you haven't—at Mrs. X's". "With this," the appellant's statement continued, "I lost my temper and picked up the hammer-head and struck her with the same on the side of the head. She fell on her knees and then rolled over on her back, her last words being, 'It's too late now, but look after the children.' She struggled just for a few moments and I could see she was too far gone to do anything. I did not like to see her lay there and suffer, so I just put both hands round her neck until she stopped breathing, which was only a few seconds." In the witness-box, the appellant was asked in cross-examination, "When you put your hands round that woman's neck and gave pressure through your fingers, you intended to take your wife's life, did you not?" and he answered, "Yes."

There was no corroboration at the trial to support the accused's statement that his wife admitted her unfaithfulness, but for the purpose of deciding whether Charles, J.'s direction to the jury was correct, it must be assumed that she did, and that either her confession or her pertinent inquiry about his own misconduct provoked him to lose his temper. The House was unanimous in holding that the direction given by the judge was correct; there were no circumstances of special aggravation, and confession of adultery, grievous as it is, cannot in itself justify the view that a reasonable man (or woman) would be so provoked as to do what this man did. The House accordingly dismissed the appeal, while taking further time to pronounce upon the more general questions of law and principle discussed in the course of the argument.

In dealing with provocation as justifying the view that the crime may be manslaughter and not murder, a distinction must be made between what the judge lays down as matter of law, and what the jury decides as matter of fact. If there is no sufficient material, even on a view of the evidence most favourable to the accused, for a jury (which means a reasonable jury) to form the view that a reasonable person so provoked could be driven, through transport of passion and loss of self control, to the degree and method and continuance of violence which produces the death, it is the duty of the judge as matter of law to direct the jury that the evidence does not support a verdict of manslaughter. If, on the other hand, the case is one in which the view might fairly be taken (a) that a reasonable person, in consequence of the provocation received, might be so rendered subject to passion or loss of control as to be led to use the violence with fatal results, and (b) that the accused was in fact acting under the stress of such provocation, then it is for the jury to determine whether on its view of the facts manslaughter or murder is the appropriate verdict. It is hardly necessary to lay emphasis on the importance of considering, where the homicide does not follow immediately upon the provocation, whether the accused, if acting as a reasonable man, had "time to cool." * * *

The whole doctrine relating to provocation depends on the fact that it causes, or may cause, a sudden and temporary loss of self-control whereby malice, which is the formation of an intention to kill or to inflict grievous bodily harm, is negatived. Consequently, where the provocation inspires an actual intention to kill (such as Holmes admitted in the present case), or to inflict grievous bodily harm, the doctrine that provocation may reduce murder to manslaughter seldom applies. Only one very special exception has been recognized, *viz.*, the actual finding of a spouse in the act of adultery. This has always been treated as an exception to the general rule. Blackstone's Commentaries, Bk. IV, p. 192, justifies the exception on the ground that "there could not be a greater provocation." But it has been rightly laid down that the exception cannot be extended, e.g., by Parke, B., in *Pearson's* case where he insisted on the condition of ocular observation. Even if Iago's insinuations against Desdemona's virtue had been true, Othello's crime was murder and nothing else.

Necessary self-defense, or action taken in the necessary defense, for example, of wife or child from outrage or maltreatment, stand apart, as in such cases there is no crime at all committed.

This brings me to the question which, as I understand, was the actual reason why the law officer's certificate was given in this case: *viz.*, whether "mere words" can ever be regarded as so provocative to a reasonable man as to reduce to manslaughter felonious homicide committed upon the speaker in consequence of such verbal provocation. * * *

It is first to be observed that provocation by "mere words" may have more than one meaning. It may mean provocation by insulting or abusive language, calculated to rouse the hearer's resentment. The contrast with provocation by physical attack is obvious. A blow may in some circumstances rouse a man of ordinary reason and control to a sudden retort in kind, but the proverb reminds us that hard words break no bones, and the law expects a reasonable man to endure abuse without resorting to fatal violence. It is in this sense that the constantly repeated statement in the old books that "mere words" (not being menace of immediate bodily harm) do not reduce murder to manslaughter is to be understood.

There is, however, a different sense which may sometimes attach to the meaning of "mere words," for they may be used, not as an expression of abuse, but as a means of conveying information of a fact, or of what is alleged to be a fact. * * *

In my view, however, a sudden confession of adultery without more can never constitute provocation of a sort which might reduce murder to manslaughter. * * * The rule, whatever it is, must apply to either spouse alike, for we have left behind us the age when the wife's subjection to her husband was regarded by the law as the basis of the marital relation, when, as BRACTON said (see Pollock and Maitland's History of English Law, 2nd Edn., Vol. II, p. 406), she was *sub virga viri sui* and when the remedies of the Divorce Court did not exist. Parliament has now conferred on the aggrieved wife the same right to divorce her husband for unfaithfulness alone as he holds against her, and neither, on hearing an admission of adultery from the other, can use physical violence against the other which results in death and then urge that the provocation received reduces the crime to mere manslaughter.

It is not necessary in this appeal to decide whether there are any conceivable circumstances accompanying the use of words without actual violence, which would justify the leaving to a jury of the issue of manslaughter as against murder. It is enough to say that the duty of the judge at the trial, in relevant cases, is to tell the jury that a confession of adultery without more is never sufficient to reduce an offence which would otherwise be murder to manslaughter and that in no case could words alone, save in circumstances of a most extreme and exceptional character, so reduce the crime. When words alone are relied upon in extenuation, the duty rests on the judge to consider whether they are of this violent provocative character, and if he is satisfied that they cannot reasonably be so regarded, to direct the jury accordingly.

There are two observations which I desire to make in conclusion. The first is that the application of common law principles in matters such as this must to some extent be controlled by the evolution of society. For example, the instance given by Blackstone's Commentaries, Bk. IV, p. 191, that if a man's nose was pulled and he thereupon struck his aggressor so as to kill him, this was only manslaughter, may very well represent the natural feelings of a past time, but I should doubt very much whether such a view should necessarily be taken nowadays. The injury done to a man's sense of honour by minor physical assaults may well be differently estimated in differing ages. And, in the same way, one can imagine in these days at any rate, words of a vile character which might be calculated to deprive a reasonable man of his customary self-control even more than would an act of physical violence. But on the other hand, as society advances, it ought to call for a higher measure of self-control in all cases.

The remaining reflection is as follows: the reason why the problem of drawing the line between murder and manslaughter, where there has been provocation, is so difficult and so important, is because the sentence for murder is fixed and automatic. In the case of lesser crimes, provocation does not alter the nature of the offence at all: but it is allowed for in the sentence. In the case of felonious homicide, the law has to reconcile respect for the sanctity of human life with recognition of the effect of provocation upon human frailty.[a]

Appeal dismissed.

a. The English Homicide Act of 1957 provides that "Where on a charge of murder there is evidence on which the jury can find that the person charged was provoked

PEOPLE v. BERRY

Supreme Court of California, 1976.
18 Cal.3d 509, 134 Cal.Rptr. 415, 556 P.2d 777.

SULLIVAN, JUSTICE.

[Defendant Berry was convicted of first degree murder for killing his wife and sentenced to life imprisonment.] * * *

Defendant contends that there is sufficient evidence in the record to show that he committed the homicide while in a state of uncontrollable rage caused by provocation * * * and therefore that it was error for the trial court to fail to instruct the jury on voluntary manslaughter as indeed he had requested.

Defendant, a cook, 46 years old, and Rachel Pessah, a 20-year-old girl from Israel, were married on May 27, 1974. Three days later Rachel went to Israel by herself, returning on July 13, 1974. On July 23, 1974, defendant choked Rachel into unconsciousness. She was treated at a hospital where she reported her strangulation by defendant to an officer of the San Francisco Police Department. On July 25, Inspector Sammon, who had been assigned to the case, met with Rachel and as a result of the interview a warrant was issued for defendant's arrest.

While Rachel was at the hospital, defendant removed his clothes from their apartment and stored them in a Greyhound Bus Depot locker. He stayed overnight at the home of a friend, Mrs. Jean Berk, admitting to her that he had choked his wife. On July 26, he telephoned Mrs. Berk and informed her that he had killed Rachel with a telephone cord on that morning at their apartment. The next day Mrs. Berk and two others telephoned the police to report a possible homicide and met Officer Kelleher at defendant's apartment. They gained entry and found Rachel on the bathroom floor. A pathologist from the coroner's office concluded that the cause of Rachel's death was strangulation. Defendant was arrested on August 1, 1974, and confessed to the killing.

At trial defendant did not deny strangling his wife, but claimed through his own testimony and the testimony of a psychiatrist, Dr. Martin Blinder, that he was provoked into killing her because of a sudden and uncontrollable rage so as to reduce the offense to one of voluntary manslaughter. He testified that upon her return from Israel, Rachel announced to him that while there she had fallen in love with another man, one Yako, and had enjoyed his sexual favors, that he was coming to this country to claim her and that she wished a divorce. Thus commenced a tormenting two weeks in which Rachel alternately taunted defendant with her involvement with Yako and at the same time

(whether by things done or by things said or by both together) to lose his self-control, the question whether the provocation was enough to make a reasonable man do as he did shall be left to be determined by the jury; and in determining that question the jury shall take into account everything both done and said according to the effect which, in their opinion, it would have on a reasonable man."—ed.

sexually excited defendant, indicating her desire to remain with him. Defendant's detailed testimony, summarized below, chronicles this strange course of events.

After their marriage, Rachel lived with defendant for only three days and then left for Israel. Immediately upon her return to San Francisco she told defendant about her relationship with and love for Yako. This brought about further argument and a brawl that evening in which defendant choked Rachel and she responded by scratching him deeply many times. Nonetheless they continued to live together. Rachel kept taunting defendant with Yako and demanding a divorce. She claimed she thought she might be pregnant by Yako. She showed defendant pictures of herself with Yako. Nevertheless, during a return trip from Santa Rosa, Rachel demanded immediate sexual intercourse with defendant in the car, which was achieved; however upon reaching their apartment, she again stated that she loved Yako and that she would not have intercourse with defendant in the future.

On the evening of July 22nd defendant and Rachel went to a movie where they engaged in heavy petting. When they returned home and got into bed, Rachel announced that she had intended to make love with defendant, "But I am saving myself for this man Yako, so I don't think I will." Defendant got out of bed and prepared to leave the apartment whereupon Rachel screamed and yelled at him. Defendant choked her into unconsciousness.

Two hours later defendant called a taxi for his wife to take her to the hospital. He put his clothes in the Greyhound bus station and went to the home of his friend Mrs. Berk for the night. The next day he went to Reno and returned the day after. Rachel informed him by telephone that there was a warrant for his arrest as a result of her report to the police about the choking incident. On July 25th defendant returned to the apartment to talk to Rachel, but she was out. He slept there overnight. Rachel returned around 11 a.m. the next day. Upon seeing defendant there, she said, "I suppose you have come here to kill me." Defendant responded, "yes," changed his response to "no," and then again to "yes," and finally stated "I have really come to talk to you." Rachel began screaming. Defendant grabbed her by the shoulder and tried to stop her screaming. She continued. They struggled and finally defendant strangled her with a telephone cord.

Dr. Martin Blinder, physician and psychiatrist, called by the defense, testified that Rachel was a depressed, suicidally inclined girl and that this suicidal impulse led her to involve herself ever more deeply in a dangerous situation with defendant. She did this by sexually arousing him and taunting him into jealous rages in an unconscious desire to provoke him into killing her and thus consummating her desire for suicide. Throughout the period commencing with her return from Israel until her death, that is from July 13 to July 26, Rachel continually provoked defendant with sexual taunts and incitements, alternating acceptance and rejection of him. This conduct was accompanied by repeated references to her involvement with another man; it led defendant to choke her on two occasions, until finally she achieved her unconscious desire and was strangled. Dr. Blinder testified that as a result of this cumulative series of provocations, defendant at the time he fatally strangled Rachel, was in a state of uncontrollable rage, completely under the sway of passion.

We first take up defendant's claim that on the basis of the foregoing evidence he was entitled to an instruction on voluntary manslaughter as defined by statute which is "the unlawful killing of a human being, without malice * * * upon a sudden quarrel or heat of passion." (§ 192.) In People v. Valentine (1946) 28 Cal.2d 121, this court * * * specifically approved the following * * * as a correct statement of the law: "In the present condition of our law *it is left to the jurors* to say whether or not the facts and circumstances in evidence are sufficient to lead them to believe that the defendant did, or to create a reasonable doubt in their minds as to whether or not he did, commit his offense under a heat of passion. The jury is further to be admonished and advised by the court that this heat of passion must be such a passion as would naturally be aroused in the mind of an ordinarily reasonable person under the given facts and circumstances, and that, consequently, no defendant may set up his own standard of conduct and justify or excuse himself because in fact his passions were aroused, unless further the jury believe that the facts and circumstances were sufficient to arouse the passions of the ordinarily reasonable man. * * * For the fundamental of the inquiry is whether or not the defendant's reason was, at the time of his act, so disturbed or obscured by some passion—not necessarily fear and never, of course, the passion for revenge—to such an extent as would render ordinary men of average disposition liable to act rashly or without due deliberation and reflection, and from this passion rather than from judgment."

We further held in *Valentine* that there is no specific type of provocation required by section 192 and that verbal provocation may be sufficient. In People v. Borchers (1958) 50 Cal.2d 321, 329, 325 P.2d 97 in the course of explaining the phrase "heat of passion" used in the statute defining manslaughter we pointed out that " 'passion' need not mean 'rage' or 'anger' " but may be any "[v]iolent, intense, high-wrought or enthusiastic emotion" and concluded there "that defendant was aroused to a heat of 'passion' by a series of events over a considerable period of time." * * * Accordingly we there declared that evidence of admissions of infidelity by the defendant's paramour, taunts directed to him and other conduct, "supports a finding that defendant killed in wild desperation induced by [the woman's] long continued provocatory conduct."

We find this reasoning persuasive in the case now before us. Defendant's testimony chronicles a two-week period of provocatory conduct by his wife Rachel that could arouse a passion of jealousy, pain and sexual rage in an ordinary man of average disposition such as to cause him to act rashly from this passion. It is significant that both defendant and Dr. Blinder testified that the former was in the heat of passion under an uncontrollable rage when he killed Rachel.

The Attorney General contends that the killing could not have been done in the heat of passion because there was a cooling period, defendant having waited in the apartment for 20 hours. However, the long course of provocatory conduct, which had resulted in intermittent outbreaks of rage under specific provocation in the past, reached its final culmination in the apartment when Rachel began screaming. Both defendant and Dr. Blinder testified that defendant killed in a state of uncontrollable rage, of passion, and there is ample evidence in the record to support the conclusion that this passion was the result of the long course of provocatory conduct by Rachel, just as the killing emerged from such conduct in *Borchers*. * * *

Reversed.

Note

In People v. Berry, the defendant complained that a manslaughter instruction should have been given, because the evidence (allegedly) might have justified a manslaughter verdict. Although the trial court should instruct on lesser included offenses where the evidence is consistent with a lesser offense, it should not do so where such an instruction merely invites the jury to compromise its doubts over guilt or innocence. For example, the evidence may show a killing of a victim in the course of an armed robbery, where the defense is alibi and mistaken identity. In that case the only proper verdicts would be guilty of murder or not guilty altogether, and it would be improper to instruct the jury on manslaughter. Sometimes the defendant wants to "roll the dice," and put the jury to a murder-or-nothing choice where the evidence would justify a manslaughter verdict. In People v. Barton, 12 Cal.4th 186, 906 P.2d 531, 47 Cal.Rptr.2d 569 (1995), the defendant shot and killed the victim in the course of a quarrel, possibly in the mistaken belief that the victim was reaching for a knife. Over objection by the defense, which argued that the killing was either murder or entirely excused, the trial judge instructed the jury on both murder and manslaughter. The jury found defendant guilty of voluntary manslaughter. The California Supreme Court affirmed the conviction, holding that "a defendant may not invoke tactical considerations to deprive the jury of the opportunity to consider whether the defendant is guilty of a lesser offense included within the crime charged. A trial court should instruct the jury on any lesser included offense supported by the evidence, regardless of the defendant's opposition." The notorious Louise Woodward case, discussed *infra*, Ch. 3, § D, which illustrates the mess a court can create when it allows a defendant to roll the dice.

PEOPLE v. CHEVALIER

Supreme Court of Illinois, 1989.
131 Ill.2d 66, 136 Ill.Dec. 167, 544 N.E.2d 942.

JUSTICE STAMOS delivered the opinion of the court:

In each of these consolidated cases, the defendant shot and killed his wife and was convicted of murder. Defendants do not dispute that they committed the killings or that the killings were not legally justified. They contend that the evidence was sufficient to warrant giving the jury an instruction on the offense of voluntary manslaughter. The issue common to both appeals is whether the provocation on the part of the victim was legally adequate to reduce the homicide from murder to voluntary manslaughter. * * * In each case, the appellate court reversed the conviction and remanded the case for a new trial.

* * * Although the details differ, the circumstances surrounding the killings are similar. In each, defendant suspected his wife of marital infidelity. Just prior to the killing, the defendant and the victim had an argument, during which the victim admitted committing adultery and either disparaged the defendant's sexual abilities (People v. Chevalier) or flaunted the fact that she slept with her lover in the marital bed (People v. Flores). The victims were shot during these arguments. * * *

In People v. Flores, the trial court refused to give defendant's tendered jury instruction on the offense of voluntary manslaughter. In People v. Chevalier, although the trial court instructed the jury on voluntary manslaughter, defendant contends that the instruction was erroneous. We need not address the accuracy of the jury instruction, however, unless Chevalier was entitled to a voluntary manslaughter instruction. As Chevalier appears to concede, if the evidence did not support such an instruction, then an erroneous instruction on the offense could not have prejudiced defendant. Accordingly, we turn to a consideration of whether defendants were entitled to a voluntary manslaughter instruction. * * *

The principles governing voluntary manslaughter based on serious provocation are well established. The only categories of serious provocation which have been recognized are: "substantial physical injury or assault, mutual quarrel or combat, illegal arrest, and adultery with the offender's spouse; but not mere words or gestures or trespass to property." The rule that mere words are insufficient provocation applies no matter how aggravated, abusive, opprobrious or indecent the language. In Illinois, adultery with a spouse as provocation generally has been limited to those instances where the parties are discovered in the act of adultery or immediately before or after such an act, and the killing immediately follows such discovery. A verbal communication that adultery has occurred or will occur falls within the rule that mere words are insufficient provocation. [Citations]

The appellate court decisions in the cases at bar * * * followed People v. Ambro (1987), 153 Ill.App.3d 1, 106 Ill.Dec. 75, 505 N.E.2d 381, which in turn relied on People v. Ahlberg (1973), 13 Ill.App.3d 1038, 301 N.E.2d 608, and People v. Carr (1980), 91 Ill.App.3d 512, 46 Ill.Dec. 955, 414 N.E.2d 1108. These cases recognized an exception to the general rule that a verbal communication of adultery is insufficient provocation.

Ahlberg was an appeal from a conviction of voluntary manslaughter. In the days preceding the homicide, defendant's wife left the couple's home and told defendant she had filed for divorce. Just before the killing, defendant's wife told him that he had never satisfied her sexually, that she had found an older man, and that she was going to get a divorce. Defendant then dragged his wife from their home, beat, kicked and stomped her, causing injuries from which she later died.

Defendant appealed, contending that he was guilty of murder or of nothing. The court disagreed, stating: "To follow unequivocally the rule that 'mere words' are insufficient to cause the provocation necessary to support a finding of guilt of voluntary manslaughter would be in keeping with precedent and an established rule; however, it would be a direct refutation of logic and a miscarriage of justice. We reach this conclusion for it is not incumbent on us to determine what could or did provoke the defendant into a state of intense passion, for by his testimony he made such determination."

In the first place, the court in *Ahlberg* was simply incorrect in its view that it need not inquire into the nature of the provocation which allegedly caused a state of passion. To the contrary, as we have stated, the law recognizes only certain categories of provocation. Under the appellate court's view in *Ahlberg,* even the slightest provocation would suffice, as long as the defendant testified that the deceased's conduct provoked intense passion. "Passion on the part of the slayer, no matter how violent, will not relieve him from liability for murder unless it is engendered by a serious provocation which the law recognizes as being reasonably adequate. If the provocation is inadequate, the crime is murder." [Citations]

Moreover, it is obvious from the *Ahlberg* opinion that the court was loath to reverse the voluntary manslaughter conviction. Defendant in that case had been acquitted of murder; therefore, reversal of the voluntary manslaughter conviction likely would mean that defendant would escape any punishment for the crime. See People v. Thompson (1973), 11 Ill.App.3d 752, 297 N.E.2d 592 (a defendant charged with murder may properly be found guilty of the lesser offense of voluntary manslaughter, but only if the evidence establishes the necessary elements of that offense; voluntary manslaughter conviction reversed). The court in *Ahlberg* stated: "Having escaped a guilty of murder conviction [defendant] now asks that we set aside a voluntary manslaughter conviction even though by his own testimony the words of his wife were such as to cause him to lose all control of himself * * *. To grant the request of the defendant would make a mockery of the law." The court candidly stated that its holding ignored precedent and established rules. The court's ruling in the *Ahlberg* case proves the old adage, "Hard cases make bad law." People v. Carr, supra, was also an appeal from a conviction for voluntary manslaughter. On facts similar to those in *Ahlberg,* the court in *Carr* followed *Ahlberg* and affirmed the conviction.

People v. Ambro, supra, unlike *Ahlberg* and *Carr,* was an appeal from a murder conviction in which defendant contended that the trial court erred in refusing to instruct the jury on the offense of voluntary manslaughter. The majority acknowledged the general rules we have set out, but thought that *Ahlberg* and *Carr* had created "an apparent exception to these general rules, based on verbal revelations of infidelity and other conduct." Since the circumstances in *Ambro* were similar to those in *Ahlberg* and *Carr* (a history of ongoing marital discord, a wife who evidenced an intent to permanently leave her husband, insulting remarks concerning the husband's masculinity, and an announcement of adultery by the wife), the court applied the exception created by Ahlberg and held it was reversible error to refuse defendant's voluntary manslaughter instruction.

Parenthetically, we fail to understand why a history of marital discord should be a factor favoring a voluntary manslaughter instruction. The [previously described] opinions all list this factor as one favoring a voluntary manslaughter instruction. Since voluntary manslaughter requires evidence of a sudden passion, a history of marital discord, particularly suspicions of adultery, if relevant at all, would undermine, not support, a defendant's claim that the evidence supports a voluntary manslaughter instruction. * * *

We conclude that the "exception" to the general rule created by the *Ahlberg* line of cases is an incorrect statement of Illinois law. * * * Whatever may be the outer limits of the general rule that only the discovery of the parties in the act of adultery, or immediately before or after the act, will suffice as provocation, neither case falls within the rule. In People v. Chevalier, during the course of the marriage, the victim left the defendant three times to live with defendant's best friend. The night before the murder, defendant discovered his wife's soiled panties in his car but said nothing to his wife. The next evening, he confronted his wife and said more than once that he knew she was "messing around" again. Similarly, in People v. Flores, defendant testified that he suspected his wife of having an affair for approximately eight months prior to the murder. Thus, neither case can possibly come within the rule. As for the insulting remarks made by the victims, the *Ahlberg* line of cases simply ignores the rule that no matter how insulting, mere words are insufficient provocation.

For these reasons, we hold that in each of the cases before us, the provocation claimed was, as a matter of law, insufficient to constitute the serious provocation necessary to reduce the homicide from murder to voluntary manslaughter. * * * The judgment of the circuit court in each case is affirmed and the convictions of murder are reinstated.

STATE v. ELLIOTT

Supreme Court of Connecticut, 1979.
177 Conn. 1, 411 A.2d 3.

LOISELLE, ASSOCIATE JUSTICE.

[Elliott was convicted of murder and sentenced to 25 years to life in prison.] * * * The jury could have found that the defendant, armed with a loaded revolver, went to the home of his brother, the victim. After failing to gain entrance at the front door, he forced his way in through the kitchen door. Once inside, he threatened his ten-year-old niece with a gun, forcing her to tell him that his brother was upstairs in bed. On the stairs, Elliott encountered his brother's wife. When she saw the defendant she ran down the hallway to the back door. Elliott pursued her down the hall pointing a gun at her. Mrs. Elliott's path was blocked by a hobbyhorse. She turned and saw that the defendant was only a few feet away from her. She then saw her husband come up from behind the defendant. He called out "Bobby." The defendant then turned around and shot him twice in rapid succession. The defendant said nothing during this whole episode. The victim died from the gunshot wounds. The defendant was apprehended shortly after the shooting about one half mile away from his brother's house.

* * * A psychiatrist interviewed the defendant about eleven months after the shooting. The psychiatrist testified that the defendant was acting under the influence of an extreme emotional disturbance caused by a combination of child custody problems, the inability to maintain a recently purchased home and an overwhelming fear of his brother. The psychiatrist placed particular emphasis on the history of conflict between the two brothers, noting that the defendant referred to his brother as a "ranger killer." The defendant told the psychiatrist that at one time his brother pulled him from a bus and chased him with a tire iron. The defendant stated that this incident was so frightening that it caused him to leave the area for a couple of years. The psychiatrist believed that this incident compounded by many other extenuating circumstances resulted in the defendant's overwhelming fear of his brother. And he testified that these circumstances taken together constituted a reasonable explanation of the defendant's extreme emotional disturbance.

The defendant's one [contention] is that the trial court erred in its charge on the defense of extreme emotional disturbance, contained in General Statutes § 53a–54a(a). We agree. In explaining the meaning of "extreme emotional disturbance," the court actually gave the substance of the traditional charge on the "heat of passion" defense, which existed prior to the enactment of the present Penal Code. The defenses of extreme emotional disturbance and heat of passion are not interchangeable.

The extreme emotional disturbance defense outlined in § 53a–54a(a) is the same as the affirmative defense that appears in the New York murder statute. The fact that a statute is almost a literal copy of a statute of a sister state is persuasive evidence of a practical reenactment of the statute of the sister state; as such it is proper to resort to the decisions of a sister court construing that statutory language.

Construing the New York statute, the United States Supreme Court upheld the designation of extreme emotional disturbance as an affirmative defense and the placing of the burden of proof upon the defendant in Patterson v. New York, 432 U.S. 197 (1977). In the present case, however, which was decided prior to the Supreme Court's ruling in *Patterson,* the trial court charged that the state had the burden of proving the nonexistence of the defense. In charging this way, the trial court was, no doubt, trying to conform to the dictates of Mullaney v. Wilbur, 421 U.S. 684 (1975) [which had held that it is unconstitutional to place upon a defendant the burden of proving the existence of a heat of passion and legally sufficient provocation under the traditional manslaughter formula.] The Supreme Court in *Patterson* distinguished *Mullaney* and went on to hold that the defense of extreme emotional disturbance was not constitutionally infirm even though the burden of proof was placed on the defendant.

The Supreme Court's reasoning for allowing the burden of proof to be placed upon the defendant was that the defense of extreme emotional disturbance does not serve to negate intent, but rather is raised to establish circumstances that mitigate culpability. * * * The Supreme Court noted that the defense of extreme emotional disturbance is a considerably expanded version of the common law defense of heat of passion or sudden provocation.

[The New York—Model Penal Code affirmative defense of extreme emotional disturbance] does not require a provoking or triggering event; or that the homicidal act occur immediately after the cause or causes of the defendant's extreme emotional disturbance; or that the defendant have lost all ability to reason. Further, the reasonable man yardstick is only used to determine the reasonableness of the explanation or excuse of the action of the defendant from the viewpoint of a person in the defendant's situation under the circumstances as the defendant believed them to be. Thus, the statute sets forth a standard that is objective in its overview, but subjective as to the defendant's belief.

Before the enactment of the [Connecticut version of the Model Penal Code], to establish the "heat of passion" defense a defendant had to prove that the "hot blood" had not had time to "cool off" at the time of the killing. A homicide influenced by an extreme emotional disturbance, in contrast, is not one which is necessarily committed in the "hot blood" stage, but rather one that was brought about by a significant mental trauma that caused the defendant to brood for a long period of time and then react violently, seemingly without provocation.

The comments accompanying the Model Penal Code attempt to explain the change from the old common law concept of killing in the "heat of passion" to the new concept of killing under the influence of an "extreme emotional disturbance." The comments seem to be contradictory in that they claim the ultimate test is objective yet the state of mind of the accused is to be evaluated from his viewpoint under the circumstances as he believes them to be. In the draft, there are no attempts to set guidelines to aid the trier of fact. The draftsmen state: "The question in the end will be whether the actor's loss of self-control can be understood in terms that arouse sympathy enough to call for mitigation in the sentence. That seems to be the issue to be faced." The Chief Reporter for the Model Penal Code has noted that "(t)he purpose was explicitly to give full scope to what amounts to a plea in mitigation based upon a mental or emotional trauma of significant dimensions, with the jury asked to show whatever empathy it can." Wechsler, "Codification of Criminal Law in the United States; The Model Penal Code," 68 Colum.L.Rev. 1425 (1968). Those comments may explain the rationale of the draftsmen but they ignore the realities of the courtroom. So the task of instructing a jury with understandable guidelines is left to the courts to determine. * * *

In People v. Shelton, 88 Misc.2d 136, 149, 385 N.Y.S.2d 708 (1976), Justice Kassal made an exhaustive analysis of the affirmative defense in question. Following *Shelton,* we hold that in determining whether the defendant has proven the affirmative defense of an extreme emotional disturbance by a fair preponderance of the evidence as a mitigation of murder to manslaughter the jury must find that: (a) the emotional disturbance is not a mental disease or defect that rises to the level of insanity as defined by the Penal Code; (b) the defendant was exposed to an extremely unusual and overwhelming state, that is, not mere annoyance or unhappiness; and (c) the defendant had an extreme emotional reaction to it, as a result of which there was a loss of self-control, and reason was overborne by extreme intense feelings, such as passion, anger, distress, grief, excessive agitation or other similar emotions. Consideration is given to whether the intensity of these feelings was such that his usual intellectual controls failed and the normal rational thinking for that individual no longer prevailed at the time of the act. In its charge, the trial court should explain that the term "extreme" refers to the greatest degree of intensity away from the norm for that individual.

The jury should be instructed that the reasonableness of a defendant's act under an extreme emotional disturbance is to be determined from the viewpoint of a person in the defendant's situation under the circumstances as the defendant believed them to be.

There is error, the judgment is set aside and a new trial is ordered.

In this opinion the other Judges concurred.

Note

"Malice aforethought" is a legal term of art in which the words are not used in their ordinary sense. It has both positive and negative elements: that is, it requires the presence of certain factors and the absence of others. Positively, it requires that the defendant at the time of the homicide have one of the following states of mind: (1) An intent to kill someone, not necessarily the victim. If A shoots at B intending to kill him, but the bullet kills C instead, then A commits an intentional killing of C under the doctrine of "transferred intent." The jury may infer that the defendant intended to kill if he intentionally used a deadly weapon upon someone. (2) An intent to commit "serious" or "grievous" bodily injury upon someone. (3) A wanton and reckless disregard of a very great risk of causing death or serious bodily injury, as where a defendant fires blindly into an occupied room or throws a heavy object off a tall building into a crowded street without caring if it hits anyone or not. The older statutes use language such as a "depraved heart" or an "abandoned and malignant heart" to refer to this type of culpability. (4) Malice is also implied when the defendant or his accomplice commits a killing in the perpetration of certain felonies. The felony-murder rule is the subject of a later section of this chapter.

Negatively, malice aforethought requires the absence of any circumstances which would "mitigate" the homicide: i.e., reduce it from murder to voluntary manslaughter. The traditional, pre-Model Penal Code rule is that a killing which would otherwise be murder is mitigated to manslaughter if the defendant acted in a "heat of passion" caused by legally sufficient provocation. The provocation must be conduct of the victim sufficient to cause a reasonable person in the defendant's situation to lose his customary self-control, and it must actually provoke the defendant into killing before he has time to "cool off."

Many judicial opinions and scholarly articles have commented upon the conceptual awkwardness of the notion that it is possible for circumstances to provoke a "reasonable person" into such a heat of passion that he or she commits a criminal homicide. If a reasonable person in the defendant's circumstances would have been so affected by the provocation as to lose his or her self control and commit a deadly attack, then why punish the defendant at all? The Model Penal Code's requirement that the defendant's extreme emotional disturbance have some "reasonable explanation or excuse" does not avoid this same conceptual awkwardness. An extreme emotional disturbance is by its nature unreasonable, and the reason for requiring the unreasonableness to have a reasonable explanation is obscure.

The conceptual awkwardness results from an ambivalence over whether it is the (relative) reasonableness of the defendant's action or its sheer irrationality which is the mitigating element. Defendants who kill in necessary self defense are guilty of no crime because reasonable people would act the same in the circumstances. Defendants who kill because they have used excessive force in a barroom brawl, or because they have caught a spouse in the act of adultery, are not justified in reacting with such violence but they are not as unjustified as people who kill for profit or to take revenge for some past injury. The presence of legally sufficient provocation in itself is not sufficient to avoid a murder conviction where the killing in intentional, however. The defendant must actually have been in a heat of passion, or subject to extreme emotional disturbance, rather than in a calm or rational state of mind. Why?

Several states such as Illinois which have used the Model Penal Code as a basis for law reform have nonetheless retained, or returned to, the requirement of legally sufficient provocation as a basis for a voluntary manslaughter conviction. Should a defendant who has been convicted of voluntary manslaughter, and acquitted of the greater charge of murder, be able to appeal the conviction on the ground that the evidence showed him to be guilty of murder? The outcome of a successful appeal on that ground is plainly absurd, since the constitutional prohibition of double jeopardy would prevent a retrial on the murder charge. In the traditional formulation voluntary manslaughter is a "lesser included offense" within the crime of murder (i.e. intentional murder without the element of malice aforethought), and a defendant who kills intentionally necessarily commits manslaughter if he commits murder. The Illinois statute defines manslaughter to include the element of "sudden and intense passion resulting from serious provocation," and so a defendant technically is not guilty of that crime in the absence of this element.

There is a substantial amount of case law in American and England on the extent to which a court should consider, or instruct the jury to consider, the peculiar characteristics of the defendant in evaluating the adequacy of the provocation. The issue has most frequently arisen in the English cases. The defendant in Bedder v. Director of Public Prosecutions, [1954] 2 All E.R. 801, was a sexually impotent man who killed a prostitute who had taunted and abused him because of his inadequacy. In affirming the resulting murder conviction, the House of Lords indicated that the standard for provocation was that of the reasonable ordinary person, and no special leniency should be shown either to the person with an unusually excitable or pugnacious temperament, or a person with some unusual physical characteristic.

Following a revision of the applicable statute, the House of Lords considered a similar question in Director of Public Prosecutions v. Camplin, [1978] 2 All E.R. 168. Defendant Camplin, who was fifteen years old at the time of the killing, asked the trial judge to instruct the jury to consider the adequacy of the provocation (an alleged sexual attack) not in terms of the reasonable man but rather the likely reaction of a reasonable boy of the defendant's age. The trial judge explicitly refused to do so, and instructed the jury to reduce the offense to manslaughter only if "the provocation was sufficient to make a reasonable man in like circumstances act as the defendant did. Not a reasonable boy * * * or a reasonable lad; it is an objective test—a reasonable man." The House of Lords allowed the appeal, indicating that the "reasonable person" with whom the defendant's conduct is to be compared is a person having the power of self-control to be expected of an ordinary person of the sex and age of the accused. Subsequently, the English Court of Appeal held that an alcoholic was not entitled to any special leniency in determining the adequacy of the provocation: The standard to be applied is that of the reasonable sober person. Regina v. Newell, 71 Crim. App. 331 (1981).

In the United States, the dispute has often been over whether psychiatric evidence is admissible on the provocation issue. A defendant might wish to offer psychiatric or other evidence of mental abnormality on at least three issues in this connection, putting aside the defense of insanity (the subject of the next chapter). First, he might wish to prove that at the time of the killing he was subjectively emotionally disturbed or in a heat of passion. Psychiatric evidence could be relevant to this issue, if it is sufficiently reliable. See Commonwealth v. McCusker, 448 Pa. 382, 292 A.2d 286 (1972). One objection to the use of such testimony is that, when a psychiatrist testifies on what the defendant's state of mind was at a particular moment in the past, he is acting as a sort of human lie detector. The psychiatrist ordinarily relies on what the defendant said in interviews, and then transforms the defendant's story into "scientific evidence," by using it as the basis for an expert opinion.

Second, the defendant might wish to argue the sufficiency of the provocation (or the reasonableness of the emotional disturbance), so that a threat addressed to an emotionally disturbed person might be considered sufficient provocation to mitigate a homicide even though the same threat addressed to a normal person would be insufficient. Most jurisdictions consider evidence of the defendant's personal mental state irrelevant on this issue, because the homicide is mitigated only if the circumstances would have provoked a reasonable person in the defendant's position. For the majority view and a thorough review of the cases, see Taylor v. State, 452 So.2d 441 (Miss.1984).

Third, the defendant might wish to show that his mental condition at the time of the homicide was such that he was unable to form an intent to kill or to realize that his actions were placing someone's life at great risk. In other words, he might argue that, due to mental abnormality, he lacked any of the positive elements of malice aforethought. For example, a diabetic man who killed his estranged wife claimed that the killing was not "intentional" because he was extremely intoxicated from a combination of excessive insulin and alcohol. A New York court held that an instruction on the lesser included offense of reckless manslaughter should have been given. People v. Morton, 100 A.D.2d 637, 473 N.Y.S.2d 66 (1984). In this type of case, the claim of lack of mens rea overlaps with the defense of legal insanity, and the related doctrine of "diminished responsibility." The majority view is that this type of claim must be made under the legal insanity defense or some other special doctrine rather than the general issue of mens rea. This issue is more thoroughly considered in the following chapter.

California Penal Code

§ 187. Murder defined; death of fetus

(a) Murder is the unlawful killing of a human being, or a fetus, with malice aforethought.

(b) This section shall not apply to [a lawful abortion].

§ 188. Malice defined

Such malice may be express or implied. It is express when there is manifested a deliberate intention unlawfully to take away the life of a fellow creature. It is implied, when no considerable provocation appears, or when the circumstances attending the killing show an abandoned and malignant heart.

When it is shown that the killing resulted from the intentional doing of an act with express or implied malice as defined above, no other mental state need be shown to establish the mental state of malice aforethought. Neither an awareness of the obligation to act within the general body of laws regulating society nor acting despite such awareness is included within the definition of malice. [This sentence repudiates the holding in People v. Poddar, 10 Cal.3d 750, 111 Cal.Rptr. 910, 518 P.2d 342 (1974).—ed.]

§ 189. Degrees of Murder

All murder which is perpetrated by means of a destructive device or explosive, knowing use of ammunition designed primarily to penetrate metal or armor, poison, lying in wait, torture, or by any other kind of willful, deliberate, and premeditated killing, or which is committed in the perpetration of, or attempt to perpetrate, arson, rape, carjacking, robbery, burglary, mayhem, kidnapping, train wrecking, or any act punishable under Section 206, 286, 288, 288a, or 289 * * *, is murder of the first degree; and all other kinds of murders are of the second degree. * * * To prove the killing was "deliberate and premeditated," it shall not be necessary to prove the defendant maturely and meaningfully reflected upon the gravity of his or her act. [This sentence repudiates the holding in People v. Wolff, 61 Cal.2d 795, 40 Cal.Rptr. 271, 394 P.2d 959 (1964).—ed.]

§ 190. Punishment for Murder

(a) Every person guilty of murder in the first degree shall suffer death, confinement in state prison for life without possibility of parole, or confinement in the state prison for a term of 25 years to life. * * *

Except as provided in subdivision (b), (c), or (d), every person guilty of murder in the second degree shall be punished by imprisonment in the state prison for a term of 15 years to life. * * *

[Sections relating to imposition of the death penalty or life imprisonment without parole for first degree murder with special circumstances, and those providing enhanced penalties for particular forms of second degree murder are omitted.—ed.]

§ 192. Manslaughter

Manslaughter is the unlawful killing of a human being without malice. It is of three kinds:

(a) Voluntary—upon a sudden quarrel or heat of passion.

(b) Involuntary—in the commission of an unlawful act, not amounting to felony; or in the commission of a lawful act which might produce death, in an unlawful manner, or without due caution and circumspection. This subdivision shall not apply to acts committed in the driving of a vehicle.

(c) Vehicular—

(1) Except as provided in Section 191.5, driving a vehicle in the commission of an unlawful act, not amounting to felony, and with gross negligence; or driving a vehicle in the commission of a lawful act which might produce death, in an unlawful manner, and with gross negligence. [§ 191.5 defines the crime of "gross vehicular manslaughter while intoxicated," which is punishable by imprisonment for 4, 6, or 10 years.—ed. As the title indicates, this section applies to intoxicated drivers who are also guilty of gross negligence in driving and cause death.]

(2) Except as provided in paragraph (3), driving a vehicle in the commission of an unlawful act, not amounting to felony, but without gross negligence; or driving a vehicle in the commission of a lawful act which might produce death, in an unlawful manner, but without gross negligence.

(3) Driving a vehicle in violation of Section 23140, 23152 or 23153 of the Vehicle Code [i.e. while intoxicated] and in the commission of an unlawful act, not amounting to felony, but without gross negligence; or driving a vehicle in violation of Section 23140, 23152 or 23153 of the Vehicle Code and in the commission of a lawful act which might produce death, in an unlawful manner, but without gross negligence. * * *

This section shall not be construed as making any homicide in the driving of a vehicle punishable which is not a proximate result of the commission of an unlawful act, not amounting to felony, or of the commission of a lawful act which might produce death, in an unlawful manner.

"Gross negligence", as used in this section, shall not be construed as prohibiting or precluding a charge of murder under Section 188 upon facts exhibiting wantonness and a conscious disregard for life to support a finding of implied malice, or upon facts showing malice, consistent with the holding of the California Supreme Court in People v. Watson, 30 Cal.3d 290, 179 Cal.Rptr. 43, 637 P.2d 279 (1981).

§ 193. Punishment of Manslaughter

(a) Voluntary manslaughter is punishable by imprisonment in the state prison for three, six, or eleven years.

(b) Involuntary manslaughter is punishable by imprisonment in the state prison for two, three or four years.

(c) Vehicular manslaughter is punishable as follows:

(1) A violation of paragraph (1) of subdivision (c) of Section 192 is punishable either by imprisonment in the county jail for not more than one year or by imprisonment in the state prison for two, four, or six years. (2) A violation of paragraph (2) of subdivision (c) of Section 192 is punishable by imprisonment in the county jail for not more than one year. (3) A violation of paragraph (3) of subdivision (c) of Section 192 is punishable either by imprisonment in the county jail for not more than

one year or by imprisonment in the state prison for 16 months or two or four years. * * *

Model Penal Code

Section 210.1. Criminal Homicide

(1) A person is guilty of criminal homicide if he purposely, knowingly, recklessly or negligently causes the death of another human being.

(2) Criminal homicide is murder, manslaughter or negligent homicide.

Section 210.2. Murder

(1) Except as provided in Section 210.3(1)(b), criminal homicide constitutes murder when:

(a) it is committed purposely or knowingly; or

(b) it is committed recklessly under circumstances manifesting extreme indifference to the value of human life. Such recklessness and indifference are presumed if the actor is engaged or is an accomplice in the commission of, or an attempt to commit, or flight after committing or attempting to commit robbery, rape or deviate sexual intercourse by force or threat of force, arson, burglary, kidnapping or felonious escape.

(2) Murder is a felony of the first degree * * *.

Section 210.3. Manslaughter

(1) Criminal homicide constitutes manslaughter when:

(a) it is committed recklessly; or

(b) a homicide which would otherwise be murder is committed under the influence of extreme mental or emotional disturbance for which there is reasonable explanation or excuse. The reasonableness of such explanation or excuse shall be determined from the viewpoint of a person in the actor's situation under the circumstances as he believes them to be.

(2) Manslaughter is a felony of the second degree.

Section 210.4. Negligent Homicide

(1) Criminal homicide constitutes negligent homicide when it is committed negligently.

(2) Negligent homicide is a felony of the third degree.

Section 210.5. Causing or Aiding Suicide

(1) Causing Suicide as Criminal Homicide. A person may be convicted of criminal homicide for causing another to commit suicide only if he purposely causes such suicide by force, duress or deception.

(2) Aiding or Soliciting Suicide as an Independent Offense. A person who purposely aids or solicits another to commit suicide is guilty of a felony of the second degree if his conduct causes such suicide or an attempted suicide, and otherwise of a misdemeanor.

Section 6.06. Sentence of Imprisonment for Felony; Ordinary Terms

A person who has been convicted of a felony may be sentenced to imprisonment, as follows:

(1) in the case of a felony of the first degree, for a term the minimum of which shall be fixed by the Court at not less than one year nor more than ten years, and the maximum of which shall be life imprisonment;

(2) in the case of a felony of the second degree, for a term the minimum of which shall be fixed by the Court at not less than one year nor more than three years, and the maximum of which shall be ten years;

(3) in the case of a felony of the third degree, for a term the minimum of which shall be fixed by the Court at not less than one year nor more than two years, and the maximum of which shall be five years.

Illinois Criminal Code of 1961

§ 9–1. Murder[a]

(a) A person who kills an individual without lawful justification commits murder if, in performing the acts which cause the death:

(1) He either intends to kill or do great bodily harm to that individual or another, or knows that such acts will cause death to that individual or another; or

(2) He knows that such acts create a strong probability of death or great bodily harm to that individual or another; or

(3) He is attempting or committing a forcible felony other than voluntary manslaughter.

* * *

§ 9–2. Voluntary Manslaughter

(a) A person who kills an individual without lawful justification commits voluntary manslaughter if at the time of the killing he is acting under a sudden and intense passion resulting from serious provocation by:

(1) The individual killed, or

a. The Illinois homicide statutes were revised in 1987 (and thereafter). The crime previously described as "murder" (§ 9–1) was renamed as "first degree murder," and voluntary manslaughter (§ 9–2) became "second degree murder." Complicated provisions relating to the death penalty and other sentencing issues were added. The statutes as currently amended are extremely lengthy, and the cases in this volume were decided under the earlier provisions. Hence the pre–1987 statutes are reproduced here rather than the current versions.—ed.

(2) Another whom the offender endeavors to kill, but he negligently or accidentally causes the death of the individual killed.

Serious provocation is conduct sufficient to excite an intense passion in a reasonable person.

(b) A person who intentionally or knowingly kills an individual commits voluntary manslaughter if at the time of the killing he believes the circumstances to be such that, if they existed, would justify or exonerate the killing under the principles stated in Article 7 of this Code, but his belief is unreasonable.

(c) Sentence.

Voluntary Manslaughter is a Class 1 felony.

§ 9–3. Involuntary Manslaughter and Reckless Homicide

(a) A person who unintentionally kills an individual without lawful justification commits involuntary manslaughter if his acts whether lawful or unlawful which cause the death are such as are likely to cause death or great bodily harm to some individual, and he performs them recklessly, except in cases in which the cause of the death consists of the driving of a motor vehicle, in which case the person commits reckless homicide.

(b) Sentence.

(1) Involuntary manslaughter is a Class 3 felony.

(2) Reckless homicide is a Class 3 felony.

New York Penal Law[b]

§ 125.10 Criminally negligent homicide

A person is guilty of criminally negligent homicide when, with criminal negligence, he causes the death of another person.

Criminally negligent homicide is a class E felony.

§ 125.15 Manslaughter in the second degree

A person is guilty of manslaughter in the second degree when:

1. He recklessly causes the death of another person; or

* * *

3. He intentionally causes or aids another person to commit suicide.

Manslaughter in the second degree is a class C felony.

b. The New York statutes are reprinted here as enacted in 1965. Subsequent amendments adding complications which need not be considered here are omitted. The crime of "murder" (§ 125.25) has become murder in the second degree, and there is a limited category of first degree murder applicable to murders by life prisoners and certain murders of police officers and prison guards. Death penalty provisions were added in March, 1995.—ed.

§ 125.20 Manslaughter in the first degree

A person is guilty of manslaughter in the first degree when:

1. With intent to cause serious physical injury to another person, he causes the death of such person or of a third person; or

2. With intent to cause the death of another person, he causes the death of such person or of a third person under circumstances which do not constitute murder because he acts under the influence of extreme emotional disturbance, as defined in paragraph (a) of subdivision one of section 125.25. The fact that homicide was committed under the influence of extreme emotional disturbance constitutes a mitigating circumstance reducing murder to manslaughter in the first degree and need not be proved in any prosecution initiated under this subdivision; * * *

Manslaughter in the first degree is a class B felony.

§ 125.25 Murder

A person is guilty of murder when:

1. With intent to cause the death of another person, he causes the death of such person or of a third person; except that in any prosecution under this subdivision, it is an affirmative defense that:

(a) The defendant acted under the influence of extreme emotional disturbance for which there was a reasonable explanation or excuse, the reasonableness of which is to be determined from the viewpoint of a person in the defendant's situation under the circumstances as the defendant believed them to be. Nothing contained in this paragraph shall constitute a defense to a prosecution for, or preclude a conviction of, manslaughter in the first degree or any other crime; or

(b) The defendant's conduct consisted of causing or aiding, without the use of duress or deception, another person to commit suicide. Nothing contained in this paragraph shall constitute a defense to a prosecution for, or preclude a conviction of, manslaughter in the second degree or any other crime; or

2. Under circumstances evincing a depraved indifference to human life, he recklessly engages in conduct which creates a grave risk of death to another person, and thereby causes the death of another person; or

3. Acting either alone or with one or more other persons, he commits or attempts to commit robbery, burglary, kidnapping, arson, rape in the first degree, sodomy in the first degree, sexual abuse in the first degree, escape in the first degree, or escape in the second degree, and, in the course of and in furtherance of such crime or of immediate flight therefrom, he, or another participant, if there be any, causes the death of a person other than one of the participants; except that in any prosecution under this subdivision, in which the defendant was not the only participant in the underlying crime, it is an affirmative defense that the defendant:

(a) Did not commit the homicidal act or in any way solicit, request, command, importune, cause or aid the commission thereof; and

(b) Was not armed with a deadly weapon, or any instrument, article or substance readily capable of causing death or serious physical injury and of a sort not ordinarily carried in public places by law-abiding persons; and

(c) Had no reasonable ground to believe that any other participant was armed with such a weapon, instrument, article or substance; and

(d) Had no reasonable ground to believe that any other participant intended to engage in conduct likely to result in death or serious physical injury.

Murder is a class A felony.

§ 70.00 Indeterminate sentence of imprisonment for felony

1. Indeterminate sentence. A sentence of imprisonment for a felony shall be an indeterminate sentence. When such a sentence is imposed, the court shall impose a maximum term in accordance with the provisions of subdivision two of this section and the minimum period of imprisonment shall be as provided in subdivision three of this section.

2. Maximum term of sentence. The maximum term of an indeterminate sentence shall be at least three years and the term shall be fixed as follows:

(a) For a class A felony, the term shall be life imprisonment;

(b) For a class B felony, the term shall be fixed by the court, and shall not exceed twenty-five years;

(c) For a class C felony, the term shall be fixed by the court, and shall not exceed fifteen years;

(d) For a class D felony, the term shall be fixed by the court, and shall not exceed seven years; and

(e) For a class E felony, the term shall be fixed by the court, and shall not exceed four years.

3. Minimum period of imprisonment. The minimum period of imprisonment under an indeterminate sentence shall be at least one year and shall be fixed as follows:

(a) In the case of a class A felony, the minimum period shall be fixed by the court and specified in the sentence. Such minimum period shall not be less than fifteen years nor more than twenty-five years;

(b) Where the sentence is for a class B, class C or class D felony and the court, having regard to the nature and circumstances of the crime and to the history and character of the defendant, is of the opinion that the ends of justice and best interests of the public require that the court fix a minimum period of imprisonment, the court may fix the minimum period. In such event, the minimum period shall be specified in the sentence and shall not be more than one-third of the maximum term imposed. When the minimum period of imprisonment is fixed pursuant to this paragraph, the court shall set forth in the record the reasons for its action; and

(c) In any other case, the minimum period of imprisonment shall be fixed by the state board of parole in accordance with the provisions of the correction law.

B. DEGREES OF MURDER: PREMEDITATION

PEOPLE v. CARUSO

Court of Appeals of New York, 1927.
246 N.Y. 437, 159 N.E. 390.

ANDREWS, J. This judgment must be reversed. * * *

Francesco Caruso, an illiterate Italian, 35 years old, came to this country about 1911. He worked as a laborer, and in the early part of 1927 was living with his wife and six small children in an apartment in Brooklyn. On Friday, February 11, one of these children, a boy of six, was ill with a sore throat. That day and the next he treated the boy with remedies bought at a drug store. The child grew worse, and at 10 o'clock of the night of the 12th he sent for a Dr. Pendola, who had been recommended to him, but with whom he was not acquainted.

What follows depends upon a statement made by Caruso and upon his testimony on the stand. Any proper inferences may be drawn therefrom. The belief that what he said was false, however, or any reasoning based upon his failure to call friendly witnesses, will not supply the want of affirmative testimony of the facts necessary to constitute the crime. These facts, if they exist, must be inferred from his own admissions.

Some time between 10:30 and 11 in the evening Dr. Pendola arrived. The child had diphtheria. Caruso was sent out to buy some antitoxin, and when he returned the doctor administered it. He then gave Caruso another prescription with instructions as to its use, and left promising to return in the morning.

Caruso watched the child all night, giving remedies every half hour. "About 4 o'clock in the morning," he testified, "my child was standing up to the bed, and asked me to, he says, 'Papa' he said, 'I am dying.' I say that time, I said, 'You don't die.' I said, 'I will help you every time.' The same time that child he will be crazy—look like crazy that time—don't want to stay any more inside. All I can do, I keep my child in my arms, and I held him in my arms from 4 o'clock until 8 o'clock in the morning. After 8 o'clock in the morning the poor child getting worse—the poor child in the morning he was"—(slight interruption in the testimony while the defendant apparently stops to overcome his emotion). "The poor child that time, and he was asking me, 'Papa,' he said, 'I want to go and sleep.' So I said, 'All right, Giovie, I will put you in the sleep.' I take my Giovie, and I put him in the bed, and he started to sleep, to wait until the doctor came, and the doctor he never came. I waited from 10 o'clock, the doctor he never came."

Then, after trying in vain to get in touch with the doctor, he sent for an ambulance from a drug store. "When I go home I seen my child is got up to the bed that time, and he says to me, 'Papa, I want to come with you.' I take my child again up in my arms, and I make him look to the backyard to the window. He looked around the yard about a couple of minutes, and after, when he looked around, he says to me, 'Papa, I want to go to sleep again.' I said, 'All right, Giovie, I will put you in the sleep.' I put my child on the bed. About a few seconds my child is on the bed, my child says to me, he says, 'Papa, I want to go to the toilet.' I said, 'All right, Giovie, I will take you to the toilet.' So I was trying to pick up the child, and make him go to the toilet, when I held that child I felt that leg—that child started to shake up in my arms. My wife know about better than me—I cannot see good myself in the face, so she tell what kind of shakes he do, and she has told me, she says, 'Listen, Frank, why, the child has died already.' I said, 'All right, you don't cry. No harm, because you make the child scared.' That time I go right away and put the child on the bed. When I put the child, before I put my hand to the pillow, my child said to me, 'Good-bye, Papa, I am going already.' So that time I put my hands to my head—I said, 'That child is dead. I don't know what I am going to do myself now.' That time I never said nothing, because I said, 'Jesus, my child is dead now. Nobody will get their hands on my child.' "

About 12 o'clock Dr. Pendola arrived. The child had been dead for some time, he was told, and then Caruso says the doctor laughed, and he "lost his head." This seems incredible. Yet Caruso apparently believed it, for his testimony on the stand is a repetition of the same charge made in his statement that same night, before it is likely that a man of Caruso's mentality would be preparing a false defense. The probability is there was, from one cause or another, some twitching of the facial muscles that might be mistaken for a smile.

Besides the delay of the doctor and the smile was another circumstance, which, if true, would exasperate Caruso. He says, and again this appears in the statement as well as in his testimony on the trial, that, when he was buying the antitoxin, the druggist told him that the dose was too large for a child of the age of his son. This he told the doctor. The latter was indignant, and paid no heed to the warning. The druggist denied any such conversation, and apparently the dose was proper. But it seems probable that something occurred that left on Caruso's mind the impression that the death of his child was caused by malpractice. At least, immediately after the death, he told an ambulance surgeon that Dr. Pendola had killed his child by an injection, and also complained of his delay in not coming that morning. And within a short time he made the same charge to others.

Then followed some talk. Caruso accused the doctor of killing his child. The doctor denied it. Caruso attacked him in anger, choked him until he fell to the floor, then went to a closet ten or twelve feet away, took a knife, and stabbed him twice in the throat, so killing him. Caruso then took his family to the janitor's apartment downstairs, and himself went to his brother's house on Staten Island, where he was arrested that night. He made no attempt whatever to conceal the facts of the homicide, and his departure cannot fairly be viewed as a flight, indicating consciousness of guilt.

The case for the people was simple. Formal identification of the dead body was required. That Caruso committed a homicide, neither excusable nor justifiable, was abundantly shown by his own statement, and, indeed, was not denied. The real issue was as to state of mind of the defendant, whether he formed the intent to kill Dr. Pendola, and, if so, whether the killing was the result of premeditation and deliberation. What Caruso in fact believed and thought, what he had in mind at the time of the homicide, is the issue—not whether his beliefs were justified. And the jury, horrified at the conceded brutality of his acts, are still to decide this issue in a judicial temper. Appeals to sympathy or prejudice can but be harmful.

Mrs. Pendola, the widow of the deceased, was a young woman, placed upon the stand by the state. The right to use her as a witness for a proper purpose is not questioned, notwithstanding the natural sympathy her presence would arouse. But she knew nothing of the circumstances of the crime. She might have been asked as to the identity of the deceased, although he could be identified by others. She might give any other material evidence, notwithstanding any influence her presence might have upon the jury. Mrs. Pendola was not called for any such purpose. She was allowed to say she had been married for 18 months; that she had one child, 6 months old; that her husband was a medical graduate; she explained why his call on Caruso was delayed on Sunday, the 13th; she gave conversations with the doctor when he received the telephone call from Caruso Saturday night, and again after his return; she told how he sat on his baby's crib and sang her to sleep. All this had no materiality upon the issues before the jury. The object of the state is clear. Although, doubtless, the result of "well intentioned though misguided zeal," it was an "unseemly and unsafe" appeal to prejudice. Nor here can we overlook it as probably unheeded. And the object of the prosecution is emphasized by questions, ruled out it is true, as to whether the defendant was a citizen, or had applied for naturalization. They were so plainly incompetent, it cannot be believed they were asked in good faith.

Testimony was given by an expert that the treatment of the child was correct, and the doses of antitoxin not excessive. The belief of Caruso as to these facts was the question, not whether his belief was mistaken. Nor did this testimony tend to corroborate the denial of the druggist that he had ever told Caruso that the dose was too large.

But, passing the two questions already discussed, which would under the circumstances of this case require a reversal, there is also a fundamental reason requiring a new trial. Conviction here of murder in the first degree is not justified by the weight of the evidence. The jury might find that the intent to kill existed. While in his testimony on the stand Caruso denies such an intent, and says that in his rage he did not know what he was doing, yet in his statement he expressly admits his intent to kill, and the inference that the intent existed might also be drawn from the two wounds in the neck inflicted with a large knife.

But was there premeditation and deliberation? This seems to have been the question which troubled the jury. They considered their verdict for six hours—twice returning for definitions of homicide and of deliberation and premeditation. Time to deliberate and premeditate there clearly was. Caruso might have done so. In fact, however, did he?

Until the Saturday evening Caruso had never met Dr. Pendola. Nothing occurred at that interview that furnished any motive for murder. Then came nervous strain and anxiety culminating in grief, deep and genuine, for the death of his child. Brooding over his loss, blaming the doctor for his delay in making the promised visit, believing he had killed the boy by his treatment, the doctor finally enters. And, when told of the child's death he appears to laugh. This, added to his supposed injuries, would fully account for the gust of anger that Caruso says he felt. Then came the struggle and the homicide.

As has been said, Caruso had the time to deliberate, to make a choice whether to kill or not to kill—to overcome hesitation and doubt—to form a definite purpose. And, where sufficient time exists, very often the circumstances surrounding the homicide justify—indeed require—the necessary inference. Not here, however. No plan to kill is shown, no intention of violence when the doctor arrived—only grief and resentment. Not until the supposed laugh did the assault begin. * * * When the supposed laugh came there was apparent cause for excitement and anger. There was enough to indicate hot blood and unreflecting action. There was immediate provocation. The attack seems to have been the instant effect of impulse. Nor does the fact that the stabbing followed the beginning of the attack by some time affect this conclusion. It was all one transaction under the peculiar facts of this case. If the assault was not deliberated or premeditated, then neither was the infliction of the fatal wound. With due consideration of all the facts presented there is insufficient evidence to justify a conviction of murder in the first degree. Doubtless, on this record the defendant might be convicted of some crime, either murder in the second degree, or, if his testimony on the stand is accepted, manslaughter in the first degree. Either verdict might be sustained on the facts. Not the one actually rendered.

The judgment of conviction is reversed, and a new trial ordered.

STATE v. BINGHAM

Supreme Court of Washington, 1986.
105 Wash.2d 820, 719 P.2d 109.

GOODLOE, JUSTICE.

[Bingham was charged with aggravated first degree (premeditated) murder, for raping and strangling Leslie Cook, a retarded adult woman.] The evidence showed that on February 15 Cook and Bingham got off a bus together in Sequim about 6 p.m. There was no evidence that they knew each other before this time. They visited a grocery store and two residences. * * * Three days later, Cook's body was found in a field [near where the two had last been seen together.]

At trial, King County Medical Examiner Reay described the results of the autopsy he performed on Cook's body. The cause of death was "asphyxiation through manual strangulation", accomplished by applying continuous pressure to the windpipe for approximately 3 to 5 minutes. Cook had a bruise on her upper lip, more likely caused by a hand being pressed over her mouth than by a violent blow. Tears were found in Cook's vaginal wall and anal ring. Spermatozoa was present. These injuries were inflicted antemortem. Also, there was a bite mark on each of Cook's breasts. Reay testified that these occurred perimortem or postmortem.

Two forensic odontologists testified that the bite mark on one breast matched Bingham's teeth. No conclusive determination could be made with respect to the other bite mark.

The prosecutor's theory was that Bingham wanted to have sex with Cook and that he had to kill her in order to do so. The prosecutor hypothesized that Bingham had started the act while Cook was alive, and that he put his hand over her mouth and then strangled her in order to complete the act. The prosecutor also told the jury that the murder would be premeditated if Bingham had formed the intent to kill when he began to strangle Cook, and thought about that intent for the 3 to 5 minutes it took her to die.

* * * The jury found Bingham guilty of aggravated first degree murder. The jury also found, in the penalty phase, that the State had failed to prove that there were insufficient mitigating circumstances to warrant leniency. The trial court therefore sentenced Bingham to life imprisonment without the possibility of release or parole.

Bingham was charged with first degree murder, which requires for conviction "a premeditated intent to cause the death of another". The element of premeditation distinguishes first and second degree murder. Washington case law further defines premeditation as "the mental process of thinking beforehand, deliberation, reflection, weighing or reasoning for a period of time, however short." We recently approved an instruction which defined premeditation as "the deliberate formation of and reflection upon the intent to take a human life."

To show premeditation, the State relied on the pathologist's testimony that manual strangulation takes 3 to 5 minutes. The State argues this is an appreciable amount of time in which Bingham could have deliberated. Bingham argues that time alone is not enough and that other indicators of premeditation must be shown. * * *

We hold that to allow a finding of premeditation only because the act takes an appreciable amount of time obliterates the distinction between first and second degree murder. Having the opportunity to deliberate is not evidence the defendant did deliberate, which is necessary for a finding of premeditation. Otherwise, any form of killing which took more than a moment could result in a finding of premeditation, without some additional evidence showing reflection. Holding a hand over someone's mouth or windpipe does not necessarily reflect a decision to kill the person, but possibly only to quiet her or him. Furthermore, here a question of the ability to deliberate or reflect while engaged in sexual activity exists. * * *

The facts of a savage murder generate a powerful drive, almost a juggernaut for jurors, and indeed for judges, to crush the crime with the utmost condemnation available, to seize whatever words or terms reflect maximum denunciation, to cry out murder "in the first degree." But it is the task and conscience of a judge to transcend emotional momentum with reflective analysis. The judge is aware that many murders most brutish and bestial are committed in a consuming frenzy or heat of passion, and that these are in law only murder in the second degree. The evidence establishes an intentional and horrible murder—the kind that could be committed in a frenzy or heat of passion. * * * We hold that manual strangulation alone is insufficient evidence to support a finding of premeditation.

[The court ordered that the defendant be sentenced for second degree murder.]

CALLOW, JUSTICE (dissenting).

* * * The rule announced by the majority seems to be that premeditation must take place before the commencement of the act that results in death. Take the farmer's son who begins to fill the bin with wheat as a joke on his brother sleeping at its bottom. Then, realizing that he will inherit the whole farm if he persists, he does so and causes his brother's death. He had time to premeditate and did so in the middle of the act. He has committed aggravated first degree murder. That a murderer originally commenced an act without intending death does not grant him a carte blanche to persist when he realizes that to do so will kill his victim. * * *

The jury heard the testimony of Dr. Reay that it takes 3 to 5 minutes to effect death by manual strangulation. Continuous and steady pressure on the victim's neck is required. The amount of pressure required is greater than the amount required to keep someone from crying out. The strangulation of Leslie Cook was cruel and brutal. The jury would be justified in concluding from the circumstances that the death was not the result of an impulsive or spontaneous act flowing from an attempt to overcome resistance or to effect sexual contact and that the defendant chose to kill in order to silence his victim and conceal a rape.

I would reinstate the first degree murder conviction. [Four of the nine Justices joined this dissent.]

STATE v. OLLENS

Supreme Court of Washington, 1987.
107 Wash.2d 848, 733 P.2d 984.

GOODLOE, JUSTICE.

Ollens was charged with aggravated murder in the first degree for the November 9, 1985 robbery/stabbing death of William Tyler, a Tacoma taxicab driver. Before trial he moved to dismiss the aggravated first degree murder charge because of lack of evidence to prove the element of premeditation. * * *

* * * The State relied on the testimony of Dr. Lacsina, the Medical Examiner. Dr. Lacsina testified that Tyler died from multiple stab wounds and resulting blood loss. * * * [describing the effects of four stab wounds to the body.]

In addition, Dr. Lacsina testified that Tyler's throat had been slit. More than one slashing motion was needed to complete the 6–inch gash which nearly transected the voice box and jugular vein. This injury was also capable of causing death. Dr. Lacsina testified, however, that Tyler could have been alive and struggling for 2 to 3 minutes after the neck wound. He stated that the stab wounds preceded the slashing of Tyler's throat, and he also noted that there were numerous defensive wounds. These wounds were inflicted when the victim was alive and indicate that the assailant and victim struggled.

At the hearing, the defense asserted that the State's main witness would testify that Ollens admitted to him that he had killed the victim when the victim made a move as if to reach for a weapon and "[Ollens] cut the man because he felt it was either the man's life or his."

Citing State v. Bingham, 105 Wash.2d 820, 719 P.2d 109 (1986) the trial court concluded that the "use of a knife to inflict more than one wound, in and of itself, is not probative of premeditation, but * * * can only be probative of intent to kill". The State appealed to this court seeking review as a matter of right pursuant to [applicable statutes.]

The issue we address is: Given multiple stab and slash wounds, is there sufficient evidence to send the question of premeditation to a jury? Specific intent to kill and premeditation are not synonymous, but separate and distinct elements of the crime of first-degree murder. Premeditation has been defined as "the deliberate formation of and reflection upon the intent to take a human life", and involves "the mental process of thinking beforehand, deliberation, reflection, weighing or reasoning for a period of however short." [Citations] Premeditation must involve more than a moment in point of time.

Ollens argues that *Bingham* is not limited to manual strangulation, as *Bingham* emphasizes the application of its analysis to other methods of death. Having the opportunity to deliberate is not evidence the defendant did deliberate, which is necessary for a finding of premeditation. Otherwise, any form of killing which took more than a moment could result in a finding of premeditation, without some additional evidence showing reflection. * * *

The issue before this court is whether *Bingham* is controlling in this situation such that given the evidence no trier of fact could find premeditation beyond a reasonable doubt. We hold that *Bingham* is distinguishable. First, manual strangulation involves one continuous act. In the case at hand, not only did Ollens stab the victim numerous times, he thereafter slashed the victim's throat. This subsequent slashing is an indication that respondent did premeditate on his already formed intent to kill. Second, a knife was used in the killing. The strangulation in *Bingham* did not involve the procurement of a weapon. Third, from the evidence a jury could find that Ollens struck Tyler from behind, a further indication of premeditation. Finally, a jury could find the presence of a motive and, therefore, it would not be left to speculate or surmise only as to the existence of premeditation.

* * * We reverse the Superior Court's dismissal of the premeditation charge and remand for the continuation of proceedings consistent with this opinion.

CALLOW, JUSTICE.

* * * Premeditated means thought over beforehand. When a person, after any deliberation, forms an intent to take human life, the killing may follow immediately after the formation of the settled purpose and it will still be premeditated. Premeditation must involve more than a moment in point of time. The law requires some time, however long or short, in which a design to kill is deliberately formed.

When the four justifications for allowing the issue of premeditation to go to the jury set forth in the majority are compared with *Bingham,* we find: (1) both attacks were prolonged, continued for an appreciable period of time and concluded with the death of the victim; (2) the absence of a weapon in *Bingham* is more than compensated for by the physical advantage of a man over a retarded female. * * * (3) The jury in *Ollens,* because they could have found that the defendant struck the victim from behind, is permitted to find that this was evidence of premeditation. The jury in *Bingham* had before it the conclusive evidence that the defendant had violently raped and then strangled his victim. This latter fact is surely as probative as speculation as to which stab wound was inflicted first and from what direction. (4) While the jury in *Ollens* is permitted to find a motive ("could find") to eliminate speculation as to premeditation, the jury in *Bingham* had before it as strong a reason to find a motive from the evidence as exists in this case.

I do not concur for the purpose of rehashing the result in *Bingham;* I concur to point out that no basis exists to make homicide by strangulation an isolated crime where premeditation cannot be proven. The majority's rationale forces this conclusion when only the defendant and the victim were present in a one-on-one situation, yet allows proof of premeditation in a one-on-one situation when a weapon is present. Sufficiency of the evidence of premeditation to allow the issue to go to the jury is present in this case, and I submit the evidence was sufficient to pass that test in the *Bingham* circumstances. * * *

GILBERT v. STATE

Florida District Court of Appeal, 1986.
487 So.2d 1185.

WALDEN, JUDGE.

Upon trial by jury, Roswell Gilbert was found guilty of the premeditated [first degree] murder of his wife, Emily. He, at age 75, was sentenced to life imprisonment. Under section 775.082, Florida Statutes (1981), there is a mandatory minimum sentence of 25 years. Thus, Mr. Gilbert would be incarcerated until he reached the age of 100 years before he would be eligible for release.

Mr. and Mrs. Gilbert lived together in a Fort Lauderdale condominium. They had been married for 51 years. Emily suffered from osteoporosis and Alzheimer's Disease. Her physician, Dr. Hidalgo, had prescribed Percodan to help alleviate the pain of the arthritis. The dosage was for moderate pain. There is no doubt that she was in pain because of the osteoporosis and sometimes confused because of the Alzheimer's.

Lillian Irvin testified that Emily was in a lot of pain because of the arthritis. One day, while Lillian was in her condominium office, Emily came in looking for appellant. She was upset and crying. He was in a condominium meeting, so Lillian called him out of the meeting to come and attend to his wife. When he arrived Emily said, "I'm so sick, I want to die, I'm so sick * * * Ros I want to die, I want to die."

On cross-examination Lillian testified that Emily would come down from her tenth floor apartment every day to either look for appellant or walk around the condominium pool. The couple also went out to lunch every day. Jacqueline Rhodes also testified for the defense. She stated that Emily had deteriorated during the last two years of their acquaintance. She was forgetful at times and in pain because of her back. In Jacqueline's opinion appellant had always been very kind and attentive to his wife. On one particular occasion, Jacqueline went to the Gilberts' apartment and saw Emily lying on the sofa crying and looking very sick. This struck Jacqueline as particularly indicative of Emily's condition.

Appellant testified in his own defense. He recounted their lives together from the first incident of osteoporosis, which was approximately eight years before her death. As time progressed the arthritis worsened and then Emily began to lose her memory. This was diagnosed as

Alzheimer's Disease. The manifestation of Emily's illness which appeared to bother appellant the most was her increased dependence on him.

She was hospitalized on 3/2

Appellant then described the events which led up to Emily's death. On March 2, Emily had another bout with osteoporosis. The next day he took her to the hospital. Emily did not want to stay there and became uncooperative and insisted on going home. Finally, appellant decided it was best to take her home. This made Emily feel better.

On March 4, the day of the killing, appellant took Emily out to lunch as usual. When they got back he gave her four Percodan tablets, put her on the sofa and went to a condominium meeting. A few minutes later Emily followed him down to the meeting. Appellant left the meeting and took Emily back to their apartment. As she lay on the sofa, she said, "Please, somebody help me. Please, somebody help me." In his own words this is how appellant killed Emily:

> Who's that somebody but me, you know, and there she was in pain and all this confusion and I guess if I got cold as icewater that's what had happened. I thought to myself, I've got to do it, it's got to be mine, I've got to end her suffering, this can't go on.
>
> I went in. The gun was up on the top shelf with a clip in it. I loaded it with one shell, pulled the clip out. I don't like to leave loaded guns laying around.
>
> Well, then I shot her in the head. I felt her pulse, I could still feel it. I thought, Oh, my God, I loused it up.
>
> I went back to the shop. This time I was shaking. I wasn't cold as ice at all. Back to the shop, put another round in the gun, came back, put another bullet in her head.
>
> The only comforting thing, the first shot there was no convulsive reaction, just her right hand shook like that fast and her head went over the impacted bullet and it slowly came down, didn't make any noise except her mouth just opened slowly like that and then, you know, I thought it hit so fast she didn't know what happened. Then I felt her pulse. It turned out I was wrong. The pulse keeps going after this episode for a few minutes anyway. I didn't know that. I just thought I had, you know—and the second time I fired I felt the pulse seemed to be gone. So I somehow got to the telephone and called the security guard downstairs and I said, "I just killed my wife," and—[His attorney continued the questioning]:
>
> [Mr. Varon:] Ros, why did you use a gun?
>
> [Appellant:] I think poison is a horrible way to die. There's no such thing as instantaneous death with poison. I know nothing about poisons but I know that and I know nothing about poisons, I didn't have any. If I did have any, I wouldn't know how to use it. * * * Firing a shot in the head will cause cessation of all consciousness in one millisecond, one thousandth of a second. I'm sure she

didn't even hear the gun go off and I've been asked that question. * * *

Q Why did you think that or did you feel that you're the only one that could have ended her suffering?

A Natural conclusion. I can't go to the medical people. They have no cure for Alzheimer's. The osteoporosis was getting worse slowly in time. Everything looked like it was converging to a climax.

I couldn't see any other end than her dying. If I put her in a nursing home, well, after that hospital thing I don't think a nursing home would take her. The hospital certainly wouldn't take her.

So I put her in a nursing home and they won't let me stay there and she's separated from me. It would be a horrible death for her. She would die. Then I can't confide in my friends without getting them involved, you know, in this sort of thing that I did. I couldn't go to the doctor. He is a professional. He is duly bound to report it to the authorities and they would pull me out of the picture.

The whole thing was a mess and the only solution to me was to terminate her suffering. That's all. * * * I didn't consider what would happen to me. The only important thing was to end her suffering. I could take care of whatever happens to me and it's happening right now and that was of no consequence to me. Sure, I know I was breaking the law but there seems to be things more important than the law, at least to me in my private tragedy. So it's murder. So what?

On cross-examination appellant testified that he had never talked with Emily about killing her and had decided to shoot her from behind so she would not see the gun.

The record reveals that up until the time of her death, Emily was always neat and well-dressed, wearing makeup, jewelry, and coordinated outfits. She also went to the hairdresser every two weeks up until the last week of her life. Her doctor testified that Emily could have lived for another five to ten years. She was never bedridden or completely incapacitated.

The appellate presentation on behalf of appellant has been skilled, sensitive and innovative. Regardless, the task facing counsel was impossible or insurmountable in light of the facts and the current state of the law. [The Court held that euthanasia or "mercy killing" is not a defense to a premeditated murder charge in Florida.]

Finally, this court notices that this aged defendant has been a peaceful, law-abiding and respected citizen up until this time. No one has suggested that he will again kill someone or enter upon a criminal career. However, the absolute rigidity of the statutory mandatory minimum sentences do not permit consideration of these factors or, for that matter, they, different from the sentencing guidelines, do not take into account any mitigating circumstances. Whether such sentences should somehow be moderated so as to allow a modicum of discretion and whether they should allow distinctions to be made in sentencing between different kinds of wrongdoers, for instance, between a hired gangster killer and one, however misguided, who kills for love or mercy, are all questions which, under our system, must be decided by the legislature and not by the judicial branch. We leave it there.

AFFIRMED.

GLICKSTEIN, JUDGE, concurring specially.

I agree in general with the reasoning of the majority, and entirely concur in the result. * * *

I have some concern about the hint in the main opinion that trial courts should be enabled to vary minimum mandatory sentences according to the "kind" of wrongdoer; e.g., hired killer versus misguided mercy killer. I do not favor opening the door to such distinctions.

My thoughts lie with the victim, who was silenced forever by appellant's criminal act. She would be no more dead if a hired gangland killer had pulled the trigger.

Can it be that we feel more comfortable about imposing severe punishment on persons we perceive to belong to a separate tribe, whom we label criminals, than on those we see as members of our own tribe? In fact, we are all members of a common humanity.

The Decalogue states categorically, "Thou shalt not murder." It draws no distinction between murder by members of the middle class and murder by members of an underclass. It draws no distinction between murder by a family member and murder by a stranger. It draws no distinction between murder out of a misguided notion of compassion and murder for hire.

The victims in all such cases are equally dead. If the act was deliberate, the minimum penalty should not vary with the actor's purported motivation. The concept of permissive mitigation of the minimum penalty based upon a claim the motive for the killing was compassion is even more difficult to accept when the offender is sophisticated, educated and mature, and has enjoyed opportunities in life to make choices.

Note

The common law never divided murder into degrees. Most American states, however, adopted the "Pennsylvania" formula, derived from a statute enacted in that state in 1794. The formula classifies as "first degree" those murders which are accompanied by "deliberation" and "premeditation," two words which seem to mean the same thing. The purpose of the formula was to provide a category of murder which would not be subject to the automatic death penalty then prevailing. The distinction survived after the death penalty for first degree murder became discretionary, however, and it persists in some jurisdictions (such as Michigan) where the death penalty has long been abolished. The formula is apparently based on the premise that a killing which is planned or considered in advance by a person in a relatively calm or dispassionate state of mind is more blameworthy than a killing committed upon the spur of the moment or under the influence of passion (even in the absence of provocation). This premise is not entirely satisfactory, because some of the most dangerous and brutal killers are individuals who spontaneously kill for little or no reason. On the other hand, there may be mitigating circumstances for a killing which is planned in advance, and such a killer may not be dangerous to other persons in the future.

Courts in Pennsylvania and a number of other states resisted the distinction between planned and unplanned murders from the start. See Keedy, History of the Pennsylvania Statute Creating Degrees of Murder, 97 U.Pa.L.Rev. 759 (1949); Wechsler & Michael, A Rationale of the Law of Homicide, 37 Col.L.Rev. 701–09 (1937). Many earlier decisions, and some recent ones, upheld convictions of first degree murder even though the intent to kill was formed very suddenly and the defendant was in a very excited state of mind. For a particularly extreme example, see Commonwealth v. Carroll, 412 Pa. 525, 194 A.2d 911 (1963). Reflecting on the fact that judicial decisions had essentially abolished the distinction between first and second degree murder in the case of intentional killings, Justice Cardozo observed that "What we have is merely a privilege offered to the jury to find the lesser degree when the suddenness of the intent, the vehemence of the passion, seem to call irresistably for the exercise of mercy. I have no objection to giving them this dispensing power, but it should be given to them directly and not in a mystifying cloud of words." Cardozo, Law and Literature and Other Essays 99 (1931).

The opinions in this subchapter show how difficult it is for courts to give some substantial content to the term premeditation, so that it means something more than just that the killing was intentional or brutal. As the Washington opinions indicate, the savagery of the manner of killing may sometimes indicate that the killer acted in a mad frenzy rather than pursuant to a premeditated plan, and thus may act as a mitigating circumstance. But if the "most brutish and bestial" murders are often unpremeditated, and if these are the murders that jurors and even judges instinctively consider to be murder "in the first degree," then why does the criminal law place so much importance on the element of premeditation or rational reflection? Possibly some other standard which is more consistent with the community's standard of blameworthiness would be more appropriate.

Many jurisdictions admit psychiatric testimony on the issue of premeditation, in an effort to provide jurors with information concerning the quality of the defendant's understanding of what he was doing. A killing by a highly irrational person, such as a paranoid, may nonetheless be planned in advance and thus premeditated, however. The California Supreme Court at one point redefined premeditation to give a greater scope for psychiatric testimony in cases where the defendant committed a planned killing for an irrational motive. The leading case was People v. Wolff, 61 Cal.2d 795, 40 Cal.Rptr. 271, 394 P.2d 959 (1964), in which the defendant was a fifteen-year-old youth who killed his mother to get her out of the way so he could use the family home for a bizarre sexual scheme. Although highly disturbed, Wolff was not legally insane under the prevailing test because he was capable of understanding the wrongfulness of his act. The California Supreme Court nonetheless reduced the verdict of first degree murder to murder in the second degree on the ground that the psychiatric evidence established that Wolff was incapable of "mature and meaningful reflection" upon the gravity of the crime. The doctrine of the *Wolff* case was subsequently repudiated by statute. See West's Ann. California Penal Code § 189, supra p. 184. The subject of "diminished responsibility" is further considered in the concluding section of the next chapter.

C. LIABILITY FOR UNINTENTIONAL KILLINGS

COMMONWEALTH v. MALONE

Supreme Court of Pennsylvania, 1946.
354 Pa. 180, 47 A.2d 445.

MAXEY, CHIEF JUSTICE.

This is an appeal from the judgment and sentence under a conviction of murder in the second degree. William H. Long, age 13 years, was killed by a shot from a 32–caliber revolver held against his right side by the defendant, then aged 17 years. These youths were on friendly terms at the time of the homicide. * * *

On the evening of February 26th, 1945, when the defendant went to a moving picture theater, he carried in the pocket of his raincoat a revolver which he had obtained at the home of his uncle on the preceding day. In the afternoon preceding the shooting, the decedent procured a cartridge from his father's room and he and the defendant placed it in the revolver.

After leaving the theater, the defendant went to a dairy store and there met the decedent. Both youths sat in the rear of the store ten minutes, during which period the defendant took the gun out of his pocket and loaded the chamber to the right of the firing pin and then closed the gun. A few minutes later, both youths sat on stools in front of the lunch counter and ate some food. The defendant suggested to the decedent that they play "Russian Poker."[1]

Long replied: "I don't care; go ahead." The defendant then placed the revolver against the right side of Long and pulled the trigger three times. The third pull resulted in a fatal wound to Long. The latter jumped off the stool and cried: "Oh! Oh! Oh!" and Malone said: "Did I hit you, Billy? Gee, Kid, I'm sorry." Long died from the wounds two days later.

The defendant testified that the gun chamber he loaded was the first one to the right of the firing chamber and that when he pulled the trigger he did not "expect to have the gun go off." He declared he had no intention of harming Long, who was his friend and companion. The defendant was indicted for murder, tried and found guilty of murder in

1. It has been explained that "Russian Poker" is a game in which the participants, in turn, place a single cartridge in one of the five chambers of a revolver cylinder, give the latter a quick twirl, place the muzzle of the gun against the temple and pull the trigger, leaving it to chance whether or not death results to the trigger puller.

the second degree and sentenced to a term in the penitentiary for a period not less than five years and not exceeding ten years. A new trial was refused and after sentence was imposed, an appeal was taken. Appellant alleges * * * that the facts did not justify a conviction for any form of homicide except involuntary manslaughter. This contention we over-rule. A specific intent to take life is, under our law, an essential ingredient of murder in the first degree. At common law, the "grand criterion" which "distinguished murder from other killing" was malice on the part of the killer and this malice was not necessarily "malevolent to the deceased particularly" but "any evil design in general; the dictate of a wicked, depraved and malignant heart"; 4 Blackstone 199. Among the examples that Blackstone cites of murder is "coolly discharging a gun among a multitude of people," causing the death of someone of the multitude.

In Pennsylvania, the common law crime of murder is divided into two degrees, and murder of the second degree includes every element which enters into first degree murder except the intention to kill. When an individual commits an act of gross recklessness for which he must reasonably anticipate that death to another is likely to result, he exhibits that "wickedness of disposition, hardness of heart, cruelty, recklessness of consequences, and a mind regardless of social duty" which proved that there was at that time in him "the state or frame of mind termed malice." This court has declared that if a driver "wantonly, recklessly, and in disregard of consequences" hurls "his car against another, or into a crowd" and death results from that act "he ought * * * to face the same consequences that would be meted out to him if he had accomplished death by wantonly and wickedly firing a gun": Com. v. Mayberry, 138 A. 686, 688, citing cases from four jurisdictions.

* * *

The killing of William H. Long by this defendant resulted from an act intentionally done by the latter, in reckless and wanton disregard of the consequences which were at least sixty per cent certain from his thrice attempted discharge of a gun known to contain one bullet and aimed at a vital part of Long's body. This killing was, therefore, murder, for malice in the sense of a wicked disposition is evidenced by the intentional doing of an uncalled-for act in callous disregard of its likely harmful effects on others. The fact that there was no motive for this homicide does not exculpate the accused. In a trial for murder proof of motive is always relevant but never necessary.

All the assignments of error are overruled and the judgment is affirmed. The record is remitted to the court below so that the sentence imposed may be carried out.

BERRY v. SUPERIOR COURT

California Court of Appeal, Sixth District, 1989.
256 Cal.Rptr. 344.[a]

AGLIANO, PRESIDING JUSTICE.

The People have charged Berry with the murder of 21/2 year old James Soto, who was killed by Berry's pit bull dog, and negligent keeping of a mischievous animal which kills a human being (Pen. Code, § 399);[b] marijuana cultivation; and misdemeanor keeping of a fighting dog. By this petition for a writ of prohibition defendant seeks dismissal of the charges of murder and Penal Code section 399. He claims the evidence taken at the preliminary hearing [fails to establish implied malice]; and there is no evidence that the animal was mischievous or was kept without ordinary care. * * * Our task is to decide whether "a person of ordinary caution or prudence would be led to believe and conscientiously entertain a strong suspicion that defendant committed the crime charged." People v. Watson (1981) 30 Cal.3d 290, 300. * * *

On June 13, 1987, James Soto, then aged two years and eight months, was killed by a pit bull dog named "Willy" owned by defendant. The animal was tethered near defendant's house but no obstacle prevented access to the dog's area. The victim and his family lived in a house which stood on the same lot, sharing a common driveway. The Soto family had four young children.

The mother left James playing on the patio of their home for a minute or so while she went into the house, and when she came out he was gone. She was looking for him when within some three to five minutes her brother-in-law, Richard Soto, called her and said defendant's dog had attacked James. Meanwhile the father, Arthur Soto, had come upon the dog Willy mauling his son. He screamed for defendant to come get the dog off the child; defendant did so. James died before an emergency crew arrived at the scene.

There was no evidence that Willy had ever before attacked a human being, but there was considerable evidence that he was bred and trained to be a fighting dog and that he posed a known threat to people. Defendant bought Willy from a breeder of fighting dogs, who informed him of the dog's fighting abilities, his gameness, wind, and exceptionally hard bite. The breeder told defendant that in a dog fight "a dog won't go an hour with Willy and live." The police searched defendant's house after the death and found many underground publications about dog

a. Acting pursuant to Rule 976 of the California Rules of Court, the California Supreme Court ordered the Court of Appeal opinion in this case not to be published in the official reports. This controversial practice allows the California Supreme Court to indicate that a lower court's opinion is not to be followed as a precedent, while leaving its result standing and without indicating what if anything is erroneous in its reasoning.—ed.

b. Penal Code section 399 makes it a felony to keep a mischievous animal, knowing its propensities, without ordinary care, when such animal kills any human being who has taken all precautions the circumstances permitted.—ed.

fighting; a pamphlet entitled "42 day keep" which set out the 6–week conditioning procedures used to prepare a dog for a match; a treadmill used to condition a dog and increase its endurance; correspondence with Willy's breeder, Gene Smith; photographs of dog fights; and a "break stick," used to pry fighting dogs apart since they will not release on command.

* * * The victim's mother testified defendant had several dogs. He told her not to be concerned about the dogs, that they would not bother her children, except for "one that he had on the side of the house" which was behind a six foot fence. Defendant further said this dangerous dog was Willy but that she need not be concerned since he was behind a fence. There was a fence where the dog was tethered on the west side of defendant's house, but the fence was not an enclosure and did not prevent access to the area the dog could reach. The police found some 243 marijuana plants growing behind defendant's house. Willy was tethered in such location that anyone wanting to approach the plants would have to cross the area the dog could reach. That area was readily accessible to anyone.

An animal control officer qualified as an expert on fighting dogs testified. He said pit bull dogs are selectively bred to be aggressive towards other animals. They attack swiftly, silently and tenaciously. Although many recently bred pit bulls have good dispositions near human beings and are bred and raised to be pets, there are no uniform breeding standards for temperament and the animal control officers consider a pit bull dangerous unless proved otherwise. * * *

Discussion

* * * People v. Watson, supra, states that the test of implied malice in an unintentional killing is actual appreciation of a high degree of risk that is objectively present. There must be a high probability that the act done will result in death and it must be done with a base antisocial motive and with wanton disregard for life. The conduct in *Watson,* held sufficient to ground a finding of malice, was reckless speeding while intoxicated. * * *

This record shows first, that Willy's owner may have been actually aware of the dog's potential danger to human beings. This mental state may be proved by showing he kept the dog chained, he warned the child's parents that the dog was dangerous to children, and he spoke of the dog as dangerous. Second, the testimony of the animal control officer could support an inference that fighting pit bull dogs are dangerous to human beings, and the record of defendant's extensive knowledge of the breed could support an inference that he knew such dogs are dangerous. * * *

Thus there is a basis from which the trier of fact could derive the two required elements of implied malice, namely existence of an objective risk and subjective awareness of that risk. Additionally, there is arguably some base and antisocial purpose involved in keeping the dog (1) because harboring a fighting dog is illegal and (2) because there is some evidence the dog was kept to guard an illegal stand of marijuana. Illegality of the underlying conduct is not an element of the charge, but may be relevant on the issue of subjective intent.

We do not know the actual probability that a death could result from defendant's conduct in keeping the dog. Presumably that is a question of fact to be submitted to the court or jury upon appropriate instructions requiring that it find a high probability that death would result from the circumstances before it can convict of murder. * * *

An interesting question the parties do not discuss is whether Penal Code section 399 is a special statute which exclusively applies, preventing any general charge of second degree murder or manslaughter arising out of the negligent keeping of the dangerous dog. If so, then the People would be limited to the punishment of three years maximum authorized by section 399. However a special statute does not replace a general statute unless it includes all the elements of the latter. [Citations] Obviously section 399 does not include the element of malice. By analogy, People v. Watson, supra, holds that the general murder statute is not preempted by vehicular manslaughter.

The petition for writ of prohibition is denied.

Note

Berry was convicted of involuntary manslaughter at trial, and sentenced to imprisonment for 3 years and 8 months.

The Kansas Supreme Court upheld a conviction of reckless murder where the defendant's three ferocious Rottweiler dogs escaped from a faulty fenced enclosure and killed an 11–year-old boy (Chris). The opinion concluded that "defendant argues that all she did was let the dogs into the fenced area, take a pill, and go to sleep. This argument conveniently ignores significant aspects of her conduct that contributed to the tragic death of Chris. The State presented evidence that she selected powerful dogs with a potential for aggressive behavior and that she owned a number of these dogs in which she fostered aggressive behavior by failing to properly train the dogs. She ignored the advice from experts on how to properly train her dogs and their warnings of the dire results which could occur from improper training. She was told to socialize her dogs and chose not to do so. She ignores the evidence of the dogs getting out on numerous occasions and her failure to properly secure the gate. She ignored the aggressive behavior her dogs displayed toward her neighbors and their children. The State presented evidence that she created a profound risk and ignored foreseeable consequences that her dogs could attack or injure someone. The State is not required to prove that defendant knew her dogs would attack and kill someone. It was sufficient to prove that her dogs killed Chris and that she could have reasonably foreseen that the dogs could attack or injure someone as a result of what she did or failed to do." The Court held that these facts were sufficient to justify the jury in finding that the defendant caused the death "unintentionally but recklessly under circumstances showing extreme indifference to the value of human life." State v. Davidson, 267 Kan. 667, 987 P.2d 335 (Kan. 1999).

PEOPLE v. REGISTER

Court of Appeals of New York, 1983.
60 N.Y.2d 270, 469 N.Y.S.2d 599, 457 N.E.2d 704.

SIMONS, JUDGE.

Defendant appeals from an order of the Appellate Division which affirmed a judgment entered after a jury trial convicting him of murder in the second degree (Penal Law, § 125.25, subd. 2 [depraved mind murder])and two counts of assault in the first degree (Penal Law, § 120.10, subd. 1). The charges arose from a barroom incident in which defendant shot and killed one man and seriously injured two others. * * *

The shootings occurred about 12:30 a.m. on January 15, 1977 in a crowded barroom in downtown Rochester. The evidence established that defendant and a friend, Duval, had been drinking heavily that day celebrating the fact that Duval, through an administrative mixup, would not have to spend the weekend in jail. Sometime between 7:00 p.m. and 8:00 p.m., the two men left home for the bar. Defendant took a loaded pistol with him and shortly after they arrived at the bar, he produced it when he got into an argument with another patron over money owed him. Apparently the dispute ended without incident and defendant continued his drinking. After midnight another argument developed, this time between Duval and Willie Mitchell. Defendant took out the gun again, shot at Mitchell but mistakenly injured Lawrence Evans who was trying to stop the fight. He then stepped forward and shot Mitchell in the stomach from close range. At that, the 40 or 50 patrons in the bar started for the doors. Some of the bystanders tried to remove Mitchell to a hospital and while they were doing so, the decedent, Marvin Lindsey, walked by defendant. Lindsey was apparently a friend or acquaintance of defendant although that was the first time he had seen him that night. For no explained reason, defendant turned and fired his gun killing Lindsey.

Defendant did not contest the shootings. In defense, his counsel elicited evidence during the prosecution's case of defendant's considerable drinking that evening and he called as his only witness a forensic psychiatrist who testified on the debilitating effects of consuming alcoholic beverages. The jury acquitted defendant of intentional murder but convicted him of depraved mind murder and the two assault counts. * * *

At the conclusion of the evidence and after the charge, defendant requested the court to instruct the jury on the effect of intoxication (see Penal Law, § 15.25).[a]

a. "Intoxication is not, as such, a defense to a criminal charge; but in any prosecution for an offense, evidence of intoxication of the defendant may be offered by

The court complied with the request when discussing the intentional murder and assault counts, but it refused to charge the jury that it could consider defendant's intoxication in determining whether he acted "[u]nder circumstances evincing a depraved indifference to human life" in causing the death of Marvin Lindsey. The court held that the *mens rea* required for depraved mind murder is recklessness and that subdivision 3 of section 15.05 of the Penal Law precludes evidence of intoxication in defense of reckless crimes because it provides that "[a] person who creates such a risk but is unaware thereof solely by reason of voluntary intoxication also acts recklessly". That ruling is assigned as error by defendant. He contends that depraved mind murder contains a different or additional element of mental culpability, namely "circumstances evincing a depraved indifference to human life", which elevates defendant's conduct from manslaughter to murder and that this additional element may be negatived by evidence of intoxication (see Penal Law, § 15.25).

The Penal Law does not expressly define the term "element". However, it does set forth what the "elements" of an offense are and identifies them, as does the common law, as a culpable mental state (*mens rea*) and a voluntary act (*actus reus*). Both are required in all but the strict liability offenses. Consistent with that provision, the statutory definition of depraved mind murder includes both a mental element ("recklessly") and a voluntary act ("engaging in conduct which creates a grave risk of death to another person") (see Penal Law, § 125.25, subd. 2; §§ 15.05, 15.10). Recklessness refers to defendant's conscious disregard of a substantial risk, and the act proscribed * * * is defined by the degree of danger presented. Depraved mind murder resembles manslaughter in the second degree (a reckless killing) but the depraved mind murder statute requires in addition not only that the conduct which results in death present a grave risk of death but that it also occur "[u]nder circumstances evincing a depraved indifference to human life." This additional requirement refers to neither the *mens rea* nor the *actus reus*. If it states an element of the crime at all, it is not an element in the traditional sense but rather a definition of the factual setting in which the risk creating conduct must occur—objective circumstances which are not subject to being negatived by evidence of defendant's intoxication. * * *

Ultimately, the only intended purpose in permitting the jury to consider intoxication in a reckless crime is to negate defendant's awareness and disregard of the risk. It is precisely that point—the inconsistency of permitting reckless and otherwise aggravating conduct to negate an aspect of the offense—that persuades us that intoxication evidence should be excluded whenever recklessness is an element of the offense. In utilitarian terms, the risk of excessive drinking should be added to and not subtracted from the risks created by the conduct of the drunken

the defendant whenever it is relevant to negative an element of the crime charged." N.Y. Penal Law § 15.25—ed.

defendant for there is no social or penological purpose to be served by a rule that permits one who voluntarily drinks to be exonerated from failing to foresee the results of his conduct if he is successful at getting drunk.

Accordingly, the order of the Appellate Division should be affirmed.

* * *

JASEN, JUDGE (dissenting).

In my view, the Legislature purposely distinguished between reckless manslaughter and depraved mind murder, intending that depraved indifference plus recklessness would connote a *mens rea* more culpable than recklessness alone and nearly as culpable as intent. The differences between the mental states set forth in the reckless manslaughter, depraved mind murder and intentional murder statutes are easily delineated, although somewhat difficult to apply. A person acts recklessly in causing the death of another when he is aware of and consciously disregards a substantial and unjustifiable risk. A person intentionally kills another when his "conscious objective" is to cause the death of the victim. A person acts with depraved indifference, however, when he engages in conduct whereby he does not intend to kill but is so indifferent to the consequences, which he knows with substantial certainty will result in the death of another, as to be willing to kill. It is at this point that reckless homicide becomes knowing homicide and the killing differs so little from an intentional killing that parity of punishment is required. This is so not because the surrounding circumstances happened to create a "grave" as opposed to a "substantial" risk, but because the accused has acted with greater culpability and a wickedness akin to that of one whose conscious objective is to kill.

By this approach, a person who acts without an awareness of the risks involved, due to intoxication or otherwise, will be punished for manslaughter, while a person who acts in a way which he knows is substantially certain to cause death, although not intending to kill, will be treated the same as a person who intentionally kills. It seems to me that this is the far more reasonable approach and the one intended by the Legislature. * * *

Finally, with respect to the majority's statement that "the risk of excessive drinking should be added to and not subtracted from the risks created by the conduct of the drunken defendant for there is no social or penological purpose to be served by a rule that permits one who voluntarily drinks to be exonerated from failing to foresee the results of his conduct if he is successful at getting drunk" I would only note that although this may be an accurate representation of what the majority believes the law should be, the Legislature has decided otherwise and it is this court's responsibility to construe the statute accordingly. * * *

Accordingly, I would reverse the conviction and order a new trial. [4–3 decision]

PEOPLE v. WHITFIELD

Supreme Court of California, 1994.
7 Cal.4th 437, 27 Cal.Rptr.2d 858, 868 P.2d 272.

GEORGE, J.

I.

[Defendant, who had an extensive prior record of drunk driving offenses, was convicted of second degree murder and lesser offenses following a traffic fatality. After driving erratically for some distance he had crossed the center line into the oncoming traffic and collided head-on with another vehicle, killing the driver. Defendant was found unconscious in his vehicle, along with empty cans of malt liquor. Tests showed his blood alcohol level to be .24 per cent, far above the level required for drunk driving. In connection with his previous convictions, defendant had watched graphic films showing the carnage caused by drunk drivers. Some of the evidence indicated that he may have passed out at the wheel just before the accident in this case occurred.]

Defendant did not dispute the prosecution's evidence establishing that he was under the influence of alcohol. To the contrary, defendant sought to prove that he did not harbor implied malice aforethought because he was so intoxicated that he was unconscious at the time the accident occurred. Accordingly, defense counsel elicited testimony demonstrating that, because the amount of alcohol in a person's system dissipates over time, defendant's blood-alcohol content would have been .27 percent about the time of the collision, and that individuals with blood-alcohol levels above .25 percent may become stuporous and lose consciousness. Defendant also introduced evidence indicating that an independent laboratory's analysis of the blood sample withdrawn at the request of the police, and an analysis by the hospital of a separate blood sample, revealed even higher blood-alcohol levels. * * *

The trial court's instructions to the jury included the following. For the crime of murder "there must exist a union or joint operation of act or conduct and a certain specific intent in the mind of the perpetrator." (CALJIC No. 3.31.) "If the evidence shows that the defendant was intoxicated at the time of the alleged crime, you should consider the fact of intoxication, including the degree of intoxication, in determining whether defendant had such specific intent or mental state." (See CALJIC No. 4.21.) "Every person who unlawfully kills a human being with malice aforethought is guilty of the crime of murder. . . ." (CALJIC No. 8.10.) " 'Malice' may be either express or implied. Malice is express when there is manifested an intention unlawfully to kill a human being. Malice is implied when: 1. The killing resulted from an intentional act, 2. The natural consequences of the act are dangerous to human life, and 3. The act was deliberately performed with knowledge of the danger to and with conscious disregard for human life." (CALJIC No. 8.11.)

"The intentional act required for 'implied malice' underlying vehicle murder is not the traffic violation which may precede a collision, but whether the defendant was driving under the influence with a conscious disregard for human life." (Special instruction requested by the prosecution.) "In order to convict defendant of second-degree murder you must examine defendant's state of mind at the time of the act. This is referred to as a subjective test. Second-degree murder based on implied malice requires that defendant acted deliberately, that defendant acted with knowledge of the danger to human life, and that defendant acted in conscious disregard for human life." (Special instruction requested by defendant.) "If a person causes another's death by doing a dangerous act in an unlawful or criminally negligent manner, without realizing the risk involved, he is guilty of manslaughter. If, on the other hand, the person realized the risk and acted in conscious disregard of the danger to human life, malice is implied and the crime is murder." (See CALJIC No. 8.51.)

In addition, the trial court carefully distinguished the mental state required for murder (implied malice) from the mental state required for the lesser offense of gross vehicular manslaughter (gross negligence). The trial court instructed the jury as follows: "Gross negligence has been defined as the exercise of so slight a degree of care as to raise a presumption of conscious indifference to the consequences. On the other hand, malice may be implied when a person knowing that his conduct endangers the life of another nonetheless acts deliberately with conscious disregard for life. Though these definitions bear a general similarity, they are not identical. Implied malice contemplates a subjective awareness of a higher degree of risk than does gross negligence and involves an element of wantonness which is absent in gross negligence." (Special instruction requested by defendant.) * * *

The trial court refused defendant's request that the jury be instructed, pursuant to CALJIC No. 8.47, that "[i]f you find that a defendant, while unconscious as a result of voluntary intoxication, killed another human being without intent to kill and without malice aforethought, the crime is involuntary manslaughter."

The jury found defendant guilty as charged on all counts, fixing the degree of the murder as second degree, and the trial court sentenced defendant to prison for a term of 18 years to life. On appeal, defendant asserted, among other contentions, that the trial court erred in refusing to instruct the jury pursuant to CALJIC No. 8.47 concerning unconsciousness caused by voluntary intoxication. * * *

II

Penal Code § 22(b) provides: "Evidence of voluntary intoxication is admissible solely on the issue of whether or not the defendant actually formed a required specific intent, premeditated, deliberated, or harbored malice aforethought, when a specific intent crime is charged." Focusing upon the final phrase of this statute—"when a specific intent crime is charged"—the Court of Appeal held that evidence of voluntary intoxication cannot establish the absence of implied malice, because second degree murder based upon implied malice is not a specific intent crime. We conclude the Court of Appeal misinterpreted section 22. * * * It is clear that the Legislature considered murder a "specific intent crime" within the meaning of the language of section 22 whether the prosecution's theory is that malice is express or implied. * * *

The circumstances of the present case demonstrate the logic of this conclusion. Defendant was charged with murder and was prosecuted on the theory that malice could be implied because, in light of defendant's experiences stemming from his prior convictions for driving under the influence and his resulting knowledge of the danger to others posed by such conduct, he performed an act dangerous to life and acted with conscious disregard for human life by driving while intoxicated. Defendant also was charged with the lesser offense of gross vehicular manslaughter while intoxicated, which does not require that the defendant harbor malice.

It was undisputed that defendant drove a vehicle while having a blood-alcohol level at least three times the legal limit, that the natural consequences of this act were dangerous to human life, and that this act resulted in the death of a human being. The sole disputed issue was whether defendant knew that his conduct endangered the life of another and acted with conscious disregard for human life. If so, malice would be implied and defendant would be guilty of second degree murder. If not, defendant would be guilty of gross vehicular manslaughter while intoxicated. The most important factor bearing upon defendant's awareness of the dangerousness of his conduct and conscious disregard of that danger was his degree of intoxication when he undertook his dangerous course of conduct. It appears obviously appropriate to permit the jury to consider defendant's degree of intoxication in determining whether he formed the mental state that distinguishes the greater offense of murder from the lesser offense of manslaughter.

The Attorney General contends it is anomalous to allow a defendant who kills another while driving under the influence to rely upon the fact of self-induced intoxication to demonstrate that he or she did not harbor malice and, therefore, is guilty only of manslaughter rather than murder. But a defendant who kills another by firing a gun may defend against a charge of murder by establishing that, due to voluntary intoxication, he or she did not harbor malice and is guilty instead of manslaughter. The laws governing prosecutions for murder must apply equally whether the defendant kills the victim by means of a firearm or an automobile.

Consider, for example, a hypothetical situation in which a defendant, with no prior history of driving under the influence, consumes alcohol at a social gathering after having arranged to be driven home by his or her spouse. The defendant's spouse unexpectedly becomes ill and the defendant, who is intoxicated, decides to drive, and causes a fatal accident. Under such circumstances, it would not be anomalous to permit the defendant to defend against a charge of murder on the ground that, due to voluntary intoxication, he or she did not appreciate the dangerousness of his or her conduct, hence did not harbor malice, and should be convicted of the lesser offense of manslaughter.

For the same reason, it was proper for defendant in the present case to attempt to establish that, due to voluntary intoxication, he did not harbor malice, but the jury, as it was entitled to do, rejected this proffered defense, impliedly finding that defendant acted with knowledge, and conscious disregard, of the danger to human life in undertaking to drive while intoxicated.

It is beyond dispute that drinking drivers exact an enormous toll on society. When a defendant drives while under the influence and thereby causes the death of another, serious punishment is warranted, but such serious punishment may be imposed without altering the long-settled requirement that a defendant not be convicted of murder unless he or she actually harbored malice. The Legislature specifically has addressed the situation in which a defendant drives under the influence and thereby causes the death of another, but does not harbor malice, by enacting § 191.5, which provides a maximum sentence of 10 years in prison for gross vehicular manslaughter while intoxicated. * * *

As the present case demonstrates, allowing the trier of fact to consider the effect of the defendant's intoxication will not preclude murder convictions when warranted. The jury in the present case considered the effect of defendant's intoxication but concluded nonetheless that he acted with implied malice. * * *

III

Having concluded that the trial court did not err in instructing the jury to consider defendant's degree of intoxication in determining whether he harbored malice, we turn to defendant's contention that the trial court erred in refusing his request that the jury be instructed, in accordance with CALJIC No. 8.47, that if "defendant, while unconscious as a result of voluntary intoxication, killed another human being without intent to kill and without malice aforethought, the crime is involuntary manslaughter." Although this instruction is a correct statement of law in the abstract, the trial court properly refused the instruction because, in the context of the present case, it erroneously implied that, if defendant was unconscious when the collision occurred, he could not be convicted of murder.

The circumstance that a defendant, when a fatal traffic collision occurs, is unconscious as a result of voluntary intoxication, does not preclude a finding that the defendant harbored malice, because malice may have been formed prior to that time. * * * In the present case, for example, it can be inferred from the presence of empty malt liquor cans in his vehicle that defendant continued to drink while he was driving. Under such circumstances, and in light of defendant's past exposure to the extreme danger posed by driving under the influence of alcohol or drugs, the jury reasonably could conclude that defendant, in undertaking this course of conduct, acted with knowledge of the dangerousness of his conduct and with conscious disregard of that danger. Because defendant knowingly embarked upon such an extremely dangerous course of conduct with conscious disregard of the danger, his malice aforethought would not be negated simply by reason of his having succeeded in rendering himself unconscious prior to the fatal collision. Accordingly, the trial court did not err in refusing defendant's proffered instruction regarding unconsciousness caused by voluntary intoxication. * * *

Moreover, even if the trial court had erred in this regard, reversal of the resulting conviction would not be required. The jury adequately was instructed that it could consider defendant's degree of intoxication in determining whether he acted with malice. By finding defendant guilty of second degree murder, rather than gross vehicular manslaughter while intoxicated, the jury necessarily concluded that, despite his intoxication, defendant actually appreciated the risk posed by his conduct and acted with conscious disregard of life. It is clear, therefore, that instructing the jury pursuant to CALJIC No. 8.47 would not have affected its verdict.

[Conviction affirmed. Concurring and dissenting opinions omitted.]

Note

Murder charges in aggravated drunk driving cases have become fairly common. See, e.g. United States v. Fleming, 739 F.2d 945 (4th Cir.1984); Essex v. Commonwealth, 228 Va. 273, 322 S.E.2d 216 (1984); People v. Watson, 30 Cal.3d 290, 179 Cal.Rptr. 43, 637 P.2d 279 (1981); Hamilton v. Commonwealth, 560 S.W.2d 539 (Ky.1977). The "vehicular murder" cases as a rule assume that the drunk driver is guilty of murder only where he drove recklessly with conscious awareness of the risk of causing a fatal injury. Hamilton v. Commonwealth is exceptional in basing liability for murder on gross negligence, in that the defendant "should have known" of the obvious risk.

Sentences in the vehicular murder cases have been severe. In Simmons v. State, 264 S.C. 417, 215 S.E.2d 883 (1975), the court upheld a sentence of life imprisonment. In Pears v. State, 672 P.2d 903 (Alaska App.1983), the defendant was warned by police officers not to drive because he was too drunk. He nonetheless returned to his truck and drove at high speed through stop signs and traffic lights until he collided with a car in an intersection, killing two people. Although he had several prior traffic offenses, he had never previously been convicted or drunk or reckless driving. Nonetheless, the Alaska Court of Appeals affirmed a 20-year sentence for second degree murder. The Alaska Supreme Court reversed and remanded for resentencing, holding that Pears' sentence should be comparable to that received by other drunk drivers who had caused fatal injuries, even though those other drivers had been convicted only of manslaughter. The highest sentences in previous cases had been 8 to 12 years imprisonment, in cases involving defendants with several previous drunk driving convictions. 698 P.2d 1198 (Alaska 1985).

COMMONWEALTH v. WELANSKY

Supreme Judicial Court of Massachusetts, 1944.
316 Mass. 383, 55 N.E.2d 902.

[Welansky owned and operated the New Cocoanut Grove, a nightclub in Boston. One evening a 16–year–old employee attempted to replace a light bulb in a darkened corner of the basement Melody Lounge, using a lighted match for illumination. He accidentally set fire to some flammable decorations, and the fire quickly spread upstairs and throughout the crowded premises. A panic resulted, and many patrons died of burns, smoke inhalation, or injuries suffered in the attempt to escape. The evidence indicated that several emergency exits were concealed or locked. Welansky himself was sick and in a hospital at the time of the fire, but the court found that he was nonetheless responsible for the condition of the premises. The manslaughter indictments upon which Welansky was convicted charged that his misconduct "consisted in causing or permitting or failing reasonably to prevent defective wiring, the installation of inflammable decorations, the absence of fire doors, the absence of proper means of egress properly maintained, and sufficient proper exits and overcrowding."]

LUMMUS, JUSTICE: * * *

The Commonwealth disclaimed any contention that the defendant intentionally killed or injured the persons named in the indictments as victims. It based its case on involuntary manslaughter through wanton or reckless conduct. The judge instructed the jury correctly with respect to the nature of such conduct.

Usually wanton or reckless conduct consists of an affirmative act, like driving an automobile or discharging a firearm, in disregard of probable harmful consequences to another. But where as in the present case there is a duty of care for the safety of business visitors invited to premises which the defendant controls, wanton or reckless conduct may consist of intentional failure to take such care in disregard of the probable harmful consequences to them or of their right to care.

To define wanton or reckless conduct so as to distinguish it clearly from negligence and gross negligence is not easy. Sometimes the word "wilful" is prefaced to the words "wanton" and "reckless" in expressing the concept. That only blurs it. Wilful means intentional. In the phrase "wilful, wanton or reckless conduct," if "wilful" modifies "conduct" it introduces something different from wanton or reckless conduct, even though the legal result is the same. Wilfully causing harm is a wrong, but a different wrong from wantonly or recklessly causing harm. If "wilful" modifies "wanton or reckless conduct" its use is accurate. What must be intended is the conduct, not the resulting harm. The words "wanton" and "reckless" are practically synonymous in this connection, although the word "wanton" may contain a suggestion of arrogance or insolence or heartlessness that is lacking in the word "reckless." But intentional conduct to which either word applies is followed by the same legal consequences as though both words applied.

The standard of wanton or reckless conduct is at once subjective and objective, as has been recognized ever since Commonwealth v. Pierce, 138 Mass. 165, 52 Am.Rep. 264. Knowing facts that would cause a reasonable man to know the danger is equivalent to knowing the danger. * * * The judge charged the jury correctly when he said, "To constitute wanton or reckless conduct, as distinguished from mere negligence, grave danger to others must have been apparent and the defendant must have chosen to run the risk rather than alter his conduct so as to avoid the act or omission which caused the harm. If the grave danger was in fact realized by the defendant, his subsequent voluntary act or omission which caused the harm amounts to wanton or reckless conduct, no matter whether the ordinary man would have realized the gravity of the danger or not. But even if a particular defendant is so stupid [or] so heedless * * * that in fact he did not realize the grave danger, he cannot escape the imputation of wanton or reckless conduct in his dangerous act or omission, if an ordinary normal man under the same circumstances would have realized the gravity of the danger. A man may be reckless within the meaning of the law although he himself thought he was careful."

The essence of wanton or reckless conduct is intentional conduct, by way either of commission or of omission where there is a duty to act, which conduct involves a high degree of likelihood that substantial harm will result to another.

* * *

The words "wanton" and "reckless" are thus not merely rhetorical or vituperative expressions used instead of negligent or grossly negligent. They express a difference in the degree of risk and in the voluntary taking of risk so marked, as compared with negligence, as to amount substantially and in the eyes of the law to a difference in kind. For many years this court has been careful to preserve the distinction between negligence and gross negligence, on the one hand, and wanton or reckless conduct on the other. * * *

Notwithstanding language used commonly in earlier cases, and occasionally in later ones, it is now clear in this Commonwealth that at common law conduct does not become criminal until it passes the borders of negligence and gross negligence and enters into the domain of wanton or reckless conduct. There is in Massachusetts at common law no such thing as "criminal negligence."

Wanton or reckless conduct is the legal equivalent of intentional conduct.

If by wanton or reckless conduct bodily injury is caused to another, the person guilty of such conduct is guilty of assault and battery. And since manslaughter is simply a battery that causes death, if death results he is guilty of manslaughter.

To convict the defendant of manslaughter, the Commonwealth was not required to prove that he caused the fire by some wanton or reckless conduct. Fire in a place of public resort is an ever present danger. It was enough to prove that death resulted from his wanton or reckless disregard of the safety of patrons in the event of fire from any cause.

* * *

Judgments affirmed.

STATE v. WILLIAMS

Washington Court of Appeals, 1971.
4 Wash. App. 908, 484 P.2d 1167.

HOROWITZ, CHIEF JUDGE.

Defendants, husband and wife, were [convicted of] manslaughter for negligently failing to supply their 17-month child with necessary medical attention, as a result of which he died on September 12, 1968. * * *

The defendant husband, Walter Williams, is a 24-year-old full-blooded Sheshont Indian with a sixth-grade education. His sole occupation is that of laborer. The defendant wife, Bernice Williams, is a 20-year-old part Indian with an 11th grade education. At the time of the marriage, the wife had two children, the younger of whom was a 14-month son. Both parents worked and the children were cared for by the 85-year-old mother of the defendant husband. The defendant husband assumed parental responsibility with the defendant wife to provide clothing, care and medical attention for the child. Both defendants possessed a great deal of love and affection for the defendant wife's young son.

The court expressly found:

> That both defendants were aware that William Joseph Tabafunda was ill during the period September 1, 1968 to September 12, 1968. The defendants were ignorant. They did not realize how sick the baby was. They thought that the baby had a toothache and no layman regards a toothache as dangerous to life. They loved the baby and gave it aspirin in hopes of improving its condition. They did not take the baby to a doctor because of fear that the Welfare Department would take the baby away from them. They knew that medical help was available because of previous experience. They had no excuse that the law will recognize for not taking the baby to a doctor.
>
> The defendants Walter L. Williams and Bernice J. Williams were negligent in not seeking medical attention for William Joseph Tabafunda.
>
> That as a proximate result of this negligence, William Joseph Tabafunda died.

From these and other findings, the court concluded that the defendants were each guilty of the crime of manslaughter as charged. Defendants take no exception to findings but contend that the findings do not support the conclusions that the defendants are guilty of manslaughter as charged. * * *

Parental duty to provide medical care for a dependent minor child was recognized at common law and characterized as a natural duty. In Washington, the existence of the duty is commonly assumed and is stated at times without reference to any particular statute. The existence of the duty also is assumed, but not always defined, in statutes that provide special criminal and civil sanctions for the performance of that duty. * * *

On the question of the quality or seriousness of breach of the duty, at common law, in the case of involuntary manslaughter, the breach had to amount to more than mere ordinary or simple negligence—gross negligence was essential. In Washington, however, [the statutes defining manslaughter] supersede both voluntary and involuntary manslaughter as those crimes were defined at common law. Under these statutes the crime is deemed committed even though the death of the victim is the proximate result of only simple or ordinary negligence.

The concept of simple or ordinary negligence describes a failure to exercise the "ordinary caution" necessary to make out the defense of excusable homicide. Ordinary caution is the kind of caution that a man of reasonable prudence would exercise under the same or similar conditions. If, therefore, the conduct of a defendant, regardless of his ignorance, good intentions and good faith, fails to measure up to the conduct required of a man of reasonable prudence, he is guilty of ordinary negligence because of his failure to use "ordinary caution." If such negligence proximately causes the death of the victim the defendant, as pointed out above, is guilty of statutory manslaughter.

* * *

In the instant case, however, the defendant husband is not the father of the minor child, nor has he adopted that child. Nevertheless, the evidence shows that he had assumed responsibility with his wife for the care and maintenance of the child, whom he greatly loved. Such assumption of responsibility, characterized in the information as that required of a "guardian and custodian," is sufficient to impose upon him the duty to furnish necessary medical care.

The remaining issue of proximate cause requires consideration of the question of when the duty to furnish medical care became activated. If the duty to furnish such care was not activated until after it was too late to save the life of the child, failure to furnish medical care could not be said to have proximately caused the child's death. Timeliness in the furnishing of medical care also must be considered in terms of "ordinary caution." The law does not mandatorily require that a doctor be called for a child at the first sign of any indisposition or illness. The indisposition or illness may appear to be of a minor or very temporary kind, such as a toothache or cold. If one in the exercise of ordinary caution fails to recognize that his child's symptoms require medical attention, it cannot be said that the failure to obtain such medical attention is a breach of the duty owed. * * *

Defendants have not assigned error to the findings either on the ground that the evidence is insufficient to prove negligence or proximate cause, or that the state has failed to prove the facts found by failing to apply the required standard of proof beyond a reasonable doubt. They contended below and on appeal that they are not guilty of the crime charged. Because of the serious nature of the charge against the parent and stepparent of a well-loved child, and out of our concern for the protection of the constitutional rights of the defendants, we have made an independent examination of the evidence to determine whether it substantially supports the court's express finding on proximate cause and its implied finding that the duty to furnish medical care became activated in time to prevent death of the child.

Dr. Gale Wilson, the autopsy surgeon and chief pathologist for the King County Coroner, testified that the child died because an abscessed tooth had been allowed to develop into an infection of the mouth and cheeks, eventually becoming gangrenous. This condition, accompanied by the child's inability to eat, brought about malnutrition, lowering the child's resistance and eventually producing pneumonia, causing the death. Dr. Wilson testified that in his opinion the infection had lasted for approximately 2 weeks, and that the odor generally associated with gangrene would have been present for approximately 10 days before death. He also expressed the opinion that had medical care been first obtained in the last week before the baby's death, such care would have been obtained too late to have saved the baby's life. Accordingly, the baby's apparent condition between September 1 and September 5, 1968 became the critical period for the purpose of determining whether in the exercise of ordinary caution defendants should have provided medical care for the minor child.

The testimony concerning the child's apparent condition during the critical period is not crystal clear, but is sufficient to warrant the following statement of the matter. The defendant husband testified that he noticed the baby was sick about 2 weeks before the baby died. The defendant wife testified that she noticed the baby was ill about a week and a half or 2 weeks before the baby died. The evidence showed that in the critical period the baby was fussy; that he could not keep his food down; and that a cheek started swelling up. The swelling went up and down, but did not disappear. In that same period, the cheek turned "a bluish color like." The defendants, not realizing that the baby was as ill as it was or that the baby was in danger of dying, attempted to provide some relief to the baby by giving the baby aspirin during the critical period and continued to do so until the night before the baby died. The defendants thought the swelling would go down and were waiting for it to do so; and defendant husband testified, that from what he had heard, neither doctors nor dentists pull out a tooth "when it's all swollen up like that." There was an additional explanation for not calling a doctor given by each defendant. Defendant husband testified that "the way the cheek looked, * * * and that stuff on his hair, they would think we were neglecting him and take him away from us and not give him back." Defendant wife testified that the defendants were "waiting for the swelling to go down," and also that they were afraid to take the child to a doctor for fear that the doctor would report them to the welfare department, who, in turn, would take the child away. "It's just that I was so scared of losing him." They testified that they had heard that the defendant husband's cousin lost a child that way. The evidence showed that the defendants did not understand the significance or seriousness of the baby's symptoms. However, there is no evidence that the defendants were physically or financially unable to obtain a doctor, or that they did not know an available doctor, or that the symptoms did not continue to be a matter of concern during the critical period. Indeed, the evidence shows that in April 1968 defendant husband had taken the child to a doctor for medical attention.

In our opinion, there is sufficient evidence from which the court could find, as it necessarily did, that applying the standard of ordinary caution, i.e., the caution exercisable by a man of reasonable prudence under the same or similar conditions, defendants were sufficiently put on notice concerning the symptoms of the baby's illness and lack of improvement in the baby's apparent condition in the period from September 1 to September 5, 1968 to have required them to have obtained medical care for the child. The failure so to do in this case is ordinary or simple negligence, and such negligence is sufficient to support a conviction of statutory manslaughter.

The judgment is affirmed.

Notes

1. Why should the criminal law *ever* punish anyone for negligently causing death or other harm? The Model Penal Code Commentary addressed this question in the Commentary to § 2.02, Tent. Draft No. 4 at 126–27:

> Of the four kinds of culpability defined, there is, of course, least to be said for treating negligence as a sufficient basis for imposing criminal liability. Since the actor is inadvertent by hypothesis, it has been argued that the "threat of punishment for negligence must pass him by, because he does not realize that it is addressed to him." So too it has been urged that education or corrective treatment not punishment is the proper social method for dealing with persons with inadequate awareness, since what is implied is not a moral defect. Hall, Principles of Criminal Law 245. We think, however, that this is to over-simplify the issue. Knowledge that conviction and sentence, not to speak of punishment, may follow conduct that inadvertently creates improper risk supplies men with an additional motive to take care before acting, to use their faculties and draw on their experience in gauging the potentialities

of contemplated conduct. To some extent, at least, this motive may promote awareness and thus be effective as a measure of control. Certainly legislators act on this assumption in a host of situations and it seems to us dogmatic to assert that they are wholly wrong. Accordingly, we think that negligence, as here defined, cannot be wholly rejected as a ground of culpability which may suffice for purposes of penal law, though we agree that it should not be generally deemed sufficient in the definition of specific crimes, and that it often will be right to differentiate such conduct for the purposes of sentence. The content of the concept, must, therefore, be treated at this stage.

But why not punish the dangerous conduct itself, rather than the negligent causing of the result? Why not draft a criminal code that simply imposes whatever penalties are thought to be appropriate for maintaining a firetrap or leaving small children unattended, without regard to the result that happened to have occurred?

2. The Washington state legislature abandoned the tort negligence standard applied in *Williams*. See State v. Norman, 61 Wash.App. 16, 808 P.2d 1159, 1162 (Wash.Ct.App.1991), where the court affirmed the defendant's conviction for first degree manslaughter for refusing to obtain medical care for his 10 year old son, causing the boy's death. The court reviewed the recent history of the relevant Washington statutes:

> * * * [W]hile the breach of duty in a common law case of involuntary manslaughter had to amount to more than ordinary or simple negligence, the law in Washington was changed by former RCW 9.48.060, which deemed the crime of manslaughter committed if the death proximately resulted from simple or ordinary negligence [citing Williams]. RCW 9.48.060, in turn, was repealed in 1975 to create two degrees of manslaughter: recklessly causing the death of another, RCW 9A.32.060, and with criminal negligence causing the death of another, RCW 9A.32.070.

The court later emphasized that although under the prior statute as interpreted in *Williams*, a person could be convicted of manslaughter for "ordinary negligence, caused by a failure to use 'ordinary caution', and which proximately caused the death of a victim," that "is no longer true." The new statutes require either "a reckless act [or] a criminally negligent act, before manslaughter can be found."

3. Assuming that *someone* should have been prosecuted for the nightclub fire described in the *Welansky* case, supra, should it have been someone other than Welansky? In such a case, is the public interest best served by a prosecution of (1) the employee whose carelessness in handling a match started the fire; (2) the owner or manager of the establishment; or (3) the public officials who failed to enforce the fire safety regulations?

4. In State v. Hazelwood, 946 P.2d 875 (Alaska 1997), the Alaska Supreme Court held that a criminal conviction may be based on proof of simple civil negligence. The defendant Joseph Hazelwood was captain of the Exxon Valdez, which ran aground in Prince William Sound, spilling eleven million gallons of oil. On remand, the Alaska Court of Appeals affirmed both his conviction and sentence. Hazelwood was sentenced to 90 days imprisonment and a $1,000 fine, the maximum penalty permitted under a statute

that made negligent discharge of oil a class B misdemeanor. The statute was subsequently amended to re-classify this crime as a class A misdemeanor or class C felony. See Hazelwood v. State, 962 P.2d 196 (Alaska App.1998)

5. See also Commonwealth v. Woodward, 427 Mass. 659, 694 N.E.2d 1277 (Mass. 1998). Eight month old Matthew Eappen died of severe head injuries which were somehow inflicted while he was under the care of Louise Woodward, a British "au pair" performing child care for the Eappen family. Circumstantial evidence indicated that she may have shaken him violently, and even slammed his head on a hard surface. Defense experts suggested that Matthew may have had a pre-existing skull fracture and blood clot which caused the death after Woodward roughly shook him. The defense decided to gamble on an "all or nothing" strategy, and persuaded the trial judge to omit a manslaughter instruction, forcing the jury to choose between second degree murder and acquittal. The jury bit the bullet and returned a murder verdict. This led to an international controversy, as British newspapers encouraged public protest against the harsh verdict. The trial judge eventually reduced the verdict to manslaughter and sentenced Woodward to "time served," thus defusing the international tension. The Massachusetts Supreme Judicial Court upheld both the reduction to manslaughter and the lenient sentence, holding also that the trial court ought to have given the manslaughter instruction in the first place, since a manslaughter verdict would clearly have been justified by the evidence. Compare, People v. Barton, *supra*, p. 174.

D. THE FELONY MURDER RULE

STATE v. HOANG

Supreme Court of Kansas, 1988.
243 Kan. 40, 755 P.2d 7.

McFarland, Justice:

A Vietnamese woman hired defendant Thai Do Hoang to burn down a building in Wichita which housed a restaurant/club business. The arson fee was to be $1,000, payable $500 in advance and the balance upon performance. Neither the owner of the building nor the operators of the business therein had given permission to defendant or anyone else to burn the building. Defendant hired three assistants, Dung Anh Tran, Thuong Nguyen, and a man known only as Soubong. The four men arrived at the building sometime between 3:00 a.m. and 4:00 a.m. on October 8, 1986. Defendant broke out one of the building's windows and Dung and Thuong crawled through to the building's interior. Defendant handed two containers of gasoline through the window to his cohorts but remained outside with Soubong. Defendant then saw flames and smoke in the building and waited for his accomplices to return to the window. The fire department arrived at approximately 5:00 a.m. Defendant and Soubong left upon hearing the approaching sirens.

The badly burned body of Dung was found in the building. Thuong was found in serious condition therein and died the next day, apparently from smoke inhalation. Burn, char, and pour patterns, as well as gasoline cans, gasoline, and timing-delay devices at the fire's point of origin established the arson causation. The defendant was arrested the following day with $500 in one pocket and $111 in another pocket. After being advised of his *Miranda* rights, defendant essentially confessed to participating in the burglary/arson but denied the act was done for money. He was subsequently charged with two counts of felony murder, and one count each of burglary and arson. [The trial judge dismissed the felony murder counts.]

The Kansas felony-murder statute, provides:

> "Murder in the first degree is the killing of a human being committed maliciously, willfully, deliberately and with premeditation or committed in the perpetration or attempt to perpetrate any felony."

Although we have never decided the precise issue before us, we have established considerable case law on felony murder. A review of these principles is appropriate.

In felony-murder cases, the elements of malice, deliberation, and premeditation which are required for murder in the first degree are deemed to be supplied by felonious conduct alone if a homicide results. To support a conviction for felony murder, all that is required is to prove that a felony was being committed, which felony was inherently dangerous to human life, and that the homicide which followed was a direct result of the commission of that felony. In a felony-murder case, evidence of who the triggerman is is irrelevant and all participants are principals. [Citations]

The purpose of the felony-murder doctrine is to deter all those engaged in felonies from killing negligently or accidentally. The underlying felony in a felony-murder case must be a forcible felony, one inherently dangerous to human life. [Citations] It is uncontroverted that arson is a felony which is inherently dangerous to human life.

In State v. Branch and Bussey, 223 Kan. 381, 573 P.2d 1041 (1978), we said: "Any participant in a life-endangering felony is guilty of first degree murder when a life is taken in the course of committing or attempting to commit a felony, regardless of whether the death was intentional or accidental." There, during the aggravated robbery of a drug dealer, Branch made advances toward the drug dealer's girlfriend. A struggle ensued, during which Bussey shot and killed the drug dealer. On appeal, defendants argued they could not be found guilty of murder because the killing was accidental. We rejected this argument, reasoning: "To apply the felony murder rule, it is only necessary to establish that defendants committed a felony inherently dangerous to human life and that the killing took place during the commission of the felony. A requirement of the felony murder rule is that the participants could reasonably foresee or expect that a life might be taken in the perpetration of the felony. It makes no difference that the killing was accidental. * * *"

For completeness State v. Mauldin, 215 Kan. 956, 529 P.2d 124 (1974), should be mentioned. In *Mauldin,* defendant sold heroin to the victim, who later injected himself and died as a result thereof. We held this conduct was not within the purview of the felony-murder statute, reasoning [that the felony had terminated when the seller and purchaser parted company].

It is argued that felony murder applies only to the deaths of "innocents" rather than co-felons. There is nothing in our statute on which to base such a distinction. * * * For this court to exclude the co-felons would constitute judicial amendment of a statute on philosophic rather than legal grounds. This would be highly improper. * * * The judgment dismissing the complaint is reversed and the case is remanded for further proceedings.

LOCKETT, JUSTICE, dissenting:

I respectfully dissent from the majority's conclusion that felony murder includes the accidental death of a co-felon in its application. * * * The majority's literal interpretation of the felony-murder statute ignores prior decisions of this court which have construed the same felony-murder statute. We have held, for example, that the underlying felony in a felony-murder case must be a forcible felony, one inherently dangerous to human life, and that whether a felony is inherently dangerous to human life must be determined when considered in the abstract only. [Citations] Clearly, there is no such limitation contained within the legislature's literal statement of the law. * * * When the interpretation of a statute according to the exact and literal import of its words would contravene the manifest purpose of the legislature in its enactment, the statute should be construed according to its spirit and reason, disregarding, as far as may be necessary, the strict letter of the law. * * *

[4–3 decision]

DOWDEN v. STATE

Court of Criminal Appeals of Texas, 1988.
758 S.W.2d 264.

ONION, PRESIDING JUDGE.

[Appellant was convicted of capital murder and sentenced to life imprisonment.] On June 28, 1974, at 1:00 a.m., the appellant's brother, Charles Ray Dowden, was arrested for robbing a 7–11 convenience store [clerk] in Orange, Texas. He was taken to the police station where he was booked and placed in the city jail on the second floor of the police station.

Appellant, who had been at the convenience store with his brother, decided to aid his brother in escaping from jail, and he drove to his brother's house, where he picked up his sister-in-law, and told her of his plan to get his brother out of jail. The appellant and his sister-in-law then drove to Clifford Blansett's house, where they picked up a rifle and a pistol, and the three drove to the police station, arriving there around 4:00 a.m. on that same morning.

Appellant and Blansett entered the police station and went to the dispatcher's booking office, where two police officers and one dispatcher were working. The appellant slammed open the door to the dispatcher's office, pointed an automatic pistol at the police officers and declared, "I have come to get Charles." The officers were stunned at the outset, but quickly regained their composure. Captain Gray (the deceased) lunged at the appellant, grabbed the hand in which he was holding the gun and, placing his other arm around the appellant's body, forced him into the hall. The door, operating on a spring closing device, closed automatically behind them. At this moment, the two men remaining in the office could not see what was happening, but they heard a shot fired in the hallway. No longer being able to see Captain Gray, they presumed that he had been shot by the appellant and was dead.

Meanwhile, the officer remaining in the dispatcher's office (Windham) drew his pistol, and the dispatcher, Denton, slipped into a small room adjoining the dispatcher's office to load a shotgun. There ensued an exchange of gunfire between the appellant and Officer Windham and Denton. After the fusillade subsided, Windham heard "moving around in the hall." Whereupon Denton hollered, "He's coming in through the door." There was more "moving around" and then another bullet came through the booking window. Following this last shot the door came "crashing open," and Windham immediately "shot twice and then again." According to Officer Windham's testimony, when he fired these shots he was on his knees at the edge of the booking counter closest to the door. The pistol was in his left hand, around the corner of the cabinet, and aimed at the door. On cross-examination, Windham admitted that he did not look before he fired because he thought that only the appellant could be coming through the door. Upon being asked why he shot without looking, he said he thought that he would be killed if he did not.

Officer Windham's three shots at the person in the doorway were the last shots fired. The two men, Windham and Denton, not knowing whether their assailants had left or whether they had taken a breather, radioed for help. It was not until Windham crawled back to join Denton in the back room that he knew that the man lying in the doorway was Captain Gray, and not the appellant. A ballistics examination revealed that Captain Gray was killed by Officer Windham. * * *

Appellant's * * * voluntary confession * * * read in part:

> "I walked up to the door to the Office, opened the door and said 'I want Charles Dowden.' I pulled the pistol out after I said that. I was standing in the doorway. One of the Officers grabbed me. I tried to hit him, but he was holding my arms. I just started shooting then. I shot through the little window. I don't know how many times I

shot, it must have been 6 or 7 times. I just kept pulling the trigger."
* * *

Appellan[t] * * * alleges that the trial court erred in not granting his motion for instructed verdict of "not guilty" as there was a fatal and fundamental variance between the State's pleading and proof. Appellant was charged with the offense of capital murder by an indictment which alleged in part:

> "... that on or about the 28th day of June, A.D. 1974, ... Billy Wayne Dowden, Sr. and Clifford S. Blansett, acting together did then and there unlawfully, intentionally, and knowingly kill Danny L. Gray by shooting him with a gun, the said Danny L. Gray being then and there, a peace officer who was then and there acting in the lawful discharge of an official duty and the said Billy Wayne Dowden, Sr. and Clifford S. Blansett, acting together, then and there knowing, and being informed that the said Danny L. Gray was then and there a peace officer."

[A]t the close of the guilt-innocence stage of trial, appellant filed his motion for an instructed verdict of "not guilty," arguing that there was insufficient evidence to warrant his conviction and that the State had failed to prove any criminal intent on his part for the offense alleged in the indictment. The evidence clearly showed that police officer Bryan Windham shot and killed Danny Gray.

Appellant also complains that the Court of Appeals Penal Code § 6.04(a), which reads:

> "A person is criminally responsible if the result would not have occurred but for his conduct, operating either alone or concurrently with another cause, unless the concurrent cause was clearly sufficient to produce the result and the conduct of the actor clearly insufficient."

The Court of Appeals cited this Court's opinion in *Blansett* [the co-defendant's case] as well as People v. Gilbert, 63 Cal.2d 690 (1965), "to conclude that there was ample basis upon which the jury could infer an intent to kill on the part of the appellant, and that the burden of proving intent, or lack thereof was not foisted on the appellant." * * *

In People v. Gilbert, supra, the defendant was convicted for the murder of his accomplice, even though the evidence showed that the accomplice was actually killed by a police officer. Writing for the majority, Chief Justice Traynor of the California Supreme Court recognized that apart from the felony-murder rule, "malice may be established when a defendant initiates a gun battle, and that under such circumstances he may be convicted of murder for a killing committed by another." People v. Gilbert, supra, (citing Judge Traynor's opinion in People v. Washington, 62 Cal.2d 777, 781–82 (1965), in which he noted that "when the defendant intends to kill or intentionally commits acts that are likely to kill with a conscious disregard for life, he is guilty of murder even though he uses another person to accomplish his objective.") * * *

In the instant case all of appellant's actions were voluntary. Under our present case law the evidence is sufficient to prove that appellant intentionally and knowingly caused the death of Captain Gray, knowing that he was a peace officer. By acting intentionally, appellant showed that he was aware of the nature of his conduct and that initiating a shoot-out in the police station would result in the death of one of the officers on duty. The evidence is also sufficient to prove that appellant acted knowingly and therefore his malicious conduct was sufficient to hold him criminally responsible for Captain Gray's resulting death. * * * We adhere to our previous ruling in Blansett, supra, and accordingly [affirm appellant's conviction for capital murder].

The judgment of the Court of Appeals is accordingly affirmed.

CLINTON, JUSTICE, dissenting.

* * * The court of appeals in the instant case relied upon our opinion in Blansett v. State, 556 S.W.2d 322 at 325 (Tex.Cr.App.1977), and, elaborating upon the California case principally cited therein, People v. Gilbert, 63 Cal.2d 690 (1965), correctly noted that in order to find an accused guilty of murder under California law for an act committed by a nonaccomplice third party, two determinations must be made. First there must be found proof of "malice aforethought," or, as the court of appeals translated it in context of our own statutory scheme, "proof of an intent to kill," on the part of the accused. Secondly, the killing must be attributable to the act of the accused or his accomplice. The court of appeals had little difficulty finding sufficient evidence of an intent to kill on appellant's part in this cause, and indeed, it is hard to argue that by firing upon the officers appellant did not manifest such an intent. However, after noting the second requirement, and quoting a germane passage from Gilbert, supra, the court of appeals failed to inquire whether in fact Officer Windham's shooting of Gray can be attributed to appellant—whether it can be said appellant "caused" Gray's death.

The majority now undertakes to resolve this latter inquiry by simply adhering to the Court's holding in *Blansett*, supra, and uncritically reviewing the California authorities cited there, and other California cases decided since. It was my understanding, however, that the Court granted appellant's petition for discretionary review in this cause in order to take a second look at *Blansett* and its progenitors, to determine whether we erred in importing California common law wholesale into our interpretation of Penal Code § 6.04(a).

Under California law, provoking a shoot-out with police may indeed constitute sufficient evidence of "malice aforethought," the required mens rea for murder. Additionally, if the policeman's act of returning fire is reasonable in response to the provocation, the provocation itself may also supply the required culpable act, inasmuch as it "caused" the act which in turn resulted in the killing. The provocation is thus a "proximate cause" of death, and the policeman's act "cannot be considered an independent intervening cause for which the defendant is not liable." People v. Gilbert, 408 P.2d at 374. So far as the cases indicate, this California doctrine is purely court-made, with no basis in statute. The doctrine implies something more restrictive than a pure "but/for" concept of causation, but the limitations are still being hammered out by the California courts. In my view there is no call for this Court to mimic the California courts' efforts to define the limits of culpable causation in this or any other context, because our § 6.04 provides its own limitation.

In § 6.04(a), notions of "proximate cause" found in our earlier caselaw were jettisoned in favor of a concept of "sufficient cause"—a result that would not have occurred in the way that it did "but for" the accused's conduct may be attributed to him "unless" there is a concurrent cause and "the concurrent cause was clearly sufficient to produce the result and the conduct of the actor clearly insufficient." In *Blansett,* supra, the Court found that "but for" the conduct of Blansett and appellant in entering the police station armed and with "a conscious disregard for life," Gray would not have been killed. Hence, Blansett "caused" his death. That Officer Windham actually shot Gray was deemed not to be a concurrent cause. At first glance this latter holding seems pure ipse dixit. Closer scrutiny reveals that it is by utilization of this notion of "proximate cause," gleaned from the California cases and Texas cases decided before enactment of the 1974 Penal Code, that the Court was able to conclude Windham's conduct was not a causal component to Gray's death. This seems to me a subversion of the statute. In order to avoid application of the new "sufficient cause" standard to determine whether Windham's conduct in actually shooting Gray would operate to exculpate Blansett of capital murder, the Court relied upon a doctrine of "proximate cause" * * * to deny what would otherwise seem intuitively obvious—that Windham's conduct was in some sense a "cause" of Gray's death, and perhaps within what the legislature meant by "concurrent cause."

I am inclined to hold not only that Windham's act of shooting was a concurrent cause of Gray's death, but also that it was "clearly sufficient" to cause that result, while appellant's conduct, even in "intentionally" entering the station "with a conscious disregard for life," was, by itself, clearly insufficient. Had Windham not fired on Gray, he would not have been killed. On the other hand, appellant's "disregard for life" would not have resulted in Gray's death if Windham had not shot Gray. It seems to me that on the facts of this case appellant cannot be prosecuted for intentionally, knowingly, recklessly or negligently "causing" Gray's death. This is not to say he could not be found guilty of attempted capital murder or aggravated assault, in that he fired upon peace officers with an apparent intent to kill. * * *

I must respectfully dissent.

STATE v. CANOLA

Supreme Court of New Jersey, 1977.
73 N.J. 206, 374 A.2d 20.

The opinion of the court was delivered by CONFORD, P.J.A.D., Temporarily Assigned.

Defendant, along with three confederates, was in the process of robbing a store when a victim of the robbery, attempting to resist the perpetration of the crime, fatally shot one of the co-felons. The sole issue is whether defendant may be held liable for felony murder. * * * The owner of a jewelry store and his employee, in an attempt to resist an armed robbery, engaged in a physical skirmish with one of the four robbers. A second conspirator, called upon for assistance, began shooting, and the store owner returned the gunfire. Both the owner and the felon, one Lloredo, were fatally shot in the exchange, the latter by the firearm of the owner. Defendant and two others were indicted on two counts of murder, one count of robbery and one count of having been armed during the robbery. The murder counts were based on the deaths of the robbery victim and the co-felon. After trial on the murder counts defendant was found guilty on both and was sentenced to concurrent terms of life imprisonment. * * *

Conventional formulations of the felony murder rule would not seem to encompass liability in this case. As stated by Blackstone about the time of the American Revolution, the rule was: "And if one intends to do another felony, and undesignedly kills a man, this is also murder." In such case the felonious intent supplies the malice requisite for murder. * * * The English courts never applied the felony murder rule to hold a felon guilty of the death of his co-felon at the hands of the intended victim. * * *

It is clearly the majority view throughout the country that, at least in theory, the doctrine of felony murder does not extend to a killing, although growing out of the commission of the felony, if directly attributable to the act of one other than the defendant or those associated with him in the unlawful enterprise. [Citations] This rule is sometimes [called] the "agency" theory of felony murder. The classic statement of the theory is found in an early case applying it in a context pertinent to the case at bar, Commonwealth v. Campbell, 89 Mass. 541, 544 (Sup.Jud. Ct.1863), as follows: "No person can be held guilty of homicide unless the act is either actually or constructively his, and it cannot be his act in either sense unless committed by his own hand or by someone acting in concert with him or in furtherance of a common object or purpose."

A contrary view, which would attach liability under the felony murder rule for any death proximately resulting from the unlawful activity—even the death of a co-felon—notwithstanding the killing was by one resisting the crime, does not seem to have the present allegiance of any court. [Citations and discussion of cases from various states where the courts first embraced and then at least partially discarded the proximate cause theory.]

To be distinguished from the situation before us here, and from the generality of the cases discussed above, and the so-called "shield" cases. The first of these were the companion cases of Taylor v. State, 41 Tex.Cr.R. 564, 55 S.W. 961 (Cr.App.1900), and Keaton v. State, 41 Tex.Cr.R. 621, 57 S.W. 1125 (Cr.App.1900). In attempting to escape after robbing a train, defendants thrust the brakeman in front of them as a shield, as a result of which he was fatally shot by law officers. The court had no difficulty in finding defendants guilty of murder. The court in *Taylor* noted the correctness of the *Campbell* case doctrine that a person could not be held liable for homicide unless the act is either actually or constructively committed by him, but indicated it was inapplicable to a case where defendants forced deceased to occupy a place of danger in order that they might carry out the crime. * * *

Most modern progressive thought in criminal jurisprudence favors restriction rather than expansion of the felony murder rule. It has frequently been observed that although the rule was logical at its inception, when all felonies were punishable by death, its survival to modern times when other felonies are not thought to be as blameworthy as premeditated killings is discordant with rational and enlightened views of criminal culpability and liability. * * * Tort concepts of foreseeability and proximate cause have shallow relevance to culpability for murder in the first degree. Gradations of criminal liability should accord with the degree of moral culpability for the actor's conduct. * * *

The judgment of the Appellate Division is modified so as to strike the conviction and sentencing of defendant for murder of the co-felon Lloredo.

SULLIVAN, J. (concurring in result only).

The practical result of the majority holding is that even though some innocent person or a police officer be killed during the commission of an armed robbery, the felon would bear no criminal responsibility of any kind for that killing as long as it was not at the hand of the felon or a confederate. The legislative intent, as I see it, is otherwise.

The thrust of our felony murder statute is to hold the criminal liable for any killing which ensues during the commission of a felony, even though the felon, or a confederate, did not commit the actual killing. The only exception I would recognize would be the death of a co-felon, which could be classified as a justifiable homicide and not within the purview of the statute.

The Legislature should act promptly to clarify the situation resulting from the majority opinion. * * *

Note

Following the decision in *Canola*, the state legislature amended New Jersey's felony murder statute, which now provides in relevant part that "homicide constitutes murder when * * * [i]t is committed when the actor, acting either alone or with one or more other persons, is engaged in the commission of, or an attempt to commit, or flight after committing or attempting to commit robbery, sexual assault, arson, burglary, kidnapping, carjacking or criminal escape, and in the course of such crime or of immediate flight therefrom, any person causes the death of a person other than one of the participants * * *." N.J.S. § 2C:11–3 (2001). Does this statute overrule Canola?

In State v. Martin, 119 N.J. 2, 573 A.2d 1359 (1990), the New Jersey Supreme Court affirmed that "Canola limited the felony-murder rule to killings committed by a participating felon acting either as a sole perpetrator or as one of multiple perpetrators." The court then concluded that by amending N.J.S. 2C:11–3, "the Legislature effectively adopted Justice Sullivan's concurring opinion and overrode so much of Canola as held that one of multiple perpetrators could not be guilty of felony murder when the death was caused by the victim."

PEOPLE v. AARON

Supreme Court of Michigan, 1980.
409 Mich. 672, 299 N.W.2d 304.

FITZGERALD, JUSTICE.

The existence and scope of the felony murder doctrine have perplexed generations of law students, commentators and jurists in the United States and England, and have split our own Court of Appeals. In these cases, we must decide whether Michigan has a felony murder rule which allows the element of malice required for murder to be satisfied by the intent to commit the underlying felony or whether malice must be otherwise found by the trier of fact. We must also determine what is the *mens rea* required to support a conviction under Michigan's first-degree murder statute.

Facts

In *Thompson*, defendant was convicted by a jury of first-degree felony murder as the result of a death which occurred during an armed robbery. The trial judge instructed the jury that it was not necessary for the prosecution to prove malice, as a finding of intent to rob was all that was necessary for the homicide to constitute first-degree murder. The Court of Appeals held that reversible error resulted from the trial court's failure to instruct the jury on the element of malice in the felony murder charge.

In *Wright*, defendant was convicted by a jury of two counts of first-degree felony murder for setting fire to a dwelling causing the death of two people. The trial court instructed the jury that proof that the killings occurred during the perpetration of arson was sufficient to establish first-degree murder. The Court of Appeals reversed the convictions, holding that it was error to remove the element of malice from the jury's consideration. Defendant Aaron was convicted of first-degree felony murder as a result of a homicide committed during the perpetration of an armed robbery. The jury was instructed that they could convict defendant of first-degree murder if they found that defendant killed the victim during the commission or attempted commission of an armed robbery.

* * *

II. History of the Felony Murder Doctrine

Felony murder has never been a static, well-defined rule at common law, but throughout its history has been characterized by judicial reinterpretation to limit the harshness of the application of the rule. Historians and commentators have concluded that the rule is of questionable origin and that the reasons for the rule no longer exist, making it an anachronistic remnant, "a historic survivor for which there is no logical or practical basis for existence in modern law."

The first formal statement of the doctrine is often said to be Lord Dacres' case, 72 Eng.Rep. 458 (KB, 1535). Lord Dacres and some companions agreed to enter a park without permission to hunt, an unlawful act, *and to kill anyone who might resist them.* While Lord Dacres was a quarter of a mile away, one member of his group killed a gamekeeper who confronted him in the park. Although Lord Dacres was not present when the killing occurred, he, along with the rest of his companions, was convicted of murder and was hanged. Contrary to the construction placed on this case by those who see it as a source of the felony-murder rule, the holding was not that Lord Dacres and his companions were guilty of murder because they had joined in an unlawful hunt in the course of which a person was killed, but rather that those not present physically at the killing were held liable as principals on the theory of constructive presence. Moreover, because they had agreed previously to kill anyone who might resist them, all the members of the group shared in the *mens rea* of the crime. Thus, because *Lord Dacres'* case involved express malice, no doctrine finding malice from the intention to commit an unlawful act was necessary or in fact utilized.

Another early case which has been cited for the origin of the felony-murder doctrine was decided after *Lord Dacres'* case. In Mansell & Herbert's case, 73 Eng.Rep. 279 (KB, 1558), Herbert and a group of more than 40 followers had gone to Sir Richard Mansfield's house "with force to seize goods under pretence of lawful authority". One of Herbert's servants threw a stone at a person in the gateway which instead hit and killed an unarmed woman coming out of Mansfield's house. The question was agreed to be whether the accused were guilty of murder or manslaughter. Since misadventure was not considered, it can be assumed that the throwing of the stone was not a careless act but that the servant who threw the stone intended at least to hit, if not kill, some person on Mansfield's side. Although the court divided, the majority held that if one deliberately performed an act of violence to third parties, and a person not intended died, it was murder regardless of any mistake or misapplication of force. The minority would have held it to be manslaughter because the violent act was not directed against the woman who died. Thus, *Herbert's* case involved a *deliberate act of violence* against a person, which resulted in an unintended person being the recipient of the violent act.

Some commentators suggest that an incorrect version of *Dacres'* case, which was repeated by Crompton, formed the basis of Lord Coke's statement of the felony-murder rule:

> If the act be unlawful it is murder. As if A. meaning to steale a deere in the park of B., shooteth at the deer, and by the glance of the arrow killeth a boy that is hidden in a bush: this is murder, for that the act was unlawfull, although A. had no intent to hurt the boy, nor knew not of him. But if B. the owner of the park had shot at his own deer, and without any ill intent had killed the boy by the glance of his arrow, this had been homicide by misadventure, and no felony.
>
> So if one shoot at any wild fowle upon a tree, and the arrow killeth any reasonable creature afar off, without any evill intent in him, this is *per infortunium* [misadventure]: for it was not unlawful to shoot at the wilde fowle: but if he had shot at a cock or hen, or any tame fowle of another mans, and the arrow by mischance had killed a man, this had been murder, for the act was unlawful.

The above excerpt from Coke is, along with *Lord Dacres'* and *Herbert's* cases, most often cited as the origin of the felony-murder doctrine. Unfortunately, Coke's statement has been criticized as completely lacking in authority. * * *

Case law of Nineteenth–Century England reflects the efforts of the English courts to limit the application of the felony-murder doctrine. See, e.g., Regina v. Greenwood, 7 Cox, Crim.Cas. 404 (1857); Regina v. Horsey, 176 Eng.Rep. 129 (1862), culminating in Regina v. Serne, 16 Cox, Crim.Cas. 311 (1887). In the latter case, involving a death resulting from arson, Judge Stephen instructed the jury as follows:

> [I]nstead of saying that any act done with intent to commit a felony and which causes death amounts to murder, it should be reasonable to say that any act known to be dangerous to life and likely in itself to cause death, done for the purpose of committing a felony which causes death, should be murder.

In this century, the felony murder doctrine was comparatively rarely invoked in England and in 1957 England abolished the felony-murder rule. Section 1 of England's 1957 Homicide Act provides that a killing occurring in a felony murder situation will not amount to murder unless done with the same malice aforethought as is required for all other murder.

Thus, an examination of the felony murder rule indicates that the doctrine is of doubtful origin. Derived from the misinterpretation of case law, it went unchallenged because of circumstances which no longer exist. The doctrine was continuously modified and restricted in England, the country of its birth, until its ultimate rejection by Parliament in 1957.

III. Limitation of the Felony Murder Doctrine in the United States

While only a few states have followed the lead of Great Britain in abolishing felony murder, various legislative and judicial limitations on the doctrine have effectively narrowed the scope of the rule in the United States. Perkins states that the rule is "somewhat in disfavor at the present time" and that "courts apply it where the law requires, but they do so grudgingly and tend to restrict its application where circumstances permit".

The draftsmen of the Model Penal Code have summarized the limitations imposed by American courts as follows:

(1) "The felonious act must be dangerous to life."

(2) and (3). "The homicide must be a natural and probable consequence of the felonious act." "Death must be 'proximately' caused." Courts have also required that the killing be the result of an act done in the furtherance of the felonious purpose and not merely coincidental to the perpetration of a felony. These cases often make distinctions based on the identity of the victim (i.e., whether the decedent was the victim of the felony or whether he was someone else, e.g., a policeman or one of the felons) and the identity of the person causing the death.

(4) "The felony must be *malum in se.*"

(5) "The act must be a common-law felony."

(6) "The period during which the felony is in the process of commission must be narrowly construed."

(7) "The underlying felony must be 'independent' of the homicide." * * *

The numerous modifications and restrictions placed upon the common-law felony murder doctrine by courts and legislatures reflect dissatisfaction with the harshness and injustice of the rule. Even though the felony murder doctrine survives in this country, it bears increasingly less resemblance to the traditional felony murder concept. To the extent that these modifications reduce the scope and significance of the common law doctrine, they also call into question the continued existence of the doctrine itself. * * *

V. The Felony Murder Doctrine in Michigan

Michigan does not have a statutory felony murder doctrine which designates as murder any *death* occurring in the course of a felony without regard to whether it was the result of accident, negligence, recklessness or willfulness. Rather, Michigan has a statute which makes a *murder* occurring in the course of one of the enumerated felonies a first-degree murder:

> Murder which is perpetrated by means of poison, lying in wait, or other wilful, deliberate, and premeditated killing, or which is committed in the perpetration, or attempt to perpetrate arson, criminal sexual conduct in the first or third degree, robbery, breaking and entering of a dwelling, larceny of any kind, extortion, or kidnapping, is murder of the first degree, and shall be punished by imprisonment for life. M.C.L. § 750.316; M.S.A. § 28.548.

The Michigan Legislature adopted verbatim the first-degree murder statute of Pennsylvania, the statute we have today. In creating the statutes which divided murder into degrees, it was the intention of the Pennsylvania Legislature to reform the penal laws of that state by making punishment more proportionate to the crime and, in particular, to narrow the category of capital offenses. It was not its apparent intention to adopt by statute the common-law felony murder rule. * * *

The prosecution argues that even if Michigan does not have a statutory codification of the felony murder rule, the common-law definition of murder included a homicide in the course of a felony. Thus, the argument continues, once a homicide in the course of a felony is proven, under the commonlaw felony murder rule a murder has been established and the first-degree murder statute then becomes applicable. This Court has ruled that the term murder as used in the first-degree murder statute includes all types of murder at common law. * * *

This Court has not been faced previously with a decision as to whether it should abolish the felony murder doctrine. Thus, the common-law doctrine remains the law in Michigan. Moreover, the assumption by appellate decisions that the doctrine exists, combined with the fact that Michigan trial courts have applied the doctrine in numerous cases resulting in convictions of first-degree felony murder, requires us to address the common-law felony murder issue. The cases before us today squarely present us with the opportunity to review the doctrine and to consider its continued existence in Michigan. Although there are no Michigan cases which specifically abrogate the felony murder rule, there exists a number of decisions of this Court which have significantly restricted the doctrine in Michigan and which lead us to conclude that the rule should be abolished. * * *

Accordingly, we hold today that malice is the intention to kill, the intention to do great bodily harm, or the wanton and willful disregard of the likelihood that the natural tendency of defendant's behavior is to cause death or great bodily harm. We further hold that malice is an essential element of any murder, as that term is judicially defined, whether the murder occurs in the course of a felony or otherwise. The facts and circumstances involved in the perpetration of a felony may evidence an intent to kill, an intent to cause great bodily harm, or a wanton and willful disregard of the likelihood that the natural tendency of defendant's behavior is to cause death or great bodily harm; however, the conclusion must be left to the jury to infer from all the evidence.

Otherwise, "juries might be required to find the fact of malice where they were satisfied from the whole evidence it did not exist".

VI. Practical Effect of Abrogation of the Common–Law Felony Murder Doctrine

From a practical standpoint, the abolition of the category of malice arising from the intent to commit the underlying felony should have little effect on the result of the majority of cases. In many cases where felony murder has been applied, the use of the doctrine was unnecessary because the other types of malice could have been inferred from the evidence. * * *

In the past, the felony murder rule has been employed where unforeseen or accidental deaths occur and where the state seeks to prove vicarious liability of co-felons. In situations involving the vicarious liability of co-felons, the individual liability of each felon must be shown. It is fundamentally unfair and in violation of basic principles of individual criminal culpability to hold one felon liable for the unforeseen and unagreed-to results of another felon. In cases where the felons are acting intentionally or recklessly in pursuit of a common plan, the felony murder rule is unnecessary because liability may be established on agency principles.

Finally, in cases where the death was purely accidental, application of the felony murder doctrine is unjust and should be precluded. The underlying felony, of course, will still be subject to punishment. The draftsmen of the Model Penal Code report that juries are not disposed to accept unfounded claims of accident in Ohio where all first-degree murder requires a purpose to kill. * * *

The first-degree murder statute will continue to operate in that all *murder* committed in the perpetration or attempted perpetration of the enumerated felonies will be elevated to first-degree murder. * * *

In *Aaron,* the judgment of conviction of murder is reversed and this case is remanded to the trial court for a new trial.

[Concurring opinions omitted.]

Note

Homicide statutes patterned on the 1794 Pennsylvania Act do not explicitly make all killings in the perpetration of felonies murder, but merely make homicides which would be murder in any event murders of the first degree where committed in perpetration of one of the named felonies. Killings that are accidental or merely negligent are murder only if the state retains the common law felony murder rule, which established "malice" for any homicide occurring in the perpetration or attempted perpetration of a dangerous felony. Compare Commonwealth ex rel. Smith v. Myers, 438 Pa. 218, 261 A.2d 550 (1970), and Warren v. State, 29 Md.App. 560, 350 A.2d 173 (1976); with State v. Galloway, 275 N.W.2d 736 (Iowa 1979). Most killings in the perpetration of robberies or burglaries would probably be first degree murder in any event, at least if we allow a concept of "conditional premeditation." Persons who participate in an armed robbery or burglary presumably intend to use their weapons if necessary to complete the crime or make a getaway. Although the need to kill may arise on the spur of the moment, the robbers or burglars contemplate the prospect of killing in advance.

The felony murder doctrine also imposes vicarious liability on participants in the felony who do not directly participate in the act of killing, such as the driver of the getaway car. If the killing was foreseeable, however, the felony murder rule probably does no more than duplicate the outcome which would follow from principles of conspiracy or complicity law in any event.

The California Supreme Court declined to follow People v. Aaron, in People v. Dillon, 34 Cal.3d 441, 194 Cal.Rptr. 390, 668 P.2d 697 (1983). Although the California murder statute, like the Michigan statute, is directly patterned upon the 1794 Pennsylvania statute, the California court held on the basis of legislative history that it incorporates the common law felony murder doctrine as well as the degree-fixing felony murder doctrine. Accordingly, even accidental killings occurring in the perpetration of the named felonies are murder in California. On the other hand, the California court held that in some circumstances the degree-fixing felony murder rule itself might violate the state's constitutional ban on cruel or unusual punishments. The defendant in *Dillon* was a seventeen-year-old high school student who went with a bunch of friends to "rip-off" a marijuana farm, taking guns for protection in the event that the owners of the marijuana appeared on the scene. When one of the owners did appear carrying a shotgun, Dillon panicked and fired nine bullets into him. Although the killing clearly was murder under any theory and could have been premeditated murder, the trial record indicated that the jury wanted to show leniency and returned a verdict of first degree murder only because it felt constrained to do so under the felony murder instructions. The California Supreme Court held that under these circumstances a first degree murder verdict violated the state constitution, and reduced the verdict to murder in the second degree. The opinion stressed the defendant's age and immaturity, as well as his lack of prior record.

PEOPLE v. PATTERSON

Supreme Court of California, 1989.
49 Cal.3d 615, 262 Cal.Rptr. 195, 778 P.2d 549.

KENNARD, JUSTICE. * * *

According to the testimony at the preliminary hearing, the victim Jennie Licerio and her friend Carmen Lopez had been using cocaine on a daily basis in the months preceding Licerio's death. On the night in question, the two women were with defendant in his motel room. There, all three drank "wine coolers," inhaled "lines" of cocaine, and smoked "coco puffs" (hand-rolled cigarettes containing a mixture of tobacco and cocaine). Defendant furnished the cocaine. When Licerio became ill, Lopez called an ambulance. Defendant stayed with the two women until the paramedics and the police arrived. The paramedics were unable to revive Licerio, who died of acute cocaine intoxication.

The People filed an information charging defendant with [murder and also with furnishing cocaine in violation of Health & Safety Code § 11532, "in that he did willfully, unlawfully and feloniously transport, import into the State of California, sell, furnish, administer, and give away, and attempt to import into the State of California and transport a controlled substance, to-wit: cocaine."]

Defendant moved to set aside that portion of the information charging him with murder, contending the evidence presented at the preliminary hearing did not establish probable cause to believe he had committed murder. In opposing the motion, the People did not suggest the murder charge was based on a theory of implied malice. Instead, they relied solely on the second degree felony-murder doctrine. [The trial court granted the motion to dismiss the murder charge, ruling that a violation of § 11532 is not an inherently dangerous felony. The Court of Appeal affirmed the dismissal.]

Discussion

1. *Second Degree Felony–Murder Doctrine*

There is no precise statutory definition for the second degree felony-murder rule. In People v. Ford (1964) 60 Cal.2d 772, 795, 36 Cal.Rptr. 620, 388 P.2d 892, we defined the doctrine as follows: "A homicide that is a direct causal result of the commission of a felony inherently dangerous to human life (other than the six felonies enumerated in Pen.Code, § 189) constitutes at least second degree murder. [Citations.] In determining whether the felony is inherently dangerous, we look to the elements of the felony in the abstract, not the particular facts of the case." [Citations]

[The opinion acknowledged that the second degree felony-murder rule has been widely and severely criticized, but noted that the legislature has refused repeated invitations from the courts to reconsider the doctrine. The court therefore declined to consider the arguments of defendant and amici curiae that the doctrine be abolished.]

We also turn down the People's invitation that we expand the second degree felony-murder doctrine by eliminating the requirement of People v. Williams, 63 Cal.2d 452, 47 Cal.Rptr. 7, 406 P.2d 647, that the elements of the offense be viewed "in the abstract," and by adopting a new standard focusing instead on the actual conduct of a defendant in determining whether the felony is inherently dangerous. In *Williams* the defendants argued with their drug dealer and stabbed him to death, assertedly in self-defense. We reversed the convictions for second degree murder because of the trial court's improper instruction to the jury that the defendants were guilty of second degree murder if the jury found the killing had occurred in the perpetration of the felony of conspiracy to possess Methedrine without a prescription. We explained that, in evaluating the inherent dangerousness of a particular felony, "we look to the elements of the felony in the abstract, not the particular facts of the case." We concluded that under this analysis the conspiracy involved in *Williams* was not a felony inherently dangerous to human life.

Sound reasons support the *Williams* rule. As we observed in People v. Burroughs, 35 Cal.3d at 830: "This form of [viewed-in-the-abstract] analysis is compelled because there is a killing in every case where the rule might potentially be applied. If in such circumstances a court were to examine the particular facts of the case prior to establishing whether the underlying felony is inherently dangerous, the court might well be led to conclude the rule applicable despite any unfairness which might redound to so broad an application: the existence of the dead victim might appear to lead inexorably to the conclusion that the underlying felony is exceptionally hazardous."

For the reasons set forth above, we are reluctant to significantly expand the scope of the second degree felony-murder rule, as the People have urged us to do. We have repeatedly said that the felony-murder rule "deserves no extension beyond its required application." [Citations] Both the People's suggestion that we expand the second degree felony-murder doctrine and defendant's suggestion that we abolish it are matters appropriately left to the Legislature.

2. *Determining "inherent dangerousness" of the felony*

* * * Because Health and Safety Code § 11352 also proscribes conduct other than furnishing cocaine, the issue still to be resolved is whether we must consider only the specific offense of furnishing cocaine or the entire scope of conduct prohibited by the statute. The Court of Appeal felt compelled to [examine § 11532 in its entirety] because of a series of recent cases where we held that, to determine a felony's inherent dangerousness, the statute as a whole had to be examined. However, unlike the situation here, each of those cases involved a statute that proscribed an essentially single form of conduct. In People v. Lopez, 6 Cal.3d 45, 98 Cal.Rptr. 44, 489 P.2d 1372 (1971), the defendant and another inmate engaged in what initially was a nonviolent escape, but which culminated in a fatal assault perpetrated by the other escaping inmate. We held the crime of escape (Pen. Code § 4532) not to be an inherently dangerous felony for purposes of applying the second degree felony-murder rule. We rejected the People's contention that because the statute's penalty for a violent escape was greater than for a nonviolent escape it could be broken into two offenses: one violent, the other nonviolent. In stressing the statute's unitary nature, we said: "The offense is escape. The circumstances of commission are relevant not to the offense committed but to the punishment to be imposed therefor."

In People v. Henderson, 19 Cal.3d 86, 137 Cal.Rptr. 1, 560 P.2d 1180 the defendant was accused of murder based on a death that had occurred in the course of aggravated false imprisonment. The crime was a felony because it had been "effected by violence, menace, fraud or deceit." (Pen. Code §§ 236, 237.) After analyzing the statutory scheme as a whole, we concluded: "While the elements of violence or menace by which false imprisonment is elevated to a felony may involve danger to human life, the felony offense viewed as a whole in the abstract is not inherently dangerous to human life." * * *

Finally, in People v. Burroughs, 35 Cal.3d 824, we held that a violation of Business and Professions Code § 2053,[7] which prohibits the practice of medicine without a license "under circumstances or conditions which cause or create a risk of great bodily harm, serious physical or mental illness, or death," was not a felony inherently dangerous to human life. We explained: "In this examination we are required to view the statutory definition of the offense as a whole, taking into account even nonhazardous ways of violating the provisions of the law which do not necessarily pose a threat to human life. The primary element of the offense is the practice of medicine without a license. The statute defines such practice as 'treating the sick or afflicted.' One can certainly conceive of treatment of the sick or afflicted which has quite innocuous results—the affliction at stake could be a common cold, or a sprained finger, and the form of treatment an admonition to rest in bed and drink fluids or the application of ice to mild swelling. Thus, we do not find inherent dangerousness at this stage. * * * "

In both *Henderson* and *Burroughs*, supra, we observed that the offense in question had a "primary element." In *Henderson*, the primary element was "the unlawful restraint of another's liberty," while in *Burroughs* it was "the practice of medicine without a license." *Lopez*, too, involved an offense with a primary element, escape. In contrast, § 11352 has no primary element. For instance, the elements of the crime of transporting a controlled substance bear no resemblance to those underlying the offense of administering such a substance; yet these two offenses are included in the same statute.

The fact that the Legislature has included a variety of offenses in § 11352 does not require that we treat them as a unitary entity. * * * There are more than 100 different controlled substances that fall within the confines of § 11352. To create statutes separately proscribing the importation, sale, furnishing, administration, etc., of each of these drugs, would require the enactment of hundreds of individual statutes. It thus appears that for the sake of convenience the Legislature has included the various offenses in one statute.

The determination whether a defendant who furnishes cocaine commits an inherently dangerous felony should not turn on the dangerousness of other drugs included in the same statute, such as heroin and peyote; nor should it turn on the danger to life, if any, inherent in the

7. Section 2053 provides: "Any person who willfully, under circumstances or conditions which cause or create risk of great bodily harm, serious physical or mental illness, or death, practices or attempts to practice, or advertises or holds himself or herself out as practicing, any system or mode of treating the sick or afflicted in this state, or diagnoses, treats, operates for, or prescribes for any ailment, blemish, deformity, disease, disfigurement, disorder, injury, or other physical or mental condition of any person, without having at the time of so doing a valid [certificate authorizing the practice of medicine] is punishable by imprisonment in the county jail for not exceeding one year or in the state prison.

"The remedy provided in this section shall not preclude any other remedy provided by law."

transportation or administering of cocaine. Rather, each offense set forth in the statute should be examined separately to determine its inherent dangerousness.

* * * Defendant argues that even the more narrow offense of furnishing cocaine is not an inherently dangerous felony and therefore the trial court acted correctly in dismissing the murder charge, despite its faulty analysis. The People have asked us to take judicial notice of various medical articles and reports that assertedly demonstrate that furnishing cocaine is sufficiently dangerous to life to constitute an inherently dangerous felony. The task of evaluating the evidence on this issue is most appropriately entrusted to the trial court, subject to appellate review. * * *

3. *Meaning of the term "inherently dangerous to human life"*

* * * Ordinarily, when a defendant commits an unintentional killing, a murder conviction requires a showing that he acted with implied malice. With the felony-murder rule, however, such malice need not be shown.

Implied malice, for which the second degree felony-murder doctrine acts as a substitute, has both a physical and a mental component. The physical component is satisfied by the performance of "an act, the natural consequences of which are dangerous to life." (People v. Watson (1981) 30 Cal.3d 290, 300, 179 Cal.Rptr. 43, 637 P.2d 279.) The mental component is that the defendant "knows that his conduct endangers the life of another and * * * acts with a conscious disregard for life." (Ibid.) The second degree felony-murder rule eliminates the need for the prosecution to establish the mental component. The justification is that when society has declared certain inherently dangerous conduct to be felonious, a defendant should not be allowed to excuse himself by saying he was unaware of the danger to life because, by declaring the conduct to be felonious, society has warned him of the risk involved. The physical requirement, however, remains the same; by committing a felony inherently dangerous to life, the defendant has committed "an act, the natural consequences of which are dangerous to life," thus satisfying the physical component of implied malice. The definition of "inherently dangerous to life" in the context of the implied malice element of second degree murder is well established. An act is inherently dangerous to human life when there is "a high probability that it will result in death." We therefore conclude—by analogy to the established definition of the term "dangerous to life" in the context of the implied malice element of second degree murder that, for purposes of the second degree felony-murder doctrine, an "inherently dangerous felony" is an offense carrying "a high probability" that death will result. A less stringent standard would inappropriately expand the scope of the second degree felony-murder rule reducing the seriousness of the act which a defendant must commit in order to be charged with murder.[9]

9. We are aware that * * * the Legislature has determined that deaths occurring in the commission of certain felonies are punishable as first degree murder. (Pen.

We share the concern Chief Justice Lucas has expressed in his dissent regarding the tragic effects that the abuse of illegal drugs, particularly crack cocaine, has on our society. However, it is the Legislature, rather than this court, that should determine whether expansion of the second degree felony-murder rule is an appropriate method by which to address this problem. * * *

We reverse the decision of the Court of Appeal, and direct that court to remand the matter to the trial court for further proceedings consistent with this opinion.

LUCAS, CHIEF JUSTICE, concurring and dissenting.

* * * Because the drug furnishing statutes must be viewed in the abstract for purposes of applying the second degree felony murder doctrine, as a practical matter the majority's new "high probability" requirement will be impossible to satisfy in any case arising under those statutes, for to my knowledge none of them involves drugs so dangerous that death is a highly probable result. At a time when our society faces a serious "crack" cocaine crisis of epidemic proportions, the majority's holding is particularly unwelcome. * * *

* * * The relevant question would be whether furnishing a particular drug such as cocaine or heroin created a substantial risk of death. Although that test may be difficult for the prosecution to meet, the majority's alternative test will entirely foreclose the possibility of a murder charge in all of these cases. The purpose of the felony murder rule is to deter the commission of inherently dangerous felonies. Certainly that purpose is furthered by deterring offenses bearing a substantial risk of death, as well as those offenses involving a greater likelihood of death. * * *

The anomalous and inconsistent nature of the majority's holding is confirmed by the fact that a defendant can be charged with first degree felony murder by committing such offenses as burglary, robbery, rape or child molestation, none of which offenses, viewed in the abstract, involves a high probability of death, although each of which may present substantial risks of death. * * *

EAGLESON and KAUFMAN, JJ., concur.

MOSK, JUSTICE, dissenting.

* * * Shortly after this court adopted the requirement [in the *Williams* case in 1965] that to determine whether a felony is inherently dangerous to human life we look to the elements of the felony in the abstract, we first confronted an attempt to depart from the statutory definition of the felony. In People v. Phillips (1966) 64 Cal.2d 574, 51 Cal.Rptr. 225, 414 P.2d 353, the defendant chiropractor persuaded the parents of a child with eye cancer to renounce planned surgery and allow

Code § 189.) The fact that the Legislature has chosen to single out those offenses in this fashion, however, provides no guidance on the appropriate reach of the second degree felony-murder doctrine in general. As noted earlier, the Legislature of course has the authority to expand or to abolish the second degree felony-murder doctrine.

him to treat her instead by chiropractic methods, charging them for his services. When the child died the defendant was convicted of second degree felony-murder, the felony being grand theft in violation of Penal Code section 484. We held that it was prejudicial error to predicate a felony-murder instruction on that offense. The Attorney General conceded that grand theft as defined in section 484 was not inherently dangerous to human life, but urged us to look at "the entire course of defendant's conduct" and to characterize the crime as "grand theft medical fraud" [which he argued was an inherently dangerous felony].

We rejected this attempt to "abandon the statutory definition of the felony as such," explaining that "To fragmentize the course of conduct of defendant so that the felony-murder rule applies if any segment of that conduct may be considered dangerous to life would widen the rule beyond calculation."

* * * The claim we rejected in *Phillips* was analytically the converse of the claim made here: in *Phillips* the Attorney General sought to expand the statutory definition of the felony by including elements ("medical fraud") not incorporated therein by the Legislature; here the Attorney General seeks instead to contract the statutory definition by excluding elements (the transportation, importation, sale, etc., of controlled substances) that the Legislature did incorporate therein. But the reasoning of *Phillips* * * * remains no less applicable to the present context. * * *

The majority's reference to the "100 different controlled substances" is a red herring: nothing actually turns on that fact. For example, Health and Safety Code § 11360 is a parallel statute whose operative wording is identical to § 11352: it, too, prohibits the acts of transporting, importing, selling, furnishing, administering, etc., a drug—but it applies only to one substance, marijuana. If a similar case were to arise under section 11360 (e.g., an accidental death following the furnishing and ingestion of an excessive quantity of marijuana), I cannot believe the majority would refuse to apply today's holding that "each offense set forth in the statute should be examined separately to determine its inherent dangerousness."[3]

* * * § 11352 can be violated in various ways that do not create a substantial risk of death. For example, it is violated by one who simply carries a small amount of cocaine home in his pocket for his personal use, or by a motorist who simply offers a ride in his car to a friend who he knows is carrying a similar amount of cocaine for his own use; no other act or intent need be proved for a conviction. * * * Because § 11352 is not a felony inherently dangerous to human life, it cannot

3. At the cost of mixing metaphors, I add that the majority's reference to the "100 different controlled substances" is also a straw man: defendant does not contend that the dangerousness of the violation of § 11352 in this case should be judged, for example, by reference to a relatively benign medication such as codeine, which is listed among the 100. Both the complaint and the information charged defendant specifically with transporting, importing, selling, furnishing, administering, etc., "a controlled substance, to wit: cocaine."

serve as a predicate for the second degree felony-murder rule; and because the prosecutor indicated to the court that felony murder was his sole theory on the homicide count, the court correctly dismissed that count in the interest of justice. * * *

I agree that for purposes of the second degree felony-murder rule a felony inherently dangerous to human life should be defined as a felony carrying a high probability that it will result in death. * * *

BROUSSARD, J., concurs.

PANELLI, JUSTICE, dissenting.

I join fully in Justice Mosk's dissenting opinion, including the approval of the "high probability of death" standard. I am writing separately to emphasize the need for legislative attention to the second degree felony-murder rule. * * *

* * * There are, or at least should be, no nonstatutory crimes in this state. The second degree felony-murder rule, however, either creates a nonstatutory crime or increases the punishment for statutory crimes beyond that established by the Legislature. We derive such authority neither from the Constitution nor from the Penal Code. My uneasiness with the second degree felony-murder rule is mirrored in the majority's adoption of the new "high probability of death" standard, which certainly will restrict the rule's future application. It may also be reflected in how often the majority mentions that the Legislature has failed to act. Today the majority expressly relies on that failure as a justification for continuing to determine the scope of this anomalous common law crime. But in view of the Legislature's long-standing declaration that "[n]o act or omission * * * is criminal or punishable, except as prescribed or authorized by [the Penal Code]" (Pen.Code, § 6), I question whether subsequent legislative inaction is a sufficient justification. * * *

I would affirm the decision of the Court of Appeal.

Note

The rationale for the second degree felony-murder doctrine is largely a matter of symmetry. If a homicide committed in the perpetration of a dangerous misdemeanor is manslaughter, and a homicide committed in the perpetration of certain listed felonies is first degree murder, then it would seem that a homicide committed in the course of other felonies must be second degree murder. This doctrine would be harsh indeed if it applied to all felonies, but the limitation to "dangerous" felonies greatly reduces its practical importance. The most commonly committed dangerous felonies are listed in the statute as supporting a conviction of first degree murder, and a homicide resulting from a dangerous felony would often be murder even in the absence of a felony-murder doctrine. Cases from a variety of jurisdictions on the felonies which are sufficiently dangerous to support a felony-murder conviction are collected in Anno. 50 A.L.R.3d 397 (1973). Some states have held as a matter of statutory or case law that sale of heroin is a dangerous felony, so that when a heroin user dies of an overdose the seller who furnished the drug is guilty of murder. For a review of authorities, see State v. Randolph, 676 S.W.2d 943 (Tenn.1984).

PEOPLE v. SMITH

Supreme Court of California, 1984.
35 Cal.3d 798, 201 Cal.Rptr. 311, 678 P.2d 886.

MOSK, JUSTICE.

[Defendant was convicted of felony child abuse and second degree felony murder.] * * * The principal issue is whether felony child abuse may serve as the underlying felony to support a conviction of second degree murder on a felony-murder theory. * * *

Defendant and her two daughters, three-and-a-half-year-old Bethany (Beth) and two-year-old Amy, lived with David Foster. On the day Amy died, she refused to sit on the couch instead of the floor to eat a snack. Defendant became angry, took Amy into the children's bedroom, spanked her and slapped her in the face. Amy then went towards the corner of the bedroom which was often used for discipline; defendant hit her repeatedly, knocking her to the floor. Foster then apparently joined defendant to "assist" in Amy's discipline. Beth testified that both Foster and defendant were striking Amy, who at that point had been at least partially undressed by defendant. Defendant and Foster used both their hands and a paddle on the child, and were also biting her. In addition, Beth testified that Foster put a wastebasket on Amy's head and hit her on the head with his fist.[3] Eventually, defendant knocked the child backwards and she fell, hitting her head on the closet door.

Amy stiffened and went into respiratory arrest. Defendant and Foster took her to the hospital, where defendant admitted that she "beat her too hard." She also stated that Foster had not come home until after the incident. Amy died that evening. Her injuries were consistent with compressive force caused by numerous blows by hands, fists, and a paddle. The severe head injury that was the direct cause of death occurred within an hour before the child was brought to the hospital.

Defendant testified that although she had spanked Amy on the day in question, she then left Amy in the children's room. Foster, believing additional discipline was warranted, went into the room, closed the door and began shouting at Amy. Although defendant heard thumping noises, she was not overly concerned because Foster had behaved similarly in the past and Amy had not been injured. After a half hour, defendant became somewhat worried and entered the room. She observed that Amy had a puffy lip, and bite marks and bruises all over her lower body. Foster left the room at defendant's request after defendant said she would continue the discipline. Defendant then shouted at Amy for 15 to 20 minutes to allow Foster time to "cool off." To avoid the possibility

3. Apparently Beth was in another room during the incident but claimed she could see "a little bit" despite her testimony that both the door to the room she was in and the door to Amy's room were closed.

that Foster might also attack Beth, she took Beth into another bedroom and closed the door. Foster returned to the children's room and began slapping Amy because she would not look at him. Defendant testified she was afraid that if she interfered she would become the object of Foster's attack. She stated that although she realized that Amy was being abused, she did not believe the child's life was in danger. Defendant eventually did intervene, at which point Amy stiffened and fainted. Defendant expressed a desire to take the child to hospital, but Foster objected because of his concern about the possible effect on his probation status. Defendant therefore agreed to take all responsibility for Amy's injuries and initially did so in her statement at the hospital. As noted above, however, defendant later denied any active involvement in the beating that led to Amy's death.

The court gave the jury the standard instructions defining murder, malice aforethought, second degree murder, second degree felony murder, and manslaughter. The second degree felony-murder instruction informed the jury that an unlawful killing, whether intentional, unintentional, or accidental, is second degree murder if it occurs during the commission of a felony inherently dangerous to human life, and that felony child abuse is such a crime. Defendant contends that on the facts of this case the crime of felony child abuse was an integral part of and included in fact within the homicide, and hence that it merged into the latter under the rule of People v. Ireland (1969) 70 Cal.2d 522, 538–540, 75 Cal.Rptr. 188, 450 P.2d 580. We agree.

Our opinions have repeatedly emphasized that felony murder, although the law of this state, is a disfavored doctrine. We have recognized that the rule is much censured because it anachronistically resurrects from a bygone age a "barbaric" concept that has been discarded in the place of its origin, and because in almost all cases in which it is applied it is unnecessary and it erodes the relation between criminal liability and moral culpability. Accordingly, we have reiterated that this highly artificial concept should not be extended beyond any rational function that it is designed to serve. Applying this principle to various concrete factual circumstances, we have sought to insure that the doctrine be given the narrowest possible application consistent with its ostensible purpose—which is to deter those engaged in felonies from killing negligently or accidentally. [Citations and quotation marks omitted.]

In accord with this policy, we restricted the scope of the felony-murder rule in *Ireland* by holding it inapplicable to felonies that are an integral part of and included in fact within the homicide. In that case the defendant and his wife were experiencing serious marital difficulties which eventually culminated in defendant's drawing a gun and killing his wife. The jury was instructed that it could find the defendant guilty of second degree felony murder if it determined that the homicide occurred during the commission of the underlying felony of assault with a deadly weapon. Like all felony-murder instructions, this instruction had the effect of relieving the jury of the necessity of finding one of the elements of the crime of murder, to wit, malice aforethought. * * * To allow such use of the felony-murder rule would effectively preclude the jury from considering the issue of malice aforethought in all cases wherein homicide has been committed as a result of a felonious assault—a category which includes the great majority of all homicides. * * *

Very soon after *Ireland* we again had occasion to consider the question of merger in People v. Wilson (1969) 1 Cal.3d 431, 82 Cal.Rptr. 494, 462 P.2d 22. There the defendant forcibly entered his estranged wife's apartment carrying a shotgun. Once inside the apartment, he fatally shot a man in the living room and proceeded to break into the bathroom where he killed his wife. The jury was instructed on second degree felony murder based on the underlying felony of assault with a deadly weapon, and convicted the defendant of second degree murder of the man. We determined that the predicate felony was a "necessary ingredient of the homicide" and reversed under Ireland, which explicitly prohibited use of the felony-murder rule in such circumstances.

The defendant was also convicted of the first degree murder of his wife, and we reversed that conviction on similar grounds. The jury was instructed on first degree felony murder on the theory that the homicide was committed in the course of a burglary because the defendant had entered the premises with intent to commit a felony, i.e., assault with a deadly weapon. We held that the felony-murder rule cannot apply to burglary-murder cases in which "the entry would be nonfelonious but for the intent to commit the assault, and the assault is an integral part of the homicide and is included in fact in the offense charged. * * * " We reasoned that "Where a person enters a building with an intent to assault his victim with a deadly weapon, he is not deterred by the felony-murder rule. That doctrine can serve its purpose only when applied to a felony independent of the homicide."

In People v. Sears (1970) 2 Cal.3d 180, 84 Cal.Rptr. 711, 465 P.2d 847, we followed *Wilson* in a slightly different factual situation. There the defendant entered a cottage with the intent to assault his estranged wife. In the course of the assault, her daughter intervened and was killed by the defendant. The People argued that this situation was distinguishable on the ground that the felony of burglary with intent to assault the wife was "independent of the homicide" of the daughter and therefore the felony-murder rule could apply. We rejected the theory, holding that "It would be anomalous to place the person who intends to attack one person and in the course of the assault kills another inadvertently or in the heat of battle in a worse position than the person who from the outset intended to attack both persons and killed one or both. Where a defendant assaults one or more persons killing one, his criminal responsibility for the homicide should not depend upon which of the victims died but should be the greatest crime committed viewing each victim of the attack individually and without regard to which in fact died. This result is reached in application of existing principles of transferred intent, and it is unnecessary to resort to the felony-murder rule." *Sears* thus reiterated our view that the felony-murder rule should be applied narrowly rather than expansively.

In addition to the offenses of assault with a deadly weapon and burglary with intent to assault, the felony of discharging a firearm at an inhabited dwelling has also been held to merge into a resulting homicide; thus, application of the felony-murder rule in this situation is similarly prohibited. * * *

Cases in which the second degree felony-murder doctrine has withstood an *Ireland* attack include those in which the underlying felony was furnishing narcotics; driving under the influence of narcotics; poisoning food, drink or medicine; armed robbery; kidnapping; and finally, felony child abuse by malnutrition and dehydration. [Citations] * * * In People v. Burton (1971) 6 Cal.3d 375, 387, 99 Cal.Rptr. 1, 491 P.2d 793, we refined the *Ireland* rule by adding the caveat that the felony-murder doctrine may nevertheless apply if the underlying offense was committed with an "independent felonious purpose." Even if the felony was included within the facts of the homicide and was integral thereto, a further inquiry is required to determine if the homicide resulted "from conduct for an independent felonious purpose" as opposed to a "single course of conduct with a single purpose" (ibid.). In cases like *Ireland,* the purpose of the conduct was the very assault which resulted in death; on the other hand, in the case of armed robbery, as well as the other felonies enumerated in section 189 of the Penal Code, there is an independent felonious purpose, namely in the case of robbery to acquire money or property belonging to another.

Our task is to apply the foregoing rules to the offense at issue here—felony child abuse defined by section 273a, subdivision (1).[4] We recognize that a violation of its terms can occur in a wide variety of situations: the definition broadly includes both active and passive conduct, i.e., child abuse by direct assault and child endangering by extreme neglect. Two threshold considerations, however, govern all types of conduct prohibited by this law: first, the conduct must be willful; second, it must be committed "under circumstances or conditions likely to produce great bodily harm or death." Absent either of these elements, there can be no violation of the statute.

The language of *Ireland, Wilson* and *Burton* bars the application of the felony-murder rule "where the purpose of the conduct was the very assault which resulted in death." In cases in which the violation of section 273a, subdivision (1), is a direct assault on a child that results in death (i.e., causing or permitting a child to suffer or inflicting thereon unjustifiable physical pain), it is plain that the purpose of the child abuse was the "very assault which resulted in death." It would be wholly illogical to allow this kind of assaultive child abuse to be bootstrapped

4. Section 273a, subdivision (1), provided: "Any person who, under circumstances or conditions likely to produce great bodily harm or death, willfully causes or permits any child to suffer, or inflicts thereon unjustifiable physical pain or mental suffering, or having the care or custody of any child, willfully causes or permits the person or health of such child to be injured, or willfully causes or permits such child to be placed in such situation that its person or health is endangered, is punishable by imprisonment in the county jail not exceeding 1 year, or in the state prison for not less than 1 year nor more than 10."

into felony murder merely because the victim was a child rather than an adult, as in *Ireland.* In the present case the homicide was the result of child abuse of the assaultive variety. Thus, the underlying felony was unquestionably an "integral part of" and "included in fact" in the homicide within the meaning of *Ireland.* Furthermore, we can conceive of no independent purpose for the conduct, and the People suggest none; just as in *Ireland,* the purpose here was the very assault that resulted in death. * * * We reiterate that the ostensible purpose of the felony-murder rule is not to deter the underlying felony, but instead to deter negligent or accidental killings that may occur in the course of committing that felony. When a person willfully inflicts unjustifiable physical pain on a child under these circumstances, it is difficult to see how the assailant would be further deterred from killing negligently or accidentally in the course of that felony by application of the felony-murder rule. * * *

The People argue that the present case is controlled by People v. Shockley (1978) 79 Cal.App.3d 669, 145 Cal.Rptr. 200, but that decision is distinguishable on its facts. In *Shockley,* the death followed from malnutrition and dehydration; by contrast, the cause of death here was unquestionably a severe beating. * * * Because of this factual distinction we need not address the question whether the merger doctrine applies when the defendant is guilty of felony child abuse of the non-assaultive variety, e.g., by extreme neglect—as in *Shockley*—or by failure to intervene when a child in his care or custody is placed in life-endangering situation.

It was therefore error to give a felony-murder instruction in this case. The People cannot show that no juror relied on the erroneous instruction as the sole basis for finding defendant guilty of murder. In these circumstances it is settled that the error must be deemed prejudicial. [Citations] Because we reverse on this ground, we need not reach defendant's alternate claim that felony child abuse is not a felony inherently dangerous to human life within the meaning of the second degree felony-murder rule. * * *

The judgment is reversed insofar as it convicts defendant of second degree murder; in all other respects the judgment is affirmed.

TODD v. STATE

Court of Appeal of Florida, Fifth District, 1992.
594 So.2d 802.

GRIFFIN, J.

On March 18, 1990, appellant entered the Lighthouse Church and stole $110 from the collection plate. The theft was witnessed by several members of the congregation, one of whom, Richard Voegltin, took off in his car in pursuit of appellant. During the pursuit, Mr. Voegltin, who had a preexisting heart condition, began to experience cardiac dysrhythmia. He lost control of his vehicle, collided with a tree at low speed and died of cardiac arrest.

The state charged appellant with manslaughter, alleging that he caused the death of Mr. Voegltin by committing the misdemeanor offense of petty theft which caused Voegltin to pursue him in order to recover the stolen property. Appellant filed a motion to dismiss, asserting that, because it cannot be said with any reasonable degree of medical certainty that Mr. Voegltin died as a result of chasing appellant, because Mr. Voegltin was at high risk of having a heart attack due to his preexisting medical condition, and because the appellant had no knowledge of this preexisting medical condition, the manslaughter charge should be dismissed. The trial court denied the motion to dismiss. [Appellant then pled guilty to the manslaughter offense under a plea agreement, reserving the right to appeal the denial of his motion to dismiss.] We reverse.

The issue, as presented to us, is whether Florida recognizes the misdemeanor manslaughter rule. Reduced to basics, the misdemeanor manslaughter rule is that an unintended homicide which occurs during the commission of an unlawful act not amounting to a felony constitutes the crime of involuntary manslaughter. It is sometimes referred to more broadly as "unlawful act manslaughter." The only express mention of the misdemeanor manslaughter rule that either party has cited in Florida case law is a passing reference in a footnote of an opinion of the Third District Court of Appeal, Rodriguez v. State, 443 So.2d 286, 290 n. 8 (Fla. 3d DCA 1983).

The misdemeanor manslaughter rule has been the subject of surprisingly little analysis, although in their *Handbook on Criminal Law*, LaFave and Scott have included a detailed discussion and critique of this theory of criminal responsibility. They suggest that "the trend today, barely underway, is to abolish altogether this type of involuntary manslaughter. . . ." The authors posit that to punish as homicide the result of an unlawful act that is unintended and produced without any consciousness of the risk of producing it is "too harsh" and "illogical". * * *

Because of the facial simplicity of the misdemeanor manslaughter rule, its application by courts has led to some rather extraordinary findings of criminal liability for homicide. For example, in 1926 a Texas court found liability for manslaughter on the following facts: The victim discovered the defendant committing adultery with the victim's wife. Adultery was a misdemeanor in Texas. The victim made a murderous attack on the defendant. In defending himself against the murderous attack, the defendant killed the victim. The court decided that since the victim's murderous attack was a foreseeable reaction to the defendant's criminal misconduct, the defendant was guilty of manslaughter. Reed v. State, 11 Tex. Ct. App. 509 (1882). In Commonwealth v. Mink, 123 Mass. 422, 425, (1877), the defendant was attempting to commit suicide, but her fiancee intervened to try to stop her and was accidentally killed by the defendant. Because suicide was an unlawful act *malum in se*, the court found defendant guilty of manslaughter.

Over time, this theory of criminal responsibility has developed many complexities. Courts differ about whether the unlawful act must amount to a criminal offense and whether different standards should apply for malum in se or malum prohibitum offenses. In this case, neither of these issues is of concern. The offense in this case is a *malum in se* misdemeanor offense under the criminal law of Florida. However, the other principal point of divergence in the development of the misdemeanor manslaughter rule—the issue of causation—is critical to this case.

The views on the requirement of causation in unlawful act manslaughter differ widely among the various jurisdictions. In some instances, no causal relationship at all has been required. At the other extreme is the requirement that there be not only a direct causal relationship between the unlawful act and the death, but that the death must be a natural and probable consequence of the offense. An example cited by Wilner is the case of Votre v. State, 138 N.E. 257 (Ind.1923) where, contrary to statute, the defendant gave whiskey to the victim, who was a minor. Consumption of the alcohol caused the victim to suffer a heart attack of which he died. The Indiana court held that the defendant was not guilty of manslaughter because the homicide must follow both as a part of the perpetration of the unlawful act and as a natural and probable consequence of it. As LaFave and Scott point out, application of this view of causation essentially converts the unlawful act type of manslaughter into culpable negligence manslaughter—a development which these commentators applaud.

In 1989 an article published in the *Solicitor's Journal* entitled "Unlawfully Occasioning Another's Death Without Physical Contact" catalogued the modern English decisions dealing with this issue. From the article, it appears that the law of manslaughter by unlawful act has developed in England along lines similar to the American experience. The author reports, however, that beginning in the mid–1960's English courts began to require that, in order to support a manslaughter conviction, the unlawful act must be such that "all sober and reasonable people would inevitably recognize it as an act which would subject the other person to at least the risk of some harm resulting therefrom, albeit not serious harm." Evidently, English courts have concluded that requiring an element of dangerousness in the unlawful act supplies the element of blameworthiness appropriate for conviction of a homicide crime.

Florida courts, by simply interpreting the statutory definition of manslaughter ("the killing of a human being by the act, procurement, or culpable negligence of another, without lawful justification . . ."), appear always to have understood the importance of causation as an element of this type of homicide. Our courts also have appreciated the foreseeability element of causation. In Tipton v. State, 97 So.2d 277 (Fla.1957), the defendants had gotten into an argument with a gas station attendant about whether he would cash a check for them. They either pushed or touched him in a threatening way. The attendant fell to the floor and died of a heart attack. The supreme court, reversing convictions for manslaughter, * * * concluded that an instruction on excusable homicide should have been given and that the lack of proof of a causal connection between the alleged "pushing, shoving and ill treatment" and the death of the deceased precluded a conviction for manslaughter.

In Phillips v. State, 289 So.2d 447 (Fla. 2d DCA), cert. denied, 294 So.2d 662 (Fla.1974), the defendant, who was under the influence of LSD, forced his way into a private home, began acting in a very bizarre manner and assaulted the elderly couple who resided there. The husband, who was 62 years old and had a chronic heart condition, was attempting to pull the defendant away from his wife when he collapsed into a chair and died of heart attack. The Second District Court found that the issue of causation on these facts was a jury question because it was foreseeable that the assaults, coupled with the bizarre conduct, would have a traumatic effect on the victims and could result in physical harm.

In 1989 the First District Court of Appeal had occasion to consider a case, Penton v. State, 548 So.2d 273 (Fla. 1st DCA), rev. denied, 554 So.2d 1169 (Fla.1989), which was in many ways similar to the case that we have under review here. There the appellant and a codefendant burglarized the garage of a private residence, stealing two bicycles. The homeowner, alerted to the burglary by barking dogs and shouts from his son that someone was stealing his bike, ran out of the house. After chasing appellant approximately twenty-five to thirty feet, the homeowner fell dead in the middle of the street, his death apparently caused by a release of fat emboli into his blood stream. The defendant was charged under the felony murder rule but was convicted by the jury of manslaughter. [The Court of Appeal held that causation was not established.]

In this case, even if it were assumed that the stress of pursuit brought on the heart attack, it cannot be said that the petty theft was the legal cause of Mr. Voegltin's death. The crime itself was a minor property offense. There is no suggestion of any touching or any threat to anyone's person. This is not even a case, like a purse snatching, where violence was necessary to produce the theft. Nor is it asserted that Mr. Voegltin died from fright or horror at witnessing the crime.[a] The state's traverse specifically asserts that it was the pursuit that caused the fatal heart attack. Although the petty theft did trigger a series of events that concluded in the death of Mr. Voegltin and was, in that sense, a "cause" of the death, the petty theft did not encompass the kind of direct, foreseeable risk of physical harm that would support a conviction of manslaughter. The relationship between the unlawful act committed (petty theft) and the result effected (death by heart attack during pursuit in an automobile) does not meet the test of causation historically or currently required in Florida for conviction of manslaughter.

REVERSED.

a. Compare, People v. Stamp, 2 Cal. App.3d 203, 82 Cal.Rptr. 598 (1969) upholding first degree felony murder convictions when the victim of an armed robbery dropped dead of a heart attack caused by fright and pre-existing heart problems.—ed.

Note

An alternative basis for liability in cases such as Commonwealth v. Welansky, discussed supra in Section C, could be the so-called misdemeanor-manslaughter doctrine, which is similar to the felony murder doctrine. If a violation of the fire safety code is a misdemeanor, then a killing proximately caused by such a violation may be manslaughter in the jurisdictions which recognize the doctrine. This approach was taken in People v. Nelson, 309 N.Y. 231, 128 N.E.2d 391 (1955). The misdemeanor-manslaughter doctrine is capable of enormously expanding the scope of liability for involuntary manslaughter, since one may commit a misdemeanor without creating the great risk of death or serious injury normally required for criminal homicidal negligence. Recognizing the potential for abuse, a number of state courts have limited the doctrine by one or more of the following devices:

(a) *Strict liability offenses.* Some cases have held the misdemeanor-manslaughter doctrine inapplicable where the misdemeanor was a crime of strict liability. See e.g. People v. Stuart, 47 Cal.2d 167, 302 P.2d 5 (1956).

(b) *Proximate cause.* In some jurisdictions, the homicide is not considered to be "proximately caused" by the misdemeanor unless death was a foreseeable consequence of the unlawful conduct. Under this rationale, courts have held that a defendant is not guilty of misdemeanor-manslaughter simply because he had no driver's license at the time his car struck and killed someone. Commonwealth v. Williams, 133 Pa.Super. 104, 1 A.2d 812 (1938). Of course, where the defendant's unlawful conduct actually creates a substantial and foreseeable risk of death, he can frequently be convicted of manslaughter without regard to the misdemeanor-manslaughter rule.

(c) Distinction between offenses that are *mala in se* and those that are *mala prohibita.* Some jurisdictions draw a distinction between unlawful conduct which is inherently wrongful and conduct which is morally neutral but happens to be forbidden by some regulatory statute. Where this somewhat cloudy distinction is drawn, the misdemeanor-manslaughter doctrine may be held applicable only where the misdemeanor is *malum in se.* More frequently, courts have held that "proximate cause" must be shown in the case of a misdemeanor which is *malum prohibitum,* but not where the misdemeanor is *malum in se.*

E. THE ACT OF HOMICIDE: CAUSING THE DEATH OF A HUMAN BEING

1. *When Does Life Begin—And End?*

WILLIAMS v. STATE

Court of Appeals of Maryland, 1989.
316 Md. 677, 561 A.2d 216.

MURPHY, CHIEF JUDGE.

Williams and Jones became embroiled in an argument over a photograph which allegedly depicted Williams engaged in sexual activity with

Jones's girlfriend. In an attempt to obtain the photograph, Jones took Williams's wallet and ran off. Williams entered his home and called the police. Upon emerging, he saw Jones approaching him with a lead pipe. After Jones swung at him three times, Williams retreated to his house. When he reemerged, Williams was armed with a bow and arrow. As he pursued Jones, he drew the arrow. He yelled to Jewel Lyles, a pedestrian, to "watch out" immediately before releasing the arrow in an apparent effort to shoot Jones. The arrow struck Lyles, lacerating her vena cava. She died from the massive loss of blood which she suffered as a result of the wound. Lyles was nine months' pregnant at the time of the shooting. Her baby was born alive an hour before Lyles died; the baby died seventeen hours later as a result of the injury inflicted upon her mother.

Williams was convicted by a jury of two counts of manslaughter and one count of carrying a weapon openly with intent to injure. He was sentenced to consecutive terms of ten, ten, and three years imprisonment. * * *

The Court of Special Appeals recognized that manslaughter is a common law felony in Maryland. It therefore focused on the common law of England, as required by Article 5 of the Maryland Declaration of Rights.[1] In determining the status of the Maryland common law, Chief Judge Gilbert, in a scholarly opinion for the court, primarily considered the writings of Lord Hale and Lord Coke. The court first acknowledged Hale's view that it was neither murder nor manslaughter if an infant, born alive, died as a result of injuries criminally inflicted upon the mother during pregnancy. * * *

Lord Coke, the intermediate appellate court noted, was of a totally opposite mind. His view of the English common law was that a criminal homicide resulted if the child, born alive, died as a result of wounds inflicted upon the mother while the child was in the mother's womb. * * *

After noting that [Blackstone and] a number of American states accepted Coke's position, the court concluded that the English common law recognized Coke's "born alive rule." Specifically, it said that "the common law of Maryland is when a child is born alive but subsequently dies as a result of injury sustained in utero the death of the child is homicide."

* * * In ascertaining the common law of this State in the absence of clear Maryland case law on the subject, we look to early English cases

1. Article 5 provides:

"That the Inhabitants of Maryland are entitled to the Common Law of England, and the trial by Jury, according to the course of that Law, and to the benefit of such of the English statutes as existed on the Fourth day of July, seventeen hundred and seventy-six; and which, by experience, have been found applicable to their local and other circumstances, and have been introduced, used and practiced by the Courts of Law or Equity; and also of all Acts of Assembly in force on the first day of June, eighteen hundred and sixty-seven; except such as may have since expired, or may be inconsistent with the provisions of this Constitution; subject, nevertheless, to the revision of, and amendment or repeal by, the Legislature of this State. . . ."

and writers on the common law, as well as cases from other jurisdictions. Coke and Blackstone's view of the common law, as espoused prior to 1776, was applied in the later English cases of Rex v. Senior, 168 Eng.Rep. 1298 (1832) and Queen v. West, 175 Eng.Rep. 329 (1848). * * *

State courts which have applied the common law in situations similar to that now before us have uniformly applied the Coke–Blackstone "born alive" rule * * * [citations] So extensive is the acceptance of this common law rule that we conclude that it was indeed the law of Maryland in 1776. We are unpersuaded by the appellant's fleeting reference to other authorities allegedly articulating a contrary view of the common law. Consequently, we find no merit in Williams's argument that should Lord Coke's version of the common law be adopted in Maryland, it should be afforded only a prospective application and not applied to his manslaughter conviction for the death of the Lyles baby.

Judgment affirmed, with costs.

PEOPLE v. DAVIS

Supreme Court of California, 1994.
7 Cal.4th 797, 30 Cal.Rptr.2d 50, 872 P.2d 591.

LUCAS, CHIEF JUSTICE

Penal Code section 187(a) provides that "Murder is the unlawful killing of a human being, or a fetus, with malice aforethought." In this case, we consider and reject the argument that viability of a fetus is an element of fetal murder under the statute. As will appear, however, we also conclude that this holding should not apply to defendant herein. Accordingly, we will affirm the judgment of the Court of Appeal [reversing defendant's conviction for murder but affirming his convictions for other crimes].

Facts

On March 1, 1991, Maria Flores, who was between 23 and 25 weeks pregnant, and her 20–month-old son, Hector, went to a check-cashing store to cash her welfare check. As Flores left the store, defendant pulled a gun from the waistband of his pants and demanded the money ($378) in her purse. When she refused to hand over the purse, defendant shot her in the chest. Flores dropped Hector as she fell to the floor and defendant fled the scene.

Flores underwent surgery to save her life. Although doctors sutured small holes in the uterine wall to prevent further bleeding, no further obstetrical surgery was undertaken because of the immaturity of the fetus. The next day, the fetus was stillborn as a direct result of its mother's blood loss, low blood pressure and state of shock. Defendant was soon apprehended and charged with assaulting and robbing Flores, as well as murdering her fetus. The prosecution charged a special circumstance of robbery-murder, [making the defendant eligible for the death penalty, or for life imprisonment without possibility of parole].

At trial, the prosecution's medical experts testified the fetus's statistical chances of survival outside the womb were between 7 and 47 percent. The defense medical expert testified it was "possible for the fetus to have survived, but its chances were only 2 or 3 percent." None of the medical experts testified that survival of the fetus was "probable."

Although § 187(a), does not expressly require a fetus be medically viable before the statute's provisions can be applied to a criminal defendant, the trial court followed several Court of Appeal decisions and instructed the jury that it must find the fetus was viable before it could find defendant guilty of murder under the statute. The trial court did not, however, give the standard viability instruction, CALJIC No. 8.10; which states that: "A viable human fetus is one who has attained such form and development of organs as to be normally capable of living outside of the uterus." The jury, however, was given an instruction that allowed it to convict defendant of murder if it found the fetus had a possibility of survival: "A fetus is viable when it has achieved the capability for independent existence; that is, when it is *possible* for it to survive the trauma of birth, although with artificial medical aid." (Italics added.)

The jury convicted defendant of murder of a fetus during the course of a robbery, assault with a firearm, and robbery. [The jury acquitted defendant of the attempted murder of Maria Flores, however.] The jury found that, in the commission of each offense, defendant personally used a firearm. The jury found true the special circumstance allegation. Accordingly, because the prosecutor did not seek the death penalty, defendant was sentenced to life without possibility of parole, plus five years for the firearm use.

On appeal, defendant contended that the trial court prejudicially erred by not instructing the jury pursuant to CALJIC No. 8.10. He relied on United States Supreme Court decisions that have defined viability of a fetus in terms of "probabilities, not possibilities" when limiting a woman's absolute right to an abortion. (See Roe v. Wade (1973) 410 U.S. 113. [defining viability as that point in fetal development when a fetus, if born, would be capable of living normally outside the womb]; Planned Parenthood v. Casey (1992) 112 S.Ct. 2791, [reaffirming Roe's viability definition].) By analogy to the abortion cases, defendant asserted that a fetus is not viable under section 187(a) unless "there is a reasonable likelihood of [its] sustained survival outside the womb, with or without artificial support." Thus, defendant claimed, rather than defining viability as a "reasonable possibility of survival," the trial court should have instructed the jury under the higher "probability" threshold described in CALJIC No. 8.10.

The People argued that no viability instruction was necessary because prosecution under section 187(a) does not require that the fetus be viable. After reviewing the wording of section 187(a), its legislative history, the treatment of the issue in other jurisdictions, and scholarly comment on the subject, the Court of Appeal agreed with the People that contrary to prior California decisions, fetal viability is not a required element of murder under the statute. Nonetheless, the court reversed defendant's murder conviction and set aside the special circumstance finding, on the ground that application to defendant of its unprecedented interpretation of section 187(a) would violate due process principles.

As explained below, we agree with the People and the Court of Appeal that viability is not an element of fetal murder under section 187(a), and conclude therefore that the statute does not require an instruction on viability as a prerequisite to a murder conviction. In addition, because every prior decision that had addressed the viability issue had determined that viability of the fetus was prerequisite to a murder conviction, we also agree with the Court of Appeal that application of our construction of the statute to defendant would violate due process and *ex post facto* principles. (People v. King (1993) 5 Cal.4th 59 [unforeseeable enlargement of a criminal statute operates in manner of *ex post facto* law].) Accordingly, we agree with the Court of Appeal that the trial court prejudicially erred when it instructed the jury contrary to then-existing law, pursuant to a modified version of CALJIC No. 8.10. Thus, we conclude we should affirm the Court of Appeal judgment in its entirety (affirming the assault and robbery counts and reversing the judgment of murder).

Discussion

Defendant asserts that section 187(a) has no application to a fetus not meeting *Roe v. Wade's* definition of viability. Essentially, defendant claims that because the fetus could have been legally aborted under Roe v. Wade at the time it was killed, it did not attain the protection of section 187(a). * * *

But *Roe v. Wade* does not hold that the state has no legitimate interest in protecting the fetus until viability. Indeed, * * * *Roe v. Wade* principles are inapplicable to a statute that criminalizes the killing of a fetus without the mother's consent. As observed by one commentator: "By holding that the Fourteenth Amendment does not cover the unborn, the Supreme Court was left with only one constitutionally mandated right, that of the mother's privacy, to be considered along with the legitimate state interest in protecting an unborn's potential life. The *Roe* decision, therefore, forbids the state's protection of the unborn's interests only when these interests conflict with the constitutional rights of the prospective parent. The Court did not rule that the unborn's interests could not be recognized in situations where there was no conflict." (Parness, "Crimes Against the Unborn: Protecting and Respecting the Potentiality of Human Life" (1985) 22 Harv. J. on Legis. 97, 144.)

Other scholarly comment agrees with Professor Parness. In her article, "The Juridical Status of the Fetus: A Proposal for Legal Protection of the Unborn" (1979) 77 Mich.L.Rev. 1647, 1678, Professor King states that, "Where the protectable interests of fully mature members do not conflict with those of less mature members, there is no justification for ignoring the latter's claims. The *Roe* opinion was correct in recognizing a state's legitimate interest in protecting the previable fetus. In ... criminal law, when that interest does not oppose a protected interest of the mature mother, the state should not hesitate to vindicate it."

Finally, as explained by Clarke Forsythe in "Homicide of the Unborn Child: The Born Alive Rule and Other Legal Anachronisms" (1987) 21 Val.U.L.Rev. 563, 616: "While the decision in *Roe* declares that the state may not protect the potential life of the human fetus from the moment of conception, it does so only in the very narrow context of the mother's abortion decision. Under Roe v. Wade, therefore, the right to abortion is encompassed within the woman's right to constitutional privacy. The fetus is not a 'person' for purposes of the Fourteenth Amendment and has no constitutional rights that would outweigh the exercise of the woman's Fourteenth Amendment rights. The fetus' rights and the state's interest, or lack of interest, in protecting maternal health and in protecting the life of the fetus, were distinctly balanced against the woman's right to privacy in the context of consensual abortion." Thus, when the state's interest in protecting the life of a developing fetus is not counterbalanced against a mother's privacy right to an abortion, or other equivalent interest, the state's interest should prevail.

Other states have adopted statutes that criminalize the killing of a fetus. Although no state has criminalized the nonconsensual killing of a "fetus," several states criminalize the nonconsensual killing of an "unborn child," characterizing it as manslaughter or murder. In these states (Arizona, Illinois, Louisiana, Minnesota, North Dakota, and Utah), the murder statutes do not require that the unborn have reached a particular stage of development.

The Illinois and Minnesota appellate courts have rejected equal protection and due process challenges to their feticide statutes. The challenges were based on the statutes' asserted failure to distinguish between viable and nonviable fetuses. As discussed below, the arguments were rejected on the ground that protection of a woman's privacy interest in the abortion context is not applicable to a nonconsensual murder of the unborn child. * * *

Like Illinois and Minnesota, California is a "code" state, (i.e., the Legislature has the exclusive province to define by statute what acts constitute a crime 6), and statutory provisions must "be construed according to the fair import of their terms, with a view to effect [their] objects and to promote justice." Under these principles, like Illinois and Minnesota, we find no impediment to our Legislature protecting the "potentiality of human life" from homicide.

Finally, [the Illinois and Minnesota cases] expressly distinguish fetal homicide from the abortion issue. Our Legislature does the same. Abortion is specifically exempted from section 187 under subdivision (b)(3), which states that section 187 shall not apply if, "The act was solicited, aided, abetted, or consented to by the mother of the fetus."

We conclude, therefore, that when the mother's privacy interests are not at stake, the Legislature may determine whether, and at what point, it should protect life inside a mother's womb from homicide. Here, the Legislature determined that the offense of murder includes the murder of a fetus with malice aforethought. Legislative history suggests "fetus" was left undefined in the face of divided legislative views about its meaning. Generally, however, a fetus is defined as "the unborn offspring in the postembryonic period, after major structures have been outlined." (Sloane–Dorland Ann. Medical–Legal Dict. (1987) p. 281.) This period occurs in humans "seven or eight weeks after fertilization" (ibid.), and is a determination to be made by the trier of fact. Thus, we agree with the above cited authority that the Legislature could criminalize murder of the postembryonic product without the imposition of a viability requirement. We need not address whether different concerns might apply to an embryo.[2] * * *

Several Courts of Appeal have erroneously implied a viability requirement into section 187(a). Although we are not faced with reconsidering our own precedent, the fact that a viability requirement has consistently been read into section 187(a), supports defendant's assertion that our proposed holding creates an unforeseeable judicial enlargement of a criminal statute. Accordingly, we now consider whether the trial court prejudicially erred by instructing the jury pursuant to a modified instruction on viability. * * *

As the Court of Appeal below observed, the wording of CALJIC No. 8.10, defining viability as "normally capable of living outside of the uterus," while not a model of clarity, suggests a better than even chance—a probability—that a fetus will survive if born at that particular point in time. By contrast, the instruction given below suggests a "possibility" of survival, and essentially amounts to a finding that a fetus incapable of survival outside the womb for any discernible time would nonetheless be considered "viable" within the meaning of section 187(a). Because the instruction given by the trial court substantially lowered the viability threshold as commonly understood and accepted we conclude that the trial court erred in instructing the jury pursuant to a modified version of CALJIC No. 8.10. * * *

We conclude that viability is not an element of fetal homicide under section 187(a). The third party killing of a fetus with malice aforethought is murder under section 187(a), as long as the state can show that the fetus has progressed beyond the embryonic stage of seven to eight weeks.

2. We do not reach the question, and it is not raised in this case, whether the doctrine of felony murder constitutionally could be applied in the circumstance where, although the fetal stage of development has been reached, the injury resulting in the death of the fetus is caused by some agency other than a defendant's direct assault on the mother. We also do not discuss the question of premeditated murder (as opposed to felony murder) of a fetus.

We also conclude that our holding should not apply to defendant and that the trial court committed prejudicial error by instructing the jury pursuant to a modified version of CALJIC No. 8.10. We therefore affirm the judgment of the Court of Appeal [reversing the murder conviction and remanding for a new trial on viability of the fetus].[3]

KENNARD, JUSTICE, concurring. 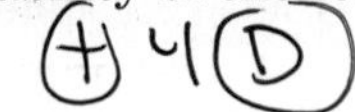

* * * The dissent raises an important concern when it points out that the lead opinion's interpretation of the statute could result in the death penalty for a defendant who lacks any intent to kill but whose conduct while committing a felony inadvertently causes a woman, early in her pregnancy, to miscarry. * * * In some such cases a penalty of death, or even life imprisonment without the possibility of parole, may be wholly disproportionate to the particular defendant's criminal culpability, and thus may violate constitutional proscriptions against cruel and unusual punishment. [Citations] * * * I concur in the lead opinion.

STONE, J. [Court of Appeal Justice sitting by assignment] concurred.

BAXTER, J., Concurring and Dissenting.

Had the trial court in this case given an instruction that a fetus need not be viable under § 187(a), or had the law in California been settled that, for purposes of section 187(a), a viable fetus meant a fetus with a "probability" or a "reasonable likelihood" of survival outside the womb, then I would not hesitate in joining the lead opinion to reverse defendant's conviction. As it stands, however, neither is the case. Therefore, while I concur in the holding that viability of a fetus is not required under section 187(a), I must dissent from the decision to reverse. * * * I would affirm the conviction. [GEORGE, J., concurred.]

[The dissenting opinion of MOSK, J. is omitted. Justice Mosk made a persuasive and well-informed argument that the legislative history of § 187(a) suggested that the legislature had only viable fetuses in mind when it amended the statute.]

COMMONWEALTH v. CRAWFORD

Supreme Judicial Court of Massachusetts, 2000.
430 Mass. 683, 722 N.E.2d 960.

SPINA, J.

The defendant, Michael L. Crawford, was convicted of the involuntary manslaughter of his girl friend and her unborn fetus. * * * In his amended motion the defendant * * * raised claims that (1) the homicide statutes are unconstitutionally vague as applied to a viable fetus, (2) the trial judge's instruction on viability unconstitutionally lowered the Com-

3. Because of the multiple opinions in this case, we believe it appropriate to observe that a majority of the court concurs in our determinations that (1) viability of a fetus is not an element of fetal murder under section 187, subdivision (a), (2) the instruction defining viability in terms of mere "possibility" of survival amounted to prejudicial error under ex post facto principles, and (3) the Court of Appeal judgment reversing the conviction of murder must be affirmed.

monwealth's burden of proof, and (3) the judge's instructions incorrectly permitted the jury to find the defendant guilty of homicide of the fetus without proof of his knowledge of its existence and viability. * * * We affirm the denial of all motions.

* * * On July 7, 1990, the defendant shot Kimberly Noblin in the face. Noblin's body was found more than four hours later, after rigor mortis had set in. At the time of the shooting, Noblin was at least seven months pregnant[3] with the defendant's baby. A medical examiner offered uncontroverted testimony that the fetus died of oxygen deprivation but had been viable, "meaning it was old enough and had mature enough systems to survive outside of the mother." * * *

In Commonwealth v. Cass, 392 Mass. 799, 807, 467 N.E.2d 1324 (1984), we announced our intent to depart from the common-law rule that the object of a homicide must be a person who had been born alive. We said, "if a person were to commit violence against a pregnant woman and destroy the [viable] fetus within her, we would not want the death of the fetus to go unpunished" (footnotes omitted). Thereafter, in Commonwealth v. Lawrence, 404 Mass. 378, 536 N.E.2d 571 (1989), we affirmed the convictions of a defendant who received consecutive sentences for the murder in the first degree of a sixteen year old girl and the involuntary manslaughter of the twenty-seven week old fetus she was carrying. Our common law expressly authorizes multiple punishment for unlawfully killing a woman and her viable fetus.

There is no merit to the defendant's contention that he may not be punished for two homicides when he fired only one shot. The "probable harmful consequences," of a single gunshot, like the fire started by a single match or the car running out of control due to a single reckless miscalculation, are not limited to one death. * * *

a. *Vagueness*. The defendant claims that the term "viability," as applied to a fetus under criminal homicide statutes, is unconstitutionally vague because it has not been defined by the Legislature or by the courts. A statute is unconstitutionally vague if "men of common intelligence must necessarily guess at its meaning." If a statute has been clarified by judicial explanation, however, it will withstand a challenge on grounds of unconstitutional vagueness. * * *

In the civil context, we defined a "viable fetus" to be a fetus "so far formed and developed that if then born it would be capable of living." In Commonwealth v. Cass, supra, decided six years before the deaths in this case, we extended protection under our criminal law to viable fetuses. By the time of these deaths in 1990, the defendant was on notice that killing a "viable fetus," as defined in the common law, is a punishable offense. As such, the term had been defined and it is not unconstitutionally vague. * * *

3. "At the time of the shooting, the male fetus weighed about two and one half pounds, was fifteen inches in length, and was between twenty-eight and thirty weeks in gestational age."

b. *Lowered burden*. The defendant claims that the Commonwealth's burden of proof was lowered when the trial judge defined viability as "having reached such a stage of development as to be potentially able of living outside the mother's womb, notwithstanding artificial aid." Relying on a California case, the defendant argues that the proper definition of viability is that the fetus must attain such form and development of organs as to be "'*normally* capable of living outside of the uterus' ... a better than even chance—a probability" (emphasis added). People v. Davis, 7 Cal. 4th 797, 814, 872 P.2d 591 (1994).

The word "potential," as defined in Black's Law Dictionary 1168 (6th ed. 1990), means "existing in possibility but not in fact. Naturally and probably expected to come into existence at some future time, though not now existing." Thus, the term "potentially" connotes a degree of probability greater than a "possibility," the term which the court in People v. Davis, supra, found lacking because it impermissibly lowered the threshold for viability to the point where a fetus incapable of surviving outside the womb would nonetheless be considered viable. Given that the trial judge's use of the term "potentially" had the effect of instructing the jury that they had to find that Noblin's fetus had a "better than even chance" for survival before they could convict the defendant, the instruction given here did not lower the Commonwealth's burden.

The Supreme Court had addressed the meaning of "viability" on two occasions before the defendant's trial. In Colautti v. Franklin, 439 U.S. 379, 388–389, 58 L. Ed. 2d 596, 99 S. Ct. 675 (1979), the Court said, "Viability is reached when, in the judgment of the attending physician on the particular facts of the case before him, there is a reasonable likelihood of the fetus' sustained survival outside the womb, with or without artificial support." In Roe v. Wade, 410 U.S. 113, 160, 35 L. Ed. 2d 147, 93 S. Ct. 705 (1973), the Court said that a fetus is viable if it is "potentially able to live outside the mother's womb, albeit with artificial aid." The issue had been sufficiently developed at the time of the defendant's trial to alert him that it was a live issue. * * *

Although we have concluded that the judge's instruction, taken from Roe v. Wade, supra, was adequate, the definition of "viability" used in Colautti v. Franklin, supra ("reasonable likelihood of the fetus' sustained survival outside the womb, with or without artificial support"), is preferable. It employs familiar language most often used in jury instructions, and should be used in trials occurring hereafter.

c. *Intent and knowledge*. The defendant's contention that the Commonwealth should be required to show that he knew of the fetus's existence and viability is without merit. The defendant was convicted of involuntary manslaughter, a crime which does not require proof of awareness of a particular victim. See Commonwealth v. Welansky, 316 Mass. 383, 401, 55 N.E.2d 902 (1944). The Commonwealth need only prove wanton and reckless conduct resulting in the death of a person.

Wantonness and recklessness are determined by the conduct involved, not the resulting harm.

The Commonwealth reasonably could not be required to prove that the defendant knew the fetus was viable because viability is an issue that involves a medical judgment. Thus, the defendant's awareness of the fetus's existence and viability was irrelevant. The issues of existence and viability also had been sufficiently developed as of the time of the defendant's trial for him to have raised it at that time. They are waived.

* * * They also are issues that appear to have had little chance of success. The defendant lived with Noblin and their four year old daughter approximately three days a week at Noblin's apartment. There was evidence that the defendant knew that Noblin was pregnant, and that he was the father of her fetus. The jury easily could have found that the defendant was aware of the existence of the fetus. The medical testimony regarding viability was uncontroverted and strong.[5] * * *

ABRAMS, J., concurring.

* * *

If a "person of ordinary intelligence" cannot determine that "his contemplated conduct is forbidden" by a law, then that law runs afoul of the due process required by our Constitution. This case * * * does not directly raise the issue of the scienter required for a conviction of homicide of a viable fetus in utero because the defendant was convicted of involuntary manslaughter. "The Commonwealth need only prove wanton and reckless conduct resulting in the death of a person. Wantonness and recklessness are determined by the conduct involved . . ."

However, the court also writes that "[t]he Commonwealth reasonably could not be required to prove that the defendant knew the fetus was viable because viability is an issue that involves a medical judgment." In support of this dictum, the court quotes my concurrence in Lawrence that "[t]he mental element needed for conviction of murder cannot depend on a medical determination that can only be made by experts after the fact."

It was the concern that a person of ordinary intelligence might not be able to determine that he or she was committing two homicides that prompted me to write the words quoted by the court. Where proof offered at a criminal trial focuses on the victim's medical status and not the defendant's acts and state of mind, I think the court strays from the purposes of the criminal laws. "The focus of a criminal trial must be on the defendant's mental state, not the victim's physical condition."

* * *

5. The medical examiner's testimony that the fetus was between twenty-eight and thirty weeks in gestational age comports with the observations in Roe v. Wade, 410 U.S. 113, 163, 35 L. Ed. 2d 147, 93 S. Ct. 705 (1973), where the Court said "viability is usually placed at about seven months (28) weeks but may occur earlier, even at 24 weeks." The fetus could have been determined to have been viable based on its age.

Note

In State v. Ashley, 701 So.2d 338 (Fla.1997), a pregnant teenager was charged with criminal homicide for murdering her own fetus. Kawana Ashley was secretly 25 or 26 weeks pregnant (early third trimester). Her 3–year-old son was being reared by his grandmother, who told Ashley she would not care for another child if Ashley became pregnant again. Ashley obtained a gun and shot herself in the abdomen. She was rushed to the hospital for surgery and survived. The fetus, which had been struck on the wrist by the bullet, was removed during surgery and died due to immaturity. Ashley gave conflicting explanations for her actions. She first told officers that she was a victim of a drive-by shooting, then said she had shot herself "in order to hurt the baby," and later said that she wanted the baby and that the gun had discharged accidently. The Florida Supreme Court held that "At common law, while a third party could be held criminally liable for causing injury or death to a fetus, the pregnant woman could not be * * *. Ultimately, immunity from prosecution for the pregnant woman was grounded in the 'wisdom of experience' * * *. [N]one of the statutes under which Ashley was charged unequivocally state that they alter the common law doctrine conferring immunity on the pregnant woman."

Is this holding consistent with the holding in People v. Davis? In Commonwealth v. Crawford?

BARBER v. SUPERIOR COURT

California Court of Appeal, Second District, 1983.
147 Cal.App.3d 1006, 195 Cal.Rptr. 484.

Compton, Associate Justice.

In these consolidated proceedings we consider petitions for writs of prohibition pursuant to Penal Code section 999a filed by two medical doctors who are charged in a complaint, now pending before a magistrate in the Los Angeles Judicial District, with the crimes of murder and conspiracy to commit murder—both felonies.

At the close of a lengthy preliminary hearing the magistrate ordered the complaint dismissed. On motion of the People, pursuant to Penal Code section 871.5, the superior court ordered the magistrate to reinstate the complaint. These proceedings followed. We issued the alternative writ, calendared the matter and heard oral argument. We have concluded that the peremptory writ should issue.

Deceased Clarence Herbert underwent surgery for closure of an ileostomy. Petitioner Robert Nejdl, M.D., was Mr. Herbert's surgeon and petitioner Neil Barber, M.D. was his attending internist. Shortly after the successful completion of the surgery, and while in the recovery room, Mr. Herbert suffered a cardio-respiratory arrest. He was revived by a team of physicians and nurses and immediately placed on life support equipment.

Within the following three days, it was determined that Mr. Herbert was in a deeply comatose state from which he was not likely to recover.

Tests and examinations performed by several physicians, including petitioners herein, each specializing in relevant fields of medicine indicated that Mr. Herbert had suffered severe brain damage, leaving him in a vegetative state, which was likely to be permanent.

At that time petitioners informed Mr. Herbert's family of their opinion as to his condition and chances for recovery. While there is some dispute as to the precise terminology used by the doctors, it is clear that they communicated to the family that the prognosis for recovery was extremely poor. At that point, the family convened and drafted a written request to the hospital personnel stating that they wanted "all machines taken off that are sustaining life" (sic). As a result, petitioners, either directly or as a result of orders given by them, caused the respirator and other life-sustaining equipment to be removed. Mr. Herbert continued to breathe without the equipment but showed no signs of improvement. The family remained at his bedside and requested of the nursing staff that Mr. Herbert not be disturbed. They even objected to certain routine procedures followed by hospital personnel in caring for comatose patients.

After two more days had elapsed, petitioners, after consulting with the family, ordered removal of the intravenous tubes which provided hydration and nourishment. From that point until his death, Mr. Herbert received nursing care which preserved his dignity and provided a clean and hygienic environment.

The precise issue for determination by this court is whether the evidence presented before the magistrate was sufficient to support his determination that petitioners should not be held to answer to the charges of murder (Pen.Code, § 187), and conspiracy to commit murder (Pen.Code, § 182).

* * *

For the purposes of this decision, we accept the superior court judge's analysis that if petitioners unlawfully and intentionally killed Mr. Herbert, malice could be presumed regardless of their motive.

The use of the term "unlawful" in defining a criminal homicide is generally to distinguish a criminal homicide from those homicides which society has determined to be "justifiable" or "excusable." Euthanasia, of course, is neither justifiable nor excusable in California. * * *

Historically, death has been defined in terms of cessation of heart and respiratory function. [Citations] Health and Safety Code section 7180(a)(2) now provides for an alternative definition in terms of irreversible cessation of all brain function.

This is a clear recognition of the fact that the real seat of "life" is brain function rather than mere metabolic processes which result from respiration and circulation.

Of course it is conceded by all that at the time petitioners terminated further treatment, Mr. Herbert was not "dead" by either statutory or historical standards since there was still some minimal brain activity. If Mr. Herbert had in fact been "brain dead," this prosecution could not have been instituted because one cannot be charged with killing another person who is already dead.

We deal here with the physician's responsibility in a case of a patient who, though not "brain dead," faces an indefinite vegetative existence without any of the higher cognitive brain functions. * * * This case, arising as it does in the context of the criminal law, belies the belief expressed by many that such decisions would not likely be subjects of criminal prosecution. To our knowledge, however, this case is the first instance in which the issue has been presented in the context of a criminal prosecution. * * *

At this juncture we observe that California has adopted the Natural Death Act which permits an adult individual to execute, in advance, a directive for the withholding or withdrawing of life sustaining procedures in the event that he or she later suffers a terminal condition. (Health & Saf.Code, § 7188.) The superior court judge relied heavily on the fact that the deceased had not previously executed a written directive pursuant to § 7188 and he viewed the family's request as a nullity. * * *

[We] conclude that Health and Safety Code section 7188 does not represent the exclusive basis for terminating life-support equipment in this state. Nor is a diagnosis of "brain dead" a condition precedent to the cessation of such treatment.

As a predicate to our analysis of whether the petitioners' conduct amounted to an "unlawful killing," we conclude that the cessation of "heroic" life support measures is not an affirmative act but rather a withdrawal or omission of further treatment.

Even though these life support devices are, to a degree, "self-propelled," each pulsation of the respirator or each drop of fluid introduced into the patient's body by intravenous feeding devices is comparable to a manually administered injection or item of medication. Hence "disconnecting" of the mechanical devices is comparable to withholding the manually administered injection or medication.

Further we view the use of an intravenous administration of nourishment and fluid, under the circumstances, as being the same as the use of the respirator or other form of life support equipment.

The prosecution would have us draw a distinction between the use of mechanical breathing devices such as respirators and mechanical feeding devices such as intravenous tubes. The distinction urged seems to be based more on the emotional symbolism of providing food and water to those incapable of providing for themselves rather than on any rational difference in cases such as the one at bench.

Medical nutrition and hydration may not always provide net benefits to patients. Medical procedures to provide nutrition and hydration are more similar to other medical procedures than to typical human ways of providing nutrition and hydration. Their benefits and burdens ought to be evaluated in the same manner as any other medical procedure.

The authority cited by the People for the holding that a murder charge may be supported by the failure to feed an infant is easily distinguishable. (People v. Burden (1977) 72 Cal.App.3d 603, 140 Cal. Rptr. 282.) The parent in that case had a clear duty to feed an otherwise healthy child. (Pen.Code, § 270.) As we will discuss, infra, the duty of a physician under the circumstances of the case at bench is markedly different.

In the final analysis, since we view petitioners' conduct as that of omission rather than affirmative action, the resolution of this case turns on whether petitioners had a duty to continue to provide life sustaining treatment.

There is no criminal liability for failure to act unless there is a legal duty to act. Thus the critical issue becomes one of determining the duties owed by a physician to a patient who has been reliably diagnosed as in a comatose state from which any meaningful recovery of cognitive brain function is exceedingly unlikely. * * *

The authorities are in agreement that any surrogate, court appointed or otherwise, ought to be guided in his or her decisions first by his knowledge of the patient's own desires and feelings, to the extent that they were expressed before the patient became incompetent.

If it is not possible to ascertain the choice the patient would have made, the surrogate ought to be guided in his decision by the patient's best interests. Under this standard, such factors as the relief of suffering, the preservation or restoration of functioning and the quality as well as the extent of life sustained may be considered. Finally, since most people are concerned about the well-being of their loved ones, the surrogate may take into account the impact of the decision on those people closest to the patient.

There was evidence that Mr. Herbert had, prior to his incapacitation, expressed to his wife his feeling that he would not want to be kept alive by machines or "become another Karen Ann Quinlan." The family made its decision together (the directive to the hospital was signed by the wife and eight of his children) after consultation with the doctors.

Under the circumstances of this case, the wife was the proper person to act as a surrogate for the patient with the authority to decide issues regarding further treatment, and would have so qualified had judicial approval been sought. There is no evidence that there was any disagreement among the wife and children. Nor was there any evidence that they were motivated in their decision by anything other than love and concern for the dignity of their husband and father.

Furthermore, in the absence of legislative guidance, we find no legal requirement that prior judicial approval is necessary before any decision to withdraw treatment can be made. * * *

[Writ prohibiting prosecution issued.]

PEOPLE v. BONILLA

New York Supreme Court, Appellate Division, 1983.
95 A.D.2d 396, 467 N.Y.S.2d 599.

RUBIN, JUSTICE.

This appeal raises the question of whether a defendant who has inflicted a mortal wound on another person can escape a homicide conviction because of the acts of hospital doctors in removing the victim's kidneys and spleen for transplant and thereafter disconnecting life support systems. * * *

[Defendant Bonilla shot the victim (Miranda) in the head, the bullet lodging in the brain. Dr. Rosenberg examined Miranda in the hospital, pronounced him "brain dead," and had his kidneys and spleen removed for transplant. Dr. Wald, the medical examiner, performed the autopsy and certified that the death was attributable solely to the bullet wound. He testified that the texture of the brain was consistent with brain death, but he could not specify when brain death occurred or how long Miranda might have survived in a vegetative state had his organs not been removed.

Dr. Beresford testified for the defense that the tests performed by Dr. Rosenberg were not adequate to determine brain death, and the Miranda may therefore have been alive when he was pronounced dead.]

On appeal here the defendant addresses the issue of his culpability under both the common law and brain death definitions. If this court subscribes solely to the traditional definition whereby cessation of heartbeat and respiration are tantamount to death, then the defendant asserts that *Miranda* did not die until his kidneys and the respirator were removed by the independent intervening acts of the hospital physicians. If, however, death is no longer solely synonymous with these observable phenomena but also rests upon a finding of brain death, defendant alternately asserts that the criteria were not met by the attending physician, Dr. Rosenberg. Therefore, the defendant contends that, by any definition, someone else "caused" Miranda's death. * * *

Criminal liability for homicide requires that the defendant's actions be a sufficiently direct cause of death, but direct does not mean immediate or unaided. It is enough that defendant's conduct forged a link in a chain of events which brought about the death. Intervention of a secondary agency constitutes a defense only if the death is solely attributable to it.

Regardless of which definition of death is followed,[a] defendant's actions were dangerous to life and were a substantial and sufficiently

a. At the time of this decision, the definition of death in New York was uncertain. Subsequently, the Court of Appeal held that death occurs when there is a complete and permanent cessation of brain function. Peo-

direct factor in the chain. He set in motion the chain of events which ultimately resulted in the victim's death. It cannot be said that there was an obscure or merely probable connection between the assault and Miranda's demise. The bullet wound to the brain was the proximate cause of death and the homicide was properly attributed to the defendant.

The organ removal was not performed to treat or remedy the victim's injuries. Furthermore, this is not an instance where the death is solely attributable to the secondary agency, and not at all induced by the primary one. The prognosis for Miranda's survival, as expressed by all three testifying experts, was very unfavorable. Organ removal would not have been initiated but for the mortal wound. This case is distinguishable from People v. Stewart, 40 N.Y.2d 692, 389 N.Y.S.2d 804, 358 N.E.2d 487, on which the defense heavily relies. In *Stewart,* operating surgeons performed unrelated surgical repair on a hernia immediately after attending to a stab wound in the victim's abdomen. One month following surgery the victim died of cardiac arrest. Testimony indicated that probably he would have survived the operation for the stab wound if the other procedure had not been performed. In addition, there was also evidence that the anesthesiologist may have been negligent in failing to oxygenate the victim and this alone could have caused the fatal result. Therefore, the defendant's actions were not a sufficiently direct cause of death and his conviction for manslaughter in the first degree was reduced to assault in the first degree.

Unlike the stab wound in *Stewart* (supra), the bullet wound to Miranda's brain was operative as the cause of death. Therefore, even if Miranda's doctors were hasty or erroneous in their diagnosis of brain death, and even if they were negligent in disconnecting the life-support systems, their intervention would not be a supervening act relieving the defendant from liability. * * * While it is true that Miranda was an ideal source for organ donation because of his young age and otherwise good health, and that speed was essential to the outcome of a successful transplant, there is no indication, as the defense posited in its summation, that untoward motivation existed to hasten the brain death determination before it was warranted. The defendant's argument cannot be accepted that one who acts in good faith, and negligently or by error of judgment shuts off life support machinery, or removes essential organs, is responsible for death instead of the culprit who acts of his own volition and inflicts a massive traumatic wound to the brain with a deadly weapon.

Defendant's identical defense strategy has been raised in other jurisdictions in cases with facts similar to those that are before us. The courts therein have all reached a similar result. * * * Judgment affirmed.

TITONE, JUSTICE PRESIDING (dissenting in part and concurring in part). * * *

ple v. Eulo, 63 N.Y.2d 341, 482 N.Y.S.2d 436, 472 N.E.2d 286 (1984)—ed.

The majority opinions resolve the troublesome issues presented by holding that the People have proven beyond a reasonable doubt that the defendant's conduct in inflicting the head wound on Miranda was the cause of the latter's death even under its common law definition. They reason that the infliction of such wound prevents a finding that the victim's death was solely attributable to the purported secondary agency of misdiagnosed brain death and the subsequent operation for organ harvesting. Proof of brain death is irrelevant since "but for" that wound the victim would not have been in a position to die from the operation.

The difficulty with this approach is that it blurs the distinction between an accused's culpable act and intervening causes. * * * Since the concept of " 'causing death' normally involves the notion of shortening life and not merely determining the manner of dying" (Hart & Honor, Causation in the Law, p. 220), "one who hastens the victim's death is a cause of his death" (LaFave & Scott, Criminal Law, § 35, p. 250). So, if the defendant has inflicted a wound which would prove fatal and a third party comes along while the victim has but hours to live and kills him instantly, the third-party's act substantially hastening death constitutes the cause of death and the defendant cannot be convicted of homicide. [Citations] True, when the culpable act produces the intervening cause the defendant remains liable for all foreseeable consequences. Medical treatment for a wound is an intervening cause of this sort because acts of ordinary medical malpractice are foreseeable. * * * After all, defendant's conduct exposed the victim to the medical procedures and it is not unjust to hold him responsible for the attendant risks.

Nonetheless, responsibility does not extend to all intervening acts to which the victim would not have been exposed "but for" the defendant. The defendant is not liable for acts of gross negligence or intentional malpractice. [Citations] He is likewise not liable for coincidences, as, for example, if the victim dies in a traffic accident attributable to the negligence of the ambulance driver who is taking the victim to the hospital The victim would not have been in the ambulance "but for" the defendant's conduct. But the traffic accident was too remote; it was not foreseeable. As LaFave and Scott point out (p. 259), for causation purposes "the medical negligence cases have usually emphasized that the negligence aggravated the wound inflicted by the defendant".

Reliance upon this theory of intervening cause is therefore misplaced. Defendant may have exposed the victim to treatment for the wound but not the organ harvesting operation because the physician's acts were intentional, not negligent. It should be self-evident that such operation hardly constitutes an accepted method of treatment for an injury. * * *

In sum, I am not willing to strain settled principles of causation solely to sustain a conviction of homicide, as opposed to assault, simply because the defendant intended to commit a brutal crime. * * *

2. *Suicide as Homicide*

STEPHENSON v. STATE

Supreme Court of Indiana, 1932.
205 Ind. 141, 179 N.E. 633.

[Defendant, formerly a leader of the powerful Indiana Ku Klux Klan, was convicted of second degree murder in the death of Madge Oberholtzer. The principal evidence against him consisted of the victim's dying declarations, the most important of which was a lengthy written statement prepared by her attorney and signed by her after her physician had told her that she was certain to die. She actually did die seventeen days after signing the statement. The statement indicated that Miss Oberholtzer, who had previously dated the defendant, went to his house at his request. There Stephenson and his henchmen forced her to get drunk, and he insisted that she accompany him on a trip to Chicago. He then drove her to the train, refusing to allow her to get out of the car. When they were in the sleeping compartment of the train, he forcibly undressed her, pushed her into the berth, and committed extraordinary acts of sex perversion. "(H)e chewed her all over her body; bit her neck and face; chewed her tongue; chewed her breasts until they bled and chewed her back, her legs and her ankles, and mutilated her all over the body."

In the morning the group got off the train in Hammond, Indiana, and checked into a hotel. Stephenson permitted Miss Oberholtzer to go shopping for a hat, accompanied by his chauffeur, and the chauffeur allowed her to go alone into a drugstore to purchase rouge. She secretly purchased a box of bichloride of mercury tablets, and at the hotel later took several of them to kill herself "in order to save her mother from disgrace." She became violently ill and told Stephenson what she had done. He suggested that she check into a hospital as his wife, but she refused. The group then set out to return to Indianapolis by car, and they made the trip without stopping although she was in agony and screaming for a doctor. One of the men left her at her home the next day, where a friend summoned a doctor.

Miss Oberholtzer died about 4 weeks after taking the poison. By that time the direct effect of the poison had largely subsided, and death was apparently caused by a combination of the poison, an infection probably stemming from one of her wounds, exhaustion, and lack of prompt medical treatment.]

PER CURIAM: * * *

Appellant very earnestly argues that the evidence does not show appellant guilty of murder. He points out in his brief that, after they reached the hotel, Madge Oberholtzer left the hotel and purchased a hat and the poison, and voluntarily returned to his room, and at the time she took the poison she was in an adjoining room to him, and that she swallowed the poison without his knowledge, and at a time when he was not present. From these facts he contends that she took her life by committing suicide; that her own act in taking the poison was an intervening responsible agent which broke the causal connection between his acts and the death; that his acts were not the proximate cause of her death, but the taking of the poison was the proximate cause of death. * * *

Bishop in his work on Criminal Law, vol. 2, (9th Ed.) page 484, says: "When suicide follows a wound inflicted by the defendant his act is homicidal, if deceased was rendered irresponsible by the wound and as a natural result of it." We do not understand that by the rule laid down by Bishop, supra, that the wound which renders the deceased mentally irresponsible is necessarily limited to a physical wound. We should think the same rule would apply if a defendant engaged in the commission of a felony such as rape or attempted rape, and inflicts upon his victim both physical and mental injuries, the natural and probable result of which would render the deceased mentally irresponsible and suicide followed, we think he would be guilty of murder.

Appellant is charged with having caused the death of Madge Oberholtzer while engaged in the crime of attempted rape. The evidence shows that appellant, together with Earl Gentry and the deceased, left their compartment on the train and went to a hotel about a block from the depot, and there appellant registered as husband and wife, and immediately went to the room assigned to them. This change from their room on the train to a room in the hotel is of no consequence, for appellant's control and dominion over the deceased was absolute and complete in both cases. The evidence further shows that the deceased asked for money with which to purchase a hat, and it was supplied her by "Shorty," at the direction of appellant, and that she did leave the room and was taken by Shorty to a shop and purchased a hat and then, at her request, to a drug store where she purchased the bichloride of mercury tablets, and then she was taken back to the room in the hotel, where about 10 o'clock a.m. she swallowed the poison. Appellant argues that the deceased was a free agent on this trip to purchase a hat, etc., and that she voluntarily returned to the room in the hotel. This was a question for the jury, and the evidence would justify them in reaching a contrary conclusion. Appellant's chauffeur accompanied her on this trip, and the deceased had, before she left appellant's home in Indianapolis, attempted to get away, and also made two unsuccessful attempts to use the telephone to call help. She was justified in concluding that any attempt she might make, while purchasing a hat or while in the drug store to escape or secure assistance, would be no more successful in Hammond than it was in Indianapolis. We think the evidence shows that the deceased was at all times from the time she was entrapped by the appellant at his home on the evening of March 15th till she returned to her home two days later, in the custody and absolute control of appellant. Neither do we think the fact that the deceased took the poison some four hours after they left the drawing-room on the train or after the crime of attempted rape had been committed necessarily prevents it from being a part of the attempted rape. Suppose they had not left the drawing-room on the train, and, instead of the deceased taking poison, she had secured possession of appellant's revolver and shot herself or thrown herself out of the window of the car and died from the fall. We can see no vital difference.

At the very moment Madge Oberholtzer swallowed the poison she was subject to the passion, desire, and will of appellant. She knew not what moment she would be subjected to the same demands that she was while in the drawing-room on the train. What would have prevented appellant from compelling her to submit to him at any moment? The same forces, the same impulses, that would impel her to shoot herself during the actual attack or throw herself out of the car window after the attack had ceased, was pressing and overwhelming her at the time she swallowed the poison. The evidence shows that she was so weak that she staggered as she left the elevator to go to the room in the hotel, and was assisted by appellant and Gentry. That she was very ill, so much so that she could not eat, all of which was the direct and proximate result of the treatment accorded her by appellant.... We therefore conclude that the evidence was sufficient and justified the jury in finding that appellant by his acts and conduct rendered the deceased distracted and mentally irresponsible, and that such was the natural and probable consequence of such unlawful and criminal treatment, and that the appellant was guilty of murder in the second degree as charged in the first count of the indictment.

* * *

COMMONWEALTH v. ATENCIO

Supreme Judicial Court of Massachusetts, 1963.
345 Mass. 627, 189 N.E.2d 223.

WILKINS, CHIEF JUSTICE.

Each defendant has been convicted upon an indictment for manslaughter in the death of Stewart E. Britch * * *.

Facts which the jury could have found are these. On Sunday, October 22, 1961, the deceased, his brother Ronald, and the defendants spent the day drinking wine in the deceased's room in a rooming house in Boston. At some time in the afternoon, with reference to nothing specific so far as the record discloses, Marshall said, "I will settle this," went out, and in a few minutes returned clicking a gun, from which he removed one bullet. Early in the evening Ronald left, and the conversation turned to "Russian roulette."

The evidence as to what happened consisted of testimony of police officers, who took statements of the defendants, and testimony of one defendant, Atencio. The evidence did not supply all the facts. For example, the source and ownership of the revolver were not made clear. The jury could have found that it was produced by the deceased and that he suggested the "game," or they might have found neither to be the fact. There was evidence that Marshall earlier had seen the revolver in the possession of the deceased, and that the latter handed it to Marshall, who put it in the bathroom under the sink. Later when the deceased accused him of stealing it, he brought it back from the bathroom, and gave it to the deceased. Any uncertainty is not of prime importance. The "game" was played. The deceased and Atencio were seated on a bed, and Marshall was seated on a couch. First, Marshall examined the gun, saw that it contained one cartridge, and, after spinning it on his arm, pointed it at his head, and pulled the trigger. Nothing happened. He handed the gun to Atencio, who repeated the process, again without result. Atencio passed the gun to the deceased, who spun it, put to his head, and pulled the trigger. The cartridge exploded, and he fell over dead.

There is no controversy as to definition. Involuntary manslaughter may be predicated upon wanton or reckless conduct. "The essence of wanton or reckless conduct is intentional conduct, by way either of commission or of omission where there is a duty to act, which conduct involves a high degree of likelihood that substantial harm will result to another." Commonwealth v. Welansky, 316 Mass. 383, 399, 55 N.E.2d 902, 910.

We are of opinion that the defendants could properly have been found guilty of manslaughter. This is not a civil action against the defendants by the personal representative of Stewart Britch. In such a case his voluntary act, we assume, would be a bar. Here the Commonwealth had an interest that the deceased should not be killed by the wanton or reckless conduct of himself and others. Such conduct could be found in the concerted action and cooperation of the defendants in helping to bring about the deceased's foolish act. The jury did not have to believe testimony that the defendants at the last moment tried to dissuade the deceased from doing that which they had just done themselves.

The defendants argue as if it should have been ruled, as a matter of law, that there were three "games" of solitaire and not one "game" of "Russian roulette." That the defendants participated could be found to be a cause and not a mere condition of Stewart Britch's death. It is not correct to say that his act could not be found to have been caused by anything which Marshall and Atencio did, nor that he would have died when the gun went off in his hand no matter whether they had done the same. The testimony does not require a ruling that when the deceased took the gun from Atencio it was an independent or intervening act not standing in any relation to the defendants' acts which would render what he did imputable to them. It is an oversimplification to contend that each participated in something that only one could do at a time. There could be found to be a mutual encouragement in a joint enterprise. In the abstract, there may have been no duty on the defendants to prevent the deceased from playing. But there was a duty on their part not to cooperate or join with him in the "game." Nor, if the facts presented such a case, would we have to agree that if the deceased, and not the defendants, had played first that they could not have been found guilty of manslaughter. The defendants were much more than merely present at a crime. It would not be necessary that the defendants force the deceased to play or suggest that he play.

We are referred in both briefs to cases of manslaughter arising out of automobiles racing upon the public highway. When the victim is a third person, there is no difficulty in holding the drivers, including the one whose car did not strike the victim (Brown v. Thayer, 212 Mass. 392, 99 N.E. 237), or in whose car a victim was not a passenger. Nelson v. Nason, 343 Mass. 220, 177 N.E.2d 887.

In two cases the driver of a noncolliding car has been prosecuted for the death of his competitor, and in both cases an appellate court has ruled that he was not guilty of manslaughter. In Commonwealth v. Root, 403 Pa. 571, 170 A.2d 310, 82 A.L.R.2d 452, the competitor drove on the wrong side of the road head-on into an oncoming truck and was killed. The court held that "the tort liability concept of proximate cause has no proper place in prosecutions for criminal homicide and more direct causal connection is required for conviction. * * * In the instant case, the defendant's reckless conduct was not a sufficiently direct cause of the competing driver's death to make him criminally liable therefor." In Thacker v. State, 103 Ga.App. 36, 117 S.E.2d 913, the defendant was indicted for the involuntary manslaughter of his competitor in a drag race who was killed when he lost control of his car and left the highway. The court said that the indictment "fails to allege any act or acts on the part of the defendant which caused or contributed to the loss of control of the vehicle driven by the deceased, other than the fact that they were engaged in a race at the time."

Whatever may be thought of those two decisions, there is a very real distinction between drag racing and "Russian roulette." In the former much is left to the skill, or lack of it, of the competitor. In "Russian roulette" it is a matter of luck as to the location of the one bullet, and except for a misfire (of which there was evidence in the case at bar) the outcome is a certainty if the chamber under the hammer happens to be the one containing the bullet. * * * [Affirmed.]

IN RE JOSEPH G.

Supreme Court of California, 1983.
34 Cal.3d 429, 194 Cal.Rptr. 163, 667 P.2d 1176.

MOSK, JUSTICE.

Joseph G., a minor, was charged in a juvenile court petition to declare him a ward of the court (Welf. & Inst.Code, § 602) with murder (Pen.Code, § 187) and aiding and abetting a suicide (Pen.Code, § 401). At the contested adjudication hearing, the court sustained the petition as to the murder count but dismissed the aiding and abetting charge as inapplicable; the court further found that the murder was in the first degree. * * *

I.

The minor and his friend, Jeff W., both 16 years old, drove to the Fillmore library one evening and joined a number of their friends who had congregated there. During the course of the two hours they spent at the library talking, mention was made of a car turnout on a curve overlooking a 300 to 350–foot precipice on a country road known as "the cliff." Both the minor and Jeff declared that they intended to "fly off the cliff" and that they meant to kill themselves. The others were skeptical but the minor affirmed their seriousness, stating "You don't believe us that we are going to do it. We are going to do it. You can read it in the paper tomorrow." The minor gave one of the girls his baseball hat, saying firmly that this was the last time he would see her. Jeff repeatedly encouraged the minor by urging, "let's go, let's go" whenever the minor spoke. One other youth attempted to get in the car with Jeff and the minor but they refused to allow him to join them "because we don't want to be responsible for you." Jeff and the minor shook hands with their friends and departed.

The pair then drove to a gas station and put air in a front tire of the car, which had been damaged earlier in the evening; the fender and passenger door were dented and the tire was very low in air pressure, nearly flat. Two of their fellow students, Keith C. and Craig B., drove up and spoke with Jeff and the minor. The minor said, "Shake my hand and stay cool." Jeff urged, "Let's go," shook their hands and said, "Remember you shook my hand." The minor then drove off in the direction of the cliff with Jeff in the passenger seat; Keith and Craig surreptitiously followed them out of curiosity. The minor and Jeff proceeded up the hill past the cliff, turned around and drove down around the curve and over the steep cliff.

Two other vehicles were parked in the turnout, from which vantage point their occupants watched the minor's car plummeting down the hill at an estimated 50 mph. The car veered off the road without swerving or changing course; the witnesses heard the car accelerate and then drive straight off the cliff. No one saw brakelights flash. The impact of the crash killed Jeff and caused severe injuries to the minor, resulting in the amputation of a foot.

Investigations following the incident revealed there were no defects in the steering or brake mechanisms. There were no skid marks at the scene, but a gouge in the pavement apparently caused by the frame of a motor vehicle coming into contact with the asphalt at high speed indicated that the car had gone straight over the cliff without swerving or skidding.

A few weeks after the crash, another friend of the minor discussed the incident with him. The minor declared he had "a quart" before driving over the cliff; the friend interpreted this to mean a quart of beer. The minor told his friend that he had "no reason" to drive off the cliff, that it was "stupid" but that he "did it on purpose." Just before the car went over the cliff, the minor told Jeff, "I guess this is it [Jeff]. Take it easy."

II.

The minor maintains that, under the peculiar circumstances presented here, he can be convicted only of aiding and abetting a suicide and not of murder. We begin by reviewing the development of the law relevant to suicide and related crimes.

At common law suicide was a felony, punished by forfeiture of property to the king and ignominious burial. Essentially, suicide was considered a form of murder. (Brenner, Undue Influence in the Criminal Law: A Proposed Analysis of the Criminal Offense of "Causing Suicide" (1982) 47 Alb.L.Rev. 62, 64 (hereafter cited as Causing Suicide).) Under American law, suicide has never been punished and the ancient English attitude has been expressly rejected. * * *

Attempted suicide was also a crime at common law. A few American jurisdictions have adopted this view, but most, including California, attach no criminal liability to one who makes a suicide attempt. * * *

The law has, however, retained culpability for aiding, abetting and advising suicide. At common law, an aider and abettor was guilty of murder by construction of law because he was a principal in the second degree to the self-murder of the other. (Williams, The Sanctity of Life and the Criminal Law (1957) p. 296 (hereafter cited as Williams).) Most states provide, either by statute or case law, criminal sanctions for aiding suicide, but few adopt the extreme common law position that such conduct is murder. Some jurisdictions instead classify aiding suicide as a unique type of manslaughter. But the predominant statutory scheme, and the one adopted in California, is to create a sui generis crime of aiding and abetting suicide. * * *

The California aiding statute, in effect since 1873, provides simply that "Every person who deliberately aids, or advises or encourages another to commit suicide, is guilty of a felony." (Pen.Code, § 401.) This statute, although creating a felony, places California among the most lenient jurisdictions in its punishment for those who assist suicide. The sole California decision which even peripherally considers criminal liability for assisting suicide under this statute is People v. Matlock (1959) 51 Cal.2d 682, 336 P.2d 505. Although by no means entirely dispositive of the issue presented here, the opinion is reviewed in some depth because of the paucity of apposite decisions.

The defendant in *Matlock* was convicted of murder and robbery. Although admitting that he strangled the victim and took his money, the defendant claimed he did so solely at the victim's insistence. According to the defendant, the victim, who had only six months to live and had been recently convicted of a federal crime, sought a way to die but could not commit suicide without forfeiting the benefits of his insurance policy; the victim therefore induced the defendant to kill him and take his property so that it would appear to be a robbery-murder.

The defendant contended that the trial court erred in refusing his requested instructions on aiding and abetting suicide under section 401 of the Penal Code. Relying on the Oregon decision in People v. Bouse (1953) 199 Or. 676, 264 P.2d 800, and State v. Fischer (1962) 232 Or. 558, 376 P.2d 418, 421, we held that the defendant's active participation in the final overt act causing the victim's death, i.e., strangling him, precluded the application of the aiding suicide statute.

In *Bouse,* the defendant's wife drowned in a bathtub; there was evidence that she had told the defendant she wanted to die and that he attempted suicide shortly after her death. On the evidence, the jury could have found that the defendant held his wife's head underwater, despite her struggles, until she died, thereby committing murder. On the other hand, the jury might have found that the defendant merely ran the water and assisted his wife into the tub, and was therefore guilty of only manslaughter under the Oregon assisting statute. In upholding the manslaughter instruction, the court reasoned that the latter statute "does not contemplate active participation by one in the overt act directly causing death. It contemplates some participation in the events leading up to the commission of the final overt act, such as furnishing the means for bringing about death—the gun, the knife, the poison, or providing the water, for the use of the person who himself commits the act of self-murder. But where a person actually performs, or actively assists in performing, the overt act resulting in death, such as shooting or stabbing the victim, administering the poison, or holding one under water until death takes place by drowning, his act constitutes murder, and it is wholly immaterial whether this act is committed pursuant to an agreement with the victim, such as a mutual suicide pact."

The reference to a suicide pact seems to relate to the evidence that the defendant made a suicide attempt after his wife's death. The type of suicide pact contemplated was apparently of the murder-suicide variety, in which, by mutual agreement, one person kills the other and then kills himself. The court noted that even given the existence of such a pact, if the defendant actively drowned his wife it would be murder. This is to be distinguished from either (1) the mutual suicide pact in which one party provides the means (e.g., poison or lethal weapons) but each individual kills himself independently pursuant to the agreement; or (2) the circumstances of the present case, in which the pact envisions both parties killing themselves simultaneously with a single instrumentality. As will be seen, in both of the latter situations the proper criminal liability to be attached is for aiding and abetting suicide rather than for murder. * * *

Traditionally under the common law the survivor of a suicide pact was held to be guilty of murder. * * * It has been suggested that the reason for imposing criminal liability upon a surviving party to a suicide pact is the "support" such a pact presents. "Surviving a suicide pact also gives rise to a suspicion that the survivor may have entered into the pact in less than good faith. Survival, either because one party backed out at the last minute or because the poison, or other agent, did not have the desired effect, suggests that the pact may have been employed to induce the other person to take his own life." (Causing Suicide, supra.) The Model Penal Code, while recognizing that "when the pact is genuine all of the arguments against treating attempted suicide as criminal apply with equal force" to the case of a suicide pact survivor, is similarly concerned with the "danger of abuse in differentiating genuine from spurious agreements" to commit suicide. (Model Pen.Code, § 210.5, supra.)

Under the facts presented here, these concerns are not particularly appropriate. First, the trial judge was satisfied there was a genuine suicide pact between Jeff and the minor. By "genuine," we mean simply that the pact was freely entered into and was not induced by force, duress or deception. There is no evidence in the present case that Jeff's participation in the pact was anything but fully voluntary and uncoerced. Second, because of the instrumentality used there was no danger of fraud: the potential consequences for the minor of driving the car off the cliff were identical to the potential consequences for Jeff, his passenger. Finally, the suicide and the attempted suicide were committed simultaneously by the same act. * * *

The anomaly of classifying the minor's actions herein as murder is further illustrated by consideration of Jeff's potential criminal liability had he survived. If Jeff, the passenger, had survived and the minor had been killed, Jeff would be guilty, at most, of a violation of Penal Code section 401. In order to commit suicide by this means, i.e., a car, only one of the parties to the pact, the driver, can be said to "control" the instrumentality. To make the distinction between criminal liability for first degree murder and merely aiding and abetting suicide turn on the fortuitous circumstance of which of the pair was actually driving serves no rational purpose. The illogic of such a distinction has been similarly recognized in the classic example of the parties to the pact agreeing to commit suicide by gassing themselves in a closed room. If the party who turns on the gas survives, he is guilty of murder; if on the other hand, the other person survives, that person's criminal liability is only that of an aider and abettor. "It would be discreditable if any actual legal consequences were made to hinge upon such distinctions." (Williams, supra, at p. 299.)

The order declaring the minor a ward of the court is reversed and the cause is remanded to the trial court for further proceedings not inconsistent with this opinion.

PEOPLE v. KEVORKIAN

Court of Appeals of Michigan, 1994.
205 Mich.App. 180, 517 N.W.2d 293.

FITZGERALD, P.J.

The prosecution appeals as of right a July 21, 1992, order of Oakland Circuit Judge David F. Breck granting defendant's motion to dismiss two counts of open murder on the ground that physician-assisted suicide is not a crime in Michigan. * * *

I

On October 23, 1991, Marjorie Wantz and Sherry Miller were reported dead by defendant. Their bodies were found in a cabin at the Bald Mountain Recreation Area. [Defendant was charged with two counts of open murder.] A preliminary examination was held on four dates between February 14 and February 28, 1992. The evidence presented showed that Ms. Wantz had complained of intense pain in the pelvic and vaginal areas for many years. Although she had undergone various operations, she had obtained no relief.

Ms. Miller was diagnosed with multiple sclerosis in 1978 or 1979. Her condition deteriorated over the years, and by 1989 she was using a wheelchair and had to be carried from place to place and put into the chair. By 1991, she was confined either to bed or to a wheelchair, did not have the use of her legs and her right arm, had only limited use of her left arm, and had problems talking and breathing.

At some point, Ms. Wantz and Ms. Miller learned of defendant's reputation as a champion of physician-assisted suicide. They contacted defendant separately on several occasions. Defendant eventually agreed to assist both individuals in taking their lives. Defendant, Ms. Wantz, Ms. Miller, and several family members or friends of each were present at the cabin on October 23, 1991. Ms. Wantz was hooked up to defendant's "suicide machine," which consisted of a board to which her arm was strapped to prevent movement, a needle to be inserted into a blood vessel, and containers of various chemicals that could be released into the needle through tubing and thus into the bloodstream. One of the chemicals was methohexital, which was described by expert witnesses as a fast-acting barbiturate used for the quick introduction of anesthesia under controlled circumstances. The drug quickly depresses respiration, and a large dose causes the recipient to stop breathing.

After defendant inserted the needle into a vein in Ms. Wantz' arm, he tied strings to two of her fingers. The strings were attached to clips on the tubing connected to the needle. The clips held back the methohexital and another drug, potassium chloride. Defendant instructed Ms. Wantz how to pull the strings attached to the clips so as to allow the drugs to flow into her bloodstream. Ms. Wantz followed defendant's instructions and died as a result of a lethal dose of methohexital.

Defendant twice attempted to connect the suicide machine to Ms. Miller, but failed. He then left the cabin and returned to his office or residence in Royal Oak where he procured a tank of carbon monoxide gas and a mask assembly. About three hours later, he returned to the cabin, where he attached a screwdriver to the gas canister to act as a lever to open the gas valve. Defendant then attached the mask to Ms. Miller's face and instructed her how to open the gas valve. Ms. Miller died from carbon monoxide poisoning.

At the close of the preliminary examination, the district court bound defendant over on two counts of open murder. * * * Defendant filed a motion in the circuit court to quash the information and dismiss the murder charges. * * * In granting defendant's motion to dismiss, the circuit court acknowledged that People v. Roberts, 178 N.W. 690 (Mich. 1920), rejected the defense that assisted suicide did not constitute the crime of murder, but held that the Court's holding was dictum in view of the fact that Roberts had pleaded guilty of open murder. The circuit court instead relied on People v. Campbell, 335 N.W.2d 27 (Mich.App. 1983), and held that, because suicide is not a crime, one cannot be criminally responsible for assisting a suicide.

II

In this case of first impression, we are asked to determine whether the murder statute applies to the conduct of a physician who assists another in voluntarily committing suicide. * * *

Under the common law, suicide was murder. See Cruzan v. Director, Missouri Dep't of Health, 497 U.S. 261, 294 (1990) (Justice Scalia, concurring). Suicide is no longer considered a criminal act, not because the act does not fall within the definition of murder, but because no punishment is provided for self-murder.[3] The American Law Institute's Model Penal Code, which is widely regarded as the greatest criminal law reform project of this century, criminalizes aiding or soliciting another to commit suicide, but does not criminalize suicide or attempted suicide. *Roberts*, supra, which held that aiding a suicide falls within the common-law definition of murder, is consistent with this view.

In *Roberts*, the defendant pleaded guilty of the murder of his wife. The defendant's wife, who had unsuccessfully attempted suicide in the past, had terminal multiple sclerosis and was in great pain. At his wife's request, the defendant made a potion of water and poison and placed it within her reach. As the defendant watched, his wife took the poison and died.

After Roberts entered a plea confessing his guilt, the court found him guilty of first-degree murder within the meaning of [the statute]. * * * On appeal, Roberts [argued that, since suicide is not a crime in Michigan, assisting a suicide is also not a crime]. The Supreme Court disagreed and upheld the defendant's conviction:

> If we were living in a purely common-law atmosphere with a strictly common-law practice, and defendant were charged with being guilty as an accessory of the offense of suicide, counsel's argument would be more persuasive than it is. But defendant is not charged with that offense. He is charged with murder and the theory of the people was that he committed the crime by means of poison. He has come into court and confessed that he mixed poison with water and placed it within her reach, but at her request. The important question, therefore, arises as to whether what defendant did constitutes murder by means of poison. * * *

3. The decriminalization of suicide occurred because the punishment—forfeiture of all property and burial in the highway with a stake through the deceased's body—is no longer considered appropriate.

We are of the opinion that when defendant mixed the paris green with water and placed it within reach of his wife to enable her to put an end to her suffering by putting an end to her life, he was guilty of murder by means of poison within the meaning of the statute, even though she requested him to do so. By this act he deliberately placed within her reach the means of taking her own life, which she could have obtained in no other way by reason of her helpless condition. [*Roberts*, supra at 195–196, 198.]

The circuit court erred in holding that the above language from *Roberts* is dictum. * * * The circuit court also erred in finding applicable this Court's decision in *Campbell*, supra. In *Campbell*, this Court was faced with the issue whether inciting a suicide was murder. The defendant and a friend were drinking heavily one night when the friend began talking about committing suicide. The friend mentioned that he did not have a gun, and the defendant offered to sell him a gun for whatever amount of money the friend had in his possession at the time. The defendant encouraged his friend to buy the gun and ridiculed him for hesitating to do so. The two men subsequently obtained a gun and ammunition from the home of the defendant's parents and returned to the original scene approximately fifteen minutes later. The defendant departed while his friend was holding the gun and the shells were on a table. The next morning the victim was found dead of a self-inflicted gunshot wound.

The defendant was charged with open murder. Relying on *Roberts*, the trial court denied the defendant's motion to quash. On appeal, this Court recognized that *Roberts* held that aiding and abetting a suicide constitutes murder, but held that Roberts no longer represented the law in Michigan because "recent cases of our Supreme Court cast doubt on [its vitality]." The opinion does not, however, explain the basis for this conclusion.

The *Campbell* opinion also concludes that the Supreme Court failed to determine in *Roberts* whether Roberts' act of placing poison within the reach of his wife constituted the crime of murder. The *Campbell* opinion thus reasons that because the term "homicide" was defined at common law as the "killing of one human being by another," the term "suicide" excludes, by definition, a homicide. In actuality, however, the *Roberts* opinion specifically responded to Roberts' allegation that there was no evidence of the commission of the crime charged because suicide is not a crime in Michigan and held that the defendant's acts constituted murder by means of poison.

Campbell is also suspect authority for two additional reasons. First, *Campbell* was based on the erroneous belief that suicide and aiding or inciting to suicide are not classified as murder or homicide under the common law. As we have noted, at common law suicide was a form of murder. If suicide is murder, then one who is an accessory to or aided and abetted in the suicide is criminally liable. Indeed, in Michigan, these distinctions have been obliterated, and both accessories before the fact and aiders and abettors are now as liable as are principals.

Secondly, the issue in *Campbell* was whether inciting a suicide is a crime. As noted by the Court, the defendant did not have a present intention to kill. Under the facts of that case, the Court was legally justified in finding that the defendant's conduct did not constitute murder. In *Roberts*, however, the issue was whether assisting a suicide with the intent to kill is a crime. It was not necessary for the Court in *Campbell* to determine whether *Roberts* still represented the law in Michigan. Were *Roberts* held to be binding, it would not have controlled the outcome in *Campbell* because the *Campbell* Court concluded that incitement to suicide did not require the degree of intention requisite to a charge of murder. Hence, *Campbell* 's conclusion that *Roberts* no longer represents the law in Michigan is dictum.

As noted above, the reasons cited in *Campbell* in support of a finding that *Roberts* no longer represents the law in Michigan are factually and legally unsupported. Our research has unveiled no authority that would support a finding that *Roberts* is no longer binding. * * * The circuit court distinguished *Roberts* on the ground that Roberts was not a physician. However, we have found no basis in either the statutes or common law for an exception for physicians who aid and abet suicide.

Rather than judicially rewrite the laws of this state, it is proper, in fact the oath we took requires nothing less, to rely on the Legislature to devise, should it choose to do so, a means to avoid the harsh penalty that is imposed when assisting a suicide is treated as murder pursuant to a literal application of [the statute].[7] * * *

We conclude that the circuit court erred in dismissing the murder charges against defendant. Reversed and remanded.

Note

The Supreme Court of Michigan ruled on the "assisted suicide" issues raised in the preceding case in People v. Kevorkian, et al., 447 Mich. 436, 527 N.W.2d 714 (1994). The Court had consolidated several cases, which it resolved in a Memorandum Opinion. Although a majority of the justices concurred "in every holding, statement, and disposition of this memorandum opinion," several wrote concurring and dissenting opinions. These lengthy opinions cannot easily be edited for casebook presentation, so the Court of Appeals opinion is preserved here as a more coherent presentation of the issues, but a summary of the Michigan Supreme Court's opinion is useful.

7. In an apparent attempt to address this concern, the Legislature passed the assistance to suicide act. The act provides that one who provides the physical means by which a person attempts to commit suicide or participates in the physical act by which another attempts to commit suicide is guilty of a felony punishable by up to four years' imprisonment. Defendant's argument that he cannot be charged with murder because the Legislature subsequently enacted a law criminalizing assisted suicide is misplaced. The Legislature is not prohibited from providing a specific and lesser penalty for actions that could be punished under another statute with a harsher penalty. * * *

The Michigan Supreme Court concluded that the "assisted suicide" statute did not violate the Michigan Constitution, and that the United States Constitution did not prohibit Michigan from "imposing criminal penalties on one who assists another in committing suicide." In reaching these conclusions, it rejected the argument that terminally ill persons have a right to assisted suicide. The court also distinguished between suicide, which "involves an affirmative act to end a life," and the "refusal or cessation of life-sustaining medical treatment [that] simply permits life to run its course, unencumbered by contrived intervention," and concluded that people who choose "to discontinue life-sustaining medical treatment are not * * * committing suicide."

The Michigan Supreme Court also overruled People v. Roberts (discussed at length in the preceding opinion), "to the extent that it can be read to support the view that the common-law definition of murder encompasses the act of intentionally providing the means by which a person commits suicide. Only where there is probable cause to believe that death was the direct and natural result of a defendant's act can the defendant be properly bound over on a charge of murder." The Court concluded that when "a defendant merely is involved in the events leading up to the death, such as providing the means, the proper charge is assisting in a suicide." In reaching its conclusion that the statute criminalizing assisted suicide applied to the latter conduct, the Michigan Supreme Court relied, in part, on the reasoning presented in *In re Joseph G.*, supra Ch. 3, § E.

Disputes about the legality of assisted suicide laws did not end with the Michigan Supreme Court's decision. Consider, for example, Compassion in Dying v. Washington, 850 F.Supp. 1454 (W.D.Wash.1994), *aff'd en banc,* 79 F.3d 790 (9th Cir.1996), *rev'd,* Washington v. Glucksberg, 521 U.S. 702 (1997). In Glucksberg, the Supreme Court found that Washington's ban on assisted suicide did not violate the Due Process Clause of the 14th Amendment. In reaching these conclusions, it rejected the argument that terminally ill persons have a right to assisted suicide. Not all states have handled the assisted suicide issue in the same way. Only a month before the Michigan Supreme Court's decision in the Kevorkian case, Oregon voters narrowly approved The Death With Dignity Act, the country's first statute authorizing terminally ill patients to request fatal drugs from their physician for the purpose of ending their lives. The Act authorized a terminally ill patient (as determined by two physicians) who "has voluntarily expressed his or her wish to die, [to] make a written request for medication for the purpose of ending his or her life in a humane and dignified manner." DEATH WITH DIGNITY ACT, OR. REV. STAT. § 127.805, et seq. (1999). The Act expressly provided that no person shall be subject to criminal, civil, or professional liability for good faith compliance with the Act, but also specified that no health care provider has a duty to provide lethal medication to anyone making a life-ending request pursuant to the Act.

Fifteen days before the Act was to take effect, a federal district court in Oregon issued an injunction halting its implementation. That court later found the Act unconstitutional under the Equal Protection Clause of the 14th Amendment, holding that it was not rationally related to any legitimate state interest. The court found the Act's "procedures designed to differentiate between the competent and incompetent are not sufficient." The Act did not require that either of the two physicians who determined a patient's status as "terminally ill" must be a mental health professional, which the court concluded could lead to misdiagnosis. Lee v. Oregon, 891 F.Supp. 1429, 1434–35 (D.Or.1995).

The Ninth Circuit Court of Appeals reversed, holding that the terminally ill patients who were the plaintiffs in the action did not have standing to assert a claim. The court never reached the constitutionality of the Act, finding that none of the plaintiffs could assert an "injury in fact." Lee v. Oregon, 107 F.3d 1382 (9th Cir.1997), *cert. denied* 522 U.S. 927 (1997).

On November 6, 2001, Attorney General Ashcroft issued AG Order No. 2534–2001, directing that for the purposes of the Federal Controlled Substances Act, 21 U.S.C. §§ 801–971 (1994 and Supp. II 1996), assisting suicide is not a "legitimate medical purpose" for dispensing, prescribing, or administering drugs covered by the Act. Under this Order, people who do administer drugs for the purpose of assisting with a suicide would be subject to the penalty provisions contained in the Federal Controlled Substances Act, including suspension or revocation of medical licenses. See 21 U.S.C. § 824(a)(4). While this edition was being prepared, a federal District Judge in Oregon issued a Permanent Injunction enjoining enforcement of the Attorney General's directive.

3. *Unexpected Consequences*

PEOPLE v. GARNER

Supreme Court of Colorado, 1989.
781 P.2d 87.

JUSTICE MULLARKEY delivered the Opinion of the Court.

I

On November 7, 1987 Garner was driving a pickup truck on a four-lane divided residential street in Colorado Springs. A small group of children was on the median, preparing to cross the street in front of Garner's vehicle. All of the children stopped, except for twelve-year-old Lisa Uhrenic who continued to cross the street. Garner, who was traveling in the left lane of traffic, swerved into the right lane in an apparent attempt to avoid the child but the right front of his truck struck and killed her. Garner was charged with vehicular homicide, driving under the influence and driving with excessive blood alcohol content.

At the preliminary hearing on the vehicular homicide charge, evidence established that Garner's blood alcohol level was .201 one hour after the collision. The defense stipulated to Garner's intoxication, to his driving the truck which hit the child, and to Lisa Uhrenic's death as a result of the accident.

An investigating officer testified on the basis of skid marks that Garner was driving an estimated 43.39 miles per hour in a posted 35 mile per hour zone. He described the point of impact as four inches from the right side of the vehicle. The officer offered his opinion that, had Garner been traveling at the posted speed limit, the vehicle would have stopped three feet after striking Uhrenic as opposed to the 26 feet which the vehicle actually traveled after the point of impact. It was the officer's opinion that the accident would have occurred even if Garner had been driving at 35 miles per hour but he could not say whether the death would have occurred under those circumstances. Another officer testified, that in his opinion, the "proximate cause" of the accident was not Garner's conduct but rather the accident resulted because Uhrenic ran between traffic and crossed in front of the vehicle.

Other eyewitnesses, who were driving directly behind Garner on the date of the accident, testified that Garner was not weaving, speeding, or driving in a careless manner. Their testimony also indicated that Garner turned to his right in an attempt to avoid hitting Uhrenic. Garner did not testify at the preliminary hearing.

At the conclusion of the hearing, the trial court dismissed the charge of vehicular homicide because it found that the speed at which Garner was driving, not his intoxication, was the proximate cause of the girl's death. The court said: "In this case the court can find as I said earlier, that the negligent activity, speeding, in the light most favorable to the People, was a cause of death of the girl but I cannot find that the intoxication of the defendant had any impact upon that, either by evidence or judicial notice."

It is from this order that the People appeal.

II

The relevant portion of the vehicular homicide statute, section 18–3–106(1)(b)(I), 8B C.R.S. (1986), states as follows:

> If a person operates or drives a motor vehicle while under the influence of any drug or intoxicant and such conduct is the proximate cause of the death of another, he commits vehicular homicide. This is a strict liability crime.

[Another section] provides that "if there was at such time 0.10 percent or more by weight of alcohol in the defendant's blood, it shall be presumed that the defendant was under the influence of alcohol." Here it is conceded that Garner was operating a vehicle while under the influence of an intoxicant at the time of the accident. The prosecution maintains that the trial court erred in narrowly interpreting the statutory language of "proximate cause" to require proof that intoxication rather than a defendant's conduct of driving while intoxicated was the proximate cause of the death. We agree. * * *

We upheld the constitutionality of this statute in People v. Rostad, 669 P.2d 126 (Colo.1983), where we discussed at length the legislature's designation of this offense as a strict liability crime and its inclusion of the proximate cause requirement. We construed the statute as requiring that the prosecution prove "voluntary conduct, as defined by section 18–1–501(9), in the operation or driving of a motor vehicle ..." We held that the proximate cause element of the crime relates to a defendant's operation of a motor vehicle and is measured by an objective test. "Voluntary act" is defined in relevant part in section 18–1–501(9), 8B C.R.S. (1986) as "an act performed consciously as a result of effort or determination...." Thus, in order to obtain a conviction under this statute, the prosecution must prove that the defendant voluntarily drove while intoxicated and that his driving resulted in the victim's death.

There is no requirement under the current statute that the prosecution also prove that the defendant's driving was negligent. Whether Garner was speeding is not relevant under the statute. In this regard, the statute represents a significant departure from prior statutes which did require such proof. * * *

Based on *Rostad*, the language of the vehicular homicide statute and its legislative history, we conclude that the conduct at issue for purposes of proximate cause is the voluntary act of driving while intoxicated. The statute does not require evidence that the intoxication affected the driver's operation in a manner that results in a collision. The clear intent of the legislature is to punish and thereby to deter the conduct of voluntarily driving while intoxicated. Thus, the trial court erred in interpreting the proximate cause element of section 18–3–106(1)(b)(I) to require proof that the intoxication of the driver was the cause of negligent conduct which resulted in the death of the victim.

III

We next consider whether the trial court abused its discretion in dismissing the vehicular homicide charge against Garner for lack of probable cause. We conclude that it did abuse its discretion.

A preliminary hearing is held for the purpose of determining whether there is probable cause to believe that the defendant committed the crime charged. The evidence presented at the hearing must be sufficient to induce a person of ordinary prudence to entertain a reasonable belief that the defendant committed the crime charged. [Citations] To establish probable cause in this case, the prosecution was required only to present evidence that the defendant voluntarily drove while he was intoxicated, and that his vehicle struck and killed the victim. The evidence presented amply supports a finding of probable cause.

We note that there also was other evidence presented at the preliminary hearing which suggested that the proximate cause of the death was the victim's own act of running in front of the vehicle. Such conduct is not an independent intervening cause which negates a conclusion that the driver's conduct was the proximate cause of the collision unless the victim's conduct amounts to gross negligence. We recognized this principle in People v. Gentry, 738 P.2d 1188 (Colo.1987), which concerned application of the same statute to a defense based on the victim's alleged negligence by stepping in front of the vehicle which struck him. We emphasized that "to qualify as an intervening cause, an event must be unforeseeable and one in which the accused does not participate."

Simple negligence on the part of the victim "is not, as a matter of law, an independent intervening cause." Assuming there was a question as to whether the victim's conduct was gross negligence, probable cause still should have been found and that question decided by the jury under an instruction conforming to the Gentry requirements.

We reverse the order of dismissal and remand the case to the district court with directions to reinstate the vehicular homicide charge.

PEOPLE v. WARNER–LAMBERT CO.

Court of Appeals of New York, 1980.
51 N.Y.2d 295, 434 N.Y.S.2d 159, 414 N.E.2d 660.

JONES, JUDGE.

Although they were aware that there was a broad, undifferentiated risk of an explosion in consequence of ambient magnesium stearate dust arising from the procedures employed in its manufacturing operations, the corporate and individual defendants may nonetheless not be held criminally liable, on the theory of either reckless or negligent conduct, for the deaths of employees occasioned when such an explosion occurred where the triggering cause thereof was neither foreseen nor foreseeable.

This case is before us on appeal from an order of the Appellate Division, which reversed an order of Supreme Court granting defendants' motion to dismiss the indictment on the ground that the evidence before the Grand Jury was not legally sufficient to establish the offenses charged or any lesser included offenses.

Defendant Warner–Lambert Co. is a manufacturing corporation which produces, among other items, Freshen–Up chewing gum. The individual defendants were officers or employees of the corporation. Defendant Kraft was vice-president in charge of manufacturing; defendant Harris was the director of corporate safety and security; defendants O'Mahoney and O'Rourke were, respectively, plant manager and plant engineer of the Warner–Lambert facility located at 30–30 Thompson Avenue in Long Island City, New York, which was the situs of the events out of which this indictment arose. The indictment charges each defendant with six counts of manslaughter in the second degree in violation of section 125.15 of the Penal Law and six counts of criminally negligent homicide in violation of section 125.10 of the Penal Law in consequence of the deaths of six employees which resulted from a massive explosion and fire at the Long Island City Warner–Lambert plant about 2:30 a.m. on November 21, 1976. On the day on which the explosion occurred, Freshen–Up gum, which is retailed in the shape of a square tablet with a jellylike center, was being produced at the Warner–Lambert plant by a process in which filled ropes of the gum were passed through a bed of magnesium stearate (MS), a dry, dustlike lubricant which was applied by hand, then into a die-cut punch (a Uniplast machine) which was sprayed with a cooling agent (liquid nitrogen), where the gum was formed into the square tablets. Both the MS (normally an inert, organic compound) and the liquid nitrogen were employed to prevent the chicle from adhering to the sizing and cutting machinery, the tendency to adhere being less if a dry lubricant was used and the punch was kept at a low temperature. The process produced a dispersal of MS dust in the air and an accumulation of it at the base of the Uniplast machine and on overhead pipes; some also remained ambient in the atmosphere in the surrounding area.

Both MS and liquid nitrogen are considered safe and are widely used in the industry. In bulk, MS will only burn or smoulder if ignited; however, like many substances, if suspended in the air in sufficient concentration the dust poses a substantial risk of explosion if ignited. The minimum concentration at which an explosion can occur is denominated the "lower explosion level" (LEL). Liquid nitrogen, with a boiling temperature of minus 422 degrees Fahrenheit, is an effective cryogenic which might play a part in the process of "liquefaction"—here, the production of liquid oxygen in the course of the condensation of air on its exposure to a source of intense cold. Liquid oxygen is highly volatile, is easily ignited and, if ignited, will explode. Among possible causes of such ignition of either liquid oxygen or ambient MS are electrical or mechanical sparks.

On November 21, 1976 defendant Warner–Lambert was operating six Uniplast machines in the production of Freshen–Up gum on the fourth floor of its Long Island City plant. The machines were in almost constant operation; however, at the time of the catastrophic explosion near the end of one of the work shifts only one machine (designated the "D" machine) was in operation and employees were engaged in removing settled MS dust from the base of that machine and from overhead pipes by broom sweeping and by the use of airhoses. Suddenly an explosion occurred in the area of the operating machine, followed almost immediately by a second, much larger explosion accompanied by flames which caused injuries to more than 50 workers in the area (six of whom did not survive) and extensive damage to the building and equipment, which was attributed to burning of ambient dust and explosion rather than general fire. Thorough postcatastrophe investigation eliminated intentional or "mancaused" ignition as the origin of the event. * * * For each of these crimes there must be "a substantial and unjustifiable risk", and "[t]he risk must be of such nature and degree that disregard thereof [or, the failure to perceive it] constitutes a gross deviation from the standard of conduct [or, care] that a reasonable person would observe in the situation." The essence of manslaughter in the second degree is awareness accompanied by disregard of the risk; for criminally negligent homicide the essence is failure to perceive the risk. With respect to each crime the culpable conduct of the defendant must have been the cause of the death of the other person or persons.

There have been relatively few reported cases (other than those involving vehicular homicide) in which judicial attention has been focused on the proof required to establish the commission of the crimes of manslaughter in the second degree or criminally negligent homicide.

None has been drawn to our attention and our research has disclosed none in which the statutory provisions were applied to deaths occurring in the course of manufacturing operations.[1]

There can be no doubt that there was competent evidence before the Grand Jury here which, if accepted as true, would have been sufficient to establish the existence of a broad, undifferentiated risk of explosion from ambient MS dust which had been brought to the attention of defendants. It may be assumed that, if it be so categorized, the risk was both substantial and unjustifiable. The issue before us, however, is whether defendants could be held criminally liable for what actually occurred, on theories either of reckless or negligent conduct, based on the evidence submitted to this Grand Jury, viewed in the light most favorable to the People. The focus of our attention must be on the issue of culpability, taking into account the conduct of defendants and the factors both of foreseeability and of causation, all of which in combination constitute the ultimate amalgam on which criminal liability may or may not be predicated.

First, we look at the evidence as to the actual event or chain of events which triggered the explosion—evidence which may only be characterized as hypothetical and speculative. There was direct testimony by eyewitnesses, confirmed by reconstruction of the physical evidence, that two explosions occurred. The first was a low-order detonation, occurring approximately two seconds before the major explosion, at the base of the "D" Uniplast machine, which was itself found to be in a substantially fragmented condition with gears, metal shafts, and other parts broken up and displaced; the second, occurring in rapid succession, was a major explosion accompanied by fire which caused the massive destruction and personal injuries. The prosecution hypothesizes that under what it describes as "the most plausible of theories" the initial detonation was attributable to mechanical sparking resulting from the breakup of the metal parts of the Uniplast machine, possibly occasioned by the machine's having become overheated or overloaded, by vibration, or by slipping of components. Testimony supporting this hypothesis included descriptions of the condition of the machine after the event, expert testimony that the physical evidence suggested mechanical failure

1. Inasmuch as we find the causation issue hereafter discussed to be decisive of this appeal, we assume for purposes of this decision, without deciding, that sections 125.10 and 125.15 of the Penal Law are broad enough to cover deaths occurring in the course of manufacturing operations. We note, however, that no case applying these sections or the predecessor sections to such operations has been found; that no legislative history which mandates that conclusion has been found, either by the parties from whom we solicited submissions on that subject prior to reargument or by our independent research; and that tenable arguments for and against it can be made. * * * The pertinent policy considerations (e.g., the protection of New York residents against injury or death knowingly or recklessly inflicted and of the State against the burden of having to care for and support persons so injured or killed on the one hand, as opposed to the possible adverse effect on the State's economy of extending criminal liability to manufacturing operations on the other) are more properly for the Legislature than for the courts (cf. Fletcher, The Theory of Criminal Negligence: A Comparative Analysis, 119 U. of Pa.L.Rev. 401). It may be that the Legislature will wish to eliminate all equivocality.

prior to the first explosion and testimony of prior instances in which the machine had become overheated or metal parts had broken off. The District Attorney adds that "ignition produced by an electrical spark or arc emission from the non-explosion proof, over loaded Uniplast motor was not ruled out either."

Another explanation for the initial explosion was offered by an expert called by the prosecution who hypothesized that liquid oxygen, produced through liquefaction as air condensed on the liquid nitrogen-cooled parts of the "D" machine, dripped onto settled MS dust at the base of the Uniplast, became trapped there and then, when subjected to the impact caused by a moving metal part, reacted violently, causing ignition of already dispersed MS.

Viewed most favorably to the People, the proof with respect to the actual cause of the explosion is speculative only, and as to at least one of the major hypotheses—that involving oxygen liquefaction—there was no evidence that that process was foreseeable or known to any of the defendants. In sum, there is no proof sufficient to support a finding that defendants foresaw or should have foreseen the physical cause of the explosion. This being so there was not legally sufficient evidence to establish the offenses charged or any lesser included offense.

It has been the position of the People that but-for causation is all that is required for the imposition of criminal liability. Thus, it is their submission, reduced to its simplest form, that there was evidence of a foreseeable and indeed foreseen risk of explosion of MS dust and that in consequence of defendants' failure to remove the dust a fatal explosion occurred. The chain of physical events by which the explosion was set off, i.e., its particular cause, is to them a matter of total indifference. On oral argument the People contended that liability could be imposed if the cause of the explosion were the lighting of a match by an uninvited intruder or the striking of a bolt of lightning. In effect they would hold defendants to the status of guarantors until the ambient dust was removed. It thus appears that the People would invoke an expanded application of proximate cause principles lifted from the civil law of torts. We have rejected the application of any such sweeping theory of culpability under our criminal law, however. We recently considered concepts of criminal culpability grounded in recklessness or negligence in People v. Kibbe, 35 N.Y.2d 407.[a]

In that case the defendants had abandoned their helplessly intoxicated robbery victim in subfreezing temperatures, without shoes or eyeglasses, by the side of an unlighted highway, and he was shortly thereafter struck and killed by a passing motorist. The critical issue in the case was whether the defendants should be held criminally liable for murder when the particular cause of death was vehicular impact rather than freezing. Under the theory now advanced by the People it would

a. For subsequent proceedings see Henderson v. Kibbe, the case immediately following.—ed.

have been irrelevant that death had been the consequence of one particular chain of causation rather than another; it would have been enough that the defendants exposed their victim to the risk of death and that he died. That, of course, was not the analysis of culpability that we adopted. Recognizing that "[a] distance separates the negligence which renders one criminally liable from that which establishes civil liability"—both as to quantum and content of proof—we held that "the defendants should not be found guilty unless their conduct 'was a cause of death sufficiently direct as to meet the requirements of the *criminal,* and not the *tort,* law'." Thus, we were concerned for the nature of the chain of particularized events which in fact led to the victim's death; it was not enough that death had occurred as the result of the defendants' abandonment of their helpless victim. To analogize the factual situation in the case now before us to that in *Kibbe* it might be hypothesized that the abandoned victim in *Kibbe* instead of being either frozen to death or killed when struck by a passing motor vehicle was killed when struck by an airplane making an emergency landing on the highway or when hit by a stray bullet from a hunter's rifle—occasions of death not reasonably to have been foreseen when the defendants abandoned their victim.

In view of our disposition of this appeal on the ground that, inasmuch as the evidence before the Grand Jury was not legally sufficient to establish the foreseeability of the actual immediate, triggering cause of the explosion, defendants cannot be held criminally culpable, we have no occasion to reach or consider whether the steps that they took with respect to the general risk of explosion were a gross deviation from the standard of care or conduct that a reasonable person would have observed in the situation. For the reasons stated, we conclude that there was not legally sufficient evidence in this case on the premise of which any jury could permissibly have imposed criminal liability on any of these defendants.

Accordingly, the order of the Appellate Division should be reversed and the indictment dismissed.

HENDERSON v. KIBBE

Supreme Court of the United States, 1977.
431 U.S. 145, 97 S.Ct. 1730, 52 L.Ed.2d 203.

MR. JUSTICE STEVENS delivered the opinion of the Court.

Respondent is in petitioner's custody pursuant to a conviction for second-degree murder. The question presented to us is whether the New York State trial judge's failure to instruct the jury on the issue of causation was constitutional error.

On the evening of December 30, 1970, respondent and his codefendant encountered a thoroughly intoxicated man named Stafford in a bar in Rochester, N.Y. After observing Stafford display at least two $100 bills, they decided to rob him and agreed to drive him to a nearby town. While in the car, respondent slapped Stafford several times, took his money, and, in a search for concealed funds, forced Stafford to lower his trousers and remove his boots. They then abandoned him on an unlighted, rural road, still in a state of partial undress, and without his coat or his glasses. The temperature was near zero, visibility was obscured by blowing snow, and snow banks flanked the roadway. The time was between 9:30 and 9:40 p.m.

At about 10 p.m., while helplessly seated in a traffic lane about a quarter mile from the nearest lighted building, Stafford was struck by a speeding pickup truck. The driver testified that while he was traveling 50 miles per hour in a 40 mile zone, the first of two approaching cars flashed its lights-presumably as a warning which he did not understand. Immediately after the cars passed, the driver saw Stafford sitting in the road with his hands in the air. The driver neither swerved nor braked his vehicle before it hit Stafford. Stafford was pronounced dead upon arrival at the local hospital.

Respondent and his accomplice were convicted of grand larceny, robbery, and second-degree murder. Only the conviction of murder, as defined in N.Y. Penal Law § 125.25(2) (McKinney 1975), is now challenged. That statute provides that "[a] person is guilty of murder in the second degree" when "[u]nder circumstances evincing a depraved indifference to human life, he recklessly engages in conduct which creates a grave risk of death to another person, *and thereby causes the death of another person*." (Emphasis added.)

Defense counsel argued that it was the negligence of the truckdriver, rather than the defendants' action, that had caused Stafford's death, and that the defendants could not have anticipated the fatal accident.[4] On the other hand, the prosecution argued that the death was foreseeable and would not have occurred but for the conduct of the defendants who therefore were the cause of death. Neither party requested the trial judge to instruct the jury on the meaning of the statutory requirement that the defendants' conduct "thereby cause[d] the death of another person," and no such instruction was given. The trial judge did, however, read the indictment and the statute to the jury and explained the meaning of some of the statutory language. He advised

4. "Let's look at this indictment. Count 1 says and I will read the important part. That the defendant, 'Felon[i]ously and under circumstances evincing a depraved indifference to human life recklessly engaged in conduct which created a grave risk of death to another person, to wit, George Stafford and thereby caused the death of George Stafford.' So, you can see by the accent that I put on reaching that, the elements of this particular crime, and which must be proven beyond a reasonable doubt.

* * *

"... [Y]ou are going to have to honestly come to the conclusion that here is three people, all three drinking, and that these two, or at least my client were in a position to perceive this grave risk, be aware of it and disregard it. Perceive that Mr. Stafford would sit in the middle of the northbound lane, that a motorist would come by who was distracted by flashing lights in the opposite lane, who then froze at the wheel, who then didn't swerve, didn't brake, and who was violating the law by speeding, and to make matters worse, he had at that particular time, because of what the situation was, he had low beams on, that is a lot of anticipation. That is a lot of looking forward. Are you supposed to anticipate that somebody is going to break the law when you move or do something? I think that is a reasonable doubt." App. 68.

the jury that a "person acts recklessly with respect to a result or to a circumstance described by a statute defining an offense *when he is aware of and consciously disregards a substantial and unjustifiable risk that such result will occur* or that such circumstance exists." (emphasis added). * * *

The New York Court of Appeals affirmed. It identified the causation issue as the only serious question raised by the appeal, and then rejected the contention that the conduct of the driver of the pickup truck constituted an intervening cause which relieved the defendants of criminal responsibility for Stafford's death. The court held that it was "not necessary that the ultimate harm be intended by the actor. It will suffice if it can be said beyond a reasonable doubt, as indeed it can be here said, that the ultimate harm is something which should have been foreseen as being reasonably related to the acts of the accused." The court refused to consider the adequacy of the charge to the jury because that question had not been raised in the trial court.

Respondent then filed a petition for a writ of habeas corpus in the United States District Court for the Northern District of New York. The District Court held that the respondent's attack on the sufficiency of the charge failed to raise a question of constitutional dimension and that, without more, "the charge is not reviewable in a federal habeas corpus proceeding."

The Court of Appeals for the Second Circuit reversed, 534 F.2d 493 (1976). In view of the defense strategy which consistently challenged the sufficiency of the proof of causation, the majority held that the failure to make any objection to the jury instructions was not a deliberate bypass precluding federal habeas corpus relief, but rather was an "obviously inadvertent" omission. On the merits, the court held that since the Constitution requires proof beyond a reasonable doubt of every fact necessary to constitute the crime, the failure to instruct the jury on an essential element as complex as the causation issue in this case created an impermissible risk that the jury had not made a finding that the Constitution requires. * * *

An appraisal of the significance of an error in the instructions to the jury requires a comparison of the instructions which were actually given with those that should have been given. Orderly procedure requires that the respective adversaries' views as to how the jury should be instructed be presented to the trial judge in time to enable him to deliver an accurate charge and to minimize the risk of committing reversible error. It is the rare case in which an improper instruction will justify reversal of a criminal conviction when no objection has been made in the trial court.

The burden of demonstrating that an erroneous instruction was so prejudicial that it will support a collateral attack on the constitutional validity of a state court's judgment is even greater than the showing required to establish plain error on direct appeal. The question in such a collateral proceeding is whether the ailing instruction by itself so infected the entire trial that the resulting conviction violates due process, not merely whether the instruction is undesirable, erroneous, or even universally condemned.

In this case, the respondent's burden is especially heavy because no erroneous instruction was given; his claim of prejudice is based on the failure to give any explanation-beyond the reading of the statutory language itself—of the causation element. An omission, or an incomplete instruction, is less likely to be prejudicial than a misstatement of the law. * * *

The New York Court of Appeals concluded that the evidence of causation was sufficient because it can be said beyond a reasonable doubt that the "ultimate harm" was "something which should have been foreseen as being reasonably related to the acts of the accused." It is not entirely clear whether the court's reference to "ultimate harm" merely required that Stafford's death was foreseeable, or, more narrowly, that his death by a speeding vehicle was foreseeable. In either event, the court was satisfied that the "ultimate harm" was one which "should have been foreseen." Thus, an adequate instruction would have told the jury that if the ultimate harm should have been foreseen as being reasonably related to defendants' conduct, that conduct should be regarded as having caused the death of Stafford.

The significance of the omission of such an instruction may be evaluated by comparison with the instructions that were given. One of the elements of respondent's offense is that he acted "recklessly." By returning a guilty verdict, the jury necessarily found, in accordance with its instruction on recklessness, that respondent was "aware of and consciously disregard[ed] a substantial and unjustifiable risk" that death would occur. A person who is "aware of and consciously disregards" a substantial risk must also foresee the ultimate harm that the risk entails. Thus, the jury's determination that the respondent acted recklessly necessarily included a determination that the ultimate harm was foreseeable to him.

In a strict sense, an additional instruction on foreseeability would not have been cumulative because it would have related to an element of the offense not specifically covered in the instructions given. But since it is logical to assume that the jurors would have responded to an instruction on causation consistently with their determination of the issues that were comprehensively explained, it is equally logical to conclude that such an instruction would not have affected their verdict.[16]

16. In fact, it is not unlikely that a complete instruction on the causation issue would actually have been favorable to the prosecution. For example, an instruction might have been patterned after the following example given in W. LaFave & A. Scott, Criminal Law 260 (1972):

"*A*, with intent to kill *B*, only wounds *B*, leaving him lying unconscious in the unlighted road on a dark night, and then *C*, driving along the road, runs over and kills *B*. Here *C*'s act is a matter of coincidence rather than a response to what *A* has done, and thus the question is whether the subsequent events were foreseeable, as they undoubtedly were in the above illustration."

Such an instruction would probably have been more favorable to the prosecution than the instruction on recklessness which

Accordingly, we reject the suggestion that the omission of more complete instructions on the causation issue "so infected the entire trial that the resulting conviction violated due process." Even if we were to make the unlikely assumption that the jury might have reached a different verdict pursuant to an additional instruction, that possibility is too speculative to justify the conclusion that constitutional error was committed.

The judgment is reversed. 

The Model Penal Code

Section 2.03. Causal Relationship Between Conduct and Result; Divergence Between Result Designed or Contemplated and Actual Result or Between Probable and Actual Result

(1) Conduct is the cause of a result when:

(a) it is an antecedent but for which the result in question would not have occurred; and

(b) the relationship between the conduct and result satisfies any additional causal requirements imposed by the Code or by the law defining the offense.

(2) When purposely or knowingly causing a particular result is an element of an offense, the element is not established if the actual result is not within the purpose or the contemplation of the actor unless:

(a) the actual result differs from that designed or contemplated, as the case may be, only in the respect that a different person or different property is injured or affected or that the injury or harm designed or contemplated would have been more serious or more extensive than that caused; or

(b) the actual result involves the same kind of injury or harm as that designed or contemplated and is not too remote or accidental in its occurrence to have a [just] bearing on the actor's liability or on the gravity of his offense.

(3) When recklessly or negligently causing a particular result is an element of an offense, the element is not established if the actual result is not within the risk of which the actor is aware or, in the case of negligence, of which he should be aware unless:

(a) the actual result differs from the probable result only in the respect that a different person or different property is injured or

the court actually gave. In its charge, the court said: "Extreme emotional disturbance means a sudden frenzy of passion of the slayer, inflamed by some provoking cause, that naturally might be expected to carry, for the moment, a reasonable man beyond the bounds of self-control.... The indignity, charge, insult or whatever it may be that provoked the impulse or passion must be sudden, unanticipated and so gross and overpowering in its character as to wipe out or away all sane self-control, and for the time being, carry the man dominated by it beyond willpower and all reason and restraint.... Moreover, if after the provocation the blood of the man subjected to it has had time to cool, ... then extreme emotional disturbance cannot be said to have caused the [homicide]."

affected or that the probable injury or harm would have been more serious or more extensive than that caused; or

(b) the actual result involves the same kind of injury or harm as the probable result and is not too remote or accidental in its occurrence to have a [just] bearing on the actor's liability or on the gravity of his offense.

(4) When causing a particular result is a material element of an offense for which absolute liability is imposed by law, the element is not established unless the actual result is a probable consequence of the actor's conduct.

Chapter 4

THE ROLE OF MENTAL ILLNESS

A. THE CONSTITUTIONAL BACKGROUND

FORD v. WAINWRIGHT

Supreme Court of the United States, 1986.
477 U.S. 399, 106 S.Ct. 2595, 91 L.Ed.2d 335.

JUSTICE MARSHALL announced the judgment of the Court and delivered the opinion of the Court with respect to Parts I and II and an opinion in Parts III, IV and V, in which JUSTICE BRENNAN, JUSTICE BLACKMUN, and JUSTICE STEVENS join.

Alvin Bernard Ford was convicted of murder in 1974 and sentenced to death. There is no suggestion that he was incompetent at the time of his offense, at trial, or at sentencing. In early 1982, however, Ford began to manifest gradual changes in behavior. They began as an occasional peculiar idea or confused perception, but became more serious over time. After reading in the newspaper that the Ku Klux Klan had held a rally in nearby Jacksonville, Ford developed an obsession focused upon the Klan. His letters to various people reveal endless brooding about his "Klan work," and an increasingly pervasive delusion that he had become the target of a complex conspiracy, involving the Klan and assorted others, designed to force him to commit suicide. He believed that the prison guards, part of the conspiracy, had been killing people and putting the bodies in the concrete enclosures used for beds. Later, he began to believe that his women relatives were being tortured and sexually abused somewhere in the prison. This notion developed into a delusion that the people who were tormenting him at the prison had taken members of Ford's family hostage. The hostage delusion took firm hold and expanded, until Ford was reporting that 135 of his friends and family were being held hostage in the prison, and that only he could help them. * * * Counsel for Ford asked a psychiatrist who had examined Ford earlier, Dr. Amin, to continue seeing him and to recommend appropriate treatment. On the basis of roughly 14 months of evaluation, taped conversations between Ford and his attorneys, letters written by Ford, interviews with Ford's acquaintances, and various medical records,

Dr. Amin concluded in 1983 that Ford suffered from "a severe, uncontrollable, mental disease which closely resembles 'Paranoid Schizophrenia With Suicide Potential' "—a "major mental disorder ... severe enough to substantially affect Mr. Ford's present ability to assist in the defense of his life."

Ford subsequently refused to see Dr. Amin again, believing him to have joined the conspiracy against him, and Ford's counsel sought assistance from Dr. Kaufman, who interviewed Ford in November 1983. Ford told Dr. Kaufman that "I know there is some sort of death penalty, but I'm free to go whenever I want because it would be illegal and the executioner would be executed." When asked if he would be executed, Ford replied, "I can't be executed because of the landmark case. I won. Ford v. State will prevent executions all over." These statements appeared amidst long streams of seemingly unrelated thoughts in rapid succession. Dr. Kaufman concluded that Ford had no understanding of why he was being executed, made no connection between the homicide of which he had been convicted and the death penalty, and indeed sincerely believed that he would not be executed because he owned the prisons and could control the Governor through mind waves. Dr. Kaufman found that there was "no reasonable possibility that Mr. Ford was dissembling, malingering or otherwise putting on a performance...." The following month, in an interview with his attorneys, Ford regressed further into nearly complete incomprehensibility, speaking only in a code characterized by intermittent use of the word "one," making statements such as "Hands one, face one. Mafia one. God one, father one, Pope one. Pope one. Leader one."

Counsel for Ford invoked the procedures of Florida law governing the determination of competency of a condemned inmate, Fla.Stat. § 922.07 (1985). Following the procedures set forth in the statute, the Governor of Florida appointed a panel of three psychiatrists to evaluate whether Ford had "the mental capacity to understand the nature of the death penalty and the reasons why it was imposed upon him." At a single meeting, the three psychiatrists together interviewed Ford for approximately 30 minutes. Each doctor then filed a separate two or three-page report with the Governor, to whom the statute delegates the final decision. One doctor concluded that Ford suffered from "psychosis with paranoia" but had "enough cognitive functioning to understand the nature and the effects of the death penalty, and why it is to be imposed on him." Another found that, although Ford was "psychotic," he did "know fully what can happen to him." The third concluded that Ford had a "severe adaptational disorder," but did "comprehend his total situation including being sentenced to death, and all of the implications of that penalty." He believed that Ford's disorder, "although severe, seem[ed] contrived and recently learned." Thus, the interview produced three different diagnoses, but accord on the question of sanity as defined by state law.

The Governor's decision was announced on April 30, 1984, when, without explanation or statement, he signed a death warrant for Ford's execution. Ford's attorneys [thereafter brought this action in federal court seeking a writ of habeas corpus.]

II

* * * There is now little room for doubt that the Eighth Amendment's ban on cruel and unusual punishment embraces, at a minimum, those modes or acts of punishment that had been considered cruel and unusual at the time that the Bill of Rights was adopted. [Citations] * * * Moreover, the Eighth Amendment's proscriptions are not limited to those practices condemned by the common law in 1789. Not bound by the sparing humanitarian concessions of our forebears, the Amendment also recognizes the "evolving standards of decency that mark the progress of a maturing society." Trop v. Dulles, 356 U.S. 86, 101 (1958) (plurality opinion). In addition to considering the barbarous methods generally outlawed in the 18th century, therefore, this Court takes into account objective evidence of contemporary values before determining whether a particular punishment comports with the fundamental human dignity that the Amendment protects.

We begin, then, with the common law. The bar against executing a prisoner who has lost his sanity bears impressive historical credentials; the practice consistently has been branded "savage and inhuman." 4 W. Blackstone, Commentaries 24–25 (1769) (hereinafter Blackstone). Blackstone explained:

> "Idiots and lunatics are not chargeable for their own acts, if committed when under these incapacities: no, not even for treason itself. Also, if a man in his sound memory commits a capital offence, and before arraignment for it, he becomes mad, he ought not to be arraigned for it: because he is not able to plead to it with that advice and caution that he ought. And if, after he has pleaded, the prisoner becomes mad, he shall not be tried: for how can he make his defense? If, after he be tried and found guilty, he loses his senses before judgment, judgment shall not be pronounced; and if, after judgment, he becomes of nonsane memory, execution shall be stayed: for peradventure, says the humanity of the English law, had the prisoner been of sound memory, he might have alleged something in stay of judgment or execution." Ibid. (footnotes omitted).

Sir Edward Coke had earlier expressed the same view of the common law of England: "By intendment of Law the execution of the offender is for example, * * * but so it is not when a mad man is executed, but should be a miserable spectacle, both against Law, and of extreme inhumanity and cruelty, and can be no example to others." E. Coke, Third Institute 6 (6th ed. 1680) (hereinafter Coke). Other recorders of the common law concurred.

As is often true of common-law principles, the reasons for the rule are less sure and less uniform than the rule itself. One explanation is that the execution of an insane person simply offends humanity; another, that it provides no example to others and thus contributes nothing to whatever deterrence value is intended to be served by capital punishment. Other commentators postulate religious underpinnings: that it is uncharitable to dispatch an offender "into another world, when he is not of a capacity to fit himself for it." It is also said that execution serves no purpose in these cases because madness is its own punishment. More recent commentators opine that the community's quest for "retribution"—the need to offset a criminal act by a punishment of equivalent "moral quality"—is not served by execution of an insane person, which has a "lesser value" than that of the crime for which he is to be punished. Hazard & Louisell, Death, the State, and the Insane: Stay of Execution, 9 UCLA L.Rev. 381, 387 (1962). Unanimity of rationale, therefore, we do not find. "But whatever the reason of the law is, it is plain the law is so." We know of virtually no authority condoning the execution of the insane at English common law.[1] * * *

B

* * * The various reasons put forth in support of the common-law restriction have no less logical, moral, and practical force than they did when first voiced. For today, no less than before, we may seriously question the retributive value of executing a person who has no comprehension of why he has been singled out and stripped of his fundamental right to life. Similarly, the natural abhorrence civilized societies feel at killing one who has no capacity to come to grips with his own conscience or deity is still vivid today. And the intuition that such an execution simply offends humanity is evidently shared across this Nation.[2] Faced with such widespread evidence of a restriction upon sovereign power, this Court is compelled to conclude that the Eighth Amendment prohibits a State from carrying out a sentence of death upon a prisoner who is insane. Whether its aim be to protect the condemned from fear and pain without comfort of understanding, or to protect the dignity of society itself from the barbarity of exacting mindless vengeance, the restriction finds enforcement in the Eighth Amendment.

III

* * * While the underlying social values encompassed by the Eighth Amendment are rooted in historical traditions, the manner in which our judicial system protects those values is purely a matter of contemporary law. Once a substantive right or restriction is recognized in the Constitution, therefore, its enforcement is in no way confined to the rudimentary

1. At one point, Henry VIII enacted a law requiring that if a man convicted of treason fell mad, he should nevertheless be executed. This law was uniformly condemned. * * *

2. Of the 50 states, 41 have a death penalty or statutes governing execution procedures. Of those, 26 have statutes explicitly requiring the suspension of the execution of a prisoner who meets the legal test for incompetence. [Citations] Others have adopted the common-law rule by judicial decision. [Citations] Still others have more discretionary statutory procedures providing for the suspension of sentence and transfer to mental facilities for convicted prisoners who have developed mental illness. [Citations] The remaining four states having a death penalty have no specific procedure governing insanity, but have not repudiated the common-law rule.

process deemed adequate in ages past. [Condemned prisoners consequently have a right to reliable and impartial fact-finding procedures on the issue of present sanity.]

IV

The first deficiency in Florida's procedure lies in its failure to include the prisoner in the truth-seeking process. Notwithstanding this Court's longstanding pronouncement that the fundamental requisite of due process of law is the opportunity to be heard, state practice does not permit any material relevant to the ultimate decision to be submitted on behalf of the prisoner facing execution. In all other proceedings leading to the execution of an accused, we have said that the factfinder must have before it all possible relevant information about the individual defendant whose fate it must determine. And we have forbidden States to limit the capital defendant's submission of relevant evidence in mitigation of the sentence. It would be odd were we now to abandon our insistence upon unfettered presentation of relevant information, before the final fact antecedent to execution has been found. Rather, consistent with the heightened concern for fairness and accuracy that has characterized our review of the process requisite to the taking of a human life, we believe that any procedure that precludes the prisoner or his counsel from presenting material relevant to his sanity or bars consideration of that material by the factfinder is necessarily inadequate. * * *

A related flaw in the Florida procedure is the denial of any opportunity to challenge or impeach the state-appointed psychiatrists' opinions. Cross-examination of the psychiatrists, or perhaps a less formal equivalent, would contribute markedly to the process of seeking truth in sanity disputes by bringing to light the bases for each expert's beliefs, the precise factors underlying those beliefs, any history of error or caprice of the examiner, any personal bias with respect to the issue of capital punishment, the expert's degree of certainty about his or her own conclusions, and the precise meaning of ambiguous words used in the report. Without some questioning of the experts concerning their technical conclusions, a factfinder simply cannot be expected to evaluate the various opinions, particularly when they are themselves inconsistent. The failure of the Florida procedure to afford the prisoner's representative any opportunity to clarify or challenge the state experts' opinions or methods creates a significant possibility that the ultimate decision made in reliance on those experts will be distorted. * * *

Perhaps the most striking defect in the [Florida statutory procedure] is the placement of the decision wholly within the executive branch. Under this procedure, the person who appoints the experts and ultimately decides whether the State will be able to carry out the sentence that it has long sought is the Governor, whose subordinates have been responsible for initiating every stage of the prosecution of the condemned from arrest through sentencing. The commander of the State's corps of prosecutors cannot be said to have the neutrality that is necessary for reliability in the factfinding proceeding. * * *

V

* * * We do not here suggest that only a full trial on the issue of sanity will suffice to protect the federal interests; we leave to the State the task of developing appropriate ways to enforce the constitutional restriction upon its execution of sentences. It may be that some high threshold showing on behalf of the prisoner will be found a necessary means to control the number of nonmeritorious or repetitive claims of insanity. Cf. Pate v. Robinson, 383 U.S. 375 (1966) (hearing on competency to stand trial required if "sufficient doubt" of competency exists). Other legitimate pragmatic considerations may also supply the boundaries of the procedural safeguards that feasibly can be provided.

Yet the lodestar of any effort to devise a procedure must be the overriding dual imperative of providing redress for those with substantial claims and of encouraging accuracy in the factfinding determination. The stakes are high, and the "evidence" will always be imprecise. It is all the more important that the adversary presentation of relevant information be as unrestricted as possible. Also essential is that the manner of selecting and using the experts responsible for producing that "evidence" be conducive to the formation of neutral, sound, and professional judgments as to the prisoner's ability to comprehend the nature of the penalty. Fidelity to these principles is the solemn obligation of a civilized society. * * *

[The case is remanded for further proceedings consistent with this opinion.]

JUSTICE POWELL, concurring in part and concurring in the judgment.

[Justice Powell agreed that the Eighth Amendment forbids the execution of the insane, but observed that the plurality opinion did not address the meaning of "insanity" in this context.] As the Court recognizes, the ancient prohibition on execution of the insane rested on differing theories. Those theories do not provide a common answer when it comes to defining the mental awareness required by the Eighth Amendment as a prerequisite to a defendant's execution. On the one hand, some authorities contended that the prohibition against executing the insane was justified as a way of preserving the defendant's ability to make arguments on his own behalf. Other authorities suggest, however, that the prohibition derives from more straightforward humanitarian concerns. * * *

The first of these justifications has slight merit today. Modern practice provides far more extensive review of convictions and sentences than did the common law, including not only direct appeal but ordinarily both state and federal collateral review. Throughout this process, the defendant has access to counsel, by constitutional right at trial, and by employment or appointment at other stages of the process whenever the defendant raises substantial claims. [Justice Powell recited in a footnote the very extensive post-trial hearings that had been afforded to this defendant in state and federal courts on a variety of issues in the 12 years following his conviction.] * * * The more general concern of the common law—that executions of the insane are simply cruel—retains its vitality. It is as true today as when Coke lived that most men and women value the opportunity to prepare, mentally and spiritually, for their death. Moreover, today as at common law, one of the death penalty's critical justifications, its retributive force, depends on the defendant's awareness of the penalty's existence and purpose. Thus, it remains true that executions of the insane both impose a uniquely cruel penalty and are inconsistent with one of the chief purposes of executions generally. * * *

Under these circumstances, I find no sound basis for constitutionalizing the broader definition of insanity, with its requirement that the defendant be able to assist in his own defense. * * * Accordingly, I would hold that the Eighth Amendment forbids the execution only of those who are unaware of the punishment they are about to suffer and why they are to suffer it. Petitioner's claim of insanity plainly fits within this standard. * * *

[Justice Powell agreed with the plurality that the Florida procedure did not comport with constitutional due process standards, but indicated that he would not require the full-scale adversary hearing on present competency that the plurality seemed to contemplate.] * * * The State should provide an impartial officer or board that can receive evidence and argument from the prisoner's counsel, including expert psychiatric evidence that may differ from the state's own psychiatric examination. Beyond these basic requirements, the States should have substantial leeway to determine what process best balances the various interests at stake. * * *

JUSTICE O'CONNOR, with whom JUSTICE WHITE joins, concurring in the result in part and dissenting in part.

I am in full agreement with JUSTICE REHNQUIST's conclusion that the Eighth Amendment does not create a substantive right not to be executed while insane. Accordingly, I do not join the Court's reasoning or opinion. Because, however, the conclusion is for me inescapable that Florida positive law has created a protected liberty interest in avoiding execution while incompetent, and because Florida does not provide even those minimal procedural protections required by due process in this area, I would vacate the judgment and remand to the Court of Appeals with directions that the case be returned to the Florida system so that a hearing can be held in a manner consistent with the requirements of the Due Process Clause. I cannot agree, however, that the federal courts should have any role whatever in the substantive determination of a defendant's competency to be executed. * * *

JUSTICE REHNQUIST, with whom THE CHIEF JUSTICE joins, dissenting.

* * * The Court places great weight on the "impressive historical credentials" of the common-law bar against executing a prisoner who has lost his sanity. What it fails to mention, however, is the equally important and unchallenged fact that at common law it was the executive who passed upon the sanity of the condemned. So when the Court

today creates a constitutional right to a determination of sanity outside of the executive branch, it does so not in keeping with but at the expense of "our common-law heritage." * * *

Creating a constitutional right to a judicial determination of sanity before that sentence may be carried out, whether through the Eighth Amendment or the Due Process Clause, needlessly complicates and postpones still further any finality in this area of the law. The defendant has already had a full trial on the issue of guilt, and a trial on the issue of penalty; the requirement of still a third adjudication offers an invitation to those who have nothing to lose by accepting it to advance entirely spurious claims of insanity. A claim of insanity may be made at any time before sentence and, once rejected, may be raised again; a prisoner found sane two days before execution might claim to have lost his sanity the next day, thus necessitating another judicial determination of his sanity and presumably another stay of his execution. Since no State sanctions execution of the insane, the real battle being fought in this case is over what procedures must accompany the inquiry into sanity. The Court reaches the result it does by examining the common law, creating a constitutional right that no State seeks to violate, and then concluding that the common-law procedures are inadequate to protect the newly created but common-law based right. I find it unnecessary to "constitutionalize" the already uniform view that the insane should not be executed, and inappropriate to "selectively incorporate" the common-law practice. I therefore dissent.

STATE v. HERRERA

Supreme Court of Utah, 1995.
895 P.2d 359.

HOWE, JUSTICE:

* * *

[Herrera and Sweezy both pleaded not guilty by reason of insanity and filed interlocutory appeals challenging the constitutionality of Utah's statutory scheme for the defense of insanity.]

ANALYSIS

I. Background

When John Hinckley was found not guilty by reason of insanity for shooting President Ronald Reagan and Press Secretary James Brady, public outrage prompted Congress and some states to reexamine their respective insanity defense laws. As a result, in 1983, Utah abolished the traditional insanity defense in favor of a new statutory scheme. Under Utah's current scheme:

> It is a defense to a prosecution under any statute or ordinance that the defendant, as a result of mental illness, lacked the mental state required as an element of the offense charged. Mental illness is not otherwise a defense.

Utah Code Ann. § 76–2–305(1). This amendment eradicated the prior law, which allowed a defendant to present an independent affirmative defense of insanity. In other words, the former statute permitted a defendant to defend on the ground that he or she committed the act but did not understand that the act was wrong. The new law limits the defense to simply that the defendant did not have the requisite mens rea of the alleged crime.

A common example is helpful to illustrate the difference between the prior law and the new law. If A kills B, thinking that he is merely squeezing a grapefruit, A does not have the requisite mens rea for murder and would be acquitted under both the prior and the new law. However, if A kills B, thinking that B is an enemy soldier and that the killing is justified as self-defense, then A has the requisite mens rea for murder and could be convicted under the new law but not under the prior law, because he knowingly and intentionally took another's life. Under the amended provision, it does not matter whether A understood that the act was wrong. The new law does away with the traditional affirmative insanity defense that the killing was perceived to be justifiable and therefore done with innocent intent. We will refer to the amended version as the mens rea model.

II. *Legislative Responsibility*

Determining accountability for criminal acts is a serious and difficult task. Government must balance society's interests in order, protection, punishment, and deterrence with the particularly arduous responsibility of caring for the insane and mentally deficient. In formulating an insanity defense, government must carry out the demands of punishment and at the same time assure that those without guilty minds are not unjustly condemned. As one state supreme court justice observed, "In a very real sense, the confinement of the insane is the punishment of the innocent; the release of the insane is the punishment of society."

This delicate balancing of public policy is better accomplished in the legislature than in the courts. * * * "[I]t is the power and responsibility of the Legislature to enact laws to promote the public health, safety, morals and general welfare of society ... and this Court will not substitute our judgment for that of the Legislature with respect to what best serves the public interest." (Citation omitted.) This sound policy of judicial restraint applies all the more when determining the culpability of the mentally ill. " 'It is not the function of this Court to evaluate the wisdom or practical necessity of legislative enactments.' "

Even if a court finds certain legislation unreasonable or unwise, that alone does not mean it has authority to invalidate it. The law must first rise to the level of violating the constitution before it can be stricken. In this instance, our role is to make such a constitutional evaluation, not to generally critique the legislation.

* * *

III. Federal Due Process Concerns

Defendants argue that the Utah mens rea model violates federal due process because a defendant cannot "rely on insanity as a basis for nonresponsibility for the crime unless he suffers from a form of insanity which serves to negate the mens rea element of the crime." Admittedly, this amended statute limits the insanity defense to a very narrow class of extremely mentally ill defendants. Defendants maintain that since they already have the opportunity to negate the statutorily required mens rea element of a crime and since the State must prove every element beyond a reasonable doubt, the traditional affirmative defense of insanity is no longer available. Its absence, they argue, offends the basic concept of "ordered liberty" protected by the Due Process Clause. Basically, defendants see Utah's mens rea model as unconstitutional because it would allow them to be convicted even if they did not consciously know the wrongfulness of their actions. As a means to reach their desired conclusion, defendants urge us to establish a combination of the M'Naghten test and the irresistible impulse rule as a minimum requirement of federal due process. * * *

In [State v. Searcy, 118 Idaho 632, 798 P.2d 914 (1990)], the Idaho Supreme Court reviewed the state's insanity defense under both state and federal due process clauses. Defendant Searcy argued that the Idaho law unconstitutionally denied him due process of law because it prevented him from pleading insanity as a defense. The court concluded, "Neither the federal nor the state Constitution[] contains any language setting forth any such right." Searcy clarified the actual effect of limiting the insanity defense to negating mens rea. The court explained that only

> three states, Idaho, Montana and Utah, have legislatively chosen to reject mental condition as a separate specific defense to a criminal charge. The statutes in these three states, however, expressly permit evidence of mental illness or disability to be presented at trial, not in support of an independent insanity defense, but rather in order to permit the accused to rebut the state's evidence offered to prove that the defendant had the requisite criminal intent or mens rea. . . .

Id. at 917. We agree with this characterization of the current Utah mens rea model. Although Utah law does not recognize as a defense that defendants did not understand the wrongfulness of their conduct, as would be allowed under an affirmative insanity defense, it still allows them to introduce rebuttal evidence that they lacked the requisite mens rea due to their mental illness.

The United States Supreme Court has never squarely addressed whether due process demands an affirmative insanity defense; neither has that Court articulated a constitutional definition of insanity. However, what little the United States Supreme Court has said suggests that there is no federal due process right to an independent defense of insanity. In Leland v. Oregon, 343 U.S. 790, 72 S. Ct. 1002, 96 L. Ed. 1302 (1952), the United States Supreme Court upheld an Oregon statute that placed the burden of proving insanity beyond a reasonable doubt on the defendant. The Court declined to adopt any specific insanity test as a requirement under federal due process, concluding that such a holding would be unwarranted given the uncertainty in the psychiatric community, the erratic history of the insanity defense, and the fact that most jurisdictions used a "[k]nowledge of right and wrong" test.

Defendants argue that this means a state is free to choose one test over another but is not permitted under the constitution to reject all of the traditional tests and apply a mens rea model. We cannot accept such a narrow reading of *Leland*. The very thrust of the Court's holding is that the law does not demand any particular approach to the insanity defense. We read Leland to allow the states some experimentation with various approaches of dealing with the insane criminal defendant. * * *

Defendants make a historical argument that an affirmative independent insanity defense is so grounded in our legal system that its abolishment offends our fundamental principles of law and justice and therefore violates due process. * * * Many different theories have surfaced, been discarded, and resurfaced as humanity has attempted to deal with the elusive concepts of mental illness and guilt. "Not surprisingly, there has resulted a wide disparity in the position taken on this issue both by legislatures and courts in the various states."

For example, although the states have taken two basic approaches to insanity, several variations of different rules exist. A majority of states follow some form of the M'Naghten test; others have adopted variations of the Model Penal Code definition. Six states have added the "irresistible impulse" test, and three states now use the mens rea model. Never has one approach been constitutionally required or universally deemed the best. Rather, jurisdictions have developed individualized systems that best serve their own public policies. * * *

IV. State Due Process Concerns

Defendants next contend that Utah's statutory scheme violates due process under the state constitution. Utah Const. art. I, § 7 ("No person shall be deprived of life, liberty or property, without due process of law.").

Defendants provide a detailed history of how Utah has been a pioneer in the treatment of the insane and mentally ill. From its territorial days to 1983, Utah has demonstrated extraordinary compassion and insight in dealing with this class of society. * * * Throughout most of its history, Utah had one of the most liberal statutory approaches governing the culpability of those with mental illness. Because of this unique history, defendants assert that the state due process protection exceeds that of its federal counterpart, at least as far as the insanity defense is concerned. Defendants argue, therefore, that the state due process clause prohibits abolishment of the traditional affirmative insanity defense. We disagree.

Defendants' reliance upon this history is misplaced. It is one thing to demonstrate that Utah has a unique background in dealing with mental illness; it is quite another to conclude that state due process must comply with this background and that any legislation that abandons Utah's historical practices violates the constitution. The legislature is allowed to reform the penal law; it is not locked into the past. * * *

Although the legislature has limited the insanity defense, it has provided the guilty and mentally ill verdict as an option. "A judgment of guilty and mentally ill does not serve to exonerate or excuse the defendant; rather, the offender found guilty and mentally ill is held accountable for his criminal conduct, yet because of his mental illness, may need specialized treatment."

* * *

The guilty and mentally ill verdict buffers some of the harsher consequences of eliminating an independent insanity defense. It affords the trial judge discretion in determining whether one found guilty and mentally ill should receive medical attention rather than traditional incarceration. This new verdict option acknowledges that a defendant can be both guilty and mentally ill, and it aids the jury in resolving the dilemma of whether to acquit due to insanity. The verdict provides a middle ground between "guilty" and "not guilty by reason of insanity." It allows for "special disposition of mentally ill offenders to a custodial or therapeutic setting for the purpose of treating the mental illness." * * *

V. *Burden of Proof*

For defendants to be convicted, due process mandates that the prosecution prove every element of the charged crimes beyond a reasonable doubt. In re Winship, 397 U.S. 358, 364, 90 S. Ct. 1068, 25 L.Ed.2d 368 (1970). Defendants assert that the Utah insanity defense scheme unconstitutionally relieves the prosecution of this burden in violation of due process. They contend that since section 76–2–305 allows them to rely on insanity only to negate the required intent, an element of the crime, in essence they are forced to prove that they lacked the requisite mens rea rather than the prosecution proving that they possess it. If true, this would shift the burden of proof. * * *

Section 76–2–305 does not shift any burden of proof. It merely enables defendants to present evidence that rebuts the State's case against them. From beginning to end, the prosecution carries the responsibility of proving each and every element of the crime beyond a reasonable doubt. * * *

We affirm the trial courts' orders denying defendants' motions to "Declare Utah Statutory Scheme Unconstitutional," and we remand both cases for trial.

STEWART, ASSOCIATE CHIEF JUSTICE, dissenting:

* * *

Today's majority opinion and the statute it sustains represent a monumental departure from, and rejection of, one of the most fundamental principles of Anglo–American criminal law that has existed for centuries. For the first time in this state's history and, with two exceptions, for the first time in the nation's history, this Court now holds that an insane person who commits an act prohibited by the criminal law is as guilty as a sane person and may be imprisoned, and even executed, as if he were a fully responsible sane person. * * * The decision flouts centuries-old legal principles of personal responsibility that evolved from Judeo–Christian moral and ethical concepts and from an expanding knowledge of the causes of human behavior. * * *

* * *

II. Section 76–2–305(1) Abolishes the Insanity Defense

To understand the radical change wrought in the law by § 76–2–305(1), it is necessary to outline the origins of the insanity defense. Beginning in the twelfth century, as the criminal law began to move from a basis of strict liability to liability based on moral culpability, both insanity and self-defense came into English criminal law. * * * Insanity, self-defense, infancy, and other defenses based on the lack of a guilty mind became part of the substantive criminal law as defenses sometime after Bracton, but at an early date. The first recorded acquittal based on insanity was in 1505.

Evolution of the insanity defense and other exculpatory defenses from the twelfth century on was the result of the assimilation of the principles of canon law and Roman law, which helped transform the basis of the law from the blood feud and vengeance to principles based on moral blameworthiness. The concept of "mens rea" or the "guilty mind" or "wrongful intent" became an essential element of a crime. Whether stated as malice aforethought, premeditation, malice pretense, guilty mind, or wrongful intent, the guilty mind concept meant more than a simple volitional or intentional act. It included the element of wrongness or malice and required a degree of moral blameworthiness, and that required the capacity for rational conduct. It included a concept of "moral blameworthiness ... predicated on the presumption of sanity."

* * * The traditional mens rea element of *wrongful* intent is, in effect, surmised on the basis that a person is charged with knowledge of the law and that one knows the inherent moral wrongfulness of malum in se crimes.

With the enactment of § 76–2–305, the Legislature abolished a defendant's right to rebut this presumption by proving insanity.

* * *

As to crimes requiring intent, an insane person will virtually always have the mental state required by the law under § 76–2–305(1), even though the defendant suffers from severe mental derangement, such as an extreme and bizarre psychotic delusion. * * *

III. Due Process

Under the due process clauses of the Fourteenth Amendment to the Constitution of the United States and of article I, section 7 of the Utah Constitution, government may not deny a person life or liberty except on principles "consistent with the fundamental principles of liberty and justice which lie at the base of all our civil and political institutions." The due process clauses protect those principles that are "implicit in the concept of ordered liberty" and without which "a fair and enlightened system of justice would be impossible."

The majority dismissively rejects the "historical argument that an affirmative independent insanity defense is so grounded in our legal system that its abolition offends our fundamental principles of law and justice and therefore violates due process." The majority argues that over the centuries, insanity has been dealt with procedurally and substantively in different ways. In truth, however, the majority simply fails to come to grips with the undisputed core fact that for centuries, the law has recognized that insanity absolves a human being of criminal responsibility for his acts, just as infancy and self-defense do. Of course, the insanity defense has evolved as moral and ethical sensitives have increased on the basis of increased scientific knowledge, but that does not alter the core fact that insanity has been a defense for centuries. * * *

In sum, for centuries the concept of moral blameworthiness has been the foundation of the criminal law and that concept is essential to the law's legitimacy and its moral authority in a free society today. The criminal law represents the conscience of society. In declaring what is unlawful, it also declares what society deems to be morally abhorrent. If the criminal law does not serve that purpose but is used only as an instrument of social control not based on moral values, society's sense of right and wrong will surely dissipate even further, and the criminal law will eventually earn the scorn and disgust of society.

The concept of criminal responsibility based on moral blameworthiness is indispensable to the fair and just treatment of persons whose cognitive impairments render them unable to perceive and react to the real world as normal people. Punishing those who suffer from such impairments serves none of the recognized penal objectives. Society has ample means other than the criminal law for protecting itself from those whose insanity makes them dangerous. Although the definition of insanity has varied over the centuries, the core principle that a civilized society does not punish insane people has not. That principle is one of those essential principles of fundamental fairness without which a "fair and enlightened system of justice would be impossible." * * *

I would hold Utah Code Ann. § 76–2–305 unconstitutional and reinstate the prior statute governing insanity in criminal cases until the Legislature decides to modify that standard.

[The dissenting opinion by Justice Durham is omitted.]

Note

Insanity may be an important issue at three different stages of the criminal process. The "insanity defense" itself relates to the defendant's sanity at the time of the commission of the criminal act, and the law relating to this defense is the subject of the materials in the section following this Note. Most jurisdictions recognize some form of the insanity defense, but as the majority held in *Herrera*, it is doubtful that they are constitutionally obligated to do so. The most frequently cited authority for the proposition that it is unconstitutional to punish a person who was insane at the time of the criminal act is an old Washington state case, State v. Strasburg, 60 Wash. 106, 110 P. 1020 (1910). The Supreme Court decision nearest in point (aside from Ford v. Wainwright, supra) is Leland v. Oregon, 343 U.S. 790 (1952) (State may require defendant to prove his own insanity beyond a reasonable doubt).

Second, a convicted person (who necessarily must have been sane at the time of the crime to be convicted) may not be put to death if he becomes insane. The state may, however, provide psychiatric treatment and then may carry out the sentence after the treatment has been successful. This doctrine was somewhat easier to understand in the context of a society dominated by religious assumptions, where it was considered of crucial importance that the condemned person be capable of repenting and receiving absolution before going before the judgment of God. When a society turns to philosophically materialistic and utilitarian notions of punishment, the reason for exempting the insane from execution is not as easy to see. If the death penalty is simply a means of getting rid of thoroughly unwanted criminals, or of giving expression to barbaric and cruel impulses to take vengeance upon murderers (as persons who oppose the death penalty frequently assert), then it is not obvious why the presently insane are not as unwanted or as appropriate targets of barbaric vengeance as other murderers. Justices who consider it equally unconstitutional to carry out the death sentence upon the sane and the insane can nonetheless rely upon tradition to justify that at least the insane are constitutionally protected.

Finally, an accused who is not presently sane may not be put on trial at all. Sanity for this purpose is defined as having the capacity to understand the charges and to cooperate with counsel in presenting a defense. The Supreme Court stated in one case that "conviction of an accused person while he is legally incompetent violates due process." Pate v. Robinson, 383 U.S. 375 (1966). Ordinarily, a finding of incapacity to stand trial results only in a continuance for a few weeks of treatment, after which the trial proceeds. If the insanity is permanent, civil commitment procedures are ordinarily available to permit the accused to be confined indefinitely in a secure mental institution. Since the commitment order is usually based upon a finding that the defendant is dangerous because he committed the crime for which he cannot be tried, the accused is in effect convicted without the safeguards of criminal due process. Moreover, the incompetent defendant may be indefinitely confined by civil commitment even when the alleged crime is a minor one for which only a short sentence would be appropriate. See Jackson v. Indiana, 406 U.S. 715 (1972).

Problems have also been encountered in a very small number of cases where the accused is incompetent but not insane. For example, a mentally retarded, illiterate deaf-mute was charged in Illinois with murder. He was apparently permanently incapable of understanding the charge or cooperating with counsel, but the civil insanity commitment statute did not appear to be applicable because he was not "insane." See Illinois v. Lang, 76 Ill.2d 311, 29 Ill.Dec. 87, 391 N.E.2d 350 (1979) (where the court judicially extended the scope of the commitment statute rather than release the incompetent defendant outright). Two distinguished legal scholars have proposed that the best way to handle such (fortunately rare) cases is to proceed with the criminal trial despite the defendant's incompetence under special procedural safeguards. See Burt and Morris, "A Proposal for Abolition of the Incompetency Plea," 40 U. Chi. L. Rev. 66 (1972).

The treatment of defendants who are incompetent to stand trial, as well as those who claim insanity at the time of the act, is currently governed in federal cases by the provisions of the Insanity Defense Reform Act of 1984. The statutory provisions are reprinted in the next section of this chapter.

B. THE INSANITY DEFENSE

UNITED STATES v. FREEMAN

United States Court of Appeals, Second Circuit, 1966.
357 F.2d 606.

KAUFMAN, CIRCUIT JUDGE:

As legislation proliferates and judicial decisions multiply, our criminal law daily takes on increased complexity and sophistication. Subtle distinctions are constantly drawn; more perfect refinements continue to evolve. At the same time, however, there are a small number of more basic questions which cut across the whole of this evolutionary process, questions so fundamental to the very notion of criminal justice that they must continue to be asked—and, insofar as possible, answered—if the criminal law is truly to reflect the moral sense of the community. This appeal poses one of those questions.

After a trial before Judge Tenney without a jury, Charles Freeman was found guilty on two counts of selling narcotics and sentenced to concurrent terms of five years on each count. Although Freeman denied commission of the substantive offense, his principal allegation at trial was that, at the time of the alleged sale of narcotics, he did not possess sufficient capacity and will to be held responsible for the criminality of his acts.[1]

In rejecting this contention, the District Court understandably relied upon the familiar M'Naghten Rules which, in their traditional formula-

1. The omission from this opinion of the phrases "criminal insanity" and "criminally insane" is deliberate. Psychiatrists generally agree that the terms are meaningless for medical purposes, and, as will be seen infra, they are sufficiently ambiguous and misleading to warrant rejection by the law as well.

tion, permit acquittal only when it is proved that, "at the time of the committing of the act, the party accused was laboring under such a defect of reason, from disease of the mind as not to know the nature and quality of the act he was doing, or, if he did know it, that he did not know he was doing what was wrong." 10 Clark and Fin. 200, 210 (1843). Since he could not find that Freeman's condition satisfied the rigid requirements of this test, Judge Tenney had no alternative but to hold the defendant guilty as charged. * * *

The Defense of Lack of Responsibility

As is not uncommon in cases in which the defense is raised, the bulk of the evidence directly relating to the issue of criminal responsibility took the form of expert psychiatric testimony of witnesses called by both the government and the defense. Freeman's expert witness at trial was Dr. Herman Denber, Associate Professor of Clinical Psychiatry at New York Medical College and Director of Psychiatric Research at Manhattan State Hospital. Dr. Denber, who had examined the defendant on the previous afternoon, testified that Freeman was not only a narcotics addict, but also a confirmed alcoholic. The Doctor noted that Freeman's body had become accustomed to the consumption of large amounts of heroin over a fourteen-year period, and that the defendant was in the habit of drinking one or two bottles of wine daily to increase the potency of the narcotics. In addition, he observed, Freeman regularly imbibed six to nine "shots" of whiskey each day.

Describing his examination in some detail, Dr. Denber testified that Freeman displayed no depth or variation in his emotional reactions, spoke in a flat monotone and paused for excessively long periods before responding to questions. Dr. Denber also noted that as a result of taking impure narcotics for so long a time, Freeman suffered from frequent episodes of toxic psychosis leading to a clouding of the sensorium (inability to know what one is doing or where one is) as well as delusions, hallucinations, epileptic convulsions and, at times, amnesia. The witness testified, moreover, that Freeman had suffered "knock-outs" on three occasions while engaging in prize fighting, and that these had led to a general vagueness about details. Finally, Dr. Denber observed that Freeman had experienced "innumerable brain traumata" which produced such organic and structural changes as destroyed brain tissue.

Restricted to stating a conclusory opinion within the confines of M'Naghten, Dr. Denber initially averred that Freeman was incapable of knowing right from wrong, even under a strict interpretation of that limited test. However, upon amplifying this conclusion, the defense expert acknowledged that Freeman had an awareness of what he was doing on the nights of June 24 and August 1 in the sense that he possessed cognition that he was selling heroin. The Doctor also added that Freeman was not in "such a state of toxicity that he did not remember the dates. He told me the story [of the narcotics transactions] clearly, but it is my feeling about him, in particular, that as far as the social implications or the nature or meaning of what this meant to him at that moment he was not aware of it."

To respond to Dr. Denber's testimony, the government called on Dr. Robert S. Carson, a former staff physician at Payne–Whitney Clinic of The New York Hospital and Clinical Instructor in Psychiatry at Cornell University. Dr. Carson testified that Freeman was able to distinguish between right and wrong within the meaning of the M'Naghten test despite his heavy use of narcotics and alcohol. He noted that Freeman possessed the capacity to enter into purposeful activity such as the sale of narcotics, and he expressed the opinion that the defendant had been aware of the wrongfulness of his acts. In support of this view, Dr. Carson pointed to the fact that on the evening of August 1, 1963, Freeman had been sufficiently fearful of being apprehended that he had suggested that the transfer of narcotics take place in the privacy of the men's room of Marvin's Bar. In summary, Dr. Carson significantly acknowledged that Freeman had "some limitations" on his ability to distinguish right from wrong, but not to the degree required by the M'Naghten test. * * *

* * * We are now concerned with whether the Court at trial should have applied a test less rigid than that provided by M'Naghten,[11] so that the essential examination and psychiatric testimony could have been directed towards Freeman's capacity to exercise will or appreciate the wrongfulness of his conduct, rather than being confined to the relatively narrow inquiry required by M'Naghten. * * *

III

M'Naghten and its antecedents can, in many respects, be seen as examples of the law's conscientious efforts to place in a separate category, people who cannot be justly held "responsible" for their acts. As far back as 1582, William Lambard of Lincolns' Inn set forth what can be viewed as the forerunner of the M'Naghten test as we know it: "If a man or a natural fool, or a lunatic in the time of his lunacy, or a child who apparently has no knowledge of good or evil do kill a man, this is no felonious act * * * for they cannot be said to have any understanding will." By 1724, the language had shifted from "good or evil" to the more familiar emphasis on the word "know." Thus, in Rex v. Arnold, 16 How.St.Tr. 695, 764 the "Wild Beast" test was enunciated. It provided for exculpation if the defendant "doth not *know* what he is doing, no more than * * * a wild beast." (Emphasis added.)

11. At sentencing the Court recommended that the defendant be given a thorough physical and psychiatric examination for the purpose of determining which institution, the United States Public Health Service Hospital, Lexington, Kentucky, or the Medical Center for Federal Prisoners, Springfield, Missouri, would be more beneficial for him. This latitude which the trial judge had at the time of sentencing was unavailable, he believed, at the trial in assessing Freeman's criminal responsibility because of the restrictive M'Naghten Rules. The trial judge explained to Freeman at the sentencing, "the defense witness [Dr. Denber] testified that [you] did know the nature and quality of [your] acts but [you] did not appreciate the extremely bad social consequences [your] acts could have, and I believe under the rules we have here that of itself is insufficient to indicate the defense of insanity."

By modern scientific standards the language of these early tests is primitive. In the 18th Century, psychiatry had hardly become a profession, let alone a science. Thus, these tests and their progeny were evolved at a time when psychiatry was literally in the Dark Ages.

In the pre-M'Naghten period, the concepts of phrenology and monomania were being developed and had significant influence on the right and wrong test. Phrenologists believed that the human brain was divided into thirty-five separate areas, each with its own peculiar mental function. The sixth area, for example, was designated "destructiveness." It was located, we are told, above the ear because this was the widest part of the skull of carnivorous animals. Monomania, on the other hand, was a state of mind in which one insane idea predominated while the rest of the thinking processes remained normal.

Of course, both phrenology and monomania are rejected today as meaningless medical concepts since the human personality is viewed as a fully integrated system. But, by an accident of history, the rule of M'Naghten's case froze these concepts into the common law just at a time when they were becoming obsolete. A discussion of M'Naghten's case will demonstrate how this came about. Daniel M'Naghten suffered from what now would be described as delusions of persecution. Apparently, he considered his major persecutor to be Robert Peel, then Prime Minister of England, for M'Naghten came to London with the intention of assassinating the chief of the Queen's government. His plan would have succeeded but for the fact that Peel chose to ride in Queen Victoria's carriage because of her absence from the city, while Drummond, his secretary, rode in the vehicle which normally would have been occupied by Peel. M'Naghten, believing that the Prime Minister was riding in his own carriage, shot and killed Drummond in error.

After a lengthy trial in 1843, M'Naghten was found "not guilty by reason of insanity." M'Naghten's exculpation from criminal responsibility was most significant for several reasons. His defense counsel had relied in part upon Dr. Isaac Ray's historic work, Medical Jurisprudence of Insanity which had been published in 1838. This book, which was used and referred to extensively at the trial, contained many enlightened views on the subject of criminal responsibility in general and on the weaknesses of the right and wrong test in particular. Thus, for example, the jury was told that the human mind is not compartmentalized and that a defect in one aspect of the personality could spill over and affect other areas. As Chief Judge Biggs tells us in his Isaac Ray lectures compiled in The Guilty Mind, the court was so impressed with this and other medical evidence of M'Naghten's incompetency that Lord Chief Justice Tindal practically directed a verdict for the accused.

For these reasons, M'Naghten's case could have been the turning point for a new approach to more modern methods of determining criminal responsibility. But the Queen's ire was raised by the acquittal and she was prompted to intervene. Mid-19th Century England was in a state of social upheaval and there had been three attempts on the life of the Queen and one on the Prince Consort. Indeed, Queen Victoria was so concerned about M'Naghten's acquittal that she summoned the House of Lords to "take the opinion of the Judges on the law governing such cases." Consequently, the fifteen judges of the common law courts were called in a somewhat extraordinary session under a not too subtle atmosphere of pressure to answer five prolix and obtuse questions on the status of criminal responsibility in England. Significantly, it was Lord Chief Justice Tindal who responded for fourteen of the fifteen judges, and thus articulated what has come to be known as the M'Naghten Rules or M'Naghten test. Rather than relying on Dr. Ray's monumental work which had apparently impressed him at M'Naghten's trial, Tindal, with the Queen's breath upon him, reaffirmed the old restricted right-wrong test despite its 16th Century roots and the fact that it, in effect, echoed such uninformed concepts as phrenology and monomania. In this manner, Dr. Ray's insights were to be lost to the common law for over one hundred years except in the small state of New Hampshire.[31]

* * *

But the principal objection to M'Naghten is not that it was arrived at by this extraordinary process. Rather, the rule is faulted because it has several serious deficiencies which stem in the main from its narrow scope. Because M'Naghten focuses only on the cognitive aspect of the personality, i.e., the ability to know right from wrong, we are told by eminent medical scholars that it does not permit the jury to identify those who can distinguish between good and evil but who cannot control their behavior. The result is that instead of being treated at appropriate mental institutions[35] for a sufficiently long period to bring about a cure or sufficient improvement so that the accused may return with relative safety to himself and the community, he is ordinarily sentenced to a prison term as if criminally responsible and then released as a potential recidivist with society at his mercy. To the extent that these individuals continue to be released from prison because of the narrow scope of M'Naghten, that test poses a serious danger to society's welfare.

Similarly, M'Naghten's single track emphasis on the cognitive aspect of the personality recognizes no degrees of incapacity. Either the defendant knows right from wrong or he does not and that is the only choice the jury is given. But such a test is grossly unrealistic; our mental institutions, as any qualified psychiatrist will attest, are filled with people who to some extent can differentiate between right and wrong,

31. Because of the influence of Dr. Ray, New Hampshire adopted a test which was a precursor of the modern *Durham* rule. See State v. Pike, 49 N.H. 399 (1870). See also, Reid, "Understanding the New Hampshire Doctrine of Criminal Insanity," 69 Yale L.Jour. 366 (1960); and Reid, "The Companion of the New Hampshire Doctrine of Criminal Insanity," 15 Vanderbilt L. Rev. 721 (1962).

35. We recognize our inability to determine at this point whether society possesses sufficient hospital facilities and doctors to deal with criminals who are found to be incompetent. But our function as judges requires us to interpret the law in the best interest of society as a whole. We therefore suggest that if there are inadequate facilities and personnel in this area, Congress, the state legislatures and federal and state executive departments should promptly consider bridging the gap.

but lack the capacity to control their acts to a substantial degree. As the commentary to the American Law Institute's Model Penal Code observes, "The law must recognize that when there is no black and white it must content itself with different shades of gray."

A further fatal defect of the M'Naghten Rules stems from the unrealistically tight shackles which they place upon expert psychiatric testimony. When the law limits a testifying psychiatrist to stating his opinion whether the accused is capable of knowing right from wrong, the expert is thereby compelled to test guilt or innocence by a concept which bears little relationship to reality. He is required thus to consider one aspect of the mind as a "logic-tight compartment in which the delusion holds sway leaving the balance of the mind intact. * * * "

Prominent psychiatrists have expressed their frustration when confronted with such requirements. Echoing such complaints, Edward de Grazia has asked, "How [does one] translate 'psychosis' or 'psychopathy' or 'dementia praecox' or even 'sociopathy' or 'mental disorder' or 'neurotic character disorder' or 'mental illness' into a psychiatric judgment of whether the accused knew 'right' from 'wrong.' " In stronger and more vivid terms, Dr. Lawrence Kolb, Director of the New York Psychiatric Institute, Professor and Chairman of the Department of Psychiatry at Columbia University and Director of the Psychiatric Service at Presbyterian Hospital, expressed a similar viewpoint when he declared that "answers supplied by a psychiatrist in regard to questions of rightness or wrongness of an act or 'knowing' its nature constitute a professional perjury."

Psychiatrists are not alone in their recognition of the unreality of M'Naghten. As long ago as 1930, Mr. Justice Cardozo observed that "everyone contends that the present definition of insanity has little relation to the truths of mental life." And Mr. Justice Frankfurter, as a witness before the Royal Commission on Capital Punishment, declared with his usual fervor: "I do not see why the rules of law should be arrested at the state of psychological knowledge of the time when they were formulated. * * * I think the M'Naghten Rules are in large measure shams. That is a very strong word, but I think the M'Naghten Rules are very difficult for conscientious people and not difficult enough for people who say, 'We'll just juggle them.' "

The tremendous growth of psychiatric knowledge since the Victorian origins of M'Naghten and even the near-universal disdain in which it is held by present-day psychiatrists are not by themselves sufficient reasons for abandoning the test. At bottom, the determination whether a man is or is not held responsible for his conduct is not a medical but a legal, social or moral judgment. Ideally, psychiatrists—much like experts in other fields—should provide grist for the legal mill, should furnish the raw data upon which the legal judgment is based. It is the psychiatrist who informs as to the mental state of the accused—his characteristics, his potentialities, his capabilities. But once this information is disclosed, it is society as a whole, represented by judge or jury, which decides whether a man with the characteristics described should or should not be held accountable for his acts. In so deciding, it cannot be presumed that juries will check their common sense at the courtroom door. As Professor Wechsler has rightly commented, "It's not to be expected that juries will lightly accept the proposition that one who seemingly knew in a true sense did not know. One would expect jury skepticism and the system is the healthier for that jury skepticism."

The true vice of M'Naghten is not, therefore, that psychiatrists will feel constricted in artificially structuring their testimony but rather that the ultimate deciders—the judge or the jury—will be deprived of information vital to their final judgment. For whatever the social climate of Victorian England, today's complex and sophisticated society will not be satisfied with simplistic decisions, based solely upon a man's ability to "know" right from wrong. It is in this respect that the vast strides made in public awareness and acceptance of psychiatry and psychiatric methods may even be more significant than the scientific developments which gave rise to them. Few areas of modern American culture—from the personnel offices of our giant corporations to the pages of our mass-circulation magazines—have been untouched by the psychiatric revolution. In this setting, a test which depends vitally on notions already discredited when M'Naghten was adopted can no longer be blandly accepted as representing the "moral sense of the community." To continue to apply such medically discarded concepts would be to follow a negative approach which is the result of a holdover of long outmoded attitudes rather than a policy decision grounded in reason or science.

IV

Efforts to supplement or replace the M'Naghten Rules with a more meaningful and workable test have persisted for generations, with varying degrees of success. Perhaps the first to receive judicial approval, however, was more an added fillip to M'Naghten than a true substitute: the doctrine which permits acquittal on grounds of lack of responsibility when a defendant is found to have been driven by an "irresistible impulse" to commit his offense. In one form or another, the "irresistible impulse" test has become encrusted on the law of several jurisdictions, including the District Courts of this Circuit, and is now a familiar part of the vocabulary of millions since it was successfully invoked by the defendant of Robert Travers' celebrated novel and motion picture, "Anatomy of a Murder."

As it has commonly been employed, however, we find the "irresistible impulse" test to be inherently inadequate and unsatisfactory. Psychiatrists have long questioned whether "irresistible impulses" actually exist; the more basic legal objection to the term "irresistible impulse" is that it is too narrow and carries the misleading implication that a crime impulsively committed must have been perpetrated in a sudden and explosive fit. Thus, the "irresistible impulse" test is unduly restrictive because it excludes the far more numerous instances of crimes committed after excessive brooding and melancholy by one who is unable to resist sustained psychic compulsion or to make any real attempt to control his conduct. In seeking one isolated and indefinite cause for every act, moreover, the test is unhappily evocative of the notions which underlay M'Naghten-unfortunate assumptions that the problem can be viewed in black and white absolutes and in crystal-clear causative terms.

In so many instances the criminal act may be the reverse of impulsive; it may be coolly and carefully prepared yet nevertheless the result of a diseased mind. The "irresistible impulse" test is therefore little more than a gloss on M'Naghten, rather than a fundamentally new approach to the problem of criminal responsibility. It is, as one professor explained, "a relatively unobnoxious attempt to improve upon M'Naghten."

With the exception of New Hampshire, American courts waited until 1954 and Judge Bazelon's opinion for the District of Columbia Circuit in Durham v. United States,[48] for legal recognition that disease or defect of the mind may impair the whole mind and not a subdivided portion of it. The *Durham* court swept away the intellectual debris of a century and articulated a test which was as simple in its formulation as its sources were complex. A defendant is not criminally responsible, wrote Judge Bazelon, "if his unlawful act was the product of mental disease or mental defect."

The advantages of *Durham* were apparent and its arrival was widely hailed. The new test entirely eliminated the "right-wrong" dichotomy, and hence interred the overriding emphasis on the cognitive element of the personality which had for so long plagued M'Naghten. The fetters upon expert testimony were removed and psychiatrists were permitted and indeed encouraged to provide all relevant medical information for the common sense application of judge or jury.

Finally, *Durham* ended to a large degree the "professional perjury" decried by psychiatrists—the "juggling" of legal standards made inevitable by M'Naghten and rightly deplored by Justice Frankfurter. Too often, the unrealistic dogma of M'Naghten had compelled expert witnesses to "stretch" its requirements to "hard cases"; sympathetic to the plight of a defendant who was not, in fairness, responsible for his conduct, psychiatrists had found it necessary to testify that the accused did not know his act was "wrong" even when the defendant's words belied this conclusion. In its frank and express recognition that criminality resulting from mental disease or defect should not bring forth penal sanctions, *Durham* brought an end to this all too-frequent practice of "winking" at legal requirements, a practice which had contributed little to the self-respect and integrity of either medicine or the law.

In the aftermath of *Durham*, however, many students of the law recognized that the new rule, despite its many advantages, also possessed serious deficiencies. It has been suggested, for example, that *Durham's* insistence that an offense be the "product" of a mental disease or defect raised near-impossible problems of causation, closely

48. Durham v. United States, 214 F.2d 862 (D.C.Cir.1954).

resembling those encountered by the M'Naghten and irresistible impulse tests.

The most significant criticism of *Durham*, however, is that it fails to give the fact-finder any standard by which to measure the competency of the accused. As a result, psychiatrists when testifying that a defendant suffered from a "mental disease or defect" in effect usurped the jury's function. This problem was strikingly illustrated in 1957, when a staff conference at Washington's St. Elizabeth's Hospital reversed its previous determination and reclassified "psychopathic personality" as a "mental disease." Because this single hospital provides most of the psychiatric witnesses in the District of Columbia courts, juries were abruptly informed that certain defendants who had previously been considered responsible were now to be acquitted. Blocker v. United States, 110 U.S.App.D.C. 41, 288 F.2d 853, 860 (1961) (Burger, J., concurring). It seems clear that a test which permits all to stand or fall upon the labels or classifications employed by testifying psychiatrists hardly affords the court the opportunity to perform its function of rendering an independent legal and social judgment.[51]

V

In 1953, a year before *Durham*, the American Law Institute commenced an exhaustive study of criminal conduct including the problem of criminal responsibility. In the ensuing months and years, under the scholarly direction of Professors Herbert Wechsler of Columbia University, its Chief Reporter, and Louis B. Schwartz of the University of Pennsylvania, Co–Reporter, the leading legal and medical minds of the country applied themselves to the task. Gradually and painstakingly a new definition of criminal responsibility began taking shape as Section 4.01 of the Model Penal Code was evolved. Before its penultimate articulation, drafts and redrafts of the section were submitted to and revised by an advisory committee comprised of distinguished judges, lawyers, psychiatrists, and penologists. After committee approval was obtained, successive drafts were debated and considered by the Council, and later by the full membership, of the Institute. Nine long years of research, exploration and consideration culminated in the definitive version of Section 4.01, which was finally adopted by the Institute in 1962.

Section 4.01 provides that "A person is not responsible for criminal conduct if at the time of such conduct as a result of mental disease or defect he lacks substantial capacity either to appreciate the wrongfulness

51. To correct many of the deficiencies of *Durham*, the Washington, D.C. Court of Appeals amplified its definition of mental disorder for the purpose of making "it very clear that neither the court nor the jury is bound by ad hoc definitions or conclusions as to what experts state is a disease or defect." To reinforce its decision, the Court redefined mental disease and defect to include "any abnormal condition of the mind which *substantially* affects mental or emotional processes and *substantially* impairs behavior controls." McDonald v. United States, 114 U.S.App.D.C. 120, 312 F.2d 847, 851 (1962) (Emphasis added). It thus adopted a formulation which closely approximates the recommendation of the American Law Institute in its Model Penal Code. See infra.

of his conduct or to conform his conduct to the requirements of law."[52] For reasons which will be more fully set forth, we believe this test to be the soundest yet formulated and we accordingly adopt it as the standard of criminal responsibility in the Courts of this Circuit.

The gravamen of the objections to the M'Naghten Rules is that they are not in harmony with modern medical science which, as we have said, is opposed to any concept which divides the mind into separate compartments—the intellect, the emotions and the will. The Model Penal Code formulation views the mind as a unified entity and recognizes that mental disease or defect may impair its functioning in numerous ways. The rule, moreover, reflects awareness that from the perspective of psychiatry absolutes are ephemeral and gradations are inevitable. By employing the telling word "substantial" to modify "incapacity," the rule emphasizes that "any" incapacity is not sufficient to justify avoidance of criminal responsibility but that "total" incapacity is also unnecessary. The choice of the word "appreciate," rather than "know" in the first branch of the test also is significant; mere intellectual awareness that conduct is wrongful, when divorced from appreciation or understanding of the moral or legal import of behavior, can have little significance. * * *

We believe, in sum, that the American Law Institute test—which makes no pretension at being the ultimate in faultless definition—is an infinite improvement over the M'Naghten Rules, even when, as had been the practice in the courts of this Circuit, those Rules are supplemented by the "irresistible impulse" doctrine. All legal definitions involve elements of abstraction and approximation which are difficult to apply in marginal cases. The impossibility of guaranteeing that a new rule will always be infallible cannot justify continued adherence to an outmoded standard, sorely at variance with enlightened medical and legal scholarship. No one would suggest that a physician-expert called to state an opinion with respect to a litigant's orthopedic or neurological condition should be restricted in his reply to a single isolated cause to the exclusion of other relevant and important findings and conclusions—much less to concepts developed at the outset of Victoria's reign. In a criminal trial, when life and liberty hang in the balance, such arbitrary limitations on expert and jury are all the less defensible.

The genius of the common law has been its responsiveness to changing times, its ability to reflect developing moral and social values. Drawing upon the past, the law must serve—and traditionally has served—the needs of the present. In the past century, psychiatry has evolved from tentative, hesitant gropings in the dark of human ignorance to a recognized and important branch of modern medicine. The

52. American Law Institute, Model Penal Code (final draft) (1962).

We have adopted the word "wrongfulness" in Section 4.01 as the American Law Institute's suggested alternative to "criminality" because we wish to include the case where the perpetrator appreciates that his conduct is criminal, but, because of a delusion, believes it to be morally justified. See People v. Schmidt, 216 N.Y. 324, 110 N.E. 945 (1916) (Cardozo, J.).

outrage of a frightened Queen has for too long caused us to forego the expert guidance that modern psychiatry is able to provide.[53]

VI

Since Freeman's responsibility was determined under the rigid standards of the M'Naghten Rules, we are compelled to reverse his conviction and remand the case for a new trial in which the criteria employed will be those provided by Section 4.01 of the Model Penal Code.

And lest our opinion be misunderstood or distorted, some additional discussion is in order. First, we wish to make it absolutely clear that mere recidivism or narcotics addiction will not *of themselves* justify acquittal under the American Law Institute standards which we adopt today. Indeed, the second clause of Section 4.01 explicitly states that "the terms 'mental disease or defect' do not include an abnormality manifested only by repeated criminal or otherwise anti-social conduct." We approve and adopt this important caveat. * * *

Secondly, in order to avoid any misapprehension as to the thrust of our opinion some mention should be made of the treatment to be afforded individuals found to lack criminal responsibility under the test we adopt. There is no question but that the security of the community must be the paramount interest. Society withholds criminal sanctions in cases of incompetence out of a sense of compassion and understanding. It would be obviously intolerable if those suffering from a mental disease or defect of such a nature as to relieve them from criminal responsibility were to be set free to continue to pose a threat to life and property.

A verdict of "not guilty by reason of incompetency" has, in the past, been equivalent in the federal judicial system to a simple "not guilty" verdict because of the existing void in provisions for commitment and treatment. As a result of the comparatively recent adoption by various federal courts of more enlightened tests of responsibility, we trust that Congress will explore its power to authorize commitment of those acquitted on these grounds. Such was the result of *Durham* in the District of Columbia; shortly after that decision, Congress provided for mandatory post-trial commitment in all cases in the District resulting in

53. We note that while the Model Penal Code permits, and, indeed, encourages the production of full psychiatric data and information at trial, such testimony can have weight only if the underlying examination of the defendant was thorough. In most instances, one hour of psychiatric examination of the defendant in the House of Detention in preparation for trial is not an adequate substitute for a complete psychiatric and neurological work-up of the defendant in a hospital under the care and guidance of a staff of experts.

Moreover, as we have indicated, for many years psychiatrists have urged, almost with one voice, the replacement of the M'Naghten rule. Their persuasive advocacy of change is now meeting with gradual success, as modern psychiatric theories of normal and deviant personality development and functioning have gained increasing acceptance. It is desirable, therefore, that the altered standard for criminal responsibility which has been adopted today should not become the *causa sine qua non* of unseemly contests between psychiatric experts. We may anticipate a weakening of public confidence in the value of psychiatric concepts and a reaction against them if this should result.

acquittals on grounds of lack of responsibility. Pending Congressional action, however, we are confident that the several states will continue to step into the breach as they have in the past. Accordingly, we suggest that those adjudged criminally irresponsible promptly be turned over to state officials for commitment pursuant to state procedures.

Effective procedures for institutionalization and treatment of the criminally irresponsible are vital as an implementation to today's decision. Throughout our opinion, we have not viewed the choice as one between imprisonment and immediate release. Rather, we believe the true choice to be between different forms of institutionalization—between the prison and the mental hospital. Underlying today's decision is our belief that treatment of the truly incompetent in mental institutions would better serve the interests of society as well as the defendant's. * * *

WATERMAN, CIRCUIT JUDGE (concurring in the result):

Though it is a bit difficult to cast aside the belief that one who plans to perform certain acts and does them according to plan should be held responsible for his conduct, I realize that that belief is out of style these days, and that modernists hold that one's will may be so meaninglessly exerted as not to have any causal relationship to conduct.

Therefore, I am happy to concur with my colleagues in promulgating for the time being the standard of responsibility for one's conduct that is set forth in the American Law Institute's May 4, 1962 Official Draft of its Proposed Model Penal Code. * * *

I say "for the time being," for though we now have been persuaded that we should be dissatisfied with the M'Naghten Rules because of the discoveries which, whether for good or ill, have in the six score years since M'Naghten changed our concepts of "mental disease," it is nevertheless also true that the scope of serious expert inquiry into the control of conduct has not halted, and tomorrow we may find that Section 4.01 needs further judicial emendation in the light of tomorrow's further discoveries.

Note

Judge Waterman was prescient.

For over a century, the dominant test of legal insanity in the United States was that set out by the English judges in Daniel M'Naghten's case in 1843. The "M'Naghten Rule" or "right-wrong test" allowed the defense only where it could be "clearly proved that, at the time of the committing of the act, the party accused was laboring under such a defect of reason, from disease of the mind, as not to know the nature and quality of the act he was doing; or if he did know it, that he did not know he was doing what was wrong." Some jurisdictions supplemented this "knowledge of wrongfulness" concept with an additional "irresistible impulse" test, which in extreme cases allowed the jury to acquit a defendant whose act resulted from a sudden and overpowering impulse.

During the two decades after its official publication in 1962, the American Law Institute's Model Penal Code influenced many courts and legislatures to broaden the insanity defense. Section 4.01 of the Code modified the traditional "M'Naghten" "knowledge of wrongfulness" test in a manner calculated to make it easier to demonstrate lack of criminal responsibility. There were two principal innovations. First, the new test excused anyone who lacked "substantial capacity to appreciate the criminality of his conduct." The purpose of using the terms "substantial capacity" and "appreciate" was to make it clear that a total lack of knowledge of the act's wrongfulness was not required, so that a defendant who "knew" only in some abstract sense that it was wrong to kill people or to steal might nonetheless be excused if his ability to understand or internalize that knowledge was seriously affected.

Second and more important, the Code introduced a "volitional" element to add to the solely "cognitive" test of the M'Naghten rule. The mentally ill defendant was to be excused not only if he could not appreciate the criminality of his conduct, but also if he lacked "substantial capacity to conform his conduct to the requirements of law." The logic of excusing persons who cannot control their own conduct is straightforward: such persons ought not to be blamed, and in any event they cannot be deterred by the threat of punishment. If we assume that some criminal acts are directed by free will and others by psychological compulsion, and that juries guided by psychiatrists can accurately distinguish freely willed acts from psychologically compelled acts, then it follows that we should punish the former and not the latter. The Code's drafters felt that the "irresistible impulse" test was an inept formulation of this principle, because its wording implied a limitation to "sudden, spontaneous acts as opposed to propulsions that are accompanied by brooding or reflection."

The history of the insanity defense after 1962 was the history of gradual adoption of the Model Penal Code's provision (commonly called the "ALI test") in jurisdiction after jurisdiction. Even the United States Court of Appeals for the District of Columbia Circuit, which in 1954 had adopted the celebrated but unworkable "disease-product" rule that for a time seemed the wave of the future, acknowledged the superiority of the ALI formula in 1972. United States v. Brawner, 471 F.2d 969 (D.C.Cir.1972). By 1982, every federal Court of Appeals and about half the states had adopted the ALI test. When the California Supreme Court belatedly adopted the ALI formulation in 1978, the Court's opinion reflected an assumption that the step was nothing more than an acknowledgement of universally accepted scientific reality, much as if the Court were to endorse the Theory of Relativity. People v. Drew, 22 Cal.3d 333, 149 Cal.Rptr. 275, 583 P.2d 1318 (1978). It seemed that the nearly impossible had been accomplished: a formulation of the insanity principle now existed which had the support of all except the most extreme determinists on one side, and the most punitive reactionary elements on the other.

That complacency was abruptly shattered in 1982 and 1983, when the American Psychiatric Association, the American Bar Association, and the American Medical Association all announced official positions decisively repudiating the ALI test, and especially its crucial volitional element. The occasion for this shift of position was the notorious verdict in the case of

John Hinckley, who wounded President Reagan and several other persons in an assassination attempt motivated by Hinckley's desire to impress a movie actress whom he had admired from a distance. Under federal law, the jury had to be instructed that they should acquit if there was a reasonable doubt about the defendant's sanity under the ALI test. If taken literally, that instruction amounted to a directed verdict of not guilty, given the fantastic motive and the fact that some distinguished psychiatrists had testified that Hinckley was insane. Frequently juries ignore the law in such cases and convict anyway, but the *Hinckley* jury surprised everyone by taking the instruction seriously and returning a not guilty verdict.

The resulting public outcry focused attention on the legal rules that seem to invite such a result. Widespread intellectual discontent with psychiatric testimony and its accompanying ideology had existed well before the *Hinckley* case, and had already influenced a major law reform effort: the "deinstitutionalization" of the mentally ill. Not very long ago, it was generally assumed that psychiatrists were capable of identifying dangerously mentally ill persons, and predicting their future behavior. Society routinely locked such persons away in institutions until "cured." Beginning in the 1960s, an unusual alliance of civil liberties lawyers, mental health professionals, and budget-cutting politicians cooperated to curtail drastically the practice of institutionalizing the mentally ill. This change was made possible by a technological innovation: the development of new drug therapies that effectively control many of the destructive symptoms of mental illness. Deinstitutionalization also had its ideological side, however, and the ideology was one of pervasive distrust of psychiatric testimony. There was no lack of ammunition. Anyone with courtroom experience knows that psychiatric judgment is sufficiently subjective that it is usually possible to retain a reputable psychiatrist to testify on either side of any controversial question. Diagnostic categories have changed enormously over the years, and on some topics (e.g. homosexuality) they have a political as well as a scientific dimension.

The campaign to protect the liberties of the mentally ill particularly called into question the ability of psychiatrists to predict dangerous behavior. In this effort as in others, the opponents of psychiatric excess found that they had powerful allies within the psychiatric profession. Psychiatrists themselves were increasingly eager to disclaim omniscience. To their credit, genuine advances in knowledge inclined them to a greater humility in the face of what remained to be learned. Today, it is perfectly orthodox to say that psychiatrists have very little ability to predict behavior, and certainly their predictions are not sufficiently accurate that they should be relied upon as a justification for taking away a person's liberty.

There has been considerable difficulty over whether we can continue to justify routine confinement of the "criminally" insane in light of the reforms in civil mental commitment law. Insanity acquittees are supposed to be not guilty, after all, and so they do not deserve to be punished. Furthermore, the verdict may only mean that there was a reasonable doubt as to the sanity of the accused at the time of the event, months or even years before the verdict. It would seem that a mental commitment order ought to be based on a determination that the former defendant is *presently* insane *and* dangerous, a conclusion that might be difficult to justify if we assume that there is no reliable method for determining dangerousness.

Judges have understandably been uncertain about whether to accept a compelling line of argument that leads to outcomes—possibly including the outright release of such as John Hinckley—that society cannot accept. In People v. McQuillan, 392 Mich. 511, 221 N.W.2d 569 (1974), the Supreme Court of Michigan held that the State's insanity acquittees could be confined for evaluation only for 60 days, after which they were entitled to the same procedural protections as any other civilly committed patient. This decision led the Michigan legislature to pass the first legislation authorizing a "guilty but insane" verdict.

On the other hand, the United States Supreme Court has upheld the constitutionality of the provisions of the District of Columbia Code which provide for automatic, indefinite commitment of defendants found not guilty by reason of insanity, with subsequent release only for those who can prove by a preponderance of the evidence that they are no longer insane and dangerous. See Jones v. United States, discussed in Foucha v. Louisiana, infra, p. 343. The Supreme Court also held that the period of commitment was not limited by the maximum term for the criminal offense for which the accused might have been convicted. The *Jones* decision was highly questionable on its facts, since the only evidence of the acquittee's dangerousness was that he had "committed" an attempted petty theft, although he stipulated that he was insane at the time of the offense. It would be still more difficult for the courts to justify automatic commitment after a trial in which the acquittee had merely raised a reasonable doubt as to his sanity.

The public reaction to the *Hinckley* verdict thus provided the occasion for a re-evaluation of psychiatric defenses which was overdue and inevitable in any case. The mental health professionals were as eager as the prosecutors to repudiate the ALI version of the insanity defense and return to a narrower formulation. Following is an extremely condensed summary of the positions taken by the major organizations:

The American Psychiatric Association (APA) Statement on the Insanity Defense took the position that the insanity defense should be retained, but drastically narrowed. Because the criminal law presumes that punishment for wrongful deeds should be predicated upon moral culpability, there must logically be a defense for defendants who do not possess free will and therefore cannot be said to have "chosen to do wrong." Although the APA thought that lack of free will is the moral basis of the insanity defense, it somewhat paradoxically recommended eliminating the ALI test, with its controversial "volitional" element, in favor of a modernized wording of the M'Naghten formula drafted by Professor Richard Bonnie. Bonnie's test would excuse the defendant only if, as a result of mental disease or retardation, he was "unable to appreciate the wrongfulness of his conduct at the time of the offense." "Mental disease" is limited to conditions that "grossly and demonstrably impair a person's perception or understanding of reality": conditions such as "psychopathic personality disturbance" are emphatically excluded. See Bonnie, "The Moral Basis of the Insanity Defense," 69 A.B.A. J. 194 (1983).

Many lawyers and judges were surprised to learn that psychiatrists no longer wished to testify as experts on the defendant's capacity to control his conduct, and preferred a narrow definition of mental disease to an open-ended one. Expansion of the insanity defense was once thought to be necessary to permit psychiatrists to explain the defendant's condition without undue legalistic restrictions. The APA Statement explained that psychiatric testimony about whether a defendant understood the wrongfulness of his act "is more reliable and has a stronger scientific basis" than does psychiatric testimony about whether a defendant could control his behavior. The APA acknowledged that "psychiatry is a deterministic discipline that views all human behavior as, to a good extent, 'caused'." On the other hand, the APA recognized that psychiatrists disagree about how this deterministic outlook should affect the moral and philosophical question of whether a person is responsible for his conduct. In the absence of a professional consensus, expert psychiatric testimony about volition is more likely to be confusing than enlightening for a jury.

The APA took no position on whether the defense or prosecution should have the burden of proof, but does observe that psychiatric issues are usually not susceptible to proof "beyond a reasonable doubt." The APA did not oppose evidentiary rules that limit psychiatric testimony to description of the defendant's condition and bar any statement on the "ultimate issue" of sanity or insanity.

Finally, the APA Statement argued that it is a mistake to treat persons acquitted of violent crimes on the grounds of insanity as if they were equivalent to mentally ill persons who have not attacked anyone. They should be confined in a secure facility and the decision to release should be made by a group similar in composition to a parole board. In other words, they should be treated much as they would be treated if they had been convicted. It is not clear that a defendant receives any benefit from an insanity acquittal under these circumstances, unless it be to escape a possible death sentence. Nonetheless, the APA Statement opposed allowing the jury to return a compromise "guilty but insane" verdict, on the ground that this too-easy alternative permits the jury to settle on a convenient label and thus avoid "grappling with the difficult moral issues inherent in adjudicating guilt or innocence," a task which serves an "important symbolic function."

The *American Bar Association* (ABA) House of Delegates approved new Standards for the insanity defense in February, 1983. Like the APA, the ABA recommended dropping the volitional prong of the ALI test and excusing only persons who are "unable to appreciate the wrongfulness" of their criminal acts. The ABA did not limit the concept of mental disease to conditions producing a gross misperception of reality, however. Instead, it merely stated that "mental disease or defect refers to impairments of mind, whether enduring or transitory, or to mental retardation which substantially affected the mental or emotional process of the defendant at the time of the alleged offense." The Commentary explained that this definition "attempts to clarify the meaning of the term 'mental disease or defect.' "One wonders what the drafters would have written had their intent been to allow the term to remain obscure.

Otherwise, the ABA Standards provided that expert testimony about mental illness could be admissible where relevant to show that the defendant did not have the specific mental state required by the definition of the defense. (The APA did not address this question.) The defendant would be required to give advance notice of any defense based on mental condition, and to submit to examination by court-appointed experts. The ABA also recommended restricting the psychiatrist from testifying on the ultimate issue of sanity, and placed the burden of persuasion by a preponderance of the evidence on the prosecution.

The American Medical Association (AMA) approved a more radical change at its 1983 annual meeting. The AMA recommended that the defense of legal insanity be abolished outright and replaced by statutes providing for acquittal when a criminal defendant, as a result of mental disease or otherwise, lacks the state of mind or mens rea required as an element of the defense charged. Defendants found not guilty on this basis would be subject to civil commitment, with a presumption of continuing dangerousness for those acquitted of offenses involving violence. They would be released only upon concurring medical certification and judicial determination that release poses no substantial public risk. Where mental illness does not serve as a defense (because it does not have the effect of causing the defendant to lack the culpability required by the definition of the offense), it could nonetheless be considered a mitigation of sentence.

The major disagreement, then, was that the organized medical profession recommended abolishing the defense altogether, while the Bar and Psychiatric Associations recommended to retain the defense but limit it fairly drastically. The AMA position explicitly endorsed the reasoning of Professor Norval Morris, whose book *Madness and the Criminal Law* (1982) argued for abolition of the special defense of legal insanity in favor of an approach directed solely to whether the defendant has satisfied the culpability requirements for the crime. See Johnson, Book Review, 50 U.Chi.L.Rev. 1534 (1983).

As applied to the *Hinckley* case, the AMA approach would have meant that mental illness was relevant only if it tended to show that Hinckley was incapable of forming an intent to kill anyone, which of course it would not. Hinckley's bizarre motive and history of irrational behavior would be considered only at sentencing, where such evidence might have a double effect. It would tend to lessen the defendant's blameworthiness, but at the same time it would tend to support confinement on the grounds of extraordinary dangerousness. In his book, Morris argued that psychiatric predictions of dangerousness are so fallible that courts should rarely rely upon them as a basis for *increasing* a sentence. Whether judges would respect that limitation in practice is doubtful.

The AMA Committee Report, relying heavily upon the writings of Norval Morris, argued that it is arbitrary to single out mental illness from other factors that effect behavior. Why should mental illness be an excuse from criminal responsibility when (for example) "gross social adversity" is not? Morris wrote that because criminal behavior is less closely correlated with psychosis than with "being born to a one parent family living on welfare in a black inner-city area," it is irrational to allow a complete defense in one case and not the other. See Morris, *Madness and the Criminal Law,* at 62–63 (1982).

Moreover, according to Morris and the AMA Report, the insanity defense does not even accomplish its stated purpose of shielding the mentally impaired from punishment. In practice it operates capriciously to exonerate a few mentally ill offenders who are either lucky or exceptionally well defended, while others with equally serious impairments go to prison. Morris thus condemned the insanity defense as "an ornate rarity, a tribute to our capacity to pretend to a moral position while pursuing profoundly different practices." This is a strong argument, particularly if one assumes that homicidal insanity acquittees are going to be locked away for at least as long as if they were convicted. How can the existence of such a defense be essential to the moral integrity of the criminal law if it makes so little tangible difference to the disposition of the offender?

Despite the strength of the argument, Morris's position is definitely a minority one among legal scholars. Most authorities would agree with the view of the APA and the ABA that recognition of an insanity defense is logically necessary to any criminal justice system based upon a premise of moral accountability. But see *State v. Herrera,* 895 P.2d 359, supra p. 307. To understand the strength of this majority position, it is useful to compare the defense of insanity with the universally recognized and uncontroversial defense of infancy.[a]

The reason that we do not hold young children accountable under the criminal law is not that they are incapable of forming an intent. Even a dog knows the difference between being kicked and being stumbled over, and children know the difference between hurting other children accidentally and "on purpose." Although a child is capable of forming an intent, we do not consider small children to be sufficiently rational to hold them fully accountable for their behavior. Similarly, through the institution of the juvenile court we give adolescents something like a defense of "partial responsibility."

If this is uncontroversial with respect to actual children, then it ought to be equally acceptable when applied to the severely mentally retarded, and to psychotics who suffer a gross misperception of reality. The point is not that psychotics or the severely retarded are more likely than other people to commit crimes. On the contrary, it is probable that the more severely retarded or psychotic one is, the more likely it is that one will be incapable of complicated purposeful action of any kind, including criminal action. After all, six year old children hardly ever commit homicide, but when they do, they are excused. The insanity defense is a logical extension of the same principle. It divides those who are sufficiently rational to be held accountable for their actions from those who have not reached that level of understanding or maturity and perhaps never will.

a. See e.g. California Penal Code § 26: Children under 14 are presumed incapable of committing crimes absent clear proof that they knew the act was wrongful when they committed it. This presumption continues to apply even though crimes by children are now prosecuted in a special "juvenile court." In re Gladys R., 1 Cal.3d 855, 83 Cal.Rptr. 671, 464 P.2d 127 (1970) The state may disprove the presumption in an individual case, by a preponderance of the evidence.

The difference between children and psychotics, of course, is that psychotics are often extremely dangerous people, although it may be difficult to say exactly how dangerous a particular psychotic is. For this reason we confine psychotics who have committed violent acts, sometimes for a longer time than if they were found to be morally responsible. The AMA Report saw this practice as evidence of social hypocrisy, and perhaps it is, but it is not illogical. The purpose of the insanity defense is not necessarily to benefit the insane offender, and certainly not to guarantee his liberty. On the contrary, a verdict of legal insanity (under a narrow definition like that proposed by the APA) labels the individual as so thoroughly irrational that he cannot be trusted with liberty or expected to benefit from it. Perhaps the difference between convicting and committing a psychotic is largely a matter of symbolism (where the death penalty is not in the picture) but symbols are not necessarily unimportant.

An insanity defense of some kind therefore fits logically in a criminal justice system that holds most but not all human beings morally responsible for their actions. It does not follow, however, that we should have an insanity defense that is so broad as to exculpate persons whom the community *does* consider morally responsible, regardless of whether a psychiatric diagnosis would appropriately include these persons within the category of the mentally ill. The ALI test contains the potential for extending the defense far beyond the limited number of persons whom the public does not in fact consider responsible for their actions. This is because the "substantial capacity" test excuses persons who are not totally irrational, and especially because inability to control one's conduct is an open-ended, speculative concept. Our prisons are full of persons with damaged personalities and a long history of lack of success in controlling their impulses.

The argument for adding a volitional element to the insanity defense was that it was thought to comport with the reality of mental illness, which may lead to a loss of behavioral control even where it does not affect the cognitive capacity to understand the wrongfulness of what one is doing. Progressive reformers in the early 1960s were not worried that the jury would fall under undue influence from psychiatrists, or be hopelessly confused by professional debate over the validity of untestable deterministic theories of human behavior. They thought that the problem was rather how to *open up* the trial process so that jurors could fully understand what the psychiatrists wanted to tell them about the psychological causes of the defendant's behavior. As the psychiatrists became more knowledgeable about the real causes of criminal conduct, they would succeed in persuading ordinary persons sitting as jurors to accept their theories. If increasing psychiatric knowledge led to an increasing number of insanity acquittals, then this would be because the community, acting through the jurors, willed it to be so. Increasingly accurate psychiatric diagnosis would also lead to increasingly effective cures, and the public's safety would be far more efficaciously protected by humane treatment of the offender than by a brutal prison system which embitters its inmates. Judge Kaufman's opinion in United States v. Freeman, supra, p. 315, is an outstanding expression of the dominant intellectual current of that time.

The dramatic turnabout that occurred on this issue after the *Hinckley* verdict is best illustrated by the 1982 APA Statement. Although lawyers who endorsed the ALI test thought that they were thereby permitting psychiatrists to testify more realistically to what they knew about the human personality and the causes of criminal behavior, the organization that represents psychiatrists came to believe that, with mostly good intentions, the lawyers were leading psychiatry into a quagmire. The familiar "battle of the experts" in insanity trials embarrassed the profession enormously by giving the impression that psychiatrists are quacks or worse.

But it is the question that the law was asking rather than the answers that the experts were giving that was primarily to blame for the situation. No one knows whether a criminal who has committed a crime for some bizarre motive could have acted otherwise if he had wished to do so. All three organizations agreed on this point. In the words of Professor Bonnie, quoted with approval in both the ABA Report and the AMA Report:

> [E]xperience confirms that there still is no accurate scientific basis for measuring one's capacity for self-control or for calibrating the impairment of such capacity. There is, in short, no objective basis for distinguishing between offenders who were undeterrable and those who were merely undeterred, between the impulse that was irresistible and the impulse not resisted, or between substantial impairment of capacity and some lesser impairment. Bonnie, "The Moral Basis of the Insanity Defense", 69 A.B.A. J. 194, 196 (1983).

The ALI insanity defense was a product of a time when intellectual leaders expected science to be as effective in remedying crime as it had been in remedying polio. Because it was irrational to punish persons for disease, mentally disturbed persons who performed criminal acts were thought to belong in a hospital where they could be cured, rather than in a prison where they would only be punished. The reformers assumed that no harm would be done by erroneous insanity acquittals, because confinement in a mental institution would adequately protect the security of the public and at the same time provide much more humane treatment to the offender than a term in prison. From this perspective, what needed to be done was to provide for as many insanity acquittals as public opinion would allow, with the jury being seen as a surrogate for public opinion.

The reaction to the *Hinckley* verdict plainly belied the notion that the public regards the jury, particularly a jury subject to manipulation by lawyers and confused by incomprehensible legal standards, as an adequate safeguard for the public interest. It even became clear that the psychiatric profession itself shared to some degree the general public's skepticism about the objectivity of psychiatric knowledge. As a result the federal Insanity Defense Reform Act of 1984 passed the Congress without substantial opposition. The main substantive section of the Act is set out immediately below; detailed procedural provisions follow a few pages later.

The Insanity Defense Reform Act Of 1984
Title 18, United States Code

§ 17. Insanity Defense

(a) Affirmative defense. It is an affirmative defense to a prosecution under any Federal statute that, at the time of the commission of the acts constituting the offense, the defendant, as a result of a SEVERE MENTAL DISEASE or defect, was unable to appreciate the nature and quality or the wrongfulness of his acts. Mental disease or defect does not otherwise constitute a defense.

(b) Burden of Proof. The defendant has the burden of proving the defense of insanity by clear and convincing evidence.

PEOPLE v. SERRAVO

Supreme Court of Colorado, 1992.
823 P.2d 128.

JUSTICE QUINN delivered the Opinion of the Court.

I

Serravo was charged in a multi-count information with crimes of attempt to commit first degree murder after deliberation, assault in the first degree, and the commission of crimes of violence. The charges arose out of the stabbing his wife, Joyce Serravo, on May 10, 1987. After the charges were filed, Serravo entered a plea of not guilty by reason of insanity and was thereafter examined by several psychiatrists. The issue of legal insanity was tried to a jury, which returned a verdict of not guilty by reason of insanity.

The evidence at the insanity trial established that the stabbing occurred under the following circumstances. On the evening of May 9, 1987, Serravo, who was a King Soopers union employee, visited striking employees at the King Soopers store near his home. Serravo returned home at approximately 12:30 a.m. on May 10. After sitting in the kitchen and reading the Bible, he went upstairs to the bedroom where his wife was sleeping, stood over her for a few minutes, and then stabbed her in the back just below the shoulder blade. When his wife awoke, Serravo told her that she had been stabbed by an intruder and that she should stay in bed while he went downstairs to call for medical help.

Police officers were later dispatched to the home. Serravo told the officers that he had gone to the King Soopers store and had left the garage door open, that the door leading to the house from the garage was unlocked, that when he returned from King Soopers and was reading the Bible he heard his front door slam, and that he went upstairs to check on his wife and children and saw that his wife was bleeding from a wound in her back. Serravo signed a consent to search his home and gave the police clothes that he was wearing at the time of his discovery of his wife's injury.

Several weeks after the stabbing Serravo's wife found letters written by Serravo. In these letters Serravo admitted the stabbing, stating that "our marriage was severed on Mother's Day when I put the knife in your back," that "I have gone to be with Jehovah in heaven for three and one-half days," and that "I must return for there is still a great deal of work to be done." After reading the letters, Serravo's wife telephoned him in order to confront him about the letters. Serravo told his wife that God had told him to stab her in order to sever the marriage bond. Mrs. Serravo informed the police of these facts and Serravo was thereafter arrested and charged.

The prosecution presented expert psychiatric testimony on Serravo's sanity at the time of the stabbing. Doctor Ann Seig, a resident psychiatrist in training at the University of Colorado Health Sciences Center, examined Serravo pursuant to a court ordered evaluation of his mental state. Serravo gave the doctor a history of having worked on a plan, inspired by his relationship to God, to establish a multi-million dollar sports complex called Purely Professionals. This facility, according to Serravo, would enable him to achieve his goal of teaching people the path to perfection. On the night of the stabbing, Serravo, according to the history given to Doctor Seig, was excited because he finally believed that he had received some positive encouragement in his endeavor from some King Soopers union members, but he was discouraged by some inner "evil spirits" who kept raising troublesome questions about how he would deal with his wife's lack of encouragement and support. Doctor Seig diagnosed Serravo as suffering either from an organic delusional disorder related to left temporal lobe damage as a result of an automobile accident some years ago or paranoid schizophrenia. Either diagnosis, in Doctor Seig's opinion, would adequately account for Serravo's delusional belief that he had a privileged relationship with God as the result of which he was in direct communication with God. Doctor Seig testified that Serravo was operating under this delusional system when he stabbed his wife and these delusions caused him to believe that his act was morally justified. Doctor Seig, however, was of the view that Serravo, because he was aware that the act of stabbing was contrary to law, was sane at the time of the stabbing.

Serravo presented four psychiatrists and a clinical psychologist on the issue of his legal insanity. The first psychiatrist, Doctor Frederick Miller, was of the opinion that on the night of the stabbing Serravo was under the psychotic delusion that it was his divine mission to kill his wife and that he was morally justified in stabbing her because God had told him to do so. Doctor Miller was not quite certain whether Serravo's psychotic disorder was paranoid schizophrenia, a paranoid delusional disorder, or an organic delusional disorder. Although uncertain of the exact diagnostic label applicable to Serravo, Doctor Miller was of the opinion that Serravo's mental illness made it impossible for him to distinguish right from wrong even though Serravo was probably aware that such conduct was legally wrong.

Another psychiatrist, Doctor Eric Kaplan, was the attending psychiatrist at the University of Colorado Health Services and a member of the faculty of the medical school. Doctor Kaplan supervised Doctor Ann Seig during her examination of Serravo and also made an independent evaluation of Serravo's mental condition. It was Doctor Kaplan's opinion that Serravo was suffering from paranoid schizophrenia at the time of the stabbing and was laboring under the paranoid delusion that his wife stood in the way of his divine mission of completing the large sports complex, that Serravo believed that the stabbing was the right thing to do, and that Serravo, as a result of his mental illness, was unable to distinguish right from wrong with respect to the stabbing. Two other psychiatrists, Doctor Geoffrey Heron and Doctor Seymour Sundell, offered the opinion that Serravo, at the time of the stabbing, was suffering from paranoid schizophrenia and a paranoid delusion about God which so affected his cognitive ability as to render him incapable of distinguishing right from wrong as normal people would be able to do in accordance with societal standards of morality.

Doctor Leslie Cohen, a clinical psychologist, also testified about Serravo's mental condition at the time of the stabbing. Having conducted extensive psychological testing of Serravo, Doctor Cohen was able to offer an opinion on Serravo's reality testing, his emotional reactivity, and his volition, all of which were relevant to the functioning of his conscience. The doctor was of the opinion that Serravo's conscience was based on a false belief or delusion about his magical powers as a result of his direct communication with God. Serravo, in the doctor's view, was suffering from a psychotic disorder that rendered him incapable of distinguishing right from wrong at the time of the stabbing. Although Doctor Cohen acknowledged that Serravo appeared to cover up his conduct when the police arrived at his home, the doctor explained that conduct as the product of a small part of his still intact reality testing. According to Doctor Cohen, Serravo is "not an incoherent man who can't figure out what's going on," but rather "senses that people don't understand his reasoning very well" and thus apparently believed that the police "wouldn't understand the complex reasoning that went behind the stabbing and that it would be better if he kept it to himself."

At the conclusion of the evidence, the trial court instructed the jury, in accordance with the statutory definition of insanity, that a person "is not accountable who is so diseased or defective in mind at the time of the commission of the act as to be incapable of distinguishing right from wrong, with respect to the act." The court also gave the following jury instruction, to which the prosecution objected, on the meaning of the phrase "incapable of distinguishing right from wrong":

> Instruction No. 5: As used in the context of the statutory definition of insanity as a criminal defense, the phrase "incapable of distinguishing right from wrong" includes within its meaning the case where a person appreciates that his conduct is criminal, but, because of a mental disease or defect, believes it to be morally right.

In objecting to the jury instruction, the prosecution stated that it would permit the jury to return an insanity verdict based solely on a purely subjective moral standard rather than a legal standard of right and wrong. The trial court, however, was of the view that, because the statutory definition of insanity was not cast in terms of either legal or moral wrong, it was appropriate to instruct the jury that legal insanity included an incapacity, due to a mental disease or defect, to distinguish right from wrong in a moral sense.

The jury returned a verdict of not guilty by reason of insanity at the time of the commission of the alleged crimes, and the court committed Serravo to the custody of the Department of Institutions until such time as he is found to be eligible for release. The prosecution appealed the district court's ruling on the challenged jury instruction to the Court of Appeals, which affirmed the district court's ruling. * * *

II

We initially consider whether the phrase "incapable of distinguishing right from wrong" should be measured by legal right and wrong, as argued by the People, or instead, should be measured by a societal standard of morality, as determined by the court of appeals. The phrase in question appears in [the applicable Colorado statute] which defines legal insanity as follows:

> The applicable test of insanity shall be, and the jury shall be so instructed: "A person who is so diseased or defective in mind at the time of the commission of the act as to be incapable of distinguishing right from wrong with respect to that act is not accountable." But care should be taken not to confuse such mental disease or defect with moral obliquity, mental depravity, or passion growing out of anger, revenge, hatred, or other motives, and kindred evil conditions, for when the act is induced by any of these causes the person is accountable to the law.

* * * We acknowledge that some cases subsequent to *M'Naghten* have interpreted the right-wrong test as limiting the insanity defense to a cognitive inability to distinguish legal right from legal wrong, with the result that a person's simple awareness that an act is illegal is a sufficient basis for finding criminal responsibility. [Citations] We believe, however, that such an analysis injects a formalistic legalism into the insanity equation to the disregard of the psychological underpinnings of legal insanity. A person in an extremely psychotic state, for example, might be aware that an act is prohibited by law, but due to the overbearing effect of the psychosis may be utterly without the capacity to comprehend that the act is inherently immoral. A standard of legal wrong would render such person legally responsible and subject to imprisonment for the conduct in question notwithstanding the patent injustice of such a disposition. Conversely, a person who, although mentally ill, has the cognitive capacity to distinguish right from wrong and is aware that an act is morally wrong, but does not realize that it is illegal, should nonetheless be held responsible for the act, as ignorance of the law is no excuse.

Construing the term "wrong" as moral wrong finds support in several cases which have basically followed the well-reasoned opinion of the New York Court of Appeals in People v. Schmidt, N.E. 945 (N.Y. 1915). [Citations] The *Schmidt* opinion, written by then Judge Benjamin

Cardozo, rejected the view that the term "wrong" means "contrary to the law of the state." After a careful analysis of *M'Naghten* and the history of the insanity defense, Judge Cardozo remarked:

> The [*M'Naghten*] judges expressly held that a defendant who knew nothing of the law would none the less be responsible if he knew that the act was wrong, by which, therefore, they must have meant, if he knew that it was morally wrong. Whether he would also be responsible if he knew that it was against the law, but did not know it to be morally wrong, is a question that was not considered. In most cases, of course, knowledge that an act is illegal will justify the inference of knowledge that it is wrong. But none the less it is the knowledge of wrong, conceived of as moral wrong, that seems to have been established by that decision as the controlling test.

* * *

In urging that the phrase "incapable of distinguishing right from wrong" in [the Colorado statute] should be limited to legal right and wrong, the People focus on that part of the insanity definition which states that "care should be taken not to confuse such mental disease or defect with moral obliquity" and argue that this statutory language manifests a legislative intent to define legal insanity in terms of an incapacity to distinguish legal right from legal wrong. We acknowledge, as asserted by the People, that the term "moral obliquity" refers to a deviation from moral rectitude. Webster's Third New International Dictionary 1557 (1986). Accepting that definition, however, does not lead us to the construction urged by the People.

The purpose served by the statutory reference to "moral obliquity" is not to provide a definitional component for legal insanity, which has been defined in the preceding sentence of [the statute] as an incapacity to distinguish right from wrong with respect to the act due to a mental disease or defect existing at the time of the commission of the act. Rather, the purpose served by the reference to "moral obliquity" is to distinguish, on the one hand, an act committed by a person capable of distinguishing right from wrong but nonetheless acting out of a perverse and culpable rejection of prevailing moral standards and, on the other hand, an act committed by a person in a state of mental illness that renders the person incapable of distinguishing right from wrong with respect to the act. * * *

Moral wrong can be measured either by a purely personal and subjective standard of morality or by a societal and presumably more objective standard. We believe that the better reasoned interpretation of "wrong" in the term "incapable of distinguishing right from wrong" refers to a wrongful act measured by societal standards of morality.

The concepts of "right" and "wrong" are essentially ethical in character and have their primary source in the existing societal standards of morality, as distinguished from the written law. A person's awareness and appreciation of right and wrong derive primarily from a variety of experiences and relationships including, but not necessarily limited to, behavioral rules endorsed by the social culture as well as ethical principles transmitted through the family, the community, the formal educational process, and religious associations. Simply put, legal insanity combines concepts of law, morality and medicine with the moral concepts derived primarily from the total underlying conceptions of ethics shared by the community at large. Defining "wrong" in terms of a purely personal and subjective standard of morality ignores a substantial part of the moral culture on which our societal norms of behavior are based.[11]

* * * We turn then to Jury Instruction No. 5, which stated that the phrase "incapable of distinguishing right from wrong" includes the case of a person who "appreciates that his conduct is criminal but, because of a mental disease or defect, believes it to be morally right." Although the court of appeals concluded that this instruction did not incorporate a "subjective moral standard to the determination of whether defendant understood right from wrong," we are of a contrary view. Jury Instruction No. 5 was cast in terms so general that it well could have been interpreted by the jury to incorporate a personal and subjective standard of moral wrong rather than a societal standard of right and wrong. The court of appeals' approval of the instruction, in our view, is inconsistent with its adoption of a societal standard of moral wrong for purposes of legal insanity.

We emphasize here that in most cases involving the defense of legal insanity there will be no practical difference between a definition of "wrong" in terms of legal wrong and a definition of "wrong" in terms of societal standards of morality. This is so because, for the most part, the proscriptions of the criminal law generally reflect the moral prohibitions of the social order. As previously discussed, however, the concept of legal insanity, while part of our positive law, incorporates psychological and moral components that are not necessarily limited by the confines of positive law. A clarifying instruction on the definition of legal insanity, therefore, should clearly state that, as related to the conduct charged as a crime, the phrase "incapable of distinguishing right from wrong" refers to a person's cognitive inability, due to a mental disease or defect, to distinguish right from wrong as measured by a societal standard of morality, even though the person may be aware that the conduct in question is criminal. Any such instruction should also expressly inform

11. The traditional reluctance to hold children under a certain age responsible for criminal acts is a good illustration of the fact that moral standards are learned through a dynamic societal process. Society has determined that both insane persons and children under a certain age are not responsible moral agents, in the former case because a mental disease or defect has prevented an adequate assimilation of societal moral standards, and in the latter case because immaturity has prevented an adequate opportunity for acquiring a moral sense of right and wrong. Like the M'Naghten test, the test for measuring infant incapacity has generally involved the inquiry of whether the child could distinguish between right and wrong. See Generally, Platt & Diamond, "The Origins of the 'Right and Wrong' Test of Criminal Responsibility and Its Subsequent Development in the United States: An Historical Survey," 54 Calif. L. Rev. 1227, 1237–47 (1966).

the jury that the phrase "incapable of distinguishing right from wrong" does not refer to a purely personal and subjective standard of morality.

III

We next consider the relationship between the so-called "deific-decree" delusion and Colorado's test of legal insanity. The court of appeals, after holding that the term "wrong" in the statutory definition of insanity refers not to legal wrong but moral wrong under societal standards of morality, held that the "deific-decree" delusion was an exception to the societal standards of moral wrong. Drawing on the opinion of the Washington Supreme Court in State v. Crenshaw, 659 P.2d 488 (Wash.1983),[12] the court of appeals limited the so-called deific-decree exception to those situations "in which a person commits a criminal act, knowing it is illegal and morally wrong according to society's standards but, because of a mental defect, believes that God has decreed the act." This exception, the court of appeals went on to conclude, must be distinguished from the case "in which a person acts in accordance with a duty imposed by a particular faith." In our view, the "deific-decree" delusion is not so much an exception to the right-wrong test measured by the existing societal standards of morality as it is an integral factor in assessing a person's cognitive ability to distinguish right from wrong with respect to the act charged as a crime.[13] * * *

IV

The question remains whether, in light of our disapproval of the trial court's jury instruction on the meaning of "wrong" in Colorado's test of legal insanity, we should remand the case for a new trial on the issue of insanity. This case was filed in the court of appeals as a prosecutorial appeal pursuant to [statutory authorization] on a question

12. In *Crenshaw*, the Supreme Court of Washington carved out the deific exception from Justice Cardozo's reference in *Schmidt*, 110 N.E. at 949, to a mother insanely obeying God's command to kill her child. The *Crenshaw* court, citing *Schmidt*, stated that although the woman who kills her infant child under an insane delusion that God has ordered the act might know "that the law and society condemn the act, it would be unrealistic to hold her responsible for the crime, since her free will has been subsumed by her belief in the deific decree." 659 P.2d at 494. *Crenshaw* appears to have judicially embroidered the *Schmidt* opinion, since *Schmidt* contains no reference to the volitional or free will aspect of the insanity defense. On the contrary, Judge Cardozo in *Schmidt* specifically states that New York's test of insanity does not contain an irresistible impulse component. It thus appears that the *Crenshaw* court added a volitional component to the "deific-decree" exception which is not supported by *Schmidt*.

13. We recognize, as did the court in People v. Schmidt, 110 N.E. 945, 950 (N.Y. 1915), that some defendants may attempt to hide behind "a professed belief that their crime was ordained by God." The *Schmidt* court, however, went on to observe that "we can safely leave such fabrications to the common sense of juries." See also State v. Crenshaw, 659 P.2d 488, 494 (Wash. 1983) (jury properly found that defendant's adherence to the Muscovite faith which requires husbands to kill unfaithful wives was a personal subjective belief rather than a "deific decree"). We agree with the *Schmidt* court's observation. The jury, functioning as the conscience of the community, is well-suited to the task of determining whether a defendant in a given case had the mental capacity to distinguish right from wrong in accordance with societal standards of morality with respect to an act charged as a crime.

of law—namely, the correctness of the jury instruction on the meaning of the term "wrong" in the statutory definition of insanity. Although we disagree with the court of appeals' conclusion that the challenged jury instruction did not apply a subjective standard of morality to the right-wrong test for legal insanity, we conclude that a retrial of the defendant would violate the federal and state constitutional prohibitions against placing an accused twice in jeopardy for the same offense.

In Colorado, while the issue of an accused's sanity must be tried separately from the issue of guilt, insanity remains an affirmative defense to a crime. Once any credible evidence of this affirmative defense is introduced into evidence, the prosecution bears the burden of proving the defendant's sanity beyond a reasonable doubt. In People ex rel. Juhan v. District Court, 439 P.2d 741, 747 (1968), this court held that "mental capacity to commit a crime is a material part of total guilt for there can be no crime without the mens rea." A jury verdict of not guilty by reason of insanity, therefore, is an adjudication on the merits which absolves the defendant of criminal responsibility, and results in a commitment of the defendant to the custody of the Department of Institutions until such time as the defendant is eligible for release. * * *

In light of the fact that the defendant was placed in jeopardy when he was adjudicated not guilty by reason of insanity, we limit appellate relief in this case as follows: we disapprove the trial court's jury instruction which defined the phrase "incapable of distinguishing right from wrong" in such a general manner as likely to be interpreted by a jury as including a purely subjective and personal standard of morality; we approve of the court of appeals' construction of the phrase "incapable of distinguishing right from wrong" as referring to an incapacity, due to a mental disease or defect, to know that an act is wrong under existing societal standards of morality; and we disapprove of the court of appeals' characterization of the deific-decree delusion as an exception to the right-wrong test for legal insanity rather than as an integral factor in assessing a person's cognitive ability to distinguish right from wrong with respect to the act charged as a crime. The judgment of the court of appeals is accordingly approved in part and disapproved in part.

[Dissenting opinion omitted.]

Note

In State v. Wilson, 242 Conn. 605, 700 A.2d 633 (Conn. 1997), the Connecticut Supreme Court explained the "appreciation of wrongfulness" test under the Connecticut version of the Model Penal Code. The defendant Wilson killed the victim while under the influence of paranoid delusions which caused him to believe that the victim and the victim's son were conspiring to ruin his life by drugging and brainwashing him. The trial judge instructed the jury that defendant would be not guilty by reason of insanity if he lacked substantial capacity to appreciate the wrongfulness of his conduct. The Connecticut Supreme Court reversed the resulting conviction and remanded for a new trial, holding that the general instruction did not adequately define "wrongfulness." The correct standard was not whether the defendant could appreciate that his act was unlawful, nor whether he personally believed it to be morally justified. Rather, the correct issue to put to the jury was whether the defendant lacked substantial capacity to appreciate that his act was contrary to *societal morality*. The court set out the following detailed instructions:

> The trial court should inform the jury that a person may establish that he was legally insane if he proves that, at the time he committed the prohibited conduct, due to mental disease or defect he suffered from a misperception of reality and, in acting on the basis of that misperception, he did not have the substantial capacity to appreciate that his actions were contrary to societal morality, even though he may have been aware that the conduct in question was criminal. The trial court should instruct the jury further that, in deciding whether the defendant had substantial capacity to appreciate that his conduct was contrary to societal morality, it must not limit its inquiry merely to the defendant's appreciation that society, objectively speaking, condemned his actions. Rather, the jury should be instructed that it must also determine whether the defendant maintained a sincere belief that society would condone his actions under the circumstances as the defendant honestly perceived them. Finally, the trial court also should instruct the jury that, if it finds that the defendant had the substantial capacity to appreciate that his conduct both violated the criminal law and was contrary to society's moral standards, *even under the circumstances as he honestly perceives them*, then he should not be adjudged legally insane simply because, as a result of mental disease or defect, he elected to follow his own personal moral code. 700 A.2d at 643.

During his second trial the defendant Wilson entered a bargained plea of guilty to murder, and received a 30-year prison sentence. The New York Times, October 15, 1999, p. B4.

FOUCHA v. LOUISIANA

Supreme Court of the United States, 1992.
504 U.S. 71, 112 S.Ct. 1780, 118 L.Ed.2d 437.

Justice White delivered the opinion of the Court, except as to Part III.

[Petitioner Foucha was charged with aggravated burglary and illegal discharge of a firearm in Louisiana in 1984. Psychiatrists reported that he was unable to distinguish right from wrong, and the trial judge found him not guilty by reason of insanity under the M'Naghten standard. In 1988 doctors at the state mental hospital recommended conditional release because there had been no evidence of mental illness during his entire time in the hospital.]

The trial judge appointed a two-member sanity commission made up of the same two doctors who had conducted the pretrial examination. Their written report stated that Foucha "is presently in remission from mental illness [but] we cannot certify that he would not constitute a menace to himself or others if released." One of the doctors testified at a hearing that upon commitment Foucha probably suffered from a drug induced psychosis but that he had recovered from that temporary condition; that he evidenced no signs of psychosis or neurosis and was in "good shape" mentally; that he has, however, an antisocial personality, a condition that is not a mental disease and that is untreatable. The doctor also testified that Foucha had been involved in several altercations at Feliciana and that he, the doctor, would not "feel comfortable in certifying that [Foucha] would not be a danger to himself or to other people."

After it was stipulated that the other doctor, if he were present, would give essentially the same testimony, the court ruled that Foucha was dangerous to himself and others and ordered him returned to the mental institution. The Court of Appeals refused supervisory writs, and the State Supreme Court affirmed, holding that Foucha had not carried the burden placed upon him by statute to prove that he was not dangerous, that our decision in Jones v. United States, 463 U.S. 354 (1983), did not require Foucha's release, and that neither the Due Process Clause nor the Equal Protection Clause was violated by the statutory provision permitting confinement of an insanity acquittee based on dangerousness alone. Because the case presents an important issue and was decided by the court below in a manner arguably at odds with prior decisions of this Court, we granted certiorari.

II

Addington v. Texas, 441 U.S. 418 (1979), held that to commit an individual to a mental institution in a civil proceeding, the State is required by the Due Process Clause to prove by clear and convincing evidence the two statutory preconditions to commitment: that the person sought to be committed is mentally ill and that he requires hospitalization for his own welfare and protection of others. Proof beyond reasonable doubt was not required, but proof by preponderance of the evidence fell short of satisfying due process.

When a person charged with having committed a crime is found not guilty by reason of insanity, however, a State may commit that person without satisfying the *Addington* burden with respect to mental illness and dangerousness. Jones v. United States, supra. Such a verdict, we observed in *Jones*, "establishes two facts: (i) the defendant committed an act that constitutes a criminal offense, and (ii) he committed the act because of mental illness," an illness that the defendant adequately proved in this context by a preponderance of the evidence. From these two facts, it could be properly inferred that at the time of the verdict, the defendant was still mentally ill and dangerous and hence could be committed.

We held, however, that "the committed acquittee is entitled to release when he has recovered his sanity or is no longer dangerous," i.e. the acquittee may be held as long as he is both mentally ill and dangerous, but no longer. We relied on O'Connor v. Donaldson, 422 U.S. 563 (1975), which held as a matter of due process that it was unconstitutional for a State to continue to confine a harmless, mentally ill person. Even if the initial commitment was permissible, "it could not constitutionally continue after that basis no longer existed." In the summary of our holdings in our opinion we stated that "the Constitution permits the Government, on the basis of the insanity judgment, to confine him to a mental institution until such time as he has regained his sanity or is no longer a danger to himself or society." *Jones*, 463 U.S., at 368, 370. The court below was in error in characterizing the above language from *Jones* as merely an interpretation of the pertinent statutory law in the District of Columbia and as having no constitutional significance. In this case, Louisiana does not contend that Foucha was mentally ill at the time of the trial court's hearing. Thus, the basis for holding Foucha in a psychiatric facility as an insanity acquittee has disappeared, and the State is no longer entitled to hold him on that basis. * * *

The State, however, seeks to perpetuate Foucha's confinement on the basis of his antisocial personality which, as evidenced by his conduct at the facility, the court found rendered him a danger to himself or others. There are at least three difficulties with this position. First, even if his continued confinement were constitutionally permissible, keeping Foucha against his will in a mental institution is improper absent a determination in civil commitment proceedings of current mental illness and dangerousness. * * * Second, if Foucha can no longer be held as an insanity acquittee in a mental hospital, he is entitled to constitutionally adequate procedures to establish the grounds for his confinement. * * * Third, the Due Process Clause contains a substantive component that bars certain arbitrary, wrongful government actions regardless of the fairness of the procedures used to implement them. * * * A State, pursuant to its police power, may of course imprison convicted criminals for the purposes of deterrence and retribution. But there are constitutional limitations on the conduct that a State may criminalize. Here, the State has no such punitive interest. As Foucha was not convicted, he may not be punished. Here, Louisiana has by reason of his acquittal exempted Foucha from criminal responsibility. * * *

III

It should be apparent from what has been said earlier in this opinion that the Louisiana statute also discriminates against Foucha in violation of the Equal Protection Clause of the Fourteenth Amendment. *Jones* established that insanity acquittees may be treated differently in some respects from those persons subject to civil commitment, but Foucha, who is not now thought to be insane, can no longer be so classified. The State nonetheless insists on holding him indefinitely because he at one time committed a criminal act and does not now prove he is not dangerous. Louisiana law, however, does not provide for similar confinement for other classes of persons who have committed criminal acts and who cannot later prove they would not be dangerous. Criminals who have completed their prison terms, or are about to do so, are an obvious and large category of such persons. Many of them will likely suffer from the same sort of personality disorder that Foucha exhibits. However, state law does not allow for their continuing confinement based merely on dangerousness. Instead, the State controls the behavior of these similarly situated citizens by relying on other means, such as punishment, deterrence, and supervised release. Freedom from physical restraint being a fundamental right, the State must have a particularly convincing reason, which it has not put forward, for such discrimination against insanity acquittees who are no longer mentally ill. * * *

For the foregoing reasons the judgment of the Louisiana Supreme Court is reversed.

JUSTICE O'CONNOR, concurring in part and concurring in the judgment.

Louisiana asserts that it may indefinitely confine Terry Foucha in a mental facility because, although not mentally ill, he might be dangerous to himself or to others if released. For the reasons given in Part II of the Court's opinion, this contention should be rejected. I write separately, however, to emphasize that the Court's opinion addresses only the specific statutory scheme before us, which broadly permits indefinite confinement of sane insanity acquittees in psychiatric facilities. This case does not require us to pass judgment on more narrowly drawn laws that provide for detention of insanity acquittees, or on statutes that provide for punishment of persons who commit crimes while mentally ill. * * *

It might therefore be permissible for Louisiana to confine an insanity acquittee who has regained sanity if, unlike the situation in this case, the nature and duration of detention were tailored to reflect pressing public safety concerns related to the acquittee's continuing dangerousness. * * * I think it clear that acquittees could not be confined as mental patients absent some medical justification for doing so; in such a case the necessary connection between the nature and purposes of confinement would be absent. Nor would it be permissible to treat all acquittees alike, without regard for their particular crimes. For example, the strong interest in liberty of a person acquitted by reason of insanity but later found sane might well outweigh the governmental interest in detention where the only evidence of dangerousness is that the acquittee committed a non-violent or relatively minor crime. Equal protection principles may set additional limits on the confinement of sane but dangerous acquittees. Although I think it unnecessary to reach equal protection issues on the facts before us, the permissibility of holding an acquittee who is not mentally ill longer than a person convicted of the same crimes could be imprisoned is open to serious question.

The second point to be made about the Court's holding is that it places no new restriction on the States' freedom to determine whether and to what extent mental illness should excuse criminal behavior. The Court does not indicate that States must make the insanity defense available. It likewise casts no doubt on laws providing for prison terms after verdicts of "guilty but mentally ill." If a State concludes that mental illness is best considered in the context of criminal sentencing, the holding of this case erects no bar to implementing that judgment.

Finally, it should be noted that the great majority of States have adopted policies consistent with the Court's holding. * * * Today's holding follows directly from our precedents and leaves the States appropriate latitude to care for insanity acquittees in a way consistent with public welfare. Accordingly, I concur in Parts I and II of the Court's opinion and in the judgment of the Court.

[Dissenting opinions omitted; Justices Kennedy, Thomas, Scalia and Chief Justice Rehnquist dissented.]

Federal Insanity Defense Reform Act of 1984 Title 18, United States Code

§ 4241. Determination of Mental Competency to Stand Trial

(a) Motion to determine competency of defendant.—At any time after the commencement of a prosecution for an offense and prior to the sentencing of the defendant, the defendant or the attorney for the Government may file a motion for a hearing to determine the mental competency of the defendant. The court shall grant the motion, or shall order such a hearing on its own motion, if there is reasonable cause to believe that the defendant may presently be suffering from a mental disease or defect rendering him mentally incompetent to the extent that he is unable to understand the nature and consequences of the proceedings against him or to assist properly in his defense.

(b) Psychiatric or psychological examination and report.—Prior to the date of the hearing, the court may order that a psychiatric or psychological examination of the defendant be conducted * * *

* * *

(d) Determination and disposition.—If, after the hearing, the court finds by a preponderance of the evidence that the defendant is presently suffering from a mental disease or defect rendering him mentally incompetent to the extent that he is unable to understand the nature and consequences of the proceedings against him or to assist properly in his defense, the court shall commit the defendant to the custody of the Attorney General. The Attorney General shall hospitalize the defendant for treatment in a suitable facility—(1) for such a reasonable period of time, not to exceed four months, as is necessary to determine whether there is a substantial probability that in the foreseeable future he will attain the capacity to permit the trial to proceed; and (2) for an additional reasonable period of time until—(A) his mental condition is so improved that trial may proceed, if the court finds that there is a substantial probability that within such additional period of time he will attain the capacity to permit the trial to proceed; or (B) the pending charges against him are disposed of according to law; whichever is earlier.

If, at the end of the time period specified, it is determined that the defendant's mental condition has not so improved as to permit the trial to proceed, the defendant is subject to the provisions of section 4246.

(e) Discharge.—When the director of the facility in which a defendant is hospitalized pursuant to subsection (d) determines that the defendant has recovered to such an extent that he is able to understand the nature and consequences of the proceedings against him and to assist properly in his defense, he shall promptly file a certificate to that effect with the clerk of the court that ordered the commitment. The clerk shall send a copy of the certificate to the defendant's counsel and to the attorney for the Government. The court shall hold a hearing * * * to determine the competency of the defendant. If, after the hearing, the court finds by a preponderance of the evidence that the defendant has recovered to such an extent that he is able to understand the nature and consequences of the proceedings against him and to assist properly in his defense, the court shall order his immediate discharge from the facility in which he is hospitalized and shall set the date for trial. * * *

§ 4242. Determination of the Existence of Insanity at the Time of the Offense

(a) Motion for pretrial psychiatric or psychological examination.—Upon the filing of a notice, as provided in Rule 12.2 of the Federal Rules of Criminal Procedure, that the defendant intends to rely on the defense of insanity, the court, upon motion of the attorney for the Government, shall order that a psychiatric or psychological examination of the defendant be conducted, and that a psychiatric or psychological report be filed with the court * * *

(b) Special verdict.—If the issue of insanity is raised by notice as provided in Rule 12.2 of the Federal Rules of Criminal Procedure on motion of the defendant or of the attorney for the Government, or on the court's own motion, the jury shall be instructed to find, or, in the event of a nonjury trial, the court shall find the defendant—

(1) guilty;

(2) not guilty; or

(3) not guilty only by reason of insanity.

§ 4243. Hospitalization of a Person Found Not Guilty Only by Reason of Insanity

(a) Determination of present mental condition of acquitted person.—If a person is found not guilty only by reason of insanity at the time of the offense charged, he shall be committed to a suitable facility until such time as he is eligible for release pursuant to subsection (e).

(b) Psychiatric or psychological examination and report.—Prior to the date of the hearing, pursuant to subsection (c), the court shall order that a psychiatric or psychological examination of the defendant be conducted, and that a psychiatric or psychological report be filed with the court * * *

(c) Hearing.—A hearing shall be conducted * * * and shall take place not later than forty days following the special verdict.

(d) Burden of proof.—In a hearing pursuant to subsection (c) of this section, a person found not guilty only by reason of insanity of an offense involving bodily injury to, or serious damage to the property of, another person, or involving a substantial risk of such injury or damage, has the burden of proving by clear and convincing evidence that his release would not create a substantial risk of bodily injury to another person or serious damage of property of another due to a present mental disease or defect. With respect to any other offense, the person has the burden of such proof by a preponderance of the evidence.

(e) Determination and disposition.—If, after the hearing, the court fails to find by the standard specified in subsection (d) of this section that the person's release would not create a substantial risk of bodily injury to another person or serious damage of property of another due to a present mental disease or defect, the court shall commit the person to the custody of the Attorney General. The Attorney General shall release the person to the appropriate official of the State in which the person is domiciled or was tried if such State will assume responsibility for his custody, care, and treatment. The Attorney General shall make all reasonable efforts to cause such a State to assume such responsibility. If, notwithstanding such efforts, neither such State will assume such responsibility, the Attorney General shall hospitalize the person for treatment in a suitable facility until—

(1) such a State will assume such responsibility; or

(2) the person's mental condition is such that his release, or his conditional release under a prescribed regimen of medical, psychiatric, or psychological care or treatment, would not create a substantial risk of bodily injury to another person or serious damage to property of another; whichever is earlier. The Attorney General shall continue periodically to exert all reasonable efforts to cause such a State to assume such responsibility for the person's custody, care, and treatment.

(f) Discharge.—When the director of the facility in which an acquitted person is hospitalized pursuant to subsection (e) determines that the person has recovered from his mental disease or defect to such an extent that his release, or his conditional release under a prescribed regimen of medical, psychiatric, or psychological care or treatment, would no longer create a substantial risk of bodily injury to another person or serious damage to property of another, he shall promptly file a certificate to that effect with the clerk of the court that ordered the commitment. The clerk shall send a copy of the certificate to the person's counsel and to the attorney for the Government. The court shall order the discharge of the acquitted person or, on the motion of the attorney for the Government or on its own motion, shall hold a hearing * * * to determine whether he should be released. * * * [Detailed provisions relating to conditional release omitted.]

§ 4244. Hospitalization of a Convicted Person Suffering From Mental Disease Or Defect

(a) Motion to determine present mental condition of convicted defendant.—A defendant found guilty of an offense, or the attorney for the Government, may, within ten days after the defendant is found guilty, and prior to the time the defendant is sentenced, file a motion for a hearing on the present mental condition of the defendant if the motion is supported by substantial information indicating that the defendant may presently be suffering from a mental disease or defect for the treatment of which he is in need of custody for care or treatment in a suitable facility. The court shall grant the motion, or at any time prior to the sentencing of the defendant shall order such a hearing on its own motion, if it is of the opinion that there is reasonable cause to believe that the defendant may presently be suffering from a mental disease or defect for the treatment of which he is in need of custody for care or treatment in a suitable facility. * * *

(d) Determination and disposition.—If, after the hearing, the court finds by a preponderance of the evidence that the defendant is presently suffering from a mental disease or defect and that he should, in lieu of being sentenced to imprisonment, be committed to a suitable facility for care or treatment, the court shall commit the defendant to the custody of the Attorney General. The Attorney General shall hospitalize the defendant for care or treatment in a suitable facility. Such a commitment constitutes a provisional sentence of imprisonment to the maximum term authorized by law for the offense for which the defendant was found guilty.

(e) Discharge.—When the director of the facility in which the defendant is hospitalized pursuant to subsection (d) determines that the defendant has recovered from his mental disease or defect to such an extent that he is no longer in need of custody for care or treatment in such a facility, he shall promptly file a certificate to that effect * * *. If, at the time of the filing of the certificate, the provisional sentence imposed pursuant to subsection (d) has not expired, the court shall proceed finally to sentencing and may modify the provisional sentence.

§ 4246. Hospitalization of a Person Due for Release But Suffering From Mental Disease or Defect

(a) Institution of proceeding.—If the director of a facility in which a person is hospitalized certifies that a person whose sentence is about to expire, or who has been committed to the custody of the Attorney General pursuant to section 4241(d), or against whom all criminal charges have been dismissed solely for reasons related to the mental condition of the person, is presently suffering from a mental disease or defect as a result of which his release would create a substantial risk of bodily injury to another person or serious damage to property of another, and that suitable arrangements for State custody and care of the person are not available, he shall transmit the certificate to the clerk of the court for the district in which the person is confined. The clerk shall send a copy of the certificate to the person, and to the attorney for the Government, and, if the person was committed pursuant to section 4241(d), to the clerk of the court that ordered the commitment. The court shall order a hearing to determine whether the person is presently suffering from a mental disease or defect as a result of which his release would create a substantial risk of bodily injury to another person or serious damage to property of another. A certificate filed under this subsection shall stay the release of the person pending completion of procedures contained in this section. * * *

(d) Determination and disposition.—If, after the hearing, the court finds by clear and convincing evidence that the person is presently suffering from a mental disease or defect as a result of which his release would create a substantial risk of bodily injury to another person or serious damage to property of another, the court shall commit the person to the custody of the Attorney General. [The remainder of this section prescribes commitment and discharge provisions similar to those in § 4243, supra. The person is discharged after the court determines by a preponderance of the evidence that he or she has recovered to the extent of no longer constituting a substantial risk.]

STATE v. JONES

Supreme Court of Washington, 1983.
99 Wash.2d 735, 664 P.2d 1216.

UTTER, JUSTICE.

This case presents the question of when a court may enter a plea of not guilty by reason of insanity (NGI) over a defendant's objection. We hold that, as long as the defendant is competent to stand trial, a court may rarely, if ever, take such action but that it does have a duty to assure the defendant's waiver of an NGI plea is intelligent and voluntary. Because the court in the present case did impose an NGI plea on a competent defendant and we find that error prejudicial, we reverse and remand for a new trial.

Petitioner, Larry Jones, was charged with second degree assault while armed with a firearm. * * *

Because Mr. Jones told a rather unusual story about fearing for his life and planning to seek political asylum in Canada, the court ordered an inquiry into his competency to stand trial. Several psychiatrists, including one retained for the defense, examined Mr. Jones and concluded he was competent to stand trial; however, all but one also indicated to the court that they believed Mr. Jones was a paranoid schizophrenic and was insane at the time of the alleged assault.

The court found Mr. Jones competent to stand trial. It then considered the State's motion that the court enter an NGI plea over Mr. Jones' objection. After hearing argument, the court granted that motion, concluding only that there was a "strong possibility" that Mr. Jones had a valid insanity defense and that there was a "substantial danger" he would be convicted if it was not asserted. The court also directed that amicus counsel be appointed to present the insanity defense. Finally, the court denied Mr. Jones' motion to bifurcate the trial into a "guilt" phase and an insanity phase, though it did rule that the State could introduce evidence of insanity only after the defense presented its case.

The trial proceeded as ordered by the court and, after Mr. Jones presented his case, the State sought to prove he was legally insane. To do this, it called two of the psychiatrists who had examined Mr. Jones to determine his competency, one a state psychiatrist and one the defense psychiatrist. Mr. Jones objected to the latter psychiatrist's testimony on the ground that it was subject to attorney-client privilege, but his objection was overruled.

The jury was instructed on both self-defense and insanity and returned the verdict described above. After being committed to Western State Hospital, Mr. Jones brought this appeal. The Court of Appeals affirmed in all respects and Mr. Jones petitioned for review by this court.

I

A

Refusing to enter an NGI plea can be viewed as both one-half of a guilty plea—since one is guilty only if one both does a proscribed act and is mentally responsible at the time—and as an aspect of defense strategy. The extent to which a defendant has a right to refuse to plead NGI is therefore intertwined with any right he has to plead guilty and/or control his own defense.

In Washington, both such rights exist. While there is no federal constitutional right to plead guilty, such a right has been established in this state by court rule. * * *

In addition, a defendant has a constitutional right to at least broadly control his own defense. In Faretta v. California, 422 U.S. 806 (1975), the Supreme Court held that a defendant has a constitutional right to represent himself at trial. * * * The language and reasoning of *Faretta* necessarily imply a right to personally control one's own defense. In particular, *Faretta* embodies the conviction that a defendant has the right to decide, within limits, the type of defense he wishes to mount. [Citations]

The rights to plead guilty and control one's own defense are not absolute, however. A defendant exercising his right of self-representation, and thus by implication a defendant exercising his right to control his own defense, must "knowingly and intelligently" relinquish the benefits he forgoes and "should be made aware of the dangers and disadvantages" of his decision. *Faretta,* 422 U.S. at 835. Similarly, a court may not accept a guilty plea unless it is intelligent and voluntary. * * *

B

Courts have taken two basic approaches to the particular question of whether a court may *sua sponte* impose an NGI plea on an unwilling defendant. The first is that taken by the District of Columbia Circuit of the United States Court of Appeals. It recognizes a broad discretion in the trial court to enter an NGI plea sua sponte whenever necessary in the pursuit of justice. See Whalem v. United States, 346 F.2d 812, 818–19 (D.C.Cir.1965). In exercising its discretion, the court is to weigh various factors, including the defendant's opposition to asserting an insanity defense, the quality of the defendant's reasoning, the viability of the defense, the court's personal observations of the defendant, and the reasonableness of the defendant's decision. United States v. Wright, 627 F.2d 1300, 1311 (D.C.Cir.1980). The rationale for the rule is that society has "[an] obligation, through the insanity defense, to withhold punishment of someone not blameworthy." *Wright,* at 1310; *Whalem,* at 818. This, the D.C. Circuit has concluded, distinguishes *Alford* and *Faretta.*

In Frendak v. United States, 408 A.2d 364 (D.C.App.1979), the District of Columbia Court of Appeals concluded that *Alford* and *Faretta* required reevaluation of the D.C. Circuit rule. [The District of Columbia Court of Appeals is the equivalent of a state appellate court, with general jurisdiction over disputes arising in the District. The United States Court of Appeals for the District of Columbia Circuit has appellate jurisdiction over cases with a specific federal element.—ed.]

> [T]he underlying philosophy of *Alford* and *Faretta* is inconsistent with *Whalem* as currently interpreted. *Whalem* and succeeding cases have laid substantially more emphasis on the strength of the evidence supporting an insanity defense than on the defendant's choice. In contrast, *Alford* and *Faretta* reason that respect for a defendant's freedom as a person mandates that he or she be permitted to make fundamental decisions about the course of the proceedings.

Frendak, at 376. Thus, the D.C. Court of Appeals concluded, any competent defendant has the absolute right to refuse an NGI plea, as long as he is competent to make and does make an intelligent and voluntary waiver.

The D.C. Circuit rejected the *Frendak* approach in United States v. Wright, supra, and questioned whether it would differ significantly in practice. Nonetheless, we believe that the approaches differ in two important respects. First, the focus in *Frendak* is solely on *present* mental condition while much, if not most, of the D.C. Circuit's focus is on the defendant's mental condition *at the time of the alleged offense.* Second, the two approaches differ in the standard by which they assess the defendant's mental condition. Under *Frendak,* the court focuses on competency to make decisions while, under the D.C. Circuit approach, the court focuses on legal insanity.

C

We favor *Frendak* for several reasons. First, we find its reasoning more in accord with *Faretta* and *Alford*. The D.C. Circuit's attempt to distinguish cases involving an insanity defense is unpersuasive. A defendant who is not guilty because of insanity is no more blameless than a defendant who has a valid alibi defense or who acted in legitimate self-defense. Yet courts do not impose these other defenses on unwilling defendants.

More generally we concur in the belief that basic respect for a defendant's individual freedom requires us to permit the defendant himself to determine his plea. As noted by the court in *Frendak,* there exist numerous reasons why a defendant might choose to forgo an NGI plea. Absent bifurcation, such a choice may be a wise tactical maneuver where the insanity defense conflicts with some other defense the defendant wishes to interpose. The defendant may find confinement in a mental institution more distasteful than confinement in prison. The stigma of insanity may in some cases be more damaging. Finally, a defendant may have legitimate philosophical reasons for opposing entry of an NGI plea. He may view such a plea as a tacit admission of guilt which he does not wish to make. Alternatively, he may admit the act but maintain its justifiability or intend it to symbolize his strong opposition to some policy of the State. The forced mental commitment of critics in other countries to discredit their dissent is well documented. * * * While we did follow the approach of the D.C. Circuit in State v. Smith, 88 Wash.2d 639, 564 P.2d 1154 (1977), we no longer find that reasoning persuasive for the reasons already described.[2]

Smith is inconsistent with the prior analysis of *Dodd* and *Johnston* as well as the subsequent decision in *Martin.* We therefore overrule *Smith* to the extent that it is inconsistent with our decision today.

II

As with waiver of all rights, waiver of an NGI plea must satisfy certain conditions in order to be constitutionally valid. In particular, the defendant must be capable of making and must actually make an intelligent and voluntary decision. This requires the trial judge to "conduct an inquiry designed to assure that the defendant has been fully informed of the alternatives available, comprehends the consequences of failing to assert the [insanity] defense, and freely chooses to raise or waive the defense." *Frendak,* at 380; State v. Khan, 175 N.J.Super. 72,

2. In addition to reiterating the reasoning of the D.C. Circuit in *Whalem,* the court in *Smith* went further to state that "[i]t would clearly be unconstitutional to permit the conviction of a defendant who was legally insane at the time of the commission of the crime." State v. Smith, 88 Wash.2d 639, 564 P.2d 1154 (1977). Yet the authority cited for this proposition, State v. Strasburg, 60 Wash. 106, 110 P. 1020 (1910), holds only that a defendant has a constitutional right to claim insanity as a defense, not that he may not waive that right. We hold today that, in addition to the right to assert an insanity defense, criminal defendants also have a right to waive the defense.

82, 417 A.2d 585 (1980). In some instances, the defendant may not be competent to make an intelligent and voluntary decision.

Among the courts adopting the *Frendak* approach, however, there is disagreement about the relationship between competency to waive the insanity defense and competency to stand trial. The split arises not from a difference of opinion regarding the level of competency necessary to waive the insanity defense but rather from differences regarding the level of competency necessary to stand trial. In *Frendak* itself, the court concluded that a greater degree of competency was necessary to waive the insanity defense because the test for competency to stand trial "is not intended to measure whether the defendant is also capable of making intelligent decisions on important matters relating to the defense." In *Khan,* supra on the other hand, the court concluded that the test for competency to waive the insanity defense and the test for competency to stand trial were identical because in New Jersey the latter does require the ability to help plan the defense.

Frendak's conclusion, that the competency standards for waiver of the insanity defense and standing trial do differ, rests upon a shaky foundation. It is premised in large part on decisions holding that the level of competency necessary to plead guilty is greater than that necessary to stand trial, because the former requires an "ability to make a reasoned choice among the alternatives presented". Sieling v. Eyman, 478 F.2d 211, 215 (9th Cir.1973), cited in *Frendak,* at 380. *Sieling* and its progeny have been severely criticized, however, and do not represent the majority view. See United States ex rel. Heral v. Franzen, 667 F.2d 633, 637–38 (7th Cir.1981) and cases cited therein. We believe the better view is that both competency standards should require an ability to make necessary decisions at trial.

In any event, the test for competency to stand trial in Washington does rise to the level of competency to waive the insanity defense. As in New Jersey, a Washington defendant must be capable of assisting in his own defense. [Citations] We construe this to include the same ability to understand and choose among alternative defenses which is necessary to intelligently and voluntarily waive the insanity defense.

Thus, the only permissible inquiries when a defendant seeks to waive his insanity defense are whether he is competent to stand trial and whether his decision is intelligent and voluntary.[3]

If the court finds that the defendant is not competent to stand trial, trial must be stayed or dismissed as required by RCW 10.77.090. If the court finds that the defendant is competent to stand trial but that his decision to forgo an NGI plea is not intelligent and voluntary, it should provide him with whatever additional information or assurances are necessary to enable such a decision. In only the rarest of cases, if ever,

3. We deal here only with waiver by defendants represented by counsel. Where a defendant represents himself, his decisions to waive various rights should be scrutinized more carefully and a higher competency standard applied. * * *

will it be impossible to make the decision intelligent and voluntary and hence be necessary to enter an NGI plea sua sponte.

III

In the present case, the trial court did find Mr. Jones competent to stand trial. Nonetheless, it entered an NGI plea sua sponte solely because it believed Mr. Jones had a viable insanity defense without which he was likely to be convicted. The plea was entered over Mr. Jones' objection and with no inquiry into whether his desire to forgo an NGI plea was intelligent and voluntary. This was error and all aspects of the judgment affected by such error must be vacated.

In these circumstances, this requires that the entire verdict, both the finding that Mr. Jones committed the assault charged and the finding that he was legally insane, must be reversed. * * *

[Dissenting opinion omitted.]

C. MENTAL ILLNESS AND CULPABILITY

KANSAS v. HENDRICKS

Supreme Court of the United States, 1997.
521 U.S. 346, 117 S.Ct. 2072, 138 L.Ed.2d 501.

JUSTICE THOMAS delivered the opinion of the Court.

In 1994, Kansas enacted the Sexually Violent Predator Act, which establishes procedures for the civil commitment of persons who, due to a "mental abnormality" or a "personality disorder," are likely to engage in "predatory acts of sexual violence." Kan. Stat. Ann. § 59–29a01 *et seq*. (1994). The State invoked the Act for the first time to commit Leroy Hendricks, an inmate who had a long history of sexually molesting children, and who was scheduled for release from prison shortly after the Act became law. * * * The Kansas Supreme Court invalidated the Act, holding that its pre-commitment condition of a "mental abnormality" did not satisfy what the court perceived to be the "substantive" due process requirement that involuntary civil commitment must be predicated on a finding of "mental illness." * * * We granted certiorari, * * * and now reverse the judgment below.

I

A

* * *

[T]he Legislature found it necessary to establish "a civil commitment procedure for the long-term care and treatment of the sexually violent predator." The Act defined a "sexually violent predator" as:

> "any person who has been convicted of or charged with a sexually violent offense and who suffers from a mental abnormality or

personality disorder which makes the person likely to engage in the predatory acts of sexual violence."

A "mental abnormality" was defined, in turn, as a "congenital or acquired condition affecting the emotional or volitional capacity which predisposes the person to commit sexually violent offenses in a degree constituting such person a menace to the health and safety of others."

[T]he Act's civil commitment procedures pertained to: (1) a presently confined person who, like Hendricks, "has been convicted of a sexually violent offense" and is scheduled for release; (2) a person who has been "charged with a sexually violent offense" but has been found incompetent to stand trial; (3) a person who has been found "not guilty by reason of insanity of a sexually violent offense"; and (4) a person found "not guilty" of a sexually violent offense because of a mental disease or defect. * * *

In addition to placing the burden of proof [beyond reasonable doubt] upon the State, the Act afforded the individual a number of other procedural safeguards. In the case of an indigent person, the State was required to provide, at public expense, the assistance of counsel and an examination by mental health care professionals. The individual also received the right to present and cross-examine witnesses, and the opportunity to review documentary evidence presented by the State.

Once an individual was confined, the Act required that "the involuntary detention or commitment . . . shall conform to constitutional requirements for care and treatment." [These included an annual review by the committing court "to determine whether continued detention was warranted."] If the court found that the State could no longer satisfy its burden under the initial commitment standard, the individual would be freed from confinement.

B

In 1984, Hendricks was convicted of taking "indecent liberties" with two 13–year-old boys. After serving nearly 10 years of his sentence, he was slated for release to a halfway house. Shortly before his scheduled release, however, the State filed a petition in state court seeking Hendricks' civil confinement as a sexually violent predator. * * *

Hendricks subsequently requested a jury trial to determine whether he qualified as a sexually violent predator. During that trial, Hendricks' own testimony revealed a chilling history of repeated child sexual molestation and abuse, beginning in 1955 when he exposed his genitals to two young girls. At that time, he pleaded guilty to indecent exposure. Then, in 1957, he was convicted of lewdness involving a young girl and received a brief jail sentence. In 1960, he molested two young boys while he worked for a carnival. After serving two years in prison for that offense, he was paroled, only to be rearrested for molesting a 7–year-old girl. Attempts were made to treat him for his sexual deviance, and in 1965 he was considered "safe to be at large," and was discharged from a state psychiatric hospital.

Shortly thereafter, however, Hendricks sexually assaulted another young boy and girl—he performed oral sex on the 8–year-old girl and fondled the 11–year-old boy. He was again imprisoned in 1967, but refused to participate in a sex offender treatment program, and thus remained incarcerated until his parole in 1972. Diagnosed as a pedophile, Hendricks entered into, but then abandoned, a treatment program. He testified that despite having received professional help for his pedophilia, he continued to harbor sexual desires for children. Indeed, soon after his 1972 parole, Hendricks began to abuse his own stepdaughter and stepson. He forced the children to engage in sexual activity with him over a period of approximately four years. Then, as noted above, Hendricks was convicted of "taking indecent liberties" with two adolescent boys after he attempted to fondle them. As a result of that conviction, he was once again imprisoned, and was serving that sentence when he reached his conditional release date in September 1994.

Hendricks admitted that he had repeatedly abused children whenever he was not confined. He explained that when he "gets stressed out," he "can't control the urge" to molest children. Although Hendricks recognized that his behavior harms children, and he hoped he would not sexually molest children again, he stated that the only sure way he could keep from sexually abusing children in the future was "to die." Hendricks readily agreed with the state physician's diagnosis that he suffers from pedophilia and that he is not cured of the condition; indeed, he told the physician that "treatment is bull—." The jury unanimously found beyond a reasonable doubt that Hendricks was a sexually violent predator. The trial court subsequently determined, as a matter of state law, that pedophilia qualifies as a "mental abnormality" as defined by the Act, and thus ordered Hendricks committed to the Secretary's custody.

Hendricks appealed, claiming, among other things, that application of the Act to him violated the Federal Constitution's Due Process, Double Jeopardy, and *Ex Post Facto* Clauses. The Kansas Supreme Court * * * held that "the Act violates Hendricks' substantive due process rights." * * *

II

A

Kansas argues that the Act's definition of "mental abnormality" satisfies "substantive" due process requirements. We agree. Although freedom from physical restraint "has always been at the core of the liberty protected by the Due Process Clause from arbitrary governmental action," *Foucha* v. *Louisiana,* 504 U.S. 71, 80, 118 L. Ed. 2d 437, 112 S. Ct. 1780 (1992), that liberty interest is not absolute. * * *

The challenged Act unambiguously requires a finding of dangerousness either to one's self or to others as a prerequisite to involuntary confinement. Commitment proceedings can be initiated only when a person "has been convicted of or charged with a sexually violent offense," and "suffers from a mental abnormality or personality disorder which makes the person likely to engage in the predatory acts of sexual violence." The statute thus requires proof of more than a mere predisposition to violence; rather, it requires evidence of past sexually violent behavior and a present mental condition that creates a likelihood of such conduct in the future if the person is not incapacitated.

* * * The Kansas Act * * * requires a finding of future dangerousness, and then links that finding to the existence of a "mental abnormality" or "personality disorder" that makes it difficult, if not impossible, for the person to control his dangerous behavior. * * *

Hendricks nonetheless argues that our earlier cases dictate a finding of "mental illness" as a prerequisite for civil commitment. He then asserts that a "mental abnormality" is *not* equivalent to a "mental illness" because it is a term coined by the Kansas Legislature, rather than by the psychiatric community. Contrary to Hendricks' assertion, the term "mental illness" is devoid of any talismanic significance. Not only do "psychiatrists disagree widely and frequently on what constitutes mental illness," but the Court itself has used a variety of expressions to describe the mental condition of those properly subject to civil confinement.

Indeed, we have never required State legislatures to adopt any particular nomenclature in drafting civil commitment statutes. * * * The legal definitions of "insanity" and "competency," for example, vary substantially from their psychiatric counterparts. Legal definitions, however, which must "take into account such issues as individual responsibility ... and competency," need not mirror those advanced by the medical profession.

* * * The mental health professionals who evaluated Hendricks diagnosed him as suffering from pedophilia, a condition the psychiatric profession itself classifies as a serious mental disorder.[3] * * * This admitted lack of volitional control, coupled with a prediction of future dangerousness, adequately distinguishes Hendricks from other dangerous persons who are perhaps more properly dealt with exclusively through criminal proceedings. Hendricks' diagnosis as a pedophile, which qualifies as a "mental abnormality" under the Act, thus plainly suffices for due process purposes.

B

We granted Hendricks' cross-petition to determine whether the Act violates the Constitution's double jeopardy prohibition or its ban on *ex post facto* lawmaking. The thrust of Hendricks' argument is that the Act

3. We recognize, of course, that psychiatric professionals are not in complete harmony in casting pedophilia, or paraphilias in general, as "mental illnesses." These disagreements, however, do not tie the State's hands in setting the bounds of its civil commitment laws. In fact, it is precisely where such disagreement exists that legislatures have been afforded the widest latitude in drafting such statutes. As we have explained regarding congressional enactments, when a legislature "undertakes to act in areas fraught with medical and scientific uncertainties, legislative options must be especially broad and courts should be cautious not to rewrite legislation."

establishes criminal proceedings; hence confinement under it necessarily constitutes punishment. He contends that where, as here, newly enacted "punishment" is predicated upon past conduct for which he has already been convicted and forced to serve a prison sentence, the Constitution's Double Jeopardy and *Ex Post Facto* Clauses are violated. We are unpersuaded by Hendricks' argument that Kansas has established criminal proceedings.

The categorization of a particular proceeding as civil or criminal "is first of all a question of statutory construction." We must initially ascertain whether the legislature meant the statute to establish "civil" proceedings. If so, we ordinarily defer to the legislature's stated intent. Here, Kansas' objective to create a civil proceeding is evidenced by its placement of the Sexually Violent Predator Act within the Kansas probate code, instead of the criminal code, as well as its description of the Act as creating a "*civil commitment procedure*." * * *

Although we recognize that a "civil label is not always dispositive," we will reject the legislature's manifest intent only where a party challenging the statute provides "the clearest proof" that "the statutory scheme [is] so punitive either in purpose or effect as to negate [the State's] intention" to deem it "civil." In those limited circumstances, we will consider the statute to have established criminal proceedings for constitutional purposes. Hendricks, however, has failed to satisfy this heavy burden.

As a threshold matter, commitment under the Act does not implicate either of the two primary objectives of criminal punishment: retribution or deterrence. The Act's purpose is not retributive because it does not affix culpability for prior criminal conduct. Instead, such conduct is used solely for evidentiary purposes, either to demonstrate that a "mental abnormality" exists or to support a finding of future dangerousness. * * *

Moreover, unlike a criminal statute, no finding of scienter is required to commit an individual who is found to be a sexually violent predator; instead, the commitment determination is made based on a "mental abnormality" or "personality disorder" rather than on one's criminal intent. The existence of a scienter requirement is customarily an important element in distinguishing criminal from civil statutes. The absence of such a requirement here is evidence that confinement under the statute is not intended to be retributive.

Nor can it be said that the legislature intended the Act to function as a deterrent. Those persons committed under the Act are, by definition, suffering from a "mental abnormality" or a "personality disorder" that prevents them from exercising adequate control over their behavior. Such persons are therefore unlikely to be deterred by the threat of confinement. * * *

Although the civil commitment scheme at issue here does involve an affirmative restraint, "the mere fact that a person is detained does not inexorably lead to the conclusion that the government has imposed punishment." The State may take measures to restrict the freedom of the dangerously mentally ill. This is a legitimate non-punitive governmental objective and has been historically so regarded. * * *

Hendricks focuses on his confinement's potentially indefinite duration as evidence of the State's punitive intent. That focus, however, is misplaced. Far from any punitive objective, the confinement's duration is instead linked to the stated purposes of the commitment, namely, to hold the person until his mental abnormality no longer causes him to be a threat to others. If, at any time, the confined person is adjudged "safe to be at large," he is statutorily entitled to immediate release.

Furthermore, commitment under the Act is only *potentially* indefinite. The maximum amount of time an individual can be incapacitated pursuant to a single judicial proceeding is one year. If Kansas seeks to continue the detention beyond that year, a court must once again determine beyond a reasonable doubt that the detainee satisfies the same standards as required for the initial confinement. * * *

Hendricks next contends that the State's use of procedural safeguards traditionally found in criminal trials makes the proceedings here criminal rather than civil. * * * The numerous procedural and evidentiary protections afforded here demonstrate that the Kansas Legislature has taken great care to confine only a narrow class of particularly dangerous individuals, and then only after meeting the strictest procedural standards. That Kansas chose to afford such procedural protections does not transform a civil commitment proceeding into a criminal prosecution.

Finally, Hendricks argues that the Act is necessarily punitive because it fails to offer any legitimate "treatment." Without such treatment, Hendricks asserts, confinement under the Act amounts to little more than disguised punishment. Hendricks' argument assumes that treatment for his condition is available, but that the State has failed (or refused) to provide it. The Kansas Supreme Court, however, apparently rejected this assumption, explaining:

> "It is clear that the overriding concern of the legislature is to continue the segregation of sexually violent offenders from the public. Treatment with the goal of reintegrating them into society is incidental, at best. The record reflects that treatment for sexually violent predators is all but nonexistent. The legislature concedes that sexually violent predators are not amenable to treatment under [the existing Kansas involuntary commitment statute]. * * *"

* * * We therefore hold that the Act does not establish criminal proceedings and that involuntary confinement pursuant to the Act is not punitive. Our conclusion that the Act is nonpunitive thus removes an essential prerequisite for both Hendricks' double jeopardy and *ex post facto* claims.

1

The Double Jeopardy Clause provides: "[N]or shall any person be subject for the same offence to be twice put in jeopardy of life or limb." Although generally understood to preclude a second prosecution for the same offense, the Court has also interpreted this prohibition to prevent the State from "punishing twice, or attempting a second time to punish criminally, for the same offense." Hendricks argues that, as applied to him, the Act violates double jeopardy principles because his confinement under the Act, imposed after a conviction and a term of incarceration, amounted to both a second prosecution and a second punishment for the same offense. We disagree.

Because we have determined that the Kansas Act is civil in nature, initiation of its commitment proceedings does not constitute a second prosecution. Moreover, as commitment under the Act is not tantamount to "punishment," Hendricks' involuntary detention does not violate the Double Jeopardy Clause, even though that confinement may follow a prison term. * * *

We hold that the Kansas Sexually Violent Predator Act comports with due process requirements and neither runs afoul of double jeopardy principles nor constitutes an exercise in impermissible *ex post facto* lawmaking. Accordingly, the judgment of the Kansas Supreme Court is reversed.

It is so ordered.

JUSTICE KENNEDY, concurring.

* * *

Notwithstanding its civil attributes, the practical effect of the Kansas law may be to impose confinement for life. At this stage of medical knowledge, although future treatments cannot be predicted, psychiatrists or other professionals engaged in treating pedophilia may be reluctant to find measurable success in treatment even after a long period and may be unable to predict that no serious danger will come from release of the detainee.

A common response to this may be, "A life term is exactly what the sentence should have been anyway," or, in the words of a Kansas task force member, "SO BE IT." The point, however, is not how long Hendricks and others like him should serve a criminal sentence. With his criminal record, after all, a life term may well have been the only sentence appropriate to protect society and vindicate the wrong. The concern instead is whether it is the criminal system or the civil system which should make the decision in the first place. If the civil system is used simply to impose punishment after the State makes an improvident plea bargain on the criminal side, then it is not performing its proper function. These concerns persist whether the civil confinement statute is put on the books before or after the offense. We should bear in mind that while incapacitation is a goal common to both the criminal and civil systems of confinement, retribution and general deterrence are reserved for the criminal system alone. * * *

JUSTICE BREYER, with whom JUSTICES STEVENS and SOUTER join, and with whom JUSTICE GINSBURG joins as to Parts II and III, dissenting.

I agree with the majority that the Kansas Act's "definition of 'mental abnormality'" satisfies the "substantive" requirements of the Due Process Clause. Kansas, however, concedes that Hendricks' condition is treatable; yet the Act did not provide Hendricks (or others like him) with any treatment until after his release date from prison and only inadequate treatment thereafter. These, and certain other, special features of the Act convince me that it was not simply an effort to commit Hendricks civilly, but rather an effort to inflict further punishment upon him. The *Ex Post Facto* Clause therefore prohibits the Act's application to Hendricks, who committed his crimes prior to its enactment. * * *

II

Kansas' 1994 Act violates the Federal Constitution's prohibition of "any ... *ex post facto* Law" if it "inflicts" upon Hendricks "a greater punishment" than did the law "annexed to" his "crimes" when he "committed" those crimes in 1984. U.S. Const., Art. I, § 10. The majority agrees that the Clause " 'forbids the application of any *new punitive measure* to a crime already consummated.' " But it finds the Act is not "punitive." With respect to that basic question, I disagree with the majority.

Certain resemblances between the Act's "civil commitment" and traditional criminal punishments are obvious. Like criminal imprisonment, the Act's civil commitment amounts to "secure" confinement, and "incarceration against one's will." In addition, a basic objective of the Act is incapacitation, which, as Blackstone said in describing an objective of criminal law, is to "deprive the party injuring of the power to do future mischief."

Moreover, the Act, like criminal punishment, imposes its confinement (or sanction) only upon an individual who has previously committed a criminal offense. And the Act imposes that confinement through the use of persons (county prosecutors), procedural guarantees (trial by jury, assistance of counsel, psychiatric evaluations), and standards ("beyond a reasonable doubt") traditionally associated with the criminal law.

These obvious resemblances by themselves, however, are not legally sufficient to transform what the Act calls "civil commitment" into a criminal punishment. Civil commitment of dangerous, mentally ill individuals by its very nature involves confinement and incapacitation. Yet "civil commitment," from a constitutional perspective, nonetheless remains civil. Nor does the fact that criminal behavior triggers the Act make the critical difference. The Act's insistence upon a prior crime, by screening out those whose past behavior does not concretely demonstrate the existence of a mental problem or potential future danger, may serve an important noncriminal evidentiary purpose. Neither is the presence of criminal law-type procedures determinative. Those procedures can serve an important purpose that in this context one might consider noncriminal, namely helping to prevent judgmental mistakes that would wrongly deprive a person of important liberty.

If these obvious similarities cannot by themselves prove that Kansas' "civil commitment" statute is criminal, neither can the word "civil" written into the statute, by itself prove the contrary. * * *

* * *

[T]he Kansas statute insofar as it applies to previously convicted offenders, such as Hendricks, commits, confines, and treats those offenders *after* they have served virtually their entire criminal sentence. That time-related circumstance seems deliberate. The Act explicitly defers diagnosis, evaluation, and commitment proceedings until a few weeks prior to the "anticipated release" of a previously convicted offender from prison. But why, one might ask, does the Act not commit and require treatment of sex offenders sooner, say soon after they begin to serve their sentences? * * *

* * * I believe the Act before us involves an affirmative restraint historically regarded as punishment; imposed upon behavior already a crime after a finding of scienter; which restraint, namely confinement, serves a traditional aim of punishment, does not primarily serve an alternative purpose (such as treatment) and is excessive in relation to any alternative purpose assigned.

* * *

Note

As Justice Kennedy pointed out in his concurring opinion, the statute at issue in *Hendricks* may in fact be the product of concern that prison sentences for those convicted of child sexual abuse are too short. From this perspective, the civil commitment statute functions as a device for supplementing inadequate criminal sentences. For example, the civil commitment statute would be unnecessary to protect the public if repeat offenders like Hendricks were sentenced to life imprisonment without possibility of parole. This analysis seems consistent with the argument made by the four dissenters in *Hendricks*, who expressed concern that the Kansas statutory scheme permitted imposition of criminal penalties disguised as civil commitments.

By characterizing the procedure as civil in nature, the Kansas legislature may have avoided an issue not addressed in the *Hendricks* opinion. Recall that the Sexually Violent Predator Act made civil commitment possible for "any person who has been convicted of or charged with a sexually violent offense and who suffers from a mental abnormality or personality disorder which makes the person likely to engage in the predatory acts of sexual violence." Arguably, the statute imposes additional confinement after completion of the criminal sentence based upon the defendant's status as a member of a class exhibiting a "mental abnormality." A criminal punishment based upon this kind of status may be unconstitutional.

In *Robinson v. California*, 370 U.S. 660 (1962), the Supreme Court struck down a statute that made the "status" of being a narcotics addict a criminal offense, and permitted conviction without proof that the defendant had used, purchased, or sold narcotics. Six years later, the Court revisited the question in *Powell v. Texas*, 392 U.S. 514 (1968). Powell was convicted under a law making it a crime to be in a public place in a state of intoxication. Powell argued that he was being punished for his status as a chronic alcoholic, which he claimed was the source of his drinking. Arguments in *Powell* corresponded to many of the issues addressed in *Hendricks*. For example, the Supreme Court acknowledged that no generally effective method for treating alcoholism was known; that experts, including psychiatrists, disagreed about the causes and treatment of alcoholism; that the states offered inadequate treatment programs and facilities; and that criminal sanctions failed to deter alcoholics from engaging in antisocial behavior. The Court held, nonetheless that Powell had been convicted for the act of being drunk in public, not for his status as an alcoholic. It concluded that this punishment was "a far cry from convicting one for being an addict, being a chronic alcoholic, being 'mentally ill, or a leper. . . . ' "

Hendricks was convicted of criminal acts of child sexual abuse. Thus his criminal punishment, like Powell's, was triggered by his conduct, not his "status." But his subsequent civil commitment, which depended upon a finding of "mental abnormality," seems more akin to incarceration, albeit civil confinement, for this "status." This would seemingly be unconstitutional if it were classified as a criminal punishment.

The Supreme Court reviewed the Kansas Sexually Violent Predator Act again in *Kansas v. Crane*, 534 U.S. 407 (2002). The Kansas Supreme Court decided that prosecutors must prove that sexual offenders have a complete or total inability to control their "dangerous" behavior to commit such offenders to a hospital for treatment under the Act. The Supreme Court concluded that the Kansas court had interpreted *Hendricks* in an "overly restrictive manner" and held that prosecutors must only prove that sexual offenders have "serious difficulty" in their ability to control their behavior.

PEOPLE v. WETMORE

Supreme Court of California, 1978.
22 Cal.3d 318, 149 Cal.Rptr. 265, 583 P.2d 1308.

TOBRINER, JUSTICE.

Charged with burglary, defendant argued that psychiatric reports showed that as a result of mental illness he lacked the specific intent required for conviction of that crime. Relying on a dictum in *People v. Wells* (1949) 33 Cal.2d 330, 202 P.2d 53, the trial court reasoned that because the reports described defendant's insanity as well as his diminished capacity, such description of defendant's condition in those reports should not be admitted to prove lack of specific intent. * * *

The only evidence submitted to the trial court in this case was the testimony of Joseph Cacciatore, the victim of the burglary, at the preliminary hearing, and three psychiatric reports. Cacciatore testified that he left his apartment on March 7, 1975. When he returned three days later, he discovered defendant in his apartment. Defendant was wearing Cacciatore's clothes and cooking his food. The lock on the front door had been broken; the apartment lay in a shambles. Cacciatore called the police, who arrested defendant for burglary. Later Cacciatore discovered that a ring, a watch, a credit card, and items of clothing were missing.[1]

The psychiatric reports submitted to the court explain defendant's long history of psychotic illness, including at least 10 occasions of hospital confinement for treatment. According to the reports, defendant, shortly after his last release from Brentwood Veteran's Hospital, found himself with no place to go. He began to believe that he "owned" property, and was "directed" to Cacciatore's apartment. When he found the door unlocked he was sure he owned the apartment. He entered, rearranged the apartment, destroyed some advertising he felt was inappropriate, and put on Cacciatore's clothes. When the police arrived, defendant was shocked and embarrassed, and only then understood that he did not own the apartment.

Defendant pled not guilty to a charge of burglary and requested court appointment of a psychiatrist to advise him whether to enter a plea based on insanity. (See Evid.Code, §§ 730, 1017.) After receiving the report from Dr. John Woodward, defendant entered a plea of not guilty by reason of insanity. The court then appointed Drs. Michael Colburn and Marshall Cherkas to examine defendant.

When the matter was called for trial defendant personally and all counsel waived trial by jury and stipulated that the cause be submitted on the transcript of the preliminary hearing, which contained only the testimony of Cacciatore, and the reports of Drs. Colburn and Cherkas. Defense counsel pointed out that burglary requires an entry with specific intent to commit larceny or felony. The reports of Drs. Colburn and Cherkas, counsel argued, indicate that defendant entered the apartment under the delusion that he owned the apartment and its contents; he thus had no intent to commit theft or any felony.

In response to counsel's argument, the court acknowledged that defendant might lack the specific intent required to commit the crime of burglary. It stated, however, that under the controlling cases, "if a defendant's mental capacity which would preclude the forming of a specific intent is that of insanity," that mental condition is "not admissible to establish the question of lack of specific intent due to diminished capacity." The court thereupon found defendant guilty of second degree burglary. Turning to the issue of insanity, the court found on the basis of the psychiatric reports that defendant was insane under the

1. At the preliminary hearing defendant appeared wearing one of Cacciatore's shirts. The magistrate directed the sheriff to provide defendant with a county shirt, and admitted Cacciatore's shirt into evidence as an exhibit.

M'Naughten test then applicable and, hence, not guilty by reason of insanity.

At a subsequent hearing the trial court found that defendant had not recovered his sanity. The court therefore ordered defendant committed to Patton State Hospital for treatment. Defendant appeals from the order of commitment.

In holding that defendant's psychiatric evidence could not be utilized to prove that he lacked the specific intent required for the offense of burglary, the trial court followed a dictum laid down in our decision in People v. Wells, *supra*. *Wells,* the seminal decision which established the doctrine of diminished capacity in California law, held that "evidence of diminished mental capacity, whether caused by intoxication, trauma, or disease, can be used to show that a defendant did not have a specific mental state essential to an offense." In dictum, however, *Wells* stated that since sanity is conclusively presumed at the guilt trial, "evidence tending to show lack of mental capacity to commit the crime because of legal insanity is barred at that stage." The *Wells* opinion later restated that conclusion in different terms: "if the proffered evidence tends to show not merely that he [defendant] *did* or *did not,* but rather that because of legal insanity he *could* not, entertain the specific intent or other essential mental state, then that evidence is inadmissible under the not guilty plea * * * ."

As we shall explain, the *Wells* dictum imposes an illogical and unworkable rule which has not been followed in subsequent cases. *Wells* spoke of excluding evidence which tended to prove "lack of mental capacity * * * because of legal insanity." Mental incapacity does not occur "because of legal insanity"; instead both insanity and diminished capacity are legal conclusions derived from evidence of defendant's mental condition. Consequently, if the evidence of a defendant's mental illness indicates that the defendant lacked the specific intent to commit the charged crime such evidence cannot reasonably be ignored at the guilt trial merely because it might (but might not) also persuade the trier of fact that the defendant is insane.

* * *

We therefore hold that evidence of diminished capacity is admissible at the guilt phase whether or not that evidence may also be probative of insanity. The trial court erred when, relying on the *Wells* dictum, it refused to consider evidence of diminished capacity in determining defendant's guilt.

Amicus Los Angeles City Attorney urges that we sustain the trial court's ruling on a different ground. He contends that a defendant should be permitted to assert the defense of diminished capacity caused by mental disease or defect only to reduce a specific crime to a lesser included offense. Claiming that there is no lesser included offense in burglary, amicus argues that the trial court correctly refused to consider evidence of defendant Wetmore's diminished mental capacity.

No decisions support amicus' contention that diminished capacity does not apply to crimes lacking lesser included offenses. To the contrary, numerous cases have stated that diminished capacity arising from mental disease or defect serves as a defense to various crimes that may lack such included offenses. Amicus argues that in some of the cases such statements are dictum.

* * * No decision, amicus concludes, has *acquitted* a defendant on the basis of diminished capacity caused by mental disease or defect.

Nevertheless, this unanimity of judicial expression reinforces our conclusion that a defense of diminished capacity arising from mental disease or defect extends to all specific intent crimes, whether or not they encompass lesser included offenses. Clearly, if a crime requires specific intent, a defendant who because of mental disease or defect lacks that intent, cannot commit that crime. The presence or absence of a lesser included offense within the charged crime cannot affect the result. The prosecution must prove all elements of the crime beyond a reasonable doubt; we do not perceive how a defendant who has in his possession evidence which rebuts an element of the crime can logically be denied the right to present that evidence merely because it will result in his acquittal.

Amicus' argument, although legally flawed, addresses a matter of real concern. A defendant whose criminal activity arises from mental disease or defect usually requires confinement and special treatment. Penal Code sections 1026 and 1026a provide such confinement and treatment for persons found not guilty by reason of insanity. A defendant acquitted because, as a result of diminished capacity, he lacked the specific intent required for the crime cannot be confined pursuant to sections 1026 and 1026a, yet often he cannot be released without endangering the public safety.

The same danger may arise, however, when a diminished capacity defense does not result in the defendant's acquittal, but in his conviction for a lesser included offense. A defendant convicted of a lesser included misdemeanor, for example, will be confined for a relatively short period in a facility which probably lacks a suitable treatment program, and may later, having served his term, be released to become a public danger. The solution to this problem thus does not lie in barring the defense of diminished capacity when the charged crime lacks a lesser included offense, but in providing for the confinement and treatment of defendants with diminished capacity arising from mental disease or defect. * * *

Before concluding, we think it appropriate to note the effect of this decision, the latest in a line of decisions establishing and refining the concept of diminished capacity, on the California statutes governing the trial and disposition of persons who plead not guilty by reason of insanity. Doubtless when the 1927 Legislature provided for the bifurcated trial, it believed that it had cleanly separated the trial of issues of objective guilt from those involving mental illness or incapacity. The rise of the defense of diminished capacity has obliterated the distinction the Legislature sought to enact. The development of that defense has brought it so close to that of insanity that we doubt that the issue of diminished capacity has currently been placed on the proper side of the judicial ledger. Indeed, when we changed the designation of the defense from diminished "responsibility" to diminished "capacity" (People v. Anderson (1965) 63 Cal.2d 351, 46 Cal.Rptr. 763, 406 P.2d 43) we approached more nearly the concept of *inability* to conform one's conduct to the requirements of law, which is now a facet of the test of insanity. We said in *Anderson* "Clearly we cannot hold defendant responsible for a crime which requires as one of its elements the presence of a state of mind which he is incapable of achieving because of subjective abnormality or impaired volitional powers."

Prior to this appeal we have been confronted with a substantial number of cases that have illustrated the overlap in evidence admissible to prove diminished capacity and evidence admissible to prove insanity; with the present decision the duplication approaches a totality. To require the jury to hear the same evidence twice, once to determine diminished capacity and once to determine insanity, appears a pointless waste of judicial time and resources.

As we did once before we again suggest that the Legislature reconsider the wisdom of the statutes providing for bifurcated trial. The evidentiary duplication inherent in the present procedure could be eliminated either by a unitary trial or by a new method of bifurcation in which issues of diminished capacity and insanity are tried together at the second phase of the trial. * * *

The judgment (order of commitment) is reversed and the cause remanded for further proceedings consistent with this opinion.

Note

The California legislature reformed the diminished capacity defense, but not in the ways suggested at the end of the opinion in *Wetmore*. In a rare unanimous vote, the California Legislature repudiated the expanded definitions of premeditation and malice aforethought which the state courts had created. See West's Ann. California Penal Code §§ 188, 189, supra. The legislature also rejected the diminished capacity defense in amendments to §§ 28 and 29 of the California Penal Code. In the 1982 election, the voters of California approved a revision of § 25 of the California Penal Code, which abolished the diminished capacity defense across the board and also repudiated the California Supreme Court's 1978 adoption of the ALI insanity test. See People v. Skinner, 39 Cal.3d 765, 217 Cal.Rptr. 685, 704 P.2d 752 (1985). (The Initiative Measure did not, however, amend California Penal Code § 26, which grants a defense to any person "who committed the act charged without being conscious thereof."). The impact of the legislation dismantling the diminished capacity defense is analyzed the following case. Although the defendant's assertion of the defense rested upon evidence of intoxication, note how the court's analysis of the diminished capacity defense lumps together intoxication and mental illness.

PEOPLE v. SAILLE

Supreme Court of California, 1991.
54 Cal.3d 1103, 2 Cal.Rptr.2d 364, 820 P.2d 588.

PANELLI, JUSTICE

We granted review in this case to resolve a conflict among the Courts of Appeal regarding the impact of legislation abolishing diminished capacity on the crime of voluntary manslaughter. Specifically, the issue is whether the law of this state still permits a reduction of what would otherwise be murder to nonstatutory voluntary manslaughter due to voluntary intoxication and/or mental disorder. In this case, the Court of Appeal held that it does not. After careful examination of the relevant statutes and legislative history, we agree.

[Defendant was convicted of first degree murder and attempted murder. He had consumed approximately 18 to 22 beers over the course of several hours and was "noticeably drunk" when a security guard asked him to leave a bar. An hour later the security guard again refused to allow defendant to enter the bar. Saille left, but said "I'm going to get a gun and kill you." Defendant went to his home, got a semiautomatic assault rifle, returned to the bar, and told the guard "I told you I would be back." The two struggled over the gun, which discharged, killing a bystander. Saille and the security guard both were wounded during the struggle. Defendant's blood alcohol level two hours after the shooting was .14 percent, and expert testimony at trial was that at the time of the shooting it was .19 percent.]

Contentions

Defendant contends the court's instructions on the effect of voluntary intoxication were inadequate. The court gave CALJIC No. 4.21, stating that voluntary intoxication could be considered in determining whether defendant *had the specific intent to kill*. The court instructed on first and second degree murder and voluntary and involuntary manslaughter. It did not, however, relate voluntary intoxication to anything other than the specific intent to kill. Defendant contends the instructions were insufficient because they did not tell the jury that voluntary intoxication, like heat of passion upon adequate provocation, could negate express malice and reduce what would otherwise be murder to voluntary manslaughter. * * *

In rejecting these contentions, the Court of Appeal based its reasoning on the legislative enactments that (1) abolished diminished capacity and (2) clarified the definition of malice aforethought. Accordingly, before we can properly assess the correctness of the Court of Appeal's interpretation of the legislation, we review the historical development of the doctrine of diminished capacity.

[The court reviewed California Supreme Court opinions that developed of the diminished capacity defense. A discussion of the defense as it evolved in this case law is included in *People v. Wetmore*, supra.]

Finally, in *People* v. *Wetmore,* * * * [w]e * * * urged the Legislature to reconsider the wisdom of the statutes providing for bifurcated trial.

In response to our request, the Joint Committee for Revision of the Penal Code held two public hearings on the subject of psychiatric evidence and the defenses of diminished capacity and insanity. These hearings led to the introduction of Senate Bill No. 54, 1981–1982 Regular Session, to abolish the defense of diminished capacity. * * *

Senate Bill No. 54 added to the Penal Code sections 28 and 29, which abolished diminished capacity and limited psychiatric testimony. It amended section 22 on the admissibility of evidence of voluntary intoxication, section 188 on the definition of malice aforethought, and section 189 on the definition of premeditation and deliberation. * * *

Section 28, subdivision (a) provides in pertinent part that evidence of mental illness "shall not be admitted to show or negate the *capacity* to form any mental state," but is "admissible solely on the issue of whether or not the accused *actually* formed a required specific intent, premeditated, deliberated, or harbored malice aforethought, when a specific intent crime is charged." (Emphasis added.) Subdivision (b) of section 28 abolishes the defenses of diminished capacity, diminished responsibility, and irresistible impulse "as a matter of public policy."

Section 29 provides that any expert testifying in the guilt phase of a criminal action "shall not testify as to whether the defendant had or did not have the required mental states, which include, but are not limited to, purpose, intent, knowledge, or malice aforethought, for the crimes charged. The question as to whether the defendant had or did not have the required mental states shall be decided by the trier of fact."

* * *

A provision abolishing the defense of diminished capacity was also included in the initiative measure adopted in June 1982 and known as Proposition 8. Section 25 was added to the Penal Code as part of Proposition 8. Subdivision (a) of section 25 provides: "The defense of diminished capacity is hereby abolished. In a criminal action, as well as any juvenile court proceeding, evidence concerning an accused person's intoxication, trauma, mental illness, disease, or defect shall not be admissible to show or negate capacity to form the particular purpose, intent, motive, malice aforethought, knowledge, or other mental state required for the commission of the crime charged."

Although there was initially some confusion about the interaction between section 25, subdivision (a) and section 28, courts and commentators now appear to agree that the two sections are complementary and that both statutes remain operative.

Scope of Voluntary Manslaughter

Defendant argues that the new legislation did not limit the ability of an accused to reduce an intentional killing to voluntary manslaughter as a result of mental illness or involuntary intoxication. He relies primarily on *People* v. *Molina* (1988) 202 Cal.App.3d 1168, 249 Cal.Rptr. 273.

In *Molina*, a psychotic mother, who was experiencing auditory hallucinations, strangled and killed her 18-month-old son and set fire to the house. The trial court refused requested instructions on the lesser offenses of voluntary and involuntary manslaughter. The defendant was convicted of second degree murder and found not guilty by reason of insanity. The Court of Appeal reversed.

The *Molina* court reviewed sections 25, 28, and 29, noting that the statutory language provides that "evidence of mental problems is inadmissible to show that a defendant *lacked the capacity to form* the requisite mental state, but is admissible to show that the defendant *actually lacked the requisite mental state*." From this the court concluded: "The inclusion of the language in subdivision (a) [of section 28] regarding actual formation of mental states shows that the Legislature did not foreclose the possibility of a reduction from murder to voluntary manslaughter where malice is lacking due to mental illness, or a further reduction to involuntary manslaughter where intent to kill is not present for the same reason."

We are unpersuaded by defendant's reliance on *Molina*, since the court's analysis failed to consider the effect on the definition of malice of the amendment to section 188, which was part of the same legislative package as sections 25, 28, and 29.

Section 188, as amended by Senate Bill No. 54 now provides: "Such malice may be express or implied. It is express when there is manifested a deliberate intention unlawfully to take away the life of a fellow creature. It is implied, when no considerable provocation appears, or when the circumstances attending the killing show an abandoned and malignant heart. [para.] *When it is shown that the killing resulted from the intentional doing of an act with express or implied malice as defined above, no other mental state need be shown to establish the mental state of malice aforethought. Neither an awareness of the obligation to act within the general body of laws regulating society nor acting despite such awareness is included within the definition of malice.*" (Emphasis added.)

The first sentence of the underscored passage limits malice to the definition set forth in section 188. This sentence clearly provides that once the trier of fact finds a deliberate intention unlawfully to kill, no other mental state need be shown to establish malice aforethought. Whether a defendant acted with a wanton disregard for human life or with some antisocial motivation is no longer relevant to the issue of express malice. No doubt about this conclusion is possible when the last sentence of section 188 is analyzed. That sentence directly repudiates the expanded definition of malice aforethought in *People* v. *Conley* and *People* v. *Poddar* that express and implied malice include an awareness of the obligation to act within the general body of laws regulating society and the capability of acting in accordance with such awareness. After this amendment of section 188, express malice and an intent unlawfully to kill are one and the same.

Pursuant to the language of section 188, when an intentional killing is shown, malice aforethought is established. Accordingly, the concept of "diminished capacity voluntary manslaughter" (nonstatutory manslaughter) recognized in *Conley,* is no longer valid as a defense.

However, while retreating from the *Conley/Poddar* definition of malice aforethought, the Legislature left unchanged the definition of voluntary manslaughter in section 192. Indeed, that definition has not changed since section 192 was first enacted in 1872. Section 192 defines voluntary manslaughter as the "unlawful killing of a human being without malice . . . [para.] . . . upon a sudden quarrel or heat of passion." Thus, pursuant to the language of section 188, when an intentional killing is shown, malice aforethought is established. Section 192, however, negates malice when the intentional killing results from a sudden quarrel or heat of passion induced by adequate provocation.

* * *

"Moreover, as defined in cases predating *Conley* and *Conley's* foundational pillars * * * the concept of malice aforethought was manifested by the doing of an unlawful and felonious act intentionally and without legal cause or excuse. The adjective 'deliberate' in section 188 consequently implies an intentional act and is essentially redundant to the language defining express malice.

"The adverb 'unlawfully' in the express malice definition means simply that there is no justification, excuse, or mitigation for the killing recognized by the law.

"We still must reconcile the narrowed definition of malice aforethought in section 188 with the language of sections 22, subdivision (b) and 28, subdivision (a). These latter sections make evidence of voluntary intoxication and mental illness admissible solely on the issue of whether the accused 'actually formed a required specific intent, premeditated, deliberated, or harbored malice aforethought, when a specific intent crime is charged.' "

* * *

[E]vidence of mental disease, disorder, or defect is still admissible on the issue of whether the accused actually formed an intent unlawfully to kill—i.e., whether the accused actually formed express malice."

Sections 22 and 28 state that voluntary intoxication or mental condition may be considered in deciding whether the defendant actually had the required mental state, including malice. These sections relate to *any* crime, and make no attempt to define what mental state is required. Section 188, on the other hand, defines malice for purposes of murder. In combination, the statutes provide that voluntary intoxication or mental condition may be considered in deciding whether there was malice as defined in section 188. Contrary to defendant's contention, we see no conflict in these provisions.

Defendant further argues that the Legislature's narrowing of the definition of express malice and the resulting restriction of the scope of voluntary manslaughter presents a due process problem. We disagree. The Legislature can limit the mental elements included in the statutory definition of a crime and thereby curtail use of mens rea defenses. If, however, a crime requires a particular mental state the Legislature may not deny a defendant the opportunity to prove he did not possess that state. The abolition of the diminished capacity defense and limitation of admissible evidence to actual formation of various mental states has been held not to violate the due process right to present a defense. If there is no due process impediment to the deletion of malice as an element of the crime of felony murder, there is likewise no problem here. In amending section 188 in 1981, the Legislature equated express malice with an intent unlawfully to kill. Since two distinct concepts no longer exist, there has been some narrowing of the mental element included in the statutory definition of express malice. A defendant, however, is still free to show that because of his mental illness or voluntary intoxication, he did not *in fact* form the intent unlawfully to kill (i.e., did not have malice aforethought). In a murder case, if this evidence is believed, the only supportable verdict would be involuntary manslaughter or an acquittal. If such a showing gives rise to a reasonable doubt, the killing (assuming there is no implied malice) can be no greater than involuntary manslaughter.

It follows from the foregoing analysis that the trial court did not err in failing to instruct that voluntary intoxication could negate express malice so as to reduce a murder to voluntary manslaughter.

* * *

The judgment of the Court of Appeal is affirmed.

Note

Before 1981, California was the state most receptive to the diminished capacity defense and other psychiatric defenses outside the traditional area of the plea of not guilty by reason of insanity, so the rejection of the diminished capacity defense by California's legislature and voters warrants some discussion. The infamous "Dan White" verdict sparked a popular revolt against the judicially-created diminished capacity doctrine. Dan White resigned his elective office as San Francisco Supervisor, but then changed his mind and asked Mayor Moscone to reappoint him to the vacancy. Moscone's decision to appoint another person so enraged White that he went to the City Hall with a loaded pistol and shot the Mayor dead. After pausing to reload, he crossed the hall and assassinated Supervisor Harvey Milk, a prominent leader of San Francisco's homosexual community and a political adversary of White. A prominent psychiatrist testified for the defense that the violent outburst resulted from White's political and financial crisis and from his habit of gorging himself on high sugar "junk food" when under stress. The jury subsequently returned a verdict of manslaughter in both homicides, and public opinion saw this "Twinkie defense" as symptomatic of the willingness of the California courts to entertain even the most far-fetched psychiatric defenses. See Johnson, Book Review, 50 U.Chi.L.Rev. 1534, 1537 (1983). White was released from prison in 1984 after serving a little over 4 years for the two homicides. The intense public reaction in California to the Dan White verdict united liberals and conservatives in opposition to the diminished capacity defense.

The federal "Insanity Defense Reform Act of 1984" also rejects the diminished capacity doctrine. 18 U.S.C.A. § 20, which defines the insanity defense, specifically provides that "Mental disease or defect does not otherwise constitute a defense." Congress also amended Rule 704 of the Federal Rules of Evidence to provide that "No expert witness testifying with respect to the mental state or condition of a defendant in a criminal case may state an opinion or inference as to whether the defendant did or did not have the mental state or condition constituting an element of the crime charged or of a defense thereto. Such ultimate issues are matters for the trier of fact alone."

STATE v. WILCOX

Supreme Court of Ohio, 1982.
70 Ohio St.2d 182, 436 N.E.2d 523.

SWEENEY, JUSTICE.

The question before the court in the instant appeal is whether appellee is entitled to a new trial at which he may present expert psychiatric testimony relating to his alleged incapacity to form the requisite specific intent to commit aggravated murder and aggravated burglary. * * *

[Defendant Wilcox participated in a burglary in which the victim was shot and killed. A court-appointed psychiatrist found that he was borderline retarded, schizophrenic, dyslexic, and suffering from organic brain syndrome. After a few months of treatment, defendant was found competent to stand trial. He introduced psychiatric testimony in support of his plea of not guilty by reason of insanity, but the trial court refused to permit additional psychiatric testimony or charge the jury on the theory that defendant's mental condition precluded him from forming the specific intent to commit aggravated murder or aggravated burglary. In Ohio, aggravated felony murder requires a purpose to kill, and aggravated burglary requires a purpose to commit theft or a felony. The jury returned a verdict of guilty and the trial court imposed a life sentence on the murder count and an additional term on the burglary count.]

I

At the outset we note that there are a number of variations on the diminished capacity theme and a variety of labels have been applied to the doctrine.[13] Inasmuch as the Court of Appeals below referred to United States v. Brawner (C.A.D.C.1972), 471 F.2d 969, for the doctrinal underpinning of its diminished capacity formulation, it is appropriate for us to use the *Brawner* model of diminished capacity to provide a working definition of the doctrine for purposes of our discussion herein.[a] According to *Brawner,* at page 998, "expert testimony as to a defendant's abnormal mental condition may be received and considered, as tending to show, in a responsible way, that defendant did not have the specific mental state required for a particular crime or degree of crime—even though he was aware that his act was wrongful and was able to control it, and hence was not entitled to complete exoneration." If the *Brawner* rule were applied to the case at bar, then appellee, even though legally sane, could present psychiatric testimony as to his abnormal mental condition (diminished capacity) to show that he did not have the specific mental state—in this instance, the purpose—required to commit the crimes with which he stands charged. However, our review of the history and policies underlying the diminished capacity concept and the experience of jurisdictions that have attempted to apply the doctrine militate against the adoption of a *Brawner*-type rule in Ohio.

The diminished capacity defense originated in Scotland more than a century ago to reduce the punishment of the "partially insane" from murder to culpable homicide, a non capital offense. The doctrine has been widely accepted overseas, but most American jurisdictions, with the notable exception of California, have been slow to embrace the concept. While a number of states followed California's lead in adopting one form or another of the diminished capacity defense, the *Brawner* court may have overstated the case when it found that the doctrine was being

13. The various names include *inter alia* diminished or partial responsibility, partial insanity, and the *Wells–Gorshen* rule (after People v. Wells, 33 Cal.2d 330, 202 P.2d 53 (1949), and People v. Gorshen, 51 Cal.2d 716, 336 P.2d 492 (1959)). Commentators have fashioned a functionally-related nomenclature that seeks to differentiate the ways in which the doctrine has been applied. See, e.g., Arenella, The Diminished Capacity and Diminished Responsibility Defenses: Two Children of a Doomed Marriage, 77 Colum.L.Rev. 827 (hereinafter "Arenella") (distinguishing the "mens rea model," "diminished capacity," and "diminished responsibility"); and Lewin, Psychiatric Evidence in Criminal Cases for Purposes Other Than the Defense of Insanity, 26 Syr.L.Rev. 1051 (hereinafter "Lewin") (distinguishing "causative partial responsibility" and "ameliorative diminished responsibility").

a. Debate over both the insanity defense and the diminished capacity doctrine has been especially intense in the District of Columbia. The federal Court of Appeals for the District of Columbia Circuit is traditionally an intellectual, elite court composed of distinguished lawyers from the nation at large. The District of Columbia Court of Appeals is more like a state appellate court, with more local input into the judicial selection process. Before 1971, the District courts were bound by federal court decisions on District law as well as federal law, but in that year a statutory revision gave the District courts full responsibility for determining the District law on non-federal matters such as local criminal law.

The federal Court of Appeals, the source of the *Brawner* decision discussed in the text, has been more receptive to generous mental illness defenses than the local court. In Bethea v. United States, 365 A.2d 64 (D.C.App.1976), the District Court rejected the diminished capacity doctrine endorsed in *Brawner.* The Ohio Supreme Court's opinion in Wilcox discusses *Bethea* and also the similar opinion of the Wisconsin Supreme Court in Steele v. State, 97 Wis.2d 72, 294 N.W.2d 2 (1980). This discussion has been deleted from the text in the interest of brevity.—ed.

"adopted by the overwhelming majority of courts that have recently faced the question." * * * At this juncture, it appears that enthusiasm for the diminished capacity defense is on the wane and that there is, if anything, a developing movement away from diminished capacity although the authorities at this point are still quite mixed in their views.

The diminished capacity defense developed as a covert judicial response to perceived inequities in the criminal law. The purported justifications for the doctrine include the following:

> "(1) it ameliorates defects in a jurisdiction's insanity test criteria; (2) it permits the jury to avoid imposing the death penalty on mentally disabled killers who are criminally responsible for their acts; and (3) it permits the jury to make more accurate individualized culpability judgments." Arenella, supra, at page 853.

In addition the diminished capacity defense has a certain logical appeal when juxtaposed against the settled rule that evidence of voluntary intoxication may be considered in determining whether an accused acted with the requisite specific intent.

* * *

Upon examination, however, we find none of the foregoing justifications for the defense of diminished capacity sufficiently compelling as to warrant its adoption, particularly in light of the problems posed by the doctrine, problems even its proponents acknowledge.[16]

A

The diminished capacity defense does serve to ameliorate the limitations of the traditional, M'Naghten, right from wrong test for insanity. It is no coincidence that California, which pioneered the diminished capacity defense, for many years adhered to a strict M'Naghten standard. * * *

The ameliorative argument loses much of its force, however, in jurisdictions that have abandoned or expanded upon the narrow M'Naghten standard. The test for insanity in Ohio is set forth in State v. Staten (1969), 18 Ohio St.2d 13, 247 N.E.2d 293, as follows:

> One accused of criminal conduct is not responsible for such criminal conduct if, at the time of such conduct, as a result of mental disease or defect, he does not have the capacity either to know the wrongfulness of his conduct or to conform his conduct to the requirements of law. * * *

(Citations omitted.)

16. See, e.g., Diamond, Criminal Responsibility of the Mentally Ill, 14 Stan. L.Rev. 59, 82–86 (hereinafter "Diamond"); Diamond, From Durham to Brawner, A Futile Journey, 1973 Wash.Univ.L.Q. 109, (hereinafter "Futile Journey"), Lewin, supra, 1089–1097; Note, A Punishment Rationale for Diminished Capacity, 18 U.C.L.A.L.Rev. 561, 570–572; Note, Keeping Wolff From the Door: California's Diminished Capacity Concept, 60 Cal.L.Rev. 1641, 1653–1655.

While this standard is arguably less expansive than that espoused by the drafters of the Model Penal Code, it is considerably more flexible than the M'Naghten rule. The record in the case at bar, which is replete with expert testimony going to the question of appellee's sanity, illustrates the relative liberality of Ohio's insanity rule. Thus we see no reason to fashion a halfway measure, e.g., diminished capacity, when an accused may present a meaningful insanity defense in a proper case.

The interplay between the diminished capacity doctrine and the insanity defense, moreover, is not limited to the supposed ameliorative effect of the former on the latter. Rather, as Dr. Diamond, among others, has observed, "experience with the diminished responsibility (or capacity) defense has been extensive in England and in California, and indicates that this defense does not just supplement the insanity defense, but tends to supersede it * * * "Dr. Diamond, a leading proponent of the diminished capacity concept whose testimony is quoted at some length in *Gorshen,* supra, attributes the supersession of the insanity defense to the fact that a diminished capacity formulation "may well be a much more rational solution to the problem of the mentally ill offender." Futile Journey, supra, at page 124. Other commentators are far less sanguine about the tendency of diminished capacity to supplant the insanity defense. * * *

Professor Arenella notes that "seriously disturbed defendants can avoid an indefinite commitment to a mental hospital for the criminally insane by relying on the diminished responsibility defense which frequently leads to a reduced term in prison." According to this view, the principal practical effect of the diminished capacity defense is to enable mentally ill offenders to receive shorter and more certain sentences than they would receive if they were adjudged insane. Having satisfied ourselves that Ohio's test for criminal responsibility adequately safeguards the rights of the insane, we are disinclined to adopt an alternative defense that could swallow up the insanity defense and its attendant commitment provisions.

B

We can quickly dispose of the argument that the diminished capacity defense alleviates the harshness of the death penalty when mentally ill but nonetheless sane defendants are convicted of capital crimes. While this rationale formerly had considerable force, and indeed may have been the underlying basis of People v. Wells, supra, recent United States Supreme Court decisions have limited capital crimes to a narrow range of cases. * * *

Mental capacity is a formal mitigating factor in capital cases under current Ohio law at the punishment stage of the now bifurcated proceedings. Thus the ameliorative purpose served by the diminished capacity defense in capital cases has largely been accomplished by other means.

C

The justifications for diminished capacity relating to the defense's potential for more accurate, individualized culpability judgments and its logical relevance are based largely on analogies to the insanity defense and the defense of intoxication, respectively. * * *

Theoretically the insanity concept operates as a bright line test separating the criminally responsible from the criminally irresponsible. The diminished capacity concept on the other hand posits a series of rather blurry lines representing gradations of culpability. As Professor Arenella notes, "the analogy to the insanity defense is misleading because the diminished responsibility doctrine asks the expert witness and the jury to make a far more subtle distinction. The insanity defense asks both to distinguish between a large group of offenders who are punishable for their acts despite their mental deficiencies, and a small class of offenders who are so mentally disabled that they cannot be held accountable because they lack the minimal capacity to act voluntarily. The diminished responsibility doctrine attempts to divide the first large group of responsible sane offenders into two subgroups: a group of 'normal' fully culpable criminal offenders, and a group of mentally abnormal but sane offenders with reduced culpability." In light of the line drawing difficulties courts and juries face when assessing expert evidence to make the "bright line" insanity determination, we are not at all confident that similar evidence will enable juries, or the judges who must instruct them, to bring the blurred lines of diminished capacity into proper focus so as to facilitate principled and consistent decision-making in criminal cases. In short, the fact that psychiatric evidence is admissible to prove or disprove insanity does not necessarily dictate the conclusion that it is admissible for purposes unrelated to the insanity defense.

The *Brawner* court emphasized the apparent illogic of permitting evidence of voluntary intoxication to be introduced to negate specific intent while precluding the introduction of evidence of an abnormal mental condition not amounting to insanity for the same purpose. While we concede that there is a superficial attractiveness to the intoxication-diminished capacity analogy, upon closer examination we, like the court in *Bethea,* find the concepts to be quite disparate. * * *

It takes no great expertise for jurors to determine whether an accused was so intoxicated as to be mentally unable to intend anything, whereas the ability to assimilate and apply the finely differentiated psychiatric concepts associated with diminished capacity demands a sophistication (or as critics would maintain a sophistic bent) that jurors (and officers of the court) ordinarily have not developed. We are convinced that these significant evidentiary distinctions preclude treating diminished capacity and voluntary intoxication as functional equivalents for purposes of partial exculpation from criminal responsibility.

II

We have examined the commonly asserted justifications for diminished capacity and have found them wanting. We have also looked at the leading California cases, which attempted to apply the diminished capacity concept in a principled manner, and have concluded that the California experience with diminished capacity does not inspire imitation. The California courts struggled to evolve a coherent diminished capacity framework but the difficulties inherent in the doctrine, e.g., its subjectivity, its non-uniform and exotic terminology, its open-endedness, and its quixotic results in particular cases, were not overcome, and therefore consistent and predictable application of the diminished capacity concept in California became an elusive and unachieved goal. * * *

We hold, therefore, that the partial defense of diminished capacity is not recognized in Ohio and consequently, a defendant may not offer expert psychiatric testimony, unrelated to the insanity defense, to show that the defendant lacked the mental capacity to form the specific mental state required for a particular crime or degree of crime.

[Conviction affirmed.]

STATE v. BROM

Supreme Court of Minnesota, 1990.
463 N.W.2d 758.

TOMLJANOVICH, J.

In the early evening of February 18, 1988, Olmsted County sheriff's deputies discovered the bodies of Paulette, Bernard, Diane, and Richard Brom on the second floor of the Brom family home. All four individuals had sustained numerous gashes in the head and upper body. Police subsequently found a blood-stained ax in the basement that forensic tests indicated was used to kill all four victims. Tests also revealed the ax handle bore appellant's palm and finger prints.

On February 19, 1988, Rochester police officers arrested appellant in connection with the deaths of his parents and siblings. Because he was 16 years old at the time, appellant was initially charged in the juvenile justice system. After a much-publicized reference hearing and appeal, however, appellant was referred for prosecution as an adult. See In re D.F.B., 433 N.W.2d 79 (Minn.1988). * * *

Because appellant pleaded both not guilty and not guilty by reason of mental illness, his trial proceeded in two phases as required by [statute]. Phase one was limited to a determination of whether appellant was guilty of first or second degree murder in connection with the deaths of his parents and siblings. During phase one, defense counsel made an offer of proof requesting permission to introduce expert psychiatric testimony regarding appellant's capacity to premeditate his actions.[4] The

4. Defense counsel stated: "The defense recognizes that under the current state of the law in Minnesota, specifically State v. Bouwman, that expert psychiatric testimo-

trial court denied this request and the defense rested without offering testimony. The jury was instructed that it should not consider evidence of appellant's mental illness in its phase one deliberations and found appellant guilty of four counts of murder in the first degree.

In phase two of his trial, appellant bore the burden of proving his legal mental illness by a preponderance of the evidence. The defense presented expert testimony from one psychiatrist who concluded that appellant did not understand that killing his parents and siblings was wrong when he did so and that, therefore, he was legally insane. The state offered expert testimony from four psychiatrists. Of these four witnesses, two concluded that appellant was not legally insane at the time he committed the murders and two did not offer an opinion as to his legal mental illness. All of the experts agreed, however, that appellant suffered some form of mental illness or impairment.

Having been instructed regarding appellant's burden of proving his legal mental illness by a preponderance of the evidence, the jury returned verdicts of guilty as to four counts of murder in the first degree. The trial court then imposed four life sentences. * * *

Appellant claimed that in prohibiting expert psychiatric testimony from the guilt phase of his bifurcated trial, the trial court precluded his defense as to the element of premeditation and thereby denied him due process of law.

Appellant's claim is not new to this court. In State v. Bouwman, 328 N.W.2d 703 (Minn.1982), we held expert psychiatric testimony inadmissible with respect to the elements of premeditation and intent. Although appellant correctly indicates that *Bouwman* focused almost exclusively on the rationale for precluding such testimony as to the element of criminal intent, we do not read *Bouwman* to permit a meaningful distinction between intent and premeditation with respect to our prohibition of psychiatric testimony.

In *Bouwman*, we reasoned that psychiatric testimony is irrelevant as to intent because intent must almost always be inferred from the circumstances surrounding a particular crime.

Essentially, the fact finder is presented with physical evidence related to a given act and asked to draw on its sensory perceptions, life experiences, and common sense to determine whether that act was indeed intentional. Because psychiatric evidence "does not relate to the physical evidence upon which the jury is to determine the issue of intent," it is irrelevant to that issue and cannot be admitted either to

ny on the subject of premeditation in phase one of a bifurcated trial is inadmissible. Recognizing that, we wish to make an offer of proof that if called to testify in phase one, Dr. Carl Malmquist, a psychiatrist, would testify in essence that if we take things in an obvious but superficial manner, it would appear that the acts of David Brom were thought about intermittently for months prior to their occurrence. However, that ignores complicated questions with respect to the nature of his thought processes, his capacity to act otherwise, and the origins and other contributing factors that led to his preoccupation with suicide and homicide. And that Dr. Malmquist has difficulty as a psychiatrist getting into the questions of premeditation."

prove or to disprove it. Id. Such evidence only becomes relevant when a criminal defendant's mental incapacity is actually put into issue—that is, in phase two of a bifurcated trial.

Bouwman does not permit a different result with respect to premeditation. Although premeditation[7] involves "more than an intent to kill," it, like intent, is "subjective" and must be inferred from "the totality of the circumstances surrounding the crime." [Citations] Indeed, both elements must be inferred from physical evidence related to a particular act. Thus, psychiatric testimony is no more relevant to determining premeditation than it is to the determination of intent. * * *

Appellant has not elucidated, and we do not now perceive, a means by which we might permit the introduction of psychiatric testimony as to premeditation without dismantling the entire bifurcated trial process. We therefore reiterate our conclusion in *Bouwman* that psychiatric testimony is inadmissible as to the element of premeditation. * * * [Convictions affirmed.]

WAHL, JUSTICE, dissenting.

The defendant admitted he committed the acts which resulted in the four deaths but sought to introduce expert psychiatric opinion to negate the element of premeditation. Premeditation, as this court has held, involves, in addition to the mere intent to kill, a pre-existing reflection and deliberation. We have stated that inferences of pre-existing reflection and deliberation are properly drawn only from physical evidence. *Bouwman*, 325 N.W.2d at 705. It cannot be said, however, that direct inquiries into impaired mental states have no relevance or value in determining whether an individual did, in fact, reflect or deliberate on an act. It is conceivable that a person whose actions are steered by powerful mental aberrations may leave behind physical evidence indicating a pre-existing reflection and deliberation, but that when the mental condition is itself directly explored, the jury may find the inference of premeditation substantially rebutted. Dr. Malmquist's proffered testimony was clearly relevant in determining the absence or presence of the requisite premeditation, under the circumstances of this case.

A finding of premeditation is to be based upon the circumstances as a whole. Defendant's mental impairment is as much a part of those circumstances as intoxication, infancy, senility and other conditions recognized by this court as probative of defendant's state of mind. Although to some extent, conditions such as intoxication or infancy are

7. "For the purposes of [murder in the first degree], 'premeditation' means to consider, plan or prepare for, or determine to commit, the act referred to prior to its commission." Minn. Stat. § 609.18 (1990).

"Premeditation means that defendant considered, planned, prepared for, or determined to commit the act before defendant committed it. Premeditation, being a process of the mind, is wholly subjective and hence not always susceptible to proof by direct evidence. It may be inferred from all the circumstances surrounding the event. It is not necessary that premeditation exist for any specific length of time. A premeditated decision to kill may be reached in a short period of time. However, an unconsidered or rash impulse, even though it includes an intent to kill, is not premeditated." 10 Minn. Dist. Judges Ass'n, Minnesota Practice, CRIMJIG 11.02 (3d ed. 1990).

capable of quantification, they, like mental illness, can only indicate the degree to which a condition impaired defendant's mental processes. All of these conditions acknowledge a mental disability of some type and all are probative as to whether a defendant formulated the required mens rea. * * *

I would reverse the convictions and remand for a new trial at which expert testimony as to defendant's state of mind at the time of the killings in order to negate the state's claim that he acted with premeditation would be admitted. This decision, as defendant's counsel has so eloquently argued, would constitute nothing more than the reaffirmation of several concepts basic to our system of jurisprudence: the presumption of innocence and the due process requirement that the state prove each element of the crime beyond a reasonable doubt and the defendant's right to present relevant evidence in his defense.

PEOPLE v. LOW

Supreme Court of Colorado, 1987.
732 P.2d 622.

ERICKSON, JUSTICE.

This is an appeal by the prosecution on a point of law following the acquittal of defendant Low in a court trial on a charge of assault in the first degree and all lesser included offenses.[a] The trial court found Low not guilty because the prosecution did not establish that he had the required specific or general intent necessary to commit assault in the first, second, or third degrees.[1] The trial court acquitted the defendant because he had consumed an excessive amount of "HOLD" cough drops which caused him to become "temporarily insane" and incapable of formulating either a specific or a general criminal intent.

I

Defendant Robert Eugene Low was president and general manager of Prime, Inc., a trucking company in Springfield, Missouri. Low and his fourteen-year old stepson Shane Low (Shane), together with several friends arranged a hunting trip to Creede, Colorado.

The hunters planned to meet in Creede on Friday, October 14, 1983. On October 13, 1983, Low worked at his trucking company all day, and then he and Shane attended a hunter's safety class that evening so that they could obtain Colorado hunting licenses. After the hunter's safety

a. Although the principle of "double jeopardy" prevents a retrial of a defendant who was acquitted after the presentation of evidence, the prosecution in some states may nonetheless appeal to obtain a legal ruling that may be important in future cases.—ed.

1. In Colorado, "all offenses ... in which the mental culpability requirement is expressed as 'intentionally' or 'with intent' are declared to be specific intent offenses." The crimes of first and second degree assault * * * are specific intent crimes.

Only those offenses that contain the mental culpability element of "knowingly" or "willfully" are general intent crimes. We use the term "general intent" to signify any crime which does not require proof of a specific intent and is not a crime of strict liability.

class, Low drove all night to be in Creede at the agreed time. Low and Shane arrived in Creede at approximately 3:00 p.m. on October 14, and after some delay, located Kim McCowan (Kim), the brother of the victim in this case, and Jerry Roller (Roller), both of whom were friends from Missouri. Kim and Roller led the way up the canyon to the campsite in a four-wheel-drive vehicle, followed by Low and Shane in Low's pickup truck.

On the trip up the mountain road, Low became increasingly anxious and apprehensive, and had feelings of unreality. He began to notice that the trees surrounding the road had a particular type of bark that was "soft and unnatural." He was paranoid and questioned his stepson about what was occurring and why he was being "tricked." At approximately the halfway point to the camp, the defendant stopped his pickup truck. When Kim and Roller stopped their truck to make sure everything was all right, Low demanded that all of the individuals kneel in prayer with him. Kim testified that he had never known Low to be "a religious person," but imagined that the beauty of the wilderness inspired Low to demand the prayer session. Upon concluding the prayer, Low insisted that Roller drive Shane to the campsite in Kim's truck, and that Kim drive Low's truck with Low as a passenger. Kim complied because Low appeared to be tired from his trip from Missouri. During the remainder of the ride to the campsite, Low speculated on whether he was alive or dead.

When the parties arrived at the campsite, Low was convinced that he was dead and had gone to hell. Kim, still believing that Low was exhausted, suggested that he rest in the small cabin at the campsite while the others unload his truck and erect his tent. Low went to the cabin and rested for five or ten minutes. While in the cabin, Low concluded that he was a corpse in a mausoleum and that it was necessary to redeem himself in order to get to heaven. He then walked out of the cabin and up a small knoll and, referring to his tent, said, "we're going to bring it up here. We're going to raise the temple here." The other members of the hunting party took Low's tent up the knoll and began to set it up. Low approached A.D. McCowan (Duane or A.D.), who was helping with the tent, and said, "You're the devil, Duane." A.D. made a response relating to Low's ingratitude and Low said, "If you're not the devil, stand up and look me in the eye." A.D. did so, and the confrontation seemingly ended.

Low went down the knoll to his truck while Kim and A.D. continued to set up the tent. He asked for his rifle and told his stepson to get him some shells for the gun. The other hunters realized by this time that Low was disturbed in some way and took the rifle from him. The defendant then unbuckled his hunting knife, went to his tent, and stabbed A.D. in the upper back. Low was immediately subdued. His friends testified that Low repeatedly called his tent a temple, and that he was acting in an irrational and "crazy" manner. McCowan suffered serious injuries and was taken to Creede, and from there he was transferred by ambulance to a hospital in Del Norte. Kim and Shane remained at the campsite to look after Low while the others took A.D. to the hospital. Low tried to stab himself when Kim attempted to take the hunting knife away from him, but Kim obtained the knife after a brief struggle. Low then returned to his truck, removed a can of kerosene from the truck bed, and went into the partially erected tent. He poured kerosene on the floor, sat in a folding chair, and ignited the tent while he was still inside of it. Kim unsuccessfully attempted to get Low out of the burning tent. Convinced that Low was "crazy," Kim grabbed a gun and ammunition and took Shane into the woods to avoid a further confrontation until help arrived. Low left the tent shortly before it was burned completely and fell asleep on the ground. After a short nap, he began questioning what had happened, and then returned to the cabin and lay down. He dozed and awakened from time to time and began feeling sensations of being cold and again questioned whether or not he was in fact dead. When the police arrived and arrested the defendant the next day, he told them that the unreal nightmare was finally over. The uncontradicted testimony was that the defendant, for several months prior to the attack on A.D. McCowan, had ingested forty to fifty "HOLD" cough drops a day. The defendant's use of the cough drops had developed over the course of five to six months. He initially took the cough drops after developing a lingering cough and cold but continued to take them as a partial substitute for chewing tobacco and in an effort to quit smoking. On his trip to Colorado, he did not sleep and consumed approximately one hundred twenty cough drops within a twenty-four-hour period. Prior to his attack on McCowan, he had never felt any adverse or intoxicating effects from the cough drops.

Dr. Lewis, a psychiatrist, examined Low in June 1984, and concluded that Low was not mentally ill at the time of the examination. "HOLD" cough drops contain the drug dextromethorphan hydrobromide. Dr. Lewis stated that Low ingested approximately one gram of dextromethorphan when he consumed twelve packages of the cough drops in the twenty-four hours preceding the attack on McCowan. In Dr. Lewis's opinion, there was very little doubt that the drug caused a psychotic disorder known as "organic delusional syndrome" or "toxic psychosis." Symptoms of toxic psychosis include a distorted perception of reality, paranoia, auditory hallucinations, and delusions. Dr. Lewis testified that Low was incapable of distinguishing right from wrong at the time of the alleged assault, and that Low did not have the ability to formulate the specific intent to commit a criminal act. * * *

Low entered a plea of not guilty and waived his right to a jury trial. Both the prosecution and the court were advised that the defendant was not entering a plea of not guilty by reason of insanity, and elected not to plead the affirmative defense of impaired mental condition. The defendant offered to submit to an examination by any certified psychiatrist selected by the prosecution.

Prior to trial, defense counsel gave a notice of defenses to the court and to the prosecutor. The affirmative defense of involuntary intoxication was raised in the notice. The defense claimed that the warning on the cough drop box did not alert the defendant to the danger of intoxication. The notice also stated that the defense would rely upon the absence of the requisite specific intent to commit the crime of assault in the first degree.

The trial judge found that the prosecution proved beyond a reasonable doubt that Low caused serious bodily injury to A.D. McCowan by means of a deadly weapon. In considering whether Low acted with the specific intent required by the first-degree assault statute, the court reviewed the affirmative defense of involuntary intoxication. However, the trial judge did not make an explicit finding of involuntary intoxication, impaired mental condition or insanity, but acquitted the defendant because the prosecution "failed to prove an element of the offense or any lesser included offense; namely, the culpability element of mens rea."

The question before us is whether the failure of the defendant to plead the defense of insanity or impaired mental condition precludes the introduction of evidence of insanity or impaired mental condition to establish the absence of mens rea.

II

* * * The only disputed factual issue in this case was whether the defendant had the requisite mental culpability to commit first-degree assault or any lesser included offense. It was stipulated that the defendant, with or by means of a hunting knife, a deadly weapon, stabbed A.D. McCowan in the back and inflicted serious bodily injury.

A. The Affirmative Defense of Intoxication

Intoxication, voluntary or involuntary, is a "disturbance of mental or physical capacities resulting from the introduction of any substance into the body." Voluntary or self-induced intoxication is "caused by substances which the defendant knows or ought to know have the tendency to cause intoxication and which he knowingly introduced or allowed to be introduced into his body. * * * "Involuntary intoxication is intoxication that is not self-induced, and by definition occurs when the defendant does not knowingly ingest an intoxicating substance, or ingests a substance not known to be an intoxicant. See § 18–1–804, 8B C.R.S. (1986).

Low claimed that the manufacturer's warning did not indicate that intoxication was a possible side effect of ingesting large quantities of the medication, and Low's previous experience with "HOLD" did not alert him to the possibility of intoxication. Expert testimony established that Low's consumption of excessive quantities of dextromethorphan hydrobromide resulted in delusional and psychotic behavior, precluding Low from conforming his conduct to the requirements of law. Had the trial court found as a factual matter that Low was involuntarily intoxicated, assuming the finding was supported by sufficient competent evidence, its judgment of acquittal would have been proper. There are no special pleading requirements for the affirmative defense of involuntary intoxication, and an involuntarily intoxicated defendant is absolved of responsibility for all criminal acts.

B. *The Affirmative Defense of Insanity*

Because the trial court did not make a finding of involuntary intoxication, we must resolve this case on grounds of insanity or impaired mental condition. Section 16–8–101, 8A C.R.S. (1986), provides in pertinent part: (1) The applicable test of insanity shall be, and the jury shall be so instructed: "A person who is so diseased or defective in mind at the time of the commission of the act as to be incapable of distinguishing right from wrong with respect to that act is not accountable. But care should be taken not to confuse such mental disease or defect with moral obliquity, mental depravity, or passion growing out of anger, revenge, hatred, or other motives, and kindred evil conditions, for when the act is induced by any of these causes the person is accountable to the law."

The General Assembly has classified insanity as an affirmative defense, and has set forth rules for pleading the defense. The consequences of failing to plead the insanity defense as required by statute are clear: "Insanity as a defense shall not be an issue in any prosecution unless it" is pleaded at arraignment. Section 18–1–802, 8B C.R.S. (1986).

A plea of insanity is akin to the common law plea of "confession and avoidance," and admits the commission of the offense but avoids or provides an excuse for criminal responsibility because the accused was insane at the time of the commission of the offense. In this context, an insane person is absolved of responsibility for all crimes, including those that do not require proof of a mens rea element.

C. *The Affirmative Defense of Impaired Mental Condition*

In our early cases, we acknowledged that evidence of a mental condition short of insanity may preclude a defendant from forming a culpable mental state. * * * [We subsequently held that evidence of an impaired mental condition may be admissible to show lack of culpability even in general intent crimes.]

"Once we accept the basic principles that an accused is presumed innocent and that he cannot be adjudicated guilty unless the prosecution proves beyond a reasonable doubt the existence of the mental state required for the crime charged, it defies both logic and fundamental fairness to prohibit a defendant from presenting reliable and relevant evidence that, due to a mental impairment beyond his conscious control, he lacked the capacity to entertain the very culpability which is indispensable to his criminal responsibility in the first instance." Hendershott v. People, 653 P.2d 385, 393–94 (Colo.1982).

The General Assembly amended the definition of impaired mental condition after *Hendershott* was announced. The new definition does not distinguish between specific and general intent crimes: "Impaired mental condition" means a condition of mind, caused by mental disease or defect, which does not constitute insanity but, nevertheless, prevents the person from forming a culpable mental state which is an essential element of a crime charged.

The impaired mental condition defense is separate and distinct from the defense of insanity. The sole effect of the defense of impaired mental condition is to negate the existence of an element of the crime charged. Thus, unlike the insanity defense, the successful assertion of impaired mental condition negatives the commission of the crime.

III

* * * The statutory scheme for raising the defenses of insanity and impaired mental condition is clear. If the defendant intends to avoid responsibility for criminal acts by pleading not guilty by reason of insanity, the plea must be entered at the time of arraignment or at any time prior to trial for good cause shown. * * * Consequently, evidence of insanity is irrelevant and inadmissible at a trial on the merits in the absence of a special plea. The defense of impaired mental condition applies where the defendant intends to contest the commission of the crime due to his alleged inability to formulate the requisite culpable mental state. Impaired mental condition also must be raised at arraignment, or it too is waived. Evidence of impaired mental condition is admissible only if the defense is pleaded as required by statute.

In this case, the trial court's findings and conclusions failed to address the defense of involuntary intoxication which was properly raised and was the primary theory of defense. Evidence of involuntary intoxication was before the trial court but Low's acquittal was not predicated on that defense. Temporary insanity is not part of the Colorado statutory framework for resolving a defendant's nonresponsibility for a criminal act, and was not a proper ground for the trial court's entry of a judgment of acquittal. The trial court permitted Low to introduce evidence of insanity and impaired mental condition to defeat the mens rea element of first-degree assault and the lesser included offenses. It is undisputed that Low did not plead the defenses of impaired mental condition or insanity at arraignment. The expert psychiatric testimony adduced at trial was inadmissible insofar as it was offered to prove Low's nonresponsibility due to insanity or inability to formulate specific or general criminal intent due to mental impairment.

Accordingly, the trial court's judgment of acquittal is disapproved.

Chapter 5

JUSTIFICATION AND EXCUSE

A. DURESS AND THE GENERAL PRINCIPLE OF JUSTIFICATION

STATE v. HUNTER

Supreme Court of Kansas, 1987.
241 Kan. 629, 740 P.2d 559.

LOCKETT, JUSTICE.

Hunter appeals his convictions of two counts of felony murder, two counts of aggravated kidnapping, one count of aggravated robbery, one count of aggravated battery on a law enforcement officer, and one count of aggravated battery. Hunter raises numerous issues, among them that the trial judge committed reversible error by refusing Hunter's requested instruction on his defense of compulsion. We reverse and remand for a new trial.

In February 1985 Hunter was hitchhiking from Texas back to the Kansas City area. On February 13, Hunter hitched a ride with Mark Walters, Lisa Dunn, and Daniel Remeta. On the way north on I–135 Remeta displayed two weapons, a .357 Magnum and an inoperative .22 pistol. Hunter repaired the .22 and Remeta fired the .22 out of the car window several times. When they reached the intersection of I–135 and I–70, Hunter asked to be let off. At that point Remeta began talking about another hitchhiker he wished he had killed and also described prior crimes he had committed including several murders.

At the Levant exchange on I–70, Dunn, Walters, Remeta, and the defendant were pulled over by a police car. The driver of the police car was Undersheriff Benjamin F. Albright, who had been asked to investigate a vehicle matching the description of the car. Albright instructed the occupants to remain in the car and put their hands on the ceiling. One of the passengers exited the car and fired two shots through Albright's windshield. Albright identified the person who fired these shots as having shoulder-length brown hair and a full beard. This description matched that of the defendant. Immediately thereafter, Albright was shot by the same person in the arm and chest. At trial, Albright identified James Hunter as his assailant. Hunter, Dunn, and Remeta all testified that it was Remeta who shot Albright. Hunter testified that, after Albright was shot, he attempted to shoot Remeta with the .22 handgun but accidentally wounded Dunn. Dunn and Remeta corroborated this testimony.

Shortly after the Albright shooting, the Remeta vehicle reached the Bartlett Elevator in Levant, Kansas. There were eight individuals at the elevator: Maurice Christie, the elevator manager; Fred Sager, the assistant manager; and Dennis Tubbs, Raymond Haremza, Rick Schroeder, Glenn Moore, and two others. The testimony concerning Hunter's activities at the Levant elevator conflicted greatly. Christie testified that he observed "a bearded man," later identified as Hunter, holding a gun in the face of Rick Schroeder and forcing him into a pickup truck. Sager testified that he saw a bearded man with a gun in his hand and that Rick Schroeder got into the pickup by himself. Dennis Tubbs testified that Hunter held Schroeder's arm and told him to get into the pickup; he further testified he saw only one person with a gun. After Rick Schroeder and Glenn Moore were taken as hostages and loaded into Moore's pickup truck, Christie, while attempting to call the sheriff from the scale house, was shot by Remeta.

Following the shooting at the elevator, the hostages were driven to a point north of U.S. Highway 24 near Colby, Kansas. Remeta testified that he killed both Schroeder and Moore and left them at the side of the road. Police caught up with the pickup truck and forced it off the road at a farm. During an exchange of gunfire, Walters was killed. Subsequently, Remeta, Dunn, and Hunter were arrested.

Remeta, Dunn, and Hunter were formally charged. * * * Prior to trial, Remeta entered a plea of guilty to all charges. Dunn and Hunter were tried by a jury, found guilty of all counts, and sentenced to consecutive terms. Hunter now appeals his conviction of two counts of felony murder (Schroeder and Moore), two counts of aggravated kidnapping (Schroeder and Moore), one count of aggravated battery on a law enforcement officer (Albright), one count of aggravated battery (Christie), and one count of aggravated robbery. * * *

Hunter contends that the trial court committed reversible error by refusing to instruct the jury on his defense of compulsion. We agree. K.S.A. 21–3209 provides for the defense of compulsion to crimes other than murder or manslaughter, stating: (1) "A person is not guilty of a crime other than murder or voluntary manslaughter by reason of conduct which he performs under the compulsion or threat of the imminent infliction of death or great bodily harm, if he reasonably believes that death or great bodily harm will be inflicted upon him or upon his spouse, parent, child, brother or sister if he does not perform such conduct. (2) The defense provided by this section is not available to one who willfully or wantonly places himself in a situation in which it is probable that he will be subjected to compulsion or threat."

Defendant's requested instruction stated: "It is a defense to the charges of Aggravated Battery Against a Law Enforcement Officer, Aggravated Robbery and Aggravated Kidnapping, if the defendant acted under compulsion or threat of immediate infliction of death or great bodily harm, and if said defendant reasonably believed that death or great bodily harm would have been inflicted upon said defendant had he or she not acted as he or she did."

The trial court refused to give the compulsion instruction because the defendant was charged with premeditated and felony murder. The judge was unsure if the instruction was applicable where an individual is charged under the felony-murder rule, but determined that one who aids and abets felony murder is not entitled to the instruction.

Whether the defense of compulsion is available to a criminal defendant charged with felony murder is an issue of first impression. Most modern statutes providing for a defense of compulsion evolved from the common-law policy that a person, when faced with a choice between suffering death or serious bodily harm and committing some lesser crime, could not be punished for committing the lesser offense. * * *

However, even early cases refused to recognize any compulsion as sufficient to excuse intentional killing. The rationale is that, when confronted by a choice between two evils of equal magnitude, the individual ought to sacrifice his own life rather than escape by the murder of an innocent.

A number of jurisdictions, including Kansas, have incorporated by statute the common law denial of the compulsion defense in crimes of murder. [Citations] While not all jurisdictions have considered the applicability of these statutes to crimes of felony murder, we note that both Arizona and Missouri have held that defendants are barred from claiming the compulsion defense in felony-murder cases. They reason that the person charged need only have the required intent to commit or participate in the underlying felony and no other mental state on his part need be demonstrated because of the strict liability imposed by the felony-murder rule. [Citations]

We are not persuaded by the reasoning of these decisions. The better view, consistently adhered to by commentators, is that any limitation to the defense of duress be confined to crimes of intentional killing and not to killings done by another during the commission of some lesser felony. As LaFave and Scott have explained:

"If A compels B at gunpoint to drive him to the bank which A intends to rob, and during the ensuing robbery A kills a bank customer C, B is not guilty of the robbery (for he was justified by duress) and so is not guilty of felony murder of C in the commission of robbery. The law properly recognizes that one is justified in aiding a robbery if he is forced by threats to do so to save his life; he should not lose the defense because his threateners unexpectedly kill someone in the course of the robbery and thus convert a mere robbery into a murder."

* * * Although some of the evidence supporting Hunter's defense of compulsion came from Hunter's own testimony, this court has held that a defendant is entitled to an instruction on his or her theory of the case even though the evidence is slight and supported only by defendant's own testimony. * * * Here, the record is replete with testimony that Daniel Remeta was a person to be feared. It was the function of the jury as the exclusive trier of fact to determine if it was believable that Hunter was afraid for his life, if such fear was reasonable, and if such fear justified any criminal acts which Hunter may have performed. When the trial judge refused the requested compulsion instruction, he effectively prevented the jury from considering the evidence presented in Hunter's defense. This denial of the jury's right to determine the facts constitutes reversible error. We reverse and remand this case for a new trial in accordance with this opinion.*

STATE v. IRONS

Court of Appeals of Kansas, 1991.
815 P.2d 1133.[a]

MEMORANDUM OPINION

Brandon N. Irons appeals his conviction of aggravated escape from custody. In 1982, at the age of 19, Brandon Irons was convicted of burglary and felony theft in Butler County, Kansas. He was sentenced to two to ten years' imprisonment. He went to the Hutchinson State Industrial Reformatory for eighteen months and was then paroled. He eventually moved to Denver, Colorado, with his wife and child, where he worked with one of his brothers as a high rise window washer.

* On retrial Hunter obtained a change of venue and was acquitted of all charges by the jury after almost 3 years in prison. According to the UPI news story dated January 21, 1988, Hunter made these comments after the acquittal:

> Asked if he was bitter, Hunter replied, "Yeah, I'm bitter. Basically at Ben Albright. I know what happened that day. He (Albright) just freaked out and lost it. He never looked up from that car. I thought that idiot was going to save my life. He's a police officer and he can't admit he turned tail."

Hunter said Remeta shot Albright as the lawman was maneuvering in his car to get out. He said the key to his acquittal was that his second trial was moved to Hays in west central Kansas and out of the northwest Kansas town of Colby. "The jury wasn't from Colby. That was the difference," he said. "I knew I would have some open-minded people for jurors instead of a lynch mob."

Hunter, who was a roofer and performed various other jobs in Amoret, said he planned to enroll in college and finish the computer technology degree he began at the Kansas State Industrial Reformatory in Hutchinson.

He said he has often wished he had taken the advice he has heard throughout life—never hitchhike. "I wouldn't do it (now) unless I got to. If a car breaks down, I can understand," he said. "I had been told for years you shouldn't hitchhike, you shouldn't hitchhike. I just wish them folks there had never stopped and picked me up."

Hunter died a week later of a heart attack at the age of 36.

a. The text at this citation only reveals that the judgment below was affirmed. Pursuant to K.S. A. § 60–2106, the Kansas Court of Appeals designated its decision in *Irons* a "memorandum opinion." Kansas Supreme Court Rule 7.04 provides that memorandum opinions are not published unless the author of a dissenting or concurring opinion requests that it be reported or the state Supreme Court orders its publication. Accordingly, the text of this opinion is available only through electronic databases.

In 1988, Irons was stopped in Colorado for driving under the influence of alcohol. He became belligerent with the police. As a consequence of this episode, his parole was revoked and he was sent back to Hutchinson.

He was sent to the Wichita Community Residential Center (CRC) in May or June of 1989. CRC was a privately owned work release facility where inmates were sent before their release. Irons was working at the Cinema at Towne West Shopping Center during the time he was at CRC. On June 8, 1990, Irons signed out to go to work. He failed to return at 7:00 a.m. the next morning, the time he was due back. Officer Sharon Willits, the shift supervisor at CRC, called Irons' workplace and learned he was not there. She then notified the Wichita police department of his escape.

Irons was charged on June 13, 1989, with one count of aggravated escape from custody. Prior to trial the State made a motion in limine requesting that the court not admit any evidence regarding Irons' motives for escaping, specifically the threats he had received from other inmates.

During the hearing on the motion in limine, Irons testified regarding threats made to him before his escape. He stated that, on June 6, 1989, he had given an interview to KAKE television regarding CRC. Although the interview lasted twenty minutes, the television station only showed a few seconds. During this interview, he stated he did not believe that CRC was "that bad of a program." This angered the other inmates because they wanted CRC closed. When Irons returned to the dormitory that night the other inmates told him he had been stupid to give the interview, and they were very angry with him. Nobody physically threatened him that night, but their anger was such that he was frightened to return to his dorm room and slept hidden between a soda machine and a wall in another part of the facility. During that night the other inmates urinated on his bunk.

The next morning Irons returned to his sleeping area. The other inmates questioned where he had been the night before and began accusing him of being a "snitch." They called him a woman and said any snitch could be turned into a woman. They told him they were going "to punk [him] out" and "dry heave" him. This was slang for sodomize. They were in his room, moving him to the back door when one said "Why don't we just take you out and why don't we just bend you over." Another one slapped him on the ear. At this point, one of his friends said a counselor was coming, causing the others to back off. Irons then went down and stood by the security office. They followed him. He signed out to go to work and when he was at the bus stop two of them appeared and began chasing him. He ran to a 7–Eleven, where they stopped chasing him but told him when he returned they were going to kill him and "dry heave his punk ass."

Irons went to work, where he first called Judge Jaworski in Butler County, the judge who had sentenced him. Judge Jaworski told him he could not do anything and suggested he call security at CRC.

Irons then called CRC and talked to Willits, who answered the phone. He told her he was having some problems and wanted to talk to the "top person." She advised him to come in and talk to them. He told her if he came back the other inmates would get him, particularly if they saw him go to a guard. He had previously witnessed one inmate beat up two guards. Willits let him talk to Mark Ryan, the assistant administrator.

Irons told Ryan what had happened and said the other inmates were going to kill him and "punk" him. Ryan said he could move Irons to another room, but Irons said they would still get him and he did not feel he could safely come back to the facility. Ryan said he could have him transferred to Topeka in about a week. Irons again said he could not come back to CRC. Ryan said he would call him later than evening at work. Irons waited until 5:00 or 6:00 p.m. and then called Ryan. He was told Ryan had left for the evening and had left no messages for Irons. Irons told CRC personnel he was not coming back and asked if his return time could be extended from 6:00 a.m. until 9:00 a.m. It was extended until 7:00 a.m.

The next morning Irons called Ryan at 7:00 a.m. at the center, but Ryan was not there. He then called at 8:00 a.m. and he was still not in. He called again at 10:00 or 10:30 a.m. and his counselor, Michelle, told him he was wanted for escape. Irons told her that Ryan was going to get him moved, but Michelle replied Ryan was in a meeting and had said simply that Irons must return. He tried to explain, but she said she was not security. He told her he was not coming back. He did not return to the center, but instead went to Texas. He remained there until he was taken into custody five months later.

The defendant argued this testimony supported his defense of compulsion. The trial court sustained the State's motion in limine, finding the threats were not "imminent", and thus, as a matter of law, the defense of compulsion was not available to the defendant. * * *

Irons was convicted by a jury on May 30, 1990. * * * Irons was sentenced to one to five years' imprisonment * * *.

Issue I: Did the Trial Court Err in Granting the State's Motion In Limine to Prohibit Evidence of Irons' Compulsion Defense?

The trial court granted the State's motion in limine to disallow evidence of compulsion because it found as a matter of law that the proffered testimony did not constitute facts which would satisfy the requirements of the defense of compulsion. Specifically, the court found the threat to Irons was not imminent. * * *

The defense of compulsion is contained in K.S.A. 21–3209, which provides:

"(1) A person is not guilty of a crime other than murder or voluntary manslaughter by reason of conduct which he performs under the compulsion or threat of the imminent infliction of death or great bodily harm, if he reasonably believes that death or great bodily harm will be inflicted upon him or upon his spouse, parent, child, brother or sister if he does not perform such conduct.

"(2) The defense provided by this section is not available to one who willfully or wantonly places himself in a situation in which it is probable that he will be subjected to compulsion or threat."

This court recently incorporated into the compulsion defense, for those defendants charged with escape, a five-part test which must be met before evidence of the defense will be admitted. *State v. Pichon,* 15 Kan. App. 2d 527, 811 P.2d 517, *rev. denied* June 27, 1991.

The five-part test is one used by many other jurisdictions. The Pichon court modified the first requirement to comply with K.S.A. 21–3209, the statute which codifies the compulsion defense. The requirements are:

(1) The prisoner is faced with a threat of imminent infliction of death or great bodily harm.

(2) There is not time for complaint to the authorities or there exists a history of futile complaints which make any result from such complaints illusory;

(3) There is not time or opportunity to resort to the courts;

(4) There is no evidence of force or violence used towards prison personnel or other 'innocent' persons in the escape; and

(5) The prisoner immediately reports to the proper authorities when he has attained a position of safety from the immediate threat.

This court held that all of the five conditions must exist before the defense is available. Other courts have held that the existence of all five is not required before the defendant may present the defense. *Esquibel v. State,* 91 N.M. 498, 576 P.2d 1129, 1132 (1978); *People v. Unger,* 66 Ill. 2d 333, 362 N.E.2d 319, 323 (1977). Those courts held that the existence or nonexistence of the factors goes only to the weight and credibility of the defendant's evidence of duress or necessity.

In the present case, the trial judge found that the threat described by Irons was not imminent. * * * Citing *State v. Milum,* 213 Kan. 581, 516 P.2d 984 (1973), the trial court stated that imminent means "right there, right now, not tomorrow, not in the future, with you right now, and I think that is what the Supreme Court says that that statute compulsion means, not something that you think might happen because of what somebody said to you in the future." The judge also noted that Irons could have turned himself in and gone to the county jail.

In *Milum,* the defendant was also charged with escaping from prison. As in the present case, the trial court did not allow the defendant to present the defense of compulsion. Milum proffered the testimony of four witnesses, each of whom would testify about four different occasions when the deputy warden told Milum if he did not leave the prison, he would have him shot. One of the witnesses testified the threats were made in June or July of 1970. Milum escaped on August 7, 1970. The Supreme Court stated, "It is apparent that the threats, if such there were, were made on several different occassions [sic] and thus could not have met the statutory requirements of imminence. At best the threats were aimed at some indefinite time in the future." It decided that threats made within one to two months of the escape were not imminent, and thus, the defendant was not entitled to the defense.

* * *

The case before this court differs from *Milum,* in that the threats were closer in time than two months. The inmates threatened Irons immediately prior to the time he left the facility and even chased him as he was waiting for the bus which would take him to work. It is true that he was gone for several hours before his escape became official, thus separating him from the time the threats were made. However, the others threatened him right up to the point he left CRC and their presence. Likewise, the threat was not for some indefinite time in the future as in *Milum* * * *. The other inmates stated they would kill and sodomize Irons when he returned from work. This was a specific time in the near future. The only reason the threat was separated from the threatened act was because Irons was allowed to leave for work. The threat to Irons was imminent. There was evidence that he had a reasonable fear of danger. The trial court erred by refusing the testimony for this reason.

However, under Pichon, four other requirements must be met before the compulsion defense is allowed. Since Pichon was filed after the trial in the present case, the trial court made no specific findings concerning all five of the tests. * * * However, since the trial court may be upheld even if it is right for the wrong reason, we will address the other requirements.

The second requirement is whether there is no time for complaint to the authorities, or there exists a history of futility when complaints are registered. Here, Irons testified that he called the institution and talked to Willits. She told him to talk to Ryan. Irons called back and talked to Ryan, who told him that he might be able to move in a week. If the other inmates made good on their threats, Irons would be killed or seriously hurt long before a week passed. He slept in a room with ten other inmates on the second floor. The doors to the rooms were not locked. There were only three or four guards for 200 inmates. At night there was only one guard stationed on the second floor. The guard sat in a booth, and another would periodically rove through the building. During the first call, Ryan told Irons he would call him back. Ryan did not call by 5:00 or 6:00 p.m., Irons called CRC and learned that Ryan had left for the day without leaving any messages. Irons tried to call twice again the next morning, but Ryan was unavailable to talk to him. There is evidence that Irons' complaints had been futile.

The third requirement is that there was no time or opportunity to resort to the courts. Irons left the facility at approximately 2:00 p.m. and was scheduled to return the next morning at 7:00 a.m. There was not time to utilize the courts for a solution.

The fourth requirement is that there is no evidence that force or violence was used in the escape. This is undisputed.

Finally, the prisoner must immediately report to the proper authorities when he has reached safety. Irons does not meet this condition. He went to Texas, where he remained until he was captured five months later. Charges were not filed in Kansas against Irons until June 13, five days after his last contact with CRC authorities. Arguably, up to the time Irons broke off contact with the CRC authorities, he had been complying with the requirements of *Pichon*. Had he continued to maintain contact with the CRC after leaving the area in an attempt to arrange for a safe surrender, his contentions of compliance with *Pichon* would have been cognizable by the court. As it is, his defense of compulsion cannot stand as he failed to report for five months after reaching the comparative security of Texas.

The trial court did not err in granting the State's motion in limine to exclude evidence supporting a compulsion defense. There was evidence that Irons was under the threat of imminent bodily harm or death and met all but one of the five conditions. However, there was no evidence he immediately reported to the proper authorities when reaching safety.

* * *

ISSUE III: DID THE TRIAL COURT ERR IN REFUSING TO GIVE AN INSTRUCTION ON THE DEFENSE OF COMPULSION?

Defendant argues that he was entitled to the compulsion instruction because the testimony of Willits regarding the telephone call was enough to support the defense.

It is true that a defendant is entitled to an instruction on his or her theory of the case even though the evidence is slight and supported only by defendant's own testimony. *State v. Hunter,* 241 Kan. 629, 646, 740 P.2d 559 (1987). However, in this case the trial court has held, and this court agrees, that Irons was not entitled to the defense. * * *

The judgment is affirmed.

DAVIS, J., dissenting. I concur with the discussion and reasoning of the majority opinion regarding the first element of Pichon that the threat to the defendant was imminent. * * *

The majority finds that all other requirements of *Pichon* were met except the last, which requires that the prisoner immediately report to the proper authorities when he or she has reached safety. * * * I believe, under the facts of this case, all conditions of *Pichon* have been satisfied and that the jury should have been instructed on the defense of compulsion.

The majority concedes that the defendant was debating whether to return under threat of imminent infliction of great bodily harm and that he reasonably believed that great bodily harm would have been inflicted upon him had he not acted as he did. It is further conceded that he did not willfully or wantonly place himself in a situation in which it was probable that he would have been subjected to compulsion or threat. He attempted to communicate with the authorities * * *.

We deal with the question of whether the evidence warranted an instruction on the defense of compulsion, not whether the defense of compulsion was established. Whether it was a viable defense depends upon the jury's determination of the evidence at trial. To say under the facts of this case that the defense of compulsion is not available is to deny the defendant a fair trial by preventing him from presenting to the jury the only theory of defense he had.

* * * In my opinion, it is not enough to say that, since the defendant did not immediately report to the proper authorities when reaching Texas, he forfeits his defense of compulsion. This is especially true under the facts of this case where the defendant sought to report the danger he perceived. The authorities offered a solution that not only failed to alleviate the danger but virtually guaranteed that the threat he perceived would be carried out if he returned. I believe that, in this case, the last requirement of *Pichon* was met by the defendant when, safe at his place of employment and before returning to the facility, he reported to the proper authorities.

Perhaps the real difficulty I have with this case is the failure of the majority to set a time limit on the last requirement of *Pichon*. * * * What is important is that the defendant, upon deciding not to return immediately, contacted the proper authorities to explain his predicament. Their answer, according to his testimony, which I might add may or may not be believed by a jury, was that the defendant return to the facility and face death or serious bodily harm and remain in that facility, with little or no protection for a week, at which time he would then be transferred to a more secure and safe institution. I would reverse and hold that the defendant satisfied all the conditions of *Pichon*.

UNITED STATES v. CONTENTO–PACHON

United States Court of Appeals, Ninth Circuit, 1984.
723 F.2d 691.

BOOCHEVER, CIRCUIT JUDGE.

This case presents an appeal from a conviction for unlawful possession with intent to distribute a narcotic controlled substance. At trial, the defendant attempted to offer evidence of duress and necessity defenses. The district court excluded this evidence on the ground that it was insufficient to support the defenses. We reverse because there was sufficient evidence of duress to present a triable issue of fact.

I. Facts

The defendant-appellant, Juan Manuel Contento–Pachon, is a native of Bogota, Colombia and was employed there as a taxicab driver. He asserts that one of his passengers, Jorge, offered him a job as the driver of a privately-owned car. Contento–Pachon expressed an interest in the job and agreed to meet Jorge and the owner of the car the next day.

Instead of a driving job, Jorge proposed that Contento–Pachon swallow cocaine-filled balloons and transport them to the United States. Contento–Pachon agreed to consider the proposition. He was told not to mention the proposition to anyone, otherwise he would "get into serious trouble." Contento–Pachon testified that he did not contact the police because he believes that the Bogota police are corrupt and that they are paid off by drug traffickers.

Approximately one week later, Contento–Pachon told Jorge that he would not carry the cocaine. In response, Jorge mentioned facts about Contento–Pachon's personal life, including private details which Contento–Pachon had never mentioned to Jorge. Jorge told Contento–Pachon that his failure to cooperate would result in the death of his wife and three year-old child.

The following day the pair met again. Contento–Pachon's life and the lives of his family were again threatened. At this point, Contento–Pachon agreed to take the cocaine into the United States.

The pair met two more times. At the last meeting, Contento–Pachon swallowed 129 balloons of cocaine. He was informed that he would be watched at all times during the trip, and that if he failed to follow Jorge's instruction he and his family would be killed.

After leaving Bogota, Contento–Pachon's plane landed in Panama. Contento–Pachon asserts that he did not notify the authorities there because he felt that the Panamanian police were as corrupt as those in Bogota. Also, he felt that any such action on his part would place his family in jeopardy.

When he arrived at the customs inspection point in Los Angeles, Contento–Pachon consented to have his stomach x-rayed. The x-rays revealed a foreign substance which was later determined to be cocaine.

At Contento–Pachon's trial, the government moved to exclude the defenses of duress and necessity. The motion was granted. We reverse.

A. *Duress*

There are three elements of the duress defense: (1) an immediate threat of death or serious bodily injury, (2) a well-grounded fear that the threat will be carried out, and (3) no reasonable opportunity to escape the threatened harm. United States v. Shapiro, 669 F.2d 593, 596 (9th Cir.1982). Sometimes a fourth element is required: the defendant must submit to proper authorities after attaining a position of safety. United States v. Peltier, 693 F.2d 96 (9th Cir.1982) (per curiam).

Factfinding is usually a function of the jury, and the trial court rarely rules on a defense as a matter of law. If the evidence is insufficient as a matter of law to support a duress defense, however, the trial court should exclude that evidence.

The trial court found Contento–Pachon's offer of proof insufficient to support a duress defense because he failed to offer proof of two elements: immediacy and inescapability.[1]

Immediacy: The element of immediacy requires that there be some evidence that the threat of injury was present, immediate, or impending. A veiled threat of future unspecified harm will not satisfy this requirement. [Citations] The district court found that the initial threats were not immediate because "they were conditioned on defendant's failure to cooperate in the future and did not place defendant and his family in immediate danger."

Evidence presented on this issue indicated that the defendant was dealing with a man who was deeply involved in the exportation of illegal substances. Large sums of money were at stake and, consequently, Contento–Pachon had reason to believe that Jorge would carry out his threats. Jorge had gone to the trouble to discover that Contento–Pachon was married, that he had a child, the names of his wife and child, and the location of his residence. These were not vague threats of possible future harm. According to the defendant, if he had refused to cooperate, the consequences would have been immediate and harsh.

Contento–Pachon contends that he was being watched by one of Jorge's accomplices at all times during the airplane trip. As a consequence, the force of the threats continued to restrain him. Contento–Pachon's contention that he was operating under the threat of immediate harm was supported by sufficient evidence to present a triable issue of fact.

Escapability: The defendant must show that he had no reasonable opportunity to escape. See United States v. Gordon, 526 F.2d 406, 407 (9th Cir.1975). The district court found that because Contento–Pachon was not physically restrained prior to the time he swallowed the balloons, he could have sought help from the police or fled. Contento–Pachon explained that he did not report the threats because he feared that the police were corrupt. The trier of fact should decide whether one in Contento–Pachon's position might believe that some of the Bogota police were paid informants for drug traffickers and that reporting the matter to the police did not represent a reasonable opportunity of escape.

If he chose not to go to the police, Contento–Pachon's alternative was to flee. We reiterate that the opportunity to escape must be reasonable. To flee, Contento–Pachon, along with his wife and three year-old child, would have been forced to pack his possessions, leave his job, and travel to a place beyond the reaches of the drug traffickers. A

1. We believe that a triable issue was presented as to the third element, that the fear be well-grounded, based on the same facts that lead us to the conclusion as to the immediacy of the threats.

juror might find that this was not a reasonable avenue of escape. Thus, Contento–Pachon presented a triable issue on the element of escapability.

Surrender to Authorities: As noted above, the duress defense is composed of at least three elements. The government argues that the defense also requires that a defendant offer evidence that he intended to turn himself in to the authorities upon reaching a position of safety. Although it has not been expressly limited, this fourth element seems to be required only in prison escape cases. Under other circumstances, the defense has been defined to include only three elements. [Citations]

The Supreme Court in United States v. Bailey, 444 U.S. 394, 413 (1980), noted that "escape from federal custody * * * is a continuing offense and * * * an escapee can be held liable for failure to return to custody as well as for his initial departure." This factor would not be present in most crimes other than escape.

In cases not involving escape from prison there seems little difference between the third basic requirement that there be no reasonable opportunity to escape the threatened harm and the obligation to turn oneself in to authorities on reaching a point of safety. Once a defendant has reached a position where he can safely turn himself in to the authorities he will likewise have a reasonable opportunity to escape the threatened harm.

That is true in this case. Contento–Pachon claims that he was being watched at all times. According to him, at the first opportunity to cooperate with authorities without alerting the observer, he consented to the x-ray. We hold that a defendant who has acted under a well-grounded fear of immediate harm with no opportunity to escape may assert the duress defense, if there is a triable issue of fact whether he took the opportunity to escape the threatened harm by submitting to authorities at the first reasonable opportunity.

B. *Necessity*

The defense of necessity is available when a person is faced with a choice of two evils and must then decide whether to commit a crime or an alternative act that constitutes a greater evil. [Citations] Contento–Pachon has attempted to justify his violation of 21 U.S.C. § 841(a)(1) by showing that the alternative, the death of his family, was a greater evil. Traditionally, in order for the necessity defense to apply, the coercion must have had its source in the physical forces of nature. The duress defense was applicable when the defendant's acts were coerced by a human force. W. LaFave & A. Scott, Handbook on Criminal Law § 50 at 383 (1972). This distinction served to separate the two similar defenses. But modern courts have tended to blur the distinction between duress and necessity.

It has been suggested that, "the major difference between duress and necessity is that the former negates the existence of the requisite mens rea for the crime in question, whereas under the latter theory there is no actus reus." United States v. Micklus, 581 F.2d 612, 615 (7th Cir.1978). The theory of necessity is that the defendant's free will was properly exercised to achieve the greater good and not that his free will was overcome by an outside force as with duress.

The defense of necessity is usually invoked when the defendant acted in the interest of the general welfare. For example, defendants have asserted the defense as a justification for (1) bringing laetrile into the United States for the treatment of cancer patients, United States v. Richardson, 588 F.2d at 1239 (9th Cir.1978); (2) unlawfully entering a naval base to protest the Trident missile system, United States v. May, 622 F.2d 1000, 1008–09 (9th Cir.1980); (3) burning Selective Service System records to protest United States military action, United States v. Simpson, 460 F.2d 515, 517 (9th Cir.1972).

Contento–Pachon's acts were allegedly coerced by human, not physical forces. In addition, he did not act to promote the general welfare. Therefore, the necessity defense was not available to him. Contento–Pachon mischaracterized evidence of duress as evidence of necessity. The district court correctly disallowed his use of the necessity defense.

II. Conclusion

Contento–Pachon presented credible evidence that he acted under an immediate and well-grounded threat of serious bodily injury, with no opportunity to escape. Because the trier of fact should have been allowed to consider the credibility of the proffered evidence, we reverse. The district court correctly excluded Contento–Pachon's necessity defense.

Reversed and remanded.

[Dissenting opinion omitted.]

PEOPLE v. CARRADINE

Supreme Court of Illinois, 1972.
52 Ill.2d 231, 287 N.E.2d 670.

UNDERWOOD, CHIEF JUSTICE.

The Cook County circuit court found Georgia Carradine to be in direct contempt of court for her refusal to testify, and sentenced her to imprisonment for six months in the Cook County jail. She appealed directly here.

On September 11, 1969, Mrs. Carradine appeared before Judge Downing as a State's witness in a criminal prosecution; she had witnessed a homicide and given a statement to an assistant State's Attorney. Having failed to respond to a subpoena, she was in court pursuant to a bench warrant, and after answering certain preliminary questions refused to testify further, indicating that she was in fear of her life and the lives of her children. No fifth-amendment privilege was arrested or available. When Mrs. Carradine persisted in her refusal to testify, despite offers of protection for her and her family and the advice of appointed counsel, a contempt order was entered. *Mittimus,* however, was stayed until September 14 to allow the contemnor to reconsider her actions. On September 15 and September 24, accompanied by counsel, she appeared before the court and still refused to testify notwithstanding offers to relocate her and her family to other sites in Chicago, this State or the continental United States; on each occasion it was ordered that she be committed to the county jail until she agreed to testify. On October 1, since Mrs. Carradine still persisted in her refusal, the trial judge entered the contempt order here in question.

The more difficult question is the contemnor's request, predicated upon the extenuating circumstances surrounding her refusal to testify, that her punishment be reduced to the two weeks already spent in jail. Those circumstances include the fact that Mrs. Carradine had been separated from her husband for some four years, had six children aged 5 to 18 at home, and was supported by payments from her husband and supplemental welfare funds; that there seems little reason to doubt her refusal to testify resulted solely from her fear of harm to herself and her children if she testified against the defendants who apparently were members of the Blackstone Rangers, a youth gang; that she believed she had been "tricked" and lied to by the assistant State's Attorney to whom she had given a statement, because, as she stated, he told her she would not have to appear and testify and that, absent this assurance, she never would have given him the statement; that she did not believe the law enforcement authorities could protect her from the "Stones" for, as she put it:

> "THE WITNESS: Well, look, Judge, I am going to tell you, I live in the middle of the slums, down in the slums. Where I live the police don't even come in there even if we call. I called the police one night about a fight. You'd think they were going to kill one another. But the police don't even come up in there where I live. So how are they going to protect me and my family when they don't even come up in the building where we live?"

Nor does she believe that relocating her family would solve the problems, for the "Stones" were "everywhere."

It is completely clear from the record that Mrs. Carradine understood the likely results of her refusal to testify and deliberately chose to incur imprisonment rather than expose herself and her family to what she considered to be the certainty of serious physical harm or death. The conscientious trial judge appointed counsel for her and patiently, clearly and repeatedly explained the situation, urging her to change her mind and reiterating the offers of protection and relocation; the proceedings were continued on several occasions in order that she might have an opportunity to reconsider her decision.

No useful purpose would be served by prolonged discussion. The reluctance of witnesses to testify is not an uncommon problem, although the circumstances here are particularly distressing. The contempt proceedings were conducted with eminent fairness, and, in our opinion, the judgment and sentence must be affirmed. The fundamental reason therefore was stated by the trial court: " * * * one of the problems that the Court has is that unless we receive the cooperation of the citizens who see certain alleged events take place these events are not going to be rooted out, nor are perpetrators of these acts going to be brought before the bar of justice unless citizens stand up to be counted, and I think this [fear] is not a valid reason for not testifying. If it's a valid reason then we might as well close the doors."

The judgment of the Cook County circuit court is affirmed.

Judgment affirmed.

Note

It is frequently said that the defense of duress is unavailable where the charge is murder or some other extremely serious crime. This limitation was called into question in Director of Public Prosecutions v. Lynch, [1975] A.C. 653. Lynch was charged as an accomplice in the assassination of a police constable in Northern Ireland. He had driven three armed members of the Irish Republican Army to a place near the scene of the crime, and then drove the killers away again after the killing. His defense was that one of the killers, a ruthless gunman, had threatened to kill him if he did not drive the car. A divided House of Lords ordered a new trial, the majority holding that on a charge of murder the defense of duress is open at least to a person who did not participate in the act of killing itself. The defense would not have been available if the defendant had voluntarily become a member of a terrorist organization such as the I.R.A., even if he had subsequently attempted to leave the organization. See G. Williams, *Textbook of Criminal Law* 627–28 (1983).

Lynch left open the question whether the killer himself can assert a defense of duress. The Judicial Committee of the Privy Council held by a narrow majority that the defense was unavailable in Abbott v. The Queen, [1976] A.C. 755. (The Judicial Committee of the Privy Council hears appeals from British Commonwealth nations; it is roughly the same body as the Appellate Committee of the House of Lords, the "Supreme Court" of Britain.) Abbott was under the domination of a murderous thug named Malik, who ran a sort of commune in Trinidad. Malik ordered the murder of the mistress of one of the members of his commune, and directed Abbott to participate. Abbott held the victim while the actual killer stabbed her repeatedly, and then participated in burying her while she was still alive. The majority held that duress was no defense under these circumstances, but observed that "there is much to be said for the view that on a charge of murder, duress, like provocation, should not entitle the accused to a clean acquittal but should reduce murder to manslaughter and thus give the court power to pass whatever sentence might be appropriate in all the circumstances of the case." This appears to be the rule in some American jurisdictions. See Wentworth v. State, 29 Md.App. 110, 349 A.2d 421 (1975); but see State v. Rumble, 680 S.W.2d 939 (Mo.1984).

The duress cases present an acute conflict between public policy and compassionate treatment of individual defendants. Mrs. Carradine's fear of the Blackstone Rangers was clearly justified, and yet to permit her to refuse to testify for this reason would make it extremely difficult to convict members of criminal gangs. If duress were easily accepted as a defense to drug smuggling, smugglers could act with impunity by submitting to coercion. The courts therefore have to decide not only whether the particular defendant's fear of death or injury was reasonable, but also whether recognition of a defense would undermine the community's interest in law enforcement to an unacceptable degree.

For an illuminating discussion of these problems, see Meir Dan–Cohen, "Decision Rules and Conduct Rules: On Acoustic Separation in Criminal Law," 97 Harv.L.Rev. 625 (1984). Professor Dan–Cohen reinvigorates a distinction originally made by Jeremy Bentham between "conduct rules" and "decision rules." The former are addressed to the general public, and the latter to officials. "Do not commit murder" is a conduct rule; "murderers shall be sentenced to life in prison" is a decision rule. Taking the *Carradine* case as an example, a court would probably find it acceptable to apply a decision rule excusing the defendant because of her reasonable fear, provided that the decision did not become known to other witnesses and thus influence their decision whether to testify or not. In other words, it is quite tolerable to excuse Mrs. Carradine (since she will not testify anyway), but it would be intolerable to set a precedent that will affect the conduct of future witnesses. The Illinois Supreme Court could not grant relief because the decision would be highly visible to lawyers and thus to prospective witnesses, although a low visibility decision releasing her might be acceptable. According to Professor Dan–Cohen, it is easiest for courts to recognize defenses of this type when their decisions are not likely to be relied upon by other persons in situations of duress in the future; i.e., when the decision rule does not become a conduct rule. The article develops this interesting thesis and applies it to a wide variety of situations.

The Model Penal Code

Section 3.02. Justification Generally: Choice Of Evils

(1) Conduct which the actor believes to be necessary to avoid a harm or evil to himself or to another is justifiable, provided that:

(a) the harm or evil sought to be avoided by such conduct is greater than that sought to be prevented by the law defining the offense charged;[a] and

a. It may be argued * * * that as applied to homicide Section 3.02 is drawn too narrowly in its requirement that the evil sought to be avoided be a greater evil than that sought to be protected by the law defining the offense. For the result is that the defense would not be available to a defendant who killed A to save B, in circumstances where had he done nothing B would have been killed and A saved, assuming, of course, that there was not such aggression on either's part as to bring into play the justifications for using protective force. Nor would the defense be available to one who acted to save himself at the expense of another, as by seizing a raft when men are shipwrecked. But whatever may be thought of such cases as presenting basis for excuse—and the problem must be faced at least in dealing with duress—they are not in principle cases of justification. In all ordinary circumstances lives in being must be assumed, * * * to be of equal value, equally deserving the protection of the law. If the values are equal, the case for a justification has not been made out. Model Penal

(b) neither the Code nor other law defining the offense provides exceptions or defenses dealing with the specific situation involved; and

(c) a legislative purpose to exclude the justification claimed does not otherwise plainly appear.

(2) When the actor was reckless or negligent in bringing about the situation requiring a choice of harms or evils or in appraising the necessity for his conduct, the justification afforded by this Section is unavailable in a prosecution for any offense for which recklessness or negligence, as the case may be, suffices to establish culpability.

The New York Penal Law

§ 35.05. Justification; Generally

Unless otherwise limited by the ensuing provisions of this article defining justifiable use of physical force, conduct which would otherwise constitute an offense is justifiable and not criminal when:

2. Such conduct is necessary as an emergency measure to avoid an imminent public or private injury which is about to occur by reason of a situation occasioned or developed through no fault of the actor, and which is of such gravity that, according to ordinary standards of intelligence and morality, the desirability and urgency of avoiding such injury clearly outweigh the desirability of avoiding the injury sought to be prevented by the statute defining the offense in issue. The necessity and justifiability of such conduct may not rest upon considerations pertaining only to the morality and advisability of the statute, either in its general application or with respect to its application to a particular class of cases arising thereunder. Whenever evidence relating to the defense of justification under this subdivision is offered by the defendant, the court shall rule as a matter of law whether the claimed facts and circumstances would, if established, constitute a defense.

The Model Penal Code

Section 2.09. Duress

(1) It is an affirmative defense that the actor engaged in the conduct charged to constitute an offense because he was coerced to do so by the use of, or a threat to use, unlawful force against his person or the person of another, which a person of reasonable firmness in his situation would have been unable to resist.

(2) The defense provided by this Section is unavailable if the actor recklessly placed himself in a situation in which it was probable that he would be subjected to duress. The defense is also unavailable if he was negligent in placing himself in such a situation, whenever negligence suffices to establish culpability for the offense charged.

Code Commentary 8–9 (Tent. Draft No. 8, 1958).

(3) It is not a defense that a woman acted on the command of her husband, unless she acted under such coercion as would establish a defense under this Section. [The presumption that a woman, acting in the presence of her husband, is coerced is abolished.]

(4) When the conduct of the actor would otherwise be justifiable under Section 3.02, this Section does not preclude such defense.

Section 2.10. Military Orders

It is an affirmative defense that the actor, in engaging in the conduct charged to constitute an offense, does no more than execute an order of his superior in the armed services which he does not know to be unlawful.[a]

Note

The defense of obedience to military orders was litigated in United States v. Calley, 22 U.S.C.M.A. 534, 1973 WL 14894 (1973). Lieutenant Calley and troops under his command massacred the inhabitants of the village of My Lai, a reported Vietcong stronghold in South Vietnam. Calley testified that the massacre was at the direct command of Captain Medina. Medina denied ordering the killing of civilians, although he admitted instructing his troops that they were to destroy the village by "burning the hootches, to kill the livestock, to close the wells and to destroy the food crops." The military judge instructed the court martial board that an order commanding the summary execution of detainees or prisoners would be unlawful, and that obedience to such an order would not be a defense if the accused knew that the order was unlawful or if a person of "ordinary sense and understanding" would have known the order to be unlawful. The United States Court of Military Appeals upheld the resulting conviction of murder, with one judge dissenting.

A United States district judge subsequently granted a writ of *habeas corpus* and ordered Calley's release, primarily on the ground that his right to a fair trial had been jeopardized by prejudicial publicity. Calley v. Callaway, 382 F.Supp. 650 (M.D.Ga.1974). The United States Court of Appeals reversed the District Court and reinstated the conviction. Calley v. Callaway, 519 F.2d 184 (5th Cir.1975), cert. denied 425 U.S. 911 (1976). The Court of Appeals opinion notes that Lieutenant Calley's life sentence had been reduced to a term of ten years by order of the Secretary of the Army.

a. "The present Manual limits the defense in military law to cases where the actor 'did not know and could not reasonably be expected to know that the act ordered was illegal.' U.S. Dept. of the Army, Field Manual: The Law of Land Warfare 182 (1956). Military courts are admonished, however, to 'take into consideration the fact that obedience to lawful orders is the duty of every member of the armed forces; that the latter cannot be expected, in conditions of war discipline, to weigh scrupulously the legal merits of the orders received,' etc. In a prosecution in a civil court, it seems unrealistic to inquire whether a defendant who did not know an order was illegal could 'reasonably be expected' to have known it. This limitation on the defense is accordingly abandoned in the view that when that question is in issue it is preferable that it should be litigated in a military court." Comment to § 2.10, Model Penal Code (P.O.D.1962).

UNITED STATES v. RIFFE

United States Court of Appeals, Sixth Circuit, 1994.
28 F.3d 565.

MERRITT, CHIEF JUDGE.

Riffe is an inmate at Michigan's Standish Maximum Correctional Facility. In 1992, a federal grand jury indicted Riffe and Stephanie Kania, Riffe's girlfriend, for conspiracy to distribute marijuana and aiding and abetting the use of the mail to facilitate distribution of marijuana. Kania pled guilty and agreed to cooperate with the government. Defendant was tried by a jury and convicted of all three counts.

The goal of defendant's scheme was to smuggle marijuana into Standish. Kania would receive packages containing marijuana or money to buy marijuana at her post office box in Carrollton, Michigan, sent by an unknown co-conspirator. Once a mailing arrangement was made, Riffe would call Kania and instruct her to retrieve the package from her post office box and deliver the marijuana to a prison guard at a location outside the prison arranged by Riffe. The guard would then deliver the marijuana to Riffe inside the prison.

* * * Riffe argues that the district court committed reversible error when it refused to give the standard Sixth Circuit jury instruction or allow the jury to pass on his defense of duress.[2] Riffe's theory of defense throughout trial was that he was under duress, including the threat of immediate harm, from a prison gang to supply marijuana to members of the gang as repayment of a debt which he owed to them because Riffe's girlfriend, Kania, had used or failed to deliver $1,300 worth of cocaine that belonged to the gang. He offered significant evidence that gang members threatened to kill him if he did not carry out this smuggling operation, and he argues that he was entitled to have the jury pass on his defense of duress rather than have it ruled out by the court.

Riffe presented evidence that he had no alternative but to comply with the demands of the prison gang to smuggle marijuana into the prison, that going to prison officials would have put him in more danger because the protective segregation was ineffective and that he would have been put in additional danger from other inmates because prison officials would have required him to identify the inmates who were threatening him. Defense witness Michael Laukas, an inmate at Stand-

2. Sixth Circuit Pattern Jury Instruction § 6.05 for coercion or duress reads:

(1) One of the questions in this case is whether the defendant was coerced, or forced, to commit the crime.

(2) Coercion can excuse a crime, but only if the defendant reasonably feared that he would immediately be killed or seriously hurt if he did not commit the crime, and there was no reasonable way for him to escape.

(3) The government has the burden of proving that the defendant was not coerced. For you to find the defendant guilty, the government must prove that his fear was unreasonable. In other words, the government must prove that it was not reasonable for him to think that committing the crime was the only way to save himself from death or serious bodily harm. Unless the government proves this beyond a reasonable doubt, you must find him not guilty.

ish, testified that he saw and heard gang members threatening Riffe with knives over the smuggling of marijuana in order to repay the $1,300 debt and that Riffe was reasonably afraid for his life. Laukas also testified that Riffe could not have obtained adequate protection by prison officials. He explained that Standish did not have an adequate protection system and that Riffe would have put himself at greater risk of harm if he had gone to prison officials for help because they would have required him to give up the names of inmates who were threatening him.

Riffe testified that gang members had threatened his life if he refused to smuggle marijuana into the prison for them. He explained that he did not report the threats to prison officials because prison officials would have required him to disclose the names of inmates making the threats and that the prison's protection system would not have adequately safeguarded his physical well-being after making such identifications. He testified that the basis for this belief was that in 1985–86 while in protective segregation after giving up a name to prison officials, Riffe had been stabbed in the chest. He also testified that a friend had been killed after a similar incident in another institution.

Postal Inspector Durand also testified that Riffe had relayed to him that he feared for his life while in the prison, and Kania testified that she was concerned with the defendant's physical safety in the prison and that the defendant had told her that he was being threatened if he did not continue to produce marijuana for inmates in the prison.

The district court refused to give the instruction because it found that the defendant had failed to meet the duress instruction requirements set forth in United States v. Singleton, 902 F.2d 471 (6th Cir.), cert. denied, 498 U.S. 872 (1990). In *Singleton*, this Court adopted five factors that control whether a jury instruction presenting a duress defense should be given. Evidence must be presented:

(1) that defendant was under an unlawful and present, imminent, and impending threat of such a nature as to induce a well-grounded apprehension of death or serious bodily injury;

(2) that the defendant had not recklessly or negligently placed himself in a situation in which it was probable that he would be forced to choose the criminal conduct;

(3) that the defendant had no reasonable, legal alternative to violating the law, a chance both to refuse to do the criminal act and also to avoid the threatened harm;

(4) that a direct causal relationship may be reasonably anticipated between the criminal action taken and the avoidance of the threatened harm.

(5) that defendant did not maintain the illegal conduct any longer than absolutely necessary.

The district court premised its refusal to give the instruction on the third factor which it interpreted as a per se rule. Although the district court found affirmatively that the defendant and Laukas "had a well founded belief that there might be dire consequences to them if they presented themselves to the administration," it applied this per se rule requiring Riffe to attempt to seek protection from prison officials in order for the duress defense to be considered by the jury. The district court compared the case to prison escape cases which generally require the escapee to turn himself in to police as soon as reasonably possible after escape in order to be entitled to consideration of the defense of duress. United States v. Bailey, 444 U.S. 394 (1980). Under this analysis, the court found that Riffe's failure to seek protection prohibited him from receiving the duress instruction under the "reasonable, legal alternative" prong of *Singleton*. We reject the application of a per se rule in a case of this type.

* * * The "no reasonable, legal alternative" prong of *Singleton* at issue in this case stems from the Supreme Court's decision in United States v. Bailey, 444 U.S. 394 (1980). In *Bailey*, the defendant escaped from federal prison because of extremely poor prison conditions and did not turn himself in to other authorities after the escape. In analyzing the duress defense, the Court stated that "if there was a reasonable, legal alternative to violating the law, 'a chance both to refuse to do the criminal act and also to avoid the threatened harm,' the defense[ ] will fail." The Court concluded that in order to be entitled to a duress instruction, the escapee must offer evidence "justifying his continued absence from custody as well as his initial departure and that an indispensable element of such an offer is testimony of a bona fide effort to surrender or return to custody as soon as the claimed duress had lost its coercive force." Id. at 412–13.

The rule in *Bailey* is not a per se rule. *Bailey* recognizes that in most escape cases, an escapee will be able to remove himself from the threatened harm or duress by turning himself in to authorities. However, the case also recognizes that the escapee might be able to offer evidence "justifying his continued absence." In other words, there might be situations in which an escapee could offer evidence justifying his remaining at large because of the coercive force or duress that caused his initial escape. Similarly here, while the typical case will require a prisoner to attempt to seek help from prison authorities as an alternative to committing the crime, there may be cases in which the prisoner will be able to offer evidence justifying his decision not to go to prison authorities: that seeking help from prison authorities would not have been a reasonable legal alternative but instead would have subjected him to continued or additional physical harm.

Riffe presented evidence of threats of immediate harm in this case, and the district court acknowledged that Riffe had a well-founded fear that going to prison officials might have placed him in more danger. In other words, seeking help might not have been a reasonable legal alternative to avoiding immediate physical harm. The district court, by erroneously applying a per se rule, abolished the reasonableness requirement set forth in *Bailey* and *Singleton*. * * *

Accordingly, the defendant's convictions are REVERSED and the case is REMANDED for a new trial.

CORNELIA G. KENNEDY, CIRCUIT JUDGE, concurring in part and dissenting in part.

I should first note that any failure to give the instruction was harmless with respect to the conspiracy count. Defendant testified that he was engaged in the conspiracy to possess with intent to distribute and distribution, and did distribute marijuana before any threats were made against him. Indeed, the threats came about because members of a prison gang overheard him discussing his ability to bring in drugs and demanded he bring in drugs for them. However, my disagreement is broader than that. I agree with the District Court that defendant failed to establish his entitlement to the requested instruction.

* * * The District Court here made a finding that the evidence of duress was insufficient in two respects. First, defendant's own prior illegal activity in smuggling marijuana into the prison placed him in the position of having to enlarge his operation to bring in drugs for those who threatened him. Thus, he had "recklessly or negligently placed himself in a situation in which it was probable he would be [forced to choose the criminal conduct]." United States v. Newcomb, 6 F.3d 1129, 1134 (6th Cir.1993) (quoting United States v. Singleton, 902 F.2d 471, 472 (6th Cir.)). Second, the District Court held that defendant had not established that he had no reasonable, legal alternative to violating the law. * * *

Defendant Riffe testified that in order to be placed in protective custody he would have to identify the persons who threatened him and that the prison authorities could not guarantee his safety. I concede that prison authorities cannot guarantee inmates' safety. The government cannot guarantee anyone's safety, but the common law defense of duress requires that a threat of imminent death or serious bodily injury exist. Although the government cannot guarantee the safety of those threatened by organized crime figures or those who live in neighborhoods dominated by vicious street gangs, we do not excuse the crimes of either group because they were committed as a result of threats, if those threats were not of an imminent danger. Defendant's unwillingness to go to the prison authorities or other law enforcement authorities was also due to the fact that for his safety he would have to remain in administrative or protective segregation and could not be released into the general prison population. The unpleasant nature of that alternative does not establish that it is unreasonable to require him to pursue that alternative.

Finally, defendant asserts that even if sent to another state institution or to a federal prison, gang members in those other institutions would seek him out. Aside from the question whether he was qualified to give an opinion on this issue, the fact that there is some risk does not remove this as a reasonable alternative. * * * If the majority is correct that the threat of some future undefined gang retaliation makes turning to the prison authority an unreasonable alternative, then it would appear to be unreasonable to incarcerate any prisoner threatened by a prison gang. We do not excuse witnesses from testifying because there is a risk that criminal defendants or their cohorts will retaliate. If we excuse prisoners from crimes they commit by reason of threats from other prisoners where the institution offers a system of protection, we greatly increase the power of the very prison gangs of which defendant complains. What gang would not be delighted to be able to tell their victims to commit the crime we demand and you'll be excused from punishment; just tell the authorities you were afraid for your personal safety and that the prison can't guarantee your future safety.

Under the majority's holding, if someone threatens a life and even though the threat is not immediate, the person threatened will be excused if he or she retaliates because society cannot guarantee that the threat will not be carried out. If we are to live in an ordered society, I believe the threatened person must take that chance and use legal means to stop the criminal from carrying out the threat. Defendant had a chance here to refuse to do the criminal act and avoid the threatened harm. He chose to commit further crimes over taking that chance. His evidence failed as a matter of law to reach the "minimum threshold" that would have required an instruction on duress.

UNITED STATES v. SCHOON

United States Court of Appeals, Ninth Circuit, 1991.
971 F.2d 193.

BOOCHEVER, CIRCUIT JUDGE

* * *

I

On December 4, 1989, thirty people, including appellants, gained admittance to the IRS office in Tucson, where they chanted "keep America's tax dollars out of El Salvador," splashed simulated blood on the counters, walls, and carpeting, and generally obstructed the office's operation. After a federal police officer ordered the group, on several occasions, to disperse or face arrest, appellants were arrested.

At a bench trial, appellants proffered testimony about conditions in El Salvador as the motivation for their conduct. They attempted to assert a necessity defense, essentially contending that their acts in protest of American involvement in El Salvador were necessary to avoid further bloodshed in that country. While finding appellants motivated solely by humanitarian concerns, the court nonetheless precluded the defense as a matter of law, relying on Ninth Circuit precedent. The sole issue on appeal is the propriety of the court's exclusion of a necessity defense as a matter of law. * * *

II

* * * To invoke the necessity defense, * * * defendants colorably must have shown that: (1) they were faced with a choice of evils and

chose the lesser evil; (2) they acted to prevent imminent harm; (3) they reasonably anticipated a direct causal relationship between their conduct and the harm to be averted; and (4) they had no legal alternatives to violating the law. *United States v. Aguilar,* 883 F.2d 662, 693 (9th Cir.1989), *cert. denied,* 111 S. Ct. 751, 112 L. Ed. 2d 771 (1991). * * *

The district court denied the necessity defense on the grounds that (1) the requisite immediacy was lacking; (2) the actions taken would not abate the evil; and (3) other legal alternatives existed. * * *

While we could affirm substantially on those grounds relied upon by the district court, we find a deeper, systemic reason for the complete absence of federal case law recognizing a necessity defense in an indirect civil disobedience case. * * * Indirect civil disobedience involves violating a law which is not, itself, the object of protest. Direct civil disobedience, on the other hand, involves protesting the existence of a law by breaking that law or by preventing the execution of that law in a specific instance * * *. This case involves indirect civil disobedience because these protestors were not challenging the laws under which they were charged. In contrast, the civil rights lunch counter sit-ins, for example, constituted direct civil disobedience because the protestors were challenging the rule that prevented them from sitting at lunch counters. * * *

While our prior cases consistently have found the elements of the necessity defense lacking in cases involving indirect civil disobedience, we have never addressed specifically whether the defense is available in cases of indirect civil disobedience. * * * Today, we conclude, for the reasons stated below, that the necessity defense is inapplicable to cases involving indirect civil disobedience.

Necessity is, essentially, a utilitarian defense. It therefore justifies criminal acts taken to avert a greater harm, maximizing social welfare by allowing a crime to be committed where the social benefits of the crime outweigh the social costs of failing to commit the crime. Pursuant to the defense, prisoners could escape a burning prison; a person lost in the woods could steal food from a cabin to survive; an embargo could be violated because adverse weather conditions necessitated sale of the cargo at a foreign port; a crew could mutiny where their ship was thought to be unseaworthy; and property could be destroyed to prevent the spread of fire.

What all the traditional necessity cases have in common is that the commission of the "crime" averted the occurrence of an even greater "harm." In some sense, the necessity defense allows us to act as individual legislatures, amending a particular criminal provision or crafting a one-time exception to it, subject to court review, when a real legislature would formally do the same under those circumstances. For example, by allowing prisoners who escape a burning jail to claim the justification of necessity, we assume the lawmaker, confronting this problem, would have allowed for an exception to the law proscribing prison escapes.

* * *

Analysis of three of the necessity defense's four elements leads us to the conclusion that necessity can never be proved in a case of indirect civil disobedience. We do not rely upon the imminent harm prong of the defense because we believe there can be indirect civil disobedience cases in which the protested harm is imminent.

A

1. Balance of Harms

It is axiomatic that, if the thing to be averted is not a harm at all, the balance of harms necessarily would disfavor any criminal action. * * *

* * * The law could not function were people allowed to rely on their *subjective* beliefs and value judgments in determining which harms justified the taking of criminal action.

The protest in this case was in the form of indirect civil disobedience, aimed at reversal of the government's El Salvador policy. That policy does not violate the Constitution, and appellants have never suggested as much. * * * The most immediate harm the appellants sought to avert was the existence of the government's El Salvador policy, which is not in itself a legally cognizable harm. Moreover, any harms resulting from the operation of this policy are insufficiently concrete to be legally cognizable as harms for purposes of the necessity defense.

* * *

2. Causal Relationship Between Criminal Conduct and Harm to be Averted

This inquiry requires a court to judge the likelihood that an alleged harm will be abated by the taking of illegal action. In the sense that the likelihood of abatement is required in the traditional necessity cases, there will never be such likelihood in cases of indirect political protest. In the traditional cases, a prisoner flees a burning cell and averts death, or someone demolishes a home to create a firebreak and prevents the conflagration of an entire community. The nexus between the act undertaken and the result sought is a close one. Ordinarily it is the volitional illegal act alone which, once taken, abates the evil.

In political necessity cases involving indirect civil disobedience against congressional acts, however, the act alone is unlikely to abate the evil precisely because the action is indirect. Here, the IRS obstruction, or the refusal to comply with a federal officer's order, are unlikely to abate the killings in El Salvador, or immediately change Congress's policy; instead, it takes another *volitional* actor not controlled by the protestor to take a further step; Congress must change its mind.

3. *Legal Alternatives*

A final reason the necessity defense does not apply to these indirect civil disobedience cases is that legal alternatives will never be deemed exhausted when the harm can be mitigated by congressional action. * * * Because congressional action can always mitigate this "harm," lawful political activity to spur such action will always be a legal alternative. * * *

The necessity defense requires the absence of any legal alternative to the contemplated illegal conduct which could reasonably be expected to abate an imminent evil. See United States v. Bailey, 444 U.S. 394, 410, 62 L. Ed. 2d 575, 100 S. Ct. 624 (1980). * * *

[The court then noted that in an earlier case it had assumed that "in the context of the democratic process * * * lawful political action [is] a reasonable alternative to indirect civil disobedience.] Thus, indirect civil disobedience can never meet the necessity defense requirement that there be a lack of legal alternatives.

B

* * *

The real problem here is that litigants are trying to distort to their purposes an age-old common law doctrine meant for a very different set of circumstances. What these cases are really about is gaining notoriety for a cause—the defense allows protestors to get their political grievances discussed in a courtroom. * * * Because these attempts to invoke the necessity defense "force the courts to choose among causes they should make legitimate by extending the defense of necessity," and because the criminal acts, themselves, do not maximize social good, they should be subject to a *per se* rule of exclusion.

Thus, we see the failure of any federal court to recognize a defense of necessity in a case like ours not as coincidental, but rather as the natural consequence of the historic limitation of the doctrine. Indirect protests of congressional policies can never meet all the requirements of the necessity doctrine. Therefore, we hold that the necessity defense is not available in such cases.

AFFIRMED. [Concurring opinion omitted.]

UNITED STATES v. OAKLAND CANNABIS BUYERS' COOPERATIVE

Supreme Court of the United States, 2001.
532 U.S. 483, 121 S.Ct. 1711, 149 L.Ed.2d 722.

JUSTICE THOMAS delivered the opinion of the Court.

The Controlled Substances Act, 21 U.S.C. § 801 et seq., prohibits the manufacture and distribution of various drugs, including marijuana. In this case, we must decide whether there is a medical necessity exception to these prohibitions. We hold that there is not.

In November 1996, California voters enacted an initiative measure entitled the Compassionate Use Act of 1996. Attempting "to ensure that seriously ill Californians have the right to obtain and use marijuana for medical purposes," Cal. Health & Safety Code Ann. § 11362.5, the statute creates an exception to California laws prohibiting the possession and cultivation of marijuana. These prohibitions no longer apply to a patient or his primary caregiver who possesses or cultivates marijuana for the patient's medical purposes upon the recommendation or approval of a physician. In the wake of this voter initiative, several groups organized "medical cannabis dispensaries" to meet the needs of qualified patients. Respondent Oakland Cannabis Buyers' Cooperative is one of these groups.

The Cooperative is a not-for-profit organization that operates in downtown Oakland. A physician serves as medical director, and registered nurses staff the Cooperative during business hours. To become a member, a patient must provide a written statement from a treating physician assenting to marijuana therapy and must submit to a screening interview. If accepted as a member, the patient receives an identification card entitling him to obtain marijuana from the Cooperative.

In January 1998, the United States sued the Cooperative and its executive director, respondent Jeffrey Jones (together, the Cooperative), in the United States District Court for the Northern District of California. Seeking to enjoin the Cooperative from distributing and manufacturing marijuana, the United States argued that, whether or not the Cooperative's activities are legal under California law, they violate federal law. Specifically, the Government argued that the Cooperative violated the Controlled Substances Act's prohibitions on distributing, manufacturing, and possessing with the intent to distribute or manufacture a controlled substance. 21 U.S.C. § 841(a). Concluding that the Government had established a probability of success on the merits, the District Court granted a preliminary injunction.

The Cooperative did not appeal the injunction but instead openly violated it by distributing marijuana to numerous persons. To terminate these violations, the Government initiated contempt proceedings. In defense, the Cooperative contended that any distributions were medically necessary. Marijuana is the only drug, according to the Cooperative, that can alleviate the severe pain and other debilitating symptoms of the Cooperative's patients. The District Court rejected this defense, however, after determining there was insufficient evidence that each recipient of marijuana was in actual danger of imminent harm without the drug. The District Court found the Cooperative in contempt and, at the Government's request, modified the preliminary injunction to empower the United States Marshal to seize the Cooperative's premises. Although recognizing that "human suffering" could result, the District Court reasoned that a court's "equitable powers [do] not permit it to ignore federal law." * * *

The Cooperative appealed * * *. Before the Court of Appeals for the Ninth Circuit decided the case, however, the Cooperative voluntarily purged its contempt by promising the District Court that it would comply with the initial preliminary injunction. Consequently, the Court of Appeals determined that the appeal of the contempt order was moot.

The denial of the Cooperative's motion to modify the injunction, however, presented a live controversy * * *. Reaching the merits of this issue, the Court of Appeals reversed and remanded. According to the Court of Appeals, the medical necessity defense was a "legally cognizable defense" that likely would apply in the circumstances. * * * Remanding the case, the Court of Appeals instructed the District Court to consider "the criteria for a medical necessity exemption, and, should it modify the injunction, to set forth those criteria in the modification order." Following these instructions, the District Court granted the Cooperative's motion to modify the injunction to incorporate a medical necessity defense.[2]

The United States petitioned for certiorari to review the Court of Appeals' decision that medical necessity is a legally cognizable defense to violations of the Controlled Substances Act. Because the decision raises significant questions as to the ability of the United States to enforce the Nation's drug laws, we granted certiorari.

II

The Controlled Substances Act provides that, "except as authorized by this subchapter, it shall be unlawful for any person knowingly or intentionally . . . to manufacture, distribute, or dispense, or possess with intent to manufacture, distribute, or dispense, a controlled substance." 21 U.S.C. § 841(a)(1). The subchapter, in turn, establishes exceptions. For marijuana (and other drugs that have been classified as "schedule I" controlled substances), there is but one express exception, and it is available only for Government-approved research projects. Not conducting such a project, the Cooperative cannot, and indeed does not, claim this statutory exemption.

The Cooperative contends, however, that notwithstanding the apparently absolute language of § 841(a), the statute is subject to addition-

2. The amended preliminary injunction reaffirmed that the Cooperative is generally enjoined from manufacturing, distributing, and possessing with the intent to manufacture or distribute marijuana, but it carved out an exception for cases of medical necessity. Specifically, the District Court ordered that "the foregoing injunction does not apply to the distribution of cannabis by [the Cooperative] to patient-members who (1) suffer from a serious medical condition, (2) will suffer imminent harm if the patient-member does not have access to cannabis, (3) need cannabis for the treatment of the patient-member's medical condition, or need cannabis to alleviate the medical condition or symptoms associated with the medical condition, and (4) have no reasonable legal alternative to cannabis for the effective treatment or alleviation of the patient-member's medical condition or symptoms associated with the medical condition because the patient-member has tried all other legal alternatives to cannabis and the alternatives have been ineffective in treating or alleviating the patient-member's medical condition or symptoms associated with the medical condition, or the alternatives result in side effects which the patient-member cannot reasonably tolerate." * * *

al, implied exceptions, one of which is medical necessity. According to the Cooperative, because necessity was a defense at common law, medical necessity should be read into the Controlled Substances Act. We disagree.

As an initial matter, we note that it is an open question whether federal courts ever have authority to recognize a necessity defense not provided by statute. A necessity defense "traditionally covered the situation where physical forces beyond the actor's control rendered illegal conduct the lesser of two evils." United States v. Bailey, 444 U.S. 394, 410, 62 L. Ed. 2d 575, 100 S. Ct. 624 (1980). Even at common law, the defense of necessity was somewhat controversial. See, e.g., Queen v. Dudley & Stephens, 14 QB 273 (1884). And under our constitutional system, in which federal crimes are defined by statute rather than by common law, it is especially so. As we have stated: "Whether, as a policy matter, an exemption should be created is a question for legislative judgment, not judicial inference." United States v. Rutherford, 442 U.S. 544, 559, 61 L. Ed. 2d 68, 99 S. Ct. 2470 (1979). Nonetheless, we recognize that this Court has discussed the possibility of a necessity defense without altogether rejecting it.[3]

We need not decide, however, whether necessity can ever be a defense when the federal statute does not expressly provide for it. In this case, to resolve the question presented, we need only recognize that a medical necessity exception for marijuana is at odds with the terms of the Controlled Substances Act. The statute, to be sure, does not explicitly abrogate the defense. But its provisions leave no doubt that the defense is unavailable.

Under any conception of legal necessity, one principle is clear: The defense cannot succeed when the legislature itself has made a "determination of values." 1 W. LaFave & A. Scott, Substantive Criminal Law § 5.4, p. 629 (1986). In the case of the Controlled Substances Act, the statute reflects a determination that marijuana has no medical benefits worthy of an exception (outside the confines of a Government-approved research project). Whereas some other drugs can be dispensed and prescribed for medical use, the same is not true for marijuana. Indeed, for purposes of the Controlled Substances Act, marijuana has "no currently accepted medical use" at all.

The structure of the Act supports this conclusion. The statute divides drugs into five schedules, depending in part on whether the

3. The Cooperative is incorrect to suggest that *Bailey* has settled the question whether federal courts have authority to recognize a necessity defense not provided by statute. There, the Court rejected the necessity defense of a prisoner who contended that adverse prison conditions justified his prison escape. The Court held that the necessity defense is unavailable to prisoners, like Bailey, who fail to present evidence of a bona fide effort to surrender as soon as the claimed necessity had lost its coercive force. It was not argued, and so there was no occasion to consider, whether the statute might be unable to bear any necessity defense at all. And although the Court noted that Congress "legislates against a background of Anglo–Saxon common law" and thus "may" have contemplated a necessity defense, the Court refused to "balance [the] harms," explaining that "we are construing an Act of Congress, not drafting it."

particular drug has a currently accepted medical use. The Act then imposes restrictions on the manufacture and distribution of the substance according to the schedule in which it has been placed. Schedule I is the most restrictive schedule. The Attorney General can include a drug in schedule I only if the drug "has no currently accepted medical use in treatment in the United States," "has a high potential for abuse," and has "a lack of accepted safety for use ... under medical supervision." Under the statute, the Attorney General could not put marijuana into schedule I if marijuana had any accepted medical use.

The Cooperative points out, however, that the Attorney General did not place marijuana into schedule I. Congress put it there, and Congress was not required to find that a drug lacks an accepted medical use before including the drug in schedule I. We are not persuaded that this distinction has any significance to our inquiry. Under the Cooperative's logic, drugs that Congress places in schedule I could be distributed when medically necessary whereas drugs that the Attorney General places in schedule I could not. Nothing in the statute, however, suggests that there are two tiers of schedule I narcotics, with drugs in one tier more readily available than drugs in the other. On the contrary, the statute consistently treats all schedule I drugs alike. * * *

The Cooperative further argues that use of schedule I drugs generally—whether placed in schedule I by Congress or the Attorney General—can be medically necessary, notwithstanding that they have "no currently accepted medical use." According to the Cooperative, a drug may not yet have achieved general acceptance as a medical treatment but may nonetheless have medical benefits to a particular patient or class of patients. We decline to parse the statute in this manner. It is clear from the text of the Act that Congress has made a determination that marijuana has no medical benefits worthy of an exception. * * *

Finally, the Cooperative contends that we should construe the Controlled Substances Act to include a medical necessity defense in order to avoid what it considers to be difficult constitutional questions. In particular, the Cooperative asserts that, shorn of a medical necessity defense, the statute exceeds Congress' Commerce Clause powers, violates the substantive due process rights of patients, and offends the fundamental liberties of the people under the Fifth, Ninth, and Tenth Amendments. As the Cooperative acknowledges, however, the canon of constitutional avoidance has no application in the absence of statutory ambiguity. Because we have no doubt that the Controlled Substances Act cannot bear a medical necessity defense to distributions of marijuana, we do not find guidance in this avoidance principle. * * *

For these reasons, we hold that medical necessity is not a defense to manufacturing and distributing marijuana. * * *

* * *

The judgment of the Court of Appeals is reversed, and the case is remanded for further proceedings consistent with this opinion.

* * *

JUSTICE STEVENS, with whom JUSTICE SOUTER and JUSTICE GINSBURG join, concurring in the judgment.

Lest the Court's narrow holding be lost in its broad dicta, let me restate it here: "We hold that medical necessity is not a defense to manufacturing and distributing marijuana." This confined holding is consistent with our grant of certiorari, which was limited to the question "whether the Controlled Substances Act forecloses a medical necessity defense to the Act's prohibition against manufacturing and distributing marijuana, a Schedule I controlled substance." * * *

Accordingly, in the lower courts as well as here, respondents have raised the medical necessity defense as a justification for distributing marijuana to cooperative members, and it was in that context that the Ninth Circuit determined that respondents had "a legally cognizable defense." The Court is surely correct to reverse that determination. Congress' classification of marijuana as a schedule I controlled substance—that is, one that cannot be distributed outside of approved research projects, makes it clear that "the Controlled Substances Act cannot bear a medical necessity defense to distributions of marijuana."[1]

Apart from its limited holding, the Court takes two unwarranted and unfortunate excursions that prevent me from joining its opinion. First, the Court reaches beyond its holding, and beyond the facts of the case, by suggesting that the defense of necessity is unavailable for anyone under the Controlled Substances Act. Because necessity was raised in this case as a defense to distribution, the Court need not venture an opinion on whether the defense is available to anyone other than distributors. Most notably, whether the defense might be available to a seriously ill patient for whom there is no alternative means of avoiding starvation or extraordinary suffering is a difficult issue that is not presented here.

Second, the Court gratuitously casts doubt on "whether necessity can ever be a defense" to any federal statute that does not explicitly provide for it, calling such a defense into question by a misleading reference to its existence as an "open question." By contrast, our precedent has expressed no doubt about the viability of the common-law defense, even in the context of federal criminal statutes that do not provide for it in so many words. See, e.g., United States v. Bailey, 444

1. In any event, respondents do not fit the paradigm of a defendant who may assert necessity. The defense "traditionally covered the situation where physical forces beyond the actor's control rendered illegal conduct the lesser of two evils." *United States* v. *Bailey,* 444 U.S. 394, 410. Respondents, on the other hand, have not been forced to confront a choice of evils—violating federal law by distributing marijuana to seriously ill patients or letting those individuals suffer—but have thrust that choice upon themselves by electing to become distributors for such patients. Of course, respondents also cannot claim necessity based upon the choice of evils facing seriously ill patients, as that is not the same choice respondents face.

U.S. 394, 415 ("We therefore hold that, where a criminal defendant is charged with escape and claims that he is entitled to an instruction on the theory of duress or necessity, he must proffer evidence of a bona fide effort to surrender or return to custody as soon as the claimed duress or necessity had lost its coercive force") * * *. Indeed, the Court's comment on the general availability of the necessity defense is completely unnecessary because the Government has made no such suggestion. * * *

The overbroad language of the Court's opinion is especially unfortunate given the importance of showing respect for the sovereign States that comprise our Federal Union. That respect imposes a duty on federal courts, whenever possible, to avoid or minimize conflict between federal and state law, particularly in situations in which the citizens of a State have chosen to "serve as a laboratory" in the trial of "novel social and economic experiments without risk to the rest of the country." In my view, this is such a case. By passing Proposition 215, California voters have decided that seriously ill patients and their primary caregivers should be exempt from prosecution under state laws for cultivating and possessing marijuana if the patient's physician recommends using the drug for treatment.[4] This case does not call upon the Court to deprive all such patients of the benefit of the necessity defense to federal prosecution, when the case itself does not involve any such patients.

* * *

COMMONWEALTH v. HUTCHINS

Supreme Judicial Court of Massachusetts, Essex, 1991.
410 Mass. 726, 575 N.E.2d 741.

O'CONNOR, J.

[Defendant was charged with possession of marijuana. Before trial, he filed a motion to dismiss the complaints "on the ground that any possession of controlled substances by the defendant is within the defense of medical necessity." The trial court ruled that medical necessity was not a defense and convicted the defendant in a bench trial.]

In support of his motion, as an offer of proof, the defendant submitted affidavits, excerpts from his medical records, literature on a disease known as progressive systemic sclerosis (scleroderma) and on the medicinal uses of marihuana and other materials. Through these materials, the defendant offered to prove the following facts: The defendant is a forty-seven year old man who has been diagnosed as having scleroderma accompanied by Raynaud's phenomenon, related to his service in the Navy. Scleroderma is a chronic disease that results in the buildup of scar tissue throughout the body. The cause of scleroderma is not known and no effective treatment or cure has been discovered. In the most severe

4. Since 1996, six other States—Alaska, Colorado, Maine, Nevada, Oregon, and Washington—have passed medical marijuana initiatives, and Hawaii has enacted a similar measure through its legislature. [citations omitted]

cases, scleroderma may result in death. The defendant's medical history includes episodes of fatigue, hypertension, loss of appetite, weight loss of up to twenty-five pounds, diarrhea, nausea, vomiting, reflux of food and stomach acid into the mouth, reduced motility and constriction of the esophagus, extreme difficulty and pain in swallowing, and swollen, painful joints and extreme sensitivity to the cold in his hands and feet. He also suffers from severe depression, related at least in part to his disease, and was briefly hospitalized after attempting suicide. As a result of his illness, the defendant has been unable to work since 1978.

According to the offer of proof, the defendant's medical condition has been unsuccessfully treated with numerous medications and therapies by physicians of the Veterans Administration. The constriction of his esophagus has been treated by dilation and in 1974 was so severe that his treating physician advised him to have his esophagus surgically removed and replaced with a piece of his own intestine. The defendant has informed his treating physicians that since 1975, with some success, he has used marihuana, in lieu of antidepressants and surgery, to alleviate certain symptoms of his illness including nausea, loss of appetite, difficulty in eating, drinking or swallowing, loss of motility of the esophagus, spasticity, hypertension, and anxiety. Two of his treating physicians state that, although they are unable to "confirm [the defendant's] claim that his use of marihuana has caused his remarkable remission, ... it does appear that his use of marihuana does alleviate the previously mentioned symptoms." These two physicians also state that "there appears to be a sufficient basis to conduct a scientific and medical investigation into the possible use of marihuana to treat the disease of scleroderma." A research study of its therapeutic potential and medical uses indicates that the use of marihuana, indeed, may be effective to treat loss of appetite, nausea, vomiting, and weight loss and may relieve severe anxiety and depression. One of the defendant's other treating physicians, however, does not find that marihuana "had any effect in [the defendant's] case" and that he is "unaware of any published or unpublished evidence of a beneficial effect of marihuana in this condition."

Through correspondence with his physicians, the Veterans Administration, and members of the Massachusetts Legislature and the United States Congress, the defendant has made numerous, albeit unsuccessful, attempts lawfully to obtain either a prescription for marihuana or permission to participate in a research study on the use of marihuana to treat scleroderma. The Massachusetts Legislature has considered a bill providing for the use of marihuana in therapeutic research on more than one occasion, but no such statute has been enacted in the Commonwealth. The Veterans Administration has determined that presently there is no research study on the use of marihuana to treat scleroderma and therefore will not dispense marihuana for the defendant's treatment. * * *

"Under the common law defense of justification by necessity, a crime committed under the pressure of imminent danger may be excused if the harm sought to be avoided far exceeds the harm resulting from the crime committed." Commonwealth v. Schuchardt, 408 Mass. 347, 349 (1990), citing Commonwealth v. Hood, 389 Mass. 581, 590 (1983), and Commonwealth v. Brugmann, 13 Mass. App. Ct. 373, 376–377 (1982). "In essence, the 'competing harms' defense exonerates one who commits a crime under the 'pressure of circumstances' if the harm that would have resulted from compliance with the law significantly exceeds the harm actually resulting from the defendant's violation of the law." At its root is an appreciation that there may be circumstances where the value protected by the law is, as a matter of public policy, eclipsed by a superseding value which makes it inappropriate and unjust to apply the usual criminal rule.

"We have ruled that 'the application of the defense is limited to the following circumstances: (1) the defendant is faced with a clear and imminent danger, not one which is debatable or speculative; (2) the defendant can reasonably expect that his [or her] action will be effective as the direct cause of abating the danger; (3) there is [no] legal alternative which will be effective in abating the danger; and (4) the Legislature has not acted to preclude the defense by a clear and deliberate choice regarding the values at issue.' "Commonwealth v. Schuchardt, supra at 349. It must be understood, however, that that oft-repeated principle, that the necessity defense is limited to certain specified circumstances, does not mean that, whenever those circumstances obtain, the defense automatically applies. Rather, the first question always is whether the harm that would have resulted from compliance with the law significantly outweighs the harm that reasonably could result from the court's acceptance of necessity as an excuse in the circumstances presented by the particular case. Only when a comparison of the "competing harms" in specific circumstances clearly favors excusing what would otherwise be punishable conduct, is it appropriate then to inquire whether the standards enumerated in the cases cited above, standards which themselves do not call for a comparison of competing harms, have been met.

We mention two illustrative cases. In Commonwealth v. Thurber, 383 Mass. 328 (1981), the defendant was convicted of escape from [prison]. At the trial, the defendant presented evidence that he had escaped because his life was in imminent danger at the prison. In discussing the necessity defense, we quoted with approval a statement in a California case of the circumstances in which an escape from prison might be excused, one of the circumstances being that the escape be accomplished without violence, and another being that "the prisoner immediately reports to the proper authorities when he has attained a position of safety from the immediate threat." People v. Lovercamp, 43 Cal.App.3d 823, 831–832 (1974). * * *

Commonwealth v. Iglesia, 403 Mass. 132 (1988), provides another illustration. There, the defendant was charged with unlawfully carrying a firearm. He testified that he was attacked by a man with a gun, that he wrested the gun from the man, and that he immediately went to the police station with it. Again, we "assumed that, when a defendant seizes a firearm from one who had expressed an immediate intention to use it, and flees to a place of safe-keeping, such possession might be lawful." In *Iglesia*, as in *Thurber*, the likely harm to society that would be likely to result from recognition of a necessity defense, carefully limited as to circumstances, would be significantly outweighed by the potential harm to the defendant, if his evidence were to be believed, if he were to comply with the law. It is fair to assume, in the absence of a specifically expressed contrary legislative intent, that judicial recognition of a necessity defense in the circumstances of the *Iglesia* case would not contradict any legislative policy determination.

Accepting the defendant's offer of proof, * * * nevertheless we rule that the defendant's proffered evidence does not raise the defense of necessity. In our view, the alleviation of the defendant's medical symptoms, the importance to the defendant of which we do not underestimate, would not clearly and significantly outweigh the potential harm to the public were we to declare that the defendant's cultivation of marihuana and its use for his medicinal purposes may not be punishable. We cannot dismiss the reasonably possible negative impact of such a judicial declaration on the enforcement of our drug laws, including but not limited to those dealing with marihuana, nor can we ignore the government's overriding interest in the regulation of such substances. Excusing the escaped prisoner in the circumstances presented by *Thurber*, or the carrier of a gun in the circumstances of *Iglesia*, is quite different from excusing one who cultivates and uses marihuana in the circumstances of this case.

Judgment affirmed.

LIACOS, C.J. (dissenting, with whom NOLAN, J., joins).

* * * While I recognize that the public has a strong interest in the enforcement of drug laws and in the strict regulation of narcotics, I do not believe that the interest would be significantly harmed by permitting a jury to consider whether the defendant cultivated and used marihuana in order to alleviate agonizing and painful symptoms caused by an illness. The court seems to suggest that we should not condone the use of marihuana, regardless of a particular individual's reasons for using the drug. Although the court appears to recognize the defense by taking this position, it fails to give sufficient consideration to the rationale behind the common law defense of necessity. That rationale is based on the recognition that, under very limited circumstances, "the value protected by the law is * * * eclipsed by a superseding value which makes it inappropriate and unjust to apply the usual criminal rule." Commonwealth v. Brugmann, 13 Mass. App. Ct. 373, 377 (1982). * * *

There is no reason to believe, as the court suggests, that allowing a defendant to present evidence of medical necessity to a jury will have a negative impact on the enforcement of drug laws. I am confident that juries would apply their wisdom and common sense in making sure that the necessity defense is not successfully utilized by defendants who use marihuana for purposes other than to alleviate agonizing and painful medical symptoms. In my view, this court's recognition of a medical necessity defense in the circumstances of this case would have a negligible impact on the enforcement of drug laws. * * * The court today once again unnecessarily interferes with the proper functions of the jury. I dissent.

Notes

1. Are the preceding cases recognizing the defense of necessity for prison escapees but rejecting claims of medical necessity for the use of marijuana by people suffering from serious medical conditions logically inconsistent, or do they rest upon rational legal and social policy choices? For example, do the medical necessity opinions rest, at least in part, on the fear that accepting this defense might encourage large numbers of people to violate the laws criminalizing marijuana cultivation, possession and use? Conversely, does the necessity defense for escapees actually create incentives for prisoners to escape?

2. Two famous nineteenth century cases rejected a defense of necessity in extreme circumstances. The defendant in United States v. Holmes, 26 Fed.Cas. 360 (C.C.E.D.Pa.1842) was a seaman on board a passenger ship who performed heroic services when the ship struck an iceberg and sank. In part due to his efforts, 32 passengers and nine crewmen made their way into the ship's leaky longboat. Subsequently, the overcrowded boat began to founder. Following the mate's orders to spare women, children, and husbands, Holmes and the other crewmen threw 14 male passengers overboard to lighten the boat. The next day the boat was sighted by a ship and all the survivors were rescued. Other members of the crew apparently were not apprehended, but Holmes was prosecuted for the manslaughter of one of the passengers. The court instructed the jury: (1) that the necessity to sacrifice some persons to save the others must be real rather than merely apparent for any defense to arise; (2) that in any case the seamen were obliged by the nature of their calling to sacrifice themselves to save the passengers rather than vice-versa; and (3) as between persons in "equal relations", the choice of whom to sacrifice must be by lot rather than by the strong choosing to sacrifice the weak. Holmes was convicted and sentenced to a term of six months in prison and a fine of twenty dollars.

The decision in Regina v. Dudley & Stephens, (1884) All E.R. 61, 14 Q.B. 273, is even more famous (For example, the Supreme Court referred to it as recently as 2001 in *United States v. Oakland Cannabis Buyers' Cooperative*, *supra* p. 415.). Dudley, Stephens and Brooks were cast adrift in a lifeboat in the South Atlantic with Parker, a 17–year–old cabin boy. After 20 days of thirst and starvation Dudley, with Stephens' assent, killed Parker for food. Brooks objected to the deed, but ate the flesh and drank the blood along with the others; later, he testified for the prosecution. Four days after the killing the three survivors were rescued, and Dudley and Stephens were charged with murder. The jury returned a special verdict reciting the facts and concluding that all four men would have died of starvation before rescue had they not sacrificed one to save the other three. The question of whether the facts established a charge of murder was left to the judgment of the court. The court held that one is not justified in taking the life of another innocent person to save his own, and found the prisoners guilty of capital murder. The Crown later commuted the sentence to six months imprisonment. The fascinating background of this case is described in Mallin, In Warm Blood: Some Historical and Procedural Aspects of Regina v. Dudley & Stephens, 34 U.Chi.L.Rev. 387 (1967); and A.W.B. Simpson, Cannibalism and the Common Law (1984).

How would *Regina v. Dudley & Stephens* be decided under Model Penal Code § 3.02, supra? The scholars who drafted the Code provided the following analysis:

> For example, in a situation like that in Regina v. Dudley and Stephens, it might be held, in support of that decision, that there is an absolute moral prohibition of directly taking human life for selfish ends, and that the shipwrecked sailors could not, therefore, justify killing the cabin boy for food as a lesser evil than the death of all aboard. To the contrary, it might be held on utilitarian grounds that if fair means had been employed in the selection of the victim, the act would have been justifiable because it was designed to achieve and adapted to achieving a net saving of life. Such a case must be decided if it arises but a legislator may consider that the course of wisdom is to go no further than to state a valid principle for its determination, without anticipating the decision to be made. Cf. Fuller, The Case of the Speluncean Explorers, 62 Harv.L.Rev. 616 (1949).

Model Penal Code Commentary, Tent. Draft No. 8, pp. 9–10 (1958).

3. Ted Patrick was charged in a New York state court with unlawful imprisonment after he assisted the parents of 20–year-old Daniel Voll to seize the young man in order to "save" him from a religious group which he had joined. The defense was partially based on New York Penal Law § 35.05, supra, in that defense counsel argued that the parents and Patrick were justified in seizing Daniel Voll because they reasonably believed that he faced psychological harm through the "indoctrination and domination" of the New Testament Missionary Fellowship. The trial judge permitted the jury to consider this defense, and the jury returned a verdict of not guilty. Daniel Voll apparently returned to the religious group. The trial is reported in The New York Times, August 7, 1973, p. 24, col. 5.

Mr. Patrick was not always successful in defending criminal prosecutions arising out of his efforts to "deprogram" members of religious groups. In People v. Patrick, 541 P.2d 320 (Colo.App.1975), the Colorado Court of Appeals upheld a conviction of false imprisonment and ruled that the trial judge properly refused to instruct the jury on "choice of evils" or justification.

B. SELF-DEFENSE

STATE v. SIMON

Supreme Court of Kansas, 1982.
231 Kan. 572, 646 P.2d 1119.

McFarland, Justice:

This is a direct appeal by the prosecution upon a question reserved pursuant to K.S.A. 22–3602(b)(3).

The issue is whether the statutory justification for the use of deadly force in defense of a person is to be determined by the trier of fact using a subjective standard (from the viewpoint of the accused's state of mind) or by using an objective standard (from the viewpoint of a reasonable man in the accused's position).

Defendant is an elderly homeowner in Wichita. Steffen Wong, a young man of Oriental extraction, rented half of the duplex next door. By virtue of Mr. Wong's racial heritage, defendant assumed he was an expert in the martial arts. Defendant was afraid of Steffen Wong, and heated words had been exchanged between the two. Defendant was fearful because more "Orientals" were moving into the neighborhood, and one had expressed interest in purchasing defendant's home.

On May 27, 1981, Mr. Wong was fired upon as he attempted to enter his own duplex. Shortly thereafter Rickey and Brenda Douglas, the residents of the other half of the duplex, pulled into their driveway and were fired upon by the defendant. Police officers arrived a few minutes later and defendant fired a number of shots at the officers who had previously identified themselves. Defendant was charged with two counts of aggravated assault for firing at Steffen Wong and Rickey Douglas. At trial defendant testified as to his general fear of Mr. Wong and that Mr. Wong had walked toward him cursing just before the incident started. The defense called a clinical psychologist who testified defendant was a "psychological invalid" who was very tense and fearful. The psychologist stated defendant's mental condition permitted him to "misjudge reality" and see himself under attack. The tentative diagnosis was "anxiety neurosis."

The jury was instructed:

> A person is justified in the use of force to defend himself against an aggressor's imminent use of unlawful force to the extent it appears reasonable to him under the circumstances then existing.

Defense counsel argued to the jury that the evidence showed defendant believed Mr. Wong was an imminent threat to him and that the firing of the gun appeared reasonable to the defendant. The jury acquitted defendant on both counts. Under the totality of the circumstances, one must assume the acquittals were occasioned in large measure by the improper instruction on self-defense. * * *

We conclude that the jury should properly have been instructed in the following language or its equivalent: A person is justified in the use of force against an aggressor when and to the extent it appears to him and he reasonably believes that such conduct is necessary to defend himself or another against such aggressor's imminent use of unlawful force. A reasonable belief implies both a belief and the existence of facts that would persuade a reasonable man to that belief.

The appeal is sustained.

STATE v. LEIDHOLM

Supreme Court of North Dakota, 1983.
334 N.W.2d 811.

VANDEWALLE, JUSTICE.

Janice Leidholm was charged with murder for the stabbing death of her husband, Chester Leidholm, in the early morning hours of August 7, 1981, at their farm home near Washburn. She was found guilty by a McLean County jury of manslaughter and was sentenced to five years' imprisonment in the State Penitentiary with three years of the sentence suspended. Leidholm appealed from the judgment of conviction. We reverse and remand the case for a new trial.

I

According to the testimony, the Leidholm marriage relationship in the end was an unhappy one, filled with a mixture of alcohol abuse, moments of kindness toward one another, and moments of violence. The alcohol abuse and violence was exhibited by both parties on the night of Chester's death.

Early in the evening of August 6, 1981, Chester and Janice attended a gun club party in the city of Washburn where they both consumed a large amount of alcohol. On the return trip to the farm, an argument developed between Janice and Chester which continued after their arrival home just after midnight. Once inside the home, the arguing did not stop; Chester was shouting, and Janice was crying.

At one point in the fighting, Janice tried to telephone Dave Vollan, a deputy sheriff of McLean County, but Chester prevented her from using the phone by shoving her away and pushing her down. At another point, the argument moved outside the house, and Chester once again was pushing Janice to the ground. Each time Janice attempted to get up, Chester would push her back again.

A short time later, Janice and Chester re-entered their home and went to bed. When Chester fell asleep, Janice got out of bed, went to the kitchen, and got a butcher knife. She then went back into the bedroom and stabbed Chester. In a matter of minutes Chester died from shock and loss of blood.

II

* * *

The first, and controlling, issue we consider is whether or not the trial court correctly instructed the jury on self-defense. Our resolution of the issue must of necessity begin with an explanation of the basic operation of the law of self-defense as set forth in Chapter 12.1–05 of the North Dakota Century Code.

Our criminal code is the product of * * * massive revision[s] which * * * are in substantial part modeled after the Proposed New Federal Criminal Code, which in turn relies heavily on the American Law Institute Model Penal Code. * * *

Conduct which constitutes self-defense may be either justified [Section 12.1–05–03, N.D.C.C.] or excused [Section 12.1–05–08, N.D.C.C.]. * * *

A defense of justification is the product of society's determination that the *actual existence* of certain circumstances will operate to make proper and legal what otherwise would be criminal conduct. A defense of excuse, contrarily, does not make legal and proper conduct which ordinarily would result in criminal liability; instead, it openly recognizes the criminality of the conduct but excuses it because the actor believed that circumstances actually existed which would justify his conduct when in fact they did not. In short, had the facts been as he supposed them to be, the actor's conduct would have been justified rather than excused.

In the context of self-defense, this means that a person who believes that the force he uses is necessary to prevent imminent unlawful harm is *justified* in using such force if his belief is a *correct* belief; that is to say, if his belief corresponds with what actually is the case. If, on the other hand, a person *reasonably* but incorrectly believes that the force he uses is necessary to protect himself against imminent harm, his use of force is *excused*.

The distinction is arguably superfluous because whether a person's belief is correct and his conduct justified, or whether it is merely reasonable and his conduct excused, the end result is the same, namely, the person avoids punishment for his conduct. Furthermore, because a correct belief corresponds with an actual state of affairs, it will always be a reasonable belief; but a reasonable belief will not always be a correct belief, viz., a person may reasonably believe what is not actually the case. Therefore, the decisive issue under our law of self-defense is not whether a person's beliefs are correct, but rather whether they are reasonable and thereby excused or justified.

Section 12.1–05–08, which sets forth the general conditions that excuse a person's conduct, states:

> "A person's conduct is excused if he believes that the facts are such that his conduct is necessary and appropriate for any of the purposes which would establish a justification or excuse under this chapter, even though his belief is mistaken. * * *"

* * * A person's conduct is excused if he *believes* that the use of force upon another person is necessary and appropriate to defend himself against danger of imminent unlawful harm, even though his belief is mistaken. Thus we have a statement of the first element of self-defense, i.e., a person must actually and sincerely believe that the conditions exist which give rise to a claim of self-defense.

[W]e may infer [from the statute] that, besides being actual and sincere, a person's belief that the use of force is necessary to protect himself against imminent unlawful harm must be reasonable. Here, we have the second element of self-defense, namely, a person must reasonably believe that circumstances exist which permit him to use defensive force.

* * *

[T]he critical issue which a jury must decide in a case involving a claim of self-defense is whether or not the accused's belief that force is necessary to protect himself against imminent unlawful harm was reasonable. However, before the jury can make this determination, it must have a standard of reasonableness against which it can measure the accused's belief.

Courts have traditionally distinguished between standards of reasonableness by characterizing them as either "objective" or "subjective." E.g., *State v. Simon*, 231 Kan. 572, 646 P.2d 1119 (1982). An objective standard of reasonableness requires the factfinder to view the circumstances surrounding the accused at the time he used force from the standpoint of a hypothetical reasonable and prudent person. Ordinarily, under such a view, the unique physical and psychological characteristics of the accused are not taken into consideration in judging the reasonableness of the accused's belief.

This is not the case, however, where a subjective standard of reasonableness is employed. See *State v. Wanrow*, 88 Wash.2d 221, 559 P.2d 548 (1977). Under the subjective standard the issue is not whether the circumstances attending the accused's use of force would be sufficient to create in the mind of a reasonable and prudent person the belief that the use of force is necessary to protect himself against immediate unlawful harm, but rather whether the circumstances are sufficient to induce in *the accused* an honest and reasonable belief that he must use force to defend himself against imminent harm.

Neither Section 12.1–05–03 nor Section 12.1–05–08 explicitly states the viewpoint which the factfinder should assume in assessing the reasonableness of an accused's belief. Moreover, this court has not yet decided the issue of whether Sections 12.1–05–03 and 12.1–05–08 should be construed as requiring an objective or subjective standard to measure the reasonableness of an accused's belief under a claim of self-defense. Finally, the legislative history of our self-defense statutes, as well as the commentaries to the codified criminal statutes which form the basis of the North Dakota Criminal Code, give no indication of a preference for an objective standard of reasonableness over a subjective standard, or vice versa.

We do, however, find guidance for our decision on this issue from past decisions of this court * * *. In 1907, the members of this court, confronted with the same issue whether to adopt an objective or subjective standard of reasonableness, unanimously decided to accept the latter standard for judging the reasonableness of an accused's belief because they believed it to be more just than an objective standard. As late as 1974, this court has confirmed that early decision.

Because (1) the law of self-defense as developed in past decisions of this court has been interpreted to require the use of a subjective standard of reasonableness, and (2) we agree * * * that a subjective standard is the more just, and (3) * * * our current law of self-defense is consistent with either a subjective or objective standard, we now decide that the finder of fact must view the circumstances attending an accused's use of force from the standpoint of the accused to determine if they are sufficient to create in the accused's mind an honest and reasonable belief that the use of force is necessary to protect himself from imminent harm.

The practical and logical consequence of this interpretation is that an accused's actions are to be viewed from the standpoint of a person whose mental and physical characteristics are like the accused's and who sees what the accused sees and knows what the accused knows. For example, if the accused is a timid, diminutive male, the factfinder must consider these characteristics in assessing the reasonableness of his belief. If, on the other hand, the accused is a strong, courageous, and capable female, the factfinder must consider these characteristics in judging the reasonableness of her belief.

In its statement of the law of self-defense, the trial court instructed the jury:

> "The circumstances under which she acted must have been such as to produce in the mind of reasonably prudent persons, regardless of their sex, similarly situated, the reasonable belief that the other person was then about to kill her or do serious bodily harm to her."

In view of our decision today, the court's instruction was a misstatement of the law of self-defense. A correct statement of the law to be applied in a case of self-defense is:

"[A] defendant's conduct is not to be judged by what a reasonably cautious person might or might not do or consider necessary to do under the like circumstances, but what he himself in good faith honestly believed and had reasonable ground to believe was necessary for him to do to protect himself from apprehended death or great bodily injury."

The significance of the difference in viewing circumstances from the standpoint of the "defendant alone" rather than from the standpoint of a "reasonably cautious person" is that the jury's consideration of the unique physical and psychological characteristics of an accused allows the jury to judge the reasonableness of the accused's actions against the accused's subjective impressions of the need to use force rather than against those impressions which a jury determines that a hypothetical reasonably cautious person would have under similar circumstances.

* * *

Leidholm argued strongly at trial that her stabbing of Chester was done in self-defense and in reaction to the severe mistreatment she received from him over the years. Because the court's instruction in question is an improper statement of the law concerning a vital issue in Leidholm's defense, we conclude it amounts to reversible error requiring a new trial.

III

* * *

Expert testimony was presented at trial on what has come to be commonly referred to as the "battered woman syndrome." Such testimony generally explains the "phenomenon" as one in which a regular pattern of spouse abuse creates in the battered spouse low self-esteem and a "learned helplessness," i.e., a sense that she cannot escape from the abusive relationship she has become a part of.

The expert witness in this case testified that Janice Leidholm was the victim in a battering relationship which caused her to suffer battered woman syndrome * * *. On the basis of the expert testimony, Leidholm offered [a] proposed instruction on battered woman syndrome[.]

* * *

There is nothing in the proposed instruction at issue which would add to or significantly alter a correct instruction on the law of self-defense. The jury's use of a subjective standard of reasonableness in applying the principles of self-defense to the facts of a particular case requires it to consider expert testimony, once received in evidence, describing battered woman syndrome and the psychological effects it produces in the battered spouse when deciding the issue of the *existence* and *reasonableness* of the accused's belief that force was necessary to protect herself from imminent harm. If an instruction given is modeled after the law of self-defense which we adopt today, the court need not include a specific instruction on battered woman syndrome in its charge to the jury.

IV

An inseparable and essential part of our law of self-defense limits the use of deadly force to situations in which its use is necessary to protect the actor against death or serious bodily injury. However, the use of deadly force by an actor in self-defense is not justified if a retreat from the assailant can be accomplished with safety to the actor and others. Thus, before it can be said that the use of deadly force is "necessary" to protect the actor against death or serious injury, it must first be the case that the actor cannot retreat from the assailant with safety to himself and others. * * *

The * * * jury must first satisfy itself that an actor could not safely retreat before it can find that the actor's use of deadly force was necessary to protect himself against death or serious injury. And the way in which the jury determines whether or not the actor could not retreat safely is by considering whether or not the actor honestly and reasonably believed that he could not retreat from his attacker with safety.

The duty to retreat, however, is not a rule without exceptions. Section 12.1–05–07(2)(b), N.D.C.C., provides, in part:

> ". . . (2) *no person is required to retreat from his dwelling*, or place of work, *unless he* was the original aggressor or *is assailed by a person who he knows also dwells* or works *there*." [Emphasis added.]

* * *

If the facts and circumstances attending a person's use of deadly force against an assailant who is a cohabitant are sufficient to create in his own mind an honest and reasonable belief that he cannot retreat from the assailant with safety to himself and others, his use of deadly force is justified or excused, and his failure to retreat is of no consequence.

[Conviction reversed]

STATE v. STEWART

Supreme Court of Kansas, 1988.
243 Kan. 639, 763 P.2d 572.

LOCKETT, JUSTICE.

A direct appeal by the prosecution[a] * * * asks whether the statutory justification for the use of deadly force in self-defense excuses a homicide committed by a battered wife where there is no evidence of a deadly threat or imminent danger contemporaneous with the killing.

Peggy Stewart fatally shot her husband, Mike Stewart, while he was sleeping. She was charged with murder in the first degree. Defendant pled not guilty, contending that she shot her husband in self-defense. Expert evidence showed that Peggy Stewart suffered from the battered woman syndrome. Based upon the battered woman syndrome, the trial judge instructed the jury on self-defense. The jury found Peggy Stewart not guilty.

The State stipulates that Stewart "suffered considerable abuse at the hands of her husband," but contends that the trial court erred in giving a self-defense instruction since Peggy Stewart was in no imminent danger when she shot her sleeping husband. We agree that under the facts of this case the giving of the self-defense instruction was erroneous. We further hold that the trial judge's self-defense instruction improperly allowed the jury to determine the reasonableness of defendant's belief that she was in imminent danger from her individual subjective view-

a. Kansas law allows the prosecution to appeal on some legal issues following a verdict of not guilty. The purpose of the appeal is only to provide a clarification of the law, because the constitutional prohibition of double jeopardy prevents the retrial of the acquitted person.

point rather than the viewpoint of a reasonable person in her circumstances.

Following an annulment from her first husband and two subsequent divorces in which she was the petitioner, Peggy Stewart married Mike Stewart in 1974. Evidence at trial disclosed a long history of abuse by Mike against Peggy and her two daughters from one of her prior marriages. Laura, one of Peggy's daughters, testified that early in the marriage Mike hit and kicked Peggy, and that after the first year of the marriage Peggy exhibited signs of severe psychological problems. Subsequently, Peggy was hospitalized and diagnosed as having symptoms of paranoid schizophrenia; she responded to treatment and was soon released. It appeared to Laura, however, that Mike was encouraging Peggy to take more than her prescribed dosage of medication.

In 1977, two social workers informed Peggy that they had received reports that Mike was taking indecent liberties with her daughters. Because the social workers did not want Mike to be left alone with the girls, Peggy quit her job. In 1978, Mike began to taunt Peggy by stating that Carla, her 12–year–old daughter, was "more of a wife" to him than Peggy.

Later, Carla was placed in a detention center, and Mike forbade Peggy and Laura to visit her. When Mike finally allowed Carla to return home in the middle of summer, he forced her to sleep in an un-air conditioned room with the windows nailed shut, to wear a heavy flannel nightgown, and to cover herself with heavy blankets. Mike would then wake Carla at 5:30 a.m. and force her to do all the housework. Peggy and Laura were not allowed to help Carla or speak to her.

When Peggy confronted Mike and demanded that the situation cease, Mike responded by holding a shotgun to Peggy's head and threatening to kill her. Mike once kicked Peggy so violently in the chest and ribs that she required hospitalization. Finally, when Mike ordered Peggy to kill and bury Carla, she filed for divorce. Peggy's attorney in the divorce action testified in the murder trial that Peggy was afraid for both her and her children's lives. One night, in a fit of anger, Mike threw Carla out of the house. Carla, who was not yet in her teens, was forced out of the home with no money, no coat, and no place to go. When the family heard that Carla was in Colorado, Mike refused to allow Peggy to contact or even talk about Carla. Mike's intimidation of Peggy continued to escalate. One morning, Laura found her mother hiding on the school bus, terrified and begging the driver to take her to a neighbor's home. That Christmas, Mike threw the turkey dinner to the floor, chased Peggy outside, grabbed her by the hair, rubbed her face in the dirt, and then kicked and beat her.

After Laura moved away, Peggy's life became even more isolated. Once, when Peggy was working at a cafe, Mike came in and ran all the customers off with a gun because he wanted Peggy to go home and have sex with him right that minute. He abused both drugs and alcohol, and amused himself by terrifying Peggy, once waking her from a sound sleep by beating her with a baseball bat. He shot one of Peggy's pet cats, and then held the gun against her head and threatened to pull the trigger. Peggy told friends that Mike would hold a shotgun to her head and threaten to blow it off, and indicated that one day he would probably do it.

In May 1986, Peggy left Mike and ran away to Laura's home in Oklahoma. It was the first time Peggy had left Mike without telling him. Because Peggy was suicidal, Laura had her admitted to a hospital. There, she was diagnosed as having toxic psychosis as a result of an overdose of her medication. On May 30, 1986, Mike called to say he was coming to get her. Peggy agreed to return to Kansas. Peggy told a nurse she felt like she wanted to shoot her husband. At trial, she testified that she decided to return with Mike because she was not able to get the medical help she needed in Oklahoma.

When Mike arrived at the hospital, he told the staff that he "needed his housekeeper." The hospital released Peggy to Mike's care, and he immediately drove her back to Kansas. Mike told Peggy that all her problems were in her head and he would be the one to tell her what was good for her, not the doctors. Peggy testified that Mike threatened to kill her if she ever ran away again. As soon as they arrived at the house, Mike forced Peggy into the house and forced her to have oral sex several times.

The next morning, Peggy discovered a loaded .357 magnum. She testified she was afraid of the gun. She hid the gun under the mattress of the bed in a spare room. Later that morning, as she cleaned house, Mike kept making remarks that she should not bother because she would not be there long, or that she should not bother with her things because she could not take them with her. She testified she was afraid Mike was going to kill her.

Mike's parents visited Mike and Peggy that afternoon. Mike's father testified that Peggy and Mike were affectionate with each other during the visit. Later, after Mike's parents had left, Mike forced Peggy to perform oral sex. After watching television, Mike and Peggy went to bed at 8:00 p.m. As Mike slept, Peggy thought about suicide and heard voices in her head repeating over and over, "kill or be killed." At this time, there were two vehicles in the driveway and Peggy had access to the car keys. About 10:00 p.m., Peggy went to the spare bedroom and removed the gun from under the mattress, walked back to the bedroom, and killed her husband while he slept. She then ran to the home of a neighbor, who called the police.

When the police questioned Peggy regarding the events leading up to the shooting, Peggy stated that things had not gone quite right that day, and that when she got the chance she hid the gun under the mattress. She stated that she shot Mike to "get this over with, this misery and this torment." When asked why she got the gun out, Peggy stated to the police: "I'm not sure exactly what * * * led up to it * * * and my head started playing games with me and I got to thinking about things and I said I didn't want to be by myself again. * * * I got the gun out because there had been remarks made about me being out there alone. It was as if Mike was going to do something again like had been done before. He had gotten me down here from McPherson one time and he went and told them that I had done something and he had me put out of the house and was taking everything I had. And it was like he was going to pull the same thing over again." Two expert witnesses testified during the trial. The expert for the defense, psychologist Marilyn Hutchinson, diagnosed Peggy as suffering from "battered woman syndrome," or post-traumatic stress syndrome. Dr. Hutchinson testified that Mike was preparing to escalate the violence in retaliation for Peggy's running away. She testified that loaded guns, veiled threats, and increased sexual demands are indicators of the escalation of the cycle. Dr. Hutchinson believed Peggy had a repressed knowledge that she was in a "really grave lethal situation."

The State's expert, psychiatrist Herbert Modlin, neither subscribed to a belief in the battered woman syndrome nor to a theory of learned helplessness as an explanation for why women do not leave an abusive relationship. Dr. Modlin testified that abuse such as repeated forced oral sex would not be trauma sufficient to trigger a post-traumatic stress disorder. He also believed Peggy was erroneously diagnosed as suffering from toxic psychosis. He stated that Peggy was unable to escape the abuse because she suffered from schizophrenia, rather than the battered woman syndrome.

At defense counsel's request, the trial judge gave an instruction on self-defense to the jury. The jury found Peggy not guilty. * * *

The State claims that under the facts the instruction should not have been given because there was no lethal threat to defendant contemporaneous with the killing. The State points out that Peggy's annulment and divorces from former husbands, and her filing for divorce after leaving Mike, proved that Peggy knew there were non-lethal methods by which she could extricate herself from the abusive relationship.

Under the common law, the excuse for killing in self-defense is founded upon necessity, be it real or apparent. Early Kansas cases held that killing in self-defense was justifiable when the defendant had reasonable grounds to believe that an aggressor (1) had a design to take the defendant's life, (2) attempted to execute the design or was in an apparent situation to do so, and (3) induced in the defendant a reasonable belief that he intended to do so immediately. In State v. Rose, 30 Kan. 501, 1 Pac. 817 (1883), we approved an instruction on self-defense which stated in part: "Before a person can take the life of another, it must reasonably appear that his own life must have been in imminent danger, or that he was in imminent danger of some great bodily injury from the hands of the person killed. No one can attack and kill another because he may fear injury at some future time." The perceived imminent danger had to occur in the present time, specifically during the time in which the defendant and the deceased were engaged in their final conflict. These common-law principles were codified in K.S.A. 21–3211, which provides: "A person is justified in the use of force against an aggressor when and to the extent it appears to him and he reasonably believes that such conduct is necessary to defend himself or another against such aggressor's imminent use of unlawful force."

The traditional concept of self-defense has posited one-time conflicts between persons of somewhat equal size and strength. When the defendant claiming self-defense is a victim of long-term domestic violence, such as a battered spouse, such traditional concepts may not apply. Because of the prior history of abuse, and the difference in strength and size between the abused and the abuser, the accused in such cases may choose to defend during a momentary lull in the abuse, rather than during a conflict. However, in order to warrant the giving of a self-defense instruction, the facts of the case must still show that the spouse was in imminent danger close to the time of the killing.

A person is justified in using force against an aggressor when it appears to that person and he or she reasonably believes such force to be necessary. A reasonable belief implies both an honest belief and the existence of facts which would persuade a reasonable person to that belief. A self-defense instruction must be given if there is any evidence to support a claim of self-defense, even if that evidence consists solely of the defendant's testimony.

Where self-defense is asserted, evidence of the deceased's long-term cruelty and violence towards the defendant is admissible. In cases involving battered spouses, expert evidence of the battered woman syndrome is relevant to a determination of the reasonableness of the defendant's perception of danger. Other courts which have allowed such evidence to be introduced include those in Florida, Georgia, Illinois, Maine, New Jersey, New York, Pennsylvania, Washington, and Wisconsin. However, no jurisdictions have held that the existence of the battered woman syndrome in and of itself operates as a defense to murder.

In order to instruct a jury on self-defense, there must be some showing of an imminent threat or a confrontational circumstance involving an overt act by an aggressor. There is no exception to this requirement where the defendant has suffered long-term domestic abuse and the victim is the abuser. In such cases, the issue is not whether the defendant believes homicide is the solution to past or future problems with the batterer, but rather whether circumstances surrounding the killing were sufficient to create a reasonable belief in the defendant that the use of deadly force was necessary. * * *

In three recent Kansas cases where battered women shot their husbands, the women were clearly threatened in the moments prior to the shootings. * * * Here, however, there is an absence of imminent danger to defendant: Peggy told a nurse at the Oklahoma hospital of her desire to kill Mike. She later voluntarily agreed to return home with Mike when he telephoned her. She stated that after leaving the hospital

Mike threatened to kill her if she left him again. Peggy showed no inclination to leave. In fact, immediately after the shooting, Peggy told the police that she was upset because she thought Mike would leave her. Prior to the shooting, Peggy hid the loaded gun. The cars were in the driveway and Peggy had access to the car keys. After being abused, Peggy went to bed with Mike at 8 p.m. Peggy lay there for two hours, then retrieved the gun from where she had hidden it and shot Mike while he slept. Under these facts, the giving of the self-defense instruction was erroneous. Under such circumstances, a battered woman cannot reasonably fear imminent life-threatening danger from her sleeping spouse.

We note that other courts have held that the sole fact that the victim was asleep does not preclude a self-defense instruction. In State v. Norman, 89 N.C.App. 384, 366 S.E.2d 586 (1988), cited by defendant, the defendant's evidence disclosed a long history of abuse. Each time defendant attempted to escape, her husband found and beat her. On the day of the shooting, the husband beat defendant continually throughout the day, and threatened either to cut her throat, kill her, or cut off her breast. In the afternoon, defendant shot her husband while he napped. The North Carolina Court of Appeals held it was reversible error to fail to instruct on self-defense. The court found that, although decedent was napping at the time defendant shot him, defendant's unlawful act was closely related in time to an assault and threat of death by decedent against defendant and that the decedent's nap was "but a momentary hiatus in a continuous reign of terror."

There is no doubt that the North Carolina court determined that the sleeping husband was an evil man who deserved the justice he received from his battered wife. Here, similar comparable and compelling facts exist. But, as one court has stated: "To permit capital punishment to be imposed upon the subjective conclusion of the [abused] individual that prior acts and conduct of the deceased justified the killing would amount to a leap into the abyss of anarchy." Jahnke v. State, 682 P.2d 991, 997 (Wyo.1984). Finally, our legislature has not provided for capital punishment for even the most heinous crimes. We must, therefore, hold that when a battered woman kills her sleeping spouse when there is no imminent danger, the killing is not reasonably necessary and a self-defense instruction may not be given. To hold otherwise in this case would in effect allow the execution of the abuser for past or future acts and conduct.

One additional issue must be addressed. In its amicus curiae brief, the Kansas County and District Attorney Association contends the instruction given by the trial court improperly modified the law of self-defense to be more generous to one suffering from the battered woman syndrome than to any other defendant relying on self-defense. We agree and believe it is necessary to clarify certain portions of our opinion in State v. Hodges, 239 Kan. 63, 716 P.2d 563.

Here, the trial judge gave the instruction approved in State v. Simon, 231 Kan. 572, 575, 646 P.2d 1119 (1982), stating:

> "A person is justified in the use of force against an aggressor when and to the extent it appears to him and he reasonably believes that such conduct is necessary to defend himself or another against such aggressor's imminent use of unlawful force. Such justification requires both a belief on the part of the defendant and the existence of facts that would persuade a reasonable person to that belief."

The trial judge then added the following: "You must determine, from the viewpoint of the defendant's mental state, whether the defendant's belief in the need to defend herself was reasonable in light of her subjective impressions and the facts and circumstances known to her."

This addition was apparently encouraged by the following language in State v. Hodges, 239 Kan. 63, 716 P.2d 563: "Where the battered woman syndrome is an issue in the case, the standard for reasonableness concerning an accused's belief in asserting self-defense is not an objective, but a subjective standard. The jury must determine, from the viewpoint of defendant's mental state, whether defendant's belief in the need to defend herself was reasonable."

The statement that the reasonableness of defendant's belief in asserting self-defense should be measured from the defendant's own individual subjective viewpoint conflicts with prior law. Our test for self-defense is a two-pronged one. We first use a subjective standard to determine whether the defendant sincerely and honestly believed it necessary to kill in order to defend. We then use an objective standard to determine whether defendant's belief was reasonable—specifically, whether a reasonable person in defendant's circumstances would have perceived self-defense as necessary. In State v. Hundley, 236 Kan. at 467, 693 P.2d 475, we stated that, in cases involving battered spouses, "the objective test is how a reasonably prudent battered wife would perceive the aggressor's demeanor."

Hundley makes clear that it was error for the trial court to instruct the jury to employ solely a subjective test in determining the reasonableness of defendant's actions. Insofar as the above-quoted language in State v. Hodges can be read to sanction a subjective test, this language is disapproved.

The appeal is sustained.

HERD, JUSTICE, dissenting:

The sole issue before us on the question reserved is whether the trial court erred in giving a jury instruction on self-defense. We have a well-established rule that a defendant is entitled to a self-defense instruction if there is any evidence to support it, even though the evidence consists solely of the defendant's testimony. It is for the jury to determine the sincerity of the defendant's belief she needed to act in self-defense, and the reasonableness of that belief in light of all the circumstances.

It is not within the scope of appellate review to weigh the evidence. An appellate court's function is to merely examine the record and determine if there is any evidence to support the theory of self-defense. If the record discloses any competent evidence upon which self-defense could be based, then the instruction must be given. In judging the evidence for this purpose, all inferences should be resolved in favor of the defendant. State v. Hill, 242 Kan. at 79, 744 P.2d 1228.

To illustrate our adherence to these rules, a discussion of cases in which self-defense was claimed is in order. In *Hill*, we held the trial court erred in refusing to instruct on self-defense although the only evidence supporting defendant's theory was testimony that the deceased, a stranger to the defendant, pushed and hit the defendant in a crowded entrance hall and then raised her hand with an unknown object in it.

In State v. Simon, 231 Kan. 572, 646 P.2d 1119 (1982), the defendant assumed the victim, who was of Oriental extraction, was proficient in the martial arts. The two had previously had a verbal argument, and the defendant testified he was afraid of the victim. He testified the victim had walked toward him, cursing, on the day of the shooting, but the defendant did not shoot him then. Instead, he waited until the victim innocently tried to enter his own duplex. We disapproved the [trial court's jury instruction] as not containing an objective standard of whether the facts were such as would persuade a reasonable person self-defense was necessary. We did not, however, conclude that no self-defense instruction should have been given; instead, we formulated a self-defense instruction which properly instructed on the law.

In State v. Kelly, 131 Kan. 357, 291 Pac. 945 (1930), the defendant sought out his wife's unarmed lover, shot him, and told his neighbor he did it "because of family trouble." At trial, however, the defendant said the victim gave him "a mean look" and withdrew his hand from his pocket; defendant then shot him from over 15 feet away. We noted that, because "self-defense was woven into" the defendant's testimony and a self-defense instruction was requested, the trial court was required to give it. * * *

It is evident from prior case law appellee met her burden of showing some competent evidence that she acted in self-defense, thus making her defense a jury question. She testified she acted in fear for her life, and Dr. Hutchinson corroborated this testimony. * * *

The majority implies its decision is necessary to keep the battered woman syndrome from operating as a defense in and of itself. It has always been clear the syndrome is not a defense itself. Evidence of the syndrome is admissible only because of its relevance to the issue of self-defense. The majority of jurisdictions have held it beyond the ordinary jury's understanding why a battered woman may feel she cannot escape, and have held evidence of the battered woman syndrome proper to explain it. The expert testimony explains how people react to circumstances in which the average juror has not been involved. It assists the jury in evaluating the sincerity of the defendant's belief she was in imminent danger requiring self-defense and whether she was in fact in imminent danger. * * *

The majority bases its opinion on its conclusion appellee was not in imminent danger, usurping the right of the jury to make that determination of fact. The majority believes a person could not be in imminent danger from an aggressor merely because the aggressor dropped off to sleep. This is a fallacious conclusion. For instance, picture a hostage situation where the armed guard inadvertently drops off to sleep and the hostage grabs his gun and shoots him. The majority opinion would preclude the use of self-defense in such a case. * * *

I would deny this appeal.

Note

In State v. Nemeth, 82 Ohio St.3d 202, 694 N.E.2d 1332 (Ohio 1998), 16–year-old Brian Nemeth was convicted of murder after he shot his mother several times in the head and neck with his compound bow and arrows. She had abused him frequently in the past, and had been threatening violence against him for hours, but was lying on a couch at the time of the killing. The trial judge refused to give instructions on either voluntary manslaughter or self-defense, or to admit expert testimony on "battered child syndrome." The Ohio Supreme Court reversed, holding that the expert testimony should have been admitted in support of both the manslaughter (provocation) and self-defense theories. Nemeth subsequently pled guilty to voluntary manslaughter

STATE v. GARTLAND

Supreme Court of New Jersey, 1997.
149 N.J. 456, 694 A.2d 564.

PER CURIAM

Ellen Gartland was convicted of reckless manslaughter for killing her husband in a bedroom of their home. In this criminal appeal, the Court addresses several issues: (1) whether the death of Ellen Gartland following the filing of her petition for certification renders her appeal moot; (2) whether the trial court erred in instructing the jury that Ellen Gartland had a duty to retreat from her separate bedroom before using deadly force; and (3) whether the trial court should have specifically instructed the jury that it could consider the history of spousal abuse to determine the reasonableness of Ellen Gartland's belief that deadly force was necessary to protect herself against death or serious bodily injury.

Ellen Gartland had been the victim of long-standing physical and emotional abuse by her husband, John Gartland, the victim. On February 8, 1993, the two became involved in an argument in their home, during the course of which neighbors heard John threaten Ellen. At some point during the argument, Ellen left the room and went upstairs to her bedroom. The two had occupied separate bedrooms for over ten years. On previous occasions, John had left Ellen alone in this room. On this occasion, however, he followed her into the bedroom. Although Ellen told John to leave her alone, he approached her, threatening to strike her. Ellen took her son's hunting shotgun from her bedroom closet and pointed it at John, telling him to stop. John then threatened to kill her and lunged at her with his fists clenched. Ellen pulled the trigger and John stepped into the hallway and fell. He ultimately died from the gunshot.

Immediately following the shooting, Ellen telephoned the operator, and asked for an ambulance, advising that she had just shot her husband. She also told the responding officers that, when she shot her husband, she had feared for her life.

At trial, the jury had twice asked for clarification of the court's charge on self-defense. On both occasions, the trial court repeated its initial instructions using the Model Jury Charge, which never specifically apprised the jury that it could consider the seventeen years of spousal abuse suffered by Ellen in determining whether she honestly and reasonably believed that deadly force was necessary to protect herself against her husband.

Prior to the charge, defense counsel objected to the court's intent to charge that Ellen had a duty to retreat before resorting to deadly force, arguing that, because Ellen had been in her own room, which her husband had never before occupied, he was not a cohabitant and under the law Ellen had no duty to retreat from her own separate dwelling. The trial court again used the Model Jury Charge in its instruction.

The jury convicted Ellen Gartland of reckless manslaughter and she was sentenced to a five-year term with a mandatory three-years imprisonment under the Graves Act. She was freed on bail pending appeal. [Ellen Garland died after the conviction. The Court held that the appeal was not moot, because the issue of a wife's duty to retreat when attacked in the marital home by the husband is a matter of significant public importance and the issue is likely to recur.] * * *

III

Did the trial court err in failing to instruct the jury that defendant had no duty to retreat if defendant's bedroom functioned as a separate dwelling and that her husband was an intruder into that separate room within the house that they shared? As noted, this was the principal objection raised at trial:

Traditionally self-defense claims require that a person who can safely retreat from the confrontation avail themselves of that means of escape. However, this requirement has since been modified, and today most courts recognize exceptions to the general retreat principle. The most notable and expansive exception has been the "castle doctrine." The castle doctrine states that if the confrontation takes place in one's home or "castle" then the requirement is suspended. This exception was established to allow individuals to defend their place of habitation. Application of this exception, however, becomes more challenging when the aggressor intruder is a co-occupant of the structure or when both parties have a legal right to occupy the dwelling. Currently, jurisdictions vary as to their willingness to extend the castle doctrine to self-defense situations where both parties legally occupy the home, but the majority of these jurisdictions extend the privilege of non-retreat to apply in these types of situations. [Beth Bjerregaard & Anita N. Blowers, Chartering a New Frontier for Self–Defense Claims: The Applicability of the Battered Person Syndrome as a Defense for Parricide Offenders, 33 U. Louisville J. Fam. L. 843, 870–71 (1995).]

New Jersey is among the minority of jurisdictions that impose a duty of retreat on a woman attacked by her cohabitant spouse. The New Jersey Code of Criminal Justice contains carefully articulated standards for determining when the use of force against another is justified. The drafters of our Code originally approached the concept of justification in terms of the subjective attitudes of the criminal actor. However, in the course of legislative modifications the self-defense provisions of the Code were altered to reestablish objective standards of self-defense:

> **Use of force justifiable for protection of the person.** Subject to the provisions of this section and of section 2C:3–9, the use of force upon or toward another person is justifiable when the actor reasonably believes that such force is immediately necessary for the purpose of protecting [the actor] against the use of unlawful force by such other person on the present occasion. [*N.J.S.A. 2C:3–4*a.]

Those general provisions are qualified in the case of the use of deadly force as that is defined in *N.J.S.A. 2C:3–11*. Concerning deadly force, the Code provides: "The use of deadly force is not justifiable under this section unless the actor reasonably believes that such force is necessary to protect [the actor] against death or serious bodily harm...." *N.J.S.A. 2C:3–4*b(2). Even if deadly force is permissible, the actor still has the duty to retreat from the scene if the actor can do so safely. *N.J.S.A. 2C:3–4*b(2)(b). One exception to this duty to retreat is if the actor is in his or her own home at the time of the attack (the so-called "castle doctrine"), unless the attacker is a cohabitant. *N.J.S.A. 2C:3–4*b(2)(b)(i) states that "the actor is not obliged to retreat from [the] dwelling, unless [the actor] was the initial aggressor or is assailed in [the actor's own] dwelling by another person whose dwelling the actor knows it to be...." *N.J.S.A. 2C:3–4*c provides special rules for the use of deadly force on an intruder into one's dwelling. For example, under this provision, deadly force may be used against an intruder to counter any level of unlawful force threatened by the intruder.

The Public Defender argues that it is ironic that Ellen Gartland could have used the shotgun against a burglar who intended to do her no serious harm but was precluded from using the same force against the true threat in her life, her husband. Instead, the law requires her to flee from her bedroom, which she had described as the only sanctuary in her chaos-filled home. * * *

That leaves for resolution whether John Gartland could be considered a cohabitant of Ellen's bedroom. Put the other way, the question is whether the upstairs bedroom in which Ellen slept was a separate dwelling. It is a close question on this record but we agree with the courts below that the bedroom was not a separate dwelling. * * *

It is true that one building may have separate apartments. However, the idea of a dwelling is that one has an exclusive right to occupy a portion of a building. In *State v. Pontery, 19 N.J. 457, 117 A.2d 473 (1955),* an estranged couple jointly owned a summer home. The wife went there to be away from her husband. When he and other family members joined her over the weekend, she could not claim that she was under no duty to retreat from the jointly-owned dwelling before inflicting deadly force. In contrast, in *State v. Lamb, 71 N.J. 545, 366 A.2d 981 (1976),* the Court exempted a wife from a duty to retreat from her husband's attack within an apartment that she exclusively occupied. He had burst in uninvited through an unlocked door. The Court stated: "In the circumstances of this case [the] defendant's estranged husband did not have as much right to be in the apartment as [the] defendant. It was her home. [The husband] was in fact an intruder and [the] defendant was under no duty to retreat." *71 N.J. at 549.* See also H.J. Alperin, Annotation, Homicide: Duty to Retreat Where Assailant and Assailed Share the Same Living Quarters, *26 A.L.R.3d 1296 (1969)* (discussing homicide prosecution cases involving duty to retreat before using deadly force where persons are attacked in homes shared with assailant). In this case, there is simply no evidence that the door to the bedroom had normally been kept locked or that John Gartland did not generally have access to the room. Defendant merely testified that because of sexual dysfunction, the couple slept in separate rooms. We cannot say that Ellen had the exclusive right to occupy this room. Hence, we agree, on this record, that the court correctly charged the statutory duty to retreat.

IV

Did the trial court err in failing specifically to instruct the jury that the evidence that defendant was abused by the decedent could be considered in assessing her claim of self-defense?

In *State v. Kelly,* 97 N.J. 178, 478 A.2d 364 (1984), this Court held that evidence of domestic abuse is relevant to a claim of self-defense. Specifically, the Court held that expert testimony concerning the battered women syndrome is relevant to the jury's determination of subjective honesty and the objective reasonableness of a defendant's belief that deadly force was necessary to protect herself against death or serious bodily harm. The Court recognized that evidence of prior abuse has the potential to confuse the jury and that expert testimony is useful to clarify and refute common myths and misconceptions about battered women. The history of prior abuse was plainly relevant to the self-defense charges. In order to acquit anyone of homicide committed in self-defense, the jury must find the defendant's belief in the need to use deadly force reasonable and honest. Like the elements of passion-provocation manslaughter, the elements of self-defense contain subjective and objective factors that focus, respectively, on the sincerity and reasonableness of the defendant's beliefs. Thus, defendant argues that because evidence of prior abuse is relevant to the issue of self-defense and because evidence of prior abuse is potentially confusing, it follows that the jury must be properly instructed concerning how to consider and give effect to such evidence in assessing a claim of self-defense. The trial court specifically instructed the jury to consider the evidence of prior abuse in determining the question of provocation. However, it did not specifically instruct the jury to consider evidence of prior abuse in determining the question of self-defense.

We agree that a better charge would have instructed the jury to consider the history of prior abuse in assessing the honesty and reasonableness of defendant's belief in the need to use deadly force. Our courts have always admitted evidence of a victim's violent character as relevant to a claim of self-defense so long as the defendant had knowledge of the dangerous and violent character of the victim. *State v. Carter, 278 N.J. Super. 629, 651 A.2d 1088 (Law Div.1994)* (citations omitted).

The issue arises in this case as one of plain error and the question is whether the absence of the specific instruction was such that it was clearly capable of producing an unjust result. R. 2:2–9. We have often emphasized that instructions to a jury are to be examined as a whole. * * * Taken as a whole, the instruction could not be understood to foreclose the jury's full and appropriate consideration of the prior abuse in assessing the honesty and reasonableness of defendant's belief.

The possibility that the jury might not have considered the prior abuse in assessing the self-defense claim appears highly attenuated in this case. A major focus of the opening and closing remarks of defense counsel was that the jury could and should consider the long-standing abuse of defendant by her husband in assessing her claim of self-defense. * * *

The court's instructions did not foreclose the jury's consideration of that prior abuse; nor were its instructions so erroneous as to confuse or mislead the jury in its consideration of self-defense. The instructions gave the members of the jury an opportunity to consider fully whether an honest and reasonable belief in the necessity to use deadly force was present. The trial court explicitly told the jurors to consider passion-provocation in the context of knowing or purposeful murder. It also told the jurors that they could not find the defendant guilty of murder or any of the lesser-included offenses if they had a reasonable doubt as to whether or not the defendant had killed her victim in the honest and reasonable belief that the use of deadly force was necessary on the occasion.

V

We now turn to consider other aspects of this case that have been neither raised nor argued by the parties, that would have been grounds for retrial in the case of a living defendant.

In a long series of cases, we have held that an essential ingredient to a fair trial is that adequate and understandable instructions be given to the jury. * * * Model jury charges are often helpful to trial courts performing this important [charging] function. However, it is not always enough simply to read the applicable provision of the Criminal Code, define the terminology, and set forth the elements of the crime. An instruction that is appropriate in one case may not be sufficient for another case. Ordinarily, the better practice is to mold the instruction in a manner that explains the law to the jury in the context of the material facts of the case.

The instructions in this case were largely devoid of reference to the specific circumstances of the case. As noted, the trial court instructed the jury that if Mrs. Gartland "knew that she could avoid the necessity of using deadly force by retreating from that house, providing ... [that] she could do so with complete safety, then the defense is not available to her." We intend no criticism of the trial court because neither party requested a charge tailored to the facts. However, an abstract charge on the duty to retreat could only have been confusing in the circumstances of this case. Exactly where could she retreat? As we understand the record, there was no other way out of the bedroom other than the doorway where her assailant stood. The charge should have asked whether, armed with a weapon, she could have safely made her way out of the bedroom door without threat of serious bodily injury to herself. * * * One of the problems in applying the retreat doctrine to the case of a battered woman is that the jurors may confuse the question of leaving the abusive partner with the duty to retreat on the occasion. Among the many myths concerning battered women is the belief "that they are masochistic and actually enjoy their beatings, that they purposely provoke their husbands into violent behavior, and, most critically ... that women who remain in battering relationships are free to leave their abusers at any time." Kelly, supra, 97 N.J. at 192.

The charge on self-defense should also have been tailored to the circumstances of the case. In *State v. Wanrow, 88 Wash. 2d 221, 559 P.2d 548 (1977)*, the Washington Supreme Court recognized that its traditional self-defense standard failed to account for the perspective of abused women. Any limitation of the jury's consideration of the surrounding acts and circumstances to those occurring at or immediately before the killing would be an erroneous statement of the applicable law. *559 P.2d at 556*. The Washington court held that a battered woman was entitled to have the jury consider her actions in the light of her own perceptions of the situation, including those perceptions that were the product of our nation's unfortunate history of sex discrimination. Id. at 559. At a minimum, the jury in Ellen Gartland's case should have been asked to consider whether, if it found such to be the case, a reasonable woman who had been the victim of years of domestic violence would have reasonably perceived on this occasion that the use of deadly force was necessary to protect herself from serious bodily injury.

In another context, the failure to relate to the facts of the case the duty to retreat and right of self-defense might not have cut so mortally into a defendant's ability to maintain a defense on the merits. However, the persistent stereotyping of the victims of domestic violence requires special concern. Both partners to the domestic tragedy are now deceased. Although we cannot fully right past wrongs, we can correct errors in the charge that were clearly capable of producing an unjust result.

The conviction of manslaughter is set aside. [All concur.]

STATE v. BOWENS

Supreme Court of New Jersey, 1987.
108 N.J. 622, 532 A.2d 215.

O'HERN, J.

In these two companion appeals both defendants contend that they were incorrectly denied jury charges on imperfect self-defense. We hold that the Code of Criminal Justice does not provide an independent category of justification, excuse, or mitigation under the concept of imperfect self-defense. We find, however, that evidence that will sustain the defense at common law is frequently relevant to the presence or absence of the essential elements of Code offenses. * * *

The doctrine of imperfect self-defense has its roots in common-law attempts to grade the degrees of murder and thus to separate capital murder from all others. * * * The characteristic effect of the doctrine is to negate the presence of malice that is predicate to a finding of first-degree or capital murder. [Citations] This effect of the defense—negation of "malice"—is not immediately relevant to a Code state that defines murder in "the minimal senses" of acting knowingly or purposely. We shall consider its relevance to our Code definition of murder.

Generally, "in order for a killer to have a perfect self-defense to homicide, he or she must: (1) be free from fault in bringing on the conflict with his or her adversary; and (2) reasonably, though not necessarily correctly, believe (a) that his adversary will, unless forcibly prevented, immediately inflict upon him or her a fatal or serious bodily injury, and (b) that the deadly force must be used upon the adversary to prevent him or her from inflicting such an injury." W. LaFave and A. Scott, Jr., Handbook on Criminal Law 583 (1972). "If one who is not the aggressor kills his adversary with these two actual and reasonable beliefs in his mind, his homicide is justified, and he is guilty of no crime—not murder, not manslaughter, but no crime." Ibid. (footnote omitted). An aggressor faced even with the reasonable belief in the necessity to kill "cannot have the defense of self-defense, for that requires both freedom from fault in the inception of the difficulty and the entertainment of beliefs which are reasonable." Ibid.

In the context of this opinion we do not deal with the first aspect of a perfect self-defense, namely, the actor's freedom from fault in the inception of the conflict; this aspect is set forth in the Code, N.J.S.A.

2C:34(b)(2)(a). Instead, we focus on the second factor of self-defense: whether the actor's beliefs are reasonable. In this context, imperfect self-defense would mean no more than an honest subjective belief on the part of the killer that his or her actions were necessary for his or her safety, even though an objective appraisal by reasonable people would have revealed not only that the actions were unnecessary, but also that the belief was unreasonable. [Some jurisdictions recognize a doctrine of imperfect self-defense to mitigate a homicide from murder to manslaughter, whereas others reject the doctrine.]

The drafters of our Code originally approached the broader concept of justification in terms of the subjective attitudes of the criminal actor. Thus, as introduced, the [New Jersey adaptation of the Model Penal Code] provided for self-defense as follows: "Subject to the provisions of this Section and of Section 2C:3–9, the use of force upon or toward another person is justifiable when the actor believes that such force is immediately necessary for the purpose of protecting himself against the use of unlawful force by such other person on the present occasion." However, in the course of legislative modifications the County Prosecutors Association and the Attorney General objected to the subjective standard of self-defense adopted in the Senate Judiciary Committee. As a result, the self-defense provisions were altered to re-establish the objective standard of self-defense: "Subject to the provisions of this section and of section 2C:3–9, the use of force upon or toward another person is justifiable when the actor *reasonably* believes that such force is immediately necessary for the purpose of protecting himself against the use of unlawful force by such other person on the present occasion." [N.J.S.A. 2C:3–4(a) (added by Senate Committee amendments) (emphasis supplied).]

At the time the self-defense provisions were modified, no change was made in N.J.S.A. 2C:3–9(b). That section provided that any actor who recklessly or negligently arrived at the belief necessary to the justifications afforded by sections 2C:3–3 to 3–8 could be found guilty of any offense "for which recklessness or negligence * * * suffices to establish culpability." Thus, at the time of the decision in State v. Powell, 419 A.2d 406 (N.J.1980), when our Court held that imperfect self-defense was available under pre-Code law to reduce second-degree murder to manslaughter, the Code was in flux. * * *

Following the decision in *Powell,* however, the Legislature deleted subsection (b) of N.J.S.A. 2C:3–9. The legislative statement annexed to the repealer stated: "As originally drafted, justification defenses (i.e. self-defense) under the code were available to a defendant if his belief in the necessity of the use of force was honestly held. In conjunction with this provision, the code also provided in 2C:3–9b that if the defendant was reckless or negligent in forming that belief, he could be convicted of a crime for which recklessness or negligence was the required mental element. As enacted, however, the code requires not only that a defendant's belief be honestly held but also that his belief in the necessity to use force be reasonable. This requirement that a defendant's belief be both honest and reasonable vis a vis a justification defense obviates the necessity for the provision in 2C:3–9b that the reckless or negligent use of force can establish criminal liability. Therefore, the amendment in section 7 would delete this provision."

The question of the continued existence of imperfect self-defense under the Code appears to have been resolved by the repealer. There remains, however, an unsettling ambiguity about the legislative statement. While the statement clearly establishes the intent to shift from subjective to objective standards of justification, it does not so clearly address the Legislature's intent with respect to mitigation. When we speak of mitigation in this context, we mean a generalized mitigation that would reduce murder to manslaughter, not specific evidence that bears on the substantive elements of an offense. We are left with this indefiniteness. * * *

We recognize the difficulty of determining the probable intent of the Legislature with respect to this issue. However, we note that other jurisdictions that have combined the Model Penal Code rubric of knowing or purposeful murder with objective principles of justification through self-defense have declined to interpret their codes to allow imperfect self-defense to establish a new and unspecified form of manslaughter. They have answered the question of the existence of imperfect self-defense bluntly: "This contention should be addressed to the Legislature. The only form of self-defense recognized in this state requires that the actor's belief that resort to self-defense is necessary be reasonable." State v. Hatley, 706 P.2d 1083 (Wash.App.1985); Balentine v. Alaska, 707 P.2d 922, 930 (Alaska App.1985) (rejecting contention that one who kills under actual but unreasonable belief that deadly force was necessary has per se acted with an insufficient degree of recklessness to be guilty of murder).

As we have recognized on other occasions, reorganizing the structure of New Jersey's criminal law was the effort of nearly a decade. It imposed numerous difficulties, some of which are not yet fully resolved. For example, we are not absolutely certain about how the Legislature would want us to resolve the dilemma posed by a case such as State v. Williams, 148 A.2d 22 (N.J.1959), in which a police officer shoots to kill in the honest but unreasonable belief that the use of force is needed in self-defense. Under the Code, the police officer might be found guilty of murder. * * *

II

* * * We shall accept for purposes of the *Rivers* appeal the version of the facts in defendant's brief. The incident began as a "pick-up" in a gay bar. Prior to arriving at the bar, defendant consumed substantial amounts of alcohol as well as some cocaine and marijuana. While at the bar he drank more alcohol. The defendant and victim subsequently left the bar to go to a restaurant where defendant worked. They went to a backroom area and engaged in sex. After they re-entered the restaurant area, the two became involved in an argument over defendant's atten-

tion to others. The defendant was seated at a bar stool. The victim allegedly picked up a knife and threatened to use it on the defendant. When the victim moved away, the defendant reached behind a counter and picked up a kitchen knife. When the victim came back at him, defendant said that he thought the victim was about to attack. The defendant stabbed the victim in the stomach, causing his death.

At trial, the court refused to charge the jury on imperfect self-defense. It did charge the jury with respect to the possible effect of alcohol on his state of mind and on the reckless manslaughter offenses. The jury acquitted the defendant of murder but found him guilty of aggravated manslaughter, unlawful possession of a knife, and possession of a knife for an unlawful purpose. He was sentenced to a fifteen-year term. * * *

The *Bowens* incident is detailed in the reported opinion below. The murder was preceded by a dispute between the defendant and the victim, John Booker. For over a year, Booker had threatened defendant on many occasions, often brandishing a knife. Defendant knew that Booker had a reputation for violence, particularly when Booker was drunk. On the day of the killing, Booker, apparently drunk, approached defendant in a manner that caused defendant to fear that Booker would attack him with the knife. The defendant showed Booker his knife and the victim retreated, but then proceeded to follow him. When Booker was about two feet away, defendant, believing he was going to be stabbed by Booker, and intending to stop Booker, stabbed him. At trial, the court denied the defendant's request for a jury charge on imperfect self-defense and instructed the jury on murder, manslaughter committed in the heat of passion, and justification based on self-defense. The jury found defendant guilty of first-degree murder, and the trial court sentenced him to life imprisonment with the required thirty-year parole disqualifier. * * * The Appellate Division reversed, finding prejudicial error in the trial court's failure to charge the jury on aggravated and reckless manslaughter. One judge dissented, finding no rational basis in the evidence to support these charges. [The prosecution appealed.]

Applying the principles outlined above to the facts in *Rivers* first, we find that the trial court was correct in refusing the instruction on imperfect self-defense. * * * In addition to its effect on self-defense, defendant was entitled to have the jury consider the evidence of his honest, if not reasonable, belief in the necessity to use force if in fact the evidence bore upon the question whether the State had proven that he acted purposely or knowingly. Did he act "purposely," as the Code defines it, in the sense of having the conscious object or design to kill, or did he act "knowingly," as the Code defines that term, in the sense of being practically certain that his conduct would cause death? The trial court gave the jury the opportunity to assess the evidence in this way when it instructed the jury on the alternate verdicts of murder, reckless manslaughter, and aggravated manslaughter, the theory the jury ultimately decided upon. [Under the New Jersey adaptation of the Model Penal Code, a criminal homicide is murder when it is committed purposely or knowingly, or in the commission of certain felonies. A reckless homicide "under circumstances manifesting extreme indifference to the value of human life" is aggravated manslaughter, not murder.] In this sense, the evidence served as a "failure-of-proof defense" in addition to its service as an exculpatory defense, a defense that the jury rejected. We therefore approve the trial court's [instructions]. * * *

In *Bowens,* the trial court correctly denied the imperfect self-defense charge but failed to permit the jury to consider the available verdicts implicated by defendant's evidence that he did not have the prerequisite for a murder conviction: the conscious object or near certainty that his attempt to defend himself would cause the victim's death. Sufficient evidence existed in the record to have the jury consider whether the defendant overreacted to the perceived menace, stabbing the victim without purposely or knowingly causing death or serious bodily harm resulting in death, but with reckless disregard of the substantial risk of death or under circumstances manifesting extreme indifference to human life. * * * In effect, the court unintentionally prevented defendant's conviction on the lesser included offenses of aggravated manslaughter or [reckless] manslaughter, and forced the jury to choose between a murder conviction and an acquittal. We therefore [affirm the judgment of the intermediate court of appeals which reversed Bowens' conviction.]

Summary and Conclusion

The statutory definitions of self-defense and manslaughter in a code like New Jersey's provide no room for [a doctrine of imperfect self-defense]. Such codes do, however, permit consideration of a defendant's state of mind. If a defendant subjectively thinks that self-defense is necessary but does not intend fatal injury, in either the sense of knowledge or purpose, such evidence is relevant to the State's case on that issue. If such a defendant is aware that his or her acts create a risk of serious harm but unreasonably disregards that risk, then, if the essential elements of the crime are present, the defendant can be found guilty of manslaughter instead of murder. In some circumstances the evidence may bear upon the question of whether the defendant who committed a homicide in the heat of passion was reasonably provoked.

For the reasons stated, both judgments are affirmed.

STATE v. MARR

Court of Appeals of Maryland, 2001.
362 Md. 467, 765 A.2d 645.

WILNER, JUDGE.

Respondent, Nathaniel Marr, was convicted in the Circuit Court for Prince George's County of the first degree premeditated murder of Arthur Carroll, the first degree assault of Jimmy Abass, and two counts of the use of a handgun in the commission of a crime of violence, for which he was given substantial consecutive sentences. The killing and the assault occurred on the evening of December 2, 1998, when Marr and a confederate, Curtis Alston, approached the rear of a waiting taxicab and opened fire on Carroll, who was about to enter the cab. Carroll was killed and Abass, the driver of the cab, was wounded.

That Marr shot Carroll and Abass was never in dispute. Abass, by all accounts, was an innocent bystander who was simply in the wrong place at the wrong time. The shooting of Carroll stemmed from an incident that occurred three days earlier, on November 29, when Carroll, Kevin Jackson, and Jerome Wright went to Marr's home with the intent to rob him. Marr was not at home, but the three came upon Marr's cousin, Ronald Muse, with whom Marr lived. In the course of searching for drugs and money, one or more of the trio shot and killed Muse. Marr later went looking for Carroll and Jackson, allegedly to inquire about their involvement in the killing of Muse. On December 2, he caught up with Carroll; on December 4, he found Jackson, who was luckier than Carroll and managed to escape in a hail of gunfire.

Marr was charged in both incidents. His defense in both was self-defense. * * * In his first statement, which was an oral one, he said nothing about self-defense. He told the officer that, believing that Carroll was responsible for his cousin's death, he and Alston went to Carroll's home, in a stolen van, "to talk to him about that," that Marr was armed with a Mac 11 semi-automatic machine pistol, and that, when he saw Carroll come out of his home and approach a waiting cab, he fired; one of the shots, he acknowledged, went into the cab. In an ensuing written statement, he claimed that he was both enraged and terrified when he learned about the earlier episode and that he went to see Carroll "to see what his feelings were and to see if things could be resolved, and if he would confess to the murder of my cousin." He and Alston were armed, he said, "for our protection." Just as they arrived, Carroll was about to enter a cab, and, apparently startled to see them, he "grabbed at his waist as if to draw a weapon." In fear of their lives, he and Alston opened fire.

In response to this evidence, which, in the Jackson case, was substantially similar, the trial court, in both cases, instructed the jury on the defenses of "perfect" and "imperfect" self-defense, using the language suggested in § 4:17.2 of the MARYLAND CRIMINAL PATTERN JURY INSTRUCTIONS, published by the Maryland State Bar Association. In both cases, Marr asked for two additional instructions, as follows:

> "In determining whether the defendant's conduct was reasonable under the circumstances, you should judge his conduct by the facts as you believe they appeared to him.
>
> A belief which may be unreasonable to a calm mind may be actually and reasonably held under the circumstances as they appeared to the defendant at the time of the incident."

In both cases, the trial court refused to give the additional instructions, and, in both cases, Marr appealed from the ensuing convictions, claiming, among other things, error in that refusal. [In the case being reviewed in this opinion, the Court of Special Appeals, Maryland's intermediate court, held that the refusal *did* constitute reversible error, a decision reversed by the Court of Appeals in the opinion presented here. In Marr's second case, the intermediate appellate court held that the failure to give the additional instructions did *not* constitute reversible error, and the Court of Appeals denied Marr's petition for *certiorari* in that case.]

Discussion

Maryland recognizes two varieties of self-defense—the traditional one, which we have sometimes termed "perfect" or "complete" self-defense, and a lesser form, sometimes called "imperfect" or "partial" self-defense. Although "perfect" self-defense is universally recognized in the United States, not all of our courts recognize the lesser variety as a separately defined defense, and there is no universal agreement on the precise elements of either variety. We shall focus, as we must, on the current state of the Maryland law, but, as we consider some of our earlier cases and cases from other States, we need to take into account the overall context in which those cases were decided.

We defined the defenses of "perfect" and "imperfect" self-defense, and the relationship between them, in *State v. Faulkner*, 301 Md. 482, 483 A.2d 759 (1984) and *Dykes v. State*, 319 Md. 206, 571 A.2d 1251 (1990). We noted that "perfect" or traditional self-defense, is a complete defense to a charge of criminal homicide—murder or manslaughter—and, if credited by the trier of fact, results in an acquittal. The elements, or requirements, of that defense, as we enumerated them in *Faulkner* and *Dykes*, are:

> "(1) The accused must have had reasonable grounds to believe himself in apparent imminent or immediate danger of death or serious bodily harm from his assailant or potential assailant;
>
> (2) The accused must have in fact believed himself in this danger;
>
> (3) The accused claiming the right of self-defense must not have been the aggressor or provoked the conflict; and
>
> (4) The force used must have not been unreasonable and excessive, that is, the force must not have been more force than the exigency demanded."

In *Faulkner*, we first adopted the concept of "imperfect" self-defense * * *. The prospect of "imperfect" self-defense arises when the actual, subjective belief on the part of the accused that he/she is in apparent imminent danger of death or serious bodily harm from the assailant, requiring the use of deadly force, is not an objectively reasonable belief. What may be unreasonable is the perception of imminent danger or the belief that the force employed is necessary to meet the danger, or both. As we said in *Faulkner*, quoting from the Court of Special Appeals opinion:

"Perfect self-defense requires not only that the killer subjectively believed that his actions were necessary for his safety but, objectively, that a reasonable man would so consider them. Imperfect self-defense, however, requires no more than a subjective honest belief on the part of the killer that his actions were necessary for his safety, even though, on an objective appraisal by a reasonable man, they would not be found to be so."

"[T]he only substantive difference between the two doctrines, other than their consequences, is that, in perfect self-defense, the defendant's belief that he was in immediate danger of death of [sic] serious bodily harm or that the force he used was necessary must be objectively reasonable. In all other respects, the elements of the two doctrines are the same." [citation omitted]

Unlike its "perfect" cousin, "imperfect" self-defense, if credited, does not result in an acquittal, but merely serves to negate the element of malice required for a conviction of murder and thus reduces the offense to manslaughter. As we explained in *Faulkner* and repeated in *Dykes*, a defendant who commits a homicide while honestly, though unreasonably, believing that he/she is threatened with death or serious harm and that deadly force was necessary does not act with malice, and, absent malice, cannot be convicted of murder. Nonetheless, because the killing was committed without justification or excuse, the defendant is not entitled to full exoneration and would be guilty of voluntary manslaughter.

* * *

The two additional instructions requested by Marr were necessarily premised on the assumption that he actually believed that he was in imminent danger of death or serious bodily harm from Carroll and that the deadly force he employed was a necessary response to that threat, and they sought to focus the jury's attention on the reasonableness of those subjective beliefs. Those instructions thus related to the defense of "perfect," rather than "imperfect," self-defense. They would have the jury determine the reasonableness of the defendant's belief as to either of those elements by looking at things solely through his eyes and mindstate, regardless of how someone else, including the imaginary reasonable person, would have viewed the situation.

Marr urges that this concept or standard is required in a self-defense analysis and that it was not fairly covered in the other instructions given by the court. * * *

* * *

* * * We do not disavow the notion that, as part of a self-defense analysis, the trier of fact must look at the circumstances as they appeared to the defendant, for that is important in understanding the defendant's explanation for his or her conduct. It provides the necessary underpinning for the defendant's subjective beliefs that (1) he/she was in imminent danger, and (2) the force used was necessary. When judging

the reasonableness of the defendant's conduct, however, that notion has some limits. Our jurisprudence, pre-dating *Faulkner*, is consistent with an objective, rather than a subjective, standard of reasonableness.[1]

It has always been a requirement of "perfect" self-defense in Maryland that the defendant's belief of imminent death or serious bodily harm and the need to respond with the amount of force used "coincide with that which would have been entertained under the same circumstances by a person of average prudence." Not only must the defendant have the subjective belief, but "the circumstances [must be] such as to warrant reasonable grounds for such belief in the mind of a man [or woman] of ordinary reason." We made clear in *Faulkner*, *supra*, that, not only must the defendant subjectively believe that his actions were necessary "but objectively, that a reasonable man would so consider them."

The objective standard does not require the jury to ignore the defendant's perceptions in determining the reasonableness of his or her conduct. In making that determination, the facts or circumstances *must* be taken as perceived by the defendant, even if they were not the true facts or circumstances, *so long as a reasonable person in the defendant's position could also reasonably perceive the facts or circumstances in that way. See State v. Simon*, 231 Kan. 572, 646 P.2d 1119, 1122 (Kan. 1982) * * *. If the fact or circumstance relied upon by the defendant to justify a belief of imminent danger or the need to use deadly force to meet that danger is so improbable that no reasonable person in the defendant's position would perceive it to be the case, the jury cannot be directed to assume that fact or circumstance in judging the reasonableness of the defendant's conduct, for that would skew the whole analysis of reasonableness.

A belief, as to either imminent danger or the amount of force necessary to meet that danger, is necessarily founded upon the defendant's sensory and ideational perception of the situation that he or she confronts, often shaded by knowledge or perceptions of ancillary or

1. Other States have wrestled with this question as well, but their conclusions, sometimes reached in the context of a self-defense law that is different from that applied in Maryland or a situation quite different from that facing us here, are not particularly helpful in light of our own well-established jurisprudence. In *State v. Leidholm*, 334 N.W.2d 811 (N.D.1983), the court observed that, in determining whether a defendant's beliefs or conduct were reasonable, there was some difference of opinion as to whether the standard of reasonableness is an objective or subjective one, the difference being whether the trier of fact was to view the circumstances surrounding the accused from the standpoint of a hypothetical reasonable person or simply to determine whether the circumstances were sufficient to induce in the accused an honest and reasonable belief that he must use force to defend himself. The North Dakota court opted for the subjective approach, that allows the jury "to judge the reasonableness of the accused's actions against the accused's subjective impressions of the need to use force." That determination, however, was made in the context of a statutory self-defense law modeled largely on the American Law Institute Model Penal Code that does not draw the same distinction between "perfect" and "imperfect" self-defense that is imposed in Maryland. * * * *Compare*, however, *State v. Simon*, 231 Kan. 572, 646 P.2d 1119, 1122 (Kan. 1982), opting for an objective standard, that "[a] reasonable belief implies both a belief and the existence of facts that would persuade a reasonable man to that belief."

antecedent events. The perception that serves as the impetus for responsive action may be incorrect for a variety of reasons, ranging from ignorance of relevant facts that, if known, would put the situation in a different light, to distortions in sensory perceptions, to judgmental errors in the instantaneous assimilation and appreciation of the apparent situation. The fact that the defendant's perception is incorrect does not necessarily make it unreasonable; human beings often misunderstand their surroundings and the intentions of other people. A defendant who is suddenly grabbed by another person at gunpoint may reasonably believe that the person is an assailant intending to do him immediate and grievous bodily harm, even though, in fact, the person is a plain clothes police officer possessing a valid warrant and properly, though forcibly, attempting to arrest him. * * *

* * *

It is not our function in this case to draft a jury instruction that properly focuses the jury's attention on the circumstances as perceived by the defendant. We simply conclude that, in light of the other instructions given by the court, the additional instructions requested by Marr did not do so and, for that reason were properly rejected.

[Judgment reversed and remanded]

HUGHES v. STATE

Court of Criminal Appeals of Texas, 1986.
719 S.W.2d 560.

CLINTON, JUDGE.

Indicted for murder, appellant was convicted by a jury of voluntary manslaughter and his punishment assessed at twenty years confinement and a fine of $10,000. The Tyler Court of Appeals reversed, holding that the trial court erred in [instructing the jury] that before appellant was entitled to use deadly force in defense of a third person it must be found that a reasonable person in his position would not have retreated under the circumstances.

I

The killing occurred on the shoulder of [a country road]. Two passersby testified that they saw a Thunderbird and a Chevrolet pickup parked along the roadside. In the driver's seat of the pickup was the deceased, Rodney Johnson, and standing beside the driver's door talking to him was Joan Goodwin. Appellant was observed leaning on the hood of the truck. Both witnesses momentarily looked away, and then, looking back, observed appellant withdrawing his upper body from the driver's window. Smoke was seen coming from the cab of the pickup, and one of the witnesses saw a pistol in appellant's hand. Appellant and Goodwin fled in the Thunderbird. When the witnesses reached Johnson's pickup, they found him on the floorboard, shot to death. Also found on the front seat was a longbarrel .22 pistol, loaded but unfired.

Joan Goodwin took the stand on behalf of appellant. She testified that Johnson had long been her friend, but that they had never been romantically involved. Nevertheless Johnson was upset that Goodwin was "seeing" appellant and asserted to her on one occasion, "If I have to kill you to get to him I will do that." Other defensive testimony showed that appellant and Goodwin had been to a party at the home of Mary Hodge on an evening earlier in January. When Johnson arrived at the party appellant rose to shake his hand, but Johnson cursed him and struck at him, precipitating a scuffle. Appellant drew a pistol but did not actually point it at Johnson, merely stating that this time he had the gun, and thus the upper hand, or words to that effect. Death threats were exchanged, but the altercation ended when Hodge ordered Johnson out of the house.

Defense witnesses testified that on the day of the killing Hodge was driving Goodwin and appellant to her house when Johnson passed them in his pickup. When Johnson turned around and began to follow them, Hodge pulled over to the side of the road. Johnson pulled up about two car lengths behind, and Goodwin and appellant got out of the Thunderbird to talk to him, while Hodge stayed in the car. It was approximately 3:00 p.m., and Goodwin and appellant had been drinking throughout the day.

According to Goodwin, the following transpired:

Q Did anyone else get out after you got out?

A John. He was behind me and I walked up there.

Q You walked up where, ma'am?

A To Rodney's pickup.

Q Okay.

A And John was right behind me. And Rodney—

Q What happened then?

A Rodney said, "I don't have anything to say to you motherfucker I just want to talk to Joan." Okay—

Q What at that point did John do if anything?

A He turned around and went back to the front of the pickup and just leaned up against the front of the pickup.

Q Okay. What happened then?

A I said, "Rodney, I don't understand why you're acting like this." I said, "If you're going to be like this we can't even be friends". And he grabbed me, Rodney grabbed me. And when he did I just—I pulled back from him and you know, just pulled my arms back from when he grabbed me and I said, "hey, what are you doing". And I looked back up in there, you know, and by the time I looked back up in there he's got a gun in his hand and I said, "he's got a gun". And that's when John turned around and shot him.

Q Did Rodney say anything prior to reaching for the gun?

A He said, "I told you if I had to kill you to get to him I would do it." * * *

Q One last question, ma'am. Did Rodney Johnson threaten to kill you and John Hughes just before John Hughes shot him?

A Yes.

The trial court charged the jury on the law of self-defense and defense of a third party. As to defense of a third party the instructions read:

> "A person is justified in using deadly force against another when and to the degree he reasonably believes such force is necessary to protect a third person if, under the circumstances as he reasonably believes them to be, he believes such force and degree of force would be immediately necessary to protect himself against the unlawful deadly force he reasonably believes to be threatening the third person he seeks to protect, if a reasonable person in his situation would not have retreated, and he reasonably believes that his intervention is immediately necessary to protect the third person." * * *

II

The requirement that an accused have made a reasonable retreat before resorting to the use of deadly force in defense of himself, though found in the common law of England, was not recognized in the statutes and decisional law of Texas prior to enactment of the 1974 Penal Code. Now, however, that requirement is expressly provided in § 9.32, which reads:

> A person is justified in using deadly force against another:
>
> (1) if he would be justified in using force against the other under § 9.31 of this code;
>
> (2) if a reasonable person in the actor's situation would not have retreated; and
>
> (3) when and to the degree he reasonably believes the deadly force is immediately necessary:
>
> (A) to protect himself against the other's use or attempted use of unlawful deadly force * * *

The State argues, as it did in the court of appeals, that § 9.33(1) incorporates the necessity to retreat if reasonable into the law of defense of third parties by virtue of its reference back to § 9.32(2). § 9.33 reads:

> A person is justified in using force or deadly force against another to protect a third person if:
>
> (1) under the circumstances as the actor reasonably believes them to be, the actor would be justified under §§ 9.31 or 9.32 of this code in using force or deadly force to protect himself against the unlawful force or unlawful deadly force he reasonably believes to be threatening the third person he seeks to protect; and

(2) the actor reasonably believes that his intervention is immediately necessary to protect the third person.

The court of appeals reasoned that to construe § 9.33 to require the accused to retreat if reasonable before coming to the aid of a third person whose safety he reasonably believes his intervention is immediately necessary to protect would countermand the obvious legislative intent in enacting the justification in the first place. The State now asserts that while the court of appeals may have correctly perceived the legislative intent, nevertheless the plain wording of § 9.33, in its reference back to § 9.32, "requires retreat before defending another." It is suggested that we uphold the instruction given in the instant case, and leave it to the Legislature to revise the provision to reflect its true purpose. In our view, however, the legislative intent as perceived by the court of appeals is reflected unambiguously in the plain wording of § 9.33.

III

Because under § 9.33(2) an accused must reasonably believe that his intervention is "immediately necessary to protect the third person," it would be paradoxical to suggest that the Legislature intended that he first be required to retreat. Clearly what the legislature did intend was to justify use of deadly force to protect a third person in any situation in which the third person would apparently be justified in using deadly force to protect himself. By positing in § 9.33(1) that "the actor would be justified under Section * * * 9.32 of this code" in using deadly force to protect himself against that force "he reasonably believes to be threatening the third person he seeks to protect," the Legislature was merely placing the accused, who is the "actor" under § 9.33 in the shoes of the third person. So long as the accused reasonably believes that the third person would be justified in using deadly force to protect himself, the accused may step in and exercise deadly force on behalf of that person. Part of what goes into the assessment of whether the third person had a right to exercise deadly force in defense of himself is whether or not a reasonable person in his position would have retreated instead. Thus, in deciding intervention is necessary, the accused must reasonably believe that "a reasonable person in [the third person's] situation would not have retreated."

The jury would correctly be instructed, then, that to find the conduct of the accused to have been justified as defense of a third person, inter alia, it must believe, or have a reasonable doubt whether the accused, from his standpoint, reasonably believed that a reasonable person in the third person's situation would not have retreated.[2] * * * The trial court erred in instructing the jury appellant could [only] be

2. Since the jury must assess the circumstances from the standpoint of the accused, so long as it is found that it reasonably appeared to him that a reasonable person in the third person's position would not have retreated before using deadly force, he would be entitled to an acquittal, even if the jury also believed that in reality a reasonable person in the third person's position would have retreated before resorting to deadly force.

acquitted "if a reasonable person in his situation would not have retreated." The judgment of the court of appeals is affirmed.

TEAGUE, JUDGE, concurring in the result only.

One of the reasons that has been given for [the increase in violent crime] in this country is that citizens became reluctant or afraid to get "involved" in deterring that violence, and refused to intervene in good faith on behalf of another person. "This reticence seemed to emanate less from fear of physical harm than from the potential consequences of a legal aftermath." Alexander v. State, 52 Md.App. 171, 447 A.2d 880 (1982). Judge Lowe, the author of that opinion, highlighted his statement with a reference to the well known case involving Katherine "Kitty" Genovese, whose screams and cries for help went unheard one night in New York City because persons in the neighborhood where she was assaulted and later murdered chose not to get involved, or intervene on Kitty's behalf, but chose, instead, to pull their window shades, and shut their windows and doors, in order not to see or hear the butchery that was then taking place. Why did those good persons not come forth to aid Kitty? Later, when interviewed, they stated that they did not intervene because they believed that the law would not protect them from possible criminal charges if they had intervened and assaulted Kitty's wrongdoer and it was later found that they were wrong in what they thought and believed they saw and heard. Thus, it was their fear of legal consequences, and not necessarily their timidity or lack of bravery, that chilled their better instincts to intervene. * * *

Is this the kind of thinking that we want our citizens to have? I, for one, think not, and I sincerely believe that those persons who subscribe to total non-intervention, regardless of the facts and circumstances, should move to a place where such views are acceptable and in vogue. Cf. People v. Young, 11 N.Y.2d 274, 229 N.Y.S.2d 1, 183 N.E.2d 319 (1962), which held that a person who in good faith and reasonable belief goes to the aid of a third person does so at his own peril, which ruling apparently shocked the consciences of the then members of the New York Legislature to such an extent that they voted to change their law. * * * [See the Note following this case.—ed.]

The majority opinion correctly affirms the decision of the Tyler Court of Appeals * * * The problem that I have with Judge Clinton's conclusion is that he appears to somehow implicate into the scenario what the person on whose behalf the defendant intervened thought or believed. If that is what he means, then I must part company with the majority opinion because if that were the case there would have been no need for the Legislature to enact § 9.33. Under § 9.33, where the defendant has killed the deceased, the question is whether the defendant reasonably believed that it was necessary to use deadly force to prevent the person he perceived to be the assailant and wrongdoer imminently committing the offense of murder of the person on whose behalf he intervened. If the jury answers the question in the affirmative, then that ends the discussion, and the defendant is entitled to be found not guilty;

if the jury does not so find, or does not have a reasonable doubt on the issue, then, as far as the defense of a third person goes, that defense just went out the window as far as the defendant is concerned. * * *

The law of retreat, as found in our law of self-defense, is simply not a part of § 9.33. § 9.33 was clearly intended to encourage and to afford protection to "good samaritans" by removing their legal doubts, which might impede crime prevention and deter those who witness violent assaults upon persons, but who otherwise would aid an apparent victim of criminal violence. * * *

MILLER, JUDGE, dissenting.

* * * Both my analysis and the majority analysis agree that the actor/defender must believe that his intervention is immediately necessary to protect the third person. Where we part ways is in the area of the actor/defender's belief concerning retreat. The majority would have the actor/defender reasonably believe that a reasonable person in the third person's shoes would not retreat. * * * My analysis would have the actor/defendant reasonably believe that he cannot retreat and still preserve the safety of the third party. The State of course would have the actor/defendant believe that he himself would have to be threatened with unlawful deadly force before he could aid a third person being similarly threatened-an analysis rejected by everyone concerned. * * *

I recognize that an apparent conflict exists between the statutes. In self-defense involving the use of deadly force, the § 9.32 duty to retreat may be logically and successfully coupled with the required belief that such force is immediately necessary to prevent the other's unlawful use of deadly force; viz., if there is no immediate need for the use of deadly force in self-defense, then retreat must also be reasonable. Though not synonymous, these two requirements, retreat and immediate need for use of deadly force, complement each other throughout the various scenarios that unfold in self-defense against deadly force situations. These two requirements, however, become paradoxical when applied to situations involving use of deadly force in defense of a third party. § 9.33 seems to require that a protector choose between retreating from an altercation that he has not even entered into or saving someone in that altercation whose life is in danger. Thus, a conflict arises. * * * Under § 9.33, the actor's use of deadly force in defense of a third person must be justified under § 9.32, before the use of such force is permitted. Under § 9.32, the actor has the duty to retreat if he can do so in complete safety. Thus, an actor is justified in using deadly force in defense of another only if he could not have reasonably retreated to prevent harm to himself.

This construction eliminates any useful application of the justification for use of deadly force in defense of another.

* * * We must determine whether there is an interpretation of the statutory language which will effectuate the object of the statutes without requiring that part of one statute be declared in fatal conflict with the other. Fortunately in this case, such an interpretation is

possible. The object of § 9.32 is self-defense. This objective, however, must not be obtained at the unnecessary cost of human life. Thus, if the actor facing deadly force attack can reasonably retreat and not exercise deadly force in counter attack, the actor is required to do so. His safety is preserved, and so is the life of the attacker. Similarly, the object of § 9.33 is preservation of the life of the third party. If that objective may be obtained without the use of deadly force, then the actor must take such action. Based upon these goals and considerations, I would therefore hold that the retreat requirement of § 9.32 is to apply to § 9.33 in the following manner: where the circumstances raise the possibility of use of deadly force in defense of a third party, and if the actor may retreat and still preserve the safety of the third party he or she seeks to protect, then the actor must retreat and not exercise deadly force against the attacker. The standard of maintaining the safety of the third person is the same standard as that of maintaining one's own personal safety in self-defense. * * *

The majority analysis, requiring that the actor believe that a reasonable person in the third person's situation would not retreat, sounds nice and neat at first blush. It works well in one of the possible scenarios; where the actor believes the third person needn't retreat and in fact does not. But what of the situation where the actor isn't sure the third person can or should retreat? It is quite foreseeable that an actor would have sufficient facts perceived to believe deadly force is immediately necessary, but not have facts to evaluate whether the third person should retreat (an entirely different matter). What of the situation where the actor thinks the third person should retreat but that person doesn't? Must the actor stand by and watch until the situation (as he perceives it—not as the third person perceives it) changes? What about the situation where the actor believes the third person needn't retreat but that person is in fact retreating? Under the majority's holding there is no answer to these scenarios that effectuates the clear legislative intent manifested by § 9.32 and § 9.33—protection of third persons against unlawful deadly force. Rather, the majority stifles the contemplated action of an actor.

For the foregoing reasons I dissent.

W.C. DAVIS, JUDGE, joins.

Note

The common law authorities limited the right to use force in defense of others to situations where the defendant was closely related in some fashion to the person attacked, so that by implication one could not intervene to protect a stranger. This limitation is obsolete, and in any event it has little practical importance. There is an independent privilege to use force to prevent the commission of a felony, and this privilege would protect the intervenor who used force in defense of a stranger who was an innocent victim of an assault.

A more important limitation on the right to use force in defense of others was the so-called "alter ego" rule. The intervenor was entitled to use only so much force as the person being rescued was entitled to use in his or her own defense. In other words, the situation was one of strict liability for the intervenor who misjudged the circumstances, however innocently, and used force to defend a party with no right to self-defense. Prosecutions were most likely to occur where the apparent victim of an assault turned out to be a criminal being arrested by plainclothes police officers. In one case following this pattern, the New York Court of Appeals reaffirmed the alter ego rule despite arguments that public policy should encourage citizens to come to the rescue of apparent crime victims rather than discourage them by imposing strict liability. People v. Young, 11 N.Y.2d 274, 229 N.Y.S.2d 1, 183 N.E.2d 319 (1962). The legislature had the last word, however. New York Penal Law § 35.15 was amended to provide that "A person may * * * use physical force upon another person when and to the extent he reasonably believes such to be necessary to defend himself or a third person from what he reasonably believes to be the use or imminent use of unlawful physical force by such other person * * *." See also, State v. Chiarello, 69 N.J.Super. 479, 174 A.2d 506 (1961).

PEOPLE v. GUENTHER

Supreme Court of Colorado, 1987.
740 P.2d 971.

Quinn, Chief Justice.

The defendant was charged with the second degree murder of Josslyn Volosin, two counts of first degree assault committed against Michael Volosin and Robbie Alan Wardwell, and one count of the commission of a crime of violence. * * * [Defendant moved to dismiss because, since] he fired the shots only after an unlawful entry had been made into his house and after it appeared that his wife was being harmed, he was immune from prosecution under [a Colorado statute.]

During the evening of April 19 and the early morning hours of April 20, 1986, a small group of people were drinking and playing pool at the home of Michael and Josslyn Volosin, which was located across the street and two houses to the north of David and Pam Guenther's home. Late in the evening three of the men left the party and went to the Guenthers'. One of the men began banging on the Guenthers' car, shouting obscenities, and challenging David Guenther to come out of the house. The men left after Pam Guenther told them her husband was not at home and she was going to call the police. The police arrived, discussed the incident with Pam Guenther, went to the Volosins' home and talked to Josslyn Volosin, and then left.

The events that followed constituted the basis for the criminal charges against the defendant and for the district court's subsequent dismissal of those charges. The witnesses' versions of these events, however, are in substantial conflict with one another. Michael Volosin stated that shortly after the police left he heard a loud noise at his front door. When he saw no one at his door, he ran to the Guenthers' house and knocked on the front door, whereupon Pam Guenther opened the door, grabbed him, threw him out onto the grass, and had him on the ground when her husband came out of the house shooting. Volosin's version was corroborated by Bonnie Smith, a neighbor who had observed the incident from her window. Smith testified that she had seen Pam Guenther standing over a figure lying next to the Guenthers' porch, shouting obscenities and trying to pick the person up off the ground.

In contrast, Pam Guenther testified that when she went to the front door and opened it, Michael Volosin grabbed her, pulled her out the door, threw her against the wall, and began to beat her up. Pam Guenther stated that as she and Michael began struggling, she screamed for her husband to get the gun. It was her further testimony that Josslyn Volosin had appeared and was trying to break up the fight when the sound of gunshots was heard. After Pam Guenther screamed for help, the defendant came to the front door of his house and, from the doorway, fired four shots from a Smith and Wesson .357 Magnum six-inch revolver. The defendant's account of the events was substantially the same as his wife's. One shot hit and wounded Michael Volosin, who was lying on the ground next to the Guenthers' porch. Robbie Alan Wardwell, a guest of the Volosins, was wounded by a second shot as he was walking across the Guenthers' front yard to help Josslyn Volosin break up the fight. A third shot killed Josslyn Volosin. There was conflicting evidence as to whether she was hit while standing near the Guenthers' front porch or in the street as she was running away. [The trial court dismissed the charges against David Guenther and the prosecution appealed.]

The issues center on section 18–1–704.5, which became effective on June 6, 1985, and provides as follows:

> (1) The general assembly hereby recognizes that the citizens of Colorado have a right to expect absolute safety within their own homes.
>
> (2) Notwithstanding the provisions of section 18–1–704,[2] any occupant of a dwelling is justified in using any degree of physical force, including deadly physical force, against another person when that other person has made an unlawful entry into the dwelling, and when the occupant has a reasonable belief that such other person has committed a crime in the dwelling in addition to the uninvited entry, or is committing or intends to commit a crime against a person or property in addition to the uninvited entry, and when the

2. Section 18–1–704, dealing with the use of physical force in defense of a person, provides that a person may use "a degree of force which he reasonably believes to be necessary" for the purpose of defending himself or a third person, but that:

(2) Deadly physical force may be used only if a person reasonably believes a lesser degree of force is inadequate and:

(a) The actor has reasonable ground to believe, and does believe, that he or another person is in imminent danger of being killed or of receiving great bodily injury; or

(b) The other person is using or reasonably appears about to use physical force against an occupant of a dwelling or business establishment while committing or attempting to commit burglary or

(c) The other person is committing or reasonably appears about to commit kidnapping, or robbery, or sexual assault or [aggravated] assault as defined [the relevant statutes].

occupant reasonably believes that such other person might use any physical force, no matter how slight, against any occupant.

(3) Any occupant of a dwelling using physical force, including deadly physical force, in accordance with the provisions of subsection (2) of this section shall be immune from criminal prosecution for the use of such force.

(4) Any occupant of a dwelling using physical force, including deadly physical force, in accordance with the provisions of subsection (2) of this section shall be immune from any civil liability for injuries or death resulting from the use of such force.

* * * We have requested the parties to submit briefs on the following questions: what is the proper procedure to be followed in determining whether a person is entitled to immunity from criminal prosecution under section 18–1–704.5(3); what is the appropriate * * * standard of proof by which that issue should be resolved; and does a denial of a pretrial motion to dismiss on grounds of immunity prohibit the defendant from raising the immunity issue as an affirmative defense at trial. * * *

II

* * * We conclude that section 18–1–704.5(3) authorizes a court to dismiss a criminal prosecution at the pretrial stage of the case when the conditions of the statute have been satisfied. * * *

Section 18–1–704.5(3) states that any occupant of a dwelling who uses physical force in accordance with the provisions of subsection (2) of the statute "shall be immune from criminal prosecution for the use of such force" In our view, this language is susceptible of only one interpretation. * * *

Although the People would have us read section 18–1–704.5(3) as creating an affirmative defense, and emphasize in support of their argument that the statute was inserted into that part of the Code which sets forth affirmative defenses, we do not believe that the People's proposed construction can be reconciled with the plain language of the statute. * * *

We find further support in the legislative history. In explaining the need for the proposed legislation, the co-sponsor of the statute, Senator Brandon, stated at a legislative committee hearing that under current Colorado law a homeowner might not be convicted in the situation addressed by the bill, but would in any event be required to hire an attorney and perhaps "put his home on the block" in order to avoid a jail sentence. This statement clearly suggests that the bill was intended to spare a homeowner the financial burden of a trial. * * *

[The court held that a defendant may raise the statutory immunity claim on a pretrial motion to dismiss the prosecution.]

* * * Since section 18–1–704.5(3) contemplates that an accused may claim an entitlement to immunity at the pretrial stage of a criminal

prosecution, we believe it reasonable to require the accused to prove his entitlement to an order of dismissal on the basis of statutory immunity. * * * We thus hold that when section 18–1–704.5(3) is invoked prior to trial as a bar to a criminal prosecution, the burden is on the defendant seeking the benefit of the statutory immunity to establish by a preponderance of evidence that: (1) another person made an unlawful entry into the defendant's dwelling; (2) the defendant had a reasonable belief that such other person had committed a crime in the dwelling in addition to the uninvited entry, or was committing or intended to commit a crime against a person or property in addition to the uninvited entry; (3) the defendant reasonably believed that such other person might use physical force, no matter now slight, against any occupant of the dwelling; and (4) the defendant used force against the person who actually made the unlawful entry into the dwelling.

* * * If a court finds that the defendant has met the burden of proof, then the court must grant immunity from prosecution and dismiss the charges. If, on the other hand, the court determines that the defendant has not met his burden of proof and denies the motion to dismiss the charges, there is nothing in section 18–1–704.5 to suggest that the defendant should somehow be precluded from raising the same statutory conditions for immunity as an affirmative defense to the charges at trial. * * * Thus, if the pretrial motion to dismiss on grounds of statutory immunity is denied, the defendant may nonetheless raise at trial, as an affirmative defense to criminal charges arising out of the defendant's use of physical force against an intruder into his home, the statutory conditions set forth in section 18–1–704.5(2). In such an instance, the burden of proof generally applicable to affirmative defenses would apply. The defendant would be required to present some credible evidence supporting the applicability of section 18–1–704.5(2); and, if such evidence is presented, the prosecution would then bear the burden of proving beyond a reasonable doubt the guilt of the defendant as to the issue raised by the affirmative defense as well as all other elements of the offense charged.

In light of these aforementioned guidelines, we consider the district court's judgment of dismissal in this case. The district court erred in concluding that the defendant was entitled to a dismissal of the charges because the prosecution had failed to disprove beyond a reasonable doubt the statutory conditions for immunity outlined in section 18–1–704.5(2). In so ruling, the court applied an erroneous standard of proof. Under the correct standard, the defendant would be entitled to immunity only if he established by a preponderance of the evidence those statutory conditions of immunity set forth in section 18–1–704.5(2). The district court also erred in concluding that section 18–1–704.5(3) immunizes from criminal prosecution an occupant of a dwelling who uses force against persons who did not actually enter the dwelling. If on remand the district court concludes that the immunity criteria of section 18–1–704.5(2) are established, then the defendant would be entitled to immunity from prosecution for any force used against any person or persons who actually entered his dwelling, but would not be immune from prosecution for any force used against non-entrants.

We reverse the district court's order of dismissal, and we remand the case for further proceedings not inconsistent with the views herein expressed.

COMMONWEALTH v. BIAGINI

Supreme Court of Pennsylvania, 1995.
540 Pa. 22, 655 A.2d 492.

MR. JUSTICE CAPPY

[Defendant Biagini was convicted of resisting arrest and of aggravated assault on a police officer.] Officer Snyder, while on a routine patrol in a residential neighborhood in North Belle Vernon at 3:00 a.m., heard a disturbance. The disturbance, a loud voice shouting, seemed to emanate from the rear of a home. Upon investigating, the officer observed Biagini stagger out of the alley between the houses, look up and down the street, and stagger back into the alley. The officer drove down the alley and encountered Biagini in the rear yard of his house with an unidentified female. The officer inquired of Biagini as to the disturbance. Biagini initially responded, in a loud voice, that there was no problem and then pointed at two other individuals across the alley. The officer told Biagini to remain where he was and went to investigate the other individuals. Biagini, however, left the yard and went into his home. The other individuals told Officer Snyder that Biagini had been screaming at them from his back yard and threw an object at them which they thought, from the sounds of the impact, to be a glass bottle. The officer returned to speak to Biagini.

As Biagini had left the alley, the officer approached the house and knocked on the door. Biagini responded by screaming at the officer "Who the [expletive] is tearing down my door?" Officer Snyder asked Biagini to come out to the patrol car and answer a few questions. Biagini refused and in vulgar terms ordered the officer off his porch. The officer then told Biagini he was under arrest for public intoxication and disorderly conduct. Biagini refused to comply with the officer's request to come quietly. Biagini shook free of the officer's hold and re-entered his home.

Officer Snyder went back to his patrol car, turned on his flashing lights, called for back-up, and again knocked on Biagini's door. Officer Snyder renewed his request that Biagini accompany him to the patrol car and Biagini renewed his vulgar refusal. The officer attempted to seize Biagini and a scuffle ensued. Officer Snyder was punched in the mouth and Biagini was subdued with the aid of the additional officers who had responded to the back-up call. Biagini was searched and a set of brass knuckles and a small amount of marijuana were found on his person.

At trial Biagini demurred to the evidence arguing that all the charges must be dismissed as the arrest was illegal. The trial court denied the demurrer. Biagini was subsequently convicted, after a non-jury trial, for public drunkenness, disorderly conduct, aggravated assault, resisting arrest, possessing prohibited offensive weapons, and possession of a small amount of marijuana. In the opinion of the trial court denying Biagini's post-trial motions the court concluded that the arrest was valid: * * * [The Superior (intermediate appellate) court held that the arrest for disorderly conduct or public intoxication was unlawful. "Being both vulgar and loud to a police officer, while in a private residence, does not constitute disorderly conduct. * * * While Biagini was allegedly intoxicated in his home and on his porch, it is apparent from the record that he had not 'appeared in any public place manifestly under the influence of alcohol to the degree that he [might] endanger himself or other persons or property, or annoy persons in his vicinity.' "]

The crime at issue is resisting arrest. [According to the Pennsylvania Crimes Code: "A person commits a misdemeanor of the second degree if, with the intention of preventing a public servant from effecting a *lawful arrest*, or discharging any other duty, the person creates a substantial risk of bodily injury to the public servant or anyone else, or employs means justifying or requiring substantial force to overcome the resistance."] Upon review of the well-reasoned opinion of the Superior Court, we accept the legal conclusion that no probable cause existed for the arrest. Accordingly, as the underlying arrest was unlawful, as effectuated in the absence of probable cause, one of the essential elements of the crime of resisting arrest was not established. The conviction of Biagini for resisting arrest must be reversed.

Thus, the initial premise of the defendant's syllogism is valid; therefore, we now turn to the secondary premise: since the underlying arrest was unlawful his resistance was justified. * * * Contrary to the assertion of the defendant, the finding of an unlawful arrest does not justify the actions of Biagini in physically resisting Officer Snyder. The determination that a Police officer placed an individual under arrest without probable cause is a legal determination; it is an issue to be resolved in a courtroom, not on a street corner. Within a civilized society rules exist to resolve disputes in an orderly and peaceful manner. Physical resistance to a police officer is not only counterproductive to the orderly resolution of controversy, but it is also specifically prohibited by statute. *18 Pa.C.S. § 505 (b)(1)(i)*. (The use of force is not justifiable to resist an arrest which the actor knows is being made by a peace officer, although the arrest is unlawful). Therefore, defendant's secondary premise, that an unlawful arrest justifies physical resistance, is invalid. * * *

First, the lawfulness of the arrest is irrelevant to the charge of aggravated assault; and second, in asserting that the physical assaults at issue were justified responses to an illegal arrest, the defendant has misinterpreted our recent decision in *Commonwealth v. French*, 531 Pa. 42, 611 A.2d 175 (1992).

The charges of aggravated assault at issue were brought under subsection (a)(3) of the statute at *18 Pa.C.S. § 2702* which reads:

(a) Offense defined.—A person is guilty of aggravated assault if he:

(3) attempts to cause or intentionally or knowingly causes bodily injury to a police officer, firefighter or county adult probation or parole officer, county juvenile probation or parole officer or an agent of the Pennsylvania Board of Probation and Parole *in the performance of duty*: (emphasis supplied).

For the narrow purposes of determining whether a person has committed aggravated assault, if the police effectuate an arrest and the arrestee physically resists the officer, and subsequently the arrest is deemed to be without probable cause, nevertheless, the arrestee is guilty of aggravated assault because the officer was within the "performance of duty" when effectuating the arrest. In 1986 the legislature amended *18 Pa.C.S. § 2702(a)(3)* and substituted the words "making or attempting to make a lawful arrest" with the phrase "in the performance of duty." This change broadened the scope of the statute, evidencing an intent to protect officers when effectuating all arrests, even those which are subsequently determined to have lacked probable cause at their inception.

Thus, a lawful arrest is not an element of the crime charged. * * *

The final aspect of the defendants' argument turns on their interpretation of this Court's recent opinion in *French*, supra. The defendants want to use *French* as a shield absolving them of responsibility for their actions. They argue that their use of force in resisting an unlawful arrest was a justifiable response to the police officers' use of force in placing them under arrest. In addition to arguing that French provides blanket protection to those who resist an unlawful arrest, the defendant * * * argues that Officer Snyder used excessive force in effectuating the arrest, thus Biagini was merely responding to that force in an effort to protect himself.

We cannot state it any more clearly: there does not exist in Pennsylvania a right to resist arrest, under any circumstances. The lawfulness of the arrest must be decided after the fact and appropriate sanctions imposed in a later judicial setting. Contrary to the position of the defendants herein, the opinion in *French* never touched upon the issue of resisting arrest when the arrestee thinks the police officer is acting without probable cause. What was at issue in *French* was the distinction between resisting arrest and the right of self-defense which would allow an individual to protect him/herself in the extreme situation where the arresting officer uses force which is so excessive that it will result in death or serious bodily harm. When the Court in *French* made reference to unlawful conduct on part of the police, the reference was to the unlawful use of excessive/deadly force in making the arrest, and not to the unlawfulness or lack of probable cause for the arrest. The defendant in *French* never contested the legality of her arrest. Rather, she argued that her attack on the Officer was justified in an effort to stop him from using excessive force in placing her boyfriend under arrest. The Court in

French was attempting to clarify that fine line between resisting arrest and self-defense.

An arrestee's use of force in self protection is justified when the arrestee reasonably believes that such force is immediately necessary to protect against an arresting officer's use of unlawful and deadly force, i.e., force which is readily capable of causing death or serious bodily injury. An arresting officer's use of excessive force capable of causing less than serious bodily injury or death can be vindicated by recourse to subsequent legal remedies. * * * The holding of *French* is limited to those rare instances when an arrestee reasonably believes it necessary to defend him/herself against the unnecessary use of unlawfully excessive or deadly force by the arresting officer.

We reverse only that part of the Order of the Superior Court which affirmed the conviction for resisting arrest. We affirm the remaining portion of the Superior Court Order which affirmed the conviction for aggravated assault and reversed the convictions for disorderly conduct, public drunkenness, prohibited offensive weapons and possession of a small amount of marijuana. Accordingly, the judgment of sentence is vacated and the matter is remanded to the trial court for the imposition of sentence consistent with this opinion.

Note

In People v. Curtis, 70 Cal.2d 347, 74 Cal.Rptr. 713, 450 P.2d 33 (1969), the defendant was arrested for burglary by an officer who had only a cursory description of the suspect. A violent struggle ensued, in which both the defendant and the arresting officer were injured. Defendant was subsequently acquitted on the burglary charge, but he was convicted of "battery on a peace officer engaged in the performance of his duties," a felony in California. Section 834a of the California Penal Code provides that "If a person has knowledge, or by the exercise of reasonable care, should have knowledge, that he is being arrested by a peace officer, it is the duty of such person to refrain from using force or any weapon to resist such arrest."

The California Supreme Court held that Section 834 is constitutional, and that it barred forcible resistance to unlawful as well as lawful arrests. Accordingly, the defendant could be convicted of a misdemeanor battery for using force to resist an unlawful arrest. The court held that he was not guilty of the felony charge, because the officer was not "engaged in the performance of his duties" if he was making an unlawful arrest. The result, in short, was a compromise: The unlawfulness of the arrest did not justify or excuse the use of force, but it reduced the charge from a felony to a misdemeanor.

The Model Penal Code

Section 3.04. Use of Force in Self-Protection

(1) Use of Force Justifiable for Protection of the Person. Subject to the provisions of this Section and of Section 3.09, the use of force upon or toward another person is justifiable when the actor believes that such force is immediately necessary for the purpose of protecting himself against the use of unlawful force by such other person on the present occasion.

(2) Limitations on Justifying Necessity for Use of Force

(a) The use of force is not justifiable under this Section:

(i) to resist an arrest which the actor knows is being made by a peace officer, although the arrest is unlawful; * * *

(b) The use of deadly force is not justifiable under this Section unless the actor believes that such force is necessary to protect himself against death, serious bodily harm, kidnapping or sexual intercourse compelled by force or threat; nor is it justifiable if:

(i) the actor, with the purpose of causing death or serious bodily harm, provoked the use of force against himself in the same encounter;[a] or

(ii) the actor knows that he can avoid the necessity of using such force with complete safety by retreating or by surrendering possession of a thing to a person asserting a claim of right thereto or by complying with a demand that he abstain from any action which he has no duty to take, except that:

(A) the actor is not obliged to retreat from his dwelling or place of work, unless he was the initial aggressor or is assailed in his place of work by another person whose place of work the actor knows it to be; and

(B) a public officer justified in using force in the performance of his duties or a person justified in using force in his assistance or a person justified in using force in making an arrest or preventing an escape is not obliged to desist from efforts to perform such duty, effect such arrest or prevent such escape because of resistance or threatened resistance by or on behalf of the person against whom such action is directed.

(c) Except as required by paragraphs (a) and (b) of this Subsection, a person employing protective force may estimate the necessity thereof under the circumstances as he believes them to be when the force is used, without retreating, surrendering possession, doing any

a. "The typical case to be imagined is this: A attacks B with his fists; B defends himself and knocks A down, then starts to batter A's head savagely against the floor. A manages to rise and, since B is still attacking him and A now reasonably fears that if he is thrown again he will be killed, he uses a knife. B is killed or seriously wounded.

"If no special rule is devised for the case, the solution under the Code provisions is as follows:

"B is entitled to defend himself against A's attack but only to the extent of using moderate, non-deadly force. He exceeds the bounds of necessary force, however, when, reducing A to helplessness he batters his head on the floor. Since this excessive force is, in its turn, unlawful, A is entitled to defend himself against it and, if he believes that he is then in danger of death or serious bodily harm without apparent opportunity for safe retreat, to use his knife in self-protection. Thus A is criminally liable for his initial battery on B but not for the ultimate homicide or wounding."

Model Penal Code Commentary 21 (Tent. Draft No. 8, 1958).

other act which he has no legal duty to do or abstaining from any lawful action.

(3) Use of Confinement as Protective Force. The justification afforded by this Section extends to the use of confinement as protective force only if the actor takes all reasonable measures to terminate the confinement as soon as he knows that he safely can, unless the person confined has been arrested on a charge of crime.

Section 3.05. Use of Force for the Protection of Other Persons

(1) Subject to the provisions of this Section and of Section 3.09, the use of force upon or toward the person of another is justifiable to protect a third person when:

(a) the actor would be justified under Section 3.04 in using such force to protect himself against the injury he believes to be threatened to the person whom he seeks to protect; and

(b) under the circumstances as the actor believes them to be, the person whom he seeks to protect would be justified in using such protective force; and

(c) the actor believes that his intervention is necessary for the protection of such other person.

(2) Notwithstanding Subsection (1) of this Section:

(a) when the actor would be obliged under Section 3.04 to retreat, to surrender the possession of a thing or to comply with a demand before using force in self-protection, he is not obliged to do so before using force for the protection of another person, unless he knows that he can thereby secure the complete safety of such other person; and

(b) when the person whom the actor seeks to protect would be obliged under Section 3.04 to retreat, to surrender the possession of a thing or to comply with a demand if he knew that he could obtain complete safety by so doing, the actor is obliged to try to cause him to do so before using force in his protection if the actor knows that he can obtain complete safety in that way; and

(c) neither the actor nor the person whom he seeks to protect is obliged to retreat when in the other's dwelling or place of work to any greater extent than in his own.

Section 3.09. Mistake of Law as to Unlawfulness of Force or Legality of Arrest; Reckless or Negligent Use of Otherwise Justifiable Force; Reckless or Negligent Injury or Risk of Injury to Innocent Persons

(1) The justification afforded by Sections 3.04 to 3.07, inclusive, is unavailable when:

(a) the actor's belief in the unlawfulness of the force or conduct against which he employs protective force or his belief in the lawfulness of an arrest which he endeavors to effect by force is erroneous; and

(b) his error is due to ignorance or mistake as to the provisions of the Code, any other provision of the criminal law or the law governing the legality of an arrest or search.

(2) When the actor believes that the use of force upon or toward the person of another is necessary for any of the purposes for which such belief would establish a justification under Sections 3.03 to 3.08 but the actor is reckless or negligent in having such belief or in acquiring or failing to acquire any knowledge or belief which is material to the justifiability of his use of force, the justification afforded by those Sections is unavailable in a prosecution for an offense for which recklessness or negligence, as the case may be, suffices to establish culpability.

(3) When the actor is justified under Sections 3.03 to 3.08 in using force upon or toward the person of another but he recklessly or negligently injures or creates a risk of injury to innocent persons, the justification afforded by those Sections is unavailable in a prosecution for such recklessness or negligence towards innocent persons.

Section 3.11. Definitions

In this Article, unless a different meaning plainly is required:

(1) "unlawful force" means force, including confinement, which is employed without the consent of the person against whom it is directed and the employment of which constitutes an offense or actionable tort or would constitute such offense or tort except for a defense (such as the absence of intent, negligence, or mental capacity; duress; youth; or diplomatic status) not amounting to a privilege to use the force. Assent constitutes consent, within the meaning of this Section, whether or not it otherwise is legally effective, except assent to the infliction of death or serious bodily harm.[b]

(2) "deadly force" means force which the actor uses with the purpose of causing or which he knows to create a substantial risk of causing death or serious bodily harm. Purposely firing a firearm in the direction of another person or at a vehicle in which another person is believed to be constitutes deadly force. A threat to cause death or serious bodily harm, by the production of a weapon or otherwise, so long as the actor's purpose is limited to creating an apprehension that he will use deadly force if necessary, does not constitute deadly force;

b. "The question of consent presents a problem of some difficulty. It is desirable, on the one hand, to exclude from the range of protective force, especially of force employed for the protection of another, most cases in which the person sought to be protected has in fact consented, and this whether or not the law would otherwise give legal effect to the consent. Thus A and B may agree to fight under such conditions that they both are guilty of a crime and that, according to some decisions, they have cross actions for battery against each other, their consent being denied legal effect. Should a third party, knowing the facts, be allowed to intervene against either A or B, as distinguished from using such force against both as may be justified by Section 3.07 to suppress the breach of the peace? Again, a girl below the age of consent is seduced; her consent is ineffective to remove the criminality of her seducer's conduct; she may have an action in tort against him. Should her father be justified in using force against the man if he discovers them in bed? Finally, to take a more dramatic illustration of the problem, if A and B make a murder-suicide pact, A to kill B and then to commit suicide, may a third party, knowing of the pact, use deadly force to prevent A from killing B? It seems clear in point of policy that here the use of deadly force should be permitted." Model Penal Code Commentary 28–29 (Tent.Draft No. 8, 1958).

(3) "dwelling" means any building or structure, though movable or temporary, or a portion thereof, which is for the time being the actor's home or place of lodging.

C. DEFENSE OF PROPERTY AND PREVENTION OF CRIME

PEOPLE v. CEBALLOS

Supreme Court of California, 1974.
12 Cal.3d 470, 116 Cal.Rptr. 233, 526 P.2d 241.

BURKE, JUSTICE.

Don Ceballos was found guilty by a jury of assault with a deadly weapon. Imposition of sentence was suspended and he was placed on probation. He appeals from the judgment, contending primarily that his conduct was not unlawful because the alleged victim was attempting to commit burglary when hit by a trap gun mounted in the garage of defendant's dwelling and that the court erred in instructing the jury. * * *

Defendant lived alone in a home in San Anselmo. The regular living quarters were above the garage, but defendant sometimes slept in the garage and had about $2,000 worth of property there.

In March 1970 some tools were stolen from defendant's home. On May 12, 1970, he noticed the lock on his garage doors was bent and pry marks were on one of the doors. The next day he mounted a loaded .22 caliber pistol in the garage. The pistol was aimed at the center of the garage doors and was connected by a wire to one of the doors so that the pistol would discharge if the door was opened several inches.

The damage to defendant's lock had been done by a 16–year–old boy named Stephen and a 15–year–old boy named Robert. On the afternoon of May 15, 1970, the boys returned to defendant's house while he was away. Neither boy was armed with a gun or knife. After looking in the windows and seeing no one, Stephen succeeded in removing the lock on the garage doors with a crowbar, and, as he pulled the door outward, he was hit in the face with a bullet from the pistol. Stephen testified: He intended to go into the garage "[f]or musical equipment" because he had a debt to pay to a friend. His "way of paying that debt would be to take [defendant's] property and sell it" and use the proceeds to pay the debt. He "wasn't going to do it [i.e., steal] for sure, necessarily." He was there "to look around," and "getting in, I don't know if I would have actually stolen."

Defendant, testifying in his own behalf, admitted having set up the trap gun. He stated that after noticing the pry marks on his garage door on May 12, he felt he should "set up some kind of a trap, something to keep the burglar out of my home." When asked why he was trying to keep the burglar out, he replied, " * * * Because somebody was trying to steal my property * * * and I don't want to come home some night and have the thief in there * * * usually a thief is pretty desperate * * * and

* * * they just pick up a weapon * * * if they don't have one * * * and do the best they can."

When asked by the police shortly after the shooting why he assembled the trap gun, defendant stated that "he didn't have much and he wanted to protect what he did have."

As heretofore appears, the jury found defendant guilty of assault with a deadly weapon. (Pen.Code, § 245.) An assault is "an unlawful attempt, coupled with a present ability, to commit a violent injury on the person of another."

Defendant contends that had he been present he would have been justified in shooting Stephen since Stephen was attempting to commit burglary, that under cases such as United States v. Gilliam, 25 Fed.Cas. p. 1319, No. 15, 205A, defendant had a right to do indirectly what he could have done directly, and that therefore any attempt by him to commit a violent injury upon Stephen was not "unlawful" and hence not an assault. The People argue that the rule in *Gilliam* is unsound, that as a matter of law a trap gun constitutes excessive force, and that in any event the circumstances were not in fact such as to warrant the use of deadly force.

The issue of criminal liability under statutes such as Penal Code section 245 where the instrument employed is a trap gun or other deadly mechanical device appears to be one of first impression in this state, but in other jurisdictions courts have considered the question of criminal and civil liability for death or injuries inflicted by such a device.

At common law in England it was held that a trespasser, having knowledge that there are spring guns in a wood, cannot maintain an action for an injury received in consequence of his accidentally stepping on the wire of such gun. (Ilott v. Wilkes (1820) 3 B. & Ald. 304.) That case aroused such a protest in England that it was abrogated seven years later by a statute, which made it a misdemeanor to set spring guns with intent to inflict grievous bodily injury but excluded from its operation a spring gun set between sunset and sunrise in a dwelling house for the protection thereof.

In the United States, courts have concluded that a person may be held criminally liable under statutes proscribing homicides and shooting with intent to injure, or civilly liable, if he sets upon his premises a deadly mechanical device and that device kills or injures another. [Citations] However, an exception to the rule that there may be criminal and civil liability for death or injuries caused by such a device has been recognized where the intrusion is, in fact, such that the person, were he present, would be justified in taking the life or inflicting the bodily harm with his own hands. * * *

Allowing persons, at their own risk, to employ deadly mechanical devices imperils the lives of children, firemen and policemen acting within the scope of their employment, and others. Where the actor is present, there is always the possibility he will realize that deadly force is not necessary, but deadly mechanical devices are without mercy or discretion. Such devices are silent instrumentalities of death. They deal death and destruction to the innocent as well as the criminal intruder without the slightest warning. * * *

It seems clear that the use of such devices should not be encouraged. Moreover, whatever may be thought in torts, the foregoing rule setting forth an exception to liability for death or injuries inflicted by such devices "is inappropriate in penal law for it is obvious that it does not prescribe a workable standard of conduct; liability depends upon fortuitous results." (See Model Penal Code (Tent. Draft No. 8), § 3.06, com. 15.) We therefore decline to adopt that rule in criminal cases.

Furthermore, even if that rule were applied here, as we shall see, defendant was not justified in shooting Stephen. Penal Code section 197 provides: "Homicide is * * * justifiable * * * 1. When resisting any attempt to murder any person, or to commit a felony, or to do some great bodily injury upon any person; or, 2. When committed in defense of habitation, property, or person, against one who manifestly intends or endeavors, by violence or surprise, to commit a felony * * *." Since a homicide is justifiable under the circumstances specified in section 197, *a fortiori* an attempt to commit a violent injury upon another under those circumstances is justifiable.

By its terms subdivision 1 of Penal Code section 197 appears to permit killing to prevent any "felony," but in view of the large number of felonies today and the inclusion of many that do not involve a danger of serious bodily harm, a literal reading of the section is undesirable. People v. Jones, 191 Cal.App.2d 478, 481, 12 Cal.Rptr. 777, in rejecting the defendant's theory that her husband was about to commit the felony of beating her (Pen.Code, § 273d) and that therefore her killing him to prevent him from doing so was justifiable, stated that Penal Code section 197 "does no more than codify the common law and should be read in light of it." *Jones* read into section 197, subdivision 1, the limitation that the felony be "some atrocious crime attempted to be committed by force." *Jones* further stated, "the punishment provided by a statute is not necessarily an adequate test as to whether life may be taken for in some situations it is too artificial and unrealistic. We must look further into the character of the crime, and the manner of its perpetration. *When these do not reasonably create a fear of great bodily harm,* as they could not if defendant apprehended only a misdemeanor assault, *there is no cause for the exaction of a human life.*"

Jones involved subdivision 1 of Penal Code section 197, but subdivision 2 of that section is likewise so limited. The term "violence or surprise" in subdivision 2 is found in common law authorities, and, whatever may have been the very early common law, the rule developed at common law that killing or use of deadly force to prevent a felony was justified only if the offense was a forcible and atrocious crime. "Surprise" means an unexpected attack—which includes force and violence, and the word thus appears redundant.

Examples of forcible and atrocious crimes are murder, mayhem, rape and robbery. * * *

Burglary has been included in the list of such crimes. However, in view of the wide scope of burglary under Penal Code section 459, as compared with the common law definition of that offense, in our opinion it cannot be said that under all circumstances burglary under section 459 constitutes a forcible and atrocious crime.[2]

Where the character and manner of the burglary do not reasonably create a fear of great bodily harm, there is no cause for exaction of human life or for the use of deadly force. The character and manner of the burglary could not reasonably create such a fear unless the burglary threatened, or was reasonably believed to threaten, death or serious bodily harm.

In the instant case the asserted burglary did not threaten death or serious bodily harm, since no one but Stephen and Robert was then on the premises. A defendant is not protected from liability merely by the fact that the intruder's conduct is such as would justify the defendant, were he present, in believing that the intrusion threatened death or serious bodily injury. There is ordinarily the possibility that the defendant, were he present, would realize the true state of affairs and recognize the intruder as one whom he would not be justified in killing or wounding. We thus conclude that defendant was not justified under Penal Code section 197, subdivisions 1 or 2, in shooting Stephen to prevent him from committing burglary. * * *

Defendant also argues that had he been present he would have been justified in shooting Stephen under subdivision 4 of Penal Code section 197, which provides, "Homicide is * * * justifiable * * * 4. When necessarily committed in *attempting*, by lawful ways and means, *to apprehend* any person for any felony committed * * *." (Italics added.) The argument cannot be upheld. The words "attempting * * * to apprehend" contain the idea of acting for the purpose of apprehending. Here no showing was made that defendant's intent in shooting was to apprehend a felon. Rather it appears from his testimony and extrajudicial statement heretofore recited that his intent was to prevent a burglary, to protect his property, and to avoid the possibility that a thief might get into his house and injure him upon his return.

Defendant * * * does not, and could not properly, contend that the intrusion was in fact such that, were he present, he would be justified under Civil Code section 50 in using deadly force. That section provides, "Any necessary force may be used to protect from wrongful injury the person or property of oneself * * *." This section also should be read in

2. At common law burglary was the breaking and entering of a mansion house in the night with the intent to commit a felony. Burglary under Penal Code section 459 differs from common law burglary in that the entry may be in the daytime and of numerous places other than a mansion house and breaking is not required. For example, under section 459 a person who enters a store with the intent of committing theft is guilty of burglary. It would seem absurd to hold that a store detective could kill that person if necessary to prevent him from committing that offense.

the light of the common law, and at common law in general deadly force could not be used solely for the protection of property. * * *

At common law an exception to the foregoing principle that deadly force could not be used solely for the protection of property was recognized where the property was a dwelling house in some circumstances. "According to the older interpretation of the common law, even extreme force may be used to prevent dispossession [of the dwelling house]." (See Model Penal Code, supra, com. 8.) Also at common law if another attempted to burn a dwelling the owner was privileged to use deadly force if this seemed necessary to defend his "castle" against the threatened harm. Further, deadly force was privileged if it was, or reasonably seemed, necessary to protect the dwelling against a burglar.

Here we are not concerned with dispossession or burning of a dwelling, and, as heretofore concluded, the asserted burglary in this case was not of such a character as to warrant the use of deadly force.

We conclude that as a matter of law the exception to the rule of liability for injuries inflicted by a deadly mechanical device does not apply under the circumstances here appearing. * * *

The judgment is affirmed.

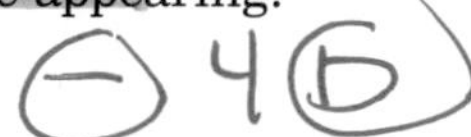

STATE v. WEDDELL

Supreme Court of Nevada, 2001.
27 P.3d 450.

AGOSTI, J.

In this case, we are asked to determine whether a private person may use deadly force in making what is commonly referred to as a citizen's arrest. Respondent Rolland P. Weddell contends that private persons have a common law right to use whatever force is necessary, including deadly force, to accomplish the arrest of and/or prevent the escape of a fleeing felon. We reject Weddell's contention for several reasons. Primarily, we conclude that the legislature indicated its disapproval of the use of deadly force by private persons when it repealed NRS 200.160(3) in 1993 and at the same time enacted NRS 171.1455. NRS 200.160(3) had been a codification of the common law fleeing felon rule. NRS 171.1455 limits the use of deadly force by police officers when making or attempting a felony arrest.[3] Furthermore, in enacting NRS 171.1455, which restricts an officer's use of deadly force and circumscribes the application of the common law fleeing felon rule to law enforcement, the legislature has disavowed the unbridled use of deadly force. We also note that the policies supporting the fleeing felon rule

3. NRS 171.1455 reads as follows:

If necessary to prevent escape, an officer may, after giving a warning, if feasible, use deadly force to effect the arrest of a person only if there is probable cause to believe that the person:

1. Has committed a felony which involves the infliction or threat of serious bodily harm or the use of deadly force; or

2. Poses a threat of serious bodily harm to the officer or to others.

have been eroded as a result of modern, more arbitrary distinctions between misdemeanors and felonies.

With these considerations in mind, we hold that a private person, when arresting another person pursuant to NRS 171.126, may use no more force than is necessary and reasonable to secure the arrest. We further hold that deadly force is, as a matter of law, unreasonable, unless the deadly force is used in defense of self or others against a threat of serious bodily injury.

Facts

Weddell operates a construction business in Carson City. On the evening of October 16, 1997, a person, whom Weddell believes was James Bustamonte, was a passenger in a late-model Chevrolet Blazer that entered his business's grounds. Not recognizing the truck, John Cole, an employee of Weddell, approached it. As he did, the truck accelerated, turned toward Cole, and struck him. The passenger threatened Cole and asked about Weddell's daughter's whereabouts. Although dazed, Cole was able to relate the incident to the police and Weddell, and was able to report a partial license plate number for the truck.

By the next day, Weddell learned that the Bustamonte brothers were looking for Weddell's daughter regarding an alleged drug transaction. Weddell learned the Bustamontes' address from his daughter and provided it to a detective at the Carson City Sheriff's Office. Unsatisfied with the detective's response, Weddell proceeded to the address. When he noticed that there was a Blazer at the residence which matched Cole's description, Weddell called police dispatch.

After fifteen minutes had passed the police had not arrived. At that time, Bustamonte and a woman exited the house and walked toward the Blazer. Weddell then parked his car behind the Blazer to prevent its departure. While pointing his gun at Bustamonte, Weddell ordered him to place his hands on the hood. After a disputed verbal exchange, Bustamonte turned and ran and Weddell shot at him several times.

Weddell was arrested and charged with assault with a deadly weapon and discharging a firearm at another. After a preliminary hearing, Weddell was bound over to the district court on both counts.

* * *

Discussion

The State contends that the district court erroneously determined that Weddell's use of deadly force to effect a citizen's arrest was permissible under Nevada law. We agree.

Nevada, like many other states, permits a private person to arrest a person suspected of committing a felony. NRS 171.126 provides that a private person may arrest another person in three situations: (1) when an offense was committed or attempted in the arrestor's presence, (2) when the person committed a felony offense although outside the arrestor's presence, and (3) when a felony has in fact been committed and the arrestor has reasonable cause to believe that the person to be arrested has committed it.

Nevada statutes and case law do not address the amount of force permissible to effect an arrest. Some amount of force is necessarily implied in the statute, however, since the act of arresting another would seem to require a modicum of force. This case requires us to determine, as a matter of first impression, what amount of force is allowed under NRS 171.126.

At common law, the fleeing felon rule permitted a private person to use deadly force to apprehend a felon.[6] The use of deadly force was permitted to prevent the commission of a felony or to arrest someone who had committed one. The rule was developed at a time when felonies were only the very serious, violent or dangerous crimes and "virtually all felonies were punishable by death." As the United States Supreme Court noted, " 'Though effected without the protections and formalities of an orderly trial and conviction, the killing of a resisting or fleeing felon resulted in no greater consequences than those authorized for punishment of the felony of which the individual was charged or suspected.' "

Today, however, many crimes which are punished as felonies do not involve dangerous conduct or violence and are not punishable by death. As the United States Supreme Court observed in Tennessee v. Garner, the modern distinction between felonies and misdemeanors is "minor and often arbitrary." For example, a person who works at a voter registration agency and who wears a "Vote for Jane Johnson" button at work is guilty of a felony. A person who steals $255 worth of bedding from a hotel is guilty of a felony. A person who buys $250 worth of food stamps from someone when not authorized to do so is guilty of a felony. These felons, like many others, will not receive the death penalty. Society would not tolerate the use of deadly force to prevent the commission of any of these crimes or to apprehend someone suspected of any of these crimes. The modern arbitrary and expanded classification of crimes as felonies has undermined the rationale for the old common law fleeing felon rule, which, as mentioned, was to prevent the escape of a felon by inflicting the punishment that was inevitably to come.

* * *

The State argues that when the legislature repealed NRS 200.160(3) and simultaneously enacted NRS 171.1455, it meant to eliminate the justified use of deadly force by private persons when arresting a felon.

Weddell argues that private persons have a common law right to use deadly force to arrest a fleeing felon. As such, he contends that the repeal of NRS 200.160(3) and enactment of NRS 171.1455 had no effect on the right to use deadly force.

[I]n repealing NRS 200.160(3), the legislature indicated its disapproval of private persons using deadly force when arresting or attempt-

6. Tennessee v. Garner, 471 U.S. 1, 12, 85 L. Ed. 2d 1, 105 S. Ct. 1694 (1985).

ing the arrest of a person suspected of a felony. In addition, by simultaneously enacting NRS 171.1455 the legislature obviously meant to limit the use of deadly force to police officers and to limit the circumstances under which police officers could employ such force. To conclude otherwise would be unreasonable. The legislature could not have meant to repose what might easily amount to vigilante justice in the hands of private persons while restricting the use of force in making an arrest by those who are charged by law with duties of public safety and protection.[22] By repealing the codification of the fleeing felon rule and leaving the citizen's arrest statute and the defense of others statute intact, the legislature has abrogated the common law fleeing felon rule while at the same time affirming that private persons may perform arrests.

Other jurisdictions similarly provide by statute that a private person may make an arrest, but do not dictate the amount of force that is allowable. While we recognize that some jurisdictions allow the use of deadly force when necessary to prevent the escape of a fleeing felon, we conclude that a rule authorizing arrest by any necessary means contravenes our legislature's clear intent to restrict private persons' use of deadly force as evidenced by its repeal of the former NRS 200.160(3). We also observe that some jurisdictions limit the use of deadly force despite the absence of an explicit legislative mandate to do so.

* * *

Given our legislature's evident disapproval of the fleeing felon doctrine, and given our concern that the rationale for the rule at common law no longer exists, and given the abandonment of this common law rule in other states, we hold that, in securing or attempting an arrest under NRS 171.126, a private person may only use the amount of force that is reasonable and necessary under the circumstances. Further, we hold that the use of deadly force is, as a matter of law, unreasonable, unless the arrestee poses a threat of serious bodily injury to the private arrestor or others. Like the affirmative defense of self-defense, the State bears the burden to prove that the use of deadly force was not reasonable and necessary.

Conclusion

The district court erred by dismissing the information filed against Weddell. Weddell has no absolute common law or statutory right to use deadly force in making an arrest. Weddell's use of deadly force to make an arrest was unreasonable, as a matter of law, unless he was threatened with serious bodily injury to himself or others. Whether Weddell was so threatened is a question of fact reserved for trial. Accordingly, we

22. While enacting A.B. 209, the legislature left intact NRS 171.126, which authorizes private persons to arrest criminal suspects in certain situations. As noted earlier, implied in an arrest is the use of force necessary to secure it. NRS 171.138 expressly permits the breaking of a door or window in order to arrest a concealed suspected felon. We presume that the legislature was aware of these statutes when it enacted A.B. 209.

reverse the district court's order and remand this matter for reinstatement of the information and for trial upon the charges.

The Model Penal Code

Section 3.07. Use Of Force In Law Enforcement

(1) Use of Force Justifiable to Effect an Arrest. Subject to the provisions of this Section and of Section 3.09,[a] the use of force upon or toward the person of another is justifiable when the actor is making or assisting in making an arrest and the actor believes that such force is immediately necessary to effect a lawful arrest.

(2) Limitations on the Use of Force.

(a) The use of force is not justifiable under this Section unless:

(i) the actor makes known the purpose of the arrest or believes that it is otherwise known by or cannot reasonably be made known to the person to be arrested; and

(ii) when the arrest is made under a warrant, the warrant is valid or believed by the actor to be valid.

(b) The use of deadly force is not justifiable under this Section unless:

(i) the arrest is for a felony; and

(ii) the person effecting the arrest is authorized to act as a peace officer or is assisting a person whom he believes to be authorized to act as a peace officer; and

(iii) the actor believes that the force employed creates no substantial risk of injury to innocent persons; and

(iv) the actor believes that:

(A) the crime for which the arrest is made involved conduct including the use or threatened use of deadly force; or

(B) there is a substantial risk that the person to be arrested will cause death or serious bodily harm if his apprehension is delayed.

(3) Use of Force to Prevent Escape from Custody. The use of force to prevent the escape of an arrested person from custody is justifiable when the force could justifiably have been employed to effect the arrest under which the person is in custody, except that a guard or other person authorized to act as a peace officer is justified in using any force, including deadly force, which he believes to be immediately necessary to prevent the escape of a person from a jail, prison, or other institution for the detention of persons charged with or convicted of a crime.

(4) Use of Force by Private Person Assisting an Unlawful Arrest.

a. Reprinted supra, Ch. 5, § B.

(a) A private person who is summoned by a peace officer to assist in effecting an unlawful arrest, is justified in using any force which he would be justified in using if the arrest were lawful, provided that he does not believe the arrest is unlawful.

(b) A private person who assists another private person in effecting an unlawful arrest, or who, not being summoned, assists a peace officer in effecting an unlawful arrest, is justified in using any force which he would be justified in using if the arrest were lawful, provided that (i) he believes the arrest is lawful, and (ii) the arrest would be lawful if the facts were as he believes them to be.

(5) Use of Force to Prevent Suicide or the Commission of a Crime.

(a) The use of force upon or toward the person of another is justifiable when the actor believes that such force is immediately necessary to prevent such other person from committing suicide, inflicting serious bodily harm upon himself, committing or consummating the commission of a crime involving or threatening bodily harm, damage to or loss of property or a breach of the peace, except that:

(i) any limitations imposed by the other provisions of this Article on the justifiable use of force in self-protection, for the protection of others, the protection of property, the effectuation of an arrest or the prevention of an escape from custody shall apply notwithstanding the criminality of the conduct against which such force is used; and

(ii) the use of deadly force is not in any event justifiable under this Subsection unless:

(A) the actor believes that there is a substantial risk that the person whom he seeks to prevent from committing a crime will cause death or serious bodily harm to another unless the commission or the consummation of the crime is prevented and that the use of such force presents no substantial risk of injury to innocent persons; or

(B) the actor believes that the use of such force is necessary to suppress a riot or mutiny after the rioters or mutineers have been ordered to disperse and warned, in any particular manner that the law may require, that such force will be used if they do not obey.

(b) The justification afforded by this Subsection extends to the use of confinement as preventive force only if the actor takes all reasonable measures to terminate the confinement as soon as he knows that he safely can, unless the person confined has been arrested on a charge of crime.

Note

Under Model Penal Code § 3.07, the use of deadly force to effect an arrest is justified only with respect to peace officers and their assistants.

Apparently, a private citizen who shot a fleeing murderer or armed robber would be guilty of a criminal homicide even if a peace officer would have been entirely justified in using deadly force in the circumstances. The Commentary justified this rule on the ground that it is wise public policy to discourage private citizens from shooting at fleeing felons, because private citizens normally have not been trained to use firearms properly and may therefore cause death or injury to innocent persons. Consider in this connection the distinction between "conduct rules" and "decision rules" developed in Meir Dan–Cohen, "Decision Rules and Conduct Rules: On Acoustic Separation in Criminal Law," 97 Harv.L.Rev. 625 (1984). For this purpose, the drafters of the Model Penal Code elected to state a *conduct* rule to discourage the citizenry from using firearms against fleeing felons. But suppose a citizen disobeys the conduct rule, and succeeds in shooting someone who really is a dangerous armed robber? Probably some way will be found to avoid a conviction in these circumstances: The police will not arrest, or the prosecutor will not prosecute, or the grand jury will not indict, or the trial jury will not convict. By some low visibility process, the *decision* rule will be that the citizen escapes conviction. Where the citizen hits an innocent bystander, or a minor offender, prosecution and conviction may follow even though a police officer might be found to have acted on reasonable grounds in the same circumstances. If this speculation is correct, the true "decision rule" under the Model Penal Code for the private citizen will be "act at your peril"—just as at common law.

The limitation on the use of deadly force provided in § 3.07(2)(b)(iv) sparked intense debate within the American Law Institute. The subject is discussed in the Model Penal Code Commentary at pp. 60–62 (Tent. Draft No. 8, 1958):

It is possible, of course, to undertake a more refined analysis and statement of the governing criteria. Professor Henry Hart of the Advisory Committee has suggested, for example, the following as a substitute for paragraph (iv):

(iv) Postponement of the arrest until it can be made with less risk of death or serious bodily harm would be contrary to the public interest for one or more of the following reasons:

First, because the officer is executing a warrant of arrest which there is no reason to believe can be executed with materially less danger of death or serious bodily harm at a later time; or

Second, because the person to be arrested is known to the officer to have a record of conviction of one or more crimes evidencing a lawless readiness to take human life or inflict serious bodily injury wilfully, or a history of association with such persons; or

Third, because there is serious risk that the person to be arrested will cause death or serious bodily harm unless apprehended; or

Fourth, because there is serious doubt that the person to be arrested can be identified if he escapes, and the crime for which the arrest is made or attempted involved conduct evidencing a lawless readiness to take human life or inflict serious bodily harm.

The Reporter's view is that it is desirable to keep the statement of the operative principle as simple as possible. The police must make a practical and often hasty judgment as to whether or not they are dealing with a person who may be a dangerous criminal, in the sense, of a threat to life or limb. They are accustomed to making such judgments and, were the draft adopted, would rarely be prosecuted when such a judgment was in fact made. Hence the Reporter recommends that the principal formulation be adopted.

It should be added that Professor Waite of the Advisory Committee disagrees with any limitation of this kind upon the use of deadly force. His reasons are as follows:

> I am convinced that only through truly effective power of arrest can law be satisfactorily enforced. Obviously until violators are brought before the courts the law's sanctions cannot be applied to them. But effectiveness in making arrests requires more than merely pitting the footwork of policemen against that of suspected criminals. An English director of public prosecutions once explained to me that the English police had no need to carry pistols because (1) no English criminal would think of killing a police officer, and (2) even if a suspected offender should outrun an officer in the labyrinth of London he could be found eventually in Liverpool or Birmingham. As the director put it, if a man offends in his own district everyone knows him; if he goes somewhere else everyone notices him.
>
> None of this is true in this country where fluidity of population and movement far exceeds anything anywhere in England. On the contrary a suspect who eludes arrest when first attempted, especially if he is a minor offender, may not be arrested at all.
>
> For this reason, I myself would carry one provision of this Article to its logical extent, and eliminate others. The Article [Section 3.04(2)(a)(i)] denies a person being arrested any privilege of resistance; he must sacrifice his right of absolute freedom to the public necessities. I believe he should also be denied the privilege of flight. I would require not only his abstention from active resistance, but also the even easier abstention from flight. His preclusion from resistance is made effective by giving the officer authority to use whatever force is needed to overcome that resistance. I would make the preclusion from flight effective by giving the officer authority to utilize necessary force there also.
>
> It should be unnecessary to say that such authorization ought in either case to be limited to situations where the character of the officer as an officer attempting arrest is clearly made known to the fugitive and the use of extreme force is a last resort. I am aware of the possibility that some innocent man resisting, or fleeing from what he justifiably supposes is a criminal attempt of robbery or assault upon him might thus meet shockingly undeserved death. It is a possibility easily conceived, but in actuality not merely improbable; virtually impossible. It is true that fugitives whom the law would not have killed, or even have imprisoned for long, if at all, have been killed in flight, but I am aware of no such case where the fugitive was not in truth a fleeing criminal of some sort who did know that he was fleeing from arrest by a known

police officer. I am convinced therefore that the dangers which can be conjured up are visionary rather than real.

And the danger to socially necessary effective law enforcement is undeniable. As I said at the Institute meeting twenty-five years ago:

> If we pass Subsection (d) we say to the criminal, "You are foolish. No matter what you have done you are foolish if you submit to arrest. The officer dare not take the risk of shooting at you. If you can outrun him, outrun him. * * * If you are faster than he is you are free, and God bless you." I feel entirely unwilling to give that benediction to the modern criminal. That subsection was even less restrictive of effective arrest than the Section here proposed. It was rejected by the meeting, and I believe would be rejected today by the great majority of people who are conversant with the difficulties of effective law enforcement. * * *

D. CONSENT

PEOPLE v. SAMUELS

Court of Appeal, First District, Division 2, 1967.
250 Cal.App.2d 501, 58 Cal.Rptr. 439.

SHOEMAKER, PRESIDING JUSTICE.

Defendant Marvin Samuels was charged by indictment with two counts of conspiracy to violate Penal Code, section 311.2 (preparing and distributing obscene matter); two counts of assault by means of force likely to cause great bodily injury (Pen.Code, § 245); and a final count of sodomy (Pen.Code, § 286). Defendant pleaded not guilty to all charges.

The jury acquitted defendant of sodomy but found him guilty on both charges of conspiracy, one charge of aggravated assault and the offense of simple assault included in the other charge of aggravated assault. The simple assault conviction was subsequently dismissed. The court suspended the imposition of sentence, fined defendant $3,000 and placed him on probation for a period of 10 years. * * *

Defendant Samuels, an ophthalmologist, testified that he recognized the symptoms of sadomasochism in himself, and his primary concern became to control and release his sadomasochistic urges in ways which were harmless. Through his hobby of photography, he participated in the production of several films on the east coast. Three of these films depicted bound individuals being whipped. Defendant wielded the whip in two of the films and acted as the cameraman, producer and director for the third film. He testified that the apparent force of the whippings was "faked" and that cosmetics were used to supply the marks of the apparent beating. Defendant produced one of these films at the trial. * * * [Defendant's cinematic career was interrupted when he sent one of his films to the Eastman Kodak Company for processing, and the Company turned the film over to the police.]

This film, which will henceforth be referred to as the "vertical" film, constituted the basis for the first conspiracy count and the aggravated assault charge. It shows a gagged and naked man strung up in an unfinished room, receiving a beating with whips and lashes administered by * * * defendant. There are marks on the victim's buttocks, the small of his back and further up on his body. The film contained no splices. * * *

Lowell Bradford, Director of the Santa Clara County Laboratory of Criminalistics and a qualified expert, testified that he had extracted certain sections from the "vertical" film by way of color slides which were then made into prints. This film, as above noted, contained no splices. His examination of the prints taken from a "representative area" of the film led him to the conclusion that the camera could not have been stopped so as to allow for the application of cosmetics and that the marks and welts which appeared on the victim during this portion of the film occurred progressively from frame to frame in slow development and were not the result of any retouching. Bradford had made a similar examination of a representative area of the "horizontal" film and had concluded that the welts on the victim had progressively developed during uninterrupted sections of the film without any indication of camera stops during which cosmetics could have been applied. There was no evidence that either the "vertical" or "horizontal" films had been retouched and Bradford was of the opinion that both films truly and correctly represented what was before the camera at the time. Edward Chong, Senior County Photographer, and Rudolph Stohr of the Eastman Kodak Company, were of the same opinion as to the absence of retouching and the accurate depiction of the scene before the camera. * * *

Defendant testified on his own behalf and admitted making both films in his home. The man who had been strung up in the "vertical" film had telephoned defendant after he had let it be known in the San Francisco "underground" that he wanted volunteers for sadomasochistic films to be sent to the Kinsey Institute. Defendant arranged to meet him at the San Jose bus depot and drove him to his Sunnyvale home. After the filming had been completed, defendant drove him back to the bus depot in the "same condition he came in." During the course of the filming, which took some four hours, defendant strung the man up with hospital restraints and struck him lightly with a riding crop, pulling his punches just before striking the man's body. He stopped the camera periodically and applied cosmetics. Defendant had coached the man to move violently so as to make the film seem realistic. * * *

[The Court reversed the conspiracy convictions because California law does not punish the preparation of obscene materials without the intent to distribute or disseminate them, and there was insufficient evidence that defendant had such an intent.]

Defendant's conviction of aggravated assault was based upon the beating depicted in the "vertical" film. Defendant contends that said film should not have been admitted into evidence over his objection that it was not properly authenticated. He also asserts that even if the film was properly admitted into evidence, the prosecution still failed, as a matter of law, to prove the commission of an aggravated, as opposed to a simple assault. We do not agree.

In the instant case, the testimony of Stohr, Chong and Bradford, upon which the People rely, was to the effect that the "vertical" film had not been retouched, showed no use of cosmetics, and accurately represented the scene before the camera. We are satisfied that the testimony of these experts, believed by the jury as demonstrated by its verdict, sufficiently authenticated the film for all purposes and that defendant's contention that it was not established that the entire beating had not been faked and the camera deceived, fails because defendant's evidence only raised a conflict which was decided adversely to him, with the result that the conviction of aggravated assault must be upheld.

Defendant also contends that the consent of the victim is an absolute defense to the charge of aggravated assault and that the trial court erred in instructing the jury to the contrary. This argument cannot be sustained.

Although both parties concede that they were unable to find any California case directly in point, consent of the victim is not generally a defense to assault or battery, except in a situation involving ordinary physical contact or blows incident to sports such as football, boxing or wrestling. (See 1 Witkin, California Crimes, § 171, p. 163, and other authorities therein cited.) It is also the rule that the apparent consent of a person without legal capacity to give consent, such as a child or insane person, is ineffective. (1 Witkin, California Crimes, § 173, p. 165.)

It is a matter of common knowledge that a normal person in full possession of his mental faculties does not freely consent to the use, upon himself, of force likely to produce great bodily injury. Even if it be assumed that the victim in the "vertical" film did in fact suffer from some form of mental aberration which compelled him to submit to a beating which was so severe as to constitute an aggravated assault, defendant's conduct in inflicting that beating was no less violative of a penal statute obviously designed to prohibit one human being from severely or mortally injuring another. It follows that the trial court was correct in instructing the jury that consent was not a defense to the aggravated assault charge. * * * The conviction as to aggravated assault is affirmed. The trial court is directed to vacate and set aside the convictions of conspiracy and the order of probation is vacated with directions to the trial court to reconsider the same in the light of our determination.

The Model Penal Code

Section 2.11. Consent

(1) In General. The consent of the victim to conduct charged to constitute an offense or to the result thereof is a defense if such consent negatives an element of the offense or precludes the infliction of the harm or evil sought to be prevented by the law defining the offense.

(2) Consent to Bodily Harm. When conduct is charged to constitute an offense because it causes or threatens bodily harm, consent to such conduct or to the infliction of such harm is a defense if:

(a) the bodily harm consented to or threatened by the conduct consented to is not serious; or

(b) the conduct and the harm are reasonably foreseeable hazards of joint participation in a lawful athletic contest or competitive sport. * * *

(3) Ineffective Consent. Unless otherwise provided by the Code or by the law defining the offense, assent does not constitute consent if:

(a) it is given by a person who is legally incompetent to authorize the conduct charged to constitute the offense; or

(b) it is given by a person who by reason of youth, mental disease or defect or intoxication is manifestly unable or known by the actor to be unable to make a reasonable judgment as to the nature or harmfulness of the conduct charged to constitute the offense; or

(c) it is given by a person whose improvident consent is sought to be prevented by the law defining the offense; or

(d) it is induced by force, duress or deception of a kind sought to be prevented by the law defining the offense.

E. ENTRAPMENT

UNITED STATES v. RUSSELL

Supreme Court of the United States, 1973.
411 U.S. 423, 93 S.Ct. 1637, 36 L.Ed.2d 366.

MR. JUSTICE REHNQUIST delivered the opinion of the Court.

Respondent Richard Russell was charged in three counts of a five count indictment returned against him and codefendants John and Patrick Connolly. After a jury trial in the District Court, in which his sole defense was entrapment, respondent was convicted on all three counts of having unlawfully manufactured and processed methamphetamine ("speed") and of having unlawfully sold and delivered that drug * * *.

There is little dispute concerning the essential facts in this case. On December 7, 1969, Joe Shapiro, an undercover agent for the Federal Bureau of Narcotics and Dangerous Drugs, went to respondent's home on Whidbey Island in the State of Washington where he met with respondent and his two codefendants, John and Patrick Connolly. Shapiro's assignment was to locate a laboratory where it was believed that methamphetamine was being manufactured illicitly. He told the respondent and the Connollys that he represented an organization in the Pacific Northwest that was interested in controlling the manufacture and distribution of methamphetamine. He then made an offer to supply the defendants with the chemical phenyl–2–propanone, an essential ingredient in the manufacture of methamphetamine, in return for one-half of the drug produced. This offer was made on the condition that Agent Shapiro be shown a sample of the drug which they were making and the laboratory where it was being produced.

During the conversation Patrick Connolly revealed that he had been making the drug since May 1969 and since then had produced three pounds of it.[2] John Connolly gave the agent a bag containing a quantity of methamphetamine that he represented as being from "the last batch that we made". Shortly thereafter, Shapiro and Patrick Connolly left respondent's house to view the laboratory which was located in the Connolly house on Whidbey Island. At the house Shapiro observed an empty bottle bearing the chemical label phenyl–2–propanone.

By prearrangement Shapiro returned to the Connolly house on December 9, 1969, to supply 100 grams of propanone and observe the chemical reaction. When he arrived he observed Patrick Connolly and the respondent cutting up pieces of aluminum foil and placing them in a large flask. There was testimony that some of the foil pieces accidentally fell on the floor and were picked up by the respondent and Shapiro and put into the flask.[3] Thereafter Patrick Connolly added all of the necessary chemicals, including the propanone brought by Shapiro, to make two batches of methamphetamine. The manufacturing process having been completed the following morning, Shapiro was given one-half of the drug and respondent kept the remainder. Shapiro offered to buy, and the respondent agreed to sell, part of the remainder for $60.

About a month later Shapiro returned to the Connolly house and met with Patrick Connolly to ask if he was still interested in their "business arrangement." Connolly replied that he was interested but that he had recently obtained two additional bottles of phenyl–2–propanone and would not be finished with them for a couple of days. He provided some additional methamphetamine to Shapiro at that time. Three days later Shapiro returned to the Connolly house with a search warrant and, among other items, seized an empty 500–gram bottle of propanone and a 100–gram bottle, not the one he had provided, that was partially filled with the chemical.

There was testimony at the trial of respondent and Patrick Connolly that phenyl–2–propanone was generally difficult to obtain. At the request of the Bureau of Narcotics and Dangerous Drugs, some chemical supply firms had voluntarily ceased selling the chemical.

At the close of the evidence, and after receiving the District Judge's standard entrapment instruction,[4] the jury found the respondent guilty

2. At trial Patrick Connolly admitted making this statement to Agent Shapiro but asserted that the statement was not true.

3. Agent Shapiro did not otherwise participate in the manufacture of the drug or direct any of the work.

4. The District Judge stated the governing law on entrapment as follows: "Where a person already has the willingness and the

on all counts charged. On appeal the respondent conceded that the jury could have found him predisposed to commit the offenses, but argued that on the facts presented there was entrapment as a matter of law. The Court of Appeals agreed, although it did not find the District Court had misconstrued or misapplied the traditional standards governing the entrapment defense. Rather, the court in effect expanded the traditional notion of entrapment, which focuses on the predisposition of the defendant, to mandate dismissal of a criminal prosecution whenever the court determines that there has been "an intolerable degree of governmental participation in the criminal enterprise." In this case the court decided that the conduct of the agent in supplying a scarce ingredient essential for the manufacture of a controlled substance established that defense.

This new defense was held to rest on either of two alternative theories. One theory is based on two lower court decisions which have found entrapment, regardless of predisposition, whenever the government supplies contraband to the defendants. United States v. Bueno, 447 F.2d 903 (C.A.5 1971); United States v. Chisum, 312 F.Supp. 1307 (C.D.Cal.1970).[a] The second theory, a nonentrapment rationale, is based on a recent Ninth Circuit decision that reversed a conviction because a government investigator was so enmeshed in the criminal activity that the prosecution of the defendants was held to be repugnant to the American criminal justice system. Greene v. United States, 454 F.2d 783 (C.A.9 1971).[b] The court below held that these two rationales constitute the same defense, and that only the label distinguishes them. In any event, it held that "[b]oth theories are premised on fundamental concepts of due process and evince the reluctance of the judiciary to countenance 'overzealous law enforcement.' " 459 F.2d, at 674, quoting Sherman v. United States, 356 U.S. 369, 381 (1958) (Frankfurter, J., concurring).

readiness to break the law, the mere fact that the government agent provides what appears to be a favorable opportunity is not entrapment." He then instructed the jury to acquit respondent if it had a "reasonable doubt whether the defendant had the previous intent or purpose to commit the offense * * * and did so only because he was induced or persuaded by some officer or agent of the government." No exception was taken by respondent to this instruction.

a. In *Bueno,* an informer in the pay of the government furnished narcotics to defendant, who was charged with selling the same narcotics to a federal agent. The defendant in *Chisum* approached a man named Metzger, whom he knew to be under indictment for counterfeiting, and offered to buy counterfeit money. Metzger introduced him to Larry, who was in fact a Secret Service Agent. Larry supplied defendant with counterfeit money and then arrested him for receiving it.—ed.

b. The defendants in *Greene* had been convicted of selling bootleg whiskey and sentenced to prison. Being incredibly stupid, they did not realize that the man to whom they had sold the whiskey, an undercover federal agent named Courtney, was responsible for their arrest and conviction. Upon their release from prison, they reestablished contact with Courtney and offered to sell him more whiskey. He urged them to go back into bootlegging, bought whiskey, and helped in numerous ways to maintain them in business for over two years. Then he arrested them. The Court of Appeals held that the defense of entrapment was inapplicable because of the defendants' obvious predisposition to commit the offense, but that the Government's involvement with the criminal activity was so pervasive that prosecution should not be allowed.—ed.

This Court first recognized and applied the entrapment defense in Sorrells v. United States, 287 U.S. 435 (1932). In *Sorrells* a federal prohibition agent visited the defendant while posing as a tourist and engaged him in conversation about their common war experiences. After gaining the defendant's confidence the agent asked for some liquor, was twice refused, but upon asking a third time the defendant finally capitulated, and was subsequently prosecuted for violating the National Prohibition Act.

Chief Justice Hughes, speaking for the Court, held that as a matter of statutory construction the defense of entrapment should have been available to the defendant. Under the theory propounded by the Chief Justice, the entrapment defense prohibits law enforcement officers from instigating criminal acts by persons "otherwise innocent in order to lure them to its commission and to punish them." Thus, the thrust of the entrapment defense was held to focus on the intent or predisposition of the defendant to commit the crime. "[I]f the defendant seeks acquittal by reason of entrapment he cannot complain of an appropriate and searching inquiry into his own conduct and predisposition as bearing upon that issue."

Justice Roberts concurred in the result but was of the view "that courts must be closed to the trial of a crime instigated by the government's own agents." The difference in the view of the majority and the concurring opinions is that in the former the inquiry focuses on the predisposition of the defendant, whereas in the latter the inquiry focuses on whether the government "instigated the crime."

In 1958 the Court again considered the theory underlying the entrapment defense and expressly reaffirmed the view expressed by the *Sorrells* majority. Sherman v. United States, 356 U.S. 369 (1958). In *Sherman* the defendant was convicted of selling narcotics to a government informer. As in *Sorrells* it appears that the government agent gained the confidence of the defendant and, despite initial reluctance, the defendant finally acceded to the repeated importunings of the agent to commit the criminal act. On the basis of *Sorrells,* this Court reversed the affirmance of the defendant's conviction. In affirming the theory underlying *Sorrells,* Chief Justice Warren for the Court, held that "[t]o determine whether entrapment has been established, a line must be drawn between the trap for the unwary innocent and the trap for the unwary criminal." Justice Frankfurter stated in a concurring opinion that he believed Justice Roberts had the better view in *Sorrells* and would have framed the question to be asked in an entrapment defense in terms of "whether the police conduct revealed in the particular case falls below standards * * * for the proper use of governmental power."

In the instant case respondent asks us to reconsider the theory of the entrapment defense as it is set forth in the majority opinions in *Sorrells* and *Sherman.* His principal contention is that the defense should rest on constitutional grounds. He argues that the level of Shapiro's involvement in the manufacture of the methamphetamine was so high that a criminal prosecution for the drug's manufacture violates the fundamental principles of due process. The respondent contends that the same factors that led this Court to apply the exclusionary rule to illegal searches and seizures, and confessions, should be considered here. But he would have the Court go further in deterring undesirable official conduct by requiring that any prosecution be barred absolutely because of the police involvement in criminal activity. The analogy is imperfect in any event, for the principal reason behind the adoption of the exclusionary rule was the government's failure to observe its own laws. * * * The government's conduct here violated no independent constitutional right of the respondent. Nor did Shapiro violate any federal statute or rule or commit any crime in infiltrating the respondent's drug enterprise.

Respondent would overcome this basic weakness in his analogy to the exclusionary rule cases by having the Court adopt a rigid constitutional rule that would preclude any prosecution when it is shown that the criminal conduct would not have been possible had not an undercover agent "supplied an indispensable means to the commission of the crime that could not have been obtained otherwise, through legal or illegal channels." Even if we were to surmount the difficulties attending the notion that due process of law can be embodied in fixed rules, and those attending respondent's particular formulation, the rule he proposes would not appear to be of significant benefit to him. For on the record presented it appears that he cannot fit within the terms of the very rule he proposes.

The record discloses that although the propanone was difficult to obtain it was by no means impossible. The defendants admitted making the drug both before and after those batches made with the propanone supplied by Shapiro. Shapiro testified that he saw an empty bottle labeled phenyl–2–propanone on his first visit to the laboratory on December 7, 1969. And when the laboratory was searched on January 10, 1970, two additional bottles labeled phenyl–2–propanone were seized. Thus, the facts in the record amply demonstrate that the propanone used in the illicit manufacture of methamphetamine not only *could* have been obtained without the intervention of Shapiro but was in fact obtained by these defendants.

While we may some day be presented with a situation in which the conduct of law enforcement agents is so outrageous that due process principles would absolutely bar the government from invoking judicial processes to obtain a conviction, the instant case is distinctly not of that breed. Shapiro's contribution of propanone to the criminal enterprise already in process was scarcely objectionable. The chemical is by itself a harmless substance and its possession is legal. While the government may have been seeking to make it more difficult for drug rings, such as that of which respondent was a member, to obtain the chemical, the evidence described above shows that it nonetheless was obtainable. * * *

The illicit manufacture of drugs is not a sporadic, isolated criminal incident, but a continuing, though illegal, business enterprise. In order to obtain convictions for illegally manufacturing drugs, the gathering of evidence of past unlawful conduct frequently proves to be an all but impossible task. Thus in drug-related offenses law enforcement personnel have turned to one of the only practicable means of detection: the infiltration of drug rings and a limited participation in their unlawful present practices. Such infiltration is a recognized and permissible means of apprehension; if that be so, then the supply of some item of value that the drug ring requires must, as a general rule, also be permissible. For an agent will not be taken into the confidence of the illegal entrepreneurs unless he has something of value to offer them. Law enforcement tactics such as this can hardly be said to violate "fundamental fairness" or be "shocking to the universal sense of justice."

Respondent also urges, as an alternative to his constitutional argument, that we broaden the nonconstitutional defense of entrapment in order to sustain the judgment of the Court of Appeals. This Court's opinions in Sorrells v. United States, supra, and Sherman v. United States, supra, held that the principal element in the defense of entrapment was the defendant's predisposition to commit the crime.... We decline to overrule these cases. *Sorrells* is a precedent of long standing that has already been once reexamined in *Sherman* and implicitly there reaffirmed. Since the defense is not of a constitutional dimension, Congress may address itself to the question and adopt any substantive definition of the defense that it may find desirable.

Critics of the rule laid down in *Sorrells* and *Sherman* have suggested that its basis in the implied content of Congress is largely fictitious, and have pointed to what they conceive to be the anomalous difference between the treatment of a defendant who is solicited by a private individual and one who is entrapped by a government agent. Questions have been likewise raised as to whether "predisposition" can be factually established with the requisite degree of certainty. Arguments such as these, while not devoid of appeal, have been twice previously made to this Court, and twice rejected by it, first in *Sorrells* and then in *Sherman*.

We believe that at least equally cogent criticism has been made of the concurring views in these cases.... [It does not] seem particularly desirable for the law to grant complete immunity from prosecution to one who himself planned to commit a crime, and then committed it, simply because government undercover agents subjected him to inducements which might have seduced a hypothetical individual who was not so predisposed. * * *

Sorrells and *Sherman* both recognize "that the fact that officers or employees of the government merely afford opportunities or facilities for the commission of the offense does not defeat the prosecution." Nor will the mere fact of deceit defeat a prosecution, for there are circumstances when the use of deceit is the only practicable law enforcement technique available. It is only when the government's deception actually implants the criminal design in the mind of the defendant that the defense of entrapment comes into play.

* * * The Court of Appeals was wrong, we believe, when it sought to broaden the principle laid down in *Sorrells* and *Sherman*. Its judgment is therefore reversed.

Reversed.

MR. JUSTICE STEWART, with whom MR. JUSTICE BRENNAN and MR. JUSTICE MARSHALL join, dissenting. * * *

In my view, this objective approach to entrapment advanced by the concurring opinions in *Sorrells* and *Sherman* is the only one truly consistent with the underlying rationale of the defense. Indeed, the very basis of the entrapment defense itself demands adherence to an approach that focuses on the conduct of the governmental agents, rather than on whether the defendant was "predisposed" or "otherwise innocent." I find it impossible to believe that the purpose of the defense is to effectuate some unexpressed congressional intent to exclude from its criminal statutes persons who committed a prohibited act, but would not have done so except for the Government's inducements. For, as Mr. Justice Frankfurter put it, "the only legislative intention that can with any show of reason be extracted from the statute is the intention to make criminal precisely the conduct in which the defendant has engaged." Since, by definition, the entrapment defense cannot arise unless the defendant actually committed the proscribed act, that defendant is manifestly covered by the terms of the criminal statute involved.

Furthermore, to say that such a defendant is "otherwise innocent" or not "predisposed" to commit the crime is misleading, at best. The very fact that he has committed an act that Congress has determined to be illegal demonstrates conclusively that he is not innocent of the offense. He may not have originated the precise plan or the precise details, but he was "predisposed" in the sense that he has proved to be quite capable of committing the crime. That he was induced, provoked, or tempted to do so by government agents does not make him any more innocent or any less predisposed than he would be if he had been induced, provoked, or tempted by a private person—which, of course, would not entitle him to cry "entrapment." Since the only difference between these situations is the identity of the tempter, it follows that the significant focus must be on the conduct of the government agents, and not on the predisposition of the defendant.

The purpose of the entrapment defense, then, cannot be to protect persons who are "otherwise innocent." Rather, it must be to prohibit unlawful governmental activity in instigating crime. * * * Whether the particular defendant was "predisposed" or "otherwise innocent" is irrelevant; and the important question becomes whether the Government's conduct in inducing the crime was beyond judicial toleration.

Moreover, a test that makes the entrapment defense depend on whether the defendant had the requisite predisposition permits the introduction into evidence of all kinds of hearsay, suspicion, and rumor—all of which would be inadmissible in any other context—in order to prove the defendant's predisposition. It allows the prosecution, in offering such proof, to rely on the defendant's bad reputation or past criminal activities, including even rumored activities of which the prosecution may have insufficient evidence to obtain an indictment, and to present the agent's suspicions as to why they chose to tempt this defendant. This sort of evidence is not only unreliable, as the hearsay rule recognizes; but it is also highly prejudicial, especially if the matter is submitted to the jury, for, despite instructions to the contrary, the jury may well consider such evidence as probative not simply of the defendant's predisposition, but of his guilt of the offense with which he stands charged.

More fundamentally, focusing on the defendant's innocence or predisposition has the direct effect of making what is permissible or impermissible police conduct depend upon the past record and propensities of the particular defendant involved. Stated another way, this subjective test means that the Government is permitted to entrap a person with a criminal record or bad reputation, and then to prosecute him for the manufactured crime, confident that his record or reputation itself will be enough to show that he was predisposed to commit the offense anyway. * * * In my view, a person's alleged "predisposition" to crime should not open him to government participation in the criminal transaction that would be otherwise unlawful.

This does not mean, of course, that the Government's use of undercover activity, strategy, or deception is necessarily unlawful. Indeed, many crimes, especially so-called victimless crimes, could not otherwise be detected. Thus, government agents may engage in conduct that is likely, when objectively considered, to afford a person ready and willing to commit the crime an opportunity to do so.

But when the agents' involvement in criminal activities goes beyond the mere offering of such an opportunity and when their conduct is of a kind that could induce or instigate the commission of a crime by one not ready and willing to commit it, then—regardless of the character or propensities of the particular person induced—I think entrapment has occurred. For in that situation, the Government has engaged in the impermissible manufacturing of crime, and the federal courts should bar the prosecution in order to preserve the institutional integrity of the system of federal criminal justice. * * *

It cannot be doubted that if phenyl–2–propanone had been wholly unobtainable from other sources, the agent's undercover offer to supply it to the respondent in return for part of the illicit methamphetamine produced therewith—an offer initiated and carried out by the agent for the purpose of prosecuting the respondent for producing methamphetamine—would be precisely the type of governmental conduct that constitutes entrapment under any definition. For the agent's conduct in that situation would make possible the commission of an otherwise totally impossible crime, and, I should suppose, would thus be a textbook example of instigating the commission of a criminal offense in order to prosecute someone for committing it.

But assuming in this case that the phenyl–2–propanone was obtainable through independent sources, the fact remains that that used for the particular batch of methamphetamine involved in all three counts of the indictment with which the respondent was charged—i.e., that produced on December 10, 1969—was supplied by the Government. This essential ingredient was indisputably difficult to obtain, and yet that used in committing the offenses of which the respondent was convicted was offered to the respondent by the government agent on the agent's own initiative, and was readily supplied to the respondent in needed amounts. If the chemical was so easily available elsewhere, then why did not the agent simply wait until the respondent had himself obtained the ingredients and produced the drug, and then buy it from him? The very fact that the agent felt it incumbent upon him to offer to supply phenyl–2–propanone in return for the drug casts considerable doubt on the theory that the chemical could easily have been procured without the agent's intervention, and that therefore the agent merely afforded an opportunity for the commission of a criminal offense.

In this case, the chemical ingredient was available only to licensed persons, and the Government itself had requested suppliers not to sell that ingredient even to people with a license. Yet the government agent readily offered and supplied that ingredient to an unlicensed person and asked him to make a certain illegal drug with it. The Government then prosecuted that person for making the drug produced *with the very ingredient* which its agent had so helpfully supplied. This strikes me as the very pattern of conduct that should be held to constitute entrapment as a matter of law.

It is the Government's duty to prevent crime, not to promote it. Here, the Government's agent asked that the illegal drug be produced for him, solved his quarry's practical problems with the assurance that he could provide the one essential ingredient that was difficult to obtain, furnished that element as he had promised, and bought the finished product from the respondent—all so that the respondent could be prosecuted for producing and selling the very drug for which the agent had asked and for which he had provided the necessary component. Under the objective approach that I would follow, this respondent was entrapped, regardless of his predisposition or "innocence." * * *

STATE v. POWELL

Supreme Court of Hawaii, 1986.
68 Hawaii 635, 726 P.2d 266.

PER CURIAM.

The incidence of thefts and robberies in the vicinity of the intersection of Wilikina Drive and Kamehameha Highway in Wahiawa prompted a police decision to institute a series of "drunk decoy" operations in the area of the reported crimes. Between November of 1984 and March of 1985 officers of the Honolulu Police Department organized such operations on eleven occasions and arrested nineteen individuals. Laverne Powell was arrested on March 21, 1985 when she pilfered a wallet containing nine dollars.

The victim on this occasion was a police officer feigning drunkenness. As he lay on his side in a fetal position with a paper bag containing a beer bottle in his hand, a wallet protruded from a rear pocket of his jeans. That the wallet contained money was rendered obvious by the partial exposure of currency. Several other officers stationed themselves at nearby vantage points and awaited possible criminal activity. Shortly after 11:00 p.m. Laverne Powell walked by the officer posing as a helpless drunkard. She then turned back, approached the apparently vulnerable victim, and stole the wallet planted on his person. Two officers who witnessed the theft sprang from cover and apprehended Ms. Powell as she left the scene. [The trial court granted a pretrial motion to dismiss the theft charge on the ground that the undisputed facts established entrapment.]

"Since the defense is not of a constitutional dimension [the legislature] may address itself to the question and adopt any substantive definition of [entrapment] that it may find desirable." *United States v. Russell,* supra. "The rationale for providing a defense based on entrapment," in the legislature's view, "does not reside in the fact that entrapped defendants are less culpable or dangerous than those who formulate their intent without outside inducement. ... The real basis for the defense ... is a purpose to deter improper conduct on the part of law enforcement officials." HRS § 702–237 (1976), Commentary. The Hawaii Penal Code's definition of "entrapment" therefore focuses "not on the [propensities and] predisposition of the defendant to commit the crime charged, but rather ... on the conduct of ... law enforcement officials." *State v. Anderson,* 58 Hawaii 479, 572 P.2d 159, 162 (1977). And by virtue of HRS § 702–237:

> [i]n any prosecution, it is an affirmative defense that the defendant engaged in the prohibited conduct or caused the prohibited result because he was induced or encouraged to do so by a law enforcement officer, or by a person acting in cooperation with a law enforcement officer, who, for the purpose of obtaining evidence of the commission of an offense....
>
> ....
>
> (b) Employed methods of persuasion or inducement which created a substantial risk that the offense would be committed by persons other than those who are ready to commit it.

Whether the defendant was entrapped or not ordinarily is a matter for the jury to decide. But when "the evidence is undisputed and ... clear" entrapment may be established as a matter of law. Here, the circuit court was neither compelled to choose between conflicting witnesses nor judge their credibility. It ruled on the basis of undisputed testimony elicited from the officer who organized the operation in question. Moreover, the findings rendered by the circuit court are not challenged by the State.

The State nonetheless argues a reversal of the court's ruling is in order because the police were "looking to interrupt ongoing criminal activity" and employed means "reasonably tailored to apprehend those involved in stealing from intoxicated persons." But we are convinced from a review of the record that the police "[e]mployed methods of . . . inducement which created a substantial risk that [theft] would be committed by persons other than those who [were] ready to commit it." HRS § 702–237(1)(b).

That the police were concerned with reports of "thefts and robberies in the area" is not to be disputed. Nor can the decision to organize covert operations be faulted. Yet as the circuit court found, the reported thefts and robberies did not "involve sleeping drunks or thefts of the same nature as the instant case." We would be hard put to contradict the court's further finding that the "drunk decoy" operations were expressly designed to ensnare anyone who would commit theft when "bait money" is placed in plain view and within easy reach.

The stealth and strategy employed here resulted in the apprehension of nineteen persons, including Laverne Powell, for "rolling drunks." Undeniably, the function of law enforcement is the prevention of crime and the apprehension of criminals. Yet, what was reported previously as happening in the vicinity were thefts of a different nature, including robberies. Manifestly, the law enforcement function does not include the manufacturing of crime. Under the circumstances, we would have to agree with the circuit court that the "drunk decoy" operation "created a substantial risk that [theft] would be committed by persons other than those who [were] ready to commit it." HRS § 702–237(1)(b).

Affirmed.

PEOPLE v. BARRAZA

Supreme Court of California, 1979.
23 Cal.3d 675, 153 Cal.Rptr. 459, 591 P.2d 947.

Mosk, J. * * *

Defendant appeals from his conviction on two counts of selling heroin (Health & Saf. Code, § 11352). The first count charged defendant with selling heroin to an undercover narcotics agent of the Los Angeles County Sheriff's Department on August 25, 1975. At trial, the agent testified that defendant sold her a yellow balloon containing heroin for $25 of county-advanced funds. Defendant, testifying in his own behalf, gave a different account of his interaction with the narcotics agent on that date, contradicting her testimony that a sale of heroin had occurred.

Count II charged a second sale of heroin on September 11, 1975; both the female agent and the defendant testified that the agent tried to contact defendant by telephoning the Golden State Mental Health Detoxification Center, where he worked as a patient care technician, several times during the three weeks between the dates of the two alleged heroin sale transactions. On September 11, the agent finally succeeded in speaking to defendant and asked him if he had "anything"; defendant asked her to come to the detoxification center. The two then met at the center and talked for some time—a few minutes according to the agent, more than an hour by the defendant's account.

The agent's version of this encounter described defendant as hesitant to deal because "he had done a lot of time in jail and he couldn't afford to go back to jail and * * * he had to be careful about what he was doing." She further testified that after she convinced defendant she "wasn't a cop," he gave her a note, to present to a woman named Stella, which read: "Saw Cheryl [the agent]. Give her a pair of pants [argot for heroin]. [signed] Cal." The agent concluded her testimony by stating that she then left defendant, used the note to introduce herself to the dealer Stella, and purchased an orange balloon containing heroin.

Defendant described a somewhat different pattern of interaction with the agent at their September 11th meeting. He related that he had asked her to come and see him because he was "fed up with her" and wanted her to quit calling him at the hospital where he worked because he was afraid she would cause him to lose his job. He insisted he told her during their conversation that he did not have anything; that he had spent more than 23 years in prison but now he had held a job at the detoxification center for four years, was on methadone and was clean, and wanted the agent to stop "bugging" him. He testified that the agent persisted in her efforts to enlist his aid in purchasing heroin, and that finally—after more than an hour of conversation—when the agent asked for a note to introduce her to a source of heroin he agreed to give her a note to "get her off * * * [his] back." According to the defendant, he told the agent that he did not know if Stella had anything, and gave her a note which read: "Saw Cheryl. If you have a pair of pants, let her have them."

[The jury found the defendant guilty on both counts. The California Supreme Court reversed the conviction on Count I because of an error in the instructions.]

Defendant urges that his conviction on the second count must be reversed because the trial court erred in failing to instruct the jury sua sponte on the defense of entrapment. His contention requires that we reexamine the entrapment doctrine to determine the manner in which the defense must be raised.

Though long recognized by the courts of almost every United States jurisdiction,[1] the defense of entrapment has produced a deep schism

1. The defense appears to have first been asserted by Eve, who complained, when charged with eating fruit of the tree of knowledge of good and evil: "The serpent beguiled me, and I did eat." (Genesis 3:13.) Though Eve was unsuccessful in asserting the defense, it has been suggested that the defense was unavailable to her because the

concerning its proper theoretical basis and mode of application. The opposing views have been delineated in a series of United States Supreme Court decisions. [The court's discussion of United States v. Russell, Sorrells v. United States, and Sherman v. United States is omitted.] * * *

Commentators on the subject have overwhelmingly favored judicial decision of the issue by application of a test which looks only to the nature and extent of police activity in the criminal enterprise. [Citations] Professor Kamisar observed that only two law review articles in the past 25 years have favored the subjective test. The Model Penal Code has adopted an objective test, and in recent years several state courts have recognized that such a test is more consistent with and better promotes the underlying purpose of the entrapment defense. [Citations] Such support for the position no doubt derives from a developing awareness that "entrapment is a facet of a broader problem. Along with illegal search and seizures, wiretapping, false arrest, illegal detention and the third degree, it is a type of lawless law enforcement. They all spring from common motivations. Each is a substitute for skillful and scientific investigation. Each is condoned by the sinister sophism that the end, when dealing with known criminals or the 'criminal classes,' justifies the employment of illegal means." (Donnelly, Judicial Control of Informants, Spies, Stool Pigeons, and Agent Provocateurs (1951) 60 Yale L.J. 1091, 1111.)

For all the foregoing reasons we hold that the proper test of entrapment in California is the following: was the conduct of the law enforcement agent likely to induce a normally law-abiding person to commit the offense? For the purposes of this test, we presume that such a person would normally resist the temptation to commit a crime presented by the simple opportunity to act unlawfully. Official conduct that does no more than offer that opportunity to the suspect—for example, a decoy program—is therefore permissible; but it is impermissible for the police or their agents to pressure the suspect by overbearing conduct such as badgering, cajoling, importuning, or other affirmative acts likely to induce a normally law-abiding person to commit the crime.

Although the determination of what police conduct is impermissible must to some extent proceed on an ad hoc basis, guidance will generally be found in the application of one or both of two principles. First, if the actions of the law enforcement agent would generate in a normally law-abiding person a motive for the crime other than ordinary criminal intent, entrapment will be established. An example of such conduct would be an appeal by the police that would induce such a person to commit the act because of friendship or sympathy, instead of a desire for personal gain or other typical criminal purpose. Second, affirmative police conduct that would make commission of the crime unusually attractive to a normally lawabiding person will likewise constitute en-

entrapping party was not an agent of the punishing authority. (Groot, The Serpent Beguiled Me and I (Without Scienter) Did Eat—Denial of Crime and the Entrapment Defense, 1973 U.Ill.L.F. 254.)

trapment. Such conduct would include, for example, a guarantee that the act is not illegal or the offense will go undetected, an offer of exorbitant consideration, or any similar enticement.[4]

Finally, while the inquiry must focus primarily on the conduct of the law enforcement agent, that conduct is not to be viewed in a vacuum; it should also be judged by the effect it would have on a normally law-abiding person situated in the circumstances of the case at hand. Among the circumstances that may be relevant for this purpose, for example, are the transactions preceding the offense, the suspect's response to the inducements of the officer, the gravity of the crime, and the difficulty of detecting instances of its commission. We reiterate, however, that under this test such matters as the character of the suspect, his predisposition to commit the offense, and his subjective intent are irrelevant.[5]

On the record of this case the trial court erred in failing to instruct the jury *sua sponte* on the defense of entrapment.[6] Defendant was entitled to such an instruction under the standards set forth in People v. Sedeno (1974) 10 Cal.3d 703, 112 Cal.Rptr. 1, 518 P.2d 913 in which we made clear that a duty to instruct *sua sponte* arises when there is substantial evidence supportive of a defense that is not inconsistent with the defendant's theory of the case.

Though controverted by the People, there is substantial evidence herein supportive of an entrapment defense, even under the subjective test previously followed. Defendant's testimony, if believed, tends to establish that he was a man who, after a long history of drug addiction and criminal behavior, was making a sincere effort to gain control of his life and to function responsibly in his community. He had held a steady job for some four years, during which time he managed to become completely free of heroin use by participating in a methadone maintenance program. His characterization of the course of conduct between himself and the undercover narcotics agent is consistent with his contention that he was a past offender trying desperately to reform himself but was prevented from doing so by an overzealous law enforcement agent who importuned him relentlessly until his resistance was worn down and overcome.

4. There will be no entrapment, however, when the official conduct is found to have gone no further than necessary to assure the suspect that he is not being "set up." The police remain free to take reasonable, though restrained, steps to gain the confidence of suspects. A contrary rule would unduly hamper law enforcement; indeed, in the case of many of the so-called "victimless" crimes, it would tend to limit convictions to only the most gullible offenders.

5. Because the test of entrapment we adopt herein is designed primarily to deter impermissible police conduct, it will be applicable, except for the present defendant, only to trials that have not yet begun at the time this decision becomes final.

6. In view of its potentially substantial effect on the issue of guilt, the defense of entrapment remains a jury question under the new test. However, for the reasons stated by Chief Justice Traynor in his dissenting opinion in People v. Moran (1970) supra, 1 Cal.3d 755, 765–766, 83 Cal.Rptr.411, 463 P.2d 763 three members of this court (Justices Mosk, Tobriner, and Newman) are of the view that claims of entrapment should be exclusively for the trial courts to decide subject to appropriate appellate review. (See also People v. D'Angelo (1977) 401 Mich. 167, 257 N.W.2d 655.)

Further, such a defense is not inconsistent with the defendant's theory on the second count. His defense of denial did not extend to the inculpatory *act* alleged—providing the agent with a note to facilitate her heroin purchase transaction with another—but only to the *intent* with which such act was committed. He claimed only that he did not intend to participate in a heroin sale when he provided the agent with the note. He does not subvert his position in arguing, "and irrespective of my intent, the overzealous law enforcement conduct directed at me constitutes entrapment." Chief Justice Traynor made it clear for this court, without dissent in People v. Perez (1965) 62 Cal.2d 769, 44 Cal.Rptr. 326, 401 P.2d 934 that a defendant need not admit his guilt, or even commission of the act, to raise a defense of entrapment.

In the circumstances of this case the issue of entrapment was not submitted to the jury under any other instructions. Accordingly, the court's error in failing to instruct *sua sponte* on this defense was prejudicial, and the conviction on count II must be set aside.

The judgment is reversed.

[Dissenting opinion omitted.]

Note

In the following passage excerpted from State v. Johnson 127 N.J. 458, 464–65, 606 A.2d 315, 318 (N.J.1992), the New Jersey Supreme Court attempted to summarize the subjective and objective theories of entrapment. Which theory seems to best accommodate both society's interest in identifying and punishing those who commit crimes and the competing interest in protecting the governed from misconduct by those who govern?

"Subjective entrapment concentrates on the criminal predisposition of the defendant wholly apart from the nature of the police conduct. The defense will fail if the defendant was ready and willing to commit the crime. The subjective approach reflects the policy that law enforcement officials should detect existing crime rather than entice the innocent into committing crime. Subjective entrapment protects the unwary innocent but not the unwary criminal.

"In contrast, objective entrapment stresses the wrongfulness of government action without regard to the defendant's criminal predisposition. 'The crucial question, not easy of answer, to which the court must direct itself is whether the police conduct revealed in the particular case falls below standards, to which common feelings respond, for the proper use of government power.' *Sherman v. United States,* 356 *U.S.* 369, 382, 78 *S.Ct.* 819, 825, 2 *L.Ed.*2d 848, 856 (1958) (Frankfurter, J., concurring). Objective entrapment seeks to deter police misconduct, even if the unwary criminal goes free.

"The determinative elements of the respective tests are the defendant's criminal predisposition and the government's conduct. The objective theory focusing on improper police conduct asks whether the government acts would have induced the average law abiding citizen to commit crime. The subjective theory stressing individual culpability asks whether the particular defendant would have committed the crime even without the government inducement. Although many courts purport to espouse either a pure subjective test or a pure objective test, '[a]s a matter of practicality, in many instances the application of the two theories overlap. *People v. Jamieson,* 436 *Mich.* 61, 461 *N.W.*2d 884, 889 (1990).' " [Other citations omitted]

How well does the Model Penal Code resolve the conflict?

The Model Penal Code

Section 2.13. Entrapment

(1) A public law enforcement official or a person acting in cooperation with such an official perpetrates an entrapment if for the purpose of obtaining evidence of the commission of an offense, he induces or encourages another person to engage in conduct constituting such offense by either:

(a) making knowingly false representations designed to induce the belief that such conduct is not prohibited; or

(b) employing methods of persuasion or inducement which create a substantial risk that such an offense will be committed by persons other than those who are ready to commit it.

(2) Except as provided in Subsection (3) of this Section, a person prosecuted for an offense shall be acquitted if he proves by a preponderance of evidence that his conduct occurred in response to an entrapment. The issue of entrapment shall be tried by the Court in the absence of the jury.

(3) The defense afforded by this Section is unavailable when causing or threatening bodily injury is an element of the offense charged and the prosecution is based on conduct causing or threatening such injury to a person other than the person perpetrating the entrapment.

UNITED STATES v. TUCKER

United States Court of Appeals, Sixth Circuit, 1994.
28 F.3d 1420.

SUHRHEINRICH, CIRCUIT JUDGE.

Defendants were indicted for purchasing, and aiding and abetting the purchase of, food stamps in violation of 7 U.S.C. § 2024(b)(1). They moved to dismiss the indictment, claiming that the government's conduct in inducing defendants to commit their crimes was so "outrageous" that it violated their due process rights. [After a hearing before a magistrate, the district court accepted the magistrate's findings and granted the dismissal motion. The government appeals.]

I. Facts

Defendants' indictment arose out of a "reverse sting," i.e., an operation in which the police pose as sellers of contraband, set up deals with would-be buyers under carefully controlled conditions, and arrest the purchasers following the sham sale. The operative in this case, Linda

Hancock, was hired by the United States Department of Agriculture to help "catch a lot of people that had been abusing the food stamp system." Hancock worked on a "commission" of sorts, keeping half the money collected from her sale of food stamps. She was not told whom she should approach, just that she should find people willing to buy the stamps below face value and secretly record the transactions.

In November of 1990, Hancock called defendant Tucker, a friend of more than ten years. Claiming that she was in dire financial need, Hancock told Tucker that she was going to have to sell her family's food stamps in order to provide a "proper Christmas" for her children. After first resisting, Tucker finally purchased the stamps when Hancock later appeared at her beauty salon dressed in a manner suggesting her financial distress. When Hancock asked who else Tucker thought might buy some stamps, Tucker sent Hancock to McDonald, one of Tucker's employees. McDonald also purchased food stamps from Hancock after listening to her tales of ill-health and financial need.[1] * * *

II. The "Due Process" Defense

Defendants argue that this court may, indeed must, undertake an independent, objective assessment of the government's methods in this case and, if we find them to be "outrageous," affirm the district court's decision to dismiss. Before engaging in the highly suspect process of labeling the conduct of a co-equal branch of our government as either "outrageous" or "not outrageous," we are compelled to determine precisely upon what authority we would do so. * * *

In *Russell* [supra, p. 440], the defendant argued that the defense of entrapment should be founded on constitutional principles rather than congressional intent. He argued that the government's involvement in creating his crime, i.e., the means and degree of inducement, was so great "that a criminal prosecution for the [crime] violates the fundamental principles of due process," his predisposition to commit the crime notwithstanding. * * * The Court soundly rejected this argument, stating that "the defense of entrapment * * * was not intended to give the federal judiciary a 'chancellor's foot' veto over law enforcement practices of which it did not approve." * * * The Court, however, went on to note the following:

> While we may some day be presented with a situation in which the conduct of law enforcement agents is so outrageous that due process principles would absolutely bar the government from invoking judicial processes to obtain a conviction, the instant case is distinctly not of that breed. * * * The law enforcement conduct here stops far short of violating that "fundamental fairness, shocking to the universal sense of justice," mandated by the Due Process Clause of the Fifth Amendment. 411 U.S. at 431

1. Several of the magistrate judge's findings of fact relating to the amount of deception employed by the undercover operative in this case were hotly disputed. The magistrate judge resolved these disputes in favor of the defendants on the basis of the credibility of the witnesses. * * *

Since this dicta was uttered, *Russell* has been cited more than two hundred times as authority for a defense based solely on an objective assessment of the government's conduct. Thus, the Court's dicta in Russell spawned the very defense which a majority of Justices in that case sought to foreclose.

Recognizing the internal inconsistency of *Russell*, then-Justice (now Chief Justice) Rehnquist, who had penned the decision in Russell, soon sought to recant its "maybe someday" dicta. In Hampton v. United States, 425 U.S. 484 (1976) (plurality opinion), Justice Rehnquist rejected the defendant's *Russell*-inspired, "due process" defense on the ground that permitting such an objective assessment of the government's conduct, while ignoring the defendant's predisposition, "would run directly contrary to our statement in *Russell*. . . ." Justice Rehnquist elaborated:

> The limitations of the Due Process Clause of the Fifth Amendment come into play only when the Government activity in question violates some protected right of the Defendant. * * * If the result of the governmental activity is to implant in the mind of an innocent person the disposition to commit the alleged offense and induce its commission * * * the defendant is protected by the defense of entrapment. If the police engage in illegal activity in concert with a defendant beyond the scope of their duties the remedy lies, not in freeing the equally culpable defendant, but in prosecuting the police under the applicable provisions of state or federal law.

Thus, "the remedy of the criminal defendant with respect of the acts of Government agents," Justice Rehnquist concluded, "lies solely in the defense of entrapment."

Justice Rehnquist's recantation of his *Russell* dicta, however, failed to gain a majority in *Hampton*. Justices Blackmun and Powell, who joined Justice Rehnquist in *Russell*, wrote separately to say that, although the facts of *Russell* and *Hampton* did not warrant dismissal under due process, they were "unwilling to conclude that an analysis other than one limited to predisposition would never be appropriate under due process principles." *Hampton*, 425 U.S. at 493 (Powell, J., concurring in the judgment).

Justices Brennan, Stewart and Marshall, steadfastly adhering to the "objective" theory of entrapment which had failed to become law in *Sorrells*, *Sherman* and *Russell*, dissented from Justice Rehnquist's plurality opinion in *Hampton*, in part, to state that courts should be able to dismiss indictments "where the conduct of law enforcement authorities is sufficiently offensive, even though the individuals entitled to invoke such a defense might be predisposed." *Hampton*, 425 U.S. at 497 (Brennan, J., dissenting).

Thus, in *Hampton*, five Justices, two in dicta and three in dissent, left open the "objective" defense door which Justice Rehnquist had unlocked in *Russell*. We note, however, that just as Justice Rehnquist's comments in *Russell* were dicta, so too were his comments (and those of Justices Powell and Blackmun) in *Hampton*. * * *

Having concluded that there is no binding authority recognizing defendants' asserted "due process" defense, we look to our sister circuits for persuasive authority. To date, however, only one appellate court has employed *Russell* to bar a prosecution. In United States v. Twigg, 588 F.2d 373 (3d Cir.1978), a government agent suggested to the defendant that they set up a drug manufacturing operation, located a site for the plant, supplied the materials and the know-how as well as the funds to "go into business." The court reversed the defendant's convictions for manufacturing the drugs, stating that "fundamental fairness does not permit us to countenance such actions by law enforcement officials and prosecution for a crime so fomented by them will be barred."

We note, however, that this holding has been disavowed by the Third Circuit on the ground that the *Twigg* court improperly relied on United States v. West, 511 F.2d 1083 (3d Cir.1975), which had been limited by Hampton and other, more recent, Third Circuit opinions. [Citations] Accordingly, we do not consider *Twigg* persuasive on the issue of whether or not a "due process" defense should be recognized.

The other courts of appeals have, like our own circuit, doggedly applied the *Russell* dicta; analyzing and rejecting numerous fact patterns in search of governmental "overreaching" which "shocks the conscience" or violates "fundamental fairness." In recent years, this defense increasingly has been subjected to ridicule, see United States v. Santana, 6 F.3d 1, 3–4 (1st Cir.1993) (defense is the "deathbed child of objective entrapment, a doctrine long since discarded in the federal courts"), and at least one circuit judge has expressly advocated that it be abandoned. See United States v. Miller, 891 F.2d 1265, 1272–73 (7th Cir.1989) (Easterbrook, J., concurring).

The lack of any sound doctrinal basis for a "due process" defense has, in our view, led to unnecessary conflict in the courts of appeals where, although the courts are all-but-unanimous in their results, contradictory standards have evolved. * * *

In sum, there is no binding Supreme Court authority recognizing a defense based solely upon an objective assessment of the government's conduct in inducing the commission of crimes. Nonbinding dicta of the Court, indicating that there may be such a defense, has been recanted by its author * * *. Moreover, this court has recognized the availability of this defense only in dicta because, in every case in which the issue has been raised, the government's conduct has been held not to have been "outrageous." The only case squarely holding that an objective assessment of the government's conduct in a particular case may bar prosecution without regard for the defendant's predisposition has been greatly criticized, often distinguished and, recently, disavowed in its own circuit. * * *

* * * Therefore, we hold that a defendant whose defense sounds in inducement is, by congressional intent and Supreme Court precedent,

limited to the defense of entrapment and its key element of predisposition. Defendants may not circumvent this restriction by couching their defense in terms of "due process" or "supervisory powers." Thus, we reject as a matter of law the theory upon which defendants based their motion to dismiss without regard to the particular facts of their case and without reaching the issue of whether or not those facts can properly be characterized as "outrageous."

To ensure that nothing we have said above is taken as having expressed an opinion as to defendants' claim of entrapment, we address that issue now. The defendants' motions to dismiss raise both the "due process" defense and entrapment as a matter of law. To warrant dismissal before trial on the ground that the defendant was entrapped as a matter of law, this court has held that the undisputed evidence must demonstrate a "patently clear" absence of predisposition. [Citations]

In the present case, although it was not necessary to reach the issue because of the disposition of the "due process" defense, the magistrate judge stated that because of the defendants' "willingness to participate in this scheme, it is not likely that the defendants would be able to mount a successful entrapment defense." The district court further noted that "but for the finding of the Magistrate [regarding the 'due process' defense] and the concurrence of this Court in that finding, it is doubtful that any defense of entrapment would prevent you from being found guilty on those offenses." The district court concluded, however, that entrapment "is something that a jury would have had to determine."

We believe the district court and the magistrate judge were correct to conclude that the question of entrapment in this case should be left to the jury. The evidence in the record before us, taken in the light most favorable to the government, is neither "undisputed" nor "patently clear" regarding whether these defendants were predisposed to commit their crimes. Therefore, the question must be resolved by the jury.

The district court's dismissal of the defendants' indictment is, for the reasons discussed above, REVERSED and this case is REMANDED for trial.

Chapter 6

THE CRIMINAL TRIAL AND APPEAL

A. THE RIGHT TO COUNSEL AND EQUAL TREATMENT

GIDEON v. WAINWRIGHT

Supreme Court of the United States, 1963.
372 U.S. 335, 83 S.Ct. 792, 9 L.Ed.2d 799.

MR. JUSTICE BLACK delivered the opinion of the Court.

Petitioner was charged in a Florida state court with having broken and entered a poolroom with intent to commit a misdemeanor. This offense is a felony under Florida law. Appearing in court without funds and without a lawyer, petitioner asked the court to appoint counsel for him, whereupon the following colloquy took place:

> The COURT: Mr. Gideon, I am sorry, but I cannot appoint Counsel to represent you in this case. Under the laws of the State of Florida, the only time the Court can appoint Counsel to represent a Defendant is when that person is charged with a capital offense. I am sorry, but I will have to deny your request to appoint Counsel to defend you in this case.
>
> The DEFENDANT: The United States Supreme Court says I am entitled to be represented by Counsel.

Put to trial before a jury, Gideon conducted his defense about as well as could be expected from a layman. He made an opening statement to the jury, cross-examined the State's witnesses, presented witnesses in his own defense, declined to testify himself, and made a short argument "emphasizing his innocence to the charge contained in the Information filed in this case." The jury returned a verdict of guilty, and petitioner was sentenced to serve five years in the state prison. Later, petitioner filed in the Florida Supreme Court this habeas corpus petition attacking his conviction and sentence on the ground that the trial court's refusal to appoint counsel for him denied him rights "guaranteed by the Constitution and the Bill of Rights by the United States Government."

Treating the petition for habeas corpus as properly before it, the State Supreme Court, "upon consideration thereof" but without an opinion, denied all relief. Since 1942, when Betts v. Brady, 316 U.S. 455, was decided by a divided Court, the problem of a defendant's federal constitutional right to counsel in a state court has been a continuing source of controversy and litigation in both state and federal courts. To give this problem another review here, we granted certiorari. * * *

The Sixth Amendment provides, "In all criminal prosecutions, the accused shall enjoy the right * * * to have the Assistance of Counsel for his defence." We have construed this to mean that in federal courts counsel must be provided for defendants unable to employ counsel unless the right is competently and intelligently waived. Betts argued that this right is extended to indigent defendants in state courts by the Fourteenth Amendment. In response the Court stated that, while the Sixth Amendment laid down "no rule for the conduct of the states, the question recurs whether the constraint laid by the amendment upon the national courts expresses a rule so fundamental and essential to a fair trial, and so, to due process of law, that it is made obligatory upon the states by the Fourteenth Amendment." In order to decide whether the Sixth Amendment's guarantee of counsel is of this fundamental nature, the Court in Betts set out and considered "[r]elevant data on the subject * * * afforded by constitutional and statutory provisions subsisting in the colonies and the states prior to the inclusion of the Bill of Rights in the national Constitution, and in the constitutional, legislative, and judicial history of the states to the present date." On the basis of this historical data the Court concluded that "appointment of counsel is not a fundamental right essential to a fair trial." It was for this reason the Betts Court refused to accept the contention that the Sixth Amendment's guarantee of counsel for indigent federal defendants was extended to or, in the words of that Court, "made obligatory upon the states by the Fourteenth Amendment." Plainly, had the Court concluded that appointment of counsel for an indigent criminal defendant was "a fundamental right, essential to a fair trial," it would have held that the Fourteenth Amendment requires appointment of counsel in a state court, just as the Sixth Amendment requires in a federal court. * * *

We accept Betts v. Brady's assumption, based as it was on our prior cases, that a provision of the Bill of Rights which is "fundamental and essential to a fair trial" is made obligatory upon the States by the Fourteenth Amendment. We think the Court in Betts was wrong, however, in concluding that the Sixth Amendment's guarantee of counsel is not one of these fundamental rights. * * *

Governments, both state and federal, quite properly spend vast sums of money to establish machinery to try defendants accused of crime. Lawyers to prosecute are everywhere deemed essential to protect the public's interest in an orderly society. Similarly, there are few defendants charged with crime, few indeed, who fail to hire the best lawyers they can get to prepare and present their defenses. That government hires lawyers to prosecute and defendants who have the money hire lawyers to defend are the strongest indications of the widespread belief that lawyers in criminal courts are necessities, not luxuries. The right of one charged with crime to counsel may not be deemed fundamental and essential to fair trials in some countries, but it is in ours. From the very beginning, our state and national constitutions and laws have laid great emphasis on procedural and substantive safeguards designed to assure fair trials before impartial tribunals in which every defendant stands equal before the law. This noble ideal cannot be realized if the poor man charged with crime has to face his accusers without a lawyer to assist him. A defendant's need for a lawyer is nowhere better stated than in the moving words of Mr. Justice Sutherland in Powell v. Alabama:

> The right to be heard would be, in many cases, of little avail if it did not comprehend the right to be heard by counsel. Even the intelligent and educated layman has small and sometimes no skill in the science of law. If charged with crime, he is incapable, generally, of determining for himself whether the indictment is good or bad. He is unfamiliar with the rules of evidence. Left without the aid of counsel he may be put on trial without a proper charge, and convicted upon incompetent evidence, or evidence irrelevant to the issue or otherwise inadmissible. He lacks both the skill and knowledge adequately to prepare his defense, even though he have a perfect one. He requires the guiding hand of counsel at every step in the proceedings against him. Without it, though he be not guilty, he faces the danger of conviction because he does not know how to establish his innocence. 287 U.S., at 68–69.

The Court in Betts v. Brady departed from the sound wisdom upon which the Court's holding in Powell v. Alabama rested. Florida, supported by two other States, has asked that Betts v. Brady be left intact. Twenty-two States, as friends of the Court, argue that Betts was "an anachronism when handed down" and that it should now be overruled. We agree.

The judgment is reversed and the cause is remanded to the Supreme Court of Florida for further action not inconsistent with this opinion.

Reversed.

DOUGLAS v. CALIFORNIA

Supreme Court of the United States, 1963.
372 U.S. 353, 83 S.Ct. 814, 9 L.Ed.2d 811.

MR. JUSTICE DOUGLAS delivered the opinion of the Court. * * *

Although several questions are presented in the petition for certiorari, we address ourselves to only one of them. The record shows that petitioners requested, and were denied, the assistance of counsel on appeal, even though it plainly appeared they were indigents. In denying petitioners' requests, the California District Court of Appeal stated that it had "gone through" the record and had come to the conclusion that "no good whatever could be served by appointment of counsel." The District Court of Appeal was acting in accordance with a California rule of criminal procedure which provides that state appellate courts, upon the request of an indigent for counsel, may make "an independent investigation of the record and determine whether it would be of advantage to the defendant or helpful to the appellate court to have counsel appointed. * * * After such investigation, appellate courts should appoint counsel if in their opinion it would be helpful to the defendant or the court, and should deny the appointment of counsel only if in their judgment such appointment would be of no value to either the defendant or the court." People v. Hyde, 51 Cal.2d 152, 154.

We agree, however, with Justice Traynor of the California Supreme Court, who said that the "[d]enial of counsel on appeal [to an indigent] would seem to be a discrimination at least as invidious as that condemned in Griffin v. People of State of Illinois * * *." In Griffin v. Illinois, 351 U.S. 12, we held that a State may not grant appellate review in such a way as to discriminate against some convicted defendants on account of their poverty. There, as in Draper v. Washington, 372 U.S. 487, the right to a free transcript on appeal was in issue. Here the issue is whether or not an indigent shall be denied the assistance of counsel on appeal. In either case the evil is the same: discrimination against the indigent. For there can be no equal justice where the kind of an appeal a man enjoys "depends on the amount of money he has." Griffin v. Illinois, supra, at p. 19.

In spite of California's forward treatment of indigents, under its present practice the type of an appeal a person is afforded in the District Court of Appeal hinges upon whether or not he can pay for the assistance of counsel. If he can the appellate court passes on the merits of this case only after having the full benefit of written briefs and oral argument by counsel. If he cannot the appellate court is forced to prejudge the merits before it can even determine whether counsel should be provided. At this stage in the proceedings only the barren record speaks for the indigent, and, unless the printed pages show that an injustice has been committed, he is forced to go without a champion on appeal. Any real chance he may have had of showing that his appeal has hidden merit is deprived him when the court decides on an *ex parte* examination of the record that the assistance of counsel is not required.

We are not here concerned with problems that might arise from the denial of counsel for the preparation of a petition for discretionary or mandatory review beyond the stage in the appellate process at which the claims have once been presented by a lawyer and passed upon by an appellate court. We are dealing only with the first appeal, granted as a matter of right to rich and poor alike, from a criminal conviction. We need not now decide whether California would have to provide counsel for an indigent seeking a discretionary hearing from the California Supreme Court after the District Court of Appeal had sustained his conviction or whether counsel must be appointed for an indigent seeking review of an appellate affirmance of his conviction in this Court by appeal as of right or by petition for a writ of certiorari which lies within the Court's discretion. But it is appropriate to observe that a State can, consistently with the Fourteenth Amendment, provide for differences so long as the result does not amount to a denial of due process or an "invidious discrimination." Absolute equality is not required; lines can be and are drawn and we often sustain them. But where the merits of the one and only appeal an indigent has as of right are decided without benefit of counsel, we think an unconstitutional line has been drawn between rich and poor.

* * *

[Judgment vacated and case remanded.]

MR. JUSTICE HARLAN, whom MR. JUSTICE STEWART joins, dissenting.

* * *

To approach the present problem in terms of the Equal Protection Clause is, I submit, but to substitute resounding phrases for analysis. I dissented from this approach in Griffin v. Illinois, and I am constrained to dissent from the implicit extension of the equal protection approach here—to a case in which the State denies no one an appeal, but seeks only to keep within reasonable bounds the instances in which appellate counsel will be assigned to indigents.

The States, of course, are prohibited by the Equal Protection Clause from discriminating between "rich" and "poor" *as such* in the formulation and application of their laws. But it is a far different thing to suggest that this provision prevents the State from adopting a law of general applicability that may affect the poor more harshly than it does the rich, or, on the other hand, from making some effort to redress economic imbalances while not eliminating them entirely.

Every financial exaction which the State imposes on a uniform basis is more easily satisfied by the well-to-do than by the indigent. Yet I take it that no one would dispute the constitutional power of the State to levy a uniform sales tax, to charge tuition at a state university, to fix rates for the purchase of water from a municipal corporation, to impose a standard fine for criminal violations, or to establish minimum bail for various categories of offenses. Nor could it be contended that the State may not classify as crimes acts which the poor are more likely to commit than are the rich. And surely, there would be no basis for attacking a state law which provided benefits for the needy simply because those benefits fell short of the goods or services that others could purchase for themselves.

Laws such as these do not deny equal protection to the less fortunate for one essential reason: the Equal Protection Clause does not impose on the States "an affirmative duty to lift the handicaps flowing from differences in economic circumstances." To so construe it would be to read into the Constitution a philosophy of leveling that would be foreign to many of our basic concepts of the proper relations between government and society. The State may have a moral obligation to eliminate the evils of poverty, but it is not required by the Equal Protection Clause to give to some whatever others can afford. * * *

ANDERS v. CALIFORNIA

Supreme Court of the United States, 1967.
386 U.S. 738, 87 S.Ct. 1396, 18 L.Ed.2d 493.

MR. JUSTICE CLARK delivered the opinion of the Court.

We are here concerned with the extent of the duty of a court-appointed appellate counsel to prosecute a first appeal from a criminal conviction, after that attorney has conscientiously determined that there is no merit to the indigent's appeal.

After he was convicted of the felony of possession of marijuana, petitioner sought to appeal and moved that the California District Court of Appeal appoint counsel for him. Such motion was granted; however, after a study of the record and consultation with petitioner, the appointed counsel concluded that there was no merit to the appeal. He so advised the court by letter and, at the same time, informed the court that petitioner wished to file a brief in his own behalf. At this juncture, petitioner requested the appointment of another attorney. This request was denied and petitioner proceeded to file his own brief *pro se.* The State responded and petitioner filed a reply brief. On January 9, 1959, the District Court of Appeal unanimously affirmed the conviction. * * *

The constitutional requirement of substantial equality and fair process can only be attained where counsel acts in the role of an active advocate in behalf of his client, as opposed to that of *amicus curiae.* The no-merit letter and the procedure it triggers do not reach that dignity. Counsel should, and can with honor and without conflict, be of more assistance to his client and to the court. His role as advocate requires that he support his client's appeal to the best of his ability. Of course, if counsel finds his case to be wholly frivolous, after a conscientious examination of it, he should so advise the court and request permission to withdraw. That request must, however, be accompanied by a brief referring to anything in the record that might arguably support the appeal. A copy of counsel's brief should be furnished the indigent and time allowed him to raise any points that he chooses; the court—not counsel—then proceeds, after a full examination of all the proceedings, to decide whether the case is wholly frivolous. If it so finds it may grant counsel's request to withdraw and dismiss the appeal insofar as federal requirements are concerned, or proceed to a decision on the merits, if state law so requires. On the other hand, if it finds any of the legal points arguable on their merits (and therefore not frivolous) it must, prior to decision, afford the indigent the assistance of counsel to argue the appeal.

This requirement would not force appointed counsel to brief his case against his client but would merely afford the latter that advocacy which a nonindigent defendant is able to obtain. It would also induce the court to pursue all the more vigorously its own review because of the ready references not only to the record, but also to the legal authorities as furnished it by counsel. The no-merit letter, on the other hand, affords neither the client nor the court any aid. The former must shift entirely for himself while the court has only the cold record which it must review without the help of an advocate. Moreover, such handling would tend to protect counsel from the constantly increasing charge that he was ineffective and had not handled the case with that diligence to which an indigent defendant is entitled. This procedure will assure penniless defendants the same rights and opportunities on appeal—as nearly as is practicable—as are enjoyed by those persons who are in a similar situation but who are able to afford the retention of private counsel.

* * *

[Judgment reversed and case remanded]

MR. JUSTICE STEWART, whom MR. JUSTICE BLACK and MR. JUSTICE HARLAN join, dissenting.

The system used by California for handling indigent appeals was described by the California Supreme Court in In re Nash, 61 Cal.2d 491:

> We believe that the requirement of the *Douglas* case is met * * * when, as in this case, counsel is appointed to represent the defendant on appeal, thoroughly studies the record, consults with the defendant and trial counsel, and conscientiously concludes that there are no meritorious grounds of appeal. If thereafter the appellate court is satisfied *from its own review* of the record in the light of any points raised by the defendant personally that counsel's assessment of the record is correct, it need not appoint another counsel to represent the defendant on appeal and may properly decide the appeal without oral argument. (Emphasis added.)

The Court today holds this procedure unconstitutional, and imposes upon appointed counsel who wishes to withdraw from a case he deems "wholly frivolous" the requirement of filing "a brief referring to anything in the record that might arguably support the appeal." But if the record did present any such "arguable" issues, the appeal would not be frivolous and counsel would not have filed a "no-merit" letter in the first place.

The quixotic requirement imposed by the Court can be explained, I think, only upon the cynical assumption that an appointed lawyer's professional representation to an appellate court in a "no-merit" letter is not to be trusted. That is an assumption to which I cannot subscribe. I cannot believe that lawyers appointed to represent indigents are so likely to be lacking in diligence, competence, or professional honesty. Certainly there was no suggestion in the present case that the petitioner's counsel was either incompetent or unethical.

But even if I could join in this degrading appraisal of the *in forma pauperis* bar, it escapes me how the procedure that the Court commands is constitutionally superior to the system now followed in California. The fundamental error in the Court's opinion, it seems to me, is its implicit assertion that there can be but a single inflexible answer to the difficult problem of how to accord equal protection to indigent appellants in each of the 50 States.

Believing that the procedure under which Anders' appeal was considered was free of constitutional error, I would affirm the judgment.

Note

Following the Supreme Court's decision in *Anders*, California responded by adopting a new procedure, which was upheld by a 5–4 vote in Smith v. Robbins, 528 U.S. 259 (2000). Under the new procedure, if an indigent's counsel concludes that an appeal is frivolous, he files a brief summarizing the case, including citations of the record. Counsel attests that he has taken several steps, including reviewing the record, explaining his evaluation of the case to his client, providing his client with a copy of the brief, and informing his client of his right to file a *pro se* supplemental brief. Counsel also requests that the appellate court conduct its own independent examination of the record. "Unlike under the *Anders* procedure, counsel * * * neither explicitly states that his review has led him to conclude that an appeal would be frivolous (although that is considered implicit, * * *) nor requests leave to withdraw. Instead, he is silent on the merits of the case and expresses his availability to brief any issues on which the court might desire briefing." Id., 528 U.S. at 265. The appellate court must review the entire case record, and if it finds the appeal frivolous, may affirm, but if it identifies a nonfrivolous issue, it will order briefing. In *Smith v. Robbins*, the Supreme court held that although this procedure varied from the procedure described in *Anders*, it nonetheless satisfied constitutional requirements. The opinion by Justice Thomas emphasized that "the *Anders* procedure is merely one method of satisfying the requirements of the Constitution for indigent criminal appeals," and that in our federalist system states should be left free to "craft procedures that, in terms of policy, are superior to, or at least as good as," the procedure announced in *Anders*. Id. at 276. The Supreme Court concluded that the new California procedure provided indigents with an adequate appellate review that ensured "that those indigents whose appeals are not frivolous receive the counsel and merits brief required by *Douglas*," while protecting the states from subsidizing frivolous appeals. Id. at 277–78.

Justice Stevens argued in dissent that the Court had effectively overruled *Anders*. Justice Souter's dissenting opinion argued that the new California procedure "fails to assure representation by counsel with the adversarial character demanded by the Constitution." Id. at 292.

UNITED STATES v. ELY

United States Court of Appeals, Seventh Circuit, 1983.
719 F.2d 902.

POSNER, CIRCUIT JUDGE.

Ely was apprehended in 1982 and at the arraignment the district judge, after ascertaining that Ely was indigent and wanted counsel, appointed a lawyer named Brady to represent him. Ely requested the judge to appoint another lawyer instead, Bartley, who at Ely's request was in the courtroom. (Both Brady and Bartley are lawyers in private practice.) Ely stated, "Mr. Bartley had represented business of mine at one time and I have—I feel a more closer relationship with Mr. Bartley in understanding what is before me * * *." Although Bartley was willing to accept the appointment and had represented other indigent criminal defendants before the district judge, the judge refused to appoint him to represent Ely: "the Court appoints an attorney for you under the program that this Court has of attorneys on its list and in some relative degree of sequence and frequency. * * * I know that Mr. Brady is [a] thoroughly competent and experienced attorney in this Court. I don't have anything different to say about Mr. Bartley, but we cannot start the practice of allowing defendants to select attorneys to be appointed." * * *

Ely argues that in denying him the counsel of his choice the judge violated the Sixth Amendment. Enacted against the background of the much criticized common law rule that forbade felony defendants to be represented by counsel, the Sixth Amendment removed that bar for federal trials and thus allowed federal criminal defendants to hire counsel—counsel of their choice. But as originally understood, the Sixth Amendment did not require the government to provide a lawyer to a criminal defendant too poor to be able to hire one. Although the Sixth Amendment has, of course, been reinterpreted in modern times to impose such a requirement, the government's constitutional obligation is exhausted "when 'the court appoints competent counsel who is uncommitted to any position or interest which would conflict with providing an effective defense.' "United States v. Davis, 604 F.2d 474, 479 (7th Cir. 1979).

Ely does not argue that Brady was incompetent or had a conflict of interest. Brady was a natural choice to represent Ely, having been his counsel when he was first charged in 1979. Although he preferred Bartley, Ely expressed no dissatisfaction with Brady. It was not that Brady was not good but that Bartley was, in Ely's opinion, better. Our decision in *Davis* approved the district judge's refusal to allow the indigent defendant to choose his own court-appointed counsel. True, Davis had expressed dissatisfaction with four lawyers offered him in lieu of the one he wanted, but as Ely expressed no dissatisfaction with his substitute counsel we do not think *Davis* is a stronger case than this one for denying the indigent the counsel of his choice.

In relation to indigent criminal defendants, the Sixth Amendment seeks not to maximize free choice of counsel but to prevent anyone from being unjustly convicted or illegally sentenced. These are distinct goals. Not only is there no indication that Ely would have fared better with Bartley at his side than with Brady; even if Bartley is the better lawyer, some other indigent criminal defendant might have been denied his assistance had he been appointed in Brady's place.

There are practical reasons for not giving indigent criminal defendants their choice of counsel. Appointed counsel are not paid at munificent rates under the Criminal Justice Act, 18 U.S.C. § 3006A(d); in the Central District of Illinois, in the most recent year for which data are available (1980), the average fee per case under the Act was only $426.31. The best criminal lawyers who accept appointments therefore limit the amount of time they are willing to devote to this relatively unremunerative type of work; some criminal lawyers, indeed, only reluctantly agree to serve as appointed counsel, under pressure by district judges to whom they feel a sense of professional obligation. The services of the criminal defense bar cannot be auctioned to the highest bidder among the indigent accused—by definition, indigents are not bidders. But these services must be allocated somehow; indigent defendants cannot be allowed to paralyze the system by all flocking to one lawyer. The district judge in this case could not, realistically, be required to arbitrate a dispute between Ely and another indigent criminal defendant who wanted to be represented by Bartley.

Neither party presented any evidence regarding the list of attorneys available for appointment that this district judge uses, or, more generally, the supply of lawyers for indigents in the Central District relative to demand. The transcript of the hearing on appointment of counsel for Ely indicates that this judge uses a rotation system for handling the appointment of counsel for indigents. If Ely wanted to show that the judge's refusal to appoint Bartley to represent him nevertheless was unreasonable, he would have to produce evidence to this effect; he failed to produce any. Ely argues, no doubt correctly, that if he were rich he could have hired Bartley. But the government is not responsible for Ely's poverty, and could not, under any reasonable system for the appointment of counsel, rectify all the consequences of the inequality of wealth among criminal defendants. In general, the best criminal lawyers are retained by the most affluent defendants, who pay them on a much more generous scale than under the Criminal Justice Act. The government cannot eliminate the consequences of poverty; it can only limit them, as it did in this case by supplying Ely with the services of competent and experienced legal counsel. * * *

[Conviction affirmed.]

Note

There are two distinct constitutional principles at work in these cases: (1) The "due process" principle that the state must provide an indigent defendant with a lawyer and whatever other resources are absolutely necessary to a fair trial; and (2) the "equal protection" principle, which requires the state to take affirmative steps to narrow the gap between the resources available to rich and poor criminal defendants. The second principle is plainly the more far-reaching, and indeed it appears to promise more than the courts and the rest of society are prepared to deliver. Fees for appointed defense counsel are typically quite low in comparison to the fees private litigants pay their lawyers. The problem is not only one of unwillingness to provide resources, however. As long as rich defendants are allowed to use all the resources at their command to retain the best lawyers and supporting services, it is difficult to see how any realistic program of public assistance could achieve anything like "equality." If we were truly dedicated to achieving this elusive goal, then we would probably have to consider "leveling down," by imposing a ceiling on what the rich can spend or by assigning defense counsel to rich and poor alike by random selection. The measures necessary to achieve equality might in themselves be unconstitutional.

The Supreme Court apparently felt it necessary to invoke the equal protection principle in the cases involving transcripts and counsel on appeal because the Constitution contains no explicit guarantee of a right to appeal. At common law there was no appeal in criminal cases, and the only remedy a convicted defendant had was executive clemency. The Supreme Court has said in *dicta* that the states are under no constitutional obligation to provide for appeal in criminal cases, although all states do. See McKane v. Durston, 153 U.S. 684 (1894). If there is no constitutional right to appeal, then it would seem that there can be no constitutional right to a transcript and a lawyer on appeal. Rather than declare that modern notions of "due process" require that there be appeal in criminal cases, the Supreme Court chose to invoke the expansive equal protection principle. One wonders what the Court would do if a state actually chose to abolish all criminal appeals.

Given the proviso that "absolute equality is not required," what must a state do beyond providing free counsel to indigents at trial and on the first appeal to satisfy the Supreme Court's ban on invidious discrimination against the poor? The Supreme Court has held that a state is not required to provide counsel for an indigent defendant to seek discretionary review in the state supreme court or in the United States Supreme Court, after his conviction has been initially affirmed in the state's intermediate court of appeals. Ross v. Moffitt, 417 U.S. 600 (1974). In its opinion, the Supreme Court observed that denial of appointed counsel at this stage would not deprive the indigent defendant of meaningful access to the state supreme court, because that court could determine whether or not to hear the case on the basis of the brief filed by appointed counsel in the intermediate court, together with the intermediate court's opinion and any supplemental materials that the defendant wished to submit *pro se.* The Court concluded that "The duty of the State under our cases is not to duplicate the legal arsenal that may be privately retained by a criminal defendant in a continuing effort to reverse his conviction, but only to assure the indigent defendant an adequate opportunity to present his claims fairly in the context of the State's appellate process." In dissent Mr. Justice Douglas noted that it would be a relatively easy matter for the attorney who had argued the first appeal to prepare a petition for further discretionary review, and repeated the admonition that "there can be no equal justice where the kind of appeal a man enjoys 'depends upon the amount of money he has.' "

Effective defense representation requires not only a lawyer and a transcript, but also in some cases resources like investigators or expert witnesses. The federal Criminal Justice Act, 18 U.S.C.A. Section 3006A (as amended, 1982), grants the courts discretion to provide such services at government expense upon defense request. State laws also ordinarily provide some such discretionary authority, although of course they do not guarantee that defendants will receive fully adequate resources, especially in comparison to the resources available to the very rich. Free lawyers and other resources are ordinarily provided only to indigents; middle class defendants must pay for their own defense. The State does not pay these costs even if the defendant is found not guilty, and so a defendant may be ruined financially by a criminal prosecution regardless of the outcome.

A defendant has a constitutional right not just to the *appointment* of counsel, but to the *effective assistance* of counsel. This principle was established long ago in the famous decision in Powell v. Alabama, 287 U.S. 45 (1932), in which the defendants were a group of black youths convicted of the capital crime of raping two white girls in Scottsboro, Alabama. In this notorious case the trial court had purported to appoint all the members of the local bar to represent the defendants collectively. The Supreme Court held that, under all the circumstances, the defendants had a constitutional right to the assistance of counsel and that the constitutional requirement was not satisfied by the collective appointment of a number of attorneys, none of whom had any specific responsibility for the case. Many subsequent lower court decisions have reversed convictions on the ground that counsel did not render effective assistance, and some have granted relief to defendants who retained their own counsel as well as defendants represented by court-appointed attorneys. On the other hand, the judicial opinions in this area also recognize that it is impractical to provide every defendant with an outstanding attorney, and that it is easy with the aid of hindsight to question the tactics of even a competent defense attorney in a losing case.

Until recently, most courts would not reverse a conviction for ineffective representation unless the attorney's advocacy was so incompetent as to reduce the proceedings to a "farce and mockery of justice." More recent decisions have dropped this language and said simply that counsel's level of performance must meet "prevailing professional standards." In most jurisdictions the defendant will not prevail unless he can show that the outcome probably would have been different if counsel had performed competently. In Strickland v. Washington, 466 U.S. 668 (1984), the Supreme Court held that "[T]he benchmark for judging any claim of ineffectiveness must be whether counsel's conduct so undermined the proper functioning of the adversarial process that the trial cannot be relied upon as having produced a just result."

Finally, the Supreme Court has held that a defendant has a constitutional right to represent himself when he "voluntarily and intelligently" elects to do so. Faretta v. California, 422 U.S. 806 (1975). In such cases, the judge typically appoints "standby counsel" to advise the defendant and possibly offer some assistance. See McKaskle v. Wiggins, 465 U.S. 168 (1984).

B. PROSECUTOR DISCRETION AND THE CHARGING PROCESS

UNITED STATES v. COX

United States Court of Appeals, Fifth Circuit, 1965.
342 F.2d 167 (en banc).

[A federal grand jury impaneled in the Southern District of Mississippi wished to indict two persons for perjury, but Hauberg, the United States Attorney, refused to prepare the necessary indictments. District Judge Cox ordered Hauberg to prepare and sign such indictments as the grand jury required but Hauberg, under instructions from Acting Attorney General Katzenbach, refused. Judge Cox found Hauberg guilty of contempt of court and ordered Katzenbach to show cause why he should not also be found guilty of contempt. Hauberg, Katzenbach, and the Department of Justice appealed.]

JONES, CIRCUIT JUDGE: * * *

The constitutional requirement of an indictment or presentment as a predicate to a prosecution for capital or infamous crimes has for its primary purpose the protection of the individual from jeopardy except on a finding of probable cause by a group of his fellow citizens, and is designed to afford a safeguard against oppressive actions of the prosecutor or a court. The constitutional provision is not to be read as conferring on or preserving to the grand jury, as such, any rights or prerogatives. The constitutional provision is, as has been said, for the benefit of the accused. The constitutional provision is not to be read as precluding, as essential to the validity of an indictment, the inclusion of requisites which did not exist at common law.

Traditionally, the Attorney for the United States had the power to enter a nolle prosequi of a criminal charge at any time after indictment and before trial, and this he could have done without the approval of the court or the consent of the accused. It may be doubted whether, before the adoption of the Federal Rules of Criminal Procedure, he had any authority to prevent the return of an indictment by a grand jury. There would be no constitutional barrier to a requirement that the signature of a United States Attorney upon an indictment is essential to its validity.

It is now provided by the Federal Rules of Criminal Procedure that the Attorney General or the United States Attorney may by leave of court file a dismissal of an indictment. Rule 48(a) Fed.Rules Crim.Proc. 18 U.S.C.A. In the absence of the Rule, leave of court would not have been required. The purpose of the Rule is to prevent harassment of a defendant by charging, dismissing and recharging without placing a defendant in jeopardy. Rule 7 eliminates the necessity for the inclusion in an indictment of many of the technical and prolix averments which were required at common law, by providing that the indictment shall be a plain, concise and definite written statement of the essential facts constituting the offense charged. The Rule also provides that "It shall be signed by the attorney for the government." Rule 7(c) Fed.Rules Crim. Proc.

The judicial power of the United States is vested in the federal courts, and extends to prosecutions for violations of the criminal laws of the United States. The executive power is vested in the President of the United States, who is required to take care that the laws be faithfully executed. The Attorney General is the hand of the President in taking care that the laws of the United States in legal proceedings and in the prosecution of offenses, be faithfully executed. The role of the grand jury is restricted to a finding as to whether or not there is probable cause to believe that an offense has been committed. The discretionary power of the attorney for the United States in determining whether a prosecution shall be commenced or maintained may well depend upon matters of policy wholly apart from any question of probable cause. Although as a member of the bar, the attorney for the United States is an officer of the court, he is nevertheless an executive official of the Government, and it is as an officer of the executive department that he exercises a discretion as to whether or not there shall be a prosecution in a particular case. It follows, as an incident of the constitutional separation of powers, that the courts are not to interfere with the free exercise of the discretionary powers of the attorneys of the United States in their control over criminal prosecutions. The provision of Rule 7, requiring the signing of the indictment by the attorney for the Government, is a recognition of the power of Government counsel to permit or not to permit the bringing of an indictment. If the attorney refuses to sign, as he has the discretionary power of doing, we conclude that there is no valid indictment. It is not to be supposed that the signature of counsel is merely an attestation of the act of the grand jury. The signature of the foreman performs that function. It is not to be supposed that the signature of counsel is a certificate that the indictment is in proper form to charge an offense. The sufficiency of the indictment may be tested before the court. Rather, we think, the requirement of the signature is for the purpose of evidencing the joinder of the attorney for the United States with the grand jury in instituting a criminal proceeding in the Court. Without the signature there can be no criminal proceeding brought upon an indictment. * * *

If it were not for the discretionary power given to the United States Attorney to prevent an indictment by withholding his signature, there might be doubt as to the constitutionality of the requirement of Rule 48 for leave of court for a dismissal of a pending prosecution.

Because, as we conclude, the signature of the Government attorney is necessary to the validity of the indictment and the affixing or withholding of the signature is a matter of executive discretion which cannot be coerced or reviewed by the courts, the contempt order must be reversed. It seems that, since the United States Attorney cannot be required to give validity to an indictment by affixing his signature, he should not be required to indulge in an exercise of futility by the preparation of the form of an indictment which he is unwilling to vitalize with his signature. Therefore he should not be required to prepare indictments which he is unwilling and under no duty to sign.

Judges Tuttle, Jones, Brown and Wisdom join in the conclusion that the signature of the United States Attorney is essential to the validity of an indictment. Judge Brown, as appears in his separate opinion, is of the view that the United States Attorney is required, upon the request of the grand jury, to draft forms of indictments in accordance with its desires. The order before us for review is in the conjunctive; it requires the United States Attorney to prepare and sign. A majority of the court, having decided that the direction to sign is erroneous, the order on appeal will be reversed. * * *

RIVES, GEWIN and GRIFFIN B. BELL, CIRCUIT JUDGES (concurring in part and dissenting in part):

* * * [T]he basic issue before this Court is whether the controlling discretion as to the institution of a felony prosecution rests with the Attorney General or with the grand jury. The majority opinion would ignore the broad inquisitorial powers of the grand jury, and limit the constitutional requirement of Amendment V to the benefit of the accused.

We agree with Professor Orfield that:

> The grand jury serves two great functions. One is to bring to trial persons accused of crime upon just grounds. The other is to protect persons against unfounded or malicious prosecutions by insuring that no criminal proceeding will be undertaken without a disinterested determination of probable guilt. The inquisitorial function has been called the more important.

Orfield, The Federal Grand Jury, 22 F.R.D. 343, 394. * * *

A federal grand jury has the unquestioned right to inquire into any matter within the jurisdiction involving violations of law and to return an indictment if it finds a reasonable probability that a crime has been committed. This it may do at the instance of the court, the District Attorney, the Attorney General or on its own initiative, from evidence it may gather or from knowledge of its members. * * *

The finding and return of the indictment are the acts of the grand jury. When a United States Attorney prepares and signs an indictment, he does not adopt, approve, or vouch for the charge, nor does *he* institute a criminal prosecution. * * *

The grand jury may be permitted to function in its traditional sphere, while at the same time enforcing the separation of powers doctrine as between the executive and judicial branches of the government. This can best be done, indeed, it is mandatory, by requiring the United States Attorney to assist the grand jury in preparing indictments which they wish to consider or return, and by requiring the United States Attorney to sign any indictment that is to be returned. Then, once the indictment is returned, the Attorney General or the United States Attorney can refuse to go forward. That refusal will, of course, be in open court and not in the secret confines of the grand jury room. To permit the district court to compel the United States Attorney to proceed beyond this point would invest prosecutorial power in the judiciary, power which under the Constitution is reserved to the executive branch of the government. It may be that the court, in the interest of justice, may require a showing of good faith, and a statement of some rational basis for dismissal. In the unlikely event of bad faith or irrational action, not here present, it may be that the court could appoint counsel to prosecute the case. In brief, the court may have the same inherent power to administer justice to the government as it does to the defendant. That question is not now before us and may never arise. Except for a very limited discretion, however, the court's power to withhold leave to dismiss an indictment is solely for the protection of the defendant.

The United States Attorney is under an affirmative and mandatory duty to lend his assistance to a grand jury in making effective its decision to institute a criminal prosecution. When the grand jury insists on finding and returning an indictment, the Attorney General must acquiesce, even though its action may be contrary to the advice of the United States Attorney. The further prosecution of the case is another matter.

We agree that proper enforcement of the law does not require that indictments should be returned in every case where probable cause exists. Public policy may in some instances require that a case not be prosecuted. Such consideration of public policy may be submitted to and acted on by the grand jury. * * * In the few cases in which the United States Attorney is unable to persuade the grand jury and the Attorney General disagrees with its action, his recourse is not to prevent the grand jury from finding and returning an effective indictment but to file a dismissal of the indictment under Rule 48(a), F.R.Crim.P.

For the Attorney General to prevent the grand jury from returning an indictment would, in effect, be to confine the grand jury to returning a mere presentment. That derogates from the grand jury its alternative power to return either "a presentment or indictment." U.S. Const. amend. V. The power of the grand jury cannot be limited in any case to a presentment; it may return an indictment.

Looking beyond the present controversy, one can foresee the grave danger inherent in such a restriction of the powers of a grand jury. If a grand jury is prevented from returning an indictment no more effective than a presentment, the statute of limitations may permanently bar prosecution for the crime. When the presentment is made public, the accused may flee or witnesses may get beyond the jurisdiction of the court. For all practical purposes, the case could be dead and there would be no point in any future Attorney General causing the presentment to be followed by an indictment. Worse still, this could be accomplished in the shadows of secrecy, with the Attorney General not being required to disclose his reasons. How much better is the constitutional system by which the grand jury can find and return an effective indictment upon which a prosecution for crime is instituted. At that point the power of the grand jury ceases. It is effectively checked and overbalanced by the power of the Attorney General, recognized in Rule 48(a), to move for a dismissal of the indictment. The court may then require such a motion to be heard in open court. Instead of a prevention in the shadows of secrecy, there would be a dismissal in a formal, public judicial proceeding.

* * *

By way of precaution, let us state that nothing here said is intended to reflect upon the present Acting Attorney General, in whose integrity we have the utmost confidence. Memory goes back, however, to days when we had an Attorney General suspected of being corrupt. There is no assurance that that will never again happen. We are establishing a precedent for other cases; we are construing a Constitution; we should retain intact that great constitutional bulwark, the institution of the grand jury.

On the cases before the Court, we agree with Judge Brown that the United States Attorney is required, upon the request of the grand jury, to draft forms of indictment in accordance with its desires. There is thus a majority of the Court in favor of that holding. We go further, and think that the United States Attorney is required to sign any indictment that may be found by the grand jury. * * * We would * * * affirm the judgment of civil contempt against the United States Attorney. * * *

[The concurring opinion of Judge John R. Brown is omitted. He argued that the trial court could properly compel the United States Attorney to prepare the indictment, but not to sign it. He reasoned that this middle course would enable the grand jury to express its conclusions in proper legal form. The United States Attorney or Attorney General could still prevent further criminal proceedings by refusing to sign the indictment, but his refusal would be public and the issue would be clearly drawn.]

WISDOM, CIRCUIT JUDGE (concurring specially): * * *

The prosecution of offenses against the United States is an executive function within the exclusive prerogative of the Attorney General. * * *

The reason for vesting discretion to prosecute in the Executive, acting through the Attorney General is twofold. First, in the interests of justice and the orderly, efficient administration of the law, some person or agency should be able to prevent an unjust prosecution. The freedom of the petit jury to bring in a verdict of not guilty and the progressive development of the law in the direction of making more meaningful the guarantees of an accused person's constitutional rights give considerable protection to the individual before and after trial. They do not protect against a baseless prosecution. This is a harassment to the accused and an expensive strain on the machinery of justice. The appropriate repository for authority to prevent a baseless prosecution is the chief law-enforcement officer whose duty, *unlike the grand jury's duty, is to collect evidence on both sides of a case.*

Second, when, within the context of law-enforcement, national policy is involved, because of national security, conduct of foreign policy, or a conflict between two branches of government, the appropriate branch to decide the matter is the executive branch. The executive is charged with carrying out national policy on law-enforcement and generally speaking, is informed on more levels than the more specialized judicial and legislative branches. In such a situation, a decision not to prosecute is analogous to the exercise of executive privilege. The executive's absolute and exclusive discretion to prosecute may be rationalized as an illustration of the doctrine of separation of powers, but it would have evolved without the doctrine and exists in countries that do not purport to accept this doctrine.

This brings me to the facts. They demonstrate, better than abstract principles or legal dicta, the imperative necessity that the United States, through its Attorney General, have uncontrollable discretion to prosecute.

The crucial fact here is that Goff and Kendrick, two Negroes, testified in a suit by the United States against the Registrar of Clarke County, Mississippi, and the State of Mississippi, to enforce the voting rights of Negroes under the Fourteenth Amendment and the Civil Rights Act.

Goff and Kendrick testified that some seven years earlier at Stonewall, Mississippi, the registrar had refused to register them or give them application forms. They said that they had seen white persons registering, one of whom was a B. Floyd Jones. Ramsey, the registrar, testified that Jones had not registered at that time or place, but had registered the year before in Enterprise, Mississippi. He testified also that he had never discriminated against Negro applicants for registration.[20] Jones testified that he was near the registration table in Stonewall in 1955, had talked with the registrar, and had shaken hands with him. The presiding judge, Judge W. Harold Cox, stated from the bench that Goff and Kendrick should be "bound over to await the action of the grand jury for perjury".

In January 1963 attorneys of the Department of Justice requested the Federal Bureau of Investigation to investigate the possible perjury. The FBI completed a full investigation in March 1963 and referred the matter to the Department's Criminal Division. In June 1963, the Crimi-

20. Judge Cox found "as a fact from the evidence that negro citizens have been discriminated against by the registrar", although he found also that there was "no pattern or practice of discrimination". In its original opinion in the Ramsey case this Court noted the "testimony which witness by witness convicts Ramsey of palpable discrimination." United States v. Ramsey, 5 Cir.1964, 331 F.2d 824, 826. In his opinion Judge Rives noted that "This case reveals gross and flagrant denials of the rights of Negro citizens to vote." 331 F.2d at 833. And on rehearing, this Court ruled that the finding that "there was no pattern or practice in the discrimination by the Registrar" was "clearly erroneous." 331 F.2d at 838. No one has suggested that Mr. Ramsey may have been guilty of perjury.

nal Division advised the local United States Attorney, Mr. Hauberg, that the matter presented "no basis for a perjury prosecution". Mr. Hauberg informed Judge Cox of the Department's decision. Judge Cox stated that in his view the matter was clearly one for the grand jury and that he would be inclined, if necessary, to appoint an outside attorney to present the matter to the grand jury. (I find no authority for a federal judge to displace the United States Attorney by appointing a special prosecutor.) On receiving this information, the Criminal Division again reviewed its files and concluded that the charge of perjury could not be sustained. General Katzenbach, then Deputy Attorney General, after reviewing the files, concurred in the Criminal Division's decision. In September 1963 General Katzenbach called on Judge Cox as a courtesy to explain why the Department had arrived at the conclusion that no perjury was involved. Judge Cox, unconvinced, requested the United States Attorney to present to the grand jury the Goff and Kendrick cases, which he regarded as cases of "palpable perjury".

* * *

[A Mississippi state grand jury indicted Goff and Kendrick for perjury for testifying falsely in the federal civil rights case, but the federal Department of Justice obtained an injunction against his prosecution. Judge Cox thereafter caused the federal grand jury to hear witnesses testify regarding the alleged perjury, and the grand jury decided to indict. Acting Attorney General Katzenbach directed the United States Attorney not to prepare or sign the indictments, and this contempt proceeding followed.]

Against the backdrop of Mississippi versus the Nation in the field of civil rights, we have a heated but bona fide difference of opinion between Judge Cox and the Attorney General as to whether two Negroes, Goff and Kendrick, should be prosecuted for perjury. Taking a narrow view of the case, we would be justified in holding that the Attorney General's implied powers, by analogy to the express powers of Rule 48(a), give him discretion to prosecute. Here there was a bona fide, reasonable exercise of discretion made after a full investigation and long consideration of the case—both sides of the case, not just the evidence tending to show guilt. If the grand jury is dissatisfied with that administrative decision, it may exercise its inquisitorial power and make a presentment in open court. It could be said, that is all there is to the case. But there is more to the case.

This Court, along with everyone else, knows that Goff and Kendrick, if prosecuted, run the risk of being tried in a climate of community hostility. They run the risk of a punishment that may not fit the crime. The Registrar, who provoked the original litigation, runs no risk, notwithstanding the fact that the district court, in effect, found that Ramsey did not tell the truth on the witness stand. In these circumstances, the very least demands of justice require that the discretion to prosecute be lodged with a person or agency insulated from local prejudices and parochial pressures. This is not the hard case that makes bad law. This is the type of case that comes up, in one way or another, whenever the customs, beliefs, or interests of a region collide with national policy as fixed by the Constitution or by Congress. It is not likely that the men who devised diversity jurisdiction expected to turn over to local juries the discretionary power to bring federal prosecutions. This case is unusual only for the clarity with which the facts, speaking for themselves, illuminate the imperative necessity in American Federalism that the discretion to prosecute be lodged in the Attorney General of the United States.

* * *

My memory, too, goes back to the days, pointedly referred to by the dissenters, when we had "an Attorney General suspected of being corrupt." But I am not aware that we have had more lawless Attorneys General than lawless juries.

Notes

1. In Inmates of Attica Correctional Facility v. Rockefeller, 477 F.2d 375 (2d Cir.1973) the plaintiffs sought to obtain a court order requiring federal and state officials to investigate and prosecute persons who allegedly had committed criminal acts in connection with the suppression of the uprising at the New York state prison. The Court of Appeals affirmed the dismissal of the action with the following comments:

> In the absence of statutorily defined standards governing reviewability, or regulatory or statutory policies of prosecution, the problems inherent in the task of supervising prosecutorial decisions do not lend themselves to resolution by the judiciary. The reviewing courts would be placed in the undesirable and injudicious posture of becoming "super-prosecutors." In the normal case of review of executive acts of discretion, the administrative record is open, public and reviewable on the basis of what it contains. The decision not to prosecute, on the other hand, may be based upon the insufficiency of the available evidence, in which event the secrecy of the grand jury and of the prosecutor's file may serve to protect the accused's reputation from public damage based upon insufficient, improper, or even malicious charges. *In camera* review would not be meaningful without access by the complaining party to the evidence before the grand jury or U.S. Attorney. Such interference with the normal operations of criminal investigations, in turn, based solely upon allegations of criminal conduct, raises serious questions of potential abuse by persons seeking to have other persons prosecuted. Any person, merely by filing a complaint containing allegations in general terms (permitted by the Federal Rules) of unlawful failure to prosecute, could gain access to the prosecutor's file and the grand jury's minutes, notwithstanding the secrecy normally attaching to the latter by law.
>
> Nor is it clear what the judiciary's role of supervision should be were it to undertake such a review. At what point would the prosecutor be entitled to call a halt to further investigation as unlikely to be productive? What evidentiary standard would be used to decide whether

prosecution should be compelled? How much judgment would the United States Attorney be allowed? Would he be permitted to limit himself to a strong "test" case rather than pursue weaker cases? What collateral factors would be permissible bases for a decision not to prosecute, e.g., the pendency of another criminal proceeding elsewhere against the same parties? What sort of review should be available in cases like the present one where the conduct complained of allegedly violates state as well as federal laws? With limited personnel and facilities at his disposal, what priority would the prosecutor be required to give to cases in which investigation or prosecution was directed by the court?

These difficult questions engender serious doubts as to the judiciary's capacity to review and as to the problem of arbitrariness inherent in any judicial decision to order prosecution. On balance, we believe that substitution of a court's decision to compel prosecution for the U.S. Attorney's decision not to prosecute, even upon an abuse of discretion standard of review and even if limited to directing that a prosecution be undertaken in good faith, would be unwise.

Id. at 380–81.

2. The laws of some states permit a court to appoint a private prosecutor in exceptional cases but in general a prosecutor's decision not to bring charges is controlled only by his own superiors and, in highly visible cases, by public opinion. Even where state law expressly or impliedly permits a private individual to initiate a criminal prosecution without the approval of the public prosecutor, the practice has tended to fall into disuse. In People v. Municipal Court, 27 Cal.App.3d 193, 103 Cal.Rptr. 645 (1972), the court refused to give a "literal" reading to a statute that appeared to allow private prosecution, explaining that it would violate the defendant's right to due process of law as well as the principle of separation of powers to permit a criminal prosecution to proceed without the approval of the District Attorney or Attorney General.

MYERS v. COMMONWEALTH

Supreme Judicial Court of Massachusetts, 1973.
363 Mass. 843, 298 N.E.2d 819.

TAURO, CHIEF JUSTICE.

This is a petition for a writ of certiorari and related relief * * * asking the court to exercise its supervisory power "to correct and prevent errors and abuses" in probable cause hearings conducted in the District Courts of the Commonwealth. The petitioner asks us to vacate a finding of probable cause in the Municipal Court of the Roxbury District and remand the case to that court for a new probable cause hearing consistent with the requirements of G.L. c. 276, § 38, which he alleges were violated in his initial preliminary hearing.

* * *

The pertinent facts may be summarized briefly. On February 23, 1973, a preliminary examination was held * * * before a judge of the Municipal Court to determine whether there was probable cause to support the prosecution of the petitioner on charges of rape, assault by means of a dangerous weapon, breaking and entering at night, and breaking and entering at night and committing rape of a person lawfully therein. At that probable cause hearing, only the complaining witness was called to testify on behalf of the Commonwealth. At the end of direct examination the petitioner's counsel began his cross-examination of the witness. When the petitioner's counsel questioned the complaining witness about her alleged belief in witchcraft, the judge stated that he had heard enough testimony to find probable cause which made further cross-examination by the petitioner's counsel unnecessary. The petitioner's counsel stated to the court that he wished to complete his cross-examination of the complaining witness, and introduce further evidence,[3] in the defendant's behalf. The judge repeated his finding of probable cause and terminated the hearing. The question before us is whether the judge's finding of probable cause before the petitioner had an opportunity to complete cross-examination of the complaining witness and to present relevant testimony and witnesses in his own behalf violated the petitioner's "substantive rights."

1. The rules governing the conduct of preliminary hearings in the Commonwealth are summarily set forth in G.L. c. 276, § 38, "The court or justice before whom a person is taken upon a charge of crime shall, as soon as may be, examine on oath the complainant and the witnesses for the prosecution, in the presence of the defendant, relative to any material matter connected with such charge. * * * *[T]he witnesses for the prisoner, if any, shall be examined on oath, and he may be assisted by counsel in such examination and in the cross examination of the witnesses in support of the prosecution*" (emphasis supplied). The Commonwealth contends that this statute should not be interpreted as granting the defendant an absolute "inflexible" right to cross-examine prosecution witnesses and present testimony in his own behalf at the preliminary hearing because the examining magistrate has the discretion to find probable cause after listening only to the witnesses for the prosecution. The petitioner argues that c. 276, § 38, grants defendants at such hearings *mandatory* fundamental procedural rights to confront their accusers and present testimony in their own behalf.

* * *

2. The judge's chief task at a preliminary hearing is to determine whether the defendant should be bound over for trial in the Superior Court. Defendants are held for trial only if the examining magistrate finds (1) "that a crime has been committed" *and* (2) "that there is probable cause to believe the prisoner guilty." G.L. c. 276, § 42 (and see

3. The petitioner's counsel told the court that he had a witness whom he wanted to present in behalf of the defendant's case, a medical report on the alleged victim which was made by the physician at the Boston City Hospital the morning of the alleged rape, and a psychiatric evaluation of the complaining witness which was conducted by a staff psychiatrist of the Roxbury Court Clinic after a motion requesting such an examination prior to the probable cause hearing had been granted by a judge of that court.

G.L. c. 276, § 41). These two requirements are designed to establish an effective bind-over standard which distinguishes between groundless or unsupported charges and meritorious prosecutions. Thus, the preliminary hearing's primary function is to screen out at this early but critical stage of the criminal process those cases that should not go to trial thereby sparing individuals from being held for trial, and from being unjustifiably prosecuted * * *.

The United States Supreme Court recognized the importance of the preliminary hearing's screening function in Coleman v. Alabama, 399 U.S. 1, where the court held that Alabama's preliminary hearing is a "critical stage" of the State's criminal process at which the accused is entitled to the aid of counsel. "Plainly the guiding hand of counsel at the preliminary hearing is essential to protect the indigent accused against an erroneous or improper prosecution. First, the lawyer's skilled examination and cross-examination of witnesses may expose fatal weaknesses in the State's case that may lead the magistrate to refuse to bind the accused over. Second, in any event, the skilled interrogation of witnesses by an experienced lawyer can fashion a vital impeachment tool for use in cross-examination of the State's witnesses at the trial, or preserve testimony favorable to the accused of a witness who does not appear at the trial. Third, trained counsel [within the limitations of relevancy] can more effectively discover the case the State has against his client and make possible the preparation of a proper defense to meet that case at the trial. Fourth, counsel can also be influential at the preliminary hearing in making effective arguments for the accused on such matters as the necessity for an early psychiatric examination or bail." * * *

Since the examining magistrate's chief task is to determine whether there is sufficient credible evidence to proceed to trial which justifies binding the defendant over, his determination of probable cause to bind over is somewhat analogous in function to the trial court's ruling on a motion for a directed verdict as to whether there is sufficient evidence to send the case to the jury. Unfortunately since this court has never defined the quantum of evidence needed to satisfy probable cause to bind over, some District Court judges have equated probable cause to bind over with probable cause for arrest (and search).

In finding probable cause to arrest, the examining magistrate has determined only that at the time *of the arrest* (or at the time when the warrant for arrest is requested), the "facts and circumstances within * * * [the officers'] knowledge and of which they had reasonably trustworthy information were sufficient to warrant a prudent man in believing that the defendant had committed or was committing an offence." Commonwealth v. Stevens, Mass., 283 N.E.2d 673. In this context, the term "probable cause" means less than evidence which would justify condemnation. Furthermore, such a finding of probable cause may rest upon hearsay evidence which is not admissible in a criminal trial. * * *

A judicial finding of probable cause to arrest validates only the initial decision to arrest the suspect, not the decision made later in the criminal process to hold the defendant for trial. Since many valid arrests are based on reliable hearsay information which could not be introduced at the defendant's trial, probable cause to arrest does not automatically mean that the Commonwealth has sufficient competent legal evidence to justify the costs both to the defendant and to the Commonwealth of a full trial. Therefore the standard of probable cause to bind over must require a greater quantum of legally competent evidence than the probable cause to arrest finding to insure that the preliminary hearing's screening standard is defined in a way that effectuates its purpose. * * *

Since the examining magistrate's determination of the minimum quantum of evidence required to find probable cause to bind over is somewhat analogous in function to the court's ruling on a motion for a directed verdict at trial as to whether there is sufficient evidence to warrant submission of the case to the jury, we have decided to adopt a "directed verdict" rule in defining the minimum quantum of credible evidence necessary to support a bind-over determination.[7] The examining magistrate should view the case as if it were a trial and he were required to rule on whether there is enough credible evidence to send the case to the jury. Thus, the magistrate should dismiss the complaint when, on the evidence presented, a trial court would be bound to acquit as a matter of law. * * *

3. We must construe G.L. c. 276, § 38, in a manner which effectuates its primary purpose of screening out an erroneous or improper prosecution, promotes its ancillary functions and avoids any serious question of constitutional infirmities. The Commonwealth's interpretation of the statute fails in each of these three respects.

The Commonwealth argues that once a prima facie showing of probable cause has been made by prosecution testimony, the examining magistrate can end the hearing before the defendant's attorney has had an opportunity to make a complete cross-examination of the prosecution witness or to present an affirmative defence. We fail to see how such a limited procedure could possibly effectuate the hearing's primary function of screening out cases that should not go to trial. To require such minimal proof of probable cause would render the hearing, in many instances, an empty ritual with a foregone conclusion. If the examining magistrate could simply rest his finding of probable cause on the ipse dixit of the prosecution, there would be little need for defence counsel's presence, let alone the defendant's. * * *

The facts of the instant case provide an excellent illustration of this point. The only witness at the petitioner's probable cause hearing was

7. According to a recent study sponsored by the American Bar Association, this "directed verdict" definition of probable cause is the most common screening standard practiced in other States which have probable cause hearings. See F. Miller, Prosecution: The Decision to Charge a Suspect With Crime (ABA study). See also Graham & Letwin, The Preliminary Hearing in Los Angeles, 18 U.C.L.A. Law Rev. 636 and American Law Institute. A Model Code of Pre–Arraignment Procedure (Tent.Draft No. 5) § 330.5(3) (Model Code). "[Probable] cause to hold the defendant for trial exists * * * when the evidence introduced at the preliminary hearing would support a guilty verdict."

the complaining witness who repeated her accusation that the petitioner had raped her. If the petitioner had been afforded his statutory rights, he would have introduced testimony challenging the complaining witness's credibility and supporting his defence of a consensual sexual relationship.[10] The examining magistrate could not have possibly made an informed judgment on the question of whether there was sufficient credible evidence of the defendant's guilt to support a bind over until he had considered all of this evidence.

In some cases, the evidence introduced in behalf of the defendant will do no more than raise a conflict which can best be resolved by a jury at the actual trial where the Commonwealth must prove the defendant's guilt beyond a reasonable doubt. But, in other cases, the evidence elicited by defence counsel on cross-examination or from the testimony of defence witnesses or from other evidence may lead the examining magistrate to disbelieve the prosecution's witnesses and discharge the defendant for lack of probable cause. * * *

5. The Commonwealth argues in its brief * * * that granting defendants inflexible statutory rights to cross-examine witnesses against them and to present testimony in their own behalf would transform the preliminary hearing into a full-blown trial with disastrous results to a criminal justice system that is already overburdened. However, past experience indicates that trial strategy usually prevents such a result as both the prosecution and the defence wish to withhold as much of their case as possible.

* * *

Since the summary manner in which the petitioner's probable cause hearing was conducted denied the petitioner his statutory right to cross-examine witnesses and present evidence before the issue of probable cause was determined, the petitioner must be given a new preliminary hearing to determine whether there is probable cause to hold him on the charges pending against him. * * *

So ordered.

Note

Traditionally, a prosecutor initiates a felony prosecution by bringing the evidence before a grand jury, which then returns an indictment or "true bill." This is still the method followed in the federal courts and in about half of the states. Although the grand jury is supposed to protect citizens from unwarranted criminal prosecutions, it is usually regarded as ineffective in

10. If permitted, the petitioner's counsel would have introduced in evidence a psychiatric evaluation of the prosecutrix which noted that she "has a hysterical neurosis, a condition in which people might make up stories and then half believe them themselves. I would question the veracity of her statements." Defence counsel also wished to introduce a "medical report on the prosecutrix which shows that she received no abdominal injury, no pelvic trauma and that a vaginal discharge test for spermatozoa performed by a physician at the Boston City Hospital the morning of the alleged rape indicated no spermatozoa."

this "screening" role. The prosecutor meets with the grand jury in secrecy, and neither the defendant nor defense counsel has a right to be present. In some jurisdictions, the prosecutor may obtain an indictment on the basis of "hearsay" evidence that is not admissible at a trial, such as police testimony summarizing the statements of the actual witnesses to the crime. See, Costello v. United States, 350 U.S. 359 (1956). In the absence of cross-examination, defense evidence, or independent legal advice, the grand jury ordinarily has little choice but to follow the recommendations of the prosecutor. Prosecutors do have a duty to refrain from inflammatory or misleading advocacy in grand jury proceedings, however, and there are a number of decisions dismissing indictments where the prosecutor violated that duty. See United States v. Hogan, 712 F.2d 757 (2d Cir.1983).

About half the states no longer require that prosecutions for serious crimes be initiated by grand jury indictment.[a] In these states the prosecutor ordinarily retains the option of seeking an indictment, but the prevailing practice is to begin the prosecution by filing a felony *complaint* in an inferior court, normally the court which handles misdemeanor trials and minor civil cases. If the magistrate in this court determines after a preliminary hearing that there is sufficient cause to believe that the defendant committed the crime, he orders the defendant held for trial in the superior court. The prosecutor may then file an *information* in the superior court: This document is the equivalent of a grand jury indictment, but, of course, it is signed only by the prosecutor and not the grand jury Foreman. In misdemeanor cases the prosecutor may file a complaint or information directly in the inferior trial court and proceed to trial without any preliminary hearing or other review of the decision to prosecute. Once the complaint, information, or indictment has been filed, the defendant must be brought to court for arraignment on the charge. At arraignment the defendant appears with counsel or counsel is appointed, a plea is ordinarily entered, and the judge sets a date for the trial.[b]

In many states, the preliminary hearing has developed into a full-fledged adversary proceeding, with the defense entitled to cross-examine prosecution witnesses and to put on witnesses for the defense. Occasionally, a defendant may be able to undermine the prosecution's case at this stage, and obtain dismissal of the charges without going through the greater ordeal of a jury trial. More often, the defense uses the preliminary hearing as an opportunity to discover the prosecution's evidence and cross-examine its witnesses for the purpose of "pinning them down" on matters of detail. In civil litigation, the parties may take the depositions of witnesses; in criminal litigation, the only comparable opportunity occurs at the preliminary hearing. Defendants who exercise their right to subpoena witnesses rarely put on a complete defense at the preliminary hearing, since it is normally better tactics not to expose the defense

a. The Fifth Amendment's requirement of an indictment in prosecutions for "infamous" crimes is not applicable to the states. Hurtado v. California, 110 U.S. 516 (1884). An infamous crime or felony is typically defined as a crime punishable by imprisonment for more than one year.

b. This description of charging procedure is intentionally brief and general; various qualifications and additions would be necessary to make it strictly accurate for any particular jurisdiction.

case before trial. Instead, they subpoena and call to testify the prosecution witnesses whom the prosecutor plans to save for the trial. The purpose usually is not so much to rebut probable cause as to find out what the witnesses will say and to build a record that may be useful in cross-examining them at the trial. A thorough preliminary hearing also helps counsel to evaluate a case for purposes of plea bargaining.

A preliminary hearing may also be held in a felony case prosecuted in the federal courts or in one of the states which still requires a grand jury indictment, but it does not fulfil the same role. Where the grand jury has returned an indictment, no preliminary hearing is held because the grand jury has already determined that probable cause exists. The official purpose of the preliminary hearing in a jurisdiction that relies upon the grand jury for the ultimate decision on whether to prosecute is merely to decide whether the defendant should be held to answer (and thus required to remain in custody or give security for his appearance) until such time as the grand jury acts. Hence the prosecutor may avoid the preliminary hearing, and thus deprive the defendant of the discovery that the hearing would incidentally give him, by obtaining an indictment before the time of the hearing. He may also be able to render moot any procedural errors occurring at the preliminary hearing by obtaining a supervening indictment.

The Supreme Court has never held that there is a federal constitutional right to a pretrial review of the decision to prosecute. The only preliminary hearing that is constitutionally required is an ex parte proceeding to determine if there is probable cause to *arrest*. There is no requirement of a hearing to determine whether there is any reasonable probability that the defendant will ultimately be convicted. If there is probable cause sufficient to justify an arrest, the defendant may be required to post a bond to insure his appearance in court, and may be held in custody if he is unable to post bond in the required amount. See Gerstein v. Pugh, 420 U.S. 103 (1975).

Pretrial detention is a form of punishment in itself, and even a defendant at liberty is apt to experience considerable psychological and financial distress from a pending criminal prosecution. From the defense point of view, these considerations justify granting defendants an effective opportunity to challenge the prosecutor's determination that sufficient evidence exists to justify a trial. Although prosecutors ordinarily have no incentive to file charges unless they have enough evidence to make a conviction reasonably likely, some prosecutors may make mistakes or abuse the authority of their office.

On the other hand, granting an adversary-type preliminary examination substantially increases the burdens on the witnesses and on the judicial system. Testifying in a criminal case may be an ordeal for a witness, particularly one who is the victim of a sexual crime or who fears retaliation from the defendant. Delays and continuances in adversary hearings are common, and witnesses may be subjected to great inconvenience and frustration as a result. From the viewpoint of the witness, the adversary preliminary hearing may appear to be merely another opportunity for harassment.

BORDENKIRCHER v. HAYES

Supreme Court of the United States, 1978.
434 U.S. 357, 98 S.Ct. 663, 54 L.Ed.2d 604.

MR. JUSTICE STEWART delivered the opinion of the Court.

* * *

The respondent, Paul Lewis Hayes, was indicted by a Fayette County, Ky., grand jury on a charge of uttering a forged instrument in the amount of $88.30, an offense then punishable by a term of two to 10 years in prison. After arraignment, Hayes, his retained counsel, and the Commonwealth's attorney met in the presence of the clerk of the court to discuss a possible plea agreement. During these conferences the prosecutor offered to recommend a sentence of five years in prison if Hayes would plead guilty to the indictment. He also said that if Hayes did not plead guilty and "save the court the inconvenience and necessity of a trial," he would return to the grand jury to seek an indictment under the Kentucky Habitual Criminal Act, which would subject Hayes to a mandatory sentence of life imprisonment by reason of his two prior felony convictions.[2] Hayes chose not to plead guilty, and the prosecutor did obtain an indictment charging him under the Habitual Criminal Act. It is not disputed that the recidivist charge was fully justified by the evidence, that the prosecutor was in possession of this evidence at the time of the original indictment, and that Hayes' refusal to plead guilty to the original charge was what led to his indictment under the habitual criminal statute.

A jury found Hayes guilty on the principal charge of uttering a forged instrument and, in a separate proceeding, further found that he had twice before been convicted of felonies. As required by the habitual offender statute, he was sentenced to a life term in the penitentiary. The Kentucky Court of Appeals rejected Hayes' constitutional objections to the enhanced sentence, holding in an unpublished opinion that imprisonment for life with the possibility of parole was constitutionally permissible in light of the previous felonies of which Hayes had been convicted,[3]

2. At the time of Hayes' trial the statute provided that "[a]ny person convicted a ... third time of felony ... shall be confined in the penitentiary during his life." Ky.Rev. Stat. § 431.190 (repealed 1975). That statute has been replaced by Ky.Rev.Stat. § 532.080 (1977 Supp.) under which Hayes would have been sentenced to, at most, an indeterminate term of 10 to 20 years. § 532.080(6)(b). In addition, under the new statute a previous conviction is a basis for enhanced sentencing only if a prison term of one year or more was imposed, the sentence or probation was completed within five years of the present offense, and the offender was over the age of 18 when the offense was committed. At least one of Hayes' prior convictions did not meet these conditions. See n. 3, infra.

3. According to his own testimony, Hayes had pleaded guilty in 1961, when he was 17 years old, to a charge of detaining a female, a lesser included offense of rape, and as a result had served five years in the state reformatory. In 1970 he had been convicted of robbery and sentenced to five

and that the prosecutor's decision to indict him as an habitual offender was a legitimate use of available leverage in the plea bargaining process.

On Hayes' petition for a federal writ of habeas corpus, the United States District Court for the Eastern District of Kentucky agreed that there had been no constitutional violation in the sentence or the indictment procedure, and denied the writ. The Court of Appeals for the Sixth Circuit reversed the District Court's judgment. While recognizing "that plea bargaining now plays an important role in our criminal justice system," the appellate court thought that the prosecutor's conduct during the bargaining negotiations had violated the principles of Blackledge v. Perry, 417 U.S. 21, which "protect[ed] defendants from the vindictive exercise of a prosecutor's discretion." Hayes v. Cowan, 547 F.2d 42, 44, 6 Cir. Accordingly, the court ordered that Hayes be discharged "except for his confinement under a lawful sentence imposed solely for the crime of uttering a forged instrument." We granted certiorari to consider a constitutional question of importance in the administration of criminal justice.

* * *

This Court held in North Carolina v. Pearce, 395 U.S. 711, that the Due Process Clause of the Fourteenth Amendment "requires that vindictiveness against a defendant for having successfully attacked his first conviction must play no part in the sentence he receives after a new trial." The same principle was later applied to prohibit a prosecutor from reindicting a convicted misdemeanant on a felony charge after the defendant had invoked an appellate remedy, since in this situation there was also a "realistic likelihood of 'vindictiveness.' "Blackledge v. Perry, supra.

In those cases the Court was dealing with the State's unilateral imposition of a penalty upon a defendant who had chosen to exercise a legal right to attack his original conviction—a situation "very different from the give-and-take negotiation common in plea bargaining between the prosecution and the defense, which arguably possess relatively equal bargaining power." Parker v. North Carolina, 397 U.S. 790, 809 (opinion of Brennan, J.). The Court has emphasized that the due process violation in cases such as *Pearce* and *Perry* lay not in the possibility that a defendant might be deterred from the exercise of a legal right, but rather in the danger that the State might be retaliating against the accused for lawfully attacking his conviction.

To punish a person because he has done what the law plainly allows him to do is a due process violation of the most basic sort, and for an agent of the State to pursue a course of action whose objective is to penalize a person's reliance on his legal rights is patently unconstitutional. But in the "give-and-take" of plea bargaining, there is no such element of punishment or retaliation so long as the accused is free to accept or reject the prosecution's offer.

years imprisonment, but had been released on probation immediately.

Plea bargaining flows from "the mutuality of advantage" to defendants and prosecutors, each with his own reasons for wanting to avoid trial. Defendants advised by competent counsel and protected by other procedural safeguards are presumptively capable of intelligent choice in response to prosecutorial persuasion, and unlikely to be driven to false self-condemnation. Indeed, acceptance of the basic legitimacy of plea bargaining necessarily implies rejection of any notion that a guilty plea is involuntary in a constitutional sense simply because it is the end result of the bargaining process. By hypothesis, the plea may have been induced by promises of a recommendation of a lenient sentence or a reduction of charges, and thus by fear of the possibility of a greater penalty upon conviction after a trial.

While confronting a defendant with the risk of more severe punishment clearly may have a discouraging effect on the defendant's assertion of his trial rights, the imposition of these difficult choices is an inevitable—and permissible—attribute of any legitimate system which tolerates and encourages the negotiation of pleas. It follows that, by tolerating and encouraging the negotiation of pleas, this Court has necessarily accepted as constitutionally legitimate the simple reality that the prosecutor's interest at the bargaining table is to persuade the defendant to forego his right to plead not guilty.

It is not disputed here that Hayes was properly chargeable under the recidivist statute, since he had in fact been convicted of two previous felonies. In our system, so long as the prosecutor has probable cause to believe that the accused committed an offense defined by statute, the decision whether or not to prosecute, and what charge to file or bring before a grand jury, generally rests entirely in his discretion. Within the limits set by the legislature's constitutionally valid definition of chargeable offenses, "the conscious exercise of some selectivity in enforcement is not in itself a federal constitutional violation" so long as "the selection was [not] deliberately based upon an unjustifiable standard such as race, religion, or other arbitrary classification." Oyler v. Boles, 368 U.S. 448, 456. To hold that the prosecutor's desire to induce a guilty plea is an "unjustifiable standard," which, like race or religion, may play no part in his charging decision, would contradict the very premises that underlie the concept of plea bargaining itself. Moreover, a rigid constitutional rule that would prohibit a prosecutor from acting forthrightly in his dealings with the defense could only invite unhealthy subterfuge that would drive the practice of plea bargaining back into the shadows from which it has so recently emerged.

There is no doubt that the breadth of discretion that our country's legal system vests in prosecuting attorneys carries with it the potential for both individual and institutional abuse. And broad though that discretion may be, there are undoubtedly constitutional limits upon its exercise. We hold only that the course of conduct engaged in by the prosecutor in this case, which no more than openly presented the defendant with the unpleasant alternatives of foregoing trial or facing charges on which he was plainly subject to prosecution, did not violate the Due Process Clause of the Fourteenth Amendment.

Accordingly, the judgment of the Court of Appeals is

Reversed.

[The dissenting opinion of MR. JUSTICE BLACKMUN, joined by JUSTICES BRENNAN and MARSHALL, is omitted.]

MR. JUSTICE POWELL, dissenting.

* * *

The prosecutor's initial assessment of respondent's case led him to forego an indictment under the habitual criminal statute. The circumstances of respondent's prior convictions are relevant to this assessment and to my view of the case. Respondent was 17 years old when he committed his first offense. He was charged with rape but pled guilty to the lesser included offense of "detaining a female." One of the other participants in the incident was sentenced to life imprisonment. Respondent was sent not to prison but to a reformatory where he served five years. Respondent's second offense was robbery. This time he was found guilty by a jury and was sentenced to five years in prison, but he was placed on probation and served no time. Although respondent's prior convictions brought him within the terms of the Habitual Criminal Act, the offenses themselves did not result in imprisonment; yet the addition of a conviction on a charge involving $88.30 subjected respondent to a mandatory sentence of imprisonment for life.[1] Persons convicted of rape and murder often are not punished so severely.

No explanation appears in the record for the prosecutor's decision to escalate the charge against respondent other than respondent's refusal to plead guilty. The prosecutor has conceded that his purpose was to discourage respondent's assertion of constitutional rights, and the majority accepts this characterization of events.

It seems to me that the question to be asked under the circumstances is whether the prosecutor reasonably might have charged respondent under the Habitual Criminal Act in the first place. The deference that courts properly accord the exercise of a prosecutor's discretion perhaps would foreclose judicial criticism if the prosecutor originally had sought an indictment under that act, as unreasonable as it would have seemed.[2] But here the prosecutor evidently made a reason-

1. It is suggested that respondent will be eligible for parole consideration after serving 15 years.

2. The majority suggests that this case cannot be distinguished from the case where the prosecutor initially obtains an indictment under an enhancement statute and later agrees to drop the enhancement charge in exchange for a guilty plea. I would agree that these two situations would be alike *only if* it were assumed that the hypothetical prosecutor's decision to charge under the enhancement statute was occasioned not by consideration of the public interest but by a strategy to discourage the defendant from exercising his constitutional rights. In theory, I would condemn both practices. In practice, the hypothetical situation is largely unreviewable. The majority's view confuses the propriety of a particular exercise of prosecutorial discretion with its unreviewability. In the instant case, however, we have no problem of proof.

able, responsible judgment not to subject an individual to a mandatory life sentence when his only new offense had societal implications as limited as those accompanying the uttering of a single $88 forged check and when the circumstances of his prior convictions confirmed the inappropriateness of applying the habitual criminal statute. I think it may be inferred that the prosecutor himself deemed it unreasonable and not in the public interest to put this defendant in jeopardy of a sentence of life imprisonment.

* * *

The plea-bargaining process, as recognized by this Court, is essential to the functioning of the criminal-justice system. It normally affords genuine benefits to defendants as well as to society. And if the system is to work effectively, prosecutors must be accorded the widest discretion, within constitutional limits, in conducting bargaining. This is especially true when a defendant is represented by counsel and presumably is fully advised of his rights. Only in the most exceptional case should a court conclude that the scales of the bargaining are so unevenly balanced as to arouse suspicion. In this case, the prosecutor's actions denied respondent due process because their admitted purpose was to discourage and then to penalize with unique severity his exercise of constitutional rights. Implementation of a strategy calculated solely to deter the exercise of constitutional rights is not a constitutionally permissible exercise of discretion. I would affirm the opinion of the Court of Appeals on the facts of this case.

Note

Plea bargaining is the most frequently criticized aspect of American criminal procedure. The Supreme Court has held that the privilege against compulsory self-incrimination is the "essential mainstay" of the American "accusatorial" system of criminal justice, and that therefore prosecutors are "constitutionally compelled to establish guilt by evidence independently and freely secured, and may not by coercion prove a charge against an accused out of his own mouth." Malloy v. Hogan, 378 U.S. 1, 7–8 (1964). In a system which places such emphasis on the right of the accused to put the state to its burden of proof, it is surprising to see that guilty pleas are routinely obtained by offering sentencing or charge concessions.

Some of the most vehement criticism of plea bargaining has come not from those who fear that the rights of defendants may not be adequately protected, but rather from those who fear that plea bargaining results in unjustifiably lenient sentences. In some jurisdictions, serious offenders like armed robbers, house burglars, and forcible rapists sometimes receive probation or sentences of no more than a few months in jail when they agree to plead guilty. The problem is not only that the period of confinement is not as long as it might be, but also that the record of conviction does not adequately reflect the seriousness of the offense. A defendant who committed several armed robberies, for example, might be allowed to plead guilty to a single count of theft. This lack of concern with the accuracy of the verdict breeds cynicism about the degree to which our legal system cares about truth.

Despite the chorus of criticism of plea bargaining from both liberal and conservative commentators, the Supreme Court held in 1970 that the practice is constitutional if the defendant is represented by competent counsel, and adequately informed of his legal rights and the consequences of pleading guilty. Brady v. United States, 397 U.S. 742 (1970). As a result of this constitutional endorsement, plea bargaining is now done openly and the courts are in the process of developing a rather specialized branch of contract law. For example, the Supreme Court has held that a defendant does not have a right to "specific performance" of a plea bargaining agreement if the prosecution withdraws its offer before the plea is officially entered. Mabry v. Johnson, 467 U.S. 504 (1984). The Supreme Court has even " 'strictly limited the circumstances under which a guilty plea may be attacked on collateral review. It is well settled that a voluntary and intelligent plea of guilty made by an accused person, who has been advised by competent counsel, may not be collaterally attacked.' " Bousley v. United States, 523 U.S. 614, 621 (1998), *quoting* Mabry, 467 U.S. at 508.

Various arguments have been given to justify the institution of plea bargaining. The fact that a defendant openly admits guilt and expresses repentance is ordinarily regarded as a mitigating circumstance, but where the admission takes the form of a guilty plea induced by a promise of leniency it is difficult to see it as anything other than calculated self-interest. When he was a law professor, Judge Frank used economic theory to support the argument that plea bargaining and other discretionary aspects of American criminal procedure are part of a rational market system which enables prosecutors to obtain the maximum amount of deterrence of crime with a minimum expenditure of scarce resources. Easterbrook, "Criminal Procedure as a Market System," 12 Journal of Legal Studies 289 (1983). Another law professor has used history to support the argument that plea bargaining plays the same role in modern American criminal justice administration that torture played in the legal system of the late Middle Ages. At that earlier time, the rules of proof were so strict that it was virtually impossible to obtain a conviction without a confession, and so torture had to be used to obtain the necessary confessions. Similarly, the American system of jury trial and appellate review has become so cumbersome and expensive that some way must be found to circumvent it. Langbein, "Torture and Plea Bargaining," 46 U.Chi.L.Rev. 3 (1978).

The most common justification for plea bargaining is simply that it is necessary because of the huge volume of crime and the limited resources available to deal with it. In a frequently quoted speech to the American Bar Association, Chief Justice Warren Burger argued that a reduction in the rate of guilty pleas from 90 percent to 80 percent would require a doubling of courtroom personnel and facilities. See, Burger, "The State of the Judiciary—1970," 56 A.B.A.J. 929, 931 (1970) (over 90 percent of all felony convictions are by guilty plea in some courts). Leading scholars have challenged this pessimistic estimate, however, and have argued that we could provide substantial additional resources by ceasing to tolerate the enormous inefficiency and waste that exists in our judicial system. Furthermore, we could provide every defendant with *some* type of reliable fact-finding procedure, even if not the expensive jury trial that we regard as appropriate for hotly contested matters. Having a bench trial in every case, perhaps with relaxed rules of evidence, would ensure that some effort was made to arrive at a reliable verdict even where the defendant was willing to waive the full rights of the adversary jury process. These issues are explored in Alschuler, "Implementing the Criminal Defendant's Right to Trial: Alternatives to the Plea Bargaining System," 50 U.Chi.L.Rev. 931 (1983); and Schulhofer, "Is Plea Bargaining Inevitable?", 97 Harv.L.Rev. 1037 (1984).

Adequate exploration of the plea bargaining controversy is beyond the scope of this book. The purpose of this part of the chapter is to acquaint the law student with the most important discretionary aspects of criminal justice administration, because the substantive criminal law cannot be adequately understood without some understanding of how it is actually administered in court. Because plea bargaining is the norm and contested trials the exception, the most important characteristic of a substantive rule is the leverage that it gives to one side or another in the plea bargaining process. For example, habitual criminal statutes are frequently invoked for the purpose of putting enormous pressure on a defendant to plead guilty to the current charge. Similarly, an important effect of a death penalty statute is to give murderers an incentive to plead guilty, and the statutes may in this sense be a powerful weapon in the hands of law enforcement even though very few murderers are put to death. On the other side of the equation, any rule that gives the defense an opportunity to delay or confuse the proceedings may increase defense leverage in the plea bargaining process. Psychiatric defenses, for example, may rarely be successful when litigated, but the prospect of a complicated trial on contested psychiatric testimony may motivate the prosecutor to offer a better bargain.

C. THE RIGHT TO TRIAL BY JURY

DUNCAN v. LOUISIANA

Supreme Court of the United States, 1968.
391 U.S. 145, 88 S.Ct. 1444, 20 L.Ed.2d 491.

MR. JUSTICE WHITE delivered the opinion of the Court.

Appellant, Gary Duncan, was convicted of simple battery in the Twenty–Fifth Judicial District Court of Louisiana. Under Louisiana law simple battery is a misdemeanor, punishable by a maximum of two years' imprisonment and a $300 fine. Appellant sought trial by jury, but because the Louisiana Constitution grants jury trials only in cases in which capital punishment or imprisonment at hard labor may be imposed,[1] the trial judge denied the request. Appellant was convicted and

1. La. Const., Art. VII, § 41:
"All cases in which the punishment may not be at hard labor shall ... be tried by the judge without jury. Cases, in which the punishment may be at hard labor, shall be tried by a jury of five, all of whom must concur to render a verdict; cases, in which the punishment is necessarily at hard labor, by a jury of twelve, nine of whom must concur to render a verdict; cases in which the punishment is necessarily at hard labor, by a jury of twelve, nine of whom must concur to render a verdict; cases in which the punishment may be capital, by a jury of twelve, all of whom must concur to render a verdict."

sentenced to serve 60 days in the parish prison and pay a fine of $150. * * *

[The state courts declined to hold that the denial of jury trial violated appellant's rights, and he appealed to the United States Supreme Court.]

Appellant was 19 years of age when tried. While driving on Highway 23 in Plaquemines Parish on October 18, 1966, he saw two younger cousins engaged in a conversation by the side of the road with four white boys. Knowing his cousins, Negroes who had recently transferred to a formerly all-white high school, had reported the occurrence of racial incidents at the school, Duncan stopped the car, got out, and approached the six boys. At trial the white boys and a white onlooker testified, as did appellant and his cousins. The testimony was in dispute on many points, but the witnesses agreed that appellant and the white boys spoke to each other, that appellant encouraged his cousins to break off the encounter and enter his car, and that appellant was about to enter the car himself for the purpose of driving away with his cousins. The whites testified that just before getting in the car appellant slapped Herman Landry, one of the white boys, on the elbow. The Negroes testified that appellant had not slapped Landry, but had merely touched him. The trial judge concluded that the State had proved beyond a reasonable doubt that Duncan had committed simple battery, and found him guilty.

* * *

The guarantees of jury trial in the Federal and State Constitutions reflect a profound judgment about the way in which law should be enforced and justice administered. A right to jury trial is granted to criminal defendants in order to prevent oppression by the Government. Those who wrote our constitutions knew from history and experience that it was necessary to protect against unfounded criminal charges brought to eliminate enemies and against judges too responsive to the voice of higher authority. The framers of the constitutions strove to create an independent judiciary but insisted upon further protection against arbitrary action. Providing an accused with the right to be tried by a jury of his peers gave him an inestimable safeguard against the corrupt or overzealous prosecutor and against the compliant, biased, or eccentric judge. If the defendant preferred the common-sense judgment of a jury to the more tutored but perhaps less sympathetic reaction of the single judge, he was to have it. Beyond this, the jury trial provision in the Federal and State Constitutions reflect a fundamental decision about the exercise of official power—a reluctance to entrust plenary powers over the life and liberty of the citizen to one judge or to a group of judges. Fear of unchecked power, so typical of our State and Federal Governments in other respects, found expression in the criminal law in this insistence upon community participation in the determination of guilt or innocence. The deep commitment of the Nation to the right of jury trial in serious criminal cases as a defense against arbitrary law enforcement qualifies for protection under the Due Process Clause of the

Fourteenth Amendment, and must therefore be respected by the States. * * *

Louisiana's final contention is that even if it must grant jury trials in serious criminal cases, the conviction before us is valid and constitutional because here the petitioner was tried for simple battery and was sentenced to only 60 days in the parish prison. We are not persuaded. It is doubtless true that there is a category of petty crimes or offenses which is not subject to the Sixth Amendment jury trial provision and should not be subject to the Fourteenth Amendment jury trial requirement here applied to the States. Crimes carrying possible penalties up to six months do not require a jury trial if they otherwise qualify as petty offenses, Cheff v. Schnackenberg, 384 U.S. 373 (1966). But the penalty authorized for a particular crime is of major relevance in determining whether it is serious or not and may in itself, if severe enough, subject the trial to the mandates of the Sixth Amendment. * * * In the case before us the Legislature of Louisiana has made simple battery a criminal offense punishable by imprisonment for up to two years and a fine. The question, then, is whether a crime carrying such a penalty is an offense which Louisiana may insist on trying without a jury.

* * *

In determining whether the length of the authorized prison term or the seriousness of other punishment is enough in itself to require a jury trial, we refer to objective criteria, chiefly the existing laws and practices in the Nation. In the federal system, petty offenses are defined as those punishable by no more than six months in prison and a $500 fine. In 49 of the 50 States crimes subject to trial without a jury, which occasionally include simple battery, are punishable by no more than one year in jail. Moreover, in the late 18th century in America crimes triable without a jury were for the most part punishable by no more than a six-month prison term, although there appear to have been exceptions to this rule. We need not, however, settle in this case the exact location of the line between petty offenses and serious crimes. It is sufficient for our purposes to hold that a crime punishable by two years in prison is, based on past and contemporary standards in this country, a serious crime and not a petty offense. Consequently, appellant was entitled to a jury trial and it was error to deny it.

The judgment below is reversed and the case is remanded for proceedings not inconsistent with this opinion.

MR. JUSTICE HARLAN, whom MR. JUSTICE STEWART joins, dissenting.

Every American jurisdiction provides for trial by jury in criminal cases. The question before us is not whether jury trial is an ancient institution, which it is; nor whether it plays a significant role in the administration of criminal justice, which it does; nor whether it will endure, which it shall. The question in this case is whether the State of Louisiana, which provides trial by jury for all felonies, is prohibited by the Constitution from trying charges of simple battery to the court alone. In my view, the answer to that question, mandated alike by our constitutional history and by the longer history of trial by jury, is clearly "no." * * *

The jury is of course not without virtues. It affords ordinary citizens a valuable opportunity to participate in a process of government, an experience fostering, one hopes, a respect for law. It eases the burden on judges by enabling them to share a part of their sometimes awesome responsibility. A jury may, at times, afford a higher justice by refusing to enforce harsh laws (although it necessarily does so haphazardly, raising the questions whether arbitrary enforcement of harsh laws is better than total enforcement, and whether the jury system is to be defended on the ground that jurors sometimes disobey their oaths). And the jury may, or may not, contribute desirably to the willingness of the general public to accept criminal judgments as just.

It can hardly be gainsaid, however, that the principal original virtue of the jury trial—the limitations a jury imposes on a tyrannous judiciary—has largely disappeared. We no longer live in a medieval or colonial society. Judges enforce laws enacted by democratic decision, not by regal fiat. They are elected by the people or appointed by the people's elected officials, and are responsible not to a distant monarch alone but to reviewing courts, including this one.

The jury system can also be said to have some inherent defects, which are multiplied by the emergence of the criminal law from the relative simplicity that existed when the jury system was devised. It is a cumbersome process, not only imposing great cost in time and money on both the State and the jurors themselves, but also contributing to delay in the machinery of justice. Untrained jurors are presumably less adept at reaching accurate conclusions of fact than judges, particularly if the issues are many or complex. And it is argued by some that trial by jury, far from increasing public respect for law, impairs it: the average man, it is said, reacts favorably neither to the notion that matters he knows to be complex are being decided by other average men, nor to the way the jury system distorts the process of adjudication. * * *

Indeed, even if I were persuaded that trial by jury is a fundamental right in some criminal cases, I could see nothing fundamental in the rule, not yet formulated by the Court, that places the prosecution of appellant for simple battery within the category of "jury crimes" rather than "petty crimes." Trial by jury is ancient, it is true. Almost equally ancient, however, is the discovery that, because of it,

> "the King's most loving Subjects are much travailed and otherwise encumbered in coming and keeping of the said six Weeks Sessions, to their Costs, Charges, Unquietness."

As a result, through the long course of British and American history, summary procedures have been used in a varying category of lesser crimes as a flexible response to the burden jury trial would otherwise impose. * * *

There is no obvious reason why a jury trial is a requisite of fundamental fairness when the charge is robbery, and not a requisite of fairness when the same defendant, for the same actions, is charged with assault and petty theft. The reason for the historic exception for relatively minor crimes is the obvious one: the burden of jury trial was thought to outweigh its marginal advantages. Exactly why the States should not be allowed to make continuing adjustments, based on the state of their criminal dockets and the difficulty of summoning jurors, simply escapes me. * * *

This Court, other courts, and the political process are available to correct any experiments in criminal procedure that prove fundamentally unfair to defendants. That is not what is being done today: instead, and quite without reason, the Court has chosen to impose upon every State one means of trying criminal cases; it is a good means, but it is not the only fair means, and it is not demonstrably better than the alternatives States might devise.

I would affirm the judgment of the Supreme Court of Louisiana.

Note

The common law criminal jury must be of exactly 12 persons, and it must agree unanimously to return a verdict of guilty or not guilty. If unanimous agreement cannot be achieved, there is a "hung jury," and the case will ordinarily be set for a new trial. After two or more hung juries the court will usually dismiss the prosecution, especially if a substantial number of jurors voted for acquittal.

Following the decision in *Duncan,* the Supreme Court had to decide whether the states are obligated to follow all the common law rules pertaining to jury trials which had been incorporated into federal law. In Baldwin v. New York, 399 U.S. 66 (1970), the Supreme Court made explicit what was suggested in *Duncan:* a state must provide a right to trial by jury for any offense where imprisonment for more than six months is authorized. Note that the Sixth Amendment provides that the accused has a right to trial "by an impartial jury" and with "the Assistance of Counsel" in all *"criminal prosecutions."* Apparently, a petty offense punishable by imprisonment for six months or less is not a "criminal prosecution," for purposes of the jury trial right. Interpreting the same constitutional language, the Supreme Court has held that the defendant's right to counsel extends to any case in which the defendant is sentenced to jail for any time whatsoever. Argersinger v. Hamlin, 407 U.S. 25 (1972). The dividing line for *this* right depends upon the jail time actually imposed rather than the penalty provided in the statute. In other words, the defendant has a right to jury trial for an offense punishable by more than six months in jail regardless of whether any jail time is actually imposed, but the same defendant has no constitutional right to the assistance of counsel for an offense punishable by a year in jail if the judge actually imposes only a fine. By refusing to appoint counsel, the judge in effect converts the offense to one punishable only by fine.

A provision of the Louisiana Constitution (see the footnote in *Duncan, supra*) provides that certain criminal cases shall be tried by a jury of 5, with a unanimous verdict, and others by a jury of 12, only 9 of whom must concur to render a verdict. Oregon also has a state constitutional provision permitting a jury to return a verdict if 10 of the 12 jurors concur. The other states require unanimous verdicts, but a number provide for six-person juries in certain types of cases. These variations created no constitutional issue as long as the Sixth Amendment right to trial by jury applied only to the federal government, but after *Duncan* their constitutionality became a close question.

In Apodaca v. Oregon, 406 U.S. 404 (1972) the Supreme Court held by a narrow vote that the Constitution requires unanimous jury verdicts in federal criminal cases but not in state cases. This decision came about because of a curious combination of votes. Eight of the nine Justices agreed that the standard for state and federal cases should be the same. Four of these eight Justices thought that the Sixth Amendment does not require unanimity in either case (although federal *statutory* law requires unanimous verdicts for federal cases), and the remaining four thought that the Sixth Amendment requires unanimous verdicts in *both* state and federal cases. Only Justice Powell thought that the constitutional requirement should be different for the federal government and for the states. His opinion argued that the Fourteenth Amendment, while requiring the states to provide jury trials for serious crimes, does not incorporate all the elements of a jury trial within the meaning of the Sixth Amendment, such as jury unanimity. There were thus five votes for imposing the unanimity requirement as a constitutional standard on the federal government, and five votes for not imposing such a requirement on the states, and so a position rejected by eight of the nine Justices became the majority position. Many persons who commented upon the *Apodaca* decision were under the impression that it heralded a major change in American jury procedure. In fact, however, it changed nothing; Oregon and Louisiana had allowed less-than unanimous jury verdicts for many years, and the other states did not choose to follow their example. England has permitted non-unanimous verdicts since 1967.

In other decisions the Supreme Court held that a jury in state cases may contain less than twelve persons but not less than six, and that a jury of six may not return a non-unanimous verdict. Ballew v. Georgia, 435 U.S. 223 (1978); Burch v. Louisiana, 441 U.S. 130 (1979).

The next excerpt, by a noted authority on comparative law, contrasts the Anglo–American jury trial with the continental mixed tribunal in which both professional and lay adjudicators deliberate together.

MIRJAN DAMAŠKA, EVIDENTIARY BARRIERS TO CONVICTION AND TWO MODELS OF CRIMINAL PROCEDURE

121 U.Pa.L.Rev. 506, 536–46 (1973).

1. Different Rules Governing Voting

The common law verdict of guilty was traditionally required to be unanimous. Of late this rule seems to be in eclipse, but is, despite some quite recent ominous signs, still retained in the majority of American jurisdictions. Continental systems never viewed the unanimity rule with favor. Even the French revolutionaries, who in 1791 were so enchanted by English institutions that they attempted a wholesale transplantation of English criminal procedure, never went so far as to require unanimous guilty verdicts from their juries. Continental adjudicators decide by a majority vote, often a bare majority. Rare indeed are voices claiming that the continental analogue of the requirement of proof of guilt beyond a reasonable doubt presupposes a voting *regime* whereby the prosecutor must overcome "reasonable doubts" of all adjudicators.

The implications of these different approaches to decisionmaking are obvious. The prosecutor will surely find it more difficult to obtain a conviction under the *regime* of unanimity than that of majority. For if only one juror refuses to convict, say, because of sympathy for the defendant, or because of very stringent views on sufficiency of the evidence presented, there will be no conviction. Consequently, where in the Anglo–American orbit the unanimity rule still prevails, the prosecutor can expect a less favorable "conviction-acquittal ratio."

2. Professional and Lay Propensities to Convict

Since the common law unanimity rule seems to be diminishing in significance, another contrast between the two systems assumes greater importance. In a jury trial the determination of guilt is made solely by lay people, whereas in the continental mixed tribunal professional judges play an active role. If lay people tend to be on average more lenient in criminal adjudication than professional adjudicators, the jury will be more reluctant to convict than the mixed tribunal, and the prosecutor trying to persuade the jury of the defendant's guilt will have a somewhat harder task before him.

That lay adjudicators are, on the whole, more lenient, seems to be an impression so widely shared that it has almost become a truism. There is empirical evidence in support of these impressions, although perhaps not enough to remove the issue entirely from the realm of speculation. Disagreements between lay and professional judges have been studied, both in America and in Europe, and the results seem to indicate that in these disagreements lay judges seem on the average to favor the defendant. Moreover—and this is of particular importance to our subsequent discussion—there is some indication in these empirical studies that those disagreements may not be entirely accounted for by such reasons as sympathy for the defendant's plight, but also, to an extent, by "higher thresholds of reasonable doubt" on the part of laymen. Lay people seem often to require *more evidence* to convict than professional adjudicators, particularly in those cases where the decision turns on mere circumstantial evidence.

Why should lay adjudicators tend on average to be more lenient? I believe that we are presented here with only an instance of a larger phenomenon observable in other areas. Max Weber has analyzed it in talking about bureaucratization; sometimes it is discussed in connection with professionalization, but it is also an aspect of any routinization of activity. In all these processes what is acquired is an ever increasing measure of self-confidence, coupled with rational detachment and matter-of-factness. So, just as in other human activities, prolonged exposure to criminal litigation will result in a degree of case-hardening. Experienced professional judges will tell us about the agony they went through before convicting their first defendant on circumstantial evidence; *cognoscenti* might perhaps tell us that even jurors find it easier to convict toward the end of their term. The longer one is involved in the business of adjudicating criminal cases, the more these cases become depersonalized, more representatives of general classes. Gradually the morning freshness of perceiving each case as a unique human drama is gone, and one becomes adjusted to the efficient performance of a routine task. This, perhaps, is the unfortunate *"default de qualite"* of any professionalization.

Assume that there is truth in these widely shared observations. It can then be demonstrated that the civil law system exhibits counterpressures to neutralize, when necessary, the differential lay predispositions in the adjudication of guilt.

Whatever influence the common law judge has on the jury is limited mostly to instructions. The jury sits alone and decides independently. What evidentiary evaluation leads to a verdict remains unknown because the jurors are not required to justify factual findings. In addition, the absence of appeals from acquittals in the overwhelming majority of common law jurisdictions removes another means of professional supervision of the jury. By contrast, the lay element on the continental panel is much more effectively controlled by professionals. The professional judge or judges retire with the lay judges, participate in the deliberation process and preside over the debate. True, the lay assessors on the bench are more often than not in the majority. Further, in most jurisdictions lay judges do play an active role and are not members of the panel for mere cosmetic purposes. Yet, few would deny that the professional judge is a towering and influential figure in the eyes of his lay colleagues. There is typically also an appeal from factual findings, and the court must state in the judgment why it gave credence to one item of evidence rather than another. The prosecutor thus knows that even if he fails to obtain a conviction on strong evidence from the original adjudicator, he will have another chance with the appellate court.

Further reflection reveals that the two procedural systems face disparate problems in trying to attune lay factfinders to actual evidentiary standards in the practical activity of deciding criminal cases. As the continental judges sit together, there is no need for the professionals to instruct their lay colleagues about the quantum of proof in advance of actual deliberations. Nor is advance information needed on how to handle possible factual doubts. If such doubts arise, the professional judge will advise the lay judges in the debate over specific facts, during *in camera* deliberations. It is, then, not surprising that very few continental systems require formal instructions on proof sufficiency for conviction. The situation on the common law side of our comparison is quite different. There is no informal exchange of views and advice between the judge and the jurors at deliberations. Instead—anticipating that some doubts concerning evidence introduced are very likely to arise—the law requires the judge to instruct jurors on the necessary quantum of proof before they retire. The instruction is in the form of a rigid and abstract formula. * * *

3. Trial Structure and Evidentiary Needs

In talking about disparate difficulties faced by prosecutors in persuading the factfinder of the defendant's guilt, a number of additional factors must be considered. They are independent of the lay-professional dichotomy, but are intimately linked to the different structures of the continental and common law type of trial. On several occasions I have mentioned that the continental trial is typically conducted in such a manner that the presiding judge is required to study the file of the case in advance of the trial. The extent to which this practice creates a danger of bias varies from country to country. It is less pronounced in those continental jurisdictions where pre-trial investigations are less thorough, and the investigating officer is not required to voice his opinion on whether the case deserves to be transferred to the court for trial. But whether from a comparative perspective the trial amounts to a verification of the record prepared by the investigator or is genuinely "creative," the impact of the dossier on guilt deliberations of the mixed panel cannot in candor be denied. While it is open to conjecture whether or not lay judges will be less open-minded than jurors as a result of the knowledge that the case has been "objectively" investigated before trial, the fact remains that the professional judge will not approach the case as a *tabula rasa.* He will have an additional edge over lay assessors at deliberations as well: he will know more about the case than his lay colleagues.

Another factor, seldom discussed, is relevant here. It is well known to experimental psychologists that different people have disparate cognitive needs; they often require different information, or ways of presenting it, in order to be persuaded of, or simply to comprehend a point. The continental trial is in a sense more attuned to this psychological phenomenon. All continental decisionmakers, lay and professional, are entitled to address questions to witnesses and take an active part during the presentation of evidence. On the other hand, common law jurors are passive observers of the examination of evidence, although, somewhat paradoxically, it is they who will have to decide the case. Their immediate cognitive needs are often unpredictable to the parties presenting evidence. It is, of course, possible that their general predispositions and needs may be elicited through voir dire or anticipated through the familiarity attorneys sometimes acquire with a small and relatively stable venire. But, on balance, more uncertainties and doubts are likely to arise, *ceteris paribus,* among jurors than among members of the mixed panel.

One can only surmise that the adversary method of presenting evidence is somewhat more conducive to uncertainties and doubts than the more organized and detached continental method. It is a truism that the more points of view we take into consideration, the harder it is for us to make a decision. When we view reality "through eyes other than our own" and are presented each side of the story in the most favorable light, it will become somewhat harder for us to become absolutely certain that only one side to an argument is in the right. Thus, it is possible to argue that the prosecutor will have somewhat more difficulty in sustaining the burden of persuasion under the adversary than under the continental style of presenting evidence.

UNITED STATES v. DOUGHERTY

United States Court of Appeals, District of Columbia Circuit, 1972.
154 U.S.App.D.C. 76, 473 F.2d 1113.

LEVENTHAL, CIRCUIT JUDGE.

Seven of the so-called "D.C. Nine" bring this joint appeal from convictions arising out of their unconsented entry into the Washington offices of the Dow Chemical Company, and their destruction of certain property therein.[a] Appellants, along with two other defendants who subsequently entered pleas of nolo contendere, were tried before District Judge John H. Pratt and a jury on a three count indictment alleging, as to each defendant, one count of second degree burglary, and two counts of malicious destruction of property valued in excess of $100. On February 11, 1970, after a six-day trial, the seven were each convicted of two counts of malicious destruction. The jury acquitted on the burglary charges but convicted on the lesser-included offense of unlawful entry. * * *

[The court reversed the convictions because the trial court refused to allow the defendants to represent themselves. It held that the denial of the defendants' statutory right to represent themselves was not harmless error, because the normal disadvantages of appearing without the assistance of counsel "may be offset by the enhanced intensity and appearance of greater sincerity of a defendant's presentation."]

Our reference to the "intensity" factor underlying the *pro se* right should not be understood as embracing the principle of "nullification" proffered by appellants. They say that the jury has a well-recognized prerogative to disregard the instructions of the court even as to matters of law, and that they accordingly have the legal right that the jury be informed of its power. We turn to this matter in order to define the nature of the new trial permitted by our mandate.

There has evolved in the Anglo–American system an undoubted jury prerogative-in-fact, derived from its power to bring in a general verdict of not guilty in a criminal case, that is not reversible by the court. The power of the courts to punish jurors for corrupt or incorrect verdicts,

a. The entry and destruction were part of a public demonstration to protest the role of the Dow Chemical Company in supplying war materials for use in Vietnam.—ed.

which persisted after the medieval system of attaint by another jury became obsolete, was repudiated in 1670 when Bushell's Case, 124 Eng.Rep. 1006 (C.P.1670) discharged the jurors who had acquitted William Penn of unlawful assembly. Juries in civil cases became subject to the control of ordering a new trial; no comparable control evolved for acquittals in criminal cases.

The pages of history shine on instances of the jury's exercise of its prerogative to disregard uncontradicted evidence and instructions of the judge. Most often commended are the 18th century acquittal of Peter Zenger of seditious libel, on the plea of Andrew Hamilton, and the 19th century acquittals in prosecutions under the fugitive slave law. The values involved drop a notch when the liberty vindicated by the verdict relates to the defendant's shooting of his wife's paramour, or purchase during Prohibition of alcoholic beverages. * * *

The existence of an unreviewable and unreversible power in the jury, to acquit in disregard of the instructions on the law given by the trial judge, has for many years co-existed with legal practice and precedent upholding instructions to the jury that they are required to follow the instructions of the court on all matters of law. There were different soundings in colonial days and the early days of our Republic. We are aware of the number and variety of expressions at that time from respected sources—John Adams; Alexander Hamilton; prominent judges—that jurors had a duty to find a verdict according to their own conscience, though in opposition to the direction of the court; that their power signified a right; that they were judges both of law and of fact in a criminal case, and not bound by the opinion of the court.

The rulings did not run all one way, but rather precipitated a number of classic exchanges on the freedom and obligations of the criminal jury. This was, indeed, one of the points of clash between the contending forces staking out the direction of the government of the newly established Republic, a direction resolved in political terms by reforming but sustaining the status of the courts, without radical change. As the distrust of judges appointed and removable by the king receded, there came increasing acceptance that under a republic the protection of citizens lay not in recognizing the right of each jury to make its own law, but in following democratic processes for changing the law. * * *

The way the jury operates may be radically altered if there is alteration in the way it is told to operate. The jury knows well enough that its prerogative is not limited to the choices articulated in the formal instructions of the court. The jury gets its understanding as to the arrangements in the legal system from more than one voice. There is the formal communication from the judge. There is the informal communication from the total culture—literature (novel, drama, film, and television); current comment (newspapers, magazines and television); conversation; and, of course, history and tradition. The totality of input generally convey adequately enough the idea of prerogative, of freedom in an occasional case to depart from what the judge says. Even indicators that would on their face seem too weak to notice—like the fact that the judge tells the jury it must acquit (in case of reasonable doubt) but never tells the jury in so many words that it must convict—are a meaningful part of the jury's total input. Law is a system, and it is also a language, with secondary meanings that may be unrecorded yet are part of its life. * * *

Rules of law or justice involve choice of values and ordering of objectives for which unanimity is unlikely in any society, or group representing the society, especially a society as diverse in cultures and interests as ours. To seek unity out of diversity, under the national motto, there must be a procedure for decision by vote of a majority or prescribed plurality—in accordance with democratic philosophy. To assign the role of mini-legislature to the various petit juries, who must hang if not unanimous, exposes criminal law and administration to paralysis, and to a deadlock that betrays rather than furthers the assumptions of viable democracy.

Moreover, to compel a juror involuntarily assigned to jury duty to assume the burdens of mini-legislator or judge, as is implicit in the doctrine of nullification, is to put untoward strains on the jury system. It is one thing for a juror to know that the law condemns, but he has a factual power of lenity. To tell him expressly of a nullification prerogative, however, is to inform him, in effect, that it is he who fashions the rule that condemns. That is an overwhelming responsibility, an extreme burden for the jurors' psyche. And it is not inappropriate to add that a juror called upon for an involuntary public service is entitled to the protection, when he takes action that he knows is right, but also knows is unpopular, either in the community at large or in his own particular grouping, that he can fairly put it to friends and neighbors that he was merely following the instructions of the court.

In the last analysis, our rejection of the request for jury nullification doctrine is a recognition that there are times when logic is not the only or even best guide to sound conduct of government. For machines, one can indulge the person who likes to tinker in pursuit of fine tuning. When men and judicial machinery are involved, one must attend to the many and complex mechanisms and reasons that lead men to change their conduct—when they know they are being studied; when they are told of the consequences of their conduct; and when conduct exercised with restraint as an unwritten exception is expressly presented as a legitimate option.

What makes for health as an occasional medicine would be disastrous as a daily diet. The fact that there is widespread existence of the jury's prerogative, and approval of its existence as a "necessary counter to case-hardened judges and arbitrary prosecutors," does not establish as an imperative that the jury must be informed by the judge of that power. On the contrary, it is pragmatically useful to structure instructions in such wise that the jury must feel strongly about the values involved in the case, so strongly that it must itself identify the case as establishing a call of high conscience, and must independently initiate and undertake an act in contravention of the established instructions. This requirement of independent jury conception confines the happening of the lawless jury to the occasional instance that does not violate, and viewed as an exception may even enhance, the over-all normative effect of the rule of law. An explicit instruction to a jury conveys an implied approval that runs the risk of degrading the legal structure requisite for true freedom, for an ordered liberty that protects against anarchy as well as tyranny.

* * *

[Reversed and remanded]

BAZELON, CHIEF JUDGE, concurring in part and dissenting in part:

I concur in the Court's discussion of the statutory right of self-representation in criminal cases. * * *

My disagreement with the Court concerns the issue of jury nullification. As the Court's opinion clearly acknowledges, there can be no doubt that the jury has "an unreviewable and unreversible power * * * to acquit in disregard of the instructions on the law given by the trial judge * * *."

The sticking point, however, is whether or not the jury should be told of its power to nullify the law in a particular case. Here, the trial judge not only denied a requested instruction on nullification, but also barred defense counsel from raising the issue in argument before the jury. The majority affirms that ruling. I see no justification for, and considerable harm in, this deliberate lack of candor. * * *

The Court reasons that a jury uninformed of its power to nullify will invoke that power only where it "feel[s] strongly about the values involved in the case, so strongly that it [will] itself identify the case as establishing a call of high conscience * * *." In other words, the spontaneous and unsolicited act of nullification is thought less likely, on the whole, to reflect bias and a perverse sense of values than the act of nullification carried out by a jury carefully instructed on its power and responsibility.

It seems substantially more plausible to me to assume that the very opposite is true. The juror motivated by prejudice seems to me more likely to make spontaneous use of the power to nullify, and more likely to disregard the judge's exposition of the normally controlling legal standards. The conscientious juror, who could make a careful effort to consider the blameworthiness of the defendant's action in light of prevailing community values, is the one most likely to obey the judge's admonition that the jury enforce strict principles of law. * * *

As for the problem of unjust acquittal, it is important to recognize the strong internal check that constrains the jury's willingness to acquit. Where defendants seem dangerous, juries are unlikely to exercise their nullification power, whether or not an explicit instruction is offered. Of course, that check will not prevent the acquittal of a defendant who may be blameworthy and dangerous except in the jaundiced eyes of a jury motivated by a perverse and sectarian sense of values. But whether a nullification instruction would make such acquittals more common is problematical, if not entirely inconceivable. In any case, the real problem in this situation is not the nullification doctrine, but the values and prejudice that prompt the acquittal. And the solution is not to condemn the nullification power, but to spotlight the prejudice and parochial values that underlie the verdict in the hope that public outcry will force a re-examination of those values, and deter their implementation in subsequent cases. Surely nothing is gained by the pretense that the jurors lack the power to nullify, since that pretense deprives them of the opportunity to hear the very instruction that might compel them to confront their responsibility.

One often-cited abuse of the nullification power is the acquittal by bigoted juries of whites who commit crimes (lynching, for example) against blacks. That repellent practice cannot be directly arrested without jeopardizing important constitutional protections—the double jeopardy bar and the jury's power of nullification. But the revulsion and sense of shame fostered by that practice fueled the civil rights movement, which in turn made possible the enactment of major civil rights legislation. That same movement spurred on the revitalization of the equal protection clause and, in particular, the recognition of the right to be tried before a jury selected without bias. The lessons we learned from these abuses helped to create a climate in which such abuses could not so easily thrive. * * *

On remand the trial judge should grant defendants' request for a nullification instruction. At the very least, I would require the trial court to permit defendants to argue the question before the jury. But it is not at all clear that defendants would prevail even with the aid of an instruction or argument. After all, this case is significantly different from the classic, exalted cases where juries historically invoked the power to nullify. Here, the defendants have no quarrel with the general validity of the law under which they have been charged. They did not simply refuse to obey a government edict that they considered illegal, and whose illegality they expected to demonstrate in a judicial proceeding. Rather, they attempted to protest government action by interfering with others—specifically, the Dow Chemical Company. This is a distinction which could and should be explored in argument before the jury. If revulsion against the war in Southeast Asia has reached a point where a jury would be unwilling to convict a defendant for commission of the acts alleged here, we would be far better advised to ponder the implications of that result than to spend our time devising strategems which let us pretend that the power of nullification does not even exist.

TURNER v. MURRAY

Supreme Court of the United States, 1986.
476 U.S. 28, 106 S.Ct. 1683, 90 L.Ed.2d 27.

JUSTICE WHITE announced the judgment of the Court and delivered the opinion of the Court with respect to Parts I and III, and an opinion with respect to Parts II and IV, in which JUSTICE BLACKMUN, JUSTICE STEVENS, and JUSTICE O'CONNOR join.

Petitioner is a black man sentenced to death for the murder of a white storekeeper. The question presented is whether the trial judge committed reversible error at *voir dire* by refusing petitioner's request to question prospective jurors on racial prejudice.

I

On July 12, 1978, petitioner entered a jewelry store in Franklin, Virginia, armed with a sawed-off shotgun. He demanded that the proprietor, W. Jack Smith, Jr., put jewelry and money from the cash register into some jewelry bags. Smith complied with petitioner's demand, but triggered a silent alarm, alerting the Police Department. When Alan Bain, a police officer, arrived to inquire about the alarm, petitioner surprised him and forced him to surrender his revolver.

Having learned that Smith had triggered a silent alarm, petitioner became agitated. He fired toward the rear wall of the store and stated that if he saw or heard any more police officers, he was going to start killing those in the store. When a police siren sounded, petitioner walked to where Smith was stationed behind a counter and without warning shot him in the head with Bain's pistol, wounding Smith and causing him to slump incapacitated to the floor.

Officer Bain attempted to calm petitioner, promising to take him anywhere he wanted to go and asking him not to shoot again. Petitioner angrily replied that he was going to kill Smith for "snitching," and fired two pistol shots into Smith's chest, fatally wounding him. As petitioner turned away from shooting Smith, Bain was able to disarm him and place him under arrest.

A Southampton County, Virginia, grand jury indicted petitioner on charges of capital murder, use of a firearm in the commission of a murder, and possession of a sawed-off shotgun in the commission of a robbery. Petitioner requested and was granted a change of venue to Northampton County, Virginia, a rural county some 80 miles from the location of the murder.

Prior to the commencement of *voir dire,* petitioner's counsel submitted to the trial judge a list of proposed questions, including the following:

> "The defendant, Willie Lloyd Turner, is a member of the Negro race. The victim, W. Jack Smith, Jr., was a white Caucasian. Will these facts prejudice you against Willie Lloyd Turner or affect your

ability to render a fair and impartial verdict based solely on the evidence?"

The judge declined to ask this question, stating that it "has been ruled on by the Supreme Court." The judge did ask the venire, who were questioned in groups of five in petitioner's presence, whether any person was aware of any reason why he could not render a fair and impartial verdict, to which all answered "no." At the time the question was asked, the prospective jurors had no way of knowing that the murder victim was white.

The jury that was empaneled, which consisted of eight whites and four blacks, convicted petitioner on all of the charges against him. After a separate sentencing hearing on the capital charge, the jury recommended that petitioner be sentenced to death, a recommendation the trial judge accepted.

Petitioner appealed his death sentence to the Virginia Supreme Court. Among other points, he argued that the trial judge deprived him of his constitutional right to a fair and impartial jury by refusing to question prospective jurors on racial prejudice. The Virginia Supreme Court rejected this argument. Relying on our decision in *Ristaino v. Ross,* 424 U.S. 589 (1976), the court stated that a trial judge's refusal to ask prospective jurors about their racial attitudes, while perhaps not the wisest decision as a matter of policy, is not constitutionally objectionable in the absence of factors akin to those in *Ham v. South Carolina,* 409 U.S. 524 (1973).[3] The court held that "[t]he mere fact that a defendant is black and that a victim is white does not constitutionally mandate * * * an inquiry [into racial prejudice]."

[Turner's petition for Federal habeas corpus was denied by the District Court, and the Court of Appeals for the Fourth Circuit affirmed.]

II

The Fourth Circuit's opinion correctly states the analytical framework for evaluating petitioner's argument: "The broad inquiry in each case must be whether under all of the circumstances presented there was a constitutionally significant likelihood that, absent questioning about racial prejudice, the jurors would not be indifferent as they stand unsworn." The Fourth Circuit was correct, too, in holding that under

3. In *Ham,* a young black man known in his small South Carolina hometown as a civil rights activist was arrested and charged with possession of marihuana. We held that the trial judge committed reversible error in refusing to honor Ham's request to question prospective jurors on racial prejudice. In *Ristaino, supra,* we specified the factors which mandated an inquiry into racial prejudice in *Ham:*

"Ham's defense was that he had been framed because of his civil rights activities. His prominence in the community as a civil rights activist, if not already known to veniremen, inevitably would have been revealed to the members of the jury in the course of his presentation of that defense. Racial issues therefore were inextricably bound up with the conduct of the trial. Further, Ham's reputation as a civil rights activist and the defense he interposed were likely to intensify any prejudice that individual members of the jury might harbor." 424 U.S., at 596–597.

Ristaino the mere fact that petitioner is black and his victim white does not constitute a "special circumstance" of constitutional proportions. What sets this case apart from *Ristaino,* however, is that in addition to petitioner's being accused of a crime against a white victim, the crime charged was a capital offense.

In a capital sentencing proceeding before a jury, the jury is called upon to make a highly subjective, unique, individualized judgment regarding the punishment that a particular person deserves. The Virginia statute under which petitioner was sentenced is instructive of the kinds of judgments a capital sentencing jury must make. First, in order to consider the death penalty, a Virginia jury must find either that the defendant is likely to commit future violent crimes or that his crime was "outrageously or wantonly vile, horrible or inhuman in that it involved torture, depravity of mind or an aggravated battery to the victim." Second, the jury must consider any mitigating evidence offered by the defendant. Mitigating evidence may include, but is not limited to, facts tending to show that the defendant acted under the influence of extreme emotional or mental disturbance, or that at the time of the crime the defendant's capacity "to appreciate the criminality of his conduct or to conform his conduct to the requirements of law was significantly impaired." Finally, even if the jury has found an aggravating factor, and irrespective of whether mitigating evidence has been offered, the jury has discretion not to recommend the death sentence, in which case it may not be imposed.

* * *

Because of the range of discretion entrusted to a jury in a capital sentencing hearing, there is a unique opportunity for racial prejudice to operate but remain undetected. On the facts of this case, a juror who believes that blacks are violence-prone or morally inferior might well be influenced by the belief in deciding whether petitioner's crime involved the aggravating factors specified under Virginia law. Such a juror might also be less favorably inclined toward petitioner's evidence of mental disturbance as a mitigating circumstance. More subtle, less consciously held racial attitudes could also influence a juror's decision in this case. Fear of blacks, which could easily be stirred up by the violent facts of petitioner's crime, might incline a juror to favor the death penalty.

III

We hold that a capital defendant accused of an interracial crime is entitled to have prospective jurors informed of the race of the victim and questioned on the issue of racial bias. The rule we propose is minimally intrusive; as in other cases involving "special circumstances," the trial judge retains discretion as to the form and number of questions on the subject, including the decision whether to question the venire individually or collectively. Also, a defendant cannot complain of a judge's failure to question the venire on racial prejudice unless the defendant has specifically requested such an inquiry.

IV

The inadequacy of *voir dire* in this case requires that petitioner's death sentence be vacated. It is not necessary, however, that he be retried on the issue of guilt. Our judgment in this case is that there was an unacceptable risk of racial prejudice infecting the *capital sentencing proceeding.* This judgment is based on a conjunction of three factors: "the fact that the crime charged involved interracial violence, the broad discretion given the jury at the death-penalty hearing, and the special seriousness of the risk of improper sentencing in a capital case." At the guilt phase of petitioner's trial, the jury had no greater discretion than it would have had if the crime charged had been noncapital murder. Thus, with respect to the guilt phase of petitioner's trial, we find this case to be indistinguishable from *Ristaino,* to which we continue to adhere.

The judgment of the Court of Appeals is reversed, and the case is remanded for further proceedings consistent with this opinion.

It is so ordered.

THE CHIEF JUSTICE concurs in the judgment.

JUSTICE BRENNAN, concurring in part and dissenting in part.

* * *

A trial to determine guilt or innocence is, at bottom, nothing more than the sum total of a countless number of small discretionary decisions made by each individual who sits in the jury box. The difference between conviction and acquittal turns on whether key testimony is believed or rejected; on whether an alibi sounds plausible or dubious; on whether a character witness appears trustworthy or unsavory; and on whether the jury concludes that the defendant had a motive, the inclination, or the means available to commit the crime charged. A racially biased juror sits with blurred vision and impaired sensibilities and is incapable of fairly making the myriad decisions that each juror is called upon to make in the course of a trial. To put it simply, he cannot judge because he has prejudged. This is equally true at the trial on guilt as at the hearing on sentencing. * * * I would reverse the conviction as well as the sentence in this case to ensure compliance with the constitutional guarantee of an impartial jury.

[The separate dissent of JUSTICE MARSHALL is omitted. The dissent by JUSTICE POWELL, joined by JUSTICE REHNQUIST, is also omitted. Powell would have affirmed both the conviction and the sentence.]

BATSON v. KENTUCKY

Supreme Court of the United States, 1986.
476 U.S. 79, 106 S.Ct. 1712, 90 L.Ed.2d 69.

JUSTICE POWELL delivered the opinion of the Court.

This case requires us to reexamine that portion of *Swain v. Alabama,* 380 U.S. 202 (1965), concerning the evidentiary burden placed on a criminal defendant who claims that he has been denied equal protection through the State's use of peremptory challenges to exclude members of his race from the petit jury.

I

Petitioner, a black man, was indicted in Kentucky on charges of second-degree burglary and receipt of stolen goods. On the first day of trial in Jefferson Circuit Court, the judge conducted *voir dire* examination of the venire, excused certain jurors for cause, and then permitted the parties to exercise peremptory challenges.[2] The prosecutor used his peremptory challenges to strike all four black persons on the venire, and a jury composed only of white persons was selected. Defense counsel moved to discharge the jury before it was sworn on the ground that the prosecutor's removal of the black veniremen violated petitioner's rights under the Sixth and Fourteenth Amendments to a jury drawn from a cross-section of the community, and under the Fourteenth Amendment to equal protection of the laws. Counsel requested a hearing on his motion. Without expressly ruling on the request for a hearing, the trial judge observed that the parties were entitled to use their peremptory challenges to "strike anybody they want to." The judge then denied petitioner's motion, reasoning that the cross-section requirement applies only to selection of the venire and not to selection of the petit jury itself.

The jury convicted petitioner on both counts. [The Kentucky Supreme Court affirmed the convictions and the Supreme Court granted certiorari.]

III

* * *

Swain required the Court to decide, among other issues, whether a black defendant was denied equal protection by the State's exercise of peremptory challenges to exclude members of his race from the petit jury. The record in *Swain* showed that the prosecutor had used the State's peremptory challenges to strike the six black persons included on the petit jury venire. While rejecting the defendant's claim for failure to prove purposeful discrimination, the Court nonetheless indicated that the Equal Protection Clause placed some limits on the State's exercise of peremptory challenges.

The Court sought to accommodate the prosecutor's historical privilege of peremptory challenge free of judicial control, and the constitutional prohibition on exclusion of persons from jury service on account of

2. The Kentucky Rules of Criminal Procedure authorize the trial court to permit counsel to conduct *voir dire* examination or to conduct the examination itself. Ky.Rule Crim.Proc. 9.38. After jurors have been excused for cause, the parties exercise their peremptory challenges simultaneously by striking names from a list of qualified jurors equal to the number to be seated plus the number of allowable peremptory challenges. Rule 9.36. Since the offense charged in this case was a felony, and an alternate juror was called, the prosecutor was entitled to six peremptory challenges, and defense counsel to nine. Rule 9.40.

race. While the Constitution does not confer a right to peremptory challenges, those challenges traditionally have been viewed as one means of assuring the selection of a qualified and unbiased jury. To preserve the peremptory nature of the prosecutor's challenge, the Court in *Swain* declined to scrutinize his actions in a particular case by relying on a presumption that he properly exercised the State's challenges.

The Court went on to observe, however, that a state may not exercise its challenges in contravention of the Equal Protection Clause. It was impermissible for a prosecutor to use his challenges to exclude blacks from the jury "for reasons wholly unrelated to the outcome of the particular case on trial" or to deny to blacks "the same right and opportunity to participate in the administration of justice enjoyed by the white population." Accordingly, a black defendant could make out a prima facie case of purposeful discrimination on proof that the peremptory challenge system was "being perverted" in that manner. For example, an inference of purposeful discrimination would be raised on evidence that a prosecutor, "in case after case, whatever the circumstances, whatever the crime and whoever the defendant or the victim may be, is responsible for the removal of Negroes who have been selected as qualified jurors by the jury commissioners and who have survived challenges for cause, with the result that no Negroes ever serve on petit juries." Evidence offered by the defendant in *Swain* did not meet that standard. While the defendant showed that prosecutors in the jurisdiction had exercised their strikes to exclude blacks from the jury, he offered no proof of the circumstances under which prosecutors were responsible for striking black jurors beyond the facts of his own case.

A number of lower courts following the teaching of *Swain* reasoned that proof of repeated striking of blacks over a number of cases was necessary to establish a violation of the Equal Protection Clause. Since this interpretation of *Swain* has placed on defendants a crippling burden of proof, prosecutors' peremptory challenges are now largely immune from constitutional scrutiny. For reasons that follow, we reject this evidentiary formulation as inconsistent with standards that have been developed since *Swain* for assessing a prima facie case under the Equal Protection Clause. * * *

The standards for assessing a prima facie case in the context of discriminatory selection of the venire have been fully articulated since *Swain*. See *Castaneda v. Partida,* 430 U.S., at 494–495; *Washington v. Davis,* 426 U.S., at 241–242; *Alexander v. Louisiana,* 405 U.S., at 629–631. These principles support our conclusion that a defendant may establish a prima facie case of purposeful discrimination in selection of the petit jury solely on evidence concerning the prosecutor's exercise of peremptory challenges at the defendant's trial. To establish such a case, the defendant first must show that he is a member of a cognizable racial group, and that the prosecutor has exercised peremptory challenges to remove from the venire members of the defendant's race. Second, the defendant is entitled to rely on the fact, as to which there can be no dispute, that peremptory challenges constitute a jury selection practice that permits those to discriminate who are of a mind to discriminate. Finally, the defendant must show that these facts and any other relevant circumstances raise an inference that the prosecutor used that practice to exclude the veniremen from the petit jury on account of their race. This combination of factors in the empanelling of the petit jury, as in the selection of the venire, raises the necessary inference of purposeful discrimination.

In deciding whether the defendant has made the requisite showing, the trial court should consider all relevant circumstances. For example, a "pattern" of strikes against black jurors included in the particular venire might give rise to an inference of discrimination. Similarly, the prosecutor's questions and statements during *voir dire* examination and in exercising his challenges may support or refute an inference of discriminatory purpose. These examples are merely illustrative. We have confidence that trial judges, experienced in supervising *voir dire,* will be able to decide if the circumstances concerning the prosecutor's use of peremptory challenges creates a prima facie case of discrimination against black jurors.

Once the defendant makes a prima facie showing, the burden shifts to the State to come forward with a neutral explanation for challenging black jurors. Though this requirement imposes a limitation in some cases on the full peremptory character of the historic challenge, we emphasize that the prosecutor's explanation need not rise to the level justifying exercise of a challenge for cause. But the prosecutor may not rebut the defendant's prima facie case of discrimination by stating merely that he challenged jurors of the defendant's race on the assumption—or his intuitive judgment—that they would be partial to the defendant because of their shared race. Just as the Equal Protection Clause forbids the States to exclude black persons from the venire on the assumption that blacks as a group are unqualified to serve as jurors, so it forbids the States to strike black veniremen on the assumption that they will be biased in a particular case simply because the defendant is black. The core guarantee of equal protection, ensuring citizens that their State will not discriminate on account of race, would be meaningless were we to approve the exclusion of jurors on the basis of such assumptions, which arise solely from the jurors' race. Nor may the prosecutor rebut the defendant's case merely by denying that he had a discriminatory motive or affirming his good faith in individual selections. If these general assertions were accepted as rebutting a defendant's prima facie case, the Equal Protection Clause would be but a vain and illusory requirement. The prosecutor therefore must articulate a neutral explanation related to the particular case to be tried. The trial court then will have the duty to determine if the defendant has established purposeful discrimination.

* * *

V

In this case, petitioner made a timely objection to the prosecutor's removal of all black persons on the venire. Because the trial court flatly rejected the objection without requiring the prosecutor to give an explanation for his action, we remand this case for further proceedings. If the trial court decides that the facts establish, prima facie, purposeful discrimination and the prosecutor does not come forward with a neutral explanation for his action, our precedents require that petitioner's conviction be reversed.

It is so ordered.

JUSTICE MARSHALL, concurring. * * *

I wholeheartedly concur in the Court's conclusion that use of the peremptory challenge to remove blacks from juries, on the basis of their race, violates the Equal Protection Clause. I would go further, however, in fashioning a remedy adequate to eliminate that discrimination. Merely allowing defendants the opportunity to challenge the racially discriminatory use of peremptory challenges in individual cases will not end the illegitimate use of the peremptory challenge.

Evidentiary analysis similar to that set out by the Court, has been adopted as a matter of state law in States including Massachusetts and California. Cases from those jurisdictions illustrate the limitations of the approach. First, defendants cannot attack the discriminatory use of peremptory challenges at all unless the challenges are so flagrant as to establish a prima facie case. This means, in those States, that where only one or two black jurors survive the challenges for cause, the prosecutor need have no compunction about striking them from the jury because of their race. See *Commonwealth v. Robinson,* 415 N.E.2d 805, 809–810 (Mass.1981) (no prima facie case of discrimination where defendant is black, prospective jurors include three blacks and one Puerto Rican, and prosecutor excludes one for cause and strikes the remainder peremptorily, producing all-white jury); *People v. Rousseau,* 179 Cal.Rptr. 892, 897–898 (Cal.App.1982) (no prima facie case where prosecutor peremptorily strikes only two blacks on jury panel). Prosecutors are left free to discriminate against blacks in jury selection provided that they hold that discrimination to an "acceptable" level.

Second, when a defendant can establish a prima facie case, trial courts face the difficult burden of assessing prosecutors' motives. See *King v. County of Nassau,* 581 F.Supp. 493, 501–502 (E.D.N.Y.1984). Any prosecutor can easily assert facially neutral reasons for striking a juror, and trial courts are ill-equipped to second-guess those reasons. How is the court to treat a prosecutor's statement that he struck a juror because the juror had a son about the same age as defendant, see *People v. Hall,* 672 P.2d 854 (Cal.1983), or seemed "uncommunicative," *King, supra,* at 498, or "never cracked a smile" and, therefore "did not possess the sensitivities necessary to realistically look at the issues and decide the facts in this case," *Hall,* 672 P.2d, at 856? If such easily generated explanations are sufficient to discharge the prosecutor's obligation to justify his strikes on nonracial grounds, then the protection erected by the Court today may be illusory.

Nor is outright prevarication by prosecutors the only danger here. "[I]t is even possible that an attorney may lie to himself in an effort to convince himself that his motives are legal." *King, supra,* at 502. A prosecutor's own conscious or unconscious racism may lead him easily to the conclusion that a prospective black juror is "sullen," or "distant," a characterization that would not have come to his mind if a white juror had acted identically. A judge's own conscious or unconscious racism may lead him to accept such an explanation as well supported. As Justice Rehnquist concedes, prosecutors' peremptories are based on their "seat-of-the-pants instincts" as to how particular jurors will vote. Yet "seat-of-the-pants instincts" may often be just another term for racial prejudice. Even if all parties approach the Court's mandate with the best of conscious intentions, that mandate requires them to confront and overcome their own racism on all levels—a challenge I doubt all of them can meet. It is worth remembering that 114 years after the close of the War Between the States and nearly 100 years after *Strauder,* racial and other forms of discrimination still remain a fact of life, in the administration of justice as in our society as a whole. * * *

The inherent potential of peremptory challenges to distort the jury process by permitting the exclusion of jurors on racial grounds should ideally lead the Court to ban them entirely from the criminal justice system.

Some authors have suggested that the courts should ban prosecutors' peremptories entirely, but should zealously guard the defendant's peremptory as essential to the fairness of trial by jury. I would not find that an acceptable solution. Our criminal justice system requires not only freedom from any bias against the accused, but also from any prejudice against his prosecution. Between him and the state the scales are to be evenly held. We can maintain that balance, not by permitting both prosecutor and defendant to engage in racial discrimination in jury selection, but by banning the use of peremptory challenges by prosecutors and by allowing the States to eliminate the defendant's peremptory as well. * * *

CHIEF JUSTICE BURGER, joined by JUSTICE REHNQUIST, dissenting.

* * *

* * * The peremptory challenge has been in use without scrutiny into its basis for nearly as long as juries have existed. It was in use amongst the Romans in criminal cases, and the *Lex Servilia* (B.C.104) enacted that the accuser and the accused should severally propose one hundred *judices,* and that each might reject fifty from the list of the other, so that one hundred would remain to try the alleged crime.

In *Swain* Justice White traced the development of the peremptory challenge from the early days of the jury trial in England:

> "In all trials for felonies at common law, the defendant was allowed to challenge peremptorily 35 jurors, and the prosecutor originally had a right to challenge any number of jurors without cause, a right

which was said to tend to 'infinite delayes and danger.' Coke on Littleton 156 (14th ed. 1791). Thus The Ordinance for Inquests, 33 Edw. 1, Stat. 4 (1305), provided that if 'they that sue for the King will challenge any * * * Jurors, they shall assign * * * a Cause certain.' So persistent was the view that a proper jury trial required peremptories on both sides, however, that the statute was construed to allow the prosecution to direct any juror after examination to 'stand aside' until the entire panel was gone over and the defendant had exercised his challenges; only if there was a deficiency of jurors in the box at that point did the Crown have to show cause in respect to jurors recalled to make up the required number. Peremptories on both sides became the settled law of England, continuing in the above form until after the separation of the Colonies." 380 U.S., at 212–213.

Peremptory challenges have a venerable tradition in this country as well:

* * *

The Court's opinion, in addition to ignoring the teachings of history, also contrasts with *Swain* in its failure to even discuss the rationale of the peremptory challenge. *Swain* observed:

> "The function of the challenge is not only to eliminate extremes of partiality on both sides, but to assure the parties that the jurors before whom they try the case will decide on the basis of the evidence placed for them, and not otherwise. In this way the peremptory satisfies the rule that to perform its high function in the best way, justice must satisfy the appearance of justice." *Id.,* at 219.

Permitting unexplained peremptories has long been regarded as a means to strengthen our jury system in other ways as well. One commentator has recognized:

> "The peremptory, made without giving any reason, avoids trafficking in the core of truth in most common stereotypes. * * * Common human experience, common sense, psychosociological studies, and public opinion polls tell us that it is likely that certain classes of people statistically have predispositions that would make them inappropriate jurors for particular kinds of cases. But to allow this knowledge to be expressed in the evaluative terms necessary for challenges for cause would undercut our desire for a society in which all people are judged as individuals and in which each is held reasonable and open to compromise. * * * [For example,] [a]lthough experience reveals that black males as a class can be biased against young alienated blacks who have not tried to join the middle class, to enunciate this in the concrete expression required of a challenge for cause is societally divisive. Instead we have evolved in the peremptory challenge a system that allows the covert expression of what we dare not say but know is true more often than not." Babcock, Voir Dire: Preserving "Its Wonderful Power," 27 Stan. L.Rev. 545, 553–554 (1975).

* * *

Instead of even considering the history or function of the peremptory challenge, the bulk of the Court's opinion is spent recounting the well-established principle that intentional exclusion of racial groups from jury venires is a violation of the Equal Protection Clause. I too reaffirm that principle, which has been a part of our constitutional tradition since at least *Strauder v. West Virginia,* 100 U.S. 303 (1880). But if today's decision is nothing more than mere "application" of the "principles announced in *Strauder,*" as the Court maintains, some will consider it curious that the application went unrecognized for over a century. * * *

A moment's reflection quickly reveals the vast differences between the racial exclusions involved in *Strauder* and the allegations before us today:

> "Exclusion from the venire summons process implies that the government (usually the legislative or judicial branch) * * * has made the general determination that those excluded are unfit to try *any* case. Exercise of the peremptory challenge, by contrast, represents the discrete decision, made by one of two or more opposed *litigants* in the trial phase of our adversary system of justice, that the challenged venireperson will likely be more unfavorable to that litigant in that *particular case* than others on the same venire.
>
> "Thus, excluding a particular cognizable group from all venire pools is stigmatizing and discriminatory in several interrelated ways that the peremptory challenge is not. The former singles out the excluded group, while individuals of all grounds are equally subject to peremptory challenge on any basis, including their group affiliation. Further, venire-pool exclusion bespeaks *a priori* across-the-board total unfitness, while peremptory-strike exclusion merely suggests potential partiality in a particular isolated case. Exclusion from venires focuses on the inherent attributes of the excluded group and infers its *inferiority,* but the peremptory does not. To suggest that a particular race is unfit to judge in any case necessarily is racially insulting. To suggest that each race may have its own special concerns, or even may tend to favor its own, is not." *United States v. Leslie,* 783 F.2d 541, 554 (C.A.5 1986) (en banc).

Unwilling to rest solely on jury venire cases such as *Strauder,* the Court also invokes general equal protection principles in support of its holding. But peremptory challenges are often lodged, of necessity, for reasons "normally thought irrelevant to legal proceedings or official action, namely, the race, religion, nationality, occupation or affiliations of people summoned for jury duty." *Swain, supra,* 380 U.S., at 220. Moreover, in making peremptory challenges, both the prosecutor and defense attorney necessarily act on only limited information or hunch. The process can not be indicted on the sole basis that such decisions are made on the basis of "assumption" or "intuitive judgment." As a result, unadulterated equal protection analysis is simply inapplicable to peremptory challenges exercised in any particular case. A clause that requires a minimum "rationality" in government actions has no application to

" 'an arbitrary and capricious right,' "*Swain, supra,* at 219, a constitutional principle that may invalidate state action on the basis of "stereotypic notions," does not explain the breadth of a procedure exercised on the " 'sudden impressions and unaccountable prejudices we are apt to conceive upon the bare looks and gestures of another.' "*Lewis v. United States,* 146 U.S., at 376 (quoting 4 W. Blackstone, Commentaries * 353).

That the Court is not applying conventional equal protection analysis is shown by its limitation of its new rule to allegations of impermissible challenge *on the basis of race;* the Court's opinion clearly contains such a limitation. * * * But if conventional equal protection principles apply, then presumably defendants could object to exclusions on the basis of not only race, but also sex, age, religious or political affiliation, mental capacity, number of children, living arrangements, and employment in a particular industry or profession. [Citations omitted.]

In short, it is quite probable that every peremptory challenge could be objected to on the basis that, because it excluded a venireman who had some characteristic not shared by the remaining members of the venire, it constituted a "classification" subject to equal protection scrutiny. * * *

The Court also purports to express "no views on whether the Constitution imposes any limit on the exercise of peremptory challenges by *defense* counsel." But the clear and inescapable import of this novel holding will inevitably be to limit the use of this valuable tool to both prosecutors and defense attorneys alike. Once the Court has held that *prosecutors* are limited in their use of peremptory challenges, could we rationally hold that defendants are not?[6] * * * Our system permits two types of challenges: challenges for cause and peremptory challenges. Challenges for cause obviously have to be explained; by definition, peremptory challenges do not. * * *

Confronted with the dilemma it created, the Court today attempts to decree a middle ground. To rebut a prima facie case, the Court requires a "neutral explanation" for the challenge, but is at pains to "emphasize" that the "explanation need not rise to the level justifying exercise of a challenge for cause." I am at a loss to discern the governing principles here. A "clear and reasonably specific" explanation of "legitimate reasons" for exercising the challenge will be difficult to distinguish from a challenge for cause. Anything short of a challenge for cause may well be seen as an "arbitrary and capricious" challenge, to use Blackstone's characterization of the peremptory. Apparently the Court envisions permissible challenges short of a challenge for cause that are just a little bit arbitrary—but not too much. While our trial judges are "experienced in supervising *voir dire,*" they have no experience in administering rules like this.

6. "[E]very jurisdiction which has spoken to the matter, and prohibited prosecution case-specific peremptory challenges on the basis of cognizable group affiliation, has held that the defense must likewise be so prohibited." *United States v. Leslie,* 783 F.2d 541, 565 (C.A.5 1986) (en banc).

An example will quickly demonstrate how today's holding, while purporting to "further the ends of justice," will not have that effect. Assume an Asian defendant, on trial for the capital murder of a white victim, asks prospective jury members, most of whom are white, whether they harbor racial prejudice against Asians. See *Turner v. Murray,* [infra p. 519]. The basis for such a question is to flush out any "juror who believes that [Asians] are violence-prone or morally inferior. * * *" Assume further that all white jurors deny harboring racial prejudice but that the defendant, on trial for his life, remains unconvinced by these protestations. Instead, he continues to harbor a hunch, an "assumption" or "intuitive judgment," that these white jurors will be prejudiced against him, presumably based on part on race. The time honored rule before today was that peremptory challenges could be exercised on such a basis. * * * The effect of the Court's decision, however, will be to force the defendant to come forward and "articulate a neutral explanation," for his peremptory challenge, a burden he probably cannot meet. This example demonstrates that today's holding will produce juries that the parties do not believe are truly impartial. This will surely do more than "disconcert" litigants; it will diminish confidence in the jury system.

A further painful paradox of the Court's holding is that it is likely to interject racial matters back into the jury selection process, contrary to the general thrust of a long line of Court decisions and the notion of our country as a "melting pot." * * *

* * * Prosecutors and defense attorney's alike will build records in support of their claims that peremptory challenges have been exercised in a racially discriminatory fashion by asking jurors to state their racial background and national origin for the record, despite the fact that such questions may be offensive to some jurors and thus are not ordinarily asked on voir dire. * * *

Even after a "record" on this issue has been created, disputes will inevitably arise. In one case, for instance, a conviction was reversed based on the assumption that no blacks were on the jury that convicted a defendant. See *People v. Motton,* 704 P.2d 176, 180 (Cal.1985). However, after the court's decision was announced, Carolyn Pritchett, who had served on the jury, called the press to state that the court was in error and that she was black. 71 A.B.A.J. 22 (Nov.1985). The California court nonetheless denied a rehearing petition. * * *

JUSTICE REHNQUIST, with whom THE CHIEF JUSTICE joins, dissenting.

* * * In my view, there is simply nothing "unequal" about the State using its peremptory challenges to strike blacks from the jury in cases involving black defendants, so long as such challenges are also used to exclude whites in cases involving white defendants, Hispanics in cases involving Hispanic defendants, Asians in cases involving Asian defendants, and so on. This case-specific use of peremptory challenges by the State does not single out blacks, or members of any other race for that matter, for discriminatory treatment.[1] Such use of peremptories is at

1. I note that the Court does not rely on the argument that, because there are fewer "minorities" in a given population than there are "majorities," the equal use of

best based upon seat-of-the-pants instincts, which are undoubtedly crudely stereotypical and may in many cases be hopelessly mistaken. But as long as they are applied across the board to jurors of all races and nationalities, I do not see—and the Court most certainly has not explained—how their use violates the Equal Protection Clause. * * *

The use of group affiliations, such as age, race, or occupation, as a "proxy" for potential juror partiality, based on the assumption or belief that members of one group are more likely to favor defendants who belong to the same group, has long been accepted as a legitimate basis for the State's exercise of peremptory challenges. Indeed, given the need for reasonable limitations on the time devoted to *voir dire,* the use of such "proxies" by both the State and the defendant may be extremely useful in eliminating from the jury persons who might be biased in one way or another. The Court today holds that the State may not use its peremptory challenges to strike black prospective jurors on this basis without violating the Constitution. But I do not believe there is anything in the Equal Protection Clause, or any other constitutional provision, that justifies such a departure from the substantive holding contained in Part II of *Swain.* Petitioner in the instant case failed to make a sufficient showing to overcome the presumption announced in *Swain* that the State's use of peremptory challenges was related to the context of the case. I would therefore affirm the judgment of the court below.

Note

A number of Supreme Court decisions have condemned racial discrimination in the selection of jury panels or "venires." Some states have employed a "key man" system for calling citizens to jury service. The jury commissioners would rely on a few prominent citizens to supply the names of persons considered suitable for jury service, and would make up the venires from these master lists. Where the jury commissioners and key men were all white persons in a segregated society, the likelihood was that at most a token number of blacks would be included. State laws also generally directed the jury commissioners to apply subjective standards in selecting persons suitable for jury service, and these standards could have the effect of creating a political test for jury service.

Where the jury commissioner system has resulted in gross under-representation of blacks on the panels, the Supreme Court has held that a presumption of discrimination exists and the burden shifts to the state to prove the absence of discrimination. The federal courts have reversed many convictions of black defendants from Southern states where members of their race were systematically excluded from grand juries or petit jury panels. See Alexander v. Louisiana, 405 U.S. 625 (1972), and the prior cases cited therein. In some ways, this anti-discrimination law is very far-reaching.

peremptory challenges against members of "majority" and "minority" racial groups has an unequal impact. The flaws in this argument are demonstrated in Judge Garwood's thoughtful opinion for the en banc Fifth Circuit in *United States v. Leslie,* 783 F.2d 541, 559 (C.A.5 1986).

The Court has been willing to reverse convictions due to grand jury discrimination, although any impropriety at the grand jury level is unlikely to have prejudiced a defendant whose guilt was later proved beyond a reasonable doubt to a properly selected petit jury. The Court has even assumed that discrimination in the selection of the foreman of a state grand jury would require that a subsequent conviction be set aside. Rose v. Mitchell, 443 U.S. 545 (1979). On the other hand, the Court later limited that ruling by holding that it did not apply to the selection of foremen for federal grand juries. Hobby v. United States, 468 U.S. 339, 350 (1984). (Holding that even assuming that "discrimination entered into the selection of federal grand jury foremen, such discrimination does not warrant the reversal of the conviction of, and dismissal of the indictment against, a white male bringing a claim under the Due Process Clause.") The vice of racial discrimination in the selection of grand jurors is not so much that it affects the outcome of particular criminal cases, as that it represents an attempt to maintain white domination of a part of the government structure. Because unconstitutional jury selection procedures cast doubt on the integrity of the whole judicial process, the Supreme Court has held that a white criminal defendant has standing to complain of discrimination against blacks in the selection of grand and petit juries. Peters v. Kiff, 407 U.S. 493 (1972). See also, Castaneda v. Partida, 430 U.S. 482 (1977).

The Supreme Court has not, however, ordered structural changes in the procedures for selecting jurors, even where complainants have proved that those procedures have been consistently abused in the past. In Carter v. Jury Commission of Greene County (Alabama), 396 U.S. 320 (1970), the plaintiffs brought a civil action alleging that the jury commissioners had systematically excluded black residents from jury service. The trial court ordered the commissioners to cease racial discrimination and to compile forthwith a complete list of qualified jurors as required by state law, but it refused: (1) to declare invalid a statute requiring the jury commissioners to select for jury service only those persons who are "generally reputed to be honest and intelligent and * * * esteemed in the community for their integrity, good character and sound judgment"; or (2) to order the Governor to cease appointing only whites to the jury commission. Appealing to the Supreme Court, the plaintiffs argued that to grant discretion to an all-white jury commission to select jurors for "good character and sound judgment" practically invites discrimination against black persons, and especially against those black persons who assert their right to legal and social equality. The Supreme Court denied further relief, concluding that the trial court had adequate power to prevent further racial discrimination in the selection process without taking the extreme steps of ordering the Governor to appoint black jury commissioners or invalidating the statute. It observed that "It has long been accepted that the Constitution does not forbid the States to prescribe relevant qualifications for their jurors. The States remain free to confine the selection to citizens, to persons meeting specified qualifications of age and educational attainment, and to those possessing good intelligence, sound judgment, and fair character."

Most states and the federal government now select jury panels by methods that involve much less subjective judgment, and therefore fewer opportunities for discrimination. The Federal Jury Selection Act of 1968, 28

U.S.C.A. § 1861 et seq., requires that panels of grand or petit jurors be selected at random from voter registration lists or other representative lists. Jurors so selected may then be disqualified only on certain limited grounds, such as conviction of a felony or inability to speak or read the English language. Random selection from voter registration lists does not, however, guarantee panels that are representative of the racial and cultural composition of the society at large. Aliens and ex-convicts are not eligible to vote or serve on juries. Many persons do not register to vote, even where it is extremely easy to do so, and others ignore the summons to jury duty. Because important groups like blacks and Hispanics continue to be under-represented on jury panels in many localities, there is a continuing controversy over whether the states and the federal government have an obligation to practice some form of "affirmative action" to obtain more representative panels.

Exclusion of women from jury service was once common. The Supreme Court barred exclusion of women from federal court juries in Ballard v. United States, 329 U.S. 187 (1946). In Hoyt v. Florida, 368 U.S. 57 (1961), a woman appealed her conviction for murdering her husband on the ground that she was tried by an all-male jury under a state statutory scheme whereby women were placed on the jury list only if they so requested. The court affirmed the conviction, stating that since "woman is still regarded as the center of home and family life," a state may permissibly "conclude that a woman should be relieved from the civic duty of jury service unless she herself determines that such service is consistent with her own special responsibilities." 368 U.S. at 62. In 1975, however, the Supreme Court overruled *Hoyt* in Taylor v. Louisiana, 419 U.S. 522 (1975). The opinion of the Court by Mr. Justice White observed that "the selection of a petit jury from a representative cross section of the community is an essential component of the Sixth Amendment right to a jury trial. * * * We think it is no longer tenable to hold that women as a class may be excluded or given automatic exemptions based solely on sex if the consequence is that criminal jury venires are almost totally male. * * * If it ever was the case that women were unqualified to sit on juries or were so situated that none of them should be required to perform jury service, that time has long since passed." See also Duren v. Missouri, 439 U.S. 357 (1979).

Some judicial opinions have assumed that a jury fairly representative of the community at large would be the "impartial" jury commanded by the Sixth Amendment. But matters are not as simple as that; the community, after all, may contain a significant percentage of prejudiced people. For this reason the attorneys are allowed to challenge prospective jurors for "cause," i.e. conscious or unconscious bias. The attorneys are also allowed a certain number of "peremptory challenges" to excuse jurors whom they think may be particularly likely to vote for the other side, even though there are no grounds for a challenge for cause. The peremptory challenge can function as an exercise in group stereotyping, with prosecutors and defense counsel both challenging jurors with group characteristics that the litigants believe might predispose them to favor one side or the other. Prosecutors are particularly concerned to strike any juror who might "hang" the jury regardless of the strength of the evidence for conviction, and this tends to mean that they will try to strike those jurors most likely to be sympathetic to the defendant. Of course, there is also the possibility that white jurors who observe the deliberate exclusion of minority group members through peremptory challenges will resent the practice, and be motivated to side with the defendant to demonstrate that they are not racially prejudiced. For this reason, often the most promising prosecution strategy is to seek to include jurors of the defendant's racial or ethnic background who have relatively conservative values. Such jurors may actually help the other members of the jury overcome whatever guilt feelings they have about convicting a member of an underprivileged minority group. Realizing this, the defense may be particularly determined to strike minority jurors of this type.

One solution to the problem of racially-based peremptory challenges is to require the prosecutor to justify the challenge in every case. If an explanation that the particular jurors seemed unsuitable for some reason is readily accepted, this remedy will be ineffective. If a high standard of justification is required, then in effect the prosecutor may be allowed to challenge minority jurors only for cause. Another solution would be to allow only a small number of peremptory challenges. Where the panel is at all representative, it should be difficult to exclude a whole class of jurors with only a handful of challenges. Rule 24 of the Federal Rules of Criminal Procedure gives each side 20 peremptory challenges in capital cases; in other felony trials the prosecution gets 6 challenges and the defense 10. In misdemeanor trials in federal court, each side gets only 3 challenges. Who benefits most from the greater number of challenges in capital cases, the prosecution or the defense?

D. THE PROSECUTION'S BURDEN OF PROOF

MULLANEY v. WILBUR

Supreme Court of the United States, 1975.
421 U.S. 684, 95 S.Ct. 1881, 44 L.Ed.2d 508.

MR. JUSTICE POWELL delivered the opinion of the Court.

The State of Maine requires a defendant charged with murder to prove that he acted "in the heat of passion on sudden provocation" in order to reduce the homicide to manslaughter. We must decide whether this rule comports with the due process requirement, as defined in In re Winship, 397 U.S. 358 (1970),[a] that the prosecution prove beyond a reasonable doubt every fact necessary to constitute the crime charged.

a. The petitioner in the *Winship* case was a juvenile who was charged with larceny in the New York Family Court. The judge acknowledged that the proof might not establish guilt beyond a reasonable doubt, but concluded that in juvenile cases guilt need only be proved by a preponderance of the evidence. Applying that standard, he found the defendant to be a juvenile delinquent and committed him to a reformatory. The Supreme Court reversed the judgment, holding that the Due Process Clause of the Fourteenth Amendment requires proof beyond a reasonable doubt in criminal cases, and that this standard is applicable to juvenile criminal proceedings. In its opinion, the Supreme Court stated that "Lest there remain any doubt about the constitutional stature of the reasonable-doubt standard, we explicitly hold that the Due Process Clause protects the accused against conviction except upon proof beyond a reasonable doubt of *every fact necessary to constitute the crime* with which he is charged." 397 U.S. at 364.—ed. [Emphasis added]

In June 1966 a jury found respondent Stillman E. Wilbur, Jr., guilty of murder. The case against him rested on his own pretrial statement and on circumstantial evidence showing that he fatally assaulted Claude Hebert in the latter's hotel room. Respondent's statement, introduced by the prosecution, claimed that he had attacked Hebert in a frenzy provoked by Hebert's homosexual advance. The defense offered no evidence, but argued that the homicide was not unlawful since respondent lacked criminal intent. Alternatively, Wilbur's counsel asserted that at most the homicide was manslaughter rather than murder, since it occurred in the heat of passion provoked by the homosexual assault.

The trial court instructed the jury that Maine law recognizes only two kinds of homicide, murder and manslaughter, and that these offenses are not subdivided into different degrees. The common elements of both are that the homicide be unlawful—i.e., neither justifiable nor excusable—and that it be intentional. The prosecution is required to prove these elements by proof beyond a reasonable doubt, and only if they are so proved is the jury to consider the distinction between murder and manslaughter.

In view of the evidence the trial court drew particular attention to the difference between murder and manslaughter. After reading the statutory definitions of both offenses, the court charged that "malice aforethought is an essential and indispensable element of the crime of murder," without which the homicide would be manslaughter. The jury was further instructed, however, that if the prosecution established that the homicide was both intentional and unlawful, malice aforethought was to be conclusively implied unless the defendant proved by a fair preponderance of the evidence that he acted in the heat of passion on sudden provocation. The court emphasized that "malice aforethought and heat of passion on sudden provocation are inconsistent things;" thus, by proving the latter the defendant would negate the former and reduce the homicide from murder to manslaughter. The court then concluded its charge with elaborate definitions of "heat of passion" and "sudden provocation."

After retiring to consider its verdict, the jury twice returned to request further instruction. It first sought reinstruction on the doctrine of implied malice aforethought, and later on the definition of "heat of passion." Shortly after the second reinstruction, the jury found respondent guilty of murder.

Respondent appealed to the Maine Supreme Judicial Court, arguing that he had been denied due process because he was required to negate the element of malice aforethought by proving that he had acted in the heat of passion on sudden provocation. He claimed that under Maine law malice aforethought was an essential element of the crime of murder—indeed that it was the sole element distinguishing murder from manslaughter. Respondent contended, therefore, that this Court's decision in *Winship* requires the prosecution to prove the existence of that element beyond a reasonable doubt.

The Maine Supreme Judicial Court rejected this contention, holding that in Maine murder and manslaughter are not distinct crimes but rather different degrees of the single generic offense of felonious homicide. State v. Wilbur, 278 A.2d 139 (1971). The court further stated that for more than a century it repeatedly had held that the prosecution could rest on a presumption of implied malice aforethought and require the defendant to prove that he had acted in the heat of passion on sudden provocation in order to reduce murder to manslaughter. With respect to *Winship,* which was decided after respondent's trial, the court noted that it did not anticipate the application of the *Winship* principle to a "reductive factor" such as the heat of passion on sudden provocation. Id., at 144–146.

Respondent next successfully petitioned for a writ of habeas corpus in federal district court. * * * [On appeal from the district court's decision that the conviction was unconstitutional,] the Court of Appeals held that the principles enunciated in *Winship* control, and that to establish murder the prosecution must prove beyond a reasonable doubt that the defendant did not act in the heat of passion on sudden provocation.

Because of the importance of the issues presented, we again granted certiorari. We now affirm. * * *

Petitioners, the warden of the Maine Prison and the State of Maine, argue that *Winship* should not be extended to the present case. They note that as a formal matter the absence of the heat of passion on sudden provocation is not a "fact necessary to constitute the *crime*" of felonious homicide in Maine. This distinction is relevant, according to petitioners, because in *Winship* the facts at issue were essential to establish criminality in the first instance whereas the fact in question here does not come into play until the jury already has determined that the defendant is guilty and may be punished at least for manslaughter. In this situation, petitioners maintain, the defendant's critical interests in liberty and reputation are no longer of paramount concern since, irrespective of the presence or absence of the heat of passion on sudden provocation, he is likely to lose his liberty and certain to be stigmatized. In short, petitioners would limit *Winship* to those facts which, if not proved, would wholly exonerate the defendant.

This analysis fails to recognize that the criminal law of Maine, like that of other jurisdictions, is concerned not only with guilt or innocence in the abstract but also with the degree of criminal culpability. Maine has chosen to distinguish those who kill in the heat of passion from those who kill in the absence of this factor. Because the former are less "blameworth[y]," State v. Lafferty, 309 A.2d, at 671, 673 (concurring opinion), they are subject to substantially less severe penalties. By drawing this distinction, while refusing to require the prosecution to establish beyond a reasonable doubt the fact upon which it turns, Maine denigrates the interests found critical in *Winship.*

The safeguards of due process are not rendered unavailing simply because a determination may already have been reached that would stigmatize the defendant and that might lead to a significant impairment of personal liberty. The fact remains that the consequences resulting from a verdict of murder, as compared with a verdict of manslaughter, differ significantly. Indeed, when viewed in terms of the potential difference in restrictions of personal liberty attendant to each conviction, the distinction established by Maine between murder and manslaughter may be of greater importance than the difference between guilt or innocence for many lesser crimes.

Moreover, if *Winship* were limited to those facts that constitute a crime as defined by state law, a State could undermine many of the interests that decision sought to protect without effecting any substantive change in its law. It would only be necessary to redefine the elements that comprise different crimes, characterizing them as factors that bear solely on the extent of punishment. An extreme example of this approach can be fashioned from the law challenged in this case. Maine divides the single generic offense of felonious homicide into three distinct punishment categories—murder, voluntary manslaughter, and involuntary manslaughter. Only the first two of these categories require that the homicidal act either be intentional or the result of criminally reckless conduct. See State v. Lafferty, 309 A.2d at 670–672 (concurring opinion). But under Maine law these facts of intent are not general elements of the crime of felonious homicide. See Petitioners' Brief, at 10 n. 5. Instead, they bear only on the appropriate punishment category. Thus, if petitioners' argument were accepted, Maine could impose a life sentence for any felonious homicide—even those that traditionally might be considered involuntary manslaughter—unless the *defendant* was able to prove that his act was neither intentional nor criminally reckless.[24]

Winship is concerned with substance rather than this kind of formalism. * * *

It has been suggested, State v. Wilbur, 278 A.2d at 145, that because of the difficulties in negating an argument that the homicide was committed in the heat of passion the burden of proving this fact should rest on the defendant. No doubt this is often a heavy burden for the prosecution to satisfy. The same may be said of the requirement of proof beyond a reasonable doubt of many controverted facts in a criminal trial. But this is the traditional burden which our system of criminal justice deems essential.

Indeed, the Maine Supreme Judicial Court itself acknowledged that most States require the prosecution to prove the absence of passion

24. Many States impose different statutory sentences on different degrees of assault. If *Winship* were limited to a State's definition of the elements of a crime, these States could define all assaults as a single offense and then require the defendant to disprove the elements of aggravation—e.g., intent to kill or intent to rob. But see State v. Ferris, 249 A.2d 523 (Me.1969) (prosecution must prove elements of aggravation in criminal assault case by proof beyond a reasonable doubt).

beyond a reasonable doubt. State v. Wilbur, 278 A.2d, at 146.[28] Moreover, the difficulty of meeting such an exacting burden is mitigated in Maine where the fact at issue is largely an "objective, rather than a subjective, behavioral criterion." In this respect, proving that the defendant did not act in the heat of passion on sudden provocation is similar to proving any other element of intent; it may be established by adducing evidence of the factual circumstances surrounding the commission of the homicide. And although intent is typically considered a fact peculiarly within the knowledge of the defendant, this does not, as the Court has long recognized, justify shifting the burden to him.

Nor is the requirement of proving a negative unique in our system of criminal jurisprudence. Maine itself requires the prosecution to prove the absence of self-defense beyond a reasonable doubt. Satisfying this burden imposes an obligation that, in all practical effect, is identical to the burden involved in negating the heat of passion on sudden provocation. Thus, we discern no unique hardship on the prosecution that would justify requiring the defendant to carry the burden of proving a fact so critical to criminal culpability. * * *

Affirmed.

MR. JUSTICE REHNQUIST, with whom THE CHIEF JUSTICE joins, concurring.

* * *

I agree with the Court that In re Winship does require that the prosecution prove beyond a reasonable doubt every element which constitutes the crime charged against a defendant. I see no inconsistency between that holding and the holding of Leland v. Oregon, 343 U.S. 790 (1952). In the latter case this Court held that there was no constitutional requirement that the State shoulder the burden of proving the sanity of the defendant.

The Court noted in *Leland* that the issue of insanity as a defense to a criminal charge was considered by the jury only after it had found that all elements of the offense, including the *mens rea* if any required by state law, had been proven beyond a reasonable doubt. Although as the state court's instructions in *Leland* recognized, evidence relevant to insanity as defined by state law may also be relevant to whether the required *mens rea* was present, the existence or nonexistence of legal insanity bears no necessary relationship to the existence or nonexistence of the required mental elements of the crime. For this reason, Oregon's placement of the burden of proof on insanity on Leland, unlike Maine's redefinition of homicide in the instant case, did not effect an unconstitutional shift in the State's traditional burden of proof beyond a reasonable doubt of all necessary elements of the offense. Both the Court's opinion and the concurring opinion of Mr. Justice Harlan in In re Winship,

28. Many States do require the defendant to show that there is "some evidence" indicating that he acted in the heat of passion before requiring the prosecution to negate this element by proving the absence of passion beyond a reasonable doubt. Nothing in this opinion is intended to affect that requirement.

supra, stress the importance of proof beyond a reasonable doubt in a criminal case as "bottomed on a fundamental value determination of our society that it is far worse to convict an innocent man than to let a guilty man go free." Having once met that rigorous burden of proof that, for example, in a case such as this, the defendant not only killed a fellow human being, but did it with malice aforethought, the State could quite consistently with such a constitutional principle conclude that a defendant who sought to establish the defense of insanity, and thereby escape any punishment whatever for a heinous crime, should bear the laboring oar on such an issue.

MARTIN v. OHIO

Supreme Court of the United States, 1987.
480 U.S. 228, 107 S.Ct. 1098, 94 L.Ed.2d 267.

JUSTICE WHITE delivered the opinion of the Court.

The Ohio Code provides that "Every person accused of an offense is presumed innocent until proven guilty beyond a reasonable doubt, and the burden of proof for all elements of the offense is upon the prosecution. The burden of going forward with the evidence of an affirmative defense, and the burden of proof by a preponderance of the evidence, for an affirmative defense, is upon the accused." An affirmative defense is one involving "an excuse or justification peculiarly within the knowledge of the accused, on which he can fairly be required to adduce supporting evidence." The Ohio courts have long determined that self-defense is an affirmative defense, and that the defendant has the burden of proving it. [Citations omitted.]

As defined by the trial court in its instructions in this case, the elements of self-defense that the defendant must prove are (1) that the defendant was not at fault in creating the situation giving rise to the argument; (2) the defendant had an honest belief that she was in imminent danger of death or great bodily harm and that her only means of escape from such danger was in the use of such force; and (3) the defendant must not have violated any duty to retreat or avoid danger. The question before us is whether the Due Process Clause forbids placing the burden of proving self-defense on the defendant when she is charged with committing aggravated murder, which, as relevant to this case, is defined by the Revised Code of Ohio as "purposely, and with prior calculation and design, caus[ing] the death of another." * * *

Petitioner Earline Martin and her husband, Walter Martin, argued over grocery money. Petitioner claimed that her husband struck her in the head during the argument. Petitioner's version of what then transpired was that she went upstairs, put on a robe, and later came back down with her husband's gun which she intended to dispose of. Her husband saw something in her hand and questioned her about it. He came at her, she lost her head and fired the gun at him. Five or six shots were fired, three of them striking and killing Mr. Martin. She was charged with and tried for aggravated murder. She pleaded self-defense and testified in her own defense. The judge charged the jury with respect to the elements of the crime and of self-defense and rejected petitioner's Due Process Clause challenge to the charge placing on her the burden of proving self-defense. The jury found her guilty. [The state appellate courts affirmed, relying on the Supreme Court's opinion in Patterson v. New York, 432 U.S. 197 (1977).]

In re Winship, 397 U.S. 358, 364 (1970), declared that the Due Process Clause "protects the accused against conviction except upon proof beyond a reasonable doubt of every fact necessary to constitute the crime with which he is charged." A few years later, we held that *Winship*'s mandate was fully satisfied where the State of New York had proved beyond reasonable doubt each of the elements of murder, but placed on the defendant the burden of proving the affirmative defense of extreme emotional disturbance, which, if proved, would have reduced the crime from murder to manslaughter. Patterson v. New York, supra. We there emphasized the preeminent role of the States in preventing and dealing with crime and our reluctance to disturb a State's decision with respect to the definition of criminal conduct and the procedures by which the criminal laws are to be enforced in the courts, including the burden of producing evidence and allocating the burden of persuasion. New York had the authority to define murder as the intentional killing of another person. It had chosen, however, to reduce the crime to manslaughter if the defendant proved by a preponderance of the evidence that he had acted under the influence of extreme emotional distress. To convict of murder, the jury was required to find beyond a reasonable doubt, based on all the evidence, including that related to the defendant's mental state at the time of the crime, each of the elements of murder and also to conclude that the defendant had not proved his affirmative defense. The jury convicted Patterson, and we held there was no violation of the Fourteenth Amendment as construed in *Winship*. * * *

As in *Patterson*, the jury was here instructed that to convict it must find, in light of all the evidence, that each of elements of the crime of aggravated murder must be proved by the State beyond reasonable doubt and that the burden of proof with respect to these elements did not shift. To find guilt, the jury had to be convinced that none of the evidence, whether offered by the State or by Martin in connection with her plea of self-defense, raised a reasonable doubt that Martin had killed her husband, that she had the specific purpose and intent to cause his death, or that she had done so with prior calculation and design. It was also told, however, that it could acquit if it found by a preponderance of the evidence that Martin had not precipitated the confrontation, that she had an honest belief that she was in imminent danger of death or great bodily harm, and that she had satisfied any duty to retreat or avoid danger. The jury convicted Martin.

We agree with the State and its Supreme Court that this conviction did not violate the Due Process Clause. The State did not exceed its authority in defining the crime of murder as purposely causing the death of another with prior calculation or design. It did not seek to shift to

Martin the burden of proving any of those elements, and the jury's verdict reflects that none of her self-defense evidence raised a reasonable doubt about the state's proof that she purposefully killed with prior calculation and design. She nevertheless had the opportunity under state law and the instructions given to justify the killing and show herself to be blameless by proving that she acted in self-defense. The jury thought she had failed to do so, and Ohio is as entitled to punish Martin as one guilty of murder as New York was to punish Patterson. It would be quite different if the jury had been instructed that self-defense evidence could not be considered in determining whether there was a reasonable doubt about the state's case, i.e., that self-defense evidence must be put aside for all purposes unless it satisfied the preponderance standard. Such instruction would relieve the state of its burden and plainly run afoul of *Winship* 's mandate. The instructions in this case could be clearer in this respect, but when read as a whole, we think they are adequate to convey to the jury that all of the evidence, including the evidence going to self-defense, must be considered in deciding whether there was a reasonable doubt about the sufficiency of the state's proof of the elements of the crime.

We are thus not moved by assertions that the elements of aggravated murder and self-defense overlap in the sense that evidence to prove the latter will often tend to negate the former. It may be that most encounters in which self-defense is claimed arise suddenly and involve no prior plan or specific purpose to take life. In those cases, evidence offered to support the defense may negate a purposeful killing by prior calculation and design, but Ohio does not shift to the defendant the burden of disproving any element of the state's case. When the prosecution has made out a prima facie case and survives a motion to acquit, the jury may nevertheless not convict if the evidence offered by the defendant raises any reasonable doubt about the existence of any fact necessary for the finding of guilt. Evidence creating a reasonable doubt could easily fall far short of proving self-defense by a preponderance of the evidence. Of course, if such doubt is not raised in the jury's mind and each juror is convinced that the defendant purposely and with prior calculation and design took life, the killing will still be excused if the elements of the defense are satisfactorily established. * * *

Petitioner submits that there can be no conviction under Ohio law unless the defendant's conduct is unlawful and that because self-defense renders lawful what would otherwise be a crime, unlawfulness is an element of the offense that the state must prove by disproving self-defense. This argument founders on state law, for it has been rejected by the Ohio Supreme Court and by the Court of Appeals for the Sixth Circuit. White v. Arn, 788 F.2d 338, 346–347 (C.A.6 1986); State v. Morris, 8 Ohio App.3d 12, 18–19, 455 N.E.2d 1352, 1359–1360 (1982). It is true that unlawfulness is essential for conviction, but the Ohio courts hold that the unlawfulness in cases like this is the conduct satisfying the elements of aggravated murder—an interpretation of state law that we are not in a position to dispute. The same is true of the claim that it is necessary to prove a "criminal" intent to convict for serious crimes, which cannot occur if self-defense is shown: the necessary mental state for aggravated murder under Ohio law is the specific purpose to take life pursuant to prior calculation and design.

As we noted in *Patterson,* the common law rule was that affirmative defenses, including self-defense, were matters for the defendant to prove. This was the rule when the Fifth Amendment was adopted, and it was the American rule when the Fourteenth Amendment was ratified. Indeed, well into this century, a number of States followed the common law rule and required a defendant to shoulder the burden of proving that he acted in self-defense. We are aware that all but two of the States, Ohio and South Carolina, have abandoned the common law rule and require the prosecution to prove the absence of self-defense when it is properly raised by the defendant. But the question remains whether those States are in violation of the Constitution; and, as we observed in *Patterson,* that question is not answered by cataloging the practices of other States. We are no more convinced that the Ohio practice of requiring self-defense to be proved by the defendant is unconstitutional than we are that the Constitution requires the prosecution to prove the sanity of a defendant who pleads not guilty by reason of insanity. We have had the opportunity to depart from Leland v. Oregon but have refused to do so. Rivera v. Delaware, 429 U.S. 877 (1976). These cases were important to the *Patterson* decision and they, along with *Patterson,* are authority for our decision today. The judgment of the Ohio Supreme Court is accordingly

Affirmed.

JUSTICE POWELL, with whom JUSTICE BRENNAN and JUSTICE MARSHALL join, and with whom JUSTICE BLACKMUN joins with respect to Parts I and III, dissenting.

I

* * * If one accepts *Patterson* as the proper method of analysis for this case, I believe that the Court's opinion ignores its central meaning. In *Patterson,* the Court upheld a state statute that shifted the burden of proof for an affirmative defense to the accused. New York law required the prosecutor to prove all of the statutorily defined elements of murder beyond a reasonable doubt, but permitted a defendant to reduce the charge to manslaughter by showing that he acted while suffering an "extreme emotional disturbance." The Court found that this burden-shifting did not violate due process, largely because the affirmative defense did "not serve to negative any facts of the crime which the State is to prove in order to convict of murder." The clear implication of this ruling is that when an affirmative defense does negate an element of the crime, the state may not shift the burden. In such a case, In re Winship requires the state to prove the nonexistence of the defense beyond a reasonable doubt.

The reason for treating a defense that negates an element of the crime differently from other affirmative defenses is plain. If the jury is told that the prosecution has the burden of proving all the elements of a crime, but then also is instructed that the defendant has the burden of disproving one of those same elements, there is a danger that the jurors will resolve the inconsistency in a way that lessens the presumption of innocence. For example, the jury might reasonably believe that by raising the defense, the accused has assumed the ultimate burden of proving that particular element. Or, it might reconcile the instructions simply by balancing the evidence that supports the prosecutor's case against the evidence supporting the affirmative defense, and conclude that the state has satisfied its burden if the prosecution's version is more persuasive. In either case, the jury is given the unmistakable but erroneous impression that the defendant shares the risk of nonpersuasion as to a fact necessary for conviction.

Given these principles, the Court's reliance on *Patterson* is puzzling. Under Ohio law, the element of "prior calculation and design" is satisfied only when the accused has engaged in a "definite process of reasoning in advance of the killing," i.e., when he has given the plan at least some "studied consideration." App. 14 (jury instructions) In contrast, when a defendant such as Martin raises a claim of self-defense, the jury also is instructed that the accused must prove that she "had an honest belief that she was in imminent danger of death or great bodily harm." In many cases, a defendant who finds himself in immediate danger and reacts with deadly force will not have formed a prior intent to kill. * * *

The Court seems to conclude that as long as the jury is told that the state has the burden of proving all elements of the crime, the overlap between the offense and defense is immaterial. This reasoning is flawed in two respects. First, it simply ignores the problem that arises from inconsistent jury instructions in a criminal case. The Court's holding implicitly assumes that the jury in fact understands that the ultimate burden remains with the prosecutor at all times, despite a conflicting instruction that places the burden on the accused to disprove the same element. * * *

Second, the Court significantly, and without explanation, extends the deference granted to state legislatures in this area. Today's decision could be read to say that virtually all state attempts to shift the burden of proof for affirmative defenses will be upheld, regardless of the relationship between the elements of the defense and the elements of the crime. * * * In the past we have emphasized that in some circumstances it may be necessary to look beyond the text of the State's burden-shifting laws to satisfy ourselves that the requirements of *Winship* have been satisfied. In Mullaney v. Wilbur, 421 U.S. 684, 698–699 (1975), we explicitly noted the danger of granting the State unchecked discretion to shift the burden as to any element of proof in a criminal case. The Court today fails to discuss or even cite *Mullaney,* despite our unanimous agreement in that case that this danger would justify judicial intervention in some cases. * * *

II

Although I believe that this case is wrongly decided even under the principles set forth in *Patterson,* my differences with the Court's approach are more fundamental. I continue to believe that the better method for deciding when a state may shift the burden of proof is outlined in the Court's opinion in *Mullaney* and in my dissenting opinion in *Patterson.* In *Mullaney,* we emphasized that the state's obligation to prove certain facts beyond a reasonable doubt was not necessarily restricted to legislative distinctions between offenses and affirmative defenses. The boundaries of the state's authority in this respect were elaborated in the *Patterson* dissent, where I proposed a two-part inquiry: "The Due Process Clause requires that the prosecutor bear the burden of persuasion beyond a reasonable doubt only if the factor at issue makes a substantial difference in punishment and stigma. The requirement of course applies a fortiori if the factor makes the difference between guilt and innocence.... It also must be shown that in the Anglo–American legal tradition the factor in question historically has held that level of importance. If either branch of the test is not met, then the legislature retains its traditional authority over matters of proof." 432 U.S., at 226–227. * * *

There are at least two benefits to this approach. First, it ensures that the critical facts necessary to sustain a conviction will be proved by the state. Because the Court would be willing to look beyond the text of a state statute, legislatures would have no incentive to redefine essential elements of an offense to make them part of an affirmative defense, thereby shifting the burden of proof in a manner inconsistent with *Winship* and *Mullaney.* Second, it would leave the states free in all other respects to recognize new factors that may mitigate the degree of criminality or punishment, without requiring that they also bear the burden of disproving these defenses.

Under this analysis, it plainly is impermissible to require the accused to prove self-defense. If petitioner could have carried her burden, the result would have been decisively different as to both guilt and punishment. There also is no dispute that self-defense historically is one of the primary justifications for otherwise unlawful conduct. Thus, while I acknowledge that the two-part test may be difficult to apply at times, it is hard to imagine a more clear-cut application than the one presented here.

III

In its willingness to defer to the State's legislative definitions of crimes and defenses, the Court apparently has failed to recognize the practical effect of its decision. Martin alleged that she was innocent because she acted in self-defense, a complete justification under Ohio law. Because she had the burden of proof on this issue, the jury could have believed that it was just as likely as not that Martin's conduct was justified, and yet still have voted to convict. In other words, even though the jury may have had a substantial doubt whether Martin committed a crime, she was found guilty under Ohio law. I do not agree that the Court's authority to review state legislative choices is so limited that it justifies increasing the risk of convicting a person who may not be blameworthy. The complexity of the inquiry as to when a state may shift the burden of proof should not lead the Court to fashion simple rules of deference that could lead to such unjust results.

APPRENDI v. NEW JERSEY

Supreme Court of the United States, 2000.
530 U.S. 466, 120 S.Ct. 2348, 147 L.Ed.2d 435.

JUSTICE STEVENS delivered the opinion of the Court.

A New Jersey statute classifies the possession of a firearm for an unlawful purpose as a "second-degree" offense. Such an offense is punishable by imprisonment for "between five years and 10 years." A separate statute, described by that State's Supreme Court as a "hate crime" law, provides for an "extended term" of imprisonment if the trial judge finds, by a preponderance of the evidence, that "the defendant in committing the crime acted with a purpose to intimidate an individual or group of individuals because of race, color, gender, handicap, religion, sexual orientation or ethnicity." The extended term authorized by the hate crime law for second-degree offenses is imprisonment for "between 10 and 20 years."

The question presented is whether the Due Process Clause of the Fourteenth Amendment requires that a factual determination authorizing an increase in the maximum prison sentence for an offense from 10 to 20 years be made by a jury on the basis of proof beyond a reasonable doubt.

I

At 2:04 a.m. on December 22, 1994, petitioner Charles C. Apprendi, Jr., fired several .22–caliber bullets into the home of an African–American family that had recently moved into a previously all-white neighborhood in Vineland, New Jersey. Apprendi was promptly arrested and, at 3:05 a.m., admitted that he was the shooter. After further questioning, at 6:04 a.m., he made a statement—which he later retracted—that even though he did not know the occupants of the house personally, "because they are black in color he does not want them in the neighborhood."

A New Jersey grand jury returned a 23–count indictment charging Apprendi with * * * shootings on four different dates, as well as the unlawful possession of various weapons. None of the counts referred to the hate crime statute, and none alleged that Apprendi acted with a racially biased purpose.

The parties entered into a plea agreement, pursuant to which Apprendi pleaded guilty to two counts of second-degree possession of a firearm for an unlawful purpose, and one count of the third-degree offense of unlawful possession of an antipersonnel bomb; the prosecutor dismissed the other 20 counts. Under state law, a second-degree offense carries a penalty range of 5 to 10 years, a third-degree offense carries a penalty range of between 3 and 5 years. As part of the plea agreement, however, the State reserved the right to request the court to impose a higher "enhanced" sentence on count 18 (which was based on the December 22 shooting) on the ground that that offense was committed with a biased purpose * * *. Apprendi, correspondingly, reserved the right to challenge the hate crime sentence enhancement on the ground that it violates the United States Constitution.

At the plea hearing, the trial judge heard sufficient evidence to establish Apprendi's guilt on counts 3, 18, and 22; the judge then confirmed that Apprendi understood the maximum sentences that could be imposed on those counts. Because the plea agreement provided that the sentence on the sole third-degree offense would run concurrently with the other sentences, the potential sentences on the two second-degree counts were critical. If the judge found no basis for the biased purpose enhancement, the maximum consecutive sentences on those counts would amount to 20 years in aggregate; if, however, the judge enhanced the sentence on count 18, the maximum on that count alone would be 20 years and the maximum for the two counts in aggregate would be 30 years, with a 15-year period of parole ineligibility.

* * * The trial judge thereafter held an evidentiary hearing on the issue of Apprendi's "purpose" for the shooting on December 22. Apprendi * * * took the stand himself, * * * denying that he was in any way biased against African-Americans, and denying that his statement to the police had been accurately described. The judge, however, found the police officer's testimony credible, and concluded that the evidence supported a finding "that the crime was motivated by racial bias." Having found "by a preponderance of the evidence" that Apprendi's actions were taken "with a purpose to intimidate" as provided by the statute, the trial judge held that the hate crime enhancement applied. Rejecting Apprendi's constitutional challenge to the statute, the judge sentenced him to a 12-year term of imprisonment on count 18, and to shorter concurrent sentences on the other two counts.

Apprendi appealed, arguing * * * that the Due Process Clause of the United States Constitution requires that the finding of bias upon which his hate crime sentence was based must be proved to a jury beyond a reasonable doubt, *In re Winship, 397 U.S. 358 (1970).* * * *

* * *

We granted certiorari * * * and now reverse.

II

* * * The constitutional question, however, is whether the 12–year sentence imposed on count 18 was permissible, given that it was above the 10–year maximum for the offense charged in that count. The finding is legally significant because it increased—indeed, it doubled—the maximum range within which the judge could exercise his discretion, converting what otherwise was a maximum 10–year sentence on that count into a minimum sentence. The sentences on counts 3 and 22 have no more relevance to our disposition than the dismissal of the remaining 18 counts.

* * *

* * * The question whether Apprendi had a constitutional right to have a jury find such bias on the basis of proof beyond a reasonable doubt is starkly presented.

Our answer to that question was foreshadowed by our opinion in *Jones v. United States, 526 U.S. 227, 143 L. Ed. 2d 311, 119 S. Ct. 1215 (1999),* construing a federal statute. We there noted that "under the Due Process Clause of the Fifth Amendment and the notice and jury trial guarantees of the Sixth Amendment, any fact (other than prior conviction) that increases the maximum penalty for a crime must be charged in an indictment, submitted to a jury, and proven beyond a reasonable doubt." The Fourteenth Amendment commands the same answer in this case involving a state statute.

III

* * *

At stake in this case are constitutional protections of surpassing importance: the proscription of any deprivation of liberty without "due process of law," and the guarantee that "in all criminal prosecutions, the accused shall enjoy the right to a speedy and public trial, by an impartial jury." Taken together, these rights indisputably entitle a criminal defendant to "a jury determination that [he] is guilty of every element of the crime with which he is charged, beyond a reasonable doubt."

As we have, unanimously, explained, the historical foundation for our recognition of these principles extends down centuries into the common law. "To guard against a spirit of oppression and tyranny on the part of rulers," and "as the great bulwark of [our] civil and political liberties," trial by jury has been understood to require that "*the truth of every accusation*, whether preferred in the shape of indictment, information, or appeal, should afterwards be confirmed by the unanimous suffrage of twelve of [the defendant's] equals and neighbours...."

Equally well founded is the companion right to have the jury verdict based on proof beyond a reasonable doubt. "The 'demand for a higher degree of persuasion in criminal cases was recurrently expressed from ancient times, [though] its crystallization into the formula "beyond a reasonable doubt" seems to have occurred as late as 1798. It is now accepted in common law jurisdictions as the measure of persuasion by which the prosecution must convince the trier of all the essential elements of guilt.' We went on to explain that the reliance on 'the reasonable doubt' standard among common-law jurisdictions 'reflects a profound judgment about the way in which law should be enforced and justice administered.' "

Any possible distinction between an "element" of a felony offense and a "sentencing factor" was unknown to the practice of criminal indictment, trial by jury, and judgment by court as it existed during the years surrounding our Nation's founding. * * *

* * *

We should be clear that nothing in this history suggests that it is impermissible for judges to exercise discretion—taking into consideration various factors relating both to offense and offender—in imposing a judgment *within the range* prescribed by statute. We have often noted that judges in this country have long exercised discretion of this nature in imposing sentence *within statutory limits* in the individual case. * * *

* * *

* * * But practice must at least adhere to the basic principles undergirding the requirements of trying to a jury all facts necessary to constitute a statutory offense, and proving those facts beyond reasonable doubt. * * *

Since *Winship*, we have made clear beyond peradventure that *Winship's* due process and associated jury protections extend, to some degree, "to determinations that [go] not to a defendant's guilt or innocence, but simply to the length of his sentence." This was a primary lesson of *Mullaney v. Wilbur* * * *.

* * * Because the "*consequences*" of a guilty verdict for murder and for manslaughter differed substantially, we dismissed the possibility that a State could circumvent the protections of *Winship* merely by "redefining the elements that constitute different crimes, characterizing them as factors that bear solely on the extent of punishment."

IV

It was in *McMillan v. Pennsylvania, 477 U.S. 79, 91 L. Ed. 2d 67, 106 S. Ct. 2411 (1986),* that this Court, for the first time, coined the term "sentencing factor" to refer to a fact that was not found by a jury but that could affect the sentence imposed by the judge. That case involved a challenge to the State's Mandatory Minimum Sentencing Act. According to its provisions, anyone convicted of certain felonies would be subject to a mandatory minimum penalty of five years imprisonment if the judge found, by a preponderance of the evidence, that the person "visibly possessed a firearm" in the course of committing one of the specified felonies. Articulating for the first time, and then applying, a multifactor set of criteria for determining whether the *Winship* protections applied to bar such a system, we concluded that the Pennsylvania statute did not run afoul of our previous admonitions against relieving the State of its burden of proving guilt, or tailoring the mere form of a criminal statute solely to avoid *Winship's* strictures.

We did not, however, there budge from the position that (1) constitutional limits exist to States' authority to define away facts necessary to constitute a criminal offense, and (2) that a state scheme that keeps from the jury facts that "expose [defendants] to greater or additional punishment," may raise serious constitutional concern. * * *

* * *

In sum, our reexamination of our cases in this area, and of the history upon which they rely, confirms the opinion that we expressed in *Jones*. Other than the fact of a prior conviction, any fact that increases the penalty for a crime beyond the prescribed statutory maximum must be submitted to a jury, and proved beyond a reasonable doubt. With that exception, we endorse the statement of the rule set forth in the concurring opinions in that case: "It is unconstitutional for a legislature to remove from the jury the assessment of facts that increase the prescribed range of penalties to which a criminal defendant is exposed. It is equally clear that such facts must be established by proof beyond a reasonable doubt."

V

The New Jersey statutory scheme that Apprendi asks us to invalidate allows a jury to convict a defendant of a second-degree offense based on its finding beyond a reasonable doubt that he unlawfully possessed a prohibited weapon; after a subsequent and separate proceeding, it then allows a judge to impose punishment identical to that New Jersey provides for crimes of the first degree, based upon the judge's finding, by a preponderance of the evidence, that the defendant's "purpose" for unlawfully possessing the weapon was "to intimidate" his victim on the basis of a particular characteristic the victim possessed. In light of the constitutional rule explained above, and all of the cases supporting it, this practice cannot stand.

* * *

Finally, this Court has previously considered and rejected the argument that the principles guiding our decision today render invalid state capital sentencing schemes requiring judges, after a jury verdict holding a defendant guilty of a capital crime, to find specific aggravating factors before imposing a sentence of death. * * *

The New Jersey procedure challenged in this case is an unacceptable departure from the jury tradition that is an indispensable part of our criminal justice system. Accordingly, the judgment of the Supreme Court of New Jersey is reversed, and the case is remanded for further proceedings not inconsistent with this opinion.

* * *

[The concurring opinions by JUSTICE SCALIA and JUSTICE THOMAS are omitted.]

JUSTICE O'CONNOR, with whom THE CHIEF JUSTICE, JUSTICE KENNEDY, and JUSTICE BREYER join, dissenting.

* * *

I

Our Court has long recognized that not every fact that bears on a defendant's punishment need be charged in an indictment, submitted to a jury, and proved by the government beyond a reasonable doubt. Rather, we have held that the "legislature's definition of the elements of the offense is usually dispositive." Although we have recognized that "there are obviously constitutional limits beyond which the States may not go in this regard," and that "in certain limited circumstances *Winship*'s reasonable-doubt requirement applies to facts not formally identified as elements of the offense charged," we have proceeded with caution before deciding that a certain fact must be treated as an offense element despite the legislature's choice not to characterize it as such. We have therefore declined to establish any bright-line rule for making such judgments and have instead approached each case individually, sifting through the considerations most relevant to determining whether the legislature has acted properly within its broad power to define crimes and their punishments or instead has sought to evade the constitutional requirements associated with the characterization of a fact as an offense element.

In one bold stroke the Court today casts aside our traditional cautious approach and instead embraces a universal and seemingly bright-line rule limiting the power of Congress and state legislatures to define criminal offenses and the sentences that follow from convictions thereunder. * * *

* * *

II

* * * [U]nder one reading, the Court appears to hold that the Constitution requires that a fact be submitted to a jury and proved beyond a reasonable doubt only if that fact, as a formal matter, extends the range of punishment *beyond the prescribed statutory maximum*. A State could, however, remove from the jury (and subject to a standard of proof below "beyond a reasonable doubt") the assessment of those facts that define narrower ranges of punishment, *within the overall statutory range*, to which the defendant may be sentenced. Thus, apparently New Jersey could cure its sentencing scheme, and achieve virtually the same results, by drafting its weapons possession statute in the following manner: First, New Jersey could prescribe, in the weapons possession statute itself, a range of 5 to 20 years' imprisonment for one who commits that criminal offense. Second, New Jersey could provide that

only those defendants convicted under the statute who are found by a judge, by a preponderance of the evidence, to have acted with a purpose to intimidate an individual on the basis of race may receive a sentence greater than 10 years' imprisonment.

* * *

Given the pure formalism of the above readings of the Court's opinion, one suspects that the constitutional principle underlying its decision is more far reaching. The actual principle underlying the Court's decision may be that any fact (other than prior conviction) that has the effect, *in real terms*, of increasing the maximum punishment beyond an otherwise applicable range must be submitted to a jury and proved beyond a reasonable doubt. The principle thus would apply not only to schemes like New Jersey's, under which a factual determination exposes defendant to a sentence beyond the prescribed statutory maximum, but also to all determinate-sentencing schemes in which the length of a defendant's sentence within the statutory range turns on specific factual determinations (*e.g.*, the federal Sentencing Guidelines). Justice Thomas essentially concedes that the rule outlined in his concurring opinion would require the invalidation of the Sentencing Guidelines.

[I]n light of the adoption of determinate-sentencing schemes by many States and the Federal Government, the consequences of the Court's and Justice Thomas' rules in terms of sentencing schemes invalidated by today's decision will likely be severe.

* * *

[Part III of this dissenting opinion and the dissenting opinion by JUSTICE BREYER are omitted.]

FRANCIS v. FRANKLIN

Supreme Court of the United States, 1985.
471 U.S. 307, 105 S.Ct. 1965, 85 L.Ed.2d 344.

JUSTICE BRENNAN delivered the opinion of the Court.

I

Respondent Franklin, then 21 years old and imprisoned for offenses unrelated to this case, sought to escape custody on January 17, 1979, while he and three other prisoners were receiving dental care at a local dentist's office. The four prisoners were secured by handcuffs to the same 8–foot length of chain as they sat in the dentist's waiting room. At some point Franklin was released from the chain, taken into the dentist's office and given preliminary treatment, and then escorted back to the waiting room. As another prisoner was being released, Franklin, who had not been reshackled, seized a pistol from one of the two officers and managed to escape. He forced the dentist's assistant to accompany him as a hostage.

In the parking lot Franklin found the dentist's automobile, the keys to which he had taken before escaping, but was unable to unlock the door. He then fled with the dental assistant after refusing her request to be set free. The two set out across an open clearing and came upon a local resident. Franklin demanded this resident's car. When the resident responded that he did not own one, Franklin made no effort to harm him but continued with the dental assistant until they came to the home of the victim, one Collie. Franklin pounded on the heavy wooden front door of the home and Collie, a retired 72–year–old carpenter, answered. Franklin was pointing the stolen pistol at the door when Collie arrived. As Franklin demanded his car keys, Collie slammed the door. At this moment Franklin's gun went off. The bullet traveled through the wooden door and into Collie's chest, killing him. Seconds later the gun fired again. The second bullet traveled upward through the door and into the ceiling of the residence.

Hearing the shots, the victim's wife entered the front room. In the confusion accompanying the shooting, the dental assistant fled and Franklin did not attempt to stop her. Franklin entered the house, demanded the car keys from the victim's wife, and added the threat "I might as well kill you." When she did not provide the keys, however, he made no effort to thwart her escape. Franklin then stepped outside and encountered the victim's adult daughter. He repeated his demand for car keys but made no effort to stop the daughter when she refused the demand and fled. Failing to obtain a car, Franklin left and remained at large until nightfall.

Shortly after being captured, Franklin made a formal statement to the authorities in which he admitted that he had shot the victim but emphatically denied that he did so voluntarily or intentionally. He claimed that the shots were fired in accidental response to the slamming of the door. He was tried on charges of malice murder[1]—a capital offense in Georgia—and kidnaping. His sole defense to the malice murder charge was a lack of the requisite intent to kill. To support his version of the events Franklin offered substantial circumstantial evidence tending to show a lack of intent. He claimed that the circumstances surrounding the firing of the gun, particularly the slamming of the door and the trajectory of the second bullet, supported the hypothesis of accident, and that his immediate confession to that effect buttressed the assertion. He also argued that his treatment of every other person encountered during the escape indicated a lack of disposition to use force.

On the dispositive issue of intent, the trial judge instructed the jury as follows:

"A crime is a violation of a statute of this State in which there shall be a union of joint operation of act or omission to act, and intention or

1. The malice murder statute at the time in question provided: "A person commits murder when he unlawfully and with malice aforethought, either express or implied, causes the death of another human being.... Malice shall be implied where no considerable provocation appears and where all the circumstances of the killing show an abandoned and malignant heart."

criminal negligence. A person shall not be found guilty of any crime committed by misfortune or accident where it satisfactorily appears there was no criminal scheme or undertaking or intention or criminal negligence. The acts of a person of sound mind and discretion are presumed to be the product of the person's will, but the presumption may be rebutted. A person of sound mind and discretion is presumed to intend the natural and probable consequences of his acts, but the presumption may be rebutted. A person will not be presumed to act with criminal intention but the trier of facts, that is, the Jury, may find criminal intention upon a consideration of the words, conduct, demeanor, motive and all other circumstances connected with the act for which the accused is prosecuted."

Approximately one hour after the jury had received the charge and retired for deliberation, it returned to the courtroom and requested reinstruction on the element of intent and the definition of accident. * * * Upon receiving the requested reinstruction, the jury deliberated 10 more minutes and returned a verdict of guilty. The next day Franklin was sentenced to death for the murder conviction. [A federal court of appeals on habeas corpus review held that the challenged jury instruction was unconstitutional, citing the Supreme Court's decision in Sandstrom v. Montana, 442 U.S. 510 (1979).]

II

The Due Process Clause of the Fourteenth Amendment protects the accused against conviction except upon proof beyond a reasonable doubt of every fact necessary to constitute the crime with which he is charged. This principle prohibits the State from using evidentiary presumptions in a jury charge that have the effect of relieving the State of its burden of persuasion beyond a reasonable doubt of every essential element of a crime. [Citations] The prohibition protects the fundamental value determination of our society that it is far worse to convict an innocent man than to let a guilty man go free. The question before the Court in this case is almost identical to that before the Court in *Sandstrom:* whether the challenged jury instruction had the effect of relieving the State of the burden of proof on the critical question of state of mind, by creating a mandatory presumption of intent upon proof by the State of other elements of the offense.

* * * The court must determine whether the challenged portion of the instruction creates a mandatory presumption, or merely a permissive inference. A mandatory presumption instructs the jury that it must infer the presumed fact if the State proves certain predicate facts.[2] A permissive inference suggests to the jury a possible conclusion to be drawn if

2. A mandatory presumption may be either conclusive or rebuttable. A conclusive presumption removes the presumed element from the case once the State has proven the predicate facts giving rise to the presumption. A rebuttable presumption does not remove the presumed element from the case but nevertheless requires the jury to find the presumed element unless the defendant persuades the jury that such a finding is unwarranted.

the State proves predicate facts, but does not require the jury to draw that conclusion.

Mandatory presumptions must be measured against the standards elucidated in *Sandstrom.* Such presumptions violate the Due Process Clause if they relieve the State of the burden of persuasion on an element of an offense. A permissive inference does not relieve the State of its burden of persuasion because it still requires the State to convince the jury that the suggested conclusion should be inferred based on the predicate facts proven. Such inferences do not necessarily implicate the concerns of *Sandstrom.* A permissive inference violates the Due Process Clause only if the suggested conclusion is not one that reason and common sense justify in light of the proven facts before the jury. * * *

Franklin levels his constitutional attack at the following two sentences in the jury charge: "The acts of a person of sound mind and discretion are presumed to be the product of a person's will, but the presumption may be rebutted. A person of sound mind and discretion is presumed to intend the natural and probable consequences of his acts, but the presumption may be rebutted." The Georgia Supreme Court has interpreted this language as creating no more than a permissive inference. * * * The question, however, is not what the State Supreme Court declares the meaning of the charge to be, but rather ... whether a reasonable juror could have understood the two sentences as a mandatory presumption that shifted to the defendant the burden of persuasion on the element of intent once the State had proved the predicate acts.

* * * The portion of the jury charge challenged in this case directs the jury to presume an essential element of the offense—intent to kill—upon proof of other elements of the offense—the act of slaying another. In this way the instructions undermine the factfinder's responsibility at trial, based on evidence adduced by the State, to find the ultimate facts beyond a reasonable doubt. The language challenged here differs from *Sandstrom,* of course, in that the jury in this case was explicitly informed that the presumptions "may be rebutted." This distinction does not suffice, however, to cure the infirmity in the charge. * * *

An irrebuttable or conclusive presumption relieves the State of its burden of persuasion by removing the presumed element from the case entirely if the State proves the predicate facts. A mandatory rebuttable presumption does not remove the presumed element from the case if the State proves the predicate facts, but it nonetheless relieves the State of the affirmative burden of persuasion on the presumed element by instructing the jury that it must find the presumed element unless the defendant persuades the jury not to make such a finding. A mandatory rebuttable presumption is perhaps less onerous from the defendant's perspective, but it is no less unconstitutional. * * *

When combined with the immediately preceding mandatory language, the instruction that the presumptions "may be rebutted" could reasonably be read as telling the jury that it was required to infer intent to kill as the natural and probable consequence of the act of firing the gun unless the defendant persuaded the jury that such an inference was unwarranted. * * *

The jury, of course, did not hear only the two challenged sentences. The jury charge taken as a whole might have explained the proper allocation of burdens with sufficient clarity that any ambiguity in the particular language challenged could not have been understood by a reasonable juror as shifting the burden of persuasion. The State argues that sufficient clarifying language exists in this case. In particular, the State relies on an earlier portion of the charge instructing the jurors that the defendant was presumed innocent and that the State was required to prove every element of the offense beyond a reasonable doubt. The State also points to the sentence immediately following the challenged portion of the charge, which reads: "[a] person will not be presumed to act with criminal intention. * * * "

As we explained in *Sandstrom,* general instructions on the State's burden of persuasion and the defendant's presumption of innocence are not rhetorically inconsistent with a conclusive or burden-shifting presumption, because the jury could have interpreted the two sets of instructions as indicating that the presumption was a means by which proof beyond a reasonable doubt as to intent could be satisfied. A reasonable juror could thus have thought that, although intent must be proved beyond a reasonable doubt, proof of the firing of the gun and its ordinary consequences constituted proof of intent beyond a reasonable doubt unless the defendant persuaded the jury otherwise. * * *

The statement "criminal intention may not be presumed" may well have been intended to instruct the jurors that they were not permitted to presume the absence of provocation or justification but that they could infer this conclusion from circumstantial evidence. Whatever the court's motivation in giving the instruction, the jury could certainly have understood it this way. A reasonable juror trying to make sense of the juxtaposition of an instruction that "a person of sound mind and discretion is presumed to intend the natural and probable consequences of his acts," and an instruction that "a person will not be presumed to act with criminal intention," may well have thought that the instructions related to different elements of the crime and were therefore not contradictory—that he could presume intent to kill but not the absence of justification or provocation. * * *

Even if a reasonable juror could have understood the prohibition of presuming "criminal intention" as applying to the element of intent, that instruction did no more than contradict the instruction in the immediately preceding sentence. * * * Language that merely contradicts and does not explain a constitutionally infirm instruction will not suffice to absolve the infirmity. A reviewing court has no way of knowing which of the two irreconcilable instructions the jurors applied in reaching their verdict. * * *

Today we reaffirm the rule of *Sandstrom* and the wellspring due process principle from which it was drawn. The Court of Appeals faithfully and correctly applied this rule and the court's judgment is therefore

Affirmed.

[The separate dissenting opinion of JUSTICE POWELL is omitted.]

JUSTICE REHNQUIST, with whom THE CHIEF JUSTICE and JUSTICE O'CONNOR join, dissenting.

In In re Winship, 397 U.S. 358 (1970), the trial judge in a bench trial held that although the State's proof was sufficient to warrant a finding of guilt by a preponderance of the evidence, it was not sufficient to warrant such a finding beyond a reasonable doubt. The outcome of the case turned on which burden of proof was to be imposed on the prosecution. This Court held that the Constitution requires proof beyond a reasonable doubt in a criminal case, and Winship's adjudication was set aside. Today the Court sets aside Franklin's murder conviction, but not because either the trial judge or the trial jury found that his guilt had not been proven beyond a reasonable doubt. The conviction is set aside because this Court concludes that one or two sentences out of several pages of jury instructions could be read as allowing the jury to return a guilty verdict in the absence of proof establishing every statutory element of the crime beyond a reasonable doubt. The Court reaches this result even though the judge admonished the jury at least four separate times that they could convict only if they found guilt beyond a reasonable doubt. The Court, instead of examining the charge to the jury as a whole, seems bent on piling syllogism on syllogism to prove that someone might understand a few sentences in the charge to allow conviction on less than proof beyond a reasonable doubt. Such fine parsing of the jury instructions given in a state court trial is not required by anything in the United States Constitution.

* * * It appears that [the majority] will reverse a conviction if a "reasonable juror" hypothetically might have understood the charge unconstitutionally to shift a burden of proof, even if it was unlikely that a single juror had such an understanding. I believe that it must at least be likely that a juror so understood the charge before constitutional error can be found. Where as here a *Sandstrom* error is alleged involving not a conclusive presumption, but a rebuttable presumption, language in the charge indicating the State's general burden of proof and the jury's duty to examine all surrounding facts and circumstances generally should be sufficient to dissipate any constitutional infirmity. * * *

I dissent and would reverse the judgment of the Court of Appeals.

E. CONFRONTATION AND CROSS–EXAMINATION OF WITNESSES

POINTER v. TEXAS

Supreme Court of the United States, 1965.
380 U.S. 400, 85 S.Ct. 1065, 13 L.Ed.2d 923.

MR. JUSTICE BLACK delivered the opinion of the Court.

The Sixth Amendment provides in part that:

> In all criminal prosecutions, the accused shall enjoy the right * * * to be confronted with the witnesses against him * * * and to have the Assistance of Counsel for his defence.

Two years ago in Gideon v. Wainwright, 372 U.S. 335, we held that the Fourteenth Amendment makes the Sixth Amendment's guarantee of right to counsel obligatory upon the States. The question we find necessary to decide in this case is whether the Amendment's guarantee of a defendant's right "to be confronted with the witnesses against him," which has been held to include the right to cross-examine those witnesses, is also made applicable to the States by the Fourteenth Amendment.

The petitioner Pointer and one Dillard were arrested in Texas and taken before a state judge for a preliminary hearing (in Texas called the "examining trial") on a charge of having robbed Kenneth W. Phillips of $375 "by assault, or violence, or by putting in fear of life or bodily injury," in violation of Texas Penal Code Art. 1408. At this hearing an Assistant District Attorney conducted the prosecution and examined witnesses, but neither of the defendants, both of whom were laymen, had a lawyer. Phillips as chief witness for the State gave his version of the alleged robbery in detail, identifying petitioner as the man who had robbed him at gunpoint. Apparently Dillard tried to cross-examine Phillips but Pointer did not, although Pointer was said to have tried to cross-examine some other witnesses at the hearing. Petitioner was subsequently indicted on a charge of having committed the robbery. Some time before the trial was held, Phillips moved to California. After putting in evidence to show that Phillips had moved and did not intend to return to Texas, the State at the trial offered the transcript of Phillips' testimony given at the preliminary hearing as evidence against petitioner. Petitioner's counsel immediately objected to introduction of the transcript, stating, "Your Honor, we will object to that, as it is a denial of the confrontment of the witnesses against the Defendant." Similar objections were repeatedly made by petitioner's counsel but were overruled by the trial judge, apparently in part because, as the judge viewed it, petitioner had been present at the preliminary hearing and therefore had been "accorded the opportunity of cross examining the witnesses there against him." The Texas Court of Criminal Appeals, the highest state court to which the case could be taken, affirmed petitioner's conviction, rejecting his contention that use of the transcript to convict him denied him rights guaranteed by the Sixth and Fourteenth Amendments. We granted certiorari to consider the important constitutional question the case involves.

In this Court we do not find it necessary to decide one aspect of the question petitioner raises, that is, whether failure to appoint counsel to represent him at the preliminary hearing unconstitutionally denied him the assistance of counsel within the meaning of Gideon v. Wainwright, supra.[a] * * *

It cannot seriously be doubted at this late date that the right of cross-examination is included in the right of an accused in a criminal case to confront the witnesses against him. And probably no one, certainly no one experienced in the trial of lawsuits, would deny the value of cross-examination in exposing falsehood and bringing out the truth in the trial of a criminal case. The fact that this right appears in the Sixth Amendment of our Bill of Rights reflects the belief of the Framers of those liberties and safeguards that confrontation was a fundamental right essential to a fair trial in a criminal prosecution. Moreover, the decisions of this Court and other courts throughout the years have constantly emphasized the necessity for cross-examination as a protection for defendants in criminal cases. * * *

Under this Court's prior decisions, the Sixth Amendment's guarantee of confrontation and cross-examination was unquestionably denied petitioner in this case. As has been pointed out, a major reason underlying the constitutional confrontation rule is to give a defendant charged with crime an opportunity to cross-examine the witnesses against him. This Court has recognized the admissibility against an accused of dying declarations, and of testimony of a deceased witness who has testified at a former trial. [Citations] Nothing we hold here is to the contrary. The case before us would be quite a different one had Phillips' statement been taken at a full-fledged hearing at which petitioner had been represented by counsel who had been given a complete and adequate opportunity to cross-examine. There are other analogous situations which might not fall within the scope of the constitutional rule requiring confrontation of witnesses. The case before us, however, does not present any situation like those mentioned above or others analogous to them. Because the transcript of Phillips' statement offered against petitioner at his trial had not been taken at a time and under circumstances affording petitioner through counsel an adequate opportunity to cross-examine Phillips, its introduction in a federal court in a criminal case against Pointer would have amounted to denial of the privilege of confrontation guaranteed by the Sixth Amendment. Since we hold that the right of an accused to be confronted with the witnesses against him must be determined by the same standards whether the right is denied in a federal or state proceeding, it follows that use of the transcript to convict

a. In a subsequent case, the Court held that a criminal defendant has a constitutional right to the assistance of counsel at his preliminary hearing. Coleman v. Alabama, 399 U.S. 1 (1970).—ed.

petitioner denied him a constitutional right, and that his conviction must be reversed.

Reversed and remanded.

Note

To a great extent, the defendant's constitutional right to confront and cross-examine witnesses incorporates the common law "hearsay" doctrine. "Hearsay evidence is testimony in court, or written evidence, of a statement made out of court, the statement being offered to show the truth of matters asserted therein, and thus resting for its value upon the credibility of the out-of-court asserter." McCormick, *Evidence* 584 (2d ed. Cleary ed. 1972). Hearsay evidence is generally excluded because it may be unreliable. As a rule, we want the person who actually observed the events to be proved to testify under oath in the presence of the jury, so that the jury can observe his demeanor and so that the opposing party can test his credibility, perception, and memory by cross-examination. Testimony by someone else relating what the witness said about the events on some former occasion is thought to be much less valuable. The hearsay rule applies to both civil and criminal trials, and to the defense as well as the prosecution.

On the other hand, some types of hearsay are extremely valuable as evidence. For example, if it is necessary to prove that the defendant withdrew a sum of money from his bank on a certain day, the best evidence of this transaction would be the bank's records made at the time and not the memory of the teller testifying at a trial months later. The records are clearly hearsay under the definition quoted above, but highly reliable in common experience and hence admissible under the "business records" exception to the hearsay rule. Even where the hearsay evidence in question is potentially unreliable, it is questionable whether it ought always to be kept from the jury if better evidence cannot be obtained. Where a witness has died before the trial, for example, it might best serve the quest for truth to allow his prior statements as evidence and trust the jury to make proper allowance in its deliberations for the fact that they have not seen the statements tested by cross-examination.

Such considerations have led the law to recognize a large number of exceptions to the rule excluding hearsay evidence, and a number of these exceptions have been held not to violate the Sixth Amendment when applied against the defendant in a criminal case. The opinion in *Pointer* specifically mentions the exception for "dying declarations" (e.g. a deathbed statement by the victim of a homicide identifying his murderer), and the exception which permits the admission of testimony recorded at a prior trial or other legal proceeding, if the opposing party had a full and fair opportunity to cross-examine the witness at the prior proceeding and if the witness has subsequently died or otherwise become unavailable. See also, Mancusi v. Stubbs, 408 U.S. 204 (1972); Barber v. Page, 390 U.S. 719 (1968). This last exception makes it possible to take the deposition of a witness in an organized crime prosecution and thereby decrease the likelihood that he may be murdered before the trial. There are many other important hearsay exceptions, including the "co-conspirator" provision. A hearsay statement of a defendant's alleged co-conspirator (i.e. one who joined with him in an agreement to commit the offense in question) is admissible against the defendant if made while the conspiracy was still active and in furtherance of its objectives. This rule has also been held to be constitutional, although it has been much criticized on the ground that statements by co-conspirators implicating each other are not necessarily very reliable. See Dutton v. Evans, 400 U.S. 74 (1970).

Although the constitutional right to confront witnesses protects only the defendant, the hearsay rule itself is theoretically applicable to the defense as well. The Sixth Amendment also grants the accused a right "to have compulsory process for obtaining witnesses in his favor," and this right has been held to limit restrictions on defense evidence in certain circumstances. In Chambers v. Mississippi, 410 U.S. 284 (1973), the Supreme Court held it unconstitutional for a state to apply its hearsay rule so strictly as to prevent a murder defendant from introducing the hearsay statements of another person who had at one time confessed to the crime. The decisions in *Chambers* and *Pointer, supra*, emphasized the importance of giving the defense an opportunity to cross-examine the government's witnesses. In a series of more recent decisions, however, the Supreme Court has blurred the distinction between hearsay rules and the constitutional right of confrontation, permitting admission of some hearsay statements by the prosecution without requiring cross-examination of the out of court declarant at trial. The more recent opinions have focused upon the trustworthiness of statements admitted under some of the exceptions to the rule against hearsay rather than upon the need to cross-examine witnesses at trial. See, e.g., Ohio v. Roberts, 448 U.S. 56 (1980); United States v. Inadi, 475 U.S. 387 (1986); Idaho v. Wright, 497 U.S. 805 (1990); White v. Illinois, 502 U.S. 346 (1992); Lilly v. Virginia, 527 U.S. 116 (1999).

F. THE PRIVILEGE AGAINST SELF–INCRIMINATION

MALLOY v. HOGAN

Supreme Court of the United States, 1964.
378 U.S. 1, 84 S.Ct. 1489, 12 L.Ed.2d 653.

MR. JUSTICE BRENNAN delivered the opinion of the Court.

In this case we are asked to reconsider prior decisions holding that the privilege against self-incrimination is not safeguarded against state action by the Fourteenth Amendment. Twining v. New Jersey, 211 U.S. 78; Adamson v. California, 332 U.S. 46.

The petitioner was arrested during a gambling raid in 1959 by Hartford, Connecticut, police. He pleaded guilty to the crime of pool selling, a misdemeanor, and was sentenced to one year in jail and fined $500. The sentence was ordered to be suspended after 90 days, at which time he was to be placed on probation for two years. About 16 months after his guilty plea, petitioner was ordered to testify before a referee appointed by the Superior Court of Hartford County to conduct an inquiry into alleged gambling and other criminal activities in the county. The petitioner was asked a number of questions related to events surrounding his arrest and conviction. He refused to answer any question "on the grounds it may tend to incriminate me." The Superior Court adjudged him in contempt, and committed him to prison until he was willing to answer the questions. * * *

[The Connecticut Supreme Court of Errors upheld the contempt citation, ruling that the Fifth Amendment's privilege against self-incrimination was not applicable in state proceedings, and that petitioner had not properly invoked the privilege available under the Connecticut Constitution. The Supreme Court granted certiorari.]

We hold today that the Fifth Amendment's exception from compulsory self-incrimination is also protected by the Fourteenth Amendment against abridgment by the States. Decisions of the Court since Twining and Adamson have departed from the contrary view expressed in those cases. We discuss first the decisions which forbid the use of coerced confessions in state criminal prosecutions.

Brown v. Mississippi, 297 U.S. 278, was the first case in which the Court held that the Due Process Clause prohibited the States from using the accused's coerced confessions against him. The Court in Brown felt impelled, in light of Twining, to say that its conclusion did not involve the privilege against self-incrimination. "Compulsion by torture to extort a confession is a different matter." 297 U.S., at 285. But this distinction was soon abandoned, and today the admissibility of a confession in a state criminal prosecution is tested by the same standard applied in federal prosecutions since 1897, when, in Bram v. United States, 168 U.S. 532, the Court held that "[i]n criminal trials, in the courts of the United States, wherever a question arises whether a confession is incompetent because not voluntary, the issue is controlled by that portion of the Fifth Amendment to the constitution of the United States commanding that no person 'shall be compelled in any criminal case to be a witness against himself.'" Under this test, the constitutional inquiry is not whether the conduct of state officers in obtaining the confession was shocking, but whether the confession was "free and voluntary; that is, [it] must not be extracted by any sort of threats or violence, nor obtained by any direct or implied promises, however slight, nor by the exertion of any improper influence. * * *" Id. In other words the person must not have been compelled to incriminate himself. We have held inadmissible even a confession secured by so mild a whip as the refusal, under certain circumstances, to allow a suspect to call his wife until he confessed. Haynes v. Washington, 373 U.S. 503.

The marked shift to the federal standard in state cases began with Lisenba v. California, 314 U.S. 219, where the Court spoke of the accused's "free choice to admit, to deny, or to refuse to answer." The shift reflects recognition that the American system of criminal prosecution is accusatorial, not inquisitorial, and that the Fifth Amendment privilege is its essential mainstay. Governments, state and federal, are thus constitutionally compelled to establish guilt by evidence independently and freely secured, and may not by coercion prove a charge against an accused out of his own mouth. Since the Fourteenth Amendment prohibits the States from inducing a person to confess through "sympathy falsely aroused," or other like inducement far short of "compulsion by torture," it follows *a fortiori* that it also forbids the States to resort to imprisonment, as here, to compel him to answer questions that might incriminate him. The Fourteenth Amendment secures against state invasion the same privilege that the Fifth Amendment guarantees against federal infringement—the right of a person to remain silent unless he chooses to speak in the unfettered exercise of his own will, and to suffer no penalty, as held in Twining, for such silence. * * *

The respondent Sheriff concedes in its brief that under our decisions, particularly those involving coerced confessions, "the accusatorial system has become a fundamental part of the fabric of our society and, hence, is enforceable against the States." The State urges, however, that the availability of the federal privilege to a witness in a state inquiry is to be determined according to a less stringent standard than is applicable in a federal proceeding. We disagree. * * * It would be incongruous to have different standards determine the validity of a claim of privilege based on the same feared prosecution, depending on whether the claim was asserted in a state or federal court. Therefore, the same standards must determine whether an accused's silence in either a federal or state proceeding is justified.

We turn to the petitioner's claim that the State of Connecticut denied him the protection of his federal privilege. It must be considered irrelevant that the petitioner was a witness in a statutory inquiry and not a defendant in a criminal prosecution, for it has long been settled that the privilege protects witnesses in similar federal inquiries. Hoffman v. United States, 341 U.S. 479. We recently elaborated the content of the federal standard in Hoffman:

> "The privilege afforded not only extends to answers that would in themselves support a conviction * * * but likewise embraces those which would furnish a link in the chain of evidence needed to prosecute. * * * [I]f the witness, upon interposing his claim, were required to prove the hazard * * * he would be compelled to surrender the very protection which the privilege is designed to guarantee. To sustain the privilege, it need only be evident from the implications of the question, in the setting in which it is asked, that a responsive answer to the question or an explanation of why it cannot be answered might be dangerous because injurious disclosure could result."

We also said that, in applying that test, the judge must be

"*perfectly clear,* from a careful consideration of all the circumstances in the case, that the witness is mistaken, and that the answer[s] *cannot possibly* have such tendency" to incriminate.

The State of Connecticut argues that the Connecticut courts properly applied the federal standards to the facts of this case. We disagree.

The investigation in the course of which petitioner was questioned began when the Superior Court in Hartford County appointed the Honorable Ernest A. Inglis, formerly Chief Justice of Connecticut, to conduct an inquiry into whether there was reasonable cause to believe that crimes, including gambling, were being committed in Hartford County. Petitioner appeared on January 16 and 25, 1961, and in both instances he was asked substantially the same questions about the circumstances surrounding his arrest and conviction for pool selling in late 1959. The questions which petitioner refused to answer may be summarized as follows: (1) for whom did he work on September 11, 1959; (2) who selected and paid his counsel in connection with his arrest on that date and subsequent conviction; (3) who selected and paid his bondsman; (4) who paid his fine; (5) what was the name of the tenant of the apartment in which he was arrested; and (6) did he know John Bergoti. The Connecticut Supreme Court of Errors ruled that the answers to these questions could not tend to incriminate him because the defenses of double jeopardy and the running of the one-year statute of limitations on misdemeanors would defeat any prosecution growing out of his answers to the first five questions. As for the sixth question, the court held that petitioner's failure to explain how a revelation of his relationship with Bergoti would incriminate him vitiated his claim to the protection of the privilege afforded by state law.

The conclusions of the Court of Errors, tested by the federal standard, fail to take sufficient account of the setting in which the questions were asked. The interrogation was part of a wide-ranging inquiry into crime, including gambling, in Hartford. It was admitted on behalf of the State at oral argument—and indeed it is obvious from the questions themselves—that the State desired to elicit from the petitioner the identity of the person who ran the pool-selling operation in connection with which he had been arrested in 1959. It was apparent that petitioner might apprehend that if this person were still engaged in unlawful activity, disclosure of his name might furnish a link in a chain of evidence sufficient to connect the petitioner with a more recent crime for which he might still be prosecuted.

Analysis of the sixth question, concerning whether petitioner knew John Bergoti, yields a similar conclusion. In the context of the inquiry, it should have been apparent to the referee that Bergoti was suspected by the State to be involved in some way in the subject matter of the investigation. An affirmative answer to the question might well have either connected petitioner with a more recent crime, or at least have operated as a waiver of his privilege with reference to his relationship with a possible criminal. We conclude, therefore, that as to each of the questions, it was "evident from the implications of the question, in the setting in which it [was] asked, that a responsive answer to the question or an explanation of why it [could not] be answered might be dangerous because injurious disclosure could result."

Reversed.

[The dissenting opinions of MR. JUSTICE HARLAN (joined by MR. JUSTICE CLARK) and MR. JUSTICE WHITE (joined by MR. JUSTICE STEWART) are omitted.]

GRIFFIN v. CALIFORNIA

Supreme Court of the United States, 1965.
380 U.S. 609, 85 S.Ct. 1229, 14 L.Ed.2d 106.

MR. JUSTICE DOUGLAS delivered the opinion of the Court.

Petitioner was convicted of murder in the first degree after a jury trial in a California court. He did not testify at the trial on the issue of guilt, though he did testify at the separate trial on the issue of penalty. The trial court instructed the jury on the issue of guilt, stating that a defendant has a constitutional right not to testify. But it told the jury:

> As to any evidence or facts against him which the defendant can reasonably be expected to deny or explain because of facts within his knowledge, if he does not testify or if, though he does testify, he fails to deny or explain such evidence, the jury may take that failure into consideration as tending to indicate the truth of such evidence and as indicating that among the inferences that may be reasonably drawn therefrom those unfavorable to the defendant are the more probable.

It added, however, that no such inference could be drawn as to evidence respecting which he had no knowledge. It stated that failure of a defendant to deny or explain the evidence of which he had knowledge does not create a presumption of guilt nor by itself warrant an inference of guilt nor relieve the prosecution of any of its burden of proof.

Petitioner had been seen with the deceased the evening of her death, the evidence placing him with her in the alley where her body was found. The prosecutor made much of the failure of petitioner to testify:

> The defendant certainly knows whether Essie Mae had this beat up appearance at the time he left her apartment and went down the alley with her.
>
> What kind of a man is it that would want to have sex with a woman that beat up if she was beat up at the time he left?
>
> He would know that. He would know how she got down the alley. He would know how the blood got on the bottom of the concrete steps. He would know how long he was with her in that box. He would know how her wig got off. He would know whether he beat her or mistreated her. He would know whether he walked away from that place cool as a cucumber when he saw Mr. Villasenor because he was conscious of his own guilt and wanted to get away from that damaged or injured woman.
>
> These things he has not seen fit to take the stand and deny or explain.

> And in the whole world, if anybody would know, this defendant would know.
>
> Essie Mae is dead, she can't tell you her side of the story. The defendant won't.

The death penalty was imposed and the California Supreme Court affirmed. The case is here on a writ of certiorari which we granted to consider whether comment on the failure to testify violated the Self-Incrimination Clause of the Fifth Amendment which we made applicable to the States by the Fourteenth in Malloy v. Hogan, 378 U.S. 1, decided after the Supreme Court of California had affirmed the present conviction.

If this were a federal trial, reversible error would have been committed. Wilson v. United States, 149 U.S. 60, so holds. It is said, however, that the Wilson decision rested not on the Fifth Amendment, but on an Act of Congress, now 18 U.S.C.A. § 3481. That indeed is the fact, as the opinion of the Court in the Wilson case states. But that is the beginning, not the end, of our inquiry. The question remains whether, statute or not, the comment rule, approved by California, violates the Fifth Amendment.

We think it does. It is in substance a rule of evidence that allows the State the privilege of tendering to the jury for its consideration the failure of the accused to testify. No formal offer of proof is made as in other situations; but the prosecutor's comment and the court's acquiescence are the equivalent of an offer of evidence and its acceptance. The Court in the Wilson case stated:

> * * * the act was framed with a due regard also to those who might prefer to rely upon the presumption of innocence which the law gives to every one, and not wish to be witnesses. It is not every one who can safely venture on the witness stand, though entirely innocent of the charge against him. Excessive timidity, nervousness when facing others and attempting to explain transactions of a suspicious character, and offenses charged against him, will often confuse and embarrass him to such a degree as to increase rather than remove prejudices against him. It is not every one, however, honest, who would therefore willingly be placed on the witness stand. The statute, in tenderness to the weakness of those who from the causes mentioned might refuse to ask to be witnesses, particularly when they may have been in some degree compromised by their association with others, declares that the failure of a defendant in a criminal action to request to be a witness shall not create any presumption against him.

If the words "Fifth Amendment" are substituted for "act" and for "statute" the spirit of the Self-Incrimination Clause is reflected. For comment on the refusal to testify is a remnant of the "inquisitorial system of criminal justice," which the Fifth Amendment outlaws. It is a penalty imposed by courts for exercising a constitutional privilege. It cuts down on the privilege by making its assertion costly. It is said, however, that the inference of guilt for failure to testify as to facts peculiarly within the accused's knowledge is in any event natural and irresistible, and that comment on the failure does not magnify that inference into a penalty for asserting a constitutional privilege. People v. Modesto, 62 Cal.2d 436, 452–453. What the jury may infer, given no help from the court, is one thing. What it may infer when the court solemnizes the silence of the accused into evidence against him is quite another. That the inference of guilt is not always so natural or irresistible is brought out in the Modesto opinion itself:

> Defendant contends that the reason a defendant refuses to testify is that his prior convictions will be introduced in evidence to impeach him and not that he is unable to deny the accusations. It is true that the defendant might fear that his prior convictions will prejudice the jury, and therefore another possible inference can be drawn from his refusal to take the stand. Id., p. 453.

We said in Malloy v. Hogan, supra, that "the same standards must determine whether an accused's silence in either a federal or state proceeding is justified." We take that in its literal sense and hold that the Fifth Amendment, in its direct application to the Federal Government and in its bearing on the States by reason of the Fourteenth Amendment, forbids either comment by the prosecution on the accused's silence or instructions by the court that such silence is evidence of guilt.

Reversed.

MR. JUSTICE STEWART, with whom MR. JUSTICE WHITE joins, dissenting.

* * *

With both candor and accuracy, the Court concedes that the question before us is one of first impression here. It is a question which has not arisen before, because until last year the self-incrimination provision of the Fifth Amendment had been held to apply only to federal proceedings, and in the federal judicial system the matter has been covered by a specific Act of Congress which has been in effect ever since defendants had been permitted to testify at all in federal criminal trials.

We must determine whether the petitioner has been "compelled * * * to be a witness against himself." Compulsion is the focus of the inquiry. Certainly, if any compulsion be detected in the California procedure, it is of a dramatically different and less palpable nature than that involved in the procedures which historically gave rise to the Fifth Amendment guarantee. When a suspect was brought before the Court of High Commission or the Star Chamber, he was commanded to answer whatever was asked of him, and subjected to a far-reaching and deeply probing inquiry in an effort to ferret out some unknown and frequently unsuspected crime. He declined to answer on pain of incarceration, banishment, or mutilation. And if he spoke falsely, he was subject to further punishment. Faced with this formidable array of alternatives, his decision to speak was unquestionably coerced.

Those were the lurid realities which lay behind enactment of the Fifth Amendment, a far cry from the subject matter of the case before us. I think that the Court in this case stretches the concept of compulsion beyond all reasonable bounds, and that whatever compulsion may exist derives from the defendant's choice not to testify, not from any comment by court or counsel. In support of its conclusion that the California procedure does compel the accused to testify, the Court has only this to say: "It is a penalty imposed by courts for exercising a constitutional privilege. It cuts down on the privilege by making its assertion costly." Exactly what the penalty imposed consists of is not clear. It is not, as I understand the problem, that the jury becomes aware that the defendant has chosen not to testify in his own defense, for the jury will, of course, realize this quite evident fact, even though the choice goes unmentioned. Since comment by counsel and the Court does not compel testimony by creating such an awareness, the Court must be saying that the California constitutional provision places some other compulsion upon the defendant to incriminate himself, some compulsion which the Court does not describe and which I cannot readily perceive.

It is not at all apparent to me, on any realistic view of the trial process, that a defendant will be at more of a disadvantage under the California practice than he would be in a court which permitted no comment at all on his failure to take the witness stand. How can it be said that the inferences drawn by a jury will be more detrimental to a defendant under the limiting and carefully controlling language of the instruction here involved than would result if the jury were left to roam at large with only its untutored instincts to guide it, to draw from the defendant's silence broad inferences of guilt?[a] The instructions in this case expressly cautioned the jury that the defendant's failure to testify "does not create a presumption of guilt or by itself warrant an inference of guilt"; it was further admonished that such failure does not "relieve the prosecution of its burden of proving every essential element of the crime," and finally the trial judge warned that the prosecution's burden remained that of proof "beyond a reasonable doubt." Whether the same limitations would be observed by a jury without the benefit of protective instructions shielding the defendant is certainly open to real doubt.

* * *

The California rule allowing comment by counsel and instruction by the judge on the defendant's failure to take the stand is hardly an idiosyncratic aberration. The Model Code of Evidence, and the Uniform Rules of Evidence both sanction the use of such procedures. The practice has been endorsed by resolution of the American Bar Association and the American Law Institute, and has the support of the weight of scholarly opinion.

* * *

a. In Carter v. Kentucky, 450 U.S. 288 (1981), the Supreme Court held that a trial judge must, upon proper request by the defense, instruct the jury not to draw any adverse inference from the failure to testify.—ed.

Some might differ, as a matter of policy, with the way California has chosen to deal with the problem, or even disapprove of the judge's specific instructions in this case. But, so long as the constitutional command is obeyed, such matters of state policy are not for this Court to decide.

I would affirm the judgment.

PORTUONDO v. AGARD

Supreme Court of the United States, 2000.
529 U.S. 61, 120 S.Ct. 1119, 146 L.Ed.2d 47.

JUSTICE SCALIA delivered the opinion of the Court.

In this case we consider whether it was constitutional for a prosecutor, in her summation, to call the jury's attention to the fact that the defendant had the opportunity to hear all other witnesses testify and to tailor his testimony accordingly.

I

Respondent's trial on 19 sodomy and assault counts and 3 weapons counts ultimately came down to a credibility determination. The alleged victim, Nessa Winder, and her friend, Breda Keegan, testified that respondent physically assaulted, raped, and orally and anally sodomized Winder, and that he threatened both women with a handgun. Respondent testified that he and Winder had engaged in consensual vaginal intercourse. He further testified that during an argument he had with Winder, he struck her once in the face. He denied raping her or threatening either woman with a handgun.

During summation, defense counsel charged Winder and Keegan with lying. The prosecutor similarly focused on the credibility of the witnesses. She stressed respondent's interest in the outcome of the trial, his prior felony conviction, and his prior bad acts. She argued that respondent was a "smooth slick character ... who had an answer for everything," and that part of his testimony "sound[ed] rehearsed." Finally, over defense objection, the prosecutor remarked:

> "You know, ladies and gentlemen, unlike all the other witnesses in this case the defendant has a benefit and the benefit that he has, unlike all the other witnesses, is he gets to sit here and listen to the testimony of all the other witnesses before he testifies.
>
> * * *
>
> "That gives you a big advantage, doesn't it. You get to sit here and think what am I going to say and how am I going to say it? How am I going to fit it into the evidence?
>
> * * *
>
> "He's a smart man. I never said he was stupid .... He used everything to his advantage."

The trial court rejected defense counsel's claim that these last comments violated respondent's right to be present at trial. The court stated that respondent's status as the last witness in the case was simply a matter of fact, and held that his presence during the entire trial, and the advantage that this afforded him, "may fairly be commented on."

Respondent was convicted of one count of anal sodomy and two counts of third-degree possession of a weapon. * * *

* * *

II

Respondent contends that the prosecutor's comments on his presence and on the ability to fabricate that it afforded him unlawfully burdened his Sixth Amendment right to be present at trial and to be confronted with the witnesses against him, and his Fifth and Sixth Amendment rights to testify on his own behalf. Attaching the cost of impeachment to the exercise of these rights was, he asserts, unconstitutional.

Respondent's argument boils down to a request that we extend to comments of the type the prosecutor made here the rationale of *Griffin* v. *California,* 380 U. S. 609 (1965), which involved comments upon a defendant's *refusal* to testify. In that case, the trial court instructed the jury that it was free to take the defendant's failure to deny or explain facts within his knowledge as tending to indicate the truth of the prosecution's case. This Court held that such a comment, by "solemniz[ing] the silence of the accused into evidence against him," unconstitutionally "cuts down on the privilege [against self-incrimination] by making its assertion costly."

We decline to extend *Griffin* to the present context. As an initial matter, respondent's claims have no historical foundation, neither in 1791, when the Bill of Rights was adopted, nor in 1868 when, according to our jurisprudence, the Fourteenth Amendment extended the strictures of the Fifth and Sixth Amendments to the States. * * *

* * *

Lacking any historical support for the constitutional rights that he asserts, respondent must rely entirely upon our opinion in *Griffin.* That case is a poor analogue, however, for several reasons. What we prohibited the prosecutor from urging the jury to do in *Griffin* was something the jury is not permitted to do. The defendant's right to hold the prosecution to proving its case without his assistance is not to be impaired by the jury's counting the defendant's silence at trial against him—and upon request the court must instruct the jury to that effect. It is reasonable enough to expect a jury to comply with that instruction since, as we observed in *Griffin,* the inference of guilt from silence is not always "natural or irresistible." A defendant might refuse to testify simply out of fear that he will be made to look bad by clever counsel, or fear "that his prior convictions will prejudice the jury." By contrast, it *is* natural and irresistible for a jury, in evaluating the relative credibility of a defendant who testifies last, to have in mind and weigh in the balance the fact that he heard the testimony of all those who preceded him. It is one thing (as *Griffin* requires) for the jury to evaluate all the *other* evidence in the case without giving any effect to the defendant's refusal to testify; it is something else (and quite impossible) for the jury to evaluate the credibility of the defendant's testimony while blotting out from its mind the fact that before giving the testimony the defendant had been sitting there listening to the other witnesses. * * *

Second, *Griffin* prohibited comments that suggest a defendant's silence is "evidence of *guilt.*" The prosecutor's comments in this case, by contrast, concerned respondent's *credibility as a witness,* and were therefore in accord with our longstanding rule that when a defendant takes the stand, "his credibility may be impeached and his testimony assailed like that of any other witness."

* * *

* * * Allowing comment upon the fact that a defendant's presence in the courtroom provides him a unique opportunity to tailor his testimony is appropriate—and indeed, given the inability to sequester the defendant, sometimes essential—to the central function of the trial, which is to discover the truth.

III

Finally, we address the Second Circuit's holding that the prosecutor's comments violated respondent's Fourteenth Amendment right to due process. * * *

Respondent * * * asserts that our decision in *Doyle* v. *Ohio,* 426 U. S. 610 (1976), requires such a holding. In *Doyle,* the defendants, after being arrested for selling marijuana, received their *Miranda* warnings and chose to remain silent. At their trials, both took the stand and claimed that they had not sold marijuana, but had been "framed." To impeach the defendants, the prosecutors asked each why he had not related this version of events at the time he was arrested. We held that this violated the defendants' rights to due process because the *Miranda* warnings contained an implicit "assurance that silence will carry no penalty."

Although there might be reason to reconsider *Doyle,* we need not do so here. "[W]e have consistently explained *Doyle* as a case where the government had induced silence by implicitly assuring the defendant that his silence would not be used against him." The *Miranda* warnings had, after all, specifically given the defendant both the option of speaking and the option of remaining silent—and had then gone on to say that if he chose the former option what he said could be used against him. * * *

* * *

[The concurring opinion by JUSTICE STEVENS is omitted.]

JUSTICE GINSBURG, with whom JUSTICE SOUTER joins, dissenting.

The Court today transforms a defendant's presence at trial from a Sixth Amendment right into an automatic burden on his credibility. I dissent from the Court's disposition. In *Griffin* v. *California*, we held that a defendant's refusal to testify at trial may not be used as evidence of his guilt. In *Doyle* v. *Ohio,* we held that a defendant's silence after receiving *Miranda* warnings did not warrant a prosecutor's attack on his credibility. Both decisions stem from the principle that where the exercise of constitutional rights is "insolubly ambiguous" as between innocence and guilt, a prosecutor may not unfairly encumber those rights by urging the jury to construe the ambiguity against the defendant.

The same principle should decide this case. Ray Agard attended his trial, as was his constitutional right and his statutory duty, and he testified in a manner consistent with other evidence in the case. One evident explanation for the coherence of his testimony cannot be ruled out: Agard may have been telling the truth. It is no more possible to know whether Agard used his presence at trial to figure out how to tell potent lies from the witness stand than it is to know whether an accused who remains silent had no exculpatory story to tell.

The burden today's decision imposes on the exercise of Sixth Amendment rights is justified, the Court maintains, because "the central function of the trial ... is to discover the truth." A trial ideally is a search for the truth, but I do not agree that the Court's decision advances that search. The generic accusation that today's decision permits the prosecutor to make on summation does not serve to distinguish guilty defendants from innocent ones. Every criminal defendant, guilty or not, has the right to attend his trial. Indeed, as the Court grants, New York law *requires* defendants to be present when tried. It follows that every defendant who testifies is equally susceptible to a generic accusation about his opportunity for tailoring. The prosecutorial comment at issue, tied only to the defendant's presence in the courtroom and not to his actual testimony, tarnishes the innocent no less than the guilty. Nor can a jury measure a defendant's credibility by evaluating the defendant's response to the accusation, for the broadside is fired after the defense has submitted its case. An irrebuttable observation that can be made about any testifying defendant cannot sort those who tailor their testimony from those who do not, much less the guilty from the innocent.

* * *

MIRJAN DAMAŠKA, EVIDENTIARY BARRIERS TO CONVICTION AND TWO MODELS OF CRIMINAL PROCEDURE

121 U.Pa.L.Rev. 506, 526–30 (1973).

1. THE DEFENDANT AS AN EVIDENTIARY SOURCE AT TRIAL

It is sometimes said that there is no privilege against self-incrimination in the continental system of criminal procedure. If, parochially oriented, we expect to find in the civil law system exactly the same procedural arrangements which in the American variant of the common law system are classified under this rubric, the above statement is obviously true. If, however, we assume that the minimum content of the privilege reduces to the idea that no person should be compelled to cause his own conviction by testifying, then the statement is generally false. Differences between the two systems appear only if we go beyond the minimum content and explore the technical implementation of the privilege, its range, and its underlying policies. These differences are important here only insofar as they apply to the defendant's position at the trial stage.

In contrast to the common law concept of the privilege, the continental defendant is not free to decide whether to take the stand and submit to the interrogation process. Questions can always be asked of him. He only has the right to refuse to answer at all, or refuse to respond to particular questions. Although, as a matter of formal doctrine, the trier of fact is usually not permitted to draw unfavorable inferences from his silence, the defendant's quite realistic concern that such inferences will, consciously or unconsciously, in fact be drawn, acts in a typical case as a psychological pressure to speak and respond to questions. Thus, it should occasion no surprise that almost all continental defendants choose to testify. The pressure to speak is, I believe, somewhat stronger than the parallel pressure in the common law trial on the defendant to take the stand, as more immediate inferences can be drawn from refusal to answer specific questions than from the general refusal to submit to the questioning process. Responding to these pressures, the guilty defendant will often resort to lies in order to escape conviction. Nevertheless, recognizing and tolerating this frequently instinctive desire of the guilty defendant to play the innocent, modern continental systems generally refuse to put the defendant on oath. Nor do any adverse *legal* consequences befall the defendant if the falsity of his testimony is established at trial, though he will, of course, hurt his credibility as an evidentiary source. It appears, then, that the continental system is not concerned about exposing the trier of fact to the defendant's unsworn testimony, although—considered as a class—it is of dubious trustworthiness. It is believed that precious information can be obtained even from false denials of guilt, detected inconsistencies, and other verbal or nonverbal expressions emanating from the defendant's person. All this information enters into the totality of data on the basis of which guilt-determination will eventually be made.

So much for the preliminary juxtaposition of the "right not to be questioned" and the "right not to answer questions" at trial. The proper dimensions of the difference in the approach of the two systems to the use of the defendant's testimony at trial can, however, not be ascertained if one ignores the time sequence. In the common law trial, of course, the defendant cannot take the stand, even if he wishes to do so, before the prosecution has established a prima facie case. Before he is given a chance to submit to questioning, he has already heard the witnesses for the prosecution. Consider the defendant's position in the continental courtroom. As there is no requirement here that the prosecution establish a credible case before the defense introduces its evidence, there is no obstacle to beginning the proof-taking stage by the interrogation of the defendant, and this in fact is the rule in continental systems. True, the continental legal folklore tells us that the defendant's interrogation comes first because it is primarily a means accorded him to contest the prosecutor's charges. But, whatever the proclaimed rationale, the fact still remains that in all continental systems the defendant is used as an evidentiary source before any other evidence has been examined at the trial. While the strategic value of this arrangement for the defense is a matter of some dispute, there is little doubt that it is advantageous to the prosecution. At the beginning of the case the prosecutor may sit back and expect that leads or evidence damaging to the defendant will come out of his interrogation. Also, the prosecutor may hope that the concocted story of a guilty defendant will crumble in the light of testimony of subsequent witnesses. In contrast, the prosecutor in the common law system must, before he can hope to obtain incriminating evidence through the trial interrogation process of the defendant, come forward with substantive proof of guilt by using items of evidence other than the defendant's statements in court.

Note

Does Mr. Justice Brennan's opinion for the Court in *Malloy v. Hogan* adequately explain why the privilege against self-incrimination is the "essential mainstay" of our "accusatorial" system of criminal justice? The privilege has always been controversial, and even its proponents have had difficulty agreeing on why it is desirable or what goals it is supposed to serve. The history of the privilege is brilliantly surveyed in Leonard Levy's *Origin of the Fifth Amendment* (1968). 8 Wigmore, Evidence § 2251 (McNaughton Rev. 1961) reviews the policy arguments that have been made for and against the privilege, and provides a helpful analysis of their relative merits. Adequate discussion of the rich history and varied purposes of the privilege cannot be attempted in these pages, but a few brief points may be helpful:

(a) The privilege has gained great prestige from its association with resistance to religious and political persecution from the Spanish Inquisition to the present day. The famous English cases that led up to the establishment of the privilege grew out of the practice of enforcing laws against religious and political dissent by examining suspected persons under oath concerning their beliefs and practices. This procedure was particularly effective in convicting conscientious dissenters who feared eternal damnation if they lied under oath. More recently, suspected communists and "fellow travellers" invoked the privilege to avoid having to disclose their political activities and associations to Congressional investigating committees. If the privilege has on occasion frustrated the enforcement of belief control laws, however, this is at the cost of impeding the enforcement of other laws as well.

(b) The most obnoxious feature of the inquisitorial procedure in the religious dissent cases (aside from the use of torture) was that the accused was often put under oath and examined generally without any prior showing that there was cause to suspect him of anything in particular. It is one thing to require a defendant to answer questions about a specific crime after substantial evidence of his guilt has been produced; it is quite another to interrogate a person who is under only a general or vague suspicion in the hope that something criminal will turn up. In modern terms, the privilege may be more necessary and desirable in Congressional or grand jury investigations than in criminal trials, where even absent the privilege the accused would presumably be questioned only on specific charges.

(c) Why should a defendant on trial for a specific crime not be required to take the stand to answer questions (or to have his refusals to answer noted by the jury) after the prosecution has presented a prima facie case? Three objections are commonly made: *First,* an innocent but nervous defendant might convict himself by a bad performance on the witness stand. The unstated premise behind this argument seems to be that we cannot trust juries to sympathize with the defendant's predicament and make proper allowance for an unimpressive demeanor. Why not? Is it likely that an innocent defendant would do himself more damage by telling the truth badly than by leaving the prosecution's case unrebutted? Would the likelihood be enormously reduced if we abolished the evidentiary rule that permits the prosecutor to use otherwise inadmissible prior felony convictions to impeach a defendant who elects to testify? *Second,* it is said to be "cruel" to force a guilty defendant to choose between contributing to his own conviction and committing perjury. The Continental European legal systems also recognize the existence of this dilemma, but respond to it differently. See the Damaška excerpt, supra. *Third,* it is argued that such compulsory testimony would upset our notion of a fair state-individual balance, which requires that the government shoulder the entire burden of proving guilt. Why should we have any such notion? Is the implication that compulsory testimony by the defendant is simply too effective a means of proving guilt, and that it therefore deprives the accused of a "fair fight"? Does the Continental European approach described by Damaška in any way violate the dignity of the human personality or any other basic value?

(d) It may be worth noting that the state may desire a confession for reasons other than its value as evidence. Professor Ehrenzweig has observed that a confession by the accused relieves the guilt feelings of the judge (and the society) that has to impose punishment. Ehrenzweig, *Psychoanalytic Justice* § 187 (1971). Consider in this connection the crucial importance of the confession in totalitarian purge trials. The rulers of a totalitarian society hardly need confessions in order to impose punishment, and in fact the individual's fate is normally sealed at the moment of arrest. Yet these rulers place the greatest importance upon the obtaining of confessions, and frequently extort statements describing vast plots and conspiracies that seem preposterous to foreign observers. Why? This subject has best been treated in such novels as Koestler's *Darkness at Noon* and Orwell's *1984,* and Solzhenitsyn's history *The Gulag Archipelago.*

Whatever its purposes, the privilege protects one only from giving testimony that may cause one's own conviction; it does not confer any general right to privacy. Hence, a witness may not invoke the privilege if the government has made a formal commitment not to use his compelled testimony or any evidence derived from it against him in a criminal prosecution. Kastigar v. United States, 406 U.S. 441 (1972). Furthermore, the accused may be required to give evidence that may lead to his conviction if the evidence is of a nontestimonial character. For example, he may be ordered to speak so that witnesses can identify his voice, to give a sample of his handwriting, or to provide a sample of his blood for chemical analysis. Schmerber v. California, 384 U.S. 757 (1966); Gilbert v. California, 388 U.S. 263 (1967). Are these limitations consistent with all the asserted policy bases of the privilege previously discussed?

It may seem obvious that a defendant has the right to testify if he wishes, but he did not always have such a right. Until late in the nineteenth century, criminal defendants were disqualified from testifying for themselves because it was thought that their interest in the outcome made their testimony unreliable. The history of this curious rule, which was merely a particular instance of the more general doctrine that the parties to a legal proceeding could not testify in their own behalf, is described in 2 Wigmore, Evidence § 579 (3d ed. 1940). This testimonial disqualification was abolished in England in 1898 over the objections of leading defense attorneys, who had found it very useful to argue to juries that their clients could have satisfactorily explained the damaging evidence if only they were allowed to testify. Where the disqualification persisted it was the practice to allow the defendant to make an unsworn statement to the jury. This procedure survived in Georgia until it was declared unconstitutional in 1961. Ferguson v. Georgia, 365 U.S. 570 (1961).

By its terms the privilege against self incrimination is applicable "in all criminal prosecutions." The Supreme Court has held that this includes interrogation of an arrested person by the police before any formal charges have been filed. The famous case of Miranda v. Arizona, 384 U.S. 436 (1966) held that the police may not interrogate a suspect under arrest without first warning him that he has a right to remain silent, that anything said can and will be used against him in court, that he has a right to have a lawyer present, and that if he is indigent a lawyer will be appointed to represent him. Only after the accused understands these rights and agrees to waive them may an interrogation proceed. The *Miranda* rule and the police interrogation practices that gave rise to it are not covered in this book because the subject is an extensive one which is treated thoroughly in courses in criminal procedure or police practices.

The Supreme Court has also held that evidence obtained in violation of the Fourth Amendment, which forbids unreasonable searches and seizures, may not be admitted at state or federal trials. Mapp v. Ohio, 367 U.S. 643 (1961). Again, this subject is left to a course in criminal procedure or police practices. The rules governing police conduct in the area of searches and arrests are extremely complicated, and adequate coverage would require at least several chapters. The cases in this chapter on the privilege against self incrimination illustrate the basic theoretical point which also underlies the decisions in Miranda v. Arizona and Mapp v. Ohio: the criminal trial is a search for truth, but it is not only that. In seeking to establish the truth, law enforcement authorities must refrain from obtaining information by procedures that do not respect the liberty and dignity of the individual.

6/4-623

Chapter 7

ATTEMPT, CONSPIRACY, AND COMPLICITY

INTRODUCTION

In some situations, criminal liability is imposed upon individuals who failed to complete their intended crimes. Attempt and conspiracy are two of the most important examples of liability for incomplete, or inchoate, crimes. Punishing people for attempts appears to have been unusual in early English law. The theory may have been that a failed attempt simply did not produce harm sufficient to justify punishment.[a] A person who fails in an attempt to commit a crime may, nonetheless, pose a threat to society. Society has an interest both in preventing crimes and punishing those individuals who would have committed crimes but for some interruption of their plans. Today prosecutions for attempted crimes are common. Our willingness to impose liability for unsuccessful attempts, however, forces us to define when conduct not achieving the target crime is sufficiently culpable to warrant punishment. Part A introduces tests commonly employed to define criminal attempts, then addresses the inchoate nature of the crime of conspiracy.

A. PREPARATORY CONDUCT

PEOPLE v. STAPLES

California Court of Appeal, Second District, 1970.
6 Cal.App.3d 61, 85 Cal.Rptr. 589.

REPPY, J.

PH

Defendant was charged in an information with attempted burglary. Trial by jury was waived, and the matter submitted on the testimony contained in the transcript of the preliminary hearing together with exhibits. Defendant was found guilty. * * *

a. "For what harm did the attempt cause, since the injury took no effect?" 2 Bracton, Legibus 465, f. 144b, 3 (Twiss ed. 1878), quoted in Jerome Hall, General Principles of Criminal Law 560 (1947).

I. The Facts

In October 1967, while his wife was away on a trip, defendant, a mathematician, under an assumed name, rented an office on the second floor of a building in Hollywood which was over the mezzanine of a bank. Directly below the mezzanine was the vault of the bank. Defendant was aware of the layout of the building, specifically of the relation of the office he rented to the bank vault. Defendant paid rent for the period from October 23 to November 23. The landlord had 10 days before commencement of the rental period within which to finish some interior repairs and painting. During this pre-rental period defendant brought into the office certain equipment. This included drilling tools, two acetylene gas tanks, a blow torch, a blanket, and a linoleum rug. The landlord observed these items when he came in from time to time to see how the repair work was progressing. Defendant learned from a custodian that no one was in the building on Saturdays. On Saturday, October 14, defendant drilled two groups of holes into the floor of the office above the mezzanine room. He stopped drilling before the holes went through the floor. He came back to the office several times thinking he might slowly drill down, covering the holes with the linoleum rug. At some point in time he installed a hasp lock on a closet, and planned to, or did, place his tools in it. However, he left the closet keys on the premises. Around the end of November, apparently after November 23, the landlord notified the police and turned the tools and equipment over to them. Defendant did not pay any more rent. It is not clear when he last entered the office, but it could have been after November 23, and even after the landlord had removed the equipment. On February 22, 1968, the police arrested defendant. After receiving advice as to his constitutional rights, defendant voluntarily made an oral statement which he reduced to writing.

Among other things which defendant wrote down were these:

> "Saturday, the 14th * * * I drilled some small holes in the floor of the room. Because of tiredness, fear, and the implications of what I was doing, I stopped and went to sleep.
>
> "At this point I think my motives began to change. The actual commencement of my plan made me begin to realize that even if I were to succeed a fugitive life of living off of stolen money would not give the enjoyment of the life of a mathematician however humble a job I might have.
>
> "I still had not given up my plan however. I felt I had made a certain investment of time, money, effort and a certain psychological commitment to the concept.
>
> "I came back several times thinking I might store the tools in the closet and slowly drill down, covering the hole with a rug of linoleum square. As time went on (after two weeks or so). My wife came back and my life as a bank robber seemed more and more absurd."

II. Discussion of Defendant's Contentions

In order for the prosecution to prove that defendant committed an attempt to burglarize as proscribed by Penal code section 664, it was required to establish that he had the specific intent to commit a burglary of the bank and that his acts toward that goal went beyond mere preparation.

The required specific intent was clearly established in the instant case. Defendant admitted in his written confession that he rented the office fully intending to burglarize the bank, that he brought in tools and equipment to accomplish this purpose, and that he began drilling into the floor with the intent of making an entry into the bank.

The question of whether defendant's conduct went beyond "mere preparation" raises some provocative problems. The briefs and the oral argument of counsel in this case point up a degree of ambiguity and uncertainty that permeates the law of attempts in this state. Each side has cited us to a different so-called "test" to determine whether this defendant's conduct went beyond the preparatory stage. Predictably each respective test in the eyes of its proponents yielded an opposite result.

Defendant relies heavily on the following language: "Preparation alone is not enough [to convict for an attempt], there must be some appreciable fragment of the crime committed, *it must be in such progress that it will be consummated unless interrupted by circumstances independent of the will of the attempter*, and the act must not be equivocal in nature." (Italics added.) (People v. Buffum, 40 Cal.2d 709, 718, 256 P.2d 317, 321.) Defendant argues that while the facts show that he did do a series of acts directed at the commission of a burglary—renting the office, bringing in elaborate equipment and actually starting drilling—the facts do not show that he was interrupted by any outside circumstances. Without such interruption and a voluntary desistence on his part, defendant concludes that under the above stated test, he has not legally committed an attempt. The Attorney General has replied that even if the above test is appropriate, the trial judge, obviously drawing reasonable inferences, found that defendant was interrupted by outside circumstances—the landlord's act of discovering the burglary equipment, resuming control over the premises, and calling the police. * * *

An examination of the decisional law reveals *at least two* general categories of attempts, both of which have been held to fall within the ambit of the statute.

In the first category are those situations where the actor does all acts necessary (including the last proximate act) to commit the substantive crime, but nonetheless he somehow is unsuccessful. This lack of success is either a "failure" or a "prevention" brought about because of some extraneous circumstances, e.g., a malfunction of equipment, a miscalculation of operations by the actor or a situation wherein circumstances were at variance with what the actor believed them to be. Certain convictions for attempted murder illustrate the first category. Some turn on situations wherein the actor fires a weapon at a person but misses; takes aim at an intended victim and pulls the trigger, but the firing mechanism malfunctions; or plants on an aircraft a homemade bomb which sputters but does not explode. [Citations omitted] * * *

In the above situations application of the rule stated in People v. Buffum, supra, would appear to be quite appropriate. After a defendant has done all acts necessary under normal conditions to commit a crime, he is culpable for an attempt if he is unsuccessful *because* of an extraneous or fortuitous circumstance.

However, it is quite clear that under California law an overt act, which, when added to the requisite intent, is sufficient to bring about a criminal attempt, need not be the last proximate or ultimate step towards commission of the substantive crime. * * * Police officers need not wait until a suspect, who aims a gun at his intended victim, actually pulls the trigger before they arrest him; nor do these officers need to wait until a suspect, who is forcing the lock of a bank door, actually breaks in before they arrest him for attempted burglary.

This rule makes for a second category of "attempts." The recognition of this separate category is well articulated by Mr. Chief Judge Learned Hand in United States v. Coplon (2d Cir.1950) 185 F.2d 629, 633 as follows: "A neat doctrine by which to test when a person, intending to commit a crime which he fails to carry out, has 'attempted' to commit it, would be that he has done all that it is within his power to do, but has been prevented by intervention from outside; in short that he has passed beyond any *locus poenitentiae*. Apparently that was the original notion, and may still be law in England; but it is certainly not now generally the law in the United States, for there are many decisions which hold that the accused has passed beyond 'preparation,' although he has been interrupted before he has taken the last of his intended steps."

* * *

Our courts have come up with a variety of "tests" which try to distinguish acts of preparation from completed attempts. "The preparation consists in devising or arranging the means or measures necessary for the commission of the offense; the attempt is the direct movement toward the commission after the preparations are made." [Citations] "The act must reach far enough towards the accomplishment of the desired result to amount to the commencement of the consummation." [Citation] "Where the intent to commit the substantive offense is clearly established, acts done toward the commission of the crime may constitute an attempt, where the same acts would be held insufficient to constitute an attempt if the intent with which they were done is equivocal and not clearly proved." [Citation]

None of the above statements of the law applicable to this category of attempts provide a litmus-like test and perhaps no such test is achievable. Such precise is not required in this case, however. There was definitely substantial evidence entitling the trial judge to find that defendant's acts had gone beyond the preparation stage. Without specifically deciding where defendant's preparations left off and where his activities became a completed criminal attempt, we can say that his "drilling" activity clearly was an unequivocal and direct step toward the completion of the burglary. It was a fragment of the substantive crime contemplated, i.e., the beginning of the "breaking" element. Further, defendant himself characterized his activity as the *actual commencement of his plan.* The drilling by defendant was obviously one of a series of acts which logic and ordinary experience indicate would result in the proscribed act of burglary.

The instant case provides an out-of-the-ordinary factual situation within the second category. Usually the actors in cases falling within that category of attempts are intercepted or caught in the act. Here, there was no direct proof of any actual interception. But it was clearly inferable by the trial judge that defendant became aware that the landlord had resumed control over the office and had turned defendant's equipment and tools over to the police. This was the equivalent of interception.

The inference of this nonvoluntary character of defendant's abandonment was a proper one for the trial judge to draw. However, it would seem that the character of the abandonment in situations of this type, whether it be voluntary (prompted by pangs of conscience or a change of heart) or nonvoluntary (established by inference in the instant case), is not controlling. The relevant factor is the determination of whether the acts of the perpetrator have reached such a stage of advancement that they can be classified as an attempt. Once that attempt is found there can be no exculpatory abandonment. "One of the purposes of the criminal law is to protect society from those who intend to injure it. When it is established that he defendant intended to commit a specific crime and that in carrying out his intention he committed an act that caused harm or sufficient danger or harm, it is immaterial that for some collateral reason he could not complete the intended crime." (People v. Camodeca, 52 Cal.2d 142, 338 P.2d 903.)

The order is affirmed.

STATE v. LATRAVERSE

Supreme Court of Rhode Island, 1982.
443 A.2d 890.

KELLEHER, JUSTICE.

The defendant, Paul A. Latraverse (Latraverse), was found guilty by a Superior Court justice, after a jury-waived trial, of attempting knowingly and maliciously to dissuade a Woonsocket police officer from giving testimony before a grand jury, a violation of the Anti-intimidation of Witnesses and Crime Victims statute. Salvatore Lombardi (Lombardi) is a member of the Woonsocket police department. As a member of the detective division, he has done undercover work numerous times using the name Frank Torro. As Frank Torro, he had purchased four stolen cars from Latraverse, who owns and operates a Woonsocket used-car dealership. Following the sale, Latraverse was arrested and arraigned in the District Court on several charges of receiving stolen goods. At the time of the incident we are about to describe, Latraverse was free on bail while awaiting the grand jury's consideration of his dealings with "Torro."

On June 26, 1980, Lombardi arrived at his Morton Avenue home sometime between 11 p.m. and midnight after completing a tour of duty. At approximately 1:40 a.m. on June 27, he and his wife were watching a television program when a car with a faulty muffler passed by. The resulting noise caused Lombardi to look out the front window. There on the street he observed a late-model Ford Thunderbird bearing a license plate assigned to Latraverse's automobile agency. Lombardi was aware that the "T-bird" belonged to Latraverse. Once the vehicle had passed by, Lombardi took his walkie-talkie, went outside his home, and secreted himself in the darkness. Lombardi told the trial justice that he kept a vigilant eye on the early-morning traffic passing by his house because he had received threats as a result of his undercover work. He also testified that on one occasion while working under cover he was asked by Latraverse if his real name was "Salvatore Lombardi."

Lombardi watched the T-bird as it proceeded along Morton Avenue and then took a left onto Bellevue Street, and within a matter of twenty to thirty seconds, he observed the T-bird coming "down" Harrison Avenue. When the vehicle came to a halt, it was parked in front of 203 Harrison Avenue. Its lights were then extinguished. Harrison Avenue runs perpendicular to Morton Avenue and is almost directly across the street from the Lombardi residence. After a wait of a minute or so, Lombardi radioed headquarters for a "backup" because, in his words, he "wasn't going to take any chances" and he "felt" that Latraverse wanted to see him injured. As the backup vehicle came onto Morton Avenue from Hamlet Avenue, its lights were on, and the vehicle was proceeding at forty miles per hour toward the Harrison Avenue–Morton Avenue intersection. As the backup headed toward the intersection, the T-bird backed up on Harrison, made a U-turn, and headed away from the Morton Avenue area toward Park Place. The backup caught up with the darkened T-bird in front of 138 Harrison Avenue.

When the police looked at the interior of the car, they saw the following items: a can of gasoline; a rag; matches; an aluminum baseball bat; a wire coat hanger that had been stretched out so that it could be used to open a car door; and a note that read, "Hi, Sal, now it's my turn asshole."

After the defense had rested without presenting any evidence, Latraverse moved for a judgment of acquittal. Thereafter, the trial justice gave a bench decision in which, after first noting that this court had yet to express itself on the subject of criminal liability for attempting to commit a crime, he referred to several cases in which various courts in

Connecticut, the District of Columbia, Maine, and Maryland had had their say in regard to whether an accused's conduct fell within the parameters of each jurisdiction's definition of what constituted criminal attempt.

Since the issues presented by Latraverse are those of first impression for this court, we shall briefly detail the evolution of the law of criminal attempt, noting as we proceed the differing views expressed through the years about what are the essential elements of the crime.

Although the criminal law is of ancient origin, the concept that there could be criminal liability for an attempt, even if ultimately unsuccessful, is of comparatively recent origin, beginning with Rex v. Scofield, Cald 397 (1784). See Sayre, Criminal Attempts, 41 Harv.L.Rev. 821 (1928). In Scofield, Lord Mansfield observed:

> "The *intent* may make an act, innocent in itself, criminal; nor is the *completion* of an act, criminal in itself, necessary to constitute criminality. Is it no offence to set fire to a train of gunpowder with intent to burn a house, because by accident, or the interposition of another, the mischief is prevented?"

The classic elements of a commonlaw attempt are an intent to commit a crime, the execution of an overt act in furtherance of the intention, and a failure to consummate the crime. However, this common-law view fails to indicate how far the accused's conduct must proceed toward the actual consummation of the crime in order to be considered an attempt to commit that crime. It is generally agreed that neither the intent to commit a crime nor mere preparation in and of itself constitutes an attempt. The difficulty is to establish a standard that excludes preparation prior to the actual attempt to commit the crime while including as punishable those acts which have reached the point where intervention by the police is justified.

In looking to the tests formulated by the various courts that have sought to distinguish preparation from perpetration, we first look to our northern New England neighbor, Vermont, where "attempt" is defined as an act which "must reach far enough towards the accomplishment of the desired result to amount to the commencement of the consummation." State v. Boutin, 133 Vt. 531, 346 A.2d 531 (1975). Again, shortly before the turn of the century in Massachusetts, Mr. Justice Oliver Wendell Holmes, in considering an appeal involving an attempted poisoning, observed that "the act done must come pretty near to accomplishing that result before the law will notice it." Commonwealth v. Kennedy, 170 Mass. 18, 48 N.E. 770 (1897). A few years later, when the question was attempted arson, he said:

> Preparation is not an attempt. But some preparations may amount to an attempt. It is a question of degree. If the preparation comes very near to the accomplishment of the act, the intent to complete it renders the crime so probable that the act will be a misdemeanor * * *. Commonwealth v. Peaslee, 177 Mass. 267, 59 N.E. 55, 56 (1901).

The learned jurist also stressed that the arson attempt was complete even though an accused had an opportunity to experience a change of mind. Twenty-four years later Mr. Justice Cardozo in People v. Werblow, 241 N.Y. 55, 148 N.E. 786 (1925), expressed the belief that acts performed in furtherance of a criminal project do not reach the stage of attempt unless "they carry the project forward within dangerous proximity to the criminal end to be attained * * *."

It should be obvious by now that much has been written trying to establish the exact placement of the dividing line where preparation ends and attempt begins, and we have no intention of contributing one whit to what has been described as the preparation-attempt "quagmire." Instead, we adopt the sensible approach to the question now before us embodied in § 5.01 of the American Law Institute's Model Penal Code. * * * [See infra, Ch. 7, § A.—ed.]

The code, with its proviso about an individual who engages in conduct with the purpose of causing a criminal result "with the belief that it will cause such result without further conduct on his part," assigns as criminal liability such conduct as that of the spouse who places a strychnine-saturated glass of milk on the other spouse's night table even though the intended victim for some unknown reason breaks with habit and leaves the glass untouched.

More to the point, however, is the substantial-step clause. Under § 5.01(1)(c) of the code, an attempt occurs when one "purposely does or omits to do anything which * * * is an act or omission constituting a substantial step in a course of conduct planned to culminate in his commission of the crime." To constitute a substantial step, the conduct must be "strongly corroborative of the actor's criminal purpose." The application of this standard will, of course, depend upon the nature of the intended crime and the facts of the particular case. A substantial step in the commission of robbery may be quite different from that in arson, rape, or some other crime, but this standard properly directs attention to overt acts of the defendant which convincingly demonstrate a firm purpose to commit a crime. In subscribing to the substantial-step doctrine, we endorse the sentiments expressed by Chief Judge Kaufman in United States v. Stallworth, 543 F.2d 1038, 1040 (2d Cir.1976), in which the court, in rejecting the defendants' contention that they could not be convicted of an attempted bank robbery because they neither entered the bank nor brandished weapons, said:

> We reject this wooden logic. Attempt is a subtle concept that requires a rational and logically sound definition, one that enables society to punish malefactors who have unequivocally set out upon a criminal course without requiring law enforcement officers to delay until innocent bystanders are imperiled.

The code's requirement of a substantial step shifts the emphasis from what remains to be done to what already has been done. Thus, liability for a relatively remote preparatory act is precluded, but at the same time dangerous individuals may be lawfully apprehended at an earlier stage of their nefarious enterprises than would be possible under the approaches subscribed to by the Vermont Supreme Court, Holmes, or Cardozo.

* * *

Having made our choice concerning the pertinent legal principles, we now turn to the merits of Latraverse's appeal. His argument is simple and straightforward. He argues that in taking the evidence adduced by the state in its best light, his actions in the early-morning hours of June 27, 1980, add up to nothing more than pure preparations that, in turn, must be considered abandoned by his decision to turn around on Harrison Avenue and leave the area.

With all due deference to Latraverse's claim of preparation and/or abandonment, the code's requirement of proof (1) that Latraverse must have been acting with the kind of culpability otherwise required for the commission of the crime he is charged with attempting and (2) that he must have been engaged in conduct which constituted a substantial step toward the commission of the crime emphasizes the importance of the necessity of encouraging early police intervention when a suspect is clearly bent on the commission of crime. There is no necessity that the police had to wait until Latraverse poured the gasoline or struck the match.

The evidence presented before the trial justice indicates that Latraverse had indeed taken substantial steps to effectuate his effort to intimidate Lombardi. There is no question that at 1:40 a.m. on the morning in question he was reconnoitering Lombardi's neighborhood and in the process continued his observation while parked in a darkened automobile 100 feet from the Lombardi household. No one disputes the fact that Latraverse carried with him a homemade tool for unlocking a motor vehicle as well as material that could cause an incendiary episode, and, the most persuasive evidence of Latraverse's intentions to enter Lombardi's property in the early-morning hours of June 27, 1980, his "billet-doux" to Lombardi in which he reminded "Sal" that it was now Latraverse's turn. We have no hesitancy whatsoever in holding that Latraverse's conduct constituted a substantial step in his endeavor to give Lombardi something to think about as the officer awaited his summons to appear before the grand jury.

The trial justice, rejecting Latraverse's abandonment defense, relied on Wiley v. State, 237 Md. 560, 207 A.2d 478 (1965), in which the Maryland Court of Appeals observed that a voluntary abandonment of a criminal attempt that had proceeded beyond mere preparation into an overt act or acts in furtherance of the commission of the attempt does not serve as a defense because the crime has already been committed. We cannot fault the trial justice for his reliance on the legal principles expressed in the *Wiley* case. There is a divergence of opinion about whether or not a defendant can rely upon the doctrine of abandonment after he or she has gone so far as to commit a criminal attempt. The *Wiley* case represents one side. The code expresses a different point of view in that it recognizes as a defense to an attempted crime the abandonment of efforts to commit the crime when circumstances manifest a complete and voluntary renunciation of criminal purpose.

The code stresses that abandonment or renunciation is not complete and voluntary if it is motivated because either (*a*) the defendant has failed to complete the attempt because of unanticipated difficulties, unexpected resistance, or circumstances that increase the probability of detection or apprehension or (*b*) the defendant fails to consummate the attempted offense after deciding to postpone his endeavors until another time or to substitute another victim or another but similar objective.

Since abandonment is an affirmative defense, Latraverse, if he wishes, has the opportunity and the burden of establishing by a preponderance of the evidence that he in fact voluntarily and completely abandoned his nefarious efforts on the evening in question when he turned around on Harrison Avenue and drove away from Lombardi's home toward Park Place. In placing the burden of abandonment upon the defendant, we perceive no constitutional limitations. Voluntary abandonment, as we view the doctrine, does not negate any element of the offense. Our adoption of the code's approach to abandonment is motivated solely by our belief that our actions are consonant with the purpose of the substantial-step rationale, which recognizes the desirability of early preventive action by the police before a defendant comes dangerously close to committing the intended crime. In like manner, the sole motivation for our recognition of an abandonment defense is the hope that individuals will desist from pursuing their criminal designs, thereby reducing the risk that the intended substantive crime will be accomplished.

Having recognized the abandonment defense, we now afford Latraverse the opportunity to establish by the fair preponderance of the evidence that his departure from Lombardi's neighborhood constituted a voluntary and complete abandonment of his criminal purposes on the evening in question. If this evidentiary hearing is not commenced within ten days of the filing date of this opinion, an order will be entered affirming the judgment of conviction entered in the Superior Court. If he accepts this mandate, the record in this case will be remanded to the Superior Court for a hearing so that the evidence may be presented forthwith to the trial justice for his evaluation. Jurisdiction will be retained by us for further appellate review if such is required.

STATE v. REEVES

Supreme Court of Tennessee, 1996.
916 S.W.2d 909.

DROWOTA, J.

On the evening of January 5, 1993, Tracie Reeves and Molly Coffman, both twelve years of age and students at West Carroll Middle School, spoke on the telephone and decided to kill their homeroom teacher, Janice Geiger. The girls agreed that Coffman would bring rat poison to school the following day so that it could be placed in Geiger's drink. The girls also agreed that they would thereafter steal Geiger's car and drive to the Smoky Mountains. Reeves then contacted Dean Foutch, a local high school student, informed him of the plan, and asked him to drive Geiger's car. Foutch refused this request.

On the morning of January 6, Coffman placed a packet of rat poison in her purse and boarded the school bus. During the bus ride Coffman told another student, Christy Hernandez, of the plan; Coffman also showed Hernandez the packet of rat poison. Upon their arrival at school Hernandez informed her homeroom teacher, Sherry Cockrill, of the plan. Cockrill then relayed this information to the principal of the school, Claudia Argo.

When Geiger entered her classroom that morning she observed Reeves and Coffman leaning over her desk; and when the girls noticed her, they giggled and ran back to their seats. At that time Geiger saw a purse lying next to her coffee cup on top of the desk. Shortly thereafter Argo called Coffman to the principal's office. Rat poison was found in Coffman's purse and it was turned over to a Sheriff's Department investigator. Both Reeves and Coffman gave written statements to the investigator concerning their plan to poison Geiger and steal her car.

Reeves and Coffman were found to be delinquent by the Carroll County Juvenile Court, and both appealed from that ruling to the Carroll County Circuit Court. After a jury found that the girls attempted to commit second degree murder in violation of Tenn. Code Ann. § 39–12–101, the "criminal attempt" statute, the trial court affirmed the juvenile court's order and sentenced the girls to the Department of Youth Development for an indefinite period. Reeves appealed from this judgment to the Court of Appeals, which affirmed the judgment of the trial court. Reeves then applied to this Court for permission to appeal. Because we have not addressed the law of criminal attempt since the comprehensive reform of our criminal law undertaken by the legislature in 1989, we granted that application.

Prior and Current Law of Criminal Attempt

Before the passage of the reform legislation in 1989, the law of criminal attempt, though sanctioned by various statutes, was judicially defined. In order to submit an issue of criminal attempt to the jury, the State was required to present legally sufficient evidence of: (1) an intent to commit a specific crime; (2) an overt act toward the commission of that crime; and (3) a failure to consummate the crime. *Bandy v. State, 575 S.W.2d 278, 281 (Tenn.1979); Gervin v. State, 212 Tenn. 653, 371 S.W.2d 449, 451 (1963); Dupuy v. State, 204 Tenn. 624, 325 S.W.2d 238, 240 (1959).*

Of the elements of criminal attempt, the second, the "overt act" requirement, was by far the most problematic. By attempting to draw a sharp distinction between "mere preparation" to commit a criminal act, which did not constitute the required overt act, and a "direct movement toward the commission after the preparations had been made," which

did, Tennessee courts construed the term "overt act" very narrowly. The best example of this extremely narrow construction occurred in *Dupuy.* In that case, the Memphis police sought to lay a trap for a pharmacist suspected of performing illegal abortions by sending a young woman to request these services from him. After the woman had made several attempts to secure his services, he finally agreed to perform the abortion. The pharmacist transported the young woman to a hotel room, laid out his instruments in preparation for the procedure, and asked the woman to remove her clothes. At that point the police came into the room and arrested the pharmacist, who then admitted that he had performed abortions in the past. The defendant was convicted under a statute that made it illegal to procure a miscarriage, and he appealed to this Court.

A majority of this Court reversed the conviction. After admitting that the defendant's "reprehensible" course of conduct would doubtlessly have resulted in the commission of the crime "had he not been thwarted in his efforts by the arrival of the police," the majority concluded that "While the defendant had completed his plan to do this crime the element of attempt [overt act] does not appear in this record. The proof shows that he did not use any of the instruments and did not touch the body of the girl in question. Under such facts we do not think that the defendant is guilty under the statute." *Dupuy,* 325 S.W.2d at 240. * * *

The sharp differentiation in Dupuy between "mere preparation" and "overt act," or the "act itself," was characteristic of the pre–1989 attempt law. See e.g., *Gervin v. State, 212 Tenn. 653, 371 S.W.2d 449 (1963)* (criminal solicitation does not constitute an attempt); *McEwing v. State, 134 Tenn. 649, 185 S.W. 688 (1915)* (conviction for attempted rape affirmed because defendant actually laid hands on the victim). In 1989, however, the legislature enacted a general criminal attempt statute, Tenn. Code Ann. § 39–12–101, as part of its comprehensive overhaul of Tennessee's criminal law. In that statute, the legislature did not simply codify the judicially-created elements of the crime, but utilized language that had up to then been entirely foreign to Tennessee attempt law. Section 39–12–101 provides, in pertinent part, as follows:

> (a) A person commits criminal attempt who, acting with the kind of culpability otherwise required for the offense:
>
> (1) Intentionally engages in action or causes a result that would constitute an offense if the circumstances surrounding the conduct were as the person believes them to be;
>
> (2) Acts with intent to cause a result that is an element of the offense, and believes the conduct will cause the result without further conduct on the person's part; or
>
> (3) Acts with intent to complete a course of action or cause a result that would constitute the offense, under the circumstances surrounding the conduct as the person believe them to be, and the conduct constitutes a substantial step toward the commission of the offense.

(b) Conduct does not constitute a substantial step under subdivision (a)(3) unless the person's entire course of action is corroborative of the intent to commit the offense.

The Substantial Step Issue

As stated above, our task is to determine whether the defendant's actions in this case constitute a "substantial step" toward the commission of second degree murder under the new statute. The "substantial step" issue has not yet been addressed by a Tennessee court in a published opinion, and the question is made more difficult by the fact that the legislature declined to set forth any definition of the term, preferring instead to "leave the issue of what constitutes a substantial step [to the courts] for determination in each particular case." § 39–12–101, Comments of Sentencing Commission.

In addressing this issue, we first note that the legislature, in enacting § 39–12–101, clearly looked to the criminal attempt section set forth in the Model Penal Code. * * *

The State argues that the striking similarity of Tenn. Code Ann. § 39–12–101 and the Model Penal Code evidences the legislature's intention to abandon the old law of criminal attempt and instead adopt the Model Penal Code approach. The State then avers that the model code contains examples of conduct which, if proven, would entitle, but not require, the jury to find that the defendant had taken a "substantial step;" and that two of these examples are applicable to this case. The section of the model code relied upon by the State, § 5.01(2), provides, in pertinent part, as follows:

(2) Conduct which may be held substantial step under paragraph (1)(c). Conduct shall not be held to constitute a substantial step under paragraph (1)(c) of this Section unless it is strongly corroborative of the actor's criminal purpose. Without negativing the sufficiency of other conduct, the following, if strongly corroborative of the actor's criminal purpose, shall not be held insufficient as a matter of law:

. . .

(e) possession of materials to be employed in the commission of the crime, which are specially designed for such unlawful use or which can serve no lawful purpose of the actor under the circumstances;

(f) possession, collection or fabrication of materials to be employed in the commission of the crime, at or near the place contemplated for its commission, where such possession, collection or fabrication serves no lawful purpose of the actor under the circumstances;

The State concludes that because the issue of whether the defendant's conduct constitutes a substantial step may be a jury question under the model code, the jury was justified in finding her guilty of attempting to commit second degree murder.

The defendant counters by arguing that despite the similarity of Tenn. Code Ann. § 39–12–101 and the Model Penal Code's attempt provision, the legislature intended to retain the sharp distinction between "mere preparation" and the "act itself" characteristic of such decisions as *Dupuy*. She supports this assertion by pointing out that although the legislature could have easily included the examples set forth in § 5.01(2) of the model code, the Tennessee statute does not include the examples. The defendant concludes that the new statute did not substantially change Tennessee attempt law, and that her conviction must be reversed because her actions constitute "mere preparation" under *Dupuy*.

Initially, we cannot accept the argument that the legislature intended to explicitly adopt the Model Penal Code approach, including the examples set forth in § 5.01(2). Although § 39–12–101 is obviously based on the model code, we agree with the defendant that the legislature could have, if it had so desired, simply included the specific examples in the Tennessee statute. That it did not do so prohibits us from concluding that the legislature explicitly intended to adopt the model code approach in all its particulars.

This conclusion does not mean, however, that the legislature intended to retain the distinction between "mere preparation" and the "act itself." Moreover, while we concede that a strong argument can be made that the conviction conflicts with *Dupuy* because the defendant did not place the poison in the cup, but simply brought it to the crime scene, we also are well aware that the *Dupuy* approach to attempt law has been consistently and effectively criticized. One persistent criticism of the endeavor to separate "mere preparation" from the "act itself" is that the question is ultimately not one of kind but of degree; the "act itself" is merely one of the termini on a continuum of criminal activity. Therefore, distinguishing between "mere preparation" and the "act itself" in a principled manner is a difficult, if not impossible, task. The other principal ground of criticism of the *Dupuy* approach bears directly on the primary objective of the law—that of preventing inchoate crimes from becoming full-blown ones. Many courts and commentators have argued that failing to attach criminal responsibility to the actor—and therefore prohibiting law enforcement officers from taking action—until the actor is on the brink of consummating the crime endangers the public and undermines the preventative goal of attempt law. [citations]

The shortcomings of the *Dupuy* rule with respect to the goal of prevention are particularly evident in this case. As stated above, it is likely that under Dupuy no criminal responsibility would have attached unless the poison had actually been placed in the teacher's cup. This rigid requirement, however, severely undercuts the objective of prevention because of the surreptitious nature of the act of poisoning. Once a person secretly places a toxic substance into a container from which another person is likely to eat or drink, the damage is done. Here, if it had not been for the intervention of the teacher, she could have been rendered powerless to protect herself from harm.

After carefully weighing considerations of *stare decisis* against the persuasive criticisms of the *Dupuy* rule, we conclude that this artificial and potentially harmful rule must be abandoned. We hold that when an actor possesses materials to be used in the commission of a crime, at or near the scene of the crime, and where the possession of those materials can serve no lawful purpose of the actor under the circumstances, the jury is entitled, but not required, to find that the actor has taken a "substantial step" toward the commission of the crime if such action is strongly corroborative of the actor's overall criminal purpose. For the foregoing reasons, the judgment is affirmed.

ADOLPHO A. BIRCH, JR., JUSTICE

I concur in the majority's statement of the rule to be applied in deciding whether a criminal attempt has occurred. I dissent, however, from their application of that rule to this case. * * * Based upon this record, I would find that the "entire course of action" of these two twelve-year-old girls was not "strongly corroborative" of intent to commit second-degree murder and that the evidence was insufficient as a matter of law. In looking at the "entire course of action," we should remember that these were twelve-year-old girls, not explosive-toting terrorists.

Note[a]

Attempt is an inchoate or preparatory crime, permitting the punishment of persons even if they never carry out their scheme or are apprehended before achieving their objective. One of the most important traditional limitations upon attempt prosecutions has been the proximity doctrine, which requires that one go beyond "mere preparation" and come somewhere near success in order to be guilty of attempting to commit a crime. The proximity doctrine seems to have originated in 1855 in the famous English case of Regina v. John Eagleton.[b]

Eagleton was a baker who contracted with the guardians of his parish to provide loaves of bread of a certain weight for the "out-door poor." He delivered the loaves directly to the paupers, and received in return from them tickets which he turned in to an officer of the board of guardians. Upon receiving the tickets, the officer credited Eagleton in his account book with the amount due, but the guardians did not actually make payment until some future date specified in the contract. After Eagleton had turned in a number of tickets but before any payment was made, the guardians discovered that he had been delivering underweight loaves, and they caused him to be prosecuted for attempting to obtain money by false promises. Until they actually made full payment in cash, the guardians retained a right to deduct from the total sum any damages for breach of contract. Eagleton's counsel argued to the Court of Crimi-

a. Adapted from Johnson, The Unnecessary Crime of Conspiracy, 61 Calif.L.Rev. 1137, 1157–64 (1973). Copyright 1973, by the California Law Review.

b. 169 Eng.Rep. 826 (Crim.App.1855).

nal Appeal that this reservation made the fact of ultimate payment so contingent or speculative that his client could not be convicted of attempt. Writing for a unanimous court, Baron Parke admitted that the judges had "great doubt on this part of the case," but concluded that the conviction for attempt was proper because the defendant had performed the last act on his part that was necessary to obtain the money. If there had remained anything further for him to do, "as the making out a further account or producing the vouchers to the Board," then his actions would not have been "sufficiently proximate" to the completed crime.

The "last act" rule of the *Regina v. Eagleton* case never became the law of England, although some authorities have supposed otherwise. Later in the same year, the same court cited *Eagleton* in upholding the conviction for attempted counterfeiting of a man who had obtained dies engraved for manufacturing Peruvian coins, although he had not made any coins or even obtained all the necessary supplies.[c]

Since that time, the courts of several nations have spent innumerable hours trying to specify how one can determine when a defendant's actions have gone beyond "mere preparation" and become "sufficiently proximate" to the completed act for conviction of attempt, with the result that considerable confusion has been added to the original uncertainty. The Model Penal Code commentary discerned six formulations in the case law, and proposed a seventh itself.[d]

Less important than the various formulations are the results that obtained in some famous cases. An English court held that a jeweler who faked a robbery for the purpose of defrauding his insurer was not guilty of attempting to obtain money by false pretenses, because he had not yet filed a claim.[e]

A New York court held that a gang of armed robbers who were apprehended as they drove around the city in search of a particular payroll clerk they intended to rob were not guilty of attempted robbery because they had not yet found the clerk.[f]

A California court reversed the conviction for attempted theft of a swindler who tried to induce his victim to withdraw his money from the bank in the course of a "bunco" scheme known as the "Jamaica switch." Because the victim luckily met his wife in the bank and did not withdraw his savings, the swindler's acts amounted only to preparation.[g]

As these cases show, the proximity approach does not consider the dangerousness of the defendant but only how close he came to completing the particular crime. A person carrying a bomb into a public building with the intent to set it off is plainly very dangerous to the community even if by chance he is apprehended before lighting the fuse. The

c. Regina v. Roberts, 169 Eng.Rep. 836 (Crim.App.1855).

d. Model Penal Code § 5.01, Comment at 39–48 (Tent.Draft No. 10, 1960).

e. Rex v. Robinson [1915] 2 K.B. 342.

f. People v. Rizzo, 246 N.Y. 334, 158 N.E. 888 (1927).

g. People v. Orndorff, 261 Cal.App.2d 212, 67 Cal.Rptr. 824 (1968).

confidence trickster whose scheme is detected before the victim is ready to hand over the money is probably a professional thief. A doctrine that leads to the acquittal of such persons is justifiable only if one views the criminal law to be dominated by the goals of retribution and deterrence. The community's desire for punishment is weaker when the potential criminal does not succeeds, or nearly succeed, in completing his crime and inflicting harm upon an identifiable victim. Punishment for attempts is also relatively unimportant in deterring crime, because the would-be criminal ordinarily expects to succeed and is deterred, if at all, by the punishment for success.

Although retribution and deterrence are by no means irrelevant to modern criminal law, today we tend to emphasize the restraint or incapacitation of dangerous individuals. We see the primary task of law enforcement as the identification and isolation or supervision of those persons who are likely to offend repeatedly unless rehabilitated or at least safely locked away. With this change in emphasis have come discretionary and indeterminate sentences, probation and parole systems, rehabilitative prison programs and a wider law of attempts. The law is conservative enough not to discard the old rules everywhere, but modern statutory reform proposals such as the Model Penal Code have increasingly taken the view that the crucial issue is the clarity and strength of the defendant's criminal purpose rather than the proximity of his actions to the completed crime.

Pursued to its logical conclusion, the modern approach would permit the conviction of anyone shown to have had a firm intention to commit a crime, whether or not he had taken any steps towards its commission. The limiting factor, however, is our reluctance to put so much trust in either the omniscience or the benevolence of those who administer the law. It is difficult to determine what someone intends to do before he does it, or at least prepares to do it. Even when an individual has plainly said what he intends to do, there remains the question of how serious or definite his intent is. Many of us at some time contemplate or even talk about committing a crime without ever doing anything to carry out the design. But if we refrain from criminal conduct (including conduct that encourages others to commit crime), we are not dangerous, and the deterrent purposes of the criminal law are fully satisfied.

For this reason the modern codes retain the requirement that a defendant go beyond merely planning or contemplating a crime before he can be convicted of an attempt. He must engage in conduct that is a sufficiently substantial step towards completion of the crime to indicate his firm criminal intent, and to identify him as a dangerous individual who would probably have gone on to complete the crime if his design had not been frustrated. Thus, although the modern formulations of attempt law retain conduct as an element of attempt, they relegate it to a lesser, evidentiary role: the defendant's actions must confirm his intent to commit a criminal act. * * * Proximity to success is no longer the crucial issue. The possibility that the actor might change his mind and not complete the crime is dealt with in an affirmative defense of renunciation.

The following materials introduce conspiracy, another crime creating inchoate liability. As you will see, conduct too preparatory to constitute an attempt might nonetheless amount to a criminal conspiracy.

STATE v. PACHECO

Supreme Court of Washington, 1994.
125 Wash.2d 150, 882 P.2d 183.

JOHNSON, J.

The Defendant, Herbert Pacheco, appeals his convictions for conspiracy to commit first degree murder and conspiracy to deliver a controlled substance. He contends he did not commit conspiracy because no genuine agreement existed between him and his sole coconspirator, an undercover police agent. We hold [that the Washington conspiracy statutes] require an actual agreement between two coconspirators, and, therefore, reverse his convictions for conspiracy to commit murder in the first degree and conspiracy to deliver a controlled substance.

Herbert Pacheco met Thomas Dillon in 1985, when Pacheco worked about 2 months for Dillon's private investigation firm. Pacheco bragged to Dillon about his involvement in illegal activities, including enforcement, collecting debts, procuring weapons, providing protection, and performing "hits".

In 1989, Dillon learned that Pacheco was a Clark County deputy sheriff. Dillon contacted the FBI and volunteered to inform on Pacheco. The FBI began an investigation of Pacheco. The Clark County Sheriff's office joined, and later directed the investigation.

The investigation involved the recording of conversations, face-to-face and over the telephone, between Dillon and Pacheco. During these conversations Dillon asked Pacheco to perform various jobs, including collections and information checks on individuals.

On March 26, 1990, according to a plan designed by the sheriff's office and the FBI, Dillon called Pacheco and told him he would like to meet to discuss a possible deal. Dillon and Pacheco met at a restaurant. Dillon said he had ties to the "Mafia" and offered Pacheco $500 in exchange for protection during a cocaine deal. Dillon told Pacheco that a buyer (an undercover FBI agent) would arrive shortly, and Pacheco was to protect Dillon during the transaction. Pacheco agreed. The undercover agent arrived and the purported drug transaction took place. Afterward, Dillon paid Pacheco $500.

The same scenario was replayed at a second purported drug transaction on April 2, 1990. Dillon again paid Pacheco $500. Later that night Dillon called Pacheco and pretended he had been shortchanged $40,000 in that afternoon's drug transaction. Dillon said he had been given $10,000 by his superiors to take care of the situation. Dillon agreed to meet Pacheco at a convenience store. At the store Pacheco offered to kill the drug buyer for $10,000. Pacheco indicated if he had to kill anyone else, it would cost more. Pacheco proposed he go get his gun while Dillon located the drug buyer at his motel.

Dillon and Pacheco met at a lounge near the motel. They decided Pacheco would go to the lobby of the motel, call the buyer and convince him to come down to the lobby where Pacheco would then shoot him. Pacheco went to the lobby with a loaded gun, but he did not call the buyer's room. As Pacheco left the lobby, sheriff's deputies arrested him. Pacheco contended he was collecting evidence to build a case against Dillon and he thought he was following police procedures.

Pacheco was charged with conspiracy to commit first degree murder, attempted first degree murder, two counts of unlawful delivery of a controlled substance, two counts of conspiracy to deliver a controlled substance, and official misconduct. The official misconduct charge was dismissed. The jury found Pacheco not guilty of attempted first degree murder, but convicted him on all other counts. The Court of Appeals affirmed the convictions. We accepted review of the conspiracy convictions, limited to the issue of whether a conspiracy exists when the sole coconspirator is an undercover agent. * * *

The Defendant argues the statute retains the common law, bilateral approach to conspiracy, which requires an actual agreement to commit a crime between the defendant and at least one other. Therefore, a government agent feigning agreement with the defendant does not constitute a conspiracy under the common law approach because no genuine agreement is reached. The Defendant asserts Washington is among those states whose statutes are patterned after the Model Penal Code but have been interpreted as adopting only a limited form of the code's unilateral approach, and retaining the requirement of a bilateral underlying agreement. E.g., People v. Foster, 457 N.E.2d 405 (Ill.1983); Williams v. State, 646 S.W.2d 221 (Tex.Crim.App.1983); State v. Grullon, 562 A.2d 481 (Conn.1989).

The State contends RCW 9A.28.040 follows the code's purely unilateral approach. Under the code, actual agreement is not required as long as the defendant believes another is agreeing to commit the criminal act. Therefore, a purported agreement between a government agent and a defendant would satisfy the code's unilateral conspiratorial agreement approach.

Adopted in 1975, as a part of the overhaul of the criminal code, RCW 9A.28.040 provides in part:

> (1) A person is guilty of criminal conspiracy when, with intent that conduct constituting a crime be performed, he agrees with one or more persons to engage in or cause the performance of such conduct, and any one of them takes a substantial step in pursuance of such agreement.
>
> (2) It shall not be a defense to criminal conspiracy that the person or persons with whom the accused is alleged to have conspired:

(a) Has not been prosecuted or convicted; or

(b) Has been convicted of a different offense; or

(c) Is not amenable to justice; or

(d) Has been acquitted; or

(e) Lacked the capacity to commit an offense.

In construing a statute, our primary objective is to carry out the intent of the Legislature. * * * As a general rule, we presume the Legislature intended undefined words to mean what they did at common law. Subsection (1) of RCW 9A.28.O40 expressly requires an agreement, but does not define the term. Black's Law Dictionary defines agreement as, "a meeting of two or more minds; a coming together in opinion or determination; the coming together in accord of two minds on a given proposition". Similarly, agreement is defined in Webster's as "1 a: the act of agreeing or coming to a mutual agreement ... b: oneness of opinion ...". Webster's Third New International Dictionary 43 (1986). The dictionary definitions thus support the Defendant's argument.

Likewise, the common law definition of the agreement required for a conspiracy is defined not in unilateral terms but rather as a confederation or combination of minds. [citations] A conspiratorial agreement necessarily requires more than one to agree because it is impossible to conspire with oneself. We conclude that by requiring an agreement, the Legislature intended to retain the requirement of a genuine or bilateral agreement.

Subsection (2) provides the conspiratorial agreement may still be found even though the coconspirator cannot be convicted. In this sense, the statute incorporates a limited form of the code's unilateral conspiracy in that it is no longer necessary that agreement be proved against both conspirators. Thus, under subsection (2)'s unilateral approach, the failure to convict an accused's sole coconspirator will not prevent proof of the conspiratorial agreement against the accused. However, this does not indicate the Legislature intended to abandon the traditional requirement of two criminal participants reaching an underlying agreement.

* * *

Additionally, the unilateral approach fails to carry out the primary purpose of the statute. The primary reason for making conspiracy a separate offense from the substantive crime is the increased danger to society posed by group criminal activity. However, the increased danger is nonexistent when a person "conspires" with a government agent who pretends agreement. In the feigned conspiracy there is no increased chance the criminal enterprise will succeed, no continuing criminal enterprise, no educating in criminal practices, and no greater difficulty of detection.

Indeed, it is questionable whether the unilateral conspiracy punishes criminal activity or merely criminal intentions. Paul Marcus, "Conspiracy: The Criminal Agreement in Theory and in Practice," 65 Geo. L.J. 925, 929–30 (1977). The "agreement" in a unilateral conspiracy is a legal fiction, a technical way of transforming nonconspiratorial conduct into a prohibited conspiracy. When one party merely pretends to agree, the other party, whatever he or she may believe about the pretender, is in fact not conspiring with anyone. Although the deluded party has the requisite criminal intent, there has been no criminal act.

The federal courts agree. In Sears v. United States, 343 F.2d 139, 142 (5th Cir.1965), the Court of Appeals established the rule that "as it takes two to conspire, there can be no indictable conspiracy with a government informer who secretly intends to frustrate the conspiracy". Every federal court which has since considered the issue has adopted this approach. [citations]

Another concern with the unilateral approach is its potential for abuse. In a unilateral conspiracy, the State not only plays an active role in creating the offense, but also becomes the chief witness in proving the crime at trial. This has the potential to put the State in the improper position of manufacturing crime. At the same time, such reaching is unnecessary because the punishable conduct in a unilateral conspiracy will almost always satisfy the elements of either solicitation or attempt. The State will still be able to thwart the activity and punish the defendant who attempts agreement with an undercover police officer.

In sum, the State has not persuaded us the Legislature intended to abandon the traditional requirement of an actual agreement. We hold [that our statutes] require the defendant to reach a genuine agreement with at least one other coconspirator. The Defendant's convictions for conspiracy to commit murder in the first degree and conspiracy to deliver a controlled substance are reversed.

DURHAM, J. (dissenting) [5–4 decision]

* * * We accepted review solely to determine whether Washington's conspiracy statute countenances unilateral conspiracies. Yet the majority fails to provide even a cursory analysis of the essential differences between the bilateral and unilateral approaches to conspiracy. The bilateral approach asks whether there is an agreement between two or more persons to commit a criminal act. Its focus is on the content of the agreement and whether there is a shared understanding between the conspirators. The unilateral approach is not concerned with the content of the agreement or whether there is a meeting of minds. Its sole concern is whether the agreement, shared or not, objectively manifests the criminal intent of at least one of the conspirators. The majority does not even mention this crucial difference, and instead merely assumes that all conspiracies must be bilateral. In other words, the majority assumes precisely what it is supposed to prove; it begs the question.

* * *

The majority portrays the unilateral approach to conspiracy as an outdated relic from a bygone era. The Model Penal Code endorses unilateral conspiracies, the majority admits, but "every federal court, which has since considered the issue" has adopted the bilateral approach. The majority neglects to mention that all the federal courts adopting bilateral conspiracy are construing a different statute, one whose language requires bilateral conspiracies. * * *

The code embodies a significant change in emphasis. In its view, the major basis of conspiratorial liability is not the group nature of the activity but the firm purpose of an individual to commit a crime which is objectively manifested in conspiring. The Washington conspiracy statute tracks the Model Penal Code's language rather than the "two or more persons" language of the general federal conspiracy statute. In any event, far from being antiquated or obsolete, the "movement toward a unilateral theory of the crime is the modern trend in conspiracy law." Patrick A. Broderick, Note, Conditional Objectives of Conspiracies, 94 Yale L.J. 895, 906 n.64 (1985). See also Dierdre A. Burgman, Unilateral Conspiracy: Three Critical Perspectives, 29 DePaul L. Rev. 75, 75 n.3 (1979) (listing 30 states that have adopted statutes conforming to Model Penal Code's unilateral approach).

A comparison of the revised Washington conspiracy statute with its predecessor is far more revealing of legislative intent than the majority's simplistic and premature resort to dictionary definitions. The predecessor statute used the phrase "whenever two or more persons shall conspire", which parallels the federal conspiracy statute and clearly requires bilateral conspiracy. The revised statute, in contrast, tracks the definitional language of the Model Penal Code, which adopts unilateral conspiracy. * * *

Next, the majority constructs a straw man by claiming that the primary purpose of conspiracy is "the increased danger to society Posed by group criminal activity." Preventing group criminal activity is the rationale behind bilateral conspiracy, but that rationale was decisively rejected by the Model Penal Code. At best, controlling group criminal activity is only one rationale for conspiracy statutes. * * *

Finally, I share the majority's concern about the potential for abuse of unilateral conspiracy. However, the majority fails to take into consideration the effect of the entrapment defense. The potential for abuse is further restricted by the statute itself, which requires not only an agreement to engage in criminal conduct but also "a substantial step in pursuance of such agreement". In the end, the majority succeeds only in providing a superfluous protection to criminal defendants at the price of hamstringing government attempts to nip criminal acts in the bud.

The Model Penal Code

Section 5.01. Criminal Attempt

(1) Definition of Attempt. A person is guilty of an attempt to commit a crime if, acting with the kind of culpability otherwise required for commission of the crime, he:

(a) purposely engages in conduct which would constitute the crime if the attendant circumstances were as he believes them to be; or

(b) when causing a particular result is an element of the crime, does or omits to do anything with the purpose of causing or with the belief that it will cause such result without further conduct on his part; or

(c) purposely does or omits to do anything which, under the circumstances as he believes them to be, is an act or omission constituting a substantial step in a course of conduct planned to culminate in his commission of the crime.

(2) Conduct Which May Be Held Substantial Step Under Subsection (1)(c). Conduct shall not be held to constitute a substantial step under Subsection (1)(c) of this Section unless it is strongly corroborative of the actor's criminal purpose. Without negativing the sufficiency of other conduct, the following, if strongly corroborative of the actor's criminal purpose, shall not be held insufficient as a matter of law:

(a) lying in wait, searching for or following the contemplated victim of the crime;

(b) enticing or seeking to entice the contemplated victim of the crime to go to the place contemplated for its commission;

(c) reconnoitering the place contemplated for the commission of the crime;

(d) unlawful entry of a structure, vehicle or enclosure in which it is contemplated that the crime will be committed;

(e) possession of materials to be employed in the commission of the crime, which are specially designed for such unlawful use or which can serve no lawful purpose of the actor under the circumstances;

(f) possession, collection or fabrication of materials to be employed in the commission of the crime, at or near the place contemplated for its commission, where such possession, collection or fabrication serves no lawful purpose of the actor under the circumstances;

(g) soliciting an innocent agent to engage in conduct constituting an element of the crime.

(3) Conduct Designed to Aid Another in Commission of a Crime. A person who engages in conduct designed to aid another to commit a crime which would establish his complicity under Section 2.06 if the crime were committed by such other person, is guilty of an attempt to commit the crime, although the crime is not committed or attempted by such other person.

(4) Renunciation of Criminal Purpose. When the actor's conduct would otherwise constitute an attempt under Subsection (1)(b) or (1)(c) of this Section, it is an affirmative defense that he abandoned his effort to commit the crime or otherwise prevented its commission, under circumstances manifesting a complete and voluntary renunciation of his criminal purpose. The establishment of such defense does not, however, affect the liability of an accomplice who did not join in such abandonment or prevention.

Within the meaning of this Article, renunciation of criminal purpose is not voluntary if it is motivated, in whole or in part, by circumstances, not present or apparent at the inception of the actor's course of conduct, which increase the probability of detection or apprehension or which make more difficult the accomplishment of the criminal purpose. Renunciation is not complete if it is motivated by a decision to postpone the criminal conduct until a more advantageous time or to transfer the criminal effort to another but similar objective or victim.

Section 5.02. Criminal Solicitation

(1) Definition of Solicitation. A person is guilty of solicitation to commit a crime if with the purpose of promoting or facilitating its commission he commands, encourages or requests another person to engage in specific conduct which would constitute such crime or an attempt to commit such crime or which would establish his complicity in its commission or attempted commission.

(2) Uncommunicated Solicitation. It is immaterial under Subsection (1) of this Section that the actor fails to communicate with the person he solicits to commit a crime if his conduct was designed to effect such communication.

(3) Renunciation of Criminal Purpose. It is an affirmative defense that the actor, after soliciting another person to commit a crime, persuaded him not to do so or otherwise prevented the commission of the crime, under circumstances manifesting a complete and voluntary renunciation of his criminal purpose.

Section 5.03. Criminal Conspiracy

(1) Definition of Conspiracy.[a] A person is guilty of conspiracy with another person or persons to commit a crime if with the purpose of promoting or facilitating its commission he:

a. "The definition of the Draft departs from the traditional view of conspiracy as an entirely bilateral or multilateral relationship, the view inherent in the standard formulation cast in terms of 'two or more persons' agreeing or combining to commit a crime. Attention is directed instead to each individual's culpability by framing the definition in terms of the conduct which suffices to establish the liability of any given actor, rather than the conduct of a group of which he is charged to be a part—an approach which in this comment we have designated 'unilateral.'

"One consequence of this approach is to make it immaterial to the guilt of a conspirator whose culpability has been established that the person or all of the persons with whom he conspired have not been or cannot be convicted. Present law frequently holds otherwise, reasoning from the definition of conspiracy as an agreement between two or more persons that there must be at least two guilty conspirators or none. The problem arises in a number of contexts.

"*First:* Where the person with whom the defendant conspired is irresponsible or has an immunity to prosecution or conviction for the crime. Section 5.04 provides that

(a) agrees with such other person or persons that they or one or more of them will engage in conduct which constitutes such crime or an attempt or solicitation to commit such crime; or

(b) agrees to aid such other person or persons in the planning or commission of such crime or of an attempt or solicitation to commit such crime.

* * *

(5) Overt Act. No person may be convicted of conspiracy to commit a crime, other than a felony of the first or second degree, unless an overt act in pursuance of such conspiracy is alleged and proved to have been done by him or by a person with whom he conspired.

(6) Renunciation of Criminal Purpose. It is an affirmative defense that the actor, after conspiring to commit a crime, thwarted the success of the conspiracy, under circumstances manifesting a complete and voluntary renunciation of his criminal purpose.

* * *

Section 5.04. Incapacity, Irresponsibility or Immunity of Party to Solicitation or Conspiracy

(1) Except as provided in Subsection (2) of this Section, it is immaterial to the liability of a person who solicits or conspires with another to commit a crime that:

(a) he or the person whom he solicits or with whom he conspires does not occupy a particular position or have a particular characteristic which is an element of such crime, if he believes that one of them does; or

(b) the person whom he solicits or with whom he conspires is irresponsible or has an immunity to prosecution or conviction for the commission of the crime.

(2) It is a defense to a charge of solicitation or conspiracy to commit a crime that if the criminal object were achieved, the actor would not be guilty of a crime under the law defining the offense or as an accomplice under Section 2.06(5) or 2.06(6)(a) or (b).

this is no defense for the responsible actor, although this result would be implicit in the basic formulation.

"*Second:* Where the person with whom the defendant conspired secretly intends not to go through with the plan. In these cases it is generally held that neither party can be convicted because there was no 'agreement' between two persons. Under the unilateral approach of the Draft, the culpable party's guilt would not be affected by the fact that the other party's agreement was feigned. He has conspired, within the meaning of the definition, in the belief that the other party was with him; apart from the issue of entrapment often presented in such cases, his culpability is not decreased by the other's secret intention. * * *

"*Third:* Where the person with whom the defendant conspired has not been apprehended or tried, or his case has been disposed of in a manner that would raise questions of consistency about a conviction of the defendant. * * * Under the Draft the failure to prosecute the only co-conspirator or an inconsistent disposition or inconsistent verdict in a different trial would not affect a defendant's liability." Model Penal Code Commentary 104–106 (Tent. Draft No. 10, 1960).

Section 5.05. Grading of Criminal Attempt, Solicitation and Conspiracy; Mitigation in Cases of Lesser Danger; Multiple Convictions Barred

(1) Grading. Except as otherwise provided in this Section, attempt, solicitation and conspiracy are crimes of the same grade and degree as the most serious offense which is attempted or solicited or is an object of the conspiracy. An attempt, solicitation or conspiracy to commit a [capital crime or a] felony of the first degree is a felony of the second degree.

(2) Mitigation. If the particular conduct charged to constitute a criminal attempt, solicitation of conspiracy is so inherently unlikely to result or culminate in the commission of a crime that neither such conduct nor the actor presents a public danger warranting the grading of such offense under this Section, the Court shall exercise its power under Section 6.12 to enter judgment and impose sentence for a crime of lower grade or degree or, in extreme cases, may dismiss the prosecution.

(3) Multiple Convictions. A person may not be convicted of more than one offense defined by this Article for conduct designed to commit or to culminate in the commission of the same crime.

Section 211.1. Assault[b]

(1) Simple Assault. A person is guilty of assault if he:

(a) attempts to cause or purposely, knowingly or recklessly causes bodily injury to another; or

(b) negligently causes bodily injury to another with a deadly weapon; or

(c) attempts by physical menace to put another in fear of imminent serious bodily injury.

Simple assault is a misdemeanor unless committed in a fight or scuffle entered into by mutual consent, in which case it is a petty misdemeanor.

(2) Aggravated Assault. A person is guilty of aggravated assault if he:

(a) attempts to cause serious bodily injury to another, or causes such injury purposely, knowingly or recklessly under circumstances manifesting extreme indifference to the value of human life; or

(b) attempts to cause or purposely or knowingly causes bodily injury to another with a deadly weapon.

b. The section has been revised in form and substance. Previous drafts called the offense "bodily injury"; we have now gone back to the traditional term "assault," on the ground that retention of the familiar term will enhance acceptability of our proposals. We have also expressly included attempts within the definition of assault. In previous drafts, the section was limited to actual batteries, and we relied on the general attempt provisions of Part I to reach unsuccessful efforts to inflict bodily injury. Again, this is not a change of substance, but a deference to the traditional scope of the "assault" concept. [From the Commentary to the Model Penal Code, Proposed Official Draft at 135 (1962).]

Aggravated assault under paragraph (a) is a felony of the second degree; aggravated assault under paragraph (b) is a felony of the third degree.

Section 211.2. Recklessly Endangering Another Person

A person commits a misdemeanor if he recklessly engages in conduct which places or may place another person in danger of death or serious bodily injury. Recklessness and danger shall be presumed where a person knowingly points a firearm at or in the direction of another, whether or not the actor believed the firearm to be loaded.

The General Federal Conspiracy Statute (18 U.S.C.A. § 371)

§ 371. Conspiracy To Commit Offense Or To Defraud United States

If two or more persons conspire either to commit any offense against the United States, or to defraud the United States, or any agency thereof in any manner or for any purpose, and one or more of such persons do any act to effect the object of the conspiracy, each shall be fined under this title or imprisoned not more than five years, or both.

If, however, the offense, the commission of which is the object of the conspiracy, is a misdemeanor only, the punishment for such conspiracy shall not exceed the maximum punishment provided for such misdemeanor.

Note[a]

Conspiracy, like attempt, is an inchoate or preparatory crime, permitting the punishment of persons who agree to commit a crime even if they never carry out their scheme or are apprehended before achieving their objective. It is in this role that the crime of conspiracy has been most strongly defended. Indeed, almost the only justification offered by the drafters of the Model Penal Code for retaining the offense was the need to punish groups which engage in preparatory conduct which cannot be reached by the law of attempt.

The Model Penal Code commentary offers perhaps the most carefully stated justification for a doctrine of conspiracy that "reaches further back into preparatory conduct than attempt":

> *First:* The act of agreeing with another to commit, like the act of soliciting, is concrete and unambiguous; it does not present the infinite degrees and variations possible in the general category of attempts. The danger that truly equivocal behavior may be misinterpreted as preparation to commit a crime is minimized; purpose must be relatively firm before the commitment involved in agreement is assumed.

a. Adapted from Johnson, *The Unnecessary Crime of Conspiracy*, 61 Calif.L.Rev. 1137, 1157–64 (1973). Copyright 1973, by the California Law Review.

Second: If the agreement was to aid another to commit a crime or it otherwise encouraged its commission, it would establish complicity in the commission of the substantive offense. * * * It would be anomalous to hold that conduct which would suffice to establish criminality, if something else is done by someone else, is insufficient if the crime is never consummated. This is a reason, to be sure, which covers less than all the cases of conspiracy, but that it covers many is the point.

Third: In the course of preparation to commit a crime, the act of combining with another is significant both psychologically and practically, the former since it crosses a clear threshold in arousing expectations, the latter since it increases the likelihood that the offense will be committed. Sharing lends fortitude to purpose. The actor knows, moreover, that the future is no longer governed by his will alone; others may complete what he has had a hand in starting, even if he has a change of heart.[b] Unfortunately, this entire argument is based on an unsound premise. The commentary seems to be justifying the Code's conspiracy provision not as a supplement to its own attempt section but as a supplement to the traditional law of attempt which the Model Penal Code rejected.

Recall that modern penal codes retain the requirement for attempt crimes that a defendant must go beyond merely planning a crime. His conduct must be sufficient to confirm his intent to commit a criminal act. His acts demonstrate that the defendant is a dangerous individual who likely would have completed the crime if his plan had not been interrupted or frustrated. Under these modern conceptions of attempt, proximity to success is no longer the crucial issue.

Against the background of a law of attempt dominated by the proximity approach, an independent inchoate crime of conspiracy made sense. Although the defendants in the New York and California cases described in the Note *supra*, page 628, could not be convicted under traditional attempt law because they did not come close enough to carrying out their crimes, they could each have been convicted of conspiracy because they worked with confederates and performed an "overt act" in furtherance of the criminal design. Each of these defendants, however, could also be convicted of attempt under the Model Penal Code attempt section. This section is also adequate to reach the leader of organized crime who hires a professional killer to murder the government's chief witness in an upcoming trial. If any doubt remains, a provision could simply be added which includes agreement with another

b. Model Penal Code § 5.03, Comment at 97 (Tent.Draft No. 10, 1960). The commentators probably were not wholly convinced by their own argument. Two pages later they quoted Professor Abraham Goldstein on the "group danger" rationale:

More likely, empirical investigation would disclose that there is as much reason to believe that a large number of participants will increase the prospect that the plan will be leaked as that it will be kept secret; or that the persons involved will share their uncertainties and dissuade each other as that each will stiffen the other's determination.

Id. at 99, quoting Goldstein, Conspiracy to Defraud the United States, 68 Yale L.J. 405, 413–14 (1959).

person to commit a crime among the enumerated types of conduct which the trier of fact may find to be a substantial step if strongly corroborative of the actor's criminal purpose.[c]

Under the conspiracy section of the Model Penal Code, however, the act of agreement *is* the forbidden conduct whether or not it strongly corroborates the existence of a criminal purpose. In justifying this *per se* rule, the Model Penal Code commentary relied heavily on the argument, quoted previously, that the act of agreeing is so decisive and concrete a step towards the commission of a crime that it ought always to be regarded as a "substantial step." Whether this point is sense or nonsense depends upon how restrictively one defines the term "agreement." Hiring a professional killer to commit murder is an agreement, and surely few would doubt that it is a substantial step toward accomplishing the killing. But the language of the Model Penal Code is broad enough to reach conduct far less dangerous or deserving of punishment than letting a contract for murder. As the Model Penal Code commentary concedes, one may be liable for agreeing with another that *he* should commit a particular crime, although this agreement might be insufficient to establish complicity in the completed offense. Furthermore, the Code would not change the well-established rule that the agreement may be tacit or implied as well as express, and that it may be proved by circumstantial evidence. In short, the term "agreement" may connote anything from firm commitment to engage in criminal activity oneself to reluctant approval of a criminal plot to be carried out entirely by others. To be sure, the Model Penal Code also requires that one enter into the agreement with the purpose of promoting or facilitating the crime, but the existence of that purpose need not be substantiated by any conduct beyond the express or implied agreement and performance in some cases of a single overt act by any party to it. This point is of particular importance in conspiracy cases involving political activity or agitation. Members of radical societies may be likely to discuss or even to begin to plan criminal activities that they have no serious intention of carrying through.

Despite these concerns, the accused's mental state is a critical issue in any prosecution for an inchoate crime. Frequently, the necessary mental state is defined in terms of intent.

B. ATTEMPT: INTENT AND IMPOSSIBILITY

PEOPLE v. HARRIS

Supreme Court of Illinois, 1978.
72 Ill.2d 16, 17 Ill.Dec. 838, 377 N.E.2d 28.

WARD, CHIEF JUSTICE.

* * *

c. The Model Penal Code also defined "solicitation" as a separate crime distinct from attempt, although solicitation of an "innocent agent" (e.g., an idiot or insane person) is an attempt. Although this distinction is analytically defensible, it seems to be unnecessary.

The defendant was convicted of the attempted murder of Joyce Baker on the night of November 18, 1975, in a country area east of Champaign. * * *

The alleged murder attempt took place while Miss Baker was sitting inside her car and the defendant was standing behind the car with a pistol in his hand. The defendant and Miss Baker had been keeping company. For much of the evening they had been engaged in an argument in which the defendant accused the victim of infidelity. As the argument became more heated, the defendant, who was driving, reached down and picked up a revolver from the floor of the car and placed it in his lap with the barrel pointed toward Miss Baker. He made several remarks which Miss Baker interpreted as threats to kill her.

Alarmed, she opened the door on her side of the car, got out and began to run away, but ran into a barbed wire fence, injuring her leg. The defendant also got out of the car. He did not pursue her, but remained standing by the car. After her collision with the fence, Miss Baker returned to the car, and made an unsuccessful attempt to capture the gun, which the defendant was holding in his hand and pointing in her general direction. Miss Baker then got into the car on the driver's side, and drove off toward a nearby farmhouse. She testified that as she drove off she looked in the rear vision mirror and saw the defendant standing behind the car. He was holding the gun with both hands, and pointing it at her. Then she heard something strike the rear window, and the broken pane of glass in the rear window fell out of its frame. There were no other witnesses, but following this episode the police were summoned, and they found the defendant walking down the road near the scene of the episode just described. When the car was located, the police officers testified, the rear glass was broken, and a bullet fragment was found on the left side of the rear seat.

The jury returned a verdict of guilty. * * * The following instructions to the jury were tendered by the State and were given, over the objection of the defendant:

> A person commits the crime of attempt who, with intent to commit the crime of murder, does any act which constitutes a substantial step toward the commission of the crime of murder. The crime attempted need not have been committed.
>
> To sustain the charge of attempt, the State must prove the following propositions:
>
> *First:* That the defendant performed an act which constituted a substantial step toward the commission of the crime of murder; and
>
> *Second:* That the defendant did so with intent to commit the crime of murder.

* * *

> A person commits the crime of murder who kills an individual if, in performing the acts which cause the death, he intends to kill or do great bodily harm to that individual.

The defendant objected to the last of the instructions on the ground that it told the jury it could find him guilty of attempted murder if the jury found that he had acted only with the intent to do great bodily harm and did not have the intent to cause death.

The Appellate Court stated that the last instruction was proper under our decision in People v. Muir (1977), 67 Ill.2d 86, 8 Ill.Dec. 94, 365 N.E.2d 332. The court therefore affirmed the conviction. * * *

The central difficulty arises out of the difference between the elements of the offense of attempt and those of the specific offense attempted, murder. The definition of attempt, contained in § 8–4(a) of the Criminal Code is:

> A person commits an attempt when, with intent to commit a specific offense, he does any act which constitutes a substantial step toward the commission of that offense.

The statutory definition of murder is found in § 9–1(a) [reprinted supra in Ch. 3, § A, p. 187]. The crime of murder is thus committed not only when a person intends to kill another individual, but also when he intends to do great bodily harm, or when he knows that his acts create a strong probability of death or great bodily harm, or when he is attempting or committing a forcible felony.

This court held in People v. Koshiol (1970), 262 N.E.2d 446, that in a trial for attempted murder it is not error to give an instruction defining the elements of murder. As was stated there, "It would seem utterly meaningless to instruct a jury on attempt to commit a specific offense without defining the specific offense." Since an attempted murder requires an intent to kill, however, the "specific offense" referred to in section 8–4(a) cannot be construed as incorporating the alternative definitions of murder contained in section 9–1(a) in their entirety. * * *

Observations of LaFave and Scott (*Criminal Law* sec. 59, at 428–29 (1972)) are representative of authority that it is not sufficient to prove attempted murder to show that the accused intended to cause serious bodily harm:

> Some crimes, such as murder, are defined in terms of acts causing a particular result plus some mental state which need not be an intent to bring about that result. Thus, if A, B and C have each taken the life of another, A acting with intent to kill, B with an intent to do serious bodily injury, and C with a reckless disregard of human life, all three are guilty of murder because the crime of murder is defined in such a way that any one of these mental states will suffice. However, if the victims do not die from their injuries, then only A is guilty of attempted murder; on a charge of attempted murder it is not sufficient to show that the defendant intended to do serious bodily harm or that he acted in reckless disregard for human

life. Again, this is because intent is needed for the crime of attempt, so that attempted murder requires an intent to bring about that result described by the crime of murder (i.e., the death of another).

* * *

[Convictions reversed. Concurring and dissenting opinion omitted.]

PEOPLE v. VALDEZ

California Court of Appeal, Second District, 1985.
175 Cal.App.3d 103, 220 Cal.Rptr. 538.

JOHNSON, ASSOCIATE JUSTICE.

Valdez appeals the judgment entered following a court trial in which he was found guilty of assault with a firearm[a] [and] sentenced to four years in state prison. * * *

At approximately 4:40 a.m. on January 13, 1984, Kenneth McKinley, an employee of a self-serve gasoline station, was at the cashier's window when appellant gave him $4 for gasoline. After appellant pumped gasoline worth $3.99, he returned to McKinley and in Spanish said something about "cinco." McKinley motioned to him to return to the pump. Appellant pumped another penny's worth of gasoline, and again returned to the window insisting that he had given McKinley "cinco dollars." McKinley denied he had been given that much money and both men began yelling. Appellant raised his jacket and McKinley saw a "45 type pistol" in appellant's belt.

Upon observing the pistol, McKinley moved to appellant's left and away from the front of the cashier's window where there was an opening. After appellant pointed the pistol in McKinley's direction, McKinley called the police on the telephone immediately behind him and about ten feet from where appellant was standing.

While McKinley was using the telephone, he heard three shots and the sound of the impact on the window. When the shots were fired, McKinley did not know where appellant was or who fired the shots. Thereafter, McKinley did see appellant jump into his vehicle and drive away. [Valdez was arrested almost immediately thereafter, in possession of a loaded .380 automatic pistol which he had recently fired.]

[A detective who investigated the shooting] saw high "puncture marks where projectiles had struck the bullet proof glass where the cashier [McKinley] sits behind." He also described the glass as "bullet resistant," and observed .380 caliber shell casings "approximately 15 feet south of the cashier's window."

In defense, appellant contended he became angry because McKinley "was not waiting" on him and instead was talking on the telephone. He

a. An assault is defined in Penal Code Section 240 as "an unlawful attempt, coupled with a present ability, to commit a violent injury on the person of another." Appellant was convicted of the aggravated offense of assault with a firearm.—ed.

admitted firing three shots but claimed McKinley was not in his line of fire. * * *

Appellant's contention there is insufficient evidence to establish he had the present ability to injure McKinley presents an issue of first impression in California. It also is a genre of issue which has provoked considerable academic interest over the years. Is the "present ability" element of the crime of assault satisfied where some outside circumstance unknown to the defendant makes it impossible for the chosen means of attack to actually inflict injury on the victim? Or, more specific to the facts of this case, does a man who fires a loaded gun at another have a "present ability" to inflict injury where the victim is behind a bulletproof window?

* * * This would be an easier case if California had followed the many jurisdictions which have moved to what Perkins characterizes as the "logical position" on the definition of the present ability element of assault. (Perkins, Criminal Law (1969) p. 121.) Under this modern view, the element of "present ability" is defined by a subjective test—did the defendant or his intended victim believe he had the ability to inflict injury at the time he made his attempt. In these jurisdictions, either by express statutory language or judicial interpretation, this element has come to require only an "apparent present ability" instead of objective present ability. Whatever might be said about appellant's actual "present ability" to injure his intended victim, he clearly entertained a subjective belief he could when he fired off the three shots from his handgun. * * *

California, on the other hand, has been committed to an "old-fashioned" version of criminal assault for at least 93 years. The three essential elements—including "present ability"—have remained unchanged since the original statute was enacted in 1856. And if there were any ambiguity about whether this law meant actual rather than apparent "present ability" it was removed by the California Supreme Court in 1892. In People v. Lee Kong, 95 Cal. 666, 30 P. 800, the Court held: "We cannot endorse those authorities, principally English, which hold that an assault may be committed by a person pointing in a threatening manner an unloaded gun at another; and this, too, regardless of the fact whether the party holding the gun thought it was loaded, or whether the party at whom it was menacingly pointed was thereby placed in great fear. Under our statute it cannot be said that a person with an unloaded gun would have the present ability to inflict an injury upon another many yards distant, however apparent and unlawful his attempt to do so might be. * * *"

Consistent with this interpretation, California courts have held attempting to shoot someone with an unloaded gun does not constitute the crime of assault because the perpetrator lacks the "present ability" to inflict injury. [Citations] Nor, obviously, does threatening someone with a toy gun or candy pistol satisfy this element. On the other hand, a defendant has been held to have a present ability to injure where he is only a moment away from being able to fire his gun. (People v. Simpson (1933) 134 Cal.App. 646, 25 P.2d 1008 [gun's magazine was loaded but no bullet in firing chamber]; People v. Ranson (1974) 40 Cal.App.3d 317, 114 Cal.Rptr. 874 [gun jammed when defendant tried to fire first round but he possessed knowledge and ability to quickly cure the jam, even though he had not done so at time attempt ended.].) * * *

The real function of this "present ability" element in common law assault as incorporated in the California statute is to require the perpetrator to have gone beyond the minimal steps involved in an attempt. That is, he must have come closer to inflicting injury than he would have to in order to satisfy the elements of an attempt. * * * Thus, because of the "present ability" element of the offense, to be guilty of assault a defendant must have maneuvered himself into such a location and equipped himself with sufficient means that he appears to be able to strike immediately at his intended victim. (Thus, the emphasis is on the word "present" as much as the word "ability.") The policy justification is apparent. When someone has gone this far he is a more imminent threat to his victim and to the public peace than if he is at an earlier stage of an attempted crime. In contrast, a defendant can be found guilty of an ordinary attempt even if intercepted on his way to a location which would be within striking distance of his intended victim, or while assembling the means to attack this target [citations].

Nothing suggests this "present ability" element was incorporated into the common law to excuse defendants from the crime of assault where they have acquired the means to inflict serious injury and positioned themselves within striking distance merely because, unknown to them, external circumstances doom their attack to failure. This proposition would make even less sense where a defendant has actually launched his attack—as in the present case—but failed only because of some unforeseen circumstance which made success impossible. Nor have we found any cases under the California law which compel this result. The decisions holding a defendant lacks "present ability" when he tries to shoot someone with an unloaded gun or a toy pistol do not support any such proposition. In those situations, the defendant has simply failed to equip himself with the personal means to inflict serious injury even if he thought he had. * * *

For these reasons of statutory construction and public policy, we hold a defendant can commit the crime of assault even though his intended victim, unknown to him, has thrown up an apparently impervious defense. We need not reach and do not decide the issue presented by a would-be assailant who knowing his victim is behind a bulletproof barrier fires merely as a joke or to release his frustrations. But this is far different from the assailant who lacks this knowledge or even one who knows of the bulletproof barrier yet blazes away like some perverted Don Quixote in the hope he might realize his impossible dream—and the victim's worst nightmare.

The judgment is affirmed.

UNITED STATES v. EVERETT

United States Court of Appeals, Third Circuit, 1983.
700 F.2d 900.

GERRY, DISTRICT JUDGE:

Appellee George Everett was convicted by a jury of attempting to distribute the drug phenyl-2-propanone (P-2-P) in violation of 21 U.S.C. § 846 (1976). The district court granted Everett's motion for judgment of acquittal on the ground that it was legally impossible for Everett to commit the crime. The United States appeals from the judgment of acquittal. We will reverse.

Facts and Proceeding Below

An undercover agent from the Drug Enforcement Administration (DEA) arranged to purchase methamphetamine and P-2-P from Mr. Ralph Horan. Both methamphetamine and P-2-P are non-narcotic controlled substances, and P-2-P has no other use than in the manufacture of methamphetamine. The government arrested Horan after he sold the agent methamphetamine but before the P-2-P deal could be consummated. Horan identified Everett as his source for the P-2-P and methamphetamine, said that the P-2-P was still in Everett's hands, and agreed to cooperate in closing the P-2-P deal.

Horan then had several telephone conversations with Everett which were tape recorded by the DEA. In those conversations the two set up a meeting at which Horan would buy six pints of Everett's P-2-P at $1250 per pint. Horan also informed Everett that Horan's "client" wanted to inspect a sample of the P-2-P before giving Everett the money. Everett agreed to provide a sample.

At the appointed time Horan, unaccompanied, entered Everett's house while DEA agents posing as the "client" remained outside in a car. Everett gave Horan one pint of the liquid as a sample. Horan took the pint to the waiting agents who performed a quick field test. The test indicated that the liquid was P-2-P. DEA agents then entered the house and placed Everett under arrest. Once in custody Everett gave a statement to DEA agents. He identified the substance as P-2-P and said that he had gotten it from Mr. Joseph Jackson, who in turn had obtained it from someone known to Everett only as Frank.

The grand jury returned an indictment charging Everett with distribution and possession of P-2-P. Subsequent tests by the DEA revealed, however, that despite strong physical resemblance to P-2-P the sample pint of liquid was not P-2-P or any other controlled substance. The government then obtained a superseding indictment * * *.[3] Count I

3. Section 846 provides:

Any person who attempts or conspires to commit any offense defined in this subchapter is punishable by imprisonment and fine or both which may not exceed the maximum punishment prescribed for the offense, the commission of which was the object of the attempt or conspiracy.

charged that Everett had conspired with Horan to distribute the methamphetamine sold to the DEA agent. Count II charged that Everett did knowingly and intentionally attempt to distribute P–2–P, [in violation of 21 U.S.C. § 846, which punishes anyone who attempts or conspires to commit any offense involving a controlled substance].

Everett pled not guilty to both counts. During trial the government introduced the tapes and the testimony of Horan and the agents. A chemist for the DEA testified that the sample pint of liquid was not P–2–P. Everett did not testify or call any witnesses. In his charge to the jury, the trial judge emphasized that to convict on Count II it must find beyond a reasonable doubt that Everett believed the pint of liquid to be P–2–P.[4]

The jury acquitted Everett on Count I. It convicted him on Count II of attempting to distribute P–2–P. Everett then moved for judgment of acquittal on Count II. The trial judge held that there was sufficient evidence in the record to support the jury's conclusion that Everett believed the pint of liquid to be P–2–P. Nonetheless, the trial judge set aside the verdict of guilty on Count II and entered judgment of acquittal on the ground that there could be no attempt as the liquid distributed by Everett was not P–2–P or any other controlled substance.

The government now takes an appeal of right pursuant to [statute] from the entry of judgment of acquittal after a jury verdict of guilty. * * *

Discussion

In his motion for judgment of acquittal, Everett claimed that the fact that the sample liquid was not P–2–P or any other controlled substance prevented his conviction [for attempt to distribute]. He argued that based on our holding in United States v. Berrigan, 482 F.2d 171 (3d Cir.1973), it was legally impossible for him to violate the statute. The district court held that it was required under *Berrigan* to reverse Everett's conviction.

In *Berrigan* a federal prisoner tried to smuggle several letters out of his penitentiary using as a courier another prisoner on study-release. The warden learned of the prisoner's first letter; the courier carried all subsequent letters with the knowledge and consent of the warden. The prisoner was then convicted of attempting to send the letters from a federal penal institution without the knowledge and consent of the

21 U.S.C. § 846 (1976).

4. The trial judge gave this summary during his charge on Count II:

Now, in order for you to convict Mr. Everett of this charge you would have to find that he in fact did some act to bring about—that he acted in a way to bring about—he acted in a way to violate the law in the distribution of P–2–P; that he did it knowingly and intentionally. And you would have to find beyond a reasonable doubt that he believed the substance to be P–2–P.

It is for you to analyze the evidence, and determine whether or not he believed the substance to be P–2–P, or whether this was merely a con, a ripoff, or an attempt to rip off Mr. Horan.

warden. The prisoner appealed his convictions for the passing of all letters but the first, arguing that the government had failed to prove all elements of the crime charged. We reversed the convictions, holding that the government did not and could not prove absence of knowledge and consent of the warden "because it was a legal impossibility."[a]

Berrigan does not control the result in this case. Unlike *Berrigan,* this case involves a statute by which Congress intended to punish attempts even when completion of the attempted crime was impossible.

* * *

We are convinced that Congress intended to eliminate the defense of impossibility when it enacted section 846. First, when Congress enacted § 846 the doctrine of impossibility had become enmeshed in unworkable distinctions and was no longer widely accepted as part of the meaning of "attempt" at common law. Second, the legislative history and purpose of § 846 provide grounds for inferring an affirmative instruction from Congress to define "attempt" to exclude the defense of impossibility. [The opinion recounted the legislative history of 21 U.S.C. § 846 in support of its conclusion that Congress had impliedly excluded the impossibility defense.]

The distribution of a noncontrolled substance believed to be a controlled substance thus constitutes an attempt to distribute a controlled substance under § 846. In this case the government established that Everett believed that the substance he distributed was P–2–P. It also proved that Everett distributed the substance knowingly and intentionally.

Of course, the crime of attempt is not established by proving "*mens rea simpliciter.*" *Berrigan,* 482 F.2d at 189 n. 39. * * * To prevent mistaken convictions the government must introduce some measure of objective evidence corroborating the attempted distribution of a controlled substance.

The Fifth Circuit has suggested the proper standard of proof to be required of the government in this case. That circuit shared our concern

a. The prisoner was Father Philip Berrigan, a Catholic priest and anti-war activist. The letters discussed a fantastic plot to kidnap Presidential Advisor Henry Kissinger and to destroy the government's underground heating system in Washington, D.C. After FBI Director J. Edgar Hoover boasted publicly about having thwarted the plot, the government was virtually forced to prosecute Berrigan and his confederates for conspiracy. The jury failed to agree on a verdict on the conspiracy charge, presumably because the plot never got beyond the talking stage, but it did convict Berrigan and the nun who received the letters of attempting to smuggle material out of a federal prison "without the knowledge *and* consent of the warden."

The federal court of appeals made the debatable assumption that the warden "consented" to the smuggling because he permitted it to continue so he could secretly read and copy the letters. The opinion then gave an enthusiastic endorsement of the legal impossibility defense, attempting without notable success to provide a coherent explanation of the distinction between legal and factual impossibility. The court's conclusion that the impossibility was legal rather than factual had no effect on Father Berrigan's sentence, which was concurrent with another, unaffected term of imprisonment, but it does seem to have saved the recipient of the letters from a year in jail.—ed.

that the crime of attempt not be used to "punish one's thoughts, desires, or motives, through indirect evidence, without reference to any objective fact." United States v. Oviedo, 525 F.2d 881, 884 (5th Cir.1976) (citing *Berrigan*). To avoid "baseless jury speculation where defendant's objective acts are equivocal," the Fifth Circuit required that

> the objective acts performed [by the defendant], without any reliance on the accompanying *mens rea*, mark the defendant's conduct as criminal in nature. The acts should be unique rather than so commonplace that they are engaged in by persons not in violation of the law.

In the instant case the government has met that strict burden. It has proven objective acts performed by Everett which are sufficient to mark his conduct as criminal without reliance on *mens rea*. The government established not only that Everett promised to sell a controlled substance and that he transferred the substance furtively, but also that immediately after arrest and proper *Miranda* warnings Everett confessed, identifying the substance he had distributed as P–2–P and revealing that he had gotten his P–2–P from Joseph Jackson who had obtained it from Frank. This statement unequivocably marked his conduct as an attempt to distribute P–2–P. * * *[19]

We remand to the district court with the direction that the jury verdict of guilty on Count II of the indictment be reinstated and for such other proceedings as are required.

STATE v. SMITH

Superior Court of New Jersey, Appellate Division, 1993.
262 N.J.Super. 487, 621 A.2d 493.

KING, J.

Defendant was a county jail inmate at the time of this criminal episode on June 11, 1989. He had, and knew he had, the human

19. The Fifth Circuit faced similar facts in *United States v. Hough, 561 F.2d 594 (5th Cir.1977).* After Hough's arrest for selling the supposed controlled substance, he had the indictment read to him. The indictment stated that Hough believed that the substance was in fact cocaine. Hough admitted the truth of the indictment and pled guilty; after *Oviedo* was decided he appealed his conviction. The Fifth Circuit found the conviction met the test set under *Oviedo,* saying:

> The *Oviedo* court's concern was that the jury had found criminal intent based solely on acts consisting with a noncriminal enterprise. 525 F.2d at 886. Had another objective fact been present, such as the confession of the defendant to a police officer after proper *Miranda* warnings, the *Oviedo* verdict would undoubtedly have withstood appellate scrutiny. Certainly an in-court admission is as corroborative of criminal intent as an out-of-court confession, the taking of money, or the defendant's unsworn personal statements that he would purchase a narcotic with that money. See 525 F.2d at 886.

561 F.2d at 595–96 (citation omitted). A district court in the First Circuit has held that a defendant's statement on arrest admitting trying to smuggle cocaine when in fact his substance was noncontrolled was an objective fact justifying conviction for attempted smuggling under the *Oviedo* standard. *Deangelis,* 430 F.Supp. at 328, 331–332; see United States v. Korn, 557 F.2d 1089 (5th Cir.1977) (payment of money is sufficient objective fact); Enker, Impossibility in Criminal Attempts—Legality and the Legal Process, 53 Minn.L.Rev. 665, 692 (1969) (sale of look-alike drug is sufficient objective fact to convict for attempted distribution); cf. United States v. Murray, 527 F.2d 401, 409 (5th Cir.1976) (finding evidence of conspiracy to distribute "controlled" substance insufficient under *Oviedo* when conspirator told undercover buyer that conspirator's supplier had "burned" them).

immunodeficiency virus (HIV). On several occasions before June 11 he had threatened to kill corrections officers by biting or spitting at them. On that day he bit an officer's hand causing puncture wounds of the skin during a struggle which he had precipitated. The jury found him guilty of attempted murder, aggravated assault and terroristic threats. The judge imposed an aggregate 25–year term with a 12½ years period of parole ineligibility.

On this appeal each of defendant's claims of error arises from his premises that (1) without dispute a bite cannot transmit HIV, and (2) defendant knew this when he bit the officers. From these premises defendant urges that he was wrongfully convicted of attempted murder because he knew that his bite could not kill the officer. He insists that he was convicted of such a serious charge because of society's discrimination against persons infected with this deadly virus. He claims that at worst he was guilty only of assaultive conduct and should have been sentenced, as a third-degree offender, to a relatively short custodial term.

From our review of this record, we conclude that neither of defendant's two premises has been established. First, if HIV cannot possibly be spread by a bite, the evidence at trial did not establish that proposition. Indeed, we doubt that the proposition is presently provable scientifically, given the current state of medical knowledge. The apparent medical consensus is that there has never been a controlled study of a sufficiently large number of cases to establish to any scientific certainty if transmission of HIV is possible by a bite, and if so, the percentage of likely infection. The proposition was surely disputed at this trial. Second, whether defendant actually believed that his bite could result in death was a question of his credibility, a question the jury obviously resolved against him.

We cannot and need not decide if a bite can transmit HIV. We have applied the elements of the attempted murder statute as we would in a case involving a more traditional criminal methodology. We conclude that the attempted murder verdict was supported by proof, which the jury reasonably could accept, that the defendant subjectively believed that his conduct could succeed in causing the officer's death, regardless of whether his belief was objectively valid. For this reason, we affirm the conviction.

[The evidence was highly disputed at the trial. Jail guards testified that defendant was a highly hostile and violent individual who repeatedly threatened to kill the officers by biting or spitting on them and who eventually bit Officer Waddington while being taken for medical treatment. Defendant denied assaulting the guards, denied threatening to kill them, and claimed that the guards assaulted him without provocation.

There was also conflicting expert testimony at the trial as to whether HIV infection can be transmitted by spitting or biting. Defendant testified that he had been informed that HIV infection could be transmitted in only three ways—"sexually, blood transfusion or using needles." He said that he believed AIDS transmission by a bite to be impossible.]

Defendant contends that Judge Mariano erroneously charged the jury that it could find him guilty of attempted murder upon proof that he intended to kill Waddington by biting him, regardless of whether it was medically possible that the bite could have transmitted HIV. Instead of focusing on his subjective belief about the effect of the bite, defendant contends the judge should have charged an objective test. Defendant claims that he can be guilty only if a "reasonable person" would have believed that the bite could be fatal. * * *

The statute governing criminal attempts is N.J.S.A. 2C:5–1. The pertinent part of that statute is the definitional subsection:

a. Definition of attempt. A person is guilty of an attempt to commit a crime if, acting with the kind of culpability otherwise required for commission of the crime, he:

(1) Purposely engages in conduct which would constitute the crime if the attendant circumstances were as a reasonable person would believe them to be;

(2) When causing a particular result is an element of the crime, does or omits to do anything with the purpose of causing such result without further conduct on his part; or

(3) Purposely does or omits to do anything which, under the circumstances as a reasonable person would believe them to be, is an act or omission constituting a substantial step in a course of conduct planned to culminate in his commission of the crime.

On its face this section creates three separate categories of attempt, two of which incorporate a reasonable-person standard—subsections (1) and (3)—and one of which looks only to defendant's own purpose—subsection (2). Judge Mariano charged on subsection (2) only, saying:

Our law provides that a person is guilty of an attempt to commit a crime if the person, acting with the same culpability or state of mind required for the commission of the substantive offense, the crime of murder in this case, does anything with the purpose of causing death, without any further conduct on his part.

The judge explained that defendant must have "done all that he believes necessary to cause the particular result," here, the death of Waddington. * * * The judge then charged that it was irrelevant whether the jury found that a bite could succeed in transmitting HIV: "I must instruct you that impossibility is not a defense to the charge of attempted murder. That is because our law, our criminal statutes punish conduct based on state of mind. It punishes purposeful actions regardless of whether the result can be accomplished. And even if the result, which would be death in this case, was a scientific or factual impossibility. In this case if you should be convinced beyond a reasonable doubt by the State's evidence that Mr. Smith's purpose was to kill Sheriff's Officer Waddington by biting him it does not matter that the chances of spreading the virus were either remote or impossible. If the State has proven purposeful conduct beyond a reasonable doubt then the State has proven the essential elements of the crime of attempted murder." * * *

Under N.J.S.A. 2C:5–1(a)(2), defendant may properly be found guilty without a concomitant finding that the bite would more probably or likely than not spread HIV. We think it sufficient that defendant himself believed he could cause death by biting his victim and intended to do so. There was ample evidence to support the jury's finding of defendant's criminal purpose to kill the correction officer. * * *

Our research and counsels' diligence disclose several similar cases from other states. In Scroggins v. State, 401 S.E.2d 13 (Ga.App.1990) defendant, who had HIV, bit a policeman trying to subdue him during a domestic disturbance. The jury found defendant guilty of aggravated assault with intent to murder. Defendant contended that the verdict was not supported by the evidence, absent proof that "the HIV virus can be transmitted by human saliva." The Georgia statute, provides that factual or legal impossibility is not a defense to attempted murder, "if such crime could have been committed had the attendant circumstances been as the accused believed them to be." The Georgia Court of Appeals found there was ample evidence supporting a finding that defendant "believed he could transmit the virus in the method used," making it immaterial "that it might have been impossible to do so." * * *

In State v. Haines, 545 N.E.2d 834, 835 (Ind.App.1989), a jury convicted defendant on three counts of attempted murder, based on evidence that he bit and spread blood from his own wounds onto a police officer and paramedics, yelling that he had AIDS and would give it to them. The evidence established that (1) defendant was, and knew he was, infected with the AIDS virus; (2) he believed his condition to be fatal; and (3) he intended to infect others "by spitting, biting, scratching and throwing blood." The trial judge vacated the conviction on the ground that the state had failed to prove that the AIDS virus could be spread by the means used by defendant. The Indiana Court of Appeals reversed, citing that state's statute expressly rejecting impossibility as a defense to an attempted crime. The court reasoned that "the State was not required to prove that Haines' conduct could actually have killed. The State needed only to show that Haines did all that he believed necessary to bring about an intended result, regardless of what was actually possible." * * *

In Weeks v. State, 834 S.W.2d 559 (Tex.Ct.App.1992) a jury convicted defendant of attempted murder, based on proof that defendant, who was HIV positive, had spit on a prison guard with the intent to infect him. Under Texas' attempted murder statute, the accused had to intend to kill his victim, and, in contrast to N.J.S.A. 2C:5–1(a)(2), he had to commit an act that "could have caused" that victim's death. The intent element was undisputed; there was conflicting medical evidence as to whether HIV was transmittable by saliva. Since the jury resolved the conflict against defendant, the Texas appellate court deferred to the jury's finding. That court rejected the defendant's invitation to take judicial notice that it is impossible to spread HIV through spitting: "Many of the AIDS experts express the opinion that it is impossible to transmit HIV through saliva. However, this has not been conclusively established and is not free from reasonable dispute." * * *

Defendant invokes the following excerpt from the commentary to the Model Penal Code as authority for his theory: "if the means selected were absurd, there is good ground for doubting that the actor really planned to commit a crime." Model Penal Code, supra, § 5.01, commentary at 315. Defendant equates his biting Waddington with a "voodoo incantation" which is medically incapable of causing death, regardless of whether a person believed to the contrary.

Again, defendant's theory founders on its premise. There was no proof at trial that biting could not possibly transmit HIV. Rather, the evidence was equivocal, with even defendant's expert conceding that there was at least a "remote" possibility of transmission. In any event, the objective likelihood of transmission is irrelevant to liability under N.J.S.A. 2C:5–1(a)(2). It is sufficient that defendant believed his attack would infect Waddington. Such a belief would not necessarily be "absurd" in the same way that a belief in the efficacy of a voodoo curse is unfounded.

Moreover, even if the voodoo analogy is apt, defendant could still be found guilty if the circumstances showed that defendant was "dangerous": "Cases can be imagined in which it might well be accurate to say that the nature of the means selected, say black magic, substantially negates dangerousness of character. On the other hand, there are many cases as well where one who tries to commit a crime by what he later learns to be inadequate methods will recognize the futility of his course of action and seek more efficacious means. There are, in other words, many instances of dangerous character revealed by 'impossible' attempts, and to develop a theory around highly exceptional situations ignores the propriety of convictions in these." [Model Penal Code, supra, § 5.01, commentary at 316 n. 88.]

In the present case defendant's violent assaults and venomous harangues before, during and after biting Waddington, all justified an inference that he bore the requisite criminal state of mind under N.J.S.A. 2C:5–1(a)(2). The judge did not err in failing to charge that the jury should consider the probable efficacy of a bite in spreading HIV. * * *

Affirmed.

COMMONWEALTH v. HENLEY

Supreme Court of Pennsylvania, 1984.
504 Pa. 408, 474 A.2d 1115.

PAPADAKOS, JUSTICE.

Appellant is the owner of the Henley Brothers Jewelry Store in Philadelphia. An informant, wired with a tape recording device, was given five specially coated chains by the police, and sent to Appellant's store. The informant entered the store and offered to sell the five gold chains to Appellant. He represented that the chains were stolen. Appellant, believing them to be stolen, purchased the chains for $30.00, took possession of them, and expressed a willingness to buy more stolen goods in the future. This conversation was recorded. The informant then left the store, met with the detective who had accompanied him, played the tape recording, and turned over the $30.00.

The detective then entered the store and arrested Appellant, charging him with the crime of theft by receiving stolen goods and receiving stolen property as a business. These charges were later amended to attempted theft by [receiving stolen property].

At the conclusion of the Commonwealth's case, Appellant demurred to the evidence, arguing that the chains were not stolen property because they were in police custody, and that, therefore, he could not be found guilty of an attempt to receive stolen property which was not stolen. The trial court found this defense of legal impossibility persuasive and granted the demurrer. * * *

Impossibility defenses were usually classified as either legal or factual in nature. "Factual impossibility denotes conduct where the objective is proscribed by the criminal law but a circumstance unknown to the actor prevents him from bringing it about. The classic example is the thief who picks an empty pocket." United States v. Conway, 507 F.2d 1047 (5th Cir.1975). Legal impossibility was said to occur where the intended acts would not amount to a crime even if completed. A frequently cited case standing for this proposition is People v. Jaffe, 185 N.Y. 497, 78 N.E. 169 (1906). The *Jaffe* Court held that where an element of the completed crime required the goods be stolen, the fact that the goods were not stolen was a defense to the completed act. Consequently, an attempt to do an act which would not be criminal if completed could not itself be criminal regardless of the actor's intent.

Factual impossibility has never been recognized as a defense to an attempt charge by any American Court, and this Court specifically rejected factual impossibility as a defense to an attempt charge in Commonwealth v. Johnson, 312 Pa. 140, 167 A. 344 (1933). Legal impossibility had been recognized in many jurisdictions as a defense to attempt charges, and this Court cited the *Jaffe* case approvingly in *Johnson,* indicating that the defense of legal impossibility was available as a defense to attempt charges in this Commonwealth.

The reasoning in the *Jaffe* line of cases has come under considerable criticism in the last twenty-five years, and in response to the criticism the defense has been uniformly rejected by the highest courts of most states where the issue has been raised.[1] Additionally, many states have passed legislation which specifically abrogated the defense. The suggested abrogation of the impossibility defense through legislation was first introduced to most state legislatures via the Model Penal Code. * * *

[The court held that Pennsylvania's revised attempt statute abolishes the defense of factual or legal impossibility. The statute, § 901, states that "It shall not be a defense to a charge of attempt that because of a misapprehension of the circumstances it would have been impossible for the accused to commit the crime attempted."]

Thus, if one forms intent to commit a substantive crime, then proceeds to perform all the acts necessary to commit the crime, and it is shown that completion of the substantive crime is impossible, the actor can still be culpable of attempt to commit the substantive crime. A defense based on the old legal or factual impossibility argument clearly is no longer available. Under the new Code, an intent to commit an act which is not characterized as a crime by the laws of the subject jurisdiction can not be the basis of a criminal charge and conviction even though the actor believes or misapprehends the intended act to be proscribed by the criminal laws. An example of this is where a fisherman believes he is committing an offense in fishing on a certain lake without a license when a fishing license is, in fact, not required in the subject jurisdiction. Since the conduct here would be perfectly legal, the actor could not be held accountable for any attempted crime. In all other cases, the actor should be held responsible for his conduct. Our reading of Section 901(b) would do just that. * * *

The Order of the Superior Court is affirmed.

[Concurring opinion omitted.]

Note

The defense of legal impossibility described in the final paragraph of the preceding opinion is the obverse of the doctrine that ignorance of the law is no defense. If a person goes fishing without a license, his ignorance of the law that prohibits unlicensed fishing is no defense. Likewise, his mistaken belief that unlicensed fishing is unlawful would not be inculpating in a jurisdiction where licenses are not required. Similarly, if a person in a heat of passion caused by legally sufficient provocation shouts "I'm going to murder you" at his tormentor and then shoots, he attempts to commit

1. The California Supreme Court repudiated the *Jaffe* Rule in People v. Rojas, 55 Cal.2d 252, 10 Cal.Rptr. 465, 358 P.2d 921 (1961); New York's Court of Appeals criticized its prior rule in People v. Rollino, 37 Misc.2d 14, 233 N.Y.S.2d 580 (1962) and requested the Legislature to remedy the rule by adopting the Model Penal Code's attempt statute [which it did]. Colorado's Supreme Court also interpreted its attempt statute to have abrogated the legal impossibility defense, as have the Supreme Courts of Nevada, Minnesota, and Kansas. [Citations]

manslaughter, not murder. What he intends is to kill under circumstances calling for a manslaughter verdict, and his mistaken notion that such a killing is murder does not supply the element of "malice aforethought" necessary for murder.

If the defendant in People v. Marrero [reprinted in Chapter One] had been a state prison guard, and had carried a firearm in the mistaken belief that such guards are not peace officers and that he was therefore violating the weapons possession law, we could say in a colloquial sense that he "attempted" to violate the law. The hypothetical example differs from the unlicensed fishing example because there is actually a criminal prohibition in existence which the actor could be charged with attempting to violate. If we accept the doctrine that an actor's mistaken notions about the meaning and scope of the criminal law do not either exculpate or inculpate, then the state prison guard is not guilty because his mistaken notion about the legality of his conduct does not supply criminal intent. This analysis admittedly appeals more to a sense of appropriate symmetry than to any analysis of the policies that might lie behind the doctrines of mistake and impossibility.

Just as there are occasions when a mistake of law should be an excuse (see e.g. the dissent in *Marrero*), there may be times when factual impossibility should also excuse. A would-be safecracker who attempts to open a safe with a can opener is so highly unlikely to succeed that he arguably presents no social danger. [See Model Penal Code § 5.05(2), supra Ch. 7, § A.] Perhaps the same reasoning applies to the defendant in *Staples,* at the beginning of this chapter. In other cases conduct which is objectively non-criminal may be regarded as insufficiently corroborative of criminal intent. In United States v. Oviedo, 525 F.2d 881 (5th Cir.1976), the court overturned a conviction for attempted sale of narcotics of a defendant who sold a nonnarcotic substance claiming it to be heroin. He may have been intending to sell genuine, heroin, or he may have been intending to commit a fraud. The court reasoned that: "When the defendant sells a substance which is actually heroin, it is reasonable to infer that he knew the physical nature of the substance, and to place on him the burden of dispelling that inference. However, if we convict the defendant of attempting to sell heroin for the sale of a non-narcotic substance, we eliminate an objective element that has major evidentiary significance and we increase the risk of mistaken conclusions that the defendant believed the goods were narcotics." A later decision interpreting *Oviedo* suggested that: "Had another objective fact been present, such as the confession of the defendant to a police officer after proper *Miranda* warnings, the *Oviedo* verdict would undoubtedly have withstood appellate scrutiny." United States v. Hough, 561 F.2d 594, 595–596 (5th Cir.1977).

Another way to handle the *Oviedo* problem is to pass a statute which independently punishes any person who consents to sell a controlled substance and then sells something else in lieu of the drug. California has such statutes, specifically Health and Safety Code §§ 11355, 11680. These sections are classified as drug offenses rather than as varieties of consumer fraud, but the penalties are lower than for sales of genuine drugs.

For a review of the case law on impossibility and an analysis of various legislative solutions see Robbins, "Attempting the Impossible: The Emerging Consensus," 23 Harv. J. on Leg. 377 (1986).

The contemporary status of the defense of impossibility was examined in United States v. Hsu, 155 F.3d 189 (3d Cir.1998). The government charged that the defendants violated the Economic Espionage Act of 1996, 18 U.S.C. § 1831, et seq. (EEA), by conspiring to steal corporate trade secrets from Bristol–Myers Squibb. The defendants sought pretrial discovery of Bristol–Myers Squibb documents, in part to attempt to develop a defense of impossibility. Defendants argued that if the documents in question did not actually contain trade secrets, it was impossible for them to have attempted or conspired to steal trade secrets. The court reviewed the current status of impossibility defenses, and concluded that "the great majority of jurisdictions have now recognized that legal and factual impossibility are 'logically indistinguishable,' and have abolished impossibility as a defense." The Third Circuit then asserted that it was the only federal circuit continuing to recognize the common law defense of legal impossibility. The court employed the analysis it had used earlier in *Everett*, supra, and decided that Congress did not intend to permit the defense of legal impossibility "to be asserted as a defense to attempt crimes created by" the EEA. The court relied upon the statute's legislative history, but also noted that the EEA "was drafted at a time when 'the doctrine of impossibility had * * * lost whatever acceptance at common law it may have possessed * * *.' "

The court held "that legal impossibility is not a defense to a charge of attempted misappropriation of trade secrets," and concluded that:

"[L]egal impossibility is not a defense to conspiracy. Although we have stated that impossibility may be a valid defense to attempt crimes, we have never recognized the defense for conspiracy charges, and we are persuaded by the views of our district courts, and by the decisions of our sister circuits, that the impossibility of achieving the goal of a conspiracy is irrelevant to the crime itself.

"It is well-settled that conspiracy and attempt serve different roles in the criminal law. The law of attempts was traditionally viewed as a way 'to deal with conduct which created a risk of immediate harmful consequences.' Even under the modern view, attempt prosecutions generally proceed only against those who have taken a 'substantial step' toward commission of a substantive crime. However, the law of conspiracy is much more preventive, aiming to nip criminal conduct in the bud before it has the chance to flourish into more ominous behavior. * * *"

"It is thus the conspiratorial agreement itself, and not the underlying substantive acts, that forms the basis for conspiracy charges. The 'illegality of the agreement does not depend on the achievement of its ends,' and it is 'irrelevant that the ends of the conspiracy were from the very inception of the agreement objectively unattainable.'

"Consequently, it is equally irrelevant that the commission of a substantive offense may have been legally impossible for the conspiracy to achieve all along. We therefore join our sister circuits, and the district courts in our own circuit, in squarely holding that legal impossibility is not a defense to conspiracy."

The court's conclusion that impossibility is not a defense to conspiracy rested upon its analysis of the elements of that crime. The traditional elements of conspiracy are examined in the following materials.

C. THE ELEMENTS OF CONSPIRACY

1. *The Agreement*

UNITED STATES v. FEOLA

Supreme Court of the United States, 1975.
420 U.S. 671, 95 S.Ct. 1255, 43 L.Ed.2d 541.

MR. JUSTICE BLACKMUN delivered the opinion of the Court.

This case presents the issue whether knowledge that the intended victim is a federal officer is a requisite for the crime of conspiracy, under 18 U.S.C. § 371 [the general federal conspiracy statute reprinted supra p. 640], to commit an offense violative of 18 U.S.C. § 111,[1] that is, an assault upon a federal officer while engaged in the performance of his official duties.

Respondent Feola and three others (Alsondo, Rosa, and Farr) were [convicted of] violations of § 371 and § 111. * * *

I

The facts reveal a classic narcotics "rip-off." The details are not particularly important for our present purposes. We need note only that the evidence shows that Feola and his confederates arranged for a sale of heroin to buyers who turned out to be undercover agents for the Bureau of Narcotics and Dangerous Drugs. The group planned to palm off on the purchasers, for a substantial sum, a form of sugar in place of heroin and, should that ruse fail, simply to surprise their unwitting buyers and relieve them of the cash they had brought along for payment. The plan failed when one agent, his suspicions being aroused, drew his revolver in time to counter an assault upon another agent from the rear. Instead of enjoying the rich benefits of a successful swindle, Feola and his associates found themselves charged, to their undoubted surprise, with conspiring to assault, and with assaulting, federal officers.

At the trial, the District Court, without objection from the defense, charged the jury that, in order to find any of the defendants guilty on either the conspiracy count or the substantive one, they were not required to conclude that the defendants were aware that their quarry were federal officers.

The Court of Appeals reversed the conspiracy convictions on a ground not advanced by any of the defendants. Although it approved the

1. "§ 111. Assaulting, resisting, or impeding certain officers or employees.

"Whoever, forcibly assaults, resists, imposes, impedes, intimidates, or interferes with any person designated in section 1114 of this title while engaged in or on account of the performance of his official duties, shall be fined not more than $5,000 or imprisoned not more than three years, or both.

"Whoever, in the commission of any such acts uses a deadly or dangerous weapon, shall be fined not more than $10,000 or imprisoned not more than ten years, or both."

Among the persons "designated in section 1114" of 18 U.S.C.A. is "any officer or employee * * * of the Bureau of Narcotics and Dangerous Drugs."

trial court's instructions to the jury on the substantive charge of assaulting a federal officer, it nonetheless concluded that the failure to charge that knowledge of the victim's official identity must be proved in order to convict on the conspiracy charge amounted to plain error. The court perceived itself bound by a line of cases, commencing with Judge Learned Hand's opinion in United States v. Crimmins, 123 F.2d 271 (C.A.2 1941), all holding that scienter of a factual element that confers federal jurisdiction, while unnecessary for conviction of the substantive offense, is required in order to sustain a conviction for conspiracy to commit the substantive offense. Although the court noted that the *Crimmins* rationale "has been criticized," and, indeed, offered no argument in support of it, it accepted "the controlling precedents somewhat reluctantly."

II

The Government's plea is for symmetry. It urges that since criminal liability [under] § 111 does not depend on whether the assailant harbored the specific intent to assault a federal officer, no greater scienter requirement can be engrafted upon the conspiracy offense, which is merely an agreement to commit the act proscribed by § 111. Consideration of the Government's contention requires us preliminarily to pass upon its premise, the proposition that responsibility for assault upon a federal officer does not depend upon whether the assailant was aware of the official identity of his victim at the time he acted.

* * *

[The Court concluded that the purpose of Congress in enacting § 111 was to allow prosecutions for assaults involving federal officers to be brought in the federal courts. Such assaults would be criminal under state laws in any event, but Congress may have feared that local and state officials would not be sufficiently vigorous in prosecuting local citizens for attacks upon federal officers, especially where the officers were engaged in enforcing locally unpopular laws. To effectuate the Congressional purpose, the statute should be construed to require only that the accused intend to assault, and not that he be aware that his victim is a federal officer.]

* * * We now consider whether the rule should be different where persons conspire to commit those acts.

III

Our decisions establish that in order to sustain a judgment of conviction on a charge of conspiracy to violate a federal statute, the Government must prove at least the degree of criminal intent necessary for the substantive offense itself. Respondent Feola urges upon us the proposition that the Government must show a degree of criminal intent in the conspiracy count greater than is necessary to convict for the substantive offense; he urges that even though it is not necessary to show that he was aware of the official identity of his assaulted victims in order to find him guilty of assaulting federal officers, the Government nonetheless must show that he was aware that his intended victims were undercover agents, if it is successfully to prosecute him for conspiring to assault federal agents. And the Court of Appeals held that the trial court's failure to charge the jury to this effect constituted plain error.

* * *

* * * In *Crimmins,* the defendant had been found guilty of conspiring to receive stolen bonds that had been transported in interstate commerce. Upon review, the Court of Appeals pointed out that the evidence failed to establish that *Crimmins* actually knew the stolen bonds had moved into the State. Accepting for the sake of argument the assumption that such knowledge was not necessary to sustain a conviction on the substantive offense, Judge Learned Hand nevertheless concluded that to permit conspiratorial liability where the conspirators were ignorant of the federal implications of their acts would be to enlarge their agreement beyond its terms as they understood them. He capsulized the distinction in what has become well known as his "traffic light" analogy:

> While one may, for instance, be guilty of running past a traffic light of whose existence one is ignorant, one cannot be guilty of conspiring to run past such a light, for one cannot agree to run past a light unless one supposes that there is a light to run past. 123 F.2d, at 273.

Judge Hand's attractive, but perhaps seductive, analogy has received a mixed reception in the courts of appeals. The Second Circuit, of course, has followed it; others have rejected it. It appears that most have avoided it by the simple expedient of inferring the requisite knowledge from the scope of the conspiratorial venture. We conclude that the analogy, though effective prose, is, as applied to the facts before us, bad law.[24]

The question posed by the traffic light analogy is not before us, just as it was not before the Second Circuit in *Crimmins.* Criminal liability, of course, may be imposed on one who runs a traffic light regardless of whether he harbored the "evil intent" of disobeying the light's command; whether he drove so recklessly as to be unable to perceive the light; whether thinking he was observing all traffic rules, he simply failed to notice the light; or whether, having been reared elsewhere, he thought that the light was only an ornament. Traffic violations generally fall into that category of offenses that dispense with a *mens rea* requirement. These laws embody the social judgment that it is fair to punish one who intentionally engages in conduct that creates a risk to others, even though no risk is intended or the actor, through no fault of his own, is completely unaware of the existence of any risk. The traffic light

24. The Government rather effectively exposes the fallacy of the Crimmins traffic light analogy by recasting it in terms of a jurisdictional element. The suggested example is a traffic light on an Indian reservation. Surely, one may conspire with others to disobey the light but be ignorant of the fact that it is on the reservation. As applied to a jurisdictional element of this kind the formulation makes little sense.

analogy poses the question whether it is fair to punish parties to an agreement to engage intentionally in apparently innocent conduct where the unintended result of engaging in that conduct is the violation of a criminal statute.

But this case does not call upon us to answer this question, and we decline to do so * * *. We note in passing, however, that the analogy comes close to stating what has been known as the "*Powell* doctrine," originating in People v. Powell, 63 N.Y. 88 (1875), to the effect that a conspiracy, to be criminal, must be animated by a corrupt motive or a motive to do wrong. Under this principle, such a motive could be easily demonstrated if the underlying offense involved an act clearly wrongful in itself; but it had to be independently demonstrated if the acts agreed to were wrongful solely because of statutory proscription. Interestingly, Judge Hand himself was one of the more severe critics of the *Powell* doctrine. * * *

The *Crimmins* rule rests upon another foundation: that it is improper to find conspiratorial liability where the parties to the illicit agreement were not aware of the fact giving rise to federal jurisdiction, because the essence of conspiracy is agreement and persons cannot be punished for acts beyond the scope of their agreement. This "reason" states little more than a conclusion, for it is clear that one may be guilty as a conspirator for acts the precise details of which one does not know at the time of the agreement. See Blumenthal v. United States, 332 U.S. 539 (1947). The question is not merely whether the official status of an assaulted victim was known to the parties at the time of their agreement, but whether the acts contemplated by the conspirators are to be deemed legally different than those actually performed solely because of the official identity of the victim. Put another way, does the identity of the proposed victim alter the legal character of the acts agreed to, or is it no more germane to the nature of those acts than the color of the victim's hair?

Our analysis of the substantive offense in Part II, supra, is sufficient to convince us that for the purpose of individual guilt or innocence, awareness of the official identity of the assault victim is irrelevant. We would expect the same to obtain with respect to the conspiracy offense unless one of the policies behind the imposition of conspiratorial liability is not served where the parties to the agreement are unaware that the intended target is a federal law enforcement official.

It is well settled that the law of conspiracy serves ends different than, and complementary to, those served by criminal prohibitions of the substantive offense. Because of this, consecutive sentences may be imposed for the conspiracy and for the underlying crime. Pinkerton v. United States, 328 U.S. 640 (1946). Our decisions have identified two independent values served by the law of conspiracy. The first is protection of society from the dangers of concerted criminal activity, That individuals know that their planned joint venture violates federal as well as state law seems totally irrelevant to that purpose of conspiracy law which seeks to protect society from the dangers of concerted criminal activity. Given the level of criminal intent necessary to sustain conviction for the substantive offense, the act of agreement to commit the crime is no less opprobrious and no less dangerous because of the absence of knowledge of a fact unnecessary to the formation of criminal intent. Indeed, unless imposition of an "anti-federal" knowledge requirement serves social purposes external to the law of conspiracy of which we are unaware, its imposition here would serve only to make it more difficult to obtain convictions on charges of conspiracy, a policy with no apparent purpose.

The second aspect is that conspiracy is an inchoate crime. This is to say, that, although the law generally makes criminal only anti-social conduct, at some point in the continuum between preparation and consummation, the likelihood of a commission of an act is sufficiently great and the criminal intent sufficiently well formed to justify the intervention of the criminal law. The law of conspiracy identifies the agreement to engage in a criminal venture as an event of sufficient threat to social order to permit the imposition of criminal sanctions for the agreement alone, plus an overt act in pursuit of it, regardless of whether the crime agreed upon actually is committed. Criminal intent has crystallized, and the likelihood of actual, fulfilled commission warrants preventive action.

Again, we do not see how imposition of a strict "anti-federal" scienter requirement would relate to this purpose of conspiracy law. Given the level of intent needed to carry out the substantive offense, we fail to see how the agreement is any less blameworthy or constitutes less of a danger to society solely because the participants are unaware which body of law they intend to violate. Therefore, we again conclude that imposition of a requirement of knowledge of those facts that serve only to establish federal jurisdiction would render it more difficult to serve the policy behind the law of conspiracy without serving any other apparent social policy.

We hold, then, that assault of a federal officer pursuant to an agreement to assault is not, even in the words of Judge Hand, "beyond the reasonable intendment of the common understanding," United States v. Crimmins, supra, 123 F.2d, at 273. The agreement is not thereby enlarged, for knowledge of the official identity of the victim is irrelevant to the essential nature of the agreement, entrance into which is made criminal by the law of conspiracy.

Again we point out, however, that the state of knowledge of the parties to an agreement is not always irrelevant in a proceeding charging a violation of conspiracy law. First, the knowledge of the parties is relevant to the same issues and to the same extent as it may be for conviction of the substantive offense. Second, whether conspirators knew the official identity of their quarry may be important, in some cases, in establishing the existence of federal jurisdiction. The jurisdictional requirement is satisfied by the existence of facts tying the proscribed conduct to the area of federal concern delineated by the statute. Federal jurisdiction always exists where the substantive offense is committed in the manner therein described, that is, when a federal officer is attacked. Where, however, there is an unfulfilled agreement to assault, it must be established whether the agreement, standing alone, constituted a sufficient threat to the safety of a federal officer so as to give rise to federal jurisdiction. If the agreement calls for an attack on an individual specifically identified, either by name or by some unique characteristic, as the putative buyers in the present case, and that specifically identified individual is in fact a federal officer, the agreement may be fairly characterized as one calling for an assault upon a federal officer, even though the parties were unaware of the victim's actual identity and even though they would not have agreed to the assault had they known that identity. Where the object of the intended attack is not identified with sufficient specificity so as to give rise to the conclusion that had the attack been carried out the victim would have been a federal officer, it is impossible to assert that the mere act of agreement to assault poses a sufficient threat to federal personnel and functions so as to give rise to federal jurisdiction. * * *

The judgment of the Court of Appeals with respect to the respondent's conspiracy conviction is reversed.

[Dissenting opinion omitted.]

GEBARDI v. UNITED STATES

Supreme Court of the United States, 1932.
287 U.S. 112, 53 S.Ct. 35, 77 L.Ed. 206.

MR. JUSTICE STONE delivered the opinion of the Court.

This case is here on certiorari, to review a judgment of conviction for conspiracy to violate the Mann Act. Petitioners, a man and a woman, not then husband and wife, were indicted in the District Court for Northern Illinois, for conspiring together, and with others not named, to transport the woman from one state to another for the purpose of engaging in sexual intercourse with the man. At the trial without a jury there was evidence from which the court could have found that the petitioners had engaged in illicit sexual relations in the course of each of the journeys alleged; that the man purchased the railway tickets for both petitioners for at least one journey; and that in each instance the woman, in advance of the purchase of the tickets, consented to go on the journey and did go on it voluntarily for the specified immoral purpose. There was no evidence supporting the allegation that any other person had conspired. The trial court gave judgment of conviction. which the Court of Appeals affirmed, on the authority of United States v. Holte, 236 U.S. 140.

[In the *Holte* case] the defendants, a man and a woman, were indicted for conspiring together that the man should transport the woman from one state to another for purposes of prostitution. In holding the indictment sufficient, the court said: "As the defendant is the woman, the district court sustained a demurrer on the ground that although the offense could not be committed without her, she was no party to it, but only the victim. The single question is whether that ruling is right. We do not have to consider what would be necessary to constitute the substantive crime under the act of 1910 [the Mann Act], or what evidence would be required to convict a woman under an indictment like this; but only to decide whether it is impossible for the transported woman to be guilty of a crime in conspiring as alleged." The court assumed that there might be a degree of co-operation which would fall short of the commission of any crime, as in the case of the purchaser of liquor illegally sold. But it declined to hold that a woman could not under some circumstances not precisely defined, be guilty of a violation of the Mann Act and of a conspiracy to violate it as well. Light is thrown upon the intended scope of this conclusion by the supposititious case which the court put: "Suppose, for instance, that a professional prostitute, as well able to look out for herself as was the man, should suggest and carry out a journey within the act of 1910 in the hope of blackmailing the man, and should buy the railroad tickets, or should pay the fare from Jersey City to New York,—she would be within the letter of the act of 1910 and we see no reason why the act should not be held to apply. We see equally little reason for not treating the preliminary agreement as a conspiracy that the law can reach, if we abandon the illusion that the woman always is the victim."

First. Those exceptional circumstances envisaged in United States v. Holte, supra, as possible instances in which the woman might violate the act itself, are clearly not present here. There is no evidence that she purchased the railroad tickets or that hers was the active or moving spirit in conceiving or carrying out the transportation. The proof shows no more than that she went willingly upon the journeys for the purposes alleged.

Section 2 of the Mann Act, violation of which is charged by the indictment here as the object of the conspiracy, imposes the penalty upon "any person who shall knowingly transport or cause to be transported, or aid or assist in obtaining transportation for, or in transporting, in interstate or foreign commerce * * * any woman or girl for the purpose of prostitution or debauchery, or for any other immoral purpose. * * *" Transportation of a woman or girl whether with or without her consent, or causing or aiding it, or furthering it in any of the specified ways, are the acts punished, when done with a purpose which is immoral within the meaning of the law.

The Act does not punish the woman for transporting herself; it contemplates two persons—one to transport and the woman or girl to be transported. For the woman to fall within the ban of the statute she must, at the least, "aid or assist" some one else in transporting or in procuring transportation for herself. But such aid and assistance must, as in the case supposed in United States v. Holte, supra, be more active than mere agreement on her part to the transportation and its immoral purpose. For the statute is drawn to include those cases in which the woman consents to her own transportation. Yet it does not specifically impose any penalty upon her, although it deals in detail with the person by whom she is transported. In applying this criminal statute we cannot infer that the mere acquiescence of the woman transported was intended to be condemned by the general language punishing those who aid and assist the transporter, any more than it has been inferred that the purchaser of liquor was to be regarded as an abettor of the illegal sale. * * *

Second. We come thus to the main question in the case, whether, admitting that the woman by consenting, has not violated the Mann Act, she may be convicted of a conspiracy with the man to violate it. * * *

As was said in the *Holte* Case an agreement to commit an offense may be criminal, though its purpose is to do what some of the conspirators may be free to do alone. Incapacity of one to commit the substantive offense does not necessarily imply that he may with impunity conspire with others who are able to commit it.[5] For it is the collective planning of criminal conduct at which the statute aims. The plan is itself a wrong which, if any act be done to effect its object, the state has elected to treat as criminal. And one may plan that others shall do what he cannot do himself.

But in this case we are concerned with something more than an agreement between two persons for one of them to commit an offense which the other cannot commit. There is the added element that the offense planned, the criminal object of the conspiracy, involves the agreement of the woman to her transportation by the man, which is the very conspiracy charged.

Congress set out in the Mann Act to deal with cases which frequently, if not normally, involve consent and agreement on the part of the woman to the forbidden transportation. In every case in which she is not intimidated or forced into the transportation, the statute necessarily contemplates her acquiescence. Yet this acquiescence, though an incident of a type of transportation specifically dealt with by the statute, was not made a crime under the Mann Act itself. Of this class of cases we say that the substantive offense contemplated by the statute itself involves the same combination or community of purpose of two persons only which is prosecuted here as conspiracy. If this were the only case covered by the act, it would be within those decisions which hold, consistently with the theory upon which conspiracies are punished, that where it is impossible under any circumstances to commit the substantive offense without co-operative action, the preliminary agreement between the

5. So it has been held repeatedly that one not a bankrupt may be held guilty * * * of conspiring that a bankrupt shall conceal property from his trustee. [Citations omitted.] These cases proceed upon the theory that only a bankrupt may commit the substantive offense * * *.

In like manner Chadwick v. United States, 72 C.C.A. 343, 141 Fed. 225 (1905), sustained the conviction of one not an officer of a national bank for conspiring with an officer to commit a crime which only he could commit.

same parties to commit the offense is not an indictable conspiracy either at common law. But criminal transportation under the Mann Act may be effected without the woman's consent as in cases of intimidation or force (with which we are not now concerned). We assume, therefore, for present purposes, as was suggested in the *Holte* Case, supra, that the decisions last mentioned do not in all strictness apply. We do not rest our decision upon the theory of those cases, nor upon the related one that the attempt is to prosecute as conspiracy acts identical with the substantive offense. We place it rather upon the ground that we perceive in the failure of the Mann Act to condemn the woman's participation in those transportations which are effected with her mere consent, evidence of an affirmative legislative policy to leave her acquiescence unpunished. We think it a necessary implication of that policy that when the Mann Act and the conspiracy statute came to be construed together, as they necessarily would be, the same participation which the former contemplates as an inseparable incident of all cases in which the woman is a voluntary agent at all, but does not punish, was not automatically to be made punishable under the latter. It would contravene that policy to hold that the very passage of the Mann Act effected a withdrawal by the conspiracy statute of that immunity which the Mann Act itself confers.

It is not to be supposed that the consent of an unmarried person to adultery with a married person, where the latter alone is guilty of the substantive offense, would render the former an abettor or a conspirator, or that the acquiescence of a woman under the age of consent would make her a coconspirator with the man to commit statutory rape upon herself. The principle, determinative of this case, is the same.

On the evidence before us the woman petitioner has not violated the Mann Act and, we hold, is not guilty of a conspiracy to do so. As there is no proof that the man conspired with anyone else to bring about the transportation, the convictions of both petitioners must be

Reversed.

Note

The opinion in *Gebardi* somewhat cryptically mentions "those decisions which hold, consistently with the theory on which conspiracies are punished, that where it is impossible under any circumstances to commit the substantive offense without cooperative action, the preliminary agreement between the same parties to commit the offense is not an indictable conspiracy either at common law." The reference is to "Wharton's Rule," named after Francis Wharton, a scholar who formulated the rule in a treatise many years ago. A current statement of the rule is "an agreement by two persons to commit a particular crime cannot be prosecuted as a conspiracy when the crime is of such a nature as to necessarily require the participation of two persons for its commission." 1 R. Anderson, Wharton's Criminal Law and Procedure § 89 p. 191 (1957). In the words of a federal court of appeals,

> The classic situations in which the Rule is said to apply are dueling, bigamy, adultery, and incest. The apparent rationale of the Rule is that

it is grossly unjust to punish two parties for the commission of a crime and for combining to commit the crime when the combination is an inherent element of the substantive offense. In the case law, the Rule has been applied almost exclusively to instances in which the object of the alleged conspiracy was a two-party crime, such as the giving and receiving of bribes, or the buying and selling of contraband goods. The Rule has been held not to apply when the number of conspirators exceeds the number of participants essential to the contemplated crime. United States v. Pacheco, 489 F.2d 554 (5th Cir.1974).

Wharton's Rule has been raised as a defense in some conspiracy cases involving special statutes aimed at organized crime. For example, 18 U.S.C.A. § 1955 punishes operation of an "illegal gambling business," and defines the type of prohibited gambling business as one which involves at least five persons in its operations. In Iannelli v. United States, 420 U.S. 770 (1975), the Supreme Court held that Wharton's Rule does not prevent convicting a defendant both of operating the illegal gambling business and of conspiring to operate that same gambling business. The majority opinion found in the language and legislative history of § 1955 evidence of a congressional intent to permit punishment for both crimes despite the fact that operation of an illegal business involving five or more persons necessarily implies the existence of a conspiracy.

In some cases, the principles of conspiracy and complicity could have the effect of contravening clearly implied legislative policies. For example, the willing victim of a statutory rape could be charged as a co-conspirator or accomplice, except that the courts understand the legislative policy to be one of protecting underage females rather than subjecting them to prosecution. Similarly, a purchaser of narcotics is technically an accomplice to the sale, but actually imposing such liability would contravene the legislative policy of punishing sellers more heavily than mere users.

The "Mann Act," was enacted early in this century in a climate of hysteria over what was then called "white slavery." It was believed that great numbers of young women were being kidnapped and forced into prostitution. Although the Act was aimed at compulsory prostitution, it was drafted extremely broadly to punish any transportation of a woman or girl "for the purpose of prostitution or debauchery, or for any other immoral purpose." The Supreme Court construed this language expansively to cover not only transportation for voluntary prostitution, but also any sexual activity outside of lawful marriage that involved travel across state lines. See Cleveland v. United States, 329 U.S. 14 (1946); Caminetti v. United States, 242 U.S. 470 (1917).

Needless to say, federal prosecutors invoked this statute selectively. Professor Patrick Hardin of the University of Tennessee Law School provided a citation which explains why Gebardi was singled out for prosecution under the Mann Act. According to Professor Hardin, the *New York Times* of July 22, 1931, at page 14, states that "Gebardi was regarded as the ace of Scarface Al's machine gun battery." He was indicted as the triggerman for all seven murders committed in the infamous St. Valentine's Day Massacre of February 14, 1929. A woman friend gave him an alibi, claiming that they were away on a pleasure trip at the time of the massacre. Unable to convict Gebardi of murder, the government indicted him and her for the Mann Act violation involved in this trip, which was doubtless fictitious. Gebardi and his friend were married by the time of the trial, which took place one week before the sentencing of Scarface Al Capone on tax evasion charges.

UNITED STATES v. ALVAREZ

United States Court of Appeals, Fifth Circuit, 1980.
610 F.2d 1250, reversed 625 F.2d 1196.

ALVIN B. RUBIN, CIRCUIT JUDGE:

The indictment named Cifarelli, Cruz and Peterson as coconspirators [with Alvarez] in a plan to import marijuana into the United States. Except for his joinder in the indictment, Alvarez is mentioned in only one other place in the indictment; it is charged as one of the overt acts that he together with Cifarelli and Cruz met two DEA agents at the Opa–Locka, Florida, airport. The indictment against Peterson was dismissed, Cifarelli pleaded guilty and Cruz was found guilty when tried jointly with Alvarez. There was ample evidence of a conspiracy between Cruz and Cifarelli to import marijuana into the United States.

Pursuant to arrangements with an undercover DEA agent, Cifarelli came to meet the agent at the Opa–Locka airport. Alvarez drove a pickup truck in which Cruz and Cifarelli were riding. The truck was loaded with some household appliances, including a washer and dryer; the DEA agent asked Cifarelli who Alvarez was and Cifarelli said Alvarez "would be at the offloading side in the United States." The agent then spoke to Alvarez in Spanish and asked him if he planned to be at the unloading site. Alvarez nodded his head, signifying "yes," smiled, and asked the DEA agent if he was going on the plane. The agent said he was. After the conversation, Alvarez unloaded the household appliances from the truck. The agent then spoke with Cruz, and, after Cruz outlined his plans for arrival of the plane and its unloading, all were arrested.

* * * [F]ederal law makes it criminal to aid and abet another in a crime although there is no general federal statute against attempts, criminal solicitation or accessorial participation before the crime. Criminal responsibility for abetting a crime requires that a defendant "associate himself with the venture, that he participate in it as in something that he wishes to bring about, that he seek by his action to make it succeed." L. Hand, J., in United States v. Peoni, 2 Cir., 100 F.2d 401, 402. When an abettor is prosecuted, the threshold question is: how much does someone have to contribute to the crime of another in order to be accountable as an abettor?

Federal prosecutors have often sidestepped the necessity of seeking the answer to this question by charging defendants involved in crime with a different criminal offense, joinder in a conspiracy. The prosecution need not even charge any completed offense because the crime of conspiracy condemns the agreement itself, treating all participants equally. Conspiracy also collapses the distinction between accessories and perpetrators through the doctrine of conspiratorial complicity, which punishes conspirators as principals in any substantive offense committed in furtherance of the conspiracy, whether or not they directly participated in that offense. See, Pinkerton v. United States, 328 U.S. 640 (1946). Thus, if a conspiracy is charged, the prosecution need not analyze whether a defendant conspirator's actions would ordinarily be sufficient to create liability as an abettor of an offense; all that is necessary is proof that the defendant joined in an unlawful agreement. * * *

The use of conspiracy as a device for prosecuting minor actors in criminal dramas is limited by the fact that conspiracy itself is not primarily a means of assessing the culpability of criminal accessories; it is a separate substantive offense. Its prohibition is directed not at its unlawful object, but at the process of agreeing to pursue that object. A defendant does not join a conspiracy merely by participating in a substantive offense, or by associating with persons who are members of a conspiracy. * * * The conspirator must knowingly agree to join others in a concerted effort to bring about a common end. [Citations] These elements of the conspiratorial offense may of course be shown by circumstantial evidence. * * *

The evidence against Alvarez is insufficient to prove that he joined in an agreement to import marijuana. Obviously, there is no direct proof of his consent. Neither is there any proof of his performance of an act directly in furtherance of the scheme. What was proved, construed most favorably to the prosecution and thus most strongly against Alvarez, is his statement that he planned to perform an act subsequent to importation, unloading the plane. That this would have been a criminal act, if done, is indisputable, but it is insufficient to prove beyond reasonable doubt that he had joined in a conspiracy to import a prohibited substance.

To justify a conviction for conspiracy, there must be evidence that Alvarez agreed to join in the unlawful plan. The evidence presented to the jury in this case permits that conclusion only by a long chain of compounded inferences: that Alvarez knew illegal activity was afoot; that Alvarez intended to unload illegal cargo upon the plane's return; that Alvarez, therefore, knew of an agreement between others to import the illegal cargo; and that, consequently, Alvarez must have joined that illegal agreement. There is direct proof only of Alvarez's intentions. That he knew the activity was criminal is a reasonable inference. The other two conclusions are logical non sequiturs. What Alvarez intended to do is culpable. But without more his statements are not punishable as conspiracy. * * *

There is one other route, seldom used, by which to implicate an accessory in a conspiracy: it is to charge that he aided and abetted the conspiracy. That charge is not made here and patently could not be, for Alvarez actually did nothing to further the conspiracy whatever he may have planned to do in the future.

For these reasons, the judgment of conviction is reversed. [The above panel decision was reversed by the Fifth Circuit en banc with the following majority opinion, found at 625 F.2d 1196:]

REAVLEY, CIRCUIT JUDGE:

* * * The government was not required to prove that Alvarez had knowledge of all the details of the conspiracy or each of its members, provided that prosecution established his knowledge of the essential of the conspiracy. [Citations] Nor can a defendant escape criminal responsibility on the grounds that he did not join the conspiracy until well after its inception; or because he plays only a minor role in the total scheme. [Citations] We agree with the panel that the evidence is sufficient to infer that Alvarez knew that criminal activity was afoot. It must also have been obvious to him that there was conspiracy to import the contraband because prior planning and concerted action would be required to load the marijuana in Colombia, fly it into this country, and unload it upon its arrival. Alvarez' joinder in the illicit compact is inferable on two fronts. First, there is direct evidence that he intended to be at the off-loading site. A jury may well conclude that his intended presence manifested a prior agreement to assist in the unloading. Alternatively, the nodded head may be viewed as assurance to Martinez, then thought to be one in confederacy with Cifarelli and Cruz, that Alvarez would be at the unloading site to insure that the aircraft was unloaded rapidly. * * *

The evidence would have been insufficient to support the conviction without the proof that Cifarelli and Alvarez assured agent Martinez that Alvarez would be on hand at the place and time of the airplane's return to Florida. That proof, combined with all of the other evidence, clearly warranted the verdict of guilt. A reasonable jury could very well conclude that only one with knowledge of the marijuana, and who had agreed to participate in the scheme to accomplish its importation, would promise to be on hand at a remote and unlikely area for the unloading of cargo. * * * The judgment of conviction is affirmed.

VANCE, CIRCUIT JUDGE, with whom FAY, RUBIN, KRAVITCH, HENDERSON, POLITZ, HATCHETT, TATE and THOMAS A. CLARK, CIRCUIT JUDGES, join, dissenting:

Alvarez nodded his head and smiled. For this he will go to the penitentiary. In another case a smile and the nod of the head may be sufficient to establish guilt. Here it clearly was not.

This is not a case where an alleged conspirator was engaged in an illegal act or in the presence of a large quantity of contraband so that it reasonably may be inferred that he knew what was afoot. Neither is it a case where he was shown to have participated in or even been present during any conspiratorial conversation. Alvarez was engaged in a completely legal act. He was loading a washing machine onto an airplane. He was asked whether he was going to be there at the unloading site when the plane got back. It was in response to this innocuous inquiry that he smiled and nodded his head. This is all the admissible evidence to which we are cited to show that Alvarez knew of the unlawful conspiracy and agreed to join in it.

The majority points to Alvarez' association with other defendants under suspicious circumstances and recounts suggestive remarks by conspirators outside Alvarez' presence. But it is not enough that he was associating with bad people. Neither will merely suspicious circumstances substitute for proof of his guilt. The conversations of participants in the conspiracy to which the majority alludes were not even admissible as to Alvarez unless it be shown that he too was a conspirator. We said that we have banished the slight evidence rule and that proof beyond a reasonable doubt that a defendant knew and intended to join a conspiracy must be based on substantial evidence. United States v. Malatesta, 590 F.2d 1379, 1382 (5th Cir.) (en banc), cert. denied, 440 U.S. 962 (1979). To be sufficient the evidence must be such that reasonable minds can conclude that it is inconsistent with every hypothesis of innocence.

Alvarez may have been a guilty coconspirator or he may have been a humble workman performing a lawful act totally unrelated to any conspiracy, who simply indicated that he would report back to work as instructed. To my mind the majority opinion suggests no way that a jury reasonably could accept one hypothesis to the exclusion of the other.

The conspiracy statutes are vitally important to the protection of society. Yet the potential for injustice in conspiracy cases is enormous. The prosecutor's net may well ensnare the innocent as well as the guilty. The presentation of evidence in such cases is sometimes almost chaotic. We should use particular care to ensure that the prosecution actually proved that the defendant was a participant in the conspiracy before he is sent to prison. Our concept of justice rests on the basic notion that it is only for personal guilt that punishment is justified. In this case the evidence simply falls short. I would reverse.

2. *Procedural Attributes of Conspiracy Cases*

KRULEWITCH v. UNITED STATES

Supreme Court of the United States, 1949.
336 U.S. 440, 69 S.Ct. 716, 93 L.Ed. 790.

MR. JUSTICE BLACK delivered the opinion of the Court.

A federal indictment charged in three counts that petitioner and a woman defendant had (1) induced and persuaded another woman to go on October 20, 1941, from New York City to Miami, Florida, for the purpose of prostitution; (2) transported or caused her to be transported from New York to Miami for that purpose; and (3) conspired to commit those offenses in violation of 18 U.S.C. § 371. Tried alone, the petitioner was convicted on all three counts of the indictment. The Court of Appeals affirmed. We granted certiorari limiting our review to consideration of alleged error in admission of certain hearsay testimony against petitioner over his timely and repeated objections.

The challenged testimony was elicited by the Government from its complaining witness, the person whom petitioner and the woman defendant allegedly induced to go from New York to Florida for the purpose of prostitution. The testimony narrated the following purported conversation between the complaining witness and petitioner's alleged co-conspirator, the woman defendant. "She asked me, she says, 'You didn't talk yet?' And I says, 'No.' And she says, 'Well, don't,' she says, 'until we get you a lawyer.' And then she says, 'Be very careful what you say.' And I can't put it in exact words. But she said, 'It would be better for us two girls to take the blame than Kay (the defendant) because he couldn't stand it, he couldn't stand to take it.' "

The time of the alleged conversation was more than a month and a half after October 20, 1941, the date the complaining witness had gone to Miami. Whatever original conspiracy may have existed between petitioner and his alleged co-conspirator to cause the complaining witness to go to Florida in October, 1941, no longer existed when the reported conversation took place in December, 1941. For on this latter date the trip to Florida had not only been made—the complaining witness had left Florida, had returned to New York, and had resumed her residence there. Furthermore, at the time the conversation took place, the complaining witness, the alleged co-conspirator, and the petitioner had been arrested. They apparently were charged in a United States District Court of Florida with the offense of which petitioner was here convicted. * * *

Although the Government recognizes that the chief objective of the conspiracy—transportation for prostitution purposes—had ended in success or failure before the reported conversation took place, it nevertheless argues for admissibility of the hearsay declaration as one in furtherance of a continuing subsidiary objective of the conspiracy. Its argument runs this way. Conspirators about to commit crimes always expressly or implicitly agree to collaborate with each other to conceal facts in order to prevent detection, conviction and punishment. Thus the argument is that even after the central criminal objectives of a conspiracy have succeeded or failed, an implicit subsidiary phase of the conspiracy always survives, the phase which has concealment as its sole objective. * * *

We cannot accept the Government's contention. There are many logical and practical reasons that could be advanced against a special evidentiary rule that permits out-of-court statements of one conspirator to be used against another. But however cogent these reasons, it is firmly established that where made in furtherance of the objectives of a going conspiracy, such statements are admissible as exceptions to the hearsay rule. * * * The Government now asks us to expand this narrow exception to the hearsay rule and hold admissible a declaration, not made in furtherance of the alleged criminal transportation conspiracy charged, but made in furtherance of an alleged implied but uncharged conspiracy aimed at preventing detection and punishment. * * * The rule contended for by the Government could have far-reaching results. For under this rule plausible arguments could generally be made in conspiracy cases that most out-of-court statements offered in evidence tended to shield co-conspirators. We are not persuaded to adopt the Government's implicit conspiracy theory which in all criminal conspiracy cases would create automatically a further breach of the general rule against the admission of hearsay evidence.

Reversed.

MR. JUSTICE JACKSON, concurring in the judgment and opinion of the Court.

This case illustrates a present drift in the federal law of conspiracy which warrants some further comment because it is characteristic of the long evolution of that elastic, sprawling and pervasive offense. Its history exemplifies the "tendency of a principle to expand itself to the limit of its logic."[1] The unavailing protest of courts against the growing habit to indict for conspiracy in lieu of prosecuting for the substantive offense itself, or in addition thereto, suggests that loose practice as to this offense constitutes a serious threat to fairness in our administration of justice.

The modern crime of conspiracy is so vague that it almost defies definition. Despite certain elementary and essential elements, it also, chameleon-like, takes on a special coloration from each of the many independent offenses on which it may be overlaid. It is always "predominantly mental in composition" because it consists primarily of a meeting of minds and an intent.

The crime comes down to us wrapped in vague but unpleasant connotations. It sounds historical undertones of treachery, secret plotting and violence on a scale that menaces social stability and the security of the state itself. "Privy conspiracy" ranks with sedition and rebellion in the Litany's prayer for deliverance. Conspiratorial movements do indeed lie back of the political assassination, the *coup d'etat,* the *putsch,* the revolution, and seizures of power in modern times, as they have in all history.

But the conspiracy concept also is superimposed upon many concerted crimes having no political motivation. It is not intended to question that the basic conspiracy principle has some place in modern criminal law, because to unite, back of a criminal purpose, the strength, opportunities and resources of many is obviously more dangerous and more difficult to police than the efforts of a lone wrongdoer. It also may be trivialized, as here, where the conspiracy consists of the concert of a loathsome panderer and a prostitute to go from New York to Florida to ply their trade, see 2 Cir., 145 F.2d 76, 156 A.L.R. 337, for details, and it would appear that a simple Mann Act prosecution would vindicate the majesty of federal law. However, even when appropriately invoked, the looseness and pliability of the doctrine present inherent dangers which should be in the background of judicial thought wherever it is sought to extend the doctrine to meet the exigencies of a particular case.

1. The phrase is Judge Cardozo's—The Nature of the Judicial Process, p. 51.

Conspiracy in federal law aggravates the degree of crime over that of unconcerted offending. The act of confederating to commit a misdemeanor, followed by even an innocent overt act in its execution, is a felony and is such even if the misdemeanor is never consummated. The more radical proposition also is well-established that at common law and under some statutes a combination may be a criminal conspiracy even if it contemplates only acts which are not crimes at all when perpetrated by an individual or by many acting severally. Thus the conspiracy doctrine will incriminate persons on the fringe of offending who would not be guilty of aiding and abetting or of becoming an accessory, for those charges only lie when an act which is a crime has actually been committed. * * *

The doctrine does not commend itself to jurists of civil law countries, despite universal recognition that an organized society must have legal weapons for combatting organized criminality. Most other countries have devised what they consider more discriminating principles upon which to prosecute criminal gangs, secret associations and subversive syndicates. * * * Of course, it is for prosecutors rather than courts to determine when to use a scatter gun to bring down the defendant, but there are procedural advantages from using it which add to the danger of unguarded extension of the concept.

An accused, under the Sixth Amendment, has the right to trial "by an impartial jury of the State and district wherein the crime shall have been committed." The leverage of a conspiracy charge lifts this limitation from the prosecution and reduces its protection to a phantom, for the crime is considered so vagrant as to have been committed in any district where any one of the conspirators did any one of the acts, however innocent, intended to accomplish its object. The Government may, and often does, compel one to defend at a great distance from any place he ever did any act because some accused confederate did some trivial and by itself innocent act in the chosen district. Circumstances may even enable the prosecution to fix the place of trial in Washington, D.C., where a defendant may lawfully be put to trial before a jury partly or even wholly made up of employees of the Government that accuses him.

When the trial starts, the accused feels the full impact of the conspiracy strategy. Strictly, the prosecution should first establish *prima facie* the conspiracy and identify the conspirators, after which evidence of acts and declarations of each in the course of its execution are admissible against all. But the order of proof of so sprawling a charge is difficult for a judge to control. As a practical matter, the accused often is confronted with a hodgepodge of acts and statements by others which he may never have authorized or intended or even known about, but which help to persuade the jury of existence of the conspiracy itself. In other words, a conspiracy often is proved by evidence that is admissible only upon assumption that conspiracy existed. The naive assumption that prejudicial effects can be overcome by instructions to the jury, all practicing lawyers know to be unmitigated fiction.

The trial of a conspiracy charge doubtless imposes a heavy burden on the prosecution, but it is an especially difficult situation for the defendant. The hazard from loose application of rules of evidence is aggravated where the Government institutes mass trials. Moreover, in federal practice there is no rule preventing conviction on uncorroborated testimony of accomplices, as there are in many jurisdictions, and the most comfort a defendant can expect is that the court can be induced to follow the "better practice" and caution the jury against "too much reliance upon the testimony of accomplices." [Citations]

A co-defendant in a conspiracy trial occupies an uneasy seat. There generally will be evidence of wrongdoing by somebody. It is difficult for the individual to make his own case stand on its own merits in the minds of jurors who are ready to believe that birds of a feather are flocked together. If he is silent, he is taken to admit it and if, as often happens, co-defendants can be prodded into accusing or contradicting each other, they convict each other. There are many practical difficulties in defending against a charge of conspiracy which I will not enumerate.

Against this inadequately sketched background, I think the decision of this case in the court below introduced an ominous expansion of the accepted law of conspiracy. * * *

It is difficult to see any logical limit to the "implied conspiracy," either as to duration or means, nor does it appear that one could overcome the implication by express and credible evidence that no such understanding existed, nor any way in which an accused against whom the presumption is once raised can terminate the imputed agency of his associates to incriminate him. Conspirators, long after the contemplated offense is complete, after perhaps they have fallen out and become enemies, may still incriminate each other by deliberately harmful, but unsworn declarations, or unintentionally by casual conversations out of court. On the theory that the law will impute to the confederates a continuing conspiracy to defeat justice, one conceivably could be bound by another's unauthorized and unknown commission of perjury, bribery of a juror or witness, or even putting an incorrigible witness with damaging information out of the way.

Moreover, the assumption of an indefinitely continuing offense would result in an indeterminate extension of the statute of limitations. If the law implies an agreement to cooperate in defeating prosecution, it must imply that it continues as long as prosecution is a possibility, and prosecution is a possibility as long as the conspiracy to defeat it is implied to continue.

* * *

There is, of course, strong temptation to relax rigid standards when it seems the only way to sustain convictions of evildoers. But statutes authorize prosecution for substantive crimes for most evildoing without the dangers to the liberty of the individual and the integrity of the judicial process that are inherent in conspiracy charges. We should disapprove the doctrine of implied or constructive crime in its entirety and in every manifestation. And I think there should be no straining to uphold any conspiracy conviction where prosecution for the substantive offense is adequate and the purpose served by adding the conspiracy charge seems chiefly to get procedural advantages to ease the way to conviction.

3. *The Scope and the Object of the Conspiracy*

UNITED STATES v. BRUNO

United States Court of Appeals, Second Circuit, 1939.
105 F.2d 921 [reversed on other grounds, 308 U.S. 287, 60 S.Ct. 198, 84 L.Ed. 257].

PER CURIAM.

Bruno and Iacono were indicted along with 86 others for a conspiracy to import, sell and possess narcotics; some were acquitted; others, besides these two, were convicted, but they alone appealed. They complain, (1) that if the evidence proved anything, it proved a series of separate conspiracies, and not a single one, as alleged in the indictment; (2) that unlawful telephone "taps" were allowed in evidence against them; (3) that the judge refused to charge the jury properly as to the effect of their failure to take the stand; and (4) that there was not enough evidence to support the verdict.

The first point was made at the conclusion of the prosecution's case: the defendants then moved to dismiss the indictment on the ground that several conspiracies had been proved, and not the one alleged. The evidence allowed the jury to find that there had existed over a substantial period of time a conspiracy embracing a great number of persons, whose object was to smuggle narcotics into the Port of New York and distribute them to addicts both in this city and in Texas and Louisiana. This required the cooperation of four groups of persons; the smugglers who imported the drugs; the middlemen who paid the smugglers and distributed to retailers; and two groups of retailers—one in New York and one in Texas and Louisiana—who supplied the addicts. The defendants assert that there were, therefore, at least three separate conspiracies; one between the smugglers and the middlemen, and one between the middlemen and each group of retailers. The evidence did not disclose any cooperation or communication between the smugglers and either group of retailers, or between the two groups of retailers themselves; however, the smugglers knew that the middlemen must sell to retailers, and the retailers knew that the middlemen must buy of importers of one sort or another. Thus the conspirators at one end of the chain knew that the unlawful business would not, and could not, stop with their buyers; and those at the other end knew that it had not begun with their sellers. That being true, a jury might have found that all the accused were embarked upon a venture, in all parts of which each was a participant, and an abettor in the sense that the success of that part with which he was immediately concerned, was dependent upon the success of the whole. * * * It might still be argued that there were two conspiracies; one including the smugglers, the middlemen and the New York group, and the other, the smugglers, the middlemen and the Texas & Louisiana group, for there was apparently no privity between the two groups of retailers. That too would be fallacious. Clearly, quoad the smugglers, there was but one conspiracy, for it was of no moment to them whether the middlemen sold to one or more groups of retailers, provided they had a market somewhere. So too of any retailer; he knew that he was a necessary link in a scheme of distribution, and the others, whom he knew to be convenient to its execution, were as much parts of a single undertaking or enterprise as to salesmen in the same shop. We think therefore that there was only one conspiracy * * *.

* * *

Judgment affirmed as to Bruno.

KOTTEAKOS v. UNITED STATES

Supreme Court of the United States, 1946.
328 U.S. 750, 66 S.Ct. 1239, 90 L.Ed. 1557.

MR. JUSTICE RUTLEDGE delivered the opinion of the Court. * * *

[Seven persons including Kotteakos were convicted of conspiring to obtain loans from the Federal Housing Administration by means of applications that fraudulently misrepresented the uses to which the borrowed money would be put. The evidence showed eight distinct loan transactions, each involving defendants who had no connection with the other loans. The only connecting element was that all the loans were obtained through the services of a single broker named Brown, who pleaded guilty and testified against all the others. The trial court ruled that the participation of Brown in every transaction established a single conspiracy among all the defendants.]

* * * As the Circuit Court of Appeals said, there were "at least eight, and perhaps more, separate and independent groups, none of which had any connection with any other, though all dealt independently with Brown as their agent." As the Government puts it, the pattern was "that of separate spokes meeting at a common center," though we may add without the rim of the wheel to enclose the spokes.

The proof therefore admittedly made out a case, not of a single conspiracy, but of several, notwithstanding only one was charged in the indictment. The Court of Appeals aptly drew analogy in the comment, "Thieves who dispose of their loot to a single receiver—a single 'fence'—do not by that fact alone become confederates: they may, but it takes more than knowledge that he is a 'fence' to make them such." It stated that the trial judge "was plainly wrong in supposing that upon the evidence there could be a single conspiracy; and in the view he took of the law, he should have dismissed the indictment." Nevertheless the appellate court held the error not prejudicial, saying among other things that "especially since guilt was so manifest, it was 'proper' to join the conspiracies," and "to reverse the conviction would be a miscarriage of justice." This is indeed the Government's entire position. It does not now contend that there was no variance in proof from the single conspiracy charged in the indictment. Admitting that separate and distinct conspiracies were shown, it urges that the variance was not prejudicial to the petitioners.

* * *

One difficulty with this is that the trial court itself was confused in the charge which it gave to guide the jury in deliberation. The court instructed: "The indictment charges but one conspiracy, and to convict each of the defendants of a conspiracy, the Government would have to prove, and you would have to find, that each of the defendants was a member of that conspiracy. You cannot divide it up. It is one conspiracy, and the question is whether or not each of the defendants or which of the defendants, are members of that conspiracy."

On its face, as the Court of Appeals said, this portion of the charge was plainly wrong in application to the proof made; and the error pervaded the entire charge, not merely the portion quoted. The jury could not possibly have found, upon the evidence, that there was only one conspiracy. The trial court was of the view that one conspiracy was made out by showing that each defendant was linked to Brown in one or more transactions, and that it was possible on the evidence for the jury to conclude that all were in a common adventure because of this fact and the similarity of purpose presented in the various applications for loans.

This view, specifically embodied throughout the instructions, obviously confuses the common purpose of a single enterprise with the several, though similar, purposes of numerous separate adventures of like character. It may be that, notwithstanding the misdirection, the jury actually understood correctly the purport of the evidence, as the Government now concedes it to have been; and came to the conclusion that the petitioners were guilty only of the separate conspiracies in which the proof shows they respectively participated. But, in the face of the misdirection and in the circumstances of this case, we cannot assume that the lay triers of fact were so well informed upon the law or that they disregarded the permission expressly given to ignore that vital difference. * * *

On those instructions it was competent not only for the jury to find that all of the defendants were parties to a single common plan, design and scheme, where none was shown by the proof, but also for them to impute to each defendant the acts and statements of the others without reference to whether they related to one of the schemes proven or another, and to find an overt act affecting all in conduct which admittedly could only have affected some. True, the Court of Appeals painstakingly examined the evidence directly relating to each petitioner and concluded he had not been prejudiced in this manner. That judgment was founded largely in the fact that each was clearly shown to have shared in the fraudulent phase of the conspiracy in which he participated. Even so, we do not understand how it can be concluded, in the face of the instruction, that the jury considered and was influenced by nothing else.

All this the Government seeks to justify as harmless error. * * *

There are times when of necessity, because of the nature and scope of the particular federation, large numbers of persons taking part must be tried together or perhaps not at all, at any rate as respects some. When many conspire, they invite mass trial by their conduct. Even so, the proceedings are exceptional to our tradition and call for use of every safeguard to individualize each defendant in his relation to the mass. Wholly different is it with those who join together with only a few, though many others may be doing the same and though some of them may line up with more than one group.

Criminal they may be, but it is not the criminality of mass conspiracy. They do not invite mass trial by their conduct. Nor does our system tolerate it. That way lies the drift toward totalitarian institutions. True, this may be inconvenient for prosecution. But our Government is not one of mere convenience or efficiency. It too has a stake, with every citizen, in his being afforded our historic individual protections, including those surrounding criminal trials. About them we dare not become careless or complacent when that fashion has become rampant over the earth.

Here toleration went too far. * * * Leeway there must be for cases * * * where proof may not accord with exact specifications in indictments. Otherwise criminal conspirators never could be brought to halt. But if the practice here followed were to stand, we see nothing to prevent its extension to a dozen, a score, or more conspiracies and at the same time to scores of men involved, if at all, only separately in them. The dangers for transference of guilt from one to another across the line separating conspiracies, subconsciously or otherwise, are so great that no one really can say prejudice to substantial right has not taken place. * * * The line must be drawn somewhere. Whether or not Berger marks the limit, for this sort of error and case, we are clear that it must lie somewhere between that case and this one.

* * *

Reversed.

BLUMENTHAL v. UNITED STATES

Supreme Court of the United States, 1947.
332 U.S. 539, 68 S.Ct. 248, 92 L.Ed. 154.

Mr. Justice Rutledge delivered the opinion of the Court. * * *

[Defendants were convicted of a single conspiracy to sell whiskey at a price above the maximum permitted under wartime price control regulations. The Francisco Distributing Company, operated by defendants Goldsmith and Weiss, obtained the lot of whiskey from its unidentified owner. Defendants Feigenbaum, Blumenthal and Abel acted as salesmen, dealing with the tavern owners who purchased the whiskey at inflated prices. There was no evidence that the individual salesmen had any dealings with each other, or that they knew of the existence of the unidentified person from whom Francisco obtained the whiskey.]

With the case thus posited, it is true the salesmen did not know of the unknown owner's existence or part in the plan. And in a hypertechnical aspect the case as a whole might be regarded as showing in one phase an agreement among Goldsmith, Weiss and the unknown owner, X, and in the other an agreement among the five defendants to which X was not a party. Thus in the most meticulous sense it might be regarded as disclosing two agreements, with Goldsmith and Weiss as figures common to both.

Indeed that may be what took place chronologically, for conspiracies involving such elaborate arrangements generally are not born full grown. Rather they mature by successive stages which are necessary to bring in the essential parties. And not all of those joining in the earlier ones make known their participation to others later coming in.

The law does not demand proof of so much. For it is most often true, especially in broad schemes calling for the aid of many persons, that after discovery of enough to show clearly the essence of the scheme and the identity of a number participating, the identity and the fact of participation of others remain undiscovered and undiscoverable. Secrecy and concealment are essential features of successful conspiracy. The more completely they are achieved, the more successful the crime. Hence the law rightly gives room for allowing the conviction of those discovered upon showing sufficiently the essential nature of the plan and their connections with it, without requiring evidence of knowledge of all its details or of the participation of others. Otherwise the difficulties, not only of discovery, but of certainty in proof and of correlating proof with pleading would become insuperable, and conspirators would go free by their very ingenuity.

Here, apart from the weight which the proof of the unknown owner's existence and participation added to the convictions of Weiss and Goldsmith, it added no essential feature to the charge against the five defendants. The whiskey was the same. The agreements related alike to its disposition. They comprehended illegal sales in the guise of legal ones. Who owned the whiskey was irrelevant to the basic plan and its essential illegality. * * *

We think that in the special circumstances of this case the two agreements were merely steps in the formation of the larger and ultimate more general conspiracy. In that view it would be a perversion of justice to regard the salesmen's ignorance of the unknown owner's participation as furnishing adequate ground for reversal of their convictions. Nor does anything in the Kotteakos decision require this. The scheme was in fact the same scheme; the salesmen knew or must have known that others unknown to them were sharing in so large a project; and it hardly can be sufficient to relieve them that they did not know, when they joined the scheme, who those people were or exactly the parts they were playing in carrying out the common design and object of all. By their separate agreements, if such they were, they became parties to the larger common plan, joined together by their knowledge of its essential features and broad scope, though not of its exact limits, and by their common single goal.

The case therefore is very different from the facts admitted to exist in the Kotteakos case. Apart from the much larger number of agreements there involved, no two of those agreements were tied together as stages in the formation of a larger all inclusive combination, all directed to achieving a single unlawful end or result. On the contrary each separate agreement had its own distinct, illegal end. Each loan was an end in itself, separate from all others, although all were alike in having similar illegal objects. Except for Brown, the common figure, no conspirator was interested in whether any loan except his own went through. And none aided in any way, by agreement or otherwise, in procuring another's loan. The conspiracies therefore were distinct and disconnected, not parts of a larger general scheme, both in the phase of agreement with Brown and also in the absence of any aid given to others as well as in specific object and result. There was no drawing of all together in a single, overall, comprehensive plan.

Here the contrary is true. All knew of and joined in the overriding scheme. All intended to aid the owner, whether Francisco or another to sell the whiskey unlawfully, though the two groups of defendants differed on the proof in knowledge and belief concerning the owner's ability. All by reason of their knowledge of the plan's general scope, if not its exact limits, sought a common end, to aid in disposing of the whiskey. True, each salesman aided in selling only his part. But he knew the lot to be sold was larger and thus that he was aiding in a larger plan. He thus became a party to it and not merely to the integrating agreement with Weiss and Goldsmith.

We think therefore that in every practical sense the unique facts of this case reveal a single conspiracy of which the several agreements were essential and integral steps, and accordingly that the judgments should be affirmed.

D. GROUP LIABILITY: COMPLICITY AND CONSPIRACY

An individual can be punished for criminal acts committed by others. Theories of complicity and conspiracy create group liability, even where not all members of the group committed the criminal acts. Part D examines both the distinctive elements of these two theories of group liability, as well as their overlapping features.

1. Aiding and Abetting

STATE v. PARKER

Supreme Court of Minnesota, 1969.
282 Minn. 343, 164 N.W.2d 633.

NELSON, JUSTICE: * * *

[Larry, a student at the University of Minnesota Law School, gave defendant Parker and two other persons a ride in his automobile. The ungrateful passengers robbed him of his wallet, watch, and car, and beat him nearly to death before he was able to escape. Parker and his two companions were stopped in Larry's automobile by police soon afterwards, and arrested after attempting to flee on foot. Larry testified that Parker personally participated in the robbery and beating. Parker testified that he had not taken part in any robbery or assault. He admitted being present during the incident, but claimed that he had simply sat and watched while another passenger assaulted Larry.]

After the trial the jury returned for instructions, asking clarification on the point of "aiding and abetting." The foreman explained:

> "* * * There is a little confusion as to how far—how much a person has to do to say that he is aiding, even at the point of can a person aid by inaction, by not leaving, if it's quite apparent to him that there is trouble * * *. Can he aid by his, say, just by his inaction at that point * * *."

The court then said:

> "The Court can do nothing but read you the law on aiding and abetting. Is that the only point that is troubling you? * * *
>
> "* * * The Court then, with the permission of counsel, will reread to the jury that portion of the instructions covering aiding and abetting. And after the Court has done so that is as far as the Court can go in assisting you with your deliberations. * * *"

* * *

> * * * 609.05 of the Statutes reads as follows: "A person is criminally liable for a crime committed by another if he intentionally aids, advises, hires, counsels, or conspires with or otherwise procures the other to commit the crime. The guilt of a defendant may be established without proof that the accused personally did every act constituting the offense charged.
>
> Whoever commits an offense or wilfully aids, abets, counsels, commands, induces or procures its commission is punishable as a principal. Whoever wilfully causes an act to be done which if directly performed by him or another would be an offense is punishable as a principal. Every person who thus wilfully participates in the commission of a crime may be found guilty of that offense. Participation is wilful if done voluntarily and purposely and with specific intent to

do some act the law forbids or with specific intent to fail to do some act the law requires to be done. That is to say, with evil motive or bad purpose either to disobey or disregard the law."

* * *

You may now resume your deliberations, ladies and gentlemen.

* * *

Defendant now contends that the foreman's question shows that the jury rejected Larry's testimony that defendant directly participated in the assault and robbery. He contends that the trial court in effect instructed the jury that defendant might in fact have owed a legal obligation to render aid to the victim. Defendant contends that he did not have such an obligation and that the failure to discharge a moral obligation to aid Larry is not enough to convict defendant of the crime charged.

1. We think it clear that the foreman's remarks fail to prove rejection by the jury of the victim's testimony about defendant's participation in the assault and robbery. The verdict indicates that the jurors resolved whatever questions they initially had. However, the question whether a person can aid by inaction may well be answered in the affirmative since inaction is often the distinguishing characteristic of the aider and abettor and is encompassed within the statute. In this regard the "lookout" is a classic example. The presence of one at the commission of a felony by another is evidence to be considered in determining whether or not he was guilty of aiding or abetting, and it has been held that presence, companionship, and conduct before and after the offense are circumstances from which one's participation in the criminal intent may be inferred.

In the instant case defendant was present during the criminal activity. He did nothing to prevent the offenses committed or the brutal beating which the victim endured. He must have known of the robbery and made no effort to stop it, and we think, under the circumstances, his presence and acts helped to make all the crimes possible. Therefore, his lack of objection under the circumstances supports his conviction.

2. It has been established that a person may aid or abet without actively participating in the overt act. If the proof shows that a person is present at the commission of a crime without disapproving or opposing it, it is competent for the jury to consider this conduct in connection with other circumstances and thereby reach the conclusion that he assented to the commission of the crime, lent to it his approval, and was thereby aiding and abetting its commission. Certainly mere presence on the part of each would be enough if it is intended to and does aid the primary actors.

* * *

We conclude that defendant's close association with the other men who appeared in the stolen car in front of the Band Box on the early morning of August 6, 1966, both before and after the crimes charged were committed, and the fact that the three of them were apprehended fleeing from the convertible stolen from the victim, all tend reasonably to justify the conclusion that defendant joined with the other two cohorts in the common purpose of assaulting the victim, robbing him, and stealing his automobile. * * * Affirmed.

STATE v. RUNDLE

Supreme Court of Wisconsin, 1993.
176 Wis.2d 985, 500 N.W.2d 916.

Opinion by: ABRAHAMSON

* * * [D]efendant, Kurt Rundle, was convicted in a jury trial of being a party to the crimes of intentional and reckless physical abuse of his daughter by intentionally aiding and abetting[1] the physical abuse inflicted by his wife, contrary to sec. 948.03(2)(b) and sec. 948.03(3)(a).[a] The court of appeals reversed the convictions, holding that the evidence was insufficient to establish the defendant's guilt as an aider and abettor to the crimes as charged. The court of appeals noted that the evidence might have supported a conviction under sec. 948.03(4), which criminalizes the failure to act to prevent a child's bodily harm.[b] The state, however, did not charge the defendant under that statute.

* * *

We conclude that the legislature intended that, in order to obtain a conviction under secs. 948.03(2)(b), 948.03(3)(a) and 939.05(2)(b), the state must prove the elements of aiding and abetting. The state must prove (1) that the defendant undertook some conduct (either verbal or overt) that as a matter of objective fact aided another person in the execution of a crime; and (2) that the defendant had a conscious desire or intent that the conduct would in fact yield such assistance. For the

1. Section 939.05 provides:

(1) Whoever is concerned in the commission of a crime is a principal and may be charged with and convicted of the commission of the crime although he did not directly commit it and although the person who directly committed it has not been convicted or has been convicted of some other crime based on the same act.

(2) A person is concerned in the commission of the crime if he:

(a) Directly commits the crime; or

(b) Intentionally aids and abets the commission of it; or

(c) Is a party to a conspiracy. . . ."

a. Section 948.03(2)(b) provided that "Whoever intentionally causes bodily harm to a child is guilty of a Class D felony. Section 948.03(3)(a) provided that "Whoever recklessly causes great bodily harm to a child is guilty of a Class D felony."—ed.

b. Under § 948.03(4) a person responsible for a child's welfare commits a felony if he fails to prevent harm to the child when he is capable of acting to prevent that harm, and he "has knowledge that another person intends to cause, is causing or has intentionally or recklessly caused great bodily harm to the child" and is capable of acting to prevent the harm. It is a more serious felony when failing to act "exposes the child to an unreasonable risk of great bodily harm by the other person or facilitates the great bodily harm to the child that is caused by the other person." When the threatened harm is not "great," the failure to act is a lesser felony.—ed.

reasons set forth, we conclude that the state did not prove aiding and abetting. Accordingly we affirm the decision of the court of appeals.

I

The material facts are not disputed for purposes of this appeal. On August 6, 1989, K.R., the three and one-half year old daughter of the defendant, was admitted to the Milwaukee County Children's Hospital. Upon her arrival at the hospital, the child was comatose, and covered with bruises and scratches of various ages. Medical personnel found that her injuries were consistent with "shaken baby syndrome," a condition marked by bleeding on the brain.[6] K.R. is blind and probably suffers from permanent brain damage and physical injuries as a result of the abuse.

Kurt Rundle was charged with four counts of child abuse, two relating to incidents in 1986 and two to incidents in 1989. Pamela Rundle was charged with two counts of child abuse relating to incidents in 1989 and one count of child abuse relating to an incident in 1988. Pamela Rundle was convicted of all charges, and the court of appeals affirmed her convictions. Kurt Rundle was acquitted of the two charges connected with incidents alleged to have taken place in 1986. He was convicted of one count of intentionally causing a child bodily harm and one count of recklessly causing a child great bodily harm as a party to the crimes.

The facts supporting the two convictions stem from two incidents which occurred between July 24, 1989, and August 6, 1989, which Kurt Rundle described to John Shlax, a social worker from the Department of Health and Social Services. The first incident occurred on July 30, 1989. On that day Pamela Rundle picked the child up and threw her several feet into the hallway of their home. Kurt Rundle, who is hearing impaired, was not present in the room at the time, but he came rushing in after feeling the vibrations from the child's fall. The second incident occurred between August 3rd and 5th in a parking lot in Madison, Wisconsin. The child had been misbehaving in the car during the return from a trip to the northern part of the state. Pamela Rundle stopped the car, pulled the child out of the car, slapped her in the face, kicked her in the knee, and dragged her by the arm so hard that she fell off her feet. Kurt Rundle told the social worker that the child might have been hurt during this incident, because he subsequently observed the child acting strangely.

Kurt and Pamela Rundle were tried together. The state's theory in prosecuting Kurt Rundle was that he aided and abetted his wife's abusive behavior. The theme of the prosecution's questioning of witnesses and closing argument was that the defendant was guilty because he "stood back" and did nothing to protect his child's physical well-being against his wife's abuse.

6. "Shaken baby syndrome" is caused by severe shaking which results in the shearing of blood vessels in the child's brain.

Much of the evidence introduced at trial detailed the constant and horrific abuse the child endured at the hands of Pamela Rundle. Family and friends of the Rundles, testifying about the child's plight, reported that they had seen Pamela Rundle slap, shake, and throw the child with as little provocation as the child's refusal to express her love for her mother.

When questioned about Kurt Rundle's role in the abuse, these same witnesses testified that the defendant did not act to prevent his wife from abusing the child. Other witnesses testified that they had discussed Pamela Rundle's abuse of the child with the defendant and that he had agreed that he should do something. One witness, Kurt Rundle's brother, testified that there were times he heard the defendant ask Pamela Rundle to stop striking the child and that at other times the defendant remained silent when his wife was slapping, striking or shaking the child.

Several witnesses who acknowledged seeing Kurt Rundle physically discipline the child on occasion testified that he did not discipline her in a forceful or injurious manner, and that he did not cause her harm. Other witnesses testified that they had never seen the defendant strike, slap or shake the child. The social worker testified that Kurt Rundle was the child's primary caretaker, that the child had a loving relation with her father, and that on one occasion the child kicked and screamed when placed in her mother's arms.

* * *

II

This case presents a single issue: To sustain a conviction for aiding and abetting intentional and reckless physical abuse of a child, must the state prove that the defendant undertook some affirmative action against the child or is it sufficient that the state prove that the defendant was a parent of the victim, was present during the administration of physical abuse by his spouse, failed to intervene to prevent physical abuse, failed to report that physical abuse, and failed to cooperate with medical personnel by not informing them how the victim sustained her injuries so that proper medical care could be undertaken?

In its case against the defendant, the state's principal theme was that Kurt Rundle did nothing to prevent his child from being abused by his wife. After eliciting evidence of the defendant's presence at the two incidents in 1989 and of his passivity, the state apparently concluded that it need not establish any further facts and ceased its inquiry. Although the burden of proof was on the state to prove every essential element of the crime charged beyond a reasonable doubt, the state made no effort to demonstrate that the defendant's behavior actually assisted his wife's physical abuse or was intended to do so, or that his behavior encouraged Pamela Rundle's abusive acts by leading her to believe he was willing to help her. * * *

* * * [R]elying on *State v. Williquette*, 129 Wis. 2d 239, 385 N.W.2d 145 (1986), the state argues that the defendant's failure to intervene constitutes aiding and abetting intentional and reckless child abuse. * * *

III

In *Williquette*, upon which the state relies, a mother of two children was convicted under the then-existing child abuse statute because she was aware that her husband was sexually and physically abusing the children, and she did nothing to prevent that abuse. The court held that a parent who fails to take any action to stop child abuse can be prosecuted * * * as a principal for exposing the child to the abuse. Section 940.201, provided as follows:

> 940.201 Abuse of children. Whoever tortures a child or subjects a child to cruel maltreatment, including, but not limited, to severe bruising, lacerations, fractured bones, burns, internal injuries or any injury constituting great bodily harm * * * is guilty of a Class E felony. * * *

The *Williquette* court concluded that * * * the phrase "subjects a child to cruel maltreatment," includes situations "in which a person with a duty toward a child exposes the child to foreseeable risk of abuse." It held that sec. 940.201 did not require an overt act of abuse to impose liability on the mother when the mother knowingly exposed her children to the risk of abusive conduct.

The state's reliance on *Williquette* is misplaced. First, *Williquette* held only that a parent who exposes a child to abuse could be convicted under 940.201 as a person who directly commits the crime. The *Williquette* court did not reach the question addressed by the court of appeals in that case, namely whether the mother had violated sec. 940.201, by aiding and abetting the father in abusing the children. In this case, the prosecution was not based on the theory that the defendant directly committed the crime; the theory of the state's case was that the defendant was an aider and abettor. Thus the *Williquette* decision, which determined who is a direct participant in the crime of child abuse under sec. 940.201, does not assist us in determining what conduct constitutes aiding and abetting child abuse.

Second, this case does not arise under the statute at issue in *Williquette*. It arises under provisions adopted in 1987, effective July 1, 1989. These provisions are part of a new chapter 948 which addresses crimes against children * * * The new child abuse law, sec. 948.03(2) and sec. 948.03(3), uses significantly different language than sec. 940.201, and now penalizes any person who intentionally or recklessly causes bodily or great bodily harm to a child. The key statutory language in sec. 940.201 * * * was eliminated in the new statutes.

* * *

Section 948.03 also includes a statutory provision explicitly criminalizing the failure of a person who is responsible for the child's welfare to act to prevent bodily harm. * * *

A legislative council memorandum explains that "the failure-to-act provisions [of sec. 948.03(4)] codify the interpretation of the current child abuse statute by the State Supreme Court in *State v. Williquette*.... The State Supreme Court in Williquette determined that a violation of the child abuse statute may occur where a parent knowingly exposes a child to a foreseeable risk of abuse or fails to act to prevent abuse."

* * *

It is apparent from the language and structure of sec. 948.03 and the statute's legislative history that the legislature intended sec. 948.03(2) and 948.03(3) to proscribe affirmative conduct and sec. 948.03(4) to proscribe acts of omission of a responsible person who is capable of taking action to prevent child abuse. The obvious purpose of drafting several subsections in sec. 948.03 was to deal separately with intentional and reckless acts which cause bodily harm or great bodily harm and the failure to act to prevent another from inflicting such harm. Addressing various types of behavior in separate subsections permitted the legislature to vary the penalties based on the nature of the conduct involved and the degree of harm caused to the child.

* * * Thus, adopting the holding of *Williquette*, the legislature declared that a parent who fails to prevent child abuse is liable as one who directly commits the crime of child abuse. The question for the court then is whether the legislature intended that the state can bypass sec. 948.03(4) by charging a defendant as a aider and abettor of intentional and reckless child abuse. In other words, when the legislature adopted sec. 948.03(4), did it intend that a defendant's failure to prevent child abuse could satisfy the requirements of aiding and abetting?

One of the elements of aiding and abetting is that the defendant engage in some conduct (either verbal or overt), that as a matter of objective fact aids another person in the execution of a crime.[18] The state reasons that in the case of a parent, who has a legal duty to protect the child, failure to act to protect the child satisfies the requirement of verbal or overt conduct under aiding and abetting. Relying on *Willi-*

18. Stated somewhat differently, "[a] person intentionally aids and abets the commission of a crime when, acting with knowledge or belief that another person is committing or intends to commit a crime, he knowingly either (a) renders aid to the person who commits the crime, or (b) is ready and willing to render aid, if needed, and the person who commits the crime knows of his willingness to aid him. However, a person does not aid and abet if he is only a bystander or spectator, innocent of any unlawful intent, and does nothing to assist or encourage the commission of a crime...." Wis. J.I. Crim. 400 (1962).

For another formulation of the aider and abettor test, *see Roehl v. State*, 77 Wis. 2d 398, 407, 253 N.W.2d 210 (1977): "[W]here one person knew the other was committing a criminal act, he should be considered a party thereto when he acted in furtherance of the other's conduct, was aware of the fact that a crime was being committed, and acquiesced or participated in its perpetration."

quette, the state contends that the special duty imposed on the defendant by virtue of his parent-child relationship with the victim brings the defendant within the provisions of sec. 948.03(2) and sec. 948.03(3) as an aider and abettor, distinguishing the defendant from a mere "bystander," and thus permitting the inference that the defendant intended to aid the commission of the crime.

* * *

* * * [W]e conclude that sec. 948.03(2) and sec. 948.03(3), read in conjunction with the aider and abettor statute, require the state to prove conduct, either verbal or overt, that as a matter of objective fact aids another person in the execution of a crime.

* * *

IV

* * *

In arguing that the defendant acted overtly because he refused to cooperate with the authorities, the state's brief relies on the defendant's statements to doctors after the 1989 incidents. The state's allegation that the defendant withheld information from medical authorities concerning the 1989 incidents seems more consistent with a theory that the defendant was an accessory after the fact than with a claim that he assisted or encouraged the abuse as it was occurring. It has been recognized that the "accessory after the fact, by virtue of his involvement only after the felony was completed, is not truly an accomplice in the felony. This category has thus remained distinct from others, and today the accessory after the fact is not deemed a participant in the felony but rather one who has obstructed justice. . . ."

* * *

The crime in this case was brutal. Pamela Rundle has been convicted of abusing her own child. Nevertheless we must conclude, as did the court of appeals, that while the evidence shows that the defendant may very well be guilty of the crime set forth in sec. 948.03(4), the evidence is insufficient to establish the defendant's guilt as an aider and abettor to the crimes as charged. We therefore affirm the decision of the court of appeals.

* * *

STEINMETZ, J. *(dissenting).*

The evidence indicating that the defendant was the victim's parent—was present when his spouse physically abused his child, failed to intervene and prevent the abuse, and failed to report the abuse to the proper authorities—was sufficient to support the jury verdict convicting Kurt Rundle of physical abuse of his daughter by aiding and abetting the physical abuse inflicted by his wife. I believe that Kurt's presence during and failure to stop his wife's abusive acts was an objective fact which aided his wife in the execution of a crime. Kurt also obviously intended his conduct to in fact render such assistance.

* * *

On July 30, 1989, Pamela Rundle threw K.R. into the hallway of the Rundle home. Although Kurt was not in the room at the time of this act, he responded to the incident because he felt the vibrations from K.R.'s landing.

Sometime between August 3rd and August 5th, 1989, in a Madison parking lot, Kurt observed Pamela slap K.R. in the face, kick K.R. in the knee, and drag K.R. until she fell to the ground. Kurt believed the child had been hurt during this incident because he subsequently observed the child acting strangely. On August 6, 1989, K.R., then three years old, arrived at the Milwaukee County Children's Hospital comatose and covered with bruises and scratches.

* * *

Kurt Rundle, who was K.R.'s father and not a mere bystander, intentionally failed to stop or report his wife's abusive acts. This behavior is consistent with his own acts toward the child in 1986, even though he was acquitted of those charges. I believe that this behavior constitutes an affirmative, overt act which aided and abetted his wife's abuse of K.R. The incident in 1988 made Kurt aware of his wife's abusive treatment prior to 1989. Despite this knowledge, Kurt failed to protect K.R. from the 1989 incidents. * * * Finally, Kurt believed that K.R. had been seriously and permanently hurt during the August 1989 incident in the Madison parking lot; nevertheless, he did nothing.

I fail to see the difference between a lookout during a burglary, who objectively aides the principal burglar by merely watching for possible danger, and Kurt's conduct in this case, which objectively aided his wife's abuse by effectively guarding against intervention by others. Similarly, a person who sits as a passenger in a stolen car knowing the car is stolen may be guilty of aiding and abetting the theft of an auto. The passenger's conduct is no more affirmative than Kurt's conduct, yet the majority concludes that Kurt is not an aider and abetter.

* * *

PEOPLE v. MONTOYA

Supreme Court of California, 1994.
7 Cal.4th 1027, 31 Cal.Rptr.2d 128, 874 P.2d 903.

GEORGE, J.

[Defendant Montoya was convicted of burglary of an inhabited dwelling. His defense at trial was that he had simply gone along with his codefendant Gaxiola, whom he understood to be removing his own property from the premises.]

I

The trial court instructed the jury as to the elements of burglary and as to liability on a theory of aiding and abetting. Defendant did not request, and the trial court did not provide, any instruction informing the jury at what point in time defendant must have formed the intent to commit, encourage, or facilitate the offense of burglary in order to be found guilty on a theory of aiding and abetting. The jury found defendant guilty of burglary of an inhabited dwelling.

On appeal, defendant contended the trial court erred in failing to instruct *sua sponte* that, in order to be found guilty on a theory of aiding and abetting, defendant must have formed the requisite intent prior to or at the time of an entry by Gaxiola into the residence. The Court of Appeal determined that the facts and circumstances of the present case were sufficiently distinguishable from those of earlier cases in which trial courts were held to have had a *sua sponte* duty to so instruct. The appellate court also held that an instruction relating to when defendant formed the requisite intent as an aider and abettor would have been inconsistent with defendant's theory that, even at the time the property was sold, he remained unaware Gaxiola had committed a burglary, and that such an instruction thus would have invited the jury to question defendant's veracity in presenting this defense. Affirming the judgment of conviction, the court therefore held that the trial court was under no obligation to provide this instruction *sua sponte*. We granted defendant's petition for review.

II

The prosecution offered two theories upon which defendant could be convicted of burglary, asserting that defendant either personally entered the residence with Gaxiola in order to commit a theft, or aided and abetted Gaxiola in the latter's commission of the offense. Before deciding whether, in light of the evidence presented at trial, the trial court erred in failing to instruct the jury *sua sponte* that an aider and abettor, prior to or at the time of an entry by the perpetrator, must have formed the intent to commit, encourage, or facilitate the commission of the offense, we first must determine the duration of the offense of burglary for purposes of the liability of an aider and abettor, because the intent of an aider and abettor must be formed before or as the offense is being committed.

Because section 31 defines as principals all who directly commit a given offense or who aid and abet in its commission, the same criminal liability attaches whether a defendant directly perpetrates the offense or aids and abets the perpetrator. (People v. Beeman (1984) 35 Cal.3d 547; People v. Brady (1987) 190 Cal.App.3d 124.) The doctrine in *Beeman* that one may be liable when he or she aids the perpetrator of an offense, knowing of the perpetrator's unlawful purpose and intending, by his or her act of aid, to commit, encourage, or facilitate commission of the offense, "snares all who intentionally contribute to the accomplishment of a crime in the net of criminal liability defined by the crime, even though the actor does not personally engage in all of the elements of the crime." (People v. Brady, supra, 190 Cal.App.3d 124, 132.) Because the aider and abettor is subject to the same criminal liability and the same potential punishment as the perpetrator, it is essential to distinguish the act and intent that constitute "aiding and abetting" the commission of a crime, from conduct that will incur the lesser liability of an "accessory" to the crime—defined as conduct by one who, "after a felony has been committed, ... aids a principal in such felony, with the intent that said principal may avoid or escape from arrest, trial, conviction or punishment, having knowledge that said principal has committed such felony or has been charged with such felony...." Penal Code § 32.

It is settled that if a defendant's liability for an offense is predicated upon the theory that he or she aided and abetted the perpetrator, the defendant's intent to encourage or facilitate the actions of the perpetrator "must be formed prior to or during 'commission' of that offense." (People v. Cooper (1991) 53 Cal.3d 1158.) Although the parties agree with this statement of the generally applicable legal principle, they disagree on the question of the duration of the offense of burglary for the purpose of establishing liability as an aider and abettor.

Defendant relies upon a line of Court of Appeal decisions that have concluded that, because the crime of burglary is complete (that is, all of the elements of the offense have been satisfied) upon the perpetrator's entry into the structure with felonious intent, a person may be found guilty as an aider and abettor only if he or she formed the requisite intent to commit, encourage, or facilitate the offense prior to or during entry by the perpetrator. [Citations] The People maintain that the reasoning of these decisions is inconsistent with the analysis contained in this court's decision in *People v. Cooper*, supra, and suggest that, under the Cooper analysis, the commission of a burglary does not terminate, for the purpose of aiding and abetting, upon the perpetrator's entry into the structure, but rather continues until the perpetrator's departure from the structure. As we explain, we conclude that our recent decision in *Cooper* supports the People's position. Accordingly, we disapprove these Court of Appeal decisions to the extent they conflict with our conclusion, explained below.

In People v. Cooper, supra, the issue of aiding and abetting arose in the context of a robbery. The defendant in *Cooper*, the driver of the getaway vehicle, contended he was unaware of the perpetrators' intent to commit the robbery until after the perpetrators already had taken the property from the immediate presence of the victim by force. The defendant asserted that, because he formed the intent to assist only after that occurrence, he could not properly be found guilty as an aider and abettor and his liability was limited to that of an accessory after the fact.

In *Cooper*, we rejected the defendant's contention, concluding that the temporal threshold for establishing guilt—a fixed point in time at which all elements of the substantive offense are satisfied so that the offense itself may be considered to have been "initially committed" rather than simply attempted—is not synonymous with the "commission" of that crime for the purpose of determining aider and abettor liability. (53 Cal.3d 1158, 1164.) We explained that in determining the duration of an offense, for the purpose of aider and abettor liability, the court must take into account the nature of the interests that the penal provision is intended to protect, emphasizing in this regard that both the victim of a crime and a potential aider and abettor frequently will not perceive an offense as "completed" simply because all elements necessary to establish guilt already have been satisfied. To illustrate this point we referred to the crime of rape, observing that "the rape victim ... would not agree that the crime was completed once the crime was initially committed (i.e., at the point of initial penetration)," but rather would consider the offense not to have ended "until all of the acts that constitute the rape have ceased." We also noted that "the unknowing defendant who happens on the scene of a rape after the rape has been initially committed and aids the perpetrator in the continuing criminal acts" reasonably would be found to have formed the intent to facilitate the rape during the commission of the rape.

Applying this analysis to the crime of robbery, we determined in *Cooper* that the crime of robbery is not completed, for aiding and abetting purposes, at the point in time at which the perpetrator has committed sufficient acts to satisfy all the elements of robbery. Instead, relying upon the circumstance that asportation (carrying away) of the stolen property is a distinct element of the crime of robbery, we concluded that, for the purpose of aiding and abetting, the duration of a robbery extends to the carrying away of the stolen property to a place of temporary safety. We held in this regard that "for conviction of the more serious offense of aiding and abetting a robbery, a getaway driver must form the intent to facilitate or encourage commission of the robbery prior to or during the carrying away of the loot to a place of temporary safety."

In the course of our discussion in *Cooper*, we noted that the crime of burglary, unlike robbery, does not include asportation as one of its elements, and thus, for the purpose of aiding and abetting, liability for burglary would not extend to a person who simply aided a burglar in the asportation of the stolen property after its removal from the burgled structure. In *Cooper*, however, we had no occasion to decide at precisely what point—the perpetrator's entry into the structure, his or her departure from the structure, or some other point—the acts constituting the crime of burglary terminate for the purpose of aiding and abetting. That question is now before us, and in resolving it we turn to the general analysis contained in our *Cooper* decision, also considering the nature of the elements of the crime of burglary and the specific interests that the law seeks to protect in defining this offense.

The crime of burglary consists of an act—unlawful entry—accompanied by the "intent to commit grand or petit larceny or any felony." (§ 459.) One may by liable for burglary upon entry with the requisite intent to commit a felony or a theft (whether felony or misdemeanor), regardless of whether the felony or theft committed is different from that contemplated at the time of entry, or whether any felony or theft actually is committed. [Citations]

It does not follow, however, that once the offense itself has been initiated, that is, the perpetrator has entered the structure with the requisite intent, an individual who, with knowledge of the perpetrator's unlawful purpose, thereafter forms the intent to commit, facilitate, or encourage commission of the offense by the perpetrator while the perpetrator still remains inside the structure, is not liable as an aider and abettor.

In People v. Gauze (1975) 15 Cal.3d 709, while observing that a burglary consists of "an entry which invades a possessory right in a building," we had occasion to review the broad underlying basis for the criminal sanction against the particular act and intent constituting burglary. Therein, we quoted the rationale set forth in People v. Lewis (1969) 274 Cal.App.2d 912, 920: "Burglary laws are based primarily upon a recognition of the dangers to personal safety created by the usual burglary situation—the danger that the intruder will harm the occupants in attempting to perpetrate the intended crime or to escape and the danger that the occupants will in anger or panic react violently to the invasion, thereby inviting more violence. The laws are primarily designed, then, not to deter the trespass and the intended crime, which are prohibited by other laws, so much as to forestall the germination of a situation dangerous to personal safety. Section 459, in short, is aimed at the danger caused by the unauthorized entry itself."

* * * Although the decisions generally have emphasized this aspect of the danger to personal safety created by the offense of burglary, other authority, involving factual circumstances in which actual danger appears not to exist or is relatively minor, and relying upon the purpose of the statute to protect against an invasion of a possessory right, has concluded that the threat to property interests alone, created by the burglar's entry and continued presence inside the structure, supports a finding of burglary. [Citations]

It is manifest that the increased danger to the personal safety of the occupant, and the increased risk of loss or damage to his or her property contemplated by the statutory proscription, do not terminate at the moment entry is accomplished, but rather continue while the perpetrator remains inside the structure. Certainly, an absent occupant could return at any moment and be faced with the danger created by the prior entry. Thus, one who learns that the perpetrator unlawfully has entered with intent to commit a felony or theft, who forms the requisite intent to assist, and who does assist—by independently contributing to the commission of the crime or by otherwise making it more likely that the crime will be successfully completed than would be the case absent such participation—logically should be liable as an aider and abettor rather than as a mere accessory.

Moreover, as long as the perpetrator remains inside the structure, the increased danger to the personal safety of the occupant and the increased risk of loss or damage to his or her property continues, whether the perpetrator commits a felony or theft different from that intended at the time of entry, or even if no felony or theft is completed. m The appearance and assistance of an aider and abettor, even if belated, contribute to and perpetuate this increased danger and risk. For example, an individual might learn of the perpetrator's earlier entry with the requisite intent, form his own intent to facilitate that offense, and commence acting as a "lookout" at the point of entry, on behalf of the perpetrator. The presence of the "lookout," by prolonging the perpetrator's presence in the structure, may increase the chance of an encounter between the perpetrator and a returning occupant.

Nor should the liability of an individual for aiding and abetting a perpetrator be negated by the circumstance that the aider and abettor forms the intent to assist in the commission of the offense only after entry by the perpetrator. We understand the concern articulated by the Court of Appeal in People v. Brady, supra, 190 Cal.App.3d 124, that, because (with some exceptions) no burglary has been committed by the perpetrator if his or her intent to commit a felony or theft arose after entry, "the culpability of the assistant to the thief, whose intent to aid does not arise until after the entry of the thief, must be judged by the same rule." Nonetheless, we believe that this comment does not fully recognize the significance of the distinct mens rea requirements for burglary and for aiding and abetting.

In People v. Croy (1985) 41 Cal.3d 1, we discussed the nature of the intent required to establish liability as an aider and abettor. Noting that "one may aid or abet in the commission of a crime without having previously entered into a conspiracy to commit it," and that an aider and abettor may be liable not only for a crime that, to one's knowledge, one's colleagues are contemplating committing, but also for the natural and reasonable consequences of any act that one knowingly aided or encouraged, we stated: "It follows that a defendant whose liability is predicated on his status as an aider and abettor need not have intended to encourage or facilitate the particular offense ultimately committed by the perpetrator. His knowledge that an act which is criminal was intended, and his action taken with the intent that the act be encouraged or facilitated, are sufficient to impose liability on him for any reasonably foreseeable offense committed as a consequence by the perpetrator. It is the intent to encourage and bring about conduct that is criminal, not the specific intent that is an element of the target offense, which *Beeman* holds must be found by the jury."

Therefore, if an individual happens upon a scene in which a perpetrator unlawfully has entered with intent to commit a felony or theft, and, upon learning of that circumstance, forms the intent to facilitate the perpetrator's illegal purpose in entering, that individual incurs the liability of an aider and abettor, commensurate with the liability of the perpetrator. This conclusion in turn compels the analogous conclusion that an aider and abettor is not liable for burglary (just as the perpetrator is not liable) where the perpetrator formed the intent to commit a felony or theft only following the entry. Contrary to the suggestion in People v. Brady, supra, 190 Cal.App.3d 124, it is this result that "preserves the symmetry of culpability of the aider and abettor" with that of the perpetrator. * * *

We conclude that a person who, with the requisite knowledge and intent, aids the perpetrator, may be found liable on a theory of aiding and abetting if he or she formed the intent to commit, encourage, or facilitate the commission of a burglary prior to the time the perpetrator finally departed from the structure. We also conclude that, in light of the record in the present case, the trial court had no duty, absent a specific request by defendant, to instruct the jury with regard to the point in time by which an aider or abettor must have formed the requisite intent. Accordingly, the judgment of the Court of Appeal is affirmed.

[Concurring opinion omitted.]

VADEN v. STATE

Supreme Court of Alaska, 1989.
768 P.2d 1102.

COMPTON, JUSTICE.

This petition arises out of convictions of two hunting guides, Douglas Vaden and Floyd Saltz, Jr., following undercover operations by the State of Alaska. * * *

I. Factual and Procedural Background

A. Vaden

In November 1983, a horse wrangler employed by Vaden during the 1983 hunting season informed Fish and Wildlife Protection officers of illegal hunting methods allegedly used by Vaden while guiding a foreign hunter. In the spring of 1984, John Snell, an undercover agent for the Alaska Department of Fish & Game posing as a hunter, contracted for guiding services from Vaden. Snell was instructed on how to conduct himself on the hunt.

During the hunt Snell shot and killed four foxes from Vaden's aircraft. The season on foxes was closed at that time. Vaden provided Snell with the shotgun used to shoot the foxes, and maneuvered the aircraft so Snell could shoot the foxes. The fox carcasses were then transported to Anchorage by Vaden. Vaden was convicted, as an accomplice, on four counts of taking foxes from an aircraft and four counts of taking foxes during closed season. He was also convicted in his own right on three counts of possession and transportation of illegally taken game. He was acquitted on several other counts, including solicitation of the agent's takings.

Vaden appealed his convictions, contending that no illegal acts were committed by Snell and thus no criminal liability could attach to Vaden for "aiding and abetting" or transportation of illegally taken game, and alternatively, if crimes had been committed by Snell, such law enforcement tactics amounted to entrapment as a matter of law and violated due process. The court of appeals upheld Vaden's convictions. * * *

B. Saltz

In October 1984, undercover agent Thomas Pagel, posing as a client, accompanied licensed assistant guide Floyd Saltz into the bush.

Initially Pagel had contracted for a fishing trip. Pagel apparently expressed a desire to hunt on the trip also and questioned Saltz about hunting. Pagel testified that Saltz responded by saying "you could not kill a caribou the same day you were airborne but that once you got in the bush you did basically what the hell you wanted to."

On October 6 the pair flew out to Talarik Creek. Pagel testified that Saltz told him the area was limited to flyfishing only and gave him a fly rod. A short time later Saltz decided the fishing was slow and gave Pagel a baited spinning rod. The pair then caught about thirty trout on spinning gear. Pagel also testified that after the trout stopped biting the pair began catching Northern Pike. According to Pagel, Saltz caught 20 to 30 pike, killed them and threw them into the lake.

On October 7 Saltz flew Pagel into an area with little air traffic for a caribou hunt. Saltz handed Pagel a rifle and pointed out which bull caribou to shoot. Pagel shot and killed the bull. Saltz also pointed out a cow caribou for Pagel to shoot. However, Pagel gave Saltz the rifle and Saltz shot the cow. They did not salvage the meat from the cow. Saltz allegedly shot at another bull, but it is not clear whether it was killed. After the two took pictures of the bull Pagel shot, they started to skin it. While working on the hindquarters, Saltz told Pagel the meat was not worth salvaging because the caribou "smelled as if it was in rut." Pagel indicated he wanted the antlers and Saltz salvaged them. The pair left the meat. Saltz testified to a different version of facts. He claimed Pagel initiated the fishing violations. He also claimed Pagel was left alone and shot the caribou while Saltz was not present, and that it was Pagel's idea to leave the meat behind.

The offenses with which Saltz was charged grew out of three basic incidents: (1) Pagel's killing and wasting of a bull caribou the same day he was airborne, (2) Saltz's killing and wasting of a cow caribou the same day he was airborne, and (3) both parties' use of illegal fishing gear and waste of fish. Saltz's pretrial motions to dismiss were denied by the trial court. At trial, the jury believed Pagel's version and convicted Saltz on all 16 counts alleged against him, including soliciting the violations.

* * *

II. Discussion

A. Legality of the Undercover Agent's Activities

Initially Vaden challenged his "aiding and abetting" and transportation convictions on the ground that the undercover agent's actions were legal. Saltz challenged his guide "aiding and abetting" and transportation convictions on the same grounds. They argue that for these convictions to be sustained, someone must have committed an illegal act. See United States v. Sanford, 547 F.2d 1085 (9th Cir.1976). (To sustain convictions under Lacey Act interstate transportation of illegally killed game, undercover agent's actions must be illegal). We agree with the court of appeals that the agents committed the offenses. However, it is irrelevant whether the agents' acts were authorized. As explained below, if the agents had a justification defense it was personal to them.

B. Applicability of Justification Defenses to Accomplices' Liability

Both Vaden and Saltz argue that they could avail themselves of the public authority justification defense available to Snell and Pagel. It is not necessary to decide whether an undercover agent in these circumstances may utilize a public authority justification defense. As the court of appeals concluded, a justification defense is personal to the undercover agent and not transferable to the accomplice.... It is clear from our statutory scheme that a principal does not need to be found guilty or even prosecuted in order to convict the accomplice. Because the accomplice's state of mind is the focus, defenses of entrapment, duress and heat of passion are not imputed to the accomplice. The entrapment defense has been likened to an immunity from prosecution based on government conduct. The public authority justification defense operates to immunize the public official from criminal liability for acts within the scope of the officials' authority. Because entrapment and the public authority justification defense are similar in this regard, even if the public authority defense were available to the undercover agents, neither Vaden nor Saltz could avail himself of the agent's defense.

[The court went on to hold that the actions of Snell and Pagel did not constitute either entrapment or outrageous government conduct in violation of due process.]

For the above reasons we affirm the convictions of Vaden and Saltz.

BURKE, JUSTICE, with whom MOORE, JUSTICE, joins, dissenting.

The danger to Alaska's resources posed by persons willing to assist others in the violation of state fish and game laws is both obvious and substantial. There must, however, be limits upon the degree of police involvement in criminal activity which will be tolerated. When the police or their agents commit criminal acts in order to charge others as accessories to those same acts, in my view the line is crossed. * * *

The accomplice liability charges should fail on another ground as well: the long-standing common law rule that the acts of a feigned accomplice may never be imputed to the targeted defendant for purposes of obtaining a conviction. In State v. Neely, 90 Mont. 199, 300 P. 561 (1931), the Montana Supreme Court applied this principle under circumstances akin to those in the case at bar. In *Neely,* a cattle owner employed a detective, Harrington, to "get in" with suspected cattle thieves during an act of cattle rustling. Harrington associated himself with the criminal enterprise, and the crime was carried out. Harrington himself, however, committed the principal offense of purloining the cattle, while the targeted suspect merely stood watch outside the premises and offered various other forms of assistance before and after commission of the offense. The court reversed Neely's conviction as an accomplice to the crime. * * *

The principle enunciated in *Neely,* which has been repeated by numerous courts under a variety of factual circumstances, is based in sound reason. It is the general rule that one who aids and abets another in criminal activity is liable for all of the "natural and probable consequences" of his accomplice's criminal acts. Thus, the potential for abuse inherent in law enforcement methods such as those employed in the case at bar is substantial. Once an agent has succeeded in persuading an individual to take some substantial act in furtherance of his general criminal scheme, the ultimate liability of the targeted defendant, if any, will depend upon which foreseeable crimes the agent chooses to commit in order to secure convictions against his criminal "accomplice."

In this case, Officer Snell shot four foxes. Vaden, as pilot of the plane from which they were shot, was charged with four separate criminal counts of taking foxes from the air out of season. Had Snell opted to shoot a fifth fox, one more count could have been added to Vaden's indictment. In my view, it is clearly inconsistent with due process principles, and manifestly unjust, that the ultimate criminal liability of a defendant should be made to depend upon the good aim and/or the good intentions of the police officer charged with securing his arrest.

I would uphold those of Saltz' convictions which were based upon his independent criminal acts. However, I would reverse those convictions, for both Saltz and Vaden, which could not have been established but for the illegal acts of the government agents in this case, i.e., the accomplice liability and transportation of illegally taken game charges. In my view, these convictions fall squarely within the parameters of the due process/outrageous conduct defense * * *. Alternatively, even if the police conduct could not be deemed sufficiently "outrageous" to satisfy the requirements of the due process defense, I would hold that the convictions for accomplice liability must fail under the common law rule prohibiting imputation of the acts of a feigned accomplice to a targeted criminal defendant.

Note

The common law recognized four distinct ways in which one could culpably participate in a felony:

(1) The *principal in the first degree* was the immediate perpetrator of the crime. He might commit the crime with his own hands, or an instrument, or by the use of an innocent agent, such as an animal, an idiot, or a child.

(2) The *principal in the second degree,* or abettor, was one actually or constructively present at the scene of the crime who aided or encouraged its commission without directly participating. The classic instance of "constructive presence" was the lookout for a gang of robbers, who was considered to be a principal in the second degree even if he remained outside or at some distance from the premises at which the robbery occurred.

(3) The *accessory before the fact* was one who aided or encouraged the commission of the felony without being actually or constructively present at the time of perpetration.

(4) The *accessory after the fact* was one who knowingly assisted the felon to escape or to avoid punishment. This type of complicity should be distinguished from the separate misdemeanor of misprision of felony. In theory at least, one could commit misprision simply by failing to report a known felony to the authorities, although one took no steps to assist the escape of the felon.

This terminology was employed only with respect to ordinary felonies. Treason was regarded as so heinous a crime that a party of any of the four types was considered to be a principal. In misdemeanor cases, parties of the first three types were described as principals, and accessories after the fact were not punished at all.

The distinction between degrees of *principals* in felony cases had no practical significance. Each could be convicted independently of whatever crime he committed. The distinction between principals and accessories had considerable procedural significance, however. The rule was that an accessory could not be convicted until a principal had been convicted, and anything that prevented conviction of the principal would thus prevent conviction of the accessory. In addition, there was a problem of jurisdiction: the principal was subject to trial in the jurisdiction where the crime occurred, but the accessory could be prosecuted only where his act of accessoryship occurred. The common law rules of principals and accessories are obsolete in most jurisdictions today. The accessory after the fact is no longer considered a party to the original felony, but is prosecuted for the separate statutory offense of obstruction of justice. Modern statutes typically describe all other accessories and abettors as principals. One who assists or encourages a crime may be prosecuted independently of the immediate perpetrator, either in the jurisdiction where the crime occurred or where his own acts were committed.

The Model Penal Code

Section 2.06. Liability for Conduct of Another; Complicity

(1) A person is guilty of an offense if it is committed by his own conduct or by the conduct of another person for which he is legally accountable, or both.

(2) A person is legally accountable for the conduct of another person when:

(a) acting with the kind of culpability that is sufficient for the commission of the offense, he causes an innocent or irresponsible person to engage in such conduct; or

(b) he is made accountable for the conduct of such other person by the Code or by the law defining the offense; or

(c) he is an accomplice of such other person in the commission of the offense.

(3) A person is an accomplice of another person in the commission of an offense if:

(a) with the purpose of promoting or facilitating the commission of the offense, he

(i) solicits such other person to commit it; or

(ii) aids or agrees or attempts to aid such other person in planning or committing it; or

(iii) having a legal duty to prevent the commission of the offense, fails to make proper effort so to do; or

(b) his conduct is expressly declared by law to establish his complicity.

(4) When causing a particular result is an element of an offense, an accomplice in the conduct causing such result is an accomplice in the commission of that offense, if he acts with the kind of culpability, if any, with respect to that result that is sufficient for the commission of the offense.

(5) A person who is legally incapable of committing a particular offense himself may be guilty thereof if it is committed by the conduct of another person for which he is legally accountable, unless such liability is inconsistent with the purpose of the provision establishing his incapacity.

(6) Unless otherwise provided by the Code or by the law defining the offense, a person is not an accomplice in an offense committed by another person if:

(a) he is a victim of that offense; or

(b) the offense is so defined that his conduct is inevitably incident to its commission; or

(c) he terminates his complicity prior to the commission of the offense and

(i) wholly deprives it of effectiveness in the commission of the offense; or

(ii) gives timely warning to the law enforcement authorities or otherwise makes proper effort to prevent the commission of the offense.

(7) An accomplice may be convicted on proof of the commission of the offense and of his complicity therein, though the person claimed to have committed the offense has not been prosecuted or convicted or has been convicted of a different offense or degree of offense or has an immunity to prosecution or conviction or has been acquitted.

The New York Penal Law

§ 20.00 Criminal Liability for Conduct of Another

When one person engages in conduct which constitutes an offense, another person is criminally liable for such conduct when, acting with the mental culpability required for the commission thereof, he solicits, requests, commands, importunes, or intentionally aids such person to engage in such conduct.

§ 20.05 Criminal Liability for Conduct of Another; no Defense

In any prosecution for an offense in which the criminal liability of the defendant is based upon the conduct of another person pursuant to section 20.00, it is no defense that:

1. Such other person is not guilty of the offense in question owing to criminal irresponsibility or other legal incapacity or exemption, or to unawareness of the criminal nature of the conduct in question or of the defendant's criminal purpose or to other factors precluding the mental state required for the commission of the offense in question; or

2. Such other person has not been prosecuted for or convicted of any offense based upon the conduct in question, or has previously been acquitted thereof, or has legal immunity from prosecution therefor; or

3. The offense in question, as defined, can be committed only by a particular class or classes of persons, and the defendant, not belonging to such class or classes, is for that reason legally incapable of committing the offense in an individual capacity.

§ 20.10 Criminal Liability for Conduct of Another; Exemption

Notwithstanding the provisions of sections 20.00 and 20.05, a person is not criminally liable for conduct of another person constituting an offense when his own conduct, though causing or aiding the commission of such offense, is of a kind that is necessarily incidental thereto. If such conduct constitutes a related but separate offense upon the part of the actor, he is liable for that offense only and not for the conduct or offense committed by the other person.[a]

§ 20.15 Convictions for Different Degrees of Offense

Except as otherwise expressly provided in this chapter, when, pursuant to section 20.00, two or more persons are criminally liable for an offense which is divided into degrees, each person is guilty of such degree as is compatible with his own culpable mental state and with his own accountability for an aggravating fact or circumstance.

a. "The kinds of reciprocal conduct and offenses with which this section deals are aptly illustrated by the correlative acts and crimes of bribe giving and bribe receiving. Under the former Penal Law, a fairly logical if strained argument could be made that a bribe giver was not only guilty of that crime but also of bribe receiving by virtue of aiding the actual receiver to commit his offense, and *vice versa;* and under the provisions of revised § 20.00, without more, the same contention might also carry some weight." New York Penal Law, Practice Commentary to § 20.10.

§ 20.20 Criminal Liability of Corporations

1. As used in this section:

(a) "Agent" means any director, officer, or employee of a corporation, or any other person who is authorized to act in behalf of the corporation.

(b) "High managerial agent" means an officer of a corporation or any other agent in a position of comparable authority with respect to the formulation of corporate policy or the supervision in a managerial capacity of subordinate employees.

2. A corporation is guilty of an offense when:

(a) The conduct constituting the offense consists of an omission to discharge a specific duty of affirmative performance imposed on corporations by law; or

(b) The conduct constituting the offense is engaged in, authorized, solicited, requested, commanded, or recklessly tolerated by the board of directors or by a high managerial agent acting within the scope of his employment and in behalf of the corporation; or

(c) The conduct constituting the offense is engaged in by an agent of the corporation while acting within the scope of his employment and in behalf of the corporation and (i) the offense is a misdemeanor or a violation, or (ii) the offense is one defined by a statute which clearly indicates a legislative intent to impose such criminal liability on a corporation.

§ 20.25 Criminal Liability of an Individual for Corporate Conduct

A person is criminally liable for conduct constituting an offense which he performs or causes to be performed in the name of or in behalf of a corporation to the same extent as if such conduct were performed in his own name or behalf.

PEOPLE v. MARSHALL

Supreme Court of Michigan, 1961.
362 Mich. 170, 106 N.W.2d 842.

SMITH, JUSTICE.

At approximately 3:00 a.m. on the morning of February 4, 1958, a car driven by Neal McClary, traveling in the wrong direction on the Edsel Ford Expressway, crashed head-on into another vehicle driven by James Coldiron. The drivers of both cars were killed. Defendant William Marshall has been found guilty of involuntary manslaughter of Coldiron. At the time that the fatal accident took place, he, the defendant William Marshall, was in bed at his place of residence. His connection with it was that he owned the car driven by McClary, and as the evidence tended to prove, he voluntarily gave his keys to the car to McClary, with knowledge that McClary was drunk.

The principal issue in the case is whether, upon these facts, the defendant may be found guilty of involuntary manslaughter. It is axiomatic that "criminal guilt under our law is personal fault." * * *

The State relies on a case, Story v. United States, 16 F.2d 342, in which the owner, driving with a drunk, permitted him to take the wheel, and was held liable for aiding and abetting him "in his criminal negligence." The owner, said the court, sat by his side and permitted him "without protest so recklessly and negligently to operate the car as to cause the death of another." If defendant Marshall had been by McClary's side an entirely different case would be presented, but on the facts before us Marshall was at home in bed. The State also points out that although it is only a misdemeanor to drive while drunk, yet convictions for manslaughter arising out of drunk driving have often been sustained. It argues from these cases that although it was only a misdemeanor for an owner to turn his keys over to a drunk driver, nevertheless a conviction for manslaughter may be sustained if such driver kills another. This does not follow from such cases as *Story,* supra. In the case before us death resulted from the misconduct of the driver. The accountability of the owner must rest as a matter of general principle, upon his complicity in such misconduct. In turning his keys over, he was guilty of a specific offense, for which he incurred a specific penalty. Upon these facts he cannot be held a principal with respect to the fatal accident: the killing of Coldiron was not counselled by him, accomplished by another acting jointly with him, nor did it occur in the attempted achievement of some common enterprise.

This is not to say that defendant is guilty of nothing. He was properly found guilty of violation of paragraph (b) of § 625 of the Michigan vehicle code which makes it punishable for the owner of an automobile knowingly to permit it to be driven by a person "who is under the influence of intoxicating liquor." The State urges that this is not enough, that its manslaughter theory, above outlined, "was born of necessity," and that the urgency of the drunk-driver problem "has made it incumbent upon responsible and concerned law enforcement officials to seek new approaches to a new problem within the limits of our law." What the State actually seeks from us is an interpretation that the manslaughter statute imposes an open-end criminal liability. That is to say, whether the owner may ultimately go to prison for manslaughter or some lesser offense will depend upon whatever unlawful act the driver commits while in the car. * * * We are not unaware of the magnitude of the problem presented, but the new approaches demanded for its solution rest with the legislature, not the courts.

PEOPLE v. WHEELER

Supreme Court of Colorado, 1989.
772 P.2d 101.

ROVIRA, JUSTICE.

The defendant, Laurie Wheeler, was convicted of criminally negligent homicide * * * Wheeler and her common-law husband, Mitchell

Anderson, lived in a triplex in Colorado Springs. Timothy Bothun, the victim, lived in another apartment in the same triplex. On the evening of September 23, 1986, Wheeler and Anderson left their apartment at about 7:30 p.m., leaving their three children in the care of Michelle Knight. During the evening Bothun and Knight talked about Wheeler. This discussion resulted in Bothun becoming angry at Wheeler.

When Wheeler and Anderson returned home, Anderson drove Knight home. During Anderson's absence, Wheeler and Bothun struck each other during the course of an argument. When Anderson returned, a fight began between him and Bothun. This fight was eventually broken up. Wheeler and Anderson entered their apartment while Bothun and a friend, Matthew Martin, who witnessed the evening's events, returned to Bothun's apartment.

A short time later, Anderson entered Bothun's apartment with a knife in his hand saying, "You hit my old lady. I'll kill you you son of a bitch." Wheeler followed Anderson into Bothun's apartment. Another fight started between Anderson and Bothun. When Anderson was on the floor with Bothun on top of him, Wheeler jumped on Bothun's back and pulled his head back by his hair. Martin, who had been present during the altercation, saw that Anderson's knife had been plunged into Bothun's side. After the knife had been withdrawn, Martin took the knife away from Anderson. Wheeler and Anderson returned to their apartment, and the police were called. Bothun died from the stab wound. At trial, Martin testified that, while Wheeler was not trying to help Anderson stab Bothun, "she wasn't trying to prevent it either." He also testified that the stabbing happened so quickly that it could not have been prevented by a bystander.

Wheeler and Anderson were charged with first degree murder, [but Wheeler's trial was severed from Anderson's at her request and the People reduced the charge against her to second degree murder.]

When the case was submitted to the jury, the trial court instructed the jury, over Wheeler's objection, on the lesser included offenses of manslaughter and criminally negligent homicide, and a complicity instruction was also given. After the jury returned a verdict of guilty to the offense of criminally negligent homicide, Wheeler moved for judgment of acquittal on the ground that it is a logical and legal impossibility to commit the crime of criminally negligent homicide by complicity.

In its order granting the motion, the trial court first noted that the prosecution relied on a complicity theory in prosecuting Wheeler, and she was found guilty of criminally negligent homicide under such a theory. The court also noted that Wheeler was acquitted of second degree murder and manslaughter. After setting out the essential elements necessary to show complicity, the court stated:

> The important requirement as it relates to this case is that the complicitor must have had knowledge that the principal intended to commit the crime. Criminally negligent homicide is an unintentional killing caused by the actor's failure to perceive a substantial and unjusti-

fiable risk that a certain result will occur.... A finding that a defendant intended to perpetrate an unintentional killing or a finding that one had knowledge that another intended to perpetrate an unintentional killing is a logical impossibility. The trial court concluded by holding that because there can be no crime of criminally negligent homicide by a complicitor, and given the fact that Wheeler was acquitted of second degree murder and manslaughter, she has been acquitted.

* * *

The trial court ruled that a verdict of guilty of criminally negligent homicide on a theory of complicity is a logical and legal impossibility because it requires a finding that a complicitor knew that the principal intended to perpetrate an unintentional killing. A careful examination of the definitions in the criminal code reveals the fallacy in this argument.

* * *

A person commits criminally negligent homicide when he causes the death of another person by performing an act if, when he does the act, he fails to perceive a substantial and unjustifiable risk that a result will occur (namely, death) through a gross deviation from the standard of care that a reasonable person would exercise.

When doing the act the principal need not intend to cause a specific result, death. What is required is that he voluntarily engage in an act and, while engaging in the act, he fails to perceive a risk that a result will occur through a gross deviation from the standard of care that a reasonable person would exercise. Therefore, for a person to be guilty of criminally negligent homicide through a theory of complicity, he need not know that death will result from the principal's conduct because the principal need not know that. However, the complicitor must be aware that the principal is engaging in conduct that grossly deviates from the standard of reasonable care and poses a substantial and unjustifiable risk of death to another. In addition, he must aid or abet the principal in that conduct and, finally, death must result from that conduct. A verdict of guilty of criminally negligent homicide on a theory of complicity, therefore, does not involve an intent to promote or facilitate an unintentional act.

Accordingly, we reverse the judgment of the trial court and remand the case for the conviction to be reinstated.

ERICKSON, JUSTICE, dissenting:

* * * The defendant's conviction does not, in my view, square with our criminally negligent homicide or complicity statutes. Under the theory of complicity, a defendant is legally accountable as a principal for the behavior of another if, with the intent to promote or facilitate the commission of the unlawful act, the defendant aids, abets, or advises the other person in planning or committing the act. * * *

The issue raised is whether the evidence would support a conviction of Anderson for criminally negligent homicide because in my view, absent such evidence, Wheeler could not be guilty of being a complicitor to that crime. The act of the principal is the measure of whether a party is accountable as a complicitor. The principal in this case, Mitchell Anderson, entered a plea of guilty to second-degree murder and was sentenced to twenty-four years in the department of corrections. Anderson took a large knife from his apartment, marched down to the decedent's apartment, told the decedent that he was going to kill him, and then proceeded to stab the victim, killing him. * * * There was nothing negligent about Anderson's conduct. Rather, his behavior evidenced an intentional, methodical plan effectively conceived and executed. * * * Since there is no evidence that Anderson committed criminally negligent homicide, Wheeler could not have assisted Anderson in the commission of that crime.

Moreover, a person cannot be a complicitor to criminally negligent homicide. * * * The critical factor in imputing criminal responsibility under the complicity doctrine is the defendant's intent to promote or facilitate the commission of the unlawful act. I share the trial judge's view that it is not logical to hold that an accused complicitor intended to promote or facilitate unintentional conduct such as criminally negligent homicide. It is incongruous to say that one person intended to facilitate an act when the actor himself did not intend to commit that act. * * * Accordingly, I would affirm the trial court's order setting aside the jury's verdict and the entry of a judgment of acquittal on the charge.

Note

In Bogdanov v. People, 941 P.2d 247 (Colo.1997), the Colorado Supreme Court emphasized that "the rule of *Wheeler* should only be applied to crimes defined in terms of recklessness or negligence, and should not be applied to dispense with the requirement that the complicitor have the requisite culpable mental state of the underlying crime with which he is charged." The court then concluded that "the Colorado complicity statute sets forth a dual mental state requirement for the complicitor. First, the complicitor must have the culpable mental state required for the underlying crime committed by the principal. Second, the complicitor must intend that his own conduct promote or facilitate the commission of the crime committed by the principal."

2. *Liability for the Acts of Co-conspirators*

Conspiracy is an independent crime. Because of its inchoate character, one who enters into a conspiracy is guilty of that crime regardless of the conspirators' success at achieving their target crimes. Conspiracy also serves as a basis for group liability. A conspirator may be liable for crimes committed by co-conspirators in which he did not participate.

a. Involvement in the Criminal Enterprise

PEOPLE v. LAURIA

California Court of Appeal, Second District, Division 2, 1967.
251 Cal.App.2d 471, 59 Cal.Rptr. 628.

FLEMING, ASSOCIATE JUSTICE.

In an investigation of call-girl activity the police focused their attention on three prostitutes actively plying their trade on call, each of whom was using Lauria's telephone answering service, presumably for business purposes.

On January 8, 1965, Stella Weeks, a policewoman, signed up for telephone service with Lauria's answering service. Mrs. Weeks, in the course of her conversation with Lauria's office manager, hinted broadly that she was a prostitute concerned with the secrecy of her activities and their concealment from the police. She was assured that the operation of the service was discreet and "about as safe as you can get." It was arranged that Mrs. Weeks need not leave her address with the answering service, but could pick up her calls and pay her bills in person.

On February 11, Mrs. Weeks talked to Lauria on the telephone and told him her business was modelling and she had been referred to the answering service by Terry, one of the three prostitutes under investigation. She complained that because of the operation of the service she had lost two valuable customers, referred to as tricks. Lauria defended his service and said that her friends had probably lied to her about having left calls for her. But he did not respond to Mrs. Weeks' hints that she needed customers in order to make money, other than to invite her to his house for a personal visit in order to get better acquainted. In the course of his talk he said "his business was taking messages."

On February 15, Mrs. Weeks talked on the telephone to Lauria's office manager and again complained of two lost calls, which she described as a $50 and a $100 trick. On investigation the office manager could find nothing wrong, but she said she would alert the switchboard operators about slip-ups on calls.

On April 1 Lauria and the three prostitutes were arrested. Lauria complained to the police that this attention was undeserved, stating that Hollywood Call Board had 60 to 70 prostitutes on its board while his own service had only 9 or 10, that he kept separate records for known or suspected prostitutes for the convenience of himself and the police. When asked if his records were available to police who might come to the office to investigate call girls, Lauria replied that they were whenever the police had a specific name. However, his service didn't "arbitrarily tell the police about prostitutes on our board. As long as they pay their bills we tolerate them." In a subsequent voluntary appearance before the Grand Jury Lauria testified he had always cooperated with the police. But he admitted he knew some of his customers were prostitutes, and he knew Terry was a prostitute because he had personally used her services, and he knew she was paying for 500 calls a month.

Lauria and the three prostitutes were indicted for conspiracy to commit prostitution, and nine overt acts were specified. Subsequently the trial court set aside the indictment as having been brought without reasonable or probable cause. (Pen.Code, § 995.) The People have appealed claiming that a sufficient showing of an unlawful agreement to further prostitution was made.

To establish agreement, the People need show no more than a tacit, mutual understanding between coconspirators to accomplish an unlawful act. Here the People attempted to establish a conspiracy by showing that Lauria, well aware that his codefendants were prostitutes who received business calls from customers through his telephone answering service, continued to furnish them with such service. This approach attempts to equate knowledge of another's criminal activity with conspiracy to further such criminal activity, and poses the question of the criminal responsibility of a furnisher of goods or services who knows his product is being used to assist the operation of an illegal business. Under what circumstances does a supplier become a part of a conspiracy to further an illegal enterprise by furnishing goods or services which he knows are to be used by the buyer for criminal purposes?

The two leading cases on this point face in opposite directions. In United States v. Falcone, 311 U.S. 205, the sellers of large quantities of sugar, yeast, and cans were absolved from participation in a moonshining conspiracy among distillers who bought from them, while in Direct Sales Co. v. United States, 319 U.S. 703, a wholesaler of drugs was convicted of conspiracy to violate the federal narcotic laws by selling drugs in quantity to a codefendant physician who was supplying them to addicts. The distinction between these two cases appears primarily based on the proposition that distributors of such dangerous products as drugs are required to exercise greater discrimination in the conduct of their business than are distributors of innocuous substances like sugar and yeast.

In the earlier case, *Falcone,* the sellers' knowledge of the illegal use of the goods was insufficient by itself to make the sellers participants in a conspiracy with the distillers who bought from them. Such knowledge fell short of proof of a conspiracy, and evidence on the volume of sales was too vague to support a jury finding that respondents knew of the conspiracy from the size of the sales alone.

In the later case of *Direct Sales,* the conviction of a drug wholesaler for conspiracy to violate federal narcotic laws was affirmed on a showing that it had actively promoted the sale of morphine sulphate in quantity and had sold codefendant physician, who practiced in a small town in South Carolina, more than 300 times his normal requirements of the drug, even though it had been repeatedly warned of the dangers of unrestricted sales of the drug. The court contrasted the restricted goods involved in *Direct Sales* with the articles of free commerce involved in *Falcone:* "All articles of commerce may be put to illegal ends," said the court. "But all do not have inherently the same susceptibility to harmful and illegal use. * * * This difference is important for two purposes. One is for making certain that the seller knows the buyer's intended illegal use. The other is to show that by the sale he intends to further, promote and cooperate in it. This intent, when given effect by overt act, is the gist of conspiracy. While it is not identical with mere knowledge that another purposes unlawful action, it is not unrelated to such knowledge. * * * The step from knowledge to intent and agreement may be taken. There is more than suspicion, more than knowledge, acquiescence, carelessness, indifference, lack of concern. There is informed and interested cooperation, stimulation, instigation. And there is also a 'stake in the venture' which, even if it may not be essential, is not irrelevant to the question of conspiracy." (319 U.S. at 710–713.)

While *Falcone* and *Direct Sales* may not be entirely consistent with each other in their full implications, they do provide us with a framework for the criminal liability of a supplier of lawful goods or services put to unlawful use. Both the element of *knowledge* of the illegal use of the goods or services and the element of *intent* to further that use must be present in order to make the supplier a participant in a criminal conspiracy.

Proof of *knowledge* is ordinarily a question of fact and requires no extended discussion in the present case. The knowledge of the supplier was sufficiently established when Lauria admitted he knew some of his customers were prostitutes and admitted he knew that Terry, an active subscriber to his service, was a prostitute. In the face of these admissions he could scarcely claim to have relied on the normal assumption an operator of a business or service is entitled to make, that his customers are behaving themselves in the eyes of the law. Because Lauria knew in fact that some of his customers were prostitutes, it is a legitimate inference he knew they were subscribing to his answering service for illegal business purposes and were using his service to make assignations for prostitution. On this record we think the prosecution is entitled to claim positive knowledge by Lauria of the use of his service to facilitate the business of prostitution.

The more perplexing issue in the case is the sufficiency of proof of *intent* to further the criminal enterprise. The element of intent may be proved either by direct evidence, or by evidence of circumstances from which an intent to further a criminal enterprise by supplying lawful goods or services may be inferred. Direct evidence of participation, such as advice from the supplier of legal goods or services to the user of those goods or services on their use for illegal purposes, such evidence as appeared in a companion case we decide today, People v. Roy, 251 Cal.App.2d 459, 59 Cal.Rptr. 636, provides the simplest case.[a] When the intent to further and promote the criminal enterprise comes from the

a. The defendant in People v. Roy also operated a telephone answering service, and also unwisely agreed to take on Stella Weeks as a client. Mrs. Roy went beyond providing telephone service, however: she introduced Mrs. Weeks to "another" prostitute, who agreed to refer business to her. The court found this additional involvement sufficient to support a conspiracy charge.—ed.

lips of the supplier himself, ambiguities of inference from circumstance need not trouble us. But in cases where direct proof of complicity is lacking, intent to further the conspiracy must be derived from the sale itself and its surrounding circumstances in order to establish the supplier's express or tacit agreement to join the conspiracy.

In the case at bench the prosecution argues that since Lauria knew his customers were using his service for illegal purposes but nevertheless continued to furnish it to them, he must have intended to assist them in carrying out their illegal activities. Thus through a union of knowledge and intent he became a participant in a criminal conspiracy. Essentially, the People argue that knowledge alone of the continuing use of his telephone facilities for criminal purposes provided a sufficient basis from which his intent to participate in those criminal activities could be inferred.

In examining precedents in this field we find that sometimes, but not always, the criminal intent of the supplier may be inferred from his knowledge of the unlawful use made of the product he supplies. Some consideration of characteristic patterns may be helpful.

1. Intent may be inferred from knowledge, when the purveyor of legal goods for illegal use has acquired a stake in the venture. For example, in Regina v. Thomas, (1957), 2 All.E.R. 181, 342, a prosecution for living off the earnings of prostitution, the evidence showed that the accused, knowing the woman to be a convicted prostitute, agreed to let her have the use of his room between the hours of 9 p.m. and 2 a.m. for a charge of £3 a night. The Court of Criminal Appeal refused an appeal from the conviction, holding that when the accused rented a room at a grossly inflated rent to a prostitute for the purpose of carrying on her trade, a jury could find he was living on the earnings of prostitution.

In the present case, no proof was offered of inflated charges for the telephone answering services furnished the codefendants.

2. Intent may be inferred from knowledge, when no legitimate use for the goods or services exists. The leading California case is People v. McLaughlin, 111 Cal.App.2d 781, 245 P.2d 1076, in which the court upheld a conviction of the suppliers of horse-racing information by wire for conspiracy to promote bookmaking, when it had been established that wireservice information had no other use than to supply information needed by bookmakers to conduct illegal gambling operations.

In Rex v. Delaval (1763) 97 E.R. 913, the charge was unlawful conspiracy to remove a girl from the control of Bates, a musician to whom she was bound as an apprentice, and place her in the hands of Sir Francis Delaval for the purpose of prostitution. Lord Mansfield not only upheld the charges against Bates and Sir Francis, but also against Fraine, the attorney who drew up the indentures of apprenticeship transferring custody of the girl from Bates to Sir Francis. Fraine, said Lord Mansfield, must have known that Sir Francis had no facilities for teaching music to apprentices so that it was impossible for him to have been ignorant of the real intent of the transaction.

In Shaw v. Director of Public Prosecutions, [1962] A.C. 220, the defendant was convicted of conspiracy to corrupt public morals and of living on the earnings of prostitution, when he published a directory consisting almost entirely of advertisements of the names, addresses, and specialized talents of prostitutes. Publication of such a directory, said the court, could have no legitimate use and serve no other purpose than to advertise the professional services of the prostitutes whose advertisements appeared in the directory. The publisher could be deemed a participant in the profits from the business activities of his principal advertisers.

Other services of a comparable nature come to mind: the manufacturer of crooked dice and marked cards who sells his product to gambling casinos; the tipster who furnishes information on the movement of law enforcement officers to known lawbreakers. (Cf. Jackson v. State of Texas, 164 Tex.Crim. 276, 298 S.W.2d 837 (App.1957), where the furnisher of signaling equipment used to warn gamblers of the police was convicted of aiding the equipping of a gambling place.) In such cases the supplier must necessarily have an intent to further the illegal enterprise since there is no known honest use for his goods.

However, there is nothing in the furnishing of telephone answering service which would necessarily imply assistance in the performance of illegal activities. Nor is any inference to be derived from the use of an answering service by women, either in any particular volume of calls, or outside normal working hours. Night-club entertainers, registered nurses, faith healers, public stenographers, photographic models, and free lance substitute employees, provide examples of women in legitimate occupations whose employment might cause them to receive a volume of telephone calls at irregular hours.

3. Intent may be inferred from knowledge, when the volume of business with the buyer is grossly disproportionate to any legitimate demand, or when sales for illegal use amount to a high proportion of the seller's total business. In such cases an intent to participate in the illegal enterprise may be inferred from the quantity of the business done. For example, in *Direct Sales,* supra, the sale of narcotics to a rural physician in quantities 300 times greater than he would have normal use for provided potent evidence of an intent to further the illegal activity. In the same case the court also found significant the fact that the wholesaler had attracted as customers a disproportionately large group of physicians who had been convicted of violating the Harrison Act. In Shaw v. Director of Public Prosecutions, supra, almost the entire business of the directory came from prostitutes.

No evidence of any unusual volume of business with prostitutes was presented by the prosecution against Lauria.

Inflated charges, the sale of goods with no legitimate use, sales in inflated amounts, each may provide a fact of sufficient moment from which the intent of the seller to participate in the criminal enterprise may be inferred. In such instances participation by the supplier of legal goods to the illegal enterprise may be inferred because in one way or another the supplier has acquired a special interest in the operation of the illegal enterprise. His intent to participate in the crime of which he has knowledge may be inferred from the existence of his special interest.

Yet there are cases in which it cannot reasonably be said that the supplier has a stake in the venture or has acquired a special interest in the enterprise, but in which he has been held liable as a participant on the basis of knowledge alone. Some suggestion of this appears in *Direct Sales,* supra, where both the knowledge of the illegal use of the drugs and the intent of the supplier to aid that use were inferred. In Regina v. Bainbridge (1959), 3 W.L.R. 656 (CCA 6), a supplier of oxygen-cutting equipment to one known to intend to use it to break into a bank was convicted as an accessory to the crime. In Sykes v. Director of Public Prosecutions [1962] A.C. 528, one having knowledge of the theft of 100 pistols, 4 submachine guns, and 1960 rounds of ammunition was convicted of misprision of felony for failure to disclose the theft to the public authorities. It seems apparent from these cases that a supplier who furnishes equipment which he *knows* will be used to commit a serious crime may be deemed from that knowledge alone to have intended to produce the result. Such proof may justify an inference that the furnisher intended to aid the execution of the crime and that he thereby became a participant. For instance, we think the operator of a telephone answering service with positive knowledge that his service was being used to facilitate the extortion of ransom, the distribution of heroin, or the passing of counterfeit money who continued to furnish the service with knowledge of its use, might be chargeable on knowledge alone with participation in a scheme to extort money, to distribute narcotics, or to pass counterfeit money. The same result would follow the seller of gasoline who knew the buyer was using his product to make Molotov cocktails for terroristic use.

Logically, the same reasoning could be extended to crimes of every description. Yet we do not believe an inference of intent drawn from knowledge of criminal use properly applies to the less serious crimes classified as misdemeanors. The duty to take positive action to dissociate oneself from activities helpful to violations of the criminal law is far stronger and more compelling for felonies than it is for misdemeanors or petty offenses. In this respect, as in others, the distinction between felonies and misdemeanors, between more serious and less serious crime, retains continuing vitality. In historically the most serious felony, treason, an individual with knowledge of the treason can be prosecuted for concealing and failing to disclose it. In other felonies, both at common law and under the criminal laws of the United States, an individual knowing of the commission of a felony is criminally liable for concealing it and failing to make it known to proper authority. But this crime, known as misprision of felony, has always been limited to knowledge and concealment of felony and has never extended to misdemeanor. A similar limitation is found in the criminal liability of an accessory [after the fact], which is restricted to aid in the escape of a principal who has committed or been charged with a *felony*. (Pen.Code, § 32.) * * *

With respect to misdemeanors, we conclude that positive knowledge of the supplier that his products or services are being used for criminal purposes does not, without more, establish an intent of the supplier to participate in the misdemeanors. With respect to felonies, we do not decide the converse, viz. that in all cases of felony knowledge of criminal use alone may justify an inference of the supplier's intent to participate in the crime. The implications of *Falcone* make the matter uncertain with respect to those felonies which are merely prohibited wrongs. But decision on this point is not compelled, and we leave the matter open.

From this analysis of precedent we deduce the following rule: the intent of a supplier who knows of the criminal use to which his supplies are put to participate in the criminal activity connected with the use of his supplies may be established by (1) direct evidence that he intends to participate, or (2) through an inference that he intends to participate based on, (a) his special interest in the activity, or (b) the aggravated nature of the crime itself.

When we review Lauria's activities in the light of this analysis, we find no proof that Lauria took any direct action to further, encourage, or direct the call-girl activities of his codefendants and we find an absence of circumstances from which his special interest in their activities could be inferred. Neither excessive charges for standardized services, nor the furnishing of services without a legitimate use, nor an unusual quantity of business with call girls, are present. The offense which he is charged with furthering is a misdemeanor, a category of crime which has never been made a required subject of positive disclosure to public authority. Under these circumstances, although proof of Lauria's knowledge of the criminal activities of his patrons was sufficient to charge him with that fact, there was insufficient evidence that he intended to further their criminal activities, and hence insufficient proof of his participation in a criminal conspiracy with his codefendants to further prostitution. Since the conspiracy centered around the activities of Lauria's telephone answering service, the charges against his codefendants likewise fail for want of proof.

In absolving Lauria of complicity in a criminal conspiracy we do not wish to imply that the public authorities are without remedies to combat modern manifestations of the world's oldest profession. Licensing of telephone answering services under the police power, together with the revocation of licenses for the toleration of prostitution, is a possible civil remedy. The furnishing of telephone answering service in aid of prostitution could be made a crime. (Cf. Pen.Code, § 316, which makes it a misdemeanor to let an apartment with knowledge of its use for prostitution.) Other solutions will doubtless occur to vigilant public authorities if the problem of call-girl activity needs further suppression.

The order is affirmed.

Notes

1. The problem discussed in the *Lauria* opinion must also be faced when the supplier of goods or services to an illegal enterprise is charged with aiding and abetting the substantive offense, as well as when he is charged with conspiracy. The cases differ on whether aid with knowledge suffices for complicity, or whether the alleged accomplice must have a purpose to assist the criminal venture or to share in the proceeds. *Compare* Backun v. United States, 112 F.2d 635 (4th Cir.1940), *with* United States v. Peoni, 100 F.2d 401 (2d Cir.1938). The New York Penal Law provides a crime of "criminal facilitation," distinct from accomplice liability, applicable to any person who, "believing it probable that he is rendering aid to a person who intends to commit a crime, * * * engages in conduct which provides such person with means or opportunity for the commission thereof and which in fact aids such person to commit a felony." McKinney's N.Y.Penal Law § 115.00. Criminal facilitation is a misdemeanor unless the crime aided is a "Class A" felony, such as murder or aggravated kidnapping. N.Y.Penal Law §§ 115.00, 115.05.

2. There is considerable support in the case law for the proposition that the "intent" required for a *conspiracy* conviction must be "corrupt" or "wrongful," i.e. that good motives or ignorance of the law might be a defense even if the object of the agreement were criminal. People v. Powell, 63 N.Y. 88 (1875); Commonwealth v. Benesch, 290 Mass. 125, 194 N.E. 905 (1935); Landen v. United States, 299 Fed. 75 (6th Cir.1924). The degree to which this "corrupt motive" or "Powell" doctrine has won acceptance in the federal courts is uncertain. See United States v. Feola, supra, for a discussion of the "Powell doctrine." The Model Penal Code rejects it. Model Penal Code § 5.03(1) (P.O.D.1962), and Commentary at 113–116 (Tent.Draft No. 10, 1960).

MERRELL v. UNITED STATES

Supreme Court of the United States, 1983.
463 U.S. 1230, 103 S.Ct. 3558, 77 L.Ed.2d 1415.

[By the Court:]

July 6, 1983. The petition for writ of certiorari is denied.

JUSTICE WHITE, with whom JUSTICE BRENNAN and JUSTICE MARSHALL join, dissenting. Between May 11, 1979, and April 19, 1980, the Federal Bureau of Investigation maintained surveillance of a certain premises in Detroit that was suspected of being the site of an illegal gambling operation. The surveillance, which entailed videotaping and recording activities and conversations, revealed an illegal dice game. As a result, 13 people were charged with violation of 18 U.S.C. § 1955* and conspiracy under 18 U.S.C. § 371. Eight co-defendants, the lessor of the premises,

* 18 U.S.C.A. § 1955 provides, in pertinent part:

Prohibition of illegal gambling businesses

(a) Whoever conducts, finances, manages, supervises, directs, or owns all or part of an illegal gambling business shall be fined not more than $20,000 or imprisoned not more than five years, or both.

(b) As used in this section—

the game operator, three dealers and three watchmen, pleaded guilty after 3 days of trial. The remaining 5 co-defendants waived a jury for the rest of the trial. Four of them were acquitted of all charges because they were "mere bettors." The evidence presented by the Government concerning petitioner established that he regularly served coffee to bettors during the gambling sessions; after the sessions he stacked tables and chairs, swept the floor, cleaned ash trays, and repositioned the tables and chairs. Petitioner was convicted of the substantive offense of conducting an illegal gambling business, but acquitted of conspiracy.

On appeal, petitioner claimed that his activities did not justify his conviction. The Court of Appeals held that the proper standard to employ in resolving petitioner's claim is whether he performed "any act, duty or function which is necessary or *helpful* in operating the enterprise." 701 F.2d 53, 55 (1983). That holding conflicts with the decision in United States v. Boss, 671 F.2d 396, 400 (C.A.10 1982), where it was held that the proper standard is whether the person performs "a function * * * necessary to the illegal gambling business." That court interpreted the term "conduct" to require "some actual involvement in the gambling operation," and found that neither a waitress, a bartender, nor a band member could be considered "conductors" under § 1955.

There is a significant difference between activities that are "necessary" to the operation of an illegal gambling establishment and those that are only "helpful." The *Boss* case involved the question whether waitresses who served drinks to the bettors in the illegal gambling establishment as well as to customers in the adjacent dance hall were "conductors" within the meaning of § 1955. The Tenth Circuit found they were not because their functions were not necessary, but merely helpful. I do not find that case distinguishable from the present one. The difference between conviction and acquittal should not rest on whether an illegal gambling establishment existed in isolation or was concealed within another, legal, establishment. If a waitress who functions solely as a waitress in an illegal gambling establishment could not be convicted under § 1955, as the Tenth Circuit has held, then a waiter/janitor who functions solely as a waiter/janitor should not be convicted either.

Because a case involving a conflict among the courts of appeals concerning the standard to be applied in determining criminal liability involves either the unjust conviction of an innocent person or the frustration of congressional intent to criminalize specific conduct, it necessarily presents an important question. This case should be granted and set for argument. I dissent.

(1) "illegal gambling business" means a gambling business which—

(i) is a violation of the law of a State or political subdivision in which it is conducted;

(ii) involves five or more persons who conduct, finance, manage, supervise, direct, or own all or part of such business and

(iii) has been or remains in substantially continuous operation for a period in excess of thirty days or has a gross revenue of $2,000 in any single day.

PEOPLE v. KESSLER

Supreme Court of Illinois, 1974.
57 Ill.2d 493, 315 N.E.2d 29.

DAVIS, JUSTICE.

Kessler was convicted on one count of burglary and two counts of attempted murder. The appellate court affirmed the burglary conviction and reversed the attempted-murder convictions, and we allowed the People's petition for leave to appeal. Defendant waited in an automobile outside a tavern while his two unarmed companions entered the building to commit the burglary. While inside the tavern, they were surprised by the owner, and one of the burglars shot and wounded him with a gun taken during the burglary. Later, while defendant's companions were fleeing on foot, one of them fired a shot at a pursuing police officer. At that time defendant was sitting in the automobile.

* * *

The People argue "that a person is responsible for all criminal violations actually committed by another if he assists another in the commission of a single criminal violation," and that "if the legislature had intended to limit accomplice liability only to further criminal acts which were specifically intended the word 'conduct' would not have been included in the language of § 5–2."

Sections 5–1 and 5–2 of the Criminal Code provide in pertinent part:

§ 5–1. Accountability for Conduct of Another.

A person is responsible for *Conduct* which is an element of an offense if the *conduct* is either that of the person himself, or that of another and he is legally accountable for such *conduct* as provided in § 5–2 or both. (Emphasis added.)

§ 5–2. When Accountability Exists.

A person is legally accountable for the *conduct* of another when:

* * *

(b) The statute defining the offense makes him so accountable; or

(c) Either before or during the commission of *an offense* and with the intent to promote or facilitate such commission, he solicits, aids, abets, agrees or attempts to aid, such other person in the planning or commission of the offense. * * * (Emphasis added.)

"Conduct" is defined as:

* * * an act or a series of acts, and the accompanying mental state.

* * *

We believe the statute means that where one aids another in the planning or commission of an offense, he is legally accountable for the conduct of the person he aids; and that the word "conduct" encompasses any criminal act done in furtherance of the planned and intended act.

An early application of this rule is found in Hamilton v. People (1885), 113 Ill. 34. The defendant and two companions invaded a watermelon patch intending to steal some melons. The owner discovered them and a scuffle or fight ensued during which the owner pinned one of the three to the ground, and when in this position another of the three fired a gun at the owner, but the shot missed the owner and struck the potential watermelon thief, who the owner had thrown to the ground. During this occurrence, the third potential watermelon thief stood by. All three of the putative watermelon thieves were charged and convicted of assault with intent to commit murder. This court stated:

> The fact is undisputed that the three defendants, one of whom was armed with a pistol, invaded the premises of the prosecuting witness with a criminal purpose. The business upon which the parties had deliberately entered was a hazardous one. They had a right to expect that in the event they were detected in stealing the melons, it would result in violence endangering life or limb,—as it actually turned out afterwards. That they were all co-conspirators in a dangerous criminal enterprise, is an undisputed fact. Such being the case, whatever was done by one, in contemplation of law was done by all, and all are therefore equally responsible.

In the case at bar, the record shows a common design to commit a robbery or burglary. * * *

A similar conclusion was reached in People v. Hubbard, 55 Ill.2d 142, 302 N.E.2d 609 (1973), where we referred to People v. Armstrong, 41 Ill.2d 390, 243 N.E.2d 825 (1968), wherein the court stated as follows:

> The next contention of defendants involves a request to depart from the long established common-design rule, i.e., that where defendants have a common design to do an unlawful act, then whatever act any one of them does in furtherance of the common design is the act of all and all are equally guilty of whatever crime is committed. * * * We have fully reiterated our support of this rule in recent cases, and we continue to do so in this case. Nor do we accept defendants' argument that the statutorily defined rules on accountability (§ 5–2) in any way modify or abrogate the common-design rule. This section provides that a person is legally accountable for the conduct of another when "(c) Either before or during commission * * * he solicits, aids, abets, or agrees or attempts to aid, such other person in the planning or commission of the offense." Applying this section to this case the attempted robbery was the offense which the defendants were jointly committing and each was legally accountable for the conduct of the other. The result was murder, the killing of an individual without lawful justification while attempting or committing a forcible felony other than voluntary manslaughter.

For the foregoing reasons, we affirm the part of the appellate court decision which affirmed the burglary conviction of the defendant, and we reverse the part of its decision which reversed the conviction of the defendant for attempted murder, and we affirm the judgment of the circuit court.

GOLDENHERSH, JUSTICE (dissenting):

I dissent. In its well-reasoned opinion the appellate court correctly reversed defendant's attempt murder convictions and its judgment should be affirmed. * * * In support of its position the majority cites People v. Armstrong, and quotes at length from People v. Hubbard. These cases are clearly not in point. They involved defendants charged with murder and fall under § 5–2(b) for the reason that § 9–1(3) creates the "felony murder" classification and obviates the need of proof of intent. * * *

The majority also quotes from Hamilton v. People. In *Hamilton* there was a common design to burglarize a watermelon patch, one of the co-defendants was armed, all were present and took part in the fight which followed their being accosted by the farmer whose melons they were stealing and the court applied a common design theory. * * *

The Committee Comments to § 5–2(c) *inter alia* state:

> Subsection 5–2(c) is a comprehensive statement of liability based on counseling, aiding and abetting and the like, which includes those situations that, at common law, involve the liability of principals in the second degree and accessories before the fact. It will be observed that liability under this subsection requires proof of an "intent to promote or facilitate * * * commission" of the substantive offense. Moreover, "conspiracy" between the actor and defendant is not of itself made the basis of accountability for the actor's conduct, although the acts of conspiring may in many cases satisfy the particular requirements of this subsection.

It should be noted that emphasis is placed on the requirement of proof of an "intent to promote or facilitate * * * commission of the substantive offense" and the Criminal Code provides:

> A person intends, or acts intentionally or with intent, to accomplish a result or engage in conduct described by the statute defining the offense, when his conscious objective or purpose is to accomplish that result or engage in that conduct. § 4–4.

The substantive offense involved is attempt murder and § 8–4(a) of the Code provides that the requisite elements of the offense of attempt are the intent to commit a specific criminal offense and the doing of an act which constitutes a substantial step toward the commission of that offense. The gist of the crime of attempt murder as defined in the Criminal Code is the specific intent to take life. As pointed out by the appellate court, had either of the intended victims died, the provisions of § 9–1(3) of the Criminal Code would have served to make the defendant accountable, but the attempt statute contains no such provision.

* * * I submit that on this record the defendant was not proved guilty of attempt murder. The evidence is uncontradicted that when his companions embarked on the burglary they were unarmed and that he was not inside the tavern when the shot was fired. Again, when the shot was fired at the pursuing officer, defendant was in the automobile, and under the circumstances neither occurrence is shown to be a consequence of any action of the defendant from which the requisite specific intent could be inferred. * * *

b. The "Pinkerton" Doctrine

STATE EX REL. WOODS v. COHEN

Supreme Court of Arizona, 1992.
173 Ariz. 497, 844 P.2d 1147.

MARTONE, J.

We are asked to decide whether a conspirator, who is responsible for the crime of conspiracy, can also be responsible for the separate criminal acts of co-conspirators when the conspirator is not an accomplice or principal to those crimes. We hold that conspiratorial responsibility does not extend that far.

Edwin C. Cohen was indicted by a grand jury for conspiracy to defraud the Arizona Health Care Cost Containment System and for various offenses committed by his co-conspirators in carrying out that conspiracy. The trial court granted Cohen's motion to remand all aspects of the indictment to the grand jury for a new determination of probable cause. The court of appeals, in a special action brought by the state, reversed and remanded the case for further proceedings based upon the existing grand jury indictment.

Count 1 of the indictment charged Cohen with conspiracy. Counts 18 through 29 of the indictment charged Cohen with various substantive offenses, including theft and fraud, committed by his co-conspirators. Cohen moved to dismiss counts 18 through 29 for lack of evidence implicating him. The trial court granted the motion and remanded those counts to the grand jury for a new determination of probable cause. The state argued that the trial court's ruling was based on a rejection of the *Pinkerton* doctrine of vicarious liability under which Cohen could be held liable for the substantive crimes of his co-conspirators even though he did not participate in those crimes. The grand jury was in fact instructed on this doctrine and the state concedes that it presented no evidence of Cohen's direct participation in the offenses which were the subject of counts 18 through 29.

The liability of an accused for acts committed by co-conspirators is often called "*Pinkerton*" liability, after the case in which the United States Supreme Court recognized the doctrine as part of federal criminal law and upheld it against a double jeopardy challenge. Pinkerton v. United States, 328 U.S. 640 (1946). The Court held that a conspirator may be found responsible for crimes committed by a co-conspirator, as long as the acts making up the crimes are reasonably foreseeable and are carried out in furtherance of the conspiracy, even though the conspirator did not participate in their commission. * * *

The court of appeals held that the Pinkerton doctrine can be found in A.R.S. § 13–1003. That section, however, defines the elements and scope of the crime of conspiracy. But Cohen's indictment for the crime of conspiracy (count 1) is not at issue. We deal here with his indictment for the crimes alleged in counts 18 through 29 committed by his co-conspirators. As noted by the court of appeals, to come within § 13–1003(A), a conspirator need not agree to personally commit a criminal act but need only agree to the commission of the act by a co-conspirator. Likewise, the overt act that constitutes an element of the crime of conspiracy under § 13–1003(A) need not be personally committed by the conspirator being prosecuted. Nevertheless, the liability which stems from the planning of crimes under § 13–1003 is liability for conspiracy, not for crimes committed by co-conspirators. The fact that one can be criminally responsible for the crime of conspiracy without committing the planned substantive offenses does not mean that one is also criminally responsible for the substantive offenses without being either an accomplice or principal to those offenses.

Nor is § 13–1003(B) a basis for Pinkerton liability. That subsection merely provides that one who conspires with another may also be a co-conspirator of an unidentified third person with whom the other has conspired.

The state argues that *Pinkerton* liability can be found within the code's vicarious liability scheme. A.R.S. § 13–303 defines vicarious liability for crimes committed by others as follows:

A. A person is criminally accountable for the conduct of another if:

1. The person is made accountable for such conduct by the statute defining the offense; or

2. Acting with the culpable mental state sufficient for the commission of the offense, such person causes another person, whether or not such other person is capable of forming the culpable mental state, to engage in such conduct; or

3. The person is an accomplice of such other person in the commission of the offense.

Liability for the acts of one's co-conspirators is not on this list. The state, however, argues that co-conspirator liability is inherent in the concept of accomplice liability listed in subsection 3, above.

"Conspiracy" is defined in § 13–1003(A) as follows:

A person commits conspiracy if, with the intent to promote or aid the commission of an offense, such person agrees with one or more persons that at least one of them will engage in conduct constituting the offense and one of the parties commits an overt act in furtherance of the offense....

"Accomplice" is defined in § 13–301 to include anyone who, intending to promote or facilitate the commission of an offense:

1. Solicits or commands another person to commit the offense; or

2. Aids, counsels, agrees to aid or attempts to aid another person in planning or committing the offense.

3. Provides the means or opportunity to another person to commit the offense.

The state argues that whenever one has conspired to commit a crime which is then actually committed by one's co-conspirators, one will inevitably come within the definition of an accomplice and can therefore be held liable for the completed crime. To put the state's case another way, if one "agrees with one or more persons that at least one of them will engage in conduct constituting" a crime, as required by the conspiracy statute, one by definition "aids, counsels, agrees to aid or attempts to aid" in the planning or commission of that crime, as required by the accomplice statute.

Although this argument has enormous appeal, we think there is a logical distinction between agreeing to the commission of a crime by another and agreeing to aid another in committing a crime, the latter being more participatory than the former. The distinction between being an accomplice and being a conspirator to a completed crime is certainly subtle when the crime conspired to is the one actually committed, but there is a difference. *Pinkerton*, in any event, goes well beyond this. Under *Pinkerton*, a conspirator may be held liable for a crime to which the conspirator never agreed, and which is committed by a co-conspirator with whom the conspirator never personally dealt, as long as the crime is reasonably foreseeable and is committed in furtherance of the conspiracy. Clearly, one who has not agreed to the commission of a crime and has not aided in its planning or commission could not be convicted of the crime as an accomplice. *Pinkerton* liability is not, therefore, the equivalent of accomplice liability. A conspirator to a completed offense is not always an accomplice to that offense. * * *

While we hold that *Pinkerton* is not the law in Arizona, the practical consequence of this holding should not be overestimated. It may well be an unusual conspirator who stops at the purely hypothetical agreement stage at which the conspiracy is committed, without doing something to promote the crime agreed upon and thus becoming an accomplice to it. Because of the broad reach of accomplice liability, our holding does not prevent the conviction of those who are culpable for the substantive offenses committed in furtherance of a conspiracy. It simply prevents a conspirator, who is not also an accomplice, from being held liable for a potentially limitless number of criminal acts which, though later determined to be "foreseeable," are at the time of their commission totally beyond the conspirator's knowledge and control. The conspirator, nevertheless, remains liable for the crime of conspiracy.

* * * We remand the case to the trial court to determine whether sufficient evidence was presented to allow the grand jury to indict Cohen on counts 18–29 based on accomplice liability, thereby making the Pinkerton instruction harmless error. If the trial court so finds, then the case may proceed on the existing indictment. If not, then remand of counts 18–29 is appropriate.

Note

One who enters into a conspiratorial relationship is liable in most jurisdictions for every reasonably foreseeable crime committed by every other member of the conspiracy in furtherance of its objectives, whether or not he knew of the crimes or aided in their commission. At first glance, this conspiracy-complicity rule seems to add little to the law of complicity or accessorial liability. No one would question that persons who plot together to commit a crime are guilty of that crime if one or more of them commits it. Some authorities limit an accomplice's liability to those crimes of his confederates which he intended to assist or encourage. Many cases like People v. Kessler, however, have held the accomplice responsible for other, unanticipated crimes if they were committed in furtherance of the original scheme. In any case, the felony murder doctrine imposes liability for unintended consequences in the most common situations: every member of a robbery or burglary gang is liable for any killing committed by any member in the perpetration of the robbery or burglary.

The important thing is not so much the conspiracy-complicity rule itself, but rather the tendency of courts to regard a conspiracy as an ongoing business relationship of indefinite scope and duration, and to consider the conspirators, as the dissenting opinion in *Pinkerton* put it, as "general partners in crime." For example, the defendant in Anderson v. Superior Court, 78 Cal.App.2d 22, 177 P.2d 315 (1947), referred several pregnant women to an abortionist and received a portion of his fees. For this the court held her to have entered into a conspiracy with him to commit abortions generally, and to be liable for subsequent abortions in which she played no part. In United States v. Bruno, supra, the federal court of appeals ruled that a single, immense conspiracy to distribute narcotics included smugglers, middlemen, and retail sellers operating in two different parts of the country. Although the defendants were charged only with conspiracy, in theory the holding implied that each smuggler was guilty of every retail sale and each retailer of every act of smuggling.

Because this pyramiding of liability seems to be justified by no conceivable penological principle, the drafters of the Model Penal Code rejected the *Pinkerton* doctrine. Under the Code, conspirators as such are liable only for conspiracy; their liability for substantive offenses committed by co-conspirators is determined under the ordinary complicity rules stated in Section 2.06, supra p. 702. The Commentary explains how the Code's approach would have affected the liability of the confederates of New York vice king Lucky Luciano:

> Luciano and others were convicted of sixty-two counts of compulsory prostitution, each count involving a specific instance of placing a girl in

a house of prostitution, receiving money for so doing or receiving money for the earnings of a prostitute, acts proved to have been done pursuant to a combination to control commercialized vice in New York City. The liability was properly imposed with respect to these defendants, who directed and controlled the combination; they commanded, encouraged and aided the commission of numberless specific crimes. But would so extensive a liability be just for each of the prostitutes or runners involved in the plan? * * * A court would and should hold that they are all parties to a single, large, conspiracy; this is itself, and ought to be, a crime. But it is one crime. Law would lose all sense of proportion if in virtue of that one crime, each were held accountable for thousands of offenses that he did not influence at all.

Note, however, that under the Code's "unilateral" definition of conspiracy it is doubtful whether there is "a single, large conspiracy." Possibly, each prostitute or runner agrees to commit only her own crimes, and only the "executives" are guilty of the overall conspiracy.

The inclination to regard a conspiracy as an ongoing business relationship in which the conspirators are treated as general partners is embedded in one of the most innovative and controversial of federal laws, the RICO statute. Many commentators and judges have concluded that the RICO statute extends the concept of group liability beyond the boundaries of traditional conspiracy theory.

E. SON OF CONSPIRACY: THE RICO STATUTE

Title 18, United States Code, Chapter 96—Racketeer Influenced and Corrupt Organizations

§ 1961. Definitions

As used in this chapter—

(1) "Racketeering activity" means (A) any act or threat involving murder, kidnaping, gambling, arson, robbery, bribery, extortion, or dealing in narcotic or other dangerous drugs, which is chargeable under State law and punishable by imprisonment for more than one year; (B) any act which is indictable under any of the following provisions of title 18, United States Code: Section 201 (relating to bribery), section 224 (relating to sports bribery), sections 471, 472, and 473 (relating to counterfeiting), section 659 (relating to theft from interstate shipment) if the act indictable under section 659 is felonious, section 664 (relating to embezzlement from pension and welfare funds), sections 891–894 (relating to extortionate credit transactions), section 1084 (relating to the transmission of gambling information), section 1341 (relating to mail fraud), section 1343 (relating to wire fraud), section 1503 (relating to obstruction of justice), section 1510 (relating to obstruction of criminal investigations), section 1511 (relating to the obstruction of State or local law enforcement), section 1951 (relating to interference with commerce, robbery, or extortion), section 1952 (relating to racketeering), section 1953 (relating to interstate transportation of wagering paraphernalia), section 1954 (relating to unlawful welfare fund payments), section 1955

(relating to the prohibition of illegal gambling businesses), sections 2314 and 2315 (relating to interstate transportation of stolen property), sections 2421–24 (relating to white slave traffic), (C) any act which is indictable under title 29, United States Code, section 186 (dealing with restrictions on payments and loans to labor organizations) or section 501(c) (relating to embezzlement from union funds), or (D) any offense involving bankruptcy fraud, fraud in the sale of securities, or the felonious manufacture, importation, receiving, concealment, buying, selling, or otherwise dealing in narcotic or other dangerous drugs, punishable under any law of the United States;

(2) "State" means any State of the United States, the District of Columbia, the Commonwealth of Puerto Rico, any territory or possession of the United States, any political subdivision, or any department, agency, or instrumentality thereof;

(3) "person" includes any individual or entity capable of holding a legal or beneficial interest in property;

(4) "enterprise" includes any individual, partnership, corporation, association, or other legal entity, and any union or group of individuals associated in fact although not a legal entity;

(5) "pattern of racketeering activity" requires at least two acts of racketeering activity, one of which occurred after the effective date of this chapter and the last of which occurred within ten years (excluding any period of imprisonment) after the commission of a prior act of racketeering activity;

(6) "unlawful debt" means a debt (A) incurred or contracted in gambling activity which was in violation of the law of the United States, a State or political subdivision thereof, or which is unenforceable under State or Federal law in whole or in part as to principal or interest because of the laws relating to usury, and (B) which was incurred in connection with the business of gambling in violation of the law of the United States, a State or political subdivision thereof, or the business of lending money or a thing of value at a rate usurious under State or Federal law, where the usurious rate is at least twice the enforceable rate.

§ 1962. Prohibited Activities

(a) It shall be unlawful for any person who has received any income derived, directly or indirectly, from a pattern of racketeering activity or through collection of an unlawful debt in which such person has participated as a principal within the meaning of section 2, title 18, United States Code, to use or invest, directly or indirectly, any part of such income, or the proceeds of such income, in acquisition of any interest in, or the establishment or operation of, any enterprise which is engaged in or the activities of which affect, interstate or foreign commerce. A purchase of securities on the open market for purposes of investment, and without the intention of controlling or participating in the control of the issuer, or of assisting another to do so, shall not be unlawful under this subsection if the securities of the issuer held by the purchaser, the members of his immediate family, and his or their accomplices in any pattern or racketeering activity of the collection of an unlawful debt after such purchase do not amount in the aggregate to one percent of the outstanding securities of any one class, and do not confer, either in law or in fact, the power to elect one or more directors of the issuer.

(b) It shall be unlawful for any person through a pattern of racketeering activity or through collection of an unlawful debt to acquire or maintain, directly or indirectly, any interest in or control of any enterprise which is engaged in, or the activities of which affect, interstate or foreign commerce.

(c) It shall be unlawful for any person employed by or associated with any enterprise engaged in, or the activities of which affect, interstate or foreign commerce, to conduct or participate, directly or indirectly, in the conduct of such enterprise's affairs through a pattern of racketeering activity or collection of unlawful debt.

(d) It shall be unlawful for any person to conspire to violate any of the provisions of subsections (a), (b), or (c) of this section.

§ 1963. Criminal Penalties

(a) Whoever violates any provision of section 1962 of this chapter shall be fined not more than $25,000 or imprisoned not more than twenty years, or both, and shall forfeit to the United States (1) any interest he has acquired or maintained in violation of section 1962, and (2) any interest in, security of, claim against, or property or contractual right of any kind affording a source of influence over, any enterprise which he has established, operated, controlled, conducted, or participated in the conduct of, in violation of section 1962.

* * *

§ 1964. Civil Remedies

(a) The district courts of the United States shall have jurisdiction to prevent and restrain violations of section 1962 of this chapter by issuing appropriate orders, including, but not limited to: ordering any person to divest himself of any interest, direct or indirect, in any enterprise; imposing reasonable restrictions on the future activities or investments of any person, including, but not limited to, prohibiting any person from engaging in the same type of endeavor as the enterprise engaged in, the activities of which affect interstate or foreign commerce; or ordering dissolution or reorganization of any enterprise, making due provision for the rights of innocent persons.

(b) The Attorney General may institute proceedings under this section. In any action brought by the United States under this section, the court shall proceed as soon as practicable to the hearing and determination thereof. Pending final determination thereof, the court may at any time enter such restraining orders or prohibitions, or take such other actions, including the acceptance of satisfactory performance bonds, as it shall deem proper.

(c) Any person injured in his business or property by reason of a violation of section 1962 of this chapter may sue therefor in any appropriate United States district court and shall recover threefold the damages he sustains and the cost of the suit, including a reasonable attorney's fee.

(d) A final judgment or decree rendered in favor of the United States in any criminal proceeding brought by the United States under this chapter shall estop the defendant from denying the essential allegations of the criminal offense in any subsequent civil proceeding brought by the United States.

UNITED STATES v. TURKETTE

Supreme Court of the United States, 1981.
452 U.S. 576, 101 S.Ct. 2524, 69 L.Ed.2d 246.

JUSTICE WHITE delivered the opinion of the Court.

* * * The question in this case is whether the term "enterprise" as used in RICO encompasses both legitimate and illegitimate enterprises or is limited in application to the former. * * *

I

Count Nine of a nine-count indictment charged respondent and 12 others with conspiracy to conduct and participate in the affairs of an enterprise engaged in interstate commerce through a pattern of racketeering activities, in violation of 18 U.S.C. § 1962(d). The indictment described the enterprise as "a group of individuals associated in fact for the purpose of illegally trafficking in narcotics and other dangerous drugs, committing arsons, utilizing the United States mails to defraud insurance companies, bribing and attempting to bribe local police officers, and corruptly influencing and attempting to corruptly influence the outcome of state court proceedings * * *." The other eight counts of the indictment charged the commission of various substantive criminal acts by those engaged in and associated with the criminal enterprise, including possession with intent to distribute and distribution of controlled substances, and several counts of insurance fraud by arson and other means. The common thread to all counts was respondent's alleged leadership of this criminal organization through which he orchestrated and participated in the commission of the various crimes delineated in the RICO count or charged in the eight preceding counts.

After a 6–week jury trial, in which the evidence focused upon both the professional nature of this organization and the execution of a number of distinct criminal acts, respondent was convicted on all nine counts. He was sentenced to a term of 20 years on the substantive counts, as well as a 2–year special parole term on the drug count. On the

RICO conspiracy count he was sentenced to a 20–year concurrent term and fined $20,000.

On appeal, respondent argued that RICO was intended solely to protect legitimate business enterprises from infiltration by racketeers and that RICO does not make criminal the participation in an association which performs only illegal acts and which has not infiltrated as attempted to infiltrate a legitimate enterprise. The Court of Appeals agreed. We reverse.

* * *

II

Section 1962(c) makes it unlawful "for any person employed by or associated with any enterprise engaged in, or the activities of which affect, interstate or foreign commerce, to conduct or participate, directly or indirectly, in the conduct of such enterprise's affairs through a pattern of racketeering activity or collection of unlawful debt." The term "enterprise" is defined as including "any individual, partnership, corporation, association, or other legal entity, and any union or group of individuals associated in fact although not a legal entity." § 1961(4). There is no restriction upon the associations embraced by the definition: an enterprise includes any union or group of individuals associated in fact. On its face, the definition appears to include both legitimate and illegitimate enterprises within its scope; it no more excludes criminal enterprises than it does legitimate ones. Had Congress not intended to reach criminal associations, it could easily have narrowed the sweep of the definition by inserting a single word, "legitimate." But it did nothing to indicate that an enterprise consisting of a group of individuals was not covered by RICO if the purpose of the enterprise was exclusively criminal. * * *

III

The statement of findings that prefaces the Organized Crime Control Act of 1970 reveals the pervasiveness of the problem that Congress was addressing by this enactment:

> The Congress finds that (1) organized crime in the United States is a highly sophisticated, diversified, and widespread activity that annually drains billions of dollars from America's economy by unlawful conduct and the illegal use of force, fraud, and corruption; (2) organized crime derives a major portion of its power through money obtained from such illegal endeavors as syndicated gambling, loan sharking, the theft and fencing of property, the importation and distribution of narcotics and other dangerous drugs, and other forms of social exploitation; (3) this money and power are increasingly used to infiltrate and corrupt legitimate business and labor unions and to subvert and corrupt our democratic processes; (4) organized crime activities in the United States weaken the stability of the Nation's economic system, harm innocent investors and

competing organizations, interfere with free competition, seriously burden interstate and foreign commerce, threaten the domestic security, and undermine the general welfare of the Nation and its citizens; and (5) organized crime continues to grow because of defects in the evidence-gathering process of the law inhibiting the development of the legally admissible evidence necessary to bring criminal and other sanctions or remedies to bear on the unlawful activities of those engaged in organized crime and because the sanctions and remedies available to the Government are unnecessarily limited in scope and impact. 84 Stat. 922–923.

In light of the above findings, it was the declared purpose of Congress "to seek the eradication of organized crime in the United States by strengthening the legal tools in the evidence-gathering process, by establishing new penal prohibitions, and by providing enhanced sanctions and new remedies to deal with the unlawful activities of those engaged in organized crime." * * *

Considering this statement of the Act's broad purposes, the construction of RICO suggested by respondent and the court below is unacceptable. Whole areas of organized criminal activity would be placed beyond the substantive reach of the enactment. For example, associations of persons engaged solely in "loan sharking, the theft and fencing of property, the importation and distribution of narcotics and other dangerous drugs," id., at 922–923, would be immune from prosecution under RICO so long as the association did not deviate from the criminal path. Yet these are among the very crimes that Congress specifically found to be typical of the crimes committed by persons involved in organized crime, and as a major source of revenue and power for such organizations. * * *

This is not to gainsay that the legislative history forcefully supports the view that the major purpose of Title IX is to address the infiltration of legitimate business by organized crime. The point is made time and again during the debates and in the hearings before the House and Senate. But none of these statements requires the negative inference that Title IX did not reach the activities of enterprises organized and existing for criminal purposes.

On the contrary, these statements are in full accord with the proposition that RICO is equally applicable to a criminal enterprise that has no legitimate dimension or has yet to acquire one. Accepting that the primary purpose of RICO is to cope with the infiltration of legitimate businesses, applying the statute in accordance with its terms, so as to reach criminal enterprises, would seek to deal with the problem at its very source. Supporters of the bill recognized that organized crime uses its primary sources of revenue and power—illegal gambling, loan sharking and illicit drug distribution—as a springboard into the sphere of legitimate enterprise. * * *

As a measure to deal with the infiltration of legitimate businesses by organized crime, RICO was both preventive and remedial. Respondent's view would ignore the preventive function of the statute. If Congress had intended the more circumscribed approach espoused by the Court of Appeals, there would have been some positive sign that the law was not to reach organized criminal activities that give rise to the concerns about infiltration. The language of the statute, however—the most reliable evidence of its intent—reveals that Congress opted for a far broader definition of the word "enterprise," and we are unconvinced by anything in the legislative history that this definition should be given less than its full effect.

The judgment of the Court of Appeals is accordingly

Reversed.

JUSTICE STEWART agrees with the reasoning and conclusion of the Court of Appeals as to the meaning of the term "enterprise" in this statute. See 632 F.2d 896. Accordingly, he respectfully dissents.

UNITED STATES v. LICAVOLI

United States Court of Appeals, Sixth Circuit, 1984.
725 F.2d 1040.

CORNELIA G. KENNEDY, CIRCUIT JUDGE.

The six defendant-appellants were convicted of conspiring to participate in the affairs of an enterprise through a pattern of racketeering activities in violation of the Racketeer Influenced and Corrupt Organizations (RICO) statute, 18 U.S.C. § 1962(c) and (d) following a jury trial, and now appeal those convictions. * * *

I. Facts

Defendant Licavoli is a leader of organized crime in Cleveland. Liberatore is his second-in-command, and Calandra also holds a position of confidence and responsibility within the organization. Carabbia and Cisternino act for the organization, carrying out the orders of the top men. Ciarcia manages a car dealership and supplies vehicles for the organization's criminal activities and also acts on behalf of the organization in other ways.

In the spring of 1976 Licavoli decided that he needed to have one Danny Greene killed. Greene was the leader of a rival criminal organization which had developed a monopoly on criminal activity in West Cleveland. Licavoli had others in his organization contact Raymond Ferritto regarding his wish to have Greene killed.[2] * * *

Licavoli had Greene's phone tapped in an effort to obtain reliable information regarding Greene's daily activities. Carabbia and Cisternino gave Ferritto the resulting tapes. One tape revealed that Greene was to go to a dentist's appointment at 2:30 p.m. on Thursday, October 6, 1977.

2. Ferritto later testified against all six defendants in their state trials for Greene's murder.

Defendants Licavoli, Cisternino and Carabbia played this tape for Ferritto on Monday, October 3.

On Thursday, the day of Greene's dentist appointment, Cisternino and Ferritto built a bomb in an apartment maintained by Cisternino. Ferritto drove to the vicinity of the dentist's office with the bomb in his car, a Plymouth. Carabbia drove a second car to the office, a Nova. This car had a special box mounted on the side in which the bomb was to be placed. Cisternino remained behind at the apartment to listen to a police scanner for calls. A few minutes after Ferritto and Carabbia arrived at the dentist's, Aratari and Guiles arrived in another car, supplied by Ciarcia as the car to be used in "the Danny Greene case." Guiles was armed with a high powered rifle. The plan was for Guiles to shoot Greene if he had the opportunity. The bomb was to be used as a backup method.

Greene arrived for his appointment, parked his car and entered the office. Guiles apparently had no opportunity to shoot. A few minutes later a parking space opened next to Greene's car. Ferritto placed the bomb in the box on the side of the Nova, parked the Nova next to Greene's car, and activated the bomb. Then he got into the driver's seat of the Plymouth, which was parked down the block. When Greene emerged from the office Ferritto began to drive away, with Carabbia in the back seat. Carabbia then detonated the bomb with a remote control device and Danny Greene was killed.

All six defendants in the present case were tried for Danny Greene's murder in state court. Cisternino, Carabbia and Ciarcia were convicted of Greene's murder.

The RICO prosecution now on appeal also relied on a separate set of events to establish a predicate criminal act. Ms. Geraldine Rabinowitz worked as a file clerk in the Cleveland office of the FBI, while her then-fiance Jeffrey Rabinowitz worked at the car dealership that Ciarcia managed. In the spring of 1977 Ciarcia asked Ms. Rabinowitz to obtain confidential information from the FBI regarding investigations of himself, Liberatore, and Licavoli. Ms. Rabinowitz complied, after some hesitation, and continued to steal confidential information for Ciarcia from time to time throughout the summer of 1977. Ciarcia assured Ms. Rabinowitz that she would in return be "covered" for a downpayment on a new home that she and her fiance planned to buy. On October 12, 1977 the Rabinowitzes met with Liberatore and Ciarcia, and the Rabinowitzes asked for $15,000 for a down payment on the home. Although Liberatore was at first unwilling to comply with this request, the next day he delivered a paper bag to Ms. Rabinowitz containing $15,000 in cash. Counsel for Liberatore characterized this payment as a "loan", but no interest was set, no repayment schedule made, and no collateral specified. The stolen FBI documents were later found at Ciarcia's car dealership. All six defendants were charged with two counts of bribery and one count of conspiracy to commit bribery and were tried in federal court.

Ciarcia pleaded guilty to all three counts, and Liberatore was convicted of the conspiracy count and one substantive count.

All six defendants were tried together in federal court for the RICO violation. The jury found all six guilty of having violated RICO. Defendants now raise a large number of issues on appeal.

II. Conspiracy to Murder May Be a Predicate Act for a RICO Conviction

The District Court instructed the jury that there were three possible acts which the jury could find to serve as predicate acts of racketeering for the RICO charge. These were: 1) conspiracy to murder Danny Greene; 2) the murder of Danny Greene; and 3) bribery. The court instructed that the bribery act applied only to defendants Liberatore and Ciarcia. The jury therefore had to find that the other four defendants both conspired to murder, and murdered Danny Greene in order to convict them of the RICO violation. These four defendants (Licavoli, Calandra, Carabbia, Cisternino) now argue that conspiracy to commit murder cannot serve as a predicate act for a RICO conviction, and that their RICO convictions therefore cannot stand.

Under 18 U.S.C. § 1961(1)(A) racketeering activity includes "any act or threat involving murder * * *." Conspiracy to murder on its face fits within this definition of racketeering activity. Conspiracy is "an act * * * involving murder." * * *

III. Murder and Conspiracy to Murder Are Separate Offenses under Ohio Law and May Both Be Predicate Acts under RICO

For a defendant to be convicted under RICO he must have committed more than one act of racketeering activity. In order for a state crime, such as murder or conspiracy to murder to serve as a predicate act, it must be "chargeable under state law and punishable by imprisonment for more than one year" under 18 U.S.C. § 1961(1)(A). Federal law holds that conspiracy to commit a substantive offense and the substantive offense itself are two separate crimes. Under Ohio law, conspiracy to murder and murder are also two separate crimes. However, a person convicted of the substantive crime "shall not be convicted of conspiracy involving the same offense." Ohio Rev.Code § 2923.01(G). Thus under Ohio law a person cannot be convicted of or sentenced for both conspiracy to commit murder and the murder crime itself. Defendants argue that the two acts consequently are not both "chargeable under state law and punishable for more than one year."

We disagree, for two reasons. First Ohio law, in both the Ohio Revised Code and the earlier case law, provides that conspiracy to commit a substantive act and the substantive act are separate offenses, both separately chargeable under state law. * * *

RICO nowhere indicates that two criminal acts otherwise qualifying as predicate acts may not both constitute predicate acts because under state law a defendant could not be convicted of or sentenced for both crimes.

Secondly, contrary to defendants' contention, it is irrelevant whether these particular defendants could have been charged under Ohio law and imprisoned for more than one year for both conspiracy to murder and murder. This argument has been raised and rejected several times in the context of state statutes of limitations, when the state statute has run on a state crime which is offered as a predicate act for a RICO violation. Courts have held that regardless of the running of the state statute the defendant is still "chargeable" with the state offense within the meaning of [the RICO statute]. * * *

IV. Acquittal in State Court of Criminal Acts Does Not Bar Their Use as Predicate Acts for a RICO Conviction

Defendants Licavoli and Calandra were acquitted in state court proceedings of murdering Greene and conspiring to murder Greene. Consequently, they argue, they were not "chargeable" with the murder or conspiracy to commit murder, as required under 18 U.S.C. § 1961(1)(A), and murder and conspiracy to commit murder could not therefore serve as predicate acts for their RICO convictions.

We disagree. United States v. Frumento, 563 F.2d 1083, (3d Cir. 1977) is directly on point. Defendants in that case were acquitted in state court on charges of bribery, extortion and conspiracy to accept bribes. They were then convicted in federal court of violating 18 U.S.C. § 1962(c) and (d), with the above crimes as predicate acts. On appeal defendants argued that the conviction was barred by the double jeopardy clause of the fifth amendment. The Third Circuit disagreed. The court said,

> [RICO] forbids "racketeering," not state offenses per se. The state offenses referred to in the federal act are definitional only; racketeering, the federal crime, is defined as a matter of legislative draftsmanship by a reference to state law crimes. This is not to say * * * that the federal statute punishes the same conduct as that reached by state law. The gravamen of § 1962 is a violation of federal law and "reference to state law is necessary only to identify the type of unlawful activity in which the defendant intended to engage. * * * "

VII. Principles of Double Jeopardy Did Not Bar the Government from Using Bribery as a Predicate Offense for the RICO Convictions

Defendants Liberatore and Ciarcia were convicted in federal court of bribing Ms. Rabinowitz. This bribery offense was also used as a predicate act for the RICO convictions of these two defendants. Liberatore and Ciarcia now claim that use of the bribery offense in the RICO prosecution violated the double jeopardy clause of the fifth amendment.

This Court has ruled on a closely related question in United States v. Morelli, 643 F.2d 402 (6th Cir.1981). Morelli was convicted of two counts of wire fraud, and these acts were used as predicate offenses for a RICO conviction. Morelli complained that he was subject to cruel and unusual punishment in violation of the eighth amendment because he was sentenced to fifteen years for the RICO violation, in addition to ten years for the wire fraud crimes. We held that Congress "may constitutionally make the commission of crimes within a specified period of time and within the course of a particular type of enterprise an independent criminal offense * * *." 643 F.2d at 413. We now hold that there was no violation of double jeopardy in trying defendants Liberatore and Ciarcia for both the federal bribery charge and the RICO charge. * * *

We affirm defendants' RICO convictions.

MERRITT, CIRCUIT JUDGE, concurring.

I concur in the clear and well reasoned opinion prepared by Judge Kennedy.

It may seem strange for a federal court to uphold convictions under a federal statute based on two underlying predicate state offenses for which a defendant has either been acquitted at state trials (the murder of Danny Greene) or for which he could not be separately convicted or punished under state law (conspiracy to murder Danny Greene). But RICO is now unique. The normal rules of construction do not apply to RICO. Although I had earlier believed that normal canons of construction applicable to other criminal statutes should be applied to RICO, the Supreme Court has now made it clear that RICO is to be given the broadest and most expansive possible interpretation in order to carry out Congressional intent aimed at eliminating organized crime. See United States v. Turkette, 452 U.S. 576 (1981); Russello v. United States, 464 U.S. 16 (1983). In *Russello,* a unanimous Supreme Court has pointed to RICO as the only federal criminal statute which should receive this kind of broad and expansive interpretation:

> The legislative history clearly demonstrates that the RICO statute was intended to provide new weapons of unprecedented scope for an assault upon organized crime and its economic roots * * *. Further, Congress directed [in the statute]: "The provisions of this title shall be liberally construed to effectuate its remedial purposes." *So far as we have been made aware, this is the only substantive federal criminal statute that contains such a directive* * * *.

104 S.Ct. at 302. (emphasis added). Thus, RICO, liberally construed as required by the Supreme Court, can reasonably be interpreted, and therefore should be interpreted, so that a defendant can be convicted even though he has already been acquitted or convicted of the two underlying offenses in state court and even though he could not be convicted or punished for both offenses together under state law.

UNITED STATES v. AULICINO

United States Court of Appeals for the Second Circuit, 1995.
44 F.3d 1102.

Opinion, KEARSE:

[Three defendants Robert Aulicino, Jr., David Cleary, and Louis Ruggiero, Jr., were convicted of various crimes by a jury. Aulicino was convicted of conspiracy to kidnap; Cleary and Ruggiero were convicted of participating in, and conspiring to participate in, the affairs of a RICO enterprise under 18 U.S.C. §§ 1962(c) and (d); Cleary was convicted on 23 other counts for violating various federal statutes, including kidnapping and conspiracy to kidnap; Ruggiero was convicted on 32 similar counts. Defendants' appeals raised several claims, including the argument that the evidence was insufficient to establish a RICO pattern.]

I. BACKGROUND

The present prosecution centered on a kidnaping ring, most of whose targeted victims were highly successful narcotics dealers. The ring was divided into two "crews." One crew, led by Steven Palmer, identified potential victims; members of the other crew, whose leaders were Ruggiero and Cleary, then impersonated law enforcement officers, purported to arrest the victim, abducted him, and ordered him to raise a ransom.

The government's case was presented principally through the testimony of more than 40 witnesses; physical evidence, including law enforcement badges, firearms, and handcuffs, seized from Cleary's home or from Ruggiero, Cleary, Aulicino, and other coconspirators; and tape recordings of conversations between coconspirators and of ransom calls made by Ruggiero to one victim's family. Three of the witnesses, Derrick Augustine, Albert Van Dyke, and William Conklin, were members of the ring who had participated in the planning or execution of the kidnaping conduct. The evidence, taken in the light most favorable to the government, was as follows.

A. *The Kidnaping Conspiracy*

Palmer conceived the kidnaping scheme in 1990. The group he led included Augustine, Van Dyke, and codefendants James Brown, Keith Green, and Robert Cherry, all of whom were or had been active in drug trafficking in Harlem and the Bronx. Augustine, who had worked for many of the most successful Harlem drug traffickers, was recruited as a member of this crew to select appropriate kidnaping victims. Palmer told his crew that he knew men who would pose as law enforcement officers to abduct the victims and extract the ransoms. For this aspect of the scheme, Palmer called upon Ruggiero and Cleary. The crew led by Ruggiero and Cleary included codefendants Anthony Castelli, Richard Olivieri, and Michael Palazzolo. Palmer, Augustine, and other members of their crew met with Ruggiero and Cleary to discuss potential victims and likely ransoms. They compiled a list of 10 targets. Over the next several months, seven attempts were made, with varying degrees of success.

Augustine testified that in late 1990 he informed Palmer that a drug dealer named Otmar Delaney was doing an active drug business at a garage in Harlem. Palmer relayed the information to Ruggiero. Ruggiero, with an associate apparently identified in the record only as "Tommy," followed Delaney to his home in Yonkers, New York; Ruggiero, stating that he was a police officer, approached Delaney and placed him under "arrest." Ruggiero and "Tommy" put Delaney into the trunk of their car and took him to a motel in New Jersey.

In the motel room, Ruggiero handcuffed Delaney to a chair and tortured him with a staple gun until he eventually agreed to pay $750,000. Ruggiero at first used Delaney's cellular telephone to arrange payment of the ransom by Delaney's half-brother. When the batteries in that telephone went dead, however, Ruggiero left the room to use a public telephone. In Ruggiero's absence, Delaney told "Tommy" he needed water, and when "Tommy" went to the bathroom to get it, Delaney, still handcuffed to the chair, escaped from the room. He explained his predicament to a truck driver in the parking lot, and the two went to the motel manager's office to summon the police. While they were there, Ruggiero entered the lobby, and Delaney retreated, saying that Ruggiero was one of his kidnapers. With one hand still handcuffed to the chair, Delaney commandeered his benefactor's truck and drove off wildly, with the truck driver clinging to the side. The truck collided with two other vehicles and came to a stop. The police arrived; Ruggiero and "Tommy" had fled.

Members of the ring met to discuss the Delaney fiasco. Palazzolo assured the Palmer crew that "nothing like that would ever happen again." The coconspirators were angry that Delaney had gotten away, and they made new attempts to extort money from him. Ruggiero and Cleary resumed surveillance of Delaney's garage. Members of both crews made telephone calls to threaten new kidnaping attempts unless Delaney paid them. At one point, Ruggiero drove into the garage "to scare them up some, to let them know that they got away but they going *[sic]* to get them again[,] and show his face." These postkidnaping extortion attempts apparently ceased when Delaney, with a false promise of payment, lured members of the Palmer crew to a meeting that ended in a shootout.

The next kidnaping victim was Alvin Cassidy Goings, for whom Augustine had sold narcotics for several years. Shortly after Christmas 1990, Ruggiero, Cleary, Castelli, Olivieri, Palazzolo, and members of the Palmer crew met outside of a laundromat owned by Goings and followed him to other locations in the Bronx. Eventually, members of the Ruggiero/Cleary crew pulled Goings over to the side of the road, flashing law enforcement badges. Cleary and Palazzolo took Goings from his car, searched and handcuffed him, and placed him in the ring members' van. The ring extracted from Goings a sizeable ransom. Members of the

Palmer crew were told by Palmer and the Ruggiero/Cleary crew that the payment was $400,000; Palmer's crew members believed, based on neighborhood rumors, that the payment might have been as high as $1 million. Cleary later confided to one witness that the ransom had been $1 million. Some of the ransom from this kidnaping was used to purchase and customize sedans to be used in further kidnapings.

On January 26, 1991, ring members kidnaped Roberto Mercedes, who previously had supplied narcotics to Augustine. Ruggiero, Olivieri, and Palazzolo conducted a close surveillance of Mercedes's sporting goods Store, with Cleary and Augustine watching from a greater distance. After Mercedes left his store and went into a barber shop, Olivieri and Palazzolo entered the barber shop and purported to arrest Mercedes. They put Mercedes into their car, and, with Ruggiero, drove off. Ruggiero made numerous ransom calls to Mercedes's family. Despite Mercedes's being tortured, his brother refused to pay the demanded ransom. Some members of the ring began to suspect the ransom demands were futile because members of Mercedes's group preferred that he not be returned.

Because Olivieri and Palazzolo were concerned that Mercedes had seen their faces in the barber shop, Palmer ordered Brown to kill Mercedes; Brown gave Cherry a gun and turned the task over to him. Cherry transported Mercedes in the trunk of a car to a vacant lot in the Bronx, planning to shoot him there. When the trunk was opened, however, Mercedes came out kicking; although shot several times, he escaped and safely reached a police station. Notwithstanding the decision to kill Mercedes, Ruggiero continued to attempt to collect ransom money from Mercedes's brother; he was still trying some 10 minutes after Mercedes had reached the police station. Ruggiero abandoned his efforts when the brother demanded to see Mercedes before making any payment.

The ring next attempted to kidnap a major Harlem narcotics dealer named Richard Simmons, for whom Augustine had worked. Palmer, Brown, Ruggiero, Cleary, Castelli, Olivieri, and Palazzolo trailed Simmons to a street corner in Harlem, where Ruggiero and Cleary attempted to "arrest" him. However, Simmons had learned of the attacks on Delaney and Goings and had heard a description of Ruggiero; when Ruggiero and Cleary approached, Simmons clung to his car and yelled for the police. The ring members fled.

* * *

On March 31, 1991, ring members kidnaped David Crumpler, a restaurant owner who dealt cocaine in the Bronx. While Ruggiero, Cleary, and Castelli waited outside of Crumpler's restaurant, Cherry and two other members of Palmer's crew entered brandishing guns and badges and brought Crumpler out in handcuffs. They took him to a nearby gas station; he was transferred to the trunk of the car occupied by Ruggiero, Cleary, and Castelli, and was then taken to New Jersey. Some hours later, Crumpler's wife received a ransom demand for

$750,000. Despite torturing Crumpler with a blackjack, a stun gun, and a staple gun, Ruggiero, Cleary, and Castelli were unable to get Crumpler or his family to pay the ransom. Ruggiero eventually asked Palmer to come get Crumpler. Palmer, Augustine, Brown, and crew member Barry Shawn took Crumpler back to New York, and Shawn shot him to death. Crumpler's handcuffed body was found in a vacant lot in the Bronx.

On April 17, 1991, Palmer was murdered. Augustine testified that he, Brown, and other Palmer crew members had decided to kill Palmer because they believed Palmer had pointed the finger at them in the Harlem community with respect to the series of kidnapings. Ruggiero, Cleary, Olivieri, and Palazzolo, however, feared that Palmer might have been killed by one of the kidnaping victims. A wiretap intercepted anxious conversations between Ruggiero and Cleary speculating that Delaney might have killed Palmer, and between Cleary and Palazzolo speculating that Simmons might have done it. In a May 22, 1991 telephone conversation with Ruggiero, Augustine attempted to encourage the belief that Palmer had been killed by one of the kidnaping victims. In addition, in that conversation, Augustine said, "I'm telling you, we need to get smart, man. One time and then leave this shit alone." Ruggiero responded "Yup," and "Maybe we will."

The surviving members of the ring attempted no further kidnapings.
* * *

B. *The Present Prosecution*

Eventually, most of the surviving ring members were arrested. * * * Defendants were charged with RICO, kidnaping, conspiracy, extortion, murder, and firearms offenses. Olivieri, Palazzolo, Castelli, and Augustine pleaded guilty to various counts prior to trial. Brown, Green, and Cherry were fugitives at the time of trial but were later apprehended: Brown and Green pleaded guilty to the RICO conspiracy count.

* * *

II. DISCUSSION

On appeal, defendants contend principally that the evidence was legally insufficient to establish a RICO pattern * * *. We find no basis for reversal.

* * *

B. *The RICO Pattern Challenge*

Ruggiero and Cleary contend that their RICO substantive and conspiracy convictions should be reversed on the ground that the government failed to prove that they engaged in a "pattern of racketeering activity" within the meaning of RICO. They argue (a) that the evidence showed that they conducted their kidnapings and attempted kidnapings only over a period of some 3 1/2 months, a period they contend is too short to show a RICO pattern, and (b) that because the enterprise ended before the present prosecution commenced, the government failed to prove any threat of continuity. We disagree.

RICO prohibits, *inter alia,* the conduct of or participation in the affairs of an enterprise "through a pattern of racketeering activity." 18 U.S.C. § 1962(c). The term "racketeering activity" includes felonious "act[s] or threat[s] involving murder, kidnaping, . . . [or] extortion." *Id.* § 1961(1). The term "pattern of racketeering activity" is defined as "requiring at least two acts of racketeering activity" within 10 years of each other. *Id.* § 1961(5). As the Supreme Court noted in *H.J. Inc. v. Northwestern Bell Telephone Co., 492 U.S. 229, 106 L. Ed. 2d 195, 109 S. Ct. 2893 (1989) ("H.J. Inc."), §* 1961(5) sets "only the minimum *number* of predicates necessary to establish a pattern; and it assumes that there is something to a RICO pattern *beyond* simply the number of predicate acts involved." The precise scope and contour of that "something . . . *beyond,"* however, have proven elusive.

In *H.J. Inc.,* the Supreme Court stated that, in order to establish a pattern of racketeering activity, a party must show that the racketeering predicate acts are not isolated or sporadic but are related, and "that the predicates themselves amount to, or that they otherwise constitute a threat of, *continuing* racketeering activity." The *H.J. Inc.* Court, reviewing a ruling that the RICO pattern element required proof of multiple "schemes," held that the pattern element did not require a plaintiff to prove that the defendant engaged in more than one scheme, stating that "what a plaintiff or prosecutor must prove is continuity of racketeering activity, or its threat, *simpliciter."* Continuity itself and the "threat" of continuity have not proven to be simple concepts.

In *H.J. Inc.,* the Court stated that continuity or its threat "may be [proven] in a variety of ways, thus making it difficult to formulate in the abstract any general test for continuity." *Id.* In general, the Court stated, "continuity"

> is both a closed-and open-ended concept, referring either to a closed period of repeated conduct, or to past conduct that by its nature projects into the future with a threat of repetition. . . . It is, in either case, centrally a temporal concept—and particularly so in the RICO context, where *what* must be continuous, RICO's predicate acts or offenses, and the *relationship* these predicates must bear one to another, are distinct requirements. A party alleging a RICO violation may demonstrate continuity over a closed period by proving a series of related predicates extending over a substantial period of time. Predicate acts extending over a few weeks or months and threatening no future criminal conduct do not satisfy this requirement: Congress was concerned in RICO with long-term criminal conduct. Often a RICO action will be brought before continuity can be established in this way. In such cases, liability depends on whether the *threat* of continuity is demonstrated.

The *H.J. Inc.* Court stated that a threat of continuity exists, for example, where the predicate acts "include a specific threat of repetition extending indefinitely into the future," or where the acts form "part of a long-term association that exists for criminal purposes," or where the acts constitute "a regular way of conducting [an] ongoing legitimate business." With respect to duration, the *H.J. Inc.* majority stated that "very short periods of criminal activity that do *not* in any way carry a threat of continued criminal activity" do not constitute racketeering to which Congress intended RICO to apply.

The *H.J. Inc.* Court preceded the above examples with an express disavowal of "any claim to cover the field of possibilities," stating that it was preferable to "deal with this issue in the context of concrete factual situations presented for decision." Since Congress intended the courts to take a "flexible approach," the sufficiency of a party's proof of a threat of continuity will "depend[ ] on the specific facts of each case."

In the wake of *H.J. Inc.,* the lower courts have struggled with the Supreme Court's view that periods of "a few weeks or months" may not be sufficient to show a RICO pattern. As discussed below, in cases where the acts of the defendant or the enterprise were inherently unlawful, such as murder or obstruction of justice, and were in pursuit of inherently unlawful goals, such as narcotics trafficking or embezzlement, the courts generally have concluded that the requisite threat of continuity was adequately established by the nature of the activity, even though the period spanned by the racketeering acts was short. In contrast, in cases concerning alleged racketeering activity in furtherance of endeavors that are not inherently unlawful, such as frauds in the sale of property, the courts generally have found no threat of continuing criminal activity arising from conduct that extended over even longer periods.

* * *

Ruggiero and Cleary zoom in on *H.J. Inc.'s* statements that Congress intended RICO to reach only activities amounting to or threatening "long-term" criminal activity, rather than "very short periods" of criminal activity that last only "a few weeks or months"; and they argue that their enterprise's series of kidnapings did not constitute a RICO pattern because their repeated conduct did not extend over a "substantial period of time," and, having been abandoned after 3 1/2 months, did not "by its nature project[ ] into the future with a threat of repetition." In effect, Ruggiero and Cleary argue that *H.J. Inc.* holds that Congress granted them a RICO-free window of opportunity to engage in numerous racketeering acts, provided that they stopped of their own volition after a few weeks or months. We reject this view.

While the history of the kidnaping enterprise at issue here does not match the continuity examples given by the *H.J. Inc.* Court, those examples were intended to be illustrative, not definitive, and *H.J. Inc.* instructs us to determine continuity with reference to the specific facts of each case. For several reasons, the facts of the present case leave no room for doubt that the ring engaged in a pattern of racketeering activity within the contemplation of Congress in enacting RICO.

First, there was nothing isolated or sporadic about the acts of racketeering performed by the enterprise in the present case. There was evidence that the ring drew up a list of 10 kidnaping targets. The ring planned to abduct its victims seriatim and aspired to ransoms of $1 million per victim. They used proceeds from their successful kidnaping to buy and customize vehicles for the kidnapings to follow. The very plan to undertake a series of inherently unlawful and interrelated racketeering acts is instinct with the threat of continuity.

Second, the kidnapings here were especially likely to involve further criminal activity. It is not uncommon for a kidnaping to result in the kidnapers' killing their victim in order to prevent his later identifying the kidnapers. The likelihood of victim identification of the kidnapers in the present scheme was heightened by the ring's modus operandi, with members of the ring pretending to be police officers and thus approaching their intended victims openly. Thus, this ring's kidnaping activities carried a high threat of further criminal activity, to wit, murder. Indeed, the coconspirators decided to kill Mercedes (which they attempted unsuccessfully) and Crumpler (successfully) precisely for fear that the victims, if allowed to go free, would be able to identify the ring members who had "arrested" them.

In addition, though actual kidnaping attempts were made only from mid-December 1990 through March 31, 1991, a period of some 3 1/2 months, there is no basis for viewing the ring's activities as having reached a natural end. The ring had begun with a list of 10 proposed victims; even assuming that the ring meant to stop after 10 kidnapings, it did not even exhaust its initial list. The ring members made attempts on only seven of its targets. Further, the circumstances were unlike those in which a defendant had a piece of property the sale of which, even if by fraudulent means, provided a natural end to his project. There was no reason the ring could not attempt to kidnap additional individuals any time the ring members wanted more money. Indeed, there was no inherent reason the ring could not attempt to kidnap the same individual more than once (assuming the victim had not been killed). For example, ring members continued to attempt to extort money from Delaney even after he escaped, and they threatened to kidnap him again.

Finally, though the last kidnaping (and last actual attempt) occurred at the end of March, Ruggiero and Augustine discussed making another attempt near the end of May. The kidnapings appear to have ended for lack of Palmer's leadership; the discussions of further attempts appear to have ended because of the fears of Ruggiero, Cleary, and Augustine that the authorities might be on their trail or because of Cleary's arrest on other charges in June and Augustine's subsequent flight from New York. The ring's activities were abandoned; they were not a discrete and finite project that came to a natural end.

* * * The jury could easily find the threat of continued criminal activity from the evidence that the ring made an average of one kidnaping attempt every two weeks for 14 weeks, made repeated extortion

attempts where the kidnapings had failed to extract ransoms, and had not exhausted its list of kidnaping targets.

* * *

[The judgments of conviction were affirmed.]

UNITED STATES v. SUTHERLAND

United States Court of Appeals, Fifth Circuit, 1981.
656 F.2d 1181.

RANDALL, CIRCUIT JUDGE:

In this case three defendants appeal their convictions for conspiracy to violate [RICO]. The defendants raise a large number of issues, one of which involves an important RICO question: whether and when conspiracies that involve the same enterprise but are otherwise unrelated may be tried together under a single RICO conspiracy count. * * *

I. The Facts

* * * The indictment charged, in brief, that the three defendants "did knowingly, wilfully, and unlawfully combine, conspire, confederate, and agree together and with each other," from November 1975 until the date of the indictment, to violate section 1962(c). The conspiracy alleged by the government consisted of an agreement to associate with and to participate in the conduct of an enterprise that affects interstate commerce (the Municipal Court of the City of El Paso) through a pattern of racketeering activity (bribery of a state official in violation of state law).

The alleged conspiracy centers around Sutherland, who at the time of these events was a judge of the Municipal Court. According to the government, the defendants agreed that Maynard and Walker would each collect traffic tickets from his or her friends and associates, along with the amount of the statutory fine plus a small premium ($10); that Maynard and Walker would deliver the tickets to Sutherland, who would have the cases transferred to his docket and would then favorably dispose of them; and that the money collected would in each case be split between Sutherland and whichever other defendant collected and delivered the ticket.

Although the indictment frames the conspiracy as a single agreement among all three defendants, the government did not attempt at trial to prove any agreement between Walker and Maynard. * * *

In each case the evidence is more than sufficient to establish an agreement to participate in the conduct of the Municipal Court through a pattern of racketeering activity. However, the government has pointed to no evidence in the record (and we have found none) that suggests that either Walker or Maynard knew or should have known of the other's similar agreement with Sutherland. The government's evidence as to these two defendants is entirely unrelated and, in fact, places the two conspiracies at different periods of time: the specific instances of bribery alleged between Walker and Sutherland all took place between 1975 and 1977, while those between Maynard and Sutherland all took place in 1979. * * *

III. The Multiple Conspiracy Doctrine and RICO

A. *The Trial of Multiple Conspiracies Under a Single RICO "Enterprise Conspiracy" Count*

It is now well settled that a material variance between the indictment and the government's evidence is created by the government's proof of multiple conspiracies under an indictment alleging a single conspiracy. [The opinion discussed the holdings of the Supreme Court in the *Kotteakos* and *Blumenthal* cases in the preceding section of this casebook, explaining the difference between multiple "wheel" conspiracies as in *Kotteakos* and single "chain" conspiracies as in *Blumenthal.*]

The government does not defend its joint trial in this case on the basis of traditional conspiracy law, i.e., by arguing either that the evidence connected the spokes of a wheel conspiracy by common knowledge or agreement, or that the evidence demonstrates a chain conspiracy. Instead, the government argues that despite the apparent relevance to this case of the traditional multiple conspiracy doctrine, the defendants were properly tried together for a single "enterprise conspiracy" under RICO. The government contends, in brief, that a single conspiracy to violate a substantive RICO provision may be comprised of a pattern of agreements that absent RICO would constitute multiple conspiracies. The government contends that this is so even where, as here, there is no agreement of any kind between the members of the two separate conspiracies. According to the government, these otherwise multiple conspiracies are tied together by the RICO "enterprise:" so long as the object of each conspiracy is participation in the same enterprise in violation of RICO, it matters not that the different conspiracies are otherwise unrelated. Thus, the government argues that it need not demonstrate any connection between Walker and Maynard because the two conspiracies at issue each involved the same RICO enterprise—the Municipal Court of the City of El Paso.

For this proposition the government relies on United States v. Elliott, 571 F.2d 880 (5th Cir.1978). We held in *Elliott* that a group of defendants who could not have been tried for a single conspiracy to violate any particular predicate crime could nevertheless be tried for a single conspiracy to violate RICO. * * *

Read out of context, without attention to the facts of the case or to the court's rationale, *Elliott* does seem to support the government's position—i.e., that the defendants' participation in the same RICO enterprise is enough to tie otherwise multiple conspiracies together even where, as here, there is no agreement of any kind between the members of the two separate conspiracies. Indeed, *Elliott* has been thus read by some courts and commentators (and, as so read, has been uniformly criticized). * * *

Taken to its logical extreme, a rule allowing the joint trial of otherwise unrelated conspiracies solely on the basis of their relationship to a common enterprise—the rule which the government advocates in this case—leads to ridiculous results.

[The government's theory could be applied to a court of very broad geographical jurisdiction, such as the United States Court of Appeals for the Fifth Circuit, with the result that "an agreement to bribe a court official in El Paso, Texas could be part of the same conspiracy as an unrelated agreement to use a judicial office for illicit profit-making purposes in Fort Lauderdale, Florida, when neither the El Paso nor the Fort Lauderdale conspirators knew of the existence of the other group."] This extreme hypothetical problem is not fundamentally different from the case now before us. Although both conspiracies in the case at bar involved the same judge, it is not that fact which the government argues ties the two conspiracies together. Rather, it is each conspiracy's relationship to the same enterprise (the Municipal Court of the City of El Paso) that is said to provide the necessary link. Thus, the theory urged by the government would bring together individual conspiracies to bribe different judges on the same court.

In this case the government has not attempted to prove that Walker and Maynard agreed with each other to participate in a bribery scheme with Sutherland, nor has it contended that the nature of each defendant's agreement with Sutherland was such that he or she must necessarily have known that others were also conspiring to commit racketeering offenses in the conduct of the Municipal Court. We must conclude, therefore, that the multiple conspiracy doctrine precluded the joint trial of the two multiple conspiracies involved in this case on a single RICO conspiracy count. In accordance with *Kotteakos* and its progeny, we must reverse the defendants' convictions if this error affected their substantial rights.

[The court held that the variance between the single conspiracy charged in the indictment and the two separate conspiracies proved at trial was not prejudicial because the number of defendants and conspiracies was small, the evidence on each charge was quite distinct, and the proof of each individual defendant's guilt was overwhelming.]

Affirmed.

UNITED STATES v. ANDREWS

United States District Court for the Northern District of Illinois, Eastern Division, 1990.
754 F.Supp. 1161.

Marvin E. Aspen, United States District Judge

The labyrinthine 305–page, 175–count indictment in this case, nearly two inches thick and weighing almost four pounds, names thirty-eight defendants, thirty-seven of whom are alleged to have been members or associates of the El Rukns, an infamous Chicago street gang. It details a maze of well over 250 factually separate criminal acts committed from 1966 to 1989 in many different locations and, for each act, alleges the participation of varying combinations of defendants and countless unindicted co-conspirators. The government's justification for including many of these otherwise unconnected criminal events in one indictment and one trial is that each was allegedly committed to attain power, control, and wealth for the street gang.

* * * [A]t least twenty-two defendants, but as many as twenty-nine, will be going to trial. Several defendants have filed motions to sever this indictment pursuant to Rule 8(b) or, in the alternative, Rule 14 of the Federal Rules of Criminal Procedure, and the issue before the Court is whether we should permit these 175 diverse charges to be tried in a single mega-trial of unprecedented projected duration. We believe that we should not. Therefore, for the reasons discussed below, although we deny the Rule 8(b) motions, the Rule 14 motions are granted.

I. Indictment

A. *Count One–RICO Conspiracy*

Count One of the indictment charges all but one of the defendants with conspiracy to violate the Racketeering Influenced and Corrupt Organizations Act ("RICO"), 18 U.S.C. § 1962(d)(1988), and alleges that the El Rukn organization is a racketeering "enterprise" as defined by 18 U.S.C. § 1961(4). It describes a cohesive organization with tightly controlled operations and a formal chain of command. As alleged, unindicted co-conspirator Jeff Fort masterminded the activities of the El Rukns and wielded ultimate and unquestioned authority. He was assisted by thirty-five defendants whom the government contends were El Rukn "generals" or "officers," the organization's second and third levels of command, respectively. The government contends that the remaining two defendants named in Count One, although not El Rukn members, were otherwise intimately associated with the organization.

Under the direction and control of Fort, the named defendants and other unindicted co-conspirators are alleged to have conducted El Rukn affairs through the commission of an astonishing number of racketeering acts, including at least twenty murders, twelve attempted murders, eleven conspiracies to murder, one act of kidnapping, wide-scale drug trafficking, and numerous acts of obstruction of justice, including one attempt to bribe a judge and several acts of witness intimidation, retaliation, and tampering. As alleged, all of these wide-ranging and diverse offenses are connected, although at times somewhat loosely, to the affairs of the El Rukn street gang.

B. *Count Two–Substantive RICO*

Count Two charges thirty-six defendants with substantive violations of RICO under 18 U.S.C. § 1962(c)and recounts 128 separate acts of racketeering, many of which are also alleged in Count One. The number of racketeering acts that each defendant is alleged to have committed ranges from as many as seventy for Melvin Mayes to only two for Isiah Kitchen. The nature of acts charged also varies. Some defendants are charged with numerous violent racketeering acts and only one or two narcotics-related acts, while other defendants are charged solely with narcotics-related acts.

1. Violent Racketeering Acts

According to the allegations in Count Two, the long string of violent racketeering acts began in May 1974, when several defendants murdered Gilbert Connors, the brother of a rival drug dealer, to prevent encroachment on the El Rukn drug trade. To facilitate a cover-up of this crime, the same defendants subsequently killed Gregory Freeman on May 22, 1974, and blamed this murder on a witness to the Connors homicide. As a result, El Rukn members were able to persuade the witness to refuse to testify and the charges in both the Connors and Freeman murder cases were subsequently dropped.

Other murders were committed to enforce and enhance Jeff Fort's control over the El Rukns. Fort ordered El Rukn members, including several defendants, to kill disloyal members and former El Rukn leaders * * *.

The El Rukns also went to extreme lengths to protect its members from criminal prosecution. In August 1977, eighteen defendants conspired to kill Audrina Thomas to prevent her from testifying against two El Rukn generals charged with murder. Then, in a case of mistaken identity, Thomas' sister, Rowena James, was shot and killed on September 1, 1977. In January of 1987, four defendants and other El Rukn members kidnapped Patricia McKinley in an attempt to prevent her from testifying against an El Rukn general charged with the murder of Maurice Coleman.

The El Rukns committed a slew of other murders and attempted murders related to narcotics activity. * * *

From about April 1981 to January 1983, as a result of a drug territorial dispute, twenty-three defendants conspired to kill the top leaders and members of the Titanic Stones, a rival gang * * *. During that same time period, Willie Bibbs and Barnett Hall were killed and George Thomas was the target of an attempted murder. In the course of the Thomas attempt, on January 23, 1983, five defendants and other gang members killed Charmaine Nathan and shot and attempted to kill Sheila Jackson.

[The opinion then recounted numerous other murders and attempted murders allegedly committed by gang members.]

2. Non–Violent Racketeering Acts

Count Two alleges ninety-seven additional racketeering acts which, with one exception, are narcotics-related offenses. The only exception, designated Racketeering Act 128, charges defendants Melvin Mayes and Alan Knox with using the telephone to facilitate the acquisition of an M–72 series Light Anti–Tank Weapon, commonly referred to as a LAW rocket, in violation of 18 U.S.C. § 1952(a)(3) (1988). The narcotics-related offenses alleged in Count Two include the possession and distribution of narcotics * * * and interstate travel with intent to further narcotics offenses * * *.

C. *Count Three–Narcotics Conspiracy*

Racketeering Act 31 is repeated as a separate "substantive" offense in Count Three. This Count describes a conspiracy to possess with intent to distribute, and to distribute, multi-kilogram quantities of heroin and cocaine, hundreds of pounds of marijuana, thousands of amphetamine pills, thousands of Talwin and Triplenamin pills, multi-liter quantities of codeine syrup, and large quantities of Phencyclidine (PCP). The government contends that, on a regular basis during the course of this conspiracy, from 1966 to 1989, various defendants purchased narcotics from sources in at least seven states, including Florida, South Carolina, Mississippi, New York, Wisconsin, Illinois, and Michigan. The government further contends that narcotics the defendants sold narcotics from numerous El Rukn-controlled buildings and territories throughout the Illinois cities of Chicago, Evanston, Skokie, and Harvey, and also from Milwaukee, Wisconsin.

D. *The Other Counts*

[The opinion listed various other offenses charged, including firearms and narcotics offenses, as well as murders, attempted murders and witness tampering.]

II. Severance Discussion

Numerous defendants have filed motions to sever this indictment claiming that they are improperly joined pursuant to Rule 8(b), or, in the alternative, that joinder is unduly prejudicial pursuant to Rule 14. We will discuss these motions in turn.

A. *Rule 8(b)*

Rule 8(b) permits joinder of an unlimited number of defendants "if they are alleged to have participated in the same act or transaction or in the same series of acts or transactions constituting an offense or offenses." Fed.R.Crim.P. 8(b). In determining whether joinder is proper under this Rule, a court must look to the face of the indictment. If the indictment alleges a conspiracy, it is well established that all members of that conspiracy are properly joined.

Although the defendants agree with this settled principal, they nonetheless argue that they are improperly joined. Relying on Kotteakos v. United States, 328 U.S. 750, 66 S. Ct. 1239, 90 L. Ed. 1557 (1946), they argue that the indictment fails to satisfy Rule 8(b) because it alleges multiple distinct conspiracies, including separate conspiracies to murder, obstruct justice, and distribute narcotics. In *Kotteakos*, the Supreme Court reversed the convictions of the petitioners where the evidence established at least eight separate conspiracies connected only by a common participant. The Court stated that a defendant has a right "not to be tried *en masse* for the conglomeration of distinct and separate offenses committed by others...." Thus, according to the defendants here, *Kotteakos* requires a finding that they are improperly joined.

While their characterization of the indictment is correct, the defendants are wrong that the allegation of separate conspiracies renders joinder improper under Rule 8(b). With the advent of RICO, Congress significantly broadened the scope of the government's authority to bring defendants together in one indictment. It conferred this broad authority without eviscerating the principals set forth in *Kotteakos* or "radically alter[ing] traditional conspiracy doctrine...." Instead, Congress simply outlawed a particular conspiratorial agreement, the object of which could include the commission of a wide array of separate and distinct offenses. Section 1962(d) of the RICO statute proscribes agreements "to conduct or participate in the affairs of an enterprise through a pattern of racketeering activity." *United States v. Neapolitan,* 791 F.2d 489, 498 (7th Cir.), *cert. denied*, 479 U.S. 940, 107 S. Ct. 422, 93 L. Ed. 2d 372 (1986). A single "pattern of racketeering activity" can include numerous distinct conspiracies. *United States v. Sutherland,* 656 F.2d 1181, 1192 (5th Cir.1981), *cert. denied*, 455 U.S. 949, 102 S. Ct. 1451, 71 L. Ed. 2d 663 (1982). Consequently, "a series of agreements that under pre-RICO law would constitute multiple conspiracies could under RICO be tried as a single 'enterprise' conspiracy" in violation of § 1962(d).[6] *Sutherland,* 656 F.2d at 1192. Therefore, consistent with the rationale of *Kotteakos*, the defendants in this case are properly joined because they are each alleged members of a *single* and unifying RICO conspiracy. The separate and distinct underlying conspiracies are simply part of the "same series of acts or transactions constituting [this] offense...." Fed.R.Crim.P. 8(b).

Some defendants argue in the alternative that joinder is improper because the indictment charges certain defendants with substantially more conspiratorial activity than others. This argument has no merit. According to the Seventh Circuit in *United States v. Whaley*:

> Various people knowingly joining together in furtherance of a common design or purpose constitute a single conspiracy. While the conspiracy may have a small group of core conspirators, other parties who knowingly participate with these core conspirators and others to achieve a common goal may be members of an overall conspiracy.

6. Many of the defendants base their motions on a misreading of the Fifth Circuit's holding in *Sutherland*. They argue that, according to *Sutherland*, an alleged RICO conspiracy cannot provide the nexus between separate conspiracies necessary to find joinder proper. This is a profound misunderstanding of that case. In fact, the case stands for precisely the opposite proposition: that an alleged RICO conspiracy is a sufficient nexus. The *Sutherland* court held that an alleged RICO conspiracy ties multiple conspiracies together, not merely because they all involve the same enterprise, but because—as in any other conspiracy—there is an "agreement on an overall objective." *Sutherland,* 656 F.2d at 1192–93; *see also Neapolitan,* 791 F.2d at 496 n. 3 (discussing Sutherland). Thus, the defendants' reliance on *Sutherland* is unavailing.

830 F.2d 1469, 1474 (7th Cir.1987) Moreover, mere ignorance of the identities of all of the conspirators or of all the details of the conspiracy is immaterial. Thus, regardless of the alleged extent of any one defendant's involvement, all of the defendants in this case are properly joined for purposes of Rule 8(b) because they each allegedly agreed to the "overall objective," namely to conduct or participate in the affairs of the so called "El Rukn Nation" through a pattern of racketeering. Indeed, the government claims that each of the moving defendants willingly held a formal leadership position, either as a "general" or "officer," and thus "operated and promoted the [racketeering] activities of the enterprise, and exercised authority over subordinate members." We conclude that these defendants are properly joined. Accordingly, their motions to sever pursuant to Rule 8(b) are denied.[9]

B. Rule 14

Having decided that the requirements of Rule 8(b) are met by the allegations in the indictment, we turn to Rule 14. As indicated above, although joinder is technically proper under Rule 8(b), Rule 14 authorizes severance if such joinder is prejudicial to the defendants. According to Rule 14:

> If it appears that a defendant or the government is prejudiced by a joinder of offenses or of defendants in an indictment or information or by such joinder for trial together, the court may order an election or separate trials of counts, grant the severance of a defendant or provide whatever relief justice requires.

* * *

[The court reviewed advantages of joint trials, including their capacity to "reduce the expenditure of judicial and prosecutorial time [and] ... the claims the criminal justice system makes on witnesses, who need not return to court for additional trials." The court then weighed these advantages against the costs associated with mega-trials in which dozens of defendants are charged with committing numerous crimes over a period of many years. It concluded that the costs outweighed the benefits. Some of its reasoning is set out below.]

It is fanciful to believe that any jury would be able, or even willing, to intelligently and thoroughly deliberate over the enormous volume of evidence expected at a single trial of this action. In its present form, the

9. This case provides a vivid example of the broad charging authority that RICO has conferred to the government. Prior to RICO, the scope of a proper indictment under Rule 8(b) was largely restricted to the number of individuals who could conspire to commit a single substantive crime. RICO removes this natural "ceiling" by making it a crime to agree to the commission of a "pattern of racketeering," which can include a limitless number of substantive crimes and, consequently, a limitless number of conspirators. Thus, RICO evades the practical limitations of group conduct that Rule 8(b) places on the scope of an indictment. *See Neapolitan,* 791 F.2d at 501 ("The government, through its ability to craft the indictment, is the master of the scope of the charged RICO conspiracy.... [It] can be broad or narrow depending on the number of predicate crimes within the scope of the agreement that the government chooses to identify.").

* * *

trial would involve twenty-two to twenty-nine defendants accused of over 150 factually separate criminal acts spanning a period of over twenty years and involving at least twenty-five different provisions of the state and federal penal codes. The government concedes that the volume of evidence at such a trial would be "massive," and we find that solely by virtue of its volume the evidence would be equally "complex." After this long and arduous trial, the jury would be required to sift through a virtual warehouse of evidence to determine what items were presented against which defendant and as to which criminal act. It would then be obliged to resolve a plethora of difficult factual issues and to strictly apply the detailed and complex law as provided by hundreds of pages of jury instructions. The inevitable length of such a trial dramatically increases the difficulty of this Herculean task. Both common sense and scientific study dictate that as the volume of evidence and corresponding length of trial increases, the degree and quality of jury comprehension decreases proportionately. To expect any jury to accurately recall and appraise the vast amount of detailed testimonial and documentary evidence it heard many months or even a year earlier is unrealistically optimistic.

* * *

C. Balance Struck in Favor of Severance

In summary, the potential prejudice against the defendants in this case and the administrative and fiscal advantages of separate trials outweigh any of the possible advantages of conducting a joint trial. Indeed, a trial of this magnitude would be appropriate in only the rarest circumstances. Nonetheless, in spite of its inherent prejudice and affront to the public interest, the mega-trial too often has been improperly tolerated and even endorsed by some participants in our judicial system.

In the first instance, of course, the decision to bring a multitude of defendants and charges within the scope of a single indictment is within the province of the prosecutor. Some courts and commentators have urged prosecutorial restraint with regard to the use of this discretion. Indeed, a prosecutor has an *obligation* to use some measure of restraint and to consider the effect of a sizable indictment on the integrity of the resulting trial. * * *

Unfortunately, prosecutors have long been willing to bring cases of this nature despite the violence they do to the notion of a fair trial. Indeed, prosecutors generally have demonstrated an increasing "penchant for drawing together evermore complex and extensive conspiracies into a single indictment." This phenomenon can be explained by the fact that prosecutors have significant incentives to bring mass indictments, not the least of which is the consequent ability to procure a large number of convictions in what they perceive to be the shortest amount of time. The regrettable truth, however, is that these incentives carry far greater weight in the charging decision than any concern for a fair and manageable trial. It seems unlikely, then, that the recent increase in mega-trials will soon be curbed at the initiative of the prosecution.

* * *

V. Conclusion

* * *

The oft-stated rule is that defendants who are charged together should be tried together. Nevertheless, * * * [t]he large number of defendants, the large number and complexity of the charges, and the projected length of the proposed mega-trial presented in this indictment mandate that we order separate trials. Were we not to so rule, the defendants could not receive fair trials, the jury would not be able to properly perform its function, the costs of appointed counsel would be exorbitant, and the damage to the orderly administration of other litigation assigned to this Court's docket would be considerable. This is too high a price to pay for the government's ill-conceived desire to prosecute all these defendants in one spectacular trial extravaganza.

* * *

Chapter 8

THEFT AND WHITE COLLAR CRIME

A. LARCENY: TRADITIONAL ELEMENTS

The law of theft is of immense practical importance, if only because of the seemingly countless number of theft crimes that occur each year. For students of criminal law, it also provides a remarkable example of the evolution of common law and statutory rules over time and in response to changing social, political, economic, and technological conditions. The historical development of the crimes of larceny, embezzlement, and false pretenses is covered at length in Hall, Theft, Law and Society (2d ed. 1952) and in the treatises. See LaFave, Criminal Law 3d Ed., ch. 8 (2000); Perkins and Boyce, Criminal Law ch. 4 (3d ed. 1982).

Larceny was a common law felony, whereas embezzlement and false pretenses were statutory innovations. Larceny came to be defined as the trespassory taking and carrying away of the personal property of another with the intent to deprive him permanently of it. Every word in this definition has significance, as the following materials illustrate. An essential, but often perplexing requirement of larceny is that the taking be "trespassory." Larceny is a crime against possession rather than ownership. One can commit larceny by stealing the ill-gotten gains of a thief, but by the same token, there is no larceny where the rightful possessor parts with possession voluntarily. In other words, larceny under its strictest definition did not reach fraud, or abuse of trust by a bailee or servant. The guiding philosophy seems to have been that rightful possessors could protect themselves against these dishonest activities by the use of due care and the pursuit of civil remedies.

The following cases illustrate some of the theoretical and practical problems arising from the requirement of a trespassory taking.

1. Possession and Custody; Larceny and Embezzlement

COMMONWEALTH v. RYAN

Supreme Judicial Court of Massachusetts, 1892.
155 Mass. 523, 30 N.E. 364.

HOLMES, J. This is a complaint for embezzlement of money. The case for the government is as follows. The defendant was employed by one Sullivan to sell liquor for him in his store. Sullivan sent two detectives to the store, with marked money of Sullivan's, to make a feigned purchase from the defendant. One detective did so. The defendant dropped the money into the money drawer of a cash register, which happened to be open in connection with another sale made and registered by the defendant, but he did not register this sale, as was customary, and afterward—it would seem within a minute or two—he took the money from the drawer. The question presented is whether it appears, as matter of law, that the defendant was not guilty of embezzlement, but was guilty of larceny, if of anything. The defendant asked rulings to that effect on two grounds: first, that after the money was put into the drawer it was in Sullivan's possession, and therefore the removal of it was a trespass and larceny; and secondly, that Sullivan's ownership of the money, in some way not fully explained, prevented the offence from being embezzlement. We will consider these positions successively.

We must take it as settled that it is not larceny for a servant to convert property delivered to him by a third person for his master, provided he does so before the goods have reached their destination, or something more has happened to reduce him to a mere custodian; while, on the other hand, if the property is delivered to the servant by his master, the conversion is larceny. [Citations]

This distinction is not very satisfactory, but it is due to historical accidents in the development of the criminal law, coupled, perhaps, with an unwillingness on the part of the judges to enlarge the limits of a capital offence.

The history of it is this. There was no felony when a man received possession of goods from the owner without violence. The early judges did not always distinguish clearly in their language between the delivery of possession to a bailee and the giving of custody to a servant, which indeed later judges some times have failed to do. When the peculiar law of master and servant was applied either to the master's responsibility or to his possession, the test seems to have been whether or not the servant was under the master's eye, rather than based on the notion of *status* and identity of person, as it was at a later day. Within his house a master might be answerable for the torts of his servant, and might have possession of goods in his servant's custody, although he himself had put the goods into the servant's hands; outside the house there was more doubt; as when a master intrusted his horse to his servant to go to market.

It was settled by St. 21 Hen. VIII, c. 7, that the conversion of goods delivered to a servant by his master was felony, and this statute has been thought to be only declaratory of the common law in later times, since the distinction between the possession of a bailee and the custody of a servant has been developed more fully, on the ground that the custody of the servant is the possession of the master. [Citations] But probably when the act was passed it confirmed the above mentioned doubt as to the master's possession where the servant was intrusted with property at a distance from his master's house in cases outside the statute, that is, when the chattels were delivered by a third person. * * * It was said that it was not within the statute if an apprentice ran off with the money received from a third person for his master's goods at a fair, because he had it not by the delivery of his master. This, very likely, was correct, because the statute only dealt with delivery by the master; but the case was taken before long as authority for the broader proposition that the act is not a felony, and the reason was invented to account for it that the servant has possession, because the money is delivered to him. * * *

The last mentioned decisions made it necessary to consider with care what more was necessary, and what was sufficient, to reduce the servant to the position of a mere custodian. An obvious case was when the property was finally deposited in the place of deposit provided by the master, and subject to his control, although there was some nice discussion as to what constituted such a place. No doubt a final deposit of money in the till of a shop would have the effect. But it is plain that the mere physical presence of the money there for a moment is not conclusive while the servant is on the spot and has not lost his power over it; as, for instance, if the servant drops it, and instantly picks it up again. Such cases are among the few in which the actual intent of the party is legally important; for, apart from other considerations, the character in which he exercises his control depends entirely upon himself.

It follows from what we have said, that the defendant's first position cannot be maintained, and that the judge was right in charging the jury that, if the defendant before he placed the money in the drawer intended to appropriate it, and with that intent simply put it in the drawer for his own convenience in keeping it for himself, that would not make his appropriation of it just afterwards larceny. The distinction may be arbitrary, but, as it does not affect the defendant otherwise than by giving him an opportunity, whichever offence he was convicted of, to contend that he should have been convicted of the other, we have the less uneasiness in applying it.

With regard to the defendant's second position, we see no ground for contending that the detective in his doings was a servant of Sullivan, or that he had not a true possession of the money, if that question were open, which it is not. The only question reserved by the exceptions is whether Sullivan's ownership of the money prevented the defendant's act from being embezzlement. It has been supposed to make a difference if the right of possession in the chattel converted by the servant has vested in the master previous to the delivery to the servant by the third person. But this notion * * * does not apply to a case like the present, which has been regarded as embezzlement in England for the last hundred years. If we were to depart from the English decisions, it would not be in the way of introducing further distinctions.

Exceptions overruled.

Note

With the growth of a commercial society, the constraints imposed by a rigid doctrine of trespass became unsatisfactory. Common law judges responded by creating what amounted to a number of exceptions to the requirement of a trespassory taking. The most important of these were the following:

(a) The *Carrier's* Case (1473) involved a defendant who contracted with a merchant to carry certain bales to Southampton, but instead broke open the bales and appropriated the contents. Although the merchant had voluntarily delivered the bales to the carrier, the judges held that the carrier had committed larceny. The case is considered to stand for the proposition that a bailee who "breaks bulk" by breaking into packages entrusted to him thereby terminates his lawful possession, and his subsequent taking of the contents is therefore from the constructive possession of the owner.

(b) When a master entrusted property to a servant, the servant was held to have only "custody" of it, and "constructive possession" remained in the master so that the servant who absconded with such property was guilty of larceny.

(c) Where one party hands over property to another as part of a transaction intended to be completed at approximately the same time and place, he transfers custody only and retains constructive possession until the completion of the transaction. Thus, if a customer hands a vendor a bill to pay for a purchase, the vendor commits larceny if he retains the bill and runs away without handing over the merchandise. Similarly, the clothing store customer who is given a coat to try on and then runs off with it without paying commits larceny.

(d) The owner who loses or mislays property retains constructive possession of it. If a finder picks it up and takes it away, he thus commits larceny if he has a clue to its ownership and if his intent at the time of the taking is to keep it for himself. Both the clue to ownership and the intent to deprive must exist at the time of the taking, however. If the finder takes the property intending to restore it to the owner, he does not commit common law larceny if he subsequently changes his mind and decides to keep it. (In many jurisdictions statutes impose liability on finders who subsequently fail to take reasonable steps to locate the owner or who subsequently misappropriate the property, regardless of their intent at the time of the finding.)

(e) A mistake as to the identity of the recipient, or the nature or amount of the property transferred, may vitiate what otherwise would be a voluntary transfer. See United States v. Rogers, infra p. 778.

(f) One who obtains possession (but not title) to personal property by deceit, intending at the time to convert it and subsequently doing so, commits larceny. The defendant in Rex v. Pear, 168 Eng.Rep. 208 (1779) rented a horse for a day and then promptly sold it and pocketed the proceeds. The judges concluded that possession obtained by trick is not really possession at all, and so possession in the legal sense remained in the owner and Pear's subsequent conversion was larceny. Had Pear purchased the horse on credit, promising to return the next week with the cash but never intending to do so, he would not be guilty of larceny by trick because he would have obtained title as well as possession of the horse. Under the traditional view, he could not even be convicted of the statutory crime of false pretenses, because that crime traditionally required a misrepresentation of present or past fact: i.e., a false promise is not a false pretense. A case turning on the distinction between possession and title is *Graham v. United States*, which is presented in the final section of this chapter. See also Chaplin v. United States, 157 F.2d 697 (D.C.Cir.1946), discussed in *People v. Ashley*, also presented later in this chapter.

When Parliament took the initiative and created the statutory crimes of embezzlement and false pretenses, the courts took the view that the statutes were intended only to cover conduct which was *not* within the expanded scope of larceny. This doctrine explains cases such as Commonwealth v. Ryan, supra, where the defendant's only defense to the charge of embezzlement was that his conduct constituted larceny.

The distinctions among the common law categories are the accidental product of history, and there is no reason to retain them in a modern penal code. Hence, a feature of every penal code revision is a consolidation of the separate crimes into a single crime of theft. Even in California, which has not revised its Penal Code for over a century, there is a general theft statute. See People v. Ashley, infra p. 828. Having a consolidated crime of "theft" eliminates the need to name the correct common law category in the indictment or information. The old distinctions may still retain some importance, however, as some of the following cases illustrate.

2. *Trespassory Taking and Carrying Away*

PEOPLE v. ROBINSON

Court of Appeals of New York, 1983.
60 N.Y.2d 982, 471 N.Y.S.2d 258, 459 N.E.2d 483.

MEMORANDUM.

On the morning of May 31, 1977, an employee of Volpe Motors in Rochester discovered that a new Lincoln Continental had been taken from the repair shop, where it was being readied for delivery. Later in the day the police found the car on a local street some distance from the dealer's place of business. Missing from the car were its wheels and tires, which had an aggregate value of $750. Defendant was arrested after the police found his fingerprints on the rear fender skirts. According to defendant's statement, he did not participate in the theft but, knowing the car had been stolen the night before from Volpe Motors, he helped two friends remove the wheels and tires and load them into their automobile. In an indictment charging grand larceny in the third degree, defendant was accused of stealing the wheels and tires. At trial, the People offered no evidence connecting defendant with theft of the car. The jury found defendant guilty of grand larceny.

The Appellate Division reversed the conviction and dismissed the indictment, concluding that while defendant might have been guilty of criminal possession of stolen property, the evidence was insufficient to establish that he committed larceny. * * * The Appellate Division ruled as a matter of law that the larceny of the car, including its wheels and tires, was complete when dominion and control of the car were assumed, and that there was insufficient evidence to establish defendant's guilt for this crime. These legal conclusions being correct, we affirm.

A person commits larceny when, "with intent to deprive another of property or to appropriate the same to himself or to a third person, he wrongfully takes, obtains or withholds such property from an owner thereof." (Penal Law, § 155.05, subd. 1.) Where a larceny is committed by trespassory taking, a thief's responsibility for the crime is not diminished because his act of carrying away the loot (asportation) is frustrated at an early stage. Thus, a shoplifter who exercises dominion and control over the goods wholly inconsistent with the continued rights of the owner can be guilty of larceny even if apprehended before leaving the store, a car thief who starts the car can commit larceny before he actually drives the automobile away, and a pickpocket can be guilty of larceny even though his removal of the victim's possessions is interrupted before completion. [Citations] By the same token, one who learns of a larceny while it is in progress and assists its perpetrator cannot avoid accomplice liability merely because such participation occurs after the principal, for purposes of his own liability, has technically completed the crime.

The Appellate Division did not misapply these principles. Contrary to the view urged upon us by the People, the court did not decide, as a matter of law, that a larceny is complete for all purposes when the principal's liability attaches. The court simply decided that in this case asportation—whether of the car, or of the wheels and tires—had ceased before defendant's involvement. Where defendant first became involved the day after theft of the car, where the original perpetrators were not being pursued in the act of carrying away the loot, and where the removal of the wheels and tires took place some distance from the dealership, we cannot say that the court below was incorrect in its conclusion that asportation had ceased before defendant's involvement.

The dissent reasons that if the original perpetrators intended only to steal the wheels and tires, the larceny would not be complete until these components were removed from the car. Under the proposed new rule of law, a larceny of parts can never be complete until they are removed from the whole, however great the passage of time or distance between the original taking and the subsequent removal, and irrespective of intervening circumstances. We decline to adopt such a rigid rule, particularly in a case where the intent of the original perpetrators was never even an issue at trial.

MEYER, JUDGE (dissenting).

The fallacy in the majority's reasoning and in that of the Appellate Division is in the insistence on viewing the theft as of the car rather than of its tires and wheels. There is, of course, no question that the original takers removed the entire car from Volpe Motors premises. But it is also true that if the intention of the original takers was to steal not the entire car but only the tires and wheels, when asportation of the car had ceased is irrelevant to defendant's criminal responsibility.

This is because by definition larceny requires not only asportation or taking of property but also the intent to deprive the owner of it or to appropriate it to the thief or to a third person (Penal Law, § 155.05, subd. 1). So far as pertinent to the present case, to "deprive" means to withhold property permanently or under such circumstances that the major portion of its economic value is lost to the owner, or to dispose of the property in such a manner or under such circumstances as to render it unlikely that the owner will recover it (Penal Law, § 155.00, subd. 3), and to "appropriate" means to control property permanently or under such circumstances as to acquire the major portion of its economic value, or to dispose of it for the benefit of oneself or a third person (Penal Law, § 155.00, subd. 4).

Whether the larceny committed by defendant's friends had been completed when the Lincoln Continental left Volpe's premises turns, therefore, on whether their intent was to deprive Volpe of, or appropriate to themselves, the entire car or only the tires and wheels. From the facts that defendant's friends had tried unsuccessfully to remove the tires and wheels before they contacted defendant and that they took with them only the tires and wheels and left the car without wheels or tires in the park, a trier of fact could infer that they intended to deprive Volpe of, or appropriate to themselves, only the tires and wheels. * * *

The indictment charged defendant with larceny of the tires and wheels only. At the close of the People's case defendant's attorney moved to dismiss on the ground that theft of the car was complete when it was taken from Volpe's premises. The Trial Judge overruled that motion and charged the jury on larceny of the tires and wheels only. No request for an instruction as to the intent of the original takers was made by defendant.

Of course, defendant's own criminal responsibility turned upon his personal knowledge and intent. Unless defendant knew that he was taking part in a recently commenced and continuing plan to steal only the tires and wheels, he could not be deemed an accomplice to the larceny of them. However, based on defendant's statement that he knew the car had been stolen the night before and that the object of his friends was to remove the tires and wheels, there was evidence from which the jury could find that he knowingly and intentionally participated in the larceny of the tires and wheels.

To consider the asportation by the original takers without considering also their intent was inconsistent with the statutory definitions quoted above and, therefore, an error of law. The order of the Appellate Division should, therefore, be reversed and the matter remitted to that court for its review of the facts.

PEOPLE v. JENNINGS

Court of Appeals of New York, 1986.
69 N.Y.2d 103, 512 N.Y.S.2d 652, 504 N.E.2d 1079.

TITONE, JUDGE.

The Sentry Armored Courier Corp. warehouse was burglarized and robbed of some $11 million by individuals unconnected to Sentry, who were later apprehended and prosecuted. In the aftermath of the robbery, the District Attorney's office focused its attention on Sentry's own business practices. A series of indictments charging Sentry and its principals with various counts of larceny and misapplication of property ensued. The six indictments collectively charge defendants Jennings, Fiumefreddo, Finnerty, and Sentry Armored Courier Corp. with several counts of grand larceny in the second degree and misapplication of property. Sentry was engaged in transporting and storing large sums of cash and performing related services on behalf of its clients. Defendant Jennings was the president of Sentry, defendant Fiumefreddo was the senior vice-president, and defendant Finnerty was the vice-president and cashier of the Hudson Valley National Bank. * * *

The Grand Jury may not indict unless the People present evidence establishing a prima facie case of criminal conduct. The sufficiency of the People's presentation is properly determined by inquiring whether the evidence viewed in the light most favorable to the People, if unexplained and uncontradicted, would warrant conviction by a petit jury. * * * Since the various counts arise from four discrete sets of facts, we will evaluate each group of charges separately.

The Repurchase Agreement Plan

[Three of the indictments] concern a business practice that the People have dubbed the "Repurchase Agreement Scheme." All of the counts in these indictments were dismissed by the trial court, and the dismissals were upheld by the Appellate Division.

* * * The evidence before the Grand Jury showed that Sentry had an agreement with its client, Chemical Bank, under which Sentry was to pick up from Chemical's Water Street offices certain "bulk deposits" that Chemical had received from its commercial customers. Sentry was to "fine count" this money in its warehouse and then deliver it within 72 hours to Chemical's account at the Federal Reserve Bank in lower Manhattan, reporting any overages or shortages discovered in the count-

ing process. In fact, Sentry was able to perform the "fine counting" task in approximately 24 hours, considerably less time than the 72 hours its agreement with Chemical allowed.

Reluctant to retain all of the cash on Sentry's premises for the full 72–hour period, defendant Jennings met with defendant Finnerty, an officer of Hudson Valley National Bank, and arranged for the "fine counted" money to be delivered to Hudson's account at the Federal Reserve Bank, with the funds to be credited to Sentry's newly created escrow account with Hudson. Once the funds were delivered, an employee of Sentry was to call Hudson and specify the amount that was to be used to buy "repurchase agreements" from that bank. Under these "repurchase agreements," which were analogous to loans or bonds, Hudson was given the right to invest the money, while Sentry's account was debited in an appropriate amount. The loan was secured by A-rated bonds held in Hudson's Federal Reserve Bank vault. At the conclusion of the 72–hour period Sentry had to deposit Chemical's money in its Federal Reserve account, Hudson would "repurchase" the bonds from Sentry by crediting Sentry's escrow account with the principal amount plus a portion of the interest Hudson had earned on its investments. On telephone orders from Sentry, Hudson would then wire transfer the principal amount to Chemical's account at the Federal Reserve Bank, leaving Sentry's account enriched by the amount of the interest payment.

The "repurchase agreement" plan was implemented in July of 1981. By late August, Chemical had noticed that its funds were being routed through Hudson and demanded an explanation. Although an officer of Sentry told Chemical's representative that the rerouting had been initiated for "insurance purposes," Chemical was evidently unsatisfied and directed Sentry orally and in writing to deliver the "fine counted" money directly to Chemical's account at the Federal Reserve Bank. Despite this admonition, Sentry continued its practice of routing the money through Hudson until November of 1981, when Chemical decided it could "fine count" its bulk deposits internally. During the period when its arrangement with Hudson was in effect, Sentry gained a total of nearly $17,000 in interest earned on over 40 repurchase agreements. The full amount of the principal belonging to Chemical, however, was always returned to its owner within the allotted 72–hour time frame.

The People have advanced several theories in support of their larceny charge, including a "breaking of the bale" and an unlawful "separation of the value of the money from its engraved ink and paper container." None of the theories the People have proffered, however, would support a larceny conviction under our modern statutes defining that crime. While Sentry's conduct may have provided a basis for civil liability in some form, that conduct did not constitute criminal larceny.

The crime of larceny consists of an unauthorized taking, coupled with the "intent to deprive another of property or to appropriate the same." The "taking" was established prima facie here, since for certain periods, however temporary, defendants exercised dominion and control over Chemical's funds in a manner that could be found to be wholly inconsistent with Chemical's ownership. Such a finding could be based on the facts that defendants used Chemical's money for their own purposes and continued to do so even after Chemical specifically directed them to stop. What is lacking here from the People's proof is evidence demonstrating an intent to deprive or to appropriate.

The gist of the People's claim is that by investing Chemical's money for periods up to 48 hours, defendants evinced an intent to deprive its true owner of the money's "economic value or benefit," that is, the interest that the money was capable of generating. The mens rea element of larceny, however, is simply not satisfied by an intent temporarily to use property without the owner's permission, or even an intent to appropriate outright the benefits of the property's short-term use.

* * * It would be inconsistent with the statutory design to treat defendants' concededly permanent taking of the interest earned on Chemical's funds as a larceny within the meaning of [the New York statutes]. It is clear that an individual who "joy-rides" and thereby deprives the automobile's owner of the value arising from its temporary use is not liable in larceny for stealing that intangible "value." By parity of reasoning, an individual who temporarily invests another's money and thereby gains interest or profit cannot be deemed guilty of larceny for appropriating that interest or profit. * * * Sentry was merely emulating the behavior of many reputable financial institutions by taking advantage of the "float" on the temporarily idle money in its possession.

We now turn to the question whether [the evidence established] the lesser crime of misapplication of property, which is defined in Penal Law 165.00(1) as follows: "A person is guilty of misapplication of property when, knowingly possessing personal property of another pursuant to an agreement that the same will be returned to the owner at a future time, he loans, leases, pledges, pawns or otherwise encumbers such property without the consent of the owner thereof in such manner as to create a risk that the owner will not be able to recover it or will suffer pecuniary loss."

The obvious thrust of this statute is to make it a crime to alienate property belonging to another under circumstances creating a risk of loss. While the created risk of loss need not rise to the level of "likelihood" or even mere "probability," the statute does require proof of a risk that is more than a farfetched or wholly speculative possibility. * * * There was no actual risk here that the money would not be repaid, since even in the unlikely event of a default by Hudson, the "loans" to Hudson were secured by A-rated bonds held in Hudson's Federal Reserve Bank vault. Indeed, these "agreements" were deemed so secure by the industry that no FDIC insurance was required. In short, however unethical defendants' conduct may have been, it did not constitute larceny or misapplication of property.

The Compensatory Balance Matter

Another set of charges against Jennings and Fiumefreddo arises from a second business arrangement that Sentry had with Chemical Bank. Under this arrangement, Sentry kept a "rolling inventory" of Chemical's dollar bills and coins in a segregated area of its money room. This money was to be delivered to various branches of Waldbaum's Supermarket, Chemical's customer, whenever a need for additional cash arose. Defendants allegedly took some $100,000 out of this "rolling inventory" and deposited it in a "compensatory balance" account at Citibank. Their apparent purpose in opening this account was to enable Sentry to obtain a lower interest rate on a refinanced equipment loan it had with Citibank. There were no restrictions on Sentry's use of the "compensatory balance" account, and Sentry's principals had full access to its funds at all times.

In late 1982, discrepancies began to appear in the amount of coins in the "rolling inventory" Sentry was storing for Chemical. An audit revealed substantial shortages in the "rolling inventory," and, as a consequence, Sentry attempted to withdraw the funds in the Citibank account. Citibank, however, refused this request and instead called in the demand portion of Sentry's equipment loan, freezing the "compensatory balance" account in an apparent preliminary attempt to set off its claim against Sentry. On January 11, 1983, Sentry returned Chemical's "rolling inventory" with a shortage of over $122,000. An additional $25,000 in dimes was returned the following day, but Chemical never recovered the remaining $97,000.

[These facts led the second Grand Jury to hand up indictment No. 369/84,] which charged Jennings and Fiumefreddo with second degree grand larceny and misapplication of property. * * * As in the case of the "repurchase agreement" indictment, the facts underlying the "compensatory balance" account indictment demonstrate, at best, a short-term taking of the money entrusted to Sentry by its true owner, Chemical Bank. By removing the money from the storage area where the "rolling inventory" was kept and placing it in a bank account in Sentry's name, defendants could be found to have exercised dominion and control over the money in a manner that was inconsistent with Chemical's ownership. The facts do not support an inference of larcenous intent. Again, what is lacking here is the intent permanently to deprive the owner of the funds or to exercise control over the money "for so extended a period or under such circumstances that the major portion of its economic value or benefit is lost". As is true with respect to their "repurchase agreement" plan, defendants' manifest intention here was to use the money they were holding for Chemical to their own advantage by placing it in a bank account rather than retaining it in a storage area, thereby obtaining some portion of the money's economic value. There is no indication, however, that they intended to appropriate the money in such a way as to sap it of the "major portion" of its economic benefit. The fact that the money was ultimately lost as a result of Citibank's exercise of its rights as a creditor does not alter this analysis, since defendants were not parties to and had apparently not even anticipated Citibank's actions.

We reach a different conclusion with respect to the count charging those defendants with misapplication of property in connection with the "compensatory balance" account matter. The elements of that count were satisfied by the evidence showing that defendants had encumbered Chemical's funds in such a manner as to place them at risk. Although there was no showing that the funds in the "compensatory balance" account were expressly deposited as security for Citibank's loan to Sentry, the bank's right of setoff made those funds the indirect equivalent of security. As a consequence, there was a sufficient basis for the Grand Jury to infer that defendants had both "encumbered" the funds within the meaning of the statute and created a tangible risk that those funds would not be recovered. * * *

Misappropriation of Insurance Proceeds

Defendant Jennings was also charged with second degree larceny for failing to remit insurance proceeds to the intended beneficiaries. * * * On September 3, 1982, one of Sentry's armored cars was robbed of more than $231,000 after having made several cash pick-ups. About two months after this robbery, which does not appear connected to the later warehouse robbery, Sentry's insurer sent it a $20,985.54 check in full settlement of its insurance claim. This check represented payment for the losses sustained by three of Sentry's clients. Sentry reimbursed one of those clients for the full amount of its $18,620 loss, but did not distribute the remainder of the insurance proceeds to its other two clients, each of which had sustained losses in excess of the $2,365 balance and had submitted proof of loss. Instead, Sentry retained the excess proceeds for itself, an act which led to the present second degree grand larceny charge against defendant Jennings.

Jennings' failure to reimburse Sentry's clients for their losses cannot serve as the basis for a larceny prosecution for the simple reason that Sentry, and not the clients, was the rightful owner of the insurance proceeds. It was Sentry that had paid for the insurance coverage, and it was Sentry, rather than its clients, that the insurer was obligated to pay in the event of loss. When the insurer met its obligation by making payment to Sentry in full satisfaction of its claim, the proceeds became Sentry's property to dispose of as it wished. While Sentry may have had a civil obligation to reimburse its clients for their loss, its failure to meet that obligation cannot be transformed into a liability for criminal larceny because nothing belonging to the clients was converted.

[The opinion went on to uphold three larceny indictments against Jennings and Fiumefreddo growing out of additional incidents. They had allegedly misused client money to pay pressing obligations of Sentry and to cover various shortages in client accounts during the period of financial difficulty following the warehouse robbery.]

SIMONS, JUDGE (dissenting in part).

I cannot concur in the majority's remarkably indulgent determination that defendants were merely emulating the practices of "reputable financial institutions" and that Sentry's use of Chemical Bank's money for esoteric investment schemes or to secure favored loan conditions for itself amounted to little more than a noncriminal financial "joy-ride." Investing the "float" may be legal in a debtor-creditor relationship, but a bailee for hire undertakes to protect and preserve the bailor's property with only such use of the property as the parties to the bailment agree upon. The bailee does not have carte blanche to risk the bailor's property for its own gain. There is no dispute in this case that Chemical Bank bailed its property to Sentry intending that Sentry securely store the funds on is premises, safely transfer them to the bailor's customer, Waldbaum, or perform related services for Chemical, such as coin counting, before depositing the funds in Chemical's account at the Federal Reserve Bank. Defendants not only performed those services badly, but while doing so they lost thousands of dollars of Chemical's funds and risked the loss of millions more by these illegal schemes and use of their bailor's insurance funds. I agree with the two Grand Juries that found that defendants' conduct was criminal, and I would sustain the indictments.

My differences with the majority are more fundamental than the significance attributed to the evidence, however. In my view, the majority has given an overly restrictive interpretation to the applicable statutes. * * *

Turning first to the larceny counts, the majority concedes, as to the repurchase agreement scheme and compensatory balance scheme, that the evidence supports the Grand Jury's finding that defendants wrongfully took substantial sums of money from Chemical Bank, the rightful owner, by depositing them in Hudson Valley National Bank and Citibank. * * * The intent to appropriate includes the intent to exercise control over property "under such circumstances as to acquire the major portion of [the] economic value or benefit [of the property]." I disagree with the majority's analysis of what constitutes "an intent to appropriate" because it fails to differentiate between a property's economic value and its economic benefit, and because it mistakenly construes the statutory definition to require a permanent or near permanent appropriation. The majority finds it necessary that the People show defendants intended to appropriate the economic value of the property although the statute clearly provides a legally sufficient alternative: the appropriation of "a major portion of its economic * * * benefit," i.e., its ability to make more money. There can be little doubt that defendants intended to use Chemical's money to their own financial advantage; they invested it with Hudson Valley National Bank, and earned $17,000 in the process, and they also used it to collateralize a loan with Citibank. This evidence was more than sufficient to establish defendants' intent to acquire the economic benefits of Chemical Bank's funds. * * *

The majority also claim that the necessary mens rea for the larceny was lacking because any intent to appropriate the economic benefit of the funds was only the intent to deprive Chemical of its property temporarily. The majority finds little difference between defendants "short term" use of the bank's money and "joy-riding" in an automobile. There is a cognizable distinction, however, between using another's property with the intent to return it and appropriating property to acquire a major portion of its economic benefit—which may never be returned—even if the appropriation is for a short time. * * *

Similarly, there was more than enough evidence to permit the jury to find defendants possessed the requisite larcenous intent when Sentry improperly took Chemical's funds and deposited them in Citibank to its own credit in its compensatory balance scheme. By so depositing the money, Sentry obtained the major portion of the economic benefit of the funds during the period of the deposit because it, in effect, collateralized its loan from Citibank with Chemical's money and it also received a reduced interest rate on the loan. * * *

Finally, I would reinstate the count charging grand larceny of insurance proceeds. There was sufficient evidence before the Grand Jury to permit it to find that the insurance proceeds belonged to the injured parties and that, contrary to their rights, defendants misappropriated some of the funds to their own use. * * * It has been settled law for at least 100 years that a bailee for hire who receives casualty insurance payments for the loss of bailed property holds those payments in trust for the bailor [Citations]. In this case, there was evidence that Sentry was contractually obligated to reimburse its clients for their losses, as well as documentary proof that Sentry's insurer had made the payment in accordance with the proof of loss submitted by those clients. This evidence was sufficient to establish prima facie that the insurance proceeds were paid to Sentry in trust for the bailor-clients who had sustained losses in the robbery, and that defendant intentionally withheld them from the bailor claimants. Given the evidence of a trust existing by operation of law, the alleged conversion by Jennings of a portion of the insurance proceeds for his own or Sentry's use would support a conviction for larceny by embezzlement That a petit jury might resolve the factual issues against the People after trial does not warrant this court in dismissing the indictment.

In conclusion, it is worth noting the concern other branches of our State government have expressed over the enormous increase in large scale white-collar crimes. * * * In contrast to this concern over the problem, the majority has trivialized the seriousness of defendants' conduct and interpreted the statutes narrowly, virtually excising important and operative language from them. * * *

New York Penal Law

§ 155.00. Larceny; Definitions of Terms

The following definitions are applicable to this title:

1. "Property" means any money, personal property, real property, computer data, computer program, thing in action, evidence of debt or

contract, or any article, substance or thing of value, including any gas, steam, water or electricity, which is provided for a charge or compensation.

2. "Obtain" includes, but is not limited to, the bringing about of a transfer or purported transfer of property or of a legal interest therein, whether to the obtainer or another.

3. "Deprive." To "deprive" another of property means (a) to withhold it or cause it to be withheld from him permanently or for so extended a period or under such circumstances that the major portion of its economic value or benefit is lost to him, or (b) to dispose of the property in such manner or under such circumstances as to render it unlikely that an owner will recover such property.

4. "Appropriate." To "appropriate" property of another to oneself or a third person means (a) to exercise control over it, or to aid a third person to exercise control over it, permanently or for so extended a period or under such circumstances as to acquire the major portion of its economic value or benefit, or (b) to dispose of the property for the benefit of oneself or a third person.

5. "Owner." When property is taken, obtained or withheld by one person from another person, an "owner" thereof means any person who has a right to possession thereof superior to that of the taker, obtainer or withholder. A person who has obtained possession of property by theft or other illegal means shall be deemed to have a right of possession superior to that of a person who takes, obtains or withholds it from him by larcenous means. A joint or common owner of property shall not be deemed to have a right of possession thereto superior to that of any other joint or common owner thereof. In the absence of a specific agreement to the contrary, a person in lawful possession of property shall be deemed to have a right of possession superior to that of a person having only a security interest therein, even if legal title lies with the holder of the security interest pursuant to a conditional sale contract or other security agreement. * * *

§ 155.05. Larceny; Defined

1. A person steals property and commits larceny when, with intent to deprive another of property or to appropriate the same to himself or to a third person, he wrongfully takes, obtains or withholds such property from an owner thereof.

2. Larceny includes a wrongful taking, obtaining or withholding of another's property, with the intent prescribed in subdivision one of this section, committed in any of the following ways:

(a) By conduct heretofore defined or known as common law larceny by trespassory taking, common law larceny by trick, embezzlement, or obtaining property by false pretenses;

(b) By acquiring lost property. A person acquires lost property when he exercises control over property of another which he knows to have been lost or mislaid, or to have been delivered under a mistake as to the identity of the recipient or the nature or amount of the property, without taking reasonable measures to return such property to the owner;

(c) By committing the crime of issuing a bad check, as defined in section 190.05;

(d) By false promise. A person obtains property by false promise when, pursuant to a scheme to defraud, he obtains property of another by means of a representation, express or implied, that he or a third person will in the future engage in particular conduct, and when he does not intend to engage in such conduct or, as the case may be, does not believe that the third person intends to engage in such conduct.

In any prosecution for larceny based upon a false promise, the defendant's intention or belief that the promise would not be performed may not be established by or inferred from the fact alone that such promise was not performed. Such a finding may be based only upon evidence establishing that the facts and circumstances of the case are wholly consistent with guilty intent or belief and wholly inconsistent with innocent intent or belief, and excluding to a moral certainty every hypothesis except that of the defendant's intention or belief that the promise would not be performed;

(e) By extortion. A person obtains property by extortion when he compels or induces another person to deliver such property to himself or to a third person by means of instilling in him a fear that, if the property is not so delivered, the actor or another will:

(i) Cause physical injury to some person in the future; or

(ii) Cause damage to property; or

(iii) Engage in other conduct constituting a crime; or

(iv) Accuse some person of a crime or cause criminal charges to be instituted against him; or

(v) Expose a secret or publicize an asserted fact, whether true or false, tending to subject some person to hatred, contempt or ridicule; or

(vi) Cause a strike, boycott or other collective labor group action injurious to some person's business; except that such a threat shall not be deemed extortion when the property is demanded or received for the benefit of the group in whose interest the actor purports to act; or

(vii) Testify or provide information or withhold testimony or information with respect to another's legal claim or defense; or

(viii) Use or abuse his position as a public servant by performing some act within or related to his official duties, or by failing or refusing to perform an official duty, in such manner as to affect some person adversely; or

(ix) Perform any other act which would not in itself materially benefit the actor but which is calculated to harm another person materially with respect to his health, safety, business, calling, career, financial condition, reputation or personal relationships.

§ 155.10. Larceny; No Defense

The crimes of (a) larceny committed by means of extortion and an attempt to commit the same, and (b) bribe receiving * * * are not mutually exclusive, and it is no defense to a prosecution for larceny committed by means of extortion of for an attempt to commit the same that, by reason of the same conduct, the defendant also committed one of such specified crimes of bribe receiving.

§ 155.15. Larceny; Defenses

1. In any prosecution for larceny committed by trespassory taking or embezzlement, it is an affirmative defense that the property was appropriated under a claim of right made in good faith.

2. In any prosecution for larceny by extortion committed by instilling in the victim a fear that he or another person would be charged with a crime, it is an affirmative defense that the defendant reasonably believed the threatened charge to be true and that his sole purpose was to compel or induce the victim to take reasonable action to make good the wrong which was the subject of such threatened charge.

§ 155.20. Larceny; Value of Stolen Property

For the purposes of this title, the value of property shall be ascertained as follows:

1. Except as otherwise specified in this section, value means the market value of the property at the time and place of the crime, or if such cannot be satisfactorily ascertained, the cost of replacement of the property within a reasonable time after the crime. * * *

§ 155.25. Petit Larceny

A person is guilty of petit larceny when he steals property. Petit larceny is a class A misdemeanor.

§ 155.30. Grand Larceny in the Fourth Degree

A person is guilty of grand larceny in the fourth degree when he steals property and when:

1. The value of the property exceeds one thousand dollars; or

2. The property consists of a public record, writing or instrument kept, filed or deposited according to law with or in the keeping of any public office or public servant; or

3. The property consists of secret scientific material; or

4. The property consists of a credit card or debit card; or

5. The property, regardless of its nature and value, is taken from the person of another; or

6. The property, regardless of its nature and value, is obtained by extortion; or

7. The property consists of one or more firearms, rifles or shotguns * * * or

8. The value of the property exceeds one hundred dollars and the property consists of a motor vehicle * * * other than a motorcycle * * *.

* * *

Grand larceny in the fourth degree is a class E felony.

§ 155.35. Grand Larceny in the Third Degree

A person is guilty of grand larceny in the third degree when he steals property and when the value of the property exceeds three thousand dollars. Grand larceny in the third degree is a class D felony.

§ 155.40. Grand Larceny in the Second Degree

A person is guilty of grand larceny in the second degree when he steals property and when:

1. The value of the property exceeds fifty thousand dollars; or

2. The property, regardless of its nature and value, is obtained by extortion committed by instilling in the victim a fear that the actor or another person will (a) cause physical injury to some person in the future, or (b) cause damage to property, or (c) use or abuse his position as a public servant by engaging in conduct within or related to his official duties, or by failing or refusing to perform an official duty, in such manner as to affect some person adversely.

Grand larceny in the second degree is a class C felony.

§ 155.42. Grand Larceny in the First Degree

A person is guilty of grand larceny in the first degree when he steals property and when the value of the property exceeds one million dollars. Grand larceny in the first degree is a class B felony.

3. *Intent to Deprive: Concurrence of Act and Mens Rea*

STATE v. BROWN

Court of Criminal Appeals of Tennessee, Middle Section, 2001.
2001 WL 385382 (Tenn.Crim.App.2001).[a]

Opinion: WOODALL, J.

Background

On August 10, 1998, at approximately 1:00 p.m., Minnie Montgomery was working at her job driving a van which delivered clothing to various stores owned by Nicholson Cleaners of Nashville. As she unloaded a delivery at the Elliston Place store, a man approached her and offered to help. She rejected his offer and continued to unload clothes until a co-worker, Michele Herman, asked her why the van was moving. She looked up to discover the van heading toward the parking lot exit. Montgomery instructed Herman to call the police and proceeded to chase after the van on foot. As she ran down the street, she was able to observe the driver. It was the same man who had offered to assist her earlier and later identified as Defendant. The man did not stop, and Montgomery watched as the van disappeared into traffic.

Shortly thereafter, a police officer arrived at the Elliston Place store. He took a description of the van and driver, then broadcast a police report containing the description to the other police officers in the vicinity. As a result, Michael Moss with the Metropolitan Police Department received the report while on patrol. The stolen van was described as having "Nicholson Cleaners" in broad letters on the side and was last seen driving northbound on Twenty-fifth Avenue. Moss immediately headed for an alley "notorious for [having] stolen vehicles dropped in it." Moss' intuition paid off. The van was found parked in the alley and backed up against a building—the suspect was still in the driver's seat. When he noticed Moss, he tried to flee through the side loading door but his escape was obstructed by a rather large pit bulldog on one side and the building on the other. Defendant was apprehended shortly thereafter, with the keys to the van still in his hand.

Fifteen minutes after the van's disappearance, Montgomery received a phone call informing her that the police had located the van three blocks away and had apprehended the suspect. Defendant was handcuffed and standing by the side of the police car when she arrived. After Montgomery identified Defendant as the person who took the vehicle, he was arrested.

Dewayne Seay testified at trial that he was the owner of Nicholson's Cleaners and confirmed that on August 10, 1998, he received a phone call that someone had stolen the "Nicholson van." Seay testified that the approximate value of the van was two thousand dollars and, according to

a. See Rule 19 of the Rules of the Court of Criminal Appeals, relating to publication of opinions and citation to unpublished opinions of this court.

his calculations, the van also contained approximately one hundred cleaning orders of clothing on the day that it was taken. Since each order averages three to four pieces of apparel, the van contained three to four hundred articles of clothing. An inventory revealed that nothing was missing when the van was recovered.

Analysis

Defendant contends that the evidence is insufficient to support a conviction for theft. Specifically, Defendant argues that the State failed to prove an essential element of the offense of theft, i.e., that he intended to "deprive" the owner of the property as defined in Tenn. Code Ann. § 39–11–106(a). Consequently, Defendant asserts that the proof adduced at trial was only sufficient to show that he committed the offense of joyriding, Tenn. Code Ann. § 39–14–106. We disagree.

When evidentiary sufficiency is questioned on appeal, we must determine "whether, after considering the evidence in a light most favorable to the prosecution, any rational trier of fact could have found the essential elements of the crime beyond a reasonable doubt." * * *

Under Tennessee law, a person commits Class D felony theft when, "with intent to deprive the owner of property, the person knowingly obtains or exercises control over the property without the owner's effective consent," and the value of the property "is one thousand dollars ($1,000) or more but less than ten thousand ($10,000)." In addition, "deprive means to: withhold property from the owner permanently or for such a period of time as to substantially diminish the value or enjoyment of the property to the owner."

By contrast, joyriding occurs when a person "takes another's automobile, airplane, motorcycle, bicycle, boat or other vehicle without the consent of the owner and the person *does not have the intent to deprive the owner thereof.*" This Court has previously observed that "the sole difference between theft of a vehicle and joyriding [is] the offender's intent." Unless the offender has "intent to deprive" as defined by statute, the offense is joyriding rather than theft.

As noted above, to obtain a conviction for theft, the State must prove (1) that Defendant knowingly obtained or exercised control over property, (2) that Defendant did not have the owner's effective consent, and (3) that Defendant intended to deprive the owner of the property. The sole dispute between the parties concerns the third element only, namely, whether Defendant had the requisite *intent to deprive* the owner of the van as defined by the statute. The intent must be to deprive the owner permanently or for such a period of time as to substantially diminish the value or enjoyment of the property to the owner. Defendant asserts that possessing the vehicle for only twelve minutes was insufficient to constitute "permanent" deprivation to the owner and, further, that twelve minutes was not a sufficient period of time to be without one's property so that the value or enjoyment of the property would be "substantially" diminished. Defendant points to the fact that he did not attempt to sell the van or hold it for "ransom" as additional proof of his lack of intent to "deprive." The State responds that Defendant's intent to deprive was proven by the fact that he took the van to a "known dumping ground for stolen vehicles."

After examining the evidence in the light most favorable to the State, we conclude that the proof was sufficient for a rational jury to find beyond a reasonable doubt that when Defendant took the van, he possessed the requisite "intent to deprive" as defined in Tenn. Code Ann. § 39–11–106(a)(8)(A). The van was parked in a known repository for stolen vehicles and Defendant leaped out of the vehicle with the keys in his hand. These facts are evidence that Defendant had the intent to permanently withhold the property from the owner. We are unpersuaded by Defendant's argument that failure to sell or ransom the van indicated the absence of intent. Clearly, the jury could infer that he was captured too early in the criminal act to accomplish either of these deeds, thanks to the efficiency of the police department and Moss' detective work. The short span of time between Defendant's commission of the offense and his capture fails to negate the State's proof concerning theft. The State was required to prove beyond a reasonable doubt only that Defendant *intended* to deprive the owner of the vehicle, not that he was 100% successful in his endeavors.

It is well-established "that a jury may infer a criminal defendant's intent from the surrounding facts and circumstances." In fact, in most cases the jury must infer the defendant's intent from circumstantial evidence. * * *

* * *

[T]he judgment of the trial court is AFFIRMED.

STATE v. BAUTISTA

Supreme Court of Hawai'i, 1997.
86 Haw. 207, 948 P.2d 1048.

Opinion: Nakayama, J.

Defendant-appellant Eryck A. Bautista appeals from his conviction on one count of theft in the first degree * * *. Because the evidence was insufficient to support a finding that Bautista had the required intent to commit theft in the first degree, we reverse his conviction.

I. BACKGROUND

* * *

On Wednesday, July 12, 1995, Bautista went to Maui Toyota and spoke with a salesperson, indicating that he was interested in purchasing a new truck. After taking a test drive, Bautista left the dealership without purchasing a vehicle. Bautista returned to Maui Toyota between 4:00 and 5:00 p.m. on Friday, July 14, 1995. He told the salesperson that he had decided to purchase a new 4–Runner. The 4–Runner that Bautista selected was prepped and ready to be driven off the lot that day. After negotiating the final selling price, Bautista wrote a check to Maui Toyota in the amount of $29,865.83. Maui Toyota did not contact Bautista's bank at that time to determine if there was adequate money in the account to cover the check. Bautista then took possession of the vehicle.

On Monday, July 17, 1995, Bautista brought the 4–Runner back to Maui Toyota in order to have optional running boards installed. Later that day, Cecilia Morris, Maui Toyota's financing and leasing manager, received a call from Maui Toyota's accounting office notifying her that Bautista's check had not been honored. She notified the salesperson, who then called Bautista, told him that the check had not cleared, and instructed him to bring the vehicle back. Bautista returned the 4–Runner that day. The vehicle had 592 miles on the odometer when it was returned. As a result of the mileage on the vehicle, it could no longer be sold as new. Bautista continued to have contact with Maui Toyota, claiming to be attempting to find a way to get the money to purchase the vehicle. Bautista did not actually apply for another loan, although he told the dealership that he had applied and that his application was denied. On July 26, 1995, Maui Toyota notified the police.

Evidence was presented at trial showing that the account upon which Bautista wrote his check was closed on February 9, 1995, over five months before Bautista wrote the check to Maui Toyota. The highest balance in that account prior to being closed was $200.

At trial, the prosecution produced two witnesses who testified that, subsequent to attempting to purchase the vehicle at Maui Toyota, Bautista went to two other car dealerships and purchased automobiles with checks written on closed accounts, returning the vehicles with large amounts of mileage as soon as it was determined that the checks were invalid.

In all of Bautista's dealings with Maui Toyota, he gave correct information as to his name, phone number and address. At trial, Bautista testified that he was unaware that Maui Toyota was going to cash his check and that he was surprised when they told him that he could take the 4–runner off the lot. Bautista stated that he gave Maui Toyota a deposit of $100 to hold the vehicle until he received financing. He claimed that he had applied for a loan with Norwest Financial, which was pending at the time he took possession of the vehicle. However, testimony from the manager of Norwest Financial revealed that Bautista never formally filed an application for a loan with that company. An investigating police officer testified that Bautista admitted that he knew the checking account was closed when he tendered the check for the vehicle.

Bautista was convicted of theft in the first degree and sentenced to ten years imprisonment. As a repeat offender, he was sentenced to serve a mandatory minimum term of imprisonment of six years and eight months. * * *

II. DISCUSSION

* * *

B. Insufficient Evidence was Presented to Prove that Bautista Intended to Commit Theft in the First Degree

* * *

The dispositive issue under the unusual facts of this case is whether, viewed in the light most strongly favoring the prosecution, substantial evidence was presented to prove that Bautista intended to deprive Maui Toyota of property valued in excess of $20,000. The prosecution cites the following evidence to support a finding that Bautista intended to commit theft in the first degree: (a) Bautista was familiar with car sales procedures because he had previously worked at a dealership; (b) Bautista knew the difference between new and used car values; (c) Bautista knew that checks took several days to clear; (d) Bautista knew that new cars driven off the lot depreciated in value; (e) Bautista knew that he did not have sufficient funds in his account to cover the check; (f) he never filled out a loan application; and (g) Bautista knew that it was unwise for a car dealership to sell a car solely on the basis of a $100 deposit and an unverified check.

Under the statutory definition of "deprive," the prosecution could meet its burden to prove Bautista's intent to commit theft in the first degree by showing that either (a) Bautista intended to permanently withhold the 4–runner from Maui Toyota; or (b) Bautista intended to withhold the 4–runner for so extended a period, or under such circumstance, that a "significant portion of its economic value, or of the use and benefit thereof," was lost to Maui Toyota. HRS § 708–800 (1993).

1. *Intent to Permanently Deprive*

After careful review of the record, we find that substantial evidence was not presented to support a finding that Bautista intended to permanently deprive Maui Toyota of the 4–Runner. Bautista gave Maui Toyota his correct name, phone number and address. He had possession of the vehicle for a period of approximately 72 hours, from Friday afternoon until Monday. When Maui Toyota contacted him to request that he return the vehicle to the dealership, he did so on that day. Further evidence of his lack of intent to keep the vehicle permanently is demonstrated by the fact that, on two subsequent occasions, he performed the same feat and each time, he returned the vehicle to the dealership.

The evidence cited by the prosecution to support a finding of intent to commit theft in the first degree is not sufficient to uphold Bautista's conviction. The evidence adduced at trial leads us to the opposite conclusion than that urged by the prosecution. The evidence indicates that Bautista intended the actual result in this case, i.e. that he would have a new vehicle to drive for the weekend and then return it when his deception was uncovered. The fact that Bautista drove the vehicle more than 500 miles over the course of the weekend further supports the conclusion that he wanted to enjoy the vehicle to the maximum extent in the short time in which he had possession of it. There is no substantial evidence that Bautista intended to permanently deprive Maui Toyota of the vehicle.

2. *Intent to Withhold Significant Portion of Economic Value, Use or Benefit*

The second definition of "deprive" has never been addressed by the Hawai'i appellate courts. The definition of "deprive" in HRS § 708–800 is essentially identical to that of the Model Penal Code, enacted in Hawai'i in 1972 and not changed substantially since that date.

The prosecution demonstrated that used cars are generally worth less than new cars. The prosecution presented evidence that a car with more than 500 miles on the odometer is considered a used car. However, in relation to the 4–Runner taken by Bautista, which was used for three days and then returned, the prosecution was unable to demonstrate any actual loss to Maui Toyota. Ms. Morris, the finance manager for Maui Toyota, testified that:

> Q [Defense Counsel]: Can—or could Maui Toyota determine the loss suffered once the car has become used? . . .
>
> A [Ms. Morris]: In some cases, yes.
>
> Q In a case such as this, would they be able to do such?
>
> A No.
>
> Q What would be the problems?
>
> A The person who purchased the vehicle after had other things done to the deal. There was a trade involved in their deal. And depending on how much we sold that trade for, what we took the trade-in for, also the preparation of the vehicle all over again.
>
> Q The actual loss suffered by Maui Toyota, that can't be determined in this particular case?
>
> A No.

Taking into consideration the evidence presented that: (1) Bautista intended to return the vehicle in a short period of time; (2) he was familiar with the operation of car dealerships; and (3) Maui Toyota was unable to demonstrate any economic loss, we must determine whether the evidence presented at trial was sufficient to support a finding that Bautista intended to deprive Maui Toyota of a significant portion of the vehicle's economic value, use, or benefit.

* * *

For the above reasons, we hold that insufficient evidence was presented at trial to uphold a finding that Bautista intended to commit theft in the first degree. Although Bautista's conduct was appalling, it does not support a conviction of theft of the vehicle.[4]

UNITED STATES v. ROGERS

United States Court of Appeals, Fourth Circuit, 1961.
289 F.2d 433.

HAYNSWORTH, CIRCUIT JUDGE.

The defendant has appealed from his conviction under the "bank robbery statute," complaining that the proof did not show the commission of larceny and that the verdict of the jury was coerced by the Court's instructions. We think the proof did support the conviction, but that a new trial should be granted because of the possibly coercive effect of the Court's instructions designed to produce agreement of the jurors upon a verdict. There was testimony showing that, at the request of his brother, the defendant took a payroll check, payable to the brother in the face amount of $97.92, to a bank where the brother maintained an account. In accordance with the brother's request, he asked the teller to deposit $80 to the credit of the brother's account and to deliver to him the balance of the check in cash. The teller was inexperienced. She first inquired of another teller whether the check could be credited to an account in part and cashed in part. Having been told that this was permissible, she required the defendant's endorsement on the check, and, misreading its date (12 06 59) as the amount payable, she deducted the $80 deposit and placed $1,126.59 on the counter. There were two strapped packages, each containing $500, and $126.59 in miscellaneous bills and change. The defendant took the $1,126.59 in cash thus placed upon the counter and departed.

There was also testimony that when the day's business was done, the teller who handled the transaction was found to be short in her accounts by $1,108.67, the exact amount of the difference between the $1,206.59, for which she had supposed the check to have been drawn, and $97.92, its actual face amount, and that her adding machine tape showed that she had accepted the check as having been drawn for $1,206.59.

There was corroboration from other witnesses of some phases of this story as told by the tellers and the bookkeeper.

The defendant agreed that he took the check to the bank for his brother, asked that $80 be credited to his brother's account, and that the excess be paid to him in cash. He stated, however, that he received in cash only the $17.92, to which he was entitled, denying that he had received the larger sum.

4. Bautista's conduct was potentially violative of other portions of the Hawai'i Penal Code. *See, e.g.* HRS § 708–857 (1993) which defines the criminal offense of negotiating a worthless negotiable instrument. However, Bautista was not charged with this misdemeanor offense.

The case was submitted to the jury under instructions that they should find the defendant guilty if they found the much larger sum was placed upon the counter and was taken by the defendant with the intention to appropriate the overpayment, or if he thereafter formed the intention to, and did, appropriate the overpayment to his own use. * * * [The discussion of the trial court's improper coercive instruction is omitted.]

Since the other questions, directed to the nature of the offense, will arise necessarily upon a retrial, we address ourselves to them.

We accept the defendant's premise that paragraph (b) of the bank robbery act reaches only the offense of larceny as that crime has been defined by the common law. It does not encompass the crimes of embezzlement from a bank, reached by another statute, or obtaining goods by false pretense. * * * [Long after the decision in this case, the Supreme Court held in Bell v. United States, 462 U.S. 356 (1983), that the Bank Robbery Act *does* reach thefts by false pretenses as well as larceny.—ed.]

The defendant's premise that the prosecution was required to show the commission of larceny does not lead, however, to the conclusion that he should have been acquitted. The indictment charged larceny and the evidence offered by the prosecution, if accepted by the jury, proved the commission of that crime, not false pretense, embezzlement or some other lesser offense.

An essential element of the crime of larceny, the "felonious taking and carrying away of the personal goods of another," is that the taking must be trespassory. It is an invasion of the other's right to possession, and therein is found the principal distinction between larceny and other related offenses.

It has long been recognized, however, that when the transferor acts under a unilateral mistake of fact, his delivery of a chattel may be ineffective to transfer title or his right to possession. If the transferee, knowing of the transferor's mistake, receives the goods with the intention of appropriating them, his receipt and removal of them is a trespass and his offense is larceny. * * *

The District Court went too far, however, when it told the jury it might convict if, though his initial receipt of the overpayment was innocent, the defendant thereafter formed the intention to, and did, convert the overpayment.

The charge as given finds support in earlier cases. [Citations] In England, a similar result was reached in Regina v. Ashwell, 16 Q.B. 190 (1883), Lord Coleridge declaring there could be in law no delivery and no receipt if giver and receiver labored under a mutual mistake as to the thing being given and received. Subsequent cases in the United States and in England, however, have consistently held that, if there is a mutual mistake and the recipient is innocent of wrongful purpose at the time of his initial receipt of the overpayment, its subsequent conversion by him cannot be larceny.

[Since the overpayment was so large and obvious to one who knew the amount of the check, the error may have been harmless. Upon the retrial, however, the jury should be properly instructed] that among the essential elements of the offense are (1) that the defendant knew when he received the money from the teller or picked it up from the counter that it was more than his due and (2) that he took it from the bank with the intention of converting it. * * *

4. *Embezzlement Revisited*

PEOPLE v. TALBOT

Supreme Court of California, 1934.
220 Cal. 3, 28 P.2d 1057.

[Defendants, the principal officers of the Richfield Oil Company, used corporate funds for speculation on the stock market in 1929. Appellant Talbot introduced evidence to prove that in 1929 he had a net worth of several million dollars, an amount far greater than the total amount of corporate funds which he was accused of misappropriating. He declared bankruptcy in 1930.]

THE COURT. A hearing was granted in this case * * * to consider the question whether the appropriation of corporate funds by the defendants was made with fraudulent intent, an element necessary to constitute embezzlement. We have painstakingly re-examined the record on this issue. Certain evidence tended to show that defendants were not conscious that their acts amounted to embezzlement even if they did constitute bad business practice. The record shows that each of the defendants and numerous employees had drawing accounts with the corporation; that the withdrawals by defendants were made openly, with no attempt at concealment; that the canceled checks were returned to the corporation; that defendants were charged on the books with all of the expenditures; and that no manipulation of accounts took place. It is further contended, and we may assume that it is true, that the practice of making advances of this sort to corporate officers and employees during this period was common, not only in the Richfield company but in other corporations as well. The prevalence of this unlawful practice cannot, of course, justify it.

These and other facts were before the trial court, and that court was permitted to draw the inference of fraudulent intent from the admitted fact that the funds were appropriated and used for the personal purposes of the defendants. In this state of the record, the appellate court may not disturb the findings and judgment.

We therefore adopt the opinion prepared by Mr. Justice *pro tem.* Archbald, of the District Court of Appeal, as the opinion of this court. It reads as follows:

* * *

Appellant contends that it had been his custom, not only in the Richfield company but in other companies of which he had been an executive, to have drawing accounts against which were charged advances made to officers and employees; that both sums of money he is charged with taking openly and without concealment or any of the other usual *indicia* of fraudulent acts.

The taking charged as grand theft was on the theory of embezzlement. Section 484 of the Penal Code, so far as material to such theory, provides: "Every person * * * who shall fraudulently appropriate property which has been entrusted to him * * * is guilty of theft". Section 503 of the same code defines embezzlement as "the fraudulent appropriation of property by a person to whom it has been entrusted". Section 504 provides that "every officer, director, trustee, clerk, servant or agent of any * * * corporation (public or private) who fraudulently appropriates to any use or purpose not in the due and lawful execution of his trust, any property which he has in his possession or under his control by virtue of his trust * * * is guilty of embezzlement". From these sections it clearly appears that fraudulent intent is an essential element of the offense of embezzlement, and such is the ruling of our courts. * * *

While secrecy or concealment is evidence of a criminal or felonious intent, nevertheless there may be embezzlement where the appropriation is openly made and consequently without concealment. * * * We think the legislature used the word "fraudulent", in its definition of embezzlement, to distinguish an "appropriation" by an agent of money or property under circumstances that might be merely tinged with suspicion as to the agent's intent, from an appropriation for purely personal uses of the agent, as contrasted with the purpose for which the money or property was entrusted to him. In other words, in every case where the officers of a corporation who are necessarily entrusted with the money and property of the concern use it, knowingly and intentionally, for their own purposes, there is a "fraudulent appropriation" thereof which is termed embezzlement by the statute, and the fact that such officers intended to restore the money or property is of no avail to them if it has not been restored before information laid or indictment found charging them with embezzlement (Pen.Code, sec. 512),[a] and even if prior to the bringing of such charges the officers *voluntarily and actually* restore the property, such fact does not constitute a defense but merely authorizes the court in its discretion to mitigate the offense (sec. 513).[b] It would seem that the legislature here has

a. "The fact that the accused intended to restore the property embezzled, is no ground of defense or mitigation of punishment, if it has not been restored before an information has been laid before a magistrate, or an indictment found by a grand jury charging the commission of the offense." West's Ann.Cal. Penal Code § 512.—ed.

b. "Whenever, prior to an information laid before a magistrate, or an indictment found by a grand jury, charging the commission of embezzlement, the person accused voluntarily and actually restores or

shown in very clear terms that it is the immediate breach of trust that makes the offense, rather than the permanent deprivation of the owner of his property. * * *

Under the evidence produced by the prosecution serious misappropriations of funds of the corporation are shown, contrary to all authority given and in violation of the trust imposed. The fact that this appellant intended to repay the money taken, or was amply able to do so, is of no avail in the face of the fact that the money was not replaced prior to indictment found. The claim that he used the money in an honest effort to stabilize the price of stock on the market, for the benefit of the corporation and its stockholders and not for the selfish purpose of making his own holdings more valuable, created but a conflict in the evidence which the court, trier of the facts, decided against him, and that determination is final so far as an appellate court is concerned. Neither does the claim that appellant had been accustomed to drawing and using the funds of the corporation for his personal needs, having such withdrawals charged to his personal account and eventually paying the money back by credits due him or payments made by him, relieve the acts from the stain of criminality. Nor can we subscribe to the doctrine that long-continued wrongdoing sanctifies or purifies such conduct. Even if all of the directors of the corporation knew of such custom, the wrong was not made right. They were each charged with the trust to use the funds of the company for company needs, and it might be seriously questioned whether an authorization or ratification by the board of such acts would not have resulted in involving the directors rather than in excusing the officers. That the trial judge understood the law as to intent clearly appears from the record, and in our opinion the evidence amply sustains the conclusion he must have reached thereon. * * *

[Affirmed.]

5. *Tangible Personal Property*

PEOPLE v. KUNKIN

Supreme Court of California, 1973.
9 Cal.3d 245, 107 Cal.Rptr. 184, 507 P.2d 1392.

WRIGHT, CHIEF JUSTICE.

The Los Angeles Free Press (Free Press), its editor and owner (Kunkin), and its reporter, (Applebaum), were each indicted on two counts of receiving stolen property (Pen.Code, § 496) for allegedly taking possession of two documents which had been removed from the Los Angeles office of the Attorney General by Jerry M. Reznick. [Reznick was tried separately and convicted on two counts of violation of Govern-

tenders restoration of the property alleged to have been embezzled, or any part thereof, such fact is not a ground of defense, but it authorizes the court to mitigate punishment, in its discretion." West's Ann.Cal. Penal Code § 513.—ed.

ment Code § 6201, which punishes theft or unauthorized removal of government records.] * * * The jury found each defendant guilty of one count of receiving stolen property, and defendants appeal from the judgment entered on the verdicts. * * *

While Reznick was employed as a mail clerk at the Los Angeles office of the Attorney General he removed a copy [apparently made on the office's duplicating machine] of a personnel roster of the Bureau of Narcotic Enforcement which listed the names, home addresses and home telephone numbers of undercover narcotics agents throughout the state. It was not marked "secret" or "confidential." The copy of such document constitutes the "property" found by the jury to have been received by defendants.

Reznick took the roster to the office of the Free Press where he met Applebaum. Reznick asked Applebaum whether the Free Press would publish the roster and Applebaum replied that he did not know. Although Applebaum feared "there might be trouble" if such a document were published, he said that he would nevertheless consult his editor. When Reznick asked if he would be paid for providing the roster, Applebaum explained that, subject to approval by his superiors, the standard fee paid for information actually used in an article was $20. Reznick then departed.

Reznick returned a week later with the roster. Although Applebaum still could not promise that the Free Press would publish the roster, Reznick left the document on the reporter's desk and insisted that the newspaper not reveal its source of information. No agent of the newspaper promised to pay for the roster and Reznick was never paid for it.

On August 8, 1969, the Free Press published the roster verbatim in its feature article. The following headlines, inter alia, accompanied the article: "Narcotics Agents Listed," "There should be no secret police," and "Know your local Narc." The text editorialized that police personnel should live openly in the community which they serve. On an ensuing television interview, Kunkin acknowledged his role in publishing the list and stated that he was satisfied as to its authenticity. He explained that the roster was appended to the editorial "for dramatic effect."

After the list was published, Reznick went to Applebaum and asked for the return of the copy of the roster he had provided. Applebaum refused but assured Reznick that the document was locked in a safe place. Following requests made by a deputy attorney general to the Free Press, an attorney of undetermined authorization delivered the copy of the roster to the Attorney General's office. Fingerprints of Reznick, Applebaum and Kunkin were found on the document.

Section 496 provides in subdivision 1: "Every person who buys or receives any property which has been stolen or which has been obtained in any manner constituting theft or extortion, knowing the property to be so stolen or obtained, or who conceals, withholds or aids in concealing or withholding any such property from the owner, knowing the property to be so stolen or obtained, is punishable by imprisonment. * * * "

A conviction for receiving stolen property cannot withstand appellate scrutiny unless substantial evidence was presented to the trier of fact that (1) the property was received, concealed, or withheld by the accused; (2) such property had been obtained by theft or extortion; and (3) the accused knew that the property had been so obtained.

We will assume, without deciding, that one of the several copies of the roster of personnel of the bureau distributed to the Los Angeles office of the Attorney General was "property" within the meaning and intended scope of § 496.[a] We will also assume, without deciding, that the receipt of the roster by defendants was a "receiving" of property within the meaning of § 496. Our discussion will focus on the evidence adduced at trial to prove the latter two elements of the crime of receiving: the received property's stolen status and the receiver's knowledge of this status.

Section 496 applies to the receipt of "any property which has been stolen or which has been obtained in any manner constituting theft or extortion." This broad language is intended to include property which has been obtained not only by common law larceny (i.e., stealing) but also by such other forms of theft as embezzlement. We note at the outset, however, that the jury in this case was instructed on the elements of theft by larceny only. Thus even though § 496 applies by its terms to the receipt of property obtained by embezzlement, the convictions below could only have been predicated on the jury's finding that the roster was stolen, not embezzled. We, of course, cannot look to legal theories not before the jury in seeking to reconcile a jury verdict with the substantial evidence rule. The immediate question, accordingly, is whether there is substantial evidence that Reznick committed a theft by larceny apart from the suggestion that, because of his employment, he might have committed theft by embezzlement.

It has been settled for at least 78 years that theft by larceny requires a specific intent permanently to deprive the rightful owner of his property. * * *

There is scant evidence in the instant case that Reznick intended a permanent deprivation. In the typical case the thief's sale of the property is persuasive proof of such an intention, but one of the many distinctive

a. In Williams v. Superior Court, 81 Cal.App.3d 330, 146 Cal.Rptr. 311 (1978), the court upheld an indictment charging three attorneys and a former insurance company claims manager with receiving stolen property. The "property" was a confidential investigatory file on a potential medical malpractice case, compiled by the Hartford insurance company. The claims manager sold a copy of the file to the other defendants, who used it to prepare a tort lawsuit. The California Court of Appeals doubted that "mere information, as distinguished from the paper on which it is printed, can be the subject of theft." It upheld the indictment, however, because the grand jury could have concluded that the claims manager either took an existing set of copies from his employer (Hartford) and delivered them to the attorneys, or photocopied a set on Hartford's premises, using its paper. The court implied that neither a theft nor a receiving of stolen property could have been charged if the disloyal employee had merely removed the documents temporarily to copy them on his own paper off the employer's premises, although the loss to the employer would have been substantially the same.—ed.

features of this case is that the alleged receiving involved no sale, at least of the stolen item itself. Reznick did leave the roster with defendants in the expectation that he would receive $20 should the roster result in a published story, but Reznick insisted in all his dealings with defendants that the roster be returned to him after they had made whatever use they cared to of the information it contained. By Reznick's uncontradicted testimony, defendants never offered to pay money for the roster or for the information it contained, nor did they actually pay Reznick any money. Thus nothing inherent in the transaction itself bears a necessary or even likely inference that Reznick intended to keep the roster away from the office of the Attorney General permanently.

It appears, however, that after Reznick testified that he had only caused the roster "to be removed," he answered in the affirmative, over objection, a prosecution question whether he had stolen it. We have heretofore recognized that words of common usage do not necessarily reflect the subtle distinctions they bear before bench and bar. Thus an affirmative answer to a leading question whether the witness stole something, when that witness himself has characterized the taking as a removal, is not dispositive of the issue whether the removal was accompanied by a specific intent to steal, that is, to remove permanently.

Were there no more evidence in the record than Reznick's acquiescence in the use of the word "steal," and his account of his tender of the roster to defendants with simultaneous insistence that it be returned to him, we would deem excruciatingly close the question whether there was substantial evidence in support of the jury's finding that the roster was stolen property. A final item of evidence convinces us, however, that there was sufficient circumstantial evidence for the finder of fact to reasonably draw the inference that Reznick took the roster with intent to steal. This dispositive circumstance is that Reznick had in fact ceased working for the office of the Attorney General at the time of his tender of the roster to defendants. Thus he was no longer in a position conveniently to return the roster to the office following its perusal by defendants. We thus conclude that there is substantial evidence in support of the finding that the property was stolen.

We turn now to the question whether there is also substantial evidence from which the jury could reasonably have drawn an inference that defendants knew the roster was stolen when Reznick tendered it to them. Crucial to consideration of this question is the fact that defendants were not made aware by Reznick that he was no longer employed by the office of the Attorney General. Besides misleading defendants about his employment status, Reznick maintained throughout his conversations with defendants that he was giving them a roster to look at only. Where the only testimony bearing on the issue is uncontradicted and negates guilty knowledge, even though it is the testimony of the defendant, a conviction of receiving stolen goods must be reversed for insufficiency of the evidence. * * *

The judgment [is] reversed.

UNITED STATES v. RIGGS

United States District Court for the Northern District of Illinois, Eastern Division, 1990.
739 F.Supp. 414.

Memorandum Order, BUA, UNITED STATES DISTRICT JUDGE

[A federal indictment charged that the defendants were computer hackers affiliated with a group of hackers that called itself the "Legion of Doom." The indictment charged violations of various federal statutes. The following excerpts from the District Court order focus upon the question of whether the computer codes allegedly stolen by the defendants constituted property which could be obtained by fraud or stolen within the meaning of the relevant statutes.]

Over the course of the past decade, advances in technology and growing respect and acceptance for the powers of computers have created a true explosion in the computer industry. Quite naturally, the growth of computer availability and application has spawned a host of new legal issues. This case requires the court to wrestle with some of these novel legal issues which are a product of the marriage between law and computers.

* * *

I. THE INDICTMENT

A. *Factual Allegations*

In about September 1988, Neidorf and Riggs devised and began implementing a scheme to defraud Bell South Telephone Company ("Bell South"), which provides telephone services to a nine-state region including Alabama, Georgia, Mississippi, Tennessee, Kentucky, Louisiana, North Carolina, South Carolina, and Florida. The objective of the fraud scheme was to steal Bell South's computer text file which contained information regarding its enhanced 911 (E911) system for handling emergency calls to policy, fire, ambulance, and other emergency services in municipalities. The text file which Riggs and Neidorf planned to steal specifically details the procedures for installation, operation, and maintenance of E911 services in the region in which Bell South operates. Bell South considered this file to contain valuable proprietary information and, therefore, closely guarded the information from being disclosed outside of Bell South and its subsidiaries. Riggs and Neidorf wanted to obtain the E911 text file so it could be printed in a computer newsletter known as "PHRACK" which Neidorf edited and published.

In about December 1988, Riggs began the execution of the fraud scheme by using his home computer in Decatur, Georgia, to gain unlawful access to Bell South's computer system located at its corporate headquarters in Atlanta, Georgia. After gaining access to Bell South's system, Riggs "downloaded" the text file, which described in detail the operation of the E911 system in Bell South's operating region. Riggs then disguised and concealed his unauthorized access to the Bell South system by using account codes of persons with legitimate access to the E911 text file.

Pursuant to the scheme he had devised with Neidorf, Riggs then transferred the stolen computer text file to Neidorf by way of an interstate computer data network. Riggs stored the stolen text file on a computer bulletin board system located in Lockport, Illinois, so as to make the file available to Neidorf. The Lockport bulletin board system was used by computer "hackers" as a location for exchanging and developing software tools and other information which could be used for unauthorized intrusion into computer systems. Neidorf, a twenty-year-old student at the University of Missouri in Columbia, Missouri, used a computer located at his school to access the Lockport computer bulletin board and thereby receive the Bell South E911 text file from Riggs. At the request of Riggs, Neidorf then edited and retyped the E911 text file in order to conceal the fact that it had been stolen from Bell South. Neidorf then "uploaded" his revised version of the stolen file back onto the Lockport bulletin board system for Riggs' review. To complete the scheme, in February 1989, Neidorf published his edited edition of Bell South's E911 text file in his PHRACK newsletter.

* * *

II. DISCUSSION

A. *Motion to Dismiss Count II*

Neidorf claims that Count II of the indictment is defective because it fails to allege a scheme to defraud, one of the necessary elements for a wire fraud claim under 18 U.S.C. § 1343. * * *

* * *

In the instant case * * * [t]he government charges Riggs and Neidorf with scheming to defraud Bell South out of *property*—the confidential information contained in the E911 text file. The indictment specifically alleges that the object of defendants' scheme was the E911 text file, which Bell South considered to be valuable, proprietary, information. The law is clear that such valuable, confidential information is "property," the deprivation of which can form the basis of a wire fraud charge under § 1343.

* * *

B. *Motion to Dismiss Counts III and IV*

Counts III and IV charge Riggs and Neidorf with violating 18 U.S.C. § 2314, which provides, in relevant part:

> Whoever transports, transmits, or transfers in interstate or foreign commerce any goods, wares, merchandise, securities or money, of the value of $5000 or more, knowing the same to have been

stolen, converted or taken by fraud ... [s]hall be fined not more than $10,000 or imprisoned not more than ten years, or both.

The government concedes that charging Neidorf under § 2314 plots a course on uncharted waters. No court has ever held that the electronic transfer of confidential, proprietary business information from one computer to another across state lines constitutes a violation of § 2314. However, no court has addressed the issue. Surprisingly, despite the prevalence of computer-related crime, this is a case of first impression. The government argues that reading § 2314 as covering Neidorf's conduct in this case is a natural adaptation of the statute to modern society. Conversely, Neidorf contends that his conduct does not fall within the purview of § 2314 and that the government is seeking an unreasonable expansion of the statute. He urges the court to dismiss the charge on two grounds.

Neidorf's first argument is that the government cannot sustain a § 2314 charge in this case because the only thing which he allegedly caused to be transferred across state lines was "electronic impulses." Neidorf maintains that under the plain language of the statute, this conduct does not come within the scope of § 2314 since electronic impulses do not constitute "goods, wares, or merchandise."

The court is unpersuaded by Neidorf's disingenuous argument that he merely transferred electronic impulses across state lines. Several courts have upheld § 2314 charges based on the wire transfer of fraudulently obtained money, rejecting the arguments of the defendants in those cases that only electronic impulses, not actual money, crossed state lines. For example, in *United States v. Gilboe*, 684 F.2d 235 (2d Cir. 1982), *cert. denied*, 459 U.S. 1201, 75 L. Ed. 2d 432, 103 S. Ct. 1185 (1983), the court held, in affirming a § 2314 conviction based on the wire transfer of funds:

> The question whether [§ 2314] covers electronic transfers of funds appears to be one of first impression, but we do not regard it as a difficult one. Electronic signals in this context are the means by which funds are transported. The beginning of the transaction is money in one account and the ending is money in another. The manner in which the funds were moved does not affect the ability to obtain tangible paper dollars or a bank check from the receiving account. If anything, the means of transfer here were essential to the fraudulent scheme.

Other circuits have followed the reasoning in *Gilboe*. In all of these cases, the courts held that money was transferred across state lines within the meaning of § 2314 because funds were actually accessible in one account prior to the transfer, and those funds were actually accessible in an out-of-state account after the transfer. The courts refused to accept the superficial characterization of the transfers as the mere transmittal of electronic impulses.

Similarly, in the instant case, Neidorf's conduct is not properly characterized as the mere transmission of electronic impulses. Through the use of his computer, Neidorf allegedly transferred proprietary business information—Bell South's E911 text file. Like the money in the case dealing with wire transfers of funds, the information in the E911 text file was accessible at Neidorf's computer terminal in Missouri before he transferred it, and the information was also accessible at the Lockport, Illinois computer bulletin board after Neidorf transferred it. Therefore, under *Gilboe* * * * the mere fact that the information actually crossed state lines via computer-generated electronic impulses does not defeat a charge under § 2314.

The question this case presents, then, is not whether electronic impulses are "goods, wares, or merchandise" within the meaning of § 2314, but whether the proprietary information contained in Bell South's E911 text file constitutes a "good, ware, or merchandise" within the purview of the statute. This court answers that question affirmatively. It is well-settled that when proprietary business information is affixed to some tangible medium, such as a piece of paper, it constitutes "goods, wares, or merchandise" within the meaning of § 2314.

Therefore, in the instant case, if the information in Bell South's E911 text file had been affixed to a floppy disk, or printed out on a computer printer, then Neidorf's transfer of that information across state lines would clearly constitute the transfer of "goods, wares, or merchandise" within the meaning of § 2314. This court sees no reason to hold differently simply because Neidorf stored the information inside computers instead of printing it out on paper. In either case, the information is in a transferrable, accessible, even salable form.

Neidorf argues in his brief that a § 2314 charge cannot survive when the "thing" actually transferred never takes tangible form. A few courts have apparently adopted this position. For example, in *United States v. Smith*, 686 F.2d 234 (5th Cir.1982), the court held that a copyright does not fit within the definition of "goods, wares, or merchandise" under § 2314. The court ruled that in order to come within that definition, "[t]he 'thing' or 'item' must have some sort of tangible existence; it must be in the nature of 'personal property or chattels.'" Similarly, in [*United States v. Bottone*, 365 F.2d 389 (2d Cir.), *cert. denied*, 385 U.S. 974, 87 S.Ct. 514, 17 L.Ed.2d 437 (1966)] where the court held that copies of documents describing a manufacturing process for a patented drug constitute "goods, wares, or merchandise" under § 2314, the court opined:

> To be sure, where no tangible objects were ever taken or transported, a court would be hard pressed to conclude that "goods" had been stolen and transported within the meaning of § 2314; the statute would presumably not extend to the case where a carefully guarded secret was memorized, carried away in the recesses of a thievish mind and placed in writing only after a [state] boundary had been crossed.

Nevertheless, this court is not entirely convinced that tangibility is an absolute requirement of "goods, wares, or merchandise" under

§ 2314. Congress enacted § 2314 to extend the National Motor Vehicle Theft Act to cover all stolen property over a certain value ($5000) which is knowingly transported across state lines. In line with this broad congressional intent, courts have liberally construed the term "goods, wares, or merchandise" as "a general and comprehensive designation of such personal property and chattels as are ordinarily the subject of commerce." Reading a tangibility requirement into the definition of "goods, wares, or merchandise" might unduly restrict the scope of § 2314, especially in this modern technological age. * * *

In any event, this court need not decide that issue to resolve this case, for even if tangibility is a requirement of "goods, wares or merchandise" under § 2314, in this court's opinion the computer-stored business information in this case satisfies that requirement. Although not printed out on paper, a more conventional form of tangibility, the information in Bell South's E911 text file was allegedly stored on computer. Thus, by simply pressing a few buttons, Neidorf could recall that information from computer storage and view it on his computer terminal. The information was also accessible to others in the same fashion if they simply pressed the right buttons on their computer. This ability to access the information in viewable form from a reliable storage place differentiates this case from the mere memorization of a formula and makes this case more similar to cases * * * where proprietary information was also stored, but in a more traditional manner—on paper. The accessibility of the information in readable form from a particular storage place also makes the information tangible, transferable, salable and, in this court's opinion, brings it within the definition of "goods, wares, or merchandise" under § 2314.

In order to sustain a charge against Neidorf under § 2314, however, the government cannot simply allege that Neidorf transferred "goods, wares, or merchandise" across state boundaries; the government must also allege that Neidorf executed the transfer knowing the goods were "stolen, converted or taken by fraud." This requirement forms the basis for Neidorf's second challenge to Counts III and IV. Relying on *Dowling v. United States*, 473 U.S. 207, 105 S.Ct. 3127, 87 L.Ed.2d 152 (1985), Neidorf maintains that the § 2314 charges should be dismissed because the "things" he allegedly transferred are not the type of property which is capable of being "stolen, converted or taken by fraud."

[In *Dowling*, the Supreme Court ruled that copyright holders possessed protectible and enforceable rights, but not the type of possessory interest that could be "stolen, converted or taken by fraud" under § 2314.]

* * * The instant case, however, is distinguishable from *Dowling* * * *. This case involves the transfer of confidential, proprietary business information, not copyrights. As *Dowling* and *Smith* recognized, the copyright holder owns only a bundle of intangible rights which can be infringed, but not stolen or converted. The owner of confidential, proprietary business information, in contrast, possesses something which

has clearly been recognized as an item of *property*. As such, it is certainly capable of being misappropriated, which, according to the indictment, is exactly what happened to the information in Bell South's E911 text file.

[The defendant's motions discussed above were denied.]

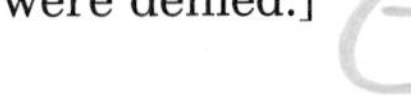

6. Property of Another

COMMONWEALTH v. MITCHNECK

Superior Court of Pennsylvania, 1938.
130 Pa.Super. 433, 198 A. 463.

KELLER, PRESIDENT JUDGE

The appellant was convicted of the offense of fraudulently converting the money of another person to his own use. * * *

The evidence produced on the part of the commonwealth would have warranted the jury in finding that the defendant, Mitchneck, operated a coal mine in Beaver township, Columbia county; that he employed certain persons, Hunsinger, Derr, Steeley, and others, as workers in and about his mine; that these employees dealt at the store of A. Vagnoni and signed orders directing their employer to deduct from their wages the amounts of their respective store bills and pay the same to Vagnoni; that the defendant agreed to do so, and pursuant to said agreement deducted from the wages due the eleven workmen, named in the indictment, an aggregate of $259.26, which he agreed to pay Vagnoni, but had failed and neglected to do so.

We are of opinion that this evidence was insufficient to support a conviction under the Fraudulent Conversion Act of 1917, and that the court erred in refusing the defendant's point for a directed verdict of acquittal.

The gist of the offense of fraudulent conversion is that the defendant has received into his possession the money or property of another person, firm, or corporation, and fraudulently withholds, converts, or applies the same to or for his own use and benefit, or to the use and benefit of any person other than the one to whom the money or property belonged. If the property so withheld or applied to the defendant's use and benefit, etc., did not belong to some other person, etc., but was the defendant's own money or property, even though obtained by borrowing the money, or by a purchase on credit of the property, the offense has not been committed. "Whatever may have been the intention of the legislature in the enactment of the statute under which the indictment in this case was drawn, it was clearly not intended to make criminal the act of one who sells his own property and it is not to be so applied as to make it an effective substitute for an action at law in the collection of a debt." Com. v. Hillpot, 84 Pa.Super. 454, at page 458.

* * *

The defendant in the present case had not received, nor did he have in his possession, any money *belonging* to his employees. True he owed them money, but that did not transfer to them the title to and ownership of the money. His deduction from their wages of the amounts of the store bills which they had assigned to Vagnoni did not change the title and ownership of the money thus withheld, nor did his agreement to pay to Vagnoni the amounts thus deducted constitute the latter the owner of the money. It effected only a change of creditors. The money, if Mitchneck actually had it, of which there was no proof, was still his own, but, after he accepted the assignments, he owed the amount due his employees to Vagnoni instead of to them. * * * Defendant's liability for the unpaid wages due his employees was, and remained, civil, not criminal. His liability for the amount due Vagnoni after his agreement to accept or honor the assignments of his employees' wages was likewise civil and not criminal. * * *

The judgment is reversed, and the appellant is discharged.

STATE v. POLZIN

Supreme Court of Washington, 1939.
197 Wash. 612, 85 P.2d 1057.

STEINERT, CHIEF JUSTICE. * * *

[Defendant Polzin owned Surety Finance Corporation (a small loan company) and Clallam Adjustment Corporation (a bill collection agency). He accepted a promissory note in the amount of $200.00 from Mrs. Braseth, giving her only $7.00 in cash for it. In return, he agreed to pay bills she owed to several creditors. He then went to two of these creditors, to whom she owed a total of $57.00, and persuaded them to retain Clallam to collect their accounts against Mrs. Braseth in return for a one-third collection fee. The creditors agreed, not knowing that Polzin was already obligated to pay over the entire amount. Polzin then remitted the $57.00 to Clallam, and Clallam paid that amount less the $19.00 fee to the creditors. Polzin was convicted of petit larceny.]

It is argued by the state that the transaction evidenced by the note was equivalent to a payment of two hundred dollars by the finance corporation direct to Mrs. Braseth and an immediate redelivery of $193 by her to it. In a sense, that is true. But we are not dealing with equivalents. We are dealing with actual facts which are alleged to constitute a criminal offense. What Mrs. Braseth did, in law, by the transaction was to establish a credit with Surety Finance Corporation to the extent of $193, with the understanding and agreement that a like amount was, in due course, to be paid by the finance corporation to certain of her creditors. Upon the execution and delivery by Mrs. Braseth of her note, the finance corporation became indebted to her, but it was not a custodian of money belonging to her. Assuming that the lender failed to make the payments as agreed, that amounted simply to a breach of part of the contract, subjecting the lender to liability in a civil action. Had Mrs. Braseth demanded that the proceeds of the note be paid directly to her, under an agreement to that effect, and had appellant then failed to make such payment, he would not thereby have been guilty of larceny; he would simply have rendered himself or the finance corporation liable upon a civil suit for breach of contract. Any judgment recovered would have been a personal one, but not a lien upon any specific fund. When, on the other hand, the proceeds were not applied as the agreement provided, it was likewise a breach of one element of the contract, for which only a civil action would lie. * * *

There is another reason, equally forceful and compelling, why appellant cannot be held criminally liable under the admitted facts. This ground meets and refutes the verdict of the jury which fixed appellant's guilt upon the retention of nineteen dollars collection charges. As already noted, the two accounts were paid in full, and Mrs. Braseth was thereupon released from further liability thereon. She lost nothing by the transaction between appellant and the two creditors. They might complain, but she cannot, for, although the collection company obtained nineteen dollars for its collection fees, that amount came from money which otherwise would have gone to, and been retained by, the two creditors, and for which Mrs. Braseth received the full benefit. Her credit has not been harmed by anything that appellant has done, for the two creditors were fully informed of the true situation before this prosecution was brought.

Appellant's conduct is not to be approved, and may even be condemned, but that is a matter of business ethics, not one of criminal liability. Appellant did not steal money belonging to Mrs. Braseth; he simply charged the creditors, and was paid, fees which, had they known the true facts, they would not have agreed to pay. They, however, are making no complaint, and the information is not drawn upon the theory that any money was stolen from them.

The judgment is reversed, and the charge is dismissed.

Note

Discussing the *Mitchneck* and *Polzin* cases, the Model Penal Code Commentary observed that "To the layman the distinction which the law makes between withholding from another money which is his and failing to pay another money which is due him must seem a tricky invention of lawyers to save some rogues from conviction for theft. * * * Once it is conceded that Polzin might have been convicted if he had handed cash to Mrs. Braseth and she had thereupon handed it back to him to pay her creditors, his acquittal in the case becomes an absurdity. * * * Likewise, if Mitchneck could have been convicted of embezzlement or fraudulent conversion, had his miners drawn their pay at one window and passed it back to Mitchneck's cashier at the next window to pay their bills, the bookkeeping shortcut actually employed hardly serves as a rational basis for exculpating Mitchneck." Model Penal Code, Tent. Draft No. 1, App. C at 113–115 (1953). Perceiving a loophole, the drafters of the Model Penal Code sought to close it with the following provision:

Section 223.8. Theft by Failure to Make Required Disposition of Funds Received

A person who purposely obtains property upon agreement, or subject to a known legal obligation, to make specified payment or other disposition, whether from such property or its proceeds or from his own property to be reserved in equivalent amount, is guilty of theft if he deals with the property obtained as his own and fails to make the required payment or disposition. The foregoing applies notwithstanding that it may be impossible to identify particular property as belonging to the victim at the time of the actor's failure to make the required payment or disposition. An officer or employee of the government or of a financial institution is presumed: (i) to know any legal obligation relevant to his criminal liability under this Section, and (ii) to have dealt with the property as his own if he fails to pay or account upon lawful demand, or if an audit reveals a shortage or falsification of accounts.

Would this provision affect the outcome of *Mitchneck* and *Polzin?* Do the holdings in those cases reflect a weakness in the law which ought to be eliminated, or do they reflect a rational doctrinal distinction that ought to be maintained?

PEOPLE v. RIGGINS

Supreme Court of Illinois, 1956.
8 Ill.2d 78, 132 N.E.2d 519.

HERSHEY, CHIEF JUSTICE.

The defendant, Marven E. Riggins, was indicted in the circuit court of Winnebago County for embezzlement. After a verdict of guilty by a jury, the court sentenced him to a term in the penitentiary of not less than two nor more than seven years.

The defendant argues for reversal on the ground that as operator of a collection agency he was an independent businessman, who at no time acted as "agent" for the complaining witness, Dorothy Tarrant, within the meaning of this embezzlement statute. * * *

At the time of the indictment (January, 1955), the defendant was the owner and operator of a collection agency in Rockford, called the Creditors Collection Service, and had been so engaged for about five years. He maintained an office, had both full and part-time employees, and during 1953 and 1954 had a clientele of some 500 persons and firms for whom he collected delinquent accounts. In February, 1953, he called on the complaining witness, Dorothy Tarrant, who operated a firm known as Cooper's Music and Jewelry. He said he was in the collection business and asked to collect the firm's delinquent accounts. As a result, they reached an oral agreement whereby the defendant was to undertake the collections.

By this agreement, the defendant was to receive one third on city accounts and one half on out-of-city accounts. It was further agreed that he need not account for the amounts collected until a bill was paid in full, at which time he was to remit by check.

There is a conflict in the evidence as to whether the defendant was to give a check for the whole amount collected and then receive his commission, or whether he was authorized to deduct his commission and account only for the net amount due.

It was further agreed that the defendant would be liable for court costs in the event he chose to file suit on any of the accounts, but the first money collected was to be applied to those costs. If no collection was made, however, the defendant was to stand the loss.

The parties operated under this agreement for almost two years. During that time the complaining witness exercised no control over the defendant as to the time or manner of collecting the accounts, and with her knowledge he commingled funds collected for all his clients in a single bank account. He also used this as a personal account, from which he drew for business, family and personal expenses.

In October, 1954, the complaining witness became aware that the defendant had collected several accounts for her in full, but had not accounted to her. She discussed the matter with him, and he assured her that he would bring his records up to date and pay what was due. After the defendant defaulted on this promise, she made further investigations and discovered new breaches of the agreement. She had further discussions with him and received additional promises to pay up, none of which were kept. Negotiations were terminated December 14, 1954, when the defendant filed a bankruptcy petition listing Cooper's Jewelry and Music, among others, as a creditor. Thereafter, the complaining witness preferred the charges against the defendant which resulted in his indictment and conviction for embezzlement. * * *

In this instance, we are particularly interested in the general embezzlement statute (par. 208) and the special statute under which defendant was indicted (par. 210). The former, applying to any "clerk, agent, servant or apprentice of any person," was originally enacted in 1827, and has existed in its present form since 1874. The latter, however, refers to "any clerk, agent, servant, solicitor, broker, apprentice or officer * * * receiving any money, * * * in his fiduciary capacity" and was not passed until 1919. For present purposes, this latter enactment is very significant, for it also provides as follows: such person "shall be punished as provided by the criminal statutes of this state for the punishment of larceny, *irrespective of whether any such* officer, *agent,* clerk, servant, solicitor, broker or apprentice *has or claims to have any commission or interest in such money,* substitute for money, or thing of value so received by him." (Italics added.)

In Commonwealth v. Libbey, 11 Metc., Mass. 64, decided in 1846, it was held that a collecting agent, who followed that as an independent business and who had the right to commingle funds, could not be convicted as an "agent" under a general embezzlement statute. This was predicated on the idea that he had a joint interest in the property said to be embezzled. This doctrine was later applied in other jurisdictions * * *.

Similarly, a 1903 decision of this court reversed the conviction of an agent who was employed to solicit subscriptions on commission and who was authorized to deduct her commissions from the amounts collected, for the reason that she was joint owner with the principal in the amounts collected. McElroy v. People, 202 Ill. 473, 66 N.E. 1058. In so deciding, the court cited with approval the *Libbey* case. In People v. O'Farrell, 247 Ill. 44, 93 N.E. 136, however, the court distinguished *McElroy* and affirmed an embezzlement conviction where under the terms of the contract creating the agency the agent was not authorized to deduct his fees from the amount collected, but accounted in full to his principal.

Briefly, then, this was the status of the law in 1919 when the special statute (par. 210) was passed, which declared that there was embezzlement "irrespective of whether" the accused "has or claims to have any commission or interest in such money." This statute expressly abrogated the doctrine enunciated in the foregoing cases and relied upon by the defendant here. Moreover, it is clear that, in accordance with said statute, the defendant was an "agent" who received money in a "fiduciary capacity."

First, the cases relied upon by the defendant to take a collection agent out of the "agent" category are based upon the notion that there can be no embezzlement where one has a joint interest in the property, not that an agent for collection is any less an agent. And, as aforesaid, the problem posed by those cases has been obviated by statute in Illinois.

Second, it can hardly be disputed but that the defendant acted as agent for the complaining witness in collecting her accounts. He undertook the collections on her behalf by virtue of authority which she delegated to him. He had no right to collect from anyone except as authorized by her and was required to render a full account of all matters entrusted to him, the same as any agent. Likewise, it is apparent that in so acting he assumed other duties ordinarily attendant upon that relationship, such as the duty to exercise good faith, make full disclosure, etc. * * *

Third, it is clear that the defendant received the funds in his fiduciary capacity. In Illinois, as in other jurisdictions, the relationship of principal and agent is a fiduciary one. One acts in a fiduciary capacity where special confidence is reposed in one who is bound in equity and good conscience to act in good faith with due regard to the interest of the person reposing the confidence.

We conclude that the defendant was an "agent" of the complaining witness, receiving money in a "fiduciary capacity" and, therefore, within the purview of said embezzlement statute. * * *

SCHAEFER, JUSTICE (dissenting).

* * * The critical question is whether the defendant was the agent of the complaining witness. Upon the record it seems to me that he was not. He maintained his own office, had his own employees, and collected

accounts for approximately 500 other individuals and firms. He was subject to no control whatsoever by any of his customers in making his collections. His customers knew that he kept all of his collections in a single account. That the defendant was not an agent would be clear, I think, if vicarious liability was sought to be asserted against Dorothy Tarrant on account of the defendant's conduct in the course of his collection activities. * * *

It is arguable of course that the conduct of the defendant in this case should be regarded as criminal. The General Assembly might wish to make it so. But it might not. It might regard the collection agency as a desirable service enterprise which should not be made unduly perilous. If the defendant in this case, with his little agency, is guilty of one embezzlement, he is guilty of 500. The General Assembly might not want to make the enterprise so hazardous. It has not done so, in my opinion, by the statute before us.

PEOPLE v. CLAYTON

Supreme Court of Colorado, 1986.
728 P.2d 723.

DUBOFSKY, JUSTICE.

I

In November 1979, Clayton and his wife Marvolene formed a partnership called Clayton Realty Company with Thomas and Donna Lee Gray. The Grays assumed a $40,000 debt and contributed an additional $20,000 in return for a 50 per cent share of the partnership. On February 13, 1981, the defendant and his wife entered into a partnership agreement with Evan C. Jones and his wife Consuelo R. Jones to form ERA Clayton Realty. Ten days later, on February 23, 1981 the Claytons and Grays dissolved the first partnership. The purpose of both partnerships was to conduct general real estate business.

As part of the dissolution of the first partnership the defendant agreed to pay the Grays $300 a month for ten years. He made five payments to the Grays, totalling $1500, from ERA Clayton Realty's partnership account. The ERA Clayton Realty partnership agreement states in relevant part:

Article X. Partners' Powers and Limitations

1. Checks shall be drawn on the partnership bank account for partnership purposes only and all checks shall be signed by any one of the partners or as may be agreed upon from time to time.

* * *

3. Each partner shall pay his separate debts punctually and shall indemnify the other partners and the capital and property of the partnership against the same and all expenses on account thereof.

Clayton was charged with felony theft under section 18–4–401, which provides:

> (1) A person commits theft when he knowingly obtains or exercises control over anything of value of another without authorization, or by threat or deception, and:
>
> (a) Intends to deprive the other person permanently of the use or benefit of the thing of value; or
>
> (b) Knowingly uses, conceals, or abandons the thing of value in such manner as to deprive the other person permanently of its use or benefit; or
>
> (c) Uses, conceals, or abandons the thing of value intending that such use, concealment, or abandonment will deprive the other person permanently of its use and benefit; * * *

After a preliminary hearing, the district court found that the defendant paid a personal debt to his former partners using funds from the ERA Clayton Realty partnership account. The court ruled, however, that a partner cannot be charged with theft of partnership property because partnership property is not a thing of value of another. The court dismissed the charge against the defendant. The People seek reinstatement of the charge, claiming that an unauthorized taking of partnership property by one of the partners constitutes theft.

II

The common law rule is that a partner cannot be guilty of embezzlement or larceny of partnership property. Jurisdictions in which partners have been found guilty of larceny or embezzlement from a partnership have statutory authority for the departure from common law. [Citations]

Colorado law is consistent with the common law. Under both the common law and the UPL, partners are joint owners of property. 401(1) provides that "[a] person commits theft when he knowingly obtains or exercises control over anything of value of another without authorization, or by threat or deception, * * *" Interpreting the language of the theft statute in People v. McCain, 191 Colo. 229, 552 P.2d 20 (1976), we refused to find a person who absconded with assets owned jointly with a church guilty of theft. * * * [The general theft provisions in the Model Penal Code defined "property of another" to include "property in which any person other than the actor has an interest which the actor is not privileged to infringe, regardless of the fact that the actor also has an interest in the property. * * *" The Colorado legislature did not include this definition in its 1971 criminal code revision.]

The misuse of partnership money, in this case to pay a debt to a former partner, is the type of partnership dispute commonly seen in civil courts. The defendant argues that the ERA Clayton Realty partnership agreement implies that the partners anticipated that separate debts of individual partners might be paid out of partnership funds because it requires prompt repayment and indemnification of the other partners and the partnership. Interpretation of the partnership agreement is best left to a civil court or to arbitration, as required by the partnership agreement. If a civil court finds that the $1500 payment constituted a misuse of partnership funds, the aggrieved partners have adequate remedies under the [partnership laws]. We affirm the ruling of the district court.

[Dissenting opinion omitted.]

B. ROBBERY AND EXTORTION

1. *Robbery*

STATE v. SEIN

Supreme Court of New Jersey, 1991.
124 N.J. 209, 590 A.2d 665.

CLIFFORD, J., writing for a majority of the Court.

On August 27, 1986, Edythe Williams cashed her unemployment check. She then placed the proceeds in the zipped compartment of a strapless, clutch-type purse that she carried under her arm. Thereafter, she headed for her car, which was parked a couple of blocks away. She went to the passenger side and put her key in the lock, while carrying her purse under her right arm. As Mrs. Williams stood in the street, Francisco Sein walked up close behind her on the left. Mrs. Williams turned her face to him thinking that he was about to speak to her. Instead Sein said nothing and reached across Mrs. Williams and slid her pocketbook from under her arm and ran away. There was no evidence that Sein used any force other than that required to slide the purse from beneath Mrs. Williams' arm.

[Sein was apprehended by the police, and was subsequently indicted for robbery. Under the statute, robbery occurs when a person, in the course of committing a theft, inflicts bodily injury or uses force upon another.] At trial, Sein moved at the conclusion of the State's case for a judgment of acquittal concerning the robbery charge, contending that the case should proceed only on the lesser-included offense of theft from the person, defined by statute as the unlawful taking or exercising of unlawful control over moveable property of another with a purpose to deprive them of that property. Sein argued that there was no evidence in the record that the taking of Mrs. Williams' purse was accompanied by the use of force against her person, a requirement for conviction of robbery. The State argued that the Legislature intended that the force used to remove the purse from the victim was sufficient to elevate the unlawful taking to a robbery. The trial court denied Sein's motion, and the jury subsequently found Sein guilty of second-degree robbery. * * *

Cases involving "snatching" have required courts to determine where to draw the line between robbery and the lesser offense of larceny from the person. A certain amount of "force" is necessary to take property from the person of another, but whether the amount necessary merely to accomplish that taking is sufficient to warrant the more serious penalties associated with robbery has vexed those courts that have considered the question.

* * * The predominant view, however, is that there is insufficient force to constitute robbery when the thief snatches property from the owner's grasp so suddenly that the owner cannot offer any resistance to the taking. See W. LaFave & A. Scott, Criminal Law § 8.11(d), at 781 (2d ed. 1986). This "majority rule" has been set forth in the following terms: "A simple snatching or sudden taking of property from the person of another does not of itself involve sufficient force to constitute robbery, though the act may be robbery where a struggle ensues, the victim is injured in the taking, or the property is so attached to the victim's person or clothing as to create resistance to the taking." [This was the rule in New Jersey before the penal code revision of 1979.] * * *

In 1979, the Legislature revamped the criminal laws by enacting the New Jersey Code of Criminal Justice. Under N.J.S.A. 2C:15–1a, as originally enacted, "[a] person [was] guilty of robbery if, in the course of committing a theft, he: (1) inflicts bodily injury upon another; or (2) threatens another with or purposely puts him in fear of immediate bodily injury; or (3) commits or threatens immediately to commit any crime of the first or second degree."

In 1981, however, the Legislature amended § 2C:15–1a(1) to read that a person is guilty of robbery if in the course of committing a theft he "inflicts bodily injury or uses force upon another." The Legislature's intention regarding the addition of the "or uses force" language is made clear by the following Statement of the Senate Judiciary Committee: "* * * [The amendment] extends the definition of robbery to cover the so-called 'blind-side' mugging. This occurs when a person commits an act of theft—for example a purse snatching—by approaching the victim from behind and using some degree of force to wrest the object of his theft from the victim. Often, however, no bodily injury is inflicted in these cases and therefore the offenses committed could be found to be theft rather than robbery."

The State contends that that Statement shows that the Legislature contemplated that a sudden, surprise snatching of property held in the grasp of another or in some way in contact with the person of another involves the use of force sufficient to elevate the taking to a robbery. To the contrary, that the Legislature intended to broaden the concept of force beyond the pre-Code understanding of that term is not at all clear. * * * As we indicated earlier, "a simple snatching or sudden taking of property from the person of another does not of itself involve sufficient force to constitute robbery" under the pre-Code statute, and nothing in the Senate Judiciary Committee Statement undercuts that standard. Although the Committee Statement refers to a "purse snatching" as an example of the conduct the amendment was intended to cover, it goes on to state that snatchings rising to the level of robbery include only those that involve "some degree of force to wrest the object" from the victim.

* * * The Legislature apparently determined that the violence associated with "wresting" is deserving of more severe punishment. It did not, however, intend to eliminate the requirement that robbery by use of force include force exerted "upon another." * * *

Because there is no evidence that defendant's conduct involved the type of force sufficient to elevate the theft to a robbery under N.J.S.A. 2C:15–1a(1), the [degree of the crime is reduced to that of larceny from the person].

[Dissenting opinion omitted.]

PEOPLE v. TUFUNGA

Supreme Court of California, 1999.
21 Cal.4th 935, 90 Cal.Rptr.2d 143, 987 P.2d 168.

BAXTER, J.

The claim-of-right defense provides that a defendant's good faith belief, even if mistakenly held, that he has a right or claim to property he takes from another negates the felonious intent necessary for conviction of theft or robbery. * * *

In *People v. Butler* (1967) 65 Cal. 2d 569 [55 Cal. Rptr. 511, 421 P.2d 703] (*Butler*), we reaffirmed that a claim-of-right defense can negate the requisite felonious intent of robbery as codified in Penal Code section 211 and extended the availability of the defense to forcible takings perpetrated to satisfy, settle or otherwise collect on a debt, liquidated or unliquidated.

In light of the strong public policy considerations disfavoring self-help through force or violence, including the forcible recapture of property, we granted review in this case to consider whether claim of right should continue to be recognized as a defense to robbery in California. * * *

* * *

I. FACTUAL AND PROCEDURAL BACKGROUND

[Defendant was convicted of battery, residential robbery, spousal abuse, and making terrorist threats based on an episode of violence against his former wife, Shelly Tufunga.]

Shelly Tufunga (Shelly) testified that around 5:00 p.m. on January 16, 1996, defendant * * * pushed Shelly to the floor and kicked her in the hip and thigh. He then threw her onto the couch * * * straddled Shelly on the couch, slapped and hit her, grabbed a pair of nine or ten-inch scissors and, making overhead stabbing motions toward her face, forehead and neck, said he was going to "mess up her face," shove the scissors up her "big fat ass" and "make it so that nobody would be able to look at" her. Afraid for her life, Shelly begged him to stop. She dodged stabs at her eyes but suffered scratches to her forehead, neck and arms before defendant finally stopped, put the scissors down, and got off of her. He continued to yell, at one point breaking a lamp in the home. [Shelly claimed that when defendant left, he took $200 in cash that her mother had brought to Shelly's house so Shelly could purchase medicine and vitamins for her.]

* * *

Jurors saw photos of Shelly's injuries taken that same day. Responding police officers testified she was crying and appeared bruised and scratched. She reported that defendant had held the scissors against the bridge of her nose. She thought he had taken the money off the couch. [Shelly's mother, Josephine, also testified at trial, corroborating most of Shelly's account.]

* * *

[Defendant offered a different account of the events. He testified that he had earned the $200, and his employer, a relative, corroborated that claim. Defendant testified that he had brought $200 to Shelly's house to pay her bills, and described the following struggle with her for the $200:]

At that point Shelly reached down, picked up the $200 from the coffee table and put it in her bra. Defendant believed the two were out to take the money, as this had happened before, and that Shelly would give it to her mother. Defendant demanded the money back and, when Shelly refused, wrestled with her, reached into her bra and took it back. As he walked out the door Josephine hit him with the phone. * * * Defendant testified he did not threaten, strike or push Shelly that day and had not broken into her apartment or stayed against her will. Defendant testified that three days later he and Shelly made up, and that he at that time gave her $160 to help pay her bills.

* * *

II. DISCUSSION

At trial, the defense requested instruction on a claim-of-right defense to the charge of robbery. The trial court concluded the facts would not support the defense and refused to instruct on it. On appeal, defendant urged that even if he had used force to take back his $200, that fact is immaterial to the existence of his bona fide belief in his right to take back the money he conditionally gave to Shelly, once he concluded in good faith that she was not going to use it to pay bills and would instead turn it over to her mother. * * *

* * *

"* * * 'Although an intent to steal may ordinarily be inferred when one person takes the property of another, particularly if he takes it by force, proof of the existence of a state of mind incompatible with an intent to steal precludes a finding of either theft or robbery. It has long been the rule in this state and generally throughout the country that a bona fide belief, even though mistakenly held, that one has a right or claim to the property negates felonious intent. A belief that the property taken belongs to the taker, or that he had a right to retake goods sold is sufficient to preclude felonious intent. Felonious intent exists only if the actor intends to take the property of another without believing in good faith that he has a right or claim to it. [Citation.]' " (*People v. Barnett* (1998) 17 Cal. 4th 1044, 1142–1143, 74 Cal. Rptr. 2d 121, 954 P.2d 384.)

* * *

At common law, claim of right was recognized as a defense to the crime of larceny because it was deemed to negate the *animus furandi*—or felonious intent to steal—of that offense. Because robbery was viewed as simply an aggravated form of larceny, it was likewise subject to the same claim-of-right defense.

When the Legislature created the first statutory scheme codifying this state's criminal law in 1850, it incorporated portions of the then-existing common law into the new statutes. * * * From this historical perspective alone, it can be inferred that the Legislature intended to incorporate the common law recognition of the defense of claim of right as negating the felonious taking or *animus furandi* element common to theft and robbery when it first codified those offenses in the 1850 statutes.

* * *

Lastly, it has long been recognized that "[t]heft is a lesser included offense of robbery, which includes the additional element of force or fear," A conclusion here that a claim of right, for policy reasons, should no longer be recognized as a defense to robbery—even where the defendant can establish that he is taking back specific property to which he has lawful title or a bona fide claim of ownership—would mean such a defendant could be convicted of robbery *based on theft of his own property*, a proposition that would stand in patent conflict with both the commonsense notion that someone cannot steal his own property, and the corollary rule that "theft," the taking of "the personal property of *another*" (§ 484, italics added), is a lesser included offense at the core of every robbery. * * *

* * *

In furtherance of the public policy of discouraging the use of forcible self-help, a majority of cases from other jurisdictions decided after *Butler* that have addressed the question whether claim of right should be available as a defense to robbery have rejected *Butler*'s expansive holding that a good faith belief by a defendant that he was entitled to the money or possessions of the victim to satisfy or collect on a debt is a defense to robbery. [The court cited decisions from many jurisdictions, including *People v. Reid*, which follows this case.]

* * *

The People in this case urge that "[t]he rationale for declining to permit a defendant to assert a claim of right defense in a robbery case is quite simple: An ordered society founded on the rule of law does not countenance self-help when it is accomplished by the use of fear, intimidation, or violence."

Justice Mosk espoused a similar viewpoint in [his dissent in Butler]: "[T]he question is ultimately one of basic public policy, which unequivocally dictates that the proper forum for resolving *debt disputes* is a court of law, pursuant to legal process—not the street, at the business end of a lethal weapon. Had this defendant been entrusted with the contents of the deceased's wallet, and had he appropriated them to his own use, believing he was entitled to keep the funds in payment of wages or a debt, that belief would have furnished him no defense to a charge of embezzlement. By parity of rationale, the claim of offset denied to the trusted employee who dips into the company cashbox should be denied to one who, like this defendant, enforces his demands at gunpoint. To hold otherwise would be to constitute him judge and jury in his own cause."

* * *

The legitimacy of the need for our laws to discourage forcible or violent self-help as a remedy seems beyond question. [However] we have concluded that California's Legislature incorporated the common law claim-of-right doctrine into the statutorily defined mens rea element of robbery when it codified that offense over 100 years ago, and that consequently, we are not free to judicially abolish it and thereby effectively expand the statutory definition of the crime.

We nonetheless conclude that *Butler* went well beyond the basic underlying notion that a thief or robber must intend to steal *another's* property when, on the facts before it, the court extended the availability of a claim-of-right defense to perpetrators who rob their victims assertedly to settle, satisfy, or otherwise collect on a debt. Specifically, we find nothing in the language of section 211 to suggest the Legislature intended to incorporate such a broad and expansive extension of the claim-of-right doctrine into the robbery statute.

* * *

We therefore hold that to the extent *Butler* extended the claim-of-right defense to robberies perpetrated to satisfy, settle or otherwise collect on a debt, liquidated or unliquidated—as opposed to forcible takings intended to recover specific personal property in which the defendant in good faith believes he has a bona fide claim of ownership or title—it is unsupported by the statutory language, further contrary to sound public policy, and in that regard is overruled.

* * *

[The court reversed defendant's robbery conviction, but affirmed the lower court's judgment "in all other respects."]

PEOPLE v. REID

Court of Appeals of New York, 1987.
69 N.Y.2d 469, 515 N.Y.S.2d 750, 508 N.E.2d 661.

SIMONS, JUDGE.

[The court considered together two separate cases (*Reid* and *Riddles*) involving the same legal issue. Reid was convicted of robbery for forcibly taking money from other persons that he said was owed to him as a result of prior unlawful drug transactions.]

* * * Defendant Riddles was convicted after a bench trial of robbery in the third degree for forcibly taking money from Genevieve Bellamy.

Bellamy and defendant both testified at trial, each providing different descriptions of events. Bellamy maintained that while she was waiting for a taxi at a street corner in The Bronx, defendant, whom she did not know, drove up to the curb and asked for directions. According to Bellamy, when she leaned into defendant's automobile to help him, defendant grabbed her, forced her into the car and demanded money from her. Bellamy stated she did not have any, but defendant struck her in the face, searched her pockets, and, upon discovering $50, took the money and ordered her out of the automobile.

Defendant disputed her story. He testified that he knew Bellamy prior to the incident and that she owed him $25. He stated that he met her on the evening of the incident and she offered to pay him $15 toward her debt if he drove her downtown so she could pick up a package. Defendant maintained that he took Bellamy downtown, as she asked, but that she was unable to obtain her package so he drove her back uptown. Defendant testified that during the return trip, Bellamy again offered to pay him $15 toward her debt, but upon seeing her counting a large sum of money, he took the full amount she owed him, $25, and no more.

In pronouncing judgment, the court stated that it credited the portion of defendant's testimony indicating that he had taken the money from Bellamy to satisfy a debt but the court held that because defendant used force he was nevertheless guilty of robbery.

A person "commits robbery when, in the course of committing a larceny, he uses or threatens the immediate use of physical force" (Penal Law § 160.00). The larceny statute, in turn, provides that an assertion that "property was appropriated under a claim of right made in good faith" is a defense to larceny. Since a good-faith claim of right is a defense to larceny, and because robbery is defined as forcible larceny, defendants contend that claim of right is also a defense to robbery. They concede the culpability of their forcible conduct, but maintain that because they acted under a claim of right to recover their own property, they were not guilty of robbery, but only some lesser crime, such as assault or unlawful possession of a weapon. Defendants' general contention is not without support. Several jurisdictions have held that one who acts under a claim of right lacks the intent to steal and should not be convicted of robbery. [Citations] That logic is tenable when a person seeks to recover a specific chattel: it is less so when asserted under the circumstances presented in these two cases: in *Reid* to recover the proceeds of crime, and in *Riddles,* to recover cash to satisfy a debt.

We have not had occasion to address the issue but the Appellate Divisions to which it has been presented have uniformly ruled that claim of right is not a defense to robbery. Their determinations ... are consistent with what appears to be the emerging trend of decisions from other jurisdictions. [Citations] We conclude that the claim of right defense is not available in these cases. We need not decide the quite different question of whether an individual who uses force to recover a specific chattel which he owns may be convicted of robbery. It should be noted, however, that because taking property "from an owner thereof" is an element of robbery, a person who recovers property which is his own (as compared to the fungible cash taken to satisfy a claimed debt in the cases before us) may not be guilty of robbery.

The claim of right defense is found in the larceny article of the Penal Law, which provides that a good-faith claim of right is a defense to trespassory larceny or embezzlement. The defense does not apply to all forms of larceny. For example, extortion is a form of larceny, but the Legislature, consistent with a prior decision of this court, has not authorized a claim of right defense to extortion. See People v. Fichtner, (p. 723 of this book). The exception is significant for extortion entails the threat of actual or potential force or some form of coercion. Thus, the inference may reasonably be drawn that in failing to authorize a claim of right defense for extortion in Penal Law § 155.15(1), and by failing to incorporate it in article 160 of the statute, which governs robbery, the Legislature recognized that an accused should not be permitted to invoke it in crimes involving force. * * *

[Affirmed.]

2. Extortion

WOODWARD v. STATE

Court of Appeals of Alaska, 1993.
855 P.2d 423.

Bryner, Chief Judge.

* * *

Woodward was convicted of extortion for threatening to physically injure George Cooper unless Cooper paid Woodward $8,000. Woodward's wife had loaned $8,000 to a man named Mike Lyle. When Lyle was ready to pay the loan back, he went to a Fairbanks bar called the Lonely Lady, where Woodward's wife worked. Woodward's wife was not there, so Lyle left the money with Cooper, who also worked at the Lonely Lady; Cooper agreed to give the money to Woodward's wife. Instead of giving the money to Woodward's wife, however, Cooper evidently spent it himself.

After Woodward learned that Lyle had paid Cooper the money but that Cooper had failed to give it to Woodward's wife, Woodward demanded $8,000 from Cooper, threatening to break Cooper's legs if he failed to pay. Cooper reported the threat to the police. The following day, Cooper made a partial payment to Woodward. The transaction was monitored by the police, who arrested Woodward immediately afterward.

Woodward was charged with extortion in violation of AS 11.41.520(a)(1), which reads, in relevant part:

> (a) A person commits the crime of extortion if the person obtains the property of another by threatening or suggesting that either that person or another may
>
> (1) inflict physical injury on anyone[.]

At trial, Woodward unsuccessfully sought to have the jury instructed to acquit him if it found that Cooper actually owed Woodward the money Woodward demanded. Woodward argued that if Cooper actually owed Woodward $8,000, Woodward had not "obtained the property of another," as required under AS 11.41.520(a)(1). Judge Hodges found this argument unpersuasive and instructed the jury that Woodward's claim of right to money from Cooper was not a defense to the extortion charge. The jury convicted Woodward.

Woodward renews his argument on appeal, insisting that he could not properly be convicted of using threats to obtain the property of another, since he was merely trying to regain his own money. * * *

Woodward's argument is not persuasive. Although the Model Penal Code proposed, some time ago, that a person who obtained property by threatening physical injury be allowed to defend against a charge of extortion by establishing a claim of right to the property, the Code's proposal has failed to gain broad acceptance, and it represents the minority view.

The Model Penal Code's proposed claim-of-right defense to extortion appears integral to the Code's view of extortion as a crime against property. The Code named the offense of extortion "theft by extortion" and classed it as one of several forms of theft included in its consolidated theft provision. All forms of theft were governed by the Code's general claim-of-right defense. In the Code's view, a good faith claim of right negates the intent to steal, thereby precluding conviction of any form of theft, including theft by extortion.[a] When the conduct involved in a theft by extortion is itself offensive, the Code would punish it separately, under provisions governing assault, reckless endangerment, or criminal coercion.

The majority view, in contrast, is that extortion is a crime against the person, not against property. Under the law of most states, and

a. The Model Penal Code includes an affirmative defense to theft charges when the defendant "acted under an honest claim of right to the property or service involved or that he had a right to acquire or dispose of it as he did." M.P.C. § 223.1(3)(b) (1980).—ed.

under federal law as interpreted by all but one of the circuit courts that have considered the issue, a person accused of extortion by threats of physical injury may not assert, as a defense to the charge, a claim of right to the property that was the subject of the extortion.

The majority view reflects the traditional view of extortion. United States v. Zappola, 677 F.2d at 268. It is a view founded on sound policy:

> A person whose property has been stolen cannot claim the right to punish the thief himself without process of law, and to make him compensate him for the loss of his property by maliciously threatening to ... do an injury to his person or property, with intent to extort property from him.

In adopting Alaska's current extortion statute, the legislature adhered to the majority view of the offense. The current extortion statute was adopted by the legislature in 1978, as part of the Alaska Revised Criminal Code. The Revised Code's forerunner, the Tentative Draft of the Revised Alaska Criminal Code, followed the Model Penal Code's approach and classified extortion as an offense against property, grouping it with theft offenses. Like the Model Penal Code, the Tentative Draft also included a claim-of-right defense that was generally applicable to all forms of theft. Nevertheless, unlike the Model Penal Code, the Tentative Draft regarded extortion as a distinct offense from theft. Analogizing extortion to robbery, the Tentative Draft specifically excluded it from the general claim-of-right defense to theft.

When the Alaska Legislature adopted the Revised Code, it made the Tentative Draft's intent even clearer, by reclassifying extortion as an offense against the person and grouping it with robbery and coercion rather than with theft offenses. No claim-of-right provision exists for this group of offenses. The extortion statute itself builds in a claim-of-right provision, but a narrow one. Subsection (a) of AS 11.41.520 describes seven distinct types of threat that will support an extortion charge:

> (a) A person commits the crime of extortion if the person obtains the property of another by threatening or suggesting that either that person or another may
>
> (1) inflict physical injury on anyone, except under circumstances constituting robbery in any degree, or commit any other crime;
>
> (2) accuse anyone of a crime;
>
> (3) expose confidential information or a secret, whether true or false, tending to subject a person to hatred, contempt, or ridicule or to impair the person's credit or business repute;
>
> (4) take or withhold action as a public servant or cause a public servant to take or withhold action;
>
> (5) bring about or continue a strike, boycott, or other collective unofficial action, if the property is not demanded or received for the

benefit of the group in whose interest the person making the threat or suggestion purports to act;

(6) testify or provide information or withhold testimony or information with respect to a person's legal claim or defense; or

(7) inflict any other harm which would not benefit the person making the threat or suggestion.

[Another statutory section restricted the claim-of-right defense to limited situations in which the charges alleged that the property was "obtained by threat of accusation, exposure, lawsuit, or other invocation of official action."]

By electing to extend the claim-of-right defense to only three of the seven types of threat in the extortion statute, the legislature made unmistakably clear its intent to withhold the defense as to the remaining four types. As adopted, and as it now stands, the claim-of-right provision set out in * * * the extortion statute does not extend to threats of physical injury charged under subparagraph (a)(1). Since this is the type of threat Woodward was charged with (and convicted of) making, we conclude that he was not entitled to assert his claim of right to Cooper's money as a defense to the extortion charge.

Woodward nevertheless maintains that, since he was only seeking to recover money that Cooper had unlawfully appropriated from him, the money was his own (Woodward's), and was not "the property of another," as required under AS 11.41.520(a). However, in threatening physical injury to Cooper if Cooper refused to pay, Woodward was not attempting to recover particular, identifiable property; he was merely seeking to collect a debt. In addressing the viability of a claim-of-right defense, courts have held that "the interest which the accused asserts under a claim of right must be to *specific property* and . . . must be in complete derogation of the victim's rights in and to the property." "[W]here, as here, the claim is to money owed, and in order to satisfy the claim, the creditor takes money or other fungible property to which he has no title or right of possession, then the intent to steal is present."

This comports with the broad reading Alaska courts have given to the term "property of another" in the context of theft cases. In *Pulakis v. State*, 476 P.2d 474 (Alaska 1970), for example, the court rejected the notion "that the state must prove, as an essential element of the crime of larceny, ownership of the property allegedly stolen." Instead, the court held that "the 'property of another' phrase in larceny statutes ordinarily refers to possession, not title."

The phrase "property of another" is not expressly defined for purposes of Alaska's extortion statute. The phrase is defined in the chapter of the criminal code that deals with offenses against property, but only as to offenses included in that chapter. Because extortion is now classified as an offense against the person rather than an offense against property, the statutory definition is not directly applicable to it.

We nevertheless find the statutory definition of "property of another" illuminating in reference to the extortion statute. Alaska Statute 11.46.990(12) broadly defines the phrase to include "property in which a person has an interest which the defendant is not privileged to infringe, whether or not the defendant also has an interest in the property and whether or not the person from whom the property was obtained or withheld also obtained the property unlawfully[.]" This definition echoes the expansive definition of "property of another" that *Pulakis* articulated as a matter of common law, and it is fully consistent with the traditional view that a claim-of-right defense cannot be asserted as to debt, but must instead involve discrete, identifiable property.

* * *

For present purposes, we need observe only that, when Woodward uttered his threats against Cooper, Cooper unquestionably had at least a possessory interest in the money Woodward demanded. This interest was sufficient to meet the "property of another" requirement of the extortion statute. Accordingly, the trial court did not err in declining to instruct Woodward's jury on the claim-of-right defense.

* * *

[Judgment affirmed] 

STATE v. BURNS

Supreme Court of Washington, 1931.
161 Wash. 362, 297 P. 212.

BEELER, J.

The appellants were convicted of the crime of extortion. They have appealed from the judgment and sentence on the verdict.

Omitting the formal parts, the information, in substance, charged: That the defendants on April 1, 1929, with intent to extort and gain the sum of $5,000, did verbally threaten to accuse Leland Frease of the crime of grand larceny, and by means of such threats did extort and gain from him the sum of $4,000.

The statute on which the information is based, provides: "Every person, who, under circumstances not amounting to robbery, shall extort or gain any money, property or advantage, . . . by means of force or any threat, . . . to accuse any person of a crime . . . shall be guilty of extortion."

[The Company which employed Frease retained the defendants to determine if money was being embezzled by any of its employees. Subsequently, defendant Burns confronted Frease and accused him of embezzling $6800. Burns claimed that he had already arranged the matter with the local judge, and that Frease would be sent to prison unless he confessed in writing to stealing $5000 and repaid the loss.

Although he denied guilt, Frease signed the confession and actually paid $4000.]

Thus it will be seen that Frease on direct examination testified that he embezzled no money from his employer, and further testified he so advised appellants at the time they extracted the written confession from him. On cross-examination appellants undertook to prove by documentary evidence (Appellants' Exhibits 1 and 2) that Frease had misappropriated money belonging to his employer which he had collected from the sale of merchandise and for which he failed to account, which proof was rejected by the court on the theory that it was immaterial whether or not Frease had embezzled money from his employer. Appellants also undertook to establish by Frease that he had stolen two sacks of corn from his employer's store, to which objection was made, and thereupon the court admonished the jury that he was admitting that particular testimony as affecting the credibility of the witness and for the purpose of impeachment only. These rulings by the trial court are assigned as error.

The question then is: Should the court have permitted appellants to cross-examine the prosecuting witness, Frease, whether he had embezzled money from his employer? Putting it more aptly: May one demand the return of money embezzled by another, and, if restitution be refused, threaten him with a criminal prosecution without violating the extortion statute, so long as the demand is limited to the specific amount embezzled? We think so. If A steals money from B, B may demand its return, and, if restitution be refused, B may threaten criminal prosecution, and, if he limits his demand to the specific amount embezzled, do no violence to the Penal Code. However, B may not demand of A more than is due him, and if B by threats and duress obtains more than rightly belongs to him he violates the statute. Nor may B in his attempt to recover what is due him, by means of threats, accuse A of the commission of another crime or threaten to expose him to public ridicule. But so long as B limits his demand to the return of the specific article stolen or to the exact amount of money embezzled the statute is not violated. Therefore, the fact whether Frease embezzled money became material as bearing on the good faith—the intent—of appellants at the time they demanded the money of Frease; hence the exhibits should have been received in evidence, and the court should not have restricted the jury in its consideration of the testimony merely as affecting the credibility of the witness Frease, or for impeachment purposes only. * * *

From the testimony of the prosecuting witness the jury could readily have found two vital facts: First, that Frease had been a faithful, industrious, and honest employee working steadily to support himself and family; Second, that he was not an embezzler. In truth, Frease stood before the jury as an object of pity who had been victimized at the hands of those tutored in the art of intrigue. Therefore, in furtherance of justice, it became important to determine whether Frease had or had not embezzled money from his employer.

If Frease embezzled no money, then appellants are guilty of extortion of the most dire type. If Frease embezzled money, but if the amount was less than that which appellants undertook to extract from him, appellants violated the extortion statute. If Frease embezzled the money which appellants undertook to collect from him, then the means they adopted were justifiable to induce him to make restitution, and proof of theft became material as bearing on the question of appellants' good faith, intent, purpose, object, and motive at the time they demanded the money from Frease, that is, whether the demand was with the intent to feloniously, illegally, and corruptly extort money from Frease or whether it was with the intent and purpose to compel Frease to repay the money he had embezzled from his employer. * * *

For the reasons assigned the case is reversed, and the cause remanded for a new trial.

Note

The New York Court of Appeals opinion in *Reid,* supra, cited a prior New York extortion case, People v. Fichtner, 281 A.D. 159, 118 N.Y.S.2d 392 (1952). The defendant in that case, a supermarket manager, caught Smith shoplifting a 53–cent jar of coffee and threatened prosecution unless Smith admitted stealing merchandise worth $75 over a period of months and paid that amount. Smith denied the additional thefts, but finally signed a paper admitting stealing $50 in merchandise. He made partial payment, and defendant turned this money over to the company. Charged with extortion, defendant testified that he had seen Smith steal merchandise worth $5.61, and that he honestly believed that Smith had stolen goods worth $75. A policeman testified that defendant admitted that it was his practice to try to get $50 or $75 from each shoplifter he caught, because he was short in his inventories. On these facts, the court held that the defendant was not entitled to an instruction that he should be acquitted if, in the judgment of the jury, he honestly believed that Smith had stolen $50 or more. A majority of the court expressed the view that "The law does not authorize the collection of just debts by threatening to accuse the debtor of crime, even though the complainant is in fact guilty of the crime. * * * (I)t makes no difference whether the indebtedness for which a defendant demands repayment is one arising out of the crime for the prosecution of which he threatens the complainant, or is entirely independent and having no connection with the crime which forms the basis of the accusation. The result in both cases is the concealment and compounding of a felony to the injury of the State. It is that result which the extortion statutes were intended to prevent." The 1965 overall revision of the New York Penal addressed this issue in § 155.15, supra p. 770.

Litigants and attorneys may be charged with extortion for using heavy-handed threats to gain an advantage in litigation. In one case a Vermont lawyer retained by the wife in a divorce case hired a prostitute to seduce the husband, burst into the hotel room and photographed the pair in bed together. The lawyer then sent a letter threatening to use the photographs in a divorce action based upon adultery [a crime in Vermont], including for good measure additional threats to the effect that the wife would seek "informer's fees" from the Internal Revenue Service if her demands were not met. The lawyer's conviction for extortion was affirmed in State v. Harrington, 128 Vt. 242, 260 A.2d 692 (1969). The court observed that "A demand for settlement of a civil action, accompanied by a malicious threat to expose the wrongdoer's criminal conduct, if made with intent to extort payment, against his will, constitutes [extortion]."

The United States Court of Appeals for the Second Circuit dealt with claim of right in extortion in a notorious case in which the victim was the famous entertainer Bill Cosby. The defendant Autumn Jackson claimed to be Cosby's daughter out-of-wedlock. Cosby denied paternity but admitted having an affair with Jackson's mother, and he provided support for the child until she became an adult. When he thereafter began to resist Jackson's repeated demands for money, she threatened to publicize the scandal unless he paid her $40 million. At Jackson's trial in federal court for transmitting threats with intent to extort, the defense theory was that Jackson was merely asking for support money to which she was entitled. The defense asked the judge to instruct the jury to find the defendant guilty only if she "had no lawful claim or right to the money or property she sought or attempted to obtain." The trial judge refused. The instructions given to the jury stated *first*, that it was irrelevant whether the defendant actually *was* Cosby's daughter (i.e., that the threat was based on true facts); and *second*, that "it makes no difference whether the defendant actually was owed any money by Bill Cosby or thought she was. This is because the law does not permit someone to obtain money or a thing of value by threatening to injure another person's reputation." United States v. Jackson, 180 F.3d 55, 65–66 (2d Cir.1999).

The Court of Appeals held this charge erroneous, ruling that extortion would not be committed if the defendant threatened a disclosure that had a nexus to a plausible claim or right. For example, it would not be extortion if a creditor threatened to expose a non-paying debtor as a deadbeat in order to collect a genuine debt. After a rehearing, the Court found the error in the instruction to be subject to a harmless error standard, and upheld the conviction. Although the defense presented expert testimony that Jackson might have been entitled to various payments in the hypothetical event that she had prevailed in a paternity suit, the appellate court found that "we are persuaded beyond a reasonable doubt that a properly instructed jury would nonetheless have found her guilty, rejecting the proposition that she had any plausible claim of right to $40 million." United States v. Jackson, 196 F.3d 383 (2d Cir.1999).

UNITED STATES v. STURM

United States Court of Appeals, First Circuit, 1989.
870 F.2d 769.

TORRUELLA, CIRCUIT JUDGE.

* * * In May 1985, Sturm obtained a $110,000 loan from the Worcester County Institution for Savings (WCIS) by signing a promissory note and granting a purchase money mortgage in connection with his

acquisition of an Aero Commander aircraft for $214,000. In addition to the aircraft, the loan was secured by other related collateral, including the plane's logbooks. Logbooks record the repair and maintenance history of a plane and are required by the FAA for all commercial aircraft. A plane without logbooks ordinarily can be used only for noncommercial purposes, and thus has a lower value.

Sturm fell behind on his loan payments in April and May 1986, but eliminated the arrears when WCIS requested him to do so. WCIS then learned that [Sturm had other financial problems.] WCIS repossessed the Aero Commander in August. The act of repossession did not include the logbooks.

[WCIS found out that it could not get a fair market price for the plane at auction unless it had the logbooks. After the auction, a WCIS officer, asked Sturm for the logbooks. He replied, "I don't know where the books are right now but I can get them for you for a price."]

Sturm called WCIS officers inquiring about the status of the aircraft on October 29 and November 26. On each occasion, he offered to help find the logbooks if he were paid a fee. When the officers explained that it was in Sturm's interest to have the plane sold at the highest possible price, Sturm disagreed, stating that he was not worried about residual indebtedness because he was going to file for bankruptcy. WCIS contacted the [FBI] after the November 26 call. All subsequent conversations were recorded.

On December 2, Sturm spoke to Phillip Zoppo, another WCIS official. He told Zoppo that he could not find the logbooks but wanted to make some money selling airplanes for WCIS at a commission. Sturm then pointed out that the logbooks would increase the value of the aircraft by more than $45,000, and therefore that the logbooks themselves were worth about $20,000. He added that he could find the books "if the price is right." Zoppo asked Sturm why WCIS should pay to recover its own property. Sturm replied, "I understand the books should go with the airplane and everything, but in fact they're not." In a subsequent conversation later the same day, Zoppo informed him that senior management had acceded to his demands; WCIS would pay him $20,000 for the logbooks.

Two days later, on December 4, Sturm called Zoppo and informed him that he had the logbooks. The next day, two FBI agents posing as WCIS officers met with Sturm. He said he had gone to the Cayman Islands to retrieve the logbooks, and offered to exchange them for $20,000 in cash. The agents reiterated that if he left with the $20,000, WCIS would be paying for property which it rightfully owned. Sturm replied, "You keep bringing that up. You don't need to." One of the agents mentioned to Sturm that the transaction reminded him of kidnapping, to which Sturm responded, "I know." Sturm was arrested in the WCIS parking lot after he showed the agents the logbooks in the trunk of his car.

[Sturm was convicted in federal court of attempted extortion in violation of the Hobbs Act, 18 U.S.C. § 1951. This federal statute, with a penalty of up to 20 years imprisonment, punishes anyone who affects interstate commerce "by robbery or extortion or attempts or conspires to do so." "Extortion" is defined as "the obtaining of property from another, with his consent, induced by wrongful use of actual or threatened force, violence, or fear, or under color of official right."]

II

* * *

[Sturm] claims that his conviction should be reversed for any one of four reasons. First, Congress did not intend the Hobbs Act to apply to actions based on a creditor's fear of nonrepayment. Second, Sturm could not be guilty of extortion because he had a claim of right to the logbooks. Third, even if Sturm did not actually have a claim of right to the logbooks he cannot be guilty of extortion because he thought he had a claim of right to the logbooks. Fourth, the trial judge failed to instruct the jury that extortion under the Hobbs Act is a crime of specific intent, requiring proof that the defendant intended to violate the Act.

A

Sturm's first claim is that Congress did not intend the Hobbs Act to apply to actions based on a creditor's fear of nonrepayment. He supports this claim by pointing to the absence of any mention of such actions in both the statute's legislative history and in cases interpreting the statute. He argues that extending the statute to include such actions would interfere with state sovereignty and squander federal judicial resources.

We find Sturm's arguments unpersuasive. The statute provides a precise definition of extortion, and there is persuasive evidence that Congress intended "to make punishable all conduct falling within the reach of the statutory language." [Citations] * * * In light of the plain language of the Act and the intent of its framers, the absence in the legislative history and prior case law of any specific mention of an action based on a creditor's fear of non-repayment is less than compelling.

Sturm's federalism arguments meet a similar fate. With respect to the enactment of the Hobbs Act, the Supreme Court has concluded that "there is no question that Congress intended to define as a federal crime conduct that it knew was punishable under state law. The legislative debates are replete with statements that the conduct punishable under the Hobbs Act was already punishable under state robbery and extortion statutes. Those who opposed the act argued that it was a grave interference with the rights of states. Congress apparently believed, however, that the states had not been effectively prosecuting robbery and extortion affecting interstate commerce and that the Federal Government had an obligation to do so." * * *

B

Sturm's second claim is that he was entitled to acquittal because he had a claim of right to the logbooks. This claim is based on two premises: first, that there is a claim of right defense to charges of extortion induced by wrongful use of economic fear, and second, that his conduct is immunized by that defense. We examine each premise in turn. The claim of right defense originated in United States v. Enmons, 410 U.S. 396 (1973), in which the defendants were charged with attempting to obtain higher wages and other benefits for striking employees through the wrongful use of actual force and violence. The main issue before the Supreme Court was whether the term "wrongful" in the statute applied to the means used or to the ends sought by the alleged extortioner. Justice Stewart, in his majority opinion for the Court, resolved this issue in the following manner:

"The term 'wrongful,' which on the face of the statute modifies the use of each of the enumerated means of obtaining property—actual or threatened force, violence, or fear—would be superfluous if it only served to describe the means used. For it would be redundant to speak of 'wrongful violence' or 'wrongful force' since, as the government acknowledges, any violence or force to obtain property is 'wrongful.' Rather, 'wrongful' has meaning in the Act only if it limits the statute's coverage to those instances where the obtaining of the property would itself be 'wrongful' because the alleged extortionist has no lawful claim to that property." *Enmons,* 410 U.S. at 399–400.

This reasoning created the claim of right defense to charges of extortion under the Hobbs Act. Despite its broad language, most federal appellate courts, including this court, have restricted *Enmons* and its claim of right defense to the labor context, fearing that a broader application "could effectively repeal the Hobbs Act." [Citations]

Although it may be appropriate not to recognize a claim of right defense in extortion cases based on the wrongful use of force or violence, different considerations apply in the context of extortion based on economic fear. Whereas the use of actual or threatened force or violence to obtain property is inherently wrongful, there is nothing inherently wrongful about the use of economic fear to obtain property. [T]his conclusion does not imply that all forms of economic fear are inherently legitimate. Although we are not aware of any cases so holding, we do not rule out the possibility that the use of wrongful economic threats to obtain property to which the defendant is legally entitled may be prosecutable as extortion under the Hobbs Act.

[U]nlike extortion cases based on the use of force and violence, extortion cases based on the use of economic fear typically will not involve allegations of wrongful means, but only allegations of wrongful ends. For these typical economic fear cases, it is self-evident that a defendant cannot be found guilty of wrongfully obtaining property through the use of a legitimate economic threat if he has a claim of right to the property. * * *

Sturm argues that he did not know where the logbooks were, and that he had no obligation to find them for WCIS. On the contrary, he asserts that he had a right to charge WCIS a fee to find the logbooks. [I]f Sturm truly did not know the whereabouts of the logbooks, he could conceivably have demanded a fee from WCIS for making extra efforts to locate them. Whether he was sincere, however, is a factual issue for the jury to decide. Judge Woodlock instructed the jury on Sturm's claim of right defense; the guilty verdict indicates that the jury resolved this factual issue against Sturm. * * *

C.

Sturm's third argument is that there was insufficient evidence to support a finding that he knew he was not legally entitled to the $20,000 fee. This claim is also based on two premises: first, that the government must prove that the alleged extortioner knew that he was not legally entitled to the property in question, and second, that there was insufficient evidence to prove that Sturm knew that he was not legally entitled to the $20,000. We again consider each premise in turn. * * *

We conclude that the term "wrongful" requires the government to prove, in cases involving extortion based on economic fear, that the defendant knew that he was not legally entitled to the property that he received. * * * The necessity of such a requirement can be demonstrated through an example: * * * A and B enter into a contract. A sincerely believes that B has breached the contract, and threatens litigation unless B abides by A's interpretation of the contract. B refuses to do so, and the judgment in the ensuing lawsuit indicates that B had not breached the contract. May A then be convicted of attempted extortion based on the threat of litigation? We think not. Even though A had no objective right to the contractual entitlement she sought, her threat of litigation does not amount to attempted extortion because A subjectively thought that she had a right to the contractual entitlement. * * * Similarly, if Sturm genuinely believed that he was entitled to charge WCIS a fee for locating the logbooks, he cannot be guilty of attempted extortion.

* * * Although there was sufficient evidence for the jury to conclude that Sturm knew he had no legal right to the $20,000 fee, we can not be certain that the jury actually made such a finding. The conviction must be vacated because the trial court did not instruct the jury that in order to convict the defendant of attempted extortion, it would have to find that Sturm knew that he was not legally entitled to a fee to help WCIS recover the logbooks. The requirement that the defendant know that he was not legally entitled to the property in question stems from the statute's use of the term "wrongful." Explaining this term, the trial court instructed the jury that "[w]rongful, as in wrongful use of fear, means that the Defendant had no lawful right to the property that he sought to obtain." The Court's definition of "wrongful" was purely objective. By making no reference to the defendant's state of mind, the instruction suggested that Sturm's mens rea was irrelevant. This omission was exacerbated by the court's subsequent instruction on specific intent. The trial court stated that "[t]he government is not required to provide, however, evidence that the Defendant knew those intentional acts were themselves illegal. In this case, ignorance of the law is no excuse." The instruction may have referred to ignorance of the Hobbs

Act itself, but * * * the jury may have concluded that it could find Sturm guilty of attempted extortion even if it found credible his claim that he sincerely believed that he was legally entitled to a fee for helping WCIS locate the logbooks. We hold that the instruction which permitted such a conclusion is erroneous. * * * [The case was remanded to the district court for a new trial.]

UNITED STATES v. COVINO

United States Court of Appeals, Second Circuit, 1988.
837 F.2d 65.

WINTER, CIRCUIT JUDGE:

Alfred Covino appeals from convictions under the Travel Act and for wire fraud. The government cross-appeals from the district court's acquittal after the jury had found Covino guilty of extortion in violation of the Hobbs Act. We affirm the Travel Act conviction, reverse the Hobbs Act acquittal, and reverse the wire fraud conviction. * * * In December 1983, after a favorable history of employment with AT & T, Covino became Director of Network Services at NYNEX Mobile Communications Co. NYNEX provided mobile telephone services and was then involved in a race with a competitor to build "cell sites," small structures containing switching gear used to relay signals from cellular phones within specific geographic areas.

Great Northeastern Building and Management Corporation was a small, newly formed contracting firm that operated out of the house of its half-owner, Robert Brennan. Its regular employees consisted of Brennan as President and his partner Joseph Boyd as Vice President. Brennan's wife helped out as a bookkeeper. Great Northeastern had originally been hired by NYNEX to provide consulting services but later became the prime contractor for the construction of certain cell sites. NYNEX's business eventually accounted for roughly ninety percent of Great Northeastern's business. Great Northeastern was thus heavily dependent upon the favor of NYNEX.

As Director of Network Services, Covino had substantial, although not absolute, control over the selection, supervision and payment of contractors hired to build cell sites. Covino usually could not act for NYNEX without the formal approval of other NYNEX executives, but he could in practice allow or disallow claims for extra work, approve or disapprove invoices and materially aid Great Northeastern in obtaining cell site construction contracts. At pertinent times, NYNEX had explicit written policies forbidding its employees from soliciting or receiving benefits from persons doing business with NYNEX. These policies did not deter Covino from taking advantage of his substantial power over Great Northeastern. In May 1984, he learned that a former employee of Great Northeastern had improperly billed $3,200 in telephone calls to a NYNEX credit card. Covino showed these bills to Brennan and warned that if Covino's superior found out about them "it wouldn't look good" for Great Northeastern. Brennan offered to pay the bills, but Covino refused the offer, saying that he would "take care of them" himself. Not long thereafter, Covino approached Brennan for help in building a sun deck for Covino's home in New Jersey. After being told by Covino to "keep in mind the phone bill," Brennan agreed to build the sun deck at a cut-rate price. Based upon plans Covino obtained from an architect (also a NYNEX subcontractor) who employed Covino's wife, Brennan built, not a sun deck, but an entire "Florida room" addition costing in excess of $20,000. To make it appear that he had actually paid for the addition, Covino asked Brennan to take a $15,000 check and then return to him the same amount in cash. Brennan declined to participate in this cover-up but nevertheless did not ask for any payment for constructing the Florida room. Later in 1984, Covino induced Brennan to arrange and pay for additional work on Covino's house, including repairs to a sump pump, refacing of a fireplace, construction of a closet in the garage, addition of a porch on the rear of the house, and construction of a deck on the Florida room.

Its consulting contract with NYNEX having been terminated in the fall of 1984, Great Northeastern became almost totally dependent upon its construction contracts with NYNEX for its commercial survival. * * * Brennan testified that he feared that if he refused to accede to Covino's demands, Covino would use his power to drive Great Northeastern out of business by withholding payments on completed work and by denying Great Northeastern any new construction work for NYNEX. In the fall of 1984, Covino shifted his demands from services to cash. Near the end of December 1984, Covino even drew up a written schedule of payments, totalling $100,000. He explained to Brennan that $5 million of construction contracts, a "once-in-a-lifetime situation," were coming up and that he, Covino, wanted his "share." Covino then asked Brennan if he wanted his "share." In response to Covino's requests, Brennan made cash payments totalling $85,000 between January and April 1985.

Discussion

1. *The Hobbs Act Acquittal.* After the jury convicted Covino on six of the eight counts charging violations of the Hobbs Act, Covino moved for [judgment of acquittal notwithstanding the verdict]. In granting the motion, the district court stated that "there was not sufficient evidence of wrongful use of fear to uphold the jury's verdict. Indeed, there was no evidence of conduct by anybody involving a threat." [Supreme Court precedents allow the government to appeal from an order of the trial judge granting a motion for acquittal after the jury has returned a verdict of guilty.]

In the view of the district court, unless a Hobbs Act defendant threatens to hurt his or her victim, the forthcoming payment is only commercial bribery, the essential element of which is "pay me and be assisted," but not extortion, the essential element of which is "pay me or be precluded." As was made clear by United States v. Capo, 817 F.2d 947 (2d Cir.1987) (in banc), the district court's statement of the law is essentially correct. We disagree, however, with his view of the sufficiency of the evidence in the instant case.

In a prosecution for extortion by the wrongful use of the fear of economic loss, the government must prove that the victim reasonably believed two things: first, that the defendant had the power to harm the victim, and second, that the defendant would exploit that power to the victim's detriment. A direct threat of future harm is not necessary to establish the reasonableness of the alleged victim's fear. [Citations] Viewed in the light most favorable to the government, the evidence of fear of economic loss was sufficient to support the jury's guilty verdict. While Covino's power over Great Northeastern's relationship with NYNEX was not absolute, Covino wielded substantial authority in contractor selection, work authorization, and payment approval. He was thus positioned to injure as well as to aid Great Northeastern. Brennan's view of Covino's power over Great Northeastern—"I was afraid if I resisted we would lose our contract," was therefore reasonable under the circumstances.

It was also reasonable for Brennan to believe that Covino was prepared to use his power to harm Great Northeastern if Brennan did not comply with Covino's demands. In particular, Covino's early statement that it would not "look good" to Covino's superiors if they were to find out about the phone bills, followed by a later reminder to "keep in mind the phone bills" when asking Brennan to build the sun deck/Florida room, would reasonably be interpreted as threats. The same is true of Covino's subsequent observation that he wanted his "share" of future NYNEX expenditures, followed by his inquiry as to whether Brennan wanted to do his "share" in the context of Covino's increasing demands for services and cash. We therefore reverse the judgment of acquittal on the Hobbs Act conviction and remand for sentencing.

2. *The Travel Act Conviction.* [The court held that Covino was properly convicted under the federal Travel Act for interstate travel in furtherance of a violation of the New York state law against commercial bribery.]

3. *The Wire Fraud Conviction.* [The indictment charged wire fraud in that Covino violated his fiduciary duty to his employer NYNEX Communications, by concealing his receipt of kickbacks from Brennan and by depriving NYNEX of his "loyal unbiased services" in regard to approving payments by NYNEX to Great Northeastern.]

The theory of the indictment and the charge to the jury were based on decisions in this circuit holding that it constituted wire or mail fraud for an employee to breach a duty to his or her employer and to fail to inform the employer of his or her breach. Covino contends, however, that his conviction may not stand in light of the Supreme Court's intervening decision in McNally v. United States, 483 U.S. 350 (1987).

McNally involved a scheme by which an insurance agency selected to procure insurance for the State of Kentucky agreed to share its commissions with other insurance agencies designated by the chairman of the state Democratic Party. The defendants, who participated in this scheme, were prosecuted for mail fraud. The element of deceit or fraud lay in the defendants' failure to disclose this scheme to persons in state government whose actions or deliberations might have been affected by such information. The prosecution was not required to prove that the Commonwealth of Kentucky, the victim of the alleged fraud, had actually been deprived of any money or property. Nor was there any claim that the Commonwealth would have paid a lower premium or secured better insurance coverage in the absence of the scheme. The Supreme Court reversed the convictions, holding that the legislative history of the mail fraud statute indicated that Congress intended § 1341's application to be "limited in scope to the protection of property rights." The Court declined to construe the statute in a way that "involves the Federal Government in setting standards of disclosure and good government," and held that mail fraud requires a finding that the victim be defrauded of money or property. Covino contends that because the wire fraud and mail fraud statutes are construed identically, *McNally* requires that his conviction be reversed. We agree.

The indictment and charge in the instant matter neither alleged nor asked the jury to find that NYNEX was defrauded of money or property. The conviction on the wire fraud counts thus rested on Covino's failure to inform NYNEX that he was soliciting and receiving money and services from Great Northeastern, not that he was defrauding NYNEX itself of its property. But for the fact that state government was involved in *McNally,* this was precisely the legal theory rejected by the Supreme Court. We therefore reverse the wire fraud counts. * * *

[T]he judgment of acquittal entered by the district court on the counts under the Hobbs Act is reversed and remanded for sentencing. The conviction on the Travel Act counts is affirmed. Finally, the conviction on the wire fraud counts is reversed.

EVANS v. UNITED STATES

Supreme Court of the United States, 1992.
504 U.S. 255, 112 S.Ct. 1881, 119 L.Ed.2d 57.

STEVENS, J., delivered the opinion of the Court, in which WHITE, BLACKMUN, and SOUTER, JUSTICES, joined, in Parts I and II of which O'CONNOR, J., joined, and in Part III of which KENNEDY, J., joined. O'CONNOR, J., AND KENNEDY, J., filed opinions concurring in part and concurring in the judgment. THOMAS, J., filed a dissenting opinion, in which REHNQUIST, C. J., and SCALIA, J., joined.

JUSTICE STEVENS delivered the opinion of the court.

I

Petitioner was an elected member of the Board of Commissioners of DeKalb County, Georgia. During the period between March 1985 and October 1986, as part of an effort by the Federal Bureau of Investigation

(FBI) to investigate allegations of public corruption in the Atlanta area, particularly in the area of rezonings of property, an FBI agent posing as a real estate developer talked on the telephone and met with petitioner on a number of occasions. Virtually all, if not all, of those conversations were initiated by the agent and most were recorded on tape or video. In those conversations, the agent sought petitioner's assistance in an effort to rezone a 25–acre tract of land for high-density residential use. On July 25, 1986, the agent handed petitioner cash totaling $7,000 and a check, payable to petitioner's campaign, for $1,000. Petitioner reported the check, but not the cash, on his state campaign-financing disclosure form; he also did not report the $7,000 on his 1986 federal income tax return. Viewing the evidence in the light most favorable to the Government, as we must in light of the verdict, see Glasser v. United States, 315 U.S. 60, 80 (1942), we assume that the jury found that petitioner accepted the cash knowing that it was intended to ensure that he would vote in favor of the rezoning application and that he would try to persuade his fellow commissioners to do likewise. Thus, although petitioner did not initiate the transaction, his acceptance of the bribe constituted an implicit promise to use his official position to serve the interests of the bribe-giver.

In a two-count indictment, petitioner was charged with extortion in violation of 18 U.S.C. § 1951 [the Hobbs Act] and with failure to report income in violation of 26 U.S.C. § 7206(1). He was convicted by a jury on both counts. With respect to the extortion count, the trial judge gave the following instruction:

"The defendant contends that the $8,000 he received from agent Cormany was a campaign contribution. The solicitation of campaign contributions from any person is a necessary and permissible form of political activity on the part of persons who seek political office and persons who have been elected to political office. Thus, the acceptance by an elected official of a campaign contribution does not, in itself, constitute a violation of the Hobbs Act even though the donor has business pending before the official.

"However, if a public official demands or accepts money in exchange for [a] specific requested exercise of his or her official power, such a demand or acceptance does constitute a violation of the Hobbs Act regardless of whether the payment is made in the form of a campaign contribution."

In affirming petitioner's conviction, the Court of Appeals noted that the instruction did not require the jury to find that petitioner had demanded or requested the money, or that he had conditioned the performance of any official act upon its receipt. 910 F.2d 790, 796 (C.A.11 1990). The Court of Appeals held, however, that "passive acceptance of a benefit by a public official is sufficient to form the basis of a Hobbs Act violation if the official knows that he is being offered the payment in exchange for a specific requested exercise of his official power. The official need not take any specific action to induce the offering of the benefit." Ibid. * * *

This statement of the law by the Court of Appeals for the Eleventh Circuit is consistent with holdings in eight other Circuits. Two Circuits, however, have held that an affirmative act of inducement by the public official is required to support a conviction of extortion under color of official right. * * *

II

It is a familiar maxim that a statutory term is generally presumed to have its common-law meaning. As we have explained, "where Congress borrows terms of art in which are accumulated the legal tradition and meaning of centuries of practice, it presumably knows and adopts the cluster of ideas that were attached to each borrowed word in the body of learning from which it was taken and the meaning its use will convey to the judicial mind unless otherwise instructed. In such case, absence of contrary direction may be taken as satisfaction with widely accepted definitions, not as a departure from them." Morissette v. United States, 342 U.S. 246, 263 (1952).

At common law, extortion was an offense committed by a public official who took "by colour of his office"[4] money that was not due to him for the performance of his official duties. A demand, or request, by the public official was not an element of the offense. Extortion by the public official was the rough equivalent of what we would now describe as taking a bribe. It is clear that petitioner committed that offense. The question is whether the federal statute, insofar as it applies to official extortion, has narrowed the common-law definition. * * *

Congress has unquestionably expanded the common-law definition of extortion to include acts by private individuals pursuant to which property is obtained by means of force, fear, or threats. It did so by implication in the Travel Act, 18 U.S.C. § 1952, see United States v. Nardello, 393 U.S. 286, 289–296 (1969), and expressly in the Hobbs Act. The portion of the Hobbs Act that is relevant to our decision today provides:

> "(a) Whoever in any way or degree obstructs, delays, or affects commerce or the movement of any article or commodity in com-

4. Blackstone described extortion as "an abuse of public justice, which consists in an officer's unlawfully taking, *by colour of his office*, from any man, any money or thing of value, that is not due to him, or more than is due, or before it is due." 4 W. Blackstone, Commentaries *141 (emphasis added). He used the phrase by colour of his office," rather than the phrase under color of official right," which appears in the Hobbs Act. Petitioner does not argue that there is any difference in the phrases. Hawkins' definition of extortion is probably the source for the official right language used in the Hobbs Act. See Lindgren, "The Elusive Distinction Between Bribery and Extortion: From the Common Law to the Hobbs Act," 35 UCLA L. Rev. 815, 864 (1988) (hereinafter Lindgren). Hawkins defined extortion as follows: "It is said, That extortion in a large sense signifies any oppression under colour of right; but that in a strict sense, it signifies the taking of money by any officer, by colour of his office, either where none at all is due, or not so much is due, or where it is not yet due." 1 W. Hawkins, Pleas of the Crown 316 (6th ed. 1787).

merce, by robbery or extortion or attempts or conspires so to do, or commits or threatens physical violence to any person or property in furtherance of a plan or purpose to do anything in violation of this section shall be fined not more than $10,000 or imprisoned not more than twenty years, or both.

"(b) As used in this section—* * *

"(2) The term 'extortion' means the obtaining of property from another, with his consent, induced by wrongful use of actual or threatened force, violence, or fear, or under color of official right." 18 U.S.C. § 1951.

The present form of the statute is a codification of a 1946 enactment, the Hobbs Act, which amended the federal Anti–Racketeering Act. In crafting the 1934 Act, Congress was careful not to interfere with legitimate activities between employers and employees. The 1946 Amendment was intended to encompass the conduct held to be beyond the reach of the 1934 Act by our decision in United States v. Teamsters, 315 U.S. 521 (1942). The Amendment did not make any significant change in the section referring to obtaining property "under color of official right" that had been prohibited by the 1934 Act. Rather, Congress intended to broaden the scope of the Anti–Racketeering Act and was concerned primarily with distinguishing between "legitimate" labor activity and labor "racketeering," so as to prohibit the latter while permitting the former. * * *

Many of those who supported the Amendment argued that its purpose was to end the robbery and extortion that some union members had engaged in, to the detriment of all labor and the American citizenry. They urged that the Amendment was not, as their opponents charged, an anti-labor measure, but rather, it was a necessary measure in the wake of this Court's decision in United States v. Teamsters. In their view, the Supreme Court had mistakenly exempted labor from laws prohibiting robbery and extortion, whereas Congress had intended to extend such laws to all American citizens. * * *

Although the present statutory text is much broader than the common-law definition of extortion because it encompasses conduct by a private individual as well as conduct by a public official, the portion of the statute that refers to official misconduct continues to mirror the common-law definition. * * *

We reject petitioner's criticism of the instruction, and conclude that it satisfies the quid pro quo requirement of McCormick v. United States, 500 U.S. 257 (1991),[a] because the offense is completed at the time when

a. The defendant in *McCormick* was a West Virginia state legislator who had sponsored a legislative program allowing foreign medical graduates to practice in the United States while studying for the state licensing exams. Some doctors practiced for years under this program because they repeatedly failed the exams. Defendant solicited cash campaign contributions from the foreign medical graduates under circumstances giving the impression that his support for the program was at stake. There was no explicit promise or undertaking as a "quid pro quo" for the contributions, however, and of the public official receives a payment in return for his agreement to perform specific official acts; fulfillment of the quid pro quo is not an element of the offense. We also reject petitioner's contention that an affirmative step is an element of the offense of extortion under color of "official right" and need be included in the instruction. As we explained above, our construction of the statute is informed by the common-law tradition from which the term of art was drawn and understood. We hold today that the Government need only show that a public official has obtained a payment to which he was not entitled, knowing that the payment was made in return for official acts. * * *

III

An argument not raised by petitioner is now advanced by the dissent. It contends that common-law extortion was limited to wrongful takings under a false pretense of official right. * * * It is perfectly clear, however, that although extortion accomplished by fraud was a well-recognized type of extortion, there were other types as well. * * *

The judgment is affirmed.

[JUSTICE O'CONNOR concurred in Parts I and II of the above opinion, and wrote that the Court did not need to address the issue discussed in Part III, which was not raised in the petition for certiorari. JUSTICE KENNEDY concurred in the judgment.]

JUSTICE THOMAS, with whom THE CHIEF JUSTICE and JUSTICE SCALIA join, dissenting.

* * * The "under color of office" element of extortion, however, had a definite and well-established meaning at common law. "At common law it was essential that the money or property be obtained under color of office, *that is, under the pretense that the officer was entitled thereto by virtue of his office.* The money or thing received must have been claimed or accepted in right of office, and the person paying must have yielded to official authority." 3 R. Anderson, Wharton's Criminal Law and Procedure § 1393, pp. 790–791 (1957) (emphasis added). Thus, although the Court purports to define official extortion under the Hobbs Act by reference to the common law, its definition bears scant resemblance to the common-law crime Congress presumably codified in 1946. * * *

The Court's historical analysis rests upon a theory set forth in one law review article. [See ante, footnote 4] Focusing on early English cases, the article argues that common-law extortion encompassed a wide range of official takings, whether by coercion, false pretenses, or bribery. Whatever the merits of that argument as a description of early English common law, it is beside the point here—the critical inquiry for our

course legislators frequently sponsor legislation that benefits campaign contributors. The Supreme Court held that solicitation of campaign contributions constitutes extortion "only if the payments are made in return for an explicit promise or undertaking by the official to perform or not to perform an official act." McCormick v. United States, 500 U.S. 257, 273 (1991).—ed.

purposes is the American understanding of the crime at the time the Hobbs Act was passed in 1946. * * *

The Court, therefore, errs in asserting that common-law extortion is the rough equivalent of what we would now describe as "taking a bribe." Regardless of whether extortion contains an "inducement" requirement, bribery and extortion are different crimes. An official who solicits or takes a bribe does not do so under "color of office"; i.e., under any pretense of official entitlement. * * * Where extortion is at issue, the public official is the sole wrongdoer; because he acts "under color of office," the law regards the payor as an innocent victim and not an accomplice. With bribery, in contrast, the payor knows the recipient official is not entitled to the payment; he, as well as official, may be punished for the offense. Congress is well aware of the distinction between the crimes; it has always treated them separately. Compare 18 U.S.C. § 872 ("Extortion by officers or employees of the United States" which criminalizes extortion by federal officials, and makes no provision for punishment of the payor), with 18 U.S.C. § 201 (which criminalizes bribery of and by federal officials). By stretching the bounds of extortion to make it encompass bribery, the Court today blurs the traditional distinction between the crimes. * * *

The Court's construction of the Hobbs Act is repugnant not only to the basic tenets of criminal justice reflected in the rule of lenity, but also to basic tenets of federalism. Over the past 20 years, the Hobbs Act has served as the engine for a stunning expansion of federal criminal jurisdiction into a field traditionally policed by state and local laws—acts of public corruption by state and local officials. See generally Ruff, Federal Prosecution of Local Corruption: A Case Study in the Making of Law Enforcement Policy, 65 Geo. L.J. 1171 (1977). That expansion was born of a single sentence in a Third Circuit opinion: [The under color of official right' language in the Hobbs Act] repeats the common law definition of extortion, a crime which could only be committed by a public official, and which did not require proof of threat, fear, or duress." United States v. Kenny, 462 F.2d 1205, 1229, cert. denied, 409 U.S. 914 (1972). As explained above, that sentence is not necessarily incorrect in its description of what common-law extortion did not require; unfortunately, it omits an important part of what common-law extortion did require. By overlooking the traditional meaning of under color of official right," *Kenny* obliterated the distinction between extortion and bribery, essentially creating a new crime encompassing both.

"As effectively as if there were federal common law crimes, the court in *Kenny* . . . amended the Hobbs Act and [brought] into existence a new crime—local bribery affecting interstate commerce. Hereafter, for purposes of Hobbs Act prosecutions, such bribery was to be called extortion. The federal policing of state corruption had begun." J. Noonan, Bribes 586 (1984).

After *Kenny*, federal prosecutors came to view the Hobbs Act as a license for ferreting out all wrongdoing at the state and local level—a special code of integrity for public officials. In short order, most other circuits followed Kenny's lead and upheld, based on a bribery rationale, the Hobbs–Act extortion convictions of an astonishing variety of state and local officials. * * *

In McNally v. United States, 483 U.S. 350 (1987)—a case closely analogous to this one—we rejected the Government's contention that the federal mail fraud statute, 18 U.S.C. § 1341, protected the citizenry's intangible right" to good government, and hence could be applied to all instances of state and local corruption. Such an expansive reading of the statute, we noted with disapproval, would leave its outer boundaries ambiguous and involve the Federal Government in setting standards of disclosure and good government for local and state officials." Prior to our decision in *McNally*, the Government's theory had been accepted by every Court of Appeals to consider the issue. We did not consider that acceptance to cure the ambiguity we perceived in the statutory language; we simply reiterated the traditional learning that a federal criminal statute, particularly as applied to state officials, must be construed narrowly. If Congress desires to go further, we said, it must speak more clearly than it has. * * *

* * * I have no doubt that today's opinion is motivated by noble aims. Political corruption at any level of government is a serious evil, and, from a policy perspective, perhaps one well suited for federal law enforcement. But federal judges are not free to devise new crimes to meet the occasion. * * * Whatever evils today's opinion may redress, in my view, pale beside those it will engender. * * * All Americans, including public officials, are entitled to protection from prosecutorial abuse. The facts of this case suggest a depressing erosion of that protection.

Petitioner Evans was elected to the Board of Commissioners of DeKalb County, Georgia, in 1982. He was no local tyrant—just one of five part-time Commissioners earning an annual salary of approximately $16,000. The Board's activities were entirely local, including the quintessentially local activity of zoning property. The United States does not suggest that there were any allegations of corruption or malfeasance against Evans.

In early 1985, as part of an investigation into allegations of public corruption in the Atlanta area," a Federal Bureau of Investigation agent, Clifford Cormany, Jr., set up a bogus firm, WDH Developers," and pretended to be a land developer. Cormany sought and obtained a meeting with Evans. From March 1985 until October 1987, a period of some two and a half years, Cormany or one of his associates held 33 conversations with Evans. Every one of these contacts was initiated by the agents. During these conversations, the agents repeatedly requested Evans' assistance in securing a favorable zoning decision, and repeatedly brought up the subject of campaign contributions. Agent Cormany eventually contributed $8,000 to Evans' reelection campaign, and Evans accepted the money. There is no suggestion that he claimed an official entitlement to the payment. Nonetheless, he was arrested and charged with Hobbs Act extortion.

The Court is surely correct that there is sufficient evidence to support the jury's verdict that Evans committed "extortion" under the Court's expansive interpretation of the crime. But that interpretation has no basis in the statute that Congress passed in 1946. If the Court makes up this version of the crime today, who is to say what version it will make up tomorrow when confronted with the next perceived rascal? * * * In my view, Evans is plainly innocent of extortion. With all due respect, I am compelled to dissent.

C. FALSE PRETENSES AND FRAUD

PEOPLE v. ASHLEY

Supreme Court of California, 1954.
42 Cal.2d 246, 267 P.2d 271.

TRAYNOR, JUSTICE:

[Defendant, manager of a corporation chartered for the purpose of "introducing people," was convicted of grand theft for fraudulently inducing two elderly ladies to lend him their life's savings. He told Mrs. Russ that he would use the money she gave him to build a theater on some property he owned, and promised her a trust deed as security. In fact, he did not own the property and his corporation was not sufficiently solvent to undertake to build the theater. He obtained loans from Mrs. Neal by representing that he would use the money to buy a theater, and would give her a trust deed on the property as security. He used all the money obtained from the two women for the operating expenses of his corporation (including a personal expense account), and the court found that there was sufficient evidence for the jury to conclude that defendant never intended to build or buy a theater.]

The case went to the jury with instructions relating to larceny by trick and device and obtaining property by false pretenses. The jurors were instructed that all would have to agree on the type of theft, if any, that was committed.[a] Defendant contends that the evidence is insufficient to support a conviction of either type of theft, that the general verdict of guilty was unlawful, and that the trial court erred in denying his motion for a new trial on these grounds.

Although the crimes of larceny by trick and device and obtaining property by false pretenses are much alike, they are aimed at different criminal acquisitive techniques. Larceny by trick and device is the appropriation of property, the possession of which was fraudulently

a. Although the court did not notice the point, this instruction was erroneous. A California jury need not agree on the "technical pigeonhole" into which the alleged theft should fall to return a general verdict of guilty of theft. People v. Nor Woods, 37 Cal.2d 584, 233 P.2d 897 (1951).—ed.

acquired; obtaining property by false pretenses is the fraudulent or deceitful acquisition of both title and possession. In this state, these two offenses, with other larcenous crimes, have been consolidated into the single crime of theft, Pen.Code, § 484, but their elements have not been changed thereby. The purpose of the consolidation was to remove the technicalities that existed in the pleading and proof of these crimes at common law. Indictments and informations charging the crime of "theft" can now simply allege an "unlawful taking." Juries need no longer be concerned with the technical differences between the several types of theft, and can return a general verdict of guilty if they find that an "unlawful taking" has been proved. The elements of the several types of theft included within § 484 have not been changed, however, and a judgment of conviction of theft, based on a general verdict of guilty, can be sustained only if the evidence discloses the elements of one of the consolidated offenses. In the present case, it is clear from the record that each of the prosecuting witnesses intended to pass both title and possession, and that the type of theft, if any, in each case, was that of obtaining property by false pretenses. Defendant was not prejudiced by the instruction to the jury relating to larceny by trick and device. Indeed, he requested instructions relating to both larceny by trick and device and obtaining property by false pretenses. Moreover, his defense was not based on distinctions between title and possession, but rather he contends that there was no unlawful taking of any sort.

To support a conviction of theft for obtaining property by false pretenses, it must be shown that the defendant made a false pretense or representation with intent to defraud the owner of his property, and that the owner was in fact defrauded. It is unnecessary to prove that the defendant benefitted personally from the fraudulent acquisition. The false pretense or representation must have materially influenced the owner to part with his property, but the false pretense need not be the sole inducing cause. If the conviction rests primarily on the testimony of a single witness that the false pretense was made, the making of the pretense must be corroborated. Pen.Code, § 1110.

The crime of obtaining property by false pretenses was unknown in the early common law, and our statute, like those of most American states, is directly traceable to [the original English statute of 1757 punishing "false pretences."] In an early Crown Case Reserved, Rex v. Goodhall, Russ. & Ry. 461 (1821), the defendant obtained a quantity of meat from a merchant by promising to pay at a future day. The jury found that the promise was made without intention to perform. The judges concluded, however, that the defendant's conviction was erroneous because the pretense "was merely a promise of future conduct, and common prudence and caution would have prevented any injury arising from it." * * * The opinion in Rex v. Goodhall was completely misinterpreted in Commonwealth v. Drew, 1837, 36 Mass. 179, in which the Supreme Judicial Court of Massachusetts declared by way of dictum, that under the statute "naked lies" could not be regarded as "false pretences." On the basis of these two questionable decisions, Wharton formulated the following generalization: " * * * the false pretense to be within the statute, must relate to a state of things averred to be at the time existing, and not to a state of things thereafter to exist." Wharton, American Criminal Law 542 [1st ed., 1846]. This generalization has been followed in the majority of American cases, almost all of which can be traced to reliance on Wharton or the two cases mentioned above. The rule has not been followed in all jurisdictions, however. Some courts have avoided the problems created by the rule by blurring the distinctions between larceny by trick and device and obtaining property by false pretenses. * * *

The Court of Appeals for the District of Columbia has, however, advanced the following reasons in defense of the majority rule: "It is of course true that then, [at the time of the early English cases cited by Wharton] as now, the intention to commit certain crimes was ascertained by looking backward from the act and finding that the accused intended to do what he did do. However, where, as here, the act complained of—namely, failure to repay money or use it as specified at the time of borrowing—is as consonant with ordinary commercial default as with criminal conduct, the danger of applying this technique to prove the crime is quite apparent. Business affairs would be materially incumbered by the ever present threat that a debtor might be subjected to criminal penalties if the prosecutor and jury were of the view that at the time of borrowing he was mentally a cheat. The risk of prosecuting one who is guilty of nothing more than a failure or inability to pay his debts is a very real consideration. . . . "

"If we were to accept the government's position the way would be open for every victim of a bad bargain to resort to criminal proceedings to even the score with a judgment proof adversary. No doubt in the development of our criminal law the zeal with which the innocent are protected has provided a measure of shelter for the guilty. However, we do not think it wise to increase the possibility of conviction by broadening the accepted theory of the weight to be attached to the mental attitude of the accused." Chaplin v. United States, 157 F.2d 697, 698–699. We do not find this reasoning persuasive. In this state, and in the majority of American states as well as in England, false promises can provide the foundation of a civil action for deceit. In such actions something more than nonperformance is required to prove the defendant's intent not to perform his promise. Nor is proof of nonperformance alone sufficient in criminal prosecutions based on false promises. In such prosecutions the People must prove their case beyond a reasonable doubt. Any danger, through the instigation of criminal proceedings by disgruntled creditors, to those who have blamelessly encountered "commercial defaults" must, therefore, be predicated upon the idea that trial juries are incapable of weighing the evidence and understanding the instruction that they must be convinced of the defendant's fraudulent intent beyond a reasonable doubt, or that appellate courts will be derelict in discharging their duty to ascertain that there is sufficient evidence to support a conviction.

The problem of proving intent when the false pretense is a false promise is no more difficult than when the false pretense is a misrepresentation of existing fact, and the intent not to perform a promise is regularly proved in civil actions for deceit. Specific intent is also an essential element of many crimes. Moreover, in cases of obtaining property by false pretenses, it must be proved that any misrepresentations of fact alleged by the People were made knowingly and with intent to deceive. If such misrepresentations are made innocently or inadvertently, they can no more form the basis for a prosecution for obtaining property by false pretenses than can an innocent breach of contract. Whether the pretense is a false promise or a misrepresentation of fact, the defendant's intent must be proved in both instances by something more than mere proof of nonperformance or actual falsity, and the defendant is entitled to have the jury instructed to that effect. * * *

If false promises were not false pretenses, the legally sophisticated, without fear of punishment, could perpetrate on the unwary fraudulent schemes like that divulged by the record in this case * * *. The inclusion of false promises within sections 484 and 532 of the Penal Code will not "materially encumber" business affairs. "Ordinary commercial defaults" will not be the subject of criminal prosecution, for the essence of the offense of obtaining property by false pretenses is (as it has always been) the fraudulent intent of the defendant. This intent must be proved by the prosecution; a showing of nonperformance of a promise or falsity of a representation will not suffice. * * *

The judgment and the order denying the motion for a new trial are affirmed.

SCHAUER, JUSTICE.

I concur in the judgment solely on the ground that the evidence establishes, with ample corroboration, the making by the defendant of false representations as to existing facts. On that evidence the convictions should be sustained pursuant to long accepted theories of law. * * *

The majority opinion strikes down a rule of law, relating to the character and competence of proof of crime, which has been almost universally respected for two hundred years—and the reasoning which has been advanced for the innovation is that creditors, grand jurors, and prosecutors must not be expected to institute any criminal charges against innocent people, and that even if they do the intelligence of trial jurors and the wisdom of appellate judges can be depended upon to right the wrong, hence the time honored rule may be scrapped. The unreality of this reasoning and the wisdom of the old rule become obvious on reflection.

In a prosecution for obtaining property by the making of a false promise, knowingly and with intent to deceive, the matter to be proved, as to its criminality, is purely subjective. It is not, like the specific intent in such a crime as burglary, a mere element of the crime; it is, in any significant sense, all of the crime. The proof will necessarily be of objective acts, entirely legal in themselves, from which inferences as to the ultimate illegal subjective fact will be drawn. But, whereas in burglary the proof of the subjective element is normally as strong and reliable as the proof of any objective element, in this type of activity the proof of such vital element can almost never be reliable; it must inevitably (in the absence of confession or something tantamount thereto) depend on inferences drawn by creditors, prosecutors, jurors, and judges from facts and circumstances which by reason of their nature cannot possibly exclude innocence with any certainty, and which can point to guilt only when construed and interpreted by the creditor, prosecutor or trier of fact adversely to the person charged. Such inferences as proof of the alleged crime have long been recognized as so unreliable that they have been excluded from the category of acceptable proof. * * *

With the rule that the majority opinion now enunciates, no man, no matter how innocent his intention, can sign a promise to pay in the future, or to perform an act at a future date, without subjecting himself to the risk that at some later date others, in the light of differing perspectives, philosophies and subsequent events, may conclude that, after all, the accused *should* have known that at the future date he could not perform as he promised—and if he, as a "reasonable" man from the point of view of the creditor, district attorney and a grand or trial jury—*should* have known, then, it may be inferred, he did know. And if it can be inferred that he knew, then this court and other appellate courts will be bound to affirm a conviction. * * *

PEOPLE v. SHIRLEY

Supreme Court of California, 1961.
55 Cal.2d 521, 11 Cal.Rptr. 537, 360 P.2d 33.

GIBSON, CHIEF JUSTICE.

After a jury trial, defendant was found guilty of grand theft under an indictment charging that she unlawfully took $1,811 of funds of Tulare County between October 1, 1958, and April 30, 1959. Imposition of sentence was suspended for three years, and she was granted probation. She has appealed from the order granting probation and from an order denying a new trial.

Defendant received welfare aid for herself and minor children periodically commencing in 1948. She was informed repeatedly that it was her duty to keep the county welfare department advised of any changes in the family status or income and that anyone moving into or out of the house would affect her welfare budget. On October 21, 1958, defendant reported to a county social worker that her only income was the money she received from the welfare department, plus the occasional earnings of two of her children, and that there were no unrelated adults living with the family. She was again advised of her duty to keep the welfare department informed regarding income and household members, and she agreed to report any change in income or other financial conditions.

The social worker visited defendant at her home on April 14, 1959, and found a Mr. Shirley there, fully clothed but wearing bedroom slippers. Two days later, at the request of the welfare department, investigators from the district attorney's office called at defendant's home about 2:30 a.m.[a] and found Shirley in bed in her bedroom. Defendant told the investigators that Shirley had been living in her home for at least six months and that during this time he had averaged spending $20 a week for household expenses and in addition had given her $10 a week in cash. Thus his total contributions during that period were approximately $800. She said that he had also helped with payments on a refrigerator. She admitted knowing that she should report all income received by her and any changes in the number of persons in the home. On April 23, 1959, she reported to the welfare department that she had married Shirley on the previous day. The department recomputed defendant's budget for the period in question and determined that she had been overpaid $1,811.

The evidence is sufficient to support the implied findings of the jury that defendant made false representations of fact with intent to defraud and that, when she promised to report any change in her household and financial condition, she had no intention of keeping her promise. It is also clear that the welfare payments were made in reliance upon the false representations and that the county was defrauded.

The jury was instructed, pursuant to § 1508 of the Welfare and Institutions Code, that where a needy child lives with his mother and stepfather, the amount of the grant shall be computed after consideration is given to the income of the stepfather and that a stepfather is bound to support, if able to do so, his wife's children if without support from such stepfather they would be needy children eligible for aid. The jury was also told that under regulations of the State Board of Social Welfare a stepfather living in the home is responsible for the support of the mother of a needy child unless incapacitated and unable to support, that a man living in the home assuming the role of spouse has the same responsibility as that of a stepfather for the mother and the needy children, and that the income of a stepfather or other man assuming the role of spouse that is to be used in determining his ability to contribute is his take-home pay plus his income from all other sources except his wife's earnings.

* * *

Under its express terms the provisions of the Welfare and Institutions Code are to be administered fairly, with due consideration not only for the needs of applicants but also for the safeguarding of public funds.

a. On the constitutionality of such unannounced "midnight visits" to welfare homes, see Parrish v. Civil Service Commission, 66 Cal.2d 260, 57 Cal.Rptr. 623, 425 P.2d 223 (1967); cf. Wyman v. James, 400 U.S. 309 (1971).—ed.

If children are not in need, they are obviously not eligible for assistance regardless of who is paying for their support. As we have seen, the welfare department is authorized by § 1508 to consider the income of a stepfather in computing the amount of aid to be granted, and it is unlikely that the financial need of a child will vary substantially depending upon the legality of the relationship between his mother and a man living in the home and assuming the role of spouse. It is reasonable to infer that a man assuming the role of spouse will contribute to the support of the mother and her needy child and will thus reduce their need, but it would be difficult and perhaps impossible for the department to ascertain the amount of contributions in each case. A practical solution of the difficulty is offered by the regulations which authorize the department to consider the income of such a man in the same manner as it would consider that of a stepfather. A decision declaring the regulations invalid would place a premium upon an illegal relationship and operate as a deterrent to marriage of the mother and the man assuming the role of spouse. The regulations are in accord with the primary purpose of the program, which is to aid needy children, and they are valid insofar as they direct the welfare department, in determining the amount of aid to be granted, to consider the man's income without regard to the existence of a lawful marriage.

To the extent that the instructions may have indicated that a man assuming the role of spouse, although not married, had an obligation to support the mother and her children, they went beyond the issues and were erroneous. It does not appear, however, how the jurors could have been misled, since the question of such a man's liability for support had no bearing on whether defendant was guilty of theft by false pretenses, and the jurors were fully informed of the elements of that offense which they must find in order to return a verdict of guilty.

The evidence of defendant's guilt is clear and convincing, and we are satisfied that there was no miscarriage of justice. The orders granting probation and denying a new trial are affirmed.

[Dissenting opinion omitted.]

NELSON v. UNITED STATES

United States Court of Appeals, District of Columbia Circuit, 1955.
227 F.2d 21.

DANAHER, CIRCUIT JUDGE.

This is an appeal from a conviction for obtaining goods by false pretenses in violation of D.C.Code § 22–1301 (1951). The trial court entered judgment of acquittal on a second count charging grand larceny. Evidence was offered to show that appellant from time to time over a period of months, for purposes of resale, had purchased merchandise from Potomac Distributors of Washington, D.C., Inc. (hereinafter referred to as Potomac Distributors). By September 18, 1952, his account was said to be in arrears more than thirty days. Late that afternoon, appellant sought immediate possession of two television sets and a washing machine, displayed his customers' purchase contracts to support his statement that he had already sold such merchandise and had taken payment therefor, and told one Schneider, secretary-treasurer of Potomac Distributors, "I promised delivery tonight." Appellant was told no further credit could be extended to him because of his overdue indebtedness in excess of $1800., whereupon appellant offered to give security for the desired items as well as for the delinquent account. He represented himself as the owner of a Packard car for which he had paid $4,260.50, but failed to disclose an outstanding prior indebtedness on the car of $3,028.08 secured by a chattel mortgage in favor of City Bank. Instead, he represented that he owed only one payment of some $55, not then due. Relying upon such representations, Potomac Distributors delivered to appellant two television sets each worth $136, taking in return a demand note for the entire indebtedness, past and present, in the total, $2,047.37, secured by a chattel mortgage on the Packard and the television sets. Appellant promised to make a cash payment on the note within a few days for default of which the holder was entitled to demand full payment. When the promised payment was not forthcoming, Schneider, by telephone calls and a personal visit to appellant's home, sought to locate appellant but learned he had left town. The Packard about that time was in a collision, incurring damage of about $1000., and was thereupon repossessed in behalf of the bank which held the prior lien for appellant's car purchase indebtedness. * * *

Appellant argues that Potomac Distributors could not have been defrauded for the car on September 18, 1952, "had an equity of between $900 and $1000 and roughly five times the value of the two television sets." That fact is immaterial. * * *

This appellant has sold two television sets, and apparently had taken payment therefor although he had no television sets to deliver to his customers. He could not get the sets from Potomac Distributors without offering security for his past due account as well as for his present purchase. In order to get them he lied. He represented that his car acquired at a cost of more than $4000 required only one further payment of $55. He now complains because his victim believed him when he lied. He argues that the misrepresentations were not material although the victim testified, and the jury could properly find, that he would not have parted with his goods except in reliance upon appellant's statements. * * *

He argues that there was no proof of an intent upon his part to defraud his victim. "Wrongful acts knowingly or intentionally committed can neither be justified nor excused on the ground of innocent intent. The color of the act determines the complexion of the intent. The intent to injure or defraud is presumed when the unlawful act, which results in loss or injury, is proved to have been knowingly committed. It is a well-settled rule, which the law applies in both criminal and civil cases, that the intent is presumed and inferred from the result of the action." This quotation from a challenged charge was found by the Supreme Court to be "unexceptionable as matter of law" in Agnew v. United States, 1897, 165 U.S. 36. * * *

Affirmed.

WILBUR K. MILLER, CIRCUIT JUDGE (dissenting).

When the essential ingredients of the crime of false pretense have been accurately ascertained, and when irrelevant facts in the evidence have been identified as such and eliminated from consideration, I believe it will be apparent that the Government failed to make out a case for submission to the jury. It will then also appear, I think, that the trial judge erroneously refused to direct a verdict of acquittal, only because he mistakenly attributed significance to the fact that appellant's automobile was damaged in a collision which occurred "early in October,"—at least two weeks after September 18, the day he purchased the two television sets and the washing machine from Potomac Distributors.

As to the ingredients of the offense. While our false pretense statute does not in express language require that the person from whom the property is obtained should be defrauded thereby, nevertheless the crime is not complete unless he is in fact defrauded. It was so held in Robinson v. United States, 1914, 42 App.D.C. 186, in accord with the general rule. In order to convict under the statute, the Government must therefore prove that in making a false pretense the defendant intended to defraud the person from whom he obtained property, and that he did thereby defraud him. The trial judge recognized this, and charged the jury accordingly.

Nelson did make a false representation; but the question is whether there was evidence from which the jury could properly be permitted to infer that he intended to defraud, and to conclude that Potomac was thereby defrauded. * * *

Differing definitions of the word "defraud" probably cause the difference in opinion between the majority and me. They seem to think it means, in connection with a purchase, to make a false pretense in the process of obtaining goods even though the purchase price is well secured. I think the word means, in connection with a purchase, to make a false pretense as a result of which the seller is deprived of his goods or of the purchase price. The difference is particularly important in a case like this one where a purchaser is charged with defrauding a seller. A purchaser can be said to have defrauded the seller of his goods only if he intended to defraud him of the purchase price for which the seller was willing to exchange them. It seems to me to follow that a purchaser who makes a false statement in buying on credit has not defrauded the seller of his goods if he nevertheless amply secures the debt. False pretense cases concerning the obtaining of property but which do not involve a situation where the *purchaser* was indicted have little application to this case. * * *

In considering the criminality *vel non* of the false statement, it must be remembered that the past due indebtedness of $1,697.87 is to play no part. That credit had already been extended generally, and with respect to it Potomac parted with nothing on September 18. Nelson was only charged with defrauding Potomac by obtaining through false pretense the articles then delivered, which had a total value of only $349.50.

What was the actual value on September 18 of the property upon which Potomac took a lien, on the strength of which it parted with property worth $349.50? The bank collection manager, testifying for the Government, said that although on September 18 Nelson still owed the bank $3,028.08, he had on that day an equity in the car worth from $900 to $1,000. The mortgaged television sets were, I suppose, worth their price of $272. Adding to this the minimum equity in the automobile proved by the prosecution, it appears that Potomac had a lien on property worth at least $1,172 to protect a debt of $349.50. The proportion was more than three to one. Such is the evidence as to what happened September 18, from which the jury was permitted to infer that Nelson then intended to defraud, and to conclude that he then did fraudulently obtain from Potomac the three articles purchased. As to intent, I suggest that it is wholly irrational to presume or infer that one intends to defraud when he buys goods on credit and safeguards that credit by giving more than triple security for it, no matter if he does falsely pretend that the security is even greater. It is equally illogical to conclude that the creditor was thereby defrauded. For that reason, my opinion is that the proof I have outlined—which was the only pertinent proof—did not warrant the trial court in submitting the case to the jury.

* * *

As to the irrelevant evidence, which produced conviction. Why then did the trial judge let the case go to the jury? He knew an actual defrauding was necessary to conviction and * * * so instructed the jury. And why, in the light of that instruction, and under Government proof which clearly showed Potomac was not defrauded, did the jury convict? Principally, I think, because of a subsequent fortuitous circumstance which Nelson could not have anticipated on September 18, and which of course was not the result of his deliberate act.

This circumstance was that some two weeks or more after the goods had been obtained, the mortgaged automobile was damaged in a collision to an extent estimated at about $1,000. If the damage was not compensated for by insurance or otherwise, the accident practically destroyed Nelson's equity in the car. The bank seized the damaged automobile and disposed of it to a transferee, who evidently saw some equity still in it, as he paid the bank's debt. Potomac seems to have stood idly by while this was going on, without taking any steps to protect its lien, which was or should have been then of record. If damages were collected by or for Nelson from a tortfeasor, Potomac's lien attached thereto. The record does not show whether such damages were or should have been recovered. It should be noted also that Potomac made no effort to enforce its lien on the television sets.

Aside from all that, however, the salient point is that the reduction in the value of the automobile caused by the collision could not properly be considered by the jury; the question was as to its value September 18, for it was that value which should have been considered in deciding whether Potomac had been defrauded. Had the trial judge observed this distinction, he would have directed a verdict of acquittal, since he was aware of the necessity that there be actual defrauding. The judge made this clear when he said in a bench colloquy: "Until I heard that there had been a wreck and the car had been repossessed I thought maybe there was sufficient equity there to cover the loss sustained; and if that were the case there would be no defrauding." I have demonstrated there was more than sufficient equity September 18 to cover the credit then extended, so there was no defrauding, even though an accident later impaired the margin of protection.

In addition to the irrelevant proof of the collision damage, which should not have been received and without which an acquittal would have been directed, there was another irrelevancy in evidence which may well have played a part in moving the jury to its verdict: the pre-existing indebtedness. Because of Nelson's misrepresentation of his equity in the car, Potomac did not get, as it thought it was getting, security for both old and new debts with a margin of more than two to one. But, as has been shown, Potomac did get more than triple security for the goods which the indictment said were fraudulently obtained. It was therefore of first importance that the jury be told to disregard Potomac's failure to get the security for the pre-existing debt which it had been led to believe it was getting, and to consider only whether Potomac had been defrauded out of goods worth $349.50. The jury should also have been told the reason for the distinction, for without it the lay jurors might have concluded—as apparently they did-that on September 18 Nelson defrauded Potomac with respect to the pre-existing indebtedness.

As I have said, Nelson was guilty of a moral wrong in falsely and grossly misrepresenting his debt to the bank, but in the circumstances he should not have been indicted and convicted because of it. The District of Columbia statute under which he was prosecuted does not make mere falsehood felonious; it only denounces as criminal a false pretense which was intended to defraud and which in fact had that result. Even a liar is entitled to the full protection of the law. I am afraid a grave injustice has been done in this case.

GRAHAM v. UNITED STATES

United States Court of Appeals, District of Columbia Circuit, 1950.
187 F.2d 87.

WASHINGTON, CIRCUIT JUDGE.

The appellant, an attorney, was indicted in two counts for grand larceny * * *. He was charged with having stolen money from Francisco Gal in the amounts of $100 and $1,900. He appeals from a judgment and conviction entered upon a verdict of guilty.

The complaining witness, Francisco Gal, consulted appellant in his professional capacity. Gal had been arrested and charged with disorderly conduct, and had forfeited $25 as collateral. He was seeking American citizenship and was apprehensive that the arrest would impede or bar his attainment of that goal. An immigrant employed as a cook, his command of the English language was far from complete. He testified that appellant Graham told him that he wasn't sure what he could do, that Graham would "have to talk to the policeman. You have to pay money for that, because the money is talk." He further testified that Graham told him he would charge him $200 for a fee; that he would have to pay an additional $2,000 for the police; that Graham said "don't mention the money for nobody and for the police either." As a result, Gal testified that he paid the appellant $300 on February 2, 1950 (of which, he said, $200 was paid as a legal fee), and $1,900 on February 3, 1950. The police officer who originally had arrested Gal testified that he came to appellant's office, and after talking with Graham, told Gal that he wasn't in any trouble. Gal testified to substantially the same effect. The officer testified that Graham did not then or at any other time offer or give him money. The appellant testified that the entire payment was intended as a fee for legal services; that he had never mentioned money for the police; that no part of the money was in fact paid to the police or anyone else, but was kept by the appellant.

Appellant's principal contentions are: First, that the evidence supports the proposition that Gal voluntarily gave Graham complete title to the money and therefore appellant is entitled to a directed verdict; and, second, that the trial court's charge to the jury was erroneous in not sufficiently distinguishing between the situation where one obtains complete title to another's property by fraud or trick and the case where possession only is obtained.

Section 2201 provides as follows: "Whoever shall feloniously take and carry away anything of value of the amount or value of $50 or upward, including things savoring of the realty, shall suffer imprisonment for not less than one nor more than ten years."

Interpreting this statute, this court has held that "one who obtains money from another upon the representation that he will perform certain service therewith for the latter, intending at the time to convert the money, and actually converting it, to his own use, is guilty of larceny". Means v. United States, 65 F.2d 206, 207. In classic terminology, "the distinction drawn by the common law is between the case of one who gives up possession of a chattel for a special purpose to another who by converting it to his own use is held to have committed a trespass, and the case of one who, although induced by fraud or trick, nevertheless actually intends that title to the chattel shall pass to the wrongdoer." United States v. Patton, 3 Cir., 1941, 120 F.2d 73, 76.

We now turn to appellant's first contention, that under the evidence in the case the court should have directed a verdict for the defendant. We think this contention without merit. If the jury believed Gal's testimony, and did not believe that of the defendant, it was possible for the jury to conclude beyond a reasonable doubt that the defendant fraudulently induced Gal to give him $2,000 to be used for a special purpose, i.e., to bribe the police, that the defendant did not intend so to use the money, and converted it to his own use. Under the rule stated above, this would be larceny by trick.

Thus, in the *Means* case, supra, the defendant was convicted of the crime of larceny under the following circumstances: After the kidnapping of the infant son of Charles Lindbergh, the defendant in an interview with Mrs. McLean persuaded her that he could assist in locating and recovering the kidnapped baby, stating that if Mrs. McLean would give him $100,000 he would use that sum to pay the ransom and secure the return of the child. On the basis of these representations he secured the money from Mrs. McLean. His representations were fraudulent and he intended at the time to convert the money to his own use, and actually so converted it. People v. Edwards, 72 Cal.App. 102, 236 P. 944, provides an even closer precedent. There the defendant took money from the complainant, representing to her that it would be used to bribe officers investigating criminal activities by her husband. The complainant did not know exactly how the defendant was going to use the money but understood that it was going to be used in some manner to corrupt the police. The court, in sustaining a conviction for larceny, held that under these circumstances title would remain in the complainant until the [money was actually delivered to the officers who were supposedly to be bribed.] * * *

[The court held that the instructions to the jury were correct.]

Affirmed.

UNITED STATES v. CLAUSEN

United States Court of Appeals, Eighth Circuit, 1986.
792 F.2d 102.

LAY, CHIEF JUDGE.

FACTS

A federal grand jury indicted Donald Clausen on three counts of wire fraud. Clausen, a dentist, opened a trading account with the Dallas, Texas, office of Conti–Commodity Services, Inc. (Conti) in 1982. On Friday, September 30, 1983, after Clausen had moved to Minneapolis, he called the Dallas office and placed a purchase order through his broker, William Thomas, for five contracts of silver futures. Clausen testified that he was experiencing severe financial difficulties at the time he placed the order and was hoping to make a profitable day trade, that is, to liquidate his position at the end of the day at a higher price. The price of silver fell throughout the day, however, and Thomas' assistant told Clausen that he would have to meet a margin call of $22,500. Clausen said he would bring in a check to the Conti office in Minneapolis on

Monday. On Monday Clausen brought a check for $22,500 to the Minneapolis office, knowing he did not have sufficient funds in his account to cover the check. He then placed another order for five contracts of silver futures. He again speculated that the price of silver would rise so that he could liquidate his ten silver contracts at the end of the day and break even. The price of silver continued to fall, however, and Clausen was faced with another margin call of $31,900. On October 5, Clausen called Thomas and said that his $22,500 check would not clear and that he could not make the second margin call. Conti immediately liquidated Clausen's ten silver contracts, resulting in a loss of $47,883.00.[3]

Clausen was indicted on three counts of wire fraud based on three separate phone calls he allegedly made from Minneapolis to the Conti office in Dallas in furtherance of the allegedly fraudulent scheme. After a trial before a jury, Clausen was convicted on all three counts.

Clausen first contends that the indictment is fatally defective because it charges him with a "scheme or artifice to defraud" which was accomplished by "false and fraudulent pretenses, representations and promises" in the form of passing an insufficient funds (NSF) check. The indictment is defective, Clausen alleges, because under Williams v. United States, 458 U.S. 279 (1982), an insufficient funds check does not constitute a false statement. Although Williams involved a prosecution for a check-kiting scheme under 18 U.S.C. § 1014 (1982), which makes it a crime to knowingly make a false statement for the purpose of influencing a financial decision of certain federal agencies, the Third Circuit extended Williams to the mail and wire fraud statutes in United States v. Frankel, 721 F.2d 917 (3d Cir.1983). In *Frankel,* the court held that an indictment charging a defendant with mail fraud based on allegations of obtaining money by means of false representations is fatally defective where the indictment alleged only that the defendant had deposited NSF checks in his bank account in order to create an artificially high balance against which checks were later drawn to pay the defendant's creditors. Under *Williams,* the *Frankel* court determined, no implicit false statement is made by knowingly presenting for deposit a check not backed by sufficient funds.

The government argues that this case is distinguishable from *Williams* and *Frankel* because in those cases the defendant presented an NSF check for deposit. In this case, Clausen gave an NSF check to Conti in payment of an obligation. We need not decide whether *Williams* also applies where an indictment alleges that a person made a misrepresentation by knowingly giving an NSF check to a third party in payment of an obligation. We find that the indictment charged Clausen with a scheme to defraud whether or not carried out by means of a misrepresentation.

3. Conti secured a civil judgment against Clausen for its loss, which Conti has attempted to collect without success. Pursuant to Conti's agreement with its brokers, Thomas was personally liable to Conti for $11,538 of the $47,883 loss.

The wire fraud statute under which Clausen was charged provides in pertinent part:

> Whoever, having devised or intending to devise any scheme or artifice to defraud, or for obtaining money or property by means of false or fraudulent pretenses, representations, or promises, transmits or causes to be transmitted by means of wire, radio, or television communication in interstate or foreign commerce, any writings, signs, signals, pictures, or sounds for the purpose of executing such scheme or artifice, shall be fined not more than $1,000 or imprisoned not more than five years, or both. 18 U.S.C. § 1343 (1982).

Courts have construed this statute to forbid both schemes to defraud, whether or not any specific misrepresentations are involved, and schemes to obtain money or property by means of false or fraudulent pretenses, representations, or promises. [Citations] In other words, a scheme to defraud need not include false representations to violate the wire fraud statute. * * * Intent to defraud need not be shown by direct evidence; rather, it may be inferred from all the facts and circumstances surrounding the defendant's actions. We agree with the government that the jury could reasonably infer Clausen's intent to defraud from his own testimony that he agreed to make margin payments that he knew he could not make. * * *

Clausen's final argument is that the district court erred in requiring him to make full restitution to Conti and Thomas as a part of his sentence without first making the necessary findings under 18 U.S.C. § 3580(a).[7] The district court had before it a presentence report disclosing Clausen's financial condition when it ordered him to make restitution to Conti and Thomas as part of his sentence. Clausen had an opportunity to respond to presentence report. He has not shown that the district court failed to consider all relevant factors before requiring him to pay approximately $48,000 in restitution. His contention that the financial condition of the victim is somehow relevant to the amount of restitution an offender may be required to pay is without merit. Simply because a large corporation is the victim of a fraudulent scheme is no justification for excusing restitution. Such a Robin Hood philosophy is hardly relevant to a system of justice based on equality under the law. We find no abuse of discretion in the order of restitution.

Affirmed.

7. The statute provides: "The court, in determining whether to order restitution under section 3579 of this title and the amount of such restitution, shall consider the amount of the loss sustained by any victim as a result of the offense, the financial resources of the defendant, the financial needs and earning ability of the defendant and the defendant's dependents, and such other factors as the court deems appropriate."

CLEVELAND v. UNITED STATES

Supreme Court of the United States, 2000.
531 U.S. 12, 121 S.Ct. 365, 148 L.Ed.2d 221.

JUSTICE GINSBURG delivered the opinion of the Court.

This case presents the question whether the federal mail fraud statute, 18 U.S.C. § 1341, reaches false statements made in an application for a state license. Section 1341 proscribes use of the mails in furtherance of "any scheme or artifice to defraud, or for obtaining money or property by means of false or fraudulent pretenses, representations, or promises." Petitioner Carl W. Cleveland and others were prosecuted under this federal measure for making false statements in applying to the Louisiana State Police for permission to operate video poker machines. We conclude that permits or licenses of this order do not qualify as "property" within § 1341's compass. It does not suffice, we clarify, that the object of the fraud may become property in the recipient's hands; for purposes of the mail fraud statute, the thing obtained must be property in the hands of the victim. State and municipal licenses in general, and Louisiana's video poker licenses in particular, we hold, do not rank as "property," for purposes of § 1341, in the hands of the official licensor.

I

Louisiana law allows certain businesses to operate video poker machines. La. Rev. Stat. Ann. §§ 27:301 to 27:324 (West Supp. 2000). The State itself, however, does not run such machinery. The law requires prospective owners of video poker machines to apply for a license from the State. The licenses are not transferable, and must be renewed annually. To qualify for a license, an applicant must meet suitability requirements designed to ensure that licensees have good character and fiscal integrity.

In 1992, Fred Goodson and his family formed a limited partnership, Truck Stop Gaming, Ltd. (TSG), in order to participate in the video poker business at their truck stop in Slidell, Louisiana. Cleveland, a New Orleans lawyer, assisted Goodson in preparing TSG's application for a video poker license. The application required TSG to identify its partners and to submit personal financial statements for all partners. It also required TSG to affirm that the listed partners were the sole beneficial owners of the business and that no partner held an interest in the partnership merely as an agent or nominee, or intended to transfer the interest in the future.

TSG's application identified Goodson's adult children, Alex and Maria, as the sole beneficial owners of the partnership. It also showed that Goodson and Cleveland's law firm had loaned Alex and Maria all initial capital for the partnership and that Goodson was TSG's general manager. In May 1992, the State approved the application and issued a license. TSG successfully renewed the license in 1993, 1994, and 1995 * * *. Each renewal application identified no ownership interests other than those of Alex and Maria.

In 1996, the FBI discovered evidence that Cleveland and Goodson had participated in a scheme to bribe state legislators to vote in a manner favorable to the video poker industry. The Government charged Cleveland and Goodson with multiple counts of money laundering under 18 U.S.C. § 1957, as well as racketeering and conspiracy under § 1962. Among the predicate acts supporting these charges were four counts of mail fraud under § 1341. The indictment alleged that Cleveland and Goodson had violated § 1341 by fraudulently concealing that they were the true owners of TSG in the initial license application and three renewal applications mailed to the State. They concealed their ownership interests, according to the Government, because they had tax and financial problems that could have undermined their suitability to receive a video poker license.

Before trial, Cleveland moved to dismiss the mail fraud counts on the ground that the alleged fraud did not deprive the State of "property" under § 1341. The District Court denied the motion, concluding that "licenses constitute property even before they are issued." A jury found Cleveland guilty on two counts of mail fraud (based on the 1994 and 1995 license renewals) and on money laundering, racketeering, and conspiracy counts predicated on the mail fraud. The District Court sentenced Cleveland to 121 months in prison.

* * *

The Court of Appeals for the Fifth Circuit * * * affirmed Cleveland's conviction and sentence * * *.

We granted certiorari to resolve the conflict among the Courts of Appeals, and now reverse the Fifth Circuit's judgment.

II

In *McNally* v. *United States*, 483 U.S. 350, 360 (1987), this Court held that the federal mail fraud statute is "limited in scope to the protection of property rights." *McNally* reversed the mail fraud convictions of two individuals charged with participating in "a self-dealing patronage scheme" that defrauded Kentucky citizens of "the right to have the Commonwealth's affairs conducted honestly." At the time *McNally* was decided, federal prosecutors had been using § 1341 to attack various forms of corruption that deprived victims of "intangible rights" unrelated to money or property. Reviewing the history of § 1341, we concluded that "the original impetus behind the mail fraud statute was to protect the people from schemes to deprive them of their money or property."

As first enacted in 1872, § 1341 proscribed use of the mails to further " 'any scheme or artifice to defraud.' " In 1896, this Court held in *Durland* v. *United States*, 161 U.S. 306, 313, that the statute covered fraud not only by "representations as to the past or present," but also by "suggestions and promises as to the future." In 1909, Congress amended § 1341 to add after "any scheme or artifice to defraud" the phrase "or for obtaining money or property by means of false or fraudulent pretenses, representations, or promises." We explained in *McNally* that the 1909 amendment "codified the holding of *Durland*," and "simply made it unmistakable that the statute reached false promises and misrepresentations as to the future as well as other frauds involving money or property." Rejecting the argument that "the money-or-property requirement of the latter phrase does not limit schemes to defraud to those aimed at causing deprivation of money or property," we concluded that the 1909 amendment signaled no intent by Congress to "depar[t] from [the] common understanding" that "the words 'to defraud' commonly refer 'to wronging one in his property rights.' "

Soon after *McNally*, in *Carpenter* v. *United States*, 484 U.S. 19, 25 (1987), we again stated that § 1341 protects property rights only. *Carpenter* upheld convictions under § 1341 and the federal wire fraud statute, 18 U.S.C. § 1343, of defendants who had defrauded the Wall Street Journal of confidential business information. Citing decisions of this Court as well as a corporate law treatise, we observed that "[c]onfidential business information has long been recognized as property."

The following year, Congress amended the law specifically to cover one of the "intangible rights" that lower courts had protected under § 1341 prior to *McNally*: "the intangible right of honest services." 18 U.S.C. § 1346. Significantly, Congress covered only the intangible right of honest services even though federal courts, relying on *McNally*, had dismissed, for want of monetary loss to any victim, prosecutions under § 1341 for diverse forms of public corruption, including licensing fraud.

III

In this case, there is no assertion that Louisiana's video poker licensing scheme implicates the intangible right of honest services. The question presented is whether, for purposes of the federal mail fraud statute, a government regulator parts with "property" when it issues a license. For the reasons we now set out, we hold that § 1341 does not reach fraud in obtaining a state or municipal license of the kind here involved, for such a license is not "property" in the government regulator's hands. Again, as we said in *McNally*, "[i]f Congress desires to go further, it must speak more clearly than it has."

To begin with, we think it beyond genuine dispute that whatever interests Louisiana might be said to have in its video poker licenses, the State's core concern is *regulatory*. Louisiana recognizes the importance of "public confidence and trust that gaming activities ... are conducted honestly and are free from criminal and corruptive elements." The video poker licensing statute accordingly asserts the State's "legitimate interest in providing strict regulation of all persons, practices, associations, and activities related to the operation of ... establishments licensed to offer video draw poker devices." The statute assigns the Office of State Police, a part of the Department of Public Safety and Corrections, the responsibility to promulgate rules and regulations concerning the licensing process. It also authorizes the State Police to deny, condition, suspend, or revoke licenses, to levy fines of up to $1,000 per violation of any rule, and to inspect all premises where video poker devices are offered for play. In addition, the statute defines criminal penalties for unauthorized use of video poker devices, and prescribes detailed suitability requirements for licensees.

In short, the statute establishes a typical regulatory program. It licenses, subject to certain conditions, engagement in pursuits that private actors may not undertake without official authorization. In this regard, it resembles other licensing schemes long characterized by this Court as exercises of state police powers.

Acknowledging Louisiana's regulatory interests, the Government offers two reasons why the State also has a property interest in its video poker licenses. First, the State receives a substantial sum of money in exchange for each license and continues to receive payments from the licensee as long as the license remains in effect. Second, the State has significant control over the issuance, renewal, suspension, and revocation of licenses.

Without doubt, Louisiana has a substantial economic stake in the video poker industry. The State collects an upfront "processing fee" for each new license application ($10,000 for truck stops), a separate "processing fee" for each renewal application ($1,000 for truck stops), an "annual fee" from each device owner ($2,000), an additional "device operation" fee ($1,000 for truck stops), and, most importantly, a fixed percentage of net revenue from each video poker device (32.5% for truck stops). It is hardly evident, however, why these tolls should make video poker licenses "property" in the hands of the State. The State receives the lion's share of its expected revenue not while the licenses remain in its own hands, but only *after* they have been issued to licensees. Licenses pre-issuance do not generate an ongoing stream of revenue. At most, they entitle the State to collect a processing fee from applicants for new licenses. Were an entitlement of this order sufficient to establish a state property right, one could scarcely avoid the conclusion that States have property rights in any license or permit requiring an upfront fee, including drivers' licenses, medical licenses, and fishing and hunting licenses. Such licenses, as the Government itself concedes, are "purely regulatory."

Tellingly, as to the character of Louisiana's stake in its video poker licenses, the Government nowhere alleges that Cleveland defrauded the State of any money to which the State was entitled by law. Indeed, there is no dispute that TSG paid the State of Louisiana its proper share of revenue, which totaled more than $1.2 million, between 1993 and 1995. If Cleveland defrauded the State of "property," the nature of that property cannot be economic.

* * *

The Government also compares the State's licensing power to a franchisor's right to select its franchisees. On this view, Louisiana's video poker licensing scheme represents the State's venture into the video poker business. Although the State could have chosen to run the business itself, the Government says, it decided to franchise private entities to carry out the operations instead. However, a franchisor's right to select its franchisees typically derives from its ownership of a trademark, brand name, business strategy, or other product that it may trade or sell in the open market. Louisiana's authority to select video poker licensees rests on no similar asset. It rests instead upon the State's sovereign right to exclude applicants deemed unsuitable to run video poker operations. A right to exclude in that governing capacity is not one appropriately labeled "property." Moreover, unlike an entrepreneur or business partner who shares both losses and gains arising from a business venture, Louisiana cannot be said to have put its labor or capital at risk through its fee-laden licensing scheme. In short, the State did not decide to venture into the video poker business; it decided typically to permit, regulate, and tax private operators of the games.

We reject the Government's theories of property rights not simply because they stray from traditional concepts of property. We resist the Government's reading of § 1341 as well because it invites us to approve a sweeping expansion of federal criminal jurisdiction in the absence of a clear statement by Congress. Equating issuance of licenses or permits with deprivation of property would subject to federal mail fraud prosecution a wide range of conduct traditionally regulated by state and local authorities. We note in this regard that Louisiana's video poker statute typically and unambiguously imposes criminal penalties for making false statements on license applications. As we reiterated last Term, " 'unless Congress conveys its purpose clearly, it will not be deemed to have significantly changed the federal-state balance' in the prosecution of crimes."

Moreover, to the extent that the word "property" is ambiguous as placed in § 1341, we have instructed that "ambiguity concerning the ambit of criminal statutes should be resolved in favor of lenity." This interpretive guide is especially appropriate in construing § 1341 because, as this case demonstrates, mail fraud is a predicate offense under RICO, and the money laundering statute. In deciding what is "property" under § 1341, we think "it is appropriate, before we choose the harsher alternative, to require that Congress should have spoken in language that is clear and definite."

* * *

IV

We conclude that § 1341 requires the object of the fraud to be "property" in the victim's hands and that a Louisiana video poker license in the State's hands is not "property" under § 1341. Absent clear statement by Congress, we will not read the mail fraud statute to place under federal superintendence a vast array of conduct traditionally policed by the States. Our holding means that Cleveland's § 1341 conviction must be vacated. Accordingly, the judgment of the United States Court of Appeals for the Fifth Circuit is reversed, and the case is remanded for further proceedings consistent with this opinion.

It is so ordered.

†

0-314-25649-0
90000
9 780314 256492